Lecture Notes in Artificial Intelligence   2972

Edited by J. G. Carbonell and J. Siekmann

Subseries of Lecture Notes in Computer Science

D1807638

Springer
Berlin
Heidelberg
New York
Hong Kong
London
Milan
Paris
Tokyo

Raúl Monroy   Gustavo Arroyo-Figueroa
Luis Enrique Sucar   Humberto Sossa (Eds.)

MICAI 2004:
Advances in
Artificial Intelligence

Third Mexican International Conference on Artificial Intelligence
Mexico City, Mexico, April 26-30, 2004
Proceedings

 Springer

Series Editors

Jaime G. Carbonell, Carnegie Mellon University, Pittsburgh, PA, USA
Jörg Siekmann, University of Saarland, Saarbrücken, Germany

Volume Editors

Raúl Monroy
ITESM - Campus Estado de México, Computer Science Department
Carretera al lago de Guadalupe km 3.5
52926 Atizapán de Zaragoza, Estado de México, Mexico
E-mail: raulm@itesm.mx

Gustavo Arroyo-Figueroa
Gerencia de Sistemas Informáticos
Instituto de Investigaciones Eléctricas
Av. Reforma 113, Col. Palmira, 62490 Cuernavaca, Morelos, Mexico
E-mail: garroyo@iie.org.mx

Luis Enrique Sucar
ITESM - Campus Cuernavaca, Computer Science Department
Av. Reforma 182-A, 62589 Temixco, Morelos, Mexico
E-mail: esucar@itesm.mx

Humberto Sossa
Centro de Investigación en Computación del IPN
Juan de Dios Batiz esq. Miguel Othon de Mendizabal
Nueva Industrial Vallejo, 07730, México, D.F. Mexico
E-mail: hsossa@cic.ipn.mx

Library of Congress Control Number: 2004103076

CR Subject Classification (1998): I.2, F.1, F.4.1, I.4

ISSN 0302-9743
ISBN 3-540-21459-3 Springer-Verlag Berlin Heidelberg New York

Springer-Verlag is a part of Springer Science+Business Media

springeronline.com

© Springer-Verlag Berlin Heidelberg 2004
Printed in Germany

Typesetting: Camera-ready by author, data conversion by PTP-Berlin, Protago-TeX-Production GmbH
Printed on acid-free paper   SPIN: 10993606   06/3142   5 4 3 2 1 0

Preface

The Mexican International Conference on Artificial Intelligence (MICAI) is a biennial conference established to promote research inartificial intelligence (AI), and cooperation among Mexican researchersand their peers worldwide. MICAI is organized by the Mexican Societyfor Artificial Intelligence (SMIA), in collaboration with the AmericanAssociation for Artificial Intelligence (AAAI) and the Mexican Society for Computer Science (SMCC).

After two successful conferences, we are pleased to present the 3rd Mexican International Conference on Artificial Intelligence, MICAI2004, which took place on April 26–30, 2004, in Mexico City, Mexico. This volume contains the papers included in the conferencemain program, which was complemented by tutorials and workshops, published in supplementary proceedings. The proceedings of past MICAI conferences, 2000 and 2002, were also published in Springer-Verlag's Lecture Notes in Artificial Intelligence (LNAI) series, volumes 1793 and 2313.

The number of submissions to MICAI 2004 was significantly higher than those of previous conferences — 254 papers from 19 different countries were submitted for consideration to MICAI 2004. The evaluation of this unexpectedly large number of papers was a challenge, both in terms of the quality of the papers and of the review workload of each PC member. After a thorough reviewing process, MICAI's Program Committee and Programs Chairs accepted 97 high-quality papers. So the acceptance rate was 38.2%. CyberChair, a free Web-based paper submission and reviewing system, was used as an electronic support for the reviewing process.

This book contains revised versions of the 94 papers presented at the conference. The volume is structured into 13 thematic fields according to the topics addressed by the papers, which are representative of the main current area of interest within the AI community.

We are proud of the quality of the research presented at MICAI 2004, and hope that this volume will become an important archival reference for the field.

April 2004

Raúl Monroy
Gustavo Arroyo-Figueroa
Luis Enrique Sucar
Humberto Sossa

Organization

MICAI 2004 was organized by the Mexican Society for Artificial Intelligence (SMIA), in collaboration with the Tecnológico de Monterrey at Estado de México, Ciudad de México and at Cuernavaca, the Instituto de Investigaciones Eléctricas, the Instituto Politécnico Nacional, the Instituto Tecnológico Autónomo de México, the Instituto Mexicano del Petróleo, and the Instituto Nacional de Astrofísica, Óptica y Electrónica.

Conference Committee

Conference Chairs	J. Humberto Sossa Azuela (CIC-IPN)
	Angel Kuri Morales (ITAM)
Program Chairs	Raúl Monroy (ITESM-CEM)
	Gustavo Arroyo Figueroa (IIE)
	L. Enrique Sucar (ITESM-CVA)
Tutorial Chair	Carlos Alberto Reyes (INAOE)
Workshop Chairs	Matias Alvarado (IMP)
	Leonid Sheremetov (IMP)
Local Chair	Alvaro de Albornoz (ITESM-CCM)

Advisory Committee

Felipe Bracho	Robert de Hoog	Pablo Noriega
Alan Bundy	Felipe Lara	Judea Pearl
Ofelia Cervantes	Christian Lemaître	Antonio Sánchez
Anthony Cohn	Jay Liebowitz	Xindong Wu
Francisco Garijo	Cristina Loyo	Wolfgang Wahlster
Randy Goebel	Donald Michie	Carlos Zozaya
Adolfo Guzmán	José Negrete	

Program Committee

José Luis Aguirre
David W. Aha
Juan Manuel Ahuactzin
James Allen
Matías Alvarado
Ronald C. Arkin
Gustavo Arroyo
Victor Ayala Ramírez
Ruth Aylett
Antonio Bahamonde
Olivia Barrón-Cano
Ildar Batyrshin
Ricardo Beausoleil
Bedrich Benes
Ramón Brena
Carlos A. Brizuela
Paul Brna
Osvaldo Cairo
Felix Calderón
Francisco Cantú
Jesus Cardeñosa
Oscar Castillo
Edgar Chávez
Carolina Chang
Carlos A. Coello
Simon Colton
Santiago E. Conant
Ulises Cortés
Carlos Cotta-Porras
Nicandro Cruz
Antonio D'Angelo
Alvaro de Albornoz
Thomas G. Dietterich
Francisco J. Diez
Juergen Dix
Carlos E. Mariano
Jesús Favela
Joaquín Fdez-Valdivia
Bob Fisher
Juan Flores
Olac Fuentes
Eduardo Gómez Ramírez
Arturo Galván
Jose A. Gamez Martín
Leonardo Garrido

Alexandre Gelbukh
Michael Gelfond
Duncan Gillies
José Luis Gordillo
Silvia Guardati
Adolfo Guzmán Arenas
N. Hernández-Gress
Arturo Hernández
Dieter Hutter
Efrain Jaime
Bruno Jammes
Nadezhda Jarushkina
Fernando Jiménez
Leo Joskowicz
Angeles Junco
Nicolás Kemper
Ingrid Kirschning
Ryszard Klempous
Mario Koeppen
Andrzej Kraslawski
Angel Kuri Morales
R. López de Mantaras
Gerhard Lakemeyer
Pedro Larrañaga
Christian Lemaître
Jim Little
Jacek Malec
Ana Ma. Martínez
Vladimir Marik
José F. Martínez
H. Martínez-Alfaro
René V. Mayorga
Chilukuri K. Mohan
María Carolina Monard
Raúl Monroy
Rafael Morales
Guillermo Morales Luna
Eduardo Morales
Rafael Murrieta
Juan A. Nolazco Flores
Konstantine M. Nyunkin
Gabriela Ochoa Meier
Mauricio Osorio
Andrés Pérez-Uribe
Helen Pain

Luis Alberto Pineda
Andre Carvalho
Alessandro Provetti
Long Quan
Maricela Quintana
Jorge Ramírez-Uresti
Fernando Ramos
Patricia Rayón
Carlos Alberto Reyes
María Cristina Riff
Roger Z. Rios
C. Rodríguez Lucatero
Katya Rodríguez
Guillermo Rodríguez
Horacio Rodríguez
Leonardo Romero
Isaac Rudomín
Alberto Sanfeliú
Eugene Santos
Onn Shehory
Leonid Sheremetov
Carles Sierra
Alexander Smirnov
Humberto Sossa
Rogelio Soto
Thomas Stuetzle
Dionisio Suárez
Enrique Sucar
Ricardo Swain
Hugo Terashima
Demetri Terzopoulos
Juan M. Torres Moreno
José Torres
Eduardo Uresti
Manuel Valenzuela
Johan van Horebeek
Maarten van Someren
Rineke Verbrugge
Felisa Verdejo
Luis Villaseñor
Toby Walsh
Alfredo Weitzenfeld
Franz Wotawa
Fritz Wysotzki

Additional Referees

Moises Alencastre
Vazha Amiranashvili
Chris Beck
Yolanda Bolea Monte
Didac Busquets
J. Carrera
Reggio Caterina
Brad Chambers
Ronaldo Cristiano Prati
Francisco Cuevas
James Davidson
Gustavo E.A.P.A. Batista
Trilce Estrada Piedra
A. Fernández-Caballero
Günter Gans
Andreas Gerber
Fernando Godínez

Miguel González-Mendoza
Federico Guedea-Elizalde
Sang-Yong Han
Hector J. Hernandez
Vera Hollink
Pablo Ibarguengoitia
Gero Iwan
Steven LaValle
Jimmy Lee
E. Lobo
Carlos-Eduardo Mariano
Patricia Melin
Erick Millán
Angélica Muñoz Meléndez
Lourdes Muñoz
Gonzalo Navarro
M. Ortiz

Miguel Perez Ramirez
Steve Prestwich
Jose M. Puerta
Josep Puyol-Gruart
Ricardo Ramirez
Claudia Regina Milare
Georg Rock
Patricia Rufino
Jordi Sabater Mir
Erika Sánchez
P. Sanongboon
A. Sriraman
Renato Tinós
Xavier Vilasis Cardona
Yingqian Zhang

Acknowledgements

We would like to thank Campus Ciudad de México of the Tecnológico de Monterrey, for their warm hospitality to MICAI 2004. We would also like to thank our sponsors for providing financial support throughout the entire conference organization. We are deeply grateful to the conference staff, and the members of both the advisory board and the program committee. We would like to express our gratitude to Manuel Franco, Fernando Godínez and Juan Carlos López, who assisted on various tasks, including software installation, database maintenance and conference registration. We would also like to express our gratitude to the Gerencia de Sistemas Informáticos from IIE, for their support on the design, development and maintenance of the conference web page. Special thanks go to the Springer-Verlag staff, for editing this volume, and to Maricela Quintana and Ricardo Swain.

Table of Contents

Knowledge Representation

Logic and Constraint Programming

Machine Learning and Data Mining

Multiagent Systems and Distributed AI

Natural Language

Uncertainty Reasoning

Vision

Evolutionary Computation

Modeling and Intelligent Control

Neural Networks

Robotics

Pattern-Based Data Compression

Ángel Kuri[1] and José Galaviz[2]

[1] Department of Computing, ITAM.
akuri@itam.mx
[2] Department of Mathematics, Facultad de Ciencias, UNAM.
jgc@fciencias.unam.mx

Abstract. Most modern lossless data compression techniques used today, are based in dictionaries. If some string of data being compressed matches a portion previously seen, then such string is included in the dictionary and its reference is included every time it appears. A possible generalization of this scheme is to consider not only strings made of consecutive symbols, but more general patterns with gaps between its symbols. The main problems with this approach are the complexity of pattern discovery algorithms and the complexity for the selection of a good subset of patterns. In this paper we address the last of these problems. We demonstrate that such problem is NP-complete and we provide some preliminary results about heuristics that points to its solution.

Categories and Subject Descriptors: E.4 [**Coding and Information Theory**]–*data compaction and compression*; F.2.2 [**Analysis of Algorithms and Problem Complexity**]: Nonnumerical Problems; I.2.8 [**Artificial Intelligence**]: Problem Solving, Control Methods, and Search–*heuristic methods*.

General Terms: Algorithms, Theory

Additional Keywords and Phrases: Genetic algorithms, optimization, NP-hardness

1 Introduction

Since the introduction of information theory in Shannon's seminal paper [7] the efficient representation of data is one of its fundamental subjects. Most of the successful modern lossless methods used today are dictionary-based such as the Lempel-Ziv family [10]. These dictionary-based methods only consider strings of consecutive symbols. In this paper we will introduce a generalization by considering "strings" with gaps, whose symbols are no necessarily consecutive. This generalization will be called *pattern* in the rest of paper. A similar concept is used in [1] for approximate string matching.

In this context a pattern is a finite and ordered sequence of symbols together with an specification of the position of each symbol. For example a pattern contained in the string It is better late than never could be:

$$p_1 = \text{I\_\_\_\_be_____t\_\_\_a.}$$

R. Monroy et al. (Eds.): MICAI 2004, LNAI 2972, pp. 1–10, 2004.

We consider two possible representations of patterns:

- An ordered pair (S, O) where S is the ordered sequence of symbols in the pattern and O is the ordered sequence of absolute positions (offsets) of symbols.
- A 3-tuple (S, D, b) where S is the ordered sequence of symbols in the pattern, b is the absolute position of the first symbol in S and D is the ordered sequence of distances between symbols (positions relative to the previous symbol).

Therefore, the pattern used as an example above could be represented as: $S = \{I, b, e, t, a\}$, $O = \{0, 6, 7, 15, 20\}$ or using: $p = 0$, $D = \{6, 0, 8, 5\}$. In general the second representation is more efficient than the first one, since absolute positions are potentially larger than the relative positions.

By identifying frequent patterns we can proceed to include such patterns in a dictionary achieving data compression.

2   Pattern-Based Data Compression

In order to apply the procedure aforementioned we need to accomplish several goals:

1. Given a sample of data S, identify frequent patterns.
2. Given the set of patterns obtained in the previous step, determine the subset of such patterns that maximizes the compression ratio.
3. Determine the best way for pattern representation and encoding, and the best way for reference encoding. The compressed sample will include the, perhaps compressed, dictionary and the compressed representation of original sample.

This paper will be focused in the second step, but we will do some annotations regarding the first.

In the first step it is needed to find patterns in the sample. Such patterns must be used frequently, that is, they must appear several times in ths sample. Evidently the most frequent patterns will be individual symbols. Therefore, we need to establish another requisite: the patterns must be as large as possible. But there is a potential conflict between the pattern size (number of symbols that contains) and its frequency. Larger patterns are rare, short patterns are common. In order to avoid this conflict, we will consider the total number of symbols that are contained in all the appearances of a given pattern p. This number will be called the *coverage* of such pattern and can be calculated by the product of the pattern frequency and the pattern size. In notation:

$$\mathrm{Cov}(p) = f(p)\, t(p) \tag{1}$$

where $f(p)$ denotes the frequency of pattern p and $t(p)$ the number of symbols in p. In our example of previous section the pattern size is $t(p_1) = 5$.

It is convenient to distinguish between the nominal coverage of some pattern: the product mentioned before, and the effective coverage of some pattern in a set of patterns: the number of symbols contained in all the appearances of the pattern and *not* contained in any previously appeared pattern.

The task for this first step must be solved by algorithms of *pattern discovery* algorithms, similar to those used in the analysis of DNA sequences and biomolecular data in general. Unfortunately the reported algorithms for the discovery of patterns of the kind we are interested in, have exponential time complexity [9].

3   Selecting Good Subset of Patterns

The second step of the aforementioned process is the selection of a good subset of the whole set of frequent patterns found in the sample. The "goodness" of a subset of patterns is given by the compression ratio obtained if such subset of patterns is the dictionary.

Obviously the best subset also must cover a considerably large amount of symbols contained in the sample, since every pattern in the subset must have a good coverage. Also it must have a low amount of data symbols multiply covered. That is, the best subset must have efficient patterns: a large amount of covered symbols but a small amount of symbols covered by another patterns or by different appearances of pattern itself.

Let S be a sample of data. We will denote by $|S|$ the number of symbols in such sample (its original size). We will denote with $T(Q)$ the size of the compressed sample using the subset of patterns Q. With P we will denote the whole set of patterns found in S, therefore $Q \subseteq P$. Using this notation we will define the compression ratio.

Definition 1. The *compression ratio* obtained by using the subset of patterns Q is:

$$G(Q) = 1 - \frac{T(Q)}{|S|} \tag{2}$$

$T(Q)$ has two components: the dictionary size $D(Q)$ and the representation of the sample itself $E(Q)$. These are given by:

$$D(Q) = z \left[\sum_{p_i \in Q} t(p_i) + r(Q) \right] \tag{3}$$

$$E(Q) = 1 + \sum_{p_i \in Q} f(p_i) \tag{4}$$

Hence:

$$T(Q) = D(Q) + E(Q) \tag{5}$$

In the expression for D, $z > 1$: since for every pattern included in the dictionary, every symbol in the pattern must also appear. The distances between them must be included and the offset of first symbol in the pattern must be included as well. We will assume that every distance or offset uses z times the space (bits for example) used for each symbol. In what follows z will be roughly estimated as $z = 2$, assuming that, for every symbol in a given pattern we need to store the symbol itself and its distance to the previous symbol in the same pattern, and both requires the same amount of data.

In expression 3, $r(Q)$ is the number of symbols not covered by patterns in Q. Such symbols must appear as a pattern in the dictionary. Once a pattern subset Q is chosen, $r(Q)$ is determined. Hence, we can equivalently think that r is included in the sum.

In the expression for E the 1 that is added to the sum at the right represents the inclusion of the "pattern" of those symbols in S not contained in any pattern of Q in the dictionary. This is the pattern with the $r(Q)$ symbols just mentioned. $E(Q)$ is the number of pattern identifiers used to represent the sample in terms of references. For every appearance of a pattern in Q, a reference must be included in the compressed sample expression. As stated a reference to the "pattern" of symbols not covered by Q must also be included in such expression.

Denoting by p_i the i-th pattern contained in a set of patterns, the coverage of a subset of patterns Q is:

$$\text{Cov}(Q) = \sum_{p_i \in Q} f(p_i)\, t(p_i) \qquad (6)$$

where $f(p_i)$ and $t(p_i)$ are the frequency and size of pattern p_i respectively.

We can now state our problem as follows:

Definition 2. OPTIMALPATTERNSUBSETPROBLEM.
Given:

- A data sample S with $|S|$ symbols.
- A set $P = \{p_1, \ldots, p_n\}$ of frequent patterns of S with frequencies $f(p_i) = f_i$ and sizes $t(p_i) = t_i$

Find a subset $Q \subset P$ that maximizes $G(Q)$ subject to the restriction:

$$\text{Cov}(Q) \leq |S| \qquad (7)$$

Hence we must find a subset of P. But there are $2^{|P|}$ of such subsets. This is a huge search space even for small values of $|P|$. In fact this is a NP-complete problem as we now prove. Similar problems have been proved NP-complete in [8,4]. However in [8] the dictionary size is not considered, and the patterns are strings of consecutive symbols. In [4] also the dictionary size is ignored and coverage of patterns is used as the only criteria to determine the best subset.

Theorem 1. OPTIMALPATTERNSUBSETPROBLEM *is NP-complete.*

Proof. First we must prove that OPSP is in NP, which means that this is verifiable in polynomial time. Given some subset $Q \subseteq P$ and the maximum compression ratio g, then we can calculate $T(Q)$ in linear time on the size of Q, therefore we can calculate $G(Q)$ also in $O(|Q|)$. That is polynomial time verifiable.

Next, in order to do the reduction we chose the (0,1) Knapsack Problem. We must prove that any given instance of such problem can be mapped, by a polynomial time algorithm, in an instance of OPSP. The solution to knapsack instance is therefore mapped in polynomial time to the solution of some OPSP instance.

In an instance of (0,1) knapsack problem there are given:

- A set of objects $\{o_1, o_2, \ldots, o_m\}$.
- A function v that assigns to every object o_i its value: $v(o_i) > 0$.
- A function w that assigns to every object o_i its weight: $w(o_i) > 0$.
- A positive integer $C > 0$ called the *capacity*.

The problem consists in finding some subset $B \subseteq O$ such that it maximizes:

$$\sum_{o_i \in B} v(o_i)$$

with the restriction:

$$\sum_{o_i \in B} w(o_i) \leq C$$

Let $B \subseteq O$. The algorithm proceeds as follows.

For every object $o_i \in B$ compute:

$$w'(o_i) = \begin{cases} \frac{(v(o_i)-C)^2}{8\,w(o_i)}, & \text{if } w(o_i) \geq \frac{(v(o_i)-C)^2}{8} \\ w(o_i), & \text{otherwise} \end{cases}$$

This means that:

$$8\,w'(o_i) < (v(o_i) - C)^2 \tag{8}$$

Now we establish the values of for sample size, the frequencies, and the sizes on the corresponding instance of OPSP:

$$C_B = \frac{C}{|B|} \tag{9}$$

$$f(o_i) = \frac{(C_B - v(o_i)) + \sqrt{(v(o_i) - C_B)^2 - 8\,w'(o_i)}}{2} \tag{10}$$

$$t(o_i) = \frac{w'(o_i)}{f(o_i)} \tag{11}$$

where (8) guarantees that the square root of (10) is real solution of:

$$f^2(o_i) + f(o_i)\,(v(o_i) - C_B) + 2\,w'(o_i) = 0$$

From this we obtain:

$$v(o_i) = \frac{C_B\,f(o_i) - 2\,w(o_i) - f^2(o_i)}{f(o_i)}$$

Finally, using (9) and (11):

$$v(o_i) = \frac{C}{|B|} - (2\,t(o_i) + f(o_i)) \tag{12}$$

Also from (11) we have:

$$w'(o_i) = f(o_i)\,t(o_i) \tag{13}$$

Therefore, in the knapsack we want to maximize:

$$\sum_{o_i \in B} v(o_i) = \sum_{o_i \in B} \left[\frac{C}{|B|} - (2t(o_i) + f(o_i)) \right] \tag{14}$$

$$= C - \sum_{o_i \in B} (2t(o_i) + f(o_i)) \tag{15}$$

If we establish $|S| = C$ for OPSP, then maximizing the last expression also maximizes:

$$\frac{\sum_{o_i \in B} v(o_i)}{|S|} = 1 - \frac{\sum_{o_i \in B}(2t(o_i) + f(o_i))}{|S|}$$

which is (2) considering (3) and (4) (excluding the terms related with the "pattern" of symbols not included in any other pattern).

The restriction is transformed as follows:

$$\sum_{o_i \in B} w'(o_i) = \sum_{o_i \in B} f(o_i)\,t(o_i) \le \sum_{o_i \in B} w(o_i) \le C = |S|$$

In terms of OPSP the restriction means that the joint coverage of patterns in B cannot be greater than the total size of the original sample.

Therefore the solution to knapsack, using the transformations above, can be mapped into the solution of OPSP in polynomial time.

$\square$

Since OPSP is NP-complete we need heuristics in order to obtain an approximate solution for large samples. In what follows we will address such heuristics.

4   Heuristics for Subset Selection

4.1   Using a Genetic Algorithm

Our first heuristic approach was the use of a genetic algorithm (GA) for the selection of a good pattern subset. The use of GA to solve NP-complete problems has been used in the past [2,3].

The first step is to define a useful domain representation. Since we need to find a subset of a set of m different patterns. We can encode every subset using a binary string of length m. The i-th pattern is included in a subset if the i-th bit of its encoding string is "1", otherwise the pattern is excluded. The number of possible binary strings of length m is 2^m, the cardinality of our search space: the power set.

The fitness function is given by (2), and the selection will be performed using a deterministic scheme called *Vasconcelos Selection* [5][1]. Such selection scheme has improved the performance of GA when combined with 2-point crossover, as is statistically proved in [6].

4.2   Using a Coverage-Based Heuristic

We propose an alternative method for the search of a good subset of patterns. The method consists in the selection of patterns using the number of symbols in the sample that are covered by them. A pattern is better the greater the number of symbols in the sample that are in the instances of such pattern. This is our concept of *coverage*. It may occur that some symbol is in the appearances of several different patterns. That is, the symbol is "overcovered". Hence we need to measure the coverage more accurately than with the product of frequency and size. Therefore, during the selection process, if some pattern covers symbols already covered by a pattern previously selected, the coverage of the last pattern should be modified to represent its *effective coverage*: the number of symbols that are covered by the pattern and not already covered by some other pattern.

Given a set of patterns P we will obtain a subset $B \subseteq P$ of selected patterns. The heuristic algorithm for the selection of subset is:

1. Set $B = \emptyset$
2. Set the current coverage $Cv = \emptyset$.
3. Select the pattern $p \in P$ with highest effective coverage (covered symbols not already in Cv).
4. Add p to B.
5. Remove p from P
6. Use the coverage of p to update the current coverage Cv.
7. Return to 3 until $|Cv|$ equals the sample size or $P = \emptyset$.

With the strategy described we will obtain the subset of patterns B with highest coverage. But good coverage does not guarantee best compression ratio, it may occur that patterns with large size and poor frequency or conversely are included in B. Since we want that the inclusion of some pattern in the dictionary will be well amortized by its use in the sample, this is not desirable.

4.3   Hillclimbing

For the improvement of the heuristic described above, we will use hillclimbing. Two different hillclimbers will be defined:

---

[1] The best individual (I_0) is mixed with the worst one (I_{N-1}), the second best is crossed with the second worst (I_1 and I_{N-2}, respectively), and so on.

MSHC *Minimum Step HillClimber.* Searching the better binary string in the neighborhood of radius 1 in Hamming distance. Given a binary string that encodes a subset, we perform a search for the best string between those that differ from the given one in only one bit.

MRHC *Minimum Replacement HillClimber.* Searching the better binary string in the neighborhood of radius 2 in Hamming distance. Given a binary string, we perform a search for the best string between those that exchanges the position of every bit with value 1 with the position with value 0.

To find a better subset than the one given by the coverage-based heuristic we run both hillclimbers: the string obtained by the heuristic is passed to MSHC, and the output of this climber is thereafter passed to MRHC. Every hillclimber is executed interatively until no further improvement is obtained.

5   Test Cases

In order to test the effectiveness of the heuristic methods above we define three simple test cases. These are only for testing, but a more robust statistical demonstration of effectiveness will be developed in the future.

The test cases are samples built with patterns defined *a priori*. Hence the expected resulting subset is the set of building patterns. The algorithm used for pattern discovery yields the whole set of patterns which is large in comparison with the subset we are looking for. The output of such algorithm is the input for the subset selection algorithm.

The characteristics of each sample are shown in table 1. The column labeled **Patterns** show the number of building patterns used for the sample. The column labeled **ComRa** contains the compression ratio obtained if uilding patterns are the whole dictionary. The column **Patt. found** contains the number of patterns found by the discovery algorithm, therefore the search space depends exponentially on the contents of this column.

For the genetic algorithm we use the parameter values shown in table 2. The GA was ran for 100 generations. A repair algorithm was used in order to restrict the maximum number of ones allowed in the chromosome (number of patterns in the proposed subset) and at the end of the GA execution the hillclimbers where executed.

The results are summarized in table 3. In the table the column labeled **ComRa** is the compression ratio as defined by expression (2) before the hillclimbers. The column labeled **HC ComRa** is the compression ratio obtained after both hillclimbers.

It is clear from table 3 that GA outperforms the results obtained by the application of cover based heuristics. But the solution proposed by this heuristic however can be improved more efficiently than the one obtained from the GA, since after the application of hillclimbers the best subset is the one obtained by the cover-based heuristic. In all cases the solution proposed by the cover-based+hillclimbers contains the patterns used to build the sample. The patterns obtained by GA contains al least 60% of such patterns.

Table 1. Characteristics of samples used.

Sample	Size	Alphabet	Patterns	ComRa	Patt. found
1	64	8	5	-0.1406	75
2	133	13	4	0.3233	309
3	185	37	7	0.3189	25

Table 2. Parameters used for GA.

Parameter	Value
Population size	100
Selection scheme	Vasconcelos
Crossover	2-point
Crossover probability	0.9
Mutation probability	0.05

Table 3. Summary of results for test cases.

	Genetic Algorithm			C-B Heuristic		
Sample	Gen	ComRa	HC ComRa	Patt	ComRa	HC ComRa	Patt
1	75	-0.2187	-0.2187	5	-0.3280	-0.1875	5
2	100	0.0225	0.3230	5	0.3082	0.3310	5
3	31	0.2756	0.2756	7	-0.0972	0.3189	7

6   Summary and Further Work

We have defined a problem whose solution is useful for a dictionary-based data compression technique: the OPTIMALPATTERNSUBSETPROBLEM. We have proved that such problem is NP-complete. Two different heuristic techniques have been proposed for its approximate solution: a genetic algorithm and a cover-based heuristic technique.

In order to refine the solutions proposed by these heuristics two different methods of hillclimbing where introduced: MSHC and MRHC. These hillclimbers are executed iteratively over the solutions proposed by the heuristics described until no better proposal is found.

Our very preliminary results show that, the best heuristic is the cover-based one. This is to be expected since the GA is not modified with special purpose operators. However a repair algorithm was included in every generation of GA in order to reduce the search space restricting the number of bits with value 1 in the chromosomes.

The cover-based heuristic technique does not outperform the GA by itself, at least not necessarily. The efficiency in the solution proposed by this heuristic was achieved through the use of hillclimbers. Also the cover-based heuristic is several times faster than the GA, since there is not an evolutionary process.

Further experimentation using the cover-based technique is required in order to provide statistically robust performance measurements, the results shown are not conclusive. However in order to provide a robust evaluation we need to solve the first phase og general compression procedure. Such evaluation can also compare the methods used with some other heuristics: tabu search, simulated annealing and memetic algorithms could be used.

Once the selection of best subset is done, the third phase must be performed. The goal is to found a set of patterns which conform a meta-symbol dictionary. A similar approach is shown in [4]. Therefore, well known encoding techniques can be used on this meta-alphabet, such as those based in information theory. Then we are able to imagine that the sample we have has been produced by an information source whose alphabet is the set of meta-symbols rather than the original one.

References

[1]   Burkhardt, Stefan and Juha Kärkkäinen, "Better Filtering with Gapped *q*-Grams", *Proceedings of 12th Annual Symposium on Combinatorial Pattern Matching CPM 2001*, Amihood Amir and Gad M. Landau (editors), Lecture Notes in Computer Science, No. 2089, 2001, pp. 73-85.

[2]   DeJong, K. and W.M. Spears. "Using genetic algorithms to solve NP-complete problems". *Proceedings of the Third International Conference on Genetic Algorithms*, J.D. Schaffer (editor), 1989, pp. 124-132.
      http://citeseer.nj.nec.com/dejong89using.html.

[3]   Jin-Kao Hao, J., F. Lardeux and F. Saubion, "Evolutionary Computing for the Satisfiability Problem", *Applications of Evolutionary Computing*, LNCS, No. 2611, 2003, pp. 259-268.
      http://citeseer.nj.nec.com/hao03evolutionary.html.

[4]   Klein, Shmuel T., "Improving Static Compression Schemes by Alphabet Extension", *Proceedings of 11th Annual Symposium Combinatorial Pattern Matching CPM 2000*, Raffaele Giancarlo and David Sankoff (editors), Lecture Notes in Computer Science, No. 1848, 2000, pp. 210-221.

[5]   Kuri, A., "A universal Eclectic Genetic Algorithm for Constrained Optimization". *Proceedings 6th European Congress on Intelligent Techniques & Soft Computing, EUFIT'98*, 1998, pp. 518-522.

[6]   Kuri, A., "A Methodology for the Statistical Characterization of Genetic Algorithms", *Proceedings of MICAI 2002*, Lecture Notes in Artificial Intelligence, No. 2313, 2002, pp. 79-89.

[7]   Shannon, Claude E., "A Mathematical Theory of Communication", *The Bell System Technical Journal*, vol. 27, July: pp. 379-423, October: pp. 623-656, 1948.

[8]   Storer, James y Thomas Szymanski, "Data Compression via Textual Substitution", JACM, Vol. 29, No. 4, october 1982, pp. 928-951.

[9]   Vilo, Jaak, *Pattern Discovery from Biosequences*, PhD Thesis, Technical Report A-2002-3, Department of Computer Science, University of Helsinki, 2002.

[10] Ziv, Jacob and Abraham Lempel, "A Universal Algorithm for Sequential Data Compression", *IEEE Transactions on Information Theory*, Vol. 23, No. 3, 1977, pp. 337-343.

Using Simulated Annealing for Paper Cutting Optimization

Horacio Martínez-Alfaro and Manuel Valenzuela-Rendón

ITESM, Center for Intelligent Systems
Monterrey, N.L. 64849 México
{hma,valenzuela}@itesm.mx
http://www-csi.mty.itesm.mx/

Abstract. This article presents the use of the Simulated Annealing algorithm to solve the waste minimization problem in roll cutting programming, in this case, paper. Client orders, which vary in weight, width, and external and internal diameter, are fully satisfied; and no cuts to inventory are additionally generated, unless, they are specified. Once an optimal cutting program is obtained, the algorithm is applied again to minimize cutting blade movements. Several tests were performed with real data from a paper company in which an average of 30% waste reduction and 100% in production to inventory are obtained compare to the previous procedure. Actual savings represent about $5,200,000 USD in four months with 4 cutting machines.

1   Introduction

Paper industry has a great product variety which can be classified in four manufacturing segments: packaging, hygienic, writing and printing, and specialties. Every segment use paper rolls as a basic input for their processes. These rolls are named as *master rolls* and they vary in their internal diameter or *center*, c, external diameter or simply *diameter*, D, and *width*, w depending on the paper type and the process it will undertake. Fig. 1(a) shows these characteristics.

Even though there are several paper manufacturing segments for paper, in a same segment there are several paper types which basic difference is density, G.

Client orders received in a paper manufacturing company are classified by paper type, then by their diameter and center. Although, each order varies in width (cm) and weight (kg). The paper manufacturing company delivers to each client a certain number of rolls (with the diameter, center and width required) that satisfy the order.

Once the orders are classified into groups by paper type (paper density), diameter, and center, each group is processed in a cutting machine with a maximum fixed width combining the order widths in order to satisfy each order weight having as objective to minimize the non used width of the master roll (W in Fig. 1(b)). The previous described optimization problem is a combinatorial one since we are interested in finding the best widths combination to cut in a master roll satisfying all orders. All cutting combinations are grouped in a *production cutting schedule*, as shown in Fig. 1(b), having a total weight or, equivalently, a total number of rolls to manufacture for each combination or item in

R. Monroy et al. (Eds.): MICAI 2004, LNAI 2972, pp. 11–20, 2004.

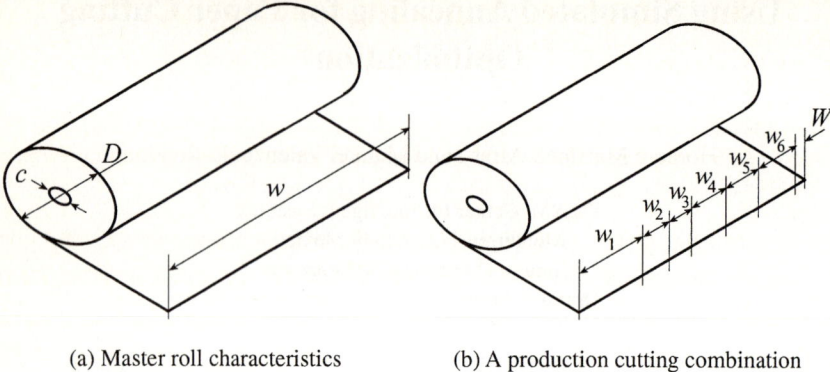

(a) Master roll characteristics　　　　(b) A production cutting combination

Fig. 1. Master rolls with and without cuts.

the cutting schedule. Bigger widths are first satisfied in the present procedure to obtain the cutting schedule.

These are the characteristics of the procedure performed in the paper manufacturing company where this research was carried out:

- Two or more people using a spreadsheet type application, i.e. MS Excel, perform the task.
- The process takes between 2.5 and 3 hours to obtain an acceptable total waste, which in this company was less than 10% of the total production weight, for four cutting machines using a very simple approximation iterative scheme.
- The smallest total waste achieved with this procedure is due to the production of some cuts that go directly to inventory, i.e., certain commonly used widths are assigned to a "virtual" client's order and created "on the fly."

By performing a deep analysis of the problem, we found the main problem was in this last characteristic since the company was generating about 30% more of the total waste as inventory production. This means that if the total waste was 9,000 ton, additionally 12,000 ton were to inventory.

The process to obtain a cutting schedule has other characteristics:

- The cutting schedule is not optimal since they measure waste as unused width (cm) and not as unused weight (kg) of a cutting combination.
- The procedure required time limits the number of times (two or three) which can be performed before deciding which cutting schedule is going to be produced.
- The process considers a $\pm 10\%$ of the order weight (ocassionally, more).
- The same people that perform the task decide the order of each combination in the cutting schedule before sending it for production.
- Cutting blade movement is not considered in the process and it is performed by the cutting machine operator.

This research shows the development of an application that:

- automates a new generating procedure to obtain a cutting schedule,
- the objective function is total waste weight,

– eliminates the need of generating cuts to inventory, and
– minimizes cutting blade movement

by using the simulated annealing algorithm [15,7,8,9,10,11,12].

2   Methodology

The first problem to solve is to create a new way of generating the cutting schedule. For that and knowing that the paper manufacturing company delivers paper rolls, we first compute the number of rolls that are equivalent to the each weight order. Master roll weight is given by the following equation:

$$p_r = (D^2 - c^2)\pi w G \tag{1}$$

where p_r is the master roll weight (in kg), D is the external diameter (in m), c is the center (internal diameter in m), w is the master roll width (in m), and G is the paper density (in kg/m^3). With this, we can compute the number of rolls for an order:

$$n_r = \left\lceil \frac{p_i/w_i}{p_r/w} \right\rceil = \left\lceil \frac{p_i w}{p_r w_i} \right\rceil \tag{2}$$

where n_r is the number of rolls for the i-th order, p_i (in kg) is the weight for the i-th order, w_i (in m) is the width of the i-th order, p_r (in kg) is the master roll weight , and w (in m) is the master roll width.

2.1   Waste Optimization

The cutting schedule procedure is performed by selecting a random order width w_i from the order set and the number of times v it will be repeated in a combination, verifying that master roll unused part W be greater or equal to the that width $w_i v$. This means that we can include in a new cut, possibly several times, in a cutting combination if the total width is smaller than the unused part of the master roll. When the unused part W of the master roll is smaller than the smallest width in not included orders in a combination, then a cutting combination has been generated. The number of rolls for this combination is determined by the smallest number of rolls or an order included in that cutting combination (repeated widths are considered). With this, the number of rolls for the orders included in the combination is updated. The process continues until every order is satisfied. Table 1 shows an order list where R is equivalent the number of rolls fot the required weight.

Table 2 shows a list of cutting combinations or cutting schedule where w_p is the total width for that combination, R is the number of rolls to manufacture for that combination, ID is the order ID (see Table 1), w_i, $(i = 1, 2, 3)$ is the width of order ID, and v_i is the number of times that width is repeated in the combination.

Once the cutting schedule is generated, the waste for each combination is computed as follows:

$$W_k = W \frac{p_r}{w} n_{\max} \tag{3}$$

Table 1. Cutting orders.

ID	Width (cm)	Weight (kg)	R	ID	Width (cm)	Weight (kg)	R
0	55.0	2035	6	19	83.0	1840	4
1	145.0	5365	6	20	68.5	20376	47
2	50.0	2267	8	21	79.0	3661	8
3	150.0	1125	2	22	69.0	3190	8
4	135.0	5108	6	23	79.0	3652	8
5	80.0	5386	11	24	83.0	3432	7
6	105.0	4030	6	25	91.5	13240	23
7	90.0	2842	5	26	85.0	5702	11
8	100.0	3158	5	27	81.0	15405	30
9	55.0	8137	24	28	24.0	1742	12
10	51.0	34295	105	29	100.0	8162	13
11	70.0	3225	8	30	64.0	15000	37
12	70.0	3225	8	31	181.0	5500	5
13	69.0	2084	5	32	181.0	20000	18
14	72.0	2175	5	33	201.0	17000	14
15	59.5	6015	16	34	195.6	20000	16
16	87.0	2026	4	35	200.0	150000	117
17	87.0	3172	6	36	201.0	80000	63
18	64.5	9529	24	37	181.0	40000	35

where W_k is the waste for k-th cutting combination, W is the master roll unused part, p_r is the master roll weight, w is the master roll width, and n_{max} is the maximum number of rolls to manufacture for that combination. The total waste W_T is the sum of each combination waste W_k:

$$W_T = \sum_k W_k \tag{4}$$

which is the *objective funtion* for our optimization problem.

Optimization is performed only with order widths which are feasible to combine, i.e., if there is an order width that satisfies:

$$w_i + w_{min} > w, \tag{5}$$

where w_{min} is the smallest order width, then, it is not considered for optimization since the waste generated by these orders is fixed with or without optimization.

2.2   Cutting Blade Movements Optimization

The initial input solution for the cutting blade movements optimization is the resulting optimized cutting schedule from the previous stage. Our new objective function is the difference in position of the cutting blades from combination i and cutting blades from combination $i + 1$, for $i = 0, \ldots, n_p - 1$, where n_p is the number of combinations in the cutting schedule.

The generation of a new solution state for this stage is similar to previous optimization stage, i.e., two cutting combinations are randomly selected with variable distance

Table 2. One possible cutting schedule for orders in Table 1.

j	w_p	R	ID	w_1	v_1	ID	w_2	v_2	ID	w_3	v_3
0	199.0	6	6	105.0	1	12	70.0	1	28	24.0	1
1	195.0	1	12	70.0	2	0	55.0	1			
2	200.0	5	8	100.0	1	29	100.0	1			
3	200.0	4	29	100.0	2						
4	198.0	8	2	50.0	1	23	79.0	1	22	69.0	1
5	197.0	5	7	90.0	1	24	83.0	1	28	24.0	1
6	174.0	1	3	150.0	1	28	24.0	1			
7	190.0	6	4	135.0	1	9	55.0	1			
8	200.5	30	20	68.5	1	27	81.0	1	10	51.0	1
9	170.0	5	26	85.0	2						
10	197.0	4	16	87.0	1	9	55.0	2			
11	196.0	6	1	145.0	1	10	51.0	1			
12	199.0	8	15	59.5	2	5	80.0	1			
13	160.0	1	5	80.0	2						
14	193.5	8	18	64.5	3						
15	185.0	5	10	51.0	1	21	79.0	1	0	55.0	1
16	198.0	3	21	79.0	1	30	64.0	1	9	55.0	1
17	196.5	17	30	64.0	2	20	68.5	1			
18	201.0	1	3	150.0	1	10	51.0	1			
19	195.0	1	26	85.0	1	9	55.0	2			
20	186.0	1	9	55.0	1	5	80.0	1	10	51.0	1
21	193.5	23	25	91.5	1	10	51.0	2			
22	195.0	2	10	51.0	1	14	72.0	2			
23	195.0	4	11	70.0	2	9	55.0	1			
24	170.0	4	17	87.0	1	19	83.0	1			
25	185.0	2	24	83.0	1	10	51.0	2			
26	153.0	3	10	51.0	3						
27	192.0	1	14	72.0	1	13	69.0	1	10	51.0	1
28	138.0	2	13	69.0	2						
29	174.0	1	17	87.0	2						

between them and then their positions are exchanged and then two different order width are randomly selected and exchange.

Simulated annealing algorithm has been successfully used in robotics [8,9] and scheduling [10,11,12] applications. The following section the algorithm is described and its requirements for implementation in our problem.

2.3 Simulated Annealing Algorithm

Simulated annealing is basically an iterative improvement strategy augmented by a criterion for occasionally accepting higher cost configurations [14,7]. Given a cost function $C(\mathbf{z})$ (analog to energy) and an initial solution or state $\mathbf{z}_0$, the iterative improvement approach seeks to improve the current solution by randomly perturbing $\mathbf{z}_0$. The Metropolis algorithm [7] was used for acceptance/rejection of the new state $\mathbf{z}'$ at a given temperature T, i.e.,

- randomly perturb $\mathbf{z}$ to obtain $\mathbf{z}'$, and calculate the corresponding change in cost $\delta C = \mathbf{z}' - \mathbf{z}$
- if $\delta C < 0$, accept the state
- if $\delta C > 0$, accept the state with probability

$$P(\delta C) = \exp\left(-\delta C / T\right), \tag{6}$$

this represents the *acceptance-rejection loop* or *Markov chain* of the SA algorithm. The acceptance criterion is implemented by generating a random number, $\rho \in [0, 1]$ and comparing it to $P(\delta C)$; if $\rho < P(\delta C)$, then the new state is accepted. The outer loop of the algorithm is referred to as the *cooling schedule*, and specifies the equation by which the temperature is decreased. The algorithm terminates when the cost function remains approximately unchanged, i.e., for n_{no} consecutive outer loop iterations.

Any implementation of simulated annealing generally requires four components:

1. **Problem configuration** (domain over which the solution will be sought).
2. **Neighborhood definition** (which governs the nature and magnitude of allowable perturbations).
3. **Cost function**.
4. **Cooling schedule** (which controls both the rate of temperature decrement and the number of inner loop iterations).

The domain for our problem is the set of cutting combinations. The objective or cost function is describe in the previous Section. The neighborhood function used for this implementation is the same used by [8] where two orders are randomly selected with the distance between them cooled, i.e. decreased as the temperature decreases. Once selected the two orders, their positions are exchange and another cutting schedule is generated. For the cutting blade movements optimization the relative distance between two randomly selected cutting combinations is also cooled. The allowable perturbations are reduced by the following limiting function

$$\epsilon = \epsilon_{\max} \frac{\log(T - T_f)}{\log(T_0 - T_f)} \tag{7}$$

where $\epsilon_{\max}$ is an input parameter and specifies the maximum distance between two elements in a list, and T, T_0, T_f are the current, initial and final temperatures, respectively.

The cooling schedule in this implementation is the same *hybrid* one introduced by [8] in which both the temperature and the inner loop criterion vary continuously through the annealing process [2]. The outer loop behaves nominally as a constant decrement factor,

$$T_{i+1} = \alpha T_i \tag{8}$$

where $\alpha = 0.9$ for this paper. The temperature throughout the inner loop is allowed to vary proportionally with the current optimal value of the cost function. So, denoting the inner loop index as j, the temperature is modified when a state is accepted, i.e,

$$T_j = \frac{C_j}{C_{\text{last}}} T_{\text{last}} \tag{9}$$

where C_{last} and T_{last} are the cost and temperature associated with the last accepted state. Note that at high temperatures, a high percentage of states are accepted, so the temperature can fluctuate by a substantial magnitude within the inner loop.

The following function was used to determine the number of acceptance-rejection loop iterations,

$$N_{\text{in}} = N_{\text{dof}} \left[2 + 8 \left(1 - \frac{\log(T - T_f)}{\log(T_0 - T_f)} \right) \right] \qquad (10)$$

where N_{dof} is the number of degrees of freedom of the system.

The initial temperature must be chosen such that the system has sufficient energy to visit the entire solution space. The system is sufficiently melted if a large percentage, i.e. 80%, of state transitions are accepted. If the initial guess for the temperature yields less than this percentage, T_0 can be scaled linearly and the process repeated. The algorithm will proceed to a reasonable solution when there is excessive energy; it is simply less computationally efficient. Besides the stopping criterion mentioned above, which indicates convergence to a global minimum, the algorithm is also terminated by setting a final temperature given by

$$T_f = \alpha^{N_{\text{out}}} T_0 \qquad (11)$$

where N_{out} is the number of outer loop iterations and is given as data to our problem.

3   Results

The source language for our implementation is in Python for Windows in a Pentium II @400 Mhz with 256 MB RAM. All tests were performed with real data given by the paper manufacturing company in which this research was carried out.

The initial data is shown in Table 1 and for a machine of 2.025 m maximum width and 3 cutting blades.

The present cutting schedule procedure generated a total waste of 17,628.5 kg and 16,742.0 kg to inventory and it took almost three hours. The system using the simulated annealing algorithm generated a total waste of 9,614.7 kg without the need of production cuts to inventory in about eight minutes. The resulting waste is about 46% less than the manual procedure and considering production to inventory also as waste, it is about 72% smaller. The total production for the test is 211,317.3 kg. This means that the total waste compare to the total production decreased from 8.34% to 4.55% with considering production to inventory as waste. If we consider it, it went down from 16.26% to 4.55%. Now, if the paper production cost of 1,000 kg is $400 USD, the SA system generated a total savings amount of $3,205 USD and considering inventory it was $9,902 USD. If we know each machine production rate, the previous savings are equivalent to $1,967 USD/day and considering the inventory to $6,075 USD/day.

The cutting blade movements optimization problem is shown in Fig. 2. The SA system generated a 41% decrease in total cutting blade movements compared to the manual procedure. Fig. 2(a) shows cutting blade movements of the resulting cutting schedule using the manual procedure and Fig. 2(b) shows the same but using the SA system. The last one shows a smoother distribution and smaller movements for the cutting schedule. Savings in cutting blade movements were an average of 48% smaller than the manual procedure due mainly to the lack of optimization in this part.

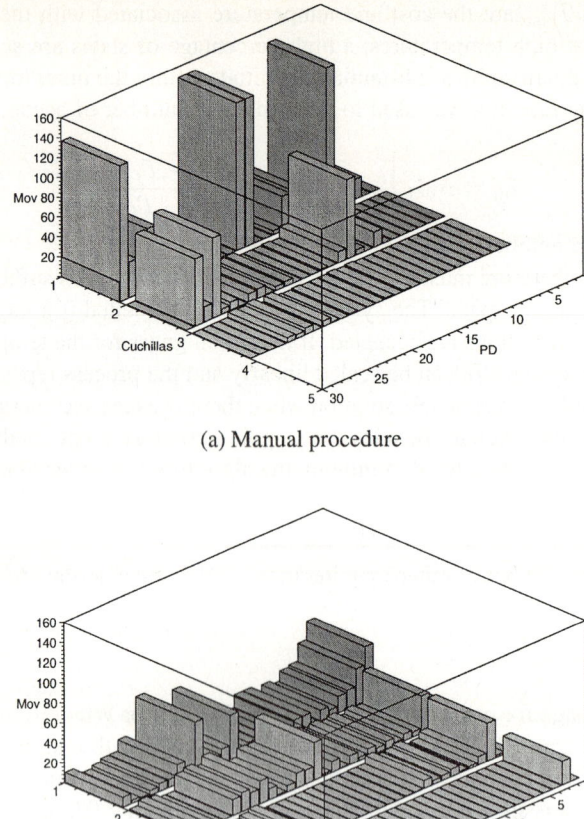

(a) Manual procedure

(b) SA system

Fig. 2. Cutting blade movements

Other test were performed with orders for four different cutting machines (main difference in maximum width) and for four months. The average savings in total waste was 900,000 kg using the SA system which represented a 22% savings compared to the manual procedure. This represents a $360,000 USD in savings. However, production that went directly to inventory was 12,000,000 kg which represents $4,800,000 USD. If we consider that the SA system does not generate production to inventory (unless it is specified), the total savings for four months with four cutting machines was **$5,160,000 USD**.

4   Conclusions

All result were validated by people in charge of obtaining the cutting schedule at the paper manufacturing company. Savings generated by the SA system allows not only an optimization of the total waste but also in the elimination of production to inventory. The production to inventory resulted as the actual problem the company had. Even though some inventory production could be sold in the future, this production was generated to minimize the total waste during the generation of the cutting schedule. By using the system, it allows people from the company to spend more time in decision making, problem analysis and/or urgent orders since to obtain a cutting schedule takes about 10 minutes.

Cutting blade movements optimization was not performed in the manual procedure. The use of the SA system for this problem generates savings due to the increase in production rate a cutting machine. However, we do not include the analysis since we do not have access to that information.

The authors are currently working in a global optimal cutting schedule generation system that will allow the use of several cutting machines (different width) to process an order list to generate the cutting schedule.

References

1. R.E. Burkard and F. Rendl. A thermodynamically motivated simulation procedure for combinatorial optimization problems. *European J. of Oper. Res.*, (17):169–174, 1984.
2. T. Elperin. Monte carlo structural optimization in discrete variables with annealing algorithm. *Int. J. for Numerical Methods in Eng.*, 1988.
3. S. B. Gelfand and S. K. Mitter. Analysis of simulated annealing for optimization. In *Proc. 24th Conf. on Decision and Control*, pages 779–786, December 1985.
4. G. G. E. Gielen, Herman C. C. Walscharts, and W. M. C. Sansen. Analog circuit design optimization based on symbolic simulation and simulated annealing. *IEEE Journal of Solid-State Circuits*, (25):707–713, June 1990.
5. S. Kirkpatrick, C.D. Gelatt, and M.P. Vecchi. Optimization by simulated annealing. *Science*, 220(4598):671–680, 1983.
6. S. Kirkpatrick and G. Toulouse. Configuration space analysis of travelling salesman problems. *J. Physique*, (46):1277–1292, 1985.
7. A. Malhotra, J. H. Oliver, and W. Tu. Synthesis of spatially and intrinsically constrained curves using simulated annealing. In *ASME Advances in Design Automation*, number 32, pages 145–155, 1991.
8. Horacio Martínez-Alfaro and Donald. R. Flugrad. Collission-free path planning of robots and/or AGVs using B-splines and simulated annealing. In *ASME 23rd Biennial Mechanisms Conference*, Minneapolis, September 1994.
9. Horacio Martínez-Alfaro and Antonio Ulloa-Pérez. Computing near optimal paths in C-space using simulated annealing. In *ASME Design Engineering Technical Conference/24th Biennial Mechanisms Conference*, Irvine, CA, 1996.
10. Horacio Martínez-Alfaro and Gerardo Flores-Terán. Solving the classroom assignment problem with simulated annealing. In *IEEE Int. Conf. On Systems, Man, & Cybernetics*, San Diego, CA, 1998.
11. Horacio Martínez-Alfaro, Homero Valdez, and Jaime Ortega. Linkage synthesis of a four-bar mechanism for n precision points using simulated annealing. In *ASME Design Engineering Technical Conferences/25th Biennial Mecanisms and Robotics Conference*, Atlanta, 1998.
12. Horacio Martínez-Alfaro, Homero Valdez, and Jaime Ortega. Using simulated annealing to minimize operational costs in the steel making industry. In *IEEE Int. Conf. On Systems, Man, & Cybernetics*, San Diego, 1998.

13. N. Metropolis, A. Rosenbluth, M. Rosenbluth, and A. Teller. Equations of state calculations by fast computing machines. *J. of Chemical Physics*, (21):1087–1091, 1953.

14. R.A. Rutenbar. Simulated annealing algorithms: An overview. *IEEE Circuits and Devices*, pages 19–26, January 1989.

15. P. J. M. van Laarhoven and E. H. L. Aarts. *Simulated Annealing: Theory and Applications*. D. Reidel Pub. Co., Dordrecht, Holland, 1987.

16. D. Vanderbilt and S.G. Louie. A monte carlo simulated annealing approach to optmization over continuous variables. *J. Comput. Phys.*, (36):259–271, 1984.

Extracting Temporal Patterns from Time Series Data Bases for Prediction of Electrical Demand

J. Jesús Rico[1], Juan J. Flores[1], Constantino Sotomane[2], and Félix Calderón[1]

[1] División de Estudios de Postgrado
Facultad de Ingeniería Eléctrica
Universidad Michoacana
Morelia, Mexico
{jerico,juanf,calderon}@zeus.umich.mx
[2] Universidade Eduardo Mondlane
Centro de Informatica
Maputo, Mozambique
sotomane@nambu.uem.mz

Abstract. In this paper we present a technique for prediction of electrical demand based on multiple models. The multiple models are composed by several local models, each one describing a region of behavior of the system, called operation regime. The multiple models approach developed in this work is applied to predict electrical load 24 hours ahead. Data of electrical load from the state of California that include an approximate period of 2 years was used as a case of study. The concept of multiple model implemented in the present work is also characterized by the combination of several techniques. Two important techniques are applied in the construction of multiple models: Regularization and the Knowledge Discovery in Data Bases (KDD) techniques. KDD is used to identify the operation regime of electrical load time series.

1 Introduction

Depending on the length of the study, forecasting of electrical demand can be divided in long-term forecasting (5 to 10 years), medium-term forecasting (months to 5 years), and short-term forecasting (hours to months) [13].

Several techniques for load forecasting have been developed over the years (e.g. regressive models, stochastic time series, time-space models, expert systems, and artificial neural networks, among others). None of them have been able to produce satisfactory models for electrical demand forecasting. Short-term demand forecasting of electricity depends mainly on the weather, which is stochastic by nature [15].

Another factor, occurring in several countries, that makes short-term forecasting very important is the new trend to produce electrical markets [13]. This situation is a natural consequence of the technological development in the electrical industry, which has reduced production costs and created a new way to produce electricity. These are the reasons why the electrical market is no longer a monopoly, as it was in the 80´s. This revolution in the electricity industry aims to a decentralized and more competitive industry [15]. This scenario has spawned the need for new, better, and more accurate, tools to model and analyze electrical demand. Modeling and analysis

R. Monroy et al. (Eds.): MICAI 2004, LNAI 2972, pp. 21–29, 2004.

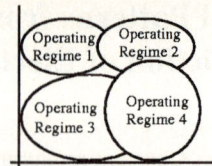

Fig. 1. Operation Regimes

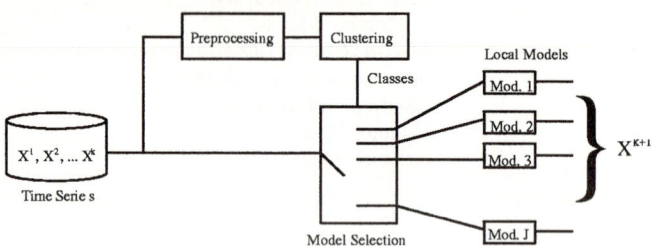

Fig. 2. Multi-models Conceptual Scheme

are important in several areas of the electrical industry; in particular in the analysis of the structure of electrical markets and forecasting the price of electricity [15].

This paper presents a methodology to predict electrical demand 24 hours ahead, using a technique called multi-models. Multi-models uses data mining to cluster the demand data and develops a local model for each cluster.

2   Operation Regimes and Multi-models

This section briefly describes the technique used to develop the forecasting model proposed in this paper. We call this methodology multi-models, for it combines several local models to form the global model of the system. This methodology assumes that systems can be decomposed in several regions, called operation regimes, exhibiting different behaviors (see Figure 1).

Figure 2 illustrates the concept of multi-models. In figure 2, X^k are the known data, X^{k+1} are the data to predict and J indicates the operation regime.

Our implementation partitions the time-series data-base in operation regimes using a clustering algorithm. Clustering, a concept borrowed from data-mining, is performed using AutoClass, a program based on stochastic classification.

Assuming that the relationship of the electrical load of those days belonging to the same operation regime is linear, and that the variation of the load characteristics of adjacent days is not large (we assume that adjacent days belong to the same operation regime), we apply a linear model for each operation regime. To achieve the second assumption, we regularize the time-series using a first order membrane filter in order to find the load tendency curve. Both assumptions lead to a great simplification in the construction of the model. The first simplification allows us to use linear models in all operation regimes; the second one allows us to use the local model for today to predict tomorrow's behavior.

The main motivation of developing multi-models is the need to find a robust and precise forecasting method for electrical load. Most forecasting methods, particularly the statistical and linear ones, are not robust to abrupt system changes. These facts indicate that those models work well only within a narrow space of operation conditions. As a solution to this problem, several models capable of adaptation to abrupt system changes have been developed. Nevertheless, those techniques require more complex models which are harder to analyze.

The basic concept of multi-models combines a set of models, where each model describes a limited part of the system that behaves specifically (an operation regime) [10]. We call local model to each model corresponding to an operation regime, and global model to a holistic model. The main advantages of the use of multi-models are (see [9] and [10]):

- Resulting models are simpler, because there are only a few relevant local phenomena. Modeling a caotic system with a holistic model can be impossible, or the accuracy of the prediction of that model would be unacceptable.
- The framework works for any kind of representation used for local models. A direct consequence of this is that the framework forms a base for the production of hybrid models.

According to [9] and [10], the multi-model problem can be decomposed into the following phases:

- Decomposition of the global system in operation regimes.
- Identification of the local model´s structures for each operation regime.
- Identification of the parameters of the local models.
- Combination of the local models to form the global model (an implicit step).

Given a time-series data-base of electrical load X^k, we estimate the values X^{k+1} that will occur in the future, assuming there exists a relation between X^{k+1} and X^k, given in general by equation 1.

$$X^{k+1} = f\left(X^k\right) \tag{1}$$

Since the system is decomposed in several operation regimes, f will be composed by a set of simpler functions f_j, each of them describing a given operation regime. Formally, this idea can be expressed as in eq. 2.

$$X^{k+1} = \begin{cases} f_1\left(X_1^k\right) \text{ if OR} = 1 \\ f_2\left(X_1^k\right) \text{ if OR} = 2 \\ \quad\cdots \\ f_J\left(X_1^k\right) \text{ if OR} = J \end{cases} \tag{2}$$

Where j=1,2, …, J are the operation regimes (OR).

3 Regularization

In this section we describe an adaptable filtering technique that allows us to estimate the low frequency components of the time-series. This technique, called regularization, is used the trend in the electrical load. That is, it decomposes the time-series in two components: a tendency signal and a signal without a tendency.

The regularized signal Z is obtained by minimizing equation 1. Where E(Z) is the energy needed to approximate the values of Z to h (see equation 3).

$$E(Z) = \sum_{k=1}^{N}\left(h^k - Z^k\right) + \lambda\sum_{k=1}^{N-1}\left(Z^{k+1} - Z^k\right) \tag{3}$$

Where N is the sample size, h is the observed signal and Z is the signal to be estimated (the trend signal). The first term of equation 3 represents the data constraints specifying that the smooth signal Z^k must not bee too different to the observed signal h^k. The second term represents the smoothing constraint, stating that neighboring values must be similar; if λ (the regularization constant) is large, Z^k will be very smooth, and therefore very different than h^k.

The smoothing constraint from equation 3 is an approximation of the gradient magnitude:

$$\left|Z^{k+1} - Z^k\right|^2 \approx \left|\nabla_z\right|^2 \tag{4}$$

By algebraic manipulation, from equation 4, we can obtain the values of Z^k that minimizes the energy E(Z), and solving for h^k we have.

$$h^k = -\lambda Z^{k-1} + (1+2\lambda)Z^k - \lambda Z^{k+1} \tag{5}$$

The trend curve is given by the values of vector Z, computed using equation 4, expressed using linear algebra.

$$Z = M^{-1}H \tag{6}$$

Note that M is a large sparce matrix. We apply the Fourier Transform to both members of equation 5, yielding equation 7.

$$H(w) = Z(w)\left[1 + \lambda\left(2 - e^{-jw} - e^{jw}\right)\right] \tag{7}$$

Simplifying,

$$F(w) = \frac{Z(w)}{H(w)} = \frac{1}{1 + 2\lambda(1 - Cos(w))} \tag{8}$$

$$Z(w) = F(w)H(w) = \frac{1}{1 + 2\lambda(1 - Cos(w))}H(w) \tag{9}$$

Equation 8 is the frequency response of the first order membrane filter, and equation 9 represents the convolution between signal h and the membrane filter.

4 Clustering

Operation regimes are detected using a clustering algorithm, taken from the field of Knowledge Discovery and Data-Mining (KDD) (for a detailed description of the KDD process, see [5, 1, and 8]). In this phase we used clustering as our Data-Mining algorithm. In general terms, clustering partitions a group of objects in subgroups, where the elements of each subgroup are similar among them and dissimilar compared to members of other subgroups [5, 3, and 15]. The concept of similarity may take different meanings; for instance, shape, color, size, etc. (see [14 and 3]). In many algorithms and applications, similarity is defined in terms of metric distances [6].

Clustering is a form of non-supervised learning, where the goal is to find structures in the data in the form of natural groups. This process requires data to be defined in terms of attributes relevant to the characteristics we want the classification to be based upon.

An example of an application that performs clustering is AutoClass. AutoClass is a clustering algorithm based on Bayesian theory, using the classical model Finite Distribution Merging (see [5]). This model states that each instance belongs to one and only one unknown class from a set C_j of J classes, with probability given by equation 10.

$$P\big(X_i \in C_j \big| PI\big) \tag{10}$$

Where X_i is an instance, C_j is class j, PI is the a priori information including the class distribution model, the set of parameters of the distribution model, and the available search space.

Assuming the number of classes is known, AutoClass tries to maximize the a posteriori likelihood of the class partition model. With no information about the class membership, the program uses a variation of the Expectation Maximization (EM) algorithm [12] to approximate the solution to the problem. Equation 11 defines weights b_{ik}, used to compute the statistical values of the unknown class.

$$b_{ik} = \frac{P\big(X_i \big| X_i \in C_j, PI\big) P\big(X_i \in C_j \big| PI\big)}{\displaystyle\sum_{i=1}^{N} P\big(X_i \big| X_i \in C_j, PI\big) P\big(X_i \in C_j \big| PI\big)} \tag{11}$$

Where

$$\alpha_i = P\big(X_i \in C_j \big| PI\big), \quad 0 \le \alpha_i \le 1, \quad \sum_{j=1}^{J} \alpha_j = 1 \tag{12}$$

Equation 12 describes the statistical values of a normal distribution (number of classes, mean, and variance).

Using the statistical values computed from equations 12 and 13, we can estimate the weights. We repeat the process until convergence leads to the proper estimation of the parameters. The probability density function with a highest a posteriori likelihood is the final result [5 and 11].

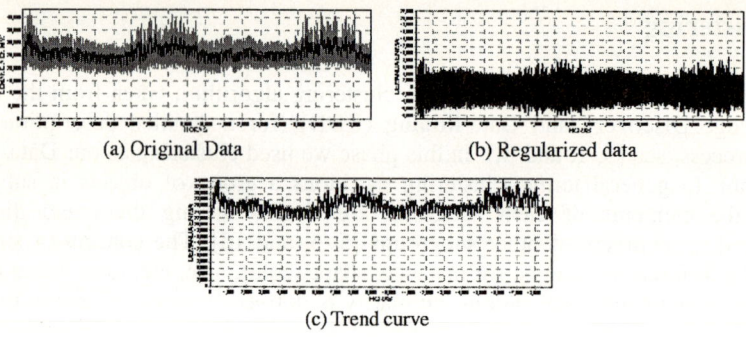

(a) Original Data   (b) Regularized data

(c) Trend curve

Fig. 3. Regularization

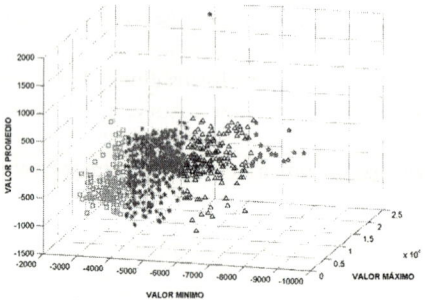

Fig. 4. Classes obtained using AutoClass

5   Case of Study

For our study case we took the data-base of the California ISO [2]; this data-base contains hourly measurements from September 1, 2000 to October 14th, 2002, for a total of 18,591 measurements. We processed and transformed the time-series into a matrix of 774 rows (days) and 3 columns (maximum, minimum, and average values). We took 744 days as the training set to predict day 745 (September 15th, 2002).

$$b_j = \sum_{i=1}^{n} b_{ij}, \quad \mu_{jk} = \frac{\sum_{i=1}^{n} b_{ij} x_{ik}}{b_j}, \quad \sigma^2_{jk} = \frac{\sum_{i=1}^{n} b_{ij}(x_{ik} - \mu_{jk})^2}{b_j} \tag{13}$$

The training set was subject to the following data-mining and forecasting process.

- Errors were corrected, missing and bad data were fixed.
- The time-series was regularized using the first order membrane filter, decomposing the time-series in trend and regularized data. Figure 3 shows the original data, the regularized data and the trend.
- The trend was predicted for day 745 using multiple-linear regression.

Using AutoClass, we found that day 745 belongs to class 1. Figure 4 shows the classification produced by AutoClass. Data mining is an iterative process; we are

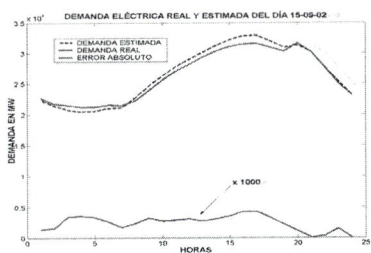

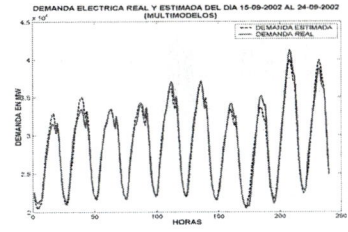

Fig. 5. Real Forecast for day 745 an Absolute Error

Fig. 6. Real and Estimated Forecast between 09/15/2002 and 09/24/2002

Table 1. Statistical parameters for the error

Parameter	σ	$\in(\%)$	ρ	$\varepsilon(\%)$	$\Sigma\in$
Value	2.31	1.78	0.9904	10.17	1227

Table 2. Statistical Parameters for the Error in the California Model

Parámetro	σ	$\in(\%)$	ρ	$\varepsilon(\%)$	$\Sigma\in$
Multi-models	2.31	1.78	0.9904	10.17	1227
California Model	2.59	2.38	0.9888	11.78	1623.3

showing here, of course, only the last iteration of the classification process. In this process, data was exposed to AutoClass using several attributes; for instance, the Fourier components of each day, up to the fifth harmonic. None of them worked as well as the final one, where the attributes were maximum, minimum, and average values for each day.

Using linear regression, we forecasted the regularized load. Then added the predicted trend and the predicted regularized load for day 745, obtaining the real forecast, presented in Figure 5.

Using the same methodology, we forecasted load for days 746 to 774. Figure 6 shows the results for the first 10 forecasted days. That is, from September 15th, to September 24th, 2002.

Table 1 shows statistical parameters for the error estimation using multi-models in the period 09/15/2002 to 10/14/2002. Where σ is the standard deviation, $\in$ the mean absolute error, ρ the correlation coefficient between real and estimated load, ε the maximum absolute error, and $\Sigma\in$ the accumulated error in the same period (that is, the area integral of the load function during a day).

Figure 7 is the forecasting error histogram for a 30 day period. This histogram shows that the most frequent errors fall in the interval from 0 to 4%.

Our results were compared with those provided by the California ISO predictor. Table 2 shows the values of statistical parameters for the error estimation for the California model, Figure 8 shows a comparison between the prediction of both models, and Figure 9 shows the error histogram for the California model.

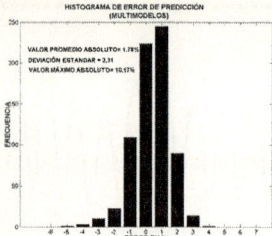
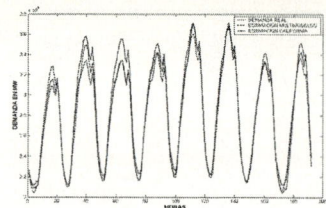

Fig. 7. Forecasting Error Histogram for a   **Fig. 8.** Comparing Predictions of Multi-models
30 Day Period   and the California Model

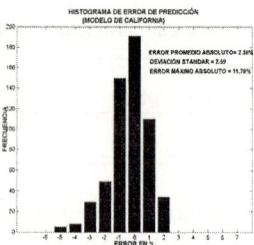

Fig. 9. Forecasting Error Histogram for a 30 Day Period for the California Model

6   Conclusions

In this work we present a technique we called multi-models. Using multi-models, we successfully forecasted a 24 hours ahead electrical demand on the California ISO model. That forecasting was done even without any weather information. The conceptual framework for developing multi-models is very general, and allows us to implement it using mixed techniques for the local models. In our implementation, we used least squares on linear models.

In order to be able to apply the concept of multi-models we needed to pre-process the time-series. First we regularized it, using a first-order membrane filter. This regularization got rid of any trend included in the signal, which was accounted for at the final step. After regularization, we applied clustering to classify the days according to their features. For each class (operation regime) a separate linear model was produced. The classification was done using Auto Class, a probabilistic clustering tool. At the end, we put together the forecast, including trend and the prediction done via a local model.

The results obtained were comparable with the model developed by the California ISO, and better in many situations.

Our next step is not to consider contiguous days in the same regime. This assumption leads to the paradoxical situation that all days must be in the same regime. Instead, we will model, perhaps using a neural network, the regime series, predicting what model to use for the next day, therefore getting even more accurate results.

References

1. Ankerst, Mihael. Visual Data Mining, http://www.dissertation.de. 2000.
2. California ISO. http://www.caiso.com.
3. Cheeseman, Peter. AutoClass Documentation. 2000.
4. Montgomery, Douglas C.; Johnson, Lynwood; Gardiner, A.; S., John, Forecasting and Time Series Analysis, second edition. Mcgraw-Hill, Singapore, 1990.
5. Fayyad, Usama M.; Piatetsky-Shapiro, Gregory; Padhraic, Smyth; Ramasamy, Uthurusamy. Advances in Knowledge Discovery and Data Mining. AAAI Press/MIT press. 1996.
6. Garcia Villanueva, Moisés. Detección de Conglomerados en Espacios Métricos. Universidad Michoacana de San Nicolás de Hidalgo, Facultad de Ingeniería eléctrica. Morelia, México. 2001.
7. Geman, S.; Geman D. Stochastic Relaxation, Gibbs Distribution and the Bayesian Restoration of Images. IEEE Trans. on Pattern Analysis and Machine Intelligence. 6, 721-741. 1994.
8. Hamilton, Haward; Gurak, Ergun; Findlater, Leah; Olive, Wayne. Knowledge Discovery in Databases. http://www.cs.uregina.ca/~dbd/cs831.html.
9. Jahansen, T. A. Operation Regime Based Process Modeling and Identification. Department of Engineering cybernetics. The Norwegian Institute of Technology. University of Trondheim. Norway. 1994.
10. Johansen, T. A.; Murray-Smith, R., Multiple Model Approach to Modeling Control. Chapter 1. http://www.dcs.gla.ac.uk/~rod/Publications.htm. 1997.
11. Li, C.; Biswas, G. Unsupervised Learning with Mixed Numeric and Nominal Data. IEEE Transactions on Knowledge and Data Engineering. Vol. 14, No. 4, pages 676-690. 2002.
12. Mclachlan, Geoffrey J.; Krishnan, Thriyambakam. The EM Algorithm and Extensions. John Wiley & sons. Canada. 1997.
13. Perry, Chris. Short-Term Load Forecasting Using Multiple Regression Analysis. Rural Electric Power conference. 1999.
14. Shen, Wei-Min. Autonomous Learning from the Environment. WH Freeman and co. 1994.
15. Weron, R.; Kozlowska, B.; Nowicka-Zragrajek. Modeling Electricity Loads in California: a Continuous-Time Approach. Physica A 299, 344-350, www.elsevier.com/locate/physa, 2001.

The Synergy between Classical and Soft-Computing Techniques for Time Series Prediction

I. Rojas[1], F. Rojas[1], H. Pomares[1], L.J. Herrera[1],
J. González[1], and O. Valenzuela[2]

[1] University of Granada, Department of Computer Architecture and Technology,
E.T.S. Computer Engineering, 18071 Granada, Spain
[2] University of Granada, Department of Applied Mathematics, Science faculty,
Granada, Spain

Abstract. A new method for extracting valuable process information from input-output data is presented in this paper using a pseudo-gaussian basis function neural network with regression weights. The proposed methodology produces dynamical radial basis function, able to modify the number of neuron within the hidden layer. Other important characteristic of the proposed neural system is that the activation of the hidden neurons is normalized, which, as described in the bibliography, provides better performance than non-normalization. The effectiveness of the method is illustrated through the development of dynamical models for a very well known benchmark, the synthetic time series Mackey-Glass.

1 Introduction

RBF networks form a special neural network architecture, which consists of three layers, namely the input, hidden and output layers. The input layer is only used to connect the network to its environment. Each node in the hidden layer has associated a centre, which is a vector with dimension equal to that of the network input data. Finally, the output layer is linear and serves as a summation unit:

$$\widetilde{F}_{RBF}(x_n) = \sum_{i=1}^{K} w_i \phi_i (x_n, c_i, \sigma_i) \tag{1}$$

where the radial basis functions ϕ_i are nonlinear functions, usually gaussian functions [9]. An alternative is to calculate the weighted average $\widetilde{F}^*_{RBF}$ of the radial basis function with the addition of lateral connections between the radial neurons. In normalized RBF neural networks, the output activity is normalized by the total input activity in the hidden layer.

The use of the second method has been presented in different studies as an approach which, due to its normalization properties, is very convenient and provides better performance than the weighted sum method for function approximation problems. In terms of smoothness, the weighted average provides better performance than the weighted sum [8,3].

R. Monroy et al. (Eds.): MICAI 2004, LNAI 2972, pp. 30–39, 2004.

Assuming that training data (x_i, y_i), $i = 1, 2, \ldots, D$ are available and have to be approximated, the RBF network training problem can be formulated as an optimization problem, where the normalized root mean squared errors (NRMSE) between the true outputs and the network predictions must be minimized with respect to both the network structure (the number of nodes K in the hidden layer) and the network parameters (center, sigmas and output weights):

$$NRMSE = \sqrt{\frac{\overline{e^2}}{\sigma_z^2}} \tag{2}$$

where σ_z^2 is the variance of the output data, and $\overline{e^2}$ is the mean-square error between the obtained and the desired output. The development of a single procedure that minimizes the above error taking into account the structure and the parameters that define the system, is rather difficult using the traditional optimization techniques. Most approaches presented in the bibliography consider a fixed RBF network structure and decompose the optimization of the parameters into two steps: In the first step the centres of the nodes are obtained (different paradigms can be used as cluster techniques, genetic algorithms, etc .) and in the second step, the connection weights are calculated using simple linear regression. Finally, a sequential learning algorithm is presented to adapt the structure of the network, in which it is possible to create new hidden units and also to detect and remove inactive units.

In this paper we propose to use a pseudo-gaussian function for the nonlinear function within the hidden unit. The output of a hidden neuron is computed as:

$$\phi_i(x) = \prod_v \varphi_{i,v}(x^v)$$

$$\varphi_{i,v}(x^v) = \begin{cases} e^{-\frac{\left(x^v - c_i^v\right)^2}{\sigma_{i,-}^v}} & -\infty < x \leq c_i^v \\ e^{-\frac{\left(x^v - c_i^v\right)^2}{\sigma_{i,+}^v}} & c_i^v < x < \infty \end{cases} \tag{3}$$

The index i runs over the number of neurons (K) while v runs over the dimension of the input space ($v \in [1, D]$). The behaviour of classical gaussian functions and the new PG-RBF in two dimensions is illustrated in Fig. 1 and Fig. 2.

The weights connecting the activation of the hidden units with the output of the neural system, instead of being single parameters, are functions of the input variables. Therefore, the w_i are given by:

$$w_i = \sum_v b_i^v x^v + b_i^0 \tag{4}$$

where b_i^v are single parameters.

The behaviour of the new PGBF in two dimensions is illustrated in Fig.1.

Therefore, the structure of the neural system proposed is modified using a pseudo-gaussian function (PG) in which two scaling parameters σ are introduced, which eliminate the symmetry restriction and provide the neurons in the hidden

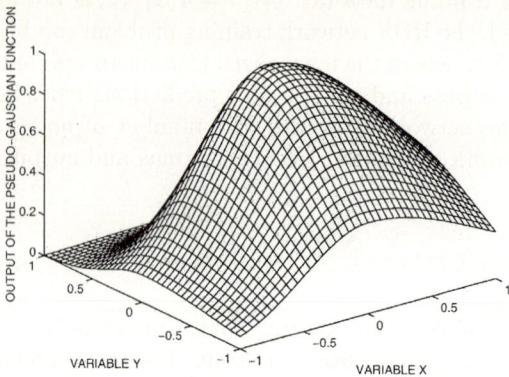

Fig. 1. 3-D behaviour of a pseudo-gaussian function for two inputs

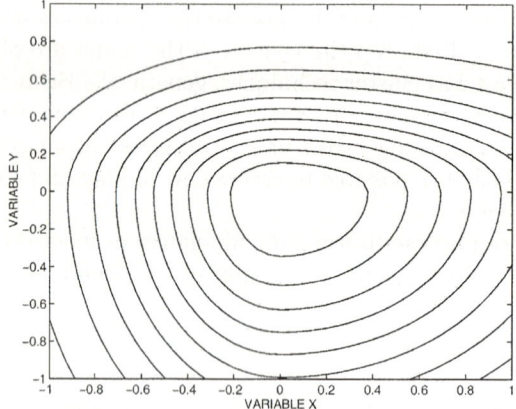

Fig. 2. Contour of a pseudo-gaussian function for two inputs

layer with greater flexibility for function approximation. Other important characteristics of the proposed neural system are that the activation of the hidden neurons is normalized and that instead of using a single parameter for the output weights, these are functions of the input variables which leads to a significant reduction in the number of hidden units compared with the classical RBF network.

2   Sequential Learning Using PGBF Network

Learning in the PGBF consists in determining the minimum necessary number of neuron units, and in adjusting the parameters of each individual hidden neuron, given a set of data (x_n, y_n)[5]. The sequential learning algorithm starts with only one hidden node and creates additional neurons based on the novelty (innovation) in the observations which arrive sequentially. The decision as to whether a datum should be deemed novel is based on the following conditions:

$$e_n = \left| y_n - \widetilde{F}^*_{RBF} \right| > \xi$$
$$\beta_{max} = \max_i (\phi_i) > \zeta \tag{5}$$

If both conditions are satisfied, then the data is considered to be novel and therefore a new hidden neuron is added to the network. This process continues until a maximum number of hidden neurons is reached. The parameters ξ and ζ are thresholds to be selected appropriately for each problem. The first condition states that the error must be significant and the second deals with the activation of the nonlinear neurons. The parameters of the new hidden node are determined initially as follows:

$$k = k + 1$$
$$b^v_K = \begin{cases} y_n - \widetilde{F}^*_{RBF} & \text{if } v = 0 \\ 0 & \text{otherwise} \end{cases}$$
$$c_K = x_n; (c^v_K = x^v_n, \forall v \in [1, D])$$
$$\sigma^v_{K,+} = \sigma^v_{K,-} = \gamma \, \sigma_{init} \min_{i=1,\ldots,K-1} \| x_n - c_i \| \tag{6}$$

where γ is an overlap factor that determines the amount of overlap of the data considered as novel and the nearest centre of a neuron. If an observation has no novelty then the existing parameters of the network are adjusted by a gradient descent algorithm to fit that observation. We propose a pruning strategy that can detect and remove hidden neurons, which although active initially, may subsequently end up contributing little to the network output. Then a more streamlined neural network can be constructed as learning progresses. For this purpose, three cases will be considered:

- (a) Pruning the hidden units that make very little contribution to the overall network output for the whole data set. Pruning removes a hidden unit i when:
$$\theta_i = \left[\sum_{n=1}^N \phi_i(x_n) \right] < \chi_1; \text{ where } \chi_1 \text{ is a threshold.}$$
- (b) Pruning hidden units which have a very small activation region. These units obviously represent an overtrained learning. A neuron i having very low values of $\sigma^v_{i,+} + \sigma^v_{i,-}$ in the different dimensions of the input space will be removed: $\sum_v \left(\sigma^v_{i,+} + \sigma^v_{i,-} \right) < \chi_2$
- (c) Pruning hidden units which have a very similar activation to other neurons in the neural system. To achieve this, we define the vectors $\psi_{i=1\ldots N}$, where N is the number of input/output vectors presented, such that: $\psi_i = [\phi_i(x_1), \phi_i(x_2), \ldots, \phi_i(x_n)]$. As a guide to determine when two neurons present similar behaviour, this can be expressed in terms of the inner product $\psi_i \cdot \psi_j < \chi_3$. If the inner product is near one then ψ_i and ψ_j are both attempting to do nearly the same job (they possess a very similar activation level for the same input values). In this case, they directly compete in the sense that only one of these neurons is selected and therefore the other one is removed.

If any of these conditions are fulfilled for a particular neuron, the neuron is automatically removed.

The final algorithm is summarized below:

Step 1: Initially, no hidden neurons exist.

Step 2: Set $n = 0$, $K = 0$, $h = 1$, where n, K and h are the number of patterns presented to the network, the number of hidden neurons and the number of learning cycles, respectively. Set the effective radius $\cdot h$ Set the maximum number of hidden neurons $MaxNeuron$.

Step 3: For each observation (x_n, y_n) compute:

a) the overall network output:

$$\widetilde{F}_{RBF}(x_n) = \frac{\sum\limits_{i=1}^{K} w_i \phi_i (x_n, c_i, \sigma_i)}{\sum\limits_{i=1}^{K} \phi_i (x_n, c_i, \sigma_i)} = \frac{\overline{Num}}{\overline{Den}} \tag{7}$$

b) the parameter required for the evaluation of the novelty of the observation; the error $e_n = \left| y_n - \widetilde{F}_{RBF}^* \right|$ and the maximum degree of activation β_{max}. If $((e_n > \xi)$ and $(\beta_{max} < \cdot h)$ and $(K < MaxNeuron))$ allocate a new hidden unit with parameters:

$$k = k + 1$$
$$b_K^v = \left\{ \begin{array}{ll} y_n - \widetilde{F}_{RBF}^* & \text{if } v = 0 \\ 0 & \text{otherwise} \end{array} \right\} \tag{8}$$
$$c_K = x_n; (c_K^v = x_n^v, \forall v \in [1, D])$$
$$\sigma_{K,+}^v = \sigma_{K,-}^v = \gamma \, \sigma_{init} \min_{i=1,\ldots,K-1} \|x_n - c_i\|$$

else apply the parameter learning for all the hidden nodes:

$$\Delta c_i^v = -\frac{\partial E}{\partial c_i^v} = -\frac{\partial E}{\partial \widetilde{F}_{RBF}^*} \frac{\partial \widetilde{F}_{RBF}}{\partial \phi_i} \frac{\partial \phi_i}{\partial c_i^v} =$$
$$= (y_n - \widetilde{F}_{RBF}^*) \frac{w_i - y_n}{Den} *$$
$$\left[2 \frac{x_n^v - c_i^v}{\sigma_{i,-}^v} e^{-\frac{(x_n - c_i^v)^2}{\sigma_{i,-}^v}} U(x_n^v; -\infty, c_i^v) + 2\frac{x_n^v - c_i^v}{\sigma_{i,+}^v} e^{\frac{(x_n^v - c_i^v)^2}{\sigma_{i,+}^v}} U(x_n^v; c_i^v, \infty) \right] \tag{9}$$

$$\Delta \sigma_{i,+}^v = -\frac{\partial E}{\partial \sigma_{i,+}^v} = -\frac{\partial E}{\partial \widetilde{F}_{RBF}^*} \frac{\partial \widetilde{F}_{RBF}}{\partial \phi_i} \frac{\partial \phi_i}{\partial \sigma_{i,+}^v} =$$
$$= (y_n - \widetilde{F}_{RBF}^*) \frac{w_i - y_n}{Den} \left[2 \frac{x_n^v - c_i^v}{\sigma_{i,+}^v} e^{\frac{(x_n^v - c_i^v)^2}{\sigma_{i,+}^v}} U(x_n^v; c_i^v, \infty) \right] \tag{10}$$

$$\Delta \sigma_{i,-}^v = (y_n - \widetilde{F}_{RBF}^*) \frac{w_i - y_n}{Den} \left[2 \frac{x_n^v - c_i^v}{\sigma_{i,-}^v} e^{-\frac{(x_n^v - c_i^v)^2}{\sigma_{i,-}^v}} U(x_n^v; -\infty, c_i^v) \right]$$

$$\Delta b_i^v = -\frac{\partial E}{\partial b_i^v} = -\frac{\partial E}{\partial \widetilde{F}_{RBF}^*} \frac{\partial \widetilde{F}_{RBF}}{\partial Num} \frac{\partial \overline{N}}{\partial w_i} \frac{\partial w_i}{\partial b_i^v} = (y_n - \widetilde{F}_{RBF}^*) \frac{1}{Den} \phi_i(x_n) x_n^v$$
$$\Delta b_i^0 = -\frac{\partial E}{\partial b_i^0} = -\frac{\partial E}{\partial \widetilde{F}_{RBF}^*} \frac{\partial \widetilde{F}_{RBF}}{\partial Num} \frac{\partial \overline{N}}{\partial w_i} \frac{\partial w_i}{\partial b_i^0} = (y_n - \widetilde{F}_{RBF}^*) \frac{1}{Den} \phi_i(x_n) \tag{11}$$

Step 4: If all the training patterns are presented, then increment the number of learning cycles ($h = h + 1$), and check the criteria for pruning hidden units:

$$\theta_i = \left[\sum_{n=1}^{N} \phi_i(x_n) \right] < \chi_1$$
$$\sum_v \left(\sigma_{i,+}^v + \sigma_{i,-}^v \right) < \chi_2 \qquad (12)$$
$$\psi_i \cdot \psi_j < \chi_3, \quad \forall j \neq i$$

Step 5: If the network shows satisfactory performance ($NRMSE < \pi^*$) then stop. Otherwise go to Step 3.

3   Using GA to Tune the Free Parameters of the Sequential Learning Algorithms

Stochastic algorithms, such as simulated annealing (SA) or genetic algorithms (GA) are more and more used for combinatorial optimization problems in diverse fields, and particularly in time series [6]. The main advantage of GA upon SA is that it works on a set of potential solutions instead of a single one; however, on particular applications, the major inconvenient lies in the difficulty of carrying out the crossover operator for generating feasible solutions with respect to the problem constraints. Insofar as this last point was not encountered in this study, a GA [2,4] has been retained.

Genetic algorithms are searching methods based upon the biological principles of natural selection and survival of the fittest introduced by Charles Darwin in his seminal work "The Origin of Species" (1859). They were rigorously introduced by [2]. GAs consist of a population of individuals that are possible solutions and each one of these individuals receives a reward, known as "fitness", that quantifies its suitability to solve the problem. In ordinary applications, fitness is simply the objective function. Individuals with better than average fitness receive greater opportunities to cross. On the other hand, low fitness individuals will have less chance to reproduce until they are extinguished. Consequently, the good features of the best individuals are disseminated over the generations. In other words, the most promising areas of the search space are explored, making the GA converge to the optimal or near optimal solution.

The 'reproduction' process by which the new individuals are derived consists in taking the chromosomes of the parents and subjecting them to crossover and mutation operations. The symbols (genes) from parents are combined into new chromosomes and afterwards, randomly selected symbols from these new chromosomes are altered in a simulation of the genetic recombination and mutation process of nature. The key ideas are thus the concept of a population of individual solutions being processed together and symbol configurations conferring greater fitness being combined in the 'offspring', in the hope of producing even better solutions.

As far as this paper is concerned, the main advantages of a GA strategy lie in:

- 1. The increased likelihood of finding the global minimum in a situation where local minima may abound.
- 2. The flexibility of the approach whereby the search for better solutions can be tailored to the problem in hand by, for example, choosing the genetic representation to suit the nature of the function being optimized.

In the Sequential learning algorithms proposed in section 2, there exist different parameter that should be tuned in order to obtain optimal solution. This parameters are: $\xi, \zeta, \chi_1, \chi_2, \chi_3$. One possibility is to make this work by trial and error, and the second possibility is to use the GA as an optimization tool that must decided the best value for this parameters. In the way described above, the relations between the different paradigms are described in figure 3:

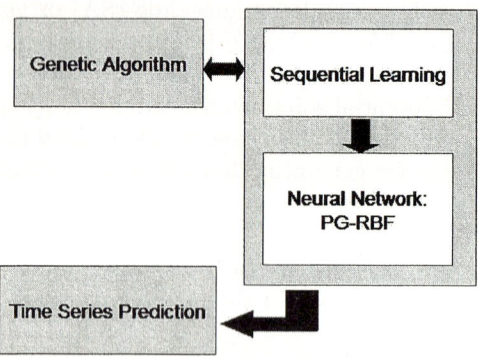

Fig. 3. Block diagram of the different paradigms used in the complete algorithm

4   Application to Time Series Prediction

In this subsection we attempt a short-term prediction by means of the algorithm presented in the above subsection with regard to the Mackey-Glass time series data. The Mackey-Glass chaotic time series is generated from the following delay differential equation:

$$\frac{dx(t)}{dt} = \frac{ax(t-\tau)}{1+x(t-\tau)^{10}} - bx(t) \tag{13}$$

When $\tau > 17$, the equation shows chaotic behaviour. Higher values of τ yield higher dimensional chaos. To make the comparisons with earlier work fair, we chose the parameters of $n = 4$ and $P = 6$.

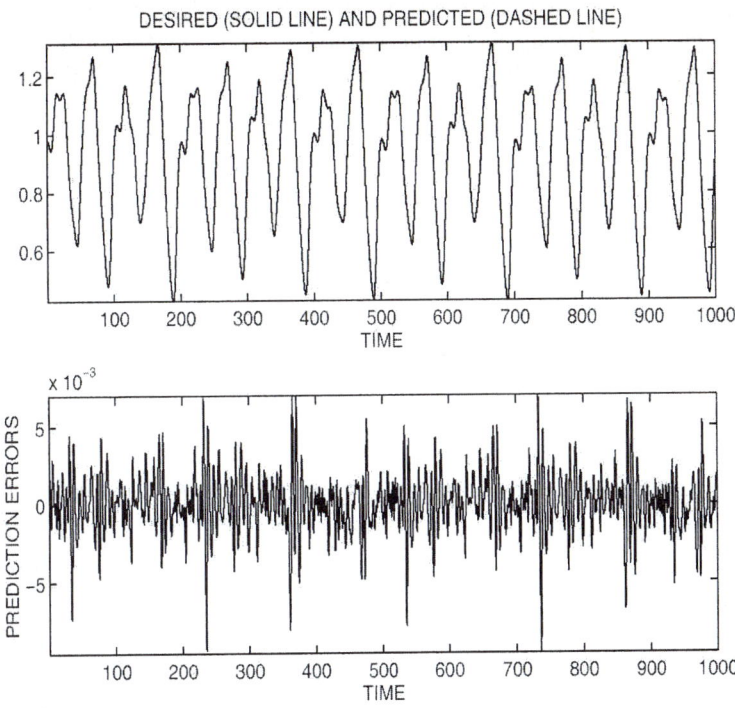

Fig. 4. 3-D Prediction step = 6 and number of neurons = 12. (a) Result of the original and predicted Mackey-Glass time series (which are indistinguishable). (b) prediction error

Table 1. Comparison results of the prediction error of different methods for prediction step equal to 6 (500 training data).

Method		Prediction Error (RMSE)
Auto Regressive Model		0.19
Cascade Correlation NN		0.06
Back-Prop. NN		0.02
6th-order Polynomial		0.04
Linear Predictive Method		0.55
Kim and Kim (Genetic Algorithm and Fuzzy System [6]	5 MFs	0.049206
	7 MFs	0.042275
	9 MFs	0.037873
ANFIS and Fuzzy System (16 rules)[6]		0.007
Classical RBF (with 23 neurons)[1]		0.0114
Our Approach (With 12 neurons)		0.0036 ± 0.0008

To compare our approach with earlier works, we chose the parameters presented in [6]. The experiment was performed 25 times, and we will show graphically one result that is close to the average error obtained. Fig4a) shows the predicted and desired values (dashed and continuous lines respectively) for both training and test data (which is indistinguishable from the time series here). As they are practically identical, the difference can only be seen on a finer scale (Fig4b)). Table 1 compares the prediction accuracy of different computational paradigms presented in the bibliography for this benchmark problem (including our proposal), for various fuzzy system structures, neural systems and genetic algorithms [4,5,6,7] (each reference use different number of decimal for the prediction, we take exactly the value presented).

5   Conclusion

This article describes a new structure to create a RBF neural network that uses regression weights to replace the constant weights normally used. These regression weights are assumed to be functions of the input variables. In this way the number of hidden units within a RBF neural network is reduced. A new type of nonlinear function is proposed: the pseudo-gaussian function. With this, the neural system gains flexibility, as the neurons possess an activation field that does not necessarily have to be symmetric with respect to the centre or to the location of the neuron in the input space. In addition to this new structure, we propose a sequential learning algorithm, which is able to adapt the structure of the network. This algorithm makes possible to create new hidden units and also to detect and remove inactive units. We have presented conditions to increase or decrease the number of neurons, based on the novelty of the data and on the overall behaviour of the neural system, respectively. The feasibility of the evolution and learning capability of the resulting algorithm for the neural network is demonstrated by predicting time series.

Acknowledgements. This work has been partially supported by the Spanish CICYT Project DPI2001-3219.

References

1. Cho, K.B.,Wang, B.H.: Radial basis function based adaptive fuzzy systems and their applications to system identification and prediction. Fuzzy Sets and Systems, vol.83. (1995) 325–339
2. Holland, J.H.: Adaptation in Natural and Artificial Systems. University of Michigan Press. (1975)
3. Benaim, M.: On functional approximation with normalized Gaussian units. Neural Comput. Vol.6, (1994)
4. Goldberg, D.E.: Genetic Algorithms in Search, Optimization & Machine Learning. Addison-Wesley (1989).

5. Karayiannis, N.B., Weiqun Mi, G.: Growing Radial Basis Neural Networks: Merging Supervised and Unsupervised Learning with Network Growth Techniques. IEEE Transaction on Neural Networks, vol.8, no.6. (1997) 1492–1506
6. Kim, D., Kim, C.: Forecasting time series with genetic fuzzy predictor ensemble. IEEE Transactions on Fuzzy Systems, vol.5, no.4. November (1997) 523–535
7. González, J., Rojas, I., Ortega, J., Pomares, H., Fernández, F.J., Díaz, A.F.: Multiobjetive evolutionary optimization of the size, shape and position parameters of radial basis function networks for function approximation. Accepted IEEE Transactions on Neural Networks,Vol.14, No.6, (2003)
8. Nowlan, S.: Maximum likelihood competitive learning. Proc. Neural Inform. Process. Systems. (1990) 574–582
9. Rojas, I., Anguita, M., Ros, E., Pomares, H., Valenzuela, O., Prieto, A.: What are the main factors involved in the design of a Radial Basis Function Network?. 6th European Symposium on Artificial Neural Network, ESANN'98.April 22-24, (1998). 1–6

A Naïve Geography Analyst System with Cognitive Support of Imagery Exploitation

Sung Baik [1], Jerzy Bala [2], Ali Hadjarian [3], and Peter Pachowicz [3]

[1] School of Computer Engineering
Sejong University, Seoul 143-747, KOREA
sbaik@sejong.ac.kr
[2] School of Information Technology and Engineering
George Mason University
Fairfax, VA 22030, U.S.A.
jbala@gmu.edu
[3] Sigma Systems Research, Inc.
Fairfax, VA 22032, U.S.A.
{ahadjarian,ppach}@sigma-sys.com

Abstract. This paper is concerned with the development of a naïve geography analyst system, which can provide the analysts with image exploitation techniques based on naïve geography and commonsense spatial reasoning. In the system approach, naïve geography information is acquired and represented jointly with imagery to form cognitively oriented interactive 3-D visualization and analysis space, and formal representations are generated by inferring a set of distributed graphical depictions representing naïve (commonsense) geographical space knowledge. The graphical representation of naïve geography information is functional in the sense that analysts can interact with it in ways that are analogous to corresponding interactions with real-world entities and settings in the spatial environments.

1 Introduction

The extraction of regions of interest from imagery relies heavily on the tedious work of human analysts who are trained individuals with an in-depth knowledge and expertise in combining various observations and clues for the purpose of spatial data collection and understanding. In particular, since the explosion of available imagery data recently overwhelms the imagery analysts and outpaces their ability to analyze it, analysts are facing the difficult tasks of evaluating diverse types of imagery, producing thoroughly analyzed and contextually based products, and at the same time meeting demanding deadline requirements. Consequently, the exploitation task is becoming the bottleneck for the imagery community. This situation generates an urgent need for new techniques and tools that can assist analysts in the transformation of this huge amount of data into a useful, operational, and tactical knowledge. To challenge the exploitation bottleneck, we need new tools that encompass a broad range of functional capabilities and utilize state-of-the-art exploitation techniques. These new techniques should greatly speed up the analysts' ability to access and integrate information. Examples of such techniques include:

R. Monroy et al. (Eds.): MICAI 2004, LNAI 2972, pp. 40–48, 2004.

1. Superimposition techniques in which symbolic information overlaid on displayed imagery could provide additional exploitation clues for analyst.
2. Automated exploitation aids which are automated target recognition (ATR) systems with a human in the exploitation loop.
3. Techniques incorporating cognitive aspects of exploitation processes.
4. Task management and interfacing techniques which incorporate mechanisms for efficiently dividing exploitation process tasks between people and computational systems.

This paper is concerned with the development of the *NG-Analyst* system, which can provide the analysts with image exploitation techniques based on Naïve Geography and commonsense spatial reasoning. Various publications related to NG (Naïve Geography) reveal a variety of explorative research activities dedicated mainly to the formalization of commonsense geographical reasoning.

Egenhofer and Mark [3] presented an initial definition of Naïve Geography, seen as the body of knowledge that people have about the surrounding geographic world. Primary theory [10] covers knowledge for which commonsense notions and scientific theories correspond. Formal models of commonsense knowledge examined by philosophers [14,15], and commonsense physics, or Naïve physics, have been an important topic in artificial intelligence for some time [5-7].

Smith claimed that the bulk of our common-sense beliefs is associated with a corresponding region of common-sense objects [13]. He suggested that it is erroneous to study beliefs, concepts and representations alone, as is done in cognitive science, and that it is necessary to study the objects and the object-domains to which the beliefs, concepts and representations relate.

Research in the area of spatial relations provides an example in which the combination and interplay of different methods generate useful results. The treatment of spatial relations within Naïve Geography must consider two complementary sources: (1) the cognitive and linguistic approach, investigating the terminology people use for spatial concepts [9,16] and human spatial behavior, judgments, and learning in general; and (2) the formal approach concentrating on mathematically based models, which can be implement on a computer[4,8,12]. The formalisms serve as hypotheses that may be evaluated with human-subject testing [11].

There has been considerable interest in the application of intelligent system techniques for the construction of Geographical Information Systems, spatial analysis and spatial decision support. Existing applications of Intelligent Systems techniques within GIS and related areas generally fall into one of three distinct classes:

1. Data access and query - Fuzzy Logic has been widely used to handle imprecision and reason about imprecise spatial concepts (e.g. near, high, etc) in text-based queries. Fuzzy spatial query is one area that has attracted a great deal of interest [17,18].
2. Spatial analysis and modeling - This is the main GIS-related application area of intelligent techniques such as Neural Networks, Genetic Algorithms, Rule-based Systems, and Intelligent front ends.
3. Expert Systems - Expert systems have been extensively assessed and used for decision support and knowledge encapsulation [2]. Fuzzy logic has also attracted a great deal of interest in recent years with, for example, applications in fuzzy spatial relations [1] and land use classification. Expert systems shells are

potentially useful as decision aids in all aspects of GIS, from the collection (sampling) and calibration of data to the analysis of these data and the construction of queries. These have been termed Intelligent GIS [2].

2 Naïve Geography Analyst

The NG-Analyst includes naïve geography formal representation structures suitable for imagery data analysis, human oriented graphical depictions of naïve geography structures, and an environment for visual integration of naïve geography depictions and imagery data. NG-Analyst consists of the following five functionalities (See Figure 1):

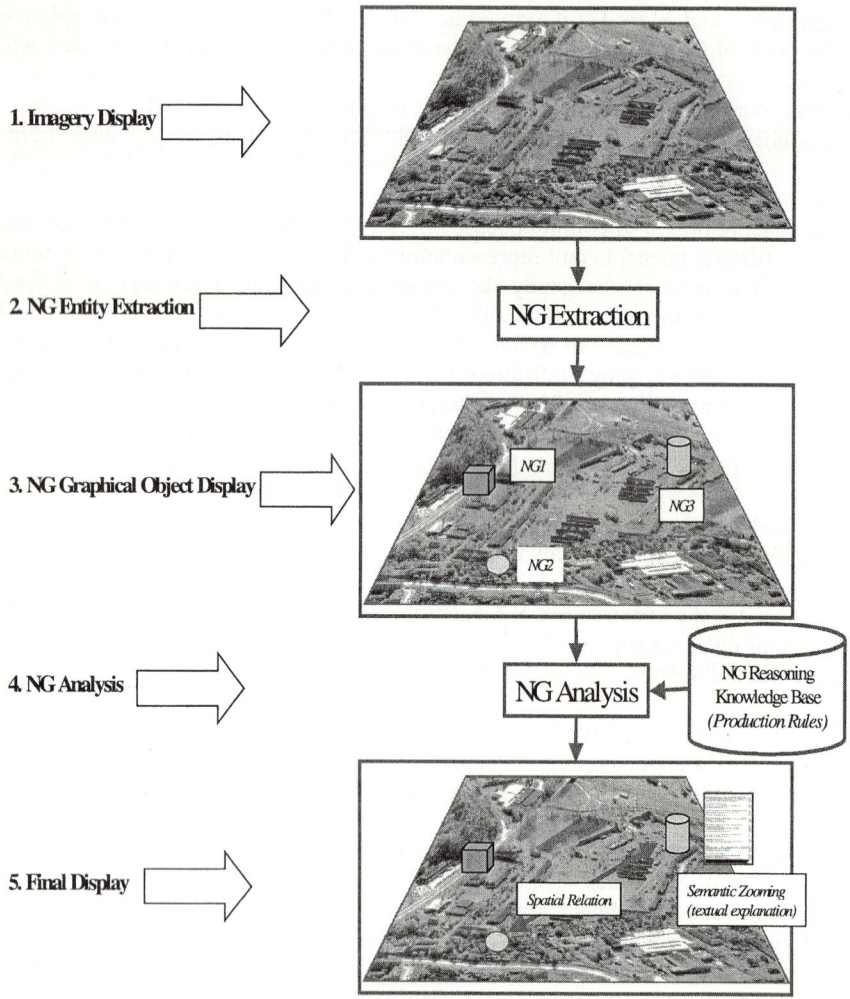

Fig. 1. Processing Steps of NG-Analyst System

1. Imagery Display: Display of imagery in a 3D visualization Graphical Interface with the user controlled zooming, rotation, and translation capabilities,
2. NG Entity Extraction: Analysis of imagery data for extraction of geographical features that can be mapped to NG entities as defined by the NG ontology,
3. NG Graphical Object Display: Rendering of graphical objects superimposed on imagery data and representing extracted NG entities,
4. NG Analysis: Processing of NG entities for their compliance with a Naïve geography-based spatial reasoning knowledge base, and
5. Final Display: Additional graphical objects are rendered and/or object graphical properties are changed in order to enhance users' cognitive capabilities for imagery analysis.

2.1 Imagery Display

The interactive visual representation of imagery and all graphical objects associated with it is referred to as the Imagery NG landscape.

The component implements the Model-View-Controller paradigm of separating imagery data (model) from its visual presentation (view). Interface elements (Controllers) act upon models, changing their values and effectively changing the views.

Such a paradigm supports the creation of applications which can attach multiple, simultaneous views and controllers onto the same underlying model. Thus, a single landscape (imagery and objects) can be represented in several different ways and modified by different parts of an application. The controller can achieve this transformation with a broad variety of actions, including filtering and multi-resolution, zooming, translation, and rotation. The component provides navigational aids that enhance user's explorative capabilities (e.g., a view from above provides a good overview of the information, and zooming-in for inspecting small items allows the user to get a detailed understanding).

2.2 NG Entity Extraction

The NG ontology set is defined as a taxonomy of NG entity classes that form a hierarchy of kinds of geographic "things". An NG entity is subject to commonsense spatial reasoning processes. Examples of these processes include such constructs as: "Towns are spaced apart", "Small towns are located between big towns", and "Gas stations are located on highways". The extraction of NG entities can be accomplished through one of the following:

- Manual annotation by users (through a graphical interface),
- Annotated maps and/or GIS systems, and
- Automated detection and annotation (e.g., using classifier systems).

In this work, the first approach has been considered and the rest will be considered in the future work. The NG entity representation used in this work is a vector representation consisting of 1) geographical feature parameters which describe various characteristics of geographical features, 2) graphical parameters which describe graphical properties of 3D objects corresponding to NG entities.

2.3 NG Graphical Object Display

The extracted NG entities are visualized by the imagery display component as graphical objects. Graphical parameters in the NG vector representation are used in this visualization process. All graphical objects, superimposed on imagery display, form an interactive graphical map of NG entities. Effective use of geometric shapes and visual parameters can greatly enhance user ability to comprehend NG entities. This interactive map is a starting point for further analysis of relations among entities and their compliance with the NG Knowledge Base.

2.4 NG Analysis

The NG Analysis component uses a production system to implement the NG Knowledge Base (NGKB). NGKB defines commonsense relations governing the set of NG entities. Figure 2 depicts the component architecture. NGKB is implemented as the database of production rules. A production rule is in an IF [condition] THEN [action] form. A set of rules requires a rule firing control system to use them and a database to store the current input conditions and the outputs. The production rule can have one of the following syntaxes:

IF [condition] THEN [action]
IF [condition1 AND condition2] THEN [action]
IF [condition1 OR condition2] THEN [action]

If the condition(s) on the left-hand side are met then the rule becomes applicable and is ready to be fired by the Control System.

Two types of production rules are considered: (1) Constraint Satisfaction Rules and (2) New NG Entity Extraction Rules. The constraint satisfaction rules govern commonsense relations among NG entities. Examples include: "A creek cannot flow uphill" and "An object cannot be in two different places at the same time." The following are examples of New NG Entity Extraction Rules:

IF (Road width > 30m) & (Number of intersections with the Road over the distance 2km > 4) & (Road is straight) & (Road is over grass/soil area)
THEN Generate an alert object Airfield Area.

IF (# of Military Buildings over area of $0.5km^2$ > 3)
THEN Allocate an object Military Complex.

IF (Distance from Building#1 to Building#2 < 30m) & (Type of Building#1 = Type of Building#2)
THEN Group objects into a new object Building Complex at higher abstraction level.

Sometimes more than one rule may be applicable so the Control System must know how to select one rule to fire out of several. The reason it must only fire one rule per cycle is that any fired rule might affect the set of facts and hence alter which rules are then applicable. The set of applicable rules is known as the Conflict Set and the process of deciding which one to use is called Conflict Resolution. There are a number of different techniques used as follows:

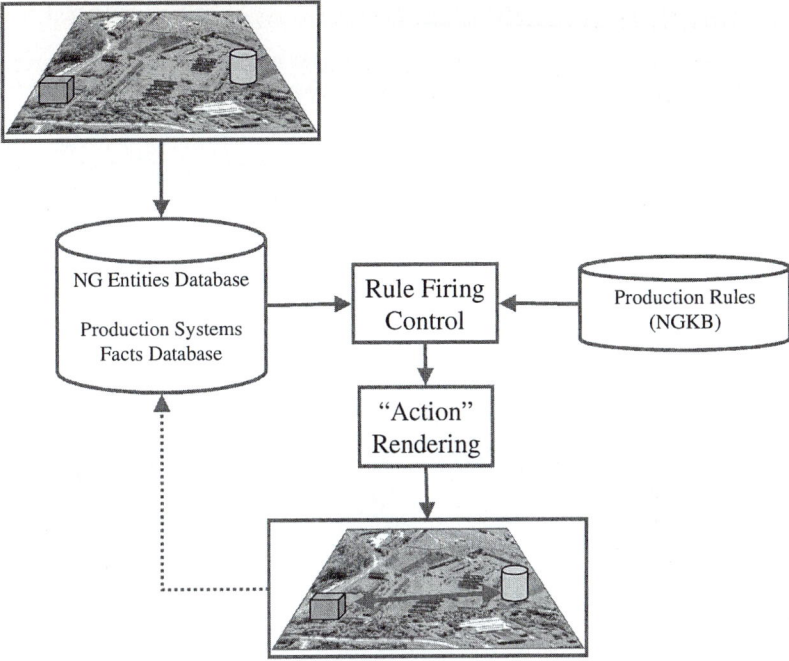

Fig. 2. NG Analyst Production Rules

Highest priority: The rules are ranked such that the highest priority rules are checked first so that as soon as one of them becomes applicable it is fired. This is obviously a very simple technique and can be quite efficient.

- Longest matching: A rule with many conditions to be met is 'stricter' than one with fewer. The longest matching strategy involves firing the 'strictest' rule of the set. This follows the premise that the stricter condition conveys more information when met.
- Most recently used: This technique takes the most recently fired rule from the conflict set and has the advantage of presenting a depth-first search that follows the path of greatest activity in generating new knowledge in the database.
- Most recently added: Use the newest rule in the conflict set. Obviously this technique is only useable in systems that create and delete rules as they go along.

2.5 Final Display

During the final display step, imagery data is rendered together with the following objects:

- Initially extracted graphical representations of NG entities,
- Graphical representation of the activated Constraint Satisfaction rules, and
- Graphical representation of the activated NG Entity Extraction rules.

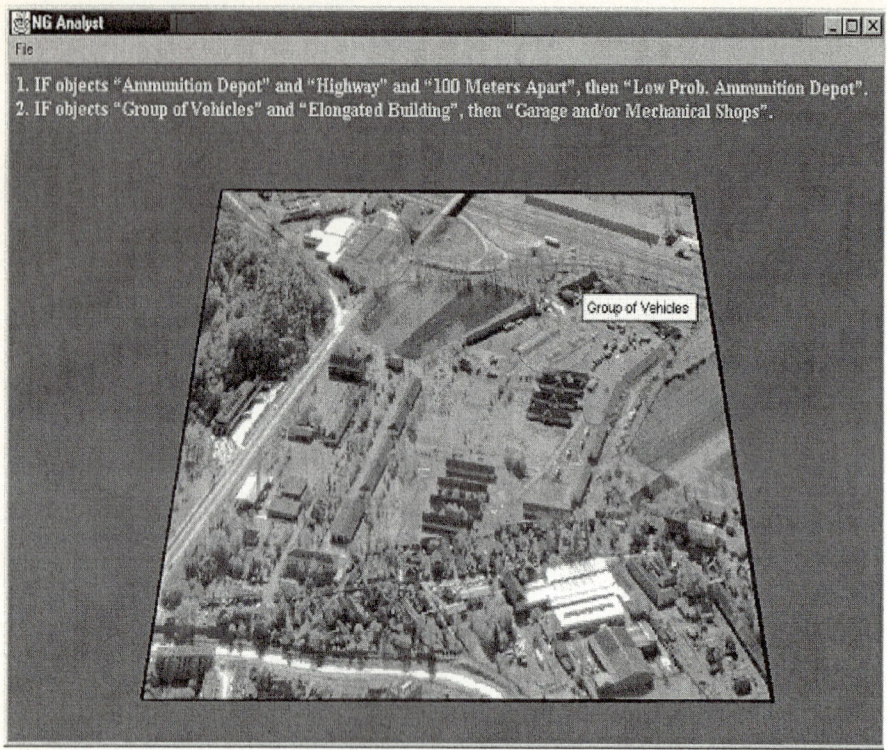

Fig. 3. NG-Analyst Visualization Interface

The highly interactive final display supports such operations as; Landscape Navigation (using mouse movement and controls the user can change views by zooming on the landscape, rotating around it, and/or translating its display), Semantic Zooming (i.e., a display of textual information) can be performed by "brushing" a given graphical object with the mouse pointer, Generation of Multiple Views (multiple landscapes can be rendered in the visualization space), Linking to Additional Information (moving the mouse pointer to a graphical object and clicking on it invokes the process of displaying additional information associated with this object).

3 System Implementation

The visualization program for the NG-Analyst system was implemented in Java and compiled using JDK1.4.1 Java environment and Java 3D class libraries[1]. The program displays an image and NG graphical objects. The user can select the image names using a pull-down menu *Load Image/Object function*. The file and folder names for each image are stored in a table of a database. The database also contains information

---

[1] © In3D Java edition by Visual Insights.

on NG entity attributes (object type, probability, size, shape, etc.) as well as properties of graphical depictions corresponding to the NG entities (e.g., color, size, textual description, and position on the image landscape). The database has been built using Microsoft Access Database. A small production rule system was also implemented in this prototype version in order to provide analytical capabilities. The user can analyze the displayed NG graphical objects for their compliance with the rule set. Figure 3 shows the visualization program interface.

4 Experimental Evaluation

The imagery database used during an experimental evaluation contained an aerial imagery set from the Kosovo operation *Allied Force*. In evaluating the initial NG-Analyst system, the following aspects were considered:

- Simplicity of use,
- Navigational locomotion,
- Compatibility and standards,
- Completeness and extensibility, and
- Maintenance.

Three evaluation approaches have been used: formal (by means of technical analysis), empirical (by means of experiments involving the users) and heuristic (judgments and opinions stated after the interaction with the system, e.g., performed by looking at the NG-Analyst interface and trying to come up with an opinion about what is complete and deficient about it).

5 Conclusion

In this paper, we present an NG-Analyst system which includes naïve geography formal representation structures suitable for imagery data analysis, human oriented graphical depictions of naïve geography structures, and an environment for visual integration of naïve geography depictions and imagery data. The NG-analyst has been developed to enhance the analysts' performance and to help to train new analysts by capturing various cognitive processes involved to human spatial data interpretation tasks. As a future plan, we will develop the automated detection/annotation approach for the extraction of NG entities instead of manual annotation by users through a graphical interface.

References

1. Altman, D., Fuzzy set theoretic approaches for handling imprecision in spatial analysis, International Journal of Geographic Information Systems, 8(3), 271- 289, 1994.
2. Burrough, P. A., Development of intelligent geographical information systems, International Journal of Geographical Information Systems, 6(1), 1-11, 1992.

3. Egenhofer, M. and D. Mark, Naïve Geography. in: A. Frank and W. Kuhn (Eds.), Spatial Information Theory-A Theoretical Basis for GIS, International Conference COSIT `95, 1-15, 1995.
4. Egenhofer, M. and R. Franzosa, Point-Set Spatial Topological Relations. International Journal of Geographical Information Systems 5(2), 161-174, 1991.
5. Hayes, P., The Naïve Physics Manifesto. in: D. Michie (Ed.), Expert Systems in the Microelectronic Age. pp. 242-270, Edinburgh University Press, Edinburgh, Scotland, 1978
6. Hayes, P., Naïve Physics I: Ontology of Liquids. in: J. Hobbs and R. Moore (Eds.), Formal Theories of the Commonsense World. pp. 71-108, Ablex, Norwood, NJ, 1985
7. Hayes, P., The Second Naïve Physics Manifesto. in: J. Hobbs and R. Moore (Eds.), Formal Theories of the Commonsense World. pp. 1-36, Ablex, Norwood, NJ, 1985.
8. Hernández, D., Qualitative Representation of Spatial Knowledge, Lecture Notes in Computer Science, Vol. 804, New York: Springer-Verlag, 1994.
9. Herskovits, A., Language and Spatial Cognition--An Interdisciplinary Study of the Prepositions in English. Cambridge, MA: Cambridge University Press, 1986.
10. Horton, R., Tradition and Modernity Revisited. in: M. Hollis and S. Lukes (Eds.), Rationality and Relativism. pp. 201-260, Blackwell, Oxford, UK, 1982.
11. Mark, D., D. Comas, M. Egenhofer, S. Freundschuh, M. Gould, and J. Nunes, Evaluating and Refining Computational Models of Spatial Relations Through Cross-Linguistic Human-Subjects Testing, COSIT `95, Semmering, Austria, Lecture Notes in Computer Science, Springer-Verlag, 1995.
12. Papadias, D. and T. Sellis, Qualitative Representation of Spatial Knowledge in Two-Dimensional Space, VLDB Journal 3(4), 479-516, 1994.
13. Smith, B., On Drawing Lines on a Map. in: A. Frank, W. Kuhn, and D.M. Mark (Ed.), Spatial Information Theory – COSIT95, Vienna, Austria, pp. 475-484, 1995.
14. Smith, B., Mereotopology: A Theory of Parts and Boundaries. Data and Knowledge Engineering 20, 287-303, 1996.
15. Smith, B., Boundaries; An Essay in Mereotopology. in: L. Hahn (Ed.), The Philosophy of Roderick Chisholm. pp. 767-795, Open Court, Chicago, IL, 1997.
16. Talmy, L., How Language Structures Space. in: H. Pick and L. Acredolo (Eds.), Spatial Orientation: Theory, Research, and Application. New York: Plenum Press, pp. 225-282, 1983.
17. Wang, F., The use of artificial neural networks in a geographical information system for agricultural land-suitability assessment, Environment and Planning A(26), 265-284, 1994.
18. Wang, F., Towards a natural language interface: an approach of fuzzy query, International Journal of Geographical Information Systems 8(2), 143-162, 1994.

Don't You Escape! I'll Tell You My Story

Jesús Ibáñez[1], Carlos Delgado-Mata[2], Ruth Aylett[2], and Rocio Ruiz-Rodarte[3]

[1] Departamento de Tecnología, Universidad Pompeu Fabra,
Passeig de Circumvallació, 8, 08003 Barcelona, Spain
`jesus.ibanez@tecn.upf.es`
[2] Centre for Virtual Environments, The University of Salford,
Business House, University Road, Salford, M5 4WT, Manchester, UK
`C.Delgado@pgr.salford.ac.uk`, `R.S.Aylett@salford.ac.uk`
[3] Instituto Tecnológico de Estudios Superiores de Monterrey,
Campus Estado de México, 52926 México
`caruiz@itesm.mx`

Abstract. This paper makes two contributions to increase the engagement of users in virtual heritage environments by adding virtual living creatures. This work is carried out on the context of models of the Mayan cities of Palenque and Calakmul. Firstly, it proposes a virtual guide who navigates a virtual world and tells stories about the locations within it, bringing to them its personality and role. Secondly, it develops an architecture for adding autonomous animals to virtual heritage. It develops an affective component for such animal agents in order to increase the realism of their flocking behaviour and adds a mechanism for transmitting emotion between animals via virtual pheromones, modelled as particles in a free expansion gas.

1 Introduction

Nowadays, virtual environments are becoming a widely-used technology as the price of the hardware necessary to run them decreases. Many recently developed virtual environments recreate real spaces with an impressive degree of realism. In such contexts, however, a lack of information for the user is frequently perceived, which makes him lose his interest in these environments. In the real world, people relate the environments that surround them to the stories they know about the places and objects in the environment. Therefore, in order to obtain more human and useful virtual environments, we need to add a narrative layer to them. We need stories related to the places and objects in the world. And finally, we need a virtual guide able to tell us these stories. Furthermore, one of the most striking features of historical investigations is the coexistence of multiple interpretations of the same event. The same historical events can be told as different stories depending on the storyteller's point of view. It would be interesting that the virtual guide who tells us stories about the virtual environment she [1] inhabits could

---

[1] In order to avoid confusion, in this paper, the virtual guide is supposed to be female, while the human guide is supposed to be male

R. Monroy et al. (Eds.): MICAI 2004, LNAI 2972, pp. 49–58, 2004.
© Springer-Verlag Berlin Heidelberg 2004

tell us these stories from her own perspective. In this sense, the first part of this paper describes the design and development of a novel proposal for storytelling in virtual environments from a virtual guide perspective.

On the other hand, in order to obtain more believable virtual environments, some research groups are trying to simulate virtual animals. In nature usually animals behave as part of social groups. Therefore, if we want to populate virtual environments with believable virtual animals, we need to emulate the behaviour of animal groups. Furthermore, our assumption of life and smartness in real animals derives from our perception of their reaction to the environment. For example, if one runs through a flock of deer, we expect them to move in order to avoid us. This reaction seems driven by emotional stimulus (most likely fear), and is communicated amongst conspecifics at an emotional level. Thus, believable virtual animals should display this kind of emotional response and communication. The second part of this paper proposes an architecture to model and simulate animals that not only "feel" emotions, that affect their decision making, but are also able to communicate them through virtual pheromones. The virtual animals also show a group behaviour, in particular a flocking behaviour based on the *boids* algorithm [11] modified so that it takes into account the animals' emotions. In this sense, the emotional communication "drives" the flocking emergence.

This paper describes the design and development of a novel proposal for storytelling in virtual environments from a virtual guide perspective and how it can be used together with animal group behaviour to add relevance to the virtual heritage instalations of Palenque and Calakmul. The structure of the paper is as follows. First we describe the proposed system for storytelling. Then we detail the architecture for the virtual deer. Next we expose the implementation and preliminary results. Finally we show the conclusions and point out future work.

2   Narrative Construction

In our model the guide begins at a particular location and starts to navigate the world telling the user stories related to the places she visits. Our guide tries to emulate a real guide's behaviour in such a situation. In particular, she behaves as a spontaneous real guide who knows stories about the places but has not prepared an exhaustive tour nor a storyline. Furthermore, our guide tells stories from her own perspective, that is, she narrates historical facts taking into account her own interests and roles. In fact, she extends the stories she tells with comments that show her own point of view. This mixture of neutral information and personal comments is what we can expect from a real guide who, on the one hand, has to tell the information he has learnt, but on the other hand, cannot hide his feelings, opinions, etc. We have designed a hybrid algorithm that models a virtual guide behaviour taking into account all the aspects described above. The mechanisms involved in the algorithm can be separated in three global processes which are carried out with every step. The next subsections detail these phases.

2.1 Finding a Spot in the Guide's Memory

Given a particular step in the navigation-storytelling process (that is, the virtual guide is at a particular location and she has previously narrated a series of story pieces), the guide should decide where to go and what to tell there. To emulate a real guide's behaviour, the virtual guide evaluates every candidate pair (*storyelement, location*) taking into account three different factors: the distance from the current location to *location*, the already told story elements at the current moment and the affinity between *storyelement* and the guide's profile.

A real guide will usually prefer nearer locations, as further away locations involve long displacements which lead to unnatural and boring delays among the narrated story elements. In this sense, our guide prefers nearer locations too. When a real guide is telling stories in an improvisational way, the already narrated story elements make him recall, by association, related story elements. In a spontaneous way, a real guide tends to tell these recently remembered stories. In this sense, our guide prefers story elements related (metaphorically remembered) to the ones previously narrated. Finally, a real guide tends to tell stories related to his own interests or roles. In this sense, our guide prefers story elements related to her own profile.

The system evaluates every candidate pair (*storyelement, location*) such that there is an entry in the knowledge base that relates *storyelement* to *location* (note that this means that *storyelement* can be narrated in *location*) and such that *storyelement* has not been narrated yet. In particular three scores corresponding to the previously commented factors are calculated. These three scores are then combined to calculate an overall score for every candidate pair. Finally the system chooses the pair with the highest overall score value.

2.2 Extending and Contextualising the Information

Figure 1a represents a part of the general memory the guide uses. This memory contains story elements that are interconnected with one another in terms of cause-effect and subject-object relations. Figure 1b shows the same part of the memory, where a story element has been selected by obtaining the best overall score described in the previous section. If the granularity provided by the selected story element is not considered to be large enough to generate a little story, then more story elements are selected. The additional story elements are chosen according to particular criteria (cause-effect and subject-object in our case). This process can be considered as navigating the memory from the original story element. Figure 1c shows the same part of the memory, where three additional story elements have been selected by navigating from the original story element.

The selected story elements are translated, if possible, from the virtual guide perspective (see figure 1d). For this task the system takes into account the guide profile and meta-rules stored in the knowledge base that are intended to situate the guide perspective. The translation process also generates guide attitudes that reflect the emotional impact that these story elements cause her. Lets see a simple example. Let us assume the following information extracted from a selected story element

```
fact(colonization, spanish, mayan)
```

meaning that the Spanish people colonized the Mayan. And let us assume the following meta-rules included in the knowledge base, aimed to situate the guide perspective

```
fact(colonization, Colonizer, Colonized) and profile(Colonized) =>
        fact(colonizedColonizacion, Colonizer, Colonized) and
        guideattitude(anger)
```

meaning that a colonizedColonization fact and anger as the guide's attitude should be inferred if a colonization fact is included in the story element and the guide profile matches the third argument of this fact, that is, the guide is the Colonized. In this example that will happen if the guide is Mayan. The new inferred fact represents the original one but from the guide's perspective.

In addition, the new translated story elements are enhanced by means of new information items generated by inferring simple commonsense rules allowing to add some comments showing her perspective. The guide uses the new contextualised story elements (figure 1d) as input for the rules that codify commonsense (figure 1e). By inferring these rules the guide obtains consequences that are added to the contextualised story elements (figure 1f), obtaining a new data structure which codifies the information that should be told. Let us continue with the previous example. Let us assume the following commonsense rule

```
fact(colonizedColonizacion, Colonizer, Colonized) =>
        fact(culturalDestruction, Colonized) and
        fact(religionChange, Colonized)
```

meaning that the colonized's view implies the destruction of the colonized's culture and the change of the colonized's religion. Therefore, if in our example the guide were Mayan, the story element to be told would be enhanced with the facts culturalDestruction and religionChange.

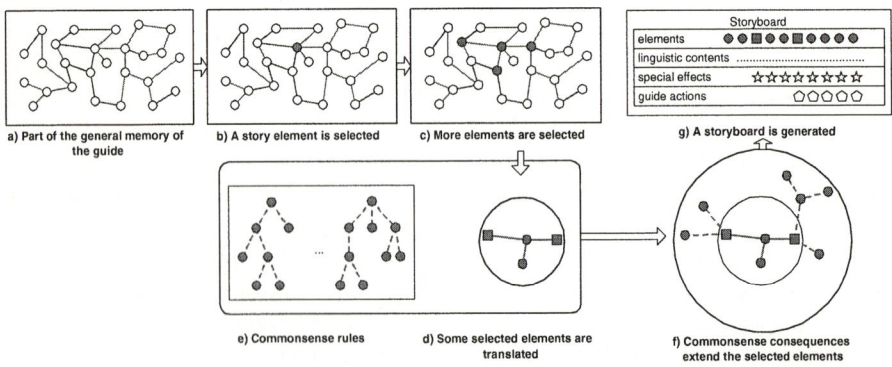

Fig. 1. Storyboard construction

2.3   Generating the Story

As a result of the previous processes, the guide obtains a set of inter-related information items to tell (figure 1f). Some elements are also related to particular guide attitudes. Now the system generates the text to tell (expressing these elements) as well as special effects and guide's actions to show while telling the story. The phases of this story generation process are as follows:

1. The first step is to order the data elements. To do so we consider three criteria: *cause-effect* (if an element Y was caused by another element X, then X should precede Y), *subject-object* (the elements whose subject/object are similar should be grouped together) and *classic climax* (the first selected story element, i.e. the one that obtained the best overall score, is supposed to be the climax of the narration, and therefore all the rest of the elements are arranged taking it into account).
2. The text corresponding to the ordered set of elements is generated. The complexity of this process depends on the particular generation mechanism (we use a template system) and the degree of granularity employed (we use a sentence per every story element).
3. A process that relies on the guide expression rules (the set of rules that translate abstract guide's attitudes in particular guide's actions) generates a set of guide actions (each one related to a particular story element).
4. Every story element is associated to particular environment conditions or special effects. Thus, finally, a storyboard like the one shown in figure 1g is obtained.

3   Communicating Emotions and Group Behaviour

3.1   Overall Architecture

The basic task of an animal brain has often been split into three sub-tasks. Our model adds a fourth sub-task, emotions. The four sub-tasks in our system are therefore: perception, emotions, action selection and motor control. Figure 2 shows a detailed diagram of the designed architecture, and the next sections describe its components.

3.2   Communicating Emotions

In the real-world, emotional transmission may well be multi-modal, with certain modes such as the perception of motion being particularly difficult to model. Thus we have limited ourselves for now to a single mode, and the one we have chosen is pheromones, to be perceived by a virtual olfaction sensor.

The nose has been linked with emotional responses and intelligence. Recent experiments [5] have shown that mammals emit pheromones through apocrine glands as an emotional response, and as means to communicate that state to conspecifics, who can adapt their behaviour accordingly; research has found that

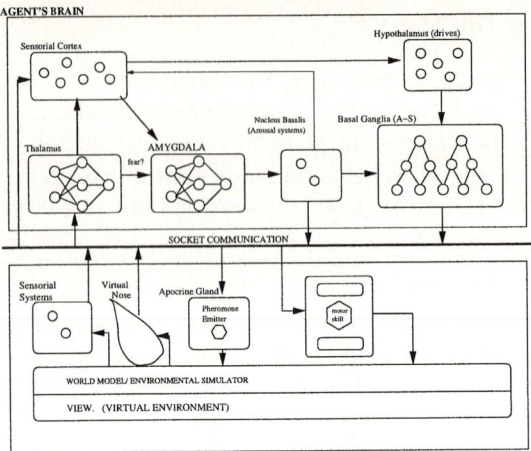

Fig. 2. Detailed architecture

odours produce a range of emotion responses in animals [6], which is adaptively advantageous because olfaction is part of the old smell-brain which can generate fast emotional-responses. Neary [10]points out that sheep will usually move more readily into the wind than with the wind, allowing them to utilise their sense of smell. In real animals chemoreceptors (exteroceptors and interoceptors) are used to identify chemical substances and detect their concentration. In our architecture we intend to model the exteroceptors which detect the presence of chemicals in the external environment.

In this work, to illustrate the use of emotion and drives to influence behaviours, deer had been selected as the exemplar creature. To support the communication of emotions, an environmental simulator has been developed, its tasks include changing the temperature and other environmental variables depending on the time of day and on the season, which depends on statistical historical data. An alarmed animal sends virtual pheromones to the environmental simulator and they are simulated using the free expansion gas formula in which the volume depends on the temperature and altitude (both simulated environmental variables). To compute the distribution of the pheromones a set of particles has been simulated using Boltzmann distribution formula 1, which is shown and described next.

$$n\left(y\right) = n_o e^{\frac{mgy}{k_b}T} \tag{1}$$

Where m is the pheromone's mass; g is the gravity; y is the altitude; k_b is the Boltzmann number; T is the temperature; n_o is N/V; N is number of molecules exhuded by the apocrine gland, which is related to the intensity of the emotional signal; and V is the Volume. The virtual animal includes a virtual nose used to detect pheromones, if any, that are near the creature. To smell a pheromone the threshold set in the current experiment is 200×10^{-16} because [8] has shown that animals have 1000 to 10000 more sensitivity than humans and Wyatt [15] claims that the threshold in humans to detect certain "emotional response odours", like those exuded from the armpits, is 200 per trillion parts, that is 200×10^{-12}.

3.3   Action Selection

The problem of action selection is that of choosing at each moment the most appropriate action out of a repertoire of possible actions. The process of making this decision takes into account many stimuli, including (in our case) the animal's emotional state. Action selection algorithms have been proposed by both ethologists and computer scientists. The models suggested by the ethologists are usually at a conceptual level, while the ones proposed by computer scientists (with some exceptions as [14] and [2]) generally do not take into account classical ethologic theories. According to Dawkins [3], a hierarchical structure represents an essential organising principle of complex behaviours. This view is shared by many ethologists [1] [13], and some action selection models follow this approach. Our action selection mechanism is based on Tyrrell's model [14]. This model is a development of Rosenblatt & Payton's original idea [12] (basically a connectionist, hierarchical, feed-forward network), to which temporal and uncertainty penalties were added, and for which a more specific rule for combination of preferences was produced. Note that among other stimuli, our action selection mechanism takes the emotional states of the virtual animal.

3.4   The Flocking Behaviour

The flocking behaviour in our system is based on *boids* [11], although we have extended it with an additional rule (escape), and, most importantly, the flocking behaviour itself is parameterised by the emotional devices output, that is, by the values of the emotions the boids feel. The escape rule is used to influence the behaviour of each boid in such a way that it escapes from potential danger (essentially predators) in its vicinity. Therefore, in our model each virtual animal moves itself along a vector, which is the resultant of four component vectors, one for each of the behavioural rules, which are: *Cohesion* (attempt to stay close to nearby flockmates), *Alignment* (attempt to match velocity with nearby flockmates), *Separation* (avoid collisions with nearby flockmates) and *Escape* (escape from potential danger, predators for example). The calculation of the resultant vector, *Velocity*, for a virtual animal A is as follows:

$$V_A = \underbrace{(Cf \cdot Cef \cdot Cv)}_{Cohesion} + \underbrace{(Af \cdot Aef \cdot Av)}_{Alignment} + \underbrace{(Sf \cdot Sef \cdot Sv)}_{Separation} + \underbrace{(Ef \cdot Eef \cdot Ev)}_{Escape} \qquad (2)$$

$$Velocity_A = limit(V_A, (MVef \cdot MaxVelocity)) \qquad (3)$$

where Cv, Av, Sv and Ev are the component vectors corresponding to the cohesion, alignment, separation and escape rules respectively. Cf, Af, Sf and Ef are factors representing the importance of the component vectors Cv, Av,

Sv and Ev respectively. These factors allow to weight each component vector independently. In our current implementation they can be varied, in real time, from a user interface. Cef, Aef, Sef and Eef are factors representing the importance of the component vectors Cv, Av, Sv and Ev respectively, given the current emotional state of the virtual animal. That is, each of this factors is a function that take the current values of the animals emotions and generate a weight for its related component vector. $MaxVelocity$ is the maximum velocity allowed to the animal. In the current implementation it can be varied from a user interface. $MVef$ is a factor whose value is calculated as a function of the current values of the animals emotions. It allows to increase and decrease the animal's $MaxVelocity$ depending on its emotional state. $limit$ is a function whose value is equal to its first parameter if this is not greater than its second one, otherwise the function value is equal to its second parameter.

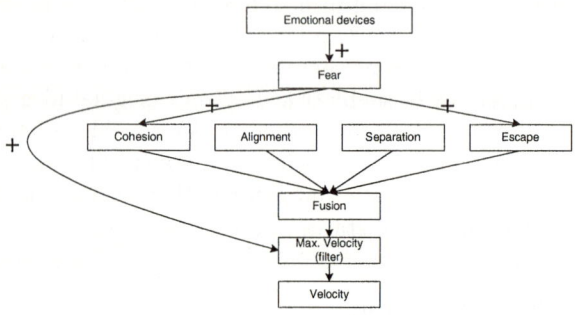

Fig. 3. How *fear* parameterises the flocking algorithm

The emotional factors (Cef, Aef, Sef, Eef, and $MVef$) reflects ethologic heuristic rules. Figure 3 shows an example of how emotions parameterise the flocking behaviour. In particular it shows how *fear* affects the component vectors of the animals' behaviour. The greater the fear an animal feels, the greater the weight of both its cohesion vector (the animal try to stay closer to nearby flockmates) and its escape vector (the boid try to stay farther from the potential danger). The resultant vector obtained by adding the four basic vectors is then scaled to not exceed the maximum speed. This maximum velocity is parameterised by the fear as well. The greater the fear an animal feels, the greater the speed it is able to reach.

4   Implementation and Preliminary Results

We have chosen Unreal Tournament (UT) engine as the platform on which our virtual guide run. As we wished our system to be open and portable, we decided to use Gamebots to connect our virtual guide to UT. Gamebots [7] is a modification to UT that allows characters in the environment to be controlled via network sockets. The core of the virtual guide is a Java application which is able to connect to UT worlds through Gamebots. This application controls the movement of the guide in the world as well as the presentation of special effects and texts which show the generated narratives. The current version uses a MySQL [9] database to store the knowledge base and Jess [4] to carry out inferences on the information. The described system has been developed (see figure 4a) and it is working properly with small and medium size knowledge bases.

On the other hand, the implementation of the emotional virtual animals architecture is three layered. Namely the agent's brain, the world model and the virtual environment. As seen in figure 2 the agents' brains are processes that runs independently on a Linux workstation and each agent's brain receives the sensorial data via network sockets and sends the selected action to the world's model which contains the agents' bodies and the environmental simulation. The changes to this model are reflected in the Palenque virtual environment (see figure 4c) which was developed using OpenGL Performer. This mechanism allows modularity and extensibility to add/modify the behaviour of the virtual animals. Furthermore, the behaviour of the deer in the Calakmul environment (see figure 4b) was prototyped in VRML and Java. The tests carried out so far, although preliminary results, show that the system is able to cope with the problem of simulating flocks of virtual animals driven by its emotional state.

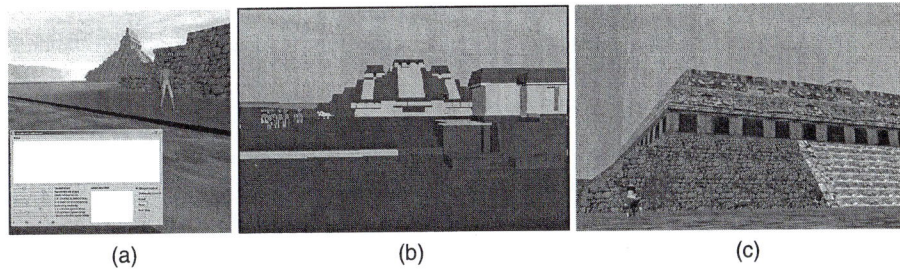

(a)   (b)   (c)

Fig. 4. User and administrator interfaces of the virtual guide (a). Snapshot of the Calakmul (b) and Palenque (c) implemented systems

5   Conclusions and Future Work

In this paper we have described work which aims to put "life" into virtual heritage environments in two distinct ways. Firstly, we discussed work towards the creation of an "intelligent guide with attitude", who tells stories in a virtual heritage environment from her distinct point of view. Work will continue in conjunction with groups in Mexico who have already produced a virtual models of the Mayan Cities of Palenque and Calakmul (whose location in the middle of a jungle makes it particularly inaccessible in the real world). We believe that the growing popularity of virtual heritage produces a growing need for intelligent guides and that this work will therefore find many potential applications.

Secondly, this work has shown that it is feasible to bring together the simple rule-based architectures of flocking with the more complex architectures of autonomous agents. Initial results suggest that populating a virtual heritage site with virtual animals can improve the experience particularly if the animals are engaged in some autonomous activity. This produces more believable and more specific flocking behaviour in the presence of predators. Further work will be carried out to more accurately characterise the changes in flocking behaviour obtained by this extended architecture. We further plan to validate this work by modelling a different flocking animal, for example the musk ox, which responds to predators by forming a horns-out circle of adult animals with the young inside.

References

1. Gerald P Baerends, *The functional organization of behaviour*, Animal Behaviour **24** (1976), 726–738.
2. Bruce Blumberg, *Action-selection in hamsterdam: Lessons from ethology*, Proceedings of the Third International Conference on Simulation of Adaptive Behavior (Brighton, England), 1994.
3. Richard Dawkins, *Hierarchical organisation: A candidate principle for ethology*, Growing Points in Ethology (Bateson & Hinde, ed.), Cambridge University Press, 1976.
4. Ernest Friedman-Hill, *Jess the rule engine for the java platform*, Available at http://herzberg.ca.sandia.gov/jess/.
5. Karl Grammer, *5-alpha-androst-16en-3alpha-one: a male pheromone ?*, Ethology and Sociobiology **14** (1993), no. 3, 201–207.
6. Carol E Izard, *Four systems for emotion activation: Cognitive and noncognitive processes*, Psychological Review **100** (1993), no. 1, 68–90.
7. G. A. Kaminka, M. M. Veloso, S. Schaffer, C. Sollitto, R. Adobbati, A. N. Marshall, A. Scholer, and S. Tejada, *Gamebots: a flexible test bed for multiagent team research*, Communications of the ACM **45** (2002), no. 1.
8. D A Marshall, L Blumer, and D G Moulton, *Odor detection curves for n-pentanoic acid in dogs and humans*, Chemical Senses **6** (1981), 445–453.
9. MySQL-AB, *Mysql*, Available at http://www.mysql.com/.
10. Mike Neary, *Sheep sense*, The Working Border Collie (2001).
11. Craig W Reynolds, *Flocks, herds, and schools: A distributed behavioral model*, Computer Graphics **21** (1987), no. 4, 25–34.
12. J.K. Rosenblatt and D.W. Payton, *A fine-grained alternative to the subsumption architecture for mobile robot control*, Proceedings of the IEEE/INNS International Joint Conference on Neural Networks (Washington DC), vol. 2, June 1989, pp. 317–324.
13. Nikolaas Tinbergen, *The study of instinct*, Oxford University Press, United Kingdom, 1969.
14. Toby Tyrrell, *Computational mechanisms for action selection*, Ph.D. thesis, University of Edinburgh, Edinburgh, Scotland, 1993.
15. Tristam D Wyatt, *Pheromones and animal behaviour*, Cambridge University Press, Cambrigde, U.K., 2003.

Querying Virtual Worlds. A Fuzzy Approach

Jesús Ibáñez[1], Antonio F. Gómez-Skarmeta[2], and Josep Blat[1]

[1] Departamento de Tecnología, Universidad Pompeu Fabra,
Passeig de Circumvallació, 8. 08003 Barcelona, Spain
{jesus.ibanez,josep.blat}@tecn.upf.es
[2] Departamento de Ingeniería de la Información y las Comunicaciones,
Universidad de Murcia. Apartado 4021, 30001 Murcia, Spain
skarmeta@dif.um.es

Abstract. In this paper we describe a querying model that allows users to find virtual worlds and objects in these worlds, using as a base a new virtual worlds representation model and a fuzzy approach to solve the queries. The system has been developed and checked in two different kinds of worlds. Both the design and current implementation of the system are described.

1 Introduction

Nowadays, virtual environments are a commonly used technology while the price of the hardware necessary to run them is decreasing. Current video games show 3D environments unimaginable some years ago. Many recently developed virtual environments recreate real spaces with an impressive degree of realism. At the same time, some digital cities are being created on the Internet including interactive 3D representations of their real cities.

Although the three-dimensional digital world offers enormous possibilities in the interaction between the user and the world of virtual objects, it has the same or more problems than the two-dimensional one. We show an example of this. If a friend tells us that she saw a web page with information about a new *Where's Wally* book authored by Martin Handford, but she forgot the web page URL, we could connect to a web search engine, Google for example, and search for *Martin Handford and Wally and 2003*. In a few minutes we would be watching the book cover. However, if she tells us she visited an interesting virtual world where Wally himself was, how could we find it? Furthermore, even if we find the world, how could we find Wally in it? Definitely, if Wally decides to hide himself in the Internet, he will be more successful if he does so in a virtual world. The problem emerges when we try to access virtual worlds defined by means of sets of three-dimensional primitives which have nothing to do with our language. Therefore it is necessary that the search process and the virtual worlds share the same kind of representation.

The problem, however, is no that simple. Let us suppose that our friend has visited a huge virtual environment where there are several Wally's. She was especially surprised by an area where there was a tiny Wally. How could we find

R. Monroy et al. (Eds.): MICAI 2004, LNAI 2972, pp. 59–68, 2004.

this location in that world? In the best case Wally's height is codified as a number, while our visual perception is imprecise. Therefore, the search mechanisms should be able to deal with imprecise queries like: *where is tiny Wally?*.

In this sense, we propose a new virtual worlds representation model that requires just a few additional efforts from the world creators, and adds a basic semantic level to the worlds which is useful to improve the interaction of the users with these worlds. We also describe a querying model that allows users to find worlds and objects in these worlds, using as a base the proposed representation and a fuzzy approach to solve the queries. Both proposed models taken together improve the current interaction with virtual worlds.

The structure of the paper is as follows. First we review related work. Next we expose our proposal by showing the virtual worlds representation model and detailing the fuzzy query mechanisms. Then we outline the current implementation and preliminary results. Finally we provide the conclusions and point out future work.

2   Related Work

There are various works [14,16,10,11] which present virtual environments with a semantic information layer. Some of them add the semantic level to the virtual environments, others add the virtual environments to pre-existing semantic information (GIS, digital cities, etc.).

On the other hand, several researchers have been working in what has been called *flexible querying*, whose objective is to provide users with new interrogation capabilities based on fuzzy criteria. Flexible querying has been applied to both the database querying and the information retrieval problems. The first fuzzy approach to database querying is probably due to Tahani [15], who defined the concept of a fuzzy relation in a database by associating a grade of membership with each tuple. He introduced the usual set operations (union, disjunction, negation and difference) and the AND and OR operators. His works were followed by numerous contributions which introduced the definitions of new operations [3,5], and the introduction of new concepts, such as the so-called *quantified queries* [23,7]. Furthermore, some works have been oriented towards the implantation of such systems in the Internet [12,13]. In the area of information retrieval several models have been proposed [4,2]. Finally, a preliminary investigation of the potential applications of fuzzy logic in multimedia database is presented in [9].

3   Proposed System

Figure 1 shows the overall architecture of the proposed system. The next subsections describe the information about the worlds that the system uses, and the query system itself.

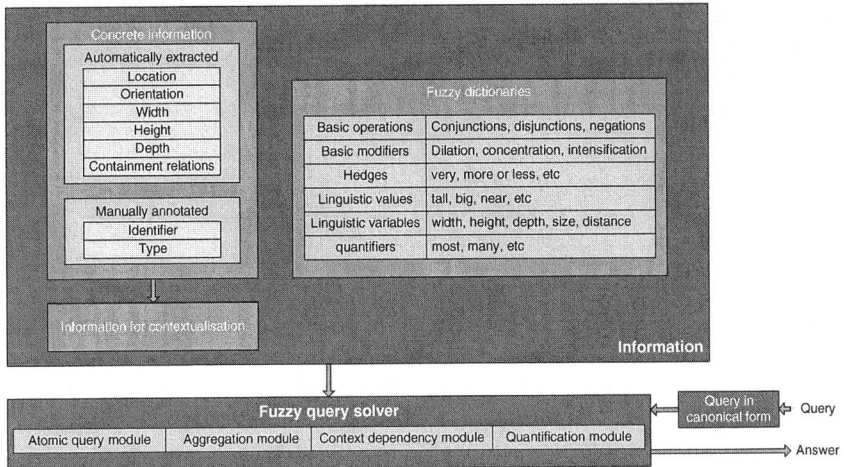

Fig. 1. Global architecture

3.1 Representing Virtual Worlds

The current description formats of virtual worlds describe mainly geometric information (points, lines, surfaces, etc.), which is required by the browsers to visualize the worlds. Our system adds a new semantic information level to the worlds representation, getting more suitable worlds for the interaction with users, and particularly more suitable to be queried in relation to their contents. The system uses concrete object information as well as general information needed to contextualise as described below.

Concrete Object Information. In particular, we annotate the following meta-contents: *location, orientation, width, height, depth, spatial containment relations, identifier* and *type*. Note that the first six are meta-contents which can be automatically extracted, while the last two should be manually annotated. Note also that additional features can be calculated from the annotated ones. For example, *object size* can be reckoned as the product of the object width, height and depth.

Information Needed to Contextualise. This information is automatically obtained from the meta-contents data. In particular, maximum and minimum values of width, height, depth and size attributes are obtained for every type of object in every context considered. The contexts we consider are the set of all the worlds, every particular world, and some objects (spaces) of particular worlds. In addition maximum possible distance in every context is calculated.

3.2 Querying Virtual Worlds

We require a modelling of a query system able to solve vague user queries working with more precise knowledge bases with some uncertainty. To model this query system we use an approach based on fuzzy set theory [19] and fuzzy logic. In fact, the main contribution of fuzzy logic is a methodology for computing with words [22].

Next we describe the main elements involved in our system. First we describe fuzzy dictionaries which encode the information the fuzzy query solver needs to work. Then we expose the canonical form to which the queries are translated to be processed by the fuzzy query solver. Finally, we show the fuzzy query solver functioning by describing how each of its modules works.

Dictionaries. The central key of the fuzzy approach is the *fuzzy set* concept, which extends the notion of a regular set in order to express classes with ill-defined boundaries (corresponding to linguistic values. e.g. tall, big, etc.). Within this framework, there is a gradual transition between non-membership and full membership. A degree of membership is associated to every element x of a referential X. It takes values in the interval $[0,1]$ instead of the pair $\{0,1\}$. Fuzzy modelling techniques make use of *linguistic hedges* as fuzzy sets transformers, which modify (often through the use of the basic *concentrator*, *dilator* and *intensifier* modifiers) the shape of a fuzzy set surface to cause a change in the related truth membership function. Linguistic hedges play the same role in fuzzy modelling as adverbs and adjectives do in language: they both modify qualitative statements. For example, *very* is usually interpreted as a concentrator using the function $f(x) = x^2$. A *linguistic variable* is a variable whose values are words or sentences in a natural or synthetic language. For example, *Height* is a linguistic variable if its values are *short, not short, very short, tall, not tall, very tall,* and so on. In general, the values of a linguistic variable can be generated from a primary term (for example, *short*), its antonym (*tall*), a collection of modifiers (*not, very, more or less, quite, not very,* etc.), and the connectives *and* and *or*. For example, one value of *Height* may be *not very short and not very tall*. Fuzzy set theory also attempts to model natural language quantifiers by operators called *fuzzy quantifiers*.

Our query system includes various dictionaries which define *basic operations* (conjunctions, disjunctions, negations), *basic modifiers* (dilation, concentration, intensification), hedges (very, more or less, etc.), *linguistic values* (tall, big, near, etc.), *linguistic variables* (width, height, depth, size, distance, etc.) and *quantifiers* (most, many, etc.).

Canonical Form. As pointed out by Zadeh [21], a proposition p in a natural language may be viewed as a collection of elastic constraints, $C_1, ..., C_k$, which restrict the values of a collection of variables $X = (X_1, ..., X_n)$. In general the constraints, as well as the variables they constrain, are implicit rather than explicit in p. Viewed in this perspective, representation of the meaning of p is, in essence, a process by which the implicit constraints and variables in p are made explicit. In fuzzy logic, this is accomplished by representing p in the so-called *canonical form* $P \rightarrow X$ is A in which A is a fuzzy predicate or, equivalently, an n-ary fuzzy relation in U, where $U = U_1 \times U_2 \times ... \times U_n$, and $U_i, i = 1, ..., n$, is the domain of X_i. We show the process of making the implicit variables and restrictions explicit through an example. Let the flexible query be *I am searching for a park which has a tall tree*. As the dictionaries relate both linguistic variables with its possible linguistic values and object attributes with linguistic variables, the system relates the linguistic value *tall* with the linguistic variable *heigth* and this in turn, with the world objects attribute *height*. Then, the system makes $X = $ Height(tree) and $A = $ TALL explicit. Therefore the explicit restriction is Height(tree) is TALL. Note that if the query is one that presents ambiguity (the linguistic value is related with various linguistic variables), it should be solved by interacting with the user.

We have defined a format to describe the queries, which is a kind of canonical form in the sense that it makes the implicit variables and restrictions explicit. The queries are translated to this format independently of the interface modality (natural language interface, graphical form interface). We show the format through an example. Let the flexible query be *I am searching for a world which has a park which has a tall tree which has many nests*; its representation is *[action: searching for, [object: world, quantity: 1, restrictions: [has: [object: park, quantity: 1, restrictions: [has: [object: tree, quantity: 1, restrictions: [height: tall, has: [object: nest, quantity: many]]]]]]]]*.

Fuzzy Query Solver. In this section we show the fuzzy query solver functioning by first describing how each of its main four modules works and then exposing the overall operation of the complete system.

Atomic Subqueries. Let the flexible query be *I am searching for a world which has a tall tree*. To calculate the degree to which a particular world fulfils the query, we have to evaluate first the satisfaction of *X is tall*, where $X = $ Height(tree), i.e. the height attribute of a tree object of the world being considered. This satisfaction degree is calculated in a two-step process. First the numeric height X of the tree object is contextualized (scaled in this case) obtaining $X_{context}$. Then $\mu_{tall}(X_{context})$ is calculated where μ_{tall} is the membership function corresponding to the fuzzy set associated with the fuzzy term *tall*.

Aggregation. Let the flexible query be *I am searching for a world which has a tall tree and a big garden*. To calculate the degree to which a particular world fulfils the query, first we calculate the degrees to which X and Y fulfil the atomic subqueries *X is tall* and *Y is big* respectively, where $X = $ Height(tree) and $Y = $ Size(garden), and tree and garden are objects of the world being considered. Then we can use the conjunction (AND) to calculate the aggregation of both degrees.

Note that the classic AND and OR connectives allow only crisp aggregations which do not capture any vagueness. For example, the AND used for aggregating n selection criteria does not allow to tolerate the unsatisfaction of a single condition; this may cause the rejection of useful items. For example, let the query be *I am searching for a room which has a bed and a wardrobe and a bedside table*. It seems obvious that the user is searching for a bedroom, however a bedroom with no bedside table will be rejected if we use the conjunction to aggregate the degrees of the atomic fulfilments. We supplement the conjunction and disjunction connectives by a family of aggregation criteria with an intermediate behaviour between the two extreme cases corresponding to the AND and to the OR. These aggregations are modelled by *means* operators and the *fuzzy linguistic quantifiers* (see below).

Context Dependency. The meaning of a fuzzy term, such as *tall*, may have several meanings among which one must be chosen dynamically according to a given context [24]. As showed above, maximum and minimum values of width, height, depth and size attributes are obtained for every type of object in every context considered. Then, these values are used to get the contextualized meaning of fuzzy terms. For example, if I search for a tall tree, being myself in a virtual park in a particular world, then the meaning of tall is obtained contextualizing its generic definition, in this particular case scaling with respect to the maximum and minimum values of the tree heights in this park.

We consider three main factors to contextualize the fuzzy terms in queries: *world immersion* (is the user in a world ?), *location in a world*, (which is the location of the user in the world she is inhabiting ? which is the minimum object (space) that contains the user ?) and *query context* (which is the context of the fuzzy term being considered in the query where it appears ?). Then, a simple algorithm decides the context of every fuzzy term in a query taking into account these factors.

Linguistic Quantifiers. Let the flexible query be *I am searching for a world which has many tall trees*. To calculate the degree by which a particular world fulfils the whole query, first we have to calculate the contextualized quantification of the degrees to which every tree object in this world fulfils the atomic subqueries X *is tall* where $X =$ Height(tree). Then the degree by which this quantification Q fulfils Q *is many* is calculated. Various interpretations for quantified statements have been proposed in literature. The classical approach is due to Zadeh. The most currently accepted derives from Yager. In [8], Bosc and Pivert compare these methods to evaluate quantified statements.

Zadeh [20] proposed viewing a fuzzy quantifier as a fuzzy characterization of an absolute or relative cardinality. The advantage of Zadeh's approach is its simplicity. However, it does not permit differentiating the case where many elements have a small membership degree and the case where few elements have a high membership degree. In [17] Yager introduced the concept of a weighted ordered averaging (OWA) operator. This operator provides a family of aggregation operators which have the conjunction at one extreme and the disjunction at the other extreme. Yager showed the close relationship between the OWA operators and the linguistic quantifiers. In particular, he suggested a methodology for associating each regular monotonic increasing quantifier with an OWA operator. Later it has been shown [6,18] that it is possible to extend this method in order to represent monotonous decreasing and increasing-decreasing quantifiers. Our system employs Yager's approach.

By using these modules, the overall system works as follows. First the query to be solved is translated to canonical form. Then every atomic subquery is contextualised and solved (that is, the degree to which every candidate solution fulfils the atomic subquery is calculated). Afterwards the compound subqueries (aggregations, quantifications) are contextualised and solved following a bottom-up order through the hierarchical structure of the canonical form. For example, let the flexible query be: I am looking for a park which contains a very tall tree and many short trees. The query is first translated to the following sentence in normal form:

```
[action: searching for,
    [object: park, quantity: 1, restrictions:
        [has:
            [composition: and
                [object: tree, quantity: 1, restrictions: [height: very tall]]
                [object: tree, quantity: many, restrictions: [height: short]]
            ]
        ]
    ]
]
```

Then, for each case, every sub-query is solved, and after that the aggregation (and in the example) is calculated. In addition, we show a list of queries, in order to illustrate the type of queries the system is able to work with: *I am looking for a tall tree; I am looking for a very tall tree; I am looking for a park containing a very tall tree; I am looking for a tall tree which is near a library; I am looking for a tall tree which is near a library and contains a nest; I am looking for a park which contains a tall tree or a tiny Wally; I am looking for a park which contains many trees.*

4   Implementation and Preliminary Results

We have developed and successfully checked the proposed system. In particular, we have implemented the fuzzy dictionaries and fuzzy query solver in SWI-Prolog [1] (a free prolog system). In addition we have developed the complete architecture shown in figure 2.

User accesses VRML virtual environments through a web browser containing a VRML plug-in (in particular we have used Cortona for our tests). The worlds contain a VRML Java Script Node which controls the user location and point of view. Furthermore, an EAI Java applet deals with the network communications and user interface.

The queries the user enters in the user interface are sent to the server where they are translated to canonical form and processed by the fuzzy query solver. The answer generated by this engine (a list of possible destinations where the

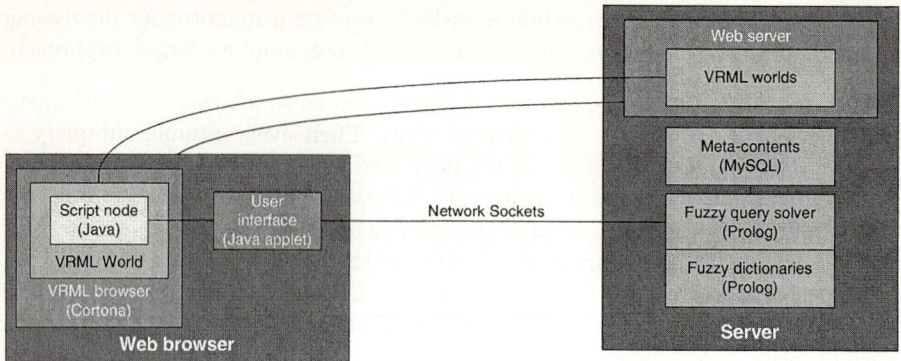

Fig. 2. Implemented architecture

objects/zones searched could be located, along with a numerical evaluation of every one) is sent back to the java applet in the user's web browser. This list is then shown on the user's interface so that she can navigate the world toward her desired target just by clicking on the preferred destination.

In order to use our system, only a few steps should be followed by the VRML world creators: install the database, save annotations about their worlds in the database, install the prolog fuzzy query engine on the server where their web server is running, and add a couple of lines of code to every VRML file so that it is controllable by the Java program.

So far we have checked the system with two different kinds of worlds. First we used the system to query in a virtual world which represents the actual Center of Environmental Education CEMACAM of the Mediterranean Savings Bank (CAM), composed by five buildings (see figure 3a). This world is a good example of the kind of virtual worlds which emulates reality. In this world queries like: *I am searching a room with many computers, I am looking for a small room with a big door*, etc. are properly solved.

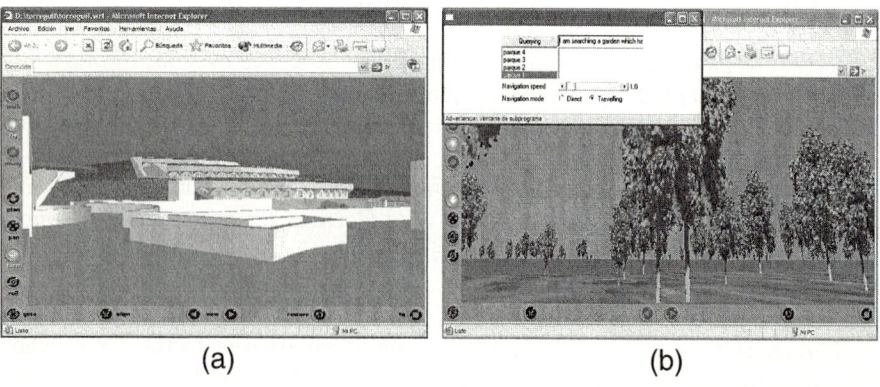

(a)   (b)

Fig. 3. Test worlds

Next we developed a Java application which automatically generates huge toy virtual worlds composed of several gardens with objects of different types and sizes. By using this application we generated several worlds which allow us to check the system in deliberately weird fictitious worlds (see figure 3b). In this world queries like: *I am searching a garden with many tall trees and a very big monument, I am looking for a very small tree near a very tall tree*, etc. are properly solved.

The tests carried out so far show that the proposed system is able to cope with the problem of querying in virtual environments. It seems that users feel more confident in the worlds when the querying system is available. At the moment we are checking the system with non experienced users, to evaluate how useful the system is.

5   Conclusions and Future Work

In this paper we have described a proposal for a new virtual worlds representation model that requires just a few additional efforts from the worlds creators, and adds a basic semantic level to the worlds which is useful to improve the interaction of the users with these worlds. We also have described a querying model that allows users to find worlds and objects in these worlds, using as a base the proposed representation, and a fuzzy approach to solve the queries. Both proposed models taken together improve the current interaction with virtual worlds. We have developed and successfully checked the system. Further work will be carried out in order to check the system with non experienced users and extend the fuzzy dictionaries (to allow more kinds of queries).

References

1. *Swi-prolog*, Available at http://www.swi-prolog.org/.
2. F. Berzal, M. J. Martin-Bautista, M. A. Vila, and H. L. Larsen, *Computing with words in information retrieval*, IFSA World Congress and 20th NAFIPS International Conference, Joint 9th, vol. 5, 2001, pp. 3088–3092.
3. G. Bordogna, P. Carrara, and G. Pasi, *Extending boolean information retrieval: a fuzzy model based on linguistic variables*, 1st IEEE International Conference on Fuzzy Systems, San Diego, CA, USA, Mar. 1992, pp. 769–779.
4. G. Bordogna and G. Pasi, *Fuzzy rule based information retrieval*, NAFIPS'99, New York, 1999.
5. P. Bosc, M. Galibourg, and G. Hamon, *Fuzzy querying with sql: Extensions and implementation aspects*, Fuzzy Sets and Systems **28** (1988), 333–349.
6. P. Bosc and L. Lietard, *On the extension of the use to the owa operator to evaluate some quantifications*, First European Congress Fuzzy and Intell.Technol, Aachen, Germany, 1993, pp. 332–338.
7. _____ , *Complex quantified statements in database flexible querying*, Biennial Conference of the North American Fuzzy Information Processing Society, NAFIPS, 1996, pp. 277–281.
8. P. Bosc and O. Pivert, *Sqlf: A relational database language for fuzzy querying*, 1995.

9. D. Dubois, H. Prade, and F. Sèdes, *Fuzzy logic techniques in multimedia database querying: A preliminary investigation of the potentials*, IEEE Transactions on Knowledge and Data Engineering **13** (2001), no. 3, 383–392.

10. N. Farenc, C. Babski, F. Garat, and D. Thalmann, *Database and virtual human representation on the web*, Advances in Databases and Multimedia for the New Century -A Swiss-Japanese Perspective-,WorldScientific, 2000.

11. T. Ishida, J. Akahani, K. Hiramatsu, K. Isbister, S. Lisowski, H. Nakanishi, M. Okamoto, Y. Miyazaki, and K. Tsutsuguchi, *Digital city kyoto: Towards a social information infrastructure*, International Workshop on Cooperative Information Agents (CIA-99), Lecture Notes in Artificial Intelligence, Springer-Verlag, vol. 1652, 1999, pp. 23–35.

12. J. Kacprzyk and S. Zadrozny, *Fuzzy querying via www: implementation issues*, IEEE International Fuzzy Systems Conference, FUZZ-IEEE '99, vol. 2, 1999, pp. 603–608.

13. _____, *Fuzzy queries against a crisp database over the internet: an implementation*, in Proc. Fourth International Conference on Knowledge-Based Intelligent Engineering Systems and Allied Technologies, vol. 2, 2000, pp. 704–707.

14. M. Soto and S. Allongue, *Semantic approach of virtual worlds interoperability*, IEEE WET-ICE '97, Cambridge, MA, IEEE Press, 1997.

15. V. Tahani, *A conceptual framework for fuzzy query processing: A step toward a very intelligent database systems*, Inf. Proc. and Manag **13** (1977), 289–303.

16. D. Thalmann, N. Farenc, and R. R. Boulic, *Virtual human life simulation and database: Why and how*, International Symposium on Database Applications in Non-Traditional Environments, DANTE'99, 1999.

17. R. R. Yager, *On ordered weigthed averaging aggregation operators in multicriteria decisionmaking*, IEEE Trans. Sys., Man Cybern. **18** (1988), 183–190.

18. _____, *Applications and extensions of owa aggregations*, Int. J. of Man-Mach. St. **37** (1991), 103–132.

19. L.A. Zadeh, *Fuzzy sets*, Informations and Control **8** (1965), 338–353.

20. _____, *A computational approach to fuzzy quantifiers in natural languages*, Comp. Math. Appl. **9** (1983), 149–183.

21. _____, *Fuzzy logic*, Computer **21** (1988), no. 4, 83–93.

22. _____, *Fuzzy logic = computing with words*, IEEE Transactions on Fuzzy Systems **4** (1996), no. 2, 103–111.

23. S. Zadrozny and J. Kacprzyk, *Multi-valued fields and values in fuzzy querying via fquery for access*, Fifth IEEE International Conference on Fuzzy Systems, vol. 2, 1996, pp. 1351–1357.

24. W. Zhang, C. T. Yu, B. Reagan, and H. Nakajima, *Context-dependent interpretations of linguistic terms in fuzzy relational databases*, ICDE, 1995, pp. 139–146.

Infant Cry Classification to Identify Hypoacoustics and Asphyxia with Neural Networks

Orion Fausto Reyes Galaviz[1] and Carlos Alberto Reyes Garcia[2]

[1] Instituto Tecnologico de Apizaco, Av. Tecnologico S/N,
Apizaco, Tlaxcala, 90400, Mexico
orionfrg@yahoo.com
[2] Instituto Nacional de Astrofisica Optica y Electronica,
Luis E. Erro 1, Tonantzintla, Puebla, 72840, Mexico
kargaxxi@inaoep.mx

Abstract. This work presents the development of an automatic recognizer of infant cry, with the objective of classifying three kinds of cry, normal, hypoacoustic and asphyxia. We use acoustic characteristics extraction techniques like LPC and MFCC, for the acoustic processing of the cry's sound wave, and a Feed Forward Input Delay neural network with training based on Gradient Descent with Adaptive Back-Propagation. We describe the whole process, and we also show the results of some experiments, in which we obtain up to 98.67% precision.

Keywords: Infant's Cry, Classification, Pattern Recognition, Neural Networks, Acoustic Characteristics.

1 Introduction

The pathological diseases in infants are commonly detected several months, often times years, after the infant is born. If any of these diseases would have been detected earlier, they could have been attended and maybe avoided by the opportune application of treatments and therapies. It has been found that the infant's cry has much information on its sound wave. For small infants this is a form of communication, a very limited one, but similar to the way an adult communicates. Based on the information contained inside the cry's wave, it can determined the infant's physical state; even detect physical pathologies, mainly from the brain, in very early stages. The initial hypothesis for this project is that if there exists this kind of relevant information inside the cry of an infant, the extraction, recognition and classification from the infant's cry can be possible through automatic means. In this work we present the design of a system that classifies different kinds of cries. These cries are recordings of normal, deaf and asphyxiating infants, of ages from one day up to one year old. In the model here presented, we classify the original input vectors, without reduction, in three corresponding classes, normal cry, hypoacoustic (deaf) and asphyxiating cries.

R. Monroy et al. (Eds.): MICAI 2004, LNAI 2972, pp. 69–78, 2004.

2 State of the Art

Although there are not many works on research related to the automatic recognition of the infants cry, recently some advances have been developed that show interesting results, and emphasize the importance of doing research in this field. Using classification methodologies based on Self-Organizing Maps, Cano et al, in [2] report some experiments to classify cry units from normal and pathological infants. Petroni used neuronal networks [3] to differentiate between pain and no pain cry. Taco Ekkel [4] tried to classify sound of newborn cry in categories called normal and abnormal (hypoxia), and reports a result of correct classification of around 85% based on a neural network of radial base. In [5] Reyes and Orozco classify cry samples from deaf and normal infants, obtaining recognition results that go from 79.05% up to 97.43%.

3 The Infant Cry Automatic Recognition Process

The infant cry automatic classification process (Fig. 1) is basically a pattern recognition problem, similar to Automatic Speech Recognition (ASR). The goal is to take the wave from the infant's cry as the input pattern, and at the end obtain the kind of cry or pathology detected on the baby. Generally, the process of Automatic Cry Recognition is done in two steps. The first step is known as signal processing, or feature extraction, whereas the second is known as pattern classification. In the acoustical analysis phase, the cry signal is first normalized and cleaned, then it is analyzed to extract the most important characteristics in function of time. The set of obtained characteristics can be represented like a vector, and each vector can be taken like a pattern. The feature vector is compared with the knowledge that the computer has to obtain the classified output.

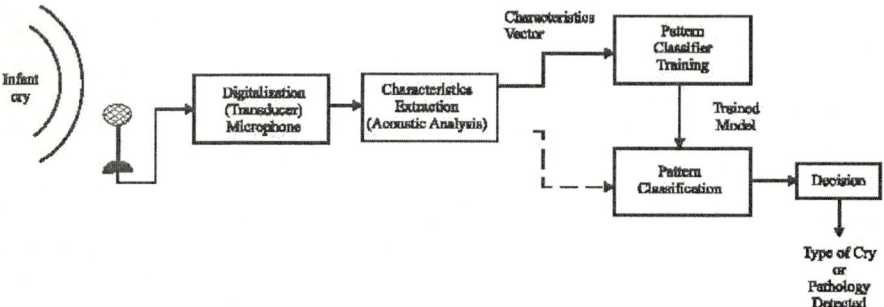

Fig. 1. Infant Cry Automatic Recognition Process

4 Acoustic Processing

The acoustic analysis implies the selection and application of normalization and filtering techniques, segmentation of the signal, feature extraction, and data compression. With the application of the selected techniques we try to describe the signal in terms of some of its fundamental components. A cry signal is complex and codifies more information than the one needed to be analyzed and processed in real time applications. For that reason, in our cry recognition system we used an extraction function as a first plane processor. Its input is a cry signal, and its output is a vector of features that characterizes key elements of the cry's sound wave. All the vectors obtained this way are later fed to a recognition model, first to train it, and later to classify the type of cry. We have been experimenting with diverse types of acoustic characteristics, emphasizing by their utility the Mel Frequency Cepstral Coefficients and the Linear Prediction Coefficients.

4.1 MFCC (Mel Frequency Cepstral Coefficients)

The low order cepstral coefficients are sensitive to overall spectral slope and the high-order cepstral coefficients are susceptible to noise. This property of the speech spectrum is captured by the Mel spectrum. The Mel spectrum operates on the basis of selective weighing of the frequencies in the power spectrum. High order frequencies are weighed on a logarithmic scale where as lower order frequencies are weighed on a linear scale. The Mel scale filter bank is a series of L triangular band pass filters that have been designed to simulate the band pass filtering believed to occur in the auditory system. This corresponds to series of band pass filters with constant bandwidth and spacing on a Mel frequency scale . On a linear frequency scale, this spacing is approximately linear up to 1KHz and logarithmic at higher frequencies. Most of the recognition systems are based on the MFCC technique and its first and second order derivative. The derivatives normally approximate trough an adjustment in the line of linear regression towards an adjustable size segment of consecutive information frames. The resolution of time and the smoothness of the estimated derivative depends on the size of the segment [6].

4.2 LPC (Linear Prediction Coefficients)

Linear Predictive Coding (LPC) is one of the most powerful speech analysis techniques, and one of the most useful methods for encoding good quality speech at a low bit rate. It provides extremely accurate estimates of speech parameters, and is relatively efficient for computation. Based on these reasons, we are using LPC to represent the crying signals. Linear prediction is a mathematical operation where future values of a digital signal is estimated as a linear function of previous samples. In digital signal processing linear prediction is often called linear predictive coding (LPC) and can thus be viewed as a subset of filter theory. In system analysis (a Sub field of mathematics), linear prediction can be viewed as a part of mathematical modeling or optimization [7]. The particular way in which data are segmented determines whether the covariance method, the autocorrelation method, or any of the so called lattice methods of LP analysis is used. The first method that we are using is the autocorrelation LP technique. As the order of the LP model increases, more details of the power spectrum of the signal can be approximated. Thus, the spectral envelope can be efficiently represented by a small number of parameters, in this cases LP coefficients [5].

5 Cry Patterns Classification

The set of acoustic characteristics obtained in the extraction stage, is represented generally as a vector, and each vector can be taken as a pattern. These vectors are later used to make the classification process. There are four basic schools for the solution of the pattern classification problem, those are: *a)* Pattern comparison (dynamic programming), *b)* Statistic Models (Hidden Markov Models HMM). *c)* Knowledge based systems (expert systems) and *d)* Connectionists Models (neural networks). For the development of the present work we used the connectionists models type, known as neural networks. We have selected this kind of model, in principle, because of its adaptation and learning capacity. Besides, one of its main functions is pattern recognition, this kind of models are still under constant experimentation, but their results have been very satisfactory.

5.1 Neural Networks

In a DARPA study [9] the neural networks were defined as a system composed of many simple processing elements, that operate in parallel and whose function is determined by the network's structure, the strength of its connections, and the processing carried out by the processing elements or nodes. We can train a neural network to realize a function in particular, adjusting the values of the connections (weights) between the elements. Generally, the neural networks are adjusted or trained so that an input in particular leads to a specified or desired output. The neural networks have been trained to make complex functions in many application areas including pattern recognition, identification, classification, speech, vision, and control systems. Nowadays the neural networks can be trained to solve problems that are hard to solve with conventional methods. There are many kinds of learning and design techniques that multiply the options that a user can take [10]. In general, the training can be supervised or not supervised. The methods of supervised training are those that are more commonly used, when labeled samples are available. Among the most popular models there are the feed-forward neural networks, trained under supervision with the back-propagation algorithm. For the present work we have used variations of these basic model, these are briefly described below.

5.2 Feed Forward Input (Time) Delay Neural Network

Cry data are not static, and any cry sample at any instance in time is dependent on crying patterns before and after that instance in time. A common flaw in the traditional Back-Propagation algorithm is that it does not take this into account. Waibel et al. set out to remedy this problem in [11] by proposing a new network architecture called the "Time-Delay-Neural Network" or TDNN. The primary feature of TDNNs is the time-delayed inputs to the nodes. Each time delay is connected to the node via its own weight, and represents input values in past instances in time. TDNNs are also known as Input Delay Neural Networks because the inputs to the neural network are the ones delayed in time. If we delay the input signal by one time unit and let the network receive both the original and the delayed signals, we have a

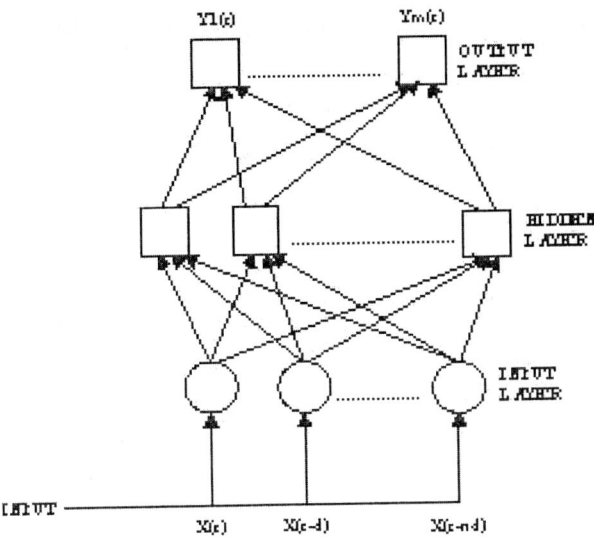

Fig. 2. A time delay neural network whose input contains a number of tapped delay lines.

simple time-delay neural network. Of course, we can build a more complicated one by delaying the signal at various lengths. If the input signal is n bits and delayed for m different lengths, then there should be *nm* input units to encode the total input. When new information arrives, it is placed in nodes at one end and old information shifts down a series of nodes like a shift register controlled by a clock. A general architecture of time-delay networks is drawn in Figure 2. [12]

The Feed-forward input delay neural network consists of *Nl* layers that use the dot product weight update function, which is a function that applies weights to an input to obtain weighed entrances. The first layer has weights that come from the input with the input delay specified by the user, in this case the delay is [0 1]. Each subsequent layer has a weight that comes from a previous layer. The last layer is the output of the network. The adaptation is done by means of any training algorithm. The performance is measured according to a specified performance function [10]. Some of the most notorious properties of TDNNs are: *i*) The Network is shift-invariant: A pattern may be correctly recognized and classified regardless of its temporal location. *ii*) The network is not sensitive to phoneme boundary misalignment: The TDNN is not only able to learn from badly aligned training data, it is even able to correct the alignment. It does this by learning where the phoneme's presence is significant within the segment of speech. This property is later used to perform recursive sample re-labeling. *iii*) The network requires small training sets: In [13] Tebelskis quotes the findings of several papers that indicate that the TDNN, when exposed to time-shifted inputs with constraint weights, can learn and generalize well even with limited amounts of training data.

5.3   Training by Gradient Descent with Adaptive Learning Rate Backpropagation

The training by gradient descent with adaptive learning rate backpropagation, proposed for this project, can train any network as long as its weight, net input, and transfer functions have derivative functions. Back-propagation is used to calculate derivatives of performance with respect to the weight and bias variables. Each variable is adjusted according to gradient descent. At each training epoch, if the performance decreases toward the goal, then the learning rate is increased. If the performance increases, the learning rate is adjusted by a decremental factor and the change, which increased the performance, is not made [10]. Several adaptive learning rate algorithms have been proposed to accelerate the training procedure. The following strategies are usually suggested: *i)* start with a small learning rate and increase it exponentially, if successive epochs reduce the error, or rapidly decrease it, if a significant error increase occurs, *ii)* start with a small learning rate and increase it, if successive epochs keep gradient direction fairly constant, or rapidly decrease it, if the direction of the gradient varies greatly at each epoch and *iii)* for each weight an individual learning rate is given, which increases if the successive changes in the weights are in the same direction and decreases otherwise. Note that all the above mentioned strategies employ heuristic parameters in an attempt to enforce the monotone decrease of the learning error and to secure the converge of the training algorithm [14].

6   System Implementation for the Crying Classification

In the first place, the infant cries are collected by recordings obtained directly from doctors of the Instituto Nacional de la Comunicación Humana (National Institute of the Human Communication) and IMSS Puebla. This is done using SONY digital recorders ICD-67. The cries are captured and labeled in the computer with the kind of cry that the collector orally mentions at the end of each recording. Later, each signal wave is divided in segments of 1 second; these segments are labeled with a pre-established code, and each one constitutes a sample. For the present experiments we have a corpus made up of 1049 samples of normal infant cry, 879 of hypo acoustics, and 340 with asphyxia. At the following step the samples are processed one by one extracting their acoustic characteristics, LPC and MFCC, by the use of the freeware program Praat [1]. The acoustic characteristics are extracted as follows: for every second we extract 16 coefficients from each 50-millisecond frame, generating vectors with 304 coefficients by sample. The neural network and the training algorithm are implemented with the Matlab's Neural Network Toolbox. The neural network's architecture consists of 304 neurons on the input layer, a hidden layer with 120 neurons, and one output layer with 3 neurons. The delay used is [0 1]. In order to make the training and recognition test, we select 340 samples randomly on each class. The number of asphyxiating cry samples available determines this number. From them, 290 samples of each class are randomly selected for training in one experiment, and 250 for another one. With these vectors the network is trained. The training is made until 2000 epochs have been completed or an 1×10^{-6} error has been reached. After the network is trained, we test it with the 50 and 90 samples of each class set apart from the original 340 samples. The recognition accuracy percentage, from each experiment, is presented in a confusion matrix.

7 Experimental Results

The classification accuracy was calculated by taking the number of samples correctly classified, divided by the total number of samples. The detailed results of two tests of each kind of acoustic characteristic used, LPC and MFCC, with samples of 1 second, with 16 coefficients for every 50 ms frame, are shown in the following confusion matrices.

Results using 290 samples to train and 50 samples to test the neural network with LPC.

Table 1. Confusion matrix showing a 93.33% precision after 2000 training epochs and an error of 1×10^2.

	normal	deaf	asphyxia
normal	45	3	2
deaf	0	50	0
asphyxia	2	0	45

Results using 250 samples to train and 90 samples to test the neural network with LPC.

Table 2. Confusion matrix showing a 92.96% precision after 2000 training epochs and an error of 1×10^2.

	Normal	deaf	asphyxia
normal	78	1	9
deaf	0	90	0
asphyxia	3	0	83

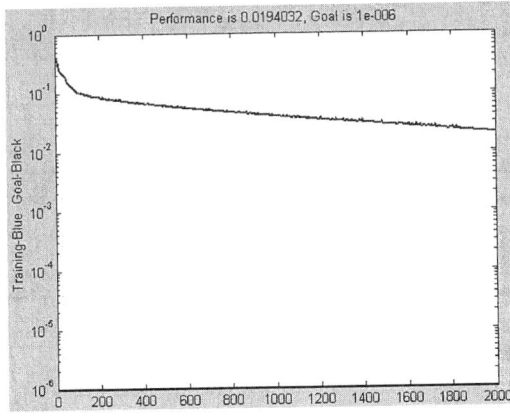

Fig. 3. Training with 250 samples and LPC feature vectors

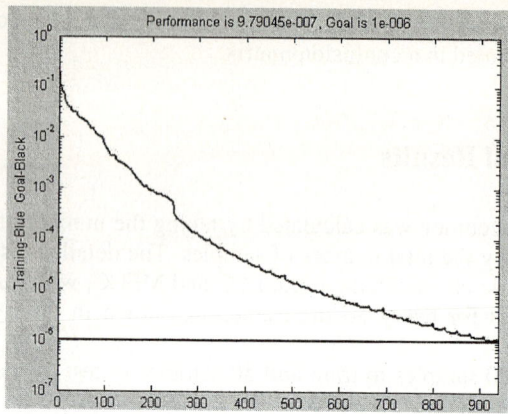

Fig. 4. Training with 290 samples and MFCC feature vectors

Results using 290 samples to train and 50 samples to test the neural network with MFCC.

Table 3. Confusion matrix showing a 98.67% precision with an error convergence of 1×10^{-6} after only 937 training epochs.

	Normal	deaf	asphyxia
normal	48	0	2
deaf	0	50	0
asphyxia	0	0	50

Results using 250 samples to train and 90 samples to test the neural network with MFCC.

Table 4. Confusion matrix showing a 96.30% precision with an error convergence of 1×10^{-6} after only 619 training epochs.

	Normal	deaf	Asphyxia
normal	83	0	5
deaf	0	90	0
asphyxia	3	0	87

7.1 Results Analysis

As we can see from Figure 3 and Figure 4, the training of the neural network with LPC is slower that the one done with MFCC. With LPC features, the neural network stops until it reaches the 2000 epochs we defined, but the error only goes down to 1×10^{-2}. On the other hand, with MFCC, the network converges when it reaches the defined error, that is 1×10^{-6}, and after the training has reached only about 950 epochs, in the case of training with 290 samples, and 619 epochs for the 250 samples case. As can also be noticed, the results shown for the two experiments for each type of features are slightly lower when the network is trained with 250 samples. Our interpretation on this is that, the classification accuracy improves with a larger number of training samples. This observation is suggesting to us that we should focus in collecting more crying samples, mainly of the asphyxia class, which is the one that, at the moment, is limiting the training set. We don't have to discard the fact that the training with LPC characteristics gave good results, the inconvenience was that the process of training was slower, the error was higher, and the classification accuracy was lower compared to the results obtained when using the MFCC features.

8   Conclusions and Future Work

This work demonstrates the efficiency of the feed forward input (time) delay neural network, particularly when using the Mel Frequency Cepstral Coefficients. It is also shown that the results obtained, of up to 98.67%, are a little better than the ones obtained in other previous works mentioned. These results can also have to do with the fact that we use the original size vectors, with the objective of preserving all useful information. In order to compare the obtained performance results, and to reduce the computational cost, we plan to try the system with an input vector reduction algorithm by means of evolutionary computation. This is for the purpose of training the network in a shorter time, without decreasing accuracy. We are also still collecting well-identified samples from the three kinds of cries, in order to assure a more robust training. Among the works in progress of this project, we are in the process of testing new neural networks, and also testing new kinds of hybrid models, combining neural networks with genetic algorithms and fuzzy logic, or other complementary models.

Acknowledgments. This work is part of a project that is being financed by CONACYT-Mexico (37914-A). We want to thank Dr. Edgar M. Garcia-Tamayo and Dr. Emilio Arch-Tirado for their invaluable collaboration when helping us to collect the crying samples, as well as their wise advice.

References

1. Boersma, P., Weenink, D. Praat v. 4.0.8. A system for doing phonetics by computer. Institute of Phonetic Sciences of the University of Amsterdam. February, 2002.
2. Sergio D. Cano, Daniel I. Escobedo y Eddy Coello, El Uso de los Mapas Auto-Organizados de Kohonen en la ClasificaciUf3n de Unidades de Llanto Infantil, Grupo de Procesamiento de Voz, 1er Taller AIRENE, Universidad Catolica del Norte, Chile, 1999, pp 24-29.
3. Marco Petroni, Alfred S. Malowany, C. Celeste Johnston, Bonnie J. Stevens, (1995). Identification of pain from infant cry vocalizations using artificial neural networks (ANNs), The International Society for Optical Engineering. Volume 2492. Part two of two. Paper #: 2492-79.
4. Ekkel, T, (2002). "Neural Network-Based Classification of Cries from Infants Suffering from Hypoxia-Related CNS Damage", Master Thesis. University of Twente, The Netherlands.

5. Orozco GarcUeda, J., Reyes GarcUeda, C.A. (2003), Mel-Frequency Cepstrum Coefficients Extraction from Infant Cry for Classification of Normal and Pathological Cry with Feed-forward Neural Networks, ESANN 2003, Bruges, Belgium.
6. Gold, B., Morgan, N. (2000), Speech and Audio Signal Processing. Processing and Perception of Speech and Music. John Wiley & Sons, Inc.
7. Wikipedia: The Free Encyclopedia, http://www.wikipedia.org/wiki/Linear_prediction.
8. Markel, John D., Gray, Augustine H., (1976). Linear prediction of speech. New York: Springer-Verlag.
9. DARPA Neural Network Study, AFCEA International Press, 1988, p. 60
10. Manual Neural Network Toolbox, Matlab V.6.0.8, Developed by MathWoks, Inc.
11. Waibel A., Hanazawa T., Hinton G., Shikano K., Lang K., Phoneme Recognition Using Time-Delay Neural Networks, IEEE Transactions on Acoustics, Speech and Signal Processing, Vol 37, No 3, March 1989, pp 328 - 339.
12. Limin Fu. (1994), Neural Networks in Computer Intelligence. McGraw-Hill International Editions, Computer Science Series.
13. Tebelskis J., (1955) Speech Recognition Using Neural Networks, PhD Dissertation, Carnegie Mellon University.
14. V.P. Plagianakos[*], M.N. Vrahatis[*], G.D. Magoulas[**], Nonmonotone Methods for Backpropagation Training with Adaptive Learning Rate; University of Patras[*] Patras, Greece; University of Athens[**] Athens, Greece.

N-best List Rescoring Using Syntactic Trigrams

Luis R. Salgado-Garza[1], Richard M. Stern[2], and Juan A. Nolazco F.[1]

[1] Computer Science Department, ITESM, Campus Monterrey
Ave. E. Garza Sada #2501 Sur, Monterrey, Nuevo León, C.P. 64849, México.
{lsalgado,jnolazco}@itesm.mx
[2] Electrical and Computer Engineering Department, Carnegie Mellon University,
5000 Forbes Avenue, Pittsburgh, PA 15213-3890, USA.
rms@cs.cmu.edu

Abstract. This paper demonstrates the usefulness of syntactic trigrams in improving the performance of a speech recognizer for the Spanish language. This technique is applied as a post-processing stage that uses syntactic information to rescore the N-best hypothesis list in order to increase the score of the most syntactically correct hypothesis. The basic idea is to build a syntactic model from training data, capturing syntactic dependencies between adjoint words in a probabilistic way, rather than resorting to the use of a rule-based system. Syntactic trigrams are used because of their power to express relevant statistics about the short-distance syntactic relationships between the words of a whole sentence. For this work we used a standarized tagging scheme known as the EAGLES tag definition, due of its ease of use and its broad coverage of all grammatical classes for Spanish. Relative improvement for the speech recognizer is 5.16%, which is statistically significant at the level of 10%, for a task of 22,398 words (HUB-4 Spanish Broadcast News).

1 Introduction

Automatic speech recognition (ASR) has progressed substantially over the past fifty years. While high recognition accuracy can be obtained even for continuous speech recognition, word accuracy deteriorates when speech recognition systems are used in adverse conditions. Therefore, new ways to tackle this problem must be tried.

Since speech recognition is a very difficult task, language knowledge has been succesfully used over many years to improve recognition accuracy. Human beings can make use of language information to predict what a person is going to say, and in adverse environments language information enables two people to follow a dialog. Similarly, language knowledge can be used to clean up the outputs of speech recognition systems.

The use of syntactic constraints is potentially especially valuable for languages like Spanish, where there are many semantically appropriate but acoustically confusable words such as the masculine and feminine forms of nouns and adjectives and the various conjugations of verbs.

R. Monroy et al. (Eds.): MICAI 2004, LNAI 2972, pp. 79–88, 2004.

This paper describes the use of a language model rescoring procedure (Fig. 1). Our system uses an N-best list to generate several potentially correct hypotheses. A postprocessing stage analyzes each entry on the N-best list and rescores it according to linguistic criteria, in our case syntactic co-occurrence. Finally, the top hypothesis in the list is selected as the new correct hypothesis.

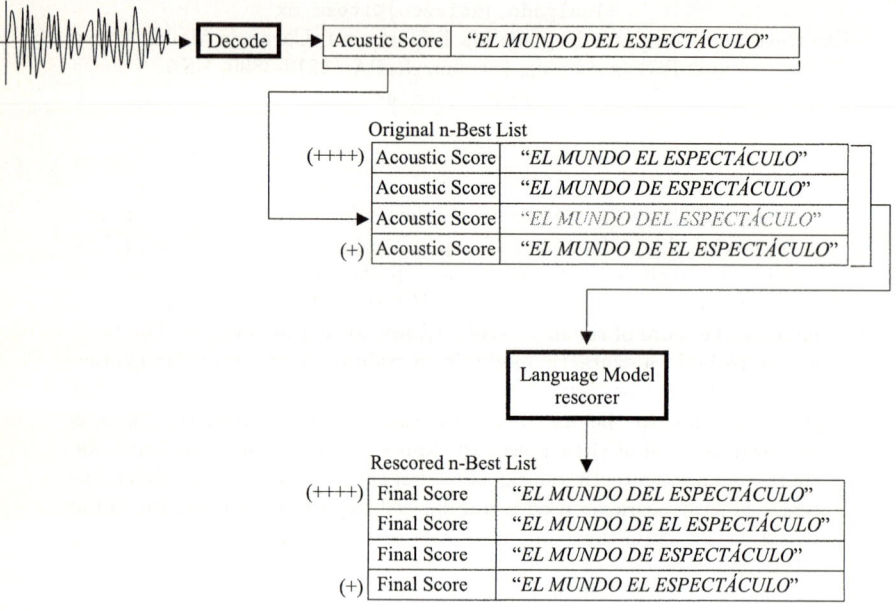

Fig. 1. Rescoring and sorting the N-best list.

In continuous speech recognition, the talker rarely uses grammatically well-constructed sentences, so attempts to use a formal language is not feasible. Probabilistic language models, on the other hand, have been very effective. Language modelling deals with the problem of predicting the next word on a utterance, given a previous known history of words. The language model definition is as follows:

$$P(W) = \prod_{i=1}^{n} P(w_i|w_1, w_2, \ldots, w_{i-1}) \tag{1}$$

where, W represents a sequence of words w_j.

The particular case of $n = 3$, which corresponds to the *trigram* language model, has been found to be very powerful even though scope is limited to a short distance. The success and simplicity of trigrams is limited by only two difficulties, local span and sparseness of data [1].

Because of the way the word trigrams build the language model (computing statistics for triplets of adjacent words), they are unable to capture long-distance dependencies. While data sparseness is a very serious problem, unseen triplets will lead to zero probability during recognition even when the acoustic probability is high [2]. Several approaches to smoothing have been proposed to ameliorate this problem. While these techniques do compensate for unseen trigrams, they also may favor incorrect grammatical constructions. Many other alternatives for language modelling have also been tried before, including the successful exponential language models [3,4], but their computational complexity is higher.

In this work we build a language model based not only on local word dependencies but also on the *syntactic structure* of the history h of previous words. This method also reduces the data sparseness problem, since during decoding we make use of correct syntactic structures derived from training, even when specific words were unseen in the training corpus.

2   Syntactic Trigrams for Prediction of a Word's Class

Inspired by the success of word trigrams, and knowing that each word has syntactic properties (or tags, see appendix A), we propose to complement the concept of word trigrams with syntactic trigram (tag trigrams), which are based on a word's attributes rather than the words themselves. Basically, a syntactic trigram is a set of the syntactic tags that describe three adjoining words. In this way, the syntactic trigrams capture the short-distance grammatical rule used of a training corpus.

In order to use the syntactic trigrams we need a tagged corpus for training the language model. During training we count each syntactic-tag trigram, using these numbers to develop probabilities that are invoked during a postprocessing stage of decoding.

Let the syntactic tags of a whole sentence W of length m words ($W = w_1, w_2, \ldots, w_m$) be denoted as $T = t_1, t_2, \ldots, t_m$. The overall correctness score for a whole sentence is computed by multiplying the syntactic trigram probabilities in a chain, according to the expression:

$$P_{synt-3g}(W) = \prod_{i=3}^{m} P(t_i | t_{i-1}, t_{i-2}) \tag{2}$$

For a whole sentence, the syntactic score is combined with the acoustical and conventional language models as follows:

$$\hat{W} = \arg \max_W \underbrace{P(X|W)}_{Acoustic\ Score} \underbrace{(P(W)^{LW} IP^m)(P_{synt-3g}(W))^{SW}}_{Language\ Model\ Score} \tag{3}$$

where IP and LW are the word-based language model parameters [5] (the insertion penalty and language weight, respectively) and SW is a *syntactic weight* that determines the effect of syntactic trigram rescoring on the N-best list. As is seen, the acoustic and word trigram language model scores are augmented (rather than replaced) by the syntactic trigram score, with the goal of improving the performance of the recognizer by implicitly encoding grammatical rules from the training corpus, and hopefully improving the score of the correct hypothesis on the N-best list.

In addition to *word error rate* (WER) we considered two additional metrics to assess the effectiveness of the syntactic trigrams: *depth reduction* and *top score total*. The first of these metrics is the average of the reduction in depth of the correct hypothesis for every sentence even when it is not promoted to the top position of the N-best list after rescoring, while the latter is the number of correct hypotheses that are raise to the top position. These numbers are computed as follows:

$$depth\ reduction = \frac{1}{N} \sum_{i=1}^{N} \left[\overbrace{depth(correct\ hyp_i)}^{after\ rescore} - \overbrace{depth(correct\ hyp_i)}^{before\ rescore} \right] \quad (4)$$

$$top\ score\ total = \frac{1}{N} \sum_{i=1}^{N} \Phi(i) \quad (5)$$

where N is the total number of sentences in the evaluation set and $\Phi(i)$ is defined by

$$\Phi(i) = \begin{cases} 1 \text{ when } correct\ hyp_i \text{ is in the topmost position of the } N\text{-best list,} \\ 0 \text{ otherwise.} \end{cases}$$

3   Experimental Results

In our experiments, we work with the CMU SPHINX-III speech recognition system to generate an N-best list for the HUB-4 Spanish Broadcast News task, a database with a vocabulary of 22,398 different words (409,927 words in 28,537 sentences), using 74 possible syntactic tags including grammatical type, gender, and number for each word.

A series of experiments was conducted to evaluate the effectiveness of the syntactic trigram language model. The first set of tests used a language weight of 9.5 and served as our baseline [6]. Since we were interested in determining an optimal value for the syntactic weight parameter we tried several possible values, the range from 0.8 to 3.0 gived the best outcomes. Specifically, the results showed that the greatest average depth reduction in depth in the N-best list for the correct hypothesis was observed for parameter values of 0.80 and 0.85 of syntactic weight, but the maximum number of correct hypothesis that moved to the top position after rescoring was achieved at 0.85 (Fig. 2).

We repeated the same syntactic weight variations for another set of tests using a language weight of 10.0 The results were slightly worst since the maximum number of correctly rescored hypothesis was lower than in the previous configuration, however the average depth reduction was almost the same (Fig. 3).

To complete the evaluation of the syntactic trigrams we rescored the N-best list generated by the lattice rescorer available in the SPHINX-III system. Using

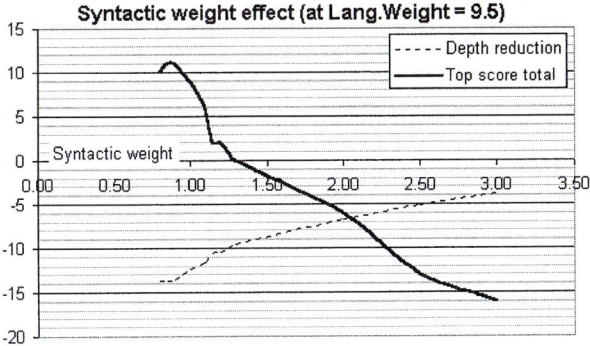

Fig. 2. Overall rescoring effectiveness of the syntactic trigrams using a language weight of 9.5.

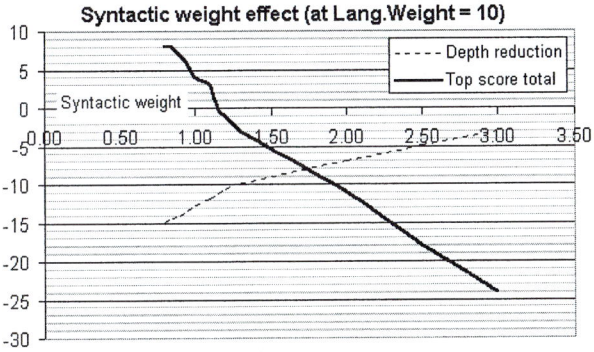

Fig. 3. Overall rescoring effectiveness of the syntactic trigrams using a language weight of 10.0.

the best configurations for syntactic weights we obtained an overall WER of the decoder using the syntactic postprocessing.

Results reported in Table 1 show a relative improvement of 4.64% (1.37% absolute) and 3.51% (0.93% absolute) using 9.5 and 10.0 as language weights, respectively. Using a simple validation test [7] we determined that all of these results are valid at a significance level of 10%. Using our best configuration (language weight of 10.0 and syntactic weight of 0.85) we note an overall improvement of 5.16% relative (1.39% absolute) over our baseline system.

Table 1. Effectiveness of the syntactic trigrams.

Experiment	Language Weight	Syntactic Weight	WER
Baseline	9.5	0.00	26.90%
Experiment 1	9.5	0.85	25.65%
Experiment 2	9.5	1.00	25.89%
Experiment 3	10.0	0.00	26.44%
Experiment 4	10.0	0.85	25.51%
Experiment 5	10.0	1.00	25.53%

4   Discussion

The results presented in the previous section show that the use of syntactic trigrams leads to a small but significant increase in recognition accuracy. Since these results taken in isolation may appear to be disappointing, we also tabulated the number of correct hypotheses that were rescored to the first two or three positions of the N-best list and compared these hypotheses to the ones above it. We performed analyses over several sentences where the mismatch was very obvious but even with rescoring, the the correct transcription never ended better than in the second position.

An interesting case to examine is the sentence sv97725b.00159.377, for which the correct transcription is different from the hypothesis chosen by the rescorer:

Hypothesis from the rescorer:

> "LA AUN ESCASA PROFESIONALIDAD DEL UN CUERPO DE POLICÍA"

Correct transcription:

> "LA AUN ESCASA PROFESIONALIDAD DEL NUEVO CUERPO DE POLICÍA"

Position of the correct transcription in the rescored N-best list: 2

Problem: "UN" (Determiner, masculine, singular)
             "NUEVO" (Adjective, masculine, singular)

Rescorer's hypothesis:

> (la DA0FS0) (aun RG) (escasa AQ0FS0) (profesionalidad NCFS000) (del SPCMS)
> (un DI0MS0) (cuerpo NCMS000) (de SPS00) (policía NCCS000)

Trigram tags	Trigram probability	Accumulated in sentence
D−FS− R− A−−FS−	1.5454e-01	1.5454e-01
R− A−−FS− N−FS−−−	1.2432e-01	1.9213e-02
A−−FS− N−FS−−− S−−MS	6.0818e-02	1.1685e-03
N−FS−−− S−−MS D−−MS−	1.2601e-02	1.4725e-05
S−−MS D−−MS− N−MS−−−	4.7826e-01	7.0425e-06
D−−MS− N−MS−−− S−−00	3.3157e-01	2.3350e-06
N−MS−−− S−−00 N−CS−−−	3.2299e-03	**7.5422e-09**

Correct transcription:

> (la DA0FS0) (aun RG) (escasa AQ0FS0) (profesionalidad NCFS000) (del SPCMS)
> (nuevo AQ0MS0) (cuerpo NCMS000) (de SPS00) (policía NCCS000)

Trigram tags	Trigram probability	Accumulated in sentence
D−FS− R− A−−FS−	1.5454e-01	1.5454e-01
R− A−−FS− N−FS−−−	1.2432e-01	1.9213e-02
A−−FS− N−FS−−− S−−MS	6.0818e-02	1.1685e-03
N−FS−−− S−−MS A−−MS−	4.0504e-02	4.7331e-05
S−−MS A−−MS− N−MS−−−	4.7115e-01	2.2300e-05
A−−MS− N−MS−−− S−−00	3.4303e-01	7.6497e-06
N−MS−−− S−−00 N−CS−−−	3.2299e-03	**2.4708e-08**

From the previous example we can see that the correct transcription got the highest score using the syntactic trigrams, but later when combined with the acoustic and word trigram language model scores, the overall results ranks the correct transcription at the second position of the rescored N-best list. This example illustrates both the effective performance of syntactic trigrams and its dependence on other stages of the decoding process. In this particular case the contributions of other knowledge sources degrade the score of the correct hypothesis. This is not observed in general, as there are also some cases where the acoustic scores indeed provide additional information to disambiguate between similar grammatical constructions. In the following example (sentence sv97725b.01337.376), the syntactic trigrams score the two different sentences as equal with equivalent grammatical constituents, as should be the case.

Hypothesis from the rescorer:

> "CREO QUE PODÍA DECIR CON TODA SEGURIDAD"

Correct transcription:

> "CREO QUE PODRÍA DECIR CON TODA SEGURIDAD"

Position of the correct transcription in the rescored N-best list: 2

Problem: "PODÍA" (Verb, 1st person, singular)
            "PODRÍA" (Verb, 1st person, singular)

Rescorer's hypothesis:

> (creo VMIP1S0) (que CS) (podía VMII1S0) (decir VMN0000) (con SPS00) (toda DI0FS0) (seguridad NCFS000)

Trigram tags	Trigram probability	Accumulated in sentence
V−−−1S0 CS V−−−1S0	6.6420e-02	6.6420e-02
CS V−−−1S0 V−−−000	1.2083e-01	8.0258e-03
V−−−1S0 V−−−000 S−−−00	2.3036e-01	1.8488e-03
V−−−000 S−−00 D−−FS−	1.9225e-01	3.5545e-04
S−−00 D−−FS− N−FS−−−	7.7827e-01	**2.7663e-04**

Correct transcription:

> (creo VMIP1S0) (que CS) (podría VMIC1S0) (decir VMN0000) (con SPS00) (toda DI0FS0) (seguridad NCFS000)

Trigram tags	Trigram probability	Accumulated in sentence
V−−−1S0 CS V−−−1S0	6.6420e-02	6.6420e-02
CS V−−−1S0 V−−−000	1.2083e-01	8.0258e-03
V−−−1S0 V−−−000 S−−00	2.3036e-01	1.8488e-03
V−−−000 S−−00 D−−FS−	1.9225e-01	3.5545e-04
S−−00 D−−FS− N−FS−−−	7.7827e-01	**2.7663e-04**

All the previous experiments were performed using an N-best list of no more than 200 entries, one list for each sentence in the test set. The lattice rescorer, however, may create a shorter list for a sentence if the A* search algorithm is exhausted before the 200 hypotheses have been generated. Using this configuration, only about 35% of the N-best lists produced after lattice rescoring include the correct hypothesis. This obviously limits the performance of the syntactic trigram whole sentence language model.

5   Conclusions

Our results demonstrate small but statistically significant improvements in the recognition accuracy of the SPHINX-III decoder, using syntactic trigrams as a post-processing language model stage. There could be still a chance for an additional reduction in WER using other configurations of language weight and syntactic weight, but we should notice that even with the optimal selection of these parameters, the syntactic language model is restricted by the performance of the lattice rescorer. In general, raising the correct hypothesis to the top of the list is not possible for syntactic trigrams unless the correct hypothesis is included in the N-best list by the lattice rescorer. In other words, the effectiveness of the language model depends on the accuracy of the A* search algorithm employed in the last stage of decoding. It is possible that additional improvements in overall performance can be obtained by considering different values of the *beam* search parameter used in the algorithm or increasing the number of hypotheses on the list.

Finally, in most of the cases where the correct hypothesis is reclassified to the second or third best position, the reason is a poor acoustic score, which vitiates the contribution of the syntactic trigrams. This suggests that incorporating this language model prior the generation of the N-best list could provide better results, as the acoustic scores, the word trigrams, and the syntactic scores could generate better hypotheses or lists of hypotheses.

Acknowledgements. This research was partially supported by NSF and CONACyT (33002-A). The authors would also like to express their gratitude to Lluis Padró (Universitat Politècnica de Cataluyna) and Marco O. Peña (ITESM) for their support during the configuration of the automatic tagger used in this work.

References

1. Rosenfeld, R., Chen, S.F., Zhu, X.: Whole-Sentence Exponential Language Models: A Vehicle for Linguistic-Statistical Integration. Computer Speech and Language, 15(1), 2001.
2. Manning, C., Schütze, H.: Fundations of Statistical Natural Language Processing, MIT Press (2001) pp 191-255.
3. Jelinek, F.: Statistical Methods for Speech Recognition, MIT Press (1994) pp 57-78.

4. Bellegarda, J., Junqua, J., van Noord, G.: Robustness in Language and Speech Technology, ELSNET/Kluwer Academic Publishers (2001) pp 101-121.
5. Huang, X., Acero, A., Hon, H.: Spoken Language Processing, Prentice-Hall (2001), pp 602-610.
6. Huerta, J.M., Chen, S., Stern, R.M.: The 1998 CMU SPHINX-3 Broadcast News Transcription System. Darpa Broadcast News Workshop, 1999.
7. Gillick, L., Cox, S.J.: Some statistical issues in the comparisson of speech recognition algorithms. In Proceedings of IEEE International Conference on Acoustics, Speech and Signal Processing (ICASSP), pp 532-535, Glasgow, May 1992.
8. Padró, L.:A Hybrid Environment for Syntax-Semantic Tagging (Ph.D. Thesis), Departament de Llenguatges i Sistemes Informàtics, Universitat Politècnica de Cataluyna, Barcelona, 1998.

A   The EAGLES Tags

The syntactic tags used in this work are based in the Expert Advisory Group on Language Engineering Standards (EAGLES) initiative [8]; this text encoding system tries to summarize the syntactic classification of each word in a code of letters and numbers to label specific attributes, such as word's class, gender, number, person, case, type, etc. In Table 2 we show the EAGLES tags used for the experiments and the particular position for gender and number (a dash means ignored attribute). Since our experiments tried to enforce the syntactic coherence in gender and number the other attributes were ignored.

Table 2. EAGLES tags.

Grammatical class	Tag	Specific attributes
Adjective	A--GN-	G → Masculine, Femenine, Common. N → Singular, Plural, Invariable.
Adverb	R-	
Article	T-GN	G → Masculine, Femenine, Common. N → Singular, Plural, Invariable.
Determiner	D--GN-	G → Masculine, Feminine, Common. N → Singular, Plural, Invariable.
Noun	N-GN---	G → Masculine, Feminine, Common. N → Singular, Plural, Invariable.
Verb	V---PNG	P → 1st person, 2nd person, 3rd person. N → Singular, Plural, Invariable. G → Masculine, Feminine, Common.
Pronoun	P-PGN---	P → 1st person, 2nd person, 3rd person. G → Masculine, Feminine, Common. N → Singular, Plural, Invariable.
Conjunction	CT	T → Coordinate, Subordinate.
Numeral	M-GN--	G → Masculine, Feminine, Common. N → Singular, Plural, Invariable.
Interjection	I	
Acronyms	Y	IGNORED
Prepositions	S--GN	G → Masculine, Feminine, Common. N → Singular, Plural, Invariable.
Punctuation marks	F	IGNORED
Week days	W	W

B   Syntactic Trigrams Counts

The following is an example of a tagged sentence and how statistics (unigrams, bigrams and trigrams) are accumulated by our system.

Utterance: *"EL MUNDO DEL ESPECTÁCULO"*
Syntactic tags:

    (el TDMS) → Article & Determiner & Masculine & Singular
    (mundo NCMS000) → Noun & Common & Masculine & Singular
    (del SPCMS) → Preposition & Contracted & Masculine & Singular
    (espectaculo NCMS000) → Noun & Common & Masculine & Singular

Unigrams:	Count(T−MS)++
	Count(N−MS−−−)++
	Count(S−−MS)++
	Count(N−MS−−−)++
Bigrams:	Count(T−MS & N−MS−−−)++
	Count(N−MS−−− & S−MS)++
	Count(S−−MS & N−MS−−−)++
Trigrams:	Count(T−MS & N−MS−−− & S−−MS)++
	Count(N−MS−−− & S−−MS & N−MS−−−)++

Continuants Based Neural Speaker Verification System

Tae-Seung Lee and Byong-Won Hwang

School of Electronics, Telecommunication and Computer Engineering, Hankuk Aviation University, 200-1, Hwajeon-dong, Deokyang-gu, Koyang-city, Kyonggi-do, 412-791, Korea
thestaff@hitel.net, bwhwang@mail.hangkong.ac.kr

Abstract. Among the techniques to protect private information by adopting biometrics, speaker verification is widely used due to its advantages in natural usage and inexpensive implementation cost. Speaker verification should achieve a high degree of reliability in verification score, flexibility in speech text usage, and efficiency in the complexity of verification system Continuants have an excellent speaker-discriminant power and the modest number of phonemes in the phonemic category. Multilayer perceptrons (MLPs) have the superior recognition ability and the fast operation speed. In consequence, the two elements can provide viable ways for speaker verification system to obtain the above properties: reliability, flexibility and efficiency. This paper shows the implementation of a system to which continuants and MLPs are applied, and evaluates the system using a Korean speech database. The results of the evaluation prove that continuants and MLPs enable the system to acquire the three properties.

Keywords: Speaker verification, biometric authentication, continuants, multiplayer perceptrons, pattern recognition

1   Introduction

Among acceptable biometric-based authentication technologies, speaker recognition has many advantages due to its natural usage and low implementation cost. Speaker recognition is a biometric recognition technique based on speech. It is classified into two types: speaker identification and speaker verification. The former enrolls multiple speakers for system and selects one speaker out of the enrolled speakers associated with the given speech. By comparison, the latter selects the speaker previously enrolled for system and claimed by a customer, and decides whether the given speech of the customer is associated with the claimed speaker. The studies for speaker verification are being conducted more widely and actively because speaker verification covers speaker identification in technical aspect [1].

For speaker verification to be influential, it is essential to have a certain degree of each of three properties: reliability in the verification score of implemented system, flexibility in the usage of speech text, and efficiency in the complexity of verification system. First, the reliability of verification score is the most important property among three in authentication system. Authentication system should give a verification score as high as possible in any adverse situation. Second, the flexibility of the usage of speech text is required for users to access the system with little effort.

R. Monroy et al. (Eds.): MICAI 2004, LNAI 2972, pp. 89–98, 2004.

To resolve the overall characteristics of a speaker, utterances with the various organ positions of vocal tract must be provided, and this burdens users with long, various, and laborious uttering [2]. Hence, it is necessary to consider that a rather short utterance might be sufficient for satisfying a high verification score. Third, for low implementation cost the efficiency of system complexity has to be achieved [3]. To prevent from being invaded by feigned accesses, many of speaker verification systems are implemented in text-prompted mode [4]. Although text-prompted mode can give immunity against the improper accesses that record the speech of an enrolled speaker and present the speech to system, it requires a speech recognition facility to recognize language units out of a text. Complex and advanced speech recognition results in increasing implementation cost of the entire system.

To content with the three properties of reliability, flexibility and efficiency, we implement a speaker verification system using continuants and multilayer perceptrons (MLPs). Continuants are in a phonemic category of which voicing is continuous and unconstraint, and have an excellent speaker-discriminant power and the small number of phonemic classes. MLPs are one of artificial neural networks in which learning of neural networks is conducted by using the error backpropagation (EBP) algorithm, and have the superior recognition ability and the fast operation speed [2], [5], [6]. Having the characteristics of continuants and the advantages of MLPs, it is expected that the system can have the three properties and achieve high speaker verification performance.

The composition of this paper hereafter is as follows. In Section 2 the feasibilities of the two ingredients of the proposed system are presented and we describe the implementation details of our speaker verification system in Section 3. The performance of the system is evaluated in Section 4. The paper is finally summarized in Section 5.

2 Continuants and MLPs for Speaker Verification

It is essential for speaker verification system to accomplish a high reliable verification score, flexible usage, and efficient system implementation. Continuants can realize the three properties in speaker verification system and MLPs help the system acquire more reliability and efficiency. In this section, we discuss briefly the feasibility of using continuants and MLPs for speaker verification system.

There are many advantages of using continuants as a major language unit in speaker verification. Speaker verification can be understood as a vocal track model adopting multiple lossless tubes [7]. In view of this model, modeling speech signal based on language information is necessary because the intra-speaker variation is bigger than the inter-speaker variation, i.e. the speaker information from the inter-speaker variation is apt to be overwhelmed by the language information from the intra-speaker variation [2]. The three properties of speaker verification system are determined by the type of language unit used. Of various language units, phonemes can reflect efficiently the reliability and the flexibility. Phonemes are atomic language units. All words are composed of phonemes and the characteristics of different speakers can be finely discriminated within a phoneme. However, the capability of speaker verification varies as to phonemic categories mainly due to their steadiness and duration of voicing. Eatock et al. and Delacretaz et al. have studied such difference in verification capability and their works are summarized in Fig. 1 [5], [8]. Continuants feature continuous and unconstraint voicing and include the best elements, nasals and vowels in Fig. 1. They show more improved verification capability than that of any other phoneme category, therefore enhance the reliability. Continuants can be easily detected by speech recognition facility because of their long voicing and the small number of kinds. As a result, continuants can largely enhance the implementation efficiency of speech recognition facility as well as the flexibility of compositions into any verification words with higher verification reliability.

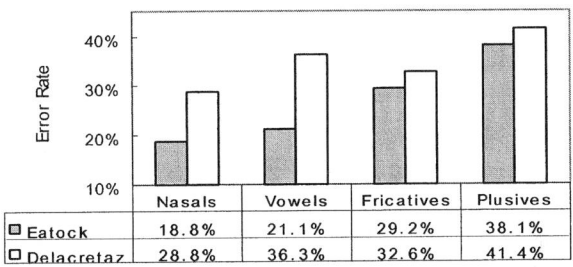

Fig. 1. Speaker identification error rates for the various phonemic categories reported in Eatock et al. and Delacretaz et al.

MLPs are the nonparametric method of classifying suitable for speaker verification due to their higher recognition rate and faster recognition speed over the parametric methods of the existing systems. MLPs learn decision boundaries to discriminate optimally between models. For speaker verification, MLPs have two models needed to classify, i.e. enrolling speaker and background speakers. Such MLPs which have only two learning models present the effectiveness similar to the cohort speakers method developed in the existing parametric-based speaker verification, in which the cohorts consist of the background speakers closest to an enrolling speaker [9]. However, the cohort speakers method based on probability density functions might derive a false recognition result according to the distribution densities of an enrolling speaker and background speakers. That is, if the density of the enrolling speaker is lower and the variance of the speaker is higher than those of any background speakers, then a speaker different to the enrolled speaker might be accepted though the speaker is far from the enrolled speaker. On the other hand, MLPs avoid that problem because it discriminates the two models on the basis of their discriminative decision boundary. Figure 2 demonstrates such a situation when the enrolled speaker is male and customer is female, and compares the cohort speakers method with MLPs. In addition to it, MLPs achieve a superior verification error rate since they need not to assume any probability distribution of underlying data [6]. It is finally noted that the reason that MLPs show faster recognition speed can be analyzed that all the background speakers are merged into a model. The merging enables for MLPs to have no need to calculate likelihoods for each background speaker at verifying identities [9].

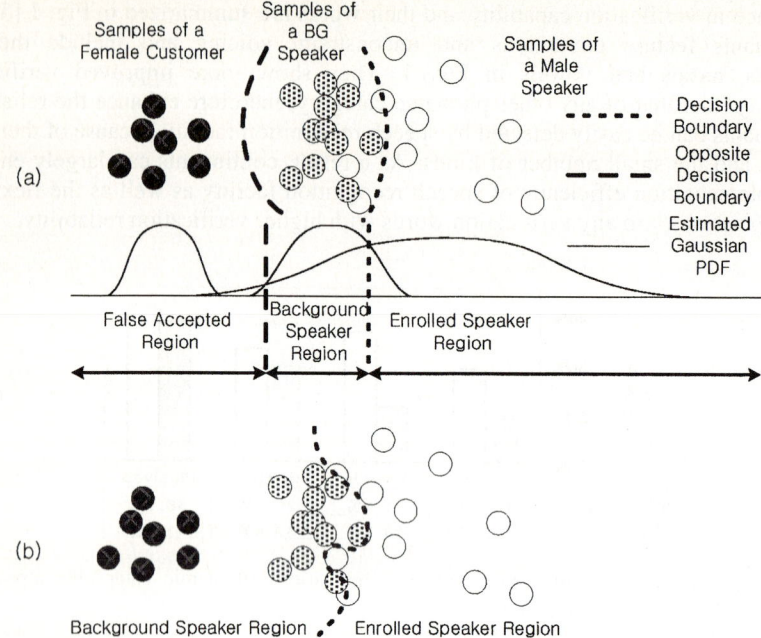

Fig. 2. A comparison of the cohort speakers method and MLPs for a specific error situation: (a) when decision boundary by Gaussian probability density functions in the cohort speakers method is used; (b) when discriminative decision boundary of MLPs is used for the same situation to (a)

3 Implemented System

In this paper we implement a speaker verification system based on continuants and MLPs. Because this system is based on continuants, which has a small phoneme set, it might be adapted easily to any of text-modes such as text-dependent, text-independent and text-prompt mode [10]. However, the text-dependent mode is adopted in this system for easy implementation, in which enrolling text should be the same to verifying text. The speaker verification system extracts isolated words from input utterances, classifies the isolated words into nine Korean continuants (/a/, /e/, /ə/, /o/, /u/, /ï/, /i/, /l/, nasals) stream, learns an enrolling speaker using MLPs for each continuant, and calculates identity scores of customers. The procedures performed in this system are described in the following:

(1) Analysis and Feature Extraction [11]
The utterance input sampled in 16 bits and 16 kHz is divided into 30ms frames overlapped every 10ms. 16 Mel-scaled filter bank coefficients are extracted from each frame and are used to detect isolated words and continuants. To remove the effect of utterance loudness from the entire spectrum envelope, the average of the coefficients from 0 to 1 kHz is subtracted from all the coefficients and the coefficients are

adjusted for the average of the whole coefficients to be zero. 50 Mel-scaled filter bank coefficients that are especially linear scaled from 0 to 3 kHz are extracted from each frame and are used for speaker verification. This scaling adopts the study arguing that more information about speakers concentrates on the second formant rather than the first [12]. As with the extraction to detect isolated words and continuants, the same process to remove the effect of utterance loudness is applied here too.

(2) Detecting Isolated Words and Continuants
Isolated words and continuants are detected using an MLP learned to detect all the continuants and silence in speaker-independent mode.

(3) Learning MLPs with Enrolling Speaker for Each Continuant
For each continuant, the frames detected from the isolated words are input to the corresponding MLP and the MLP learns enrolling speaker with background speakers.

(4) Evaluating Speaker Score for Each Continuant
For each continuant, all the frames detected from the isolated words are input to the corresponding MLP. All the outputs of the MLPs are averaged.

(5) Comparing Speaker Score with Threshold
The final reject/accept decision is made by comparing a predefined threshold with the average from the step (4).

Since this speaker verification system uses the continuants as speaker recognition units, the underlying densities show mono-modal distributions [2]. It is, therefore, enough for each MLP to have two layers structure that includes one hidden layer [5], [13]. Since the number of models for the MLPs to learn is two, one is enrolling speaker and the other background speakers, the MLPs can learn the models using only one output node and two hidden nodes. Nine MLPs in total are provided for nine continuants.

4   Performance Evaluation

To evaluate the performance of the implemented speaker verification system, an experiment is conducted using a Korean speech database. This section records the results of the evaluation.

4.1   Speech Database

The speech data used in this experiment are the recording of connected four digits spoken by 40 Korean male and female speakers, which the digits are Arabic numerals each corresponding to /goN/, /il/, /i/, /sam/, /sa/, /o/, /yug/, /cil/, /pal/, /gu/ in Korean pronunciation. Each of the speakers utters totally 35 words of different digit strings four times, and the utterances are recorded in 16 bits resolution and 16 kHz sampling.

Three of the four utterances are used to enroll speakers, and the last utterance to verify. As background speakers for MLPs to learn enrolling speakers discriminatively, 29 Korean male and female speakers except for the above 40 speakers are participated.

4.2 Experiment Condition

In this evaluation, MLP learning to enroll a speaker is set up as follows [6]:

- MLPs are trained by the online mode EBP algorithm.
- Input patterns are normalized such that the elements of each pattern are into the range from -1.0 to +1.0.
- The objectives of output node, i.e., learning targets, are +0.9 for an enrolling speaker and -0.9 for background speakers to obtain faster EBP learning speed.
- Speech patterns of the two models are presented in an alternative manner during learning. In most cases, the numbers of patterns for the two models are not the same. Therefore, the patterns of the model having fewer patterns are repetitively presented until all the patterns of the model having more patterns are once presented, and it completes one learning epoch.
- Since learning might be fallen in a local minimum, the maximum number of learning epochs is limited to 1000.

Each of the 40 speakers is regarded as both enrolling speaker and true test speaker, and when a speaker out of them is picked as true speaker the other 39 speakers are used as imposters. As a result, for each test speaker 35-time tests are performed for true speaker and 1,560-time tests for imposter. As a whole, 1,400 trials of test for true speaker and 54,600 trials for imposter are performed in the experiment.

The experiment is conducted on a 1 GHz personal computer machine. In the experiment result, the error rate designates the equal error rate (EER), the number of learning epochs the averaged number of epochs used to enroll a speaker for a digit string word, and the learning duration the overall duration taken to learn these patterns. The values of error rate, the number of learning epochs, and learning durations are the averages for the results of three-time learning each with the same MLP learning condition to compensate for the effect of the randomly selected initial weights.

4.3 Evaluation Results

The experiment to evaluate the performance of the proposed system consists of two stages. First, the overall performance for the experimental speech database is measured. To do so, the parameters involved to train MLPs are searched to record error rates and the numbers of learning epochs when the best learning is achieved. Then, the learning records are analyzed for the advantages from the use of MLPs and continuants discussed in Section 2. To argue the merits of MLPs over the cohort speaker method, the EERs are divided into ones for the same sex and for the different sex. To analyze the advantages of continuants, the EERs according to the number of the extracted continuants and the number of frames in the extracted continuants for each digit string are measured.

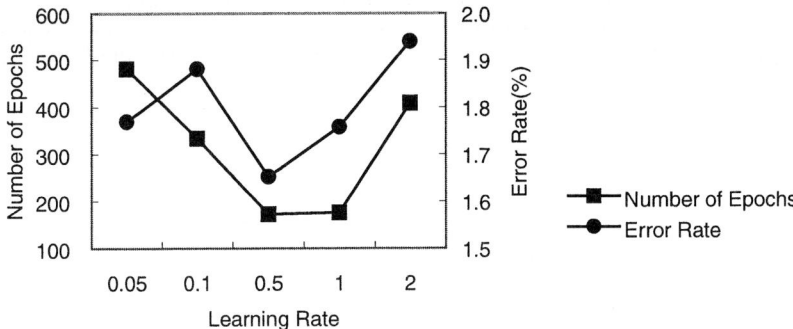

Fig. 3. The performance points of the system with different learning rates

The learning parameters in the MLP learning using the EBP algorithm include learning rate and learning objective error energy [6]. Learning rate is the parameter to adjust the updating step-length of the internal weight vector in MLPs. The learning rate that is too small or large value tends to prolong learning duration and becomes a cause to increase error rate. It is because a small value grows the number of learning epochs until the objective is reached and a large value makes learning oscillate around the optimal learning objective. Error energy gauges the difference between the desired output vector and the current output vector of an MLP, and learning objective error energy is the objective that MLPs must get to for the given learning data. Although error rate must be decreased as low learning objective error energy is taken, the number of learning epochs increases along with error rate. It is even possible for the error rate to get worse for the large number of epochs. As a consequence, it needs to determine the proper learning objective error energy and learning rate in the MLP learning using the EBP.

The performance change of the implemented system as to various learning rates for the EBP algorithm is depicted in Fig. 3. Those values in the figure are to pursue the trajectories of the numbers of the learning epochs and the verification errors when learning objective error energy is fixed to 0.01. As seen in the figure, when the best learning is achieved, i.e. the number of learning epochs is 172.3, and the error rate 1.65 %, the point of learning rate is 0.5.

The performance change of the implemented system as to various learning objective error energies is depicted in Fig. 4. Those values in the figure are to pursue the trajectories of the numbers of the learning epochs and the verification errors when learning rate is fixed to 0.5 as determined in Fig. 3. As seen in the figure, when the optimal learning is achieved, i.e. the number of learning epochs is 301.5, and the error rate 1.59 %, the point of learning objective error energy is 0.005. The best performance achieved is summarized in Table 1.

To demonstrate the suitability of MLPs to speaker verification, the experimental results are analyzed for reliability and efficiency. The high reliability of MLPs is derived from their discriminative decision boundary. The discriminative decision boundary is to protect the verification system from the error by the difference of distribution densities between speakers of the two types: enrolling and background speakers. To verify this, the experimental speaker set is rearranged to examine two different experimental conditions; one is such that the sex of enrolling speakers is the

Table 1. The best performance of the implemented system

EER (%)	Number of Epochs	Enrolling Duration (sec)	Verifying Duration (millisec)
1.59	301.5	2.7	0.86

Table 2. Comparison of the error rates for the same sexes and for different sexes at enrolling and verifying speakers

	Entire Database	Same Sex	Different Sex
EER (%)	1.59	2.29	0.78

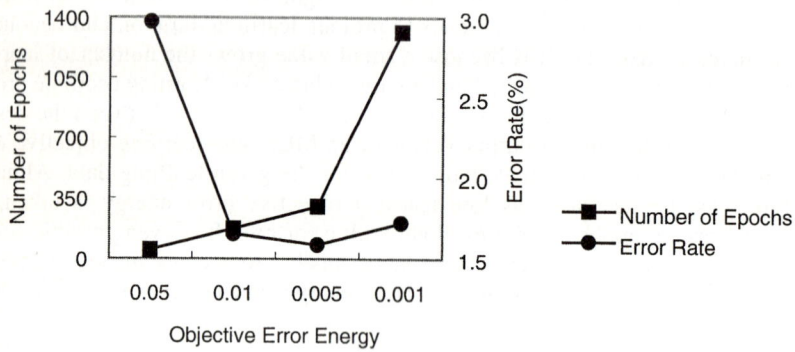

Fig. 4. The performance points of the system with different learning objective error energies

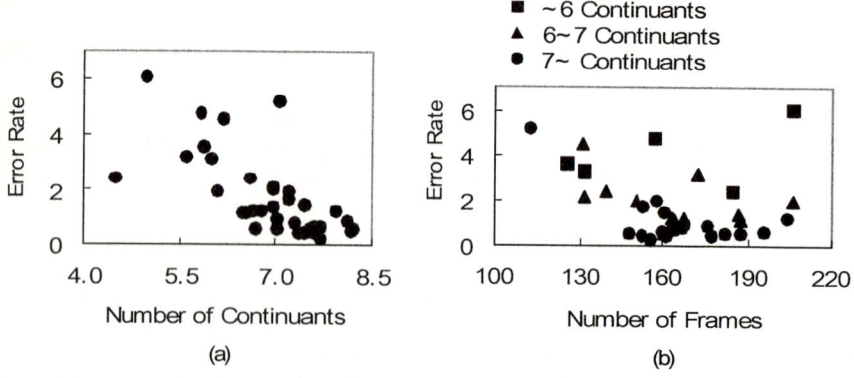

Fig. 5. Experiment result analyses: (a) Distribution of error rates according to the numbers of the extracted continuants for each verifying digit string; (b) Distribution of error rates according to the numbers of frames in the extracted continuants for each verifying digit string

same to those of verifying speakers and the other vice versa. The results of the rearrangement are presented in Table 2 and enable us to know that the high EER for the same sex and the low EER for the different sex are obtained over the EER for the entire database.

To illustrate the superior properties of continuants for speaker verification, the experiment results are analyzed for reliability in error rate, flexibility in utterance duration and efficiency in the number of recognition units. Figures (a) and (b) of Fig. 5 represent the distribution of error rates according to the numbers of the extracted continuants for each digit string of identity verifying and the distribution to the numbers of frames in the extracted continuants, respectively. The result of figure (a) informs that error rate decreases near linearly as the number of continuants increases and the error rate less than 1 % can be obtained when over 7.5 out of 9 continuants are included in verifying utterance. Figure (b) means that only the level of 2 to 4 seconds in utterance duration, when the duration of unit frame is 10 ms, is sufficient to achieve fairly low error rate, even though it needs to be born in mind that the verifying utterance includes consonants and other phonemes besides continuants. The results of Fig. 5 say that it is more important to get many continuants rather than to keep the utterance of the same continuant long when the duration is over some level. It is finally noted that the complexity of speech recognition module to identify continuants will be eased from the fact that the number of continuants to be recognized is only up to 9.

5 Conclusion

The measurements and analyses for the experiment brought out the credibility, elasticity and practicality that continuants and MLPs can show for the application to speaker verification. To make an appeal, speaker verification should achieve a high degree of credibility in verification score, elasticity in speech text usage, and practicality in verification system complexity. Continuants have an excellent speaker-discriminant power and the small number of classes, and multilayer perceptrons have the high recognition ability and the fast operation speed. In consequence, the two provide feasible means for a speaker verification system to obtain the above three properties. In this paper we implemented the speaker verification system to which continuants and MLP were applied, and measured and analyzed the system for performance evaluation using the Korean continuously spoken four-digit speech database. The results of the experiment ascertain that continuants are very effective to achieve all the three properties and MLPs enable the system to acquire more credibility and practicality.

References

1. Li, Q., Juang B., Lee C., Zhou, Q., Song, F.: Recent Advancements in Automatic Speaker Authentication. IEEE Robotics & Automation Magazine 6 (1999) 24-34
2. Savic, M., Sorensen, J.: Phoneme Based Speaker Verification. IEEE International Conference on Acoustics, Speech, and Signal Processing 2 (1992) 165-168

3. Lodi, A., Toma M., Guerrieri, R.: Very Low Complexity Prompted Speaker Verification System Based on HMM-Modeling. IEEE International Conference on Acoustics, Speech, and Signal Processing 4 (2002) IV-3912-IV-3915
4. Che, C. W., Lin, Q., Yuk, D. S.: An HMM Approach to Text-Prompted Speaker Verification. IEEE International Conference on Acoustics, Speech, and Signal Processing 2 (1996) 673-676
5. Delacretaz, D. P., Hennebert, J.: Text-Prompted Speaker Verification Experiments with Phoneme Specific MLPs. IEEE International Conference on Acoustics, Speech, and Signal Processing 2 (1998) 777-780
6. Bengio, Y.: Neural Networks for Speech and Sequence Recognition. International Thomson Computer Press, London Boston (1995)
7. O'Shaughnessy, D.: Speech Communications: Human and Machine. 2nd edn. IEEE Press, New York (2000)
8. Eatock, J. P., Mason, J. S.: A Quantitative Assessment of the Relative Speaker Discriminating Properties of Phonemes. IEEE International Conference on Acoustics, Speech, and Signal Processing 1 (1994) 133-136
9. Rosenberg, A. E., Parthasarathy, S.: Speaker Background Models for Connected Digit Password Speaker Verification. IEEE International Conference on Acoustics, Speech, and Signal Processing 1 (1996) 81-84
10. Furui, S.: An Overview of Speaker Recognition Technology. In: Lee, C. H. (eds.): Automatic Speech and Speaker Recognition. Kluwer Academic Publishers, Massachusetts (1996)
11. Becchetti, C., Ricotti, L. P.: Speech Recognition: Theory and C++ Implementation. John Wiley & Sons, Chinchester New York Weinheim Brisbane Singapore Toronto (1999)
12. Cristea, P., Valsan, Z.: New Cepstrum Frequency Scale for Neural Network Speaker Verification. IEEE International Conference on Electronics, Circuits and Systems 3 (1999) 1573-1576
13. Lippmann, R. P.: An Introduction to Computing with Neural Nets. IEEE Acoustics, Speech, and Signal Processing Magazine 4 (1987) 4-22

Agent Protocols as Executable Ontologies

Manuel José Contreras M. and Alan Smaill

School of Informatics, University of Edinburgh
{M.Contreras,A.Smaill}@ed.ac.uk

Abstract. Agent protocols are difficult to specify, implement, share and reuse. In addition, there are not well developed tools or methodologies to do so. Current efforts are focused in creating protocol languages with which it is possible to have formal diagrammatic representations of protocols. What we propose is a framework to use ontology technology to specify protocols in order to make them shareable and reusable.

1 Introduction

Agent protocols are very complex and have different elements which need to be carefully combined and well understood in order to make them useful. They need to be unambiguous and readable by both humans and agents. This is not an easy task because even most simple agent protocols can be very complex and difficult to implement. In addition, there are not well developed tools to make it easy. For instance, in [6] the author says that *Perhaps the major challenge from a technical point of view was the design of the protocols. . .* and this is because even in big implementations the protocols are built from scratch and there are not shared and reusable libraries or methodologies to create a protocol for a specific purpose. If there are some, it may be not be worth trying to use them because —at the current stage of protocols development— it is less risky and easier to create the desired protocol from scratch.

Protocols are complex because they have several components that need to work well and smoothly together. For instance, unknown agents aiming to have a conversation need to agree about the language to use and its semantics. In addition, they need to share the knowledge needed to use that language in a specific matter or ontology. If we are talking about non centralised protocols, the coherence of the conversations relies on the ability of every agent to understand and interpret properly all the protocol components.

What we propose here is a framework that uses ontology technology to specify protocols. What we do is to create the ontologies with an ontology editor (e.g. Protégé[8]) and convert them to the Resource Description Framework (RDF) model. In this way it is possible to generate protocol instantiations from reusable specifications. The challenge here is to create a framework which supports languages sufficiently expressive to specify protocols and their formal diagrammatic specification. In this paper we address the following issues:

1. Is it possible to keep in an ontology all the features that protocol languages provide?
2. What do we gain from using this approach to specify the protocols?

R. Monroy et al. (Eds.): MICAI 2004, LNAI 2972, pp. 99–108, 2004.

2   Background

An Agent Communication Protocol aimed to be a communication channel between unknown, autonomous and heterogeneous agents would ideally have most of the following characteristics:

- It needs to be specified in such a way that there is no room for ambiguities which lead the developers to different interpretations of the protocol.
- The specification language needs to be expressive enough to state all the required features in a protocol of this kind.
- The specification needs to be as easy as possible to read/understand and able to be run in different computer languages and platforms. That means that the way to specify the protocol needs to be a standard or a widely used language.
- The specification needs to be easy to maintain, share and reuse.
- The specification needs to support concurrency.

Protocols in agent communication have been specified in many different ways. We can find specifications based on the combination of natural language and AUML[1] diagrams[4]. This is a very general specification of the type of messages (i.e. the performative to use) and the sequence that agents should follow to exchange them in a context with a high level of generality. For complex conversations agents need to have more information than that. For instance, the possible reason why the other participants or themselves are reacting in a particular way. If an agent is aiming to have conversations with unknown and heterogeneous agents, it needs to be able to solve aspects of the protocol that are not well defined in this kind of specification. And the developers are forced to interpret the lack of information (or ambiguity) in their own way to equip their agents with the complete machinery needed to run the protocol[1].

There is work going on to tackle this issue. Much of the recent effort focuses on techniques that allow protocols to be specified in two different ways. The first one is a formal language with enough expressiveness to create unambiguous protocols which do not leave room for different interpretations. The second is to find a diagrammatic representation with which it is possible to represent a protocol without losing expressiveness. In [7] the authors propose the ANML protocol language and a diagrammatic representation which combines an extension of statechart notation and some ANML features. In [9] the author describes a formal method using rewrite rules to specify asynchronous and concurrent agent executable dialogues. This description allows the specification of formally concurrent protocols.

Although these approaches present executable descriptions of protocols, the problem of interoperability is not solved. In addition, we would like to have a mechanism to specify protocols which has features from both languages, for instance, concurrency and diagrammatic representation.

---

[1] Agent-based Unified Modelling Language

3 Protocols as Ontologies

If we take a well known and general definition of what an ontology is we may say that it is an explicit specification of a conceptualisation[5]. From this view it would be possible to specify any concept. A protocol is a concept, therefore it can be specified in this way. However, ontologies have been traditionally used for specifying objects, not processes or exchange of messages. A major difference between a protocol and an object is that the protocol needs to be executable. That is, a protocol is a specification that can lead an agent to perform some actions and to put itself in a specific position within a group of agents. When we talk about heterogeneous computer programs (i.e, software agents) which have some degree of autonomy and may or not have interacted before —to collaborate or perhaps to compete—, that is not a trivial issue.

What we propose here is to specify the protocols using ontology technology. One advantage of this approach is that agent technology is dealing with the issue of how agents should understand, share and handle ontologies and these efforts are being done separately from agent protocols. We can assume that agents will have to extend their capabilities of ontology management to be able to cope with these *executable ontologies*. In fact, we see agent protocols as a special case of ontologies.

4 Architecture

In order to specify the protocol as an ontology it is necessary to identify which are the main elements that are always present in any protocol. Doing this we are able to make a generic ontology which can be used as a template to create instantiations from it. The main elements that we can find in protocols are:

Roles are assigned to agents. They define the set of states and transitions that the agent is allowed to pass through and the actions that the agent is allowed and perhaps, obligated to perform.

States may be explicitly or implicitly stated. Every agent is always in a particular state related to the role it is playing. States may be specified in a hierarchical way which specifies that $X \subset Y$ where X and Y are states.

Transitions are links between states and are used by the agents to go from one state to another. They need to be triggered by preconditions. They are often related to processes that should be executed when the transition has been triggered. They have a direction that specifies the origin state and the target sate.

Actions are specific processes that the agents need to execute at some point in the protocol. They may be executed within a state or a transition.

Operators relate transitions and actions to lead the agents to the next step to perform.

Messages are the units of information that agents send and receive among them. The agents may send messages during a process within a state or during a transition. Messages may be received at any time.

Decision points are places where agents need to make decisions in order to carry on with the protocol. They involve operators, transitions and actions. This point is central to the ambiguity problem since some protocol specifications do not say how the agents may/should take decisions.

4.1   The High Level Set of Ontologies

In this section we describe in a top-down way the high level architecture of the different ontologies we put together to get a template from which we can create instantiations. The whole architecture is based on ontologies. That is, all the elements described are ontologies or properties of an ontology. An element of an ontology may be an ontology or an atomic value. We describe ontologies as tuples in the form $o = \{e_1, \ldots, e_n\}$ where n is the number of elements in o. We describe the structure of an ontology as a record type $Ontology = \{A_1 : O_1, \ldots, A_m : O_m\}$ with m fields named $A_1, \ldots A_m$; each field type may be an ontology or an atomic type $AtomicType$ that is defined as

$$Ontology.AtomicType ::= integer|float|symbol|uri|ip|boolean|\ldots$$

where the left hand side of the dot represents the ontology and the right hand side the type. It is possible to have a wide range of atomic types. We assume that there are ontologies that describe lists and sets where the elements may be atomic values or ontologies. The ontology $Protocol$ is defined as

$$Protocol = \{Name, URI, Roles, States, Processes, Transitions, Messages\}$$

where $Name$ is a symbol that identifies a particular kind of protocol, for instance $Name = english\_auction$. This information helps the interoperability since these symbols may become a standard among agent community. If a new type of protocol is created, it is an easy task to create a new symbol for it. URI is an Uniform Resource Identifier[11] which helps to identify a specific instantiation of a particular protocol. For example, $URI = whereagentsare.org{:}26000/ABC123$ describes a particular machine and port where the agents need to request to participate in the protocol $ABC123$. This protocol may be held just for a few hours or days and once finished that URI will be no longer valid to participate in any other protocol. Instead, the URI may be used to retrieve the history of the protocol (e.g. identity of the participants and the result of the protocol) as necessary.

$Roles$ is an ontology which specifies all roles that may be assumed by the agents and those agents who can assume those roles. We say that

$$Roles = \{RName, SetOfAgents, SetOfStates\}$$

where $RName$ is a symbol and $SetOfAgents$ is an ontology that describes the agents allowed to assume the role and how many agents can assume the role at the same time. $SetOfAgents$ is described as

$$SetOfAgents = \{Agents, MaxNumber\}$$

where $Agents$ is an ontology that describes a set of agents. Every agent is described as

$$Agent = \{AName, IP, Port\}$$

where $AName$ is a unique[2] symbol, IP is an Internet Protocol Address and $Port$ is and integer that specifies the port where the agent can be reached at that IP. This information allows identification of a particular agent on the Internet. This implies that the same agent may reside in another IP/port at the same moment of performing the protocol allowing the agents to be mobile and ubiquitous. $MaxNumber$ is the maximum number of agents that can assume this role at once. If $MaxNumber = -1$ the maximum number is not defined and there is no limit.

$SetOfStates$ is an ontology describing the set of states that a particular role is allowed to pass through in the protocol. Every state is specified as

$$States = \{SName, Ancestor, TransIn, TransOut, TransFormulae\}$$

where $SName$ is a symbol, $Ancestor$ is defined as

$$Ancestor ::= SName|nil$$

that allows to have a hierarchical structure of states which can have a root ancestor. $TransIn$ and $TransOut$ are sets of transitions which allow agents to enter and leave the sate. These are defined as:

$$Transitions = \{TName, StateFrom, StateTo, ProcFormulae, Parameters\}$$

where $TName$ is a symbol, $StateFrom$ and $StateTo$ are sets of state names which specify the states that are linked by the transition. $ProcFormulae$ is a formula that defines the way the processes that are involved in the transition should be executed. When the formula is evaluated, there is a boolean output. $Parameters$ defines the parameters that should be passed to every process involved in $ProcFormulae$. Before explaining how these two elements work, we describe $TransFormulae$ which is an element of $States$ ontology and that is the upper level formula.

$TransFormulae$ is the decision point in every state. When agents enter a state, they should evaluate this formula in order to know the next step to do. That is, which transition(s) they should follow. The decision point is not deterministic since the evaluation's result may vary depending on the agents' beliefs and capabilities.

The transition operators we describe here are: $\triangle$ which describes an *or* in the sense that if T_a is *true* in $T_a \triangle T_b$ then T_b is not evaluated; $\triangledown$ describes an *or* with the meaning that both operands will be evaluated and will return *true* if either of them is *true*; the operator *par* works as described in [9] where

---

[2] The issue of how to make these symbols unique is outside the scope of this paper but is very relevant for the interoperability problem.

both transitions will be evaluated concurrently; the operator $\wedge\diamond$ has the syntax $A \wedge \diamond B$ [9] where if A is true, B will be evaluated at some point in the future; the operator $\vee par$ evaluates both operands concurrently and when one of them is true will stop evaluating the other. *TransFormulae* is defined as

$$TransFormulae ::= boolean|nil|TOp'['FP \quad FP']'$$
$$TOp ::= \triangle|\,\triangledown\,|par|\wedge\diamond|\vee\,par$$
$$FP ::= TransFormulae|PName$$

In figure 1 we present a diagrammatic representation of the transition operators as defined above. The little dots at the end of the lines between transitions show the precedence in which every transitions should be evaluated.

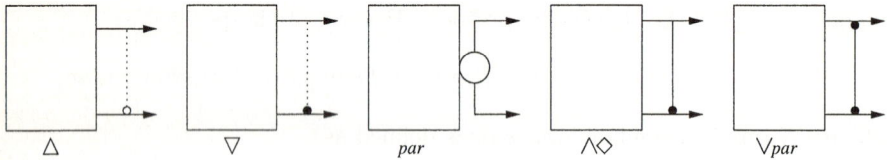

Fig. 1. Transition Operators

PName is a process name explained below. The processes are defined as

$$Process = \{PName, ParamStructure, Output,$$
$$Description, SampleCode\}$$

where *PName* is a symbol, *ParamStructure* is an ontology describing the process' parameters (e.g. order and type), $Output ::= Ontology.AtomicType$. *Description* is a brief explanation of the functionality of the process stated in natural language and *SampleCode* is a small programming language code to illustrate the process. These two last properties are omitted in this paper for reasons of space. We now come back to *ProcFormulae* which is a formula that specifies how processes are evaluated and is defined as

$$ProcFormulae ::= nil|boolean|Comparison|LogicOperator'['PC \quad PC']'$$
$$PC ::= ProcFormulae|Comparison$$
$$LogicOperator ::= \vee|\,\wedge$$
$$Comparison ::= ComparisonOp'['PAT \quad PAT']'$$
$$PAT ::= PName|Ontology.AtomicType$$
$$ComparisonOp ::= =\,|\neq|\leq|\geq$$

where we have two logical operators and four comparison operators. Every time a process is present in *ProcFormulae*, it has a set of parameters specified in

Parameters. If a process is specified more than once, the order of the sets of parameters matches with the order of precedence in *ProcFormulae.*

$$Parameters ::= {'['}(PName'['ParamList^{*}']')^{*}']'$$
$$ParamList ::= Ontology.AtomicType$$

Messages is an ontology based in the FIPA ACL[3] Message Structure Specification[3]. For simplicity, we are not using all the fields.

$$Messages = \{Performative, Sender, Receivers, Ontology,$$
$$Protocol, Content, Language\}$$
$$Performative ::= request|inform$$
$$Sender ::= Agent$$
$$Receivers ::= {'['}Agent^{+}']'$$
$$Ontology ::= uri$$
$$Protocol ::= uri$$

Content is the content of the message and is what the agent who sends the message wants to communicate to the receivers. *Language* is the language used to express the content.

5   Example

We present the simplified case for one of the protocols of *Agenteel*, a system that we are implementing and with which we are exploring the ideas presented here. Agenteel is a multi agent framework which architecture requires an agent called *yellowPages* and a set of agents called *nodes*. The main function of *yellowPages* is to stay online in the same point on the web. In the protocol, where to find *yellowPages* is stated. So any *node* capable of finding, reading and executing the protocol can find it easily. The issue of where to find the specification is not discussed in this example: we assume that the agents know where to find the protocol's specification. When a *node* wants to be incorporated in the framework, makes contact with *yellowPages* and obtains the information about where the other agents are and gives the information of where it can be found. In addition, *yellowPages* propagates to the other nodes the address of the new *node*. So our first definition is

$$Protocol = \{agenteel, whereagentsare.org : 26000/001,$$
$$\{\{yellowPages, \{yp, whereagentsare, 26000\}, 1\},$$
$$\{listening, attendMessage\}\},$$
$$\{node, \{\}, -1\},$$
$$\{initialising, waitingConfirmation, online, offline\}\}$$
$$States, Processes, T, Messages\}$$

---

[3] Agent Communication Language

where the role $yellowPages$ can be enacted by a single agent which should be specifically the agent yp. This issue of authority in protocols is important: who can take what roles? In contrast, there is room for any number of nodes. Any agent may execute the protocol and assume the $node$ role. The states are defined as

$$States = \{\{listening, nil, \{t_1\}, \{t_1, t_2\}, decision_1\},$$
$$\{attendMessage, nil, \{t_2\}, nil, nil\},$$
$$\{initialising, nil, nil, \{t_3\}, decision_2\},$$
$$\{waitingConfirmation, nil, \{t_3\}, \{t_4, t_5\}, decision_3\},$$
$$\{online, nil, \{t_4\}, nil, nil\},$$
$$\{offline, nil, \{t_5\}, nil, nil\}\}$$

With this information an agent can have an idea of the paths that is possible to take not just for the role it will assume but for the other roles. In addition, it is possible to know where are the decision points. The transitions are defined as

$$T = \{\{t_1, listening, listening, = [receivedMessage \quad true], nil\},$$
$$\{t_2, listening, attendMessage,$$
$$= [getMessage \quad inform], [getMessage[performative \quad M]]\},$$
$$\{t_3, initialising, waitingConfirmation,$$
$$= [sendMessage \quad true], [sendMessage[yp \quad M]]\},$$
$$\{t_4, waitingConfirmation, online,$$
$$\wedge[= [getMessage \quad inform] \quad = [getMessage \quad accepted]],$$
$$[getMessage[performative \quad M] \quad getMessage[content \quad M]]\},$$
$$\{t_5, waitingConfirmation, offline, \geq [timeOut \quad 10], [timeOut[T]]\}\}$$

The transitions' specification gives the agent the necessary information to know how the processes should be performed and what conditions are needed to trigger the transitions.

$$Processes = \{\{getMessage, [symbol], message.abstract\},$$
$$\{receivedMessage, [], boolean\},$$
$$\{sendMessage, [agent \quad message], boolean\},$$
$$\{timeOut, [time], boolean\}\}$$

The processes' specification completes the information that the agents need to know if they are capable of performing the processes in order to assume a specific role. Agents need to answer the question: am I capable of assuming this role? In the processes we have omitted $Description$ and $SampleCode$ to simplify the example. In $ParamStructure$ we have defined only the parameters' type. $message.abstract$ assumes that all the fields in the ontology $Messages$ have been inherited from an abstract type that allows the output to be of any field found in it. The decisions points are

$$decision_1 = \wedge \diamond [t_1 \quad par[t_1 \quad t_2]]$$
$$decision_2 = t_3$$
$$decision_3 = \vee par[t_4 \quad t_5]$$

where there are three decision points. In $decision_1$, $yellowPages$ acts as a server listening for new incoming messages and when a message arrives it breaks the execution in two threads; one to go back to keep listening and the other to attend the message. In $decision_2$ the agent does not have any choice, when it is initialising the protocol, it should send a message to $yellowPages$. In $decision_3$ the agent evaluates both transitions and waits until it receives a confirmation that it has been included in the framework. On the other hand, if the process $timeOut$ reaches its limit the agent is not included in the framework. In this case, to get into the framework, the agent would need to start the protocol from the beginning again. In figure 2 are depicted the two simplified diagrammatic representations —one for each role— that together comprise the whole protocol.

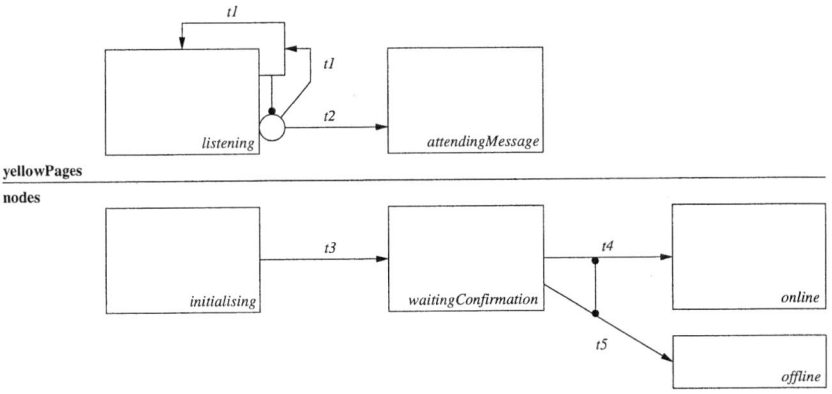

Fig. 2. Agenteel Protocol

6   Current Work and Conclusions

We are using Protégé[8] to create this kind of protocol and to convert them to the RDF model. This model is divided in two parts. The first one is the structure of the ontology and the second is the instantiation of it. This allows the agents to read the instantiation of the protocol and to reason about any term found in it using the structure's specification. Agenteel is created using the Mozart Programming Language[10]. We are using a XML parser[2] that has the capability of reading RDF specifications and parse them into Mozart's internal data structures. This shows that it is possible to specify protocols using ontology technology and to execute them using a programming language. Agenteel supports protocols which are held by only one agent. That is, the agents internal behaviour is controlled by internal protocols or soliloquies.

Even though there is much more work to do we believe that it is possible to specify protocols using ontologies and keep the features needed by the agent community. This will improve agent interoperability. What we gain doing so is that instead of tackling the problems of ontologies and protocols separately we have a bigger picture of a problem that we think embraces both issues. In addition to this, we contribute to the task of creating shareable and reusable protocols. Reusability is a feature that software technology has been developing as one of its most important characteristics. As part of software improvement it is necessary that agent developers evaluate the possibilities that programming languages offer in order to implement agent protocols which are very demanding.

References

1. Stephen Cranfield, Martin Purvis, Mariusz Nowostawski, and Peter Hwang. On-tologies for Interaction Protocols. Technical Report f-in-00076, Department of Information Science, University of Otago, 2002.
2. Denys Duchier. http://www.mozart-oz.org/mogul/info/duchier/xml/parser.html.
3. FIPA. FIPA ACL Message Structure Specification. Technical Report PC00061E, Foundation for Intelligent Physical Agents, 2001.
   http://www.fipa.org/specs/fipa00061/XC00061E.pdf.
4. FIPA. FIPA Request Interaction Protocol Specification. Technical Report SC00026H, Foundation for Intelligent Physical Agents, 2002. http://www.fipa.org.
5. Gruber T.R. A Translation Approach to Portable Ontology Specifications. *Knowledge Acquisition*, 5(2):21–66, 1998.
6. Pablo Noriega. In Institut d'Investigació en Intel-ligència Artificial and Consell Superior d'Investigacions Cintífiques, editor, *Agent Mediated Auctions: The Fishmarket Metaphor*, number 8 in Monografies del L'IIIA. Institut d'Investigació en Intel-ligència Artificial, 1999.
7. S. Paurobally, J. Cunningham, and N. R. Jennings. Developing Agent Interaction Protocols Using Graphical and Logical Methodologies. In *AAMAS'03*, 2003.
8. Protégé. http://protege.stanford.edu/.
9. Dave Robertson. A Lightweight Method for Coordination of Agent Oriented Web Services. Technical report, University of Edinburgh, 2003.
10. Mozart Programming System. http://www.mozart-oz.org/.
11. Semantic Web. http://www.w3.org/addressing.

Evaluation of RDF(S) and DAML+OIL Import/Export Services within Ontology Platforms

Asunción Gómez-Pérez and M. Carmen Suárez-Figueroa

Laboratorio de Inteligencia Artificial
Facultad de Informática
Universidad Politécnica de Madrid
Campus de Montegancedo sn.
Boadilla del Monte, 28660. Madrid, Spain
asun@fi.upm.es
mcsuarez@delicias.dia.fi.upm.es

Abstract. Both ontology content and ontology building tools evaluations play an important role before using ontologies in Semantic Web applications. In this paper we try to assess ontology evaluation functionalities of the following ontology platforms: OilEd, OntoEdit, Protégé-2000, and WebODE. The goal of this paper is to analyze whether such ontology platforms prevent the ontologist from making knowledge representation mistakes in concept taxonomies during RDF(S) and DAML+OIL ontology import, during ontology building and during ontology export to RDF(S) and DAML+OIL. Our study reveals that most of these ontology platforms only detect a few mistakes in concept taxonomies when importing RDF(S) and DAML+OIL ontologies. It also reveals that most of these ontology platforms only detect some mistakes in concept taxonomies during building ontologies. Our study also reveals that these platforms do not detect any taxonomic mistake when exporting ontologies to such languages.

1 Introduction

Ontology content should be evaluated before using or reusing it in other ontologies or software applications. To evaluate the ontology content, and the software used to build ontologies are important processes to take into account before integrating ontologies in final applications. Ontology content evaluation should be performed during the whole ontology life-cycle. In order to carry out such evaluation, ontology development tools should support content evaluation during the whole process.

The goal of ontology evaluation is to determine what the ontology defines correctly, what it does not define or defines incorrectly. Up to now, few domain-independent methodological approaches [4, 8, 11, 13] have been reported for building ontologies. All the aforementioned approaches identify the need for ontology evaluation. However, such evaluation is performed differently in each one of them.

The main efforts on ontology content evaluation were made by Gómez-Pérez [6, 7] and by Guarino and colleagues with the OntoClean method [9].

In the last years, the number of tools for building, importing, and exporting ontologies has increased exponentially. These tools are intended to provide support

R. Monroy et al. (Eds.): MICAI 2004, LNAI 2972, pp. 109–118, 2004.

for the ontology development process and for the subsequent ontology usage. Examples of such platforms are: OilEd [2], OntoEdit [12], Protégé-2000 [10], and WebODE [3, 1].

Up to now, we do not know of any document that describes how different ontology platforms evaluate ontologies during the processes of import, building and export. In this paper we study whether the previous ontology platforms prevent the ontologist from making knowledge representation mistakes in concept taxonomies.

We have performed experiments with 24 ontologies (7 in RDF(S)[1, 2] and 17 in DAML+OIL[3]) that are well built from a syntactic point of view, but that have inconsistencies and redundancies. These knowledge representation mistakes are not detected by the current RDF(S) and DAML+OIL parsers [5]. We have imported these ontologies into the previous ontology platforms. We have also built 17 ontologies with inconsistencies and redundancies using the editors provided by the previous platforms. After that, we have exported such ontologies to RDF(S) and DAML+OIL.

This paper is organized as follows: section two describes briefly the method for evaluating taxonomic knowledge in ontologies. Section three gives an overview of the ontology platforms used. Section four exposes the results of importing, building and exporting RDF(S) and DAML+OIL ontologies with taxonomic mistakes in the ontology platforms. And, section five concludes with further work on evaluation.

2   Method for Evaluating Taxonomic Knowledge in Ontologies

Figure 1 shows a set of the possible mistakes that can be made by ontologists when modeling taxonomic knowledge in an ontology [6].

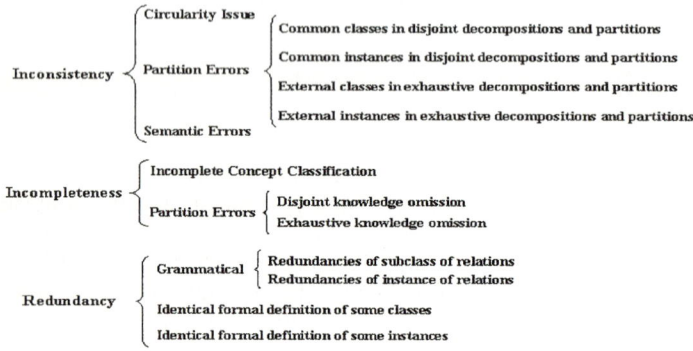

Fig. 1. Types of mistakes that might be made when developing taxonomies

In this paper we have focused only on inconsistency mistakes (circularity and partition) and grammatical redundancy mistakes, and have postponed the analysis of the others for further works.

---

[1] http://www.w3.org/TR/PR-rdf-schema
[2] http://www.w3.org/TR/REC-rdf-syntax/
[3] http://www.daml.org/2001/03/daml+oil-walkthru.html

We would like to point out that concept classifications can be defined in a disjoint (*disjoint decompositions*), a complete (*exhaustive decompositions*), and a disjoint and complete manner (*partitions*).

3   Ontology Platforms

In this section, we provide a broad overview of the tools we have used in our experiments: OilEd, OntoEdit, Protégé-2000, and WebODE.

OilEd[4] [2] was initially developed as an ontology editor for OIL ontologies, in the context of the IST OntoKnowledge project at the University of Manchester. However, OilEd has evolved and now is an editor of DAML+OIL and OWL ontologies. OilEd can import ontologies implemented in RDF(S), OIL, DAML+OIL, and in the SHIQ XML format. OilEd ontologies can be exported to DAML+OIL, RDF(S), OWL, to the SHIQ XML format, and to DIG XML format.

OntoEdit[5] [12] was developed by AIFB in Karlsruhe University and is now being commercialized by Ontoprise. It is an extensible and flexible environment and is based on a plug-in architecture, which provides functionality to browse and edit ontologies. Two versions of OntoEdit are available: Free and Professional. OntoEdit Free can import ontologies from FLogic, RDF(S, DAML+OIL, and from directory structures and Excel files. OntoEdit Free can export to OXML, FLogic, RDF(S, and DAML+OIL.

Protégé-2000[6] [10] was developed by Stanford Medical Informatics (SMI) at Stanford University, and is the latest version of the Protégé line of tools. It is an open source, standalone application with an extensible architecture. The core of this environment is the ontology editor, and it holds a library of plug-ins that add more functionality to the environment (ontology language import and export, etc.).

Protégé-2000 ontologies can be imported and exported with some of the back-ends provided in the standard release or provided as plug-ins: RDF(S, DAML+OIL, OWL, XML, XML Schema, and XMI.

WebODE[7] [3, 1] is an ontological engineering workbench developed by the Ontology Engineering Group at Universidad Politécnica de Madrid (UPM). It is an ontology engineering suite created with an extensible architecture. WebODE is not used as a standalone application but as a Web application. Three user interfaces are combined in the WebODE ontology editor: an HTML form-based editor for editing all ontology terms except axioms and rules; a graphical user interface, called OntoDesigner, for editing concept taxonomies and relations; and the WebODE Axiom Builder (WAB) [3], for creating formal axioms and rules.

There are several services for importing and exporting ontologies: XML, RDF(S), DAML+OIL, OIL, OWL, XCARIN, FLogic, Jess, Prolog, and Java.

---

[4] http://oiled.man.ac.uk
[5] http://www.ontoprise.de/com/start_downlo.htm
[6] http://protege.stanford.edu/plugins.html
[7] http://webode.dia.fi.upm.es/

4 Comparative Study of Ontology Platforms

At present, there are a great number of ontologies in RDF(S) and DAML+OIL, and most of the RDF(S) and DAML+OIL parsers are not able to detect knowledge representation taxonomic mistakes in ontologies implemented in such languages [5]. Therefore, we have decided to analyze whether ontology platforms presented in section 3 are able to detect this type of mistakes during RDF(S) and DAML+OIL ontology import, ontology building, and ontology export to RDF(S) and DAML+OIL.

The results of our analysis are shown in the tables using the following symbols:

✓   The ontology platform detects the mistake.

☑   The ontology platform allows inserting the mistake, which is only detected when the ontology is verified.

✗   The ontology platform does not detect the mistake.

☺   The ontology platform does not allow representing this type of mistake.

--   The mistake cannot be represented in this language.

⊖   The ontology platform does not allow inserting the mistake.

4.1 Detecting Knowledge Representation Mistakes during Ontology Import

To carry out this experiment, we have built a testbed of 24 ontologies (7 in RDF(S) and 17 in DAML+OIL), each of which implements one of the possible problems presented in section 2. In the case of RDF(S) we have only 7 ontologies because partitions cannot be defined in this language. This testbed can be found at *http://minsky.dia.fi.upm.es/odeval*. We have imported these ontologies using the import facilities of the ontology platforms presented in section 3. The results of this experiment are shown in table 1. Figure 2 shows the code of two of the ontologies used in this study: circularity at distance 2 in RDF(S) and external instance in a partition in DAML+OIL.

```
<rdfs:Class rdf:ID="ClassA">
   <rdfs:subClassOf rdf:resource="#ClassB" />
</rdfs:Class>

<rdfs:Class rdf:ID="ClassB">
   <rdfs:subClassOf rdf:resource="#ClassC" />
</rdfs:Class>

<rdfs:Class rdf:ID="ClassC">
   <rdfs:subClassOf rdf:resource="#ClassA" />
</rdfs:Class>
```

```
<daml:Class rdf:ID="ClassA" />
<daml:Class rdf:ID="ClassP1" />
<daml:Class rdf:ID="ClassP2" />

<ClassA rdf:ID="Instance_A" />

<daml:Class rdf:about="#ClassA">
   <daml:disjointUnionOf rdf:parseType="daml:collection">
      <daml:Class rdf:about="#ClassP1"/>
      <daml:Class rdf:about="#ClassP2"/>
   </daml:disjointUnionOf>
</daml:Class>
```

a) Loop at distance 2 in RDF(S)   b) External instance in partition in DAML+OIL

Fig. 2. Examples of RDF(S) and DAML+OIL ontologies

The main conclusions of the RDF(S) and DAML+OIL ontology import are:

Circularity problems at any distance are the only problems detected by most of ontology platforms analyzed in this experiment. However, OntoEdit Free does not detect circularities at distance zero, but it ignores them.

Table 1. Results of the RDF(S) and DAML+OIL ontology import

		OilEd		OntoEdit Free		Protégé-2000		WebODE	
		RDF(S)	DAML+OIL	RDF(S)	DAML+OIL	RDF(S)	DAML+OIL	RDF(S)	DAML+OIL
Inconsistency: Circularity Problems	At distance zero	✓	✓	✗	✗	✓	✓	✓	✓
	At distance one	✓	✓	✓	✓	✓	✓	✓	✓
	At distance n	✓	✓	✓	✓	✓	✓	✓	✓
Inconsistency: Partition Errors	Common classes in disjoint decompositions — Direct	--	✗	--	✗	--	✗	--	☺
	Common classes in disjoint decompositions — Indirect	--	✗	--	✗	--	✗	--	☺
	Common classes in partitions	--	✗	--	☺	--	✗	--	☺
	Common instances in disjoint decompositions — Direct	--	✗	--	✗	--	☺	--	☺
	Common instances in disjoint decompositions — Indirect	--	✗	--	✗	--	☺	--	☺
	Common instances in partitions	--	✗	--	☺	--	☺	--	☺
	External classes in exhaustive decompositions	--	✗	--	☺	--	✗	--	☺
	External classes in partitions	--	✗	--	☺	--	✗	--	✓
	External instances in exhaustive decompositions	--	✗	--	☺	--	✗	--	☺
	External instances in partitions	--	✗	--	☺	--	✗	--	✓
Redundancy: Grammatical Problems	Redundancies of subclass-of relations — Direct	✗	✗	✗	✗	✗	✗	✗	✗
	Redundancies of subclass-of relations — Indirect	✗	✗	✗	✗	✗	✗	✓	✓
	Redundancies of instance-of relations — Direct	✗	✗	✗	✗	☺	☺	☺	☺
	Redundancies of instance-of relations — Indirect	✗	✗	✗	✗		☺	☺	☺

Regarding *partition errors*, we have only studied DAML+OIL ontologies because this type of knowledge cannot be represented in RDF(S). Most of ontology platforms used in this study cannot detect partition errors in DAML+OIL ontologies. Only WebODE using the ODEval[8] service detects some partition errors.

Grammatical redundancy problems are not detected by most of ontology platforms used in this work. However, some ontology platforms ignore direct redundancies of 'subclass-of' or 'instance-of' relations. As in the previous case, only WebODE using the ODEval service detects indirect redundancies of 'subclass-of' relations in RDF(S) and DAML+OIL ontologies.

4.2 Detecting Knowledge Representation Mistakes during Ontology Building

In this section we analyze whether the editors of the ontology platforms detect concept taxonomy mistakes. We have built 17 ontologies using such ontology platforms. Each of which implements one of the problems presented in section 2.

Figure 3 shows two of the ontologies used in this study: the first represents an indirect common instance in a disjoint decomposition and the second represents an indirect redundancy of 'subclass-of' relation.

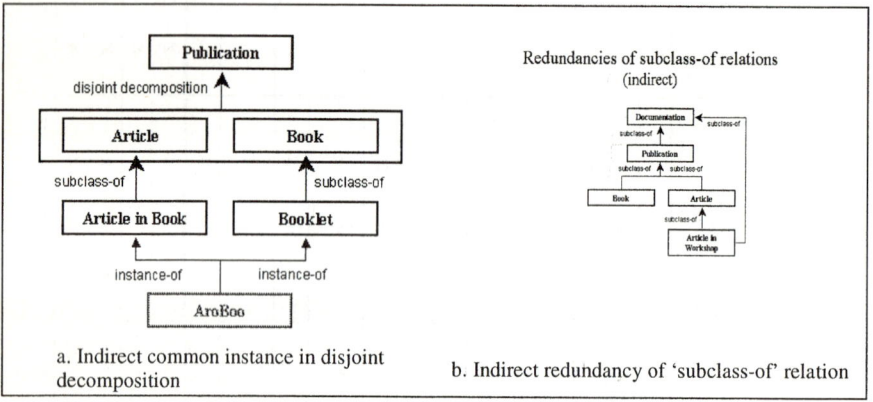

Fig. 3. Examples of ontologies built in the ontology editors

The results of analyzing the editors of the ontology platforms are shown in table 2. The main conclusions of this study are:

Circularity problems are the only ones detected by most of ontology platforms used in this study. However, OntoEdit Free detects neither circularity at distance one nor at distance 'n'. Furthermore, OntoEdit Free and WebODE have mechanisms to prevent ontologists from inserting circularity at distance zero.

As for *partition errors*, WebODE detects only external classes in partitions. OilEd and Protégé-2000 detect some partition errors when the ontology is verified, but these types of mistakes can be inserted in those ontology platforms. Most of partition errors are not detected by the platforms or cannot be represented in the platforms.

---

[8] http://minsky.dia.fi.upm.es/odeval

Table 2. Results of the ontology building

			OilEd	OntoEdit Free	Protégé-2000	WebODE HTML form-based	WebODE OntoDesigner
Inconsistency: Circularity Problems	At distance zero		✓	①	✓	①	✓
	At distance one		✓	✗	✓	✓	✓
	At distance n		✓	✗	✓	✓	✓
	Common classes in disjoint decompositions	Direct	☑	✗	☑	✗	✗
		Indirect	✗	✗	☑	✗	✗
	Common classes in partitions		☑	①	☑	✗	✗
	Common instances in disjoint decompositions	Direct	✗	①	①	①	①
		Indirect	✗	✗	①	①	①
Inconsistency: Partition Errors	Common instances in partitions		✗	①	①	①	①
	External classes in exhaustive decompositions		✗	①	☑	①	①
	External classes in partitions		✗	①	☑	✓	✓
	External instances in exhaustive decompositions		✗	①	✗	①	①
	External instances in partitions		✗	①	✗	✗	①
Redundancy: Grammatical Problems	Redundancies of subclass-of relations	Direct	✗	①	✓	✓	✓
		Indirect	✗	✗	✓	✗	✗
	Redundancies of instance-of relations	Direct	✗	✗	①	①	①
		Indirect	✗	✗	①	①	①

Table 3. Results of the RDF(S) and DAML+OIL ontology export

			OilEd		OntoEdit Free		Protégé-2000		WebODE	
			RDF(S)	DAML+OIL	RDF(S)	DAML+OIL	RDF(S)	DAML+OIL	RDF(S)	DAML+OIL
Inconsistency: Circularity Problems	At distance zero		×	×	⊘	⊘	⊘	⊘	⊘	⊘
	At distance one		×	×	×	×	⊘	⊘	⊘	⊘
	At distance n		×	×	×	×	⊘	⊘	⊘	⊘
Inconsistency: Partition Errors	Common classes in disjoint decompositions	Direct	–	×	–	×	–	×	–	×
		Indirect	–	×	–	×	–	×	–	×
	Common classes in partitions		–	×	–	⊙	–	×	–	⊙
	Common instances in disjoint decompositions	Direct	–	×	–	×	–	×	–	×
		Indirect	–	×	–	×	–	×	–	×
	Common instances in partitions		–	×	–	⊙	–	×	–	⊙
	External classes in exhaustive decompositions		–	×	–	⊙	–	×	–	⊙
	External classes in partitions		–	×	–	⊙	–	×	–	×
	External instances in exhaustive decompositions		–	×	–	⊙	–	×	–	⊙
	External instances in partitions		–	×	–	⊙	–	×	–	×
Redundancy: Grammatical Problems	Redundancies of subclass-of relations	Direct	×	×	⊘	⊘	⊘	⊘	×	×
		Indirect	×	×	×	×	×	×	×	×
	Redundancies of instance-of relations	Direct	×	×	×	×	⊙	×	⊙	⊙
		Indirect	×	×	×	×	⊙	×	⊙	⊙

Regarding *grammatical redundancy problems*, direct redundancies of 'subclass-of' relations are detected by Protégé-2000 and WebODE, but are forbidden by OntoEdit Free. Protégé-2000 also detects indirect redundancies of 'subclass-of' relations. Other grammatical problems are not detected or cannot be represented in the platforms.

4.3 Detecting Knowledge Representation Mistakes during Ontology Export

To analyze whether the export facilities of the ontology platforms detect concept taxonomy mistakes, we have exported to RDF(S) and DAML+OIL the 17 ontologies built in the previous experiment. After exporting these ontologies, we have analyzed 7 RDF(S) files and 17 DAML+OIL files. Since RDF(S) cannot represent partition knowledge, this type of knowledge is lost when we export to RDF(S).

The results of analyzing the RDF(S) and DAML+OIL export facilities of these ontology platforms are shown in table 3. The main conclusions of this study are:

Circularity problems are not detected by RDF(S) and DAML+OIL export facilities of ontology platforms. Furthermore, some ontology platforms do not allow inserting this type of problems, therefore the ontologies exported do not contain these mistakes.

With regard to *partition errors*, no ontology platforms detect these mistakes. Furthermore, some partition errors cannot be represented in ontology platforms.

Grammatical redundancy problems are not detected by the ontology platforms used in this study. OntoEdit Free and Protégé-2000 do not allow inserting direct redundancies of 'subclass-of' relations; therefore, neither RDF(S) nor DAML+OIL exported files can contain this type of mistake. Furthermore, some grammatical problems cannot be represented in the ontology platforms studied.

5 Conclusions and Further Work

In this paper we have shown that only a few taxonomic mistakes in RDF(S) and DAML+OIL ontologies are detected by ontology platforms during ontology import. We have also shown that most editors of ontology platforms detect only a few knowledge representation mistakes in concept taxonomies during ontology building. And we have also shown that current ontology platforms are not able to detect such mistakes during ontology export to RDF(S) and DAML+OIL.

Taking into account these results, we consider that it is necessary to check possible anomalies that can be made during ontology building in ontology platforms. Therefore it is important that these platforms help the ontologist build ontologies without making knowledge representation mistakes. We also consider that it is necessary to evaluate ontologies during the import and export processes.

We also consider that we need tools for giving support to the evaluation activity during the whole life-cycle of ontologies. These tools should not only evaluate concept taxonomies, but also other ontology components (relations, axioms, etc.).

Acknowledgements. This work has been supported by the Esperonto project (IST-2001-34373), the ContentWeb project (TIC-2001-2745), and a research grant from UPM ("Beca asociada a proyectos modalidad B"). We are very greatful to Óscar Corcho, Rosario Plaza and José Ángel Ramos for their revisions and intelligent comments.

References

1. Arpírez JC, Corcho O, Fernández-López M, Gómez-Pérez A (2003) *WebODE in a nutshell.* AI Magazine 24(3): 37-48. Fall 2003.
2. Bechhofer S, Horrocks I, Goble C, Stevens R (2001) *OilEd: a reason-able ontology editor for the Semantic Web.* In: Baader F, Brewka G, Eiter T (eds) Joint German/Austrian conference on Artificial Intelligence (KI'01). Vienna, Austria. (Lecture Notes in Artificial Intelligence LNAI 2174) Springer-Verlag, Berlin, Germany, pp 396–408.
3. Corcho O, Fernández-López M, Gómez-Pérez A, Vicente O (2002) *WebODE: an Integrated Workbench for Ontology Representation, Reasoning and Exchange.* In: Gómez-Pérez A, Benjamins VR (eds) 13th International Conference on Knowledge Engineering and Knowledge Management (EKAW'02). Sigüenza, Spain. (Lecture Notes in Artificial Intelligence LNAI 2473) Springer-Verlag, Berlin, Germany, pp 138–153.
4. Fernández-López M, Gómez-Pérez A, Pazos-Sierra A, Pazos-Sierra J (1999) *Building a Chemical Ontology Using METHONTOLOGY and the Ontology Design Environment.* IEEE Intelligent Systems & their applications 4(1) (1999) 37-46.
5. Gómez-Pérez A, Suárez-Figueroa MC (2003) *Results of Taxonomic Evaluation of RDF(S) and DAML+OIL Ontologies using RDF(S) and DAML+OIL Validation Tools and Ontology Platforms Import Services.* Evaluation of Ontology-based Tools (EON2003) 2nd International Workshop located at the 2nd International Semantic Web Conference (ISWC 2003) Sundial Resort, Sanibel Island, Florida, USA. PP: 13-26.
6. Gómez-Pérez A (1996) *A Framework to Verify Knowledge Sharing Technology.* Expert Systems with Application. Vol. 11, N. 4. PP: 519-529.
7. Gómez-Pérez A (1994) *Some Ideas and Examples to Evaluate Ontologies.* Technical Report KSL-94-65. Knowledge System Laboratory. Stanford University. Also in Proceedings of the 11th Conference on Artificial Intelligence for Applications. CAIA94.
8. Grüninger M, Fox MS (1995) *Methodology for the design and evaluation of ontologies.* In Workshop on Basic Ontological Issues in Knowledge Sharing (Montreal, 1995).
9. Guarino N, Welty C (2000) *A Formal Ontology of Properties* In R. Dieng and O. Corby (eds.), Knowledge Engineering and Knowledge Management: Methods, Models and Tools. 12th International Conference, EKAW2000, LNAI 1937. Springer Verlag: 97-112.
10. Noy NF, Fergerson RW, Musen MA (2000) *The knowledge model of Protege-2000: Combining interoperability and flexibility.* In: Dieng R, Corby O (eds) 12th International Conference in Knowledge Engineering and Knowledge Management (EKAW'00). Juan-Les-Pins, France. (Lecture Notes in Artificial Intelligence LNAI 1937) Springer-Verlag, Berlin, Germany, pp 17–32.
11. Staab S, Schnurr HP, Studer R, Sure Y (2001) *Knowledge Processes and Ontologies,* IEEE Intelligent Systems, 16(1). 2001.
12. Sure Y, Erdmann M, Angele J, Staab S, Studer R, Wenke D (2002) *OntoEdit: Collaborative Ontology Engineering for the Semantic Web.* In: Horrocks I, Hendler JA (eds) First International Semantic Web Conference (ISWC'02). Sardinia, Italy. (Lecture Notes in Computer Science LNCS 2342) Springer-Verlag, Berlin, Germany, pp 221–235.
13. Uschold M, Grüninger M (1996) *ONTOLOGIES: Principles, Methods and Applications.* Knowledge Engineering Review. Vol. 11; N. 2; June 1996.

Graduated Errors in Approximate Queries Using Hierarchies and Ordered Sets

Adolfo Guzman-Arenas and Serguei Levachkine

Centro de Investigación en Computación, Instituto Politécnico Nacional.
07738 Mexico City, MEXICO
a.guzman@acm.org, palych@cic.ipn.mx

Abstract. Often, qualitative values have an ordering, such as (very-short, short, medium-height, tall) or a hierarchical level, such as (The-World, Europe, Spain, Madrid), which are used by people to interpret mistakes and approximations among these values. Confusing Paris with Madrid yields an error smaller than confusing Paris with Australia, or Paris with Abraham Lincoln. And the "difference" between very cold and cold is smaller than that between very cold and warm. Methods are provided to measure such confusion, and to answer *approximate queries* in an "intuitive" manner. Examples are given. Hierarchies are a simpler version of *ontologies,* albeit very useful. Queries have a blend of errors by order and errors by hierarchy level, such as "what is the error in confusing very cold with tall?" or "give me all people who are somewhat like (John (*plays* baseball) (*travels-by* water-vehicle) (*lives-in* North-America))." Thus, retrieval of approximate *objects* is possible, as illustrated here.

1 Introduction

The type of mistakes and misidentification that people make give clues to how well they know a given subject. Confusing Ramses with Tutankamon is not as bad as confusing Ramses with George Washington, or with Greenland. Indeed, teachers often interpret these mistakes to assess the extent of the student's learning.

The paper formalizes the notion of *confusion* between elements of a hierarchy. Furthermore, this notion is extended to hierarchies where each node is an ordered set. *These are the main trusts of the paper.*

Some definitions follow.

Qualitative variable. A single-valued variable that takes symbolic values. ◆ As opposed to numeric, vector or quantitative variables. Its value cannot be a set, although such symbolic value may represent a set. Example: the qualitative variables (written in *italics*) *profession, travels-by, owns, weighs;* the symbolic values (written in normal font) lawyer, air-bone-vehicle, horse, heavy.

Partition. K is a partition of set S if it is both a covering for S and an exclusive set. ◆ The members of K are mutually exclusive and collectively exhaust S. Each element of S is in exactly one K_j.

Ordered set. An element set whose values are ordered by a < ("less than") relation. ◆ Example: {short, medium-length, long}. Example: {Antartica, Australia, Brazil, Ecuator, Nicaragua, Mexico, Germany, Ireland, Iceland}, where the relation "<" is "South of".

R. Monroy et al. (Eds.): MICAI 2004, LNAI 2972, pp. 119–128, 2004.

1.1 Hierarchy

For a node n in a tree, relations **father_of(n), son_of(n), brother_of, ascendant_of...** are defined, as expected. ♦

A **hierarchy** H is a tree whose root is a set S, and, if a node has sons, then these sons form a partition of their father. ♦ This paper deals with hierarchies whose set S is formed by symbolic values. Often, we give names (symbolic values, strings) to the different subsets of S. Often, we name the hierarchy H after the set S, and we speak of "the hierarchy S". Example: The Hierarchy H_1 of means of travel or transportation vehicles, whose root is the set S = {animal, foot, bike, motor-bike, 2-seat-car, 4-seat-car; van, bus, train, boat, ship, helicopter, airplane} is shown in Figure 1.

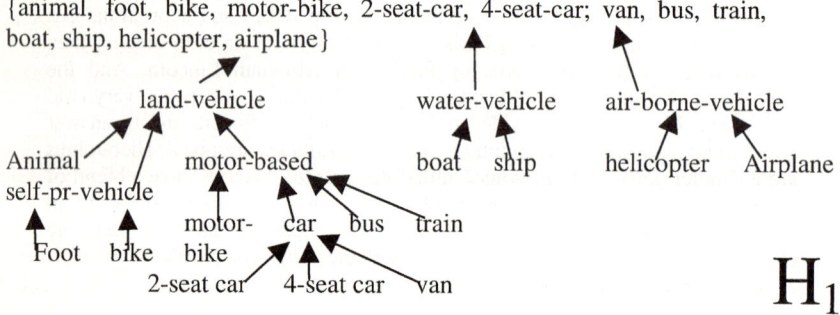

Fig. 1. A hierarchy H_1 of transportation vehicles. Some qualitative values, like air-borne-vehicle, represent sets: {helicopter, airplane} in our example

Hierarchies make it easier to compare qualitative values belonging to the same hierarchy (§2), and even to different hierarchies [COM in 4, 9].

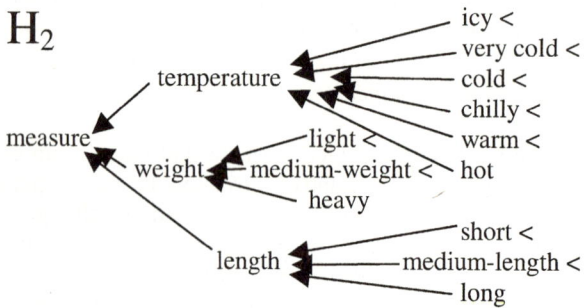

Fig. 2. A hierarchy having some ordered sets: (short < medium-length < long), (light < medium-weight < heavy), (icy < very cold < cold < chilly < warm < hot)

A **hierarchical variable** is a qualitative variable whose values are nodes of a hierarchy. ♦ The data type of a hierarchical variable is hierarchy.

Example: *travels-by,* whose values are nodes of H_1 (figure 1). Example: *weighs,* whose values are nodes weight, light, medium and heavy of H_2. Note: hierarchical variables are single-valued. Thus, a value for *travels-by* can be water-vehicle, but not {boat, ship} although water-vehicle represents {boat, ship}.

It is also possible for a hierarchy to have some nodes that are ordered nodes. Example: Hierarchy H_2 of figure 2.

1.2 Previous Related Work

Hierarchies are used in data warehousing and data mining; see, for instance, the H-sets of [1]. The paper [7] enlarges these notions with greater mathematical background. [6] studies hierarchies where the relative proportion of each set in its father set is known. On the other hand, [9] deals mainly with *ontologies,* more elaborate data structures used for knowledge representation, of which CYC [2] was an early attempt to build an ontology for common concepts. A companion paper in this book [4], matches similar concepts in different ontologies. The thesis [8] describes how to map concepts from one ontology to another. A practical use of hierarchies is Clasitex [3], which finds the themes of an article written in Spanish or English. It uses the concept tree, and a word (not in the tree) *suggests the topic of* one or more concepts in the tree. BiblioDigital [5], a recent development, uses a large taxonomy (although not a hierarchy) to classify text documents.

Work described here is similar to Pattern Classifiers, but these classify *objects* according to the values of their properties, whereas hierarchies help to classify these *values,* when they are non-numeric.

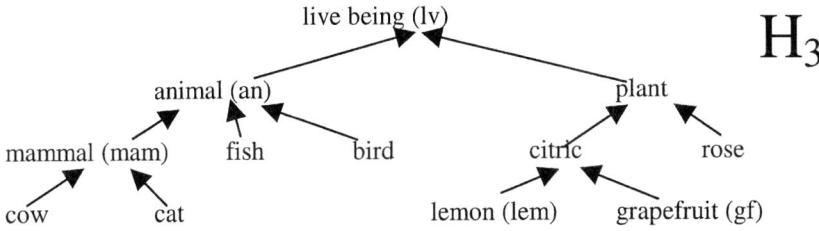

Fig. 3. A hierarchy H_3 of living creatures (*lv*). *an* stands for animal; *mam* for mammal; *lem* for lemon, and *gf* for grapefruit. See table 1 below

2 Confusion in Hierarchies

Who was the first Emperor of Mexico? "Agustin de Iturbide" is the correct answer; "Maximilian of Hapsburg" is a close miss, "Benito Juarez" a fair error, and "Mexico City" a gross error. What is closer to a cat, a dog or an orange? Can we measure these errors or similarities? Yes, with hierarchies of symbolic values.

2.1 Confusion in Using r Instead of s, for a Hierarchy H

If r, s ∈ H, then the **confusion** in using r instead of s, written conf(r, s), is:

- conf (r, r) = conf (r, s) = 0, when s is any ascendant of r.
- conf (r, s) = 1 + conf (r, father_of(s)). ♦

To measure conf, move from r to s in the hierarchy, and count the *descending* links from r to s, the replaced value. conf is not a distance, nor ultradistance.

Table 1. conf(r, s), Confusion in using r instead of s, for hierarchy H_3. r runs down, while s runs to the right. Thus, the black **2** is the confusion of using an animal (*an*) instead of a cow, while the confusion of using a cow instead of an animal is 0. Values (nodes) of H_3 are ordered *width-first* in the table

	lv	an	plant	mam	fish	bird	citric	rose	cow	cat	lem	gf
lv	0	1	1	2	2	2	2	2	3	3	3	3
an	0	0	1	1	1	1	2	2	**2**	2	3	3
plant	0	1	0	2	2	3	1	1	3	3	2	2
mam	0	0	1	0	1	1	2	2	1	1	3	3
fish	0	0	1	1	0	1	2	2	2	2	3	3
bird	0	0	1	1	1	0	2	3	2	2	3	3
citric	0	1	0	2	2	2	0	1	3	3	1	1
rose	0	1	0	2	2	2	1	0	3	3	2	2
cow	0	0	1	0	1	1	2	2	0	1	3	3
cat	0	0	1	0	1	1	2	2	1	0	3	3
lem	0	1	0	2	2	2	0	1	3	3	0	1
gf	0	1	0	2	2	2	0	1	3	3	1	0

Example: conf(r, s) in the hierarchy of Figure 3 is given in Table 1.
conf resembles our sense of "closeness" between these concepts. Examples:

conf (citric, plant) = 0; if I use citric instead of plant, the confusion is 0, since citrics are plants.

conf (plant, citric) = 1; giving a plant when I wanted a citric is a "small" error; giving a cow when I wanted a citric is a larger error (value 2). Using these gradations in errors, the paper later will produce responses to queries that are "very similar to x", or "somewhat similar to x", where x is a node or a predicate.

The confusion among two brothers, such as cow and cat, is 1. The confusion in using a son instead of its father is 0; the confusion in using a father instead of its son is 1. conf is not a symmetric function. In the next section we modify the confusion among two brothers to be a number ≤ 1, for brothers that belong to an ordered set.

Points to ponder. The confusion in using a live being instead of a plant is 1. Thus, conf (animal, plant) = conf (mammal, plant) = conf (cow, plant) = 1. This may seem odd, but it is not: cow, mammal, and animal are examples of live beings, and the confusion of using a live being instead of a plant is 1. Another example will perhaps be more convincing: Say that "wine" and "beer" are brothers, so that conf (wine, beer) = 1: if I am given wine when I wanted beer, the confusion is 1. But this is exactly the same confusion if I am given red wine instead of beer, or Riesling wine instead of beer, or chilled dry Riesling wine vintage 1999 instead of beer. It is always 1, no matter how "specialized" the wine or the live being is.

In the other direction, conf (citric, plant) = 0: if I am given a citric when I want a plant, the confusion is 0, because a citric *is* a plant. Another example: If I am given a cold beer when I want a beer, the confusion is 0. Similarly, conf (Corona_beer, beer) = conf (chilled_Corona_beer, beer) = 0, since all these "specialized" types of beer are, nevertheless, beer.

Thus, conf (r, s), takes into account the relative position of nodes r and s in the hierarchy, *but only when going down* in our journey from r to s. When going up, no matter how far apart s is from r, conf is 0 "in the upwards part of the journey from r to s."

2.2   Confusion in Using r instead of s, for a Hierarchy with Some Ordered Sets

In §2.1, the confusion between any two brother nodes is 1. For ordered sets, the confusion between any two brothers depends on how far they are in their ordering. If the ordered set has only one element e, then conf (e, e) = 0. If it has two elements, then conf (e1, e2) = 1. For ordered sets with more than two elements, n>2, the confusion between two contiguous elements is 1/(n-1). Figure 4 shows an example.

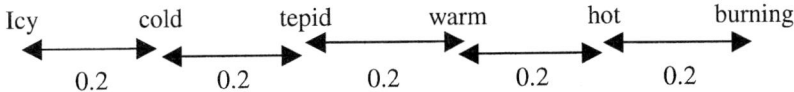

Fig. 4. A set showing the confusion between its elements

Thus, conf (icy, cold) = conf (cold, icy) = 0.2; conf (cold, warm) = 0.4

For a hierarchy composed of sets some of which have an ordering relation (such as H_2), the confusion in using r instead of s, conf (r, s), is defined as follows:

- conf (r, r) = conf (r, s) = 0, when s is any ascendant of r.

- If r and s are distinct brothers,
  conf (r, s) = 1 if the father is not an ordered set; else,
  conf (r, s) = the relative distance from r to s = the number of steps needed to jump from r to s in the ordering, divided by the cardinality-1 of the father.

- conf (r, s) = 1 + conf (r, father_of(s)). ◆

This is like conf for hierarchies formed by (unordered) sets (§0; more at [6, 7]), except that there the error between two brothers is 1, and here it may be a number between 0 and 1. Example (for H_2): conf (short, measure) = 0; conf (short, length) = 0; conf (short, light) = 2; conf (short, medium-length) = 0.5; conf (short, long) = 1.

3 Queries and Graduated Errors

This section explains how to pose and answer queries where there is a permissible error due to confusion between values of hierarchical variables.

3.1 The Set of Values That Are Equal to Another, up to a Given Confusion

A **value u is equal to value v, within a given confusion ε**, written $u =_\varepsilon v$, iff conf(u, v) ≤ ε. ◆ It means that value u can be used instead of v, within error ε.

Example: If v = lemon (Figure 2), then
the set of values equal to v with confusion 0 is {lemon};
the set of values equal to v with confusion 1 is {citric lemon grapefruit};
the set of values equal to v with confusion 2 is {plant citric rose lemon grapefruit}.

Notice that $=_\varepsilon$ is neither symmetric nor transitive.

These values can be obtained from table 1 by watching column v ("lemon") and collecting as u's those rows that have conf ≤ ε.

That two values u and v have confusion 0 does not mean that they are identical (u = v). For example, the set of values equal to mammal with confusion 0 is {cow mammal cat}, and the set of values equal to live being (the root) with confusion 0 contains all nodes of H_3, since any node of H_3 is a live being.

3.2 Identical, Very Similar, Somewhat Similar Objects

Objects are entities described by a set of (property, value) pairs, which in our notation we refer to as (variable, value) pairs. They are also called (relationship, attribute) pairs in databases. An object o with k (variable, value) pairs is written as (o $(v_1\ a_1)$ $(v_2\ a_2)$... $(v_k\ a_k)$).

We want to estimate the error in using object o' instead of object o. For an object o with k erhaps hierarchical) variables $v_1, v_2,.., v_k$ and values $a_1, a_2, ..., a_k$, we say about another object o' with same variables $v_1...v_k$ but with values $a_1', a_2',... a_k'$, the following statements:

o' is **identical** to o if $a_i' = a_i$ for all $1 \le i \le k$. All corresponding values are identical.
◆ If all we know about o and o' are their values on variables $v_1,...v_k$, and both objects have these values pairwise identical, then we can say that "for all we know," o and o' are the same.

o' is **a substitute** for o if conf $(a_i', a_i) = 0$ for all $1 \le i \le k$. ◆ All values of o' have confusion 0 with the corresponding value of o. There is no confusion between a value of an attribute of o' and the corresponding value for o.

o' is **very similar** to o if Σ conf $(a_i', a_i) = 1$. ◆ The sum of all confusions is 1.

o' is **similar** to o if Σ conf $(a_i', a_i) = 2$. ◆

o' is **somewhat similar** to o if Σ conf $(a_i', a_i) = 3$. ◆

In general, o' is **similar**$_n$ to o if Σ conf $(a_i', a_i) = n$. ◆

These relations are not symmetric.

Table 2. Relations between objects of Example 1. This table gives the relation obtained when using object o' (running down the table) instead of object o' (running across the table)

	Ann	Bob	Ed	John
Ann	identical	$similar_4$	somewhat similar	$similar_5$
Bob	very similar	identical	very similar	$similar_6$
Ed	similar	$similar_{3.5}$	identical	$similar_6$
John	substitute	$similar_4$	$similar_{2.5}$	identical

Example 1 (We use hierarchies H_1, H_2 and H_3). Consider the objects
    (Ann   (*travels-by* land-vehicle)   (*owns* animal) (*weighs* weight))
    (Bob   (*travels-by* boat)   (*owns* bird)   (*weighs* heavy))
    (Ed   (*travels-by* water-vehicle) (*owns* plant)   (*weighs* medium-weight))
    (John (*travels-by* car)   (*owns* cow)   (*weighs* light)).

Then Ann is $similar_4$ to Bob; Bob is very similar to Ann; Ann is somewhat similar to Ed; Ed is $similar_{3.5}$ to Bob;[1] Bob is $similar_6$ to John, etc. See Table 2.

Hierarchical variables allow us to define objects with different degrees of precision. This is useful in many cases; for instance, when information about a given suspect is gross, or when the measuring device lacks precision. *Queries* with "loose fit" permit handling or matching objects with controlled accuracy, as exposed below.

3.3 Queries with Controlled Confusion

A table of a data base stores objects like Ann, Bob... defined by (variable, value) pairs, one object per row of the table. We now extend the notion of queries to tables with hierarchical variables,[2] by defining the objects that have property P within a given confusion ε, where $\varepsilon \geq 0$.

P holds for object o with confusion ε, written P_ε *holds for o*, iff

- If P_ε is formed by non-hierarchical variables, iff P is true for o.

- For *pr* a hierarchical variable and P_ε of the form (*pr* c),[3] iff for value v of property *pr* in object o, $v =_\varepsilon c$. [if the value v can be used instead of c with confusion ε]

- If P_ε is of the form P1 $\vee$ P2, iff $P1_\varepsilon$ holds for o or $P2_\varepsilon$ holds for o.

- If P_ε is of the form P1 $\wedge$ P2, iff $P1_\varepsilon$ holds for o and $P2_\varepsilon$ holds for o.

- If P_ε is of the form $\neg$P1, iff $P1_\varepsilon$ does not hold for o. ◆

The definition of P_ε *holds for o* allows control of the "looseness" of P or of some parts of P; for instance, the predicate (*plays* guitar)$_0$ will match people who play guitar

---

[1] conf (water-vehicle, boat) = 1; conf (plant, bird) = 2; conf (medium-weight, heavy) = 0.5; they add to 3.5.

[2] For non hierarchical variables, a match in value means conf = 0; a mismatch means conf = ∞

[3] (*pr* c) in our notation means: variable *pr* has the value c. Example: (*profession* Engineer). It is a predicate that, when applied to object o, returns T or F.

or any of the variations (sons) of guitar (refer to Figure 5); $(plays$ guitar)$_1$ will match those people just mentioned as well as people who play violin and harp.

What do we mean by "P holds for o" when we do not specify the confusion of P? If P and o are *not* formed using hierarchical variables, the meaning is the usual meaning given in Logic. Nevertheless, if P or o use hierarchical variables, then by "P holds for o" we mean "P_0 holds for o". This agrees with our intuition: predicate $(owns$ chord-instrument), given without explicitly telling us its allowed confusion, is interpreted as $(owns$ chord-instrument)$_0$, which will also match with a person owning an electric-guitar, say.

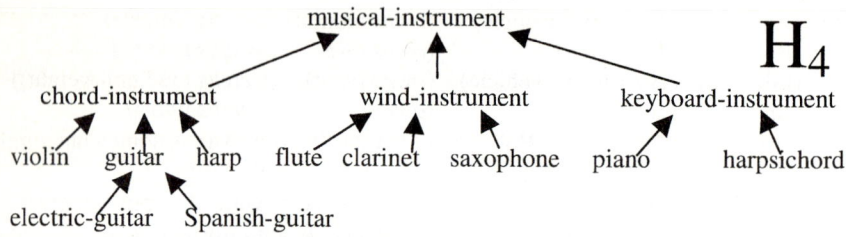

Fig. 5. A hierarchy of musical instruments

Example 2 (refer to hierarchies and persons of Example 1). Let the predicates
  P = $(travels$-by bike) $\vee$ $(owns$ cow),
  Q = $(travels$-by helicopter) $\wedge$ $(owns$ cat),
  R = $\neg$ $(travels$-by water-vehicle).
Then we have that P_0 holds for John; P_1 holds for John, P_2 holds for {Ann, Bob, John}, P_3 holds for {Ann, Bob, Ed, John}., as well as P_4, P_5,...
We also have that Q_0 holds for nobody; Q_1 holds for nobody; Q_2 holds for {Ann, Bob, John}; Q_3 holds for {Ann, Bob, Ed, John}, as well as Q_4, Q_5...
We also have that R_0 holds for {Ann, John}; R_1 holds for nobody, as well as R_2, R_3, R_4...

From the definition of P_ε *holds for o*, it is true that $(P \vee Q)_\varepsilon = (P_\varepsilon \vee Q_\varepsilon)$. This means that for $(P \vee Q)_a = (P_b \vee Q_c)$, a = min (b, c). Similarly, for $(P \wedge Q)_a = (P_b \wedge Q_c)$, we have a = max (b, c).

Accumulated confusion. For compound predicates, a tighter control of the error or confusion is possible if we require that the accumulated error does not exceed a threshold ε. This is accomplished by the following definition.

P holds for object o with accumulated confusion ε, written P^ε *holds for o*, iff

- If P^ε is formed by non-hierarchical variables, iff P is true for o.

- For pr a hierarchical variable and P^ε of the form $(pr$ c), iff for value v of property pr in object o, v $=_\varepsilon$ c. [if the value v can be used instead of c with confusion ε]

- If P^ε is of the form P1 $\vee$ P2, iff P1$^\varepsilon$ holds for o or P2$^\varepsilon$ holds for o.

- If P^ε is of the form P1 $\wedge$ P2, iff there exist confusions a and b such that a+b = ε and P1^a holds for o and P2^b holds for o.

- If P^ε is of the form $\neg$P1, iff P1$^\varepsilon$ does not hold for o. ♦

Example 3: For Q = (*travels-by* helicopter) $\wedge$ (*owns* cat), we see that Q^0 holds for nobody; Q^1 holds for nobody; Q^2 holds for nobody; Q^3 holds for John; Q^4 holds for {Ann, Bob, John}; Q^5 holds for {Ann, Bob, Ed, John}, as well as Q^6, Q^7...

Closeness. An important number that measures how well object o fits predicate P_ε is the smallest ε for which $P_\varepsilon(o)$ is true. This leads to the following definition.

The **closeness** of an object o to a predicate P_ε is the smallest ε which makes P_ε true.
♦ The smaller this ε is, the "tighter" P_ε holds.

Example: (refer to hierarchies, persons and predicates of Example 2) The closeness of P_ε to John is 0; its closeness to Ann is 2; to Bob is 2, and to Ed is 3. This means that John fits P_ε better than Ed. See Table 3.

Table 3. Closeness of an object to a predicate. Persons, hierarchies and predicates are those of example 2

	P_ε	Q_ε	R_ε
Ann	2	2	0
Bob	2	2	∞
Ed	3	2	∞
John	0	3	0

4 Conclusions

The paper shows a way to introduce ordered sets into hierarchies.
Hierarchies can be applied to a variety of jobs:

To compare two values, such as Madrid and Mexico City, and to measure their *confusion* (§0), for instance in answering query "What is the capital of Spain?"

To compare two objects for similarity, like Ann and Ed (§0), giving rise to the notions of **identical, very similar, similar...** objects (not *values*).

To find out how closely an object o fits a predicate P_ε (definition of **closeness**, §0).

To retrieve objects that fit imperfectly a given predicate to a given threshold, using P_ε *holds for* o (confusion, §0 and example 2), and P^ε *holds for* o (accumulated confusion, §0 and example 3).

To handle partial knowledge. Even if we only know that Ed *travels-by* water-vehicle, we can productively use this value in controlled searches (Example 1 of §0).

Hierarchies make a good approximation to the manner in which people use gradation of qualitative values (ordered sets), to provide less than crisp, but useful, answers.

Ordered sets add a further refinement to the precision with which confusion can be measured and used.

Hierarchies can also be used as an alternative to fuzzy sets, defining a membership function for a set with the help of closeness.

They can also be employed as a supervised pattern classifier, by using definitions of §0 that measure how close two objects are, and by using definitions of P_ε and P^ε (§0).

In [7] we describe a mathematical apparatus and further properties of functions and relations for hierarchies. Instead, [4, 9] explain similar functions, relations and examples for *ontologies*.

Acknowledgments. Useful exchanges were held with CIC-IPN professors Jesus Olivares and Alexander Gelbukh, and with Dr. Victor Alexandrov, SPIIRAS-Russia. This work was partially supported by Project CGPI-IPN 18.07 (20010778) and NSF-CONACYT Grant 32973-A. The authors have a *National Scientist* Award from SNI-CONACYT.

References

1.   Bhin, N. T., Tjoa, A. M, and Wagner, R. Conceptual Multidimensional data model based on meta-cube. In *Lecture Notes in Computer Science* **1909**, 24-31. Springer. (2000)
2.   Lenat, D. B., and Guha, R. V. *Building large knowledge-based systems.* Addison Wesley. (1989)
3.   Guzman, A. Finding the main themes in a Spanish document. *Journal Expert Systems with Applications*, Vol. **14**, No. 1/2, 139-148, Jan./Feb. (1998)
4.   Guzman, A., and Olivares, J. Finding the most similar concepts in two different ontologies. Accepted in *MICAI 04.*
5.   Guzman, A., and De Gyves, V. *BiblioDigital. A distributed digital library.* Work in progress. SoftwarePro International, Inc.
6.   Levachkine, S., and Guzman, A. Confusion between hierarchies partitioned by a percentage rule. Submitted to *AWIC 04.*
7.   Levachkine, S., and Guzman, A. Hierarchies as a new data type for qualittive variables. Submitted to Data and Knowledge Engineering. (2003)
8.   Olivares, J. *An Interaction Model among Purposeful Agents, Mixed Ontologies and Unexpected Events.* Ph. D. Thesis, CIC-IPN. In Spanish. Available on line at http://www.jesusolivares.com/interaction/publica (2002)
9.   Olivares, J. and Guzman, A. *Measuring the comprehension or understanding between two agents.* CIC Report in preparation.

Finding the Most Similar Concepts in Two Different Ontologies

Adolfo Guzman-Arenas and Jesus M. Olivares-Ceja

Centro de Investigación en Computación, Instituto Politécnico Nacional
07738 Mexico City, MEXICO
{a.guzman,jesuso}@acm.org

Abstract. A concise manner to send information from agent A to B is to use phrases constructed with the *concepts* of A: to use the *concepts* as the atomic tokens to be transmitted. Unfortunately, tokens from A are not understood by (they do not map into) the ontology of B, since in general each ontology has its own address space. Instead, A and B need to use a *common communication language*, such as English: the transmission tokens are English words.
An algorithm is presented that finds the concept c_B in O_B (the ontology of B) most closely resembling a given concept c_A. That is, given a concept from ontology O_A, a method is provided to find the *most similar concept* in O_B, as well as the similarity *sim* between both concepts. Examples are given.

1 Introduction and Objectives

How can we communicate our *concepts,* what we really mean? Two persons (or agents) A and B can communicate through previously agreed stereotypes, such as the *calling sequence* between a caller program and a called subroutine. This requires previous agreement between A and B. This paper deals with communication with little previous consensus: A and B agree only to share a given *communication language*. The purpose of the communication is for A and for B to fulfill its objectives or goals. That is, we shall define a successful communication if A and B are closer to their goals as the result of such communication.

What can an agent do to meaningfully communicate with other agents (or persons), even when they had not made any very specific comitment to share a private ontology and communication protocol? Concept communication can not be fulfilled through direct exchange of concepts belonging to an ontology, since *they do not share* the same ontology. Instead, communication should be sought through a common language. Lucky agents can agree on a language whose words have a *unique meaning*. Others need to use an ambiguous language (such as a natural language) to share knowledge. This gives rise to imperfect understanding and confusion. This is the trust of this paper.

The objective of this work is to find the most similar (in meaning) object in B's ontology corresponding to a given object in A's ontology, and to measure their similarity. Example: Assume A wants to transmit its concept grapefruit[1] to B.

---

[1] In this paper, concepts appear in Courier font.

R. Monroy et al. (Eds.): MICAI 2004, LNAI 2972, pp. 129–138, 2004.

To this end, A translates it into word grapefruit, which is then transmitted to B. But B has no such word in its ontology. Thus, B asks A "what is a grapefruit?" A answers "it is a citric" (by seeing that `citric` is the father of `grapefruit` in O$_A$). Unfortunately, B has no concept to map word "citric". So B asks A "what is a citric?" A answers "it is a fruit". Now, O$_B$ has concept `fruit` denoted by word fruit. But `fruit`$_B$ (the subindex B means "in O$_B$") has several children: B knows several fruits. Now B has to determine wich of the children of `fruit`$_B$ most resembles `grapefruit`$_A$. It may do so by seeing which child of `fruit`$_B$ has children quite similar to those children of `grapefruit`$_A$. Or by seeing which fruits in O$_B$ have skin, bone, weight... similar to those of `grapefruit`$_A$. Unfortunately, the problem is recursive: what is `skin` for B is `epidermis` for A, and `peel` for C. `weight`$_A$ is in kilograms, whereas `weight`$_B$ is in pounds. So the comparison has to continue recursively. §2 gives a precise description of the algorithm.

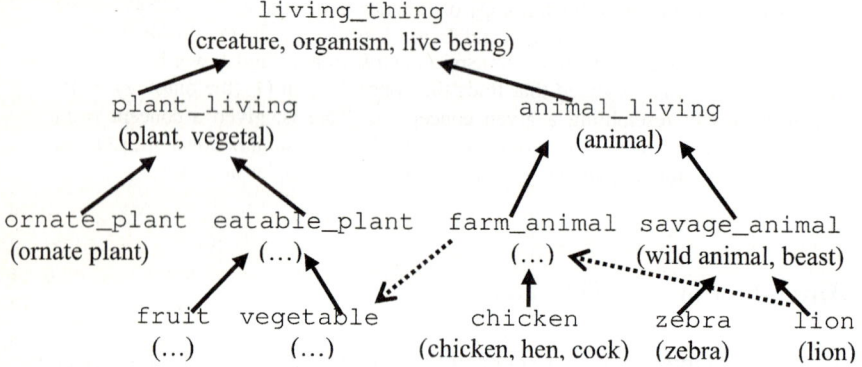

Fig. 1. An ontology consists of a tree of concepts (nodes) under the *subset* relation (solid arrows), with other relations such as *eats* (dotted arrows), and with words associated to each concept (in parenthesis after each concept; some are omitted). Nodes also have (property, value) pairs, not shown in the figure

1.1 Ontologies

Knowledge is the concrete internalization of facts, attributes and relations among real-world entities ♦ It is stored as concepts; it is *measured* in "number of concepts."

Concept. An object, relation, property, action, idea, entity or thing that is well known to many people, so that it has a name: a word(s) in a natural language. ♦ Examples: `cat-chien`, `to_fly_in_air`, `angry_mad`. So, *concepts have names*: those words used to denote them. A concept is unambiguous, by definition. Unfortunately, the names given by different people to a concept differ and, more unfortunately, the same word is given to two concepts (examples: words mole; star; can). Thus, *words are ambiguous,* [2] *while concepts are not.* A person or agent, when receiving words from some speaker, has to solve their ambiguity in order to

---

[2] Some symbols or words are unambiguous: 3, Abraham Lincoln, π, (30°N, 15°W).

understand the speaker, by mapping the words to the "right" concept in his/her/its own ontology. The mapping of words to concepts is called *disambiguation*.

If two agents do not share a concept, at least partially, they can not communicate it or about it. A concept has (property, value) pairs associated with it.

Ontology. It is a formal explicit specification of a shared conceptualization [5].♦ It is a hierarchy or taxonomy of the concepts we know.[3] We represent an ontology as a tree, where each node is a concept with directed arcs (representing the relation `subset` and, at the leaves, perhaps the relation `member_of` instead of `subset`) to other concepts. Other relations (such as `part_of`, `eats-ingests`, `lives_in`, ...) can be drawn, with arcs of different types (figure 1). In general, these relations are also nodes in another part of the ontology.

Associated words. To each concept (node) there are several English words[4] associated: those who denote it or have such concept as its meaning. Example: concept `mad_angry` has associated (is denoted by) words angry, crossed, pissed-of, mad, irritated, incensed. Example: Word mole denotes a `small_rodent`, a `spy_infiltrator` and also a `blemish_in_skin`.

1.2   Related Work

[12] represents concepts in a simpler format, called a *hierarchy*. Most works (for instance [11]) on ontologies involve the construction of a single ontology, even those that do collaborative design [8]. Often, ontologies are built for man-machine interaction [10] and not for machine-machine interaction. [1] tries to identify conceptually similar documents, but uses a single ontology. [3, 4] do the same using a topic hierarchy: a kind of ontology. [9] seeks to communicate several agents sharing a single ontology. The authors have been motivated [6, 7] by the need of agents to communicate with unknown agents, so that not much *a priori* agreement between them is possible. With respect to concept comparison, an ancestor of our COM (§2, appears first in [13]) matching mechanism is [2], based on the theory of analogy.

2   Most Similar Concepts in Two Different Ontologies

The most similar concept c_B in O_B to concept c_A in O_A is found by the COM algorithm using the function $sim(c_A)$ (called "hallar (c_A)" in [13]) as described in the four cases below. It considers a concept, its parents and sons. In this section, for each case, a tree structure shows the situation and a snapshot of a screen presents an example. Assume that agent A emits (sends) to B words[5] corresponding to c_A, and also sends words corresponding to the father of c_A, denoted by p_A. COM finds $c_B = sim(c_A)$, the concept in O_B most similar to c_A. *sim* also returns a similarity value *sv*, a number between 0 and 1 denoting how similar such returned concept c_B was to c_A.

---

[3] Each concept that I know and has a name is shared, since it was named by somebody else.

[4] Or word phrases, such as "domestic animal".

[5] Remember, an agent can not send a node to another agent, just words denoting it.

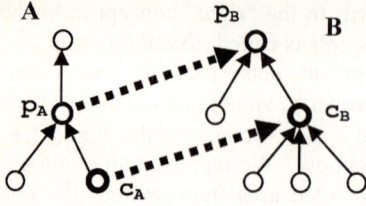 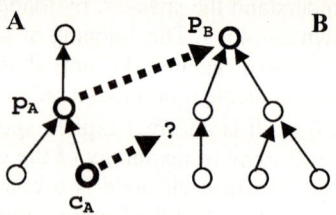

Fig. 2. Case (a). Words from c_A and p_A match words from c_B and p_B

Fig. 3. Case (b). Words from p_A match words from p_B but c_A has no equivalence

Case a) We look in O_B for two nodes p_B and c_B, such that: (1) the words associated to c_B coincide with most of the words (received by B from A)[6] of c_A; and (2) the words associated to p_B coincide with most of the words[6] corresponding to p_A; and (3) p_B is the father, grandfather or great-grandfather[7] of c_B.

If such p_B and c_B are found, then c_B is the nearest concept to c_A; the answer is c_B and the algorithm finishes returning $sv = 1$. Figure 2 represents this situation. Figure 4 shows the screenshot of COM when seeking in B the concept most similar to $apple_A$. The answer is concept $apple_B$ in B with $sv = 1$.

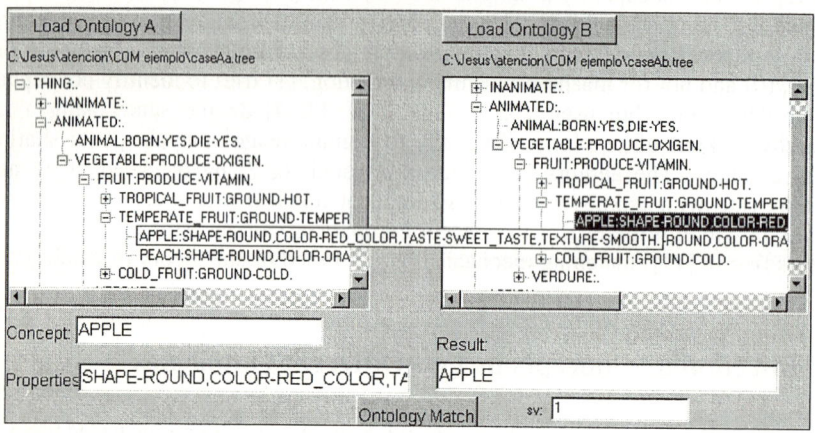

Fig. 4. Case (a). Screen with the execution of COM for the case shown in Fig. 2

Case b) This case occurs when (2) of case (a) holds, but (1) and (3) do not. p_B is found in O_B but c_B is not. See Figure 3. In this case, *sim* (which Olivares calls *hallar*) is called recursively, and we try to compute $p_B' = sim(p_A)$ to confirm that p_B is the ancestor of concept of interest (c_A).

---

[6] We have found useful the threshold 0.5: more than half of the compared entities must coincide.

[7] If p_B is found more than three levels up, the "semantic distance" is too high and *sim* says "no match."

(1) If the p_B' found is thing, the root of O_B, the algorithm returns not_found and concludes; $sv = 0$;

(2) Otherwise, a special child of p_B, to be called c_B', is searched in O_B, such that:

    A. Most[6] of the pairs (property, value) of c_B' coincide with the corresponding pairs of c_A. Children of p_B with just a few matching properties[6] or values are rejected. If the candidate c_B' analyzed has children, they are checked (using *sim* recursively) for a reasonable match[6] with the children of c_A. If a c_B' is found with the desired properties, the algorithm reports success returning c_B' as the concept in O_B most similar to c_A. $sv =$ the fraction of pairs of c_B' coinciding with corresponding pairs of c_A.

    B. Otherwise c_B' is sought among the sons of the father (in B) of p_B; that is, among the brothers of p_B; if necessary, among the sons of the sons of p_B; that is, among the grandsons of p_B. If found, the answer is c_B'. $sv =$ the sv returned by c_B' multiplied by 0.8 if c_B' was found among the sons of p_B,[8] or by $0.8^2 = 0.64$ if found among the grandsons of p_B.

    C. If such c_B' is not found, then the node nearest to c_A is some son of p_B, therefore *sim* returns the remark (son_of p_B) and the algorithm concludes. $sv = 0.5$ (an arbitrary but reasonable value). For example, if A sends words that correspond to the pair (c_A = kiwi, p_A = fruit), and B has the concept fruit but doesn't have the concept kiwi nor any similar fruit, in this case, the concept kiwi (of A) is translated by B into (son_of fruit), which means "some fruit I don't know" or "some fruit I do not have in my ontology."

Figure 5 shows the execution of COM for case (b)2(A). In this case concept kiwi$_A$ has no equivalent in B. Here rare_fruit$_B$ is chosen from B as the most similar concept because parents coincide and properties of kiwi$_A$ and rare_fruit$_B$ are similar (that was calculated using COM recursively for each property-value). $sv = 0.8$ because the exact equivalent concept in B was not found.

Case c) This case occurs when (1) of case (a) holds but (2) and (3) do not. See figure 6. c_B is found but p_B is not. We try to ascertain whether the grandfather (in O_B) of c_B has words that match[6] those of p_A (corresponding words that are equal exceed 50%), or if the great-grandfather of c_B in O_B has such matching[6] words.

(1) If that is the case, the concept in O_B more similar to p_A is the grandfather (or the great-grandfather) of c_B, and the algorithm finishes returning c_B. $sv = 0.8$ for the grandfather case, and 0.8^2 for the great-grandfather case.

(2) Otherwise (parents do not match), we verify two conditions:

    A. Most[6] of the properties (and their corresponding values) of c_B should coincide (using *sim*) with those of c_A ; and

    B. Most of the children of c_A should coincide (using *sim*) with most[6] of the children of c_B.

If the properties in (A) and the children in (B) coincide, the algorithm concludes with response c_B, although it did not find in O_B the p_B that corresponds to the concept p_A in O_A. $sv =$ the fraction of properties and children of c_B matching with corresponding entities of c_A.

---

[8] We have found that 0.8 allows for a fast decay as one moves up from father to grandfather and up.

(3) If even fewer properties and children are *simi*lar then response is (probably c_B) and the algorithm finishes. *sv* is computed like in (2)B.

(4) If neither properties nor children are *simi*lar, response is not_found and the algorithm finishes. $sv = 0$.

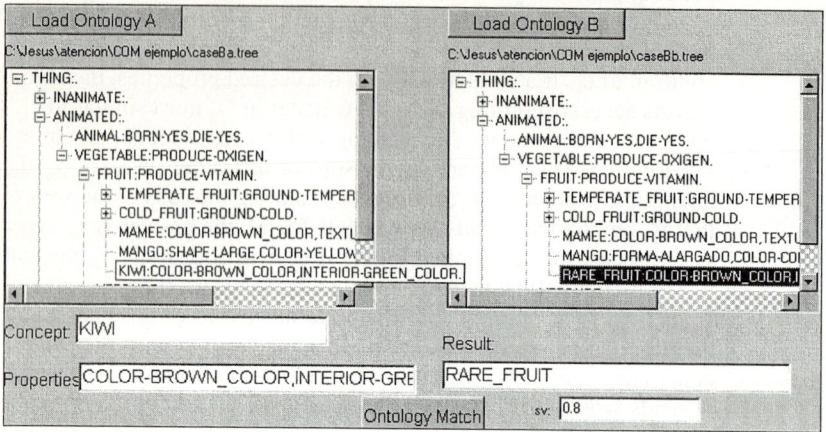

Fig. 5. Case (b). Screen with the execution of COM corresponding to Figure 3

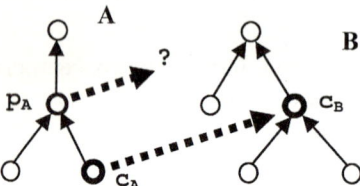

Fig. 6. Case (c). Words from c_A match with words of c_B but there is no equivalence for words of p_A. See Figure

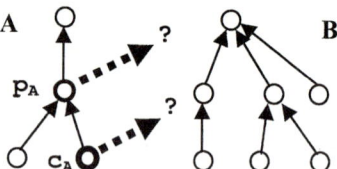

Fig. 7. Case (d). There are no words from c_A nor p_A that match with words of B.

Figure 8 shows an example of case (c)(2). In this case we use COM to seek in B the most similar concept to apple$_A$. Here concepts match but parents do not (fruit$_A$, food$_B$) (words are different for each parent), therefore similarity of the properties are used (calling recursively to COM). $sv = 0.8$ because parents do not coincide.

Case d) If neither c_B nor p_B are found, the algorithm concludes returning the response not_found. $sv = 0$. c_A could not find a similar node in O_B. The agents may have different ontologies (they know about different subjects) or they do not share a common communication language. See figures 7 and 9.

Figure 9 shows the execution of case (d). Observe that ontology O_A is mainly about fruits while O_B is mainly about Computer Science. There are some concepts in common, but not the involved concepts. $sv = 0$.

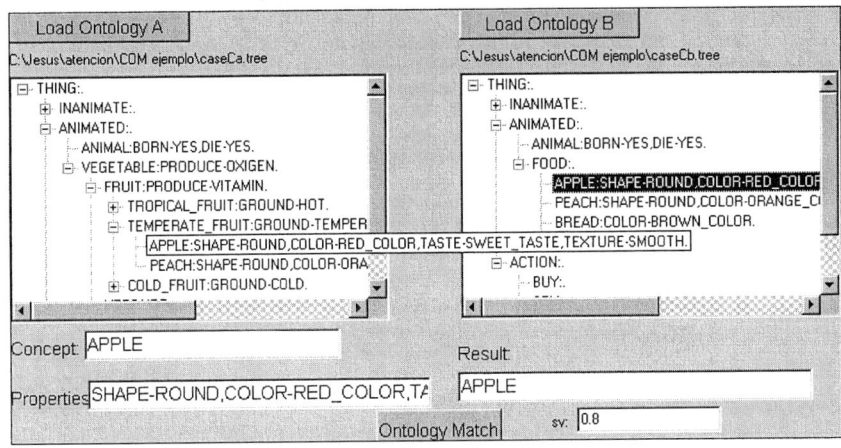

Fig 8. Case (c). Screen with the execution of COM corresponding to figure 6

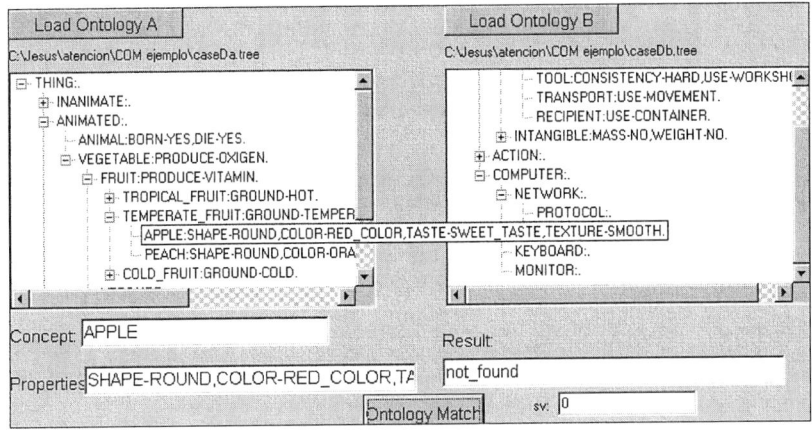

Fig 9. Case (d). Screen with the execution of COM for case (d). Ontologies refer mostly to different areas. COM returns not_found with $sv = 0$

sim is not symmetric. If c_B is the concept most similar to c_A, it is not necessarily true that c_A is the concept most similar to c_B. Example: O_A knows ten kinds of hammer$_A$, while O_B only knows hammer$_B$ (a general hammer). Then, COM maps each of the ten hammer$_A$ into hammer$_B$, while hammer$_B$ best maps into, say, hammer_for_carpenter$_A$ [12].

The function *sim* is only defined between a concept c_A in O_A and *the most similar concept c_B in O_B*.

```
                        Ontology A
thing: .
     living_creature: .
          animal: .
          plant_living:color-green_color,produce-
oxigen.
               melon: .
               bean: .
     tool: .
          screwdriver: .
          key_tool: .
     data: .
          field: .
               integer_field: .
               real_field: .
               double_field: .
               float_field: .
          key_data: .
               foreign_key: .
               Primary_key: .
```

Fig. 10. Ontology A. Used to compute similarity to concepts in ontology B

2.1 Examples of Similarity

Now we give examples for *sim,* the similarity between two concepts, each from one ontology. Here we assume that properties like relations and colors are part of both ontologies. For simplicity properties are shown only where needed. Properties appear after the colon as relation-value pairs. For ontologies A and B (Figures 10 and 11):

$sim(\text{field}_A) = \text{field}_B$ with $sv = 1$ because words of concepts and parents coincide. This is an example of case (a).

$sim(\text{key\_tool}_A) = \text{key\_tool}_B$ with $sv = 1$. This is an example of case(a), where words of the parent and concept in A match words of corresponding nodes in B. Although word 'key' denotes (belongs to the *associated words* of) both concepts key_data$_B$ and key_tool$_B$, the words of tool$_A$ only map into those of tool$_B$ and key_tool$_B$ is selected without ambiguity.

$sim(\text{screwdriver}_A) = (\text{son\_of tool}_B)$ with $sv = 0.5$. This is case (b): parents coincide, but in ontology B there is no concept similar to screwdriver$_A$, therefore the algorithm detects that agent A is referring to a son of concept tool$_B$.

$sim(\text{plant\_living}_A) = \text{vegetable}_B$ with $sv = 0.8$. This an example of case (b) when parents coincide but the concepts do not. In this case properties of concepts are used to establish the similarity among concepts. The similarity of the properties is calculated using the COM recursively for each property and value.

$sim(\text{double\_field}_A) = \text{not\_found}$ and $sv = 0$. This is an example of case (d) when no concept nor parent are found in B. The ontology A has sent B a concept of which B has no idea.

```
                              Ontology B
thing:.
    living_creature:.
        animal:.
        vegetable:color-green_color,produce-oxigen.
            apple:.
            bean:.
    tool:.
        hammer:.
        key_tool:.
    data:.
        field:.
        key_data:.
```

Fig. 11. Ontology B. Used to compute similarity to concepts in ontology A

$sim(\text{melon}_A) = \text{not\_found}$ and $sv = 0$. This is other example of case (d) where words sent to B from A do not match a pair parent-concept in B.

2.2 Conclusions

Methods embodied in a computer program are given to allow concept exchange and understanding between agents with different ontologies, so that there is no need to agree first on a standard set of concept definitions. Given a concept, a procedure for finding the most similar concept in another ontology is shown. The procedure also finds a measure of the similarity sv between concepts c_A and c_B. Our methods need further testing against large, vastly different, or practical ontologies.

In contrast, most efforts to communicate two agents take one of these approaches:
1. The same person or programmer writes (generates) both agents, so that pre-established *ad hoc* communicating sequences ("calling sequences," with predefined order of arguments and their meaning) are possible. This approach, of course, will fail if an agent is trying to communicate with agents built by somebody else.
2. Agents use a common or "standard" ontology to exchange information. This is the approach taken by CYC [11]. Standard ontologies are difficult and slow to build (they have to be designed by committee, most likely). Another deficiency: since new concepts appear each day, they slowly trickle to the standard ontology, so that it always stays behind current knowledge.

Even for approach (2), a language to convey other entities built out of concepts: complex objects (which do not have a name), actions, desires, plans, algorithms... (not just concepts) is needed. Such language is beyond this paper; hints of it at [13].

Our approach allows communication in spite of different ontologies, and needs neither (1) nor (2).

Acknowledgments. Work herein reported was partially supported by NSF-CONACYT Grant 32973-A and Project CGPI-IPN 18.07 (20010778). Olivares received a PIFI research assistantship from CGPI-IPN. Guzman-Arenas has a SNI *National Scientist* Award from SNI-CONACYT.

References

1. John Everett, D Bobrow, R Stolle, R Crouch, V de Paiva, C Condoravdi, M van den Berg, and L Polyani. (2002) Making ontologies work for resolving redundancies across documents. *Communication of the ACM* **45**, 2, 55-60. February.
2. K. Forbus, B. Falkenhainer, D. Gentner. (1989) The structure mapping engine: algorithms and examples. *Artificial Intelligence* **41**, 1, 1-63.
3. A. Gelbukh, G. Sidorov, and A. Guzman-Arenas. (1999) Use of a weighted document topic hierarchy for document classification. *Text, Speech, Dialogue*, 133-138. Pilsen, Chech Republic, September 13-17.
4. A. Gelbukh, G. Sidorov, and A. Guzman-Arenas. (1999) Document comparison with a weighted topic hierarchy. *DEXA-99*, 10th International Conference on Database and Expert System applications, Workshop on Document Analysis and Understanding for Document Databases, 566-570. Florence, Italy, August 30 to September 3.
5. Thomas R. Gruber (1993) Toward Principles for the Design of Ontologies Used for Knowledge Sharing, in *Formal Ontology in Conceptual Analysis and Knowledge Representation*, Nicola Guarino and Roberto Poli (eds.), Kluwer Academic Publishers.
6. A. Guzman, Jesus Olivares, Araceli Demetrio and Carmen Dominguez, (2000) Interaction of purposeful agents that use different ontologies. *Lecture Notes in Artificial Intelligence (LNAI)* **1793**, 557-573. Osvaldo Cairo, Enrique Sucar, F. J. Cantu (eds). Springer Verlag.
7. A. Guzman, C. Dominguez, and J. Olivares. (2002) Reacting to unexpected events and communicating in spite of mixed ontologies In *LNAI* **2313**, 377-386.
8. Cloyde W. Holsapple and K. D. Joshi. (2002) A collaborative approach to ontology design. *Comm. ACM* **45**, 2, 42-47. February.
9. M. N. Huhns; M. P. Singh. and T. Ksiezyk (1997) Global Information Management Via Local Autonomous Agents. In *Readings in Agents,* M. N. Huhns, Munindar P. Singh, (eds.). Morgan Kauffmann Publishers, Inc. San Francisco, CA
10. Henry Kim. (2002) Predicting how ontologies for the semantic web will evolve. *Comm. ACM* **45**, 2, 48-54. February.
11. Douglas B. Lenat, R. V. Guha, Karen Pittman, Dexter Pratt and Mary Shepherd (1990) Cyc: Toward Programs with Common Sense, *Comm. ACM* **33**, 9, 30 – 49.
12. Serguei Levachkine, A. Guzman-Arenas (2002) Hierarchy as a new data type for qualitative variables. Submitted to *Data and Knowledge Engineering*.
13. Jesus Olivares (2002) *An Interaction Model among Purposeful Agents, Mixed Ontologies and Unexpected Events*. Ph. D. Thesis, CIC-IPN. In Spanish. Available on line at http://www.jesusolivares.com/interaction/publica

ADM: An Active Deductive XML Database System

Oscar Olmedo-Aguirre, Karina Escobar-Vázquez, Giner Alor-Hernández, and
Guillermo Morales-Luna

Computer Science, CINVESTAV-IPN, Av. IPN 2508, Mexico City, Mexico,
{oolmedo,gmorales}@cs.cinvestav.mx,
{kescobar,galor}@computacion.cs.cinvestav.mx

Abstract. As XML is becoming widely accepted as a mean of storing, searching and extracting information, a larger number of Web
applications will require conceptual models and administrative tools to
organize their collections of documents. Recently, event-condition-action
(ECA) rules have been proposed to provide reactive functionality into
XML document databases. However, logical inference mechanisms to
deliver multiagent-based applications remain unconsidered in those
models. In this paper, we introduce ADM, an active deductive XML
database model that extends XML with logical variables, logical
procedures and ECA rules. ADM has been partially implemented in an
open distributed coordination architecture written in Java. Besides of
coupling the rational and reactive behavioral aspects into a simple and
uniform model, a major contribution of this work is the introduction
of sequential and parallel rule composition as an effective strategy to
address the problem of scheduling rule selection and execution.

Keywords: XML, Semantic Web, Deductive Databases, Active
Databases.

1 Introduction

The motivation behind this work is in the increasing use of the *Extensible Markup
Language*, XML, as a mean of storing structured information that cannot be conveniently stored using the available database technology. Examples of handling
XML document collections are recent Web-based recommendation systems that
have increasingly adopted the publish/subscribe model to disseminate relevant
new information among an users community. Actually, in the active database
community it has been proposed to extend the persistent storage functionality
of databases to support rule production systems [2]. By extending the relational database model with expert systems technology, a number of application-
independent tasks can be undertaken by the *Active Database Management System*, active DBMS, e.g. enforcement of data integrity constraints and data pro-
tection, versioning maintenance and data monitoring for knowledge discovery
and acquisition. Recently, XML active DBMS have been suggested to mirror
major results of active DBMS to the XML document management domain [1].

R. Monroy et al. (Eds.): MICAI 2004, LNAI 2972, pp. 139–148, 2004.
© Springer-Verlag Berlin Heidelberg 2004

Another substantial amount of research has been devoted to deductive database systems [6]. Those systems are similar to relational database systems in that both are passive, responding only to user queries. Deductive DBMS extend a relational DBMS with a Prolog-like inference engine to answer possibly recursive queries in order to derive conclusions logically entailed in the database content. As the expressive power of both the query model and the language becomes richer then the deductive DBMS is a more convenient mean to describe the complex conditions used in production rules.

The *DARPA Agent Markup Language*, DAML [4], has been developed as an extension of XML by using ontologies to describe objects and their relations to other objects. We follow, instead, a theorem prover approach.

In this work, we introduce ADM to address the problem of coupling XML active databases with deductive databases to support multiagent-based applications. The adopted approach consists on extending XML with logical variables, logical procedures and ECA rules. The extensions allow a user to annotate XML documents with logical constraints among other related features to enforce integrity. Event annotations allow an user to describe where the insertion or deletion events take place, making available the content of the document involved to test the integrity constraints. The experimental system developed so far can be considered an open distributed coordination architecture that enables third-party applications to use the already created XML documents. It provides basic language constructs to coordinate document content flow in Web-based applications. ADM is built upon LogCIN-XML, an experimental deductive XML database developed by the first two authors of the current paper, that in turn has been written in Prolog-Cafe [3], a WAM-like Prolog engine that sits on the Java Virtual Machine. While the Prolog-Cafe provides the basic automated inferencing capabilities, a set of Java servlets provide the core functionality for coordination and communication among clients and servers.

2   Extensional Databases

XML extensional databases are collections of standard XML documents maintained on a distributed directory structure across the Internet. ADM preserves the open character of extensional databases by keeping apart language extensions from the data created by third-party applications. From a logic programming point of view, XML elements roughly correspond to ground terms. Nonetheless, XML elements have a more complex structure than those of first order logical languages due to the presence of a list of attribute-value pairs. Assuming that such a list is in ascending order by the name of the attribute, the structure of an XML element can be rewritten into a syntactically equivalent Prolog term. As an example, Table 1 shows a collection of XML documents containing family relations information in which all documents share the same simple structure. The root element fatherof contains two child elements father and son describing the role of the participants. Thus, bob and tom are two persons related by the fatherof relation, having the roles father and son respectively.

Table 1. A family relations extensional XML database.

⟨fatherof ⟩⟨father ⟩bob⟨/father⟩ ⟨son ⟩joe⟨/son⟩⟨/fatherof⟩
⟨fatherof ⟩⟨father ⟩bob⟨/father⟩ ⟨son ⟩tom⟨/son⟩⟨/fatherof⟩
⟨fatherof ⟩⟨father ⟩joe⟨/father⟩ ⟨son ⟩doe⟨/son⟩⟨/fatherof⟩

3   Intentional Databases

Intentional databases are collections of logical procedures and ECA rules called
programs. The reason for maintaining language extensions isolated from data is
twofold: firstly, to create a low-level conceptual layer of the fundamental concepts
that underlie the application, and secondly, to create an upper-level conceptual
layer to describe the integrity constraints and consistency-preserving rules that
can be logically derived from the extensional database contents.

XML elements are extended with logical variables to introduce the notion
of XML *terms*. Logical variables are used to define the integrity constraints
imposed on the document contents and to formulate queries to bind values to
variables. Logical variables can be of either type *string* (prefixed by a '\$') or
term (prefixed by a '#') and they may occur in elements and in attributes. The
function var : XMLTerm $\rightarrow$ **P** XMLVariable is defined to obtain the set of variables
occurring in a term (here **P** stands for the *power set* operator).

Integrity constraints are introduced by means of logical procedures. A log-
ical procedure has the form $\langle$b $b_1 = T_1 \cdots b_n = T_n\rangle B_1 \cdots B_m \langle$/b$\rangle$ comprising
a *head* and a *body*. The head $\langle$b $b_1 = T_1 \cdots b_n = T_n\rangle$ consists of a procedure
name b and a list of parameter names $b_1 \cdots b_n$ associated with their respective
terms $T_1 \cdots T_n$. The body $B_1 \cdots B_m$ consists of a sequence of procedure calls.
A procedure call has either the form $\langle$b $b_1 = S_1 \cdots b_n = S_n/\rangle$ or the form
$\langle$b $b_1 = S_1 \cdots b_n = S_n\rangle A_1 \cdots A_k \langle$/b$\rangle$ where $S_1 \cdots S_n$ are the XML terms passed
to the procedure and $A_1, \ldots, A_m$ are XML terms. The former case corresponds to
a call to a defined procedure, whereas the latter case corresponds to a consult to
the extensional database. In any case, unification is used for parameter passing,
and equality comparison between documents with complex structure.

The consistency-preserving and reactive behavior are described by ECA
rules. Any ECA rule has the structure given in Table 2. When a collection
of XML documents changes by inserting or deleting a document, an event E
occurs, and then one or more rules may be selected. In this case, condition C is
checked and if it is satisfied within the database, then the actions of deleting B
or inserting A the argument document are executed. Ordering of actions can be
defined by composing rules R either sequentially or in parallel.

As an example of an intentional database, Table 3 shows the logical procedures fatherof and cousinof and the ECA rule partyInvitation. The logical
procedures describe the father-of and cousin-of relations between two persons,
called in the procedure the subject and the object, respectively. In the logical

Table 2. ECA rule structure.

```
⟨rule ⟩⟨on ⟩E⟨/on⟩⟨if ⟩C⟨/if⟩
⟨do ⟩
⟨delete ⟩B⟨/delete⟩opt
⟨insert ⟩A⟨/insert⟩opt
⟨seq ⟩R⟨/seq⟩opt
⟨par ⟩R⟨/par⟩opt
⟨/do⟩
⟨/rule⟩
```

procedure `brotherof`, logical variables `$X` and `$Y` are respectively associated to parameter names `subject` and `object`. The call to the system-defined procedure `notequal` tests whether the ground terms bound to variables `$X` and `$Y` are not identical. Table 3 also shows the ECA rule `partyInvitation` that notifies the good news to all cousins of having a new member.

Table 3. A family relations document in the XML intensional database.

```
⟨brotherof subject="$X"   object="$Y" ⟩
⟨notequal subject="$X"   object="$Y" /⟩
⟨fatherof ⟩⟨father ⟩$Z⟨/father⟩⟨son ⟩$X⟨/son⟩⟨/fatherof⟩
⟨fatherof ⟩⟨father ⟩$Z⟨/father⟩⟨son ⟩$Y⟨/son⟩⟨/fatherof⟩
⟨/brotherof⟩
```

```
⟨cousinof subject="$X"   object="$Y" ⟩
⟨fatherof ⟩⟨father ⟩$Z1⟨/father⟩⟨son ⟩$X⟨/son⟩⟨/fatherof⟩
⟨fatherof ⟩⟨father ⟩$Z2⟨/father⟩⟨son ⟩$Y⟨/son⟩⟨/fatherof⟩
⟨brotherof subject="$Z1"   object="$Z2" /⟩
⟨/cousinof⟩
```

```
⟨rule name="partyInvitation"⟩
⟨on ⟩⟨insert ⟩
⟨fatherof ⟩⟨father ⟩$X⟨/father⟩⟨son ⟩$Y⟨/son⟩⟨/fatherof⟩
⟨/insert⟩⟨/on⟩
⟨if ⟩⟨cousinof subject="$Y"   object="$Z"   /⟩⟨/if⟩
⟨do ⟩⟨insert ⟩
⟨invitation ⟩⟨host ⟩$Y⟨/host⟩⟨guest ⟩$Z⟨/guest⟩⟨/invitation⟩
⟨/insert⟩⟨/do⟩⟨/rule⟩
```

3.1   Rule Activation

A rule is activated when a new document is inserted. Table 4 shows the new document that has the structure defined by the rule's event section.

An alerter agent notifies the system that an insertion event occurs. The alerter sends the document content to the ADM rule manager to select an appropriate rule.

Table 4. Inserted XML document.

...
⟨fatherof ⟩⟨father ⟩tom⟨/father⟩ ⟨son ⟩tim⟨/son⟩⟨/fatherof⟩

3.2   Rule Response

After ADM receives the document involved in the event from the alerter, it selects a rule and checks the condition. If condition holds, the rule is executed.

Table 5. Document generated by rule partyInvitation.

...
⟨invitation ⟩⟨host ⟩tim⟨/host⟩ ⟨guest ⟩doe⟨/guest⟩⟨/invitation⟩

In the rule, the event section uses a document template to retrieve the required information. The logical variables $X and $Y are used to extract the pieces of information that match their position with the event document. A substitution that include the bindings $X = "tom" and $Y = "tim" is applied to the rule to obtain an instance of the rule. Then, a solution $Z = "doe" of the query ⟨cousinof subject="$Y"   object="$Z"   /⟩ is deduced. As the query succeeds, the action of inserting the document shown in Table 5 is performed.

4   Operational Semantics

4.1   Basic Definitions

In this section a few basic definitions for XML terms are given to formally introduce the operational semantics of ADM. The XML term $\langle$a $a_1 = T_1 \cdots a_m = T_m \rangle \cdots \langle$/a$\rangle$ is *normalized* if its list of attribute-value pairs is lexicographically ordered by the name of the attribute in increasing order: $a_i \leq a_j$ if $i \leq j$, $i, j \in \{1, \ldots, m\}$. The set of *substitutions* Σ consists of the partial functions XMLVariable $\rightarrow$ XMLTerm defined recursively in Table 6. Computed answers to queries are obtained by the *composition* of substitutions. The *null substitution* ϵ is the identity for substitution composition $\epsilon\sigma = \sigma\epsilon = \sigma$. A *ground substitution* does not introduce any variable. The *natural extension* σ : XMLTerm $\rightarrow$ XMLTerm of a substitution defined over variables to XML terms is denoted by the same name. The *instance* of an XML term x under substitution σ is denoted by xσ and its inductive definition on the structure of the XML term is given in Table 6. Instances of XML terms under ground substitutions are called *ground instances*.

An *unifier* σ for the XML terms T and S is a substitution that produces syntactically identical instances Tσ = Sσ. The *most general unifier* (*mgu*) is an

Table 6. Variable substitution on XML terms.

$$x\sigma = x \quad x \in \texttt{XMLString} \cup \texttt{XMLText}$$
$$x\sigma = \sigma(x) \quad x \in \texttt{XMLVariable}$$
$$\langle \texttt{a } a_1 = T_1 \cdots a_m = T_m /\rangle \sigma = \langle \texttt{a } a_1 = T_1\sigma \cdots a_m = T_m\sigma /\rangle$$

$\langle \texttt{a } a_1 = T_1 \cdots a_m = T_m \rangle$		$\langle \texttt{a } a_1 = T_1\sigma \cdots a_m = T_m\sigma \rangle$
$\cdots T \cdots$	$\sigma =$	$\cdots T\sigma \cdots$
$\langle /\texttt{a} \rangle$		$\langle /\texttt{a} \rangle$

unifier that cannot be obtained as the composition of any other. The *unification algorithm*, shown in Table 7, essentially corresponds to that introduced by Martelli-Montanari [7], producing either a most general unifier if it exists or a failure otherwise.

Table 7. Unification of XML terms.

$A =$	$\langle \texttt{a } a_1 = S_1 \ldots a_m = S_m \rangle$	$B =$	$\langle \texttt{a } a_1 = T_1 \ldots a_m = T_m \rangle$
	$E_1 \cdots E_n$		$F_1 \cdots F_n$
	$\langle /\texttt{a} \rangle$		$\langle /\texttt{a} \rangle$

$$\overline{(C \cup \{A\text{=}B\}, \sigma) \triangleright (C \cup \{S_1 = T_1, \ldots, S_m = T_m, E_1 = F_1, \ldots, E_n = F_n\}, \sigma)}$$

$$\frac{A = \langle \texttt{a } a_1 = S_1 \ldots a_m = S_m /\rangle \quad B = \langle \texttt{a } a_1 = T_1 \ldots a_m = T_m /\rangle}{(C \cup \{A\text{=}B\}, \sigma) \triangleright (C \cup \{S_1 = T_1, \ldots, S_m = T_m\}, \sigma)}$$

$$(C \cup \{T = T\}, \sigma) \triangleright (C, \sigma)$$
$$(C \cup \{T = x\}, \sigma) \triangleright (C \cup \{x = T\}, \sigma)$$
$$(C \cup \{x = T\}, \sigma) \triangleright (C\sigma, \sigma\{x \mapsto T\}) \quad x \notin vars(T)$$
$$(C \cup \{x = T\}, \sigma) \triangleright \text{failure} \qquad x \in vars(T)$$

$$\frac{(\{T = S\}, \epsilon) \triangleright^* (\epsilon, \sigma)}{mgu(T, S) = \sigma}$$

The most general unifier is defined as the reflexive and transitive closure of the binary relation $\triangleright \subseteq (\texttt{XMLTerm} \times \Sigma) \times (\texttt{XMLTerm} \times \Sigma)$. Unification of XML terms provides an uniform mechanism for parameter passing, construction and selection of the information contained in the XML document.

4.2   Deductive Database Model

The meaning of a logical procedure is given by the interpretation of an SLD-resolution[1] step of a procedure call [5]. Conversely, the declarative reading of a logical procedure establishes the validity of the call to the procedure head whenever all the conditions forming the procedure body are valid. An SLD resolution step of the logical procedure $\langle \texttt{b } b_1 = T_1 \cdots b_n = T_n \rangle B_1 \cdots B_m \langle /\texttt{b} \rangle$ in the query $\langle \texttt{query} \rangle A_1 \cdots A_n \langle /\texttt{query} \rangle$ is obtained by replacing an instance of the body

---
[1] Linear resolution for Definite programs with Selection rule

$B_1\sigma' \cdots B_m\sigma'$ under the most general unifier σ of the first call A_1 in the query and the head $\langle b\ b_1 = T_1 \cdots b_n = T_n\ /\rangle$ of the procedure.

Table 8. SLD inference relation.

$$\frac{\langle b\ b_1 = T_1 \cdots b_n = T_n\ \rangle B_1 \cdots B_m \langle /b\rangle \in \texttt{XMLProgram} \quad \exists \sigma'.\ \sigma' = mgu(head(A_1), \langle b\ b_1 = T_1 \cdots b_n = T_n\ \rangle)}{(\langle \texttt{query}\ \rangle A_1 A_2 \cdots A_n \langle /\texttt{query}\rangle, \sigma) \Rightarrow (\langle \texttt{query}\ \rangle B_1\sigma' \cdots B_m\sigma' A_2\sigma' \cdots A_n\sigma' \langle /\texttt{query}\rangle, \sigma\sigma')}$$

An SLD resolution step is thus defined as the relation $\Rightarrow \subseteq (\texttt{XMLTerm} \times \Sigma) \times (\texttt{XMLTerm} \times \Sigma)$ that transforms the query $(\langle \texttt{query}\ \rangle A_1 A_2 \cdots A_n \langle /\texttt{query}\rangle, \sigma)$ into the query $(\langle \texttt{query}\ \rangle B_1\sigma' \cdots B_m\sigma' A_2\sigma' \cdots A_n\sigma' \langle /\texttt{query}\rangle, \sigma\sigma')$ by replacing the procedure call $A_1\sigma'$ by the instance of the procedure body $B_1\sigma' \cdots B_m\sigma'$ under σ'.

Table 9. Correctness of SLD inference.

$$\frac{(\langle \texttt{query}\ \rangle C_1 \cdots C_k \langle /\texttt{query}\rangle, \epsilon) \rightarrow^* (\langle \texttt{query}\ \rangle\ \langle /\texttt{query}\rangle, \sigma)}{\models_\sigma \langle \texttt{query}\ \rangle C_1 \cdots C_k \langle /\texttt{query}\rangle}$$

The computed answer of a query consists of zero, one or more SLD resolution steps beginning from the initial query. The query execution terminates when there are no more goals to be solved. The computed answer is obtained from the composition of the substitutions used in each resolution step. Table 6 states that the computed answer is indeed the correct answer, i.e. the substitution that is the solution of the query. A well known result from logic programming [5] asserts that a computed answer σ obtained by the SLD resolution calculus is a model for both the program P and the query $\langle \texttt{query}\ \rangle C_1 \cdots C_k \langle /\texttt{query}\rangle$. Therefore, the computed answers are those that satisfy the logical constraints of the program.

4.3   Active Database Model

ECA rules integrate the event-directed rule processing into the knowledge-based model of deductive databases. The ECA rule model closely follows the perception-deduction-action cycle of multiagent-based systems.

The operational semantics of rule execution, given in Table 10, defines the reduction relation $\longrightarrow \subseteq (\mathbf{M}\,\texttt{XMLTerm} \times \Sigma) \times (\mathbf{M}\,\texttt{XMLTerms} \times \Sigma \cup \mathbf{M}\,\texttt{XMLTerms})$ where $\mathbf{M}\,\texttt{XMLTerm}$ denotes multisets of XML terms, including logical procedures and ECA rules. After observing event E, if there is a computed answer σ' for both the extended program with the event $P \cup \{E\}$ and the condition $\langle \texttt{query}\ \rangle C_1 \cdots C_k \langle /\texttt{query}\rangle$, then the collection of documents in both the extensional and intensional databases are modified by deleting the instance of documents $B_1\sigma', \ldots, B_n\sigma'$ and inserting the instance of documents $A_1\sigma', \ldots, A_m\sigma'$ under σ'. The difference $\ominus$ and union $\oplus$ operators for multisets of documents are used instead of the corresponding operators over sets due to the importance of documents multiplicity. The order in which documents are deleted or inserted is

Table 10. Reduction relation of active rules.

$$
\begin{array}{|l|}
\hline
\langle\texttt{rule }\rangle \\
\langle\texttt{on }\rangle\texttt{E}\langle\texttt{/on}\rangle \\
\langle\texttt{if }\rangle\texttt{C}_1\cdots\texttt{C}_k\langle\texttt{/if}\rangle \\
\langle\texttt{do }\rangle \\
\langle\texttt{delete }\rangle\texttt{B}_1\cdots\texttt{B}_m\langle\texttt{/delete}\rangle \\
\langle\texttt{insert }\rangle\texttt{A}_1\cdots\texttt{A}_n\langle\texttt{/insert}\rangle \\
\langle\texttt{/do}\rangle \\
\langle\texttt{/rule}\rangle \\
\hline
\end{array}\;\in P
$$

$$
\frac{\exists\sigma'\in\Sigma.P\cup\{E\}\models_{\sigma'}\langle\texttt{query }\rangle\texttt{C}_1\cdots\texttt{C}_k\langle\texttt{/query}\rangle}{(P,\sigma)\longrightarrow(P\ominus\{B_1\sigma',\dots,B_n\sigma'\}\oplus\{A_1\sigma',\dots,A_m\sigma'\},\sigma\sigma')}
$$

not specified. By using instance of documents under substitutions, the semantics captures the propagation of values among logical variables across documents.

Table 11. Termination condition.

$$
\begin{array}{|l|}
\hline
\langle\texttt{rule }\rangle \\
\langle\texttt{on }\rangle\texttt{E}\langle\texttt{/on}\rangle \\
\langle\texttt{if }\rangle\texttt{C}_1\cdots\texttt{C}_k\langle\texttt{/if}\rangle \\
\langle\texttt{do }\rangle\cdots\langle\texttt{/do}\rangle \\
\langle\texttt{/rule}\rangle \\
\hline
\end{array}\;\in P
$$

$$
\frac{\neg\exists\sigma'\in\Sigma.P\cup\{E\}\models_{\sigma'}\langle\texttt{query }\rangle\texttt{C}_1\cdots\texttt{C}_k\langle\texttt{/query}\rangle}{(P,\sigma)\longrightarrow P}
$$

The operational semantics for the termination condition of the execution of a rule is given in Table 11. After observing the event E that triggers a rule, the rule does not execute if the current contents of the XML databases does not entail the rule condition. In this case, the reduction relation $\longrightarrow$ leads to the program singleton P.

Though ECA rules are powerful, an unpredictable behavior may arise since the rules may interfere with each other preventing their execution. In order to reduce the non-determinism in the ordering of actions, the sequential and parallel composition of rules are introduced to schedule their execution. The operational semantics of sequential composition is given in Table 12.

The first rule describes the termination condition of two rules under sequential composition. If rule P terminates at state σ, then sequential composition of rules P and Q behaves like Q at the same state σ. The second rule describes the progress condition of two rules under sequential composition. If at state σ rule P reduces to rule P', then the sequential composition of P and Q reduces to the sequential composition of P' and Q.

Table 12. Reduction relation for the sequential composition of rules.

$$\frac{(P,\sigma) \longrightarrow P}{(\langle \mathsf{seq}\,\rangle P\ Q\langle/\mathsf{seq}\rangle,\sigma) \longrightarrow (Q,\sigma)}$$

$$\frac{(P,\sigma) \longrightarrow (P',\sigma')}{(\langle \mathsf{seq}\,\rangle P\ Q\langle/\mathsf{seq}\rangle,\sigma) \longrightarrow (\langle \mathsf{seq}\,\rangle P'\ Q\langle/\mathsf{seq}\rangle,\sigma\sigma')}$$

Table 13 shows the rules of parallel composition of programs. The function $docset : \mathbf{M}\,\mathtt{XMLTerm}\times \Sigma \to \mathbf{M}\,\mathtt{XMLTerms}$ gets the multiset consisting of document instances (possibly including logical variables) under a given substitution. The first two rules apply only if they share a non-empty multiset of documents. In that case, either rule P or Q may develop its behavior but not simultaneously.

Table 13. Reduction relation for parallel composition of rules.

$$\frac{(P,\sigma) \longrightarrow (P',\sigma') \quad docset(P,\sigma) \cap docset(Q,\sigma') \neq \emptyset}{(\langle \mathsf{par}\,\rangle P\ Q\langle/\mathsf{par}\rangle,\sigma) \longrightarrow (\langle \mathsf{par}\,\rangle P'\ Q\langle/\mathsf{par}\rangle,\sigma\sigma')}$$

$$\frac{(Q,\sigma) \longrightarrow (Q',\sigma') \quad docset(P,\sigma) \cap docset(Q,\sigma') \neq \emptyset}{(\langle \mathsf{par}\,\rangle P\ Q\langle/\mathsf{par}\rangle,\sigma) \longrightarrow (\langle \mathsf{par}\,\rangle P\ Q'\langle/\mathsf{par}\rangle,\sigma\sigma')}$$

$$\frac{(P,\sigma) \longrightarrow (P',\sigma_1) \quad (Q,\sigma) \longrightarrow (Q',\sigma_2) \quad docset(P,\sigma) \cap docset(Q,\sigma) = \emptyset}{(\langle \mathsf{par}\,\rangle P\ Q\langle/\mathsf{par}\rangle,\sigma) \longrightarrow (\langle \mathsf{par}\,\rangle P'\ Q'\langle/\mathsf{par}\rangle,\sigma\sigma_1\sigma_2)}$$

$$\frac{(P,\sigma) \longrightarrow P \quad (Q,\sigma) \longrightarrow Q}{(\langle \mathsf{par}\,\rangle P\ Q\langle/\mathsf{par}\rangle,\sigma) \longrightarrow P \cup Q}$$

Third rule for parallel composition applies only if rules P and Q do not share a collection of documents. In that case, if both rules independently exhibit some progress, then under parallel composition they do not interfere. Finally, last rule describe the termination condition under parallel composition of rules. If two programs P and Q terminate at state σ, the they also terminate under parallel composition at the same state.

5   Conclusions

A simple and uniform model for active and deductive XML databases has been proposed in this paper. The ADM language extends the XML language by introducing logical variables, logical procedures and ECA rules. An experimental distributed system with layered architecture has been implemented that maintains the openness of the XML data by keeping apart the language extensions. As future work, we plan to develop analysis methods and tools to face the most difficult aspects of controlling and predicting rule execution.

References

1. J. Bailey, A. Poulovassilis, P. T. Wood, Analysis and optimization of event-condition-action rules on XML. *Computer Networks*, 39:239-259. 2002.
2. N. W. Paton, O. Diaz, Active database systems. *ACM Computing Surveys*, 31(1): 64-103. 1999.
3. M. Bambara, N. Tamura, Translating a linear logic programming language into Java. In *Proceedings of ICLP'99 Workshop on Parallelism and Implementation Technology for (Constraint) Logic Programming Languages*. pp. 19-39, Dec 1999.
4. The DARPA Agent Markup Language Homepage, http://www.daml.org/
5. J. W. Lloyd, *Foundations of Logic Programming*. Springer-Verlag, 1987.
6. M. Liu, G. Dobbie, T. W. Ling, A logical foundation for deductive object-oriented databases, *ACM Transactions on Database Systems*, 27(1), pp. 117-151. 2002
7. A. Martelli, U. Montanari, An efficient unification algorithm, *ACM Transactions on Programming Language and Systems*, 4(2): 258-282, April, 1982.

Web-Based Intelligent Service for Coalition Operation Support in Networked Organizations

Alexander Smirnov, Mikhail Pashkin, Nikolai Chilov,
Tatiana Levashova, and Andrew Krizhanovsky

St.Petersburg Institute for Informatics and Automation of the Russian Academy of Sciences
39, 14ᵗʰ Line, St Petersburg, 199178, Russia
{smir,michael,nick,oleg,aka}@mail.iias.spb.su

Abstract. Nowadays, organizations must continually adapt to market and organizational changes to achieve their most important goals. The migration to business services and service-oriented architectures provides a valuable opportunity to attain the organization objectives. The migration causes evolution both in organizational structure and technology enabling businesses to dynamically change vendors or services. The paper proposes a view integrating the concept of *networked organization* & *Web intelligence* & *Web Services* into a collaboration environment of a networked organization. An approach to knowledge logistics problem based on the concepts of Web intelligence and Web services in the networked intelligent organization environment is described. Applicability of the approach is illustrated through a "Binni scenario"-based case study of portable hospital configuration as an e-business & e-government coalition operation.

1   Introduction

Nowadays, organizations must continually adapt to market and organizational changes to achieve their most important goals: lowering costs, expanding revenues, and retaining customers. The migration to business services and service-oriented architectures provides a valuable opportunity to attain the organization objectives [1]. The migration causes evolution both in organizational structure and technology enabling businesses to dynamically change vendors or services.

Among forms of organizational structures the form of *networked organization* has been developed. This form denotes an organization that uses information and communication technologies to extend its boundaries and physical location [2]. Such the organization can be considered as an *intelligent organization* with a distributed network structure. The *nodes* of a networked organization represent any objects of the environment (people, teams, organizations, etc.) acting independently and forming multiple *links* across boundaries to work together for a common purpose [3].

Behaviour of a networked organization corresponds to the behaviour of an intelligent organization. The latter "behaves as an open system which takes in information, material and energy from the environment, transforms these resources into knowledge, processes, and structures that produce goods or services which are in turn consumed by the environment" [4]. Such the behaviour assumes a presence of

R. Monroy et al. (Eds.): MICAI 2004, LNAI 2972, pp. 149–158, 2004.

organization 'intellectual abilities', i.e., abilities to create, exchange, process and infer knowledge, and to learn.

Such technologies as *Web intelligence* (e.g., *business intelligence*) provide for strategies enabling to implement main behavioural principles of networked intelligent organization. The purpose of business intelligence is an effective support of consumer and business processes. An attainment of this goal involves development of services for consumer needs recognition, information search, and evaluation of alternatives [5]. Web intelligence deals with advancement of Web-empowered systems, services, and environments. It includes issues of Web-based knowledge processing and management; distributed inference; information exchange and knowledge sharing [6].

Described in the paper approach has been developed to solve knowledge logistics problem. *Knowledge logistics* [7] addresses activities over the knowledge delivery. These activities concern acquisition, integration, and transfer of the right knowledge from distributed sources located in an information environment and its delivery in the right context, to the right person, in the right time for the right purpose. The aim of knowledge logistics has much in common with the purposes of business intelligence and Web intelligence. The proposed approach combines technologies of artificial intelligence appearing in business intelligence and Web intelligence as intelligent agents, profiling, ontology and knowledge management with constraint satisfaction problem.

In the context of the paper the approach offers Web-based intelligent services for a networked organization by an example of a coalition operation support. The choice of coalition operations is governed by the structure and activities of cooperation supporting such the operations. The cooperation is made up of a number of different, quasivolunteered, vaguely organized groups of people, non-governmental organizations, and institutions providing humanitarian aid. Its activities are oriented on support of e-health / humanitarian operations. The cooperation structure is close to one of a networked organization. The cooperation is formed for problem solving by all cooperation members. The task of forming the cooperation and the problem solving itself can be considered as the above cited 'common purpose'.

The rest of the paper is organized as follows. Section 0 describes a framework of the proposed approach. Main approach implementation features significant to networked organization and cooperative problem solving are presented in Section 0. Application of the approach is illustrated in Section 0 through a case study.

2   KSNet-Approach: Framework

The being described approach considers the knowledge logistics problem as a problem of a Knowledge Source Network (KSNet) configuration, in this connection it has been referred to as KSNet-approach [8]. Knowledge sources (KSs) comprise end-users / customers, loosely coupled knowledge sources / resources, and a set of tools and methods for information / knowledge processing. In the context of the paper the configured KSNet is thought of as a networked organization, where the listed above constituents of the KSNet correspond to the organization nodes.

Since knowledge logistics assumes dealing with knowledge containing in distributed and heterogeneous KSs the approach is oriented to ontological model providing a common way of knowledge representation. The methodology addresses

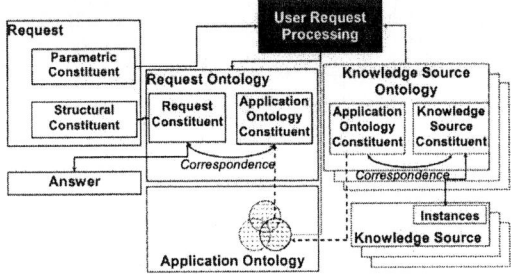

Fig. 1. Framework of ontology-driven methodology

user needs (problems) identification and solving these problems (Fig. 1). User needs are introduced by a request. The methodology considers request processing as a configuration of a network of KSs containing information relevant to the request, generation of an appropriate solution relying on this information, and presenting the solution to the user represented by a Web-service client (service requestor).

At the heart of the framework a fundamental ontology providing a common notation lies. This is implemented through an ontology library. It is a knowledge storage assigning a common notation and providing a common vocabulary to ontologies that it stores. Main components of the ontology library are domain, tasks & methods, and application ontologies. All these ontologies are interrelated according to [9] in such a way that an application ontology (AO) is a specialization of both domain and tasks & methods ontologies.

AO plays a central role in the request processing. It represents shared knowledge of a user (request constituent in Fig. 1) and knowledge sources (knowledge source constituent in Fig. 1). AO is formed through merging parts of domain and tasks & methods ontologies relevant to the request into a single ontology. Requested information from KSs is associated with the same AO that is formed for the request processing [7].

For the translation between user terms, KS terms, and the vocabulary supported by the ontology library request ontologies and knowledge source ontologies are used. These ontologies represent correspondences between terms of AO which are words of the ontology library vocabulary and request / knowledge source terms.

The KSNet-approach is based on the idea that knowledge corresponding to individual user requirements and knowledge peculiar to KSs are represented by restrictions on the shared knowledge described by AO. That was the main reason to use an approach oriented to constraint satisfaction / propagation technology for problem solving. As the common notation formalism of object-oriented constraint networks has been chosen [7]. According to the formalism ontology is described by sets of classes, attributes of the classes, domains of the attributes, and constraints.

Because of distributed structure of networked organization, its behaviour of open system, and orientation on the Internet as the e-business environment the technology of Web-services for the approach implementation has been applied. As a constraint-based tool ILOG tool has been chosen [10]. The system implementing the approach inherits its name and is referred to as the system "KSNet". The detailed description of the multiagent system architecture and its functionalities can be found in [11]. Main features of the system which are significant for networked intelligent organization and cooperative problem solving are described in the next section.

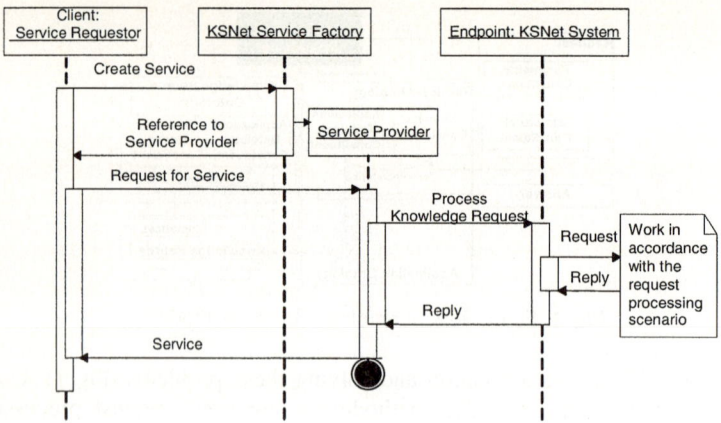

Fig. 2. Service-based scenario for the system "KSNet"

3 Service Model of the System "KSNet"

The general aim on the course to Web services is to turn the Web into a collection of computational resources, each with a well-defined interface for invoking its services. Thereby Web Services can be defined as software objects that can be assembled over the Internet using standard protocols to perform functions or solve tasks.

The Web service-oriented model applied to the system "KSNet" is organized as follows. The system acts as a service provider for knowledge customer services and at the same time as a service requestor for knowledge suppliers (OKBC-compliance knowledge representation systems). The proposed scenario is presented in (Fig. 2). The main specific is that the service passes the request into the system where it goes through all the stages of the request processing scenario. The service requestor sends a request to the KSNet service factory for a service creation. KSNet service factory defines a service provider and returns a reference to it to the requestor. After that the requestor sends a request for the service to the service provider and the latter interacts with the system "KSNet" for the purpose of the requested service. When the system finds an answer for the request the reply gets to the service provider and then it is passed to the requestor.

The key to Web Services is on-the-fly software creation through the use of loosely coupled, reusable software components [12]. For this purpose the described approach implements adaptive services. These services may modify themselves when solving a particular task. For example, within the KSNet-approach there is a service attached to an application that is responsible for configuration problem solving based on existing knowledge. Upon receiving a task the application loads an appropriate AO and generates an executable module for its solving "on-the-fly".

Referring to the approach framework a request defines a task statement (goal) which, in turn, defines what ontologies describe knowledge relevant to the request and what KSs contain information to generate the answer. Knowledge relevant to the request is described by an AO. Thereby, a triple <G, AO, KS> where G – goal, AO – application ontology for the request processing, and KS – available KSs containing

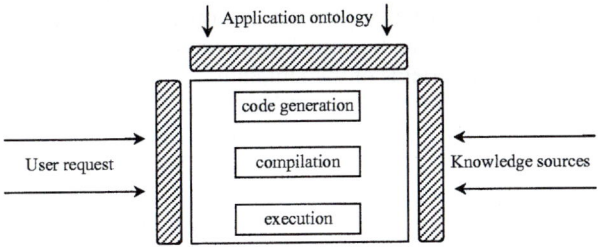

Fig. 3. Solver "on-the-fly" compilation mechanism

requested information can be considered as an abstract structure. Depending on a particular request this structure can be refilled with information revealed from the request. The "on-the-fly" compilation mechanism enables ILOG code generation according to the filled structure. It is based on the following aspects (Fig. 3): (1) a pre-processed request defines which ontologies of the ontology library are relevant to the request and which KSs are to be used; (2) C++ code is generated on the base of the filled triple <G, AO, KS>; (3) the compilation is performed in an environment of the prepared in advance C++ project; (4) failed compilations/executions are not to fail the system functioning instead an appropriate message is generated.

Services preceding the "on-the-fly" compilation are supported by ILOG Configurator. The essence of the proposed "on-the-fly" compilation mechanism is in writing the AO elements (classes, attributes, domains, constraints) to a C++ file directly. Based on these elements a C++ file is created and the created source code is inserted into an existing source code served as a template. The program is compiled and an executable DLL file is created. After that the function from DLL to solve the task is called.

4   Case Study

As an application domain for verification and validation of the approach a coalition formation problem in the Binni region was chosen. The aim of the used Binni scenario [13] is to provide a rich environment, focusing on new aspects of coalition problems and new technologies demonstrating the ability of distributed systems for intelligent support to supply services in an increasingly dynamic environment. The considered within the framework of the paper task is a mobile hospital configuration in the Binni region.

Because of the space limit in the paper a request of the template-based structure is considered. Descriptions of the problems relating to the goal identification; the request, KSs and ontology vocabularies alignment; and steps on the AO composition go beyond the paper. The template and the case study scenario were developed based on results of the parsing several requests concerning the mobile hospital configuration task. Below, a general request is considered. Request terms defined in the template are italicized.

Define *suppliers, transportation routes* and *schedules* for *building* a *mobile hospital* of *given capacity* at *given location* by *given time*.

The term *given* generalizes values for the assumed number of patients, desirable hospital sites, and deadlines of the hospital formation used in the parsed requests. This term corresponds to the input fields of the template.

A service requestor represented by a Web-service client sends a request to the system via the standard SOAP-based interface. It has been implemented using PHP [14] and NuSOAP Web Services Toolkit [15]. This combination enables rapid development of such applications as web-services

Request terms corresponding to the structural request constituent are: *suppliers, transportation routes, schedules, building, mobile hospital, capacity, location, time*. A parametric request constituent consists of the values represented by the term "*given*".

Parts of ontologies corresponding to the described task were found in Internet's ontology libraries [16 – 21] by an expert. These ontologies represent a hospital in different manners. Firstly, the ontologies were imported from the source formats into the system notation by means of a developed tool for the ontology library management. The tool supports ontology import from / export to external knowledge representation formats [22]. After that, they were included into the ontology library, henceforth they can be reused for the solution of similar problems. Next, ontology parts relevant to the request were combined into a single ontology. Principles underlying AO composition are described in [23]. The resulting AO is shown in Fig. 4. In the figure firm unidirectional arrows represent hierarchical relationships "is-a", dotted unidirectional arrows represent hierarchical relationships "part-of", double-headed arrows show associative relationships. Ontology part corresponding to AO included into the case study is represented by the shaded area.

No ontologies corresponding to configuration tasks were found out in known ontology libraries and servers. An ontology for the hospital configuration task (the class "hospital configuration" in Fig. 4) was elaborated by knowledge engineers and ontology engineers. The ontology is expanded in Fig. 5. In the figure "part-of" relationships between the classes are represented. In the considered example the method for staff definition is not taken into account as class "Staff" related to it is not included in the part of the case study being under consideration.

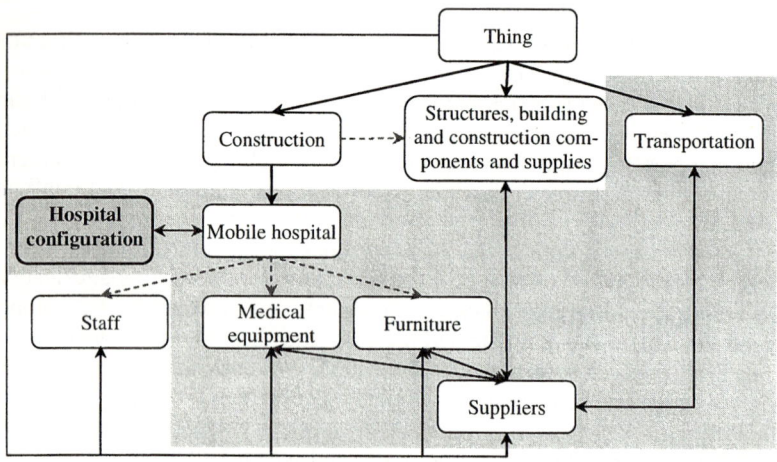

Fig. 4. "Mobile hospital" application ontology

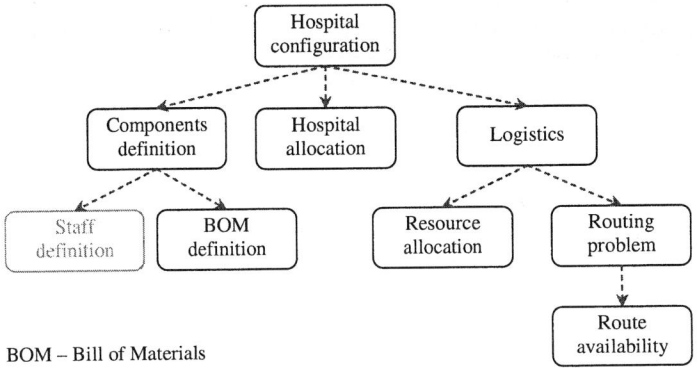

Fig. 5. Task ontology "Hospital configuration"

After the request enters the system a set of KSs containing information relevant to the request is identified. To solve the case study task the system using AO gathers requirement information from distributed KSs the knowledge map refers to. The knowledge map is an expandable knowledge storage holding references to KS locations. Since the problem of an automatic knowledge seeking is future research for the case study a list of KSs containing information for the request processing was prepared by an expert team.

As all the components ILOG needs for the request processing (see the framework in Fig. 1) are specified the parametric constituent, AO (Fig. 4), and information containing in a set of knowledge sources related to this AO are processed by ILOG.

As shown in Fig. 5 the "Hospital configuration" task has the explicit hierarchical structure that allows decomposing this task. In the framework of the case study the "on-the-fly" mechanism is used for the solving the task "Resource allocation" (choice of suppliers based on suppliers' availability of commodities, suppliers' locations, routes availability, etc.). The application of the mechanism enables reuse of the developed module even if the parametric constituent of the request or AO have been changed.

In the paper as an example the solution for the subtask "Hospital allocation" is given. The solution is illustrated by a map of the Binni region with cities, and chosen transportation routes as shown in Fig. 6. The figure uses the following notations. Small dots are the cities of the region. The city indicated with a pin (Aida) is the closest to the disaster (indicated with a cross) city where the mobile hospital is to be built. The bigger dots are the cities where suppliers are situated and they have to be visited (Libar, Higgville, Ugwulu, Langford, Nedalla, Laki, Dado). Transportation routes are shown as lines. The lines with trucks denote routes of particular vehicle groups (indicated with appropriate callouts). Other lines are routes that are not used for transportation in the solution. Lines attached to the closed cities (indicated with thunderstorms next to them) are not available for transportation.

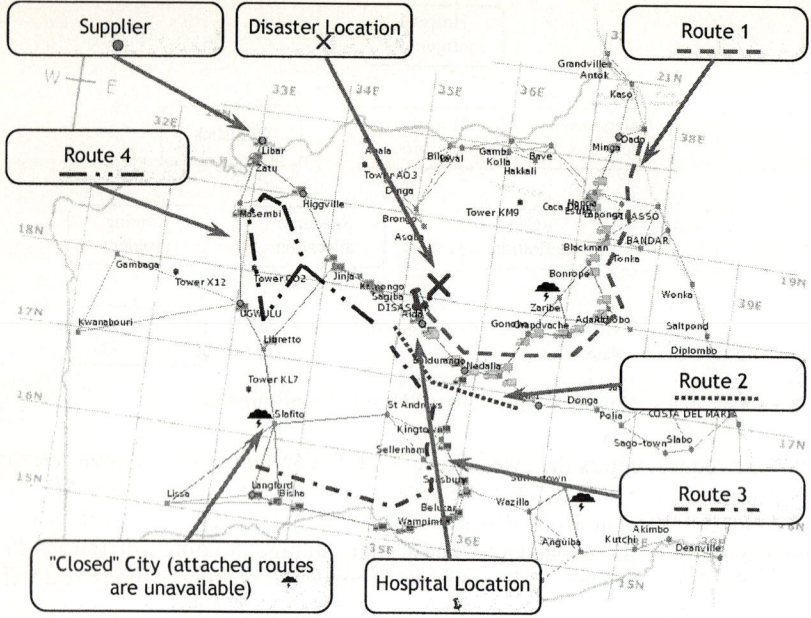

Fig. 6. Example results of request processing

5 Conclusion

The paper describes an ontology-driven approach to knowledge logistics problem and its applicability to a collaboration environment of a networked organization. The approach addresses the ontology-driven methodology for problem solving through a knowledge source network configuration. It is based on object-oriented constraint networks theory as a fundamental / representation ontology and technology of constraint satisfaction / propagation. Due to the incorporated in the approach technologies of Web Intelligence and Web Services it well suits to use in the Web-environment as the e-business and thereby networked organization environment.

The considered in the case study coalition operation scenario includes problems similar to ones of such application domain as e-business, logistics, supply chain management, configuration management, e-government, etc. and thereby the scenario can be reapplied to different domains.

Acknowledgements. Some parts of the research were done as parts of the ISTC partner project # 1993P funded by Air Force Research Laboratory at Rome, NY, the project # 16.2.44 of the research program "Mathematical Modelling and Intelligent Systems" & the project # 1.9 of the research program "Fundamental Basics of Information Technologies and Computer Systems" of the Russian Academy of Sciences, and the grant # 02-01-00284 of the Russian Foundation for Basic Research and the grant from Ford Motor Company. Some prototypes were developed using software granted by ILOG Inc.

References

1. CommerceNet Consortium Web-site (2003) URL: http://www.commerce.net/cnservices/index.html.
2. Laudon, K.C., Laudon, J.P.: Management Information Systems: Organisation and Technology in the Networked Enterprise. Prentice Hall International, New York (2000).
3. The Networked Organization. In: Management *Insights*. David Skyrme Associates, 1 (2002) http://www.skyrme.com/insights/1netorg.htm.
4. Chun Wei Choo: Information Management for the Intelligent Organization, 2nd ed. Information Today Inc., Medford, New Jersey, USA (1998).
5. Vrechopoulos, A.P., Pramataris K.C., Doukidis, G.I.: Utilizing information processing for enhancing value: towards a model for supporting business and consumers within an Internet retailing environment. In: Proceedings of 12th International Bled Electronic Commerce Conference, Bled, Slovenia, June 7—9 (1999).
6. Zhong, N., Liu, J., Yao, Y.: In Search of the Wisdom Web. In: Computer, 11, Vol. 35 (2002) 27—31.
7. Smirnov, A., Pashkin, M., Chilov, N., Levashova, T., Haritatos, F.: Knowledge Source Network Configuration Approach to Knowledge Logistics. In: International Journal of General Systems, 3, Vol. 32. Taylor & Francis Group (2003) 251—269.
8. Smirnov, A., Pashkin, M., Chilov, N., Levashova, T.: KSNet-Approach to Knowledge Fusion from Distributed Sources. In: Computing and Informatics, Vol. 22 (2003) 105—142.
9. Guarino, N.: Formal Ontology and Information Systems. In: Proceedings of FOIS'98. Trento, Italy. Amsterdam, IOS Press (1998) 3—15.
10. ILOG Corporate Web-site (2003) URL: http://www.ilog.com.
11. Smirnov A., Pashkin M., Chilov N., Levashova T.: Multi-agent Architecture for Knowledge Fusion from Distributed Sources. In: Lecture Notes in Artificial Intelligence, Vol. 2296. Springer (2002) 293—302.
12. Maedche, A., Staab, S.: Services on the Move — Towards P2P-Enabled Semantic Web Services. In: Proceedings of the 10th International Conference on Information Technology and Travel & Tourism. Helsinki, Finland (2003) http://www.aifb.uni-karlsruhe.de/WBS/-sst/Research/Publications/enter2003-maedche-staab.pdf.
13. Rathmell R.A.: A Coalition Force Scenario "Binni – Gateway to the Golden Bowl of Africa". In: A. Tate (ed.): Proceedings on the International Workshop on Knowledge-Based Planning for Coalition Forces/ Edinburgh, Scotland (1999) 115—125.
14. PHP (2003) http://www.php.net
15. NuSOAP Web Services Toolkit (2003) http://dietrich.ganx4.com/nusoap
16. Clin-Act (Clinical Activity). The ON9.3 Library of Ontologies: Ontology Group of IP-CNR (a part of the Institute of Psychology of the Italian National Research Council (CNR)) (2000) http://saussure.irmkant.rm.cnr.it/onto/.
17. Hpkb-Upper-Level-Kernel-Latest: Upper Cyc / HPKB IKB Ontology with links to SENSUS, Version 1.4. Ontolingua Ontology Server. (1998) http://www-ksl-svc.stanford.edu:5915.
18. Weather Theory. Loom ontology browser. Information sciences Institute, The University of Southern California (1997) http://sevak.isi.edu:4676/loom/shuttle.html.
19. North American Industry Classification System code. DAML Ontology Library, Stanford University (2001) http://opencyc.sourceforge.net/daml/naics.daml.
20. The UNSPSC Code (Universal Standard Products and Services Classification Code). DAML Ontology Library, Stanford University (2001) http://www.ksl.stanford.edu/projects/DAML/UNSPSC.daml.
21. WebOnto: Knowledge Media Institute (KMI). The Open University, UK (2002) http://eldora.open.ac.uk:3000/webonto.

22. Smirnov A., Pashkin M., Chilov N., Levashova T., Krizhanovsky A. In: R., Meersman, Z., Tari, D.C., Schmidt et al. (eds.): Ontology-Driven Knowledge Logistics Approach as Constraint Satisfaction Problem. On the Move to Meaningful Internet Systems 2003: CoopIS, DOA, and ODBASE. Proceedings of the International Conference on Ontologies, Databases and Applications of Semantics Information Reuse and Integration (ODBASE'2003). November 3—7, 2003. Catania, Sicily, Italy. Lecture Notes in Computer Science, Vol. 2888. Springer (2003) 535—652.
23. Smirnov, A., Pashkin, M., Chilov, N., Levashova, T.: Knowledge Source Network Configuration in e-Business Environment. In: Proceedings of the 15th IFAC World Congress (IFAC'2002). Barcelona, Spain, July 21—26 (2002). URL: http://bioinfo.cpgei.cefetpr.br/anais/IFAC2002/data/content/01278/1278.pdf.

Knowledge Acquisition and Management System for an Intelligent Planner

Elí B. Zenteno and Pablo H. Ibargüengoytia

Instituto de Investigaciones Eléctricas
Av. Reforma 113, Cuernavaca, Mor., 62490, México
ebuzemor@yahoo.com.mx, pibar@iie.org.mx

Abstract. Intelligent planning helps to solve a great amount of problems based on efficient algorithms and human knowledge about a specific application. However, knowledge acquisition is always a difficult and tedious process. This paper presents a knowledge acquisition and management system for an intelligent planning system. The planning system is designed to assist an operator of a power plant in difficult maneuvers such as the presence of faults. The architecture of the planner is briefly describes as well as the representation language. This language is adequate to represent process knowledge but it is difficult for an expert operator to capture his/her knowledge in the correct format. This paper presents the design of a knowledge acquisition and management system and describes a case study where it is being utilized.

1 Introduction

Intelligent planning is an area of artificial intelligence (AI) that has been influenced by the increasing tendency for applications in real problems. Briefly, a typical planning problem is one that can be characterized by the representation of the following elements:

- the state of the world, including initial and goal state,
- the actions that can be executed in this world.

If these representations can be made formally, then the planner is a program whose output is a sequence of actions that, when applied to the established initial state, produces the established goal state [10,4]. However, the acquisition and representation of all the knowledge required to solve a problem is always a tedious and complicated process. Specially in the application presented in this paper where the planning system assists an operator of a power plant in difficult and rare maneuvers.

This work forms part of a larger project dedicated to the diagnosis and planning of a power plant. The diagnosis system detects and isolates a faulty component that makes the process behave abnormally [3], and the planning system assists the operator to minimize the effects of the failure and to coexist with it in a safe way until the maintenance can be achieved. The maneuvers are composed

R. Monroy et al. (Eds.): MICAI 2004, LNAI 2972, pp. 159–168, 2004.
© Springer-Verlag Berlin Heidelberg 2004

by several actions that the operator executes, e.g., closing valves, starting pumps, opening switches, etc. The state of the process is obtained utilizing sensors and other sources of information like personnel reports.

The diagnosis system reports the detection of a faulty component. The planner receives this information and designs a plan that will advise the operator in order to keep the process in the most useful and safe state. For example, if the diagnosis detects a failure in one of the temperature sensors, the operator may decrement the load and keep the unit generating in lower temperatures while the failure is fixed. On the contrary, if temperature readings are uncertain, then some operators may shut down the turbine in order to avoid damage. The opportune advice to the operator may keep the availability index of the plant.

Consequently, the planning system must be provided with all the knowledge that deals with all the possible detectable failures. This knowledge includes all the possible actions that can be recommended, considering the current state of the generation process. However, this knowledge belongs to the operators and plant managers but they are not familiar with the notation of the representation language. The knowledge acquisition and management system (KAMS) represent a useful tool in two basic ways:

1. it permits the acquisition of knowledge in a *fill the blanks* form, keeping the user out of the semantic restrictions of the representation language, and
2. it maintains coherence and completeness of the knowledge base, and determines the required variables from the real time database.

The knowledge base is a complete set of actions that the operator can execute, together with the preconditions and purposes of these actions. The actions are represented in a language inspired in the *ACT* formalism, developed at Stanford Research Institute (SRI) [9]. In this formalism, the set of ACTs form the knowledge base from which the plan would be defined.

Similar efforts are been developed in the international community, specially in the community of ontologies. For example, the Protégé system [6] is a knowledge acquisition tool that produces ontologies and knowledge bases that other programs can read. The inference engine is the Jess system [7] (a Java implementation of CLIPS [2] shell). Thus, Protégé system carries out its duty for Jess while KAMS performs for the dynamic planner system developed for this research group. Other proposals include WebODE [1], and OntoEdit [5].

This paper is organized as follows. The next section briefly describes the architecture of the planning system. Next, section 3 describes the representation language in which all the knowledge is captured. Section 4 describes the design and implementation of the knowledge acquisition and management system and section 5 describes the consistency checking procedures carried out by the KAMS. Section 6 presents one example of the use of the system in a case study and discusses some results. Finally, section 7 concludes the paper and addresses the future work in this area.

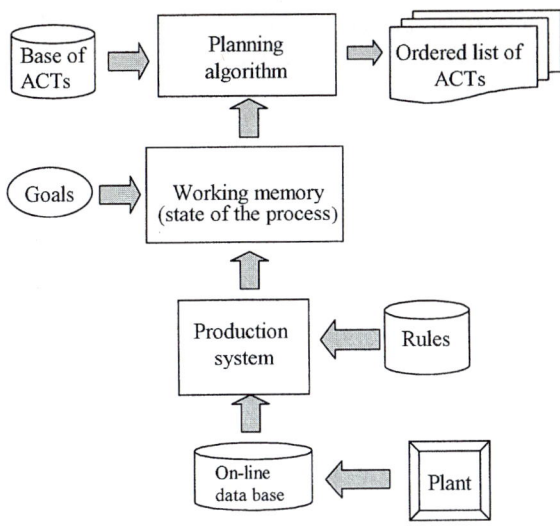

Fig. 1. Architecture of the planning system.

2   Architecture of the System

Figure 1 shows the architecture for the plan generation agent. This architecture has two modules: the data to knowledge mapper and the searching algorithm module. The mapper is formed by the production system, the working memory and the rules. The production system consults the value of the variables and triggers the corresponding rules that produce logical expressions stored in the working memory. This working memory represents the current state of the process. For example, when the variable VL65 has the value of logic one, the formula $(main - switch\ state\ ON)$ can be inferred. Additionally, a set of rules can be included to store a theory of causality in the domain. For example, if the formula $(main - switch\ state\ ON)$ is included in the working memory, then it can also be inferred that $(400KV - bus\ state\ ON)$ and $(main - transformer\ state\ ON)$. Thus, the knowledge base includes all the rules that may generate a complete theory that reflects the current state of the plant. This theory is stored in the working memory of the production system. Also Fig. 1 shows a goal module that can be considered as part of the working memory. The goal formulas are a determinant part of the theory that is utilized by the searching algorithm in the formation of a plan.

The searching or planning algorithm uses the working memory with the state of the plant, the current goals and the knowledge base of the operations of the plant codified in the formalism described below. The searching algorithm uses all these elements in order to find the plan. In the first prototype of this planner, the planning algorithm executes an exhaustive search . The searching is made between the conditions and purposes of all possible actions in the knowledge base. The plan is simply a list of the actions that has to be followed by the operator, in response to a specific current state with a specific goal. A deeper description of this module can be consulted in [8].

3   Representation Language

The representation language utilized in this project is based on knowledge units (KU). The KUs are inspired in the *ACT* formalism, developed at Stanford Research Institute (SRI) [9]. By definition, a KU describes a set of actions that can be executed in order to achieve an established purpose in certain conditions. The following example shows how a typical piece of expert knowledge can be represented in one KU.

> The conversion between a gas turbine in rotating mode to the generating mode can be obtained closing the field generator switch

Here, the purpose is to get the gas turbine in the generating mode. This can be achieved if the environment conditions include the gas turbine in the rotating mode. The action that can be executed is the closing of the field generator switch. In general, the actions are all those atomic operations than can be executed in the plant, e.g., close a switch. The purpose is the condition that will be present in the process when the actions have been executed. The conditions refer to the state of the process that must be present before the actions can be executed.

In this KU formalism, all the concepts mentioned above (actions, purposes and conditions) are represented utilizing the following elements: logic formulas, predicates and goal expressions. The logic formulas are utilized to reference all the objects in the plant including their characteristics, properties, attributes and values. A logic formula can be expressed in two formats: {object, attribute, value} or {variable ID, value}. For example, (*turbine state normal*) or (*Valve*1 1) are logical formulas. The predicates are always applied to the logic formulas for the representation of actions and goals. Thus, a goal expression is a predicate applied to a logic formula. For example, the representation of the action for opening a valve can be: (*achieve*(*GasValve state open*)) and the expression to verify if the valve is open can be: (*test*(*valve*1 1)). This will be true if the valve is open and false otherwise. Here, *achieve* and *test* are the predicates applied to the logical formulas (*GasValve state open*) and (*valve*1 1) to indicate an action (*achieve*) or a verification (*test*). More complex expressions can be represented to verify certain conditions in the plant. For example, the expression:

(test (and (gas-turbine state hot-standby)
(heat-recovery state hot-standby)
(steam-turbine state hot-standby))

can be utilized to test if the main equipment of the plant are in the stand by mode, ready to work in the normal mode.

Summarizing, the KU formalism is utilized in this project to represent all the needed knowledge for the planning system. The KU formalism utilizes goal expressions to represent actions, goals and conditions.

Syntactically, a KU is formed with the three elements:

name: a unique ID for the KU,

environment: a set of goal expressions that define the environment conditions that hold before and after a KU is executed,

plot: a network of activities where the nodes represent the atomic activities that need to be executed to complete the KU goal. The arcs represent temporal relations between the different activities.

The plot can be seen as the lowest level of abstraction of the activities carried out in the control of the plant. At the same time, a KU can be seen as the representation of activities with a higher level of abstraction. An example of a KU is shown in the Fig. 2.

```
(TG1G
  (environment
    (cue (achieve(turbine1 state generating)))
    (preconditions (test(turbine1 state stand-by))))
  (plot
    (tg1gi (type conditional)
      (orderings (next tg1g1)))
    (tg1g1 (type conditional)
      (achieve (Swtg1 0))
      (orderings (next tg1gf))
    (tg1gf (type conditional)))))
```

Fig. 2. An example of a KU.

The elements of the *plot* section are the representation of a network. The syntax of the nodes includes a name, a type, the ordering and other elements. The type can be *conditional* or *parallel*. In the parallel node, all the trajectories that include that node must be executed, while in the conditional node, just one of the paths can be executed. The *orderings* field indicates the temporal order in which the action must be executed. In the example of Fig. 2, there is an arc from node *tg1gi* to the node *tg1g1*.

As can be seen in Fig. 2, the syntax of KUs is complicated and difficult to use for an expert in turbines. The next section presents a proposal to overcome this problem.

4   Knowledge Acquisition and Management

The KAMS is a system that acquires and manages knowledge. It has been designed to perform two main functions: (i) acquisition of knowledge, and (ii) management and validation of it. Therefore, the following functional modules forms the KAMS:

Capture panel: special windows for the capture of all the required information.

Mapper rules: display of the captured information that will be used in the data to knowledge mapper.

Real time data base: display of the identifiers of all the captured variables that participate in the planning process.

Consistency checking: revision of the completeness and consistency of all the captured knowledge.

The following sections describe these modules separately.

4.1   Capture Panel

The capture panel shows three sections: (i) the capture of the environment conditions, (ii) the capture of nodes of the plot section, and (iii) the construction of the rules required in the mapper.

Figure 3 shows (in Spanish) the panel that captures the environment conditions at the left, and the plot nodes at the right. The left panel contains two sections. First, the capture of the post-conditions and second, the preconditions. In both cases, the conditions consists in logical formulas with the format $\{object, attribute, value\}$. The post-conditions allow the capture of one or the conjunction of several conditions. Two buttons allow adding or removing conditions from this section.

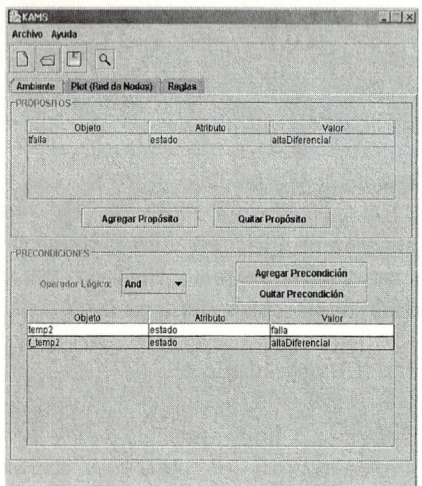 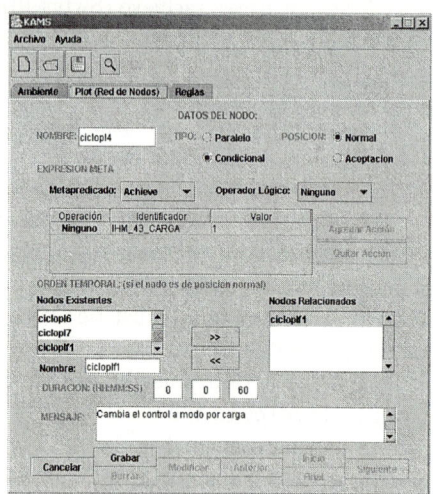

Fig. 3. Capture of the environment section and the plot nodes of the KUs.

The preconditions section is similar to the post-conditions with the only difference that several conditions can be combined in other logical functions besides the conjunction. In Fig. 3, an KU with a precondition

$$(temp2\ estado\ falla)\ \ and\ \ (f\_temp2\ estado\ altaDiferencial)$$

and a purpose of

$$(tfalla\ estado\ altaDiferencial)$$

is being captured. The right panel captures all the fields that compound the plot nodes, namely the action, the time required to execute the action, the type of node, the message that will be issued to the operator and the links to other nodes. The type of nodes can be parallel or conditional and normal or acceptation. The action executed can be expressed with the logical relation of logical expressions. The logical operator that can be included are *and*, *or*, *not* and arithmetic comparators as $>$, $=$, $>$, etc.

A text window is included to capture the message that will be issued to the operator once the action should be carried out. In the Fig. 3 at the right, an example of a normal, conditional node is being captured. The node require to achieve that the variable IHM_43_CARGA reaches the state 1, and this will be obtained once that the operator follows the message included. In this example, he/she must change the control mode through the activation of a control switch in the console.

4.2   Mapper Rules

The environment conditions are logical formulas expressed in the format {object, attribute, value} or OAV format. They express the preconditions that need to be present in order to execute a KU, and the conditions that will be present after the KU is executed. These expressions are not directly inferred but need to be detected from the real variables. This is the mapper function. However, the user should provide with the rules that maps data to knowledge. The KAMS acquire all the environment conditions and the real variables of the real time data base, so it matches both entities to define the rules. Every environment condition must be included in the conclusion side of a rule whose premise is based on the variables of the data base. KAMS generates a table with the entire pairs premise-conclusion that form the mapper rules.

For example, the condition $(temp2\ estado\ falla)$ require to infer its value based on some real variables. This can be obtained with the following rule, also captured in KAMS:

IF f_ttxd2 $= 2$, THEN temp2 estado falla

The KAMS enunciates all the logical formulas captured in the environment conditions and expects that the user generates the *left hand side* of the rule that will produce the corresponding condition.

4.3   Real Time Data Base

When defining the mapper rules explained above, a list with all the variables is obtained. This list is compared with the real time data base. It is very common to reference variables with different identifiers. This module holds all the variables that will be validated in the consistency checking procedure explained below.

5   Consistency Checking

The consistency checking process verifies the completeness and correspondence of all the elements of the knowledge base. They are: (i) Logical formulas in the OAV format, used in the representation of knowledge. (ii) Logical formulas in the $\{id, value\}$ format, used in the representation of raw information. (iii) Rules, for the conversion between raw information and knowledge. (iv) Rules, for the representation of a causal theory of the domain, and (v) real time data base.

The verification process is developed as follows.

1. The environment conditions and the preconditions are written in the OAV format. This is the main knowledge acquisition activity.
2. KAMS verifies if all the $OAVs$ are included in the right hand side of some rule.
3. Once that all the logical formulas are detected in some rule, the verification of the left hand side of the rules is needed. This verification is made between these left hand sides and the real time data base. It is a common mistake to spell the identifiers of variables differently in their appearances.

Summarizing, completeness refers to the verification that all logical formulas are included either in the rules or in the data base. Correspondence refers to the equivalence of elements in the different parts of the knowledge base. The example followed during this paper would be checked as follows: The user captures the precondition *(temp2 estado falla)*. KAMS then searches for this formula and finds the rule *(IF f_ttxd2 = 2, THEN temp2 estado falla)*. If there exists a variable with an id = f_ttxd2 in the real time data base, then the condition can be accomplished.

Once that all the elements of the knowledge base are complete and validated, the planner is ready to be executed in a real application.

6   Use of KAMS

The system was developed in a first prototype, and was tested in a simple case. This is, the detection of a failure in one temperature sensor of a gas turbine in a power plant. A brief description follows.

The planner designed at the IIE is coupled with an intelligent diagnosis system, also being developed in this laboratory. When the diagnosis system founds an abnormal behavior in the monitored variables, for example in the temperature sensor 2, it writes a code in the f_ttxd2 variable of the real time data base. The planner contains a rule that explains that if the f_ttxd2 variable has a number 2, then a condition must be issued that establishes that the temperature sensor 2 is in a state of failure. Once that the mapper declares this failure, then the planner starts building a plan based on the environment conditions of the Kus in the knowledge base. Figure 3 left shows the capture of the first KU in a plan that deals with this problem. The main action in this plan is to decrement

```
(ciclopl
  (environment
    (cue (achieve(temp2 estado correcto)))
    (preconditions (achieve (operador estado informadoFallaAD))))
  (plot
    (espera1 (type parallel)(normal)
      (time–window inf inf inf inf eps 5)
      (orderings (next ciclopl2)(next ciclopl3)))
    (ciclopl2 (type conditional)(normal)
      (test (IHM_43_TEMP 1))
      (time-window inf inf inf inf eps 600)
      (orderings (next ciclopl4)))
    (ciclopl3 (type conditional)(normal)
      (test (IHM_43_CARGA 1))
      (time–window inf inf inf inf eps 600)
      (orderings (next nulo)))
    (ciclopl4 (type conditional)(normal)
      (achieve (IHM_43_CARGA 1))
      (time–window inf inf inf inf eps 60)
      (orderings (next nulo)))
    (nulo (type conditional)(normal)
      (time–window inf inf inf inf eps 1)
      (orderings (next ciclopl5)))
    (ciclopl5 (type parallel)(normal)
      (achieve (* operador 1))
      (orderings (next ciclopl2)(next checafin)))
    (checafin (type conditional)(normal)
      (test (f_ttxd2 0))
      (orderings (next ciclopf)))
    (ciclopf (type parallel)(aceptation)
      (achieve (* falla 0)))))
```

Fig. 4. A KU resulted from the use of the system.

the load in order to decrease the magnitude of the temperature problem. This is obtained with the plot section of the *KU* as the one shown in Fig. 3 right.

Figure 4 shows an example of the use of the KAMS in the codification of complex *KU*.

This is a ascii file that contains all the captured information in a format required by the planner system. First, the identifier of the *KU* is included: *ciclopl*. In the following three lines, the environment conditions are included. Third, the nodes of the *plot* section is produced in a format that can be normally utilized by the monitor of the execution [8]. Notice the difficulty for a power plant operator to keep track of all the parenthesis that the syntax of *KU* requires.

The planner has been utilized in the capture and validation of knowledge for the diagnosis and corrective plans for gas turbines in power plants.

7   Conclusions and Future Work

This paper has presented a knowledge acquisition and management system, designed to support the capture of the experience of an operator of a power plant. The knowledge was initially represented using the *KU* formalism. However, serious difficulties were found for the experts in the correct utilization of this language. Just a parenthesis not closed, caused frustration and loose of time. Also, the knowledge engineers discovered difficulties in the logic of the processes.

The KAMS has been used in the capture of knowledge that is required by the diagnosis system of gas turbines. The diagnosis founds different failures and the planning system issues the correct recommendations that can take the power unit back to normal state or the minimization of effects due to the failures. Work is being done in the utilization of the system in a more complex process of the plant.

References

1. J.C. Arpirez. Webode: A workbench for ontological engineering. In *Proceedings of the 1th International Conference Knowledge Capture (K–CAP 2001)*, pages 6–13, ACM Press, 2001.
2. Software Technology Branch. *CLIPS reference Manual*. Lyndon B. Johnson Space Center, NASA, 1991.
3. Luis de Jesús González-Noriega and Pablo H. Ibargüengoytia. An architecture for on–line diagnosis of gas turbines. In *Advances in Artificial Intelligence - IB-ERAMIA 2002, LNAI 2527*, pages 795–804, Sevilla, Spain, 2002. Springer.
4. M. E. desJardins, C.L. Ortiz E.H. Durfee, and M.J. Welverton. A survey research in distributed, continual planning. *AI Magazine*, 20(4):13–22, 1999.
5. Henrik Eriksson. Automatic generation of ontology editors. In *Proceedings of the 12th Workshop Knowledge Acquisition, Modeling, and Management*, pages 4.6.1–4.6.20, University of Calgary, Canada, 1999.
6. Henrik Eriksson. Using jesstab to integrate protégé and jess. *IEEE Intelligent Systems*, 18(2):43–50, 2003.
7. E.J. Friedman-Hill. Jess in action: Java rule–based system. *Manning*, 2003.
8. Pablo H. Ibargüengoytia and Alberto Reyes. Continuous planning for the operation of power plants. In *Proc. ENC-01 Encuentro Internacional de Ciencias de la Computación*, pages 199–208, Aguascalientes, Ags., México, 2001.
9. K. L. Myers and D. E. Wilkins. The act formalism", version 2.2b. Technical report, SRI International Artificial Intelligence Center, 1997.
10. S.J. Russell and P. Norvig. *Artificial intelligence: a modern approach*. Prentice Hall, Englewood Cliffs, New Jersey, U.S.A., 1995.

Stability Analysis for Dynamic Constraint Satisfaction Problems

Manuel Iván Angles-Domínguez and Hugo Terashima-Marín

Center for Intelligent Systems, ITESM Campus Monterrey
Ave. Eugenio Garza Sada 2501 Sur, C.P. 64849
Monterrey, Nuevo Leon., Mexico, Tel. +52 (81) 8328 4379
iangles@consultant.com, terashima@itesm.mx

Abstract. Problems from various domains can be modeled as dynamic constraint satisfaction problems, where the constraints, the variables or the variable domains change overtime. The aim, when solving this kind of problems, is to decrease the number of variables for which their assignment changes between consecutive problems, a concept known as distance or stability. This problem of stability has previuosly been studied, but only for variations in the constraints of a given problem. This paper describes a wider analysis on the stability problem, when modifying variables, domains, constraints and combinations of these elements for the resource allocation problem, modeled as a DCSP. Experiments and results are presented related to efficiency, distance and a new parameter called global stability for several techniques such as solution reuse, reasoning reuse and a combination of both. Additionaly, results show that the distance behavior is linear with respect to the variations.

1 Introduction

A Constraint Satisfaction Problem (CSP) is a problem composed by a finite set of variables, each of them associated to a finite domian, and a set of constraints limiting the values that the variables can simultaneously take. Formally [1], a CSP is a triple $Z = (V, D, C)$, where $V = \{v_1, \ldots, v_n\}$ is a set of variables; $D = \{D_{v_1}, \ldots, D_{v_n}\}$ is a set of variable domains, one for each variable, and C is a set of constraints, each being a pair $c = (Y, R)$, where $Y = \{v_{i1}, \ldots, v_{ik}\}$ is a set of variables intervening in the constraint and R is an existing relation over the domains of those variables, that is, $R \subset D_{v_{i1}} \times \ldots \times D_{v_{ik}}$. A solution to a CSP is an assignment of a value in its domain for each variable, in such a way that all constraints are satisfied at the same time.

A Dynamic Constraint Satisfaction Problem (DCSP) [2] is a series of static CSPs that change overtime, due to the evolution of its componenents (variables, domains and constraints), given certain changes produced in the environment (change in the set of tasks to be executed and/or of their execution conditions, similar to the assignment problem), a change produced by the user (if dealt with an interactive problem), or variations in a process (the DCSP only represents part of a bigger problem, and a different entity solving the global problem

R. Monroy et al. (Eds.): MICAI 2004, LNAI 2972, pp. 169–178, 2004.

changes the way on how the solving process can be performed; for instance, a distributed multiagent problem). In their original work, Dechter and Dechter [2] consider only modifications on the constraints of CSPs. There exist six possible alterations between CSPs in a DSCP: increase or decrease of variables, increase or decrease of values in a domain, or increase or decrease of constraints. Jonsson and Frank [1] present a formal definition of all these possible alterations:

> Let $Z = (V, D, C)$ be a CSP. Any problem of the form $Z' = (V', D', C')$ such that $V' \supseteq V$ (i.e. there are more variables), $D'_v \subseteq D_v$ for each $v \in V$ (i.e. there are less values in the domain) and $C' \supseteq C$, (i.e. there are more constraints between variables) is a constraint in Z. A problem of the form $Z' = (V', D', C')$ such that $V' \subseteq V$ (i.e. there are less variables), $D'_v \supseteq D_v$ for each $v \in V$ (i.e. there are more values in the domain) and $C' \subseteq C$, (i.e. there are less constraints between variables) is a relaxation in Z. A DCSP is a sequence of CSPs $C_0, C_1, \ldots$, such that each problem C_i is either a constraint or relaxation of C_{i-1}.

Solving a DCSP consists in finding a solution to everyone of the CSPs in the sequence. A way of doing this, is solving each CSP back to back, from the beginning, approach with two main drawbacks: inefficiency and lack of stability. In many cases, some of the work carried out to the previous CSP can be reused to solve the new CSP, since for real time applications, time is limited. With respect to stability, if the solution to the previous CSP represent an assigment currently under execution, any new solution should minimize the effort necessary to apply that current assignment. For interactive or descentralized problems, it is better to have less modifications as possible to the current solution. The lack of stability in the solutions (known also as distance between solutions) is a relevant and important problem, due to the cost in both money and effort, to modify the current assignment, in order to meet the new requirements; especially when, typically, there is no model of future events, that is, knlowledge about when and what modifications will appear is limited, making difficult to develop robust solutions.

For tackling these problems, there exist two approaches that take advantage of features in a CSP to solve the next one [3]. The first one of them, called solution reuse, uses a previous solution (if there is one) to determine the new solution. Verfaillie and Schiex [4] developed an algorithm called *LocalChanges*, inspired in the techniques of *Backjumping* (if the current variable violates a constraint, the assignment of the other conflicting variable is revised, not necessarily the previous one) and iterative repair [5], which consists in using a previous assignment and repair it with a sequence of local modifications. The second approach, reasoning reuse, intends to keep an approximate description of the boundary of the solution space, and justifications of that boundary in terms of a set of constraints. Schiex and Verfaillie [6] developed a method called *NogoodBuilder*, which generates a set of *nogoods* from the constraints in the CSP. *nogoods* are partial instantiations of variables that cannot be extended to a solution for the complete set of variables. These *nogoods* can be added as constraints for the next generated CSP.

These models have been previously examined for variations on the constraints of a CSP, but, a more detailed analysis has not been discussed in the literature. The main interest in this paper is to analyze the performance of these methods, in relation to efficiency and stability, when modifying variables, domains, and constraints, but additionaly, proposing and analyzing new ways to integrate the two approaches, in order to improve the performance.

This article is organized as follows. Section 2 establishes the methodology followed to analyze the various approaches for solving DCSPs. Section 3 presents the experimental setup and the analysis of results. Finally, in Section 4 our conclusions are included.

2   Methodology

The first step in the methdology was modeling the Resource Allocation Problem (RAP) as a DCSP. Further, a problem generator was implemented. Based on the original algorithms of solution reuse and reasoning reuse, two new hybrid algorithms were developed that integrate both approaches. Then, the stability analysis was performed on the four algorithms considering the sensibility and the distance parameters.

2.1   Resource Allocation Problem

Assigning resources to tasks is an important problem with a wide variety of applications (satellite telecommunications [7], dynamic routing in computer networks [8]). The Resource Allocation Problem [9] consists in allotting resources to a set of tasks, scheduled for certain time intervals, in such a way that a resource is not assigned to two different tasks at the same time. This problem is NP-complete [10], meaning that for problems with real dimensions is not feasible to find a solution in polynomial time. Formally: Variables: $\{v_1, \ldots, v_n\}$; where v_i represents a task i from the n tasks; Domains: $D_{v_i} = \{R_1, \ldots, R_m\}$; where R_j represents the resource j from as total of m resources that can be assigned to task v_i; and, Constraints: $v_i \neq v_j$ if $i \neq j$; it establishes that the tasks v_i and v_j cannot be at the same resource at the same time. This model was extended in order to include two additional constraints: $>$ and $<$. So, the RAP modeled as a DCSP, consists in a series of CSPs definded by the previous model, each one may suffer alterations in variables, domains or constraints. A generator of DCSPs was developed, to create random instances of binary CSPs, based on the features of a RAP. It is possible to increase or decrease the sizes of the set of variables, the domains or the number of constrains or any combination of these three. The smallest size of a variable domain is 2 for experimental purposes.

2.2   Analyzed Algorithms

Along to the algorithms *LocalChanges* [4] and *NogoodBuilder* [6], two additional algorithms were implemented. The first of them, *Lopt* is based on *LocalChanges*,

and together with a method for generating *nogoods* implicit in the technique of
iterative repair, it does reasoning reuse as well. Its process for generating *nogoods*
prunes the search space, more than what the *NogoodBuilder* algorithm does.
The second algorithm developed, called *Nopt*, complements the *NogoodBuilder*
algorithm with solution reuse, taking advantage of its recursive nature. These
two algorithms use solution reuse when there exist relaxations in the DCSP, and
reasoning reuse in the case of constraints, avoiding to start all over any CSP in
the DCSP.

2.3   Sensibility and Distance Analysis

The sensibility in the algorithms was measured according to the following parameters:

(a) Stability (Distance): Distance between two succesive solutions, that is, the
    number of variables with different asssignment between solutions of two con-
    tiguous CSPs.
(b) Null Generation: Number of times the distance between two contiguous
    CSPs is zero. Currently, the concept of stability considers only those vari-
    ables whose assignment varies between solutions of two contiguous CSPs,
    regardless how many times such variation is present during the complete
    solution of the DCSP. Due to this, a new metric is proposed to measure also
    the frequency during the solving process of the DCSP.
(c) Consistency Checks: Number of times an algorithm determines if a potential
    value for a variable violates a constraint with any other variable. This is a
    common parameter to measure the efficiency of algorithms.

In order to have a better perspective in relation to the performance of the
algorithms, and specialize them according to the types of variations that a DCSP
can have, their sensibility to the changes was evaluated for the following modifications in the DCSP: number of variables (V), domain size (D), number of constraints (C), number of variables and domain size (V, D), domain size and number of constraints (D, C), number of variables and number of constraints (V, C),
and number of variables, domain size, and number of constraints (V, D, C). Considering that in practice, the domain size of variables changes relatively slow, it
was empirically established that the maximum number of changes between two
CSPs is three (for any combination). A set of 30 DCSP was generated to test
each modification. Each DCSP is formed with 20 binary CSPs. The intial CSP
has 40 variables, domain size of 5, and 14 constraints. With this, it is expected
an average number of changes of 2, and that in 10 out of the 20 CSP problems
the number of variables is increased. There is a relationship between the domain
size and the number of constraints selected for the test problems. The idea was
to obtain a 50% of chance of solving the DCSP, that is, that at least 10 of the
CSPs in the DCSP were solvable. After certain experimentation, it was observed
that solving a CSP took around 850 CPU miliseconds. This time was used to set
up maximum time limit for solving CSP_i before proceeding to the next CSP_{i+1}.

The aim of the Distance Analysis is to determine the way in which the distance between two CSPs varies. The case of constraints between CSPs was taken into account, since, as mentioned in a previous section, when relaxing, the solution to the previous CSP is taken, and then the distance between solutions is zero. The distance was evaluated for the following modifications in the DCSP: increase in the number of variables in 2, 4, 6, 8, 10, 12, 14, 16, 18 and 20 variables. Increase in the number of variables whose domain was modified in 2, 4, 6, 8, 10, 12, 14, 16, 18 and 20 variables. The number of values decreased from a variable domain was randomly generated for each variable. Increase in the number of constraints in 1, 2, 3, 4, 5, 6 and 7 constraints. This modifications were selected intending to to have a total variation of 50% with respect to the initial parameters. For each of the proposed modifications, 300 DCSP, modeled as a RAP, were evaluated, handling contraints of the type $>, <, \neq$. Each DCSP was formed with two CSPs. The initial CSP has 40 variables, domain size of 5, and 14 constraints. The reasons for selecting these parameters are explained later. The effect of the distance was analyzed comparing the hybrid algorithm *Lopt* (with solution and reasoning reuse) against the *LocalChanges* algorithm (with solution reuse only). For these experiments, there was no time limit for solving a CSP.

3   Experimental Results and Discussion

The sensibility analysis explores the behavior of the algorithms with respect to efficiency, stability (or distance), and null generation; varying the variables, the domains, the constraints or any combination of them. The second set of experiments is oriented to the distance analysis, with the purpose to compute the number of assignment changes between two solutions of CSPs.

3.1   Sensibility Analysis

The sensibility analysis was carried out over a set of 30 randomly generated DCSPs. In the case of the distance, for each DCSP, it is considered an average of the number of times the distance was not zero.

Efficiency. Figure 1 shows the consistency checks perfomed by the tested algorithms for each of the possible modifications. In general, it is observed that *NogoodBuilder* and *Nopt* take more consistency checks than *LocalChanges* and *Lopt*. This is due to the process of consistency elimination in each algorithm, *Backjumping* for *NogoodBuilder* and *Nopt*, and iterative repair for *LocalChanges* and *Lopt*. *Lopt* is the algorithm with the least number of consistency checks as shown in Figure 1. This reduction in the number of consistency checks is due to the solution reuse and reasoning reuse. The difference between *NogoodBuilder* and *Nopt* represents the work that *Nopt* is avoiding by using solution reuse, and that is around 50% less consistency checks than those produced by *Nogood-builder*. *Lopt* saves around 30% of the work done by *LocalChanges* due to the use of solution reuse. The biggest reduction is produced when reasoning reuse

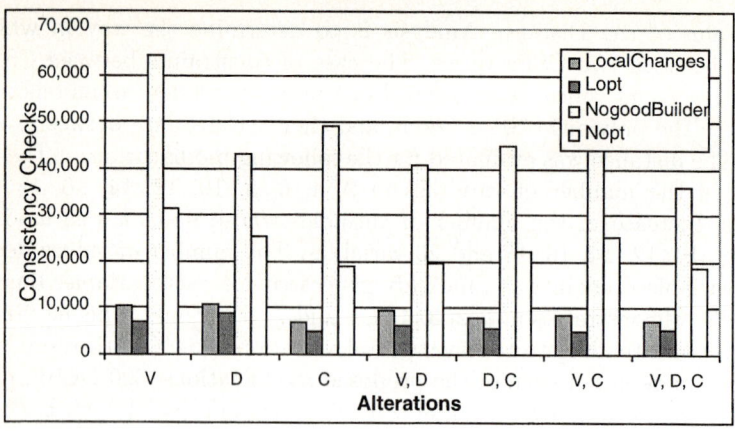

Fig. 1. Results for efficiency in the sensibility analysis.

is used since this technique prunes the complete tree when having relaxations between the CSPs in the DCSP.

Distance. Figure 2 shows the average distance obtainde by the tested algorithms in relation to each of the modifications in the DCSP. It can be observed that *LocalChanges* and *Lopt* generate larger distance between contiguous solutions. It seems that the search process in each algorithm is causing this behavior, *Backjumping* for *NogoodBuilder* and iterative repair for *Lopt* and *LocalChanges*. There is a small difference between *LocalChanges* and *Lopt*, basically produced by the use of reasoning resue in *Lopt*, since using *nogoods* implies eliminating some values in the domains, and forcing to assign other values to the variables. This increases the distance between solutions. Instead, the solution reuse in *Nopt* does not affect its performance in comparison to *NogoodBuilder*, since this reuse avoids precisely the distance between solutions.

Null Generation. Figure 3 presents the number of CSPs whose solution did not change with respect to the solution of the previous CSP. There is a slight difference between *LocalChanges* and *Lopt*, caused by the use of reasoning resue in *Lopt*. Let us assume that the CSP_i does not have a solution, but a partial instantiation of variables is generated right before failing to find a consistent assignment. For *LocalChanges* in CSP_{i+1}, the new modification may allow the algorithm to assign new values to variables before the inconsistency. When comparing these, it is noted that they are different and that there is a decrease in the null generation. However, *Lopt* generates nogoods that allow to determine from the beginning that the CSP_{i+1} does not have a solution, avoiding any process to modify variables, and keeping the null generation. In average *Lopt* has an increase of 17% in the null generation with respect to *LocalChanges*. *Nopt* has an increase of around 14% with respect to *NogoodBuilder* due to the solution reuse.

The sensibility analysis has shown that using a hybrid mechanism for combining solution and reasoning reuse produce better performance than using a

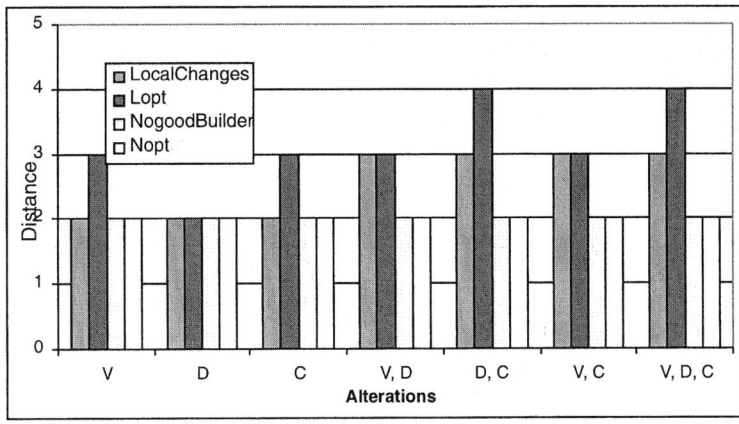

Fig. 2. Results for distance in the sensibility analysis.

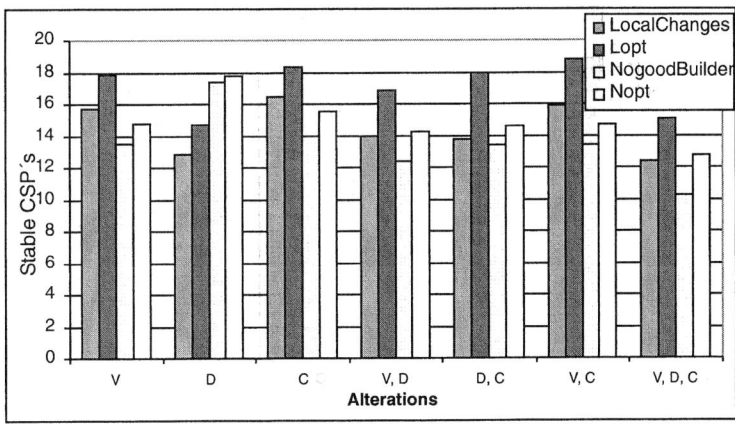

Fig. 3. Results for null generation in the sensibility analysis.

single method. Given that solution reuse eliminates consistency checks and produces zero distance between solutions increasing the null generation, it is an approach that any algorithm for solving DCSP should use. We can realize, by paying attention to the case of constraints, that a combination of the use of *nogoods* and a systematic approach to iterative repair would be a good option. A proposal for achieving this is to adjust iterative repair to start looking for solutions close to that established by the *nogoods*, and from there expand its search scope. Results obtained are independent of the DCSP size (20 CSPs in this case), since measurements are computed over contiguous CSPs, regardless on the number of CSPs in the DCSP. Let us consider a DCSP whose initial CSP has 100 variables. The behavior of the algorithms initiating with this CSP, is similar to that when the algorithms face the same problem that was produced later in the process after having initiated in a CSP, let us say, with 40 variables.

We can conclude also that for CSPs with higher number of variables the results
of the analysis presented in this research are consistent. A comparable analysis
can be carried out for the domain size and the number of constraints.

3.2   Distance Analysis

Figure 4 shows how the distance increases when the number of varables is increased. For instance, if the number of variables increases by 40%, the distance
raises around 20%. In this way, for a CSP with 40 variables, if a modification produces a new CSP with 16 new variables, in average, it could produce a distance
of 8 variables with different value amongst the solutions.

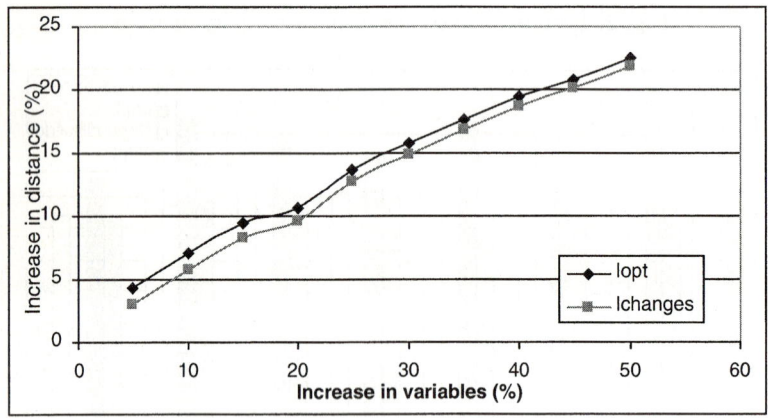

Fig. 4. Behavior of distance when varying the number of variables.

Figure 5 presents the distance behavior when varying the number of variables
when their domain was modified. In this case there is larger increase compared
to that reported when varying the number of variables. Figure 6 illustrates the
increase in distance when varying the number of constraints.

By observing the last three figures, we can conlude that in general, the distance behaves linearly for any of the three analyzed cases. This is a test that
makes possible to determine, in terms of number of the varying elements, the
distance that will be produced between solutions. Let us recall nevertheless, that
these results were produced when using the RAP. It would be interesting to experiment with other problems modeled as a DSCP, and also for other algorithms.
The fact that for *LocalChanges* the relationship is linear, implies that any other
algorithm that improves on it, will have to generate a relationship with smaller
slope, or in its best case, a constant relationship. This empirical relationship
could be used as a heuristic within an algorithm of the kind of A* for example,
that would allow to minimize the distance.

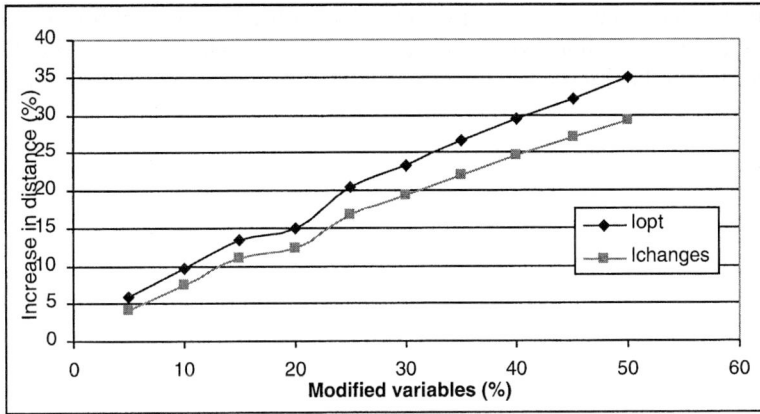

Fig. 5. Behavior of distance when varying the domain size.

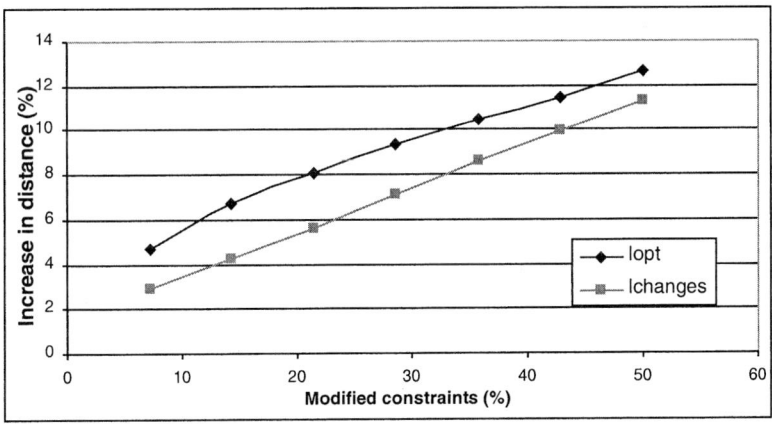

Fig. 6. Behavior of distance when varying the number of constraints.

4   Conclusions

This paper has presented an empirical study to perform the stability analysis over four algorithms for solving DCSP. Results show that no algorithm obtains best performance for all three comparison measures. In the case of efficiency, the iterative repair of *Lopt* and *Localchanges* produces better results than the *Backjumping* technique integrated in *NogoodBuilder* and *Nopt*. However, *Backjumping* produces less distance between solutions than iterative repair. In particular, it has been observed that the desired features in an algorithm for solving DCSPs are: solution reuse for relaxations, and reasoning resue in combination with iterative repair for constraints. It has also been verified that an algorithm that produces good stability, does not always produce less distance between solutions. In this way, the null generation allows to select, according to the application domain, what algorithm is more convenient depending if more stability is required during the entire solving process or just in few occasions. Based on the distance analysis, it has been empirically proved that there is a linear relationship between the increase in the distance and the variation in the number of variables, the domain size and the number of constraints. This relationship helps to determine, in average, the distance between solutions, that can improve the decision making process if the modifications are performed manually. The analysis was performed over randomly generated instances of the RAP modeled as a DCSP. Future extensions to this work may include: perform sensibility analysis for other similar problems which handle different types of constraints or domain size; perform a detailed analysis for establishing lower and upper bounds on the distance behavior; and additionaly, develop theoretical analysis for more general problem types and modifications.

Acknowledgments. This research is supported by ITESM under the Research Chair CAT-010.

References

1. A.K. Jonsson and J. Frank. A framework for dynamic constraint reasoning using procedural constraints. In *European Artificial Intelligence Conference*, 2000.
2. R. Dechter and A. Dechter. Belief maintenance in dynamic constraint networks. In *Proceedings of the Sixth National Conference on Artificial Intelligence*, pages 37–42, 1988.
3. T. Schiex and G. Verfaillie. Two approaches to the solution maintenance problem in dynamic constraint satisfaction problems. 1993.
4. G. Verfaillie and T. Schiex. Solution reuse in dynamic constraint satisfaction problems. In *AAAI, Vol. 1*, pages 307–312, 1994.
5. S. Minton, M. D. Johnston, A. B. Philips, and P. Laird. Minimizing conflicts: A heuristic repair method for constraint satisfaction and scheduling problems. *Artificial Intelligence*, 58(1-3):161–205, 1992.
6. T. Schiex and G. Verfaillie. Nogood recording for static and dynamic constraint satisfaction problems. 1993.
7. C. Plaunt, A.K. Jonsson, and J. Frank. Run-time satellite tele-communications call handling as dynamic constraint satisfaction. In *Proceedings of the IEEE Aerospace Conference 1999*, pages 165–174, 1999.
8. Murat Alanyali and Bruce Hajek. On simple algorithms for dynamic load balancing. In *INFOCOM (1)*, pages 230–238, 1995.
9. B. Y. Choueiry, G. Noubir, and B. Faltings. Blending AI and mathematics: the case of resource allocation. In *Fourth International Symposium on Artificial Intelligence and Mathematics*, pages 32–37, Fort Lauderdale, Florida, 1996.
10. C. P. Gomes and J. Hsu. ABA: An assignment based algorithm for resource allocation. *SIGART Bulletin*, 7(1):2–8, 1996.

Evaluation-Based Semiring Meta-constraints*

Jerome Kelleher and Barry O'Sullivan

Cork Constraint Computation Centre
Department of Computer Science, University College Cork, Ireland
{j.kelleher,b.osullivan}@4c.ucc.ie

Abstract. Classical constraint satisfaction problems (CSPs) provide an expressive formalism for describing and solving many real-world problems. However, classical CSPs prove to be restrictive in situations where uncertainty, fuzziness, probability or optimisation are intrinsic. Soft constraints alleviate many of the restrictions which classical constraint satisfaction impose; in particular, soft constraints provide a basis for capturing notions such as vagueness, uncertainty and cost into the CSP model. We focus on the semiring-based approach to soft constraints. In this paper we present a new evaluation-based scheme for implementing meta-constraints, which can be applied to any existing implementation to improve its run-time performance.

1 Introduction

Classical constraint satisfaction problems (CSPs) provide an expressive formalism for stating and solving many real-world problems. CSPs allow us to express relations over variables in a problem, which can be seen as declaring the allowed combinations of instantiated values for variables. In this way we can declaratively state problems and pass the burden of finding solutions to these problems onto the constraint solver. However, classical CSPs prove to be restrictive in any problems where uncertainty, fuzziness, probability or optimisation are intrinsic. *Soft* constraints alleviate many of these restrictions which classical constraint satisfaction impose.

We introduce the term semiring meta-constraints (constraints which depend on other constraints) in this paper as a useful means of referring to a class of constraints defined in the literature. We advocate the use of these meta-constraints to reduce the complexity of defining algorithms to efficiently solve soft constraint problems without relying on local consistency techniques, which severely limit the scope of a soft constraint solver. Such algorithms have been defined in the system given in [2], which are unfortunately highly inefficient due to the representation of meta-constraints used.

In this paper we discuss the specification and implementation of semiring meta-constraints. We show how the currently dominant compilation-based conceptualisation of meta-constraints is fundamentally flawed as it results in any algorithm which utilises these useful abstractions having exponential time and space complexity. We show how these problems can be very simply resolved by instead adopting an *evaluation*-based approach to specifying and implementing these constraints. Therefore, the

---

* This work has received support from Enterprise Ireland under their Basic Research Grant Scheme (Grant Number SC/02/289).

R. Monroy et al. (Eds.): MICAI 2004, LNAI 2972, pp. 179–189, 2004.
© Springer-Verlag Berlin Heidelberg 2004

primary contribution of this paper is the new evaluation-based scheme for implementing meta-constraints, which can be applied to any existing implementation to alleviate problems of unnecessary space usage.

The paper is organised as follows. Section 2 presents the semiring framework of Bistarelli et al. [3] and illustrates how it can unify many disparate models of constraint satisfaction by using a semiring structure to represent consistency levels and the operations needed to combine and compare those levels. We describe semiring meta-constraints and provide some pedagogical examples of *evaluation*-based meta-constraints. Section 3 reviews the existing implementations of the semiring framework. Section 4 presents our scheme for the implementation of evaluation-based meta-constraints and Section 5 presents some basic results of the runtime efficiency that can be expected for evaluating these constraints over problems of different tightness. Finally, Section 6 summarises the ideas presented in this paper.

2   Semiring Framework

The semiring framework for constraint satisfaction is based on one key insight, that is, a semiring (a set together with two binary operators which satisfy certain properties) is all that is needed to describe many constraint satisfaction schemes. The semiring set provides the levels of consistency which can be interpreted as cost, degrees of preference, probabilities or any other criteria consistent with the requirements of the framework. The two operations then allow us to combine ($\times$) and to compare ($+$) consistency levels from this set.

In the interest of brevity we will restrict our discussion of the semiring framework under the functional formulation [4] to a brief statement of the basic ideas involved. For a more detailed and rigorous treatment of the subject the reader is referred to the literature [1,3,4], where many key results pertaining to this framework are proven.

2.1   Semirings

A c-semiring (constraint-semiring) is a tuple $\langle A, +, \times, \mathbf{0}, \mathbf{1} \rangle$ such that:

- A is the set of all consistency values and $\mathbf{0}, \mathbf{1} \in A$. $\mathbf{0}$ is the lowest consistency value and $\mathbf{1}$ is the highest consistency value;
- $+$, the additive operator, is a closed, commutative, associative and idempotent operation such that $\mathbf{1}$ is its absorbing element and $\mathbf{0}$ is its unit element;
- $\times$, the multiplicative operator, is a closed and associative operation such that $\mathbf{0}$ is its absorbing element, $\mathbf{1}$ is its unit element and $\times$ distributes over $+$.

The c-semirings for some typical instances of the semiring framework are:

- Crisp CSP: $\langle \{false, true\}, \vee, \wedge, false, true \rangle$;
- Fuzzy CSP: $\langle \{x \mid x \in [0,1]\}, max, min, 0, 1 \rangle$;
- Probabilistic CSP: $\langle \{x \mid x \in [0,1]\}, max, \times, 0, 1 \rangle$;
- Weighted CSP: $\langle \mathcal{R}^+, min, +, +\infty, 0 \rangle$;
- Set-based CSP: $\langle \wp(A), \cup, \cap, \emptyset, A \rangle$.

2.2 Constraint Problems

Given a semiring $S = \langle A, +, \times, \mathbf{0}, \mathbf{1} \rangle$ and an ordered set of variables V over a finite domain D, a *constraint* is a function which, given an assignment $\eta : V \to D$ of the variables, returns a value of the semiring. Using this notation we define $\mathcal{U} = \eta \to A$ as the set of all possible constraints that can be built starting from S, D and V.

In this *functional* formulation of the semiring framework each constraint is a function (as defined in [4]) and not a pair (as defined in [3]). Each constraint function involves all the variables in V, but it depends on the assignment of only a finite subset of them. For example, a binary constraint $c_{x,y}$ over variables x and y, is a function $c_{x,y} : V \to D \to A$, but it depends only on the assignment of variables $\{x, y\} \subseteq V$. This subset is known as the *support* of the constraint. The assignment of a domain value d to a variable v as a modification to a particular instantiation η is denoted by $\eta[v := d]$.

A soft constraint satisfaction problem is a pair $\langle C, con \rangle$ where $con \subseteq V$ and C is a set of constraints; con is the set of variables of interest for the set of constraints.

2.3 Semiring Meta-constraints

In this paper we introduce the term *semiring meta-constraints* (or simply meta-constraints) as a convenient means of referring to constraint functions defined over other constraints in the semiring framework. Several classes of meta-constraints have been defined in the literature, including *combination* constraints, *projection* constraints, *solution* constraints and *blevel* (best-level) constraints [1,3,4]. In this paper we will focus on combination and projection meta-constraints as both solution and blevel meta-constraints are defined in terms of these primitives.

Combination Meta-Constraints. Given the set $\mathcal{U}$, the combination function $\bigotimes$ is defined as $(\bigotimes C)\eta = \prod_{c \in C} c\eta$. This function takes a set of constraints and returns a combination meta-constraint. This definition is the straightforward extension of the $\otimes$ function [4] to sets of constraints.

Informally, a combination meta-constraint represents the constraint which is equivalent to all of the constraints in C combined together. This is a very useful abstraction as it allows us to perform all reasoning over single constraints instead of cumbersome sets of constraints. To evaluate a given combination meta-constraint for an instantiation of the variables η simply involves evaluating all of its constituent constraints under η and combining the individual consistency values using the semiring $\times$ operator.

Projection Meta-Constraints. Given a constraint $c \in \mathcal{U}$ and a variable $v \in supp(c)$, the *projection* function $\Downarrow$ is defined as $(c \Downarrow_{(supp(c) - \{v\})})\eta = \sum_{d \in D} c\eta[v := d]$. This function takes a constraint and set of variables as parameters and returns the constraint which is equivalent to the original constraint with its support reduced to the specified set of variables.

Informally, projecting a constraint c over the set of variables $(supp(c) - \{v\})$ returns a constraint c' which is equivalent to c with the variable v removed from the support. This is done by evaluating $c\eta[v := d]$ (for the instantiation of interest) for all domain values d in the domain of v, and returning the sum of all of these individual consistency values using the semiring additive operator $+$. Effectively then, the value returned from evaluating $c'\eta$ is the best consistency value possible for the instantiation of variables η if we can choose any value for the instantiation of v.

2.4   Example Soft Constraint Problem

In this section we present an example soft constraint problem, defined over the semiring $S = \langle \mathcal{R}^+, min, +, 0, +\infty \rangle$ which describes Weighted CSPs. In this problem we have two variables, x and y, defined over the domain $D = \{1, 2, 3, 4, 5\}$. In a problem of this type we have a set of cost functions defined over the variables of interest; each individual cost function describes the cost of one specific section of a configuration under a particular instantiation of the variables. For simplicity we define a generic cost function $cost(a, n) = (n - a)^2$ to enable us to easily demonstrate the ideas in question.

In particular, we will define three constraints denoted c_x, c_y and $c_{x,y}$ defined as follows:

$$c_x\eta = cost(2, x),$$
$$c_y\eta = cost(4, y),$$
$$c_{x,y}\eta = cost(1, y - x).$$

Unary constraints c_x and c_y are intended to represent the costs associated with an instantiation deviating from an ideal value. For instance, the ideal value for x according to c_x is 2 and any instantiation where x is not set to this value will be penalised proportional to the square of its distance from this value. Binary constraint $c_{x,y}$ is used to illustrate the idea that we can easily model complex inter-relationships between variable instantiations.

The constraint problem in this example is then given by $P = \langle \{c_x, c_y, c_{x,y}\}, \{x, y\} \rangle$. To allow us to demonstrate the ideas of evaluation based meta-constraints introduced in this paper we will give examples of combination and projection meta-constraints over this problem.

Combination. In this example we demonstrate the evaluation of a combination meta-constraint. To evaluate a combination meta-constraint for a particular instantiation we must evaluate each of the constituent constraints under the instantiation in question and find the product of these values using the semiring multiplicative operator.

In particular, we demonstrate the evaluation of the combination of the constraints c_x, c_y and $c_{x,y}$, $\bigotimes\{c_x, c_y, c_{x,y}\}$, under the instantiation where x has the value 1 and y has the value 5 ($\eta[x := 1, y := 5]$), i.e.,

$$
\begin{aligned}
(\bigotimes\{c_x, c_y, c_{x,y}\})\eta[x := 1, y := 5] &= \\
c_x\eta[x := 1, y := 5] &= cost(2, 1) = 1 \\
&\times_s \\
c_y\eta[x := 1, y := 5] &= cost(4, 5) = 1 \\
&\times_s \\
c_{x,y}\eta[x := 1, y := 5] &= cost(1, 4) = 9.
\end{aligned}
$$

As the semiring multiplicative operator in this case is addition over reals, the overall cost associated with this instantiation of the variables $\eta[x := 1, y := 5]$ is 11.

Projection. In this example we demonstrate the evaluation of the projection of the constraint $c_{x,y}$ over the set $\{x\}$, i.e. the meta-constraint where we remove y from the support of $c_{x,y}$. Specifically then, we will evaluate $c_{x,y} \Downarrow_{\{x\}}$ under the instantiation $\eta[x := 1, y := 5]$, i.e., the instantiation where x has the value 1 and y has the value 5.

To evaluate a projection meta-constraint for a particular instantiation, we must evaluate the constraint in question for all domain values of variables which have been removed from its support. We then find the sum of all of the individual consistency values using the semiring additive operator, $+_s$, i.e.,

$$
\begin{aligned}
(c_{x,y} \Downarrow_{\{x\}})\eta[x := 1, y := 5] \;&= \\
c_{x,y}\eta[x := 1, y := 1] \;&=\; cost(1,0) = 1 \\
+_s& \\
c_{x,y}\eta[x := 1, y := 2] \;&=\; cost(1,1) = 0 \\
+_s& \\
c_{x,y}\eta[x := 1, y := 3] \;&=\; cost(1,2) = 1 \\
+_s& \\
c_{x,y}\eta[x := 1, y := 4] \;&=\; cost(1,3) = 4 \\
+_s& \\
c_{x,y}\eta[x := 1, y := 5] \;&=\; cost(1,4) = 9.
\end{aligned}
$$

As the semiring additive operator for the weighted semiring is the *min* function over reals, the result of evaluating this constraint is 0.

One important idea illustrated in this example is the concept of the support of a constraint. In this example, the support of $c_{x,y} \Downarrow_{\{x\}}$ is $\{x\}$. This means that this constraint depends only on the assignment of values to variable x. This is demonstrated in the example when we evaluate the constraint $c_{x,y} \Downarrow_{\{x\}}$ under the instantiation $\eta[x := 1, y := 5]$, but we evaluate the constraint that it depends on, $c_{x,y}$, for all instantiations where $x := 1$ and $y := d$.

3   Existing Implementations

In this section we discuss the published implementations of the semiring framework. There are a number of issues with these implementations: these range from limitations on the types of semirings that can be handled to runtime efficiency issues.

3.1   clp(FD,s)

In [7] the authors present an extension of the clp(FD) [5] system, clp(FD,s). This system provides an efficient means of solving constraint problems defined over a subset of the semirings in the semiring framework. However, no implementation of the combination and projection meta-constraints is provided.

In this system, the authors explicitly restrict the scope of the solver to those semirings in which × is idempotent, and hence do not support the full generality of the semiring framework. Many of the techniques used to gain efficiency utilise properties only present in semirings where the multiplicative operation is idempotent. This may seem like a reasonable compromise; however, this design decision prevents problems defined over the Probabilistic and Weighted semirings from being solved on this system.

3.2   Soft CHR

In [2] the authors present an implementation of the semiring framework based on CHRs [6]. CHRs allow for the simplification and propagation of constraints and have been successfully deployed in dozens of projects to implement various crisp solvers. However, as propagation cannot be applied to instantiations where the multiplicative operation is not idempotent, the usefulness of CHRs is limited in this context.

However, the system does provide several algorithms which can be used over all instances of the semiring framework, including Branch and Bound algorithms with both variable and constraint labelling, as well as a Dynamic Programming search algorithm. Unfortunately, the implementation of meta-constraints in this system severely limits the utility of these algorithms.

In this system all meta-constraints are represented *extensionally* as a list of tuple-consistency pairs using the compilation-based scheme (see Section 4). Savings in space usage are attained by not storing tuples with consistency of zero. However, in general, a k-ary meta-constraint will require exponential time and space to compile and store. Moreover, many of the more complex operations for this system - such as the dynamic-programming solver - use this operation heavily, ensuring that these operations require exponential time and space also.

In the next section we present a simple method to solve this problem of exponential time and storage. Hopefully, this can be integrated into this system, which may allow the useful general purpose algorithms provided in the system be applied to non-trivial problems.

4   Implementing Meta-constraints

While a large amount of work has been published on the theoretical aspects of soft constraints, apart from the two implementations mentioned in Section 3, very little has been published on the subject of practical implementation of soft constraints. We advocate the use of semiring meta-constraints as a useful abstraction to reduce the complexity of developing efficient algorithms to solve soft constraint problems in general.

However, currently meta-constraints are not viable as they are both specified and implemented using a compilation-based approach. By compilation-based we mean that when a meta-constraint function is created a lookup table of all possible input values and their corresponding output results is computed and stored. This approach is extraordinarily wasteful of both computing time and space. For instance, if we had a binary meta-constraint function over variables with domains of size twenty, we would need to compile a lookup table with 20^2 entries. In general, if we have a compilation-based meta-constraint function over a set of variables V with domain D, then we will require

Table 1. Compilation-based function $f(x, y) = x^2 + y^3$ defined over domain $\{1, \dots, 5\}$.

	$f(x, y)$	
x	y	$x^2 + y^3$
1	1	1
1	2	9
1	3	28
$\vdots$	$\vdots$	$\vdots$
5	5	150

a lookup table with $|D|^{|V|}$ entries to fully encode the function. This means we need *exponential* time and space to construct these functions.

For example, consider the function $f(x, y)$ shown in Table 1. In this example we show a function which is composed of two functions over different variables with their respective results added together. This is analogous to a combination meta-constraint, which is a function composed of a number of separate functions over different variables with their results combined together using some simple operation. The variables in this function x and y are defined over the domain $D = \{1, \dots, 5\}$. Even with this tiny domain it is necessary to contract the lookup table which we are using for explanatory purposes.

An Alternative Approach. A far more economical and simpler method of implementing meta-constraint functions is to simply store the original constraint functions that are involved and evaluate these as required with the instantiation of interest. In this way we can create a new meta-constraint function in constant time and with space linear in the number of constraints involved. This is the *evaluation*-based method of implementing meta-constraints.

One possible criticism of this evaluation-based approach is that there may be situations where we need know the value of all possible instantiations for a particular meta-constraint, and furthermore, we may need to find out the value of a particular instantiation many times. However, these situations are hard to imagine and still do not warrant the *storage* of all possible instantiations. If we wish to find the value of every possible instantiation for a given meta-constraint we can simply iterate through all possible instantiations and evaluate the constraint for that instantiation. If the value of an instantiation will be needed many times, it is the responsibility of the specific algorithm which requires this property to determine if it worthwhile caching the value, *not* the function which calculates it.

Furthermore, if we make the not-unreasonable assumption that in the majority of constraint processing algorithms we define we will want to find the value of the least number of instantiations possible, the compilation scheme is highly undesirable. To sum up, *any* algorithm that we define in terms of compilation-based meta-constraints will have exponential time and space complexity, regardless of the semantics of the algorithm itself.

Algorithm 1 CombinationEvaluate(η)

$\quad a \leftarrow 1$
$\quad$**for all** $c \in C$ **do**
$\quad\quad a \leftarrow a \times c\eta$
$\quad\quad$**if** $a = 0$ **then**
$\quad\quad\quad$**return** 0
$\quad\quad$**end if**
$\quad$**end for**
$\quad$**return** a

Combination Evaluation. Combination meta-constraints are an extremely useful abstraction as they allow us to treat a set of constraints as a single constraint. Thus, any reasoning or operations that deal with constraints can be defined over a single constraint as we can refer to any set of constraints by their combination as a single constraint. This simplifies both theoretical and practical work with constraints.

Combination is a universal operation in constraint satisfaction. Any form of constraint processing which deals with distinct sets of constraints can all be expressed in terms of this operation. Therefore any improvements we make in the time or space efficiency of this operation will have knock-on effects on any other more sophisticated constraint processing that we do.

To evaluate a combination meta-constraint defined over the set of constraints C at runtime for a given instantiation η we use Algorithm 1. In this algorithm we simply iterate through all of the constraints in C and evaluate each one under the instantiation in question. To prevent unnecessary computation, we use the fact that 0 is the absorbing element of the $\times$ operation. In this way, we know that if any single function evaluates to 0 then the entire combination constraint will also evaluate to 0 and we can therefore immediately return 0.

As this lazy-evaluation leverages the full generality of the semiring framework, it applies to *all* instances. For example, in the crisp semiring, this optimisation reduces to the lazy evaluation of the boolean AND operation; over the fuzzy semiring, it reduces to the lazy evaluation of the min function defined over the interval $[0, 1]$.

5 Experimental Evaluation

In this section we present some basic foundational results on semiring meta-constraints. In particular, in Section 5.1 we discuss results for applying the lazy evaluation presented in Section 4 and in Section 5.2, we compare the performance of a Branch and Bound search for the set of best solutions using compilation-based and evaluation-based combination constraints.

In both sections we use random soft constraint problems. To achieve this we follow the methodology adopted in [8], in which binary fuzzy CSPs are generated with four specific properties: the number of variables n, the number of domain values per variable m, the density d and the tightness t. The tightness of a problem is defined as the ratio of the number of instantiations which evaluate to semiring 0 over the total number of possible instantiations. The remaining instantiations are then assigned a consistency value from

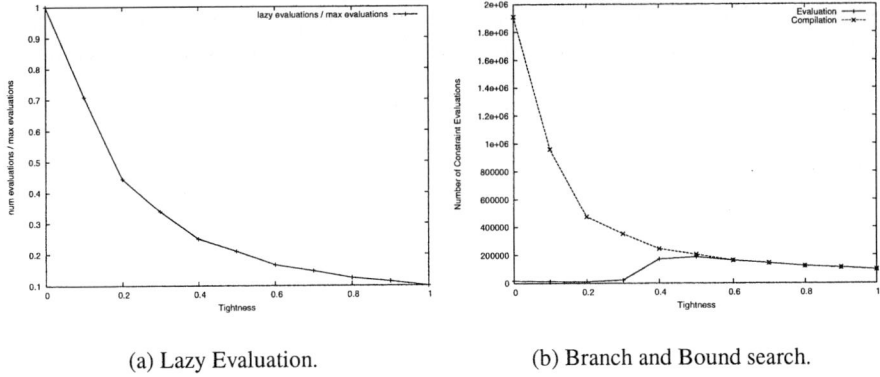

(a) Lazy Evaluation.   (b) Branch and Bound search.

Fig. 1. Experimental results for problems of varying tightness.

the interval $(0, 1]$ which is randomly generated with a uniform distribution [8]. To ensure that anomalous results are not reported, we performed ten-fold cross validation over the results obtained, i.e., we generated ten random problems with the required specifications and report the average result over all of these problems.

5.1 Lazy Evaluation

In the problems generated for this experiment, the number of variables is fixed at 5, density at 1.0 and the number of domain values is also 5. Results reported are the number of constraint evaluations using lazy evaluation divided by the number of constraint evaluations where no lazy evaluation is used. This can be seen as the gain in running time obtained by applying the lazy evaluation.

Specifically, for each set of constraint problems generated, we evaluate the the meta-constraint representing the combination of all constraints in the problem under all possible instantiations. Results reported are given as the ratio of the number of constraint evaluations required using the lazy evaluation method in Algorithm 1 and the number of constraint evaluations required without using this method, which is a constant for a problem with a given specification. These results are shown in Figure 1(a).

If we examine Figure 1(a), we see that at low tightness levels (i.e., where the number of instantiations which evaluate to **0** is small), the lazy evaluation has little or no effect. However, as the tightness of the problems increases, the likelihood of the lazy evaluation coming into effect also increases, and has a significant effect on the average time required to evaluate a combination constraint.

5.2 Branch and Bound Search

For this experiment we generated random problems with 7 variables, 5 domain value and with density 1.0. It was necessary to use small numbers of variables and small domains as the size of the compilation-based meta-constraints required for this experiment prohibited the use of larger values. The results are obtained by counting the number of (problem) constraint evaluations required to find the set of best solutions (i.e. the set of instantiations for which the semiring value is highest when evaluated over the entire problem) in a Branch and Bound algorithm which utilises combination meta-constraints. We then compare the number of constraint evaluations required when using the current compilation-based approach and our new evaluation-based approach.

Figure 1(b) shows that our evaluation-based approach is *never* outperformed by the compilation-based approach. This is because the compilation approach to implementing meta-constraints will often compile a great deal of information which is not required for a specific task. This is most clearly shown when the tightness of a problem is low and a great number of branch cuts can be performed by the algorithm. As the compilation-based approach exhaustively compiles each meta-constraint, there is no benefit gained from these branch cuts. As each variable is instantiated in the search algorithm, the compilation-based approach will exhaustively generate the entire cross product for this variable in conjunction with all of the previously instantiated variables. On the other hand, as the evaluation-based approach only evaluates constituent constraints of a combination meta-constraint *as required*, Figure 1(b) shows that great savings in the number of constraint evaluations are obtained by utilising branch cuts.

As the tightness increases, we see that the number of constraint evaluations required for the compilation-based approach actually decreases. This is due to the lazy-evaluation shown in Algorithm 1 which we used to compute the values when compiling the combination constraints, ensuring a fair comparison of the two methodologies. This is the main reason for the convergence of the two methodologies: as the number of constraint evaluations required to compile the meta-constraint decreases, the number of constraint evaluations required to find the set of best solutions increases using the evaluation-based methodology.

To conclude, the time required to compile any given meta-constraint outweighs the benefits of constant access time which are gained by this approach, and certainly does not warrant the inordinate amount of space required to store them. As Branch and Bound is a systematic and complete search algorithm we will never need to find the value of a particular instantiation of the variables on a given combination constraint more than once; it makes little sense in this case to store all instantiation valuations.

6   Conclusions

Classical constraint satisfaction problems (CSPs) provide an expressive formalism for expressing and solving many problems in a declarative fashion. Soft constraints alleviate many of the restrictions which classical constraint satisfaction impose. In particular, soft constraints provide a basis for capturing notions such as vagueness, uncertainty and cost into the CSP model. In this paper we have focused on the semiring-based approach to soft constraints. Furthermore, we focused on some critical issues related to the implementation of semiring-based constraint solvers. We presented a new *evaluation-based* scheme for implementing meta-constraints, which can be applied to any existing implementation to improve its run-time performance.

References

1. S. Bistarelli. *Soft Constraint Solving and programming: a general framework.* PhD thesis, Dipartimento di Informatica, Università di Pisa, Italy, mar 2001. TD-2/01.
2. S. Bistarelli, T. Fruehwirth, M. Marte, and F. Rossi. Soft constraint propagation and solving in constraint handling rules. In *Proc. of ACM SAC*, pages 1–5, 2002.
3. S. Bistarelli, U. Montanari, and F. Rossi. Semiring-based Constraint Solving and Optimization. *Journal of the ACM*, 44(2):201–236, Mar 1997.
4. S. Bistarelli, U. Montanari, and F. Rossi. Soft concurrent constraint programming. In *Proc. ESOP, April 6 - 14, 2002, Grenoble, France*, LNCS, pages 53–67. Springer-Verlag, 2002.
5. Philippe Codognet and Daniel Diaz. Compiling constraints in clp(FD). *Journal of Logic Programming*, 27(3):185–226, 1996.
6. Thom Frühwirth. Theory and practice of constraint handling rules. *Journal of Logic Programming, Special Issue on Constraint Logic Programming*, 37(1-3):95–138, October 1998.
7. Y. Georget and P. Codognet. Compiling semiring-based constraints with clp(FD,S). In *Proc. of CP-98*, LNCS 1520, pages 205–219, 1998.
8. F. Rossi and I. Pilan. Abstracting soft constraints: Some experimental results. In *Proceedings of the Joint Annual Workshop of the ERCIM Working Group on Constraints and the CoLogNET area on Constraint and Logic Programming*, 2003.

Invariant Patterns for Program Reasoning

Andrew Ireland, Bill J. Ellis, and Tommy Ingulfsen

School of Mathematical & Computer Sciences
Heriot-Watt University, Edinburgh, Scotland, UK
a.ireland@hw.ac.uk, bill@macs.hw.ac.uk, tommying@online.no

Abstract. We address the problem of integrating standard techniques for automatic invariant generation within the context of program reasoning. We propose the use of *invariant patterns* which enable us to associate common patterns of program code and specifications with invariant schemas. This allows crucial decisions relating to the development of invariants to be delayed until a proof is attempted. Moreover, it allows patterns within the program to be exploited in patching failed proof attempts.

1 Introduction

Within the context of program reasoning, we address the problem of automating loop invariant generation. There are two basic kinds of invariant generation techniques. Firstly, *bottom-up* analysis techniques generate inductive invariants by analysing program code. Secondly, *top-down* analysis techniques use specifications (assertions) as the basis for generating inductive invariants. In practice, a third kind of analysis, what we will call *proof-failure* analysis, also plays a crucial role within invariant generation.

We propose the use of *invariant patterns* as a means of achieving a effective integration of these three kinds of analyses. An invariant pattern represents an invariant schema together with a selection criteria. We build upon *proof planning* [3], a technique for automating theorem proving. In particular, we use *middle-out reasoning* [4] which supports an incremental style of invariant discovery and *proof critics* [9,11] which supports proof-failure analysis. The context for our work is the application of proof planning to the verification of programs written in SPARK [1], a programming language designed for the development of critical software systems. SPARK is derived from Ada and includes an annotation language which supports flow analysis and formal proof. In §2, §3, and §4 we outline our general approach, while in §5, we present a detailed application.

2 Bottom-Up Analysis

Traditional bottom-up analysis techniques generate light-weight invariant properties, such as relationships between loop counter variables. Such invariants are typically required in order to complete a proof. In addition to generating invariants, our extended bottom-up analysis technique generates information that

R. Monroy et al. (Eds.): MICAI 2004, LNAI 2972, pp. 190–201, 2004.
© Springer-Verlag Berlin Heidelberg 2004

mono_dec(V, W): Means that V is a loop counter which monotonically decreases during the execution of loop W.

mono_inc(V, W): Means that V is a loop counter which monotonically increases during the execution of loop W.

constant(V, W): Means that V is a loop counter which is constant during the execution of loop W.

Fig. 1. Meta predicates

supports both top-down and proof-failure analyses. This involves identifying common patterns in terms of how program variables and data structures are used within an algorithm. Such patterns can be used in guiding the discovery of invariants. By way of illustration, invariant discovery involves identifying the relationship between "work done" and "work still to do" during a computation. Within the context of array based programs, this relationship typically corresponds to partitioning an array, where partition boundaries are defined in terms of loop counter variables. Knowing how counter variables change during a computation provides guidance in determining the structure of invariants. We explicitly represent these changes by means of predicates as defined in figure 1. Making these notions explicit means that the information can be exploited by our top-down and failure-analysis techniques, as will be illustrated later. Note that where loops are nested an outer-loop counter will typically remain unchanged during the execution of an inner-loop. This notion is expressed by the predicate *constant*. It is envisaged that this set of predicates will evolve as new patterns between algorithms and invariants are identified.

3   Top-Down Analysis

Our top-down analysis technique is novel in that it generates schematic invariants. To illustrate the general mechanism, consider the following pattern of postcondition for an array based program:

$$(\forall q : int. \, ((l \leq q) \wedge (q \leq u)) \rightarrow P(q)) \tag{1}$$

Note that l and u denote the lower and upper bounds on q respectively. Typically these bounds will correspond to the array bounds and the predicate $P(q)$ will define a property of the array. Weakening a postcondition corresponding to (1) can be achieved by restricting the range of q. We call this pattern of invariant *range restriction*. In order to tailor this pattern to a particular algorithm we use the information generated via bottom-up analysis. Let us assume that the predicate P specifies a property of an array t, moreover that t is partitioned with respect to a loop counter i with accessible range l to i. If i is monotonically increasing then this suggests that (1) should be weakened by replacing u, the upper bound on q. Determining the identity of the replacement term is a key problem. The conventional strategy involves generate and test, where test involves a theorem prover. Here we propose the use of meta-variables, this allows us to delay the choice until we plan the proof. In terms of (1), this gives an invariant schema of the form:

$$(\forall q : int. \,((l \leq q) \wedge (q \leq F_1(i)))) \rightarrow P(q))$$

Note that F_1 denotes a second-order meta-variable. If the accessible range associated with i was i to u and i was monotonically decreasing, then the l would have been replaced by $F_1(i)$. Within the context of nested loops, invariant schemas are generated for an outer-loop before its inner-loop. An inner-loop will inherit the invariant schemas generated for its outer-loop.

4   Proof-Failure Analysis

Given a failed proof attempt, a common theorem proving strategy is to conjoin the failed goal onto the original conjecture (invariant) and attempt the proof again. We extend this strategy by introducing two alternative generalization steps. We describe each generalization in terms of a proof critic.

4.1   Range Generalization Critic

Using a "picture" notation, consider the following array:

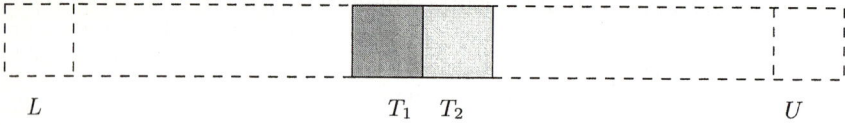

Note that the elements indexed by T_1 and T_2 are adjacent while L and U denote the lower and upper bounds on the array respectively. When proving a relationship between adjacent elements it is often the case that one needs to consider a range of elements rather than just the individuals, *i.e.*

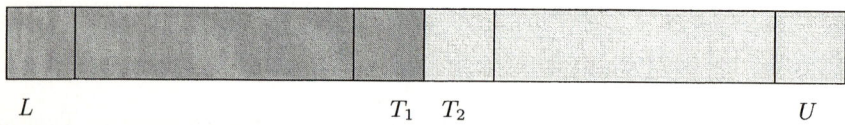

Considering a range of elements provides a stronger invariant (inductive) hypothesis. Here we represent this observation as a proof critic. The preconditions for what we call the *range generalization critic* are as follows[1]:

1. A goal is unprovable within the current proof context and matches the following pattern:

$$\underbrace{ele(A, [T_1]) \; Rel \; ele(A, [T_2])}_{\text{blocked}}$$

---

[1] Note that $ele(X, [Y])$ denotes the value of element Y within array X.

where A denotes an array, terms T_1 and T_2 index adjacent elements within the array A and Rel denotes a transitive relation.

2. Terms T_1 and T_2 contain a counter variable in common.

Note that precondition 2 exploits the meta predicates outlined in §2. The associated patch involves generalizing with respect to both T_1 and T_2, *i.e.*

$$(\forall X : int.((L \le X) \land (X \le T_1)) \to$$
$$(\forall Y : int.((T_1 < Y) \land (Y \le U)) \to ele(A, [X]) \; Rel \; ele(A, [Y])))$$

This generalized goal represents an auxiliary invariant which is then conjoined onto the original invariant. We envisage situations where a weaker generalization may be appropriate. For instance, if T_1 denotes a constant then only T_2 would be generalized, and vice versa.

4.2   Difference Generalization Critic

Our second generalization critic builds upon the *rippling* proof plan. Rippling is a rewriting technique in which annotations are used to guide the selection of rewrite rules. Selection is based upon a difference reduction heuristic. The difference between a goal and a hypothesis are annotated, where the annotations are called *wave-fronts*. Annotated rewrite rules, known as *wave-rules*, are used to reduce the differences between goal and hypothesis. Rippling is successful if a match between the goal and the hypothesis is made possible. This matching is known as *fertilization*. A completely formal account of the ripple method can be found in [2,5]. Our second generalization critic is motivated by the observation that an unproven goal resulting from a successful fertilization often requires a subsequent ripple proof. This in turn involves annotating the differences between the post-fertilization goal and another hypothesis (invariant) within the proof context. This change of the "rippling focus" breaks down if the proof context is missing the hypothesis (invariant) that is necessary for the ripple proof to proceed. The patch uses the available wave-rules (background theory) to guide the discovery of the missing hypothesis (invariant), *i.e.* we look for wave-rule matches that fail because of missing wave-front annotations within the goal. The preconditions to the critic are as follows:

1. A post-fertilization goal is unprovable within the current proof context, *i.e.*

$$\underbrace{f(g(c(a, b)))}_{\text{blocked}}$$

2. There exists a wave-rule that matches modulo missing wave-front annotations, *i.e.*

$$g(\boxed{c(a, b)}^{\uparrow}) \Rightarrow \boxed{h(g(a))}^{\uparrow}$$

3. Application of the wave-rule would progress the proof planning.

Note that shading is used to represent wave-front annotations. Here annotations are missing from the goal, preventing the application of the wave-rule. With regards to precondition 2, a criteria for evaluating the closeness of a near-miss would be necessary in order to rank candidate wave-rules. Note that precondition 3 is not essential, but further constrains the search for an auxiliary invariant by looking ahead into the proof planning. The associated patch involves eliminating the terms within the unproven goal that correspond to the missing wave-front annotations. In the general case this gives $f(g(a))$. This modified formula represents an auxiliary invariant that is then conjoined to the original invariant. Where multiple sources for the missing wave-front annotations exist then alternative schemas need to be considered. Using *rippling in reverse*[2] alternative sources for the missing annotations can be identified. Each alternative gives rise to an unique candidate invariant schema. Again information gathered during bottom-up analysis can be used to impose an ordering on the schemas, as will be illustrated later.

5   Verification of a Bubble Sort Program

We now apply the ideas described above to the verification of bubble sort. The SPARK version of bubble sort, which is verified, is given in figure 5.3. Note that the code is annotated with preconditions and postconditions, but no loop invariants are specified. Moreover, given that the code involves nested loops then two loop invariants will be required in order to prove partial correctness.

5.1   Bottom-Up Analysis

In terms of proof construction, our bottom-up analysis of the bubble sort code generates a couple of invariant properties. Firstly, the analysis identifies the bounds on loop counter I: $1 \leq i \wedge i \leq last$. Secondly, bounds on loop counter J are also identified: $i \leq j \wedge j \leq last$. Note that the second invariant is with respect to the inner-loop only. These are generated by analysing the initial and final values of both loop counters. In terms of proof search, the following properties are established:

$$mono\_inc(i, for\_loop\_i) \tag{2}$$
$$mono\_dec(j, for\_loop\_j) \tag{3}$$
$$constant(i, for\_loop\_j) \tag{4}$$

Note that these meta predicates are defined in figure 1.

---

[2] This is analogous to the *induction revision critic* (see [11]) where *rippling in reverse* is used to determine alternative induction schemas.

5.2   Top-Down Analysis

We now turn to the specification of bubble sort. The predicate Ordered, that forms part of the postcondition, is defined as follows:

$$ordered(A, L, U) \leftrightarrow (\forall P : int.(L \leq P \wedge P < U) \rightarrow ele(A, [P]) \leq ele(A, [P+1])) \quad (5)$$

Unfolding using (5), the Ordered predicate becomes:

$$(\forall p : int.((0 \leq p) \wedge (p < last)) \rightarrow ele(table, [p]) \leq ele(table, [p+1])) \quad (6)$$

This is a candidate for the range restriction invariant pattern. From our bottom-up analysis of the bubble sort code (see §5.1), we identify nested loops. The outer-loop is associated with a single partition defined by (2), while the inner-loop is associated with partitions defined by (3) and (4). As mentioned above, we consider the outer most loop first, then the second outer most loop and so on. So in weakening (6) we consider the partition defined by I. By (2), we know that I monotonically increases during the execution of the outer-loop, which suggests replacing $last$ by $F_1(i)$ to give an outer-loop invariant schema of the form:

$$(\forall p : int.((0 \leq p) \wedge (p < F_1(i))) \rightarrow ele(table, [p]) \leq ele(table, [p+1])) \quad (7)$$

This invariant schema is inherited by the inner-loop. By (4) we known that I remains constant within the inner-loop. As a consequence we only consider a partition defined by (3) as the basis for a further weakening of (7). By (3), we know that J monotonically decreases during the execution of the inner-loop, which suggests replacing 0 by $G_1(j)$ within (7) to give:

$$(\forall p : int.((G_1(j) \leq p) \wedge (p < F_1(i))) \rightarrow ele(table, [p]) \leq ele(table, [p+1])) \quad (8)$$

Clearly the more meta-variables that appear within a schema, the greater the search control problems. To minimize these problems we organize the search by ordering schemas according to the number of meta-variables they contain. For instance, schema (7) has less meta-variables than schema (8), so proof planning with respect to (8) will only be undertaken if the proof planning for (7) is not successful.

5.3   Proof Planning and Proof-Failure Analysis

The proof planning requires a number of attempts, where each attempt refines the candidate invariants. Success corresponds to the generation of a concrete set of invariants (proof annotations) and proof tactics for the associated verification conditions (VCs).

First Proof Planning Attempt: The analysis outlined above gives rise to a set of schematic VCs. We focus on the Ordered predicate. Following a rippling style of proof, we have schematic hypothesis (7) and an annotated goal of the form:

```
package BubbleSort is
subtype Index_Type is Integer range 0..9;
type Array_Type is array (Index_Type) of Integer;
...
procedure Bubble_Sort(Table: in out Array_Type);
--# derives Table from Table;
--# pre  true;
--# post Ordered(Table, 0, Index_Type'Last) and
--#      Perm(Table, Table~);
end BubbleSort;
```

```
package body BubbleSort is
  procedure Bubble_Sort(Table: in out Array_Type) is
    T: Integer;
  begin
    for I in Index_Type range 1..Index_Type'Last loop
      for J in reverse Index_Type range I..Index_Type'Last loop
        if Table(J-1) > Table(J) then
          T:= Table(J-1); Table(J-1):= Table(J); Table(J):= T;
        end if;
      end loop;
    end loop;
  end Bubble_Sort;
end BubbleSort;
```

Fig. 2. A SPARK implementation of Bubble Sort

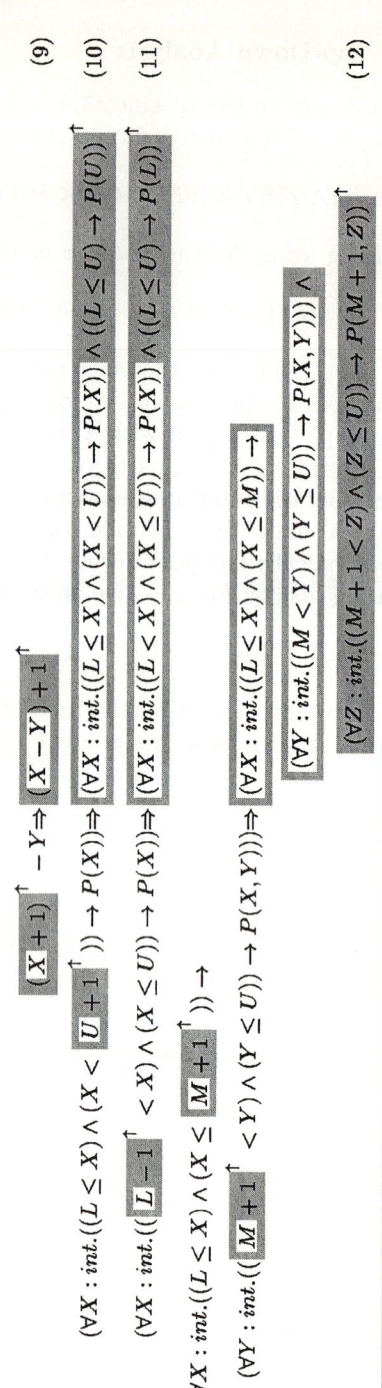

Fig. 3. Wave-rules

First Proof Planning Attempt: The analysis outlined above gives rise to a set of schematic VCs. We focus on the `Ordered` predicate. Following a rippling style of proof, we have schematic hypothesis (7) and an annotated goal of the form:

$$(\forall p : int.((0 \leq p) \wedge (p < F_1(\boxed{(i+1)}^{\uparrow}))) \rightarrow ele(table, [p]) \leq ele(table, [p+1]))$$

$$(13)$$

Using wave-rules (9) and (10) rippling rewrites (13) to give:

$$(\forall p : int.((0 \leq p) \wedge (p < i - F_2(\boxed{i+1}^{\uparrow}))) \rightarrow ele(table, [p]) \leq ele(table, [p+1])) \wedge$$

$$(0 \leq (i - F_2(i+1))) \rightarrow ele(table, [i - F_2(i+1)]) \leq ele(table, [i - F_2(i+1)+1]) {}^{\uparrow}$$

Note that as a side-effect, F_1 is partially instantiated, *i.e.* F_1 becomes $\lambda x.x - F_2(x)$. Fertilization with hypothesis (7) would leave a residue of the form:

$$(0 \leq (i - F_2(i+1))) \rightarrow ele(table, [i - F_2(i+1)]) \leq ele(table, [i - F_2(i+1)+1])$$

Decomposing the implication gives rise to a new hypothesis

$$0 \leq (i - F_2(i+1))$$

$$(14)$$

and a goal of the form:

$$\underbrace{ele(table, [i - F_2(i+1)]) \leq ele(table, [i - F_2(i+1)+1])}_{\text{blocked}}$$

$$(15)$$

Note that this goal is *blocked* as no proof methods are applicable, *i.e.* rippling, simplification or fertilization. Proof-failure analysis applies the range generalization critic. The associated proof patch generates the following auxiliary invariant schema:

$$(\forall p : int.((0 \leq p) \wedge (p \leq i - F_2(i+1))) \rightarrow$$
$$(\forall q : int.((i - F_2(i+1) < q) \wedge (q \leq last)) \rightarrow ele(table, [p]) \leq ele(table, [q])))$$

$$(16)$$

The proof patching process is completed by conjoining (16) onto the refined outer-loop invariant schema, from which a revised set of VCs are generated.

Second Proof Planning Attempt: With the refined outer-loop invariant, the proof context on the second proof attempt contains (16). Proof proceeds initially, as described for the first attempt. However, where the proof previously was blocked, hypothesis (16) can be specialized (using (14)) in order to prove (15). To complete the proof of goal (13) we need to complete the instantiation of the schema. To achieve this we have to exploit constraints imposed by other parts of the proof. Testing a candidate invariant on loop entry will typically detect over generalizations[3]. For instance, on entry to the outer-loop I has the value 1 and schema (16) becomes:

$$(\forall p : int.((0 \le p) \wedge (p \le 1 - F_2(2))) \rightarrow$$
$$(\forall q : int.((1 - F_2(2) < q) \wedge (q \le last)) \rightarrow ele(table, [p]) \le ele(table, [q])))$$

This schematic goal is trivial to prove if F_2 is instantiated to be $\lambda x.2$, We return to the mechanization of such a step in §7. Note that the instantiated invariant schema asserts that the array *table* is *partitioned* such that elements below $i - 2$ (inclusive) are less than or equal to the elements above $i - 2$.

Third Proof Planning Attempt: We now consider the proof of the *partitioned* invariant discovered above. In particular, we focus on the VC corresponding to the path from the inner-loop invariant to the outer-loop invariant, *i.e.* where i is equal to j and we have a hypothesis of the form

$$(\forall p : int.((0 \le p) \wedge (p \le i - 2)) \rightarrow$$
$$(\forall q : int.((i - 2 < q) \wedge (q \le last)) \rightarrow ele(table, [p]) \le ele(table, [q]))) \quad (17)$$

and an annotated goal of the form:

$$(\forall p : int.((0 \le p) \wedge (p \le \boxed{(i+1)}^{\uparrow} - 2)) \rightarrow$$

$$(\forall q : int.((\boxed{(i+1)}^{\uparrow} - 2 < q) \wedge (q \le last)) \rightarrow ele(table, [p]) \le ele(table, [q])))$$
$$(18)$$

Using wave-rules (9) and (10) rippling rewrites (18) to give:

$$\boxed{(\forall p : int.((0 \le p) \wedge (p \le i - 2)) \rightarrow}$$

$$\boxed{(\forall q : int.((i - 2 < q) \wedge (q \le last)) \rightarrow ele(table, [p]) \le ele(table, [q]))) \wedge}$$

$$\boxed{(\forall q' : int.(((i - 2) + 1 < q') \wedge (q' \le last)) \rightarrow ele(table, [i - 2 + 1]) \le ele(table, [q']))}^{\uparrow}$$

Fertilization with hypothesis (17) leaves a residue which simplifies to give:

$$\underbrace{(\forall q' : int.((i - 1 < q') \wedge (q' \le last)) \rightarrow ele(table, [i - 1]) \le ele(table, [q']))}_{\text{blocked}}$$
$$(19)$$

No proof methods are applicable so the goal is *blocked*. Motivated by a partial match with wave-rule (11), proof-failure analysis applies the difference generalization critic. Given that i and j are equal, two alternative invariant schemas can be generated. The first asserts a notion of *minimum* element based upon i:

$$(\forall q' : int.((i < q') \wedge (q' \le last)) \rightarrow ele(table, [i]) \le ele(table, [q']))$$

---

[3] This is analogous to testing base cases within the context of proof by mathematical induction in order to guard against an over generalization.

The second makes a similar assertion for j:

$$(\forall q' : int.((j < q') \wedge (q' \leq last)) \rightarrow ele(table, [j]) \leq ele(table, [q'])) \qquad (20)$$

Note that from our bottom-up analysis we know that i denotes the upper boundary of a partition (see (2)) while j denotes the lower boundary of a partition (see (3)). Consequently, (20) is most closely aligned with the bubble sort algorithm. By this combination of proof-failure and bottom-up analysis, (20) is selected as a second auxiliary invariant. Note that (20) asserts that for the partition above j, the element indexed by j is the *minimum*. The proof patching process is completed by conjoining (20) onto the inner-loop invariant schema, from which a revised set of VCs are generated.

Fourth and Fifth Proof Planning Attempts: With the refined inner-loop invariant, the proof context on the fourth proof attempt contains (20). Proof proceeds initially as described for the third attempt. However, where the proof previously was blocked (see (19)), hypothesis (20) provides the basis for a simple rippling proof. To complete the reasoning, (20) must be shown to be invariant with respect to the inner-loop, again a relatively simple application of rippling is required.

5.4 Summary of Invariant Discovery Results

Bottom-up analysis generated counter variable properties which contributed to both the outer-loop and inner-loop invariants. Top-down analysis, constrained by bottom-up analysis, generated an invariant schema. Through proof-failure analysis, this schema was refined to give the *partitioned* invariant, *i.e.* (17). Proof-failure analysis also generated the *minimum* invariant, *i.e.* (20).

6 Comparison with Related Work

Research into heuristic rules for both bottom-up and top-down analysis have a long history [15,16,18,19]. The work of Wegbreit led to the development of a prototype system called VISTA [7]. The VISTA system, and the later RUNCHECK [6] system used the strategy of conjoining failed goals onto a conjecture. The VISTA system was also able to extract information from failed proofs. Our proof critics extend theses ideas. In particular, there are two key differences between our approach and previous approaches. Firstly, the use of schematic invariants which allows an incremental style of generation (cf generate-and-test). Secondly, the use of program knowledge in constraining proof patches during proof planning.

7 Current Implementation and Future Work

Our bottom-up analysis techniques have been implemented and tested within a prototype called AutoGap [8]. The application of rippling presented here is not new and we have a proof planner that supports the incremental instantiation of schematic conjectures and proof patching [10,11,12,13,17,14]. The implementation of the proposed generalization proof critics is under-way. In terms of future work, the style of proof planning outlined above requires the ability to opportunistically switch between VCs. Moreover, the ability to exploit counter-examples in instantiating invariant schemas (see second proof planning attempt §5.3) is an area that requires further investigation.

8   Conclusion

We propose an integration of invariant discovery techniques. The approach relies upon the incremental instantiation of invariant schemas and the use of program patterns during the patching of failed proof attempts. Our implementation work is ongoing, but we believe that this work will demonstrate the synergies that can be achieved through the integration of static analysis techniques.

Acknowledgements. Thanks to Peter Amey, Alan Bundy, Rod Chapman, Jonathan Hammond and Ian O'Neill for their feedback and support. The research is funded by EPSRC grant GR/R24081 and is a collaboration with Praxis Critical Systems Ltd.

References

1. J. Barnes. *High integrity software: the SPARK approach to safety and security.* Addison-Wesley, 2003.
2. D. Basin and T. Walsh. A calculus for and termination of rippling. *Journal of Automated Reasoning*, 16(1–2):147–180, 1996.
3. A. Bundy. The use of explicit plans to guide inductive proofs. In *CADE-9*, Springer-Verlag, 1988.
4. A. Bundy, A. Smaill, and J. Hesketh. Turning eureka steps into calculations in automatic program synthesis. In *Proceedings of UK IT 90*, IEE, 1990.
5. A. Bundy, A. Stevens, F. van Harmelen, A. Ireland, and A. Smaill. Rippling: A heuristic for guiding inductive proofs. *Artificial Intelligence*, 62:185–253, 1993.
6. S.M. German. Automating proof of the absence of common runtime errors. In *Proceedings of 5th ACM Conference on Principles of Programming Languages*. 1978.
7. S.M. German and B. Wegbreit. A synthesizer of inductive assertions. *IEEE Trans. on Software Engineering*, SE-1(1), 1975.
8. T. Ingulfsen. *Automatic generation of algorithmic properties: AutoGAP*. BSc undergraduate dissertation project, School of Mathematical and Computer Sciences, Heriot-Watt University, Edinburgh, 2003.
9. A. Ireland. The use of planning critics in mechanizing inductive proofs. In *LPAR 92*, LNAI No. 624. Springer-Verlag, 1992.
10. A. Ireland and A. Bundy. Extensions to a generalization critic for inductive proof. In *CADE-13*. LNAI No. 1104. Springer-Verlag, 1996.
11. A. Ireland and A. Bundy. Productive use of failure in inductive proof. *Journal of Automated Reasoning*, 16(1–2), 1996.

12. A. Ireland and A. Bundy. Automatic verification of functions with accumulating parameters. *Journal of Functional Programming: Special Issue on Theorem Proving & Functional Programming*, 9(2):225–245, March 1999.

13. A. Ireland and J. Stark. On the automatic discovery of loop invariants. In *Proceedings of LFM-97, NASA Conference Publication 3356*, 1997.

14. A. Ireland and J. Stark. Proof planning for strategy development. *Annals of Mathematics and Artificial Intelligence*, 29(1-4):65–97, February 2001.

15. S.M. Katz and Z. Manna. A heuristic approach to program verification. In *Proceedings of IJCAI-73*. 1973.

16. S.M. Katz and Z. Manna. Logical analysis of programs. *Communications of the ACM*, 19(4):188–206, 1976.

17. J. Stark and A. Ireland. Invariant discovery via failed proof attempts. In *LOPSTR-98*, LNCS No. 1559. Springer-Verlag, 1998.

18. B. Wegbreit. Heuristic methods for mechanically deriving inductive assertions. In *Proceedings of IJCAI-73*, 1973.

19. B. Wegbreit. The synthesis of loop predicates. *Comm. ACM*, 17(2):102–122, 1974.

Closing the Gap between the Stable Semantics and Extensions of WFS

Mauricio Osorio, Veronica Borja, and Jose Arrazola

Universidad de las Américas, CENTIA.
Sta. Catarina Mártir, Cholula, Puebla
72820 México
josorio@mail.udlap.mx
http://mailweb.udlap.mx/~josorio

Abstract. In order to really understand all aspects of logic-based program development of different semantics, it would be useful to have a common solid logical foundation. The stable semantics has one already based on intuitionistic logic I and using the notion of completions. Since S4 expresses I then the stable semantics can be fully represented in S4. We propose the same approach to define extensions of the WFS semantics. We distinguish a particular semantics that we call AS-WFS wich is defined over general propositional theories, can be defined via completions using S4. Interesting AS-WFS seems to satisfy most of the principles of a well behaved semantics. Our general goal is to propose S4 and completions to study the formal behavior of different semantics.

Keywords: Stable semantics, WFS, FOUR, Modal logics.

1 Introduction

A-Prolog (Stable Logic Programming [9] or Answer Set Programming) is the realization of much theoretical work on Nonmonotonic Reasoning and AI applications of Logic Programming (LP) in the last 15 years. This is an important logic programming paradigm that has now great acceptance in the community. Efficient software to compute answer sets and a large list of applications to model real life problems justify this assertion. The two most well known systems that compute stable models are DLV [1] and SMODELS[2]. It has been recently provided a characterization of answer sets by intuitionistic logic I as follows: a literal is entailed by a disjunctive program in the stable model semantics if and only if it belongs to every I complete and consistent extension of the program formed by adding only negated atoms. [16]. We adopted the following formal notation to express this fact: M is an answer set of a disjunctive program P if and only if $P \cup \neg \widetilde{M} \Vdash_I M$.

---

[1] http://www.dbai.tuwien.ac.at/proj/dlv/
[2] http://saturn.hut.fi/pub/smodels/

R. Monroy et al. (Eds.): MICAI 2004, LNAI 2972, pp. 202–211, 2004.

This logical approach provides the foundations to define the notion of nonmonotonic inference of any propositional theory (using the standard connectives) in terms of a monotonic logic (namely intuitionistic logic I), see [13,14, 15,16]. Notions such as conservative extensions, conservative transformations, equivalence, strong equivalence (see [10,13]), among others are now better understood thanks to this logical approach. These notions are very important if one wants to push forward a logic-based program development approach.

The well founded semantics is also a very well known paradigm originated at the same time that stable semantics [18]. The main difference between STABLE and WFS is in the definition of the former, a *guess* is made and then a particular (2-valued) model is constructed and used to justify the guess or to reject it. However, in the definition of WFS, more and more atoms are declared to be true (or false): once a decision has been drawn, it will never be rejected. WFS is based on a single 3-valued intended model.

Several authors have recognized the interest in semantics with closed behavior to classical logic see [4,5,6,7,17]. They have extend the WFS semantics by putting an additional mechanism on top of its definition. Dix noticed that the new semantics sometimes have a more serious shortcomings than WFS and hence he defined a set of principles where all semantics should be checked against [6]. It is worth to mention that such notions helped Dix to propose the concept of well behaved semantics. We think that is important to understand well such concept if one wants to follow any serious methodology for logic-based program development. We introduce an extension of WFS that we will call AS-WFS with the following properties:

1. It is defined based on completions (as the stable semantics) but using the well known S4 logic. In our notation, M is an AS-WFS set of P if and only if $P \cup \neg \widetilde{M} \Vdash_{S4} M$. This is our scenarios semantics. We can define our sceptical AS-WFS semantics as usual. The STABLE semantics is defined as completions using I, namely $P \cup \neg \widetilde{M} \Vdash_{I} M$. Since S4 can express I (using the Gödel translation [1]) then S4 also defines stable [14].
2. AS-WFS is defined for propositional theories based in basic formula.
3. Using the knowledge ordering ($\leq_k$, see [5]), we have that WFS < AS-WFS < STABLE for normal programs. The well known WFS$^+$ defined by Dix also satisfies this property.
4. AS-WFS can also be defined using modal logic S5. Moreover, AS-WFS can also be defined using the well known billatice FOUR. The stable semantics can also be defined using FOUR [3].
5. The known counter examples for the well behavior of several known extensions of WFS (such as GWFS and EWFS) do not apply for AS-WFS. It seems, but we do not know yet, that AS-WFS satisfies several of the principles given for well behaved semantics [2].
6. AS-WFS is different from GWFS, EWFS, WFS$^+$.

We expect the reader to have some familiarity with modal logics, many valued logics and logic programming.

2   Background

We consider a formal (propositional) language built from an alphabet containing: a denumerable set $\mathcal{L}$ of elements called atoms, the standard 2-place connectives $\wedge, \vee, \rightarrow$, and the 1-place connective $\neg$. Formulas and theories are constructed as usual in logic. In this paper we only consider finite theories. We will later define other connectives, but only for temporal use.

We define the class of *basic formulas* recursively as follows:

$$\neg a, a \quad \text{if } a \text{ is an atom.}$$
$$\alpha \vee \beta \quad \text{if } \alpha, \beta \text{ are basic formulas.}$$
$$\alpha \wedge \beta \quad \text{if } \alpha, \beta \text{ are basic formulas.}$$
$$\alpha \rightarrow \beta \text{ if } \alpha, \beta \text{ are basic formulas.}$$

A *normal program* is a set of rules of the form

$$A_1 \wedge ... \wedge A_m \wedge \neg A_{m+1} \wedge ... \wedge \neg A_n \rightarrow A_0$$

We use the well known definition of a stratified program, see [12]. We use the notation $\vdash_X F$ to denote that the formula F is provable (a theorem or tautology) in logic X. If T is a theory we use the symbol $T \vdash_X F$ to denote $\vdash_X (F_1 \wedge \cdots \wedge F_n) \rightarrow F$ for some formulas $F_i \in T$. We say that a theory T is *consistent* if it has a model in the given logic. We also introduce, if T and U are two theories, the symbol $T \vdash_X U$ to denote that $T \vdash_X F$ for all formulas $F \in U$. We will write $T \Vdash_X U$ to denote the fact that (i) T is consistent and (ii) $T \vdash_X U$.

Given a class of programs C, a *semantic operator* Sem is a function that assigns to each program $P \in C$ a set of sets of atoms $M \subseteq \mathcal{L}_P$. These sets of atoms are usually some "preferred" two valued models of the program P each of them is called a *Sem model* of P. Sometimes, we say, that this is the scenarios semantics [7]. Given a scenarios semantics Sem, we define the sceptical semantics of a program P as: $\text{Sem}(P) = \bigcap(\{M \cup \neg \widetilde{M} : M \text{ is a Sem model of } P\}$, where $\widetilde{M} = \mathcal{L}_P \setminus M$ and $\neg M = \{\neg a : a \in M\}$.

Given two semantics S_1 and S_2, we define: $S_1 \leq S_2$ if for every program P is true that $S_1(P) \subseteq S_2(P)$. We can easily define $S_1 = S_2$ and $S_1 < S_2$. We say that a semantics is stronger than another one according to this order.

2.1   Non Monotonic Reasoning via S5

Consider modal logic S5 with its standard connectives that we will denote as: $\sim$, $\rightarrow, \vee, \wedge$. McDermott and Doyle introduced a non-monotonic version of S5. They define the X-expansions E of a theory T as those sets satisfying the equation:

$$E = Cn_x(T \cup \{\sim \Box \psi \notin E\}) \tag{1}$$

where C_{n_X} is the inference operation of the modal logic X. Depending on the approach, an arbitrary selected X-expansion for T or the intersection of all X-expansions for T is considered as a set of nonmonotonic consequences of T. McDermott proved that S5 coincides with its non-monotonic version, hence it is not very interesting. However, he considered formulas to complete the theory. If we only consider adding simple formulas of the form $\sim \Box a$ (a an atom), the story changes. In fact, Gelfond [8] was able to characterize stable models of stratified normal programs using this idea and the following translation: A normal clause:

$$A_1 \wedge ... \wedge A_m \wedge \neg A_{m+1} \wedge ... \wedge \neg A_n \rightarrow A_0$$

becomes

$$A_1 \wedge ... \wedge A_m \wedge \sim \Box A_{m+1} \wedge ... \wedge \sim \Box A_n \rightarrow A_0$$

3   Definition via S4

Consider modal logic S4 with its standard connectives that we will denote as: $\sim, \rightarrow, \vee, \wedge$.

Let $\neg\alpha$ be the abbreviation form of the modal formula $\sim \Box \alpha$. Gelfond in [8] gives a definitions of similar semantics to AS-WFS, but it covers only the class of stratified programs, we generalized this concept in the following definition:

Definition 1. *Let P be a theory based on basic formula and M be a set of atoms. We define M to be an AS-WFS model of P iff $P \cup \neg\widetilde{M} \Vdash_{S4} M$. We denote the sceptical semantics of P as AS-WFS(P).*

Hence, this definition opens the research line of defining other WFS extensions via different modal logics. For example, modal logic K behaves 'closer' (but still different) to the stable semantics. Consider the following example: $\neg a \rightarrow b, \neg b \rightarrow a, \neg p \rightarrow a, \neg p \rightarrow p$. Then AS-WFS has two models, namely $\{a,p\}, \{b,p\}$. But using modal logic K we obtain no models.

If we consider S5 instead, we obtain the same semantics.

Lemma 1. *Let P be a theory based on basic formula and M be a set of atoms. Then M is an AS-WFS model of P iff $P \cup \neg\widetilde{M} \Vdash_{S5} M$.*
(See proof in Appendix).

Is well known that STABLE and WFS agree in the class of normal stratified programs. Gelfond showed [8] that the stable models of stratified programs can be characterized using S5 completions under his proposed translation. Hence, we have the following result.

Corollary 1. *If P is a stratified normal program, WFS(P)= AS-WFS(P)= STABLE(P).*

4   Results

We first show that AS-WFS is different to some well known semantics and then present its characterization using S4. We will also introduce some families of semantics and finish this section presenting a brief comment on well behaved semantics.

4.1   Comparing AS-WFS with Other Semantics

Consider the EWFS semantics, the CUT rule and the following example all of them taken from [5]:

$$\neg a \rightarrow a, \neg x \wedge a \rightarrow b, \neg b \rightarrow y, \neg y \rightarrow z$$

Here $EWFS(P) = \{a, b, \neg x\}$, however $EWFS(P \cup \{b\}) = \{a, b, z, \neg x, \neg y\}$. This example shows that EWFS does not satisfies CUT. $AS\text{-}WFS(P) = \{a, b, z, \neg x, \neg y\}$ as well as AS-WFS $(P \cup \{b\}) = \{a, b, z, \neg x, \neg y\}$. Hence AS-WFS is different to EWFS.

Consider the following two program examples taken from [5]:

$$\neg b \rightarrow p, c \rightarrow b, (p \wedge \neg a) \rightarrow c, \neg b \rightarrow a$$

and

$$\neg b \rightarrow p, (p \wedge \neg a) \rightarrow b, \neg b \rightarrow a$$

One may expect the same semantics of both programs w.r.t. the common language. However, GWFS infers p in the first program, but it does not in the second program. AS-WFS gives the same answer in both programs which consists in deriving only $\neg c$ in both programs. Hence, AS-WFS is different to GWFS.

Consider the following program example taken from [7]:

$$\neg b \rightarrow a, \neg a \rightarrow b, \neg a \rightarrow x, \neg b \rightarrow x$$

Note that $WFS^+(P) = \{\}$, but $AS\text{-}WFS(P) = \{x\}$.

In [7] we have that WFS^+ is an stronger extension of WFS, then comparing the semantics we proposed and the results obtained in [5], we have that WFS < AS-WFS < STABLE. This can be formalized as follows:

Lemma 2. *Let P be a normal program, then $WFS(P) < AS\text{-}WFS(P) < STABLE(P)$.*

4.2   Well Behaved Semantics

We conjecture that AS-WFS satisfies all principles involved in the definition of a well behaved semantics as long as we reject to interpret $P \cup M$ as P^M. Note that the notion P^M is a syntactic transformation, not required when $P \cup M$ has a logical meaning. Take for instance, the following program P from [6]:

$b \rightarrow a, \neg a \rightarrow b$. This example is used to show that WFS$^+$ does not satisfies the Extended Cut principle. While WFS$^+(P) = \{a, \neg b\}$, WFS$^+(P \cup \{\neg b\}) = \{\neg a, \neg b\}$. Moreover, $\{\neg a, \neg b\}$ is neither a 2-valued model, nor a 3-valued model of the program $P \cup \{\neg b\}$. However, this happens because WFS$^+$ does not have a "logical" definition for the semantics of programs extended with constraints (negated formulas). Hence, Dix interprets $P \cup \{\neg b\}$ as $P^{\{\neg b\}}$. $P^{\{\neg b\}} := b \rightarrow a$. Now $\{\neg a, \neg b\}$ is a model of $P \cup \{\neg b\}$. AS-WFS has a definition for semantics of any basic propositional theory that allows the use of constraints. In this example we get AS-WFS(P) = ASP-WFS$(P \cup \{\neg b\})$ = $\{a, \neg b\}$. Hence, we propose to reconsider Dix's work on well-behaved semantics, towards a direction of making it more general and logical based.

5   Characterization of ASP-WFS via FOUR

The logical role that the four-valued estructure has among Ginsberg's well known bilattices is similar to the role that the two-valued algebras has among Boolean algebras. Four valued semantics is a very suitable setting for computerized reasoning acording to Belnap and in fact the original motivation of Ginsberg for introducing bilattices was to provide a uniform approach for a diversity of applications in AI. Bilattices were furter investigated by Fitting, who showed that they are useful also for providing semantics to logic programs, hence our interest is focus on relating FOUR with ASP-WFS.

5.1   The FOUR-Valuation Bilattice

Belnap introduced a logic for dealing in an useful way with inconsistent and incomplete information. This logic is based on a structure called FOUR, see [3]. This structure has four truth values, the classical t and f, and two new $\top$ that intuitively denotes lack of information (no knowledge), and $\bot$ that indicates inconsistency ("over"-knowledge). These values have two different natural orderings.

- Measuring the truth:
  The minimal element is f, the maximal element is t and values $\top$ and $\bot$ are incomparable. Here we have the inverse involution $\sim_{tr}$, the meet and join operators denoted respectively as $\wedge_{tr}$ and $\vee_{tr}$.
- Reflecting differences in the amount of knowledge or information:
  The minimal element is $\bot$, the maximal element is $\top$ and values f and t are incomparable. Here we have inverse involution $\sim_{kn}$, the meet and join operators denoted respectively as $\wedge_{kn}$ and $\vee_{kn}$.

5.2   The AS-WFS Semantics

We first explain how are we going to use FOUR to define our semantics.
    We read the bilattice FOUR identifying $\bot$ as 0, $\top$ as 3, f as 1 and t as 2. We have the following tables for the connectives $\sim$ and $\rightarrow$, and if we give the other

table as a valuation for the *assertion* connective $\Box$. Later, will become more clear why are we selecting a "typical" modal operator symbol for this purpose.

The idea of this last connective is due to the Russian logician Bochvar. It intends to represent the "external assertion" of a proposition p, that is, $\Box p$ can be considered as the assertion "p is true" in a two valued metalanguage. We define the operators $\sim, \rightarrow, \Box$ as follows:

A	$\sim A$
0	3
1	2
2	1
3	0

$\rightarrow$	0	1	2	3
0	3	3	3	3
1	2	3	2	3
2	1	1	3	3
3	0	1	2	3

A	$\Box A$
0	0
1	0
2	0
3	3

It is important to note that these connectives are abbreviation forms using the standard language of FOUR as it is shown in the following table.

$$
\begin{aligned}
\sim \alpha &:= \sim_{kn} \sim_{tr} \alpha \\
\alpha \rightarrow \beta &:= \sim_{kn} \sim_{tr} \alpha \vee_{kn} \beta \\
\Box \alpha &:= \alpha \wedge_{kn} \sim_{tr} \alpha \\
\bot &:= \sim_{kn} \sim_{tr} a \wedge_{kn} a \, for \, a \, given \, atom \, a. \\
\alpha \vee \beta &:= \alpha \vee_{kn} \beta \\
\alpha \wedge \beta &:= \alpha \wedge_{kn} \beta
\end{aligned}
\tag{2}
$$

As before, we define our main negation operator ($\neg$): $\neg p$ as $\sim \Box p$.

Using the reading of FOUR and the valuation defined in the tables tautologies will be the formulas whose truth value is 3. Examples of some tautologies are: $(\neg a \rightarrow a) \rightarrow a, a \vee \neg a, \neg\neg a \rightarrow a, a \rightarrow a$). Note that $a \rightarrow \neg\neg a$ is not a tautology.

Theorem 1. *Let P be a theory based on basic formula and M be a set of atoms. M is an AS-WFS model of P iff $P \cup \neg\widetilde{M} \Vdash_{FOUR} M$.*
(See proof in Appendix)

6 Conclusions

There is still actual interest in extensions of WFS ([4,7]). We need however to find a logical framework to define such extensions if one really believes in a logic-based program development approach. We propose an approach to define extensions of the WFS semantics based on completions with the same spirit of STABLE, hence closing the gap between both approaches. As a result, we gain a better understanding of those semantics as well as the relation among them. We have that AS-WFS is sound with respect to stable models semantics and it can be used to approximate stable entailment. Still it is left work to do with respect to this semantics and our future work is to continue going deep in this semantics to see what properties of the well-behaved semantics it satisfies.

References

1. Dirk van Dalen. *Intuitionistic Logic* Handbook of Philosophical Logic, Volume III: Alternatives to Classical Logic, D. Gabbay and F. Guenthner (eds.) D. Reidel Publishing Co. 1986.

2. Gerard Brewka, Jürgen Dix and Kurt Konolige. Non Monotonic Reasoning An Overview. Center for the Study of Languages and Information Stanford California, 1997.

3. Avron Arnon. *On the Expressive Power of the Three-Valued and FOUR-Valued LanguajesLanguages.*. Journal of Logic and Computation 9. 1999.

4. Marc Denecker, Nikolay Pelov, and Maurice Bruynooghe. *Ultimate Well-Founded and Stable Semantics for Logic Programs with Aggregates.* Logic programming. *Proceedings of the 17th International Conference, ICLP 2001*, pages 212-226 LNCS 2237, Springer, November/December 2001.

5. Jürgen Dix. A Classification Theory of Semantics of Normal Logic Programs: I. Strong Properties. Fundamental Informaticae XXII (3)* 227-255, 1995.

6. Jürgen Dix. A Classification Theory of Semantics of Normal Logic Programs: II. Weak Properties. Fundamental Informaticae XXII (3)* 257-288, 1995.

7. Jürgen Dix, Mauricio Osorio, and Claudia Zepeda. A general theory of confluent rewriting systems for logic programming and its applications. *Annals of Pure and Applied Logic*, 108(1–3):153–188, 2001.

8. Michael Gelfond. *On stratified auto-epistemic theories.* In Proceedings of AAAI-87.pp 207-211. Morgan Kaufmann, 1987.

9. Michael Gelfond, Vladimir Lifschitz. The stable model semantics for logic programs. Proceedings of the Fifth International Conference on Logic Programming MIT Press. Cambridge, Ma. 1988. pp.1070-1080.

10. Vladimir Lifschitz, David Pearce, and Agustin Valverde. Strongly equivalent logic programs. ACM Transactions on Computational Logic, 2:526-541, 2001.

11. Drew McDermott. *Nonmonotonic Logic II: nonmonotonic Modal Theories.* Journal of the Association for Computing Machinery. Vol 29 No. 1 January 1982 pages 33-57.

12. John W. Lloyd. *Foundations of Logic Programming.* Springer, Berlin, second edition, 1987.

13. Mauricio Osorio, Juan Antonio Navarro, José Arrazola. "Equivalence in Answer Set Programming (extended version)", Proceedings of LOPSTR 01, LNCS 2372, pp57-75, Springer-Verlag, Paphos, Cyprus, November 2001.

14. Mauricio Osorio, Juan Antonio Navarro, José Arrazola. "Applications of Intuitionistic Logic in Answer Set Programming", accepted in *Journal of TPLP*, 2003.

15. Mauricio Osorio, Juan Antonio Navarro, José Arrazola. "A Logical Approach to A-prolog.", 9th. Workshop on Logic Language and Information. Brazil, 2002.

16. David Pearce. Stable inference as intuitionistic validity. *Logic Programming*, 38:79–91, 1999.

17. John S. Schlipf. Formalizing a Logic for Logic Programming. *Annals of Mathematics and Artificial Intelligence.* 5:279-302, 1992.

18. Allen van Gelder, Kenneth A. Ross, and John S. Schlipf. The well-founded semantics for general logic programs. *Journal of the ACM*, 38:620–650, 1991.

Appendix

We define a $K - basic\ formula$ as the modal formula result of the translation of Gelfond [8] of a basic formula. Then if α is a K-basic formula the scope of the modal operator $\Box$ will be only atoms.

Proof Lemma 1.

$P \cup \neg \widetilde{M} \Vdash_{S4} M$ i.e. $\vdash_{S4} \bigwedge(P \cup \neg \widetilde{M}) \to \bigwedge M$. As P is a theory based on basic formula and M be a set of atoms, then $\bigwedge(P \cup \neg \widetilde{M}) \to \bigwedge M$ is a $K -$ basic formula.

    If α a K-basic formula then $\vdash_{S4} \alpha$ iff $\vdash_{S5} \alpha$. To prove it, the sufficiency follows immediately, so it is enough to check necessity. Suppose $\nvdash_{S4}\alpha$ then exists $\mathcal{M} = (R, S, V)$ model of $S4$ such that $\mathcal{M} \nvDash \alpha$. Let be $\mathcal{M}' = (R', S, V)$ where $R' = R \cup \{(x, x) \mid x \in S\}$, then $\mathcal{M}'$ is a model of $S5$. By a direct induction over the number of connectives of α we have that $\mathcal{M}' \nvDash \alpha$ i.e. $\nvdash_{S5}\alpha$. Then $\vdash_{S5} \alpha$ implies $\vdash_{S4} \alpha$.

Logic $S5_2$ is constructed by adding to logic $S5$ the following axiom:

$$\mathbf{F_2} : \Diamond A_1 \wedge \Diamond A_2 \wedge \Box\neg(A_1 \wedge A_2) \to \Box(A_1 \vee A_2)$$

Proof Theorem 1.

Applying Lemma 1 we have $P \cup \neg\widetilde{M} \Vdash_{S5} M$, equivalent to $\vdash_{S5} \bigwedge(P \cup \neg\widetilde{M}) \to \bigwedge M$ where $\bigwedge(P \cup \neg\widetilde{M}) \to \bigwedge M$ is a K-basic formula. We have the following two lemmas:

Lemma 3. *If α is a K-basic formula then $\vdash_{S5} \alpha$ iff $\vdash_{S5_2} \alpha$.*
(See proof in Appendix).

Lemma 4. *Let be α a modal formula $\vdash_{S5_2} \alpha$ iff $\vDash_{FOUR} \alpha$.*
(See proof in Appendix).

    Then by Lemmas 3 and 4 $\vDash_{FOUR} \bigwedge(P \cup \neg\widetilde{M}) \to \bigwedge M$ and $P \cup \neg\widetilde{M} \Vdash_{FOUR} M$.

Proof Lemma 3.

We first define the model $\mathcal{M}'_t$ based on a model $\mathcal{M} = (R, S, V)$ and t a fixed element of S. We suppose that S has at least two elements.
We define:
$S' = S/\{t\} = \{\{t\}, T\}$ where $T = \{s \in S \mid s \neq t\}$
$R' = S' \times S'$

$$V'(p) = \begin{cases} S' & if\ \forall r \in S \quad V_r(p) = true \\ \{\{t\}\} & if\ V(p) = \{t\} \quad and \quad \exists r \in T \quad V_r(p) = false \\ \{T\} & if\ t \notin V(p) \quad and \quad \exists t' \in T \quad t' \in V(p) \\ \emptyset & otherwise \end{cases}$$

Then $\mathcal{M}' = (R', S', V')$ is a model of $S5_2$ by construction. We have the following corollary about the relation between this new model and models of $S5$.

Corollary 2. *Let be $\mathcal{M}$ a model of $S5$ with at least two elements and s a fixed element of S and α a K-basic formula then: $\mathcal{M} \models_s \alpha$ iff $\mathcal{M}'_s \models_{\{s\}} \alpha$*

The proof is a direct induction on the size of α.

Sufficiency of our Lemma 3 follows immediately. Let us check necessity: Suppose $\nvdash_{S5} \alpha$ and $\vdash_{S5_2} \alpha$. Then exists $\mathcal{M}$ a model of $S5$ (with at least three elements, otherwise the proof is trivial) such that $\mathcal{M} \nvDash \alpha$ then exists $s \in S$ such that $\mathcal{M} \nvDash_s \alpha$ then by the Corollary 2 $\mathcal{M}'_s \nvDash_{\{s\}} \alpha$. But $\vdash_{S5_2} \alpha$ and $\mathcal{M}'_s$ is a model of $S5_2$ then $\mathcal{M}'_s \models_{\{s\}} \alpha$ which leads to a contradiction.

Proof Lemma 4.
Let $\mathcal{F} = < \{1,2\}, \{1,2\} \times \{1,2\} >$ and $\mathcal{M} = < \{1,2\} \times \{1,2\}, \{1,2\}, V >$. Suppose that $\gamma \in Form(\phi)$, let $\mathcal{L}_\gamma = \{a_1, a_2, ..., a_k\} \subseteq \phi$ atoms of language and any valuation $V : \phi \to 2^{\{1,2\}}$ of the atomic formulas, we define $g : \{0, 1, 2, 3\} \to \{\emptyset, \{1\}, \{2\}, \{1,2\}\}$ as
$$g(0) = \emptyset \qquad g(2) = \{2\} \qquad g(1) = \{1\} \qquad g(3) = \{1,2\}$$
Then we have the tetra-valuation V_{FOUR} defined as follows

1. If a is an atom $V_{FOUR}(a) = g^{-1}(V(a))$
2. If α is not atomic V_{FOUR} is defined recursively over the valuation of the operators $\sim, \to, \square$ given in section 5.2.

Of the above definitions we have the following lemma about the relation between the valuation and the frames.

Corollary 3. *Let be V_{FOUR} the valuation FOUR extended to the modal operators as we have defined then $V_{FOUR}(\alpha) = i$ iff $\mathcal{M} \models_{g(i)} \alpha$.* [3]

In other words, if we denote $V_{FOUR}(\alpha) = 3$ as $\models_{FOUR} \alpha$ we have that: $\mathcal{F} \models \alpha$ iff $\models_{FOUR} \alpha$.

As $S5_2$ is determined by the class of frames based in a set with two elements and a reflexive, transitive, symmetric, serial and euclidean relation then $\vdash_{S5_2} \alpha$ iff $\mathcal{F} \models \alpha$. Then if V_{FOUR} is the valuation FOUR extended to the modal operators as we have defined $\vdash_{S5_2} \alpha$ iff $\models_{FOUR} \alpha$

---

[3] The proof of this corollary is available by request via e-mail.

A Framework for Agent-Based Brokering
of Reasoning Services

Jürgen Zimmer*

Mathematical Reasoning Group, School of Informatics, University of Edinburgh,
Appleton Tower, Edinburgh EH8 9LE, Scotland
jzimmer@mathweb.org

Abstract. Many applications have shown that the combination of specialized reasoning systems, such as deduction and computation systems, can lead to synergetic effects. Often, a clever combination of different reasoning systems can solve problems that are beyond the problem solving horizon of single, stand-alone systems. Current platforms for the integration of reasoning systems typically lack abstraction, robustness, and automatic coordination of reasoners. We are currently developing a new framework for reasoning agents to solve these problems. Our framework builds on the FIPA specifications for multi-agent systems, formal service descriptions, and a central brokering mechanism. In this paper we present the architecture of our framework and our progress with the integration of automated theorem provers.

1 Introduction

Automated reasoning systems[1] have reached a high degree of maturity in the last decade. However, reasoning systems are highly specialized and, typically, they can only solve problems in a particular domain such as, for instance, proof by induction, reasoning on first-order logic with equality, or computation in group theory. Many case studies have shown that the combination of reasoning specialists can help to solve problems that are beyond the problem solving horizon of single, stand-alone systems (see, e.g., [1,2]).

In our research group we have developed the MathWeb Software Bus [3] for the integration of heterogeneous reasoning systems. The main idea behind the MathWeb-SB is to extend existing reasoning systems, such as automated theorem provers (ATPs), computer algebra systems (CASs), model generators, and constraint solvers, with a generic interface that allows them to communicate over a common software bus. The MathWeb-SB has proven very successful for the integration of reasoning specialists on the system level [4,5], and is in everyday use in different research groups. Despite this success, problems occurred in certain applications that are hard to solve without fundamental changes in the architecture of the MathWeb-SB. Among others we faced the following problems:

---

* The author is supported by the CALCULEMUS IHP grant HPRN-CT-2000-00102.
[1] Throughout this paper, the term reasoning system denotes deduction systems as well as symbolic computation systems.

R. Monroy et al. (Eds.): MICAI 2004, LNAI 2972, pp. 212–221, 2004.
© Springer-Verlag Berlin Heidelberg 2004

1. The access of reasoning systems has to be performed on the system level, i.e. developers of client applications for the MathWeb-SB still have to know which reasoning system is suitable for a problem at hand, and how to access the system.
2. Many problems cannot be solved by one single reasoning system but only by a co-ordinated interplay between different systems. A coordination of reasoning systems by the MathWeb-SB is not possible. Thus, client applications have to coordinate the systems needed to solve a problem.
3. The client-broker-server architecture of the MathWeb-SB is not designed for asynchronous communication. Synchronous communication is not flexible enough for modern applications of distributed reasoning.

To overcome these problems, we are developing a new framework for distributed automated reasoning based on agent-oriented programming. In our framework the capabilities of reasoning systems are described in the Mathematical Service Description Language (MSDL) [6], an XML language developed in the MONET project [7]. The central agents in our framework are *brokers* that act as middle-agents between the service providing agents (the reasoning agents) and the service requesting agents. Our brokers will reason on MSDL service descriptions to find suitable sequences of available services to tackle a given problem.

For our framework we use existing standards wherever possible. In particular, we employ the specifications of the Foundation for Intelligent Physical Agents (FIPA) [8] for the interaction and coordination of agents. We use the languages OPENMATH [9] and OMDoc [10] for the encoding of mathematical content. Furthermore, we use OMDoc and the language TSTP [11] for theorem proving problems and proofs. For the definition of ontologies we use the Web Ontology Language (OWL) [12].

In [13] we described first ideas for our framework. Since then we have made progress in integrating first-order ATPs as reasoning agents. We can now describe the service offered by these agents in MSDL using an ontology we have developed. We also implemented a prototypical broker which analyzes a given theorem proving problem and chooses the best available prover to tackle the problem.

The remainder of this paper is structured as follows: In section 2 we present the overall structure of our reasoning agent framework, our ontology for the description of theorem proving services, and the description of first-order ATP services with MSDL. In section 3 we show an example for advanced brokering of reasoning services. We conclude and discuss some related work in section 4.

2   A Framework for Reasoning Agents

Our work on the brokering of reasoning services can be split into three major parts: 1) The development of the system of reasoning agents and a brokering mechanism, 2) the development of an ontology for reasoning service descriptions, and 3) MSDL descriptions of the services needed for our case-studies. In this section we describe our work on these issues.

2.1   The Agent Platform

As we have already mentioned in section 1 we base our reasoning agents, the communication between them, and the encoding mathematical content on existing standards. The Foundation for Intelligent Physical Agents (FIPA) has produced many specifications for the inter-operation of heterogeneous software agents. FIPA specifies the agent communication language FIPA-ACL, the communicative acts between agents, and several interaction protocols for agents, such as the Contract Net Protocol[2]. For our work we employ the Java Agent DEvelopment Framework (JADE) [14] which is a widely used implementation of the FIPA specifications.

Reasoning agents are specialized JADE agents which encapsulate reasoning systems and manage conversations with other reasoning agents. They translate incoming FIPA-ACL messages into calls of the underlying reasoning system and wrap results into response messages. Reasoning agents advertise MSDL descriptions of their capabilities to a local broker which stores all advertised services in its service directory.

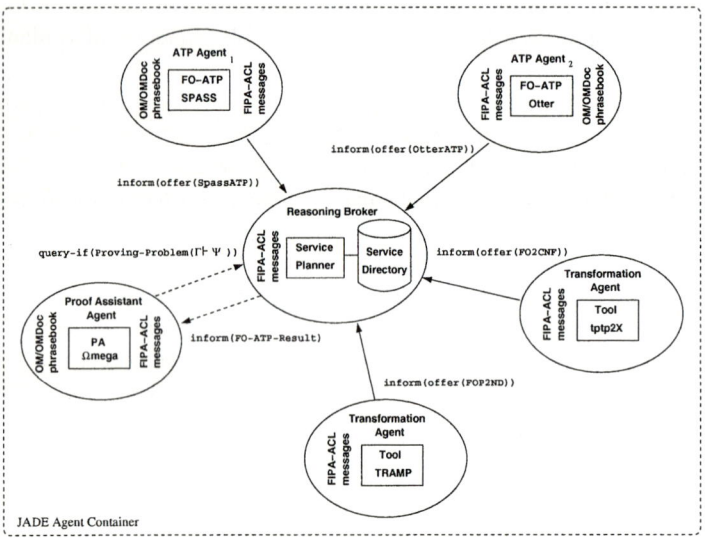

Fig. 1. Reasoning agents informing a central reasoning *broker* about the services they offer, and the *Proof Assistant Agent* ΩMEGA asking for a proof of a conjecture

Fig. 1 shows a scenario in which several agents inform a local broker about the reasoning services they offer using the communicative act **inform** of the FIPA-ACL. For instance, the agent ATP Agent₁, which encapsulates the theorem prover SPASS, informs the broker that it offers the first-order theorem proving service SpassATP (see section 2.3). The proof assistant ΩMEGA [15] does not offer any service but uses the

---

[2] These protocols will become interesting in a later state of our project where we intend to investigate whether they can be used for the coordination of distributed reasoning agents.

query-if performative to send an open conjecture (Proving-Problem($\Gamma \vdash \psi$)) to the broker asking whether the conjecture holds. JADE agents are grouped in agent containers. We are planning to start one broker in each agent container because of our positive experience with dynamic networks of brokers [3]. At the moment we only work with one broker in one agent container. However, in the future, brokers in different agent containers will connect to each other to exchange information about available services.

Every agent can send queries, i.e. open reasoning problems, to the broker of their agent container. Currently, our broker only accepts first-order theorem proving problems. In [16] Sutcliffe and Suttner distinguish six important features of first-order problem (e.g., whether the problem contains the equality predicate or not). Our broker analyzes incoming proving problems according to these features and annotates the problem with the result of this analysis. Then the annotated problem is matched against the available services. Up to now, the broker uses a very simple matching based on the tuProlog engine [17]. In the future the broker will employ a more sophisticated reasoning process which is capable of combining several services to tackle a problem. This is also going to incorporate reasoning on our ontology (cf. section 2.2). In section 3 we describe how reasoning on service descriptions could be used to solve the proving problem sent by ΩMEGA (see Fig. 1).

At first sight, our brokering mechanism seems to be similar to Polya's four phases of problem solving [18]. But, as opposed to Polya, our broker does not have a "understanding" of a problem in the sense of an intelligent mathematician. Up to now, it only finds syntactical features of problems. However, some of Polya's ideas, such as theorem lookup (in a database), the use of analogy, and independent proof checking, are also interesting for brokering as it has been described above.

Different deduction systems typically rely on different logics and consequence relations. Therefore, we are investigating the possible use of the LF logical framework, and its implementation in the TWELF system [19] as a logical basis for brokers. Different logics and calculi can be encoded in TWELF's type theory and the system offers partial transformations of proofs from one deductive system to another. These transformations might become useful in future applications of our framework. In particular, a combination of LF with the TRAMP tool [20] described in section 3 would be very useful for our work and other research projects.

2.2   An Ontology for Reasoning Service Descriptions

We are currently developing two ontologies: 1) a brokering ontology which is used in service advertisements sent to the broker, and 2) a reasoning ontology which is used in MSDL service descriptions and problem descriptions. In this paper we focus on the latter. We decided to use the Protégé-2000 Tool [21] which, lately, supports the development of ontologies in OWL. The Protégé tool is particularly useful for our purposes as it allows us to automatically generate ontology classes for JADE which can be used instantaneously by our reasoning agents. Due to space limitations, and to preserve readability, we present only the fragment of the reasoning ontology that is important for this paper. Our ontology consists of concepts (classes), slots (attributes), and pre-defined instances of concepts. Fig. 2 shows the "is-a" (subclass) relationship between concepts as solid arrows. Slots and their cardinality restrictions are denoted with dashed lines. Instances are connected

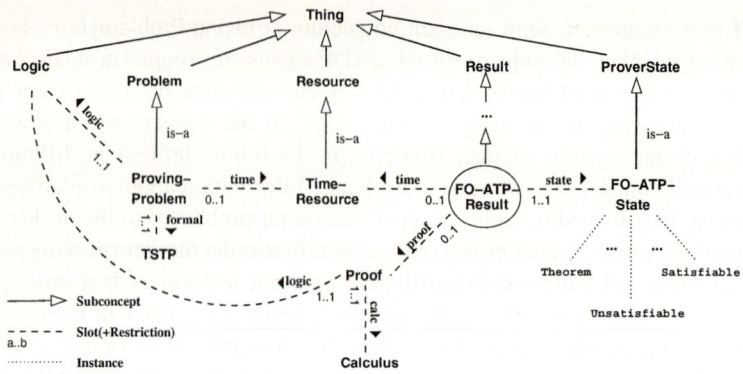

Fig. 2. The fragment of an ontology for reasoning services

to their concepts by dotted lines. Fig. 2 contains some of the concepts needed to describe first-order theorem proving services and their results. One crucial concept for this paper (circled in Fig. 2) is the FO-ATP-Result which denotes results of first-order ATPs. A FO-ATP-Result can have a *time* slot which contains an instance of a time resource description (Time-Resource), and a *proof* of a conjecture (an instance of Proof). Most important, the *state* slot of a FO-ATP-Result always contains one of the valid states of first-order ATPs that we developed jointly with Geoff Sutcliffe and Stephan Schulz [11]. This state defines the prover's result for the conjecture given. For instance, the state Theorem says that the prover has found out that the given conjecture is a theorem of the given axioms.

2.3 Service Descriptions

In our framework, reasoning agents offer services specified in the service description language MSDL. Up to now, we distinguish three different types of services. *Proving and computing services* are services that solve given reasoning problems. Examples include theorem provers that try to prove a given formula, or computer algebra systems that simplify terms or solve differential equations. *Transformation and translation services* are used to change the representation of a problem or a result such as, for instance, the translation of first-order logic problems into clause normal form (CNF), or the transformation of a resolution proof into Natural Deduction calculus [20]. *Classification services* are services that come up with a refined classification of a given problem. Examples are services that, given a proving problem, recognize that the problem is essentially a propositional problem, belongs to the guarded fragment of first-order logic, or consists solely of horn clauses. These characteristics of proving problem are important for the choice of a suitable theorem prover to tackle the problem [16].

The projects *MathBroker* [22] and MONET [7] intend to offer mathematical services, described in MSDL, as web services in the Semantic Web. Although MSDL aims at describing all kinds of mathematical services, the two projects have only investigated the description of symbolic and numeric computation services. We are using our expertise in deduction systems to extend the use of MSDL to deduction services. We started with first-order ATP services because they have been successfully used in many applications [3,4].

An MSDL document describes many different facets of a reasoning service. We briefly describe these facets with an example: the MSDL description of the first-order proving service SpassATP offered by the ATP Agent₁ (shown in Fig. 1). We only present the most important parts of the rather verbose service description. Due to space limitations we abstract from MSDL's XML and present the SpassATP service in a table:

Service: SpassATP	
classification:	`http://www.mathweb.org/proving-services\#F0-ATP`

problem:
  input parameters:
  output parameters:
  pre-conditions:
 	
  post-conditions:
	
	name: $problem$, signature: Proving-Problem
	name: $result$, signature: FO-ATP-Result
	$essentiallyPropositional(problem) \wedge$ (OpenMath)
	$noEquality(problem) \wedge$
	$fofForm(problem)$
	$true$

service interface:	**agent**(_, %client, $problem) =
	  query-if($problem) $\Rightarrow$ **agent**(_, %prover) **then**
	  waitfor inform($result) $\Leftarrow$ **agent**(_, %prover)
	  timeout (e)

implementation details:	Information about hardware, software (implementation)

First, a **classification** of a service is given via a URI[3] which serves as a reference to a problem description library or to an existing taxonomy of services. Then, the service is further classified by the abstract mathematical **problem** it can tackle. The abstract problem solved by the service SpassATP expects only one input: a Proving-Problem as it is described in the ontology in Fig. 2. The output of the service is a FO-ATP-Result. The **pre-conditions** of the service say that the service should be used if the problem is essentially propositional, contains no equality, and it is presented as first-order formulas (as opposed to clause normal form). There are no **post-conditions** on the output of this service.

The **service interface** provides information on how to access the service. MSDL has been designed to describe the semantics of web services. Therefore, the **service interface** typically contains a document written in the Web Service Description Language (WSDL). However, since our agents communicate via FIPA-ACL messages we are experimenting with the use of the MAP language [23] to describe the protocol which guides the invocation of a service. In case of the SpassATP service this protocol simply states that any agent that acts as a client (has the role **%client**) should send a **query-if** message containing the proving problem to the agent providing the service. Then the client has to wait for an **inform** message which contains the result of the proving attempt. The timeout "e" indicates that there is no timeout given.

Finally, the **implementation details** of the service contain information about the underlying reasoning system, the hardware the service is running on, etc.

---

[3] Note that Uniform Resource Identifiers (URI) (as opposed to URLs) do not necessarily point to existing web resources.

3 Example for Advanced Brokering

Currently, our broker is limited to first-order theorem proving problems and it has only basic brokering capabilities. However, we plan to extend our broker to also find sequences of services that might solve a problem, in case a single service is not sufficient. In this section, we describe a scenario in which this advanced form of brokering is needed.

Typically, the user of a proof assistant like ΩMEGA [15] has to tackle many sub-problems occurring in a large proof development. The user may therefore be interested in asking a broker within our reasoning service network to tackle some of these problems. More specifically, we now assume that the subproblem consists of a set of (local) proof assumptions Γ and a conclusion ψ in order-sorted type theory, the logic underlying ΩMEGA. The user or the proof assistant could, for instance, be interested in the following query to a broker:

Query: Given Γ and ψ, determine whether ψ is a logical consequence of Γ in order-sorted type theory. If so, find a Natural Deduction (ND) derivation (proof object) of $\Gamma \vdash \psi$. We denote this query with the sequent $\Gamma \vdash_{HO}^{P(ND)?} \psi$, where $P(ND)?$ means that the user is asking for a proof object in ND calculus.

For our example, we also assume that some reasoning agents have already advertised descriptions of the following reasoning services to the broker:

FO-ATP$_{1,2}$: Classical resolution-based first-order theorem proving services as described in section 2.3.

HO-ATP: A higher-order proving service offered, e.g., by the theorem prover LEO. It takes a Proving-Problem (in type theory) and delivers a proof in ND calculus (HO-ND-Proof).

HO2FO: Transforms, if possible, problems in type theory into first-order logic problems. Such a service is, for instance, implemented in the ΩMEGA system.

FOP2ND: Transforms a first-order resolution proof into a ND proof. This service is, for instance, offered by the TRAMP system [20].

The broker uses the advertised services in his service directory and the service planner to find possible sequences of services that may answer ΩMEGA's query. Fig. 3 shows all promising sequences in a disjunctive tree. The problem might be solved directly by the available higher-order theorem prover. It might also essentially be a first-order problem and is therefore transformable using HO2FO. After this transformation, the problem can be sent to one of the available first-order ATPs. The resulting FO-ATP-Results can be used as input for the service FOP2ND. This service will produce an ND proof in case FO-ATP$_1$ or FO-ATP$_2$ could find a resolution proof.

After plan formation the broker could first try to execute the first branch of a plan. If a service application in this branch fails, the broker should try another branch as an alternative solution path. Disjunctive plans could also be used to model parallel service invocations either to obtain a second, independent result for a problem, or to increase the overall performance of the system.

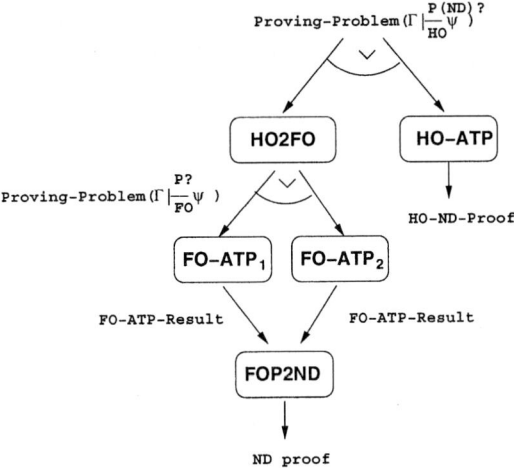

Fig. 3. Possible sequences of service calls to answer the query of ΩMEGA

4   Conclusions and Related Work

We have presented a new framework for reasoning agents that we are developing on top of the JADE agent platform. Our framework is based on formal descriptions of mathematical services and problems in MSDL. Using our new framework we can already overcome some of the problems we faced with the MathWeb Software Bus. So far, we have implemented first-order theorem proving agents and a prototypical broker in JADE. Furthermore, we have developed the ontology needed to describe the services of first-order ATPs in MSDL. We propose the employment of a plan-based brokering mechanism which finds suitable sequences of services to solve a given problem. In the near future, we are going to implement this brokering mechanism. However, we are not yet sure which reasoning technique is most suitable for reasoning on service descriptions. Future case studies in distributed reasoning might require the flexibility of planning techniques similar to proof planning. But it might also be the case that much simpler techniques, such as lookup-tables or production systems, are sufficient.

Furthermore, we might extend our framework by integrating more services, such as transformation tools and proof checkers. We are also going to investigate how much of our work on first-order ATPs can be used to describe higher-order ATPs. We also intend to integrate the work of the *MathBroker* project on symbolic computation services. However, for the integration of computation services with deduction systems (e.g., as described in [5]) a more centralized approach such as in the ΩMEGA system, seems to be more appropriate than the decentralized approach presented here.

Franke and others have already motivated the use of agent-oriented programming and the agent communication language KQML for the integration of distributed mathematical services [24]. However, their ideas have never been realized in an actual system. We think that our work goes further than the ideas presented in [24] for two reasons:

1) The core of our framework will be the brokering of reasoning services described in a formal service description language, and 2) we generally use state of the art Internet and multi-agent standards wherever possible.

A sound combination of deduction systems is particularly difficult because different systems are based on different logics and consequence relations. At the current stage of our project, we are not addressing this problem. However, the above-mentioned LF logical framework might be a suitable meta-logic for our broker.

The *Logic Broker Architecture* (LBA) [25] is a system (quite similar to the Math-Web-SB) which also aims at a sound integration of logic services using a logic service matcher and logic morphisms. The question of how different theorem provers can be easily combined in a single environment has led to the concept of Open Mechanized Reasoning Systems [26]. In OMRS, a mathematical software system is described in three layers: the logic layer, the control layer, and the interaction layer.

The Semantic Web community [27] aims at developing languages and tools for annotating web resources, such as web pages and online services, with semantic markup. The goal is to develop better search engines for the web and registries for web services. The ontology languages OWL and OWL-S are first outcomes of the Semantic Web initiative.

Acknowledgements. Many thanks to Christoph Benzmüller, Serge Autexier, Geoff Sutcliffe, and Paul Libbrecht for their important contributions to this work.

References

1. Homann, K., Calmet, J.: Combining Theorem Proving and Symbolic Mathematical Computing. In Calmet, J., Campbell, J.A., eds.: Integrating Symbolic Mathematical Computation and Artificial Intelligence; Proc. of the second International Conference;. Volume 958 of LNCS., Springer Verlag (1995) 18–29
2. Harrison, J., Théry, L.: A Skeptic's Approach to Combining HOL and Maple. Journal of Automated Reasoning **21** (1998) 279–294
3. Zimmer, J., Kohlhase, M.: System Description: The Mathweb Software Bus for Distributed Mathematical Reasoning. [28] 139–143
4. Zimmer, J., Franke, A., Colton, S., Sutcliffe, G.: Integrating HR and tptp2x into Mathweb to Compare Automated Theorem Provers. In: Proc. of PaPS'02 Workshop. DIKU Technical Report 02-10. Department of Computer Science, University of Copenhagen (2002) 4–18
5. Melis, E., Zimmer, J., Müller, T.: Integrating Constraint Solving into Proof Planning. In Kirchner, H., Ringeissen, C., eds.: Frontiers of Combining Systems – Third International Workshop. Volume 1794 of LNAI., Springer (2000) 32–46
6. Dewar, M., Carlisle, D., Caprotti, O.: Description Schemes For Mathematical Web Services. In: Proc. of EuroWeb 2002 Conference: The Web and the GRID, St Anne's College Oxford, British Computer Society Electronic Workshops in Computing (eWiC) (2002)
7. Consortium, T.M.: The MONET Project. http://monet.nag.co.uk/cocoon/monet/index.html (2002)
8. Fipa: The Foundation for Itelligent Physical Agents Specifications. http://www.fipa.org/ (2003)
9. Caprotti, O., Cohen, A.M.: Draft of the Open Math standard. The Open Math Society, http://www.nag.co.uk/projects/OpenMath/omstd/ (1998)

10. Kohlhase, M.: OMDoc: Towards an Internet Standard for the Administration, Distribution and Teaching of mathematical knowledge. In: Proc. AISC'2000. (2000)
11. Sutcliffe, G., Zimmer, J., Schulz, S.: Communcation Formalisms for Automated Theorem Proving Tools. In Sorge, V., Colton, S., Fisher, M., Gow, J., eds.: Proc. of the Workshop on Agents and Automated Reasoning, 18th International Joint Conference on Artificial Intelligence. (2003)
12. Smith, M.K., Welty, C., McGuinness, D.L.: Web Ontology Language (2003) Available at http://www.w3.org/TR/owl-guide/.
13. Zimmer, J.: A New Framework for Reasoning Agents. In Sorge, V., Colton, S., Fisher, M., Gow, J., eds.: Proc. of the Workshop on Agents and Automated Reasoning, 18th International Joint Conference on Artificial Intelligence. (2003)
14. Telecom Italia Lab: Java Agent DEvelopment Framework (JADE). Available at http://sharon.cselt.it/projects/jade/ (2003)
15. Siekmann, J., et al.: Proof Development with ΩMEGA. [28] 144–149
16. Sutcliffe, G., Suttner, C.: Evaluating General Purpose Automated Theorem Proving Systems. Artificial Intelligence **131** (2001) 39–54
17. Denti, E., Omicini, A., Ricci, A.: tuprolog: A light-weight prolog for internet applications and infrastructures. In Ramakrishnan, I., ed.: Practical Aspects of Declarative Languages (PADL'01). Number 869 in LNCS (2001)
18. Polya, G.: How to Solve it. Princeton University Press, Princeton, NJ (1945)
19. Pfenning, F., Schürmann, C.: System description: Twelf - a meta-logical framework for deductive systems. In: Proc. of the 16th International Conference on Automated Deduction. Number 1632 in LNAI, Springer (1999) 202–206
20. Meier, A.: System description: TRAMP: Transformation of machine-found proofs into ND-proofs at the assertion level. In McAllester, D., ed.: Automated Deduction – CADE-17. Number 1831 in LNAI, Springer Verlag (2000) 460–464
21. Noy, N.F., Sintek, M., Decker, S., Crubezy, M., Fergerson, R.W., Musen, M.A.: Creating Semantic Web Contents with Protege-2000. IEEE Intelligent Systems **2** (2001) 60–71
22. Schreiner, W., Caprotti, O.: The MathBroker Project. http://poseidon.risc.uni-linz.ac.at:8080/index.html (2001)
23. Walton, C.: Multi-Agent Dialogue Protocols. In: Proc. of the Eighth International Symposium on Artificial Intelligence and Mathematics, Fort Lauderdale, Florida (2004)
24. Franke, A., Hess, S.M., Jung, C.G., Kohlhase, M., Sorge, V.: Agent-oriented Integration of Distributed Mathematical Services. J. of Universal Computer Science **5** (1999) 156–187
25. Armando, A., Zini, D.: Towards Interoperable Mechanized Reasoning Systems: the Logic Broker Architecture. In Poggi, A., ed.: Proc. of the AI*IA-TABOO Joint Workshop 'From Objects to Agents: Evolutionary Trends of Software Systems', Parma, Italy (2000)
26. Giunchiglia, F., Pecchiari, P., Talcott, C.: Reasoning Theories – Towards an Architecture for Open Mechanized Reasoning Systems. In Baader, F., Schulz, K., eds.: Frontiers of Combining Systems. Volume 3 of Applied logic series., Kluwer, Netherlands (1996) 157–174
27. Berners-Lee, T., Hendler, J., Lassila, O.: The Semantic Web. Scientific American **284(5)** (2001) 34–43
28. Voronkov, A., ed.: Proc. of the 18th International Conference on Automated Deduction. Number 2392 in LNAI, Springer Verlag (2002)

Faster Proximity Searching in Metric Data[*]

Edgar Chávez[1] and Karina Figueroa[1,2]

[1] Universidad Michoacana, México.
{elchavez,karina}@fismat.umich.mx
[2] DCC Universidad de Chile, Chile

Abstract. A number of problems in computer science can be solved efficiently with the so called *memory based* or *kernel* methods. Among this problems (relevant to the AI community) are multimedia indexing, clustering, non supervised learning and recommendation systems. The common ground to this problems is satisfying proximity queries with an abstract metric database.

In this paper we introduce a new technique for making practical indexes for metric range queries. This technique improves existing algorithm based on pivots and signatures, and introduce a new data structure, the *Fixed Queries Trie* to speedup metric range queries. The result is an $O(n)$ construction time index, with query complexity $O(n^\alpha), \alpha \leq 1$. The indexing algorithm uses only a few bits of storage for each database element.

1 Introduction and Related Work

Proximity queries are those extensions of the exact searching where we want to retrieve objects from a database that are *close* to a given query object. The query object is not necessarily a database element. The concept can be formalized using the metric space model, where a distance function $d(x, y)$ is defined for every site in a set $\mathbb{X}$. The distance function d has *metric* properties, i.e. it satisfies $d(x, y) \geq 0$ (positiveness), $d(x, y) = d(y, x)$ (symmetry), $d(x, y) = 0$ iff $x = y$ (strict positiveness), and the property allowing the existence of solutions better than brute-force for similarity queries: $d(x, y) \leq d(x, z) + d(z, y)$ (triangle inequality).

The database is a set $\mathbb{U} \subseteq \mathbb{X}$, and we define the query element as q, an arbitrary element of $\mathbb{X}$. A similarity query involves additional information, besides q, and can be of two basic types of proximity queries: $(q, r)_d = \{u \in \mathbb{U} : d(q, u) \leq r\}$. *Metric Range* queries and $nn_k(q)_d = \{u_i \in \mathbb{U} : \forall v \in \mathbb{U}, d(q, u_i) \leq d(q, v)$ *and* $|\{u_i\}| = k\}$. *K nearest neighbor* query.

The problem have received a lot of attention in recent times, due to an increasing interest in indexing multimedia data coming from the web. For a detailed description of recent trends in the also called *distance based indexing* the reader should see [6]. If the objects are vectors (with coordinates), then a recent kd-tree improvement can be used [7], we are interested in the rather more general case of non-vectorial data.

---

[*] Partially supported by CONACyT grant R-36911A and CYTED VII.19 RIBIDI.

R. Monroy et al. (Eds.): MICAI 2004, LNAI 2972, pp. 222–231, 2004.

1.1   Related Work

There are two basic paradigms for distance based indexing, pivot-based algorithms and local partition algorithms, as described in [6], there the authors state the general idea for *local partition algorithms* which is to build a locality-preserving hierarchy, and then to map the hierarchy levels to a tree. *Pivoting algorithms*, on the other hand, are based on a mapping to a vector space using the distance to a set of distinguished sites in the metric space. Since our algorithm is also pivot-based we concentrate on this family of algorithms.

An abstract view of a pivot based algorithm is as follows. We select a set of l pivots $\{p_1, \ldots, p_l\}$. At indexing time, for each database element a, we compute and store $\Phi(a) = (d(a, p_1)...d(a, p_l))$. At query time, for a query $(q, r)_d$, we compute $\Phi(q) = (d(q, p_1)...d(q, p_l))$. Now, we can discard every $a \in \mathbb{U}$ such that, for some pivot p_i, $|d(q, p_i) - d(a, p_i)| > r$, or which is the same, we discard every a such that

$$\max_{1 \leq i \leq l} |d(q, p_i) - d(a, p_i)| \ = \ L_\infty(\Phi(a), \Phi(q)) \ > \ r \ .$$

The underlying idea of pivot based algorithms is to project the original metric space into a vector space with a contractive mapping. We search in the new space with the same radius r, which guarantees that no answer will be missed. There is, however, the chance of selecting elements that should not be in the query outcome. This false positives are filtered using the original distance. The more pivots used, the more accurate is the mapping and the number of distance computations is closer to the number of elements in the query ball. The differences between each indexing algorithm is how is implemented the search in the mapped space. A naive solution is to search exhaustively in the mapped space[9], or to use a generic spatial access method like the R-tree[8]. Both of this solutions are acceptable if the dimension of the mapped space is maintained low, but can be worse if the dimension of the mapped space is high.

A natural choice for measuring the complexity of a proximity query in metric spaces is the number of distance computations, since this operation has leading complexity. The distance computations are in turn divided in inner and outer complexity, the later is the size of the candidate list and the former the distances to the pivots. A more realistic setup must include what is called *side computations* or the cost of searching in the tree (or data structure in general) to collect the list of candidates.

Some of the pivoting algorithms[2,4,10] have no control on the number of pivots used. If we want to have an effective control in reducing the size of the candidate list we must have arbitrarily taller trees, or a fixed number of pivots in the mapping. This is the approach of the Fixed Height Fixed Queries Trees (FHQT) [1], where the height of the tree is precisely the number of pivots, or the dimension of the mapped space. A serious drawback of the FHQT is the amount of memory used, because even if a branch in the tree collapses to a single path for each additional node we must save the distance and some additional node information.

Actual instances of datasets show that the optimum number of pivots (balancing the external and internal complexity) cannot be reached in practice. For example, when indexing a dictionary of 1,000,000 English words we can use as much as 512 pivots without increasing the number of distance computations.

The Fixed Queries Array [5] showed a dramatic improvement (lowering) on the size of the index induced by completely eliminating the tree, and working only with an ordered array representing the tree. In this approach every tree traversal can be simulated using binary search, hence adding a $\log n$ penalty in the side computations but notably decreasing the *external complexity* or the size of the candidate list.

In this paper we will show a further improvement on the FQA algorithm, eliminating the logarithmic factor in the searching. This will be done by designing a way to manipulate whole computer words, instead of fetching bytes inside them.

1.2   Basic Terminology

The set of pivots $\mathbb{K} = \{p_1, \cdots, p_k\}$ is a subset of the metric space $\mathbb{X}$.

A discretization rule is an injective function $\delta_p : \mathbb{R}^+ \times \mathbb{K} \rightarrow \{0, \cdots, 2^{b_p} - 1\}$ mapping positive real numbers into 2^{b_p} discrete values. The discretization rule depends on the particular pivot p. The preimage of the function defines a partition of $\mathbb{R}^+$. We assume $\delta_p(r)$ will deliver a binary string of size b. Defining the discretization rule as pivot-depending allows to emphasize the importance of a particular pivot. For simplicity the same rule may be applied to all the pivots.

A signature function for objects will be a mapping $\delta^* : \mathbb{X} \rightarrow \{0, 1\}^m$ with $m = \sum_{i=1}^{k} b_{p_i}$, given by the rule $\delta^*(o) = \delta_{p_1}(d(o, p_1)) \cdots \delta_{p_k}(d(o, p_k))$.

An infinite number of discretization rules may be defined for b bytes. Some of them will lead to better filtering methods and some of them will not filter at all. The definition of the discretization rule is not essential for the *correctness* of the filtering method, but for its efficiency. We can generalize the signature function for intervals, in the same way a function is extended from points to sets.

A discretization rule for intervals is denoted $\delta_p([r_1, r_2]) = \{\delta_p(r) | r \in [r_1, r_2]\}$. Formally δ_p is defined for positive real numbers. This definition may be extended to the domain of real values, assuming $\delta([r_1, r_2]) = \delta([0, r_2])$ if $r_1 < 0$.

A signature function for queries will be a function $\delta^* : \mathbb{X} \times \mathbb{R}^+ \rightarrow 2^{(\{0,1\}^m)}$, mapping queries $(q, r)_d$ into a signature set. The signature of a query will be given by the following expression

$$\delta^*((q, r)_d) = \{\delta_{p_1}([d(q, p_1) - r, d(q, p_1) + r])\} \tag{1}$$
$$\{\delta_{p_2}([d(q, p_2) - r, d(q, p_2) + r])\} \cdots \tag{2}$$
$$\{\delta_{p_k}([d(q, p_k) - r, d(q, p_k) + r])\} \tag{3}$$

which is *any* ordered concatenation of the signature sets for the corresponding intervals in each pivot.

Claim 1. If an object $o \in \mathbb{X}$ satisfies a query $(q, r)_d$, then $\delta^*(o) \in \delta^*((q, r)_d)$.

To prove the above claim, it is enough to observe that $\delta^*((q, r)_d))$ is an extension of $\delta^*(\cdot)$, and hence $o \in (q, r)_d$ implies $\delta^*(o) \in \delta^*((q, r)_d)$.

The candidate list is the set $[q, r]_d = \{o | \delta^*(o) \in \delta^*((q, r)_d)\}$. Note that the candidate list is a superset of the query outcome, in other words, $(q, r)_d \subseteq [q, r]_d$.

Remark 1. Computing the candidate list $[q, r]_d$ implies only a constant number of distance evaluations, namely the number of pivots.

Remark 2. The candidate list asymptotically approaches the size of the query outcome, as the number of pivots increases. This fact has been proved in [6] but it is easily verified, observing that $(q, r)_d \subseteq [q, r]_d$ and that increasing the number of pivots never increases the size of $[q, r]_d$. For any finite sample $\mathbb{U}$ of $\mathbb{X}$, if we take all the elements of $\mathbb{U}$ as pivots, then $(q, r)_d = [q, r]_d$ provided $(q, r)_d \subseteq \mathbb{U}$. This proves the assertion.

Remark 3. Increasing the number of pivots increases the number of distance evaluations in computing $\delta^*((q, r)_d)$. This is trivially true, since computing $\delta^*(\cdot)$ implies k distance computations. If we take as pivots all of $\mathbb{U}$, then we are changing one exhaustive search for another.

2   The Index

The goal of an indexing algorithm is to obtain the set $(q, r)_d$ using as few distance computations as possible. The indexing algorithm consist in preprocessing the data set (a finite sample $\mathbb{U}$ of the metric space $\mathbb{X}$) to speed up the querying process. Let us define some additional notation to formally describe the problem and the proposed solution.

The index of $\mathbb{U}$ denoted as $\mathbb{U}^*$ is the set of all signatures of elements of $\mathbb{U}$. $\mathbb{U}^* = \delta^*(\mathbb{U}) = \{\delta^*(o) | o \in \mathbb{U}\}$.

Remark 4. $|\mathbb{U}^*| \leq |\mathbb{U}|$. The repeated signatures are factored out and all the matching objects are allocated in the same bucket.

With this notation $[q, r]_d$ may be computed as $[q, r]_d = \delta^*(\mathbb{U}) \cap \delta^*((q, r)_d)$. To satisfy a query we exhaustively search over $[q, r]_d$ to discard false positives. The complete algorithm is described in figure 1.

We assume a blind use of $\delta_p(\cdot)$, the discretization function (optimizing $\delta_p(\cdot)$ has been studied empirically in [5]), since we are interested in a fast computation of $[q, r]_d$. Nevertheless a fair choice is to divide the interval of minimum to maximum distances in 2^b equally spaced slices.

2.1   Lookup Tables

The core of the searching problem with signatures consist in computing $[q, r]_d$. Observe that there are exponentially many elements in $\delta^*((q, r)_d)$. The signatures are obtained as an ordered concatenation of signatures for each pivot. If each pivot produces ν_{p_i} signatures for its range, then we will have up to $\Pi_{i=1}^{k} \nu_{p_i}$ signatures. For example, for 32 pivots generating as few as 2 signatures for a query, the number of signatures is 2^{32}. Instead we can split each signature in t computer words. A query signature may be represented as t arrays with at most 2^w elements. A signature $a_1 \cdots a_m$ $a_i \in \{0, 1\}$ is splitted in t binary strings of size

---

Generic Metric Range Search
$(\mathbb{X}, d)$ the metric space, $\mathbb{U}$ is a database (a sample of $\mathbb{X}$) of size n
$\mathbb{K} = \{p_1, \cdots, p_k\}$ is the set of pivots. $k = |\mathbb{K}|$, b_{p_i} the number of
bits for each pivot $\delta(\cdot)$ the discretization rule, $q \in \mathbb{X}$ the query object
Startup: $(\mathbb{U}, \mathbb{K}, \{b_{p_i}\}, \delta(\cdot))$
   1.   Compute $\mathbb{U}^*$
Search: (q, r)
  2.   Compute $[q, r]_d$
        for each $o \in [q, r]_d$ do
            if $d(q, o) \leq r$
                $(q, r)_d \leftarrow o$
       fi
    od

Fig. 1. A generic indexing algorithm based on signatures. The index is $\mathbb{U}^*$, the objective is to compute $(q, r)_d$ given q and r.

w of the form $A_1 \cdots A_t$ with A_i computer words. Each A_i is called a coordinate of a signature. A query signature will be represented as t sets of coordinates.
A lookup table for query signatures is an array $L_j[]$ of 2^w booleans, $1 \leq j \leq t$. $L_j[i] = true$ if and only if i appears in the j-th set of coordinates. Note that computing $L_j[]$ can be done in constant time (at most 2^w).
Remark 5. We can decide if a particular signature is in the signature of the query by evaluating the boolean AND expression $L_j[A_1] \otimes \cdots \otimes L_j[A_t]$, which takes at most t table fetches for an evaluation, on the average we may use fewer than t operations.

2.2   Sequential Scan

Remark 5 leads to a direct improvement of the sequential scan (FQS). We will compare the straight sequential scan with two better alternatives. If the query $(q, r)_d$ has low selectivity the size of the candidate list $[q, r]_d$ will be very large. An clever (sublinear) algorithm for finding the candidate list will be time consuming. Figure 2 illustrates the procedure to obtain the candidate list.

2.3   The Fixed Queries Array with Lookup Tables

The Fixed Queries Array (FQA) was proposed in [5] to increase the filtering power of a pivoting algorithm. Unlike sequential scan the approach is sublinear. The general idea of FQA is to keep an ordered array of the signatures. For the first pivot the query signature will be an interval in the array of signatures. This interval may be found using binary search with an appropriate mask. The process in repeated recursively for the successive pivots, which will appear as sub-intervals. The FQA may be improved using the lookup tables, allowing whole word comparisons (which is faster than fetching many times a few bits inside).

```
Compute [q, r]_d using Sequential Scan (FQS)
U* is the signature set n, L_j[] is the lookup table for the query (q, r)_d
  1.    Compute [q, r]_d
        for each signature s = A_1 ··· A_t ∈ U* do
            for j=1 to t do
                if not L_j[A_j]
                    next s
                fi
            od
            [q, r]_d ← Object(s)
        od
```

Fig. 2. A sequential scan to compute $[q, r]_d$. The complexity is linear on the size of the database $\mathbb{U}$. If the query has low selectivity the sequential scan beats a clever (sublinear) approach.

Given a query $(q, r)_d$, the **signature vector** for the i-th coordinate will be denoted as $A_i[]$. Figure 3 describes the recursive procedure to compute $[q, r]_d$. The FQA implementation with lookup tables is faster in practice than the plain algorithm in [5], and has the same theoretical $O(\log(n))$ penalty.

```
Compute [q, r]_d using FQA
U* is the signature set n, which is ordered by coordinates.
{A_i[]} are the signature vectors of query (q, r)_d
Compute [q, r]_d
  1.    function FQA(int j, V*)
            if j=t then
                for each A ∈ A_t[] do
                    [q, r]_d ← Object(Select(V, A, t))
                od
                return
            fi
            for each A ∈ A_j[] do
                FQA(j+1,Select(V, A, j))
            od
```

Fig. 3. Computing $[q, r]_d$ using a recursive binary search. The function **Select**(V, A, j) obtains the signatures in $\mathbb{V}$ whose j-th coordinate matches A. It may be implemented in logarithmic time if $\mathbb{V}$ is ordered, which takes no extra memory, but a $n \log(n)$ penalty for signature ordering.

2.4   The Fixed Queries Trie

Since we are using the signatures as strings, and want to find matching strings we have a plethora of data structures and algorithms from the string pattern matching community. Among them we selected a *trie* to index the signatures set $\mathbb{U}^*$. We will denote this trie as Fixed Queries Trie or *FQh*, the lowercase to distinguish between the trie and the tree (the Fixed Queries Tree) FQT described in [2].

Building the FHQt is even faster than building the FQA, the reason is that we don't need to use a sort, inserting each site's signature is done in time proportional to the signature length. The construction complexity, measured in distance computations, is then $O(n)$ (as the FQA). Nevertheless the side computations for the construction is $O(n)$ instead of $O(n \log n)$.

A trie is an m-ary tree with non-data nodes (routing only) and all the data at the leafs [3]. Searching for any string takes time proportional to the string size, independent of the database size. For our purposes the basic searching algorithm is modified to allow multiple string searching, and we make heavy use of the lookup table for routing. Our string set will be represented as a lookup table, this lead to a slightly different rule for following a node. Instead of following a node matching the i-th character of the string (i the trie level) we will follow the node if *any* coordinate in the set matches the node label. In other words, we will follow the node if the lookup table is *true* for the corresponding node and level.

The number of operations for this search will be proportional to the number of successful searches, or the number of leafs visited, times the length of the strings. In other words the complexity will be $O(|[q, r]_d| t)$. This represent a $\log(n)$ factor, with respect to the FQA implementation.

The space requirements for the FQt may be smaller than that of FQA. The number of paths in the FQt is the number of elements in the signature array, but the trie will factor out matching coordinates and will use additional memory for pointers. The net result is that the trie will use *about* the same amount of memory, is built faster and uses less time for matching queries.

3   Experimental Results

The FHQt is exactly equivalent to the FQA and the FQS, from the point of view of selectivity, internal and external complexity. The same parametric decisions can be made using exactly the same analysis. We remark that the only difference is in the amount of extra work to find the candidate list. In that view we only will make an experimental validation of the algorithms improved with lookup tables, and hence will compare only the *side computations* and in a single experiment will compare the overall complexity. A more complete experimental study of the algorithm will be reported with the final version of this paper.

The three algorithms were implemented using lookup tables. The algorithms are only compared themselves, since it has been proved that FQA's may beat any indexing algorithm just by using more pivots. This is also true for FQt an

---

Compute $[q,r]_d$ **using FQt**
$\mathbb{U}^*$ is the signature set n, which is arranged in a trie. $\{L_i[]\}$
are the lookup tables of the query $(q,r)_d$ Each node of the trie is labeled
after a coordinate U
Compute $[q,r]_d$
  1.   function **FQt**(**node** U, i)
          if i *geq* t then
             if $L_t[U]$ then
                $[q,r]_d \leftarrow$ Object(U.signature)
                return
             fi
          for each $U - > node$ do
             if $L_i[U]$ then
                FQt($U - > node, i+1$)
             fi
          od

Fig. 4. Computing $[q,r]_d$ using a trie. The trie is faster than the FQA because the recursion is done without searching.

FQS, hence the interest is between the three surviving alternatives. The previous implementations of the FQA (using bit masks) are beaten by the lookup table implementation by a large factor.

    Ee indexed a vocabulary of the English dictionary, obtained from the TREC collection of the Wall Street Journal under the edit distance. This is a known difficult example of proximity searching, with high intrinsic dimension, as described in [6]. Figure 5 shows the overall time needed to compute a query of radius 1 and 2. Each point in the plots, for each experiment, were obtained by averaging 200 queries in the database. It can be noticed that as the query becomes less selective, the overall time of the algorithms FQA, FQS and FQS becomes practically the same. This is explained because the three algorithms have the same filtering power and the time to compute the candidate list makes a tiny difference. Figure 6 (top) shows the differences between the three filtering algorithms, at the left the overall time, and at the right only the time for filtering. Figure 6 (bottom) shows the performance of the indexes for medium and low selectivity queries (with radius one and two respectively). The time plotted is only the filtering time, since the number of distance computations will be the same for all of them. The lookup tables are computed for the three algorithms, the construction is slightly more costly for fewer bits.

4   Final Remarks

Pivoting algorithms have proved to be very efficient and sound for proximity searching. They have two control parameters, the number of pivots and the number of bits in the representation. Using lookup tables to implement the

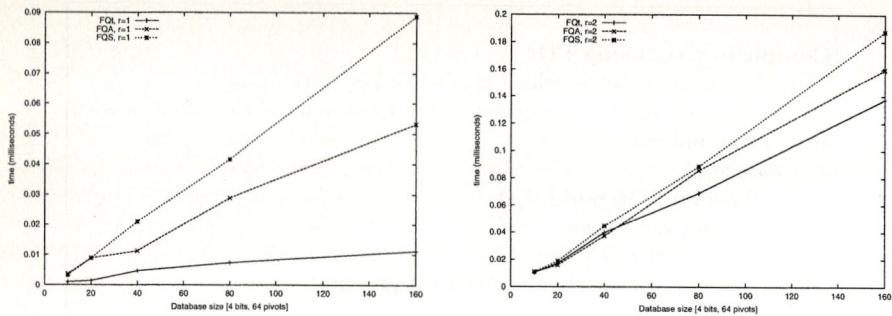

Fig. 5. The overall time needed to satisfy a queries of radius one (left) and two (right). The database is a sample of vocabulary of the TREC WSJ collection, under the edit distance.

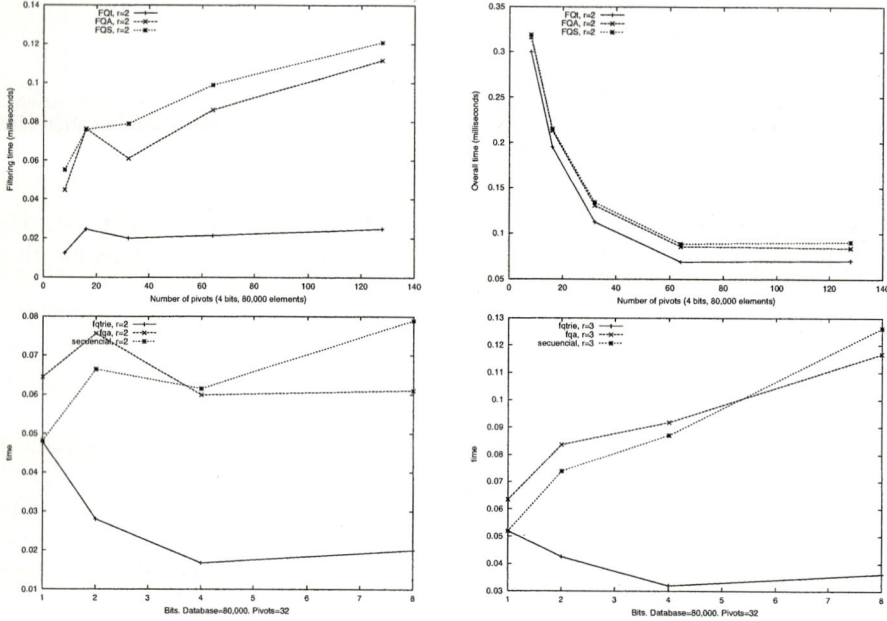

Fig. 6. (TOP) If we increase the number of pivots the time to obtain the candidate list is increased. The FQA and the FQS will use about the same time (about linear) for low selectivity queries, while the FQt increases very slowly. (BOTTOM)The role of the number of bits in the filtering time. For a fixed number of pivots, and a fixed database size.

three alternatives presented in this paper gives a faster filtering stage. We also saw a strictly decreasing overall time for a particularly difficult example. The experimental evidence and the analysis allows to favor the use of the FQt over the FQA or FQS in most realistic environments. Additionally the FQA and FQS don't accept insertion or deletions, unlike the FQh where insertion or deletions (of non-pivot objects) can be carried out trivially.

References

1. R. Baeza-Yates. Searching: an algorithmic tour. In A. Kent and J. Williams, editors, *Encyclopedia of Computer Science and Technology*, volume 37, pages 331–359. Marcel Dekker Inc., 1997.
2. R. Baeza-Yates, W. Cunto, U. Manber, and S. Wu. Proximity matching using fixed-queries trees. In *Proc. 5th Combinatorial Pattern Matching (CPM'94)*, LNCS 807, pages 198–212, 1994.
3. R. Baeza-Yates and B. Ribeiro-Neto. *Modern Information Retrieval*. Addison-Wesley, 1999.
4. W. Burkhard and R. Keller. Some approaches to best-match file searching. *Comm. of the ACM*, 16(4):230–236, 1973.
5. Edgar Chávez, José Luis Marroquín, and Gonzalo Navarro. Fixed queries array: A fast and economical data structure for proximity searching. *Multimedia Tools and Applications (MTAP)*, 14(2):113–135, 2001.
6. Edgar Chávez, Gonzalo Navarro, Ricardo Baeza-Yates, and José Luis Marroquín. Proximity searching in metric spaces. *ACM Computing Surveys*, 33(3):273–321, September 2001.
7. Mark Derthick, James Harrison, Andrew Moore, and Steven Roth. Efficient multi-object dynamic query histograms. In *Proceedings of the IEEE Symposium on Information Visualization*, pages 84–91. IEEE Press, 1999.
8. A. Guttman. R-trees: a dynamic index structure for spatial searching. In *Proc. ACM SIGMOD International Conference on Management of Data*, pages 47–57, 1984.
9. L. Micó, J. Oncina, and E. Vidal. A new version of the nearest-neighbor approximating and eliminating search (AESA) with linear preprocessing-time and memory requirements. *Pattern Recognition Letters*, 15:9–17, 1994.
10. P. Yianilos. Data structures and algorithms for nearest neighbor search in general metric spaces. In *Proc. 4th ACM-SIAM Symposium on Discrete Algorithms (SODA'93)*, pages 311–321, 1993.

Data Mining with Decision Trees and Neural Networks for Calcification Detection in Mammograms

Beatriz A. Flores and Jesus A. Gonzalez

National Institute of Astrophysics, Optics and Electronics
Luis Enrique Erro #1
Tonantzintla, Puebla, Mexico
baflores@ccc.inaoep.mx, jagonzalez@inaoep.mx

Abstract. One of the best prevention measures against breast cancer is the early detection of calcifications through mammograms. Detecting calcifications in mammograms is a difficult task because of their size and the high content of similar patterns in the image. This brings the necessity of creating automatic tools to find whether a mammogram presents calcifications or not. In this paper we introduce the combination of machine vision and data-mining techniques to detect calcifications (including micro-calcifications) in mammograms that achieves an accuracy of 92.6 % with decision trees and 94.3 % with a back-propagation neural network. We also focus in the data-mining task with decision trees to generate descriptive patterns based on a set of characteristics selected by our domain expert. We found that these patterns can be used to support the radiologist to confirm his diagnosis or to detect micro-calcifications that he could not see because of their reduced size.

1 Introduction

Breast cancer is the second cause of death in women with cancer after cervical-uterine cancer; this is why breast cancer is considered a public health problem. Statistical data from INEGI shows that in 2001, breast cancer was the 12th cause of death for Mexican women with 3,574 deaths.

Early diagnosis of breast cancer is the best-known solution for the problem [5]. The level of affection of cancer is related to the size of the tumor. In the case of small patterns (not palpable), we need another reference such as a mammogram. With the use of mammograms, the mortality caused by breast cancer has decreased in a 30% [9].

A mammogram study consists of a set of four images, two craniocaudal and two lateral images. The radiologist has to look in the images for calcifications and make a diagnosis that is consistent with the images. This is a difficult task that only trained experts can do with high confidence. Even when an expert makes the diagnosis, there are factors that may affect his decision such as tiredness. One way to make this process more objective consists on creating an automatic way to detect calcifications in a mammogram to give the radiologist a second opinion. In this way, the automatic system may confirm the radiologist's diagnosis or may suggest that a suspicious area in the mammogram can be a calcification. The automatic method presented in this paper is based on the combination of machine vision and data mining technologies

R. Monroy et al. (Eds.): MICAI 2004, LNAI 2972, pp. 232–241, 2004.

and can be used to create an automatic system to provide a second opinion for the diagnosis of the radiologist.

A lot of efforts have been done to solve this problem. In [11], the authors use a Bayesian network to find and classify regions of interest. In this research they use a segmentation algorithm based on wavelet transforms and the use of a threshold that corresponds to the local minimum of the image. In [1], the authors use data mining techniques to detect and classify anomalies in the breast. They use neural networks and association rules as the data mining algorithms. They also use a histogram equalization process to enhance the image contrast, and then they perform a feature extraction process and include those features combined with patients' information (such as age of the patient) for the classification task. Their results were of 82.248 % with neural networks and 69.11 % with association rules. In [3], the authors present a method for feature extraction of lesions in mammograms using an edge based segmentation algorithm. In [8], we find an evaluation of different methods that can be used to get texture features from regions of interest (calcifications) extracted from mammogram images. In [10], we can see how the wavelet transformation has been used to detect groups of micro-calcifications in digital mammograms. In this paper, the authors only use the wavelet transformation to detect those groups of micro-calcifications without the help of any other algorithm.

Through this paper, we will present our method starting in section 2 with a brief description of the mammograms database that we used for our experiments. In section 3 we introduce our methodology with all its components. In section 4 we present our experiments and results and finally, in section 5 we show our conclusions and future work.

2   Mammograms Database

For our experiments we are creating a mammograms database in coordination with our domain expert, Dr. Nidia Higuero, a radiologist from the ISSSTEP hospital. Until now we have a set of 84 cases of mammograms (one case per patient), each case contains four images, one craniocaudal and one oblique view of each breast. The images were digitized with an Epson Expression 1680 fire-wire scanner at 400 dpi's, with a size of 2,500 x 2,500 pixels in bmp format. From the 84 cases, 54 have calcifications and 30 are normal (with no calcifications). Figure 1a shows an example of a mammogram of a healthy breast and figure 1b shows a magnified area of a mammogram with calcifications (the bright areas in figure 1b correspond to calcifications). Detecting a calcification is a difficult task because calcifications can

a) 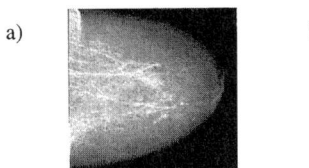   b)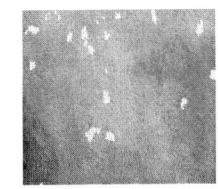

Fig. 1. Mammogram Images. a) Image of a healthy breast, b) Magnified area of a mammogram with calcifications

be very similar to other areas of the image (this is not the case of figure 1b where we chose a region where calcifications could be easily identified). Our domain expert selected the set of cases and gave them to us for scanning. After the images were digitized, Dr. Higuero put marks to those images with calcifications in the places where those were found; we will refer to these marked images as positive mammograms. We needed these marked images for training purposes, as we will mention in the methodology section.

3 Methodology

The combination of machine vision and data mining techniques to find calcifications in mammograms is shown in figure 2. Figure 2a shows the knowledge discovery in databases (KDD) process that we use to find patterns that describe calcifications from known images (those images for which we know if they contain calcifications or not). The process starts with the image database that consists of the original and marked mammograms. As we mentioned before, marked mammograms identify where calcifications are located in a positive mammogram. An image preparation process is applied to these images to make calcifications easier to detect. After this, a segmentation algorithm is applied to each positive image in order to get our positive Regions Of Interest (ROI's) corresponding to calcifications. A different segmentation algorithm is used to get our negative ROI's, that is; regions of interest of areas that are very similar to calcifications but that are not. After this step we have a ROI's database where each ROI is classified as positive or negative. Next, we apply a feature extraction process to each region of interest to create a feature database that will be used to train the data mining algorithms. In our case we use a back-propagation neural network and a decision tree for the data-mining step. After applying the data-mining algorithm, we get patterns to be evaluated in the pattern evaluation step. In the case of

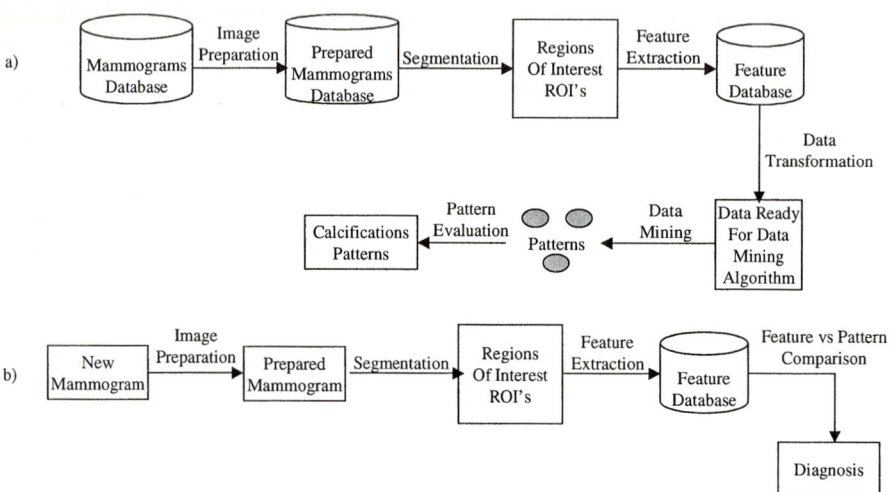

Fig. 2. KDD Process Applied to Find Calcifications in Mammograms. a) Training Phase, b) Diagnosis Phase

the decision trees, our patterns are human understandable as we will show in the data mining section but the patterns found with the neural network are difficult to interpret because they are hidden in the neural network weights and architecture. The patterns found in the training phase will be used in the diagnosis phase shown in figure 2b. The diagnosis starts with the image to be analyzed. We first perform the image preparation filter and then use a segmentation algorithm to find our ROI's (in this case we do not have a marked image) that correspond to possible calcifications. Once we have our ROI's, we execute the feature extraction algorithm to get our feature database, where a feature vector represents each ROI. In the next step, we compare each ROI (represented by its feature vector) with the patterns found in the training phase and if the ROI matches any of the positive patterns we diagnose that ROI as positive or a calcification and as negative otherwise. In the following sections we give more detail about each of the steps shown in figure 2. In section 3.1 we describe the image processing steps and in section 3.2 we describe the data mining algorithms used.

3.1 Image Processing

In order to find patterns that distinguish a calcification from other tissues, we need to get examples of those parts of the image that correspond to calcifications and also examples of parts of images that look like calcifications but that are not. We call these parts of images regions of interest (ROI). In order to make more effective the ROI´s identification we need to include a noise reduction process that is achieved with the wavelet transformation [10, 11]. Once we found our ROI's, we extract characteristics (or features) that will be used as a representation of the ROI's for the data mining algorithms. Section 3.1.1 describes the algorithm used to find regions of interest and section 3.1.2 describes the features that are extracted from each ROI.

Regions of Interest. Finding ROI's in a mammogram is a difficult task because of the low contrast with other regions and the differences in types of tissues. ROI's in the training phase are found using the segmentation algorithm shown in figure 3. The algorithm receives as input the set of original images and the set of marked images. As we mentioned in section 2, the set of marked images corresponds to the images where our domain expert marked the calcifications that she found. In line 2 of the algorithm, we initialize the ROIS variable to be the empty set. In lines 4 and 5 we apply the symmlet wavelet transformation to each pair of original and marked images in order to stress the places where a calcification might be found and to make a more defined background. In lines 6 to 9, we find the position of the area of each marked calcification and get the region of interest from the original image for that position and keep storing each ROI in the ROIS variable until we have processed every pair of images. Once we generated the complete set of regions of interest, we are ready for the feature extraction process explained in the following section.

The algorithm used to find negative ROI's and also to find ROI's in new images differs from the algorithm in figure 3 because there are not marked images for those cases. As shown in figure 4, the testing segmentation algorithm starts with a wavelet filter application to the original image (see line 2 of figure 4) as we described for the training segmentation algorithm. In line 4, we use a global threshold segmentation

```
1.  TrainingSegmentation (SetOfOriginalImages, SetOfMarkedImages)
2.  ROIS = {φ}
3.  For each pair of images: OriginalImage, MarkedImage
4.     WOriginalImage = SymsWavelet(OriginalImage)
5.     WMarkedImage = SymsWavelet(MarkedImage)
6.     For each calcification mark in WMarkedImage
7.        Position = LocateCalcificationArea(WMarkedImage)
8.        ROIS = ROIS ∪ GetCalcificationArea(WOriginalImage)
9.     EndFor
10. EndFor
11. End Segmentation
```

Fig. 3. Training Segmentation Algorithm

```
1.  TestingSegmentation (OriginalImage,MinSize,MaxSize)
2.  WOriginalImage = SymsWavelet(OriginalImage)
3.  ROIS = {φ}
4.  ROIS = GlobalThresholdSegmentation(WOriginalImage,Threshold)
5.  For each ROI in ROIS
6.     If Area(ROI) < MinSize
7.        ROIS = ROIS - ROI
8.     EndIf
9.     If Area(ROI) > MaxSize
10.       ROIS = ROIS - ROI
11.       ROISInNodule = EdgeSegmentation(ROI)
12.       ROIS = ROIS + ROISInNodule
13.    EndIf
14. EndFor
15. For each ROI in ROIS
16.    LocalThresholdSegmentation(ROI)
17.    FinalROIS = FinalROIS + ROI
18. EndFor
19. Return FinalROIS
```

Fig. 4. Testing Segmentation Algorithm

algorithm to find ROI's. After this, we eliminate those small ROI's that, because of their size cannot be a calcification, not even a micro-calcification (lines 5 to 8). We keep those ROI's that have a size in the range of the size of those ROI's in the training set. Next, we apply a local edge segmentation algorithm to those ROI's that are too large to be considered a calcification but that could contain one or more calcifications inside, these regions are called nodules and we also get those ROI's inside a nodule as possible calcifications (lines 9 to 13 in figure 4). Then, in lines 15 to 18, we keep all ROI's that might be calcifications and apply to them a local threshold segmentation algorithm to eliminate small imperfections in the image called artifices and also improve the quality of the edges of calcifications. Finally, we perform the feature extraction task over these ROI's to create a feature database of negative ROI's for the training case or a feature database for the diagnosis case.

Feature Extraction Algorithm. The feature extraction algorithm shown in figure 5 receives as input the set of ROI's found with the segmentation algorithms shown in figures 3 and 4. This algorithm processes each region of interest to extract the characteristics: area, diameter, density, convexity, internal ellipse radius, external

```
1.   FeatureExtraction (ROIS)
2.   FeatureVector[|ROIS|]  = [φ]
3.      For i = 1 to |ROIS|
4.         FeatureVector[i] = GetFeatures(ROIS[i])
5.      EndFor
1.   End FeatureExtraction
```

Fig. 5. Feature Extraction Algorithm

ellipse radius, orientation, circularity, eccentricity, roundness, and contour length. We chose these characteristics with the help of our domain expert trying to consider what she uses at the time she does a diagnosis. We experimented with texture features [2] but we got better results with the features recommended by our domain expert. All the features extracted from each ROI are stored in a feature vector database that will be used to feed our data mining algorithms in the next phase of the process.

3.2 Data Mining

Data mining is the task of finding interesting, useful, and novel patterns from databases [4]. In our case we want to find patterns that describe calcifications in mammograms so that we can use them to predict whether a new mammogram has calcifications or not. As we mentioned before, we use a backpropagation neural network and a decision tree as our data mining algorithms. Neural networks have the property of achieving high accuracies for the classification task but what they learn is not easy to understand. On the other hand, decision trees are known to achieve high accuracies in the classification task and are also easy to understand.

Neural Networks. For a long time researchers have tried to simulate how the human brain works with mathematical models called neural networks. A neural network is composed of a set of cells that are interconnected in a layer fashion. The first layer is called the input layer and its function is to pass the input signals to the next layer. Each cell in the next layer (intermediate cells) receives a signal from each cell in the previous layer modified by a weight factor. The intermediate cells calculate their output signal according to a function over its input signals, in the case of the backpropagation algorithm [7]; the output signal is calculated with the sigmoid function and then passed to the next layer cells. Once the signals reach the output cells, the result is compared with the real classification of the input feature vector and the error is propagated to the previous layers by adjusting the weights of each connection between cells. In our experiments, we use a Neural Network (NN) with 11 input nodes, 1 hidden layer with 5 nodes and two output nodes. As we can see in figure 6, the input nodes receive the feature vector of each ROI and the output nodes show the classification of the NN for the given input vector. The possible classifications are positive (the feature vector corresponds to a calcification) or negative (the feature vector does not correspond to a calcification). The NN is trained with the backpropgation algorithm with a learning rate of 0.01 and for 500 epochs comparing the actual output of the network with the real output for each ROI and changing the weights of the network.

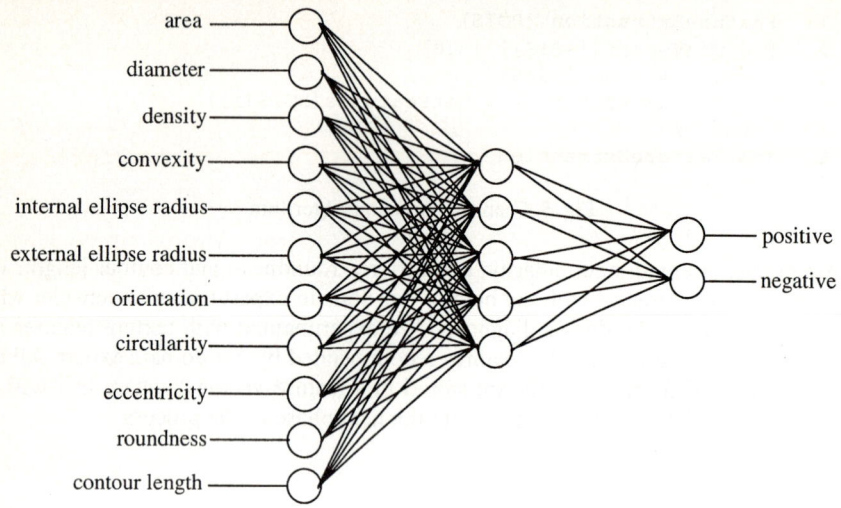

Fig. 6. Neural Network Architecture

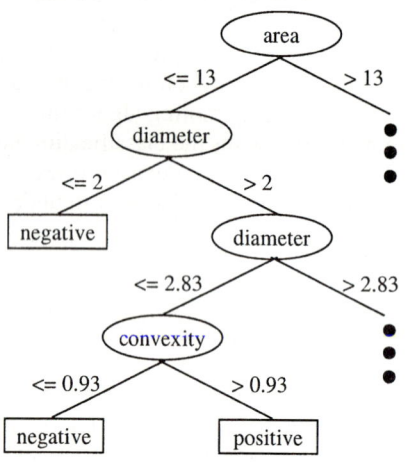

Fig. 7. Partial Decision Tree

Decision Trees. Decision trees are a classification method that generates a tree to classify a set of input examples according to their class [6]. Each branch in the tree represents a decision. Each node in the tree refers to a particular attribute. Edges connecting nodes are labeled with attribute values and leave nodes give a classification that applies to the examples that were reached through that branch. At each step of the tree construction a node is selected according to a statistical measure called information gain, that measures how well a node (attribute) distributes the input examples with respect to their class. Figure 7 shows part of an example of a decision tree for our domain. As we can see, the root node for the tree is the area node. If area has a value of less or equal to 13, we verify the value of the diameter attribute. If diameter has a value of less or equal to 2 then the class of the example is negative. If

Table 1. 10-Fold Cross Validation Results

Algorithm	10-FoldCV Result	Standard Deviation
Neural Networks	94.3 %	1.7127
Decision Trees	92.6 %	0.2662

1)   If area <= 13, and diameter <= 2, then calcification = negative
2)   If roundness > 0.68, and contour length > 10.49, then calcification = positive
3)   If density > 6.60, then calcification = negative
4)   If external ellipse radius <= 1.19, then calcification = positive

Fig. 8. Decision Rules from the Calcification Detection Domain

the value for diameter is greater than 2, we verify again the value of the diameter attribute and if it is less or equal to 2.83, we verify the convexity attribute. If the convexity attribute has a value of less or equal to 0.93, the class is negative, otherwise the class is positive. For our experiments with decision trees we used the c4.5 algorithm described in [6].

In the following section we will show our experimental results using the machine vision and data mining algorithms for the task of calcification detection in mammograms.

4   Experiments and Results

For our experiments we follow the process described in figure 2. We find positive and negative regions of interest from 70 craniocaudal mammogram images with calcifications and 60 mammogram images with no calcifications. We mentioned before that we had 54 cases with calcifications but this does not mean that both craniocaudal images of a case have calcifications; this is why we only have 70 mammogram images with calcifications. From these images, we obtained a total of 653 ROI's, from which 326 are positive (calcifications) and 327 are negative (non calcifications). We performed the feature extraction process to these ROI's and trained our data mining algorithms with them. We used the 10 fold cross validation technique (that is, we used 90% of the examples for training and the remaining 10% for testing in each of the 10 trials) to evaluate the algorithms performance and got the results shown in table 1.

As we can see in table 1, we got better accuracy results with the neural network algorithm than with the decision tree, but we can also see that the standard deviation with the neural network is higher than with the decision tree. The only problem with neural networks is that they are not easy to understand and we needed to show the learned patterns to our domain expert. This is why we generated rules from the decision tree and asked our domain expert to study them. Dr. Higuero found the rules very interesting and told us that she was relating them to the way she does her diagnosis. Figure 8 shows some examples of these rules. The first rule says that if the area of the ROI is less or equal to 13, and its diameter is less or equal to 2, then it might not be a calcification. Rule 2 says that if the roundness of the ROI is greater than 0.68, and its contour length is greater than 10.49, then it might be a calcification.

Rule 3 states that if the density of the ROI is greater than 6.60, it might not be a calcification. Finally, rule 4 says that if the external ellipse radius of a ROI is less or equal to 1.19, then it might be a calcification. In a different experiment with Dr. Higuero we discovered that the system could detect very small microcalcifications that she could miss because of their reduced size.

5 Conclusion

The experimental results show that our method combining machine vision and data mining techniques for the calcification detection task from mammograms has been successful achieving an accuracy of 94.3% with a neural network trained with the backpropagation algorithm and an accuracy of 92.6% with decision trees. The accuracy was calculated using the 10-fold cross validation technique. Our domain expert also told us that the accuracy achieved was good enough to implement our method as a Computer Aid Diagnosis (CAD) system to give a second opinion to the radiologist. She also told us that our method had found calcifications that she was not able to see because of their reduced size (micro-calcifications). Our next step is to implement the CAD system using the process discussed in figure 2b and this will allow us to compare our method's accuracy with the physician's accuracy for the prediction of calcifications in mammograms. We also want to try other algorithms such as Bayesian networks to see if we can improve the efficiency achieved with the backpropagation and decision trees algorithms.

Acknowledgements. This research work was done with the assistance of our radiology domain expert, Dr. Nidia Higuero from the ISSSTEP hospital.

References

1. Antonie, Maria-Luisa, Zaiane, Osmar R., and Coman, Alexandru. Application of Data Mining Techniques for Medical Image Classification. Proceedings of the International Workshop on Multimedia Data Mining, San Francisco, CA. (2001) 94-101.
2. Bovis, K., Singh, S. Detection of Masses in Mammograms using Texture Measures. Fifteenth International Conference on Pattern Recognition. Barcelona. IEEE Press. vol 2 (2000) 267-270.
3. Bottigli, U. and Golosio, B. Feature Extraction from Mammographic Images Using Fast Matching Methods. Nuclear Instruments and Methods in Physics Research. ELSEVIER, A 487, (2002) 209-215.
4. Fayyad, Usama M., Gregory Piatetsky-Shapiro, and Padhraic Smyth. From Data Mining to Knowledge Discovery in Databases: An Overview. In Advances of Knowledge Discovery and Data Mining, eds. U.M. Fayyad, G. Piatetsky-Shapiro, P. Smyth, and R. Uthurusamy, AAAI Press/The MIT Press, Menlo Park, CA., (1996) 1-34.
5. López-Carrillo, Lizbeth; Torres-Sánchez, Luisa; López-Cervantes, Malaquías; and Rueda-Neria, Celina. Identification of Malignant Breast Lesions in Mexico. Salud Pública de México. Vol. 43, No. 3, (2001) 199-202.
6. Quinlan, J. R. Improved Use of Continuous Attributes in C4.5, Journal of Artificial Intelligence Research, Vol. 4, (1996) 77-90.

7. Rumelhart, David E., Widrow, Bernard, and Lehr, Michael A. The Basic Ideas in Neural Networks. Communications of the ACM, Vol. 37, No. 3 (1994) 87-92.
8. Sharma, M and Singh, S. Evaluation of Texture Methods for Image Analysis. Proceedings of the 7th Australian and New Zeland Intelligent Information Systems Conference. Perth, November, (2001) 18-21.
9. Tabar L, Fagerbgerg G, Gad A, et al. Reduction in Mortality from Breast Cancer after Mass Screening with Mammography. Lancet. 1 (1985) 829-832.
10. Yoshida, H.; Doi, K.; Nishikawa, R.; Muto, K. and Tsuda, M. Application of the Wavelet Transform to Automated Detection of Clustered Microcalcifications in Digital Mammograms. Academic Reports of Tokyo Institute of Polytechnics, 16, (1994) 24-37.
11. Zhang, Xiao-Ping and Desai, Mita D. Wavelet Based Automatic Thresholding for Image Segmentation. In Proceedings of the ICIP'97 conference, Santa Barbara, CA. (1997) 26-29.

An Optimization Algorithm Based on Active and Instance-Based Learning

Olac Fuentes and Thamar Solorio

Instituto Nacional de Astrofísica, Óptica y Electrónica
Luis Enrique Erro 1
Santa María Tonantzintla, Puebla, México 72840

Abstract. We present an optimization algorithm that combines active learning and locally-weighted regression to find extreme points of noisy and complex functions. We apply our algorithm to the problem of interferogram analysis, an important problem in optical engineering that is not solvable using traditional optimization schemes and that has received recent attention in the research community. Experimental results show that our method is faster than others previously presented in the literature and that it is very accurate for the case of noiseless interferograms, as well as for the case of interferograms with two types of noise: white noise and intensity gradients, which are due to slight missalignments in the system.

Keywords: Optimization, active learning, instance-based learning, locally-weighted regression

1   Introduction

Optimization in poorly modelled, noisy and complex domains is an important problem that is faced in many scientific and engineering areas. In such domains, traditional optimization algorithms, such as the Simplex method [1] or the Levenberg-Marquardt algorithm [2], do not yield satisfactory results and are usually very sensitive to the starting search points provided by the user. For these reasons, non-traditional optimization algorithms, including simulated annealing [3], genetic algorithms [4,5], evolution strategies [6,7] and hybrid evolutionary-classical algorithms [8], have been proposed. While good results have been reported, the running times of these algorithms are often high, and they are not well suited to all domains. Thus, more efficient and complementary algorithms are desirable.

In this paper we propose an efficient algorithm to perform optimization in complex domains. Our algorithm is based on the observation that the candidate solutions generated by an optimization algorithm, which are normally discarded by both traditional and non-traditional schemes, can be used as a training set for a learning algorithm, which in turn can predict the parameters of an optimal solution to the problem. An advantage of this approach is that, if we want to find the solutions to several similar problems, we can process them concurrently

R. Monroy et al. (Eds.): MICAI 2004, LNAI 2972, pp. 242–251, 2004.

and integrate all the candidate solutions in a single training set. Since the training set is continuously changed, we need a learning algorithm that requires a small training time. Instance-based learning algorithms, whose training consists of simply storing the training data, fulfill this requirement. In our work we used the locally-weighted regression algorithm [9], an instance-based learning algorithm that has been found to yield similar accuracy as neural networks in many application domains while preserving the short training times inherent to this class of methods.

We illustrate our method with an application to the problem of interferogram analysis, which has received recent attention in the literature. This is an interesting domain, as there are published attempted solutions using both traditional optimization schemes and evolutionary algorithms [10,11].

The organization of the remainder of this paper is as follows. In Section 2 we describe the proposed optimization algorithm, the main contribution of this paper. Section 3 presents background material about interferometry, the application area we use to illustrate the algorithm. Section 4 gives details about the adaptation of the algorithm to the problem. Section 5 shows the main results, and Section 6 presents conclusions and suggests directions for future work.

2 Outline of the Optimization Algorithm

We are interested in the problem of finding the parameters of a known analytic function that best match an observation. Let $\mathbf{o}$ be the observed (multidimensonal) variable, let $\mathbf{f}(\mathbf{x})$ be a function with the same dimensionality as $\mathbf{o}$. The goal of the optimization procedure is to obtain the value of $\mathbf{x}$ that minimizes $|\mathbf{o} - \mathbf{f}(\mathbf{x})|$. Typically, this problem is solved by an iterative process: in iteration i we generate $\mathbf{x_i}$, evaluate the target function $|\mathbf{o} - \mathbf{f}(\mathbf{x_i})|$ and based on the value of the target function, as well as its first and second derivatives (if they are available), we generate the next candidate value $\mathbf{x_{i+1}}$, which is expected to be closer to the optimum.

This work deals with the problem where we have several observations $\mathbf{o_1}, \ldots, \mathbf{o_n}$, and we want to find the vectors $\mathbf{x_1}, \ldots, \mathbf{x_n}$ that minimize the errors $e_i = |\mathbf{o_i} - \mathbf{f}(\mathbf{x_i})|$. Clearly, this can be solved by solving the n optimization problems separately. However, we propose a method to solve the problem more efficiently, posing it as a learning problem, where a learning algorithm learns the inverse function $\mathbf{f^{-1}}(\mathbf{x})$. The training set used by the algorithm is formed by the pairs of values $\langle \mathbf{f}(\mathbf{x_i}), \mathbf{x_i} \rangle$ previously generated in the search, its test set consists of the values $\mathbf{o_1}, \ldots, \mathbf{o_n}$ and it outputs an estimate of $\mathbf{x_1}, \ldots, \mathbf{x_n}$ that is expected to minimize $e_1, \ldots e_n$. When a new set of solutions $\mathbf{x_1}, \ldots, \mathbf{x_n}$ is proposed by the algorithm, we compute their corresponding $\mathbf{f}(\mathbf{x_1}), \ldots, \mathbf{f}(\mathbf{x_n})$ and use the new pairs $\langle \mathbf{f}(\mathbf{x_i}), \mathbf{x_i} \rangle$ to augment the training set, and continue this iterative process until convergence is attained. Since this type of active learning adds to the training set examples that are progressively closer to the points of interest, the errors are guaranteed to decrease in every iteration. The outline of the algorithm can be described by the following pseudocode:

1. Generate randomly an initial set of values $\mathbf{x_1}, \ldots, \mathbf{x_m}$ and compute their corresponding $\mathbf{f(x_1)}, \ldots, \mathbf{f(x_m)}$.
2. Let $R = \{\langle \mathbf{f(x_1)}, \mathbf{x_1} \rangle, \ldots, \langle \mathbf{f(x_m)}, \mathbf{x_m} \rangle\}$ be the initial training set.
3. Let $T = \mathbf{o_1}, \ldots, \mathbf{o_n}$ be the test set.
4. While T is not empty
   a) Train an approximator $\mathbf{A}$ using R as training set
   b) For each $\mathbf{o_i} \in T$
      i. Generate $\mathbf{A(o_i)}$
      ii. $R = R \cup \{\langle \mathbf{f(A(o_i))}, \mathbf{A(o_i)} \rangle\}$
      iii. If $|\mathbf{o_i} - \mathbf{f(A(o_i))}| < threshold$, remove $\mathbf{o_i}$ from T.

Here, $\mathbf{A(o_i)}$ can be seen as the best current guess for the value of $\mathbf{x}$ such that $\mathbf{f(x)} = \mathbf{o_i}$. For the algorithm to be efficient, we need to minimize the time taken to train A. This can easily be done if we use an instance-based learning algorithm, such as the locally-weighted regression algorithm (explained in the next subsection). The other potentially time consuming step is the application of $\mathbf{A}$ to compute $\mathbf{A(o_i)}$, as it normally takes time proportional to the size of the training set to find the nearest neighbors of each example in the test set. However, since the algorithm is applied repeatedly to the same test set, we can cache the nearest neighbors of each example in the test set, and every time the training set is augmented (step 4.b.ii) we can check if the example added to the training set becomes a nearest-neighbor of any of them.

2.1 Locally-Weighted Regression

Locally-Weighted Regression (LWR) belongs to the family of instance-based learning algorithms. In contrast to most other learning algorithms, which use their training examples to construct explicit global representations of the target function, instance-based learning algorithms simply store some or all of the training examples and postpone any generalization effort until a new instance must be classified. They can thus build query-specific local models, which attempt to fit the training examples only in a region around the query point. In this work we use a linear model around the query point to approximate the target function.

Given a query point $\mathbf{x_q}$, to predict its output parameters $\mathbf{y_q}$, we find the k examples in the training set that are closest to it, and assign to each of them a weight given by the inverse of its distance to the query point: $w_i = \frac{1}{|\mathbf{x_q} - \mathbf{x_i}|}$. Let W, the weight matrix, be a diagonal matrix with entries $w_1, \ldots, w_n$. Let X be a matrix whose rows are the vectors $\mathbf{x_1}, \ldots, \mathbf{x_k}$, the input parameters of the examples in the training set that are closest to $\mathbf{x_q}$, with the addition of a "1" in the last column. Let Y be a matrix whose rows are the vectors $\mathbf{y_1}, \ldots, \mathbf{y_k}$, the output parameters of these examples. Then the weighted training data are given by $Z = WX$ and the weighted target function is $V = WY$. Then we use the estimator for the target function $\mathbf{y_q} = \mathbf{x_q}^T (Z^T Z)^{-1} Z^T V$.

Thus, locally weighted linear regression is very similar to least-squares linear regression, except that the error terms used to derive the best linear approximation are weighted by the inverse of their distance to the query point. Intuitively, this yields much more accurate results than standard linear regression because the assumption that the target function is linear does not hold in general, but is a very good approximation when only a small neighborhood is considered.

3 Interferometry

Interferometry is a laboratory technique very commonly used to test the quality of optical systems. To perform interferometry, two beams, one passing through a reference surface and the other passing through the test surface, are combined and made to interfere, which results in a pattern, called interferogram, that characterizes the quality of the test surface. A schematic diagram of a simple interferometer is shown in figure 1. Experienced technicians can diagnose the flaws of the test surface by careful analysis of the interferogram, however, this is a time consuming task, and when there is a need to analyze more than a few interferograms, it becomes impractical. Thus, there is a need for techniques to automate this process.

The problem of automatically characterizing an interferogram has received recent attention in the literature. This is a difficult problem, and traditional optimization schemes based on the least-squares method often provide inconclusive results, specially in the presence of noisy data [12,13]. For this reason, nontraditional optimization schemes, such as evolutionary algorithms, have been proposed to solve this problem [11]. While evolutionary algorithms provide very accurate results in the case of both noiseless and noisy data, their running time is high, taking several minutes to analyze a single interferogram. Clearly, if we need to analyze a large number of interferograms, this approach becomes unfeasible.

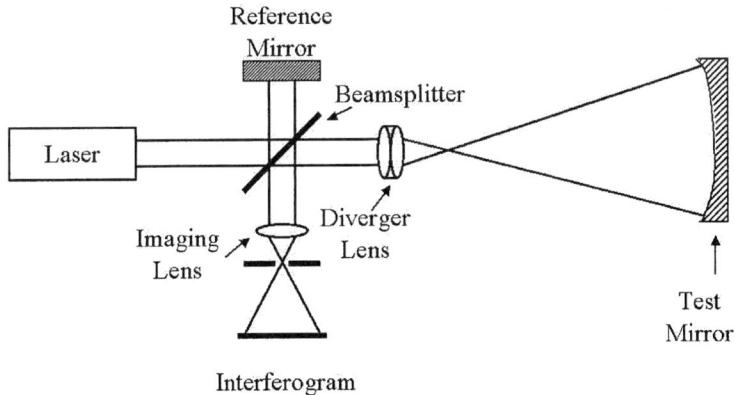

Fig. 1. A simple interferometer

3.1   Interferogram Simulation

To obtain the simulated interferograms we use Kingslake's formulation [14], where the intensity in the interferogrametric image is given by

$$I(x,y) = cos(\frac{2\pi}{\lambda} W(x,y)) + G(x,y) + N(x,y) \tag{1}$$

where λ is the wavelength of the light source, N is white noise which we represented as a random number obtained from a Gaussian distribution with zero mean, G is a noise term due to slight missalignments in the system and appears in the image as an intensity gradient and can be defined by three parameters γ_1, γ_2 and γ_3:

$$G(x,y) = \gamma_1 + \gamma_2 x + \gamma_3 y \tag{2}$$

$W(x,y)$ is the optical path difference (OPD) between the reference and test surfaces, and it is represented by a polynomial using the Seidel aberration formulation:

$$W(x,y) = A(x^2+y^2)^2 + By(x^2+y^2) + C(x^2+3y^2) + D(x^2+y^2) + Ey + Fx \tag{3}$$

where A is the spherical aberration coefficient, B, C and D are the comma coefficient, astigmatism and defocusing coefficients, respectively, E is the tilt about the y axis, and F is the tilt about the x axis.

Clearly, it is easy to obtain an interferogram I given the vector of aberration coefficients $v = [A, B, C, D, E, F]$ and the vector of intensity gradients $\gamma = [\gamma_1, \gamma_2, \gamma_3]$. However, we are interested in the inverse problem, that is, obtaining the vector of aberration coefficients and intensity gradient from the corresponding interferogram, which, as mentioned before, is a very difficult optimization problem. The following section will describe our proposed solution to this problem.

4   Automated Interferogram Analysis

The problem of finding the parameters that characterize an optical system is known as interferogram analysis. In this section we show the application of our proposed optimization method to the problem of interferogram analysis.

4.1   Preprocessing

The input to our system is a set of interferograms and the output is a vector of aberration and gradient coefficients that characterize them. Before we apply the optimization algorithm, we can greatly reduce the dimensionality of the learning task using a principal component analysis preprocessing stage to compress the high-dimensional interferograms into a more manageable size with minimal loss of information.

Principal Component Analysis. The formulation of standard PCA is as follows. Consider a set of m vectors $\mathbf{v_1}, \mathbf{v_2}, \ldots, \mathbf{v_m}$, where the mean object of the set is defined by

$$\mu = \frac{1}{m} \sum_{i=1}^{m} \mathbf{v_i} \tag{4}$$

Each object differs from the mean by the vector

$$\theta_\mathbf{i} = \mathbf{v_i} - \mu \tag{5}$$

Let $A = [\theta_1, \theta_2, \ldots, \theta_m]$. C, the covariance matrix, is given by

$$C = \sum_{i=1}^{m} \sum_{j=1}^{m} \theta_i \theta_j^T = AA^T \tag{6}$$

The principal components are then the eigenvectors of C. If we sort these eigenvectors by decreasing order of their corresponding eigenvalues, a projection onto the space defined by the first k eigenvectors ($1 \leq k \leq m$) is optimal with respect to information loss. That is, let P be the matrix whose columns are the first k eigenvectors of C, then the optimal projection of $\mathbf{v_i}$ is given by

$$\mathbf{p_i} = P^T \theta_i \tag{7}$$

4.2   Optimization Algorithm

The algorithm to perform automated interferogram analysis can be described as follows. First we generate randomly k parameter vectors $\mathbf{x_o} \ldots, \mathbf{x_k}$, where $\mathbf{x_i} = [A_i, B_i, C_i, D_i, E_i, F_i, \gamma_{1i}, \gamma_{2i}, \gamma_{3i}]$ contains aberration and gradient coefficients. For each $\mathbf{x_i}$ we construct the corresponding interferogram $I(\mathbf{x_i})$ applying equations 1, 2 and 3. Then we perform PCA on a matrix $J = [I(\mathbf{x_1}), \ldots, I(\mathbf{x_k})]$, obtaining P, the matrix of principal components, and μ, the mean vector, as described in 4.1. The projection of each interferogram into the eigenspace is then given by $\mathbf{p_i} = P^T(I(\mathbf{x_i}) - \mu)$. We can now use the set of pairs $R\langle \mathbf{p_i}, \mathbf{x_i} \rangle$ as initial training set to the algorithm.

Given a set of test $T_1, \ldots T_m$ interferograms, we first project them to the eigenspace created in the previous step, $\mathbf{t_i} = P^T(T_i - \mu)$, and we give these projections as the test set to the learning algorithm described in Section 2.

5   Experimental Results

In this section we describe the experiments performed with our optimization algorithm applied to the problem of predicting the vectors of aberration coefficients and intensity gradients. First, we generated a thousand aberration vectors, a thousand intensity gradient vectors and their corresponding interferograms, using an 81 by 81 resolution. For this experiment we dealt with noiseless interferograms (that is, the noise terms G and N were set to zero). Using principal

Table 1. Mean Absolute Errors for Simulated Interferograms

Coefficients	Mean Absolute Error	Standard Deviation
A	0.0011	0.0010
B	0.0015	0.0011
C	0.0006	0.0005
D	0.0010	0.0009
E	0.0002	0.0002
F	0.0004	0.0005

Table 2. Mean Absolute Errors for Noisy Simulated Interferograms

Coefficients	Mean Absolute Error	Standard Deviation
A	0.1109	0.1525
B	0.0887	0.0829
C	0.0398	0.0697
D	0.0591	0.0506
E	0.0250	0.0526
F	0.0463	0.0800
γ_1	0.0080	0.0023
γ_2	0.0100	0.0024
γ_3	0.0030	0.0010

component analysis we reduced the dimensionality of the task, keeping 47 eigenvectors, which preserve about 95% of the information in the original data. Then we randomly divided the data into ten equally sized subgroups, one group was used for testing and the remainder nine were considered the training set. Ten different experiments were performed, each one using a different group for testing. We repeated this procedure ten times, and the overall average are the results presented here. Table 1 shows averaged mean absolute errors and standard deviations for each aberration coefficient. As the experimental results show, our method is very accurate with the simulated interferograms. On average, each interferogram took 1.6 seconds to process, which is much faster than the results reported in recent works dealing with the same problem. For example, [11] reports that evolution strategies took about 3 minutes to find the parameters of each interferogram, using the same resolution and similar computing hardware.

Real data always pose the challenge of managing noise. In order to evaluate the noise sensibility of our method, we performed experiments on interferograms with simulated noise, using both Gaussian noise and an intensity gradient, as described in Section 3. Table 2 shows errors in aberration coefficients and intensity gradients. In Figure 2 we can see a visual comparison between noisy interferograms and the interferograms obtained from the predicted aberrations. It can be

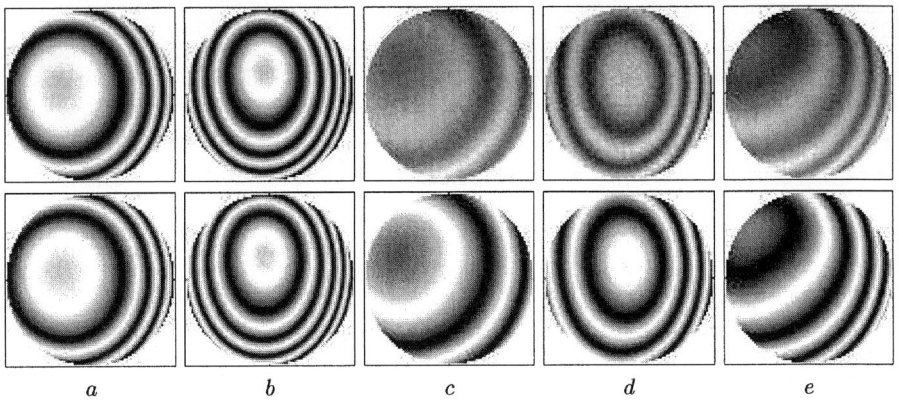

Fig. 2. The top row shows five of the interferograms used for testing and the bottom row shows the best matches found by the algorithm. Columns a and b show noiseless interferograms; it can be seen that the matches found by the algorithm are virtually undistinguishable from the test interferograms. Columns c, d and e show noisy interferograms; the matches found by the algorithm show almost identical interferograms, except that the noise has been removed.

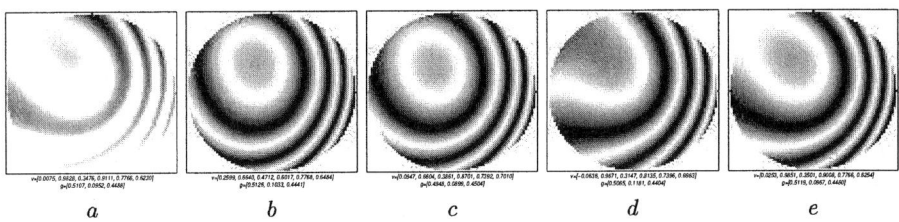

Fig. 3. A detailed trace of the optimization algorithm using a noiseless interferogram as input. The test interferogram is shown in a; b shows the result of applying LWR using only the original (randomly generated) training data. Figures c and d show successive approximations given by the algorithm as it iterates toward a solution, finally, the best result found is shown in e.

seen that our method's performance was not damaged by the noise in the test data. For this case, due to the fact that the parameter space is increased, the running time is also increased, taking 9 seconds to find the optimal parameters of each interferogram, on average. As this is, to the best of our knowledge, the first attempt to approximate interferograms using a noise model that is more complex than simple Gaussian noise, we cannot compare our results with previous approaches, however, the running time is still much smaller than that taken by the method that only deals with noiseless interferograms.

In Figure 3 we present a detailed execution trace of the algorithms, using a randomly chosen noiseless test example. We can see how the algorithm is gradually converging to a set of parameters that generate an interferogram that is

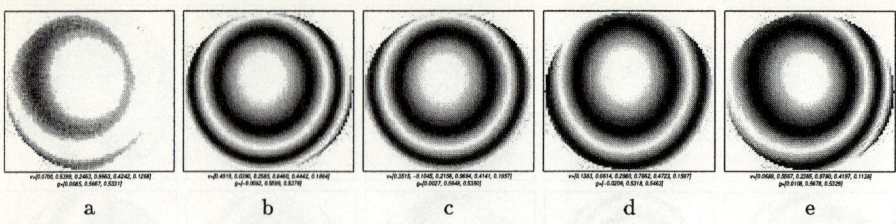

Fig. 4. A detailed trace of the optimization algorithm using a noisy interferogram as input. The test interferogram is shown in *a*; *b* shows the result of applying LWR using only the original (randomly generated) training data. Figures *c* and *d* show successive approximations given by the algorithm as it iterates toward a solution, finally, the best result found is shown in *e*.

virtually undistinguishable from the test interferogram. Figure 4 shows a similar trace, except that the input is now a noisy interferogram. The output of the algorithm is again an almost exact match to the test interferogram, except that the noisy has been eliminated.

6   Conclusions

In this paper we have presented an optimization algorithm that has a very strong feature: the ability of extending the training set automatically in order to best fit the target function for the test data. There is no need for manual intervention, and if new test instances need to be classified the algorithm will generate as many training examples as needed.

We have shown experimental results of the application of our method to solve the problem of, given a large set of interferograms, finding their corresponding vectors of aberration coefficients. The method yields very accurate results, even in the presence of noise, and also, it is faster by two orders of magnitude than other methods introduced earlier.

Present and future work includes:

- Testing the method using real interferograms.
- Extending the algorithm to handle higher-order aberrations.
- Testing the applicability of the method to other optimization problems in optics, as well as in other areas of science.

Acknowledgements. We would like to thank CONACYT for partially supporting this work and Sergio Vázquez y Montiel and Jaime Sánchez Escobar for stimulating discussions.

References

1. J. Nelder and R. Mead. A simplex method for function minimization. *Computer Journal*, 7:308–313, 1965.
2. K. Levenberg. A method for the solution of certain problems in least squares. *Quarterly Journal on Applied Mathematics*, 2:164–168, 1944.
3. S. Kirkpatrick, C. D. Gelatt, and M. P. Vecchi. Optimization by simulated annealing. *Science*, 220(4598):671–680, 1983.
4. John Holland. *Adaptation in Natural and Artificial Systems*. University of Michigan Press, Ann Arbor, MI, 1975.
5. David E. Goldberg. *Genetic Algorithms in Search, Optimization and Machine Learning*. Addison-Wesley, 1989.
6. Hans-Per Schwefel. *Numerical Optimization of Computer Models*. John Wiley & Sons, Ltd., 1981.
7. Thomas Bäck, Frank Hoffmeister, and Hans-Paul Schwefel. A survey of evolutionary strategies. In *Proceedings of the Fourth International Conference on Genetic Algorithms*. Morgan Kaufmann Publishers, Inc, 1991.
8. Nicholas J. Radcliffe and Patrick D. Surry. Formal memetic algorithms. In *Evolutionary Computing, AISB Workshop*, pages 1–16, 1994.
9. Christopher G. Atkeson, Andrew W. Moore, and Stefan Schaal. Locally weighted learning. *Artificial Intelligence Review*, 11:11 73, 1997.
10. A. Cordero-Dávila, A. Cornejo-Rodríguez, and O. Cardona-Núñez. Polynomial fitting of interferograms with gaussian errors on fringe coordinates. I: Computer simulations. *Applied Optics*, 33:7343–7349, 1994.
11. S. Vázquez y Montiel, J. Sánchez, and O. Fuentes. Obtaining the phase of an interferogram using an evolution strategy, part I. *Applied Optics*, 41(17):3448–3452, June 2002.
12. D. Dutton, A. Cornejo, and M. Latta. A semiautomatic method for interpreting shearing interferograms. *Applied Optics*, 7:125–131, 1968.
13. J. Y. Wang and D. E. Silva. Wave-front interpretation with Zernike polynomials. *Applied Optics*, 19:1510–1518, 1980.
14. R. Kingslake. *Applied Optics and Optical Engineering*. Academic Press, 1979.

MultiGrid-Based Fuzzy Systems for Function Approximation

Luis Javier Herrera[1], Héctor Pomares[1], Ignacio Rojas[1], Olga Valenzuela[2], and Mohammed Awad[1]

[1] University of Granada, Department of Computer Architecture and Technology, E.T.S. Computer Engineering, 18071 Granada, Spain
http://atc.ugr.es
[2] University of Granada, Department of Applied Mathematics, Science faculty, Granada, Spain

Abstract. In this paper we make use of a modified Grid Based Fuzzy System architecture, which may provide an exponential reduction in the number of rules needed. We also introduce an algorithm that automatically, from a set of given I/O training points, is able to determine the pseudo-optimal architecture proposed as well as the optimal parameters needed (number and position of membership functions and fuzzy rule consequents). The suitability of the algorithm and the improvement in both performance and efficiency obtained are shown in an example.

1 Introduction

The estimation of an unknown model from a set of input/output data is a crucial problem for a number of scientific and engineering areas where lots of research efforts have been employed on. The objective is to obtain a model from which to obtain the expected output given any new input data. Regression or function approximation problems deal with continuous input/output data while classification problems deal with discrete, categorical output data. In this paper we are concerned with function approximation problems in which we want to obtain the model that approximates better the desired continuous output given any input data.

Several authors have worked with fuzzy systems to deal with the problem of function approximation. One of the first studies in this context was carried out by Wang and Mendel [1] presenting a general method for combining numerical and linguistic information into a fuzzy rule-table. A procedure was proposed in which each datum generates a rule, though this approach produces an enormous number of rules when the input data set is considerable. Other approaches have also attempted to solve function approximation problems by means of clustering techniques [2,9]. In general, two main approaches might be taken for the partitioning of the input space:

On the one hand, the use of fuzzy clusters (see *fig 1a*)) performs a marginal subdivision of the input space depending obviously on the number of rules taken to reach the objective. This approach has the disadvantage that the whole input

R. Monroy et al. (Eds.): MICAI 2004, LNAI 2972, pp. 252–261, 2004.

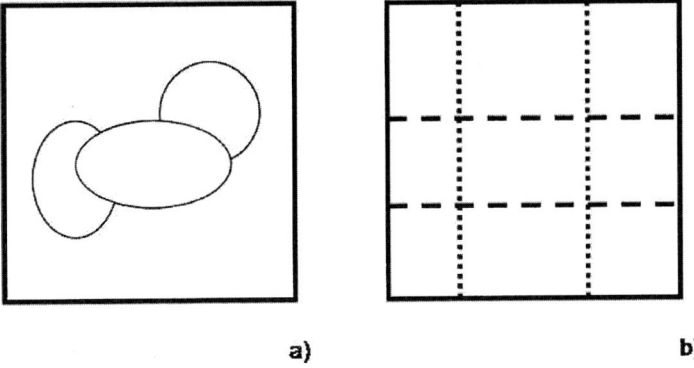

a)   b)

Fig. 1. a) Clustering Techniques for function approximation. b) Grid techniques for function approximation

space might not be covered properly. Some input space regions might be kept uncovered by any rule. Besides, the use of clustering for function approximation problems generally does not take into account the interpolation properties of the approximator system [3].

On the other hand, Grid-Based Fuzzy Systems (see *fig 1b)*) provide a thorough coverage of the whole input space which makes them especially well-suited for low-dimension function approximation problems. Several previous works and papers have shown the great performance that might be reached using this kind of partitioning of the input space. Nevertheless in this last approach, the number of rules used by the fuzzy system increases exponentially with the number of input variables and with the number of membership functions per variable. This increase derives in a loss of effectiveness and in a loss of one of the main properties of the fuzzy systems, the understanding and interpretability of the system.

In this paper we use a very simple structure to overcome the problem of the curse of dimensionality for Grid-Based Fuzzy Systems. Apart from presenting this simple and convenient sort of fuzzy systems, we also will provide an algorithm that, when possible, will select the group of variables that will form each sub-grid, resulting to a MultiGrid structure. Also once we know the hard-structure of our multigrid system, we will provide an adaptative algorithm to select the optimal parameters and fine-structure of the system, to obtain the final optimal function approximator for the given data set.

2   MultiGrid-Based Fuzzy System (MGFS) Architecture

When we have a high number of input variables, a N-dimensional grid might seem useless for our aim of obtaining an approximation of the input points, since having too many rules as well as too many antecedents on each rule, results in an incomprehensible huge model. Also managing so many parameters may reach an efficiency bottleneck, resulting impossible to optimize.

Now considering a high dimensional space, we propose to use systems in the form [4]:

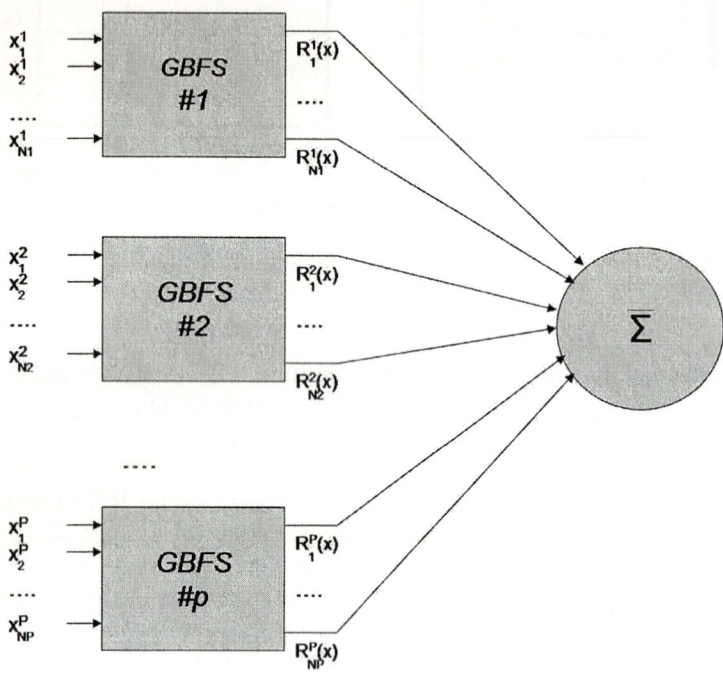

Fig. 2. MultiGrid-Based Fuzzy System (MGFS)

Each group of variables are used to define a Grid-Based Fuzzy System (GBFS) from which a set of rules is obtained in the form [5]:

$$\text{IF } x_1 \text{ is } X_1^{i_1} \text{ AND } \ldots \text{ AND } x_N \text{ is } X_N^{i_N} \text{ THEN } R_i^p = R_{i_1 i_2 \ldots i_N} \qquad (1)$$

being R_i^p the $i-th$ rule of the $p-th$ GBFS. Thus, all the rules from all the GBFS form the whole MGFS, whose output is obtained by normalizing according to the number of GBFS. Therefore the final output of the system for any input value $\vec{x} = (x_1, x_2, \ldots, x_N)$, can be expressed as follows:

$$F(\vec{x}, MF, R, C) = \frac{\sum\limits_{p=1}^{P} \sum\limits_{j=1}^{R_p} R_j^p \prod\limits_{m=1}^{N_p} \mu_m^{j_p}(x_m)}{\sum\limits_{p=1}^{P} \sum\limits_{j=1}^{R_p} \prod\limits_{m=1}^{N_p} \mu_m^{j_p}(x_m)} \qquad (2)$$

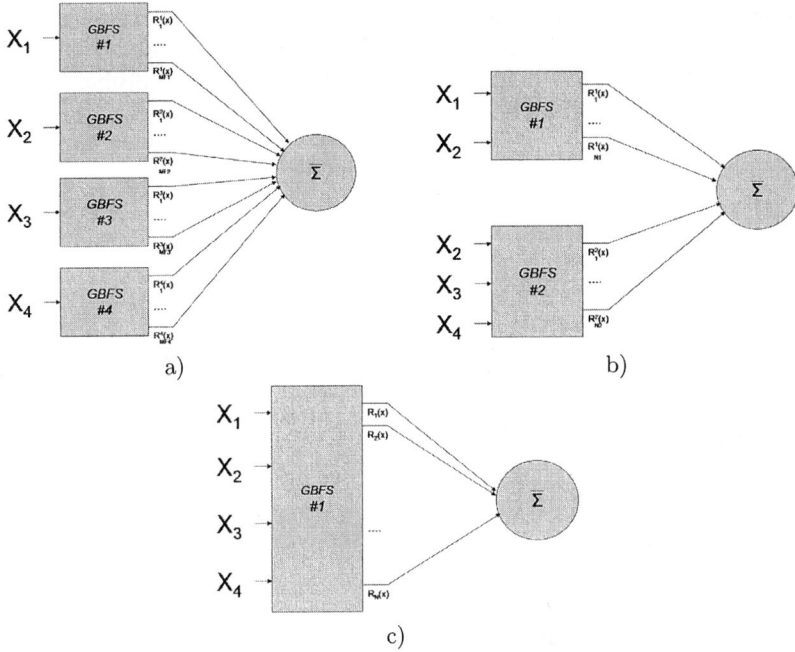

Fig. 3. MGFS Different topologies a) one simple topology considers one GBFS per variable, therefore having simple rules with only one antecedent, one for each membership function of each variable. b) a high number of more complex topologies might take place, here we present a two-GBFS topology; the first GBFS has variables x_1, x_2 while the second GBFS has variables x_2, x_3, x_4. See how one single variable might appear in several GBFS with different membership functions distribution. c) the most expensive topology has a single GBFS for all the variables. The number of rules here might be too high in terms of interpretability and efficiency.

where explicit statement is made on the dependency of the output function with the structure of membership functions of the system MF, with the consequents of the whole set of rules R, and with the hard structure of the system $C = \{\{x_1^1, x_2^1, \ldots x_{N1}^1\}, \{x_1^2, x_2^2, \ldots x_{N2}^2\}, \ldots, \{x_1^P, x_2^P, \ldots x_{Np}^P\}\}$, i.e, the input variables entering each individual GBFS.

Several architecture forms are therefore possible for any given problem with a set of input variables (see $Fig.3$). The simplest case is when each variable forms a single set (maybe some variables are even not present if they don't have influence on the output of the system), then each rule on each set of variables has a single antecedent.

Many more complex configurations are possible for all the combinations (permutations on the number of input variables) until keeping only one set of the whole number of input variables, that is the case of having a (single) *grid based fuzzy system* (**GBFS**).

Now that we have an architecture that, when possible, might reduce the number of rules exponentially, we will study how we can calculate the subjacent data model structure to group the variables and form the optimal MultiGrid-Based Fuzzy System (**MGFS**).

3   Hard-Structure Identification

In this section we present a very effective algorithm to determine the GBFSs that will comprise the system hard-structure, the final MGFS, as shown in $Fig.2$. Notice the high difficulty to guess the GBFSs that could form the structure of the system. For 4 variables for example, 4 GBFSs of 1 variable + 6 GBFSs of two variables + 4 GBFSs of three variables (+1 GBFS of one variable) are candidate elements to form the structure. Now we would have to choose from every possible grouping of these 15 GBFSs, which one perform best with the less number of rules possible to form the final MGFS, giving thousands of possible combinations even for this simple problem.

To tackle this problem, a Top-Down algorithm is presented now. It starts from a whole, complete and effective, grid fuzzy system, proceeding to decrease its complexity step by step while possible. Then it goes step by step, building a simpler MGFS each time, leaving this optimal number of membership functions per variable, and recalculating the consequents of new rules. On each step of the algorithm, if the error obtained is "similar" to the more complete GBFS previous one, we will take the new simpler configuration as the chosen one. Similarly here we mean that the error does not increase over a tolerance level. If the error obtained is higher, another alternative will be chosen. This will go working until no simpler GBFS can be obtained without keeping the error level. The detailed algorithm is presented now:

Top-Down Algorithm

1: **Initialize** the fuzzy system with a complete grid, setting optimal number of membership functions per input variable.
2: **while** further steps can be performed **do**
3:    NumberOfGroups = the number of variable groups in this moment
4:    **for** I = 1:NumberOfGroups **do**
5:       **Decompose** the group 'I' into all the possibilities having one variable less and add them temporary to the group of variables, taking away the group 'I'
6:       Take away temporary any groups included in other one bigger.
7:       **Evaluate** the system configuration and take the overall error.
8:       **if** the new error $\leq$ previous error + tolerance. **then**
9:          Make definitive the previous decomposition
10:          **for** J = 1:NumberOfNewAddedSubGroups **do**
11:             Take away the subgroup J temporary
12:             Take away temporary any groups included in other one bigger

13:          **Evaluate** the system configuration and take the overall error.
14:          **if** The new error ≤ previous error + tolerance **then**
15:              Make definitive the elimination of subgroup J.
16:          **else**
17:              Undo the previous elimination of subgroup J.
18:          **end if**
19:      **end for**
20:      **else**
21:          **Undo** the previous decomposition.
22:      **end if**
23: **end for**
24: **end while**
25: **Return** the Final optimal configuration for the MultiGrid-Based Fuzzy System.

In steps 7 and 13 we *EVALUATE* by optimizing the consequents and evaluating the error using the data set of input/output points. The system configuration is obtained by taking the number of membership functions per input variable, setting the membership functions equally-distributed on each variable input domain and forming the rules for each sub-grid. Considering the data set D, we perform a Least Square Error (LSE) algorithm to optimize the rules consequents [6].

The well-known expression for the square error given, the data set D, the distribution of membership functions MF, the rule consequents R, and the MGFS configuration C, is:

$$J(D, MF, R, C) = \sum_{x \in D} (y_k - F(\vec{x}, MF, R, C))^2 \qquad (3)$$

Differentiating J over each rule consequent give us a lineal equations system with R parameters and R equations. This procedure to calculate the rule consequents is independent of the form and distribution of the membership functions. Singular Value Decomposition (SVD) will be the method used to solve the equations system [7]. Due to the high redundancy that might appear in the system equations matrix, this method suits fine for our problem.

Once the rule consequents have been optimally calculated, the error of the MGFS will be measured using the *Normalized Root-Mean-Square Error* (*NRMSE*) [6].

Alter applying the whole algorithm we will have the pseudo-optimal structure of groups of variables. Now it remains to perform a final parameter tuning to have the system completely fitted according to the dataset D.

4   Parameter Tuning

Now that we have the final MultiGrid structure, now let's perform the parameter adjustment so that the error is completely minimized for a given membership function configuration.

For this, we will use a triangular partition configuration [5,9] and make use of the method presented in [6]. We have already explained how to calculate the consequents of the rules for a given MF configuration (number and position of the membership functions). Now let's study how we can set the position of the centers of the MFs.

A two-step algorithm is performed to optimize the position of the centers of the MFs. First an initialization is done to set the centers to pseudo-optimal values through a heuristic that we'll explain now. Secondly a gradient-based methodology is performed to obtain the local minimum for the given initial configuration.

The first step is an iterative process with another two phases for calculating a slope parameter for each center and adjust the centers. The objective of this step is to have at each side of each membership function the same amount of error according to the dataset D. In each iteration, for each center c_m^{im} we calculate the value p_m^{im}:

$$p_m^{im} = \frac{1}{\sigma_y^2} \left(\sum_{\substack{k \in D \\ x_m \in \left[c_m^{im-1}, c_m^{im} \right]}} e^2(\vec{x}_k) - \sum_{\substack{k \in D \\ x_m \in \left[c_m^{im}, c_m^{im+1} \right]}} e^2(\vec{x}_k) \right) \qquad (4)$$

A positive value of the parameter p_m^{im} means that the contribution of the left side of the MF to the error is higher than the right side one; therefore we would have to move the center of the MF to the left, and vice versa.

Afterwards we perform the following movement of the centers:

$$\triangle c_m^{im} = \begin{cases} \dfrac{c_m^{im-1} - c_m^{im}}{b} \dfrac{p_m^{im}}{p_m^{im} + \frac{1}{T_m^{im}}}, & \text{if } p_m^{im} \geq 0 \\[3mm] \dfrac{c_m^{im+1} - c_m^{im}}{b} \dfrac{|p_m^{im}|}{|p_m^{im}| + \frac{1}{T_m^{im}}}, & \text{if } p_m^{im} < 0 \end{cases} \qquad (5)$$

Here b is the active radius, which is the maximum variation distance and is used to guarantee that the order of the membership function location remains unchanged (a typical value is $b=2$); T_m^{im} is the temperature which indicates how far the center will be moved. This step of the algorithm will work iteratively moving the centers until a balance takes place in the error on each side of each center.

The last step is to find a local minimum from this initial configuration. For this purpose, it can be chosen any of the gradient-based methods that we can encounter in the literature (steepest descent, conjugate gradient, Levenberg-Marquardt algorithm, etc.)

Now we have described a tool that for a given MultiGrid configuration and for a given membership function configuration, allows us to find pseudo-optimal parameter values for the whole MGFS. But, as in [8], here we will go one step further and try to optimize the number of membership functions associated with each input variable of each MGBS that forms the MGFS. This is the task that is accomplished in the next section.

5   Fine-Structure Identification

We have explained two important phases for our approach for function approximation. The MultiGrid structure algorithm has been presented, we have the key to reduce in many cases the complexity of our system exponentially. A parameter adjustment algorithm has also been obtained for a given MultiGrid structure and a fixed number of membership functions per input variable. Now let's explain how we can adjust the number of membership functions per input variable according to a final error objective. Too complex systems might be useless though also give much less error, and too simple systems might not perform well enough. The algorithm we explain here will give us the last key to obtain the system that fits best to the NRMSE we want for our system with the less complexity possible.

This part of the whole algorithm will work together with parameter tuning to try to obtain the simpler but more effective system according to a limit in the error that we will impose. The idea is to begin from a topology where all the variables in all the sub-grids begin for example with two membership functions per input variable. The parameter identification sub-algorithm is performed to check if the system in this moment fits the error goal.

Step by step, we check which sub-grid and in which variable adding a new membership function decreases most the error. There we will add a new membership function, and will execute again the parameter identification sub-algorithm to check if the error goal has been passed.

6   Simulations

Now that we have all the tools for the whole method for function approximation, let's execute the whole algorithm for a representative example:

We will demonstrate how the proposed algorithm works with the following example taken from the literature [4,8].

$$F\left(x_1, x_2, x_3, x_4\right) = 10sin\left(\pi x_1 x_2\right) + 0x_3 + 5x_4 + \xi$$
$$\text{with } x_1, x_2, x_3, x_4, \in [0, 1] \tag{6}$$

We have 10.000 training points generated using this function and we will introduce a random error ξ with variance 0.1. We will first evaluate how the structure would be detected. The initial configuration will be a whole grid fuzzy system having 5 membership functions for each variable. We show in table 1, the steps that the algorithm would follow.

Now from this execution we see how the algorithm goes discarding most of the possibilities, taking on each step the only possible configuration according to the stability of the training error. Notice that in fact, from the thousand of possibilities to form a MGFS for 4 input variables, only less than 15 possibilities need to be tested following the algorithm steps to get the optimal MGFS configuration. A final configuration having one grid of two variables (x_1 and x_2) and one grid of one variable (x_4) is taken for parameter adjustment.

Table 1. Trace and results for the Top-Down algorithm for the example

Step of the algorithm	Variable Groups	NRMSE
1	$\{1,2,3,4\}$	0.025
2, 4, 5	$\{2,3,4\}$, $\{1,3,4\}$, $\{1,2,4\}$, $\{1,2,3\}$	0.025
9, 11	$\{1,3,4\}$, $\{1,2,4\}$, $\{1,2,3\}$	0.025
15, 11	$\{1,2,4\}$, $\{1,2,3\}$	0.025
15, 11	$\{1,2,3\}$	0.406
17, 11	$\{1,2,4\}$	0.025
15, 2, 4, 5	$\{2,4\}$,$\{1,4\}$, $\{1,2\}$	0.025
9,11	$\{1,4\}$, $\{1,2\}$	0.025
15,11	$\{1,2\}$	0.406
17,11	$\{1,4\}$	0.715
17, 2, 4, 5	$\{1,2\}$, $\{4\}$	0.025
9,11	$\{1,2\}$	0.406
17, 4, 5	$\{4\}$, $\{1\}$, $\{2\}$	0.435
21, 2, 25	$\{1,2\}$, $\{4\}$	0.025

Notice that this algorithm not only performs the groups' selection but also a task of variable selection is accomplished. In the case where any of the variables does not affect the output of the system, it will be immediately detected and discarded, decreasing even more the complexity of our system for a fine parameter tuning, and final interpretability and usability of the resulting MGFS.

Next let's check the results for the parameter and fine-structure tuning. Setting a limit of 0.01 for the NRMSE, after applying the whole algorithm, the final number of membership functions needed per input variable is 6 for the variables 1 and 2, (0 for the variable 3 that was already discarded by the algorithm of MGFS selection), and 2 for variable number 4. The algorithm works adding membership functions to the first two input variables and without adding anyone to the variable 4, since as noticed in reference [8], the lineal dependence of this variable is easily identified with two membership functions.

7   Conclusions

In this paper we have presented the utility of a MultiGrid-Based Fuzzy System (MGFS) architecture to reduce the complexity of a fuzzy system model when the number of input variables grow up. Besides, it has been presented an algorithm capable of finding a suitable MGBS topology together with the pseudo-optimal parameters defining it, in order to model the underlying system expressed from a set of given I/O data points. As parameters of the MGBS model, it is meant not only the position of the membership functions of every GBFS but also the optimal number of them for a given target accuracy error. Finally, the functioning of the method has been demonstrated through a simple but rather instructive example.

Acknowledgements. This work has been partially supported by the Spanish CICYT Project DPI2001-3219.

References

1. Wang, L.X., Mendel, J.M.: Generating fuzzy rules by learning from examples. IEEE Trans. Syst. Man and Cyber. November/December(1992) 1414–1427
2. Bezdek,J.C.: Pattern Recognition with Fuzzy Objective Function Algorithms. Plenum Press, New York, (1981)
3. Gonzalez, J., Pomares, H., Rojas, I., Ortega, J., Prieto, A.: A New Clustering Technique for Function Approximation. IEEE Trans. on Neural Networks, Vol.13, No.1. (2002) 132–142
4. Gunn, S.R., Brown, M., Bossley:Network Performance Assesment for Neurofuzzy Data Modeling. Lect Not. C.S. (1997) 313–323
5. Rojas, I., Pomares, H., Ortega, J., Prieto, A.: Self-Organized Fuzzy System Generation from Training Examples. IEEE Trans. Fuzzy Systems, vol.8, no.1. February (2000) 23–36
6. Pomares, H., Rojas, I., Ortega, J., Prieto, A.: A systematic approach to a self-generating fuzzy rule-table for function approximation. IEEE Trans. Syst., Man, Cybern. vol.30. (2000) 431–447
7. Golub, G., Loan, C.V.: Matrix Computations. The Johns Hopkins University Press, Baltimore. (1989)
8. Pomares, H., Rojas, I., Gonzalez, J., Prieto, A.: Structure Identification in Complete Rule-Based Fuzzy Systems. IEEE Trans. Fuzz. Vol.10, no. 3. June (2002) 349–359
9. Ruspini, E.H.: A new approach to Clustering, Info Control, no.15,. (1969) 22–32

Inducing Classification Rules from Highly-Structured Data with Composition

René MacKinney-Romero[1] and Christophe Giraud-Carrier[2]

[1] Departmento de Ingeniería Eléctrica, Universidad Autónoma Metropolitana
México D.F. 09950, México
rene@xanum.uam.mx http://xamanek.uam.mx/rene/
[2] ELCA Informatique SA
Lausanne, Switzerland
cgc@elca.ch

Abstract. This paper elaborates on two techniques, deconstruction and composition, to handle complex data in order to learn from it. We propose typed higher-order logic as a suitable representation formalism for domains with complex structured data. Both techniques derive naturally from such framework. A naive sequential covering algorithm which uses both techniques is applied on well known learning datasets (simple and structured) to test them with good results. A further experiment on the change of knowledge representation is presented to showcase the robustness of our approach.

1 Introduction

Inductive learning focuses on techniques for supervised learning from examples. Traditionally, inductive learners have used the attribute-value language to represent training examples and induced hypotheses. The relative simplicity of this attribute-value language representation allows the implementation of efficient learning systems. However, it also makes difficult to apply such systems to domains with complex structure such as molecular biology, where data is rich in structure and the structural information may provide clues essential in inducing insightful concepts. Although not designed primarily to overcome such problems the learning paradigm of Inductive Logic Programming (ILP) [11] allows to tackle such domains. Since ILP is based on first order logic still some work must be done to represent highly structured data in order to learn from it.

It can be argued that, from a knowledge representation point of view, it would be more desirable to be able to capture physical structures in the data with corresponding abstract structures in its representation. For instance, to represent a molecule, which is a collection of connected atoms, as a graph; or a collection of figures, as a set. Then, if we can design learning algorithms capable of manipulating such representations directly, it would be possible to apply machine learning directly and naturally to domains rich in structure. Clearly, the additional expressiveness of the representation may lead to an increase of the search space, which must be constrained in some way. Furthermore, the emphasis should be

R. Monroy et al. (Eds.): MICAI 2004, LNAI 2972, pp. 262–271, 2004.

on gaining insight from the data. Because the quality of the induced knowledge, as measured by both accuracy and comprehensibility, is more important than processing time.

We use these arguments as our motivation for using a typed higher-order logic for knowledge representation, and for upgrading existing learning model classes (e.g., decision tree induction, rule induction, etc.) to this richer representation. Here we elaborate on two techniques presented separately before [9,8] and how combined can be used to induce rules. Further details on the representation are in [3,4,2,12]. A decision tree learning algorithm based on it is described in [4,2] and a genetic programming system that uses this basis is described in [6].

The paper is organised as follows. Section 2 discusses knowledge representation using typed higher-order closed terms. Section 3 briefly discusses deconstruction as a means to obtain characteristic features of examples. Section 4 discusses in more detail predicate construction through function composition and briefly presents a naive sequential covering algorithm based on composition and deconstruction. Section 5 presents experimental results and section 6 presents an experiment on the importance of knowledge representation on the learning process and how our approach handles it. Finally, in section 7 some concluding remarks are presented.

2   Typed Higher-Order Knowledge Representation

In order to capture complex structures we need correspondingly complex abstract data structures or types. Our representation formalism, whose details are in [4], is expressive enough to allow the representation of arbitrary structures as closed terms of the corresponding type. Thus, all information is typed.

We note here that, in this sense, our formalism is a natural extension of the attribute-value framework. Indeed, in the attribute-value language, each attribute has a type (e.g., nominal, real) and examples are tuples (another simple type) of constants drawn from the domains of the corresponding types. The efficiency of learners using this simple representation is in large measure a direct result of its strong typing, as types act as constraints on the search space. Interestingly, ILP has focused on first-order representations implemented in Prolog which has risen the necessity to create an ad-hoc typing system. We believe that this approach, which has proved very valuable [13], still falls short of handling complex data in a straight forward manner.

In contrast, we wish to make types an intrinsic part of first and higher-order representations. This enables the examination of possible relations among distinct elements that have the same type whilst limiting the associated increase of the search space. Of course, it is possible to simulate lack of types by using the same type for all elements of a type (e.g., a tuple). We use the programming language Escher [7] as the vehicle for typed higher-order logic knowledge representation. Escher is an integrated functional and logic programming language, based on Church's theory of types. The syntax of Escher coincides with that of Haskell for the functional subset and includes extensions for quantifiers and set constructs. A formal account of Escher is beyond the scope of this paper. For our purposes here, it is sufficient to state that Escher implements the necessary computational machinery to handle standard abstract data types such as tuples, lists, sets, multisets, trees and graphs. In fact, one can in principle construct any arbitrary abstract data type with its associated structure and operations.

As mentioned above, examples are represented as closed terms of the abstract data type that "best" captures the structure of the domain. We give a few examples to illustrate the approach trying to use standard mathematical (or familiar) notation here to improve readability.

Example 1 *Consider the Mushroom Database available at UCI[1]. Each example describes a mushroom belonging to the Agaricus and Lipidota Family. We can represent examples as tuples using:*

type Mushroom = (CapShape, CapSurface, CapColor, Odor, Bruises)

Note we are using a sample of all the attributes available. Base types can then be declared as follows.[2]

data CapShape = Bell | Conical | Convex | Flat | Knobbed | Sunken
data CapSurface = Fibrous | Grooves | Scaly | Smooth
data CapColor = Brown | Buff | Cinnamon | Gray | Green | Red
data Odor = Almond | Anise | Creosote | Fishy | Foul | None
type Bruises = Boolean

The following is an example of a mushroom.

mushroom = (Convex, Fibrous, Red, None, False)

Example 2 *Consider Michaelsky East-West Challenge [10] involving trains made up of load-carrying cars. Each car has several attributes: shape, length, number of wheels, roof and kind. Each car carries a number of cargo objects as well. We can model such trains as a* list *of cars, i.e.,*

type Train = [Car]

Each car can in turn be represented by a tuple *consisting of its attributes and its load, i.e.,*

type Car = (Shape, Length, Wheels, Kind, Roof, Load)

and each load as a tuple *consisting of an object and number of elements, i.e.,*

type Load = (Object, Number)

The following is the first train going east.

ftrain = [(Rectangular,Long,2,Open,None,(Square,3)),
          (Rectangular,Short,2,Closed,Peaked,(Triangle,1)),
          (Rectangular,Long,3,Open,None,(Hexagon,1)),
          (Rectangular,Short,2,Open,None,(Circle,1))]

Note that this representation has the advantage that all the information relevant to an example is localised but the potential disadvantage that some information may be repeated.

---

[1] http://www.ics.uci.edu/~mlearn/MLRepository.html

[2] Note that the keyword **data** indicates the declaration of a type and the data constructors of that type, whilst the keyword **type** indicates a type synonym.

3 Deconstruction

Now that we have a language to represent structured data as abstract data types, we need mechanisms to manipulate this representation and use it in learning. We first consider the extraction of components or characteristic features from examples.

In order to construct useful hypotheses from examples, we must be able to access their constituent parts in order to discover features relevant to a given classification task. The technique we use to obtain such components is called deconstruction[3]. We will briefly discuss it here and further details can be obtained in [9].

The objective of deconstruction is to take a single term and return the set of its constituent elements. Each abstract data type has, associated with it, a set of *accessor* functions, which essentially perform the inverse operation of its constructor. The user can provide as well any other type declaring its accesor functions. Given a term, deconstruction is applied recursively to it until a base type is encountered. The deconstruction process creates a set of tuple of the form

$$(term, type, value, predicate)$$

where the predicate asserts the membership of a sub-term to the term. To illustrate how deconstruction works, we show the deconstruction of the two examples of section 2. Note that there are no predicates when we are only using the accessor functions.

Example 3 *Some elements of the deconstruction of the sample* mushroom *term in Example 1 are:*
```
(v1, Mushroom, (Convex, Fibrous, Red, False, None), true)
(projCapShape(v1), CapShape, Convex, true)
(projCapSurface(v1), CapSurface, Fibrous, true)
```

Example 4 *Some elements of the deconstruction of the sample* ftrain *term in Example 2 are:*
```
(head(v1), Car, (Rectangular,Long,2,Open,None,(Square,3)), true)
(head(v3), Car, (Rectangular,Short,2,Closed,Peaked,(Triangle,1),
v3 == tail(v1))
(projShape(v4), Shape, Rectangular, v4 == head(v3))
```

Since a term is essentially a tree structure, there is a single *deconstructor chain* for each sub-term, *i.e.* a conjunction of predicates that link each sub-term to the top-level term.

Example 5 *The deconstructor chain of the sub-term* Rectangular *in Example 4 is* v3 == tail(v1) && v4 == head(v3)

---

[3] In [9] the term decomposition was used. With hindsight, we realised this was not a good choice since it may lead to confusion with the notion of composition defined later.

4   Composition

Composition was briefly presented in [8]. We give here further details. Using deconstruction, we can show now how our higher-order framework allows complex conditions to be built on terms using composition. Composition is the (higher-order) function '.' having signature $(.) : (\beta \to \gamma) \to (\alpha \to \beta) \to (\alpha \to \gamma)$ and defined by `(f.g)(x) = f(g(x))` where α, β and γ are types.

In addition to its accessor functions (see section 3), each abstract data type also has a set of *observer* and *modifier* functions[4], which permit the building of conditions on terms. The user provides, in general, observer and modifier functions to suit a particular application domain. There are, however, some general functions that can be supplied for basic types. For instance, the following functions for sets are provided

- *Size.* The function `card: {T} -> Int` that returns the number of elements in a set.
- *Filter.* The function `filter: (T -> Bool) x [T] -> [T]` that takes a predicate and a set as arguments and returns the set obtained from the original one by removing those items that do not satisfy the predicate.
- *Map.* The function `map: (T -> A) x [T] -> [A]` that takes a function and a set as arguments and returns the set obtained from applying the function to all members of the set.

Given a set of functions and a bound on how much to compose them we take each of the functions and try to compose it with another. Once we have performed all possible compositions we decrease the bound. If it reaches zero we stop, otherwise we start again with the augmented set and the new bound.

Note the utility of our higher-order framework as some of these functions take predicates and/or other functions as parameters. By composing accessor, observer and modifier functions, it is possible to construct complex conditions on terms, as illustrated in the following example.

Example 6 *Consider the trains of Example 2. We can test whether a car carries at least one object with the composition*
`(>0).projNumber.projLoad`
Note that this is equivalent using lambda notation to
`(\x -> projNumber (projLoad x)) > 0`
We can test whether a train has less than 3 cars with more than 2 wheels with the composition
`(<3).length.(filter ((>2).projWheels))`
Finally, assume that we are given the functions
`sum: [Int] -> Int`
`map: (T -> S) x [T] -> [S]`
where `sum` *adds up the values of the items in a list of integers and* `map` *takes a*

---

[4] In [4], accessor, observer and modifier functions are treated uniformly as transformations. The distinction highlights the generality of the approach to arbitrary abstract data types

function and a list as arguments and returns the list obtained by applying the function to each item in the original list. Then, we can test complex conditions, such as whether the total cargo of a train is at least 10 objects with the composition

```
(>10).sum.(map (projNumber.projLoad))
```

Finally, note that the building of new functions and predicates through composition is akin to the processes of constructive induction and predicate invention.

4.1   ALFIE

ALFIE, A Learner for Functions In Escher [8,9] is a sequential covering algorithm based on the concepts presented so far. It uses examples as beaming guides in the search for useful properties and induces concepts in the form of decision lists, i.e.,

```
if E1 then t1 else if E2 then t2 else ... if En then tn else t0
```

where each Ei is a Boolean expression and the tj's are class labels. The class t0 is called the *default* and is generally, although not necessarily, the majority class.

ALFIE first uses composition as a pre-processing step to augment its original set of available functions. Given a set of *seed* functions and a depth bound, ALFIE constructs all allowable compositions of functions of up to the given depth bound.

Then the algorithm uses the deconstruction set (see section 3) of the first example and from it finds the E_1 with the highest accuracy (measured as the information gain on covering). It then computes the set of examples that are not yet covered, selects the first one and repeats this procedure until all examples are covered.

Examples are represented as closed terms and the type structure of the top-level term automatically makes available the corresponding accessor, observer and modifier functions. In addition to these, the user may provide a set of functions that can be applied to the components of the examples (e.g., see the functions sum and map in Example 6). Such functions represent properties that may be present in the sub-parts of the structure of the data, as well as auxiliary functions able to transform components. They constitute the *background knowledge* of the learner and may be quite complex.

5   Experiments

The main goal of the experiments was to test how deconstruction and composition can be used to learn from a variety of problems. Therefore we performed experiments on well known datasets both simple and complex.

The outcome was very satisfactory since results were on par with other learning systems. Furthermore, even for well known datasets our approach came up with different, interesting answers.

Table 1. Results for Attribute-value Datasets

Dataset	CN2		ALFIE	
	Training	Test	Training	Test
Mushroom	100.00%	100.00%	98.90%	98.20%
Iris	97.00%	94.00%	97.00%	94.00%
Zoo	100.00%	82.40%	100.00%	97.00%

Table 2. Results for Highly-structured Datasets

Dataset	Progol	ALFIE
Mutagenesis	83.00%	88.00%
Mutagenesis SO	67.00%	83.00%
Mutagenesis RU	81.40%	76.00%
PTE	72.00%	73.90%

5.1 Attribute-Value

We used the learning system *CN2* [5] since it produces a decision list making the comparison easier to the results provided by ALFIE.

Table 1 presents the results obtained for attribute-value datasets. All of them can be obtained from UCI machine learning repository. They appear in the literature often as benchmarks for learning systems. We used the subset of UCI datasets included in the package MLC++. They have the advantage that they have been split using the utility GenXVFILES 3-fold to produce approximately $\frac{2}{3}$ of the examples that are used for training and the rest are used for testing.

In the *Zoo* problem, accuracy is increased given that ALFIE produces conditions in which the value of the attribute hair must be equal to the value of the attribute backbone for crustaceans. This condition simply states the high correlation between the two attributes. Although it may seem strange it points out to interesting facts about the dataset overlooked by CN2.

5.2 Complex Structure

These are the kind of problems we are most interested in. We focused on two well known problems of molecular biology: Mutagenesis [13] and PTE [1]. We used the *Progol* system to benchmark against since the datasets we used have the knowledge representation ready for Progol. We performed experiments on three variants of Mutagenesis: plain, using structural information only and Mutagenesis with regression unfriendly data. In all cases a ten fold cross validation experiment was carried out. The results presented correspond to the average of the ten folds. Table 2 presents the results obtained for these datasets.

We would like to stress the fact that we didn't provide background knowledge that the Progol learning system had at its disposal. Further background knowledge about the rings in the molecule is provided in the Progol dataset. We did not include such information in ALFIE because we were more interested in exploring what was possible to learn just from the highly structured data.

It is interesting to note that the algorithm "invented" the negation as in the property

```
card (filter \x -> (iselS(elemP x)) (atomSetP v1)) <= 0
```

which indicates the absence of Sulphur atoms in a molecule.

6   Knowledge Representation Change

Our main motivation was to develop a framework to handle complex data in a straight forward manner. That is to say that the learning system should be able to cope with different knowledge representations that the user may come up with. The following experiment tests such scenario.

The White King and White Rook versus Black King is a well known dataset in the machine learning community. It consists of examples of chess boards with the positions of the pieces on it. The learning task is to obtain rules that allow to determine when such a board has an illegal configuration.

Although this is an attribute value problem, since examples can be expressed as tuples of six elements, our interest on it was to explore the impact on the learning system if the representation was to be different.

The problem as first stated was simply a collection of predicates stating whether a board was illegal

```
illegal(WKingRank,WKingFile,WRookRank,WRookFile,BKingRank,BRookFile).
```

This was changed to a representation that has a board as three tuple each representing the position of a piece. In Prolog that was represented as

```
illegal(Board).
whiteking(Board,WKingRank,WKingFile).
whiterook(Board,WRookRank,WRookFile).
blacking(Board,BKingRank,BKingFile).
```

Additionally a predicate adjacent has been defined that is able to determine whether a piece is next to another. In Escher the representation is

```
type PosWKing = (WKingRank, WKingFile)
type PosWRook = (WKingRank, WRookFile)
type PosBKing = (BKingRank, BKingFile)
type Board = (PosWKing, PosWRook, PosBKing)
```

Given this representation ALFIE search space contains elements such as

```
((adjacent (fileP (whiteKingP v1)) (fileP (blackKingP v1)))
  && ((fileP (whiteRookP v1)) == (fileP (blackKingP v1))))
((adjacent (fileP (whiteKingP v1)) (fileP (blackKingP v1)))
  && (adjacent (rankP (whiteKingP v1)) (rankP (whiteRookP v1))))
```

ALFIE tries to produce hypothesis involving the positions of the pieces straight away. In contrast Progol search space contains

```
[C:-65,65,71,0 illegal(A)  :- wk(A,B,B).]
[C:5,506,499,0 illegal(A)  :- bk(A,B,C).]
[C:-35,176,185,0 illegal(A)  :- wr(A,B,C), bk(A,B,D).]
[C:59,66,55,0 illegal(A)  :- wr(A,B,C), B=4.]
[C:51,66,55,0 illegal(A)  :- wr(A,B,C), B=4, adj(C,C).]
[C:81,74,57,0 illegal(A)  :- wr(A,B,C), C=6, adj(B,B), adj(C,C).]
[C:4,506,499,0 illegal(A)  :- wr(A,B,C), adj(B,B).]
[C:41,57,49,0 illegal(A)  :- bk(A,B,C), B=4.]
```

It can be observed that because of the variables involved, Progol must try a large number of combinations. Moreover, there is no clear relation between the different variables and Progol attempts to find a solution. The search space is not bounded as in ALFIE by deconstruction.

Solutions. The solution found by Progol with the 6-tuple representation contains the following predicates clauses.

```
illegal(A,B,C,D,E,F)  :- adj(E,A), adj(B,F).
illegal(A,B,C,D,C,E).
```

For the structured problems the following clauses are found among other. There is no clear relation between both solutions.

```
illegal(A)  :- wk(A,B,C), wr(A,D,E), bk(A,F,C), adj(E,B), adj(E,F).
illegal(A)  :- wk(A,B,C), wr(A,D,E), bk(A,F,F), adj(E,D).
illegal(A)  :- wr(A,B,7), bk(A,C,D), adj(D,B).
```

In the case of ALFIE we obtain for the unstructured case the first rule

```
if (v2,v3,v4,v5,v6,v7) = v1 && adjacent v3 v7 then illegal
```

And for the structured case the first rule

```
if adjacent (fileP (whiteKingP v1)) (fileP (blackKingP v1))
   then illegal
```

Note that both conditions are the same.

7   Conclusion

A different approach to handling highly-structured examples in inductive learning has been presented. This approach relies on the complementary techniques of deconstruction and function composition. Deconstruction makes it possible to access the components of a structure and composition provides a powerful means of constructing complex conditions on both the components and the structure of the examples. These techniques allow to learn from highly structured data.

A learning system, ALFIE, that uses both deconstruction and function composition was described, together with experimental results. The results show our approach learning from both simple and highly structured data. Furthermore, we were able to test our approach coping with different knowledge representations.

Acknowledgements. This work was supported in part by EPSRC Grant GR/L21884, and grants from the CONACYT and the Universidad Autónoma Metropolitana (México). Special thanks to Tony Bowers for his implementation of the Escher interpreter.

References

1. S.H. Muggleton M.J.E. Sternberg A. Srinivasan, R.D. King. Carcinogenesis predictions using ilp. In *Proceedings of the 7th International Workshop ILP-97*, pages 273–287, 1997.
2. C. Giraud-Carrier A.F. Bowers and J.W. Lloyd. Classification of individuals with complex structure. In *Proceedings of the Seventeenth International Conference on Machine Learning*, 2000.
3. C. Kennedy J.W. Lloyd A.F. Bowers, C. Giraud-Carrier and R. MacKinney-Romero. A framework for higher-order inductive machine learning. In *Proceedings of the COMPULOGNet Area Meeting on Representation Issues in Reasoning and Learning*, pages 19–25, 1997.
4. A. F. Bowers, C. Giraud-Carrier, and J. W. Lloyd. Classification of individuals with complex structure. In *Proceedings of the Seventeenth International Conference on Machine Learning (ICML'2000)*, pages 81–88. Morgan Kaufmann, 2000.
5. P. Clark and T. Niblett. The CN2 induction algorithm. *Machine Learning*, 3:261–283, 1989.
6. C. Kennedy and C. Giraud-Carrier. An evolutionary approach to concept learning with structured data. In *Proceedings of the Fourth International Conference on Artificial Neural Networks and Genetic Algorithms*, pages 331–336, 1999.
7. J.W. Lloyd. Programming in an integrated functional and logic language. *Journal of Functional and Logic Programming*, 1999(3), 1999.
8. R. MacKinney-Romero. Learning using higher-order functions. In *Proceedings of ILP'99 Late-Breaking Papers*, pages 42–46, 1999.
9. R. MacKinney-Romero and C. Giraud-Carrier. Learning from highly-structured data by decomposition. In *Proceedings of the Third European Conference on Principles and Practice of Knowledge Discovery in Databases*, pages 436–441, 1999.
10. R. S. Michalski and J.B. Larson. Inductive inference of VL decision rules. pages 33–44. Workshop on Pattern-directed Inference Systems, 1977.
11. S. Muggleton and L. De Raedt. Inductive logic programming: Theory and methods. *Journal of Logic Programming*, 19/20:629–679, 1994.
12. C. Giraud-Carrier P.A. Flach and J.W. Lloyd. Strongly-typed inductive concept learning. In *Proceedings of the Eighth International Conference on Inductive Logic Programming*, pages 185–194, 1998.
13. A. Srinivasan R.D. King, S. Muggleton and M. Sternberg. Structure-activity relationships derived by machine learning: The use of atoms and bonds and their connectivities to predict mutagenicity in inductive logic programming. In *Proceedings of the National Academy of Sciences*, pages 93:438–442, 1996.

Comparing Techniques for Multiclass Classification Using Binary SVM Predictors

Ana Carolina Lorena and André C.P.L.F. de Carvalho

Laboratório de Inteligência Computacional (LABIC),
Instituto de Ciências Matemáticas e de Computação (ICMC),
Universidade de São Paulo (USP),
Av. do Trabalhador São-Carlense, 400 - Centro - Cx. Postal 668
São Carlos - São Paulo - Brasil
{aclorena,andre}@icmc.usp.br

Abstract. Multiclass classification using Machine Learning techniques consists of inducing a function $f(\mathbf{x})$ from a training set composed of pairs $(\mathbf{x}_i, y_i)$ where $y_i \in \{1, 2, \ldots, k\}$. Some learning methods are originally binary, being able to realize classifications where $k = 2$. Among these one can mention Support Vector Machines. This paper presents a comparison of methods for multiclass classification using SVMs. The techniques investigated use strategies of dividing the multiclass problem into binary subproblems and can be extended to other learning techniques. Results indicate that the use of Directed Acyclic Graphs is an efficient approach in generating multiclass SVM classifiers.

1   Introduction

Supervised learning consists of inducing a function $f(\mathbf{x})$ from a given set of samples with the form $(\mathbf{x}_i, y_i)$, which accurately predicts the labels of unknown instances [10]. Applications where the labels y_i assume k values, with $k > 2$, are named multiclass problems.

Some learning techniques, like Support Vector Machines (SVMs) [3], originally carry out binary classifications. To generalize such methods to multiclass problems, several strategies may be employed [1,4,8,14]. This paper presents a study of various approaches for multiclass classification with SVMs. Although the study is oriented toward SVMs, it can be applied to other binary classifiers, as all the strategies considered divide the problem into binary classification subproblems.

A first standard method for building k class predictors form binary ones, named *one-against-all* (1AA), consists of building k classifiers, each distinguishing one class from the remaining classes [3]. The label of a new sample is usually given by the classifier that produces the highest output.

Other common extension to multiclass classification from binary predictions is known as *all-against-all* (AAA). In this case, given k classes, $k(k-1)/2$ classifiers are constructed. Each of the classifiers distinguishes one class c_i from another class c_j, with $i \neq j$. A majority voting among the individual responses

R. Monroy et al. (Eds.): MICAI 2004, LNAI 2972, pp. 272–281, 2004.

can then be employed to predict the class of a sample $\mathbf{x}$ [8]. The responses of the individual classifiers can also be combined by an Artificial Neural Network (ANN) [6], which weights the importance of the individual classifiers in the final prediction. Another method to combine such kind of predictors, suggested in [14], consists of building a *Directed Acyclic Graph* (DAG). Each node of the DAG corresponds to one binary classifier. Results indicate that the use of such structure can save computational time in the prediction phase.

In another front, Dietterich and Bariki [4] suggested the use of error-correcting output codes (ECOC) for representing each class in the problem. Binary classifiers are trained to learn the "bits" in these codes. When a new pattern is submitted to this system, a code is obtained. This code is compared to the error-correcting ones with the Hamming distance. The new pattern is then assigned to the class whose error-correcting codeword presents minimum Hamming distance to the code predicted by the individual classifiers.

As SVMs are large margin classifiers [15], that aim at maximizing the distance between the patterns and the decision frontier induced, Allwein et al. [1] suggested using the margin of a pattern in computing its distance to the output codes (*loss-based* ECOC). This measure has the advantage of providing a notion of the reliability of the predictions made by the individual SVMs.

This paper is organized as follows: Section 2 presents the materials and methods employed in this work. It describes the datasets considered, as well as the learning techniques and multiclass strategies investigated. Section 3 presents the experiments conducted and results achieved. Section 4 concludes this paper.

2   Materials and Methods

This section presents the materials and methods used in this work, describing the datasets, learning techniques and multiclass strategies employed.

2.1   Datasets

The datasets used in the experiments conducted were extracted from the UCI benchmark database [16]. Table 1 summarizes these datasets, showing the numbers of instances (♯ Instances), of continuous and nominal attributes (♯ Attributes), of classes (♯ Classes), the majority error (ME) and if there are missing values (MV). ME represents the proportion of examples of the class with most patterns on the dataset.

Instances with missing values were removed from the "bridges" and "posoperative" datasets. This procedure left 70 and 87 instances in the respective datasets. For the "splice" dataset, instances with attributes different from the base pairs Adenine, Cytosine, Guanine and Thymine were eliminated. The other values of attributes present reflects the uncertainty inherent to DNA sequencing processes. This left a total of 3175 instances.

Almost all datasets have been pre-processed so that data had zero mean and unit variance. The exceptions were "balance" and "splice". In "balance", many

Table 1. Datasets summary description

Dataset	♯ Instances	♯ Attributes (cont., nom.)	♯ Classes	ME	MV
Balance	625	4 (0, 4)	3	46.1%	no
Bridges	108	11 (0, 11)	6	32.9%	yes
Glass	214	9 (9, 0)	6	35.5%	no
Iris	150	4 (4, 0)	3	33.3%	no
Pos-operative	90	8 (0, 8)	3	71.1%	yes
Splice	3190	60 (0, 60)	3	50.0%	no
Vehicle	846	18 (18, 0)	4	25.8%	no
Wine	178	12 (12, 0)	3	48.0%	no
Zoo	90	17 (2, 15)	7	41.1%	no

attributes became null, so the pre-processing procedure was not applied. In the "splice" case, a coding process suggested in the bioinformatics literature, which represents the attributes in a canonical format, was employed instead [13]. Thus, the number of attributes used in "splice" was of 240.

2.2   Learning Techniques

The base learning technique employed in the experiments for comparison of multiclass strategies was the Support Vector Machine (SVM) [3]. Inspired by the Statistical Learning Theory [17], this technique seeks an hyperplane $\mathbf{w} \cdot \mathbf{x} + b = 0$ able of separating data with a maximal margin.

For performing this task, it solves the following optimization problem:

$$\textbf{Minimize: } \|\mathbf{w}\|^2$$
$$\textbf{Restrictions: } y_i(\mathbf{w} \cdot \mathbf{x}_i + b) \geq 1$$

where $\mathbf{x}_i \in \Re^m$, $y_i \in \{-1, +1\}$ and $i = 1, \dots, n$.

In the previous formulation, it is assumed that all samples are far from the decision border from at least the margin value, which means that data have to be linearly separable. Since in real applications the linearity restriction is often not complied, slack variables are introduced [5]. These variables relax the restrictions imposed to the optimization problem, allowing some patterns to be within the margins. This is accomplished by the following optimization problem:

$$\textbf{Minimize: } \|\mathbf{w}\|^2 + C \sum_{i=1}^{n} \xi_i$$

$$\textbf{Restrictions: } \begin{cases} \xi_i \geq 0 \\ y_i (\mathbf{w} \cdot \mathbf{x_i} + b) \geq 1 - \xi_i \end{cases}$$

where C is a constant that imposes a tradeoff between training error and generalization and the ξ_i are the slack variables.

The decision frontier obtained is given by Equation 1.

$$f(\mathbf{x}) = \sum_{\mathbf{x_i} \in \text{SV}} y_i \alpha_i \mathbf{x_i} \cdot \mathbf{x} + b \tag{1}$$

where the constants α_i are called "Lagrange multipliers" and are determined in the optimization process. SV corresponds to the set of support vectors, patterns for which the associated lagrange multipliers are larger than zero. These samples are those closest to the optimal hyperplane. For all other patterns the associated lagrange multiplier is null, so they do not participate on the determination of the final hypothesis.

The classifier represented in Equation 1 is still restricted by the fact that it performs a linear separation of data. This can be solved by mapping the data samples to a high-dimensional space, also named feature space, where they can be efficiently separated by a linear SVM. This mapping is performed with the use of Kernel functions, that allow the access to spaces of high dimensions without the need of knowing the mapping function explicitly, which usually is very complex. These functions compute dot products between any pair of patterns in the feature space. Thus, the only modification necessary to deal with non-linearity is to substitute any dot product among patterns by the Kernel product.

For combining the multiple binary SVMs generated in some of the experiments, Artificial Neural Networks (ANNs) of the Multilayer Perceptron type were considered. These structures are inspired in the structure and learning ability of a "biological brain" [6]. They are composed of one or more layers of artificial neurons, interconnected to each other by weighted links. These weights codify the knowledge of the network. This weighted scheme may be an useful alternative to power the strength of each binary SVM in the final multiclass prediction, as described in the following section.

2.3 Multiclass Strategies

The most straightforward way to build a k class multiclass predictor from binary classifiers is to generate k binary predictors. Each classifier is responsible to distinguish a class c_i from the remaining classes. The final prediction is given by the classifier with the highest output value [3]. This method is called *one-against-all* (1AA) and is illustrated in Equation 2, where $i = 1, \ldots, k$ and $\boldsymbol{\Phi}$ represents the mapping function in non-linear SVMs.

$$f(\mathbf{x}) = \max_i(\mathbf{w}_i \cdot \boldsymbol{\Phi}(\mathbf{x}) + b_i) \tag{2}$$

Other standard methodology, called *all-against-all* (AAA), consists of building $k(k-1)/2$ predictors, each differentiating a pair of classes c_i and c_j, with $i \neq j$. For combining these classifiers, a majority voting scheme (VAAA) can be applied [8]. Each AAA classifier gives one vote for its preferred class. The final result is given by the class with most votes.

Platt et al. [14] points some drawbacks in the previous strategies. The main problem is a lack of theory in terms of generalization bounds. To overcome this, they developed a method to combine the SVMs generated in the AAA methodology, based on the use of *Directed Acyclic Graphs* (DAGSVM). The authors provide error bounds on the generalization of this system in terms of the number of classes and the margin achieved by each SVM on the nodes.

A Directed Acyclic Graph (DAG) is a graph with oriented edges and no cycles. The DAGSVM approach uses the SVMs generated in an AAA manner in each node of a DAG. Computing the prediction of a pattern using the DAGSVM is equivalent to operating a list of classes. Starting from the root node, the sample is tested against the first and last classes of the problem, which usually corresponds to the first and last elements of the initial list. The class with lowest output in the node is then eliminated from the list, and the node equivalent to the new list obtained is consulted. This process proceeds until one unique class remains. Figure 1 illustrates an example where four classes are present. For k classes, $k - 1$ SVMs are evaluated on test. Thus, this procedure speeds up the test phase.

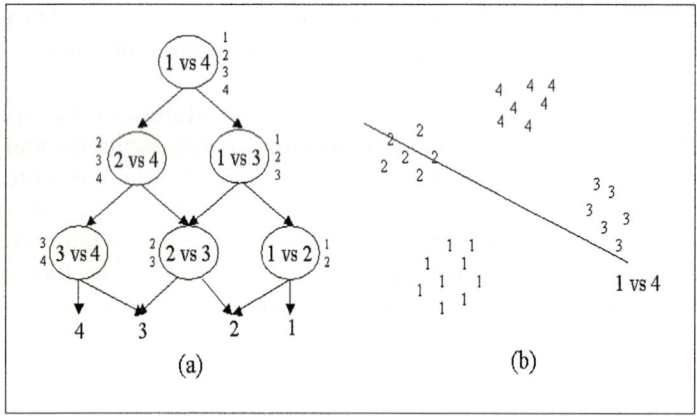

Fig. 1. (a) DAGSVM of a problem with four classes; (b) illustration of the SVM generated for the 1 vs 4 subproblem [14]

This paper also investigates the use of ANNs in combining the AAA predictors. The ANN can be viewed as a technique to weight the predictions made by each classifier.

In an alternative multiclass strategy, Dietterich and Bariki [4] proposed the use of a distributed output code to represent the k classes in the problem. For each class, a codeword of length l is assigned. These codes are stored on a matrix $M \in \{-1, +1\}^{kXl}$. The rows of this matrix represents the codewords of each class and the columns, the l binary classifiers desired outputs. A new pattern $\mathbf{x}$ can be classified by evaluating the predictions of the l classifiers, which generates a string s of length l. This string is then compared to the rows of M. The sample is assigned to the class whose row is closest according to some measure, like the Hamming distance [4]. Commonly, the size of the codewords has more bits than needed to represent each class uniquely. The additional bits can be used to correct eventual classification errors. For this reason, this method is named *error-correcting output coding* (ECOC).

Allwein et al. [1] points out that the use of the Hamming distance ignores the loss function used in training, as well as confidences attached to the predictions made by each classifier. The authors claim that, in the SVM case, the use of the margins obtained in the classification of the patterns for computing the distance measure can improve the performance achieved by ECOC, resulting in the *loss-based ECOC method* (LECOC). Given a problem with k classes, let M be the matrix of codewords of lengths l, r a label and $f_i(\mathbf{x})$ the prediction made by the i-th classifier. The loss-based distance of a pattern $\mathbf{x}$ to a label r is given by Equation 3.

$$d_M(r, \mathbf{x}) = \sum_{i=1}^{l} \max\{(1 - M(r,i)f_i(\mathbf{x})), 0\} \tag{3}$$

Next section presents the experiments conducted using each of the described strategies for multiclass classification.

3   Experiments

To obtain better estimates of the generalization performance of the multiclass methods investigated, the datasets described in Section 2.1 were first divided in training and test sets following the *10-fold cross-validation* methodology [10]. According to this method, the dataset is divided in ten disjoint subsets of approximately equal size. In each train/test round, nine subsets are used for training and the remaining is left for test. This makes a total of ten pairs of training and test sets. The error of a classifier on the total dataset is then given by the average of the errors observed in each test partition.

For ANNs, the training sets obtained were further subdivided in training and validation subsets, in a proportion of 75% and 25%, respectively. While the training set was applied in the determination of the network weights, the validation set was employed in the evaluation of the generalization capacity of the ANN on new patterns during its training. The network training was stopped when the validation error started to increment, in a strategy commonly referred as *early-stopping* [6]. With this procedure, overfitting to training data can be reduced. The validation set was also employed in the determination of the best network architecture. Several networks with different architectures were generated for each problem, and the one with lower validation error was chosen as the final ANN classifier. In this work, the architectures tested were one-hidden-layer ANNs completely connected with 1, 5, 10, 15, 20, 25 and 30 neurons on the hidden layer. The standard back-propagation algorithm was employed on training with a learning rate of 0.2 and the SNNS (*Stuttgart Neural Network Simulator*) [19] simulator was used in the networks generation.

The software applied in SVMs induction was the SVMTorch II tool [2]. In all experiments conducted, a Gaussian Kernel with standard deviation equal to 5 was used. The parameter C was kept equal to 100, default value of SVMTorch II. Although the best values for the SVM parameters may differ for each multiclass strategy, they were kept the same to allow a fair evaluation of the differences between the techniques considered.

The codewords used in the ECOC and LECOC strategies were obtained following a heuristic proposed in [4]. Given a problem with $3 \leq k \leq 7$ classes, k codewords of length $2^{k-1} - 1$ are constructed. The codeword of the first class is composed only of ones. For the other classes c_i, where $i > 1$, it is composed of alternate runs of 2^{k-i} zeros and ones.

Following, Section 3.1 summarizes the results observed and Section 3.2 discusses the work conducted.

3.1   Results

Table 2 presents the accuracy (percent of correct classifications) achieved by the multiclass strategies investigated. The first and second best accuracies obtained in each dataset are indicated in boldface and italic, respectively.

Table 2. Multiclass strategies accuracies

Dataset	1AA	VAAA	AAA-ANN	DAGSVM	ECOC	LECOC
Balance	96.5±3.1	97.9±2.0	**99.2±0.8**	*98.4±1.8*	90.7±4.7	96.5±3.1
Bridges	58.6±19.6	60.0±17.6	58.6±12.5	**62.9±16.8**	58.6±20.7	*61.4±19.2*
Glass	64.9±14.2	67.3±10.3	*68.2±9.7*	**68.7±11.9**	65.3±14.5	65.8±14.6
Iris	*95.3±4.5*	**96.0±4.7**	**96.0±4.7**	**96.0±4.7**	94.7±6.1	*95.3±4.5*
Pos op.	*63.5±18.7*	**64.6±19.3**	62.2±17.1	61.3±26.7	61.3±18.9	*63.5±18.7*
Splice	**96.8±0.9**	**96.8±0.7**	83.4±1.7	**96.8±0.7**	93.6±1.7	**96.8±0.9**
Vehicle	85.4±4.5	85.5±4.0	84.4±5.3	**85.8±4.0**	81.9±4.7	*85.5±3.6*
Wine	**98.3±2.7**	**98.3±2.7**	*97.2±3.9*	**98.3±2.7**	97.2±4.1	**98.3±2.7**
Zoo	**95.6±5.7**	*94.4±5.9*	*94.4±5.9*	*94.4±5.9*	**95.6±5.7**	**95.6±5.7**

Similarly to Table 2, Table 3 presents the mean time spent on training, in seconds. All experiments were carried out on a dual Pentium II processor with 330 MHz and 128 MB of RAM memory.

Table 4 shows the medium number of support vectors of the models (♯ SVs). This value is related to the processing time required to classify a given pattern. A smaller number of SVs leads to faster predictions [9].

In the case of the AAA combination with ANNs, other question to be considered in terms of classification speed is the network architecture. Larger networks lead to slower classification speeds. Table 5 shows, for each dataset, the number of hidden neurons of the best ANN architectures obtained in each dataset.

3.2   Discussion

According to Table 2, the accuracy rates achieved by the different multiclass techniques are not much different. Applying the corrected resampled t-test statistic described in [12] to the first and second best results in each dataset, no statistical significance can be detected at 95% of confidence level. However, the results suggests that the most successful strategy is the DAGSVM. On the other side, the

Table 3. Training time (seconds)

Dataset	1AA	VAAA	AAA-ANN	DAGSVM	ECOC	LECOC
Balance	5.7±1.1	**4.2±1.1**	33.7±1.0	**4.2±1.1**	*4.3±0.5*	*4.3±0.5*
Bridges	**11.3±1.1**	43.4±1.9	50.3±10.8	43.4±1.9	64.3±3.4	64.3±3.4
Glass	**10.2±0.8**	*38.7±2.0*	42.1±3.2	*38.7±2.0*	72.5±2.0	72.5±2.0
Iris	**1.7±1.2**	1.9±1.0	11.7±7.0	1.9±1.0	*1.8±1.2*	*1.8±1.2*
Pos op.	**3.6±0.8**	4.4±0.7	7.3±1.2	4.4±0.7	*3.7±0.7*	*3.7±0.7*
Splice	476.7±17.1	**205.9±1.2**	*388.2±4.2*	**205.9±1.2**	497.4±41.5	497.4±41.5
Vehicle	*21.9±0.9*	**17.4±1.1**	96.7±1.3	**17.4±1.1**	45.2±1.3	45.2±1.3
Wine	*4.9±0.6*	**4.7±0.7**	13.5±19.0	**4.7±0.7**	5.0±0.0	5.0±0.0
Zoo	**12.3±1.2**	*36.8±3.5*	50.3±2.1	*36.8±1.2*	108.6±1.9	108.6±1.9

Table 4. Mean number of Support Vectors (SVs)

Dataset	1AA	VAAA	AAA-ANN	DAGSVM	ECOC	LECOC
Balance	208.2±10.7	*115.3±6.5*	*115.3±6.5*	**69.8±3.5**	208.2±10.7	208.2±10.7
Bridges	*129.6±4.1*	175.3±3.4	175.3±3.4	**59.3±2.7**	879.4±29.7	879.4±29.7
Glass	275.5±7.5	*252.2±6.2*	*252.2±6.2*	**100.6±5.3**	2160.4±67.9	2160.4±67.9
Iris	40.8±2.7	*24.5±1.4*	*24.5±1.4*	**16.7±1.3**	40.7±2.8	40.7±2.8
Pos op.	106.8±7.6	*61.0±6.1*	*61.0±6.1*	**54.2±4.9**	107.3±7.5	107.3±7.5
Splice	5043.0±16.4	*3625.2±10.3*	*3625.2±10.3*	**2577.1±9.0**	5043.0±16.4	5043.0±16.4
Vehicle	669.0±11.1	*469.2±5.0*	*469.2±5.0*	**232.1±9.7**	1339.5±22.7	1339.5±22.7
Wine	75.2±1.5	*54.3±3.4*	*54.3±3.4*	**35.3±3.2**	75.2±1.5	75.2±1.5
Zoo	*132.9.6±4.5*	191.2±6.8	191.2±6.8	**62.0±4.8**	1608.4±65.8	1608.4±65.8

Table 5. Number of hidden neurons in the AAA-ANN architectures

Balance	Bridges	Glass	Iris	Pos op.	Splice	Vehicle	Wine	Zoo
1	5	5	10	1	1	5	30	5

ECOC method presents, in general, the lowest performance. It must be observed that the simple modification of this technique with the use of a distance measure based in margins (LECOC) improves its results substantially. In a comparison among the methods with best and worse accuracy in each dataset, a statistical significance of 95% can be verified in the following datasets: "balance", "splice" and "vehicle".

Comparing the three methods for AAA combination, no statistical significance at 95% of confidence level can be verified in terms of accuracy - except on the "splice" dataset, where the ANN integration was worst. It should be noticed that the ANN approach presents a tendency in some datasets towards lowing the standard deviation of the accuracies obtained, indicating some stability gain.

Concerning training time, in general the faster methodology was 1AA. The ECOC and LECOC approaches, on the other hand, were generally slower in this phase. The lower training time achieved by VAAA and DAGSVM in some datasets is due to the fact that this method trains each SVM on smaller subsets of data, which speeds it up. In the AAA-ANN case, the ANN training time has to be taken into account, which gives a larger time than those of VAAA or DAGSVM.

From Table 4 it can be observed that the DAGSVM method had the lower number of SVs in all cases. This means that the DAG strategy speeds up the classification of new samples. VAAA figures as the method with second lowest number of SVs. Again, the simpler data samples used in the binary classifiers induction in this case can be the cause of this result. It should be noticed that, although AAA-ANN has the same number of SVs of VAAA, the ANN prediction stage has to be considered.

4   Conclusion

This work evaluated several techniques for multiclass classification with SVMs, originally binary predictors. There are currently works generalizing SVMs to the multiclass case directly [7,18]. However, the focus of this work was on the use of SVMs as binary predictors, and the methods presented can be extended to other Machine Learning techniques.

Although some differences were observed among the methods in terms of performance, in general no technique can be considered the most suited for a given application. When the main requirement is classification speed, while maintaining a good accuracy, the results observed indicate that an efficient alternative for SVMs is the use of the DAG approach.

As future research, further experiments should be conducted to tune the parameters of the SVMs (Gaussian Kernel standard deviation and the value of C). This could improve the results obtained in each dataset.

Acknowledgements. The authors would like to thank the financial support provided by the Brazilian research councils FAPESP and CNPq.

References

1. Allwein, E. L., Shapire, R. E., Singer, Y.: Reducing Multiclass to Binary: a Unifying Approach for Margin Classifiers. Proceedings of the 17th International Conference on Machine Learning, Morgan Kaufmann (2000) 9–16
2. Collobert, R., Bengio, S.: SVMTorch: Support vector machines for large scale regression problems. Journal of Machine Learning Research, Vol. 1 (2001) 143–160
3. Cristianini, N., Taylor, J. S.: An Introduction to Support Vector Machines. Cambridge University Press (2000)
4. Dieterich, T. G., Bariki, G.: Solving Multiclass Learning Problems via Error-Correcting Output Codes. Journal of Artificial Intelligence Research, Vol. 2 (1995) 263–286
5. Cortes, C., Vapnik, V. N.: Support Vector Networks. Machine Learning, Vol. 20 (1995) 273–296

6. Haykin, S.: Neural Networks - A Compreensive Foundation. Prentice-Hall, New Jersey (1999)

7. Hsu, C.-W., Lin, C.-J.: A comparison of methods for multi-class support vector machines. IEEE Transactions on Neural Networks, Vol. 13 (2002) 415–425

8. Kreßel, U.: Pairwise Classification and Support Vector Machines. In Scholkopf, B., Burges, C. J. C., Smola, A. J. (eds.), Advances in Kernel Methods - Support Vector Learning, MIT Press (1999) 185–208

9. Mayoraz, E., Alpaydm, E.: Support Vector Machines for Multi-class Classification. Technical Report IDIAP-RR-98-06, Dalle Molle Institute for Perceptual Artificial Intelligence, Martigny, Switzerland (1998)

10. Mitchell, T.: Machine Learning. McGraw Hill (1997)

11. Müller, K. R. et al.: An Introduction to Kernel-based Learning Algorithms. IEEE Transactions on Neural Networks, Vol. 12, N. 2 (2001) 181–201

12. Nadeau, C., Bengio, Y.: Inference for the Generalization Error. Machine Learning, Vol. 52, N. 3 (2003) 239–281

13. Pedersen, A. G., Nielsen, H.: Neural Network Prediction of Translation Initiation Sites in Eukaryotes: Perspectives for EST and Genome Analysis. Proceedings of ISMB'97 (1997) 226–233

14. Platt, J. C., Cristianini, N., Shawe-Taylor, J.: Large Margin DAGs for Multiclass Classification. In: Solla, S. A., Leen, T. K., Müller, K.-R. (eds.), Advances in Neural Information Processing Systems, Vol. 12. MIT Press (2000) 547–553

15. Smola, A. J. et al.: Introduction to Large Margin Classifiers. In Advances in Large Margin Classifiers, Chapter 1, MIT Press (1999) 1–28

16. University of California Irvine: UCI benchmark repository - a huge collection of artificial and real-world datasets. http://www.ics.uci.edu/~mlearn

17. Vapnik, V. N.: The Nature of Statistical Learning Theory. Springer-Verlag (1995)

18. Weston, J., Watkins, V.: Multi-class Support Vector Machines. Technical Report CSD-TR-98-04, Department of Computer Science, University of London, 1998.

19. Zell, A. et al.: SNNS - Stuttgart Neural Network Simulator. Technical Report 6/95, Institute for Parallel and Distributed High Performance Systems (IPVR), University of Stuttgart (1995)

Analysing Spectroscopic Data Using Hierarchical Cooperative Maximum Likelihood Hebbian Learning

Donald MacDonald[1,2], Emilio Corchado[1,2], and Colin Fyfe[2]

[1] Department of Civil Engineering, University of Burgos, Spain.
escorchardo@ubu.es
[2] Applied Computational Intelligence Research Unit, University of Paisley, Scotland
{Donald.MacDonald,Colin.Fyfe}@paisley.ac.uk

Abstract. A novel approach to feature selection is presented in this paper, in which the aim is to visualize and extract information from complex, high dimensional spectroscopic data. The model proposed is a mixture of factor analysis and exploratory projection pursuit based on a family of cost functions proposed by Fyfe and MacDonald [12] which maximizes the likelihood of identifying a specific distribution in the data while minimizing the effect of outliers [9,12]. It employs cooperative lateral connections derived from the Rectified Gaussian Distribution [8,14] to enforce a more sparse representation in each weight vector. We also demonstrate a hierarchical extension to this method which provides an interactive method for identifying possibly hidden structure in the dataset.

1 Introduction

We introduce a method which is closely related to factor analysis and exploratory projection pursuit. It is a neural model based on the Negative Feedback artificial neural network, which has been extended by the combination of two different techniques. Firstly by the selection of a cost function from a family of cost functions which identify different distributions. This method is called Maximum-Likelihood Hebbian learning [6]. Secondly, cooperative lateral connections derived from the Rectified Gaussian Distribution [8] were added to the Maximum-Likelihood method by Corchado et al. [14] which enforced a greater sparsity in the weight vectors.

In this paper we provide a hierarchical extension to the Maximum-likelihood method.

2 The Negative Feedback Neural Network

The Negative Feedback Network [4,5] is the basis of the Maximum-Likelihood model. Consider an N-dimensional input vector, $\mathbf{x}$, and a M-dimensional output vector, $\mathbf{y}$, with W_{ij} being the weight linking input j to output i and let η be the learning rate.

R. Monroy et al. (Eds.): MICAI 2004, LNAI 2972, pp. 282–291, 2004.

The initial situation is that there is no activation at all in the network. The input data is fed forward via weights from the input neurons (the **x**-values) to the output neurons (the **y**-values) where a linear summation is performed to give the activation of the output neuron. We can express this as:

$$y_i = \sum_{j=1}^{N} W_{ij} x_j, \ \forall i \tag{1}$$

The activation is fed back through the same weights and subtracted from the inputs (where the inhibition takes place):

$$e_j = x_j - \sum_{i=1}^{M} W_{ij} y_i, \ \forall j, \tag{2}$$

After that simple Hebbian learning is performed between input and outputs:

$$\Delta W_{ij} = \eta e_j y_i \tag{3}$$

Note that this algorithm is clearly equivalent to Oja's Subspace Algorithm [7] since if we substitute Equation 2 in Equation 3 we get:

$$\Delta W_{ij} = \eta e_j y_i = \eta \left(x_j - \sum_k W_{kj} y_k \right) y_i \tag{4}$$

This network is capable of finding the principal components of the input data [4] in a manner that is equivalent to Oja's Subspace algorithm [7], and so the weights will not find the actual Principal Components but a basis of the Subspace spanned by these components.

Factor Analysis is a technique similar to PCA in that it attempts to explain the data set in terms of a smaller number of underlying factors. However Factor Analysis begins with a specific model and then attempts to explain the data by finding parameters which best fit this model to the data. Charles [2] has linked a constrained version of the Negative Feedback network to Factor Analysis. The constraint put on the network was a rectification of either the weights or the outputs (or both). Thus if the weight update resulted in negative weights, those weights were set to zero; if the feedforward mechanism gives a negative output, this was set to zero. We will use the notation $[t]^+$ for this rectification: if t<0, t is set to 0; if t>0, t is unchanged.

3 ε-Insensitive Hebbian Learning

It has been shown [10] that the nonlinear PCA rule

$$\Delta W_{ij} = \eta \left(x_j f(y_i) - f(y_i) \sum_k W_{kj} f(y_k) \right) \tag{5}$$

can be derived as an approximation to the best non-linear compression of the data.

Thus we may start with a cost function

$$J(W) = 1^T E\left\{\left(\mathbf{x} - Wf\left(W^T\mathbf{x}\right)\right)^2\right\} \tag{6}$$

which we minimise to get the rule(5). [12] used the residual in the linear version of (6) to define a cost function of the residual

$$J = f_1(\mathbf{e}) = f_1(\mathbf{x} - W\mathbf{y}) \tag{7}$$

where $f_1 = \|.\|^2$ is the (squared) Euclidean norm in the standard linear or nonlinear PCA rule. With this choice of $f_1(\ )$, the cost function is minimized with respect to any set of samples from the data set on the assumption that the residuals are chosen independently and identically distributed from a standard Gaussian distribution [15].

We may show that the minimization of J is equivalent to minimizing the negative log probability of the residual, $\mathbf{e}$ if $\mathbf{e}$ is Gaussian. Let:

$$p(\mathbf{e}) = \left(\frac{1}{Z}\right)\exp(-\mathbf{e}^2) \tag{8}$$

The factor Z normalizes the integral of $p(\mathbf{y})$ to unity.

Then we can denote a general cost function associated with this network as

$$J = -\log p(\mathbf{e}) = (\mathbf{e})^2 + K \tag{9}$$

where K is a constant. Therefore performing gradient descent on J we have

$$\Delta W \propto -\frac{\partial J}{\partial W} = -\frac{\partial J}{\partial \mathbf{e}}\frac{\partial \mathbf{e}}{\partial W} \approx \mathbf{y}(2\mathbf{e})^T \tag{10}$$

where we have discarded a less important term (see [11] for details).

In general[9], the minimisation of such a cost function may be thought to make the probability of the residuals greater dependent on the probability density function (pdf) of the residuals. Thus if the probability density function of the residuals is known, this knowledge could be used to determine the optimal cost function.

[12] investigated this with the (one dimensional) function:

$$p(\mathbf{e}) = \frac{1}{2+\varepsilon}\exp\left(-|\mathbf{e}|_\varepsilon\right) \tag{11}$$

where

$$|\mathbf{e}|_\varepsilon = \begin{cases} 0 \_ \forall |\mathbf{e}| < \varepsilon \\ |\mathbf{e}| - \varepsilon \_ otherwise \end{cases} \tag{12}$$

with ε being a small scalar ≥ 0.

[12] described this in terms of noise in the data set. However we feel that it is more appropriate to state that, with this model of the pdf of the residual, the optimal $f_1(\ )$ function is the ε-insensitive cost function:

$$f_1(\mathbf{e}) = |\mathbf{e}|_\varepsilon \tag{13}$$

In the case of the Negative Feedback Network, the learning rule is

$$\Delta W \propto -\frac{\partial J}{\partial W} = -\frac{\partial f_1(e)}{\partial e}\frac{\partial e}{\partial W} \tag{14}$$

which gives:

$$\Delta W_{ij} = \begin{cases} 0 & if\,\left|e_j\right| < \varepsilon \\ \eta y_i\left(sign(e_j)\right) & otherwise \end{cases} \tag{15}$$

The difference with the common Hebb learning rule is that the sign of the residual is used instead of the value of the residual. Because this learning rule is insensitive to the magnitude of the input vectors **x**, the rule is less sensitive to outliers than the usual rule based on mean squared error.

4   Maximum Likelihood Hebbian Learning

Now the ε-insensitive learning rule is clearly only one of a possible family of learning rules which are suggested by the family of exponential distributions. Let the residual after feedback have probability density function

$$p(\mathbf{e}) = \left(\frac{1}{Z}\right)\exp(-|\mathbf{e}|^p) \tag{16}$$

Then we can denote a general cost function associated with this network as

$$J = -\log p(\mathbf{e}) = |\mathbf{e}|^p + K \tag{17}$$

where K is a constant. Therefore performing gradient descent on J we have

$$\Delta W \propto -\frac{\partial J}{\partial W} = -\frac{\partial J}{\partial e}\frac{\partial e}{\partial W} \approx y(p\,|\mathbf{e}|^{p-1}\,sign(\mathbf{e}))^T \tag{18}$$

where T denotes the transpose of a vector. We would expect that for leptokurtotic residuals (more kurtotic than a Gaussian distribution), values of p<2 would be appropriate, while for platykurtotic residuals (less kurtotic than a Gaussian), values of p>2 would be appropriate. Therefore the network operation is:

Feedforward:
$$y_i = \sum_{j=1}^{N} W_{ij}x_j, \;\; \forall_i \tag{19}$$

Feedback:
$$e_j = x_j - \sum_{i=1}^{M} W_{ij}y_i \tag{20}$$

Weight change:
$$\Delta W_{ij} = \eta.y_i.sign(e_j)|e_j|^{p-1} \tag{21}$$

[12] described their rule as performing a type of PCA, but this is not strictly true since only the original (Oja) ordinary Hebbian rule actually performs PCA. It might be

more appropriate to link this family of learning rules to Principal Factor Analysis since this method makes an assumption about the noise in a data set and then removes the assumed noise from the covariance structure of the data before performing a PCA. We are doing something similar here in that we are basing our PCA-type rule on the assumed distribution of the residual. By maximising the likelihood of the residual with respect to the actual distribution, we are matching the learning rule to the pdf of the residual. This method has been linked to the standard statistical method of Exploratory Projection Pursuit (EPP) [4,13,16]. EPP also gives a linear projection of a data set but chooses to project the data onto a set of basis vectors which best reveal the interesting structure in the data.

5   The Rectified Gaussian Distribution

5.1   Introduction

The Rectified Gaussian Distribution [8] is a modification of the standard Gaussian distribution in which the variables are constrained to be non-negative, enabling the use of non-convex energy functions.

The multivariate normal distribution can be defined in terms of an energy or cost function in that, if realised samples are taken far from the distribution's mean, they will be deemed to have high energy and this will be equated to low probability. More formally, we may define the standard Gaussian distribution by:

$$p(\mathbf{y}) = Z^{-1}e^{-\beta E(\mathbf{y})}, \tag{22}$$

$$E(\mathbf{y}) = \left(\tfrac{1}{2}\right)\mathbf{y}^T \mathbf{A}\mathbf{y} - \mathbf{b}^T \mathbf{y} \tag{23}$$

The quadratic energy function $E(\mathbf{y})$ is defined by the vector $\mathbf{b}$ and the symmetric matrix $\mathbf{A}$. The parameter $\beta = \frac{1}{T}$ is an inverse temperature. Lowering the temperature concentrates the distribution at the minimum of the energy function.

5.2   The Energy Function and the Cooperative Distribution

The quadratic energy function $E(\mathbf{y})$ can have different types of curvature depending on the matrix $\mathbf{A}$. Consider the situation in which the distribution of the firing of the outputs of our neural network follows a Rectified Gaussian Distribution.

Two examples of the Rectified Gaussian Distribution are the competitive and the cooperative distributions. The modes of the competitive distribution are well-separated by regions of low probability. The modes of the cooperative distribution are closely spaced along a non-linear continuous manifold. Our experiments focus on a network based on the use of the cooperative distribution.

Neither distribution can be accurately approximated by a single standard Gaussian. Using the Rectified Gaussian, it is possible to represent both discrete and continuous variability in a way that a standard Gaussian cannot.

The sorts of energy function that can be used are only those where the matrix A has the property:

$$\mathbf{y}^T \mathbf{A} \mathbf{y} > 0 \quad \text{for all} \quad \mathbf{y} : y_i > 0, i = 1...N \tag{24}$$

where N is the dimensionality of **y**. This condition is called co-positivity. This property blocks the directions in which the energy diverges to negative infinity.

The cooperative distribution in the case of N variables is defined by:

$$A_{ij} = \delta_{ij} + \frac{1}{N} - \frac{4}{N} \cos\left(\frac{2\pi}{N}(i-j)\right) \tag{25}$$

$$b_i = 1 \tag{26}$$

where δ_{ij} is the Kronecker delta and i and j represent the identifiers of output neuron.

To speed learning up, the matrix **A** can be simplified [3] to:

$$A_{ij} = \left(\delta_{ij} - \cos(2\pi(i-j)/N)\right) \tag{27}$$

and is shown diagrammatically in Figure 1. The matrix **A** is used to modify the response to the data based on the relation between the distances between the outputs.

5.3 Mode-Finding

Note that the modes of the Rectified Gaussian are the minima of the energy function, subject to non-negativity constraints. However we will use what is probably the simplest algorithm, the projected gradient method, consisting of a gradient step followed by a rectification:

$$y_i(t+1) = [y_i(t) + \tau(b - Ay)]^+ \tag{28}$$

where the rectification $[\ ]^+$ is necessary to ensure that the y-values keep to the positive quadrant. If the step size τ is chosen correctly, this algorithm can provably be shown to converge to a stationary point of the energy function [1]. In practice, this stationary point is generally a local minimum.

The mode of the distribution can be approached by gradient descent on the derivative of the energy function with respect to **y**. This is:

$$\Delta \mathbf{y} \propto -\frac{\partial E}{\partial \mathbf{y}} = -(\mathbf{Ay} - \mathbf{b}) = \mathbf{b} - \mathbf{Ay} \tag{29}$$

which is used as in Equation 28.

Now the rectification in Equation 28 is identical to the rectification which Corchado [14] used in the Maximum-Likelihood Network.

We use the standard Maximum-Likelihood Network but now with a lateral connection (which acts after the feed forward but before the feedback). Thus we have

Feedforward:
$$y_i = \sum_{j=1}^{N} W_{ij} x_j, \quad \forall i \tag{30}$$

Lateral Activation Passing: $y_i(t+1) = [y_i(t) + \tau(b - Ay)]^+$ (31)

Feedback: $e_j = x_j - \sum_{i=1}^{M} W_{ij} y_i,$ (32)

Weight change: $\Delta W_{ij} = \eta . y_i . sign(e_j) | e_j |^{p-1}$ (33)

where the parameter τ represents the strength of the lateral connections.

6   Generating a Reduced Scatterplot Matrix Using Cooperative Maximum Likelihood Learning

When researchers initially investigated spectroscopic data they looked for structure by generating a scatterplot matrix in which they plotted each dimension of the data against one another. This technique rapidly became less viable as the dimensionality of the data increased.

Investigators later used techniques such as PCA to provide a single projection which tried to provide as much information as possible. In our method, unlike PCA we have no ordering in our projections, but we reduce the number of factors back down to a manageable level where we can generate this scatterplot matrix and look for the structure by eye. As ML looks for correlations or clusters, it will generate factors which are a linear combination of the data, resulting in fewer factors than the dimensions of the data.

7   Hierarchical Cooperative Maximum Likelihood Method (HCML)

ML and FA can only provide a linear projection of the data set. There may be cases where the structure of the data may not be captured by a single linear projection. In such cases a hierarchical scheme may be beneficial. In this method we project the data, and then perform brushing to select data within regions of interest which we then re-project.

This can be done in two ways, firstly by projecting the data using the ML method, select the data points which are interesting and re-run the ML network on the selected data. Using this method only the projections are hierarchical.

A second more interesting adaptation is to use the resulting projected data of the previous ML network as the input to the next layer. Each subsequent layer of the network identifying structure among fewer data points in a lower dimensional subspace.

The Hierarchical Cooperative Maximum Likelihood method can reveal structure in the data which would not be identified by a single Maximum Likelihood projection as each subsequent projection can analyse different sections of the subspace spanned by the data.

8   The Spectroscopic Stain Glass Data

The data used to illustrate our method is composed of samples from 76 different sections of the window. The window has 6 colours which are green, red, blue, yellow, pink and white. After a morphological study the structure of the red stain glass sections were found to consist of two layers, one transparent and the other coloured. This resulted in the re-sampling of the red glass as two separate samples, one red and the other transparent. After this the data contained 450 data vectors obtained from 90 samples each having been analysed 5 times. The data is 1020 dimensions, which after normalisation was reduced to 390 dimensions.

9   Results and Conclusions

In this section we show the results obtained on the spectroscopic data and highlight the differences in the projections obtained by PCA and ML. We also demonstrate the HCML Method.

Comparison of PCA and ML on the Spectroscopic Data

In Figure 1 we show the comparison of PCA and ML projections of the spectroscopic data on the first 4 eigenvectors/factors respectively. ML (Figure 1a) clearly shows more structure and greater separation between clusters than is achieved with PCA (Figure 1b).

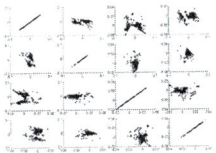   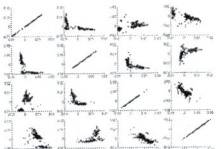

a. ML on spectroscopic data.   b. PCA on spectroscopic data.

Fig. 1. ML and PCA on spectroscopic data.

Figure 2 shows a comparison of the first 2 eigenvector pairs (Figures 2b, 2d) against the ML first two factor pairs (Figures 2a, 2c). In Figure 2a the projection is more spread out with a large separation between the two main clusters. There is a very strongly grouped central cluster in the Figure 2c, which contains glass from class 28. Class 10 is at the top of the right most cluster and class 4 at the right part of other cluster. The first eigenvector pair in Figure 2b shows two distinct clusters. In the center between these two clusters we can see classes 28 and 70 together,18 on its own again and 70 and 52 are almost distinct from the left cluster. We can see that there is some structure in the clusters which hints at further sub-clusters. Unlike Figure 2a, Class 10 in the bottom left of the Figure 2b is not completely distinct from class 23, which is spread throughout the cluster from the top to the bottom.

ML factor pair 1-3 (Figure 2c) is more defined than any other eigenvector/factor pair, showing much greater definition of sub-clusters, separation of class 18, 70 as a cluster, 28 as a cluster, 47 is in the center of the projection, distinct if spread out along the y-axis. In the right most cluster we can see very distinct structure which suggests 9 sub-clusters, upon investigation these give quite distinct and sensible groupings. Table 1 shows some of the classes in each of these sub-clusters.

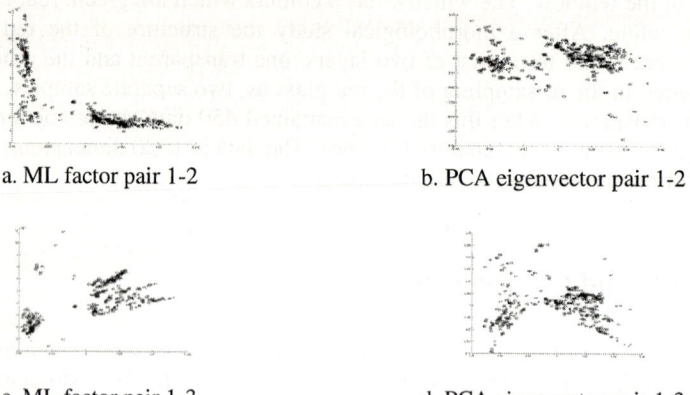

a. ML factor pair 1-2   b. PCA eigenvector pair 1-2

c. ML factor pair 1-3   d. PCA eigenvector pair 1-3

Fig. 2. A comparison of the ML factor 1-2, 1-3 pair and PCA eigenvector 1-2, 1-3 pair.

Table 1. Classes belonging to 6 of the sub-clusters found in the right most cluster of Figure 2c.

Cluster	1	2	3	4	5	6
Classes	19, 24	11,46, 49,70	3, 5, 7, 60	22, 44, 64	51, 51t	53, 59

PCA eigenvector pair 1-3 (Figure 2d) suggests some sub-clustering in the right most cluster but upon investigation these sub-clusters are not well defined, containing an uninterpretable mix of classes.

Results of HCML on Spectroscopic Data

Figure 3 shows the result of HCML on the right most cluster of Figure 2c, the outputs of the 4 ML factors we used as the inputs to the second layer of the HCML network, this resulted in the greater separation between the clusters, Figure 3.

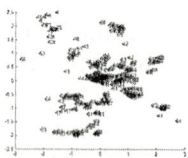

Fig. 3. Result of HCML on right cluster in Figure 2c.

In Figure 3, we can see that the HCML shows new clusters in the hierarchical projection of the original factors from Figure 2c. The projection identifies separate clusters and a central mass which after a separate projection gives more clusters still. The HCML method has the advantage that the selection of regions of interest can occur repeatedly until the structure in the data has been fully identified.

We have developed a new method for the visualization of data which can be used as a complementary technique to PCA.

We have shown that the combination of the scatter plot matrices with HCML providing a method for selecting a combination of factor pairs which identify strong structure in the data. By then selecting these points and projecting through the HCML network and re-projecting in a further layer the network can identify further structure in the data.

References

1. D.P. Bertsekas, Nonlinear Programming. Athena Scientific, Belmont, MA, (1995)
2. D. Charles, and C. Fyfe, Modeling Multiple Cause Structure Using Rectification Constraints. Network: Computation in Neural Systems, 9:167-182, May (1998)
3. D. Charles, Unsupervised Artificial Neural Networks for the Identification of Multiple Causes in Data. PhD thesis, University of Paisley. (1999)
4. C. Fyfe, Negative Feedback as an Organising Principle for Artificial Neural Networks, PhD Thesis, Strathclyde University. (1995)
5. C. Fyfe A Neural Network for PCA and Beyond, Neural Processing Letters, 6:33-41. 1996.
6. C. Fyfe, and E. Corchado, Maximum Likelihood Hebbian Rules. European Symposium on Artificial Neural Networks. (2002)
7. E. Oja, Neural Networks, Principal Components and Subspaces, International Journal of Neural Systems, 1:61-68. (1989)
8. H.S. Seung, N.D. Socci, and D. Lee, The Rectified Gaussian Distribution, Advances in Neural Information Processing Systems, 10. 350 (1998).
9. A.J. Smola and B. Scholkopf, A Tutorial on Support Vector Regression. Technical Report NC2-TR-1998-030, NeuroCOLT2 Technical Report Series. (1998)
10. L. Xu, Least Mean Square Error Reconstruction for Self-Organizing Nets", Neural Networks, Vol. 6, pp. 627-648. (1993)
11. J. Karhunen, and J. Joutsensalo, Representation and Separation of Signals Using Non-linear PCA Type Learning, Neural Networks, 7:113-127. (1994)
12. C. Fyfe, and D. MacDonald, ε-Insensitive Hebbian learning", Neuro Computing, (2002)
13. J. Friedman and J. Tukey. A Projection Pursuit Algorithm for Exploratory Data Analysis. IEEE Transaction on Computers, (23): 881-890. (1974)
14. E. Corchado and C. Fyfe, Orientation Selection Using Maximum Likelihood Hebbian Learning, International Journal of Knowledge-Based Intelligent Engineering Systems Volume 7 Number 2, ISSN: 1327-2314. Brighton, United Kingdom. April (2003)
15. C.M. Bishop, Neural Networks for Pattern Recognition, Oxford,(1995)
16. E. Corchado, D. MacDonald, and C. Fyfe, Maximum and Minimum Likelihood Hebbian Learning for Exploratory Projection Pursuit, Data mining and Knowledge Discovery, Kluwer Academic Publishing, (In press)

Feature Selection-Ranking Methods in a Very Large Electric Database

Manuel Mejía-Lavalle[1], Guillermo Rodríguez-Ortiz[1], Gustavo Arroyo[1], and Eduardo F. Morales[2]

[1] Instituto de Investigaciones Eléctricas, Gerencia de Sistemas Informáticos
Reforma 113, 62490 Cuernavaca, Morelos, México,
{mlavalle,gro,garroyo}@iie.org.mx
[2] ITESM - Cuernavaca
eduardo.morales@itesm.mx

Abstract. Feature selection is a crucial activity when knowledge discovery is applied to very large databases, as it reduces dimensionality and therefore the complexity of the problem. Its main objective is to eliminate attributes to obtain a computationally tractable problem, without affecting the quality of the solution. To perform feature selection, several methods have been proposed, some of them tested over small academic datasets. In this paper we evaluate different feature selection-ranking methods over a very large real world database related with a Mexican electric energy client-invoice system. Most of the research on feature selection methods only evaluates accuracy and processing time; here we also report on the amount of discovered knowledge and stress the issue around the boundary that separates relevant and irrelevant features. The evaluation was done using *Elvira* and *Weka* tools, which integrate and implement state of the art data mining algorithms. Finally, we propose a promising feature selection heuristic based on the experiments performed.

1 Introduction

Data mining is mainly applied to large amounts of stored data to look for the implicit knowledge hidden within this information. In other words, it looks for tendencies or patterns of behavior that allow to improve actual organizational procedures of marketing research, production, operation, maintenance, invoicing and others. To take advantage of the enormous amount information currently available in many databases, algorithms and tools specialized in the automatic discovery of hidden knowledge within this information have been developed; this process of non-trivial extraction of relevant information that is implicit in the data is known as Knowledge Discovery in Databases (KDD), where the data mining phase plays a central role in this process [1].

It has been noted, however, that when very large databases are going to get mined, the mining algorithms get very slow, requiring too much time to process the information and sometimes making the problem intractable. One way to attack this problem is to reduce the amount of data before applying the mining process [2]. In particular, the pre-processing method of feature selection applied to the data before mining has shown to be successful, because it eliminates the irrelevant or redundant

R. Monroy et al. (Eds.): MICAI 2004, LNAI 2972, pp. 292–301, 2004.

attributes that cause the mining tools to become inefficient, but preserving the classification quality of the mining algorithm. Sometimes the percentage of instances correctly classified gets even higher when using feature selection, because the data to mine are free of noise or data that cause that the mining tool to generate overfitted models [3].

In general, wrapper and filter methods have been applied to feature selection. Wrapper methods, although effective to eliminate irrelevant and redundant attributes, are very slow because they apply the mining algorithm many times, changing the number of attributes each execution time, as they follow some search and stop criteria [4]. Filter methods are more efficient using existing techniques such as decision trees algorithms, neuronal networks, nearest neighborhood, etc., that take into account dependencies between attributes. Another technique, called ranking method, uses some type of information gain measurement between individual attributes and the class, and it is very efficient [5]; however, because it measures the relevance of each isolated attribute, they cannot detect if redundant attributes exist, or if a combination of two attributes, apparently irrelevant when analyzed independently, can be transformed into relevant [6].

On the other hand, CFE (Federal Commission of Electricity in Mexico) faces the problem to accurately detecting customers that illicitly use energy, and consequently to reduce the losses due to this concept. At present time, a lot of historical information is stored in the Commercial System (SICOM), whose database was developed and it is maintained by CFE. SICOM was created mainly to register the users contract information, and the invoicing and collection data; this database has several years of operation and has a great amount of accumulated data (millions of records).

To make feasible the mining of this large database, in an effective and efficient way, in this paper we present an evaluation of different filter-ranking methods for supervised learning. The evaluation takes into account not only the classification quality and the processing time obtained after the filter application of each ranking method, but also it considers the discovered knowledge size, which, the smaller, the easier to interpret.

Also the boundary selection topic to determine which attributes must be considered relevant and which irrelevant is approached, since the ranking methods by themselves do not give this information, this decision is left without criterion. We propose an extension, simple to apply, that allows unifying the criterion for the attributes boundary in the different evaluated ranking methods.

Finally, based on the experimentation results, we propose a heuristic that looks for the efficient combination of ranking methods with the effectiveness of the wrapper methods. Although our work focuses on the SICOM data, the lessons learned can be applied to other real world databases with similar problems.

2 Related Work

The emergence of Very Large Databases (VLDB) leads to new challenges that the mining algorithms of the 90´s are incapable to attack efficiently. This is why new specialized mining algorithms for VLDB are required. According to [7], from the point of view of the mining algorithms, the main lines to deal with VLDB (scaling up algorithms) are: a) to design fast algorithms, optimizing searches, reducing complexity, finding approximate solutions, or using parallelism; b) to divide the data based on the variables involved or the number of examples; and c) to use relational representations instead of a single table.

In particular, these new approaches in turn give origin to Data Reduction or Dimensional Reduction. Data Reduction tries to eliminate variables, attributes or instances that do not contribute information (or they do not contribute much information) to the KDD process, or to group the values that a variable can take (discretizing). These methods are generally applied before the actual mining is performed. Although in the 90´s the pre-processing was minimum, and almost all the discovery work was left to the mining algorithm, every day we see more and more Data Pre-processing activities. This pre-processing allows the mining algorithm to do its work more efficiently (faster) and effectively (better quality).

In fact, the specialized literature mentions the *curse of dimensionality*, referring to the fact that the processing time of many induction methods grows dramatically (sometimes exponentially) with the number of attributes. Searching for improvements on VLDB processing power (necessary with tens of attributes and hundreds of thousands of instances), two main groups of methods have appeared: wrappers and filters.

The wrapper methods basic approach is to use the same induction algorithm to select the relevant variables and then to execute the classification task or mining process. The mining algorithm executes as many times as it changes the number of attributes for each run. With a 100 attribute dataset the total number of possible states and runs would reach 1.26×10^{30}, which tells us that to use an exhaustive method is out of consideration, except for databases with very few attributes.

On the other hand, filter methods use algorithms that are independent to the mining algorithm and they are executed previous to the mining step. Among filter methods are those algorithms for relevant variable selection, generally called feature selection, and the instance sampling methods, also known as sub sampling algorithms [8].

A great variety of filter methods exist for feature selection. Some authors consider the ID3 algorithm [9] (and its extensions) as one of the first proposed approaches to filter, even so ID3 is more used as a mining algorithm. Among the pioneering filter methods and very much cited are FOCUS [10], that makes an exhaustive search of all the possible attribute subgroups, but this is only appropriate for problems with few attributes, and RELIEF [11] that has the disadvantage of not being able to detect redundant attributes.

Koller [12] uses a distance metric called cross-entropy or KL-distance, that compares two probability distributions and indicates the error, or distances, among them, and obtains around 50% reduction on the number of attributes, maintaining the quality of classification and being able to significantly reduce processing times (for example, from 15 hours of a wrapper scheme application, to 15 minutes for the proposed algorithm). The final result is "sub optimal" because it assumes independence between attributes, which it is not always true. Piramuthu [6] evaluates 10 different measures for the attribute-class distance, using Sequential Forward Search (SFS) that includes the best attributes selected by each measure into a subset, such that the final result is a "better" attribute subset than the individual groups proposed by each method. However, the results are not compared with the original attribute set, and so it is not possible to conclude anything about the effectiveness of each measure, and although SFS manages to reduce the search space, multiple mining algorithm runs varying the attribute subsets are necessary to validate the scheme, and this is computationally expensive.

SOAP is a method that operates only on numerical attributes [13] and has a low computational cost; it counts the number of times the class value changes with respect to an attribute whose values have been sorted into ascending order. SOAP reduces the number of attributes as compared to other methods; nevertheless it does not handle discrete attributes and the user has to supply the number of attributes that will be used in the final subset. Another filter scheme, SAPPP [5], handles continuous and discrete attributes; initially SAPPP selects an attribute subset and each time that increases the number of attributes uses a decision tree construction algorithm to evaluate if the added attributes in the subset are more relevant with respect to the previous tree. It verifies if they affect the classification quality (accuracy) and if they do not affect it, they are discarded (because they are irrelevant) and the process stops. A 30% reduction in processing time was obtained, maintaining the classification accuracy. In spite of everything, work must be done to solve how many instances to use at the beginning and the increment selection for each step.

Molina [14] tried to characterize 10 different methods to select attributes by measuring the impact of redundant and irrelevant attributes, as well as of the number of instances. Significant differences could not be obtained, and it was observed that, in general, the results of the different methods depended on the data being used. Stoppiglia [15] proposes to introduce an additional random variable to the database, such that, after the attribute ranking time, all those variables that obtained less scores than the random variable, will be considered irrelevant. This criterion represents an alternative to the statistical Fisher´s test. The results show that the method obtains a good attributes selection, comparable to other techniques. This method is attractive because of simplicity, although more experiments are needed to prove its effectiveness, for example, it could be that most of the time the random variable manages only to eliminate or discriminate very few attributes (or none), so that the power to select attributes would be reduced. In section 4.3, we will explore this and other subjects.

Other proposals for feature selection explore the use of neural networks, fuzzy logic, genetic algorithms, and support vector machines [3], but they are computationally expensive. In general, it is observed that the methods that have been proposed: a) are verified with small, academic or simulated databases; b) obtain results that vary with the domain of the application; c) obtain greater quality of the result applying greater computational cost; d) depend on suitable tuning; and e) they do not evaluate the size of the extracted knowledge, which is a key factor to understand the phenomenon underlying the data.

3   The Application Domain

One the main CFE functions is to distribute to the costumers the electrical energy produced in the different generating plants in Mexico. Related to distribution, CFE faces different problems that prevent it to recover certain amount of "lost income" from the 100% of the total energy for sale. At present CFE loses approximately 21% of the energy for distribution. These losses are mainly due to two kinds of problems: a) technical, and b) administrative. The technical energy losses are usually in the range of 10% and a great investment in new technologies would be needed in the distribution equipment to be able to reduce this percentage. The other 11% of the losses are due to administrative control problems, and they are classified in three categories of anomalies: a) invoicing errors, b) measurement errors, and c) illicit energy use or fraud. The first two have a minimum percentage impact so the big problem is the illicit use of energy, that is to say, people who steal the energy and therefore they do not pay for it.

CFE has faced this problem applying different actions (as to increase the frequency of measurement equipment readings of suspect customers, or to install equipment for automatic readings) and has managed to reduce the percentage due to illicit use losses, which represents a recovery of several million dollars. Since the problem has not been completely solved, it is important to attack it with other technologies and actions, using a knowledge discovery approach based on data mining to obtain patterns of behavior of the illicit customers. This alternative solution does not require a great deal of investment and it has been proven to be effective in similar cases, like credit card fraud detection [16].

The subject information to analyze is a sample of the SICOM database, a legacy system developed with the COBOL language, it contains around twenty tables with information about contracts, invoicing, and collection from customers across the nation. This system was not designed with the illicit users discovery in mind; nevertheless, it contains a field called *debit-type* in which a record is made if the debit is due to illicit use of energy. After joining three tables, including the one that has the *debit-type* field, a "mine" with 35,983 instances was obtained with the following attributes: *Permanent customer registry (RPU), Year, Month, debit-type, Digit, kWh, Energy, Cve-invoicing, Total, Status, Turn, Tariff, Name, Installed-load, Contract-load*, and others that altogether add up to 21 attributes. One of the values that the attribute *debit-type* can be assigned is "9", which indicates an illicit use, and it is our class attribute. Various experiments were executed with this database to evaluate the different ranking methods as described next.

4   Evaluating Ranking Methods

4.1   Measuring the Attributes Degree of Relevance

The application of filter-ranking methods to select features of a VLDB is adequate due to its low computational cost. We use *Elvira* [17] and *Weka* [18] tools, since they provide suitable and updated platforms for the easy execution of multiple experiments in a PC environment. In the presentation of the experiments the processing time has been left out because it was always very small, for example, *Elvira* obtains, in less of a second, the Mutual Information distance to measure the relevance of 21 attributes using 35,983 instances. The result is shown in the left column of Table 1.

Although in this case the attributes appear ordered according to their relevance, we lack of a uniform criterion to decide which attributes to select. We used the Stoppiglia criterion [15], but modifying it as follows: instead of using a single random variable, we added three, to observe how the ranking method maintains together, or not, the random variables in the set of ranked attributes, avoiding a possible bias introduced to the result by a single random variable, that in fact is a computational pseudo-random

Table 1. Ranking using *Elvira* (Mutual Information distance)

Traditional Ranking		Ranking with three random variables	
fctura	0.09097299304149882	fctura	0.09097299304149882
status	0.06121332572180206	status	0.06121332572180206
kwEen	0.051186334426340505	kwEen	0.051186334426340505
cCEto	0.045967636246832214	cCEto	0.045967636246832214
kwMen	0.0443061751909163	RAND3	0.04450328124055651
toMkw	0.04376718990743937	kwMen	0.0443061751909163
enrgia	0.04325196857770465	toMkw	0.04376718990743937
kwMcI	0.04308595013830481	enrgia	0.04325196857770465
toMcI	0.04302669641028058	kwMcI	0.04308595013830481
kwh	0.04259503495345594	toMcI	0.04302669641028058
total	0.042438776707532586	RAND2	0.04295118668801855
mes	0.04204718796227498	kwh	0.04259503495345594
toMcC	0.04163309856095569	total	0.042438776707532586
cIEen	0.038549970847028533	mes	0.04204718796227498
toMen	0.03831938680147813	toMcC	0.04163309856095569
cgInst	0.036173176514204305	RAND1	0.04031876955965204
cgCont	0.034291607355202744	cIEen	0.038549970847028533
cIMcC	0.02679884377613058	toMen	0.03831938680147813
anio	0.004512035977610684	cgInst	0.036173176514204305
tarifa	0010537446951081608	cgCont	0.034291607355202744
digito	7.321404042019974E-4	cIMcC	0.02679884377613058
		anio	0.004512035977610684
		tarifa	0.0010537446951081608
		digito	7.321404042019974E-4

variable. The obtained result is shown in the right column of Table 1, where variables RAND3, 2 and 1 are the boundaries of the four subsets of attributes.

Following the same procedure, we applied different ranking methods to the database (a detailed explanation of the used "distances" can be found in [6] and [14]); the results are shown in Table 2. Also, the methods: Principal Component Analysis (PCA), Information Gain, Gain Ratio and Symmetrical were explored, and they produced similar results as Chi-Square, which means that they did not obtain a significant reduction on the number of attributes. From Table 2 we observe that, although some ranking methods agree in the selection of some attributes, in general, each method produces different attribute ordering, including the position for the three random variables. (This is a very interesting result, as we will see in Table 3).

4.2 Performance Evaluation of the Methods

In order to evaluate the methods, we applied the *J4.8* tree induction classifier (the Weka implementation of the last public version of *C4.5*) to the database "projected" on the attributes selected by each method. Table 3 shows the results. In all the cases, we always used the Weka's default parameters and the attributes of the first subset identified by the appearance of the first random variable (in section 4.3 we analyze this in more detail). The feature reduction column measures the number of attributes selected against the total number of attributes. The processing time is expressed in relation to the time required to obtain a tree that includes all the attributes of the

Table 2. Application of different ranking measures

Euclidean distance	Matusita distance	Kullback-Leibler 1	Kullback-Leibler 2	Shannon entropy	Bhatta-charyya	Relief	OneR	Chi-Square
fctura	fctura	fctura	fctura	kwh	kwEen	anio	factra	factra
mes	kwEen	status	mes	enrgia	fctura	mes	status	status
cIMcC	kwMen	kwEen	status	total	kwMen	factra	anio	mes
anio	RAND3	cCEto	cgInst	tarifa	RAND3	digito	tarifa	kwEen
RAND3	status	RAND3	cgInst	cgInst	toMkw	RAND3	digito	kwMcI
tarifa	cCEto	kwMen	cCEto	cgInst	toMcI	RAND2	mes	kwh
digito	toMkw	toMkw	cIMcC	kwEen	enrgia	RAND1	cIMcC	toMcI
status	enrgia	enrgia	anio	toMcI	cCEto	status	cgCont	toMcC
RAND2	toMcI	kwMcI	kwEen	kwMen	total	cgInst	cgInst	total
cIEen	total	toMcI	RAND2	toMen	RAND2	tarifa	RAND1	toMen
cgInst	kwMcI	RAND2	RAND3	toMkw	kwMcI	cgCont	toMkw	enrgia
cgCont	RAND2	kwh	toMkw	kwMcI	toMcC	cCEto	RAND2	kwMen
RAND1	kwh	total	kwh	toMcC	RAND1	cIEen	cCEto	toMkw
cCEto	toMcC	mes	kwMen	cCEto	kwh	cIMcC	kwh	cCEto
toMcC	RAND1	toMcC	cIEen	cIEen	toMen	kwEen	toMcI	cIEen
kwMcI	toMen	RAND1	enrgia	status	mes	toMen	RAND3	cgInst
toMkw	mes	cIEen	total	cIMcC	status	total	total	cgCont
toMen	cIEen	toMen	kwMcI	RAND2	cIEen	toMcC	toMen	anio
kwMen	cgInst	cgInst	RAND1	RAND1	cgInst	toMcI	kwEen	cIMcC
toMcI	cgCont	cgCont	tarifa	RAND3	cgCont	kwh	enrgia	tarifa
kwEen	cIMcC	cIMcC	digito	digito	cIMcC	kwMcI	kwMen	RAND2
total	anio	anio	toMcC	mes	anio	kwMen	cIEen	RAND3
enrgia	tarifa	tarifa	toMcI	fctura	tarifa	toMkw	kwMcI	RAND1
kwh	digito	digito	toMen		digito	enrgia	toMcC	digito

database (complete case). The size of the discovered knowledge is measured by the number of leaves and the number of nodes of the induced tree. The classification quality appears as the percentage of instances correctly classified using the training data (accuracy) and also using a 10-fold cross validation test. A column is included that considers cost-benefit that it would be obtained if the discovered knowledge were applied by the organization, and assuming that each inspection has a cost of −2.5 units and that the obtained benefit of a correct prediction of an illicit is of +97.5 units. The reported cost-benefit corresponds to the application of the above mentioned 10-fold cross validation test and it is calculated considering that the complete case obtains a 1000 units of benefit, and the results of the other methods are normalized with respect to the complete case.

In Table 3, we observe that most of the methods obtain a reduction of the number of attributes greater than 0.50 and reduce the mining algorithm processing time in an order of magnitude; a special case is Relief, that unlike the other methods whose processing time is small, Relief requires a proportion of time 9721 times greater than the time required to induce the tree by using all the attributes. With respect to the size of the discovered knowledge it is observed that almost all the methods produce trees smaller than the complete case. On the other hand, although apparently all the methods do not affect too much on the accuracy of the discovered knowledge, the cost-benefit column highlights those methods that better impact on the prediction of the illicit energy use patterns.

Table 3. Evaluating ranking methods by inducing J4.8 trees

Method	Feature reduction	Time	Leaves / Nodes	Acc train / test	Cost-benefit (test)
Complete case	0	100	21 / 41	98.41 / 97.25	1000
Mutual Information	0.80	12	5 / 9	90.86 / 90.10	444
Euclidean distance	0.80	11	3 / 5	93.89 / 93.89	520
Matusita distance	0.86	8	2 / 3	90.58 / 90.21	507
Kullback-Leibler 1	0.80	11	5 / 9	90.86 / 90.10	444
Kullback-Leibler 2	0.57	14	17 / 33	98.26 / 97.50	1001
Shannon entropy	0.14	92	23 / 45	95.52 / 93.71	876
Bhattacharyya	0.86	9	2 / 3	90.18 / 90.21	507
Relief	0.80	12 + 9721	3 / 5	93.89 / 93.89	520
OneR	0.57	15	12 / 23	96.64 / 95.95	892

Table 4. Using feature subsets to induce *J4.8 trees*

Feature subsets	Feature reduction	Time	Leaves / Nodes	Acc train / test	Cost-benefit (Test)
begin – RAND2	0.57	14	17 / 33	98.26 / 97.50	1001
RAND3–RAND1	0.66	12	1 / 1	79.42 / 79.45	-910
RAND1-end	0.76	11	1 / 1	79.42 / 79.42	-913
begin-RAND1	0.23	16	17 / 33	98.26 / 97.43	1001
RAND3-end	0.42	18	1 / 1	79.42 / 79.45	-910
begin-RAND2/RAND1-end	0.33	17	21 / 41	98.41 / 97.18	992

4.3 Combination of Ranking and Wrapper Methods

Although the ranking methods are very efficient, they have a flaw in that they do not take into account the possible interdependences between attributes. Observing the obtained results mention above, we propose a heuristic that looks for to overcome such a deficiency, combining the efficiency of the ranking methods, with the effectiveness of the wrapper methods. The heuristic involves the induction of a number of decision trees considering all subsets of attributes that a method produces (the subsets appear limited by the three random variables in Table 2). Applying the previous idea, we can observe, in a computationally economic way, if some combination of attributes exists in the subsets that improves the obtained results as compared when using only the first attribute subset. For example, the application of KL-2 with three random variables produces three subsets. The induction trees produced by *J4.8* using the three subsets and a combination of these subsets are shown in Table 4. It is observed that, for this case, it does not exist a combination that significantly improves the results of the first subset, and this is why we can conclude that we have found a good solution, one that manages to reduce to the processing time and the knowledge size, without affecting the tree quality of prediction.

5   Conclusions and Future Work

The feature selection ranking methods are very efficient because they only need to calculate the relevance of each isolated attribute to predict the class attribute. The disadvantages of these methods are that no uniform criterion is provided to decide which attributes are more relevant than others, and that no mechanism is included to detect the possible interdependences between attributes. In this article the integration of three random variables to the database is proposed to avoid a possible bias introduced to the result if a single random variable is used. We observed that, although some ranking methods agree in the selection of some attributes, in general, each method produces different attribute ordering, including the position for the three random variables. This is a very interesting result. The three variables serve as subset boundaries and help to decide which attributes to select. Also, we propose to analyze the possible interdependences between attributes using the induction trees constructed on these subsets. These ideas have been proven to be successful in a real world electrical energy customer-invoice database. In the future these ideas are going to be applied to other databases and classifiers. In particular we are going to perform more sumulations using the inclusion of multiple random variables to observe its utility like criterion within the feature selection area.

References

1. Frawley, W. et.al., Knowledge Discovery in DBs: An Overview, in Knowledge Discovery in Databases, Piatetsky-Shapiro, G. eds., Cambridge, MA, AAAI/MIT, 1991, pp. 1-27.
2. Pyle, D., Data preparation for data mining, Morgan Kaufmann, Sn Fco, California,1999.
3. Guyon, I., Elisseeff, A., An introduction to variable and feature selection, Journal of machine learning research, 3, 2003, pp. 1157-1182.
4. Kohavi, R., John, G., Wrappers for feature subset selection, Artificial Intelligence Journal, Special issue on relevance, 1997, pp. 273-324.
5. Leite, R., Brazdil, P., Decision tree-based attribute selection via sub sampling, Workshop de minería de datos y aprendizaje, Herrera, F., Riquelme, J. (eds), VIII Iberamia, Sevilla, Spain, Nov, 2002, pp. 77-83.
6. Piramuthu, S., Evaluating feature selection methods for learning in data mining applications, Proc. 31st annual Hawaii Int. conf. on system sciences, 1998, pp. 294-301.
7. Mitra, S., et.al., Data mining in soft computing framework: a survey, IEEE Trans. on neural networks, vol. 13, no. 1, January, 2002, pp. 3-14.
8. Domingos, P., When and how to sub sample, SIGKDD Explorations, Vol. 3, Issue 2, 2001, pp. 74-75.
9. Quinlan, J., Unknown attribute values in ID3, Int. conf. Machine learning, 1989, pp. 164-168.
10. Almuallim, H., Dietterich, T., Learning with many irrelevant features, Ninth nat. conf. on AI, MIT Press, 1991, pp. 547-552.

11. Kira, K., Rendell, L., The feature selection problem: traditional methods and a new algorithm, Tenth nat. conf. on AI, MIT Press, 1992, pp. 129-134.
12. Koller, D., Sahami, M., Toward optimal feature selection, Int. conf. on machine learning, 1996, pp. 284-292.
13. Ruiz, R., Aguilar, J., Riquelme, J., SOAP: efficient feature selection of numeric attributes, VIII Iberamia, workshop de minería de datos y aprendizaje, Spain, 2002, pp. 233-242.
14. Molina, L., Belanche, L., Nebot, A., Feature selection algorithms, a survey and experimental evaluation, IEEE Int. conf. on data mining, Maebashi City Japan, 2002, pp. 306-313.
15. Stoppiglia, H., Dreyfus, G., et.al., Ranking a random feature for variable and feature selection, Journal of machine learning research, 3, 2003, pp. 1399-1414.
16. S. Stolfo, W. Fan, W. Lee, A. Prodromidis, and P. Chan. Credit card fraud detection using meta-learning: Issues and initial results. Working notes of AAAI Workshop on AI Approaches to Fraud Detection and Risk Management, 1997.
17. www. ia.uned.es/~elvira/ , 2003.
18. www. cs.waikato.ac.nz/ml/weka , 2003.

Automatic Case Adaptation with a Hybrid Committee Approach

Claudio A. Policastro, André C.P.L.F. de Carvalho, and
Alexandre C.B. Delbem

Institute of Mathematical and Computer Sciences – University of Sao Paulo.
Av. Trabalhador Sao-Carlense, 400 – 13560-970 – Sao Carlos, Sao Paulo, Brazil.
{capoli,andre,acbd}@icmc.usp.br

Abstract. When Case Based Reasoning systems are applied to real-world problems, the retrieved solutions in general require adaptations in order to be useful in new contexts. Therefore, case adaptation is a desirable capability of Case Based Reasoning systems. However, case adaptation is still a challenge for this research area. In general, the acquisition of knowledge for adaptation is more complex than the acquisition of cases. This paper explores the use of a hybrid committee of Machine Learning techniques for automatic case adaptation.

1   Introduction

Case Based Reasoning (CBR) is a methodology for problem solving based on past experiences. This methodology tries to solve a new problem by retrieving and adapting previously known solutions of similar problems. However, retrieved solutions, in general, require adaptations in order to be applied to new contexts. One of the major challenges in CBR is the development of an efficient methodology for case adaptation. In contrast to case acquisition, knowledge for case adaptation is not easily available and is hard to obtain [7,20].

The most widely used form of adaptation employs handcoded adaptation rules, which demands a significant effort of knowledge acquisition for case adaptation, presenting a few difficulties [7]. Smyth and Keane [17], for example, propose a case adaptation that is performed in two stages: first, it employs general adaptation specialists to transform a solution component target. Then, it uses general adaptation strategies to handle problems that can arise from the activities of the specialists. These adaptation specialists and strategies are handcoded knowledge packages acquired specifically for a particular application domain. An alternative to overcome the difficulties in acquiring adaptation knowledge has been the use of automatic learning. This paper proposes a hybrid committee approach for case adaptation that automatically learns adaptation knowledge from a Case Base (CB) and applies it to adapt retrieved solutions.

This paper is organized as follows: Section 2 briefly introduces the CBR paradigm. Section 3 presents some considerations about case adaptation. Section 4 introduces the proposed for case adaptation. Section 5 shows the evaluation of the proposed system. Section 6 presents the final considerations.

R. Monroy et al. (Eds.): MICAI 2004, LNAI 2972, pp. 302–311, 2004.

2   Case Based Reasoning

CBR is a methodology for problem solving based on past experiences. This methodology tries to solve a new problem by employing a process of retrieval and adaptation of previously known solutions of similar problems. CBR systems are usually described by a reasoning cycle (also named CBR cycle), which has four main phases [1]:

1. *Retrieval*: according to a new problem provided by the user, the CBR system retrieves, from a CB, previous cases that are similar to the new problem;
2. *Reuse*: the CBR system adapts a solution from a retrieved case to fit the requirements of the new problem. This phase is also named *case adaptation*;
3. *Revision*: the CBR system revises the solution generated by the *reuse* phase;
4. *Retention*: the CBR system may learn the new case by incorporating it into in the CB, which is named *case learning*. The fourth phase can be devided into the following procedures: relevant *information selection* to create a new case, *index composition* for this case, and *case incorporation* into the CB.

CBR is not a technology developed for specific proposes; it is a general methodology of reasoning and learning [1,19]. CBR allows unsupervised and incremental learning by updating the CB when a solution for a new problem is found [1].

3   Case Adaptation

When CBR systems are applied to real-world problems, retrieved solutions rarely can be directly used as adequate solutions for each new problem. Retrieved solutions, in general, require adaptations (second phase of the CBR cycle) in order to be applied to new contexts. Several strategies for case adaptation have been proposed in the literature [9,16]. They can be classified into three main groups: *substitutional adaptation*, *transformational adaptation*, and *generative adaptation*.

Case adaptation is one of the major challenges for CBR [7,20] and there is still much to be done concerning it. Case adaptation knowledge is harder to acquire and demands a significant knowledge engineering effort. An alternative to overcome such difficulties has been the use of automatic learning, where case adaptation knowledge is extracted from previously obtained knowledge, the CB. For example, Wiratunga et al. [20] proposed an inductive method for automatic acquisition of adaptation knowledge from a CB. The adaptation knowledge extracted from the CB is used to train a committee of Rise algorithms [4] by applying Boosting [6] to generate different classifiers. However, the knowledge generation process proposed is specific for certain design domains due the specific encoding employed for the adaptation training patterns and the extraction of differences between description attributes and between component solution attributes.

4   Proposed Approach

This work proposes the use of committees of Machine Learning (ML) algorithms to adapt cases retrieved from a CB (second phase of the CBR cycle). The committees investigated are composed of ML algorithms, here named *estimators*, based on different paradigms. One ML algorithm, here named *combiner*, combines the outputs of the individual estimators to produce the output of the committee. The estimators and the combiner are used to perform adaptations in domains with symbolic *components* (in this work, the case solution attributes are named components), extending the approaches presented in [12,13]. The committee is composed by the following ML algorithms: The ML algorithms are:

- Estimators – a *Multi Layer Perceptron* (MLP) neural network [8]; a symbolic learning algorithm C4.5 [14]; a *Support Vector Machine* (SVM) technique [18], based on the statistical learning theory.
- Combiner: in this work we investigated 2 ML algorithms as the combiner of the committee – a MLP neural network and the SVM technique. The combiner receives the outputs from the other three algorithms as input, combines the results, and produces the output of the committee.

MLP networks are the most commonly used Artificial Neural Network model for pattern recognition. A MLP network usually presents one or more hidden layers with nonlinear activation functions (generally sigmoidal) that carry out successive nonlinear transformations on the input patterns. In this way, the intermediate layers can transform nonlinearly separable problems into linearly separable ones [8].

C4.5 is a symbolic learn algorithm that generates decision trees [14]. It builds a decision tree from a training data set by applying a divide-and-conquer strategy and a greedy approach. It uses a gain ratio to divide the training instances into subsets corresponding to the values of the selected attribute and calculate the gain ratio of the attribute from these subsets. This process is repeated for all input attributes of the training patterns, until a given subset contains instances of only one class. After the construction, the model may be complex or specific to the training data. Afterward, the model needs to be pruned in order to improve its performance. This process is carried out by eliminating those nodes that do not affect the prediction [14].

SVM is a family of learning algorithms based on statistical learning theory [18]. It combines generalization control with a technique that deals with the dimensionality problem[1] [18]. This technique basically uses hyperplanes as decision surface and maximizes the separation borders between positive and negative classes. In order to achieve these large margins, SVM follows a statistical principle named *structural risk minimization* [18]. Another central idea of SVM algorithms is the use of kernels to build support vectors from the training data set.

---

[1] Machine Learning algorithms can have a poor performance when working on data sets with a high number of attributes. Techniques of attribute selection can reduce the dimensionality of the original data set. SVM is a ML Algorithm capable of obtaining a good generalization even for data sets with many attributes.

The proposed approach for case adaptation employs two modules. The first module (adaptation pattern generation) produces a data set of adaptation patterns. This data set is then used by the second module (case adaptation mechanism) that trains a committee of ML algorithms to automatically perform case adaptation. This approach extends the approach proposed in [12,13] by exploring the use of a hybrid committee of ML algorithms as case adaptation mechanism. This approach assumes that a CB is representative [15], i.e. the CB is a good representative sample of the target problem space. Therefore, no re-training of the adaptation mechanism is required when the system creates new cases during the reasoning process.

4.1 Adaptation Pattern Generation

The data set generation module proposed is capable of extracting implicit knowledge from a CB. This module employs an algorithm that is similar to that proposed in [12,13] (see Algorithm 1).

Algorithm 1 Adaptation Pattern Generation

---
function AdaptationPatternGenerate (CasesNumber, Component)
   for each cases from the original case base **do**
      ProofCase ⇐ ProofCaseExtract ()
      ProofDescrpt ⇐ DescriptionExtract (ProofCase)
      ProofSolution ⇐ SolutionExtract (ProofCase, Component)
      RetrievedCases ⇐ Retrieve (ProofDescrpt, CasesNumber)
      for each RetrievedCases **do**
         RetDescrpt ⇐ DescriptionExtract (RetrievedCases(i))
         RetSolution ⇐ SolutionExtract (RetrievedCases(i), Component)
         MakeAdaptationPattern (ProofDescrpt, RetDescrpt, RetSolution, ProofSolution)
      end for
   end for
end function

Initially, the pattern generation algorithm extracts a case from the original CB and uses it as a new problem (*ProofCase*) to be presented to the CBR system. The remaining cases compose a new CB without the proof case. Next, the algorithm extracts, from the proof case, the attributes of the problem (*ProofDescrpt*) and a component (indicated by *Component*) of the solution (*ProofSolution*). Then, this algorithm returns the *CasesNumber* most similar cases from the *ProofDescrpt* (*RetrievedCases*), where *CasesNumber* is a predefined value. For each retrieved case, the attributes of the problem (*RetDescrpt*) and a component of the corresponding solution (indicated by *Component*) are extracted (*RetSolution*). Next, the algorithm generates the adaptation patterns using as input attributes: the problem description stored in the proof case, the problem description stored in the retrieved case, a component solution stored in the retrieved case; and as output attribute: a solution component stored in the proof case. Finally, the generated data sets are used to train the committee of ML algorithms. First, the MLP, the SVM, and C4.5 are trained individually using the adaptation pattern data set generated. Next, the output of these three ML algorithms are combined to produce a training data set for the the combiner of the committee (MLP or SVM).

4.2 Case Adaptation Mechanism

The proposed case adaptation mechanism allows the learning of the modifications that need to be performed in the components values of the retrieved solutions in order to achieve an adequate solution for a new problem. The most important characteristic of this mechanism is the employment of implicit knowledge obtained from the CB with a minimum effort for the knowledge acquisition. The case adaptation process is shown in the Algorithm 2.

Algorithm 2 Case Adaptation Mechanism

---

function Adaptation (Description, RetrievedCase, Component)
   RetDescription $\Leftarrow$ DescriptionExtract (RetrievedCase)
   RetSolution $\Leftarrow$ SolutionExtract (RetrievedCase, Component)
   InputPattern $\Leftarrow$ MakeInputPattern (Description, RetDescription, RetSolution)
   Acts $\Leftarrow$ AdaptationMechanism (Normalization(InputPattern), Component)
   NewSolution $\Leftarrow$ ApplyActs (RetSolution, Acts, Component)
   return NewSolution
end function

When a new problem is presented to the CBR system, the most similar case stored in the CB is obtained by a retrieval mechanism [5,10]. This case (*RetrievedCase*) is sent to the adaptation mechanism together with the problem description (*Description*). The adaptation algorithm, in turn, extracts the attributes from the new problem (*RetDescription*). Next, for each component of the retrieved solution (indicated by *Component*), the algorithm extracts the corresponding solution and generates an adequate input pattern for the committee of ML algorithms developed for this component. Then, the committee indicates the modifications in the component of the retrieved solution (*Acts*). Finally, these modifications are applied to the current component in order to obtain the solution for the new problem (*NewSolution*). The proposed adaptation approach works only with a single component of the solution of a case. This approach can be easily extended for domains where the solution of the cases has more than one component, by treating each solution component as a distinct problem. This strategy keeps this approach independent of the structure of the case solution.

5   Empirical Evaluation

This Section presents a set of experiments carried out to explore the use of committees os ML algorithms and investigate if it introduces more precision and stability to the the system. For such, the performances obtained with the use of committees of ML algorithms are compared to those obtained by using individual ML algorithms for case adaptation: a MLP new……、 a C4.5 algorithm and a SVM technique. In order to show that the automatic case adaptation may result in considerable gain in the prediction of desired values for the solution attribute, both case adaptation approaches, using committees of ML algorithms and individual ML algorithms, have their performance compared with the performances obtained by the individual ML algorithms for the prediction of the solution attribute values. For the evaluation of the knowledge extraction algorithm, a data set from the UCI Machine Learning repository [2] was used. The

Table 1. Pittsburgh bridges case structure.

	Attribute	Values
	RIVER	a, m, o
	LOCATION	1..52
	ERECTED	1818..1986
Problem	PURPOSE	walk, aqueduct, rr, highway
	LENGTH	804..4558
	LANES	1, 2, 4, 6
	CLEAR-G	N, G
	T-OR-D	through, deck
	MATERIAL	wood, iron, steel
Solution	SPAN	short, medium, long
	REL-L	S, S-F, F
	TYPE	wood, suspen, simple-t, arch, cantilev, cont-t

selected domain was the Pittsburgh bridges data set. This data set is originally composed of 108 cases. However, some cases contain missing values for some solution attributes. After removing cases with missing solution attributes values, the data set was reduced to 89 cases. The input missing attributes were filled by mean and median values. The case structure contains 5 discrete input attributes, 2 continuous input attributes and 5 discrete output attributes (see Table 1). In this domain, 5 output attributes (design description) are predicted from 7 input attributes (specification properties).

A sample of a case and of a adaptation pattern generated for the solution component *MATERIAL* is shown in the Figure 1. The adaptation pattern input is composed by the attributes of the problem description from the proof case and the retrieved case. The adaptation pattern output is composed by the value of the solution component from the proof case:

The topology of the MLP networks employed as estimator has 29 to 33 input units (depending on the solution component), a hidden layer with 30 neurons and 1 output neuron. The MLP networks were trained using the momentum backpropagation algorithm, with moment term equal to 0.2 and learning rate equal to 0.3. The C4.5 algorithm was trained using default parameters. The SVM Algorithm was trained using the Radial Basis Function kernel and default parameters. The MLP networks and C4.5 algorithm were simulated using the WEKA library[2]. The SVM algorithm was simulated using the LIBSVM library[3]. Three different adaptation pattern data sets were created by generating adaptation patterns using 1, 3, and 5 similar cases (see *CasesNumber* in Algorithm 1).

The numerical values were normalized (see *Normalization* in Algorithm 2) for the interval [0...1]. For the MLP, SVM, and C4.5 techniques, the input symbolic values were transformed into orthogonal vectors of binary values. For the MLP and SVM, the symbolic solution components were also transformed in the same way. Additionally, the original data set was balanced using a technique of

---

[2] Available in http://www.cs.waikato.ac.nz/ml/weka/index.htm

[3] Available in http://www.csie.ntu.edu.tw/c̄jlin/libsvm

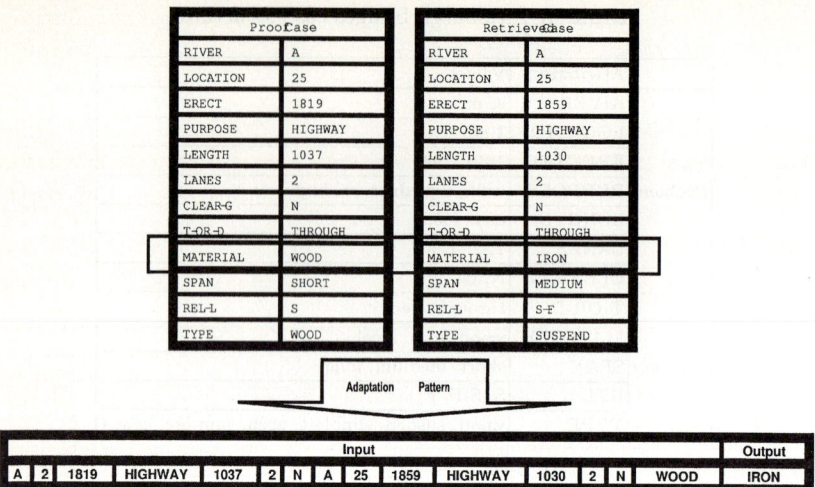

Fig. 1. Adaptation Pattern Sample.

over-sampling [3]. This is by the fact that ML algorithms may fail learning on unbalanced data sets. However, further investigation is required to comprove if it is necessary. The tests followed the *10-fold-cross-validation* strategy. The patterns were randomly divided into 10 groups (*folds*) with similar size. One *fold* was used as a *test-fold* (a set of new problems to be presented to the system) and the remaining 9 *folds* were considered as a *training-fold* (a set of previously stored cases). Before the training of a ML algorithm using the *training-fold*, the over-sampling technique was applied to the *training-fold*. After the training of a ML algorithm using the over-sampled *training-fold*, the *test-fold* was presented to the system and the average absolute error was calculated. This process was repeated for the remaining 9 *folds*. Next, the average and standard deviation of the absolute error for each training session were calculated. Table 2 shows the results of the tests carried out with the hybrid CBR systems, with individual classifiers and with committees, using the three settings for the parameter *CasesNumber* (see Algorithm 1), indicated by for the column named K. The results obtained by the individual techniques employed alone (MLP, C4.5, and SVM) are also shown.

In order to confirm the performance of the proposed approach, the authors used the t test for bilateral procedures which 99% of certainty [11]. The results achieved are shown in Table 3.

Although the results show that the use of Committees do not outperform the best CBR with individual ML algorithm adaptation mechanism, the result show that, in general, committees of classifiers reduce the standard deviation of the results (introduces more stability to the system). The results obtained by the committees could be better if more estimators were employed. Additionally, the results show that the hybrid CBR approaches proposed obtained better prediction of the problems solution than the classifiers techniques used individually.

Table 2. Average error rates and standard deviation for the proposed approach. The two best results for each column are indicated with an (*). Comm. means Committee.

Model	K	Average Absolute Error and standard deviation (%)					
		t-or-d	rel-l	span	material	type	global
CBR (C4.5)	1	$31,11 \pm 9,02$	$65,24 \pm 9,98$	$45,74 \pm 7,98$	$32,30 \pm 6,95$	$53,19 \pm 8,02$	$45,52 \pm 8,39$
CBR (C4.5)	3	$28,39 \pm 7,07$	$54,27 \pm 11,06$	$50,27 \pm 8,05$	$33,03 \pm 3,54$	$53,18 \pm 9,98$	$43,83 \pm 7,94$
CBR (C4.5)	5	$31,11 \pm 8,34$	$55,17 \pm 9,00$	$52,17 \pm 7,21$	$35,03 \pm 5,43$	$56,09 \pm 11,50$	$45,91 \pm 8,30$
CBR (SVM)	1	$16,00 \pm 7,73$	$*31,33 \pm 9,59$	$41,22 \pm 9,25$	$24,22 \pm 5,51$	$48,22 \pm 13,70$	$32,20 \pm 9,16$
CBR (SVM)	3	$6,00 \pm 5,59$	$*31,33 \pm 9,59$	$36,22 \pm 10,58$	$13,22 \pm 6,77$	$47,22 \pm 12,21$	$*26,80 \pm 8,95$
CBR (SVM)	5	$*6,00 \pm 5,59$	$50,89 \pm 15,56$	$*36,22 \pm 10,58$	$*10,00 \pm 5,33$	$*46,22 \pm 13,41$	$29,87 \pm 10,10$
CBR (MLP)	1	$23,84 \pm 4,97$	$55,27 \pm 12,76$	$45,74 \pm 7,98$	$34,12 \pm 6,69$	$56,99 \pm 7,32$	$43,19 \pm 7,94$
CBR (MLP)	3	$24,75 \pm 4,77$	$56,08 \pm 7,88$	$50,27 \pm 8,05$	$29,39 \pm 4,58$	$57,71 \pm 8,03$	$43,64 \pm 6,66$
CBR (MLP)	5	$24,75 \pm 4,77$	$49,74 \pm 10,57$	$52,17 \pm 7,21$	$31,12 \pm 4,78$	$55,80 \pm 8,85$	$42,72 \pm 7,23$
CBR (Comm.MLP)	1	$23,84 \pm 3,60$	$55,27 \pm 12,76$	$44,01 \pm 8,75$	$34,12 \pm 6,69$	$62,25 \pm 12,37$	$43,90 \pm 8,83$
CBR (Comm.MLP)	3	$25,66 \pm 5,60$	$54,27 \pm 11,06$	$50,27 \pm 8,05$	$30,21 \pm 5,75$	$53,08 \pm 12,41$	$42,70 \pm 8,57$
CBR (Comm.MLP)	5	$26,57 \pm 7,89$	$49,74 \pm 10,57$	$51,26 \pm 5,54$	$31,12 \pm 4,78$	$54,09 \pm 10,88$	$42,56 \pm 42,56$
CBR (Comm.SVM)	1	$*6,00 \pm 5,59$	$43,67 \pm 16,17$	$*35,33 \pm 10,07$	$17,33 \pm 8,87$	$*46,44 \pm 6,56$	$29,75 \pm 9,45$
CBR (Comm.SVM)	3	$7,00 \pm 5,40$	$42,56 \pm 10,25$	$36,33 \pm 10,70$	$13,22 \pm 6,77$	$51,33 \pm 11,81$	$30,09 \pm 8,99$
CBR (Comm.SVM)	5	$7,00 \pm 5,40$	$33,33 \pm 9,24$	$36,67 \pm 11,31$	$*10,00 \pm 5,33$	$48,22 \pm 11,44$	$*27,04 \pm 8,55$
C4.5		$28,38 \pm 9,22$	$61,61 \pm 7,95$	$45,74 \pm 7,98$	$31,39 \pm 6,95$	$59,69 \pm 7,54$	$45,36 \pm 7,93$
SVM		$19,00 \pm 7,96$	$31,33 \pm 10,30$	$39,22 \pm 11,35$	$24,22 \pm 5,51$	$57,44 \pm 11,56$	$34,24 \pm 9,33$
MLP		$25,66 \pm 6,56$	$50,63 \pm 13,04$	$45,74 \pm 7,98$	$31,30 \pm 6,43$	$64,35 \pm 10,32$	$43,54 \pm 8,87$

Table 3. Results for the t Test.

Compared Models	Conclusion
CBR (Committee SVM - 5) and CBR (SVM - 3)	Similar Performance
CBR (SVM - 3) and MLP	CBR (SVM - 3) better than MLP
CBR (SVM - 3) and SVM	CBR (SVM - 3) better than SVM
CBR (SVM - 3) and M5	CBR (SVM - 3) better than M5

This suggest that the adaptation pattern data set extracted from the CB contains patterns that are consistent (not conflicting) with each other. Therefore, this approach for adaptation knowledge learning may be a useful technique for real-world problem solving.

6   Conclusions

One of the major challenges in designing CBR systems is the acquisition and modelling of the appropriate adaptation knowledge [7]. In this work, a CBR system that uses a hybrid approach for case adaptation was proposed. This approach uses a hybrid committee for case adaptation in a domain with symbolic solution components, extending the proposal described in [12,13], where a similar approach was tested using a single ML algorithm. The proposed approach employs a process of adaptation pattern generation that can reduce the effort for knowledge acquisition in domains that require substitutional adaptation (see

Section 3). Besides, the hybrid approach proposed is not computationally expensive, since the generation of the adaptation patterns demands no comparisons between solution components. Preliminary results show that the committees do not outperform the best CBR with individual ML adaptation mechanism. This suggest the investigation of committees with a larger number of estimators, reducing the influence of individual estimators on the final response of a committees. It would also be interesting to investigate the use of such committees for other domains.

Acknowledgments. The authors would like to thank CNPq and FAPESP, Brazilian Fund Agencies, for the support received.

References

1. Aamodt,A., Plaza,E. : Case Based Reasoning: Foundational issues, methodological variations, and systems approaches. AI Communications. **7** (1994) 39–59
2. Blake,C.L. and Merz,C.J.: UCI Repository of machine learning databases. http://www.ics.uci.edu/~mlearn/MLRepository.html. University of California, Irvine, Dept. of Information and Computer Sciences (1998)
3. Chawla, N. V., Bowyer, K. W., Hall, L. O., Kegelmeyer, W. P.: SMOTE: Synthetic Minority Over-sampling Technique. Journal of Artificial Intelligence Research **16**, 321–357. (2002)
4. Domingos,P.: Unifying Instance-Based and Rule-Based Induction. Machine Learning. **24** (1996) 141–168
5. Duda,R., Hart,P., Stork,D.: Pattern Classification. Wiley-Interscience. (2001)
6. Freund,Y. and Schapire,R.: Experiments with a New Boosting Algorithm. 13th. International Conference on Machine Learning, Bari, Italy. Saitta, L. eds. Morgan Kaufmann. (1996) 148–156
7. Hanney,K.: Learning adaptation rules from cases. Master's thesis. University College Dublin. (1996)
8. Haykin,S.: Neural Networks: A Comprehensive Foundation. Prentice Hall. (1999)
9. Kolodner,J.: Adaptation methods and strategies. Case-Based Reasoning. Chapter 11. Morgan Kaufmann. (1993) 393–468
10. Lenz,M., Burkhard,H.-D.: Case Retrieval Nets: Basic Ideas and Extensions. 4th. German Workshop on Case-Based Reasoning: System Development and Evaluation, Berlin, German. Burkhard,H.-D. and Lenz,M. eds. (1996) 103–110
11. Mason,R., Gunst,R., Hess,J.: Statistical design and analysis of experiments. John Wiley & Sons. (1989)
12. Policastro,C., Carvalho,A. Delbem,A. : Hybrid Approaches for Case Retrieval and Adaptation. 26th German Conference on Artificial Inteligence. Hamburg, German. Günter,A. et al eds. LNAI. Springer Verlag (2003)520–527
13. Policastro,C., Carvalho,A. Delbem,A. : Hybrid Approaches for Case Adaptation. To be published in the proceedings of the 3rd International Conference on Hybrid Intelligent Systems. Melbourne, Australia. (2003)
14. Quinlan,R.: C4.5: Programs for Machine Learning. Morgan Kaufmann. (1993)
15. Smyth,B.: Case Base Maintenance. 12th. International Conference on Industrial and Engineering Applications of Artificial Intelligence and Expert Systems, Cairo, Egypt. Mira,J., Pobil,A. eds. Springer Verlag (1998) 507–516

16. Smyth,B., Cunningham,P.: Complexity of adaptation in real-world case-based reasoning systems. 8th Irish Conference on Artificial Intelligence and Cognitive Science. Belfast, Ireland. (1993) 228–240
17. Smyth,B., Keane,M.: Retrieval & Adaptation in DeJa Vu, a Case-Based Reasoning System for Software Design. AAAI Fall Symposium on AI Applications in Knowledge Navigation and Retrieval. Cambridge, USA. Burke,R. ed. (1995)
18. Vapnik,V.: Statistical learning theory. John Wiley & Sons. (1998)
19. Watson,I.: CBR is a methodology not a technology. Knowledge-Based Systems. **12**(1999) 303–308
20. Wiratunga,N., Craw,S., Rowe,R.: Learning to Adapt for Case-Based Design. 6th European Conference on Case-Based Reasoning. Aberdeen, Scotland, Uk. Craw,S., Preece,A. eds. Springer Verlag. (2002) 421–435

Class Imbalances *versus* Class Overlapping: An Analysis of a Learning System Behavior

Ronaldo C. Prati, Gustavo E.A.P.A. Batista, and Maria C. Monard

Laboratory of Computational Intelligence - LABIC
Department of Computer Science and Statistics - SCE
Institute of Mathematics and Computer Science - ICMC
University of São Paulo - Campus of São Carlos
P. O. Box 668, 13560-970, São Carlos, SP, Brazil
Phone: +55-16-273-9692. FAX: +55-16-273-9751.
{prati,gbatista,mcmonard}@icmc.usp.br

Abstract. Several works point out class imbalance as an obstacle on applying machine learning algorithms to real world domains. However, in some cases, learning algorithms perform well on several imbalanced domains. Thus, it does not seem fair to directly correlate class imbalance to the loss of performance of learning algorithms. In this work, we develop a systematic study aiming to question whether class imbalances are truly to blame for the loss of performance of learning systems or whether the class imbalances are not a problem by themselves. Our experiments suggest that the problem is not directly caused by class imbalances, but is also related to the degree of overlapping among the classes.

1   Introduction

Machine learning methods have advanced to the point where they might be applied to real world problems, such as in data mining and knowledge discovery. By being applied on such problems, several new issues that have not been previously considered by machine learning researchers are now coming into light. One of these issues is the class imbalance problem, *i.e.*, the differences in class prior probabilities. In real world machine learning applications, it has often been reported that the class imbalance hinder the performance of some standard classifiers. However, the relationship between class imbalance and learning algorithms is not clear yet, and a good understanding of how each one affects the other is lacking. In spite of a decrease in performance of standard classifiers on many imbalanced domains, this does not mean that the imbalance is the sole responsible for the decrease in performance. Rather, it is quite possible that beyond class imbalances yield certain conditions that hamper classifiers induction.

Our research is motivated by experiments we had performed over some imbalanced datasets, for instance the sick dataset [9], that provided good results (99.65% AUC) even with a high degree of imbalance (only 6.50% of the examples belong to the minority class). In addition, other research works seems to agree with our standpoint [8].

R. Monroy et al. (Eds.): MICAI 2004, LNAI 2972, pp. 312–321, 2004.

In this work, we develop a systematic study aiming to question whether class imbalances hindrance classifier induction or whether these deficiencies might be explained in other ways. To this end, we develop our study on a series of artificial datasets. The idea behind using artificial datasets is to be able to fully control all the variables we want to analyze. If we were not able to control such variables, the results may be masked or difficult to understand and interpret, under the risk of producing misleading conclusions. Our experiments suggest that the problem is not solely caused by class imbalances, but is also related to the degree of data overlapping among the classes.

This work is organized as follow: Section 2 introduces our hypothesis regarding class imbalances and class overlapping. Section 3 presents some notes related to evaluating classifiers performance in imbalanced domains. Section 4 discusses our results. Finally, Section 5 presents some concluding remarks.

2   The Role of Class Imbalance on Learning

In the last years, several works have been published in the machine learning literature aiming to overcome the class imbalance problem [7,12]. There were even two international workshops, the former was sponsored by AAAI [5] and the latter was held together with the Twentieth International Conference on Machine Learning [1]. There seems to exist an agreement in the Machine Learning community with the statement that the imbalance between classes is the major obstacle on inducing classifiers in imbalanced domains.

Conversely, we believe that class imbalances are not always the problem. In order to illustrate our conjecture, consider the decision problem shown in Figure 1. The problem is related to building a Bayes classifier for a simple single attribute problem that should be classified into two classes, positive and negative. It is assumed perfect knowledge regarding conditional probabilities and priors. The conditional probabilities for the two classes are given by Gaussian functions, with the same standard deviation for each class, but the negative class having mean one standard deviation (Figure 1(a)) and four standard deviations (Figure 1(b)) apart from the positive class mean. The vertical lines represent optimal Bayes splits.

From Figure 1, it is clear that the influence of changing priors on the positive class, as indicated by the dashed lines, is stronger in Figure 1(a) than in Figure 1(b). This indicates that it is not the class probabilities the main responsible for the hinder in the classification performance, but instead the degree of overlapping between the classes. Thus, dealing with class imbalances will not always help classifiers performance improvement.

3   On Evaluating Classifiers in Imbalanced Domains

The most straightforward way to evaluate classifiers performance is based on the confusion matrix analysis. Table 1 illustrates a confusion matrix for a two class problem having class values **positive** and **negative**.

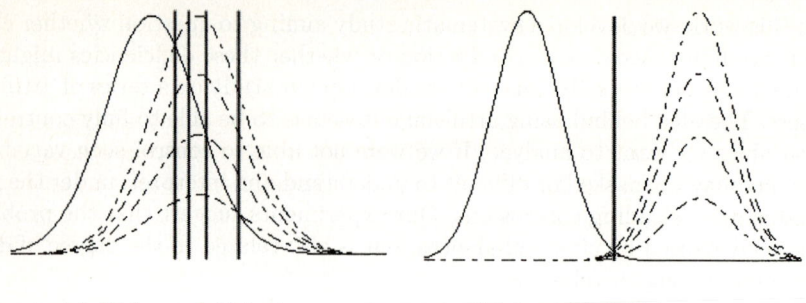

(a) High overlaid instances   (b) Low overlaid instances

Fig. 1. A Simple Decision Problem

Table 1. Confusion matrix for a two-class problem.

	Positive Prediction	Negative Prediction
Positive Class	True Positive (TP)	False Negative (FN)
Negative Class	False Positive (FP)	True Negative (TN)

From such matrix it is possible to extract a number of widely used metrics for measuring learning systems performance, such as Classification Error Rate, defined as $Err = \frac{FP+FN}{TP+FN+FP+TN}$, or, equivalently, Accuracy, defined as $Acc = \frac{TP+TN}{TP+FP+FN+TN} = 1 - Err$.

However, when the prior classes probabilities are highly different, the use of such measures might produce misleading conclusions. Error rate and accuracy are particularly suspect as performance measures when studying the effect of class distribution on learning since they are strongly biased to favor the majority class. For instance, it is straightforward to create a classifier having an accuracy of 99% (or an error rate of 1%) in a domain where the majority class proportion correspond to 99% of the instances, by simply forecasting every new example as belonging to the majority class.

Other fact against the use of accuracy (or error rate) is that these metrics consider different classification errors as equally important. However, highly imbalanced problems generally have highly non-uniform error costs that favor the minority class, which is often the class of primary interest. For instance, a sick patience diagnosed as healthy might be a fatal error while a healthy patience diagnosed as sick is considered a much less serious error since this mistake can be corrected in future exams.

Finally, another point that should be considered when studying the effect of class distribution on learning systems is that the class distribution may change. Consider the confusion matrix shown in Table 1. Note that the class distribution (the proportion of positive to negative instances) is the relationship between the first and the second lines. Any performance metric that uses values from both columns will be inherently sensitive to class skews. Metrics such as accuracy and error rate use values from both lines of the confusion matrix. As class distribution changes these measures will change as well, even if the fundamental classifier performance does not.

All things considered, it would be more interesting if we use a performance metric that disassociates the errors (or hits) that occurred in each class. From Table 1 it is possible to derive four performance metrics that directly measure the classification performance on positive and negative classes independently:

- **False negative rate:** $FN_{rate} = \frac{FN}{TP+FN}$ is the percentage of positive cases misclassified as belonging to the negative class;
- **False positive rate:** $FP_{rate} = \frac{FP}{FP+TN}$ is the percentage of negative cases misclassified as belonging to the positive class;
- **True negative rate:** $TN_{rate} = \frac{TN}{FP+TN}$ is the percentage of negative cases correctly classified as belonging to the negative class;
- **True positive rate:** $TP_{rate} = \frac{TP}{TP+FN}$ is the percentage of positive cases correctly classified as belonging to the positive class;

These four performance measures have the advantage of being independent of class costs and prior probabilities. The aim of a classifier is to minimize the false positive and negative rates or, similarly, to maximize the true negative and positive rates. Unfortunately, for most real world applications, there is a tradeoff between FN_{rate} and FP_{rate} and, similarly, between TN_{rate} and TP_{rate}. The ROC[1] graphs [10] can be used to analyze the relationship between FN_{rate} and FP_{rate} (or TN_{rate} and TP_{rate}) for a classifier.

A ROC graph characterizes the performance of a binary classification model across all possible trade-offs between the classifier sensitivity (TP_{rate}) and false alarm (FP_{rate}). ROC graphs are consistent for a given problem even if the distribution of positive and negative instances is highly skewed. A ROC analysis also allows the performance of multiple classification functions to be visualized and compared simultaneously. A standard classifier corresponds to a single point in the ROC space. Point (0, 0) represents classifying all instances as negative, while point (0, 1) represents classifying all instances as positive. The upper left point (0, 1) represents a perfect classifier. One point in a ROC diagram dominates another if it is above and to the left. If point A dominates point B, A outperforms B for all possible class distributions and misclassification costs [2].

Some classifiers, such as the Naïve Bayes classifier or some Neural Networks, yield a score that represents the degree to which an instance is a member of a class. Such ranking can be used to produce several classifiers, by varying the threshold of an instance pertaining to a class. Each threshold value produces a different point in the ROC space. These points are linked by tracing straight lines through two consecutive points to produce a ROC curve[2]. For Decision Trees, we could use the class distributions at each leaf as score or, as proposed

---

[1] ROC is an acronym for *Receiver Operating Characteristic*, a term used in signal detection to characterize the tradeoff between hit rate and false alarm rate over a noisy channel.

[2] Conceptually, we may imagine varying a threshold from $-\infty$ to $+\infty$ and tracing a curve through the ROC space

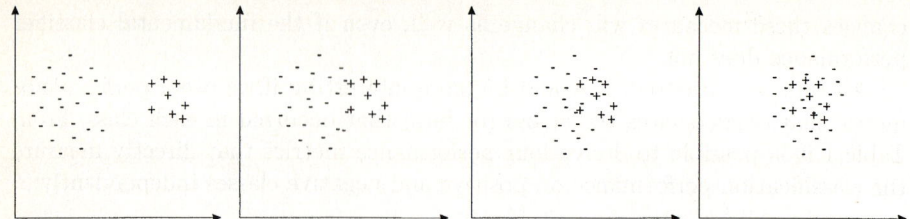

Fig. 2. Pictorial representation of some instances of the artificial datasets employed in the experiments.

in [3], by ordering the leaves by its positive class accuracy and producing several trees by re-labelling the leaves, once at time, from all forecasting negative class to all forecasting positive class in the positive accuracy order.

The area under the ROC curve (AUC) represents the expected performance as a single scalar. The AUC has a known statistical meaning: it is equivalent to the Wilconxon test of ranks, and is equivalent to several other statistical measures for evaluating classification and ranking models [4]. In this work, we use the AUC as the main method for assessing our experiments. The results of these experiments are shown in the next section.

4   Experiments

As the purpose of our study is to understand when class imbalances influence the degradation of performance on learning algorithms, we run our experiments on a series of artificial datasets whose characteristics we are able to control, thus allowing us to fully interpret the results. This is not the case when real datasets are used, as we stated before.

The artificial datasets employed in the experiments have two major controlled parameters. The first one is the distance between the centroids of the two clusters, and the second one is the grade of imbalance. The distance between centroids let us control the "level of difficulty" of correctly classifying the two classes. The grade of imbalance let us analyze if imbalance is a factor for degrading performance by itself.

The main idea behind our experiments is to analyze if class imbalance, by itself, can degrade the performance of learning systems. In order to perform this analysis, we created several datasets. These datasets are composed by two clusters: one representing the majority class and the other one representing the minority class. Figure 2 presents a pictorial representation of four possible instances of these datasets in a two-dimensional space.

We aim to answer several question analyzing the performance obtained on these datasets. The main questions are:

- Is class imbalance a problem for learning systems as it is being stated in several research works? In other words, will a learning system present low performance with a highly imbalanced dataset even when the classes are far apart?

— The distance between the class clusters is a factor that contributes to the poor performance of learning systems in an imbalanced dataset?

— Supposing that the distance between clusters matters in learning with imbalanced datasets, how class imbalance can influence the learning performance for a given distance between the two cluster?

The following section provides a more in deep description of the approach we used to generate the artificial datasets used in the experiments.

4.1   Experiments Setup

To evaluate our hypothesis, we generated 10 artificial domains. Each artificial domain is described by 5 attributes, and each attribute value is generated at random, using a Gaussian distribution, with standard deviation 1. Jointly, each domain has 2 classes: positive and negative. For the first domain, the mean of the Gaussian function for both classes is the same. For the following domains, we stepwise add 1 standard deviation to the mean of the positive class, up to 9 standard deviations. For each domain, we generated 12 datasets. Each dataset has 10.000 instances, but having different proportions of instances belonging to each class, considering 1%, 2.5%, 5%, 10%, 15%, 20%, 25%, 30%, 35%, 40%, 45% and 50% of the instances in the positive class, and the remainder in the negative class.

Although the class complexity is quite simple (we generate datasets with only two classes, and each class is grouped in only one cluster), this situation is often faced by machine learning algorithms since most of them, for classification problems, follow the so-called separate-and-conquer strategy, which recursively divides and solves smaller problems in order to induce the whole concept. Furthermore, Gaussian distribution might be used as an approximation of several statistical distributions.

To run the experiments, we chose the algorithm for inducing decision trees C4.5 [11]. C4.5 was chosen because it is quickly becoming the community standard algorithm when evaluating learning algorithms in imbalanced domains. All the experiments were evaluated using 10-fold cross validation. As discussed in Section 3, we used the area under the ROC curve (AUC) as a quality measure. We also implemented the method proposed in [3] to obtain the ROC curves and the corresponding AUCs from the standard classifiers induced by C4.5.

4.2   Results

The results obtained by applying C4.5 in the artificially generated datasets are summarized in Table 2, which shows the mean AUC value and the respective standard deviation in parenthesis, of the classifiers induced by C4.5 for all the datasets having different class priors and different distances between the positive and negative class centroids. We omitted the values of AUC for the datasets

Table 2. AUC obtained from classifiers induced by C4.5 varying class priors and class overlapping

Positive instances	Distance of Class Centroids				
	0	1	2	3	9
1%	50.00% (0.00%)	64.95% (9.13%)	90.87% (6.65%)	98.45% (2.44%)	99.99% (0.02%)
2.5%	50.00% (0.00%)	76.01% (6.41%)	95.82% (3.11%)	97.95% (2.12%)	99.99% (0.02%)
5%	50.00% (0.00%)	81.00% (2.86%)	98.25% (1.45%)	98.95% (1.11%)	100.00% (0.00%)
10%	50.00% (0.00%)	86.69% (2.11%)	98.22% (1.14%)	99.61% (0.55%)	99.99% (0.02%)
15%	50.00% (0.00%)	88.41% (2.37%)	98.92% (0.75%)	99.68% (0.49%)	99.99% (0.02%)
20%	50.00% (0.00%)	90.62% (1.44%)	99.08% (0.42%)	99.90% (0.21%)	99.99% (0.02%)
25%	50.00% (0.00%)	90.88% (1.18%)	99.33% (0.32%)	99.90% (0.14%)	99.98% (0.03%)
30%	50.00% (0.00%)	90.75% (0.81%)	99.24% (0.29%)	99.86% (0.14%)	99.99% (0.02%)
35%	50.00% (0.00%)	91.19% (0.94%)	99.36% (0.43%)	99.91% (0.08%)	99.99% (0.02%)
40%	50.00% (0.00%)	90.91% (0.99%)	99.46% (0.10%)	99.90% (0.13%)	99.99% (0.03%)
45%	50.00% (0.00%)	91.73% (0.79%)	99.44% (0.22%)	99.90% (0.09%)	99.98% (0.04%)
50%	50.00% (0.00%)	91.32% (0.68%)	99.33% (0.19%)	99.87% (0.13%)	99.99% (0.03%)

having a distance of class centroids greater or equal than 4 standard deviations since the results are quite similar to the datasets having a distance of 3 standard deviations. Furthermore, for those datasets the difference of AUC are statistically insignificant, with 95% of confidence level, for any proportion of instances in each class. The results with the dataset having class centroids 9 standard deviations apart is included in order to illustrate the small variation between them and the previous column.

As expected, if both positive and negative classes have the same centroids, we have a constant AUC value of 50%, independently of class imbalance. This AUC value means that all examples are classified as belonging to the majority class.

Consider the column where the centroids of each class are 1 standard deviation appart. If this column is analyzed solely, someone may infer that the degree of class imbalance on its own is the main factor that influences the learning process. The AUC has an upward trend, increasing from nearly 65% when the proportion of instances of positive class is 1% to more than 90% when the proportion of positive and negative instances are the same. However, when the class centroids distance goes up to 2 standard deviations, we can see that the influence of the class priors becomes weaker. For instance, the value of AUC for the classifiers induced with the dataset having 1% and 2.5% of instances in the positive class and the centroid of this class 2 standard deviations apart the centroid of the negative class is still worst than the classifiers induced changing the class distribution and the same centroids, but the values of AUC are closer than the values with the same proportion and the difference of the centroids is 1 standard deviation.

For classifiers induced with datasets having 3 or more standard deviations apart, the problem becomes quite trivial, and the AUC values are nearly 100% regardless of the class distribution.

For a better visualization of the overall trends, these results are shown graphically in Figure 3 and 4. These graphs show the behavior of the C4.5 algorithm assessed by the AUC metric in both class imbalance and class overlapping.

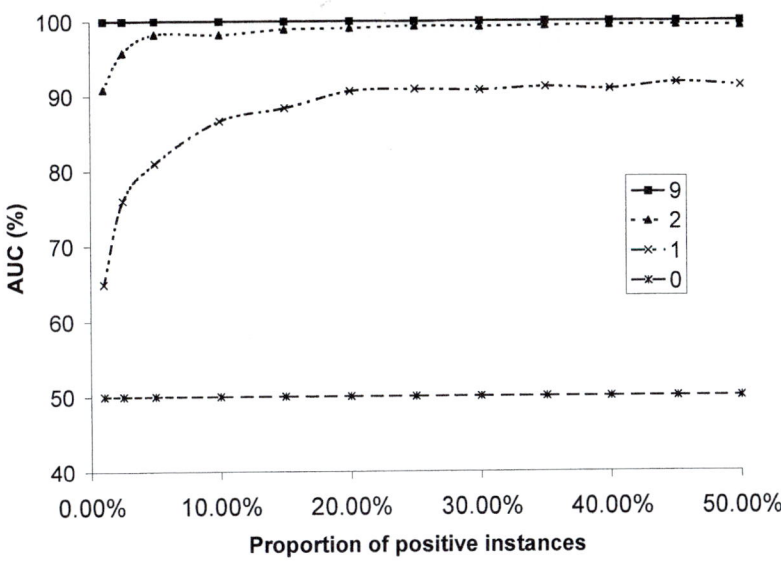

Fig. 3. Variation in the proportion of positive instances *versus* AUC

Figure 3 plots the percentage of positive instances in the datasets *versus* the AUC of the classifiers induced by C4.5 for different centroids of positive class (in standard deviations) from the negative class. The curves with centroids of positive class 3 to 8 standard deviations apart are omitted for a better visualization, but the curves are quite similar to the curve with centroid 9 standard deviations apart the negative class. Consider the curves of positive class where the class centroids are 2 and 3 standard deviations apart. Both classifiers have good performances, with AUC higher than 90%, even if the proportion of positive class is barely 1%. Particularly, the curve where the positive class centroid is 9 standard deviations from the negative class centroid represents almost a perfect classifier, independently of the class distribution.

Figure 4 plots the variation of centroids distances *versus* the AUC of the classifiers induced by C4.5 for different class imbalances. The curves that represent the proportion of positive instances between 20% and 45% are omitted for visualization purposes since they are quite similar to the curve that represents equal proportion of instances in each class. In this graph, we can see that the main degradation in the classifiers performances occurs mainly when the difference between the centre of the positive and negative class is 1 standard deviation. In this case, the degradation is significantly higher for highly imbalanced datasets, but decreases when the distance between the centre of the positive and negative class increases. The differences in performance of classifiers are statistically insignificant when the difference between the centers goes up 4 standard deviations, independently on how many instances belongs to the positive class.

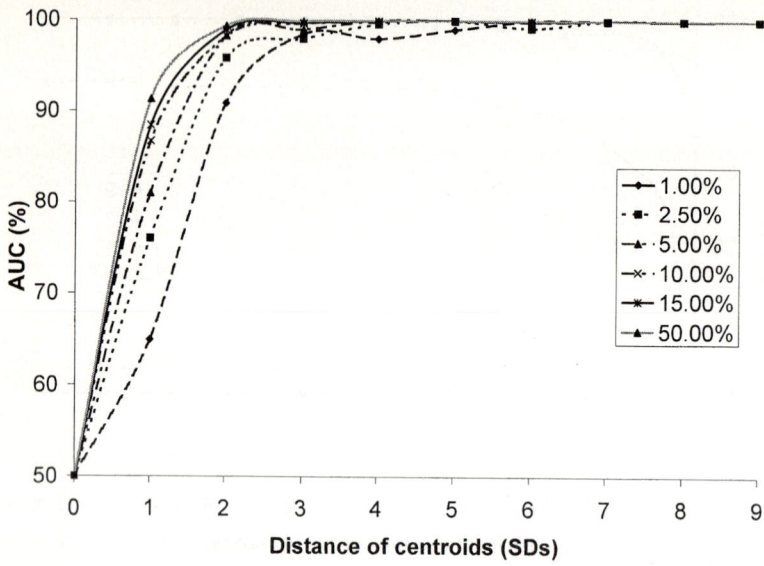

Fig. 4. Variation in the centre of positive class *versus* AUC

Analyzing the results, it is possible to see that class overlapping have an important role in the concept induction, even stronger than class imbalance. Those trends seem to validate our formerly hypothesis, presented in Section 2.

5   Conclusion and Future Work

Class imbalance is often reported as an obstacle to the induction of good classifiers by machine learning algorithms. However, for some domains, machine learning algorithms are able to achieve meaningful results even in the presence of highly imbalanced datasets. In this work, we develop a systematic study using a set of artificially generated datasets aiming to show that the degree of class overlapping has a strong correlation with class imbalance. This correlation, to the best of our knowledge, has not been previously analyzed elsewhere in the machine learning literature. A good understanding of this correlation would be useful in the analysis and development of tools to treat imbalanced data or in the (re)design of learning algorithms for practical applications.

In order to study this question in more depth, several further approaches can be taken. For instance, it would be interesting to vary the standard deviations of the Gaussian functions that generate the artificial datasets. It is also worthwhile to consider the generation of datasets where the distribution of instances of the minority class is separated in several small clusters. This approach can lead the study of the class imbalance problem together with the small disjunct problem, as proposed in [6]. Another point to explore is to analyze the ROC curves obtained from the classifiers. This approach might produce some useful insights in order to develop or analyze methods for dealing with class imbalance. Last but not least, experiments should also be conducted on real-world datasets in order to verify that the hypothesis presented in this work does apply to them.

Acknowledgements. This research is partially supported by Brazilian Research Councils CAPES and FAPESP.

References

1. N. Chawla, N. Japkowicz, and A. Kolcz, editors. *ICML'2003 Workshop on Learning from Imbalanced Data Sets (II)*, 2003. Proceedings available at `http://www.site.uottawa.ca/~nat/Workshop2003/workshop2003.html`.
2. C. Drummond and R. C. Holt. Explicity representing expected cost: An alternative to roc representation. In *Proceedings of the Sixth ACM SIGKDD International Conference on Knowledge Discovery and Data Mining*, pages 198–207, 2000.
3. C. Ferri, P. Flach, and J. Hernández-Orallo. Learning decision trees using the area under the ROC curve. In C. S. A. Hoffman, editor, *Nineteenth International Conference on Machine Learning (ICML-2002)*, pages 139–146. Morgan Kaufmann Publishers, 2002.
4. D. J. Hand. *Construction and Assessment of Classification Rules*. John Wiley and Sons, 1997.
5. N. Japkowicz, editor. *AAAI Workshop on Learning from Imbalanced Data Sets*, Menlo Park, CA, 2003. AAAI Press. Techical report WS-00-05.
6. N. Japkowicz. Class imbalances: Are we focusing on the right issue? In *Proc. of the ICML'2003 Workshop on Learning from Imbalanced Data Sets (II)*, 2003.
7. N. Japkowicz and S. Stephen. The class imbalance problem: A systematic study. *Intelligent Data Analysis*, 6(5):429–450, 2002.
8. J. Laurikkala. Improving Identification of Difficult Small Classes by Balancing Class Distributions. Technical Report A-2001-2, University of Tampere, Finland, 2001.
9. C. J. Merz and P. M. Murphy. UCI Repository of Machine Learning Datasets, 1998. `http://www.ics.uci.edu/~mlearn/MLRepository.html`.
10. F. J. Provost and T. Fawcett. Analysis and Visualization of Classifier Performance: Comparison under Imprecise Class and Cost Distributions. In *Knowledge Discovery and Data Mining*, pages 43–48, 1997.
11. J. R. Quinlan. *C4.5 Programs for Machine Learning*. Morgan Kaufmann, San Mateo, CA, 1993.
12. G. M. Weiss and F. Provost. The Effect of Class Distribution on Classifier Learning: An Empirical Study. Technical Report ML-TR-44, Rutgers University, Department of Computer Science, 2001.

Advanced Clustering Technique for Medical Data Using Semantic Information*

Kwangcheol Shin[1], Sang-Yong Han[1], and Alexander Gelbukh[1,2]

[1] School of Computer Science and Engineering, Chung-Ang University,
221 HukSuk-Dong, DongJak-Ku, Seoul, 156-756, Korea
kcshin@archi.cse.cau.ac.kr, hansy@cau.ac.kr
[2] Center for Computing Research,
National Polytechnic Institute, Mexico City, Mexico
{gelbukh,igor}@cic.ipn.mx, www.Gelbukh.com

Abstract. MEDLINE is a representative collection of medical documents supplied with original full-text natural-language abstracts as well as with representative keywords (called MeSH-terms) manually selected by the expert annotators from a pre-defined ontology and structured according to their relation to the document. We show how the structured manually assigned semantic descriptions can be combined with the original full-text abstracts to improve quality of clustering the documents into a small number of clusters. As a baseline, we compare our results with clustering using only abstracts or only MeSH-terms. Our experiments show 36% to 47% higher cluster coherence, as well as more refined keywords for the produced clusters.

1 Introduction

As science and technology continues to advance, the number of related documents rapidly increases. Today, the amount of related stored documents is incredibly massive. Information retrieval on the numerous documents has become an active field for study and research.

MEDLINE database maintained by the National Library of Medicine (http://www.nlm.gov/) contains ca. 12 million abstracts on biology and medicine collected from 4,600 international biomedical journals, stored and managed in the format of eXtensible Markup Language (XML). MeSH (Medical Subject Headings) are manually added to each abstract to describe its content for indexing. Currently, MEDLINE supports various types of search queries.

However, query-based information search is quite limited on performing searches for biological abstracts. The query-based search method may be appropriate for content-focused querying, but this is so only on the condition that the user is an expert in the subject and can choose the keywords for the items they are searching for. Thus it is very confusing and time-consuming for users who are not experts in biology or

---

* Work done under partial support of the ITRI of Chung-Ang University, Korean Government (KIPA Professorship for Visiting Faculty Positions in Korea), and Mexican Government (CONACyT, SNI, IPN). The third author is currently on Sabbatical leave at Chung-Ang University.

R. Monroy et al. (Eds.): MICAI 2004, LNAI 2972, pp. 322–331, 2004.

medicine to search using queries because new techniques and theories pour out continuously in this particular field. Even expert users have troubles when they need to quickly find specific information because it is impossible to read every found document from the beginning to the end. We see that query based search method is not so efficient in both cases [1].

Unlike the general query-based search method, document clustering automatically gathers highly related documents into groups. It is a very important technique now that efficient searching must be applied to massive amounts of documents. Generally, unsupervised machine learning [2] method is applied for clustering. Then the features included in the instance are provided as input of the clustering algorithm in order to group together highly similar documents into a cluster.

In recent years, concerns on processing biological documents have increased but were mostly focused on the detection and extraction of relations [3][4] and the detection of keywords [5][6]. Up to now, few studies on clustering of biological documents have been done, except for the development of TextQuest [1], which uses the method of reducing the number of terms based on the abstract of the document. Namely, this is simple method uses a cut-off threshold to eliminate infrequent terms and then feeds the result into an existing clustering algorithm.

The present study proposes an improvement to clustering technique using the semantic information of the MEDLINE documents, expressed in XML. For the proposed method the XML tags are used to extract the so-called MeSH, the terms that represent the document, and give additional term weights to the MeSH terms in the input of a clustering algorithm. The greater the additional term weight given to the MeSH, the greater the role of the MeSH terms in forming clusters. This way the influence of the MeSH on the clusters can be controlled by adjusting the value of the additional term weighting parameter.

For this study, the vector space model [7] with the cosine measure was used to calculate the similarity between the documents. The formula for calculating the coherence of the cluster was applied to evaluate the quality of the formed clusters, and the cluster key words were extracted based on the concept vector [8] for summarizing the cluster's contents.

2 Basic Concepts

This section will present the theoretical background: the vector space model, which is the basis for document searching, the measurement of coherence for evaluating the quality of the clusters, and the extraction of keywords that represent the cluster.

2.1 Vector Space Model

The main idea of the vector space model [7] is expressing the documents by the vector of its term frequency with weights. The following procedure is used for expressing documents by vectors [9]:

- Extract all the terms from the entire document collection.
- Exclude the terms without semantic meaning (called stopwords).

- Calculate the frequency of terms for each document.
- Treat terms with very high or low frequency as stopwords.
- Allocate indexes from 1 to d to each remaining term, where d is the number of such terms. Allocate indexes from 1 to n to each document. Then the vector space model for the entire group of documents is determined by the $d \times n$-dimensional matrix $w = | w_{ij} |$, where w_{ij} refers to the *tf-idf* (term frequency—inverse document frequency) value of the i-th term in j-th document.

Measuring the similarity between two documents in the process of clustering is as important as the selection of the clustering algorithm. Here we measure the similarity between two documents by the cosine expression widely used in information retrieval and text mining, because it is easy to understand and the calculation for sparse vectors is very simple [9].

In this study, each of the document vector $x_1, x_2, \ldots, x_n$ was normalized in the unit of the L_2 norm. The normalization here only maintains the terms' direction, to have the documents with the same subject (i.e., those composed of similar terms) converted to similar document vectors. With this, the cosine similarity between the document vectors x_i and x_j can be derived by using the inner product between the two vectors:

$$s(x_i, x_j) = x_i^T x_j = \| x_i \| \| x_j \| \cos(\theta(x_i, x_j)) = \cos(\theta(x_i, x_j))$$

The angle formed by the two vectors is $0 \leq \theta(x_i, x_j) \leq \pi/2$.

When n document vectors are distributed into k disjoint clusters $\pi_1, \pi_2, \ldots, \pi_k$, the mean vector, or centroid, of the cluster π_j is

$$m_j = \frac{1}{|\pi_j|} \sum_{x \in \pi_j} x \tag{1}$$

Then, when the mean vector m_j is normalized to have a unit norm, the concept vector c_j can be defined to possess the direction of the mean vector [8].

$$c_j = \frac{m_j}{\|m\|} \tag{2}$$

The concept vector c_j defined in this way has some important properties, such as the Cauchy-Schwarz inequality applicable to any unit vector z:

$$\sum_{x \in \pi_j} x^T z \leq \sum_{x \in \pi_j} x^T c_j \tag{3}$$

Referring to the inequality above, it can be perceived that the concept vector c_j has the closest cosine similarity with all document vectors belonging to cluster π_j.

2.2 Cluster Quality Evaluation Model

As a measure of quality of obtained clusters we use the coherence of a cluster π_j ($1 \leq j \leq k$), which based on formula (3) can be measured as

$$\frac{1}{|\pi_j|} \sum_{x \in \pi_j} x^T c_j \tag{4}$$

If the vectors of all the documents in a cluster are equal, its coherence is 1, the highest possible value. On the other hand, if the document vectors in a cluster are spread extremely wide apart from each other, the average coherence would be close to 0. The coherence of cluster system $\pi_1, \pi_2, ..., \pi_k$ is measured using the objective function shown below [8]:

$$Q(\{\pi_j\}_{j=1}^k) = \sum_{j=1}^k \sum_{x_i \in \pi_j} x_i^T c_j \qquad (5)$$

The coherence measure can be successfully used when the number of clusters is fixed, as it is in our case (with a variable number of clusters it favors a large number of small clusters).

2.3 Extracting Cluster Summaries

To present the clusters to the user, we provide cluster summaries, for the user to understand easier the contents of the documents in the cluster and to be able to select the cluster of interest by examining only these summaries. As summaries we use representative keyword sets.

Given n document vectors divided into k disjoint clusters $\pi_1, \pi_2, ..., \pi_k$, denote the keywords of the document cluster π_j by $words_j$. A term is included in the summary $word_j$ if its term weight in the concept vector c_j of cluster π_j is greater that its term weight in the concept vectors of other clusters [8]:

$$words_j = \{k^{th} \text{ word}: 1 \le k \le d, c_{k,j} \ge c_{k,m}, 1 \le m \le c, m \ne j\}, \qquad (6)$$

where d is the total number of terms and $c_{k,j}$ is the weight of the j-th term of k-th cluster. Such summary $word_j$ has the property of having the concept vector localized to the matching cluster. Because of this, it gives comparably good keywords.

3 Term Weighing

This section presents our method of advanced clustering technique combining the structured semantic information assigned to the MEDLINE documents with their full-text information.

3.1 Medical Subject Headings (MeSH)

MeSH is an extensive list of medical terminology. It has a well-formed hierarchical structure. MeSH includes major categories such as *anatomy/body systems, organisms, diseases, chemicals and drugs* and *medical equipment*. Expert annotators of the National Library of Medicine databases, based on indexed content of documents, assign subject headings to each document for the users to be able to effectively retrieve the information that explains the same concept with different terminology.

MeSH terms are subdivided into Major MeSH headings and MeSH headings. Major MeSH headings are used to describe the primary content of the document, while MeSH headings are used to describe its secondary content. On average, 5 to 15 subject headings are assigned per document, 3 to 4 of them being major headings.

MeSH annotation scheme also uses subheadings that limit or qualify a subject heading. Subheadings can also be major subheadings and subheadings according to the importance of the corresponding terms.

3.2 Extraction of MeSH Terms from MEDLINE

MEDLINE annotated documents are represented as XML documents. An XML document itself is capable of supporting tags with meaning. The MEDLINE documents are formed with Document Type Description (DTD) that works as the document schema, namely, NLM MEDLINE DTD (www.nlm.nih.gov/database/dtd/ nlmcommon.dtd). In the DTD, information on the MeSH is expressed with the <MeshHeadingList> tag as shown in Fig. 1. Fig. 2 shows the MeSH expressed by using the DTD of Fig. 1.

```
<!ELEMENT MeshHeadingList (MeshHeading+)>
<!ELEMENT MeshHeading (Descriptor, QualifierName* )>
<!ELEMENT Descriptor (#PCDATA)>
<!ATTLIST Descriptor MajorTopicYN (Y | N) "N">
<!ELEMENT QualifierName (#PCDATA)>
<!ATTLIST QualifierName MajorTopicYN (Y | N) "N">
```

Fig. 1. NLM MEDLINE DTD (MeSH)

```
<MeshHeadingList>
<MeshHeading><Descriptor MajorTopicYN="Y">Acetabulum</Descriptor></MeshHeading>
<MeshHeading><Descriptor MajorTopicYN="N">Adolescence</Descriptor></MeshHeading>
<MeshHeading><Descriptor MajorTopicYN="N">Adult</Descriptor></MeshHeading>
<MeshHeading><Descriptor MajorTopicYN="N">Aged</Descriptor></MeshHeading>
<MeshHeading><Descriptor MajorTopicYN="N">Arthroscopy</Descriptor></MeshHeading>
<MeshHeading><Descriptor MajorTopicYN="N">Cartilage, Articular</Descriptor>
        <QualifierName MajorTopicYN="Y">injuries</QualifierName>
        <QualifierName MajorTopicYN="N">surgery</QualifierName></MeshHeading>
<MeshHeading><Descriptor MajorTopicYN="N">Case Report</Descriptor></MeshHeading>
<MeshHeading><Descriptor MajorTopicYN="N">Female</Descriptor></MeshHeading>
<MeshHeading><Descriptor MajorTopicYN="N"">Human</Descriptor></MeshHeading>
<MeshHeading><Descriptor MajorTopicYN="N">Male</Descriptor></MeshHeading>
<MeshHeading><Descriptor>Rupture</Descriptor></MeshHeading>
<MeshHeading><Descriptor  MajorTopicYN="Y">Surgical Procedures, Endoscopic</Descriptor>
</MeshHeading>
</MeshHeadingList>
```

Fig. 2. MEDLINE Data Sample (MeSH)

As observed in Fig. 1 and Fig. 2, the information on MeSH in DTD can be classified largely into two types, which can in turn be divided into two more specific types each. The first type refers to the terms appearing under the tag <Descriptor> with *MajorTopicYN* attribute *Y* or *N*, which indicates that the terms appearing under the tag are major MeSH or MeSH, accordingly. The second type refers to terms appearing under the tag <QualifierName> with the *MajorTopicYN* attribute *Y* or *N*, which indicates that the terms appearing under the tag are major subheadings or subheadings.

In order to extract the four types of terms described above, the XML document is parsed and the DOM (www.w3.org/DOM) tree is produced. The terms extracted in this process are used to adjust the term weights in the document vector.

3.3 Combining Abstract Terms with MeSH Terms

MEDLINE documents include both full-text abstract taken from the original document (a scientific article published in a journal) as well as the MeSH terms. The MeSH terms represent important information about the document, since they are assigned by experts with great care and consideration. Thus it can be expected (and our experiments confirmed this) that clustering the documents according to their MeSH information would give better clusters than clustering using the original abstracts.

However, combining the two types of information can lead to even better results. We combine the two sources of information by adjusting term weights in the document vectors used as feature weight by the clustering algorithm.

Indeed, clustering results are highly influenced by the term weights assigned to individual terms; for better results, more important terms are to be assigned greater weight. Since MeSH terms are known to be more important, the original term weights w_{ij} for the words appearing under the corresponding headings are adjusted as follows:

$$w_{ij} \leftarrow \begin{cases} w_{ij} + (\rho + \dfrac{\rho}{4 + \ln(\rho)}); & < Decriptor \; MajorTopic \; YN = "Y" > \\[2ex] w_{ij} + (\rho + \dfrac{\rho}{2 \times (4 + \ln(\rho))}); & < Decriptor \; MajorTopic \; YN = "N" > \\[2ex] w_{ij} + (\rho - \dfrac{\rho}{2 \times (4 + \ln(\rho))}); & < SubHeading \; MajorTopic \; YN = "Y" > \\[2ex] w_{ij} + (\rho - \dfrac{\rho}{4 + \ln(\rho)}); & < SubHeading \; MajorTopic \; YN = "N" > \end{cases} \quad (7)$$

In this formula, a coefficient ρ is used to control de degree in which the abstracts or the MeSH terms participate in the resulting weighting. With ρ close to 0, the MeSH terms do not receive any special treatment, so that the results are close to those of clustering using only abstracts. With very large ρ, the results are close to those of clustering using only MeSH terms. With intermediate values of ρ, the two types of information are combined. Our experimental results show that the best clusters are obtained with some intermediate values of ρ.

The specific expressions in formula (7) were found empirically in such a way that the formula gives slightly different additional values to the terms according to their significance: about 33% and 16% of the value of ρ is added or subtracted from its original value. For example, when $\rho = 0.3$, additional term weights are $0.3 + 0.107$, $0.3 + 0.054$, $0.3 - 0.054$, and $0.3 - 0.107$, respectively.

After the term weights are modulated by the above formula, they are re-normalized since the former normalized value had been changed, see Fig. 3.

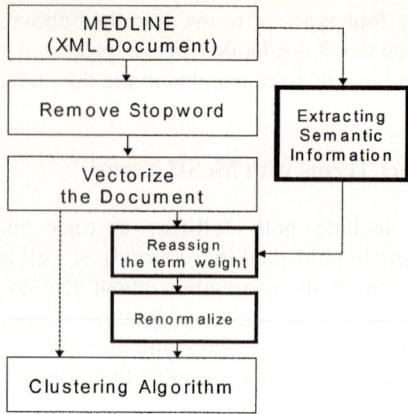

Fig. 3. The Main Algorithm.

4 Experimental Results

For the experiment, 4,872 documents have been extracted from MEDLINE edition published in 1996. Two groups of documents were formed: one group contained documents with abstract only and another one those with both abstract and MeSH terms.

The MC program [10], which produces vectors from a given group of documents, was used to vectorize the documents. Stopwords and the terms with frequency lower than 0.5% and higher than 15% were excluded. With this, the document group with abstracts only had 2,792 terms remaining and that with both abstract and MeSH, 3,021. Then the *tf-idf* value was calculated for each of the document groups and normalized to the L_2 norm to form 4,872 document vectors.

To verify the proposed method, the MeSH terms were extracted from the document group with both abstract and MeSH and then for the extracted terms, the term weights of the corresponding terms of each document vector were modulated by (3-1). Then they were normalized to the L_2 norm.

The standard spherical *k*-means algorithm was implemented for testing these data. This is an efficient clustering algorithm that quickly produces the fixed number of clusters specified by the user.

We clustered our test document set into a fixed number of 3 to 6 clusters (these numbers are of major interest for user interfaces providing document collection navigation support) and using different values of the parameter ρ, varying smoothly from abstract-only to MeSH-only strategies. The abstract-only strategy was used as a baseline. The quality of the clusters was measured as inter-cluster coherence, as explained in Section 2.2. The test results are as shown in Table 1, where the gain ratio is calculated relative to the abstract-only strategy. The best values in each column are emphasized. Fig. 4 shows the average (over different number of clusters; the right-most column of Table 1) coherence obtained with different values of the parameter ρ.

As can be observed in the figure, there is a wide area of the values of ρ providing optimal values of coherence. In particular, such optimal values are 36 to 47% better than those obtained with abstracts only and 10 to 15% better than with MeSH terms only. This justifies our idea of combination of these two sources of information in a non-trivial manner.

Table 1. Experimental Results.

N stands for the number of clusters, C for average coherence of the obtained clusters, and R for gain rate relative to the abstract-only clustering.

ρ	N = 3		N = 4		N = 5		N = 6		Average	
	C	R	C	R	C	R	C	R	C	R
Abstracts only	1065	0%	1126	0%	1157	0%	1234	0%	1146	0%
$\rho = 0$	1185	11.3%	1217	8.1%	1280	10.6%	1327	7.5%	1252	9.3%
$\rho = 1$	1480	39.0%	1561	38.6%	1619	39.9%	1679	36.1%	1585	38.3%
$\rho = 5$	1535	44.1%	1560	38.5%	1650	42.6%	1717	39.1%	1616	41.0%
$\rho = 10$	1557	46.2%	1631	44.8%	1684	45.5%	1720	39.4%	1648	43.8%
$\rho = 20$	1560	46.5%	1616	43.5%	1692	46.2%	1716	39.1%	1646	43.7%
$\rho = 100$	**1570**	47.4%	**1641**	45.7%	**1699**	46.8%	**1746**	**41.5%**	**1664**	45.3%
$\rho = 500$	1550	45.5%	1619	43.8%	1685	45.6%	1743	41.2%	1649	44.0%
$\rho = 1000$	1558	46.3%	1585	40.8%	1664	43.8%	1738	40.8%	1636	42.8%
$\rho = 2000$	1563	46.8%	1601	42.2%	1688	45.9%	1655	34.1%	1627	42.0%
MeSH only	1361	27.8%	1422	26.3%	1535	32.7%	1561	26.5%	1470	28.3%

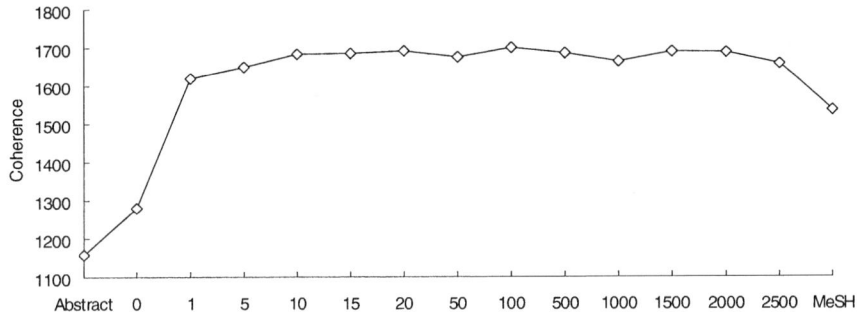

Fig. 4. Experimental Results: Average coherence as function of the parameter ρ.

As an additional evidence of the improvement in cluster quality, we extracted the keyword summaries from the clusters produced with the baseline procedure and with our method, accordingly. For this, we used the formula (6). Table 2 represents the summaries for the five clusters obtained using abstracts only and Table 3 for the clusters obtained with $\rho = 100$, which gives the best clusters according to the coherence measure. Fifteen key words with the greatest term weight were extracted from the five clusters.

One can easily observe that the keyword summary is more consistent and natural for the clusters obtained with a non-trivial value of the parameter ρ.

Table 2. Keyword summaries for clustering based only on abstracts.

Cluster	Key Words
1	*cells, protein, cell, dna, proteins, expression, receptor, gene, beta, binding, alpha, human, acid, activity, kinase*
2	*care, health, medical, united, states, usa, medicine, apr, management, clin, research, cancer, nursing, dis, nurse*
3	*hiv, mice, virus, peptide, infected, california, muscle, model, signaling, mucosal, wild, differentiation, class, produced, signal*
4	*patients, group, treatment, clinical, cases, trial, study, patient, disease, surgery, risk, years, age, hospital, children*
5	*heart, coronary, rats, cardiac, ventricular, cardiology, artery, aim, myocardial, pressure, failure, atrial, flow, exercise, blood*

Table 3. Keyword summaries for clustering by abstracts and MeSH terms ($\rho = 100$).

Cluster	Key Words
1	*cell, cells, mice, pathology, expression, growth, factor, tumor, cultured, kinase, induced, antigens, hiv, membrane, beta*
2	*human, health, care, united, states, medical, nursing, drug, agents, medicine, disease, research, patient, therapy, hospital*
3	*diagnosis, female, male, age, case, adult, middle, aged, radiography, diseases, heart, child, neoplasms, ultrasonography, adolescence*
4	*animal, rats, support, receptors, chemical, effects, brain, activity, wistar, sprague, dawley, inhibitors, antagonists, muscle, rat*
5	*sequence, dna, proteins, protein, molecular, acid, amino, binding, data, gene, structure, base, genetic, recombinant, genes*

5   Conclusion

Medical documents in the MEDLINE database contain both original full-text natural-language abstract and structured keywords manually assigned by expert annotators. We have shown that a combination of these two sources of information provides better features for clustering the documents than each of the two sources independently. We have shown a possible way of their combination, depending on a parameter that determines the degree of contribution of each source. Namely, we combined them by adjusting the term weights of the corresponding terms in the document vectors, which were then used as features by a standard clustering algorithm.

Our experimental results show that there exists a wide area of the values of the parameter that gives a stable improvement in the quality of the obtained clusters, both in internal coherence of the obtained clusters and in the consistency of their keyword summaries. This implies, in particular, that our method is not sensible to a specific selection of the parameter.

The improvement observed in the experiments was 36 to 47% in comparison with taking into account abstracts only and 10 to 15% in comparison with taking into account MeSH terms only.

References

[1]   Iliopoulos I, Enright A, Ouzounis C.: Textquest: document clustering of medline abstracts for concept discovery in molecular biology. Pac. Symp. on Biocomput. 384-395. 2001.

[2]   Kubat M., Bratko I. and Michalski R.S., In Machine Learning and Data Mining: methods and applications,: A review of machine learning methods, Ed. Michalski R.S., Bratko I. and Kubat M., John Wiley & Sons, New York NY, 1997.

[3]   Sekimizu T., Park H. S. and Tsujii J.,: Identifying the interaction between genes and gene products based on frequently seen verbs in Medline abstracts, Genome Informatics Workshop, Tokyo, p. 62, 1998.

[4]   Thomas J., Milward D., Ouzounis C., Pulman S. and Carroll M.,: Automatic extraction of protein interactions from scientific abstracts, Pac. Symp. Biocomput, p. 538-549, 2000.

[5]   Andrade M.A. and Valencia A.,: Automatic extraction of keywords from scientific text: application to the knowledge domain of protein families, Bioinformatics 14, 600, 1998.

[6]   Proux D., Rechenmann F., Julliard L., Pillet V. and Jacq B.,: Detecting gene symbols and names in biological texts: a first step toward pertinent information extraction, Genome Informatics Workshop, Tokyo, p.72-80, 1998.

[7]   Salton G. and. McGill M. J.,: Introduction to Modern Retrieval, McGraw-Hill Book Company, 1983.

[8]   Dhillon I. S. and Modha, D. S.: Concept Decomposition for Large Sparse Text Data using Clustering, Technical Report RJ 10147(9502), IBM Almaden Research Center, 1999.

[9]   Frakes W. B. and Baeza-Yates R.: Information Retrieval : Data Structures and Algorithms, Prentince Hall, Englewood Cliffs, New Jersey, 1992.

[10]   Dhillon I. S., Fan J., and Guan Y.,: Efficient Clustering of Very Large Document Collections. Data Mining for Scientific and Engineering Applications, Kluwer Academic Publishers, 2001.

Strict Valued Preference Relations and Choice Functions in Decision-Making Procedures

Ildar Batyrshin[1], Natalja Shajdullina[2], and Leonid Sheremetov[1]

[1]Mexican Petroleum Institute, Eje Central Lazaro, 152, Mexico, D.F., 07730
{batyr,sher}@imp.mx
[2]Kazan State Technological University, K. Marx st., 68, Kazan, Russia
batyr1@hotbox.ru

Abstract. Fuzzy (valued) preference relations (FPR) give possibility to take into account the intensity of preference between alternatives. The refinement of crisp (non-valued) preference relations by replacing them with valued preference relations often transforms crisp preference relations with cycles into acyclic FPR. It gives possibility to make decisions in situations when crisp models do not work. Different models of rationality of strict FPR defined by the levels of transitivity or acyclicity of these relations are considered. The choice of the best alternatives based on given strict FPR is defined by a fuzzy choice function (FCF) ordering alternatives in given subset of alternatives. The relationships between rationality of strict FPR and rationality of FCF are studied. Several valued generalizations of crisp group decision-making procedures are proposed. As shown on examples of group decision-making in multiagent systems, taking into account the preference values gives possibility to avoid some problems typical for crisp procedures.

1 Introduction

The problem of decision-making (DM) may be considered as the problem of ranking of elements of some set of alternatives X or looking for the "best" alternatives from this set [6, 9]. Different approaches to these problems are varying in the structure of the set X, in the initial information about these elements, in the criteria used for ranking and evaluation of the "best" alternatives, etc. Most of intelligent systems include as a part some DM procedures, e.g. crisp and valued preference relations are used for modeling decision making in multiagent systems [5, 11, 12].

Valued (fuzzy) preference relations (FPR) give possibility to take into account the intensity of preference between alternatives. Different models of DM based on FPR have been considered in literature [1-3, 5-8, 10-12]. These models are usually based on a weak fuzzy preference relation $R:X{\times}X{\to}L$ defined on the set of alternatives X such that for all alternatives x,y the value $R(x,y)$ is understood as a degree to which the proposition "a not worse than b" is true, or as intensity of preference of x over y etc. Usually it is supposed that the set of true values L coincides with interval $[0,1]$. In this case the operations on the set of FPR may be defined by means of fuzzy logic operations given on L. Generally L may denote some linearly ordered set of preference values [2, 7] For example, L may be a set of numerical values, the set of

R. Monroy et al. (Eds.): MICAI 2004, LNAI 2972, pp. 332–341, 2004.
© Springer-Verlag Berlin Heidelberg 2004

scores $\{0, 1, 2, 3, 4, 5, 6\}$ or the set of linguistic evaluations such as "very small preference", "small preference", "strong preference" etc.

Usually a weak FPR and associated with it strict, indifference and incomparability fuzzy relations are considered [5, 6]. The properties of rationality of DM procedures are related with the properties of consistency of underlying FPR. These consistency properties are usually formulated in the form of transitivity or acyclicity of weak FPR and associated strict FPR. The types of consistency of strict FPR in the form of types of transitivity and acyclicity of these relations are considered in this work. The absence of desired requirement of consistency may be used for correction of given strict FPR by some formal procedure or for overestimation of preference values for some pair of alternatives.

The more traditional approach considers the rationality of fuzzy choice function (FCF) with respect to the crisp set of non-dominated alternatives, which may be obtained as a result of the use of FCF [2, 3, 6, 8, 10]. The existence of such non-dominated set of alternatives is related with acyclicity of underlying FPR [2, 3]. This approach really reduces the problem to a non-valued, crisp choice functions and crisp acyclic relations and makes little use of information about valued preferences. In our work, we consider FCF as a ranking function and rationality conditions of FCF are formulated as rationality of rankings on all possible subsets of alternatives.

The paper is organized as follows. The properties of consistency of strict fuzzy preference relations in terms of possible types of transitivity and acyclicity are studied in Section 2. The rationality conditions for FCF are considered in Section 3. The relationships between the consistency properties of strict FPR and rationality conditions of FCF are studied in Section 4. Example of application of DM procedures in multiagent systems is discussed in Section 5. Finally the conclusions and further directions of extension of proposed models are discussed.

2   Strict Valued Preference Relations

A valued relation on a universal set of alternatives Ω is a function $P{:}\Omega{\times}\Omega{\rightarrow}L_p$, where L_p is a linearly ordered set of preference values with minimum and maximum elements denoted as 0 and I respectively. We will consider here the set of preference values $L_p= [0,1]$ used in fuzzy logic with ordering relation $<$ defined by the linear ordering of real numbers, and with $0 = 0$, $I = 1$. Generally, many results related with strict FPR and FCF may be extended on the case of finite scale $L_p= \{a_0, a_1, ..., a_n\}$ with linearly ordered grades $a_0 < a_1< ...< a_n$. Such a scale may contain numerical grades like $L_p= \{0,1,2,3,4,5,6\}$ or linguistic grades $L_p = \{absence\ of\ preference,\ very\ small\ preference,\ small\ preference,\ average\ preference,\ strong\ preference,\ very\ strong\ preference,\ absolute\ preference\}$. For this reason we will consider here the terms valued preference relation and fuzzy preference relation as synonyms [2, 7]. The linear ordering relation $<$ on L defines the operations $\wedge$ and $\vee$ on L: $a{\wedge}b=a$ and $a{\vee}b=b$ iff $a \leq b$ (i.e. $a < b$ or $a=b$) for all a,b from L. The negation operation $'$ may be introduced on L_p as follows: $a' = 1 - a$ for $L_p= [0,1]$ and $a_k' = a_{n-k}$ for finite scale with $n+1$ grades. The operations on L_p satisfy De Morgan laws: $(a{\wedge}b)'=a'{\vee}b'$ and $(a{\vee}b)'=a'{\wedge}b'$ and the involution law: $a_k''= a_k$.

P will be called a FPR if it satisfies on Ω the asymmetry condition: $P(x,y) \wedge P(y,x) = 0$. We will write $P(x,y) \geq 0$ if $P(y,x) = 0$. $P(x,y)$ will be understood as a preference degree or intensity of preference of x over y.

The following types of transitivity reflect the different types of consistency of P:
- Weak transitivity: WT. From $P(x,y) > 0$ and $P(y,z) > 0$ it follows $P(x,z) > 0$.
- Negative transitivity: NT. From $P(x,y) \geq 0$ and $P(y,z) \geq 0$ it follows $P(x,z) \geq 0$.
- Transitivity: T. From $P(x,y) > 0$ and $P(y,z) > 0$ it follows $P(x,z) \geq P(x,y) \wedge P(y,z)$.
- Strong transitivity: ST. From $P(x,y) \geq 0$ and $P(y,z) \geq 0$ it follows $P(x,z) \geq P(x,y) \vee P(y,z)$.
- Quasi-series: QS. From $P(x,y) \geq 0$ and $P(y,z) \geq 0$ it follows $P(x,z) = P(x,y) \vee P(y,z)$.
- Super-strong transitivity: strong transitivity together with the property
  SST. From $P(x,y) > 0$ and $P(y,z) > 0$ it follows $P(x,z) > P(x,y) \vee P(y,z)$.

Suppose P is a strict FPR P on Ω and $x_0, x_1, ..., x_n$ ($n \geq 2$) are some elements of Ω. Consider the following types of cycles, which may by induced by P in Ω:
- 0-cycle: $P(x_0,x_1) > 0$, $P(x_1,x_2) > 0$, ..., $P(x_{n-1},x_n) > 0$, $P(x_n,x_0) > 0$;
- a-cycle: $P(x_0,x_1) \geq a$, $P(x_1,x_2) \geq a$, ... $P(x_{n-1},x_n) \geq a$, $P(x_n,x_0) \geq a$, where $a \in L$, $a > 0$;
- max-cycle: $P(x_0,x_1) = P(x_1,x_2) = ... = P(x_{n-1},x_n) = P(x_n,x_0) = a \geq P(x_i,x_k)$ for some $a \in L$, $a \geq 0$, and all $i,k \in \{0, 1, ..., n\}$.

As a special case of a-cycle with $a = I$, I-cycle will be considered. It is clear that any I-cycle is a max-cycle. We will say that a strict FPR P satisfies one of the properties acyclicity (0-AC), a-acyclicity (a-AC), I-acyclicity (I-AC) and max-acyclicity (MAC) if it does not contain correspondingly 0-cycles, a-cycles, I-cycles and max-cycles.

Proposition 1. The transitive and acyclic classes of strict FPR are partially ordered by inclusion as follows:

$QS \subseteq ST \subseteq NT \subseteq WT$, $SST \subseteq ST \subseteq T \subseteq WT \subseteq 0\text{-}AC \subseteq a_i\text{-}AC \subseteq a_j\text{-}AC \subseteq I\text{-}AC$,
$MAC \subseteq I\text{-}AC$, where a_i and a_j are elements of L such that $0 \leq a_i \leq a_j \leq I$.

The fuzzy quasi-series is a direct fuzzification of crisp quasi-series considered in [2, 10]. A fuzzy quasi-series is related with a fuzzy quasi-ordering relation [13] and defines some hierarchical partition of the set of alternatives on the ordered classes of alternatives. The class of these relations due to their special structure is the narrowest class of strict FPR, whereas the class of I-AC is the widest class of strict FPR.

3 Fuzzy Choice Functions

Suppose L_C is a linearly ordered set of evaluations of the respective quality of alternatives in the sets of alternatives $X \subseteq \Omega$. The minimum 0 and the maximum I elements of L_C will be considered as evaluations of the "worst" and the "best" alternatives in X. Generally we will suppose that such the "worst" and the "best" alternatives may be absent in X which may contain for example only "good" or "not bad" alternatives. The set L_C will be considered as a set of possible values of FCF related with the fuzzy preference relation P defined on Ω. For this reason L_C will be tied with the set of values L_P of correspondent FPR. In fuzzy context, it will be supposed that $L_C = [0,1]$, but generally it may be a set of scores $L_C = \{0, 1, 2, 3, 4, 5, 6\}$ or a set of suitable linguistic values.

A fuzzy choice function C is a correspondence which defines for each finite set of alternatives $X \subseteq \Omega$ the function $C_X : X \to L_C$. In such definition, the FCF is really a score function measuring alternatives in the scale L_C and defining some linear ordering of alternatives from given set X. The possible properties of rationality of these orderings on different sets of alternatives $X \subseteq \Omega$ are discussed in [2]. We consider here several new conditions of rationality of FCF. In the following, for any FCF the fulfillment of the trivial choice property will be required:

TC. $(\forall x \subseteq \Omega)\ C_{\{x\}}(x) = I.$

This condition says that any element x is "the best" in the set containing only this element. Another, more strong condition requires that in any set of alternatives "the best" alternative exists:

BC. $(\forall X \subseteq \Omega)(\exists x \in X)\ C_X(x) = I.$

This axiom is a very strong requirement because the set of "the best" alternatives in general may be empty. As shown in DM theory, the choice functions generated by preference relations fulfill the similar condition if the correspondent preference relation is acyclic [2, 3]. This problem will be discussed also below.

The following two conditions are some weakening of the previous one.

b-UAC. $(\forall X \subseteq \Omega)(\exists x \in X)\ C_X(x) > b,$

where $b \in L,\ (b \geq 0)$ is some level of unacceptability of the quality of alternatives chosen from a given set of alternatives. The "good" alternative should have the quality, which is greater than this level. The next special case of the previous condition requires the existence of "*not the worst*" alternatives:

NWC. $(\forall X \subseteq \Omega)(\exists x \in X)\ C_X(x) > 0.$

This rationality condition requires that in any set of alternatives the rational choice function can select "*not the worst*" alternatives. Another possible requirement on FCF requires the existence of nontrivial ordering of alternatives:

NTO. $(\forall X \subseteq \Omega)\ ((\,|X|\geq 2) \to (\exists x, y \in X)\ (x \neq y)\&(C_X(x) > C_X(y)).$

The stronger condition on FCF requires that the "best" alternatives should be "standard" element:

ES. $(\forall X \subseteq \Omega)\ (\forall x \in X)((C_X(x)=I) \to (\forall y \in X)(C_X(y) = C_{\{x,y\}}(y))).$

This condition is very strong. For choice functions satisfying this condition it follows, for example, that if we have "the best" element in some set X then for evaluating the quality of another alternatives in X it is sufficient to compare these alternatives only with this standard (or "ideal") element and other alternatives in X may not be considered in this evaluation.

The condition of dependence of strict orderings:

DSO. $(\forall X, Y \subseteq \Omega)(\forall x, y \in X \cap Y)((C_X(x) > C_X(y)) \to (C_Y(x) > C_Y(y))),$

requires that if x has a higher level of choice function than y in some set X then such situation takes place also in any set Y containing both alternatives.

Proposition 2. BC $\subseteq$ b$_j$-UAC $\subseteq$ b$_i$-UAC $\subseteq$ NWC, NTO$\subseteq$ NWC, ES$\cap$BC$\subseteq$DSO, where b_i and b_j are elements of L such that $0 \le b_i \le b_j \le I$.

As shown in the following section, if the FCF is generated by strict FPR then all these conditions are characterized by some requirements on transitivity or acyclicity of this relation.

4   Choice Functions Generated by Strict FPR

Fuzzy choice functions may be generated by some FPR [10, 2] as follows:

$$C_X(x) = (\max_{y \in X} P(y,x))' = \min_{y \in X} (P(y,x))'.$$

It is clear that the properties of choice function and strict preference relation generating this choice function are interrelated. It is clear also from asymmetry of fuzzy strict preference relations P and from definition of choice function that any choice function satisfies the property *TC*. We will need also in the following condition of **weak completeness** of linguistic strict preference relation:

WC. From $x \ne y$ it follows $P(x,y) \vee P(y,x) > 0$.

Theorem 3. The diagram on Fig. 1 characterizes the FCFs and fuzzy strict preference relations generating these choice functions.

On this diagram, A $\leftrightarrow$ B denotes that the choice function satisfies the property A if and only if the strict preference relation generating this choice function satisfies the property B. A$\rightarrow$ B denotes that from A follows B. For example, choice function satisfies the condition of *b-UAC* iff the strict preference relation P generating this choice function is *a*-acyclic with $a = b'$.

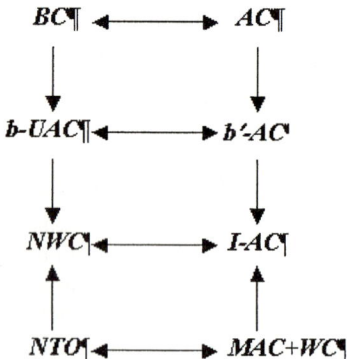

Fig.1. Relationships between the classes of choice functions and linguistic strict preference relations generating these choice functions.

5 Group Decisions

In group DM, the intensity of preferences often plays important role. Consider an example. Five friends want to make decision where to go in the evening. Three of them slightly prefer bar to restaurant but other two strongly prefer restaurant to bar. If the intensity of preferences is not taken into account then applying for example simple majority rule, bar should be chosen. But usually, the intensity of preferences influences on the group decision and in this case, the restaurant may be chosen if the intensities of preference of restaurant by two friends are very strong. Different methods of aggregation of preference intensities have been proposed [6, 7]. Several methods of aggregation of FPR, which generalize the classical crisp methods, are considered further in this section. As shown by Arrow, a group decision procedure satisfying several axioms or rationality does not exist. Any such proposed procedure may be criticized from one or another point of view. The generalizations of some of these procedures on the case of valued preferences are not free from critique as well but they give the possibility to take into account the intensity of preferences and as a result, to diminish the drawbacks of crisp procedures.

5.1 Valued Simple Majority Rule

The draft formulation of the simple majority rule is the following: an alternative is a winner if it is placed on the first position by majority of agents. It may happen that several alternatives receive equal number of votes. In this case, some additional procedure of resolving such situations may be used [4]. The possible generalization of this method on fuzzy preference relations for linguistic evaluations of intensity was considered in [7]. We propose here a new method, which uses the fuzzy evaluations of intensity in strict FPR.

The crisp simple majority rule takes into account only information about the best alternatives and may be considered as a procedure operating with the individual choice functions. The alternative x receives the vote $V_i(x) = 1$ if it belongs to the choice function of i-th agent. The sum of these votes defines the winner. The vote that alternative received from some agent may be considered as the value of characteristic function of choice function defined by linear ordering of all alternatives by this agent. Table 1 shows example of preference profile for 5 agents $a_1, \ldots, a_5$ on the set of three alternatives $X = \{x, y, z\}$, where, for example the first column denotes the ordering $x > y > z$ of alternatives correspondent to the agent a_1. Here x and y have the maximum scores equal 2 correspondent to the number of their location on the first place in the preference profile. Table 2 contains the correspondent values of votes of alternatives in this preference profile.

Table 1. Profile of 5 preferences

a_1	a_2	a_3	a_4	a_5
x	y	z	x	y
y	z	x	y	z
z	x	y	z	x

Table 2. Choice functions and sum of votes for profile from Table 1.

	a_1	a_2	a_3	a_4	a_5	$SUM_i(V_i)$
x	1	0	0	1	0	2
y	0	1	0	0	1	2
z	0	0	1	0	0	1

Consider possible fuzzy generalization of simple majority rule based on the profile of strict FPR. Each strict FPR is replaced by a correspondent FCF, linearly ordering alternatives with respect to the value of choice function. The averaged sum of membership values in the FCFs for each alternative obtained for all agents is calculated. The alternative with the maximum value is considered as the solution of the group decision problem.

For example of group decision problem for 5 friends considered above, the crisp and fuzzy simple majority rules give the following results. Suppose the fuzzy strict preferences between *bar* and *restaurant* for these 5 friends have the following values: $P_1(bar, restaurant) = 0.2$, $P_2(bar, restaurant) = 0.3$, $P_3(bar, restaurant) = 0.2$, $P_4(restaurant, bar) = 0.8$, $P_5(restaurant, bar) = 0.7$. The corresponding matrixes of fuzzy strict preference relations are presented on Table 3. Table 4 contains corresponding crisp ranking when the intensity of preferences is not taken into account. Table 5 contains the scores obtained by all alternatives by the crisp simple majority rule. Table 6 contains FCFs defined by FPRs and the resulting scores of alternatives. As it can be seen, the crisp and fuzzy simple majority rules give different results because the fuzzy approach gives possibility to take into account the intensity of preferences which are not considered by the crisp approach.

Table 3. Example of 5 fuzzy strict preference relations

P_1	bar	rest.	P_2	bar	rest.	P_3	bar	rest.
bar	0	0.2	bar	0	0.3	bar	0	0.2
rest.	0	0	rest.	0	0	rest.	0	0
P_4	bar	rest.	P_5	bar	rest.			
bar	0	0	bar	0	0			
rest.	0.8	0	rest.	0.7	0			

Table 4. Profile of crisp preferences corresponding to Table 3

a_1	a_2	a_3	a_4	a_5
bar	bar	bar	restaurant	restaurant
restaurant	restaurant	restaurant	bar	bar

Table 5. Crisp choice functions and sum of votes for profile from Table 4

	a_1	a_2	a_3	a_4	a_5	$SUM_i(V_i)$
bar	1	1	1	0	0	3
restaurant	0	0	0	1	1	2

Table 6. Fuzzy choice functions and sum of votes for profile from Table 3

	a_1	a_2	a_3	a_4	a_5	$SUM_i(V_i)$
bar	1	1	1	0.2	0.3	3.5
restaurant	0.8	0.7	0.8	1	1	4.3

Table 7. Example on fuzzy Condorcet winner rule

P	x	y	z
x	0	1/5	0
y	0	0	3/5
z	1/5	0	0
C	**4/5**	**4/5**	**2/5**

5.2 Fuzzy Condorcet Winner

The crisp Condorcet winner rule directly uses the information about pair-wise preferences. For given preference profile, an alternative x is a Condorcet winner if in more than half preference relations from the profile it is more preferable than each other alternative. Unfortunately the Condorcet winner does not always exist. This situation happens for the example presented in Table 1. The alternative that is better than all other alternatives for more than 2 agents does not exist: the alternative x is better than y for 3 agents, y is better than z for 4 agents and z is better that x for 3 agents. We obtain the circle: $x > y, y > z, z > x$ which does not give us the possibility to select or reject one of three alternatives. But if we consider valued preference relations then one alternative may be rejected.

Let us define strict valued preference relation on the set of alternatives in the following way. Denote $V(x,y)$ the number of agents which say that x is better than y. Define $P(x,y) = max\{0, V(x,y)-V(y,x)\}/N$, where N is a total number of agents. Then for our example, we receive the strict valued preference relation shown in Table 7. The obtained strict FPR satisfies max-acyclicity *MAX* and weak completeness *WC* conditions and according to the Theorem 3 the choice function of this strict FPR satisfies the non-trivial ordering *NTO* condition and contains alternatives with different values of FCF. The FCF of this FPR is shown in the last string of Table 7. In comparison with x and y, the alternative z obtains the lower value of FCF and may be rejected. We should note that for the considered fuzzy Condorcet winner rule it is also possible to receive a strict FPR, which does not satisfy *MAC* condition such that all alternatives compose circle of preferences with equal values. But the possibility of such situation is much less than in the case of crisp Condorcet winner rule. It may be shown that for some classes of preference profiles the fuzzy Condorcet winner rule always will give FPR satisfying *MAC* condition and hence the correspondent FCF will satisfy the non-trivial ordering condition.

6 Conclusions

In the paper, we have presented the models of valued strict preferences, which can be used by agents addressing the problems of ranking and aggregation of their fuzzy opinions. We considered the consistency properties of strict FPR separately from the properties of some weak FPR. First, it gives us the possibility to analyze more fine structures of FPR related with the rationality properties of DM procedures. Second, many situations exist when initially given information about preferences may be presented directly in the form of strict FPR, i.e. as asymmetric FRP. Such FPR may be received, for example, as a result of pair-wise comparison of all alternatives and replying on two questions: 1) What alternative from considered pair is more preferable? 2) If one of alternatives is more preferable, then what is the intensity of this preference? We think that for expert it is easier to evaluate his pair-wise preferences in a form given by strict FPR than to evaluate two intensities of preference: alternative *a* over *b* and alternative *b* over *a* for obtaining weak FPR.

Another distinctive feature of considered approach is the way in which we study the rationality of the FCF. More traditional approach to FCF considers only crisp set of non-dominated alternatives, which lead to acyclicity of some underlying crisp preference relation and does not deal much with the intensity of preferences. Our approach really takes into account the information about intensity of pair-wise preferences in underlying FPR and gives a possibility to consider as the "good" alternatives, the alternatives dominated with a "low" value of intensity. This set of alternatives may be considered as a solution of a DM problem when the set of the "best", non-dominated alternatives is empty. Our approach can give solution to the DM problem when more traditional approach does not work. The existence of the set of "good" alternatives is related with the properties of "weak" acyclicity of underlying strict FPR, which essentially use the intensity of pair-wise preferences. Such "weak" acyclicity properties admit some types of fuzzy circles in the strict FPR such that the choice of "good" alternatives may be done in the presence of such circles. The circles in crisp preference relations arise usually in multi-criteria evaluation of alternatives or like in Condorcet paradox when these relations are obtained as a result of aggregation of individual preference relations. In this case, the use of DM procedures based on strict FPR will decrease the possibility of arising circles in aggregated preference relation when the rational decision cannot be done.

Central to this model is the incomparability relation that occurs when agents have conflicting information preventing them to come to a consensus. Here we have shown how the valued strict preferences can decrease the number of cycles and this way the number of conflicts for multi-agent DM. This model was shown to be applicable to both a single and multi-agent multi-criteria DM problem setting. Several generalizations of crisp group DM procedures have been proposed that give possibility to avoid some problems typical for crisp models.

Acknowledgements. Partial support for this research work has been provided by the IMP, project D.00006 "Distributed Intelligent Computing", and by RFBR grant 03-01- 96245.

References

1.   Abaev, L.: Choice of variants in a fuzzy environment: binary relations and fuzzy decomposition, in: I. Batyrshin, I., Pospelov D. (eds.): Soft Models in Decision-Making. Special Issue of International Journal of General Systems. 30 (2001) 53–70
2.   Averkin, A., Batyrshin, I., Blishun, A. et al.: Fuzzy Sets in the Models of Control and Artificial Intelligence. Nauka Publ., Moscow (1986) (in Russian)
3.   Bouyssou, D.: Acyclic fuzzy preference and the Orlovsky choice function: a note. Fuzzy Sets and Systems 89 (1997) 107-111

4. Danilov, V.I., Sotskov, A.I.: Mechanisms of Group Choice. Nauka Publ., Moscow (1991) (in Russian).

5. Faratin, P., Van de Walle B.: Agent Preference Relations: Strict, Equivalent and Incomparables. in: Autonomous Agents and Multi-Agent Systems. Italy: AAAI Press (2002) 1317-1324.

6. Fodor, J., Roubens, M.,: Fuzzy Preference Modelling and Multicriteria Decision Support. Dordrecht: Kluwer Academic Publishers (1994)

7. García-Lapresta, J.L.: A general class of simple majority decision rules based on linguistic opinions. Information Sciences (2003)(in print).

8. Kulshreshtha, P., Shekar, B.: Interrelationships among fuzzy preference-based choice functions and significance of rationality conditions: A taxonomic and intuitive perspective. Fuzzy Sets and Systems 109 (2000) 429–4459

9. Mirkin B.G.: The Problem of Group Choice. Nauka Publ., Moscow (1974) (in Russian)

10. Orlovsky, S.A.: Decision-making with a fuzzy preference relation. Fuzzy Sets and Systems, 1 (1978) 155 – 167

11. Sheremetov, L., Romero-Cortés, J.: Fuzzy Coalition Formation Among Rational Cooperative Agents. LNAI (Revised Papers of CEEMAS'03), Springer Verlag (2003)

12. Yager, R.: Fusion of multi-agent preference orderings. Fuzzy Sets and Systems 117 (2001) 1-12

13. Zadeh, L.A.: Similarity relations and fuzzy orderings. Inform. Sciences 3 (1971) 177-200

Adaptation in the Presence of Exogeneous Information in an Artificial Financial Market

José L. Gordillo[1], Juan Pablo Pardo-Guerra[2], and Christopher R. Stephens[3]

[1] Dirección Gral. de Serv. de Cómputo Académico, UNAM.
jlgr@super.unam.mx
[2] Facultad de Ciencias, UNAM.
jpardog@prodigy.net.mx
[3] Instituto de Ciencias Nucleares, UNAM.
stephens@nuclecu.unam.mx

Abstract. In recent years, agent-based computational models have been used to study financial markets. One of the most interesting elements involved in these studies is the process of learning, in which market participants try to obtain information from the market in order to improve their strategies and hence increase their profits. While in other papers it has been shown how this learning process is determined by factors such as the adaptation period, the composition of the market and the intensity of the signals that an agent can perceive, in this paper we shall discuss the effect of external information in the learning process in an artificial financial market (AFM). In particular, we will analyze the case when external information is such that it forces all participants to randomly revise their expectations of the future. Even though AMFs usually use sophisticated artificial intelligence techniques, in this study we show how interesting results can be obtained using a quite elementary genetic algorithm.

1 Introduction

In recent years it has become ever more popular to consider financial markets (FMs) from an evolutionary, rather than the traditional *rational expectations*, point of view [1,2]. In particular, there has been a substantial increase in studies that use agent-based, evolutionary computer simulations, known as Artificial Financial Markets (AFM) [3]. In this paper we use a particular AFM — the NNCP [4] — whose design was motivated by the desire to study relatively neglected elements in other AFMs (for instance, the Santa Fe Virtual Market [5]), such as the effect of organizational structure on market dynamics and the role of *market makers* and information. All of these elements are crucial in the formation of market microstructure [6].

Among the most interesting aspects one can study in an AFM — and constituting the central topic of this work — is the process of learning, a set of mechanisms which allows agents to modify their buy/sell strategy with the aim of adapting to the conditions imposed by the market. In particular, in this paper

R. Monroy et al. (Eds.): MICAI 2004, LNAI 2972, pp. 342–351, 2004.

we study the effect of external information on the learning process. For this purpose we have analyzed the extreme case where the arrival of information forces all participants to change their perception about the state of the market and therefore their expectations about its future evolution.

Though the NNCP allows us to include many features that influence the behavior of the market, in this study we used only a small number of elements: informed and uninformed agents, adaptive agents, and information "shocks" in the market's development. Despite this relatively modest diversity of behaviors and simplicity of elements, it was possible to conduct experiments that produced significant results.

The structure of the next paper is as follows. In section 2 we describe the general form of the elements used in the NNCP, namely the market organization, the market participants, the information processes ("shocks"), and the learning mechanisms. In section 3 we explain the experiments conducted, along with a discussion of their main results. Finally, we give our conclusions, as well as some general ideas for future lines of research.

2   The Building Blocks of the NNCP

The workings of the NNCP are, in general terms, as follows: a simulation is carried out for a prescribed number of *ticks* on a single risky asset. An agent can divide his/her wealth between this risky asset and a riskless asset ("cash"). At each *tick* an agent —or a set of agents — takes a position (buy/sell/neutral). Shares are bought in fixed size lots of one share. Resources are finite and hence traders have portfolio limits associated with either zero cash or zero stock. Short selling is not permitted.

2.1   Market Organization

The market clearing mechanism we used for all our simulations in this particular study is a simple double auction, where at every *tick* each trader takes a position with an associated volume and at a given price, each trader being able to value the asset independently but with prices that are not too different. In this model price changes are induced only via the disequilibrium between supply and demand. Specifically:

1. At time (or "tick") t one lists all the positions taken by the agents and the associated volume and price. The agents' bids and offers are obtained via a Gaussian distribution with mean $\bar{p} = p(t-1)$.
2. A bid and an offer are matched only if they overlap, i.e. $p_b(t) > p_o(t)$. To realize a transaction we used: *"best bid/offer"*, where the highest bid and the lowest offer are matched at their midpoint successively until there are no overlapping bids and offers.

After each *tick* price is updated exogeneously via a supply/demand type law as in Eq. (1).

$$p(t+1) = p(t)[1 + \eta(B(t) - O(t))] \tag{1}$$

In this equation, which is common to many AFMs, $p(t)$ is price at *tick* t and $B(t)$ and $O(t)$ are the demand and supply at t, while η is a tuning parameter. Note that $D(t) = (B(t) - O(t))$ depends not only on the positions taken by the agents but also on the mechanism used to match their trades, e.g. at what price two contrary trades will be matched. In this sense one may think of a "bare" $D(t)$, $D_B(t)$, that represents the imbalance in supply and demand associated purely with the desired trades of the agents while $D(t)$ represents the residual imbalance after matching those orders that can be matched under a given clearing mechanism.

2.2   Market Participants

We will divide traders into various classes. Two of the principal classes are informed and uninformed, or liquidity, traders. The latter make random decisions, buying or selling with equal probability irrespective of the market price. Informed agents on the other hand have a higher probability to buy than sell. One can try to rationalize this behavior in different ways, each rationalization being equally legitimate in the absence of further information. One can, for instance, imagine that informed agents have a better understanding of the market dynamics in that they "know" that in the presence of uninformed traders the excess demand the informed trader's bias generates will translate itself, via Eq. (1), into a price increase which will augment their portfolio values at the expense of the uninformed. Alternatively, one may simply imagine that the informed traders believe the market will rise. We will, in fact, consider a one-parameter family of informed traders described by a "bias", d, where the position probabilities are:

$$P(c) = \frac{2d}{3}, \qquad P(n) = \frac{1}{3}, \qquad P(v) = \frac{2(1-d)}{3} \qquad (2)$$

where c represents Buy, v Sell and n Hold. For example, when $d = 1/2$ then the corresponding probabilities are $1/3$, $1/3$, $1/3$; which actually corresponds to an uninformed trader, i.e. a trader having no statistical bias in favour of one position versus another. In contrast, a trader with $d = 1$ has probabilities $2/3$, $1/3$, 0 and corresponds to a trader with a strong belief that the market will rise or, alternatively, to a trader who believes that there are many uninformed traders in the market that can be exploited by selling while the informed trader drives the price up. We will denote a trading strategy from this one-parameter family by the pair $(100d, 100(1 - d))$. Thus, an uninformed, or liquidity, trader is denoted by $(50, 50)$ and a maximally biased one by $(100, 0)$. Essentially, the different traders have different belief systems about the market. As mentioned, due to the simplicity of the model we may not ask how it is that the different traders arrive at these different expectations. It may be that they have different information sets, or it may be due to the fact that they process the same information set in different ways, or, more realistically, a combination of these.

Given that we wish to compare the relative profitability of the different trading strategies we need to define profits. Here, the profits of agents are given in terms of a "moving target" where excess profit during timestep t is related to the increase in the market value of an active trading portfolio in the timestep t relative to the increase in the market value of a buy and hold portfolio in the same timestep. In this way an excess profit for a given trader over the timestep t can only arise when there has been a net change in the trader's portfolio holdings in the asset *and* a net change in the asset's price. This choice of benchmark always refers the market dynamics to a "zero sum" game, while with other benchmarks this is not the case. More concretely, we define the "excess" profit of a trader i in the time interval $t-1$ to t to be

$$e_i(t, t-1) = \delta n_i(t) \delta p(t), \tag{3}$$

where $\delta n_i(t)$ is the change in portfolio holdings over the timestep $\delta t = t - (t-1)$ of the trader i and $\delta p(t)$ is the change in asset price over this timestep. The excess profit earned between times t' and t is

$$E_i(t, t') = \sum_{n=t'}^{n=t} e_i(n, n-1) \tag{4}$$

2.3 Adaptation and Learning in the Presence of Endogeneous and Exogeneous Information

In the context of only informed and uninformed whose strategies remain static there can be no adaptation in the market, nor any learning. In order to caricature these elements we introduce adaptive agent strategies wherein an adapting agent may copy the strategy of the most successful agent currently in the market (the *copycat* strategy). In this sense the copycat agents have to both learn or infer what is the best strategy to copy, and then adapt their own strategy in the light of this new knowledge. The manner in which they do this is via standard "roulette wheel selection" as commonly used to represent the selection operator in Genetic Algorithms [7], to update their strategies using accumulated excess profits as the "fitness" function. In other words, a copycat copies the strategy of agent i with probability

$$P_i(t) = E_i(t, t') / \sum_i E_i(t, t') \tag{5}$$

where $E_i(t, t')$ is defined in Eq. (4). They observe the market, updating their information at a fixed frequency, for example, every 100 ticks, and copy the agent's strategy that wins the roulette wheel selection process. Given that the roulette wheel selection is stochastic it may be that a copycat does not copy the strategy with the most excess profit. It is important to clarify that we are not interested in pinpointing the agent which is copied in so far as we are interested in identifying the strategy that is picked during the process. This way we can conceive the selection mechanism as a roulette divided not in small regions representing individual agents, but rather in bigger slices that account for each of the strategies present in the market; Eq. (6) depicts this situation

$$P_i(t) = S_i(t, t') / \sum_{j=1}^{m} S_j(t, t') \tag{6}$$

where $S_j(t, t')$ is the sum of accumulated profits (Eq. (4)) of all the agents with strategy j, and where m is the total number of strategies present in the market.

The more successful a strategy is relative to others, the more likely it is that this is the strategy copied. The stochastic nature of the copying process reflects the inefficiencies inherent in the learning process.

In the above we described how copycats learn and adapt in the presence of endogeneous information, i.e. information intrinsic to the market itself, this information being the relative profits of the different trading strategies in the market. This information is dynamic and so the copycats change their expectations and beliefs about what will happen in the future. In real markets, however, new exogeneous information frequently arrives. In this context one must ask how the different traders will react to this information. Such exogeneous information is usually taken to be random. We will follow this paradigm here, imagining the exogeneous information to be in the form of information "shocks". In this case we assume that the participants are forced to change their perception of the state of the market — and therefore their buy/sell strategy. At this point, two interesting questions can be raised: First, how is the learning process affected by these information shocks? And second, is the information prior to a shock useful in the learning process?

3   Experimental Results

We will answer the above questions in the context of various simulations carried out using the NNCP artificial market. However, before presenting the experiments with their results, we will discuss some aspects of the copycat's adaptation process. As it has been mentioned previously, in order to adapt their strategies to the market's conditions, copycats must "play" a roulette formed from the profits of each strategy in the market (Eq. 6). It is convenient to recognize the stochastic effects of this game, in particular those produced by the composition of the market. We can illustrate this by thinking of a market where the copycats copy via roulette wheel selection the most popular strategy. Suppose the roulette is formed by the number s of agents that possess a strategy given by

$$P_i(t) = s_i(t)/\sum_j^m s_j(t) \, ; \tag{7}$$

One question we can answer is how many copycats will adopt strategy i at time t. Let C be the number of copycat agents, I the initial number of agents with strategy i and T the total number of agents (i.e. $\sum_j^m s_j(t)$). When $t = 1$ (the first adaptation) it follows that

$$X_i(1) = C * P_i(1) = I * C/T \, ; \tag{8}$$

where $X_i(t)$ is the average number of copycats that adopt strategy i at time t. Now, when $t = 2$, the number of agents with strategy i is $I + X_i(1)$, and in general, after K adaptations, one has

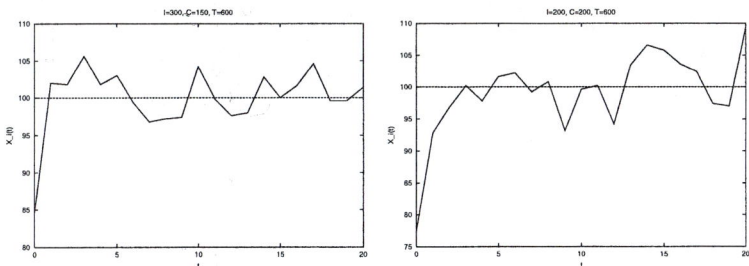

Fig. 1. Number of copycats that learn strategy i in simulations with different values of $\{I,C,T\}$. The values are $\{300,150,600\}$ (left) and $\{200, 200, 600\}$ (right).

$$X_i(K) = C*P_i(t-1) = I*C/T+I*C^2/T^2+\ldots+I*C^n/T^n = I*\sum_j^k C^j/T^j \quad (9)$$

Obviously, $C < T$, and therefore

$$X_i(t)_{t\to\infty} = I*C/(T-C). \quad (10)$$

which is the expected maximum number of copycats that will copy the most popular strategy. In Figure 1 we show the result of the first 20 adaptations in markets with different values of I, C and T, where copycats adapt every tick and the most popular strategy is associated with informed $(51, 49)$ agents. The graphs are a result of averaging over 10 different runs. In Figure 1 we see how the number of correct copycats asymptotes to a value close to that given by Eq. (10). There is a slight difference in that the graphs are for copycats that copy the most profitable strategy. However, for weak bias we see that Eq. (10) gives a good approximation. More generally, it gives a lower bound for the number of correct copycats.

Returning to the problem of learning: The objective of a copycat is to acquire the optimal strategy (i.e. the strategy that maximizes profits constrained to existing market conditions); conversely, the objective of the biased traders is to create an excess demand. This excess demand thus drives the price via the price evolution equation (Eq. 1) along with the profits of informed agents, as has been noted in previous work [4,8]. Additionally, both the excess demand and the profits of the informed traders depend on the composition of the entire population as well as on the distribution of biases. In this scenario, copycats try to copy informed traders to find the optimal strategy. This activates the learning process. However, complete learning is by no means guaranteed in the sense that they do not necessarily identify the best strategy. The quality of the learning depends on the signal to noise ratio (i.e. the size of the different regions in the roulette), which in its turn depends on the agent biases and the market composition. Note that the learning might be incomplete even in the case where there is only one other strategy to learn. As an illustration of the latter consider Figure 2, where we show the number of copycats that learn the correct strategy

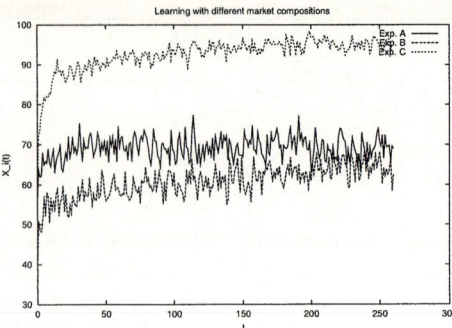

Fig. 2. Incompleteness of learning: number of copycats that learn strategy i in experiments with different market compositions

in three different experiments. In the first case (Experiment A), the market is composed of 20 agents of each of the following strategies: $(50, 50)$, $(60, 40)$, $(70, 30)$, $(80, 20)$, $(90, 10)$, 100 $(99, 1)$ agents, and 100 copycats. In Experiment B the market is formed by 100 uninformed agents (i.e. with a $(50, 50)$ strategy), 100 $(60, 40)$ agents and 100 copycats. Finally, Experiment C was composed of 100 $(50, 50)$ agents, 100 $(99, 1)$ agents and 100 copycats. The roulette at time t was built using $E_i(t, 0)$, that is, the profits calculated since the beginning of the experiment.

In Experiment A, the optimal strategy is $(99, 1)$. However, the presence of other strategies with lesser yields confuses the copycats in such a way that only about 70% of them present successful learning, i.e. that identify the optimal strategy, (the average due purely to the composition of the market is 50% in all cases; this can be derived through simple probabilistic arguments with the use of the roulette). In Experiment B we can observe that the interaction of the $(50, 50)$ and $(60, 40)$ strategies generates only a relatively small signal, hence explaining why the number of copycats that learn the best strategy is only slightly bigger than the average of the market's composition. Experiment C shows the imperfection of the learning process, even in a market with a very large difference in biases, i.e. that due to the stochastic nature of the roulette wheel complete learning cannot take place. We see in general then that the efficiency of learning depends on the market biases and the diversity of strategies in the market as well as the stochastic nature of the roulette wheel selection.

3.1   Simulating Markets with Exogeneous Shocks

As mentioned earlier, we model the effect of an information shock by changing the perception of all the market participants. This is done by means of a random re-selection of strategies among the agents at the moment of the shock. Specifically, by labeling the agents as either informed (I) or uninformed (U), we can visualize an information shock as a moment t_s in which all the market's participants select a strategy again, either U or I. Thus, an agent that prior to a shock is informed may become uninformed with a certain probability s or may remain in his original state with a probability $1 - s$[1]. With this scheme, over a period that contains several shocks an agent can no longer be tagged as being either informed or uninformed. However, we can label them with a chain that represents the different states they have occupied over a certain interval of time[2]. For instance, an agent may be defined by the sequence $IUUI$, which means that, starting out as an informed, it changed into a uninformed at the first shock, remained in this state after the following shock and returned to an informed strategy after the third shock. This simulation of information processes clearly creates a new level of complexity in the system since now we face many more options than the ones present in a static market.

Taking this into account, after a shock an evolutionary agent must re-learn what is the optimal strategy under the new market conditions. An interesting problem is determining how much endogeneous information an evolutionary agent needs to learn the best strategy, given the dynamic conditions of the market. In the examples presented in the first part of this section, each evolutionary agent used all the history of the trader's profits to make a decision, i.e. each agent had "long-term" memory. However, with the introduction of shocks into the system, the evolutionary agents now face new difficulties in processing the available information. In this sense, the amount of data used for inference becomes a crucial matter: it is not the same considering a multi-shock time window when the strategies can shift between informed and uninformed than when they remain static. And so, we may pose the following question: Will the same information be as useful in a system with changing perceptions? In Figure 3 we show the results of two experiments that shed some light on this question. In Experiment D the copycats try to copy a strategy using only the information generated by the market after each shock. Thus, they have only "short-term" memory as they do not keep in their memory any information prior to the shock. In contrast, Experiment E depicts the case in which copycats have long-term memory, preserving the entire information of the market's history without distinguishing data obtained before and after shocks. In these experiments the traders change their perception of the market to one of two possible states: either an informed or an uninformed strategy. In other words, despite the shocks, during all the periods of the experiment, the optimal strategy is invariant, i.e. to be constantsly informed; what changes are the perceptions of the participants which affects the strategy that they choose and therefore the profits they have accumulated. At the same time, after each shock an arbitrary agent has the same chance of ending in the set of the informed as in the set of the uninformed, in such a way that the composition of the market in each period is, on average, always the same.

---

[1] In the experiments presented in this paper that involve shocks, s takes a value of $\frac{1}{2}$, unless otherwise indicated.

[2] Since the definitions of informed and uninformed are mutually exclusive, we can consider them as states that describe the actual strategy of an agent. This way, if an agent is informed, we can say that he is in state I or, in other words, that he is occupying state I.

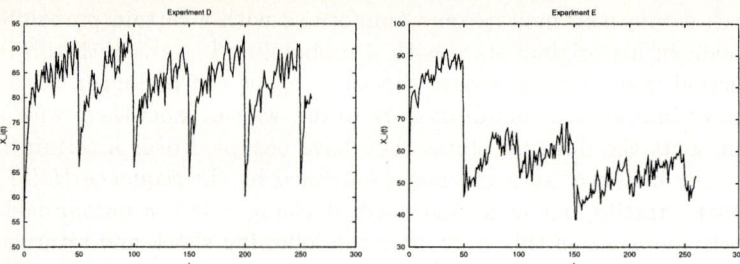

Fig. 3. Learning in markets with exogeneous shocks: copycats with long-term (right) and short-term (left) memory

We can see in this figure that the learning process where traders only use as their learning information set market information from the last shock until the present moment better adapt to the new market conditions. This is especially true in the present case where the first shock arrives when the learning process is almost finished; the shock produces a reset of the process but the learning process itself stays the same. After each shock the copycats realize that they must adjust their perceptions in the new market conditions by relearning everything. Meanwhile, in the case of learning with long-term memory, it is much more difficult for the copycats to identify the correct strategy after each shock as they are using past information that is no longer relevant. For example, they end up copying a strategy that was useful and therefore accumulated significant profit before the shock but is suboptimal after the shock. By the time the copycat has realized that the strategy is no longer optimal it has made significant losses.

4   Conclusions

We have shown here that it is possible to produce very interesting results utilizing only a fairly simple computational model. Although the model itself has little complexity and is relatively small — a significant benefit that expresses itself in small run times — our work on the NNCP has given us some interesting ideas on how financial markets might deal with external information. Among the most important findings, we can identify the role of memory during the learning process. As shown in section 3.1, the relevance of information considered during the selection of a strategy is of vital significance when it comes to optimizing profits: using irrelevant information from before the shock to determine the optimal post-shock strategy results in poor learning and a more efficient market.

And though the identification of shock-like structures in real financial markets is still somewhat controversial, results like these might translate into practical trading techniques in the future. We have also shown that learning is very much a statistical inference process in the context of a financial market and have exhibited some of the factors on which the efficiency of the learning depends.

There is, however, much more work ahead. The configuration of NNCP, as used in this paper, is quite simple, so it is not implausible to have left a large collection of behaviors out of the simulations. In this sense, we can consider several improvements to the model aimed at better describing the nature of financial markets, or at least at refining our approximations of their description. For instance, future models might consider more complex mechanisms of learning as well as sophisticated information shocks that do not affect the entire market. Equally important, the participation methods of the artificial agents could be enhanced into more than stochastic rules defined by a probabilistic bias. Nonetheless, all these approaches demand a better understanding of the system (from the mechanisms of learning to the role of market structure) as well as increased computational requirements.

Acknowledgments. This work was supported by DGAPA grants IN100201 and IN114302 and CONACyT grant 41221-F. We are grateful to the Dept. of Supercomputing, DGSCA, UNAM for access to computational resources. We are also grateful for useful conversations to Prof. Harald Benink.

References

1. Bedau M., Joshi S.: An Explanation of Generic Behavior in an Evolving Financial Market. Preprint 98-12-114E, Santa Fe Institute (1998).
2. Farmer J. D.: Market Force, Ecology and Evolution. Working Paper 98-12-117E, Santa Fe Institute (1998).
3. Chan N., Lebaron B., Lo A., Poggio T.: Agent Based Models of Financial Markets: a Comparison with Experimental Markets. Working Paper, Brandeis University (1999).
4. Gordillo J.L.: Análisis de Mercados Financieros mediante el Mercado Financiero Artificial NNCP. Tesis de Maestría. IIMAS-UNAM (2000).
5. Palmer R.G., Arthur W.B., Holland J.H., Lebaron B., Tayler P.: Artificial Economic Life: a Simple Model of a Stock Market. Physica D 73 (1994).
6. O'Hara M.: Market Microstructure Theory. Blackwell Publishers Inc (1997).
7. Goldberg D.G.: Genetic Algorithms in Search, Optimization and Machine Learning. Addison Wesley (1989).
8. Gordillo J.L, Stephens C.R.: Strategy Adaptation and the Role of Information in an Artificial Financial Market. Late Breaking Papers, GECCO (2001).
9. Gordillo J.L, Stephens C.R.: Analysis of Financial Markets with the Artificial Agent-based Model-NNCP. Encuentro Nacional de Ciencias de la Computación. Sociedad Mexicana de Ciencias de la Computación. Mexico (2001).

Design Patterns for Multiagent Systems Design

Sylvain Sauvage[1,2]

[1] GREY — CNRS UMR 6072, université de Caen (France)
[2] IIUN — université de Neuchâtel (Switzerland)
Sylvain.Sauvage@info.unicaen.fr

Abstract. Capitalizing and diffusing experience about multiagent systems are two key mechanisms the classical approach of methods and tools can't address. Our hypothesis is that, among available techniques that collect and formalise experience, design patterns are the most able technique allowing to express the agent concepts and to adapt itself to the various MAS developing problems.
In this paper, we present several agent oriented patterns, [1], in order to demonstrate the feasibility of helping MAS analysis and design through design patterns. Our agent patterns cover all the development stages, from analysis to implementation, including re-engineering (through antipatterns, [2]).

1 Introduction

Analysis and design are becoming an important subject of research in multiagent systems (MAS). Now MAS are more and more used, the need for tools and methods allowing the quick and reliable realisation of MAS is clearly appearing. This need is appearing in the MAS community itself but it's also a necessity to empower a larger community to use the agent paradigm.

Present attempts of the community focus on MAS design methodology. In fact, MAS paradigm development is restricted by the gap between the apparent ease to seize the basic concepts (as agent, role, organisation, or interaction) and the difficulty to create a MAS which resolves or helps to resolve a real world problem. Then, to help the MAS designer, we seek a new formalisation.

As agents are often implemented by the way of object programming, the idea to use object-oriented analysis and design methods is appealing. But those methods are not applicable, simply because objects and agents do not pertain to the same logical and conceptual levels – for example, one can program a MAS in a functional language. Nevertheless, we can draw our inspiration from object methods and from their development to create methods for MAS.

Reuse has three targets: structures, processes, and concepts. Each of these targets can be viewed at different abstraction levels, for example, structures address both the code, the organisation of the code and the architecture of the concepts. As shown on Table 1 on page 353, among the reusing techniques, the design patterns, [1], cover all three targets and, even if the coding part is a little less covered than with components, the method (*i.e.*, the path from the problem to its solution) is much more covered.

R. Monroy et al. (Eds.): MICAI 2004, LNAI 2972, pp. 352–361, 2004.

Table 1. Reuse in reusing techniques

	Structures	Processes	Concepts
Duplication	code	—	—
Functions library	code	algorithms	—
Classes library	code	comportment	classes
Components	code, architecture	comportment	classes
Frameworks	code, architecture	algorithms	(classes)
Design patterns	(code), architecture	algorithms, method	classes, models
Design methods	—	method!	models

Those reasons show that design patterns are strongly appropriate to resolve the MAS design problems. In fact, design patterns are the perfect means to spread the concepts, the models, and the techniques used in the MAS design and in their implementation.

In the following section, in order to demonstrate the feasibility of helping MAS analysis and design through design patterns, we will expose shortened versions of various agent oriented design patterns.

2   Agent Oriented Design Patterns

We describe here eleven agent oriented design patterns. The fields we use to formalise our patterns are the following: its *name*, a *sysnopsis*, the contextual *forces* of its application, real *examples* of its usage, the *solution* it proposes, some *implementation* issues, an *examination* of its advantages and disadvantages, and *associated patterns*, as design patterns are tied together (co-operation, use, delegation, or conflict).

We class our patterns in four categories: metapatterns, metaphoric patterns, architectural patterns and antipatterns.

2.1   MetaPatterns

Metapatterns are so called because they are patterns of higher conceptual level than other patterns. Their scope is wider, they address problems at all stages of the design process, from analysis to implementation. Moreover, they also cover children patterns, which are more specific patterns that use and detail the concepts and the solution proposed by the associated metapattern.

For their formalisation, the *forces* field is replaced by *concepts*.

Organisation schemes explains the concepts associated with organisation and describes their numerous uses.

Concepts

- *Agent:* an autonomous entity.
- *Role:* a function an *agent* can take in an *organisation*. This function can have a short life (undertook and shortly after abandonned) or a long life

(the function survives the agent as several agents follow each other at its charge). Each role defines associated behaviours, interactions and relations.
- *Organisation:* a structure grouping several agents which undertake roles in the *organisation scheme* from which this *organisation* is modelled.
- *Organisation scheme:* an abstract structure grouping role descriptions. It's a class of organisations.

Examples of the usage of *organisation schemes* are various. They spread from analysis and design, [3, 4, 5, 6, 7], to implementation, [8, 9].

The Solution. This patterns proposes for the analysis of a MAS is to use organisation schemes as a lecture grid: organisations in the MAS are discovered and described by the comparison with a catalog of organisation schemes ([10] could be a sketch for such a catalog).

In MAS design, this pattern proposes to integrate and describe roles and organisations in the UML class diagrams of the designed MAS. This integration allows to virtualize the services the roles represent: relations between roles only depend on the roles, not on the agents undertaking the roles.

In MAS implementation, this pattern proposes to embody roles and organisations as objects, so that agents could be able to use and control them.

The Examination of this pattern shows us various advantages. Among them is the ability this pattern gives the designer to integrate, through high level concepts, *real world* knowledge into the description of the MAS he is designing.

Another advantage is the ability, by dividing the system into various organisations, to divide and conquer the analysis and design of the system.

This pattern also has a disadvantage: it fixes the system's organisation, though limiting its reactivity and adaptability by restricting its ability of auto-reorganisation.

Associated patterns to this patterns are, of course, its children patterns: patterns about specific organisation structures and models that explain specific roles, their associated behaviours and interactions.

Protocols covers the concepts associated to interaction and communication protocols.

Concepts
- *Agent:* an autonomous entity.
- *Message:* an information object transmitted by an *agent* to another one. This concept also addresses speech acts, [11].
- *Interaction:* communication, perturbation or influence link between agents. In a communication protocol, it's a *conversation*.
- *Role:* a function an agent undertake in an interaction. Each role defines the messages the agent can send.
- *Protocol:* a set of rules allowing two or more agents to coordinate. A protocol defines the order and the type of messages and actions.

Examples of the use of *Protocols* are numerous in analysis and design, [12, 13, 14, 15, 16].

The Solution. This pattern proposes is to find messages, conversations and interactions in the system and to abstract them into protocols. Another complementary way of using protocols is to use a catalog of protocols as a grid to analyse the system (such a catalog can be written from the list of protocols the FIPA proposes: `http://www.fipa.org`).

Examination. Identifying protocols at an early stage allows a better identification of the roles and the interactions of the system, and of the messages agents can send.

In another hand, as design patterns already do, protocols form a common vocabulary that enables a better analysis and a better description of the system.

Associated patterns to this one are its children patterns: patterns explaining the application context and the constraints resolved by a particular protocol. *Organisation schemes* is associated to this pattern as they both share the main concept of *role*. *Influences* and *Marks* are also associated patterns: communications between agents are a form of influences and marks are a form of messages.

2.2   Metaphoric Patterns

Metaphoric patterns are widely used is MAS. They describe the use of a solution that is inspired from a discipline which, at the first glance, seems to be totally exotic to multi-agent systems and to their design.

As they have external origins, a new fied, *origins,* is added to their formalisation.

Marks is a pattern about the metaphor of pheromones, a model of communication through the environment.

Forces

- Agents have limited memory capabilities.
- Agents have limited communication capacities.
- Agents are situated: there are constraints affecting their positions, their moves.
- There are constraints affecting the resources agents can use: limited speed, energetic autonomy, and time.
- Informations that need to be kept or shared have spatial characteristic (they are only locally relevant).

The Origins of this metaphor are biological. The principle is especially used by insect species. As an example, an ant deposits slight quantities of a chemical matter (called *pheromone*) which enables it to make a track of its path (external memory) and to point out this path to its congeners (communication and recruitment medium). Pheromones directly induce a specific behaviour for the individual perceiving them – it's a *reaction,* as in the *reactive–cognitive* opposition of the agent literature. Pheromones act in the same way as the nervous system chemical transmitters.

Examples. Communication by marks and especially by pheromones has been studied and used in various works, [17, 18, 19, 20].

Solution. The agent deposits marks in the environment. These marks are low granularity objects and have a minimal size. They have some strength that allows the agent to *sense* their presence at a known distance. Once they are deposited, the environment takes care of their mutation: evaporation, dissemination/propagation, and perception. Those marks are perceived in a limited zone and in a limited way (mainly related to associated agent sensors).

The *marks* allow the agents to communicate without message exchange: depositing some quantity of a known *mark* is a modification of the environment every agent perceives.

Implementation. If the goal is to have agents living in the real world (*e.g.* robots), therefore marks are slight quantities of a product that agents are able easily and distinctly to perceive. It's unlikely that a chemical matter be used, but one can use marks which will be easy to distinct and which will be persistent to their emission.

If the agents live in a simulated world, therefore the environment has to be pro-active to manage the marks' life-cycle: evaporation, dissemination (due to the wind, other agents' moves), masking (by other marks), disappearance (even removal).

Examination. There also are problems due to the use of this pattern. Its implementation in a real world (that is, with robots) is not so easy: there are some troubles to find the good *product* – that implies troubles with the sensors, with their sensitivity and accuracy.

Concerning the difficulties of the simulation, the required memory and computational resources can't be neglected. This pattern also gives a great role to the environment.

However, this pattern has plenty of advantages, in addition to resolving the constraints exposed in the field *Forces.* Marks are simple messages – as much by their form than by their handling – and the fact that they are deposited allows integrating a locality notion to the information they carry. Moreover, this integration is done in an indirect way for the agent: he does not need a coordinate system, marks are deposited where they have a signification.

Associated patterns to this one are mainly *Influences* and *Protocols:* the attraction/repulsion effect of marks is mainly an influence and marks are somewhat a type of message.

Influences allow separating causes and effects of primitive actions to overcome simultaneous actions conflicts.

Forces

- There are global influences and forces.
- There may be simultaneous actions.
- An agent can perturbate another one whithout going through the second agent's cognitive mechanisms (no asynchronous message, physical and social levels are disctinct).

The Origins of this metaphor are physics: influences are forged from physical forces. Objects (and though agents) don't modify each other, instead, they create forces that, once combined, have an action.

Examples of using *influences* are various, [21, 22, 23, 24].

The Solution proposed consists in distinguishing the action an agent apply to another agent and the action this other agent undergoes.

The Implementation of this solution can use the algorithm defined in [22]. It can also use gradients and a discrete space algorithm to compute them: the wave gradient algorithm, [25].

Examination. Concurrent actions conflicts are frequent and difficult to handle. Moreover, it is often convenient to have a mechanism to handle global influences. *Influences* are also suitable to handle inertia, noise or friction.
    The main disadvantage of this pattern is that the combination of influences and the calculus of their effects have to be done by a mechanism that is outside the agents. It then leads to a global action controller, though being in contradiction to the principle of MAS: control distribution.

Associated patterns. The *Marks* pattern can benefit from this pattern as a mark is a source of attraction/repulsion. The three antipatterns we expose below *(Discretisation, Iniquity and Physical entity)* can be applied to implement this one, as *Command* and *Composite* can be, [1, pp. 86, 233].

2.3   Architectural Patterns

Architectural patterns descibe the internal architecture of an agent. As an agent often has many tasks to accomplish and as these tasks require skills of different cognition levels – some are reactive tasks, some are deliberations –, the structure of an agent is often decomposed into several modules. The architectural patterns show different ways to discover and arrange these modules and their interactions.

For now, we can see four main agent architecture types: BDI, Vertical, Horizontal, and Recursive architectures.

BDI architecture mainly embobies the BDI model used, for example, in [26, 27,28]. The principle of this architecture dwells in four knowledge bases: beliefs, desires, intention and plans.

Vertical architecture proposes to layer the modules in knowledge levels, each module having its own knowledge base, [29, 30, 31].

Horizontal architecture parallelizes the modules so they can deliberate and act all together, each one for its own purpose and/or at his own knowledge purpose, [32, 33, 34].

Recursive architecture sees an agent as a multiagent system. In other words, the modules composing the agent are seen as micro-agents acting all together in a micro-environment, which is the macro-agent itself, [35, 36, 37].

2.4   Antipatterns

Antipatterns, [2], are somewhat special patterns as they don't explain how to design a system but how to redesign and correct common mistakes. These mistakes are explained in the field we called *DysSolution*.

Iniquity is what happens when parallel calculus is inappropriately simulated: resources are not equally managed.

Discretisation is a partial loss of information, especially with numerical data.

Physical entity is to be used when, for practical reasons, the agent handles the physical actions applied to itself with its deliberative modules. That is, when there is no separation between the agent's physical part of its rational part.

3   Conclusions

Different works about agent patterns exist. Some are short or more object-like, [38, 39, 40, 41]. Some are interesting, as Aridor's, Kendall's, Deugo's, or Aarsten's [42, 43, 44, 45, 46], but it's a consideration not to limit the MAS application of the pattern technique to the simple use of patterns in a particular domain that MAS are. Indeed, some papers submit patterns presenting agents and agent techniques in an object-oriented way, *i.e.* as object techniques, leaving out the fact that agents are much more than objects – as autonomy, finality, interaction, and the fact they form a multiagent system.

That's why the eleven agent oriented patterns we have just presented shortened versions are of a higher abstraction level than object oriented design patterns usually are.

We think that patterns can help to develop MAS, as much in analysis, design or implementation as in teaching and spreading of the agent paradigm. Presenting as patterns the models and concepts of the MAS paradigm, as well as the techniques used to implement them, would enable us to structure, spread and constructively extend the knowledge of the agent paradigm we now have. Indeed, more than their *uniform* structure, patterns allow to understand more easily the concepts – for they emerge from experience and widely used examples, but also for they integrate theory to examples and they explain the conceptual reasons behind implementation techniques.

For now, our main goal is to present our agent patterns, as in [47], submit them to discussion and enhancement, and show their use through the development of MAS.

References

1. E. Gamma, R. Helm, R. Johnson, and J. Vlissides. *Design Patterns: Elements of Reusable Object-Oriented Software*. Addison Wesley, Reading (USA), 1994.
2. H. W. McCormick, R. Malveaux, T. Mowbray, and W. J. Brown, *AntiPatterns: Refactoring Software, Architectures, and Projects in Crisis*. John Wiley & Sons, Chichester, 1998.
3. E. Le Strugeon, R. Mandiau, and G. Libert. "Proposition d'organisation dynamique d'un groupe d'agents en fonction de la tâche." In JFIADSMA [48], pp. 217–227.
4. O. Gutknecht and J. Ferber. "Un méta-modèle organisationnel pour l'analyse, la conception et l'exécution de systèmes multi-agents." In Barthès et al. [49], pp. 267–280.
5. E. A. Kendall. "Agent Roles and Role Models: New Abstractions for Intelligent Agent Systems Analysis and Design." In *AIP'98*, 1998.
6. M. Wooldridge, N. R. Jennings, and D. Kinny. "The Gaia Methodology for Agent-Oriented Analysis and Design." *Journal of Autonomous Agents and Multi-Agent Systems*, 2000.
7. F. Zambonelli, N. R. Jennings, A. Omicini, and M. Wooldridge. "Agent-Oriented Software Engineering for Internet Applications." In A. Omicini, F. Zambonelli, M. Klusch, and R. Tolksdorf, editors, *Coordination of Internet Agents: Models, Technologies and Applications*, chapter 13. Springer-Verlag, Heidelberg (Germany), 2000.
8. B. Durand. *Simulation multi-agent et épidémiologie opérationnelle. Étude d'épizooties de fièvre aphteuse*. Thèse de doctorat (informatique), université de Caen (France), June 1996.
9. O. Gutknecht and J. Ferber. http://www.madkit.org. MadKit official web site.
10. J. C. Collis and D. T. Ndumu. *The Role Modelling Guide*, August 1999.
11. J. L. Searle. *Speech Acts*. Cambridge University Press, 1969.

12. R. Depke, R. Heckel, and J. M. Küster. "Agent-Oriented Modeling with Graph Transformation." In AOSE'2000, Limerick (Ireland), June 10 2000.

13. A. Omicini. "SODA: Societies and Infrastructures in the Analysis and Design of Agent-based Systems." In AOSE'2000, Limerick (Ireland), June 10 2000.

14. M. F. Wood and S. A. DeLoach. "An Overview of the Multiagent Systems Engineering Methodology." In AOSE'2000, Limerick (Ireland), June 10 2000.

15. J. Odell, H. Van Dyke Parunak, and B. Bauer. "Extending UML for Agents." In AOSE'2000, Limerick (Ireland), June 10 2000.

16. C. Oechslein, F. Klügl, R. Herrler, and F. Puppe. "UML for Behaviour-Oriented Multi-Agent Simulations." In Dunin-Kęplicz and Nawarecki [50], pp. 217–226.

17. M. Booth and J. Stewart. "Un modèle de l'émergence de la communication." In JFIADSMA [48], pp. 9–18.

18. A. Drogoul. De la simulation multi-agent à la résolution collective de problèmes. Une étude de l'émergence de structures d'organisation dans les SMA. Thèse de doctorat (informatique), université Paris 6 (France), 1993.

19. F. Klügl, F. Puppe, U. Raub, and J. Tautz. "Simulating Multiple Emergent Phenonema — Exemplified in an Ant Colony." In C. Adami et al., editors, Artificial Life VI, UCLA, June 27–29 1998. A Bradford book, MIT Press, Cambridge (USA).

20. P. Ballet. Intérêts mutuels des SMA et de l'immunologie — Application à l'immunologie, l'hématologie et au traitement d'images. Thèse de doctorat (informatique), université de Bretagne occidentale (France), January 28 2000.

21. J. Ferber and J.-P. Müller. "Influences and Reaction: a Model of Situated Multi-agent Systems." In ICMAS'96, Kyoto (Japan), December 1996.

22. R. Canal. "Environnement et réaction en chaîne — Le cas des systèmes multi-agents situés." In Barthès et al. [49], pp. 235–250.

23. P. Gruer, V. Hilaire, and A. Koukam. "Towards Verification of Multi-Agents Systems." In ICMAS'2000, pp. 393–394, Boston (USA), July 10–12 2000.

24. M. Amiguet. MOCA : un modèle componentiel dynamique pour les systèmes multi-agents organisationnels. Thèse de doctorat (informatique), université de Neuchâtel (Switzerland), 2003.

25. S. Sauvage. Conception de systèmes multi-agents : un thésaurus de motifs orientés agent. Thèse de doctorat (informatique), université de Caen (France), université de Neuchâtel (Switzerland), October 2003.

26. A. L. Lansky and M. P. Georgeff. "Reactive Reasoning and Planning." In AAAI, pp. 677–682, Seattle (USA), 1987.

27. A. S. Rao and M. P. Georgeff. "Modeling Rational Agents within a BDI-architecture." technical note 14, Australian Artificial Intelligence Institute, February 1991.

28. M. P. Singh, A. S. Rao, and M. P. Georgeff. "Formal Methods in DAI: Logic-Based Representation and Reasoning." In Gerhard Weiß, editor, Multiagent Systems — A Modern Approach to Distributed Artificial Intelligence, chapter 8, pp. 331–376. MIT Press, Cambridge (USA), 1999.

29. E. Gat. "Integrating Planning and Reacting in a Heterogeneous Asynchronous Architecture for Controlling Real-World Mobile Robots." In AAAI'92, 1992.

30. R. J. Firby, R. E. Kahn, P. N. Prokopowicz, and M. J. Swain. "An Architecture for Vision and Action." In IJCAI'95, pp. 72–79, August 1995.

31. J. P. Müller and M. Pischel. "The Agent Architecture InteRRaP: Concept and Application." research report RR-93-26, DFKI GMBH (Germany), 1993.

32. R. A. Brooks. "A Robust Layered Control System for a Mobile Robot." IEEE Journal of Robotics and Automation, 2(1):14–23, April 1986.

33. I. A. Ferguson. *TouringMachines: An Architecture for Dynamic, Rational, Mobile Agents*. PhD thesis, university of Cambridge, United Kingdom, November 1992.

34. A. Sloman and R. Poli. "SIM_AGENT: A toolkit for exploring agent designs." In M. Wooldridge, J. P. Müller, and M. Tambe, editors, *Intelligent Agents II, ATAL'95*, volume 1037 of *LNAI*, pp. 392–407. Springer-Verlag, Heidelberg (Germany), 1995.

35. M. Occello and Y. Demazeau. "Vers une approche de conception et de description récursive en univers multi-agent." In J. Quinqueton, M.-C. Thomas, and B. Trousse, editors, *JFIADSMA'97*, Nice (France), 1997. Hermès, Paris (France).

36. K. Fernandes and M. Occello. "Une approche multi-agents hybride pour la conception de systèmes complexes à raisonnement intégré." In *RJCIA'2000*, Lyon, September 10–13 2000.

37. F. Girault. *L'Environnement comme espace de cognition*. Thèse de doctorat (informatique), université de Caen (France), December 2002.

38. R. Tolksdorf. "Coordination Patterns of Mobile Information Agents." In M. Klusch and G. Weiß, editors, *Cooperative Information Agents II*, volume 1435 of *LNAI*, pp. 246–261. Springer-Verlag, Heidelberg (Germany), 1998.

39. E. Hung and J. Pasquale. "Agent Usage Patterns: Bridging the Gap Between Agent-Based Application and Middleware." technical report CS1999-0638, Department of Computer Science and Engineering, University of California, San Diego (USA), November 17 1999.

40. A. Silva and J. Delgado. "The Agent Pattern for Mobile Agent Systems." In *EuroPLoP'98*, Irsee (Germany), 1998.

41. M. Occello and J.-L. Koning. "Multiagent Oriented Software Engineering: An Approach Based on Model and Software Reuse." In P. Petta and J. P. Müller, editors, *Second International Symposium From Agent Theory to Agent Implementation*, Vienna (Austria), April 25–28 2000.

42. Y. Aridor and D. B. Lange. "Agent Design Patterns: Elements of Agent Application Design." In P. Sycara and M. Wooldridge, editors, *Agents'98*. ACM Press, May 1998.

43. E. A. Kendall, P. V. Murali Krishna, C. V. Pathak, and C. B. Suresh. "Patterns of Intelligent and Mobile Agents." In P. Sycara and M. Wooldridge, editors, *Agents'98*. ACM Press, May 1998.

44. D. Deugo, F. Oppacher, J. Kuester, and I. Von Otte. "Patterns as a Means for Intelligent Software Engineering." In *IC-AI'99*, pp. 605–611. CSREA Press, 1999.

45. D. Deugo, E. A. Kendall, and M. Weiß. "Agent Patterns." http://www.scs.carleton.ca/~deugo/Patterns/Agent/Presentations/AgentPatterns, November 21 1999.

46. A. Aarsten, D. Brugali, and G. Menga. "Patterns for Cooperation." In *PLoP'96*, Monticello (USA), September 1996.

47. S. Sauvage. "MAS Oriented Patterns." In Dunin-Kęplicz and Nawarecki [50], pp. 283–292.

48. *Premières journées francophones IAD & SMA*. Hermès, Paris (France), 1993.

49. J.-P. Barthès, V. Chevrier, and C. Brassac, editors. *JFIADSMA'98*, Pont-à-Mousson (France), November 18–20 1998. Hermès, Paris (France).

50. B. M. Dunin-Kęplicz and E. Nawarecki, editors. *CEEMAS 2001*, volume 2296 of *LNCS*. Springer-Verlag, Heidelberg (Germany), 2002.

A Faster Optimal Allocation Algorithm in Combinatorial Auctions

Jin-Woo Song and Sung-Bong Yang

Dept. of Computer Science
Yonsei University, Seoul, 120-749, Korea
{fantaros,yang}@cs.yonsei.ac.kr

Abstract. In combinatorial auctions, a bidder may bid for arbitrary combinations of items, so combinatorial auction can be applied to resource and task allocations in multiagent systems. But determining the winners of combinatorial auctions who maximize the profit of the auctioneer is known to be *NP-complete*. A branch-and-bound method can be one of efficient methods for the winner determination.

In this paper, we propose a faster winner determination algorithm in combinatorial auctions. The proposed algorithm uses both a branch-and-bound method and Linear Programming. We present a new heuristic bid selection method for the algorithm. In addition, the upper-bounds are reused to reduce the running time of the algorithm in some specific cases. We evaluate the performance of the proposed algorithm by comparing with those of CPLEX and a known method. The experiments have been conducted with six datasets each of which has a different distribution. The proposed algorithm has shown superior efficiency in three datasets and similar efficiency in the rest of the datasets.

1   Introduction

Combinatorial auctions(CAs) allow a bidder to tender a bidding on a combination of distinguishable items. However, determining the bidders in CAs whose bids give the auctioneer the highest profit is *NP*-complete[11]. The problem of determining such bidders is known as *the winner determination problem*. Solving this problem can be applicable to various practical auctions for airport landing slots, transportation exchanges, spectrum licenses, pollution permits, computational resources, and so on[2][3][7][8].

There are two important characteristics of biddings in CAs. One is *complementarity* - the valuation of a set of items that a bidder wants is more than the sum of the individual items. The other is *substitutability* - the valuation of a set of items that a bidder wants is less than the sum of the individual items. So CAs can be applied to resource and task allocations in multiagent systems in which items have the above characteristics.

The winner determination problem can be defined formally as follows. Let there be n bidders and m items. We denote the set of bidders as $B = \{b_1, b_2, \ldots, b_n\}$ and the set of items as $S = \{1, 2, \ldots, m\}$. Let $b_i = (s_i, p_i)$ be

R. Monroy et al. (Eds.): MICAI 2004, LNAI 2972, pp. 362–369, 2004.

the bid for a bidder b_i, where s_i is a nonempty subset of S and p_i is the price that b_i will pay for the items in s_i. Then the winners are determined with the following equation under the condition that each item can be allocated into at most one bidder, where if b_i is a winner then $x_i = 1$, otherwise $x_i = 0$ for $i = 1, 2, \ldots, n$.

$$\max \sum_{i=1}^{n} x_i p_i \quad s.t. \quad \sum_{i|j \in s_i} x_i \leq 1 \ , \forall j \in S \tag{1}$$

$$x_i = 0 \ or \ 1, for \ i = 1, 2, \ldots, n.$$

When the items are allowed to be allocated partially to the winners, Equation (1) can be converted into the following equation; that is, the winner determination problem can be reduced to a linear programming(LP).

$$\max \sum_{i=1}^{n} x_i p_i \quad s.t. \quad \sum_{i|j \in s_i} x_i \leq 1 \ , \forall j \in S \tag{2}$$

$$0 \leq x_i \leq 1, for \ i = 1, 2, \ldots, n.$$

The above equation helps a branch-and-bound method with pruning the search space to reduce the search time[9].

Andersson et al.[1] showed that the winner determination problem can be reduced to a mixed integer programming(MIP). They used CPLEX to solve MIP. Sandholm et al.[12] presented an optimal allocation algorithm called *CABOB*, in which a branch-and-bound method is used to guarantee the optimal solutions, LP is employed to get the upper-bounds, and some heuristic methods are proposed to improve its performance. BOB[15] is the original model of CABOB, and introduces various methods appeared in CABOB. CASS[5] constructs a data structure called *BIN* to exploit the characteristics of CAs and explores the search space with DFS for the optimal solution. In [5], [10], and [13], several approximation algorithms for the problem are given. [9], [11], and [13] provided some other methods to limit the bids.

In this paper we propose a faster optimal allocation algorithm for CAs that uses both a branch-and-bound method and LP. In the proposed algorithm we introduce a new heuristic bid selection method. It also reuses the upper-bounds to reduce the computation time. The experiments have been conducted with six datasets as in [12] each of which has a different distribution. The proposed algorithm has shown better performance than CPLEX and CABOB for three datasets and showed similar performance for the rest of the datasets.

The rest of this paper is organized al follows. In Section 2 describes the proposed algorithm in detail. Experimental results are given in Section 3. Finally the conclusions are made in Section 4.

2   The Proposed Algorithm

The proposed algorithm exploits a branch-and-bound method with BFS(best-first-search) to traverse the search space globally, while it uses DFS(depth-first-search) locally within a portion of the search space in which there are only a certain amount of remaining bids to be searched. The reason we introduce a hybrid search of BFS and DFS is that we could overcome memory shortage during search when only BFS is used and could avoid longer search time when only DFS is deployed.

Algorithm 2.1

1. PriorityQueue Q;
2. Node u, v; Opt_value $= 0$;
3. **If** (the input is *the complete case*) **then**
4.   **return** the winner from the complete case;
5. Initialize v with the initial bid;
6. Insert v into Q;
7. **While** (Q is not empty) **do**
8.   Dequeue v from Q;
9.   Upper_bound $= Bound(v)$;   //compute the upper-bound with LP//
10.   **If** (Upper_bound $>$ Opt_value) **then**
11.   **If** (the number of remaining bids $<$ 10% of the total number of bids)**then**
12.   Search the remaining bids with DFS;
13.   **else**
14.   **If** (v is the integer case) **then** solve integer programming;
15.   Select a bid b with the proposed heuristic bid selection method;
16.   Create nodes u_1 and u_2 such that u_1 includes b and u_2 does not;
17.   Opt_value $= \max\{$Opt_value, $value(u_1)$, $value(u_2)\}$;
18.   **If** ($Bound(u_i) >$ Opt_value) **then** insert u_i into Q, for $i = 1, 2$;
19. **end while**

The proposed algorithm, first, checks if the input is *the complete case* in which there is only one winner and the biddings from the rest of bidders conflict each other. If so, we terminate the algorithm with the winner (Line 4). Otherwise, we continue to the next step of the algorithm. There is another special case called *the integer case* in which, for each b_i, Equation (1) results in either $x_i = 0$ or $x_i = 1$.

Then we initialize v with the initial bids and insert v into Q. Note that a node v holds the bids selected so far, the rejected bids, the upper-bound, the x values, and $value(v)$ which is the sum of the prices of the selected bids. Next, the algorithm performs the **while-loop** unless Q is empty. Within the **while-loop**, node v is dequeued from Q (Line 8). $Bound(v)$ returns the upper-bound for v using LP with Equation (2). If $Bound(v)$ is greater than Opt_value which is the optimal value found so far, we check if the number of remaining bids is less than 10% of the total number of bids. If so, we perform DFS for the rest of the bids (Line 12). During DFS, we calculate the upper-bound of each node and update Opt_value, if the upper-bound is greater than Opt_value. Otherwise, the algorithm carries out BFS. Although BFS takes shorter time, it needs an exponential amount of memory. Hence, we used DFS along with BFS. Note that DFS has shown that its execution time is longer, while it uses smaller amount of memory.

Hence we need to find a proper percentage of BFS among the entire search to save memory without affecting the execution time. We have tested various percentages of BFS from 5% to 30% incrementing 5% at a time. The test results have shown that when 10% of the search is done by BFS we obtained better results. Before branching from v, if v is the integer case, we solve integer programming to obtain $value(v)$. Otherwise, we select a new bid from the rest of the bids using the proposed heuristic bid selection method (Line 15). After creating u_1 and u_2 (Line 15), for u_1 and u_2, we find the upper-bound to see if it is greater than Opt_value. If so, we insert it into Q for the next iteration of the **while-loop**. The loop is terminated when Q is empty. In the rest of this section, we describe a new heuristic bid selection method and explain the reuse of the upper-bounds.

2.1   A New Heuristic Method for Bid Selection

We propose a new heuristic bid selection method in which the bids that are not selected are searched with a branch-and-bound method in order to select the bids that may belong to the optimal solution. Some heuristic bid selection methods appeared in the previous work utilize the coefficients of LP or the information (bid prices and the number of items) submitted by bidders[6][9][12]. Some other method uses a graph, in which each node represents a bid and each edge links two bids that bid the same item, to utilize the degrees of nodes in selecting the bids[12].

In this paper we use both the coefficients of LP and a bid graph approach. Let $c_{ij} = 0$ if $i = j$ or if b_i and b_j bid on different items, $c_{ij} = 1$ if b_i and b_j bid on at least one common item; we say that b_i and b_j conflict each other.

We now describe the proposed heuristic method called *Conflict Bids Sum(**CBS**)* for bid selection. For b_i, if $x_i \geq 0.5$, we obtain cbs_i by summing up the x values for all the bids conflicting against b_i. Otherwise, $cbs_i = x_i$. CBS selects the bid with the highest cbs_i.

$$cbs_i = \begin{cases} \sum_{j=1}^{n}(x_j \times c_{ij}) & , x_i \geq 0.5 \\ x_i & , otherwise \end{cases} \tag{3}$$

CBS treats the bids with their x values greater than or equal to 0.5 as if they have the same x value and uses the sum of the x values of the conflicting bids against them for determining the priority in selection. Therefore, even though b_i has a higher x value, bid b_i is not likely to be selected if cbs_i is small. *CBS* tends to select bids with both higher x values and higher cbs values. *CBS* selects first the bids with values close to 0.5 and then selects the bids with indecisive x values so that *CBS* can reach the integer cases faster.

Fig. 1 shows an example of a bid graph. For each b_i, we can obtain its cbs_i using Equation (3):

$cbs_1(x_1 < 0.5) = x_1 = 0.0$, $cbs_2(x_2 \geq 0.5) = x_1 + x_3 + x_5 = 0.0 + 0.3 + 0.0 = 0.3$, $cbs_3(x_3 < 0.5) = x_3 = 0.3$, $cbs_4(x_4 \geq 0.5) = x_5 = 0.0$, $cbs_5(x_5 < 0.5) = x_5 = 0.0$, $cbs_6(x_6 < 0.5) = x_6 = 0.2$, $cbs_7(x_7 \geq 0.5) = x_3 + x_6 = 0.3 + 0.2 = 0.5$. In this example, b_7 is selected as the bid to branch, since it has the highest cbs value among others.

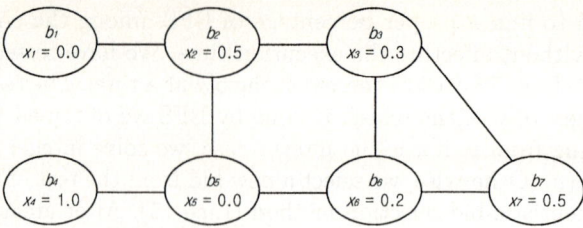

Fig. 1. An example of a bid graph

2.2   The Reuse of the Upper-Bounds

There are two cases in searching with a branch-and-bound method; that is, branching after either including the bid selected by the bid selection method into the solution set or not(Line 16 of Algorithm 2.1). For both cases, we may reuse the previous upper-bounds without calculating the upper-bounds with LP.

- Case 1: (Including the bid selected by the bid selection method) When the x value of the selected bid is 1, the upper-bound at the time of branching is the same as the upper-bound before branching minus the price of the selected bid, because the x value of the selected bid and those of its conflicting bids are all zeroes and the conflicting bids are not considered when computing the upper-bound at the time of branching.
- Case 2: (Excluding the bid selected by the bid selection method) The conflicting bids against the selected bid are not excluded from the candidate bids. If the x value of the selected bid is 0, the upper-bound for the remaining bids is the same as that before branching. So we do not calculate the upper-bound again[6].

3   Experimental Results

The Experiments have been conducted on a PC of a Pentium IV-1.0GHz processor with memory of 512MB on Windows 2000. We used the CPLEX version 7.0. The input datasets have been created according to Sandholm et al.[12]. There are six different datasets - random, weighted random, decay, uniform, bounded-low and bounded-high datasets. Except the uniform dataset, the number of items in each dataset is one tenth of the number of bids. The following describes each dataset:

◇ Random dataset: Select the items randomly from m items. Although there may be some duplicate items in the selected items, we do not select items for any replacement. A price is created by choosing a real number between 0 and 1 and multiplying it 10,000.
◇ Weighted random dataset: Select randomly the items as in the random dataset. A price is created by choosing a real number between 0 and the number of selected items and multiplying it 10,000.

◇ Decay dataset: Select randomly one item from m items and select an item with a probability α repeatedly until no further items can be selected.
◇ Uniform dataset: For each bid, select the same number of items randomly. A price is created by choosing a real number between 0 and 1 and multiplying it 10,000. The number of bids for the experiment is set to 450.
◇ Bounded-low dataset: Select k items, where k is chosen randomly between the lower and upper bounds. A price is created by choosing a real number between 0 and the number of selected items and multiplying it 10,000. The lower and upper bounds of the bounded-low dataset are 0 and 5, respectively.
◇ Bounded-high dataset: Select the bids and determine the price as in the bounded-low dataset. The lower and upper bounds of the bounded-high dataset are 20 and 25, respectively.

We implemented our proposed algorithm and CPLEX(version 7.0) for the experiments. Note that we obtained the results of CABOB from their work for the sake of fairness in comparison. That is, there are many unknown factors and parameters for us to implement CABOB. Therefore, we referred to the results of CABOB appeared in [12] for the comparison. CABOB was implemented on a Pentium III-933MHz with 512MB of memory. In an effort to compare CABOB with ours and CPLEX fairly, we used the same datasets as those CABOB tested. We have also compared the results on the algorithm using only DFS with others.

Before we show the experimental results, we introduce a preprocessing of the datasets to speedup the entire processing. In the preprocessing, we filter out the bids that can never be the winners. For example, we can get rid of all the bids whose prices are lower than the highest price of a bid on the same item set. We can also remove more bids in the following situation. Assume that b_i and b_j want the items s_i and s_j, and their prices are p_i and p_j, respectively. If $s_i \subset s_j$ and $p_i > p_j$, then b_j can be removed in the preprocessing.

Table 1 shows the average percentage of bids removed in the preprocessing for each dataset. We could remove a great amount of bids from the random and the decay datasets. However, we exclude the time for preprocessing in measuring the overall processing time for each dataset as CABOB did.

Each point in the Fig. 2, Fig. 3 and Fig. 4 shows the average of the results on 100 different test data for the same number of bids. The proposed algorithm has shown better performance than both CPLEX and CABOB except for the weighted random and the decay datasets. But observe that the differences among these algorithms are not quite big especially for the weighted random dataset.

Table 1. The average percentage of bids removed in the preprocessing

Dataset	Avg. percentage of bids removed
Random	79.72
Weighted Random	12.27
Decay	61.92
Uniform	0.17
Bound	5.98

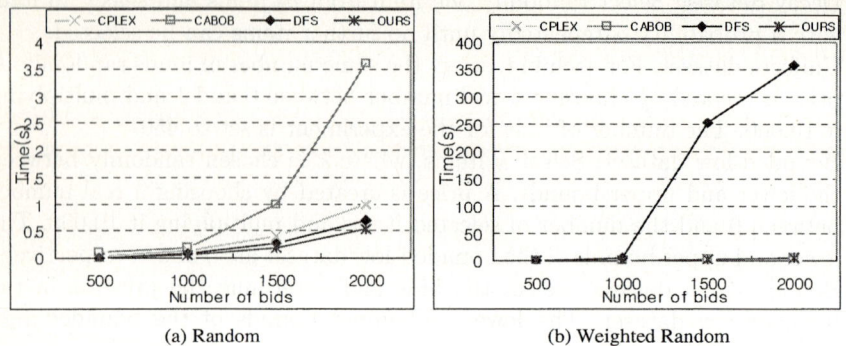

Fig. 2. Random and Weighted random datasets

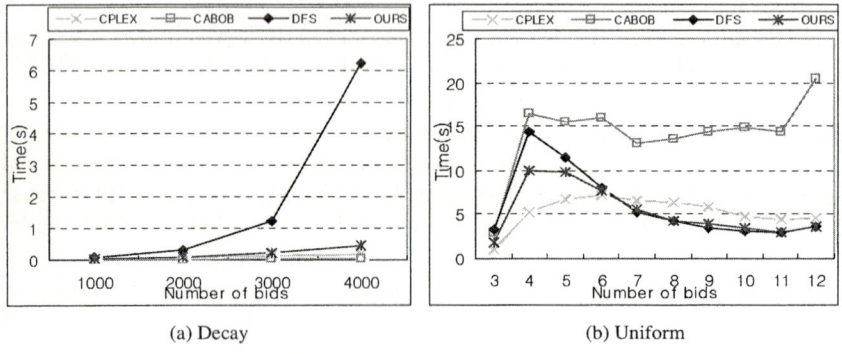

Fig. 3. Decay and uniform datasets

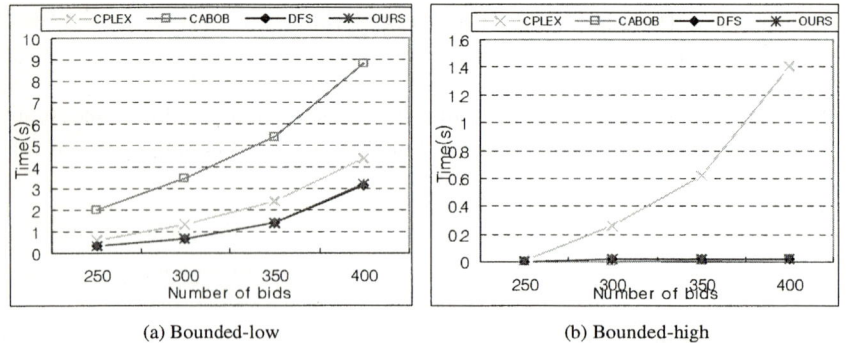

Fig. 4. Bounded-low and bounded-high datasets

4   Conclusion

Multiagent systems need efficient resource and task allocations for complementary and substitutable items. Combinatorial auctions can be employed to satisfy the needs. In this paper, we have proposed a faster allocation algorithm for the winner determination in combinatorial auctions. The proposed algorithm utilizes a branch-and-bound method and LP for searching the optimal solution. In this algorithm we have introduced a new heuristic bid selection method that considers not only the x value of each bid but also those of the conflicting bids at the same time. The experimental results show that the proposed allocation algorithm showed better performance than CPLEX and CABOB for the random, the uniform and bounded-low datasets and showed similar performance for the rest of the datasets.

References

1. A. Andersson, M. Tenhunen, F. Ygge: Integer Programming for Combinatorial Auction Winner Determination. Proceedings of the Fourth International Conference on MultiAgent Systems (ICMAS). (2000) 39–46
2. P. J. Brewer, C. R. Plott: A Binary Conflict Ascending Price (BICAP) Mechanism for the Decentralized Allocation of the Right to Use Railroad Tracks. Int.Journal of Industrial Organization. **14** (1996) 857–886
3. S. H. Clearwater (ed.) : Market-Based Control: a Paradigm for Distributed Resource Allocation. World Scientific (1996)
4. S. de Vries, R. Vohra: Combinatorial Auctions: A Survey. Draft, (2000)
5. Y. Fujishima, K. Leyton-Brown, Y. Shoham: Taming the Computational Complexity of Combinatorial Auctions: Optimal and Approximate Approaches. Proceedings of the Sixteenth International Joint Conference on Artificial Intelligence(IJCAI). (1999) 548–553
6. R. Gonen, D. Lehmann: Linear Programming Helps Solving Large Multi-unit Combinatorial Auctions. Electronic Market Design Workshop, July 11-13. (2001)
7. A. Lazar, N. Semret: The Progressive Second Price Auction Mechanism for Network Resource Sharing. 8th International Symposium on Dynamic Games, Maastricht, The Netherlands, July 5-8. (1998)
8. P. Milgrom: Putting Auction Theory to Work: The Simultaneous Ascending Auction. Journal of Political Economy. **108** (2000) 245–272
9. N. Nisan: Bidding and Allocation in Combinatorial Auctions. ACM Conference on Electronic Commerce. (2000) 1–12
10. S. J. Rassenti, V. L. Smith, R. L. Bulfin: A combinatorial Auction Mechanism for Airport Time Slot Allocation. Bell Journal of Economics. **13** (1982) 402–417
11. M. H. Rothkopf, A. Pekec, R. M. Harstad: Computationally Manageable Combinatorial Auctions. Management Science, Vol.**44**. No.8 (1995) 1131–1147
12. T. Sandholm, S. Suri, A. Gilpin, D. Levine: CABOB: A Fast Optimal Algorithm for Combinatorial Auctions. Proceedings of the Seventeenth International Joint Conference on Artificial Intelligence (IJCAI). (2001) 1102–1108
13. M. Tennenholtz: Some Tractable Combinatorial Auctions. AAAI. (2000)
14. E. Zurel, N. Nisan: An Efficient Approximate Allocation Algorithm for Combinatorial Auctions. ACM Conference on Electronic Commerce. (2001) 125–136
15. T. Sandholm and S. Suri: BOB: Improved Winner Determination in Combinatorial Auctions and Generalizations. Artificial Intelligence, **145**(1-2) (2003) 33–58

An Agent Based Framework for Modelling Neuronal Regulators of the Biological Systems

Antonio Soriano Payá, Juan Manuel García Chamizo,
and Francisco Maciá Pérez

Department of Computing and Information Technology, University of Alicante,
P.O. 99, Alicante, Spain
{soriano,juanma,pmacia}@dtic.ua.es
http://www.ua.es/i2rc

Abstract. The neuronal regulators of biological systems are very difficult to deal with since they present nonstructured problems. The agent paradigm can analyze this type of systems in a simple way. In this paper, a formal agent-based framework that incorporates aspects such as modularity, flexibility and scalability is presented. Moreover, it enables the modeling of systems that present distribution and emergence characteristics. The proposed framework provides a definition of a model for the neuronal regulator of the lower urinary tract. Several examples of the experiment have been carried out using the model as presented, and the results have been validated by comparing them with real data. The developed simulator can be used by specialists in research tasks, in hospitals and in the field of education.

1 Introduction

At the moment, the theories developed to control complex systems that incorporate nonlinear aspects and that present unknown parameters are the optimal control, the adaptive control, the robust control [1]. The common characteristic of these theories is its sound mathematical basis.

The neuronal regulators of the biological systems cannot be merely described by means of mathematical models and because of this, the data available are incomplete and vague and besides, most of the information is qualitative. The situation gets still more complex if distributed systems and emergent behaviour intervene as is the case with the neuronal regulators. It is in this context where the agent paradigm adds a greater level of abstraction allowing the solution of complex problem to be reached in a simpler way.

Several mathematical models of the lower urinary tract have been published [2], [3], [4], [5]. They focus on solving the problem from a global approach. In this present study, we deal with the problem from a distributed viewpoint, with emergent characteristics. We consequently define a framework-based on agents which will enable us to model the lower urinary tract neuronal regulator showing a particular structure and performance.

Multiagent systems provide a paradigm capable of supplying reasonable sufficient expressive capacity to tackle the development of such distributed systems, accounting

R. Monroy et al. (Eds.): MICAI 2004, LNAI 2972, pp. 370–379, 2004.

for a wide range of contingencies, emerging behavior, and the possibility of structure modification as new advances are made in neurological research.

In the following sections, we analyze an agent-based formal framework which will enable us to define the model of the neuronal regulator of the biological system. In section 3, we eventually define the model once the characteristics are presented and the functioning of the system is explained. The results are included in section 4, and in section 5, we extract our conclusions, and offer an outline of the different areas of work we are currently involved.

2 The Framework

At general level, we assume that a biological system is made up of a mechanical system (MS), a neuronal regulator system (NRS) that controls the mechanical part and an interface ($^{MS}I_{NRS}$) communicating both systems. Formally,

Biological_System = $\langle MS, NRS, {}^{MS}I_{NRS}\rangle$ (1)

Next we define each one of the elements that forms the biological system.

2.1 Interface of the Systems ($^{MS}I_{NRS}$)

The interface regards the biological system as a system of actions and reactions, using the following structure:

$${}^{MS}I_{NRS} = \langle \Sigma, \Gamma, P \rangle \tag{2}$$

where Σ represents the group of possible states of the system. Γ identifies the group made up of the possible intentions of actions on the system. The entities do not have overall control of the system and they also have to combine their objectives with those of other entities so that the result of each action will be represented as an intention of action on the system. Finally, P is the set of all the possible actions that the entities can perform on the system.

The states of the system (Σ) can be expressed by the values of the different sensor and actuator signals that act as an interface with the others systems. Each state $\sigma_i \in \Sigma$ is defined as a list of pairs (signal, valueSignal):

$$\sigma_i = \langle (sig_1, val_1), (sig_2, val_2), ..., (sig_u, val_u) \rangle \tag{3}$$

On the other hand, the system can change before different actions are made on it. The set of the possible influences or attempts of action of the different entities in reference to the present state from the system is defined as:

$$\Gamma = \{\gamma_1, \gamma_2, ..., \gamma_n\} \tag{4}$$

in which γ_i is a list of pairs from an element together with its value.

The entities must carry out actions to be able to act on the system. The set of all the possible actions that can be performed in a certain system can be defined as:

$$P = \{p_1, p_2, ..., p_n\} \tag{5}$$

Each action (p_i) is defined in terms of a name, a precondition that describes the conditions that must verify the action to be executed, and a postcondition that makes inferences on the set of influences that converge on the action being executed.

2.2 Entities of the Neuronal Regulator System (NRS)

The entities of the neuronal regulator system (NRS) are modeled as cognitive agents that present a PDE (Perception-Deliberation-Execution) architecture [6] with a modified execution function [7]. The capacity to memorize has been incorporated to those agents in order to obtain a richer and more powerful deliberation:

$$NRS = \langle \alpha_1, \alpha_2, ..., \alpha_v \rangle \tag{6}$$

An agent $\alpha \in NRS$ can be formally described using the structure:

$$\alpha = \langle \Phi_\alpha, S_\alpha, Percept_\alpha, Mem_\alpha, Decision_\alpha, Exec_\alpha \rangle \tag{7}$$

where Φ_α corresponds to the set of perceptions, S_α to the set of internal status, $Percept_\alpha$ provides the centre with information about the state of the system, Mem_α allows the centre to show awareness of the state, $Decision_\alpha$ selects the next influence, and $Exec_\alpha$ represents the agent's intention of acting on the system. These functions present a general structure that depends on each agent's specified sets and functions [8]. We can appreciate the internal structure of an agent in the fig. 1.

For an agent, perception is the quality of being able to classify and to distinguish states of the system. The perception is defined as a function that associates a set of values, denominated perceptions or stimuli, with a set of states of the system:

$$Percept_\alpha : \Sigma \rightarrow \Phi_\alpha \tag{8}$$

The set of the possible perceptions associated with the agent is defined as:

$$\Phi_\alpha = \langle \phi_1, \phi_2, ..., \phi_m \rangle \tag{9}$$

where each ϕ_i is a structure composed of a list of pairs formed by an element and its value corresponding to the state of the system previously defined.

Each agent has an internal state that confers the capacity to memorize and to develop a complex behavior. The set of internal states of a certain agent is defined as:

$$S_\alpha = \{ s_1, s_2, ..., s_p \} \tag{10}$$

On the other hand, the decision function submits an action to the perception in a determined internal state of the agent:

$$Decision_\alpha : \Phi_\alpha \times S_\alpha \rightarrow P \tag{11}$$

The decision function depends on the precondition decision function $(PreD_\alpha(\phi,s))$ that relates a true or false value to a perception in a given internal state, a function $(FunD_\alpha(\phi,s))$ associates a list of actuators signals the new values the agent has acquired a perception function.

The memorization function of information happens when switching to another internal state; that is, it will relate an internal state of the agent to a perception in a given internal state:

$$Mem_\alpha : \Phi_\alpha \times S_\alpha \rightarrow S_\alpha \tag{12}$$

The memorization function depends on a precondition memorization function $(PreM_\alpha(\phi,s))$ that relates a true or false value to a perception in a particular internal state, a function $(FunD_\alpha(\phi,s))$ that associates a new internal state with a perception in a given internal state.

Once the agent has decided what action to take, it must execute. The actions on the system are carried out by means of the execution function defined as

$$Exec_\alpha : P \times \Phi_\alpha \rightarrow \Gamma \tag{13}$$

where P is the set of actions that can be made on the system, Φ_α is the set of the possible perceptions that the agent α can have of the system and Γ is the set of influences of the different agents.

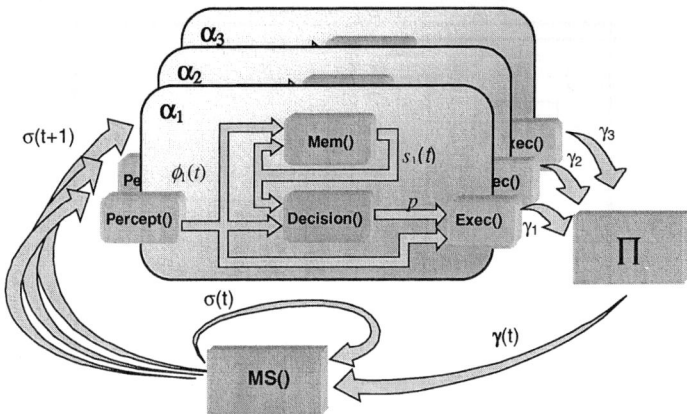

Fig. 1. Representation of the system. Agents perceive how the world is from the state of the system (σ(t)). With the perception (ϕ_i(t)) and the internal state (s_i(t)) it will change to another internal state (s_i(t+1)) and it will decide what action to take (p). The execution of that action will generate an influence (γ_i) that will try to act on the system

2.3 Mechanical System (MS)

This paper focuses on the neuronal regulator of a biological system. However, since the mechanical system (MS) and the neuronal regulator system are so closely connected, let's introduce the function of the mechanical system in this context: what it does is to generate afferent signal from a given set of efferent signals. This function complies with the dynamics of the mechanical system and is carried out through accomplishment of actions with the aim of transforming one state into another. This change is regarded as reaction of the system under different influences.

Function MS provides the information about the current state of the system subjected to the influences from different entities:
$$MS : \Sigma \times \Gamma \to \Sigma \tag{14}$$

Taking into account the above definition for agent, and the perception of the environment at a certain point, the new state of the system results as the assessment of influences from the different agents when they are concurrently performing their tasks:

$$\sigma(t+1) = MS(\sigma(t), \prod_i^v Exec_i \,(Decision_i(\phi_i(t), s_i(t)), \phi_i(t))) \; s_1(t+1) =$$
$$Mem_i(\phi_1(t), s_1(t)); \quad \dots \quad ; s_v(t+1) = Mem_n(\phi_v(t), s_v(t)) \tag{15}$$

Fig. 1 shows graphically to the structure of the system where the agents and their relations are established.

3 The Biological System

The previous section has set the general framework. This section will analyze a model of the neuronal regulator of the lower urinary tract using the proposed general framework.

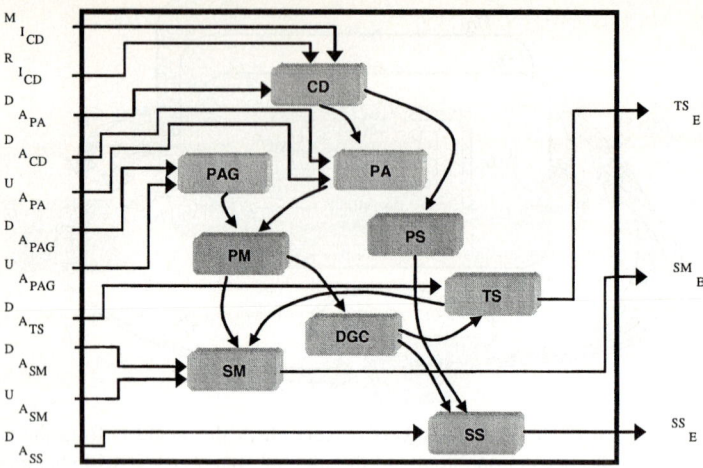

Fig. 2. Structure of the biological neuronal regulator. Afferent (A), efferent (E), voluntary (I) and internal signals. CD - cortical diencephalic, AP reoptic area, PAG - periacqueductal grey area, PS - pontine storage, PM - pontine micturition, SM - sacral micturition, SS - sacral storage, DGC - dorsal grey commissure, TS - thoracolumbar storage

3.1 Overview of the Biological System

The lower urinary tract (LUT) is made up of a mechanical part, comprising the bladder and the urethra that allow urine to be stored and expelled from the body, and a neuronal part that controls these two functions. The complexity of the neuronal regulator of the LUT can easily be appreciated if we take into account that both reflex and voluntary mechanisms are involved in its functioning [9].

The biological neuronal regulator of the LUT is made up of neuronal centers and communicating paths. The latter connects the mechanical system and the neuronal centers [10]. Information streams from the mechanical system to the neuronal centers where it is processed and forwarded to the mechanical system so as to contract or relax the muscles involved [8]. Fig. 2 shows the structure of the neuronal regulator of the lower urinary tract.

One of the most important centers is the sacral micturition (SM). It is a neuronal centre related to the regulating biological function of urine emptying [8]. Several inputs and outputs are identified in the SM [11]. Associated to the SM centre, two involuntary facilitator loops are identified at sacral level: the vesicoparasympathetic loop that is activated when the signal $^{D}A_{SM}$ goes beyond the threshold $^{D}H_{SM}$ and the uretrovesicalparasympathetic loop that is activated when the signal $^{U}A_{SM}$ goes beyond the threshold $^{U}H_{SM}$.

3.2 Model of the Biological System

On the ground of the formal framework already proposed in section 2, we formally define the lower urinary tract (LUT) using the tupla:

$$LUT = \langle MLUT, RLUT, {}^{MLUT}I_{RLUT} \rangle \tag{16}$$

in which the MLUT models the mechanical part of the lower urinary tract, the RLUT the neuronal regulator of the lower urinary tract, and finally the ${}^{MLUT}I_{RLUT}$ the relation between both parts.

The neural regulator of the lower urinary tract consist of the set of neuronal centers (NC) that are constantly perceiving, deliberating and executing.

The states of system (σ_i) are list of pairs composed of the afferent and efferent neuronal signals with their corresponding values.

The influences of an agent (γ_i) are stated by a list of pairs of its efferent neuronal signals together with the new values that the agent wants to obtain.

The tasks performed by an agent at a certain moment are associated with the influence the agent wants to exert on the system.

On the other hand, bearing in mind that the neuronal centers are constantly registering information from the mechanical system and from other centers, and that they act as autonomous entities by means of efferent signals on the mechanical system and by means of internal neuronal signals on other centers, we model the centers as PDE agents. By example, the sacral micturition centre (SM) is defined by:

$$SM = \langle \Phi_{SM}, S_{SM}, Percept_{SM}, Mem_{SM}, Decision_{SM}, Exec_{SM} \rangle \tag{17}$$

The perception function associated with the SM ($Percept_{SM}$) provides the group of signals of the state of the world whose origin or destination is this neuronal centre.

The internal state of the SM is formed by the internal neuronal signals of origin or destination; that is, the input and the output neuronal signals.

According to its current state and what it perceives, the centre will be able to change to a new state and decide what action to take. The decision function ($Decision_{SM}$) presents a general structure that depends on its internal functions ($PreD_{SM}(\phi,s)$ and $FunD_{SM}(\phi,s)$) [11]. As is the case with the decision function, the memorization function (Mem_{SM}) also presents a general structure dependent on its internal functions ($PreM_{SM}(\phi,s)$ and $FunD_{SM}(\phi,s)$) [11]. These functions are defined in table 1.

Table 1. Internal functions of decision and memorization. ϕ - perception; s - internal state; $ts()$ - translation function; 1 - $PreD_{SM}(\phi,s)$; 2 - $FunD_{SM}(\phi,s)$; 3 - $PreM_{SM}(\phi,s)$; 4- $FunD_{SM}(\phi,s)$

$\phi.{}^{D}A$	$\phi.{}^{U}A_i$	$s.{}^{PM}I_s$	$s.{}^{TS}I_s$	$ts(t)$	1	2	3	4	$ts(t+1)$
$<{}^{D}H_{SM}$	$<{}^{U}H_{SM}$	0	0	I,M	False	$<(\phi^{SM}E,0)>$	False	$\langle\,\rangle$	I
$\geq{}^{D}H_{SM}$	$<{}^{U}H_{SM}$	0	0	I,MB,MA	True	$<(\phi^{SM}E,0.2)>$	True	$\langle\,\rangle$	MB
$<{}^{D}H_{SM}$	$\geq{}^{U}H_{SM}$	0	0	I,MM,MA	True	$<(\phi^{SM}E,0.25)>$	True	$\langle\,\rangle$	MM
$\geq{}^{D}H_{SM}$	$\geq{}^{U}H_{SM}$	0	0	I,MA,MM	True	$<(\phi^{SM}E,0.45)>$	True	$\langle\,\rangle$	MA
X	X	0	1	MB,R	True	$<(\phi^{SM}E,0)>$	True	$\langle\,\rangle$	R
X	X	1	X	R,M	True	$<(\phi^{SM}E,1)>$	True	$\langle\,\rangle$	M

By means of a translation function, ts(t), the internal states of the centre are associated with the different segments of the vesical pressure curve, identified by the different phases of the system [8] (I corresponds to a inactive state; MB, MM, MA and M to a micturition state; R is a retention state), thus simplifying its current state.

4   Experiments

To validate the model of the LUT, a simulator has been developed using Java as the programming language together with the support of a graphical representation tool. We have carried out different LUT simulations with data regarding both healthy individuals and those with dysfunctions due to neuronal causes.

4.1   Situation without Dysfunctions

The result of the tests in average working conditions, without dysfunctions, can be observed in fig. 3. In the storage phase, the centre remains inhibited, allowing the bladder to be filled. During the emptying phase, the person activates the micturition centers to contract the detrusor to expel the urine.

In the first part of the storage phase, we can observe that an increase in urine generates exponential increases in pressure because of the initial stretching of the muscle. When the micturition begins, a contraction of the detrusor takes place generating a great increase in vesical pressure, reaching values of 40 cm of H_2O. At the end of the process, the bladder will have practically emptied, maintaining a basal pressure. The urine flows out when the external sphincter is opened. It can be seen how the output flow of urine increases to 23 ml/seg. As can be observed, urodynamic curves fall within the permitted ranges for the International Continence Society [12].

4.2   Situation with Neuronal Dysfunctions

When there is a lesion that affects interaction among the sacral centers and the rest of the neuronal centers (thoracolumbar centre, pontine centre and suprapontine centers), interaction ceases. The LUT no longer controls voluntary and involuntary areas, but the vesicosomatic guarding reflex and the vesicosimpatic and urethralparasympathetic reflexes of micturition remain. A lesion of this type usually generates a detrusor-sphincter disinergy [13]. Fig. 4 shows the urodynamic curves of a suprasacral lesion. In it, detrusor-sphincter disinergy can be observed. When detrusor pressure is greater than sphincter pressure, urine loss takes place.

Urodynamic data provided by the simulator show similarities to real clinical data and are alike as far as dynamics is concerned [12].

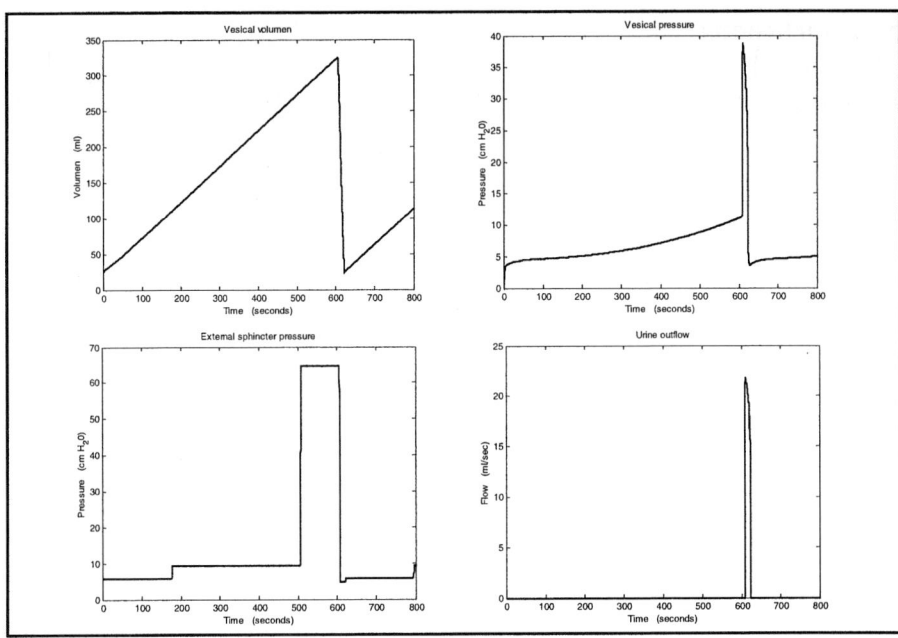

Fig. 3. Urodynamic data (vesical volume, vesical pressure, external sphincter pressure, urine outflow) obtained by the simulator in a situation without dysfunctions

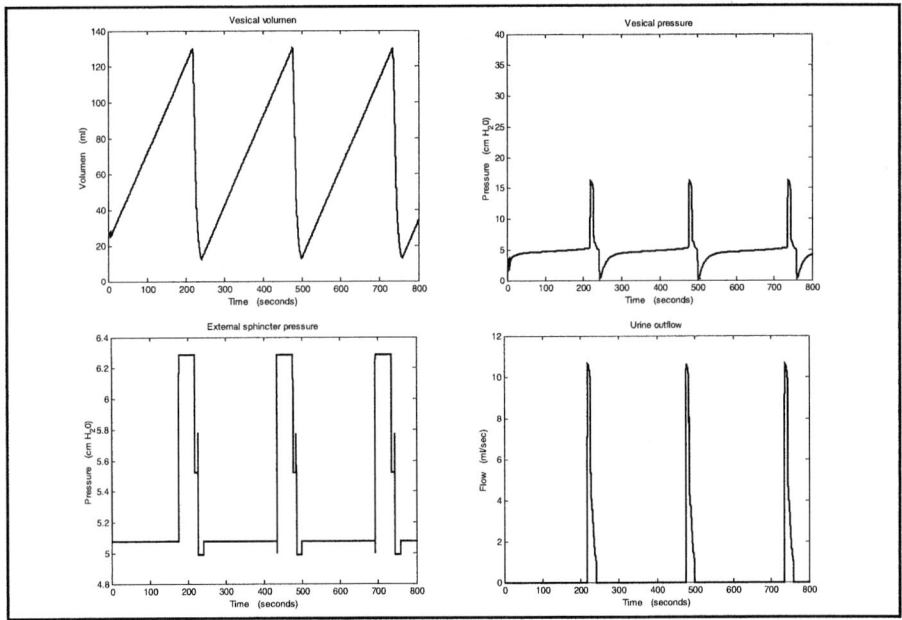

Fig. 4. Urodynamic data (vesical volume, vesical pressure, external sphincter pressure, urine outflow) obtained by the simulator in suprasacral dysfunctions

5 Conclusions

In this paper an agent paradigm-based framework is presented. This paradigm, widely used in other fields such as robotics or communications, share interesting features that cover the implicit requirements common to the majority of biological control models: distribution, adaptability, emergence, etc.

The discussed framework delivers a model of the neuronal regulator of the lower urinary tract. The model presents an independent formulation of the present knowledge. Moreover, its modular conception makes it not only versatile but also capable of being enriched by further development in the field.

A simulator has been used to validate the model and with it, urodynamic graphs have been obtained and comparisons have been made with real data obtained from healthy individuals and others with simulated disorders. This simulator can either be used by specialists in research tasks to discover new information about the mechanical neuronal operation of the lower urinary tract or to complement existing data. In hospitals, it can be of use as a nucleus of a monitoring and diagnostic aid tool. In the field of education, it can be used to discuss pathological disorders connected to the lower urinary tract.

Our most immediate task is to enlarge the model by improving the cognitive capacity of the agents in order to create an artificial system capable of self-regulating and of reducing the problems posed by the biological regulator. Eventually, the outcome of this piece of research will hopefully be used as a basis for designing control device to be implanted in the human body.

Acknowledgements. This study has been supported as part of the research project CTIDIA/2002/112 by the Office of Science and Technology of the Autonomous Government of Valencia (Spain).

References

1. Aström, K.J. (ed.): Control of Complex Systems. Spinger-Verlag (2000)
2. Bastiaanssen, E.H.C., van Leeuwen, J.L., Vanderschoot, J., Redert, P.A.: A Myocybernetic Model of the Lower Urinary Tract. J. Theor Biol. Vol. 178 (1996) 113-133
3. van Duin, F., Rosier, P.F., Bemelmans, B.L., Wijkstra, H., Debruyne, F.M., van Oosterom, A.: Comparison of Different Computer Models of the Neural Control System of the Lower Urinary Tract. Neurourol Urodyn. Vol. 19 (2000) 203-222
4. Soriano, A., García, J.M., Ibarra, F., Maciá, F.: Urodynamic Model of the Lower Urinary Tract. Proceedings of Computational Intelligence for Modelling, Control & Automation (1999) 123-128
5. Valentini, F.A., Besson, G.R., Nelson, P.P., Zimmern, P.E.: A mathematical micturition model to restore simple flow recordings in healthy and symptomatic individuals and enhance uroflow interpretation. Neurourol Urodyn. Vol. 19 (2000) 153-176
6. Ferber, J.: Multi-Agent Systems. An Introduction to Distributed Artificial Intelligence. Addison-Wesley (1999)
7. Maciá, F.: Modelos de Administración de Redes Heterogéneas de Computadores. Sistema de Regeneración de Nodos de Red. Thesis of University of Alicante (2000)
8. Soriano, A.: Modelado y Simulación del Regulador Neuronal del Tracto Urinario Inferior. Thesis of University of Alicante (2001)

9. Kinder, M.V., Bastiaanssen, E.H.C., Janknegt, R.A., Marani, E.: The Neuronal Control of the Lower Urinary Tract: A Model of Architecture and Control Mechanisms. Archives of Physiology. 107 (1999) 203-222
10. Micheli, F., Nogués, M.A., Asconapé, J.J., Pardal, M.M.F., Biller, J.: Tratado de Neurología Clínica. Ed. Panamericana (2002)
11. García, J.M., Soriano, A., Maciá, F., Ruiz, D.: Modelling of the Sacral Micturition Centre Using a Deliberative Intelligent Agent. Proceedings of the IV International Workshop on Biosignal Interpretation (2002) 451-454
12. Salinas, J., Romero, J.: Urodinámica clínica. Aspectos básicos. Luzán 5, S.A. (2002)
13. Sotolongo, J.R.: Causes and treatment of neurogenic bladder dysfunction. In Krane, R.J. et al (eds): Clinical Urology. J.B. Lippincott Company (1994) 558-568

Possibilistic Reasoning and Privacy/Efficiency Tradeoffs in Multi-agent Systems*

Richard J. Wallace[1], Eugene C. Freuder[1], and Marius Minca[2]

[1] Cork Constraint Computation Center, University College Cork, Cork, Ireland
{r.wallace,e.freuder}@4c.ucc.ie
[2] Ecora, Inc., Portsmouth, NH, USA
mminca@ecora.com

Abstract. In cooperative problem solving, while some communication is necessary, privacy issues can limit the amount of information transmitted. We study this problem in the context of meeting scheduling. Agents propose meetings consistent with their schedules while responding to other proposals by accepting or rejecting them. The information in their responses is either a simple accept/reject or an account of meetings in conflict with the proposal. The major mechanism of inference involves an extension of CSP technology, which uses information about possible values in an unknown CSP. Agents store such information within 'views' of other agents. We show that this kind of possibilistic information in combination with arc consistency processing can speed up search under conditions of limited communication. This entails an important privacy/efficiency tradeoff, in that this form of reasoning requires a modicum of actual private information to be maximally effective. If links between derived possibilistic information and events that gave rise to these deductions are maintained, actual (meeting) information can be deduced without any meetings being communicated. Such information can also be used heuristically to find solutions before such discoveries can occur.

1 Introduction

Constraint satisfaction is a powerful technology that has been successfully extended to distributed artificial intelligence problems [1]. Within the multi-agent setting new problems arise when agents have a degree of independence. Most systems of this sort have been built on the assumption that agents will be completely open about communicating information that might be relevant to solving a problem [2] [3]. This may not always be the case in such settings; agents may want to maintain their privacy as much as possible while still engaging in collaborative problem solving [4]. Since holding back information may impair the efficiency of problem solving, there is a potentially important tradeoff between privacy and efficiency that must be considered.

In any 'real-world' situation, privacy issues are tied up with agent intentions (as described, for example, in [5]). This means that any agent's agenda (its goals or intentions) potentially involves minimizing the loss of its own private information and/or gaining

* This work was supported in part by NSF Grant No. IIS-9907385 and Nokia, Inc and by Science Foundation Ireland Grant No. 00/PI.1/C075.

R. Monroy et al. (Eds.): MICAI 2004, LNAI 2972, pp. 380–389, 2004.

information about other agents. Here, we assume both goals are in operation; the question then is, how to manage problem solving given these intentions. More specifically, we study how search can be conducted under conditions of limited communication, as well as the degree of privacy loss actually incurred under such conditions.

Because of privacy concerns, agents may need to operate under conditions of partial ignorance. In such cases, even though critical information may not be known, agents may be able to reason in terms of sets of possibilities, such as the set of possible values for a known variable. In this paper we show how this can be accomplished. This entails the use of a new formal structure that supports consistency reasoning under conditions of partial ignorance. The soundness of this approach is proven in detail elsewhere [6]. This paper demonstrates the effectiveness of this approach under conditions where agents would otherwise need to proceed more or less blindly.

We demonstrate the efficacy of our methods by examining a simplified situation, which we think can be extended to more realistic scenarios. We use an independent agent paradigm, where agents communicate with each other to solve a problem of mutual interest. Rather than solving parts of a single problem, as in the distributed CSP paradigm [1], here each agent has its own problem to solve, but portions of the individual solutions must be mutually consistent. The specific application is a type of meeting-scheduling problem, where agents have pre-existing schedules and need to add a new meeting that all can attend.

We first consider the kinds of information that agents can derive about other agents' schedules in the course of a meeting scheduling session. We show that such information can be encoded using ideas from standard modal logic, in which terms with modal properties are treated as as kind of CSP value. We show that such information gathering can be enhanced by consistency processing based on general temporal relations assumed to hold for any schedule.

Regarding the privacy/efficiency tradeoff, we find that if agents reveal private information (portions of their schedules) without being able to reason about it (via consistency processing), there is no gain in efficiency, i.e. no tradeoff. If they can reason in this way, then efficiency can be markedly improved provided that agents reveal small amounts of private information; thus, under these conditions there is a clear tradeoff. We also show that more sophisticated reasoning techniques can be used *either* to gain private information under conditions of limited communication *or* to reduce search while revealing very little information. This raises new issues in regard to privacy loss and tradeoffs with efficiency.

Section 2 describes the basic problem for our agents. Section 3 introduces the idea of "shadow CSPs" based on possibilistic information, that can represent an agent's current knowledge about another agent's schedule. Section 4 describes a testbed and experiments that test effects of different levels of communication and forms of knowledge (actual and possible) on efficiency and privacy loss. Section 5 describes the basic experimental results. Section 6 shows how knowledge of possibilities linked to communications that gave rise to it can be used to deduce actual information about a schedule and to support heuristics for gaining efficiency without such loss. Section 7 gives conclusions.

2   A Meeting Scheduling Problem

In the scheduling problem we are considering, each of k agents has its own calendar, consisting of appointments in different cities at different times of the week. The problem is to find a meeting time that all agents can attend given their existing schedules and constraints on travel time. Agents communicate on a 1:1 basis; the basic protocol is for one agent to suggest a meeting time in a certain city to each of the other agents, who then tell the first agent whether the choice is acceptable or not given their existing schedules.

For analysis and experimentation, we devised a simplified form of this problem. First, we assume a fixed set of cities where meetings can be held: London, Paris, Rome, Moscow and Tbilisi. We also restrict meeting times to be one hour in length and to start on the hour between 9 AM and 6 PM, inclusive, on any day of the week. These restrictions apply to pre-existing schedules as well as the new meeting assignment.

The basic constraints are the times (in hours) required for travel between meetings in different cities, shown in Figure 1. Times between cities within one region (Western Europe or the former Eastern Bloc) are shown beside arcs connecting cities; the arc between the two ellipses represents constraints between any two cities in the different regions.

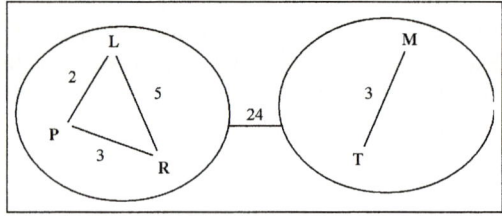

Fig. 1. Time constraint graph. Cities are London, Paris, Rome, Moscow and Tbilisi.

3   Communication and Inference (About Other Agents' Schedules)

In the situation we are considering there are three basic kinds of message: proposals, consisting of a city, day and hour ("Paris on Monday at 3 PM"), acceptances, and rejections. In addition, under some experimental conditions agents give reasons for their rejection by communicating one or all conflicts ("I have a meeting in Rome on Monday at 5 PM."). This allows agents to reveal small amounts of private information, which has the potential to speed up search. This kind of communication can be considered as a strategy that is tied specifically to privacy management and whose goal is to handle any privacy/efficiency tradeoff. A similar but less focused strategy, that of exchanging partial calendars, was used for this purpose in [4].

In the present situation, a solution to each agent's problem depends on $k-1$ other problems that it does not know directly. However, information about these problems can be represented in "views" of other agents' schedules. A view can be updated after each communication from another agent. Since an agent does not actually know the other schedules, but it does know the basic constraints and meeting locations, it can deduce facts about other schedules in terms of *possible* values at any point in the session. This information can be used to guide selection of proposals, both deterministically (by deducing that meetings are unavailable) and heuristically (by avoiding proposals that conflict with possible existing meetings).

Deductions are made on the basis of the communications. From proposals and acceptances, the agent that receives the message can deduce that the other agent has an open time-slot. It can also deduce that certain meetings that might have been in the other agent's schedule are, in fact, not possible; otherwise, given the travel constraints, the agent could not have proposed (or accepted) a given meeting in that slot. From a rejection a simple reduction in the set of possibilities can be made that refers to the meeting just proposed. In addition, the agent receiving this message can also deduce a disjunctive set of possible causes for this rejection. Finally, if even a small number of actual meetings are communicated, then many more possibilities can be excluded.

The approach we use to carry out these deductions combines CSP ideas with basic concepts from modal logic. In addition to gathering actual information about other agents' schedules, agents keep track of possibilities regarding other agents' meetings. This information is maintained in CSP-like representations, where time-slots are again taken as variables. In one type of CSP we have possible values for meetings that another agent may already have in its schedule, which we call "possible-has-meeting" values. In another, values represent meetings that an agent might be able to attend, termed "possible-can-meet" values. Considered more generally, the former represent possible existing assignments in an unknown CSP, while the latter represent possible future assignments in the same CSP. A third type represents possible causes for any rejection made by the other agent, termed "possible-cause" or "possible-conflict" values.

To indicate the close semantic relation between these CSPs, which represent possible values, and the actual CSP of the other agent, we call the former "shadow CSPs". Appropriately, shadow CSPs cannot be said to exist on their own, as can ordinary CSPs. Moreover, they do not have solutions in the ordinary sense. However, they can be described as a tuple, $P = (V, D, C)$, consisting of variables V, domains D and constraints, C, just like ordinary CSPs.

The possibilistic character of domain values of shadow CSPs can be represented by the possibility operator, $\Diamond$, from standard modal logic (cf. [7]). We, therefore, refer to these values as "modal values". In this paper, specific modal values are always referred to in conjunction with the modal operator, e.g. $\Diamond x$. Inferences involving such values are subject to the rules of modal logic as well as ordinary truth-functional logic. (The connection to modal logic is described in more detail in [6].)

In this situation, we can make deductions from actual to possible values under a closed world assumption, in that CSP domains can be considered closed worlds. In this case, $\neg x$, entails $\Box \neg x$, where $\Box$ is the necessity operator. But, by a standard modal equivalence, $\Box \neg x \equiv \neg \Diamond \neg \neg x \equiv \neg \Diamond x$. Under this assumption, therefore, an agent can make deductions from whatever 'hard' information it can glean during the scheduling session in order to refine domains in the shadow CSPs.

For instance, when another agent makes or accepts a proposal, up to five possible-has-meeting values can be deleted, since under closed world assumptions $\neg x$ entails $\neg \Diamond x$. Moreover, if x implies $\neg y$, then we can also deduce $\neg \Diamond y$; hence, arc consistency based on the original constraint graph can be used to delete possible-has-meeting values for other variables (i.e. other cities in nearby time slots).

For possible has-meetings, inferences can also be made back to the actual values. This is because $\neg \Diamond x$ implies $\neg x$ under standard assumptions. If, for all cities x associated with a single time-slot, we have inferred $\neg \Diamond x$, we can then infer that the agent has no meeting at that time, i.e. it has an open slot.

From a simple rejection, an agent can only infer that one possible-can-meet value is invalid. However, if an existing meeting is given as a reason, it is possible to remove up to five possible-can-meet and four possible-has-meeting values from that time slot, and, using arc consistency reasoning, to delete other possible-can-meet and possible-has-meeting values based on the known constraints between hard values.

From a rejection, an agent can also use arc consistency to deduce possible-cause values, i.e. it can deduce the set of possible causes for that rejection. Unfortunately, the set of possible causes for a rejection forms a disjunctive relation, in contrast to sets of inferred possible-has-meeting and possible-can-meet values, which are conjunctive. However, since possible-cause values must be included in the set of possible-has-meeting values, this subset relation allows agents to prune values of the former kind, so that knowledge about another agent's schedule can be refined.

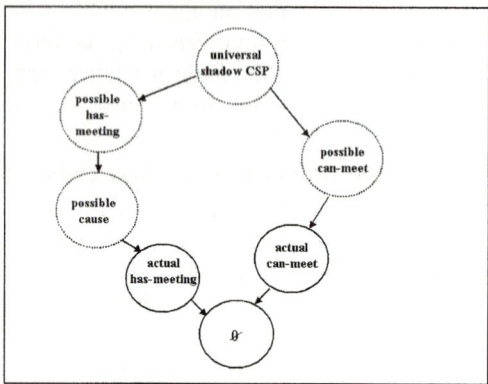

Fig. 2. Structure of shadow CSP system for the meeting-scheduling problem. Arrows represent set inclusion (or "realization") relations holding between domains of super- and subordinate CSPs.

To show that this deductive machinery is valid, we establish a system composed of the actual and shadow CSPs, establish certain requirements for the system to be well-structured, and show that these requirements are satisfied at every stage of the search process. We add to the present set of CSPs a supremum whose domains contain the set of all possible domain values and an infimum which in this case is composed of null sets. Then, the corresponding domains of these CSPs can in each case be arranged in a partial order under the relation of set inclusion (see Figure 2). (Corresponding domains are those associated with the same variable.) The proof that the system remains well-structured shows that, with the present communications and rules of inference, this relation remains achievable at every step in search [6]. In particular, this means that we cannot deduce an actual value that is not (potentially) contained in the corresponding domain of all superordinate shadow CSPs. In other respects, the system is sound because it relies on standard logic, plus the closed world assumption.

At the beginning of a session when an agent knows nothing about other agents' schedules, all domains of the possible-has-meeting and possible-can-meet CSPs, as well as the "universal" shadow CSP, have five modal values, corresponding to the five possible cities. The possible-cause shadow and the actual CSP have empty domains. As search proceeds, values are deleted from the domains of the first two CSPs and added to the last two. The soundness of the deduction rules insures that the system remains potentially well-structured throughout search.

4   An Experimental Testbed

4.1   System Description

Although the previous section and the work referred to demonstrates the soundness of our deductive system, we still need to know how well it will perform in practice. Will reasoning based on possibilities improve efficiency? Under what conditions and to what degree? And how will it affect the privacy/efficiency tradeoff?

To study these issues, a testbed system was built in Java. The system allows the user to select the number of agents and initial meetings. In addition, the user can select the:

- level of communication (xor): (i) a 'mimimum' level consisting of the three basic messages, propose, accept and reject, (ii) a level in which each rejection is accompanied by one reason, i.e. one meeting that conflicts with the proposal, (iii) a level in which all such reasons are given.
- knowledge to be gathered about other agents (ior): actual knowledge (meetings and open slots), possible-can-meet nogoods, possible-has-meeting nogoods, and possible-cause values.
- optional use of arc consistency processing (as described above).
- proposal strategy (xor): (i) blind guessing, where agents choose any time slot allowed by their own schedules without remembering them, (ii) guessing where previous, rejected proposals (by any agent) are avoided, (iii) proposals are guided by accumulated knowledge, of whatever kind chosen to be gathered, (iv) proposals are also guided by heuristics based on this knowledge.
- protocol (xor): (i) round robin, where each agent makes a proposal in turn, (ii) "one coordinator", where all proposals are made by one agent.

4.2   Design of Experiments

Most experiments reported here involve three agents, where the number of initial meetings varies from 5 to 40 in steps of 5. In each experiment, an individual test run begins with random generation of schedules followed by a series of proposals which continue until one is found that is acceptable to all agents. The present experiments use the "round-robin" protocol, which is democratic and allows agents to update their knowledge efficiently. A similar protocol was used in [4].

At each step of an experimental run, candidate proposals are generated for one agent by choosing a time slot and city at random to ensure unbiased sampling. This is repeated until the candidate fits the proposer's schedule. Then depending on the experimental settings, further tests may be made against this agent's knowledge, for example, knowledge of other agents' actual meetings, current possible-has-meeting's, etc. The first proposal that passes all these tests is communicated to all the other agents, and the latter reply with an acceptance or rejection (with or without reasons) to the proposer alone.

During a run, modal values are deleted from the possible-has-meeting and possible-can-meet shadow CSPs; in the implementation they are stored as nogoods. Nogoods are generated either by direct inference or through arc consistency processing after a message has been received, as described in Section 3.

In these experiments, the efficiency measure is number of proposals per run, averaged over all 500 runs of an experiment. The measures of privacy lost are number of meetings identified, number of open slots identified, and number of modal values removed from the shadow CSPs for possible-can-meet's and possible-has-meeting's. Privacy tallies are averaged per agent view per run. (There are two views per pair of agents, or $n \times (n-1)$) views for n agents.) In addition, number of solutions per agent was determined as well as the number of common solutions. Differences in means are evaluated statistically, using t-tests or analyses of variance.

5   Efficiency and Privacy: Empirical Results

Figure 3 shows measures of efficiency and privacy loss for the "baseline" condition of minimal communication, where no knowledge is used except past proposals. (For later comparisons, actual and possibilistic knowledge was collected but not used to guide proposals.) The curvilinear relation between number of initial meetings and number of proposals required to find a solution is due to the relation between number of common solutions and number of average personal solutions which decreased at different rates. Note the large number of possible has-meeting's discarded in relation to the number of can-meet's.

Effects of varying conditions of communication and inference are shown in Figure 4 for 15 initial meetings. The same pattern of results was found with other numbers of initial meetings. The main conclusions from these experiments are as follows (statistical comparisons are with the corresponding baseline condition):

- explicit communication about meetings *does not* improve efficiency, despite the giving up of 'hard' information ("1" or "all conflicts", $t(499) \leq 1.24$, ns.)
- efficiency is not improved by deriving modal information even when this is enhanced by arc consistency reasoning ("knowledge" and "know+AC", $t(499) \leq .36$, ns), which allows deduction of many more possible-has-meeting nogoods.
- a combination of explicit information interchanged, information in the form of modal values, and arc consistency processing results in a marked improvement in efficiency

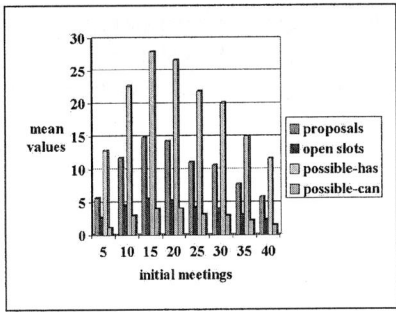

Fig. 3. Efficiency and privacy measures in 'baseline' experiments, where no explicit meeting information is communicated and no information is used except previous proposals.

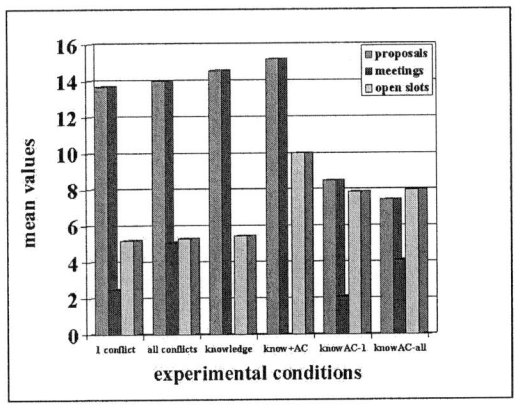

Fig. 4. Efficiency and loss of 'hard' information concerning meetings and open slots under varying conditions with respect to level of communication, knowledge, and consistency reasoning. Experiments with three agents and 15 initial meetings.

("know AC-1" and "-all", $t(499) \geq 8.59, p \ll .01$). In this case, large numbers of possible-can-meet nogoods are deduced.

6   Linking Possibilities to Causes (Specific Communications)

If derived information is classified by the kind of event that gave rise to it, this can affect both privacy loss and efficiency. For example, if possible-has-meeting nogoods deduced from conflicts are distinguished from those deduced from proposals and acceptances, then open slots deduced from the former are times when an agent cannot meet. Subsequent proposals should, therefore, not involve those time-slots. This extension (and the next) can be easily incorporated into the shadow CSP system in a way that maintains its soundness [6].

Another form of deduction based on a similar strategy involves possible-cause values. If the relation between possible-cause values and the rejection that gave rise to them is retained, then values associated with a specific rejection can be pruned. If such a set is reduced to one value, it can be concluded that this meeting must be in the schedule of the agent that made the rejection. Thus, it is possible to deduce a meeting of another agent even when no explicit meeting information is exchanged. In empirical tests, agents using this strategy discovered a number of actual meetings. For 15-25 initial meetings, the means were $> .1$ per agent view, while for the longest runs up to 2-3 meetings were found *per view*. Efficiency was not improved, however, because of the number of proposals required to gain such information.

Possible-cause values stored in this manner can also be used to heuristically guide proposal selection. Given a candidate proposal, if any possible-cause values associated with the nearest rejections before or after would also conflict with the new proposal, then the latter is (temporarily) avoided.

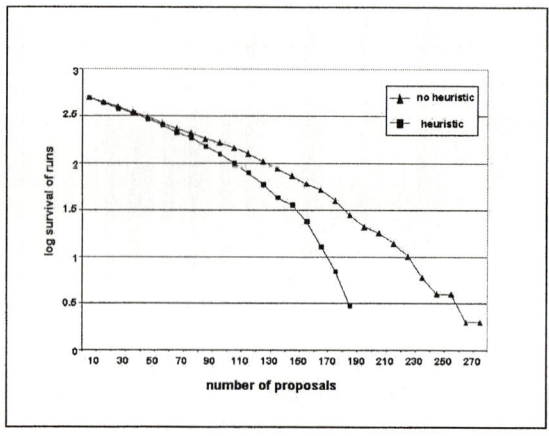

Fig. 5. Performance with and without heuristic based on possible causes for problems with 20 agents having 7 initial meetings. Log survivorship curves show number of unfinished runs after k proposals. Each curve is based on a total of 500 runs.

This heuristic does improve efficiency, without actual meetings being deduced, e.g. for 15 initial meetings, there was an average improvement of 20% ($t(499) = 3.27$, $p < .01$). More importantly, the range of values for number of proposals across all runs is drastically reduced. This occurs because the precision of the heuristic improves dramatically as possible-cause lists are reduced. This is shown in Figure 5 for a much harder problem involving 20 agents and seven initial meetings. In this experiment the maximum number of proposals was 275 without and 188 with the heuristic. In addition, total runtime was reduced by a factor of 2-3.

7 Conclusions

Work on modeling agents has considered models that incorporate ideas from modal logic. However, these models have been concerned with representing agent cognition in order to demonstrate consistency between beliefs and goals and similar issues [8]. There seems to be little work done on agent views that corresponds to the present research.

Perhaps the most significant aspect of this work is that we have shown how consistency reasoning can allow agents to find solutions more efficiently under conditions of ignorance. In doing so, we have developed a new CSP formalism that makes the possibilistic aspects of such reasoning more explicit and more coherent.

Significant improvements in efficiency were obtained either by giving up a limited amount of private information in communications or by linking modal information to specific causes (here, communications), which could in turn be associated with specific CSP elements in the form of candidate proposals. In both cases, possibilistic information was essential. In the former case, the critical feature was the deduction of possible-can-meet nogoods; in the latter case, it was a combination of possible-cause and possible-has-meeting values.

In the present situation we discovered some ways to improve efficiency, and in so doing we also established some parameters for privacy/efficiency tradeoffs. Most importantly, we found that such tradeoffs do not emerge unless communication is accompanied by effective reasoning. Under these conditions, the tradeoff can be modulated by variations in communication and even to a degree finessed by sophisticated heuristic techniques.

References

1. Yokoo, M.: Distributed Constraint Satisfaction. Foundations of Cooperation in Multi-Agent Systems. Springer, Berlin (1998)
2. Luo, X., Leung, H., Lee, J.H.: Theory and properties of a selfish agent protocol for multi-agent meeting scheduling using fuzzy constraints. In: Proc., 14th European Conference on Artificial Intelligence, ECAI-00, Amsterdam, IOS (2000) 373–377
3. Sen, S.: Developing an automated distributed meeting scheduler. IEEE Expert **12** (1997) 41–45
4. Garrido, L., Sycara, K.: Multi-agent meeting scheduling: Preliminary experimental results. In: Proc., Second International Conference on Multi-Agent Systems, ICMAS-96, Menlo Park, CA, AAAI Press (1996)
5. Woolridge, M.: An Introduction to MultiAgent Systems. John Wiley & Sons, Chichester (2002)
6. Wallace, R.J.: Representing possibilities in relation to constraints and agents. In: Logics in Artificial Intelligence, JELIA 2002, LNCS 2424, Berlin, Springer (2002) 407–418
7. Hughes, G.E., Cresswell, M.J.: An Introduction to Modal Logic. Routledge, London and New York (1968)
8. Rao, A.S., Georgeff, M.P.: Modeling rational agents with a bdi-architecture. In: Proc. Second International Conference on Principles of Knowledge Representation and Reasoning, KR'91, San Mateo, CA, Morgan Kaufmann (1991) 473–484

A Biologically Motivated and Computationally Efficient Natural Language Processor

João Luís Garcia Rosa

Centro de Ciências Exatas, Ambientais e de Tecnologias
Pontifícia Universidade Católica de Campinas - PUC-Campinas
Rodovia D. Pedro I, km. 136 - Caixa Postal 317
13012-970 - Campinas - SP - Brazil
joaoluis@puc-campinas.edu.br

Abstract. Conventional artificial neural network models lack many physiological properties of the neuron. Current learning algorithms are more concerned to computational performance than to biological credibility. Regarding a natural language processing application, the thematic role assignment – semantic relations between words in a sentence –, the purpose of the proposed system is to compare two different connectionist modules for the same application: (1) the usual simple recurrent network using backpropagation learning algorithm with (2) a biologically inspired module, which employs a bi-directional architecture and learning algorithm more adjusted to physiological attributes of the cerebral cortex. Identical sets of sentences are used to train the modules. After training, the achieved output data show that the physiologically plausible module displays higher accuracy for expectable thematic roles than the traditional one.

1 Introduction

Several connectionist natural language processing systems often employ recurrent architectures instead of feedforward networks. These systems with "reentrancy" are expected to be more adequate to deal with the temporal extension of natural language sentences, and, at the same time, they seem to be physiologically more realistic [1]. Other biological features are being taken into account in order to achieve new models that restore the artificial neural systems first concerns. Connectionist models based on neuroscience are about to be considered the next generation of artificial neural networks, inasmuch as nowadays models are far from biology, mainly for mathematical simplicity reasons [2].

In this paper, it is compared two distinct connectionist modules of a system about the thematic role assignment in natural language sentences: a conventional simple recurrent network employing the backpropagation learning algorithm (TRP-*BP*) with a bi-directional architecture using a biologically plausible learning algorithm, adapted from the Generalized Recirculation algorithm [3] (TRP-*GR*). Through the same set of test sentences, it is shown that, for the same training set, the neurophysiological module reflects better the thematic relationships taught to the system.

R. Monroy et al. (Eds.): MICAI 2004, LNAI 2972, pp. 390–399, 2004.

2   Thematic Roles

Linguistic theory [4] refers to the roles words usually have in relation to the predicate (often the verb) as thematic roles, so that the verb *break*, for instance, in one possible reading of sentence (1), assigns the thematic roles agent, patient, and instrument, because the subject *man* is supposed to be deliberately responsible for the action of breaking (the "agent"), the object *vase* is the "patient" affected by the action, and the complement *stone* is the "instrument" used for such action.

$$\text{The man broke the vase with the stone .} \qquad (1)$$

But the thematic structure can change for some verbs. So, in sentence (2), there is a different thematic grid ([CAUSE, PATIENT]) assigned by the same verb *break*, since the subject *ball* causes the breaking, but in an involuntary way.

$$\text{The ball broke the vase .} \qquad (2)$$

Verbs presenting two or more thematic grids depending on the sentence they take place, like the verb *break*, are named here as *thematically ambiguous* verbs. In a componential perspective, it is possible to have a representation for verbs independently of the sentence in which they occur. Considering sentences (1) and (2) again, it seems that the nouns employed as subjects make the distinction between AGENT and CAUSE. In other words, thematic roles must be elements with semantic content [5].

One of the reasons that the thematic assignment is chosen for a connectionist natural language processing application is because of its componential feature. Details can be found in [6].

2.1   Word Representation

In the system presented, word representation is adapted from the classical distributed semantic microfeature representation [7]. Twenty three-valued logic semantic microfeature units account for each verb and noun. Table 1 and table 2 display the semantic features for verbs and nouns, respectively. See also the microfeatures for two different readings of the thematically ambiguous verb *break* on table 3 [8].

It is important to notice here that the microfeatures for verbs are chosen in order to contemplate the semantic issues considered relevant in a thematic frame. The microfeatures outside this context are not meaningful. They only make sense in a system where the specification of semantic relationships between the words in a sentence plays a leading role [6].

3   TRP-*BP*

The Thematic Role Processor (TRP) is a connectionist system designed to process the thematic roles of natural language sentences, based on its symbolic-connectionist hybrid version [9]. For each input sentence, TRP gives as output, its thematic grid.

Table 1. The ten semantic microfeature dimensions for verbs. For thematically unambiguous verbs, only one feature in each dimension is *on*

"positive" feature	"negative" feature
control of action	no control of action
direct process triggering	indirect process triggering
direction to source	direction to goal
impacting process	no impacting process
change of state	no change of state
psychological state	no psychological state
objective	no objective
effective action	no effective action
high intensity of action	low intensity of action
interest on process	no interest on process

Table 2. The seven semantic microfeature dimensions for nouns, separated in rows. Only one value in each dimension is *on* for each unambiguous noun (adapted from [7])

human			non-human		
soft			hard		
small		medium		large	
1-D/compact		2-D		3-D	
pointed			rounded		
fragile/breakable			unbreakable		
value	furniture	food	toy	tool/utensil	animate

Table 3. The semantic microfeatures for the thematically ambiguous verb *break*, with the default reading and two alternative readings (*break1* and *break2*). The "?" sign represents ambiguity [8]

microfeature	break	break1	break2
control of action	?	yes	no
process triggering	?	direct	indirect
direction	goal	goal	goal
impacting process	yes	yes	yes
change of state	yes	yes	yes
psychological state	no	no	no
objective	?	yes	no
effective action	yes	yes	yes
intensity of action	high	high	high
interest on process	?	yes	no

TRP is deployed in two modules with completely different approaches: *BP* and *GR*. TRP-*BP* learns through backpropagation algorithm and employs an architecture representing a four-layer simple recurrent neural network with forty input units (A), fifteen hidden units (B), fifteen context units (D), and ten output units (C), one for each of the ten thematic roles: AGENT, PATIENT, EXPERIENCER, THEME, SOURCE, GOAL, BENEFICIARY, CAUSE, INSTRUMENT, and VALUE (figure 1).

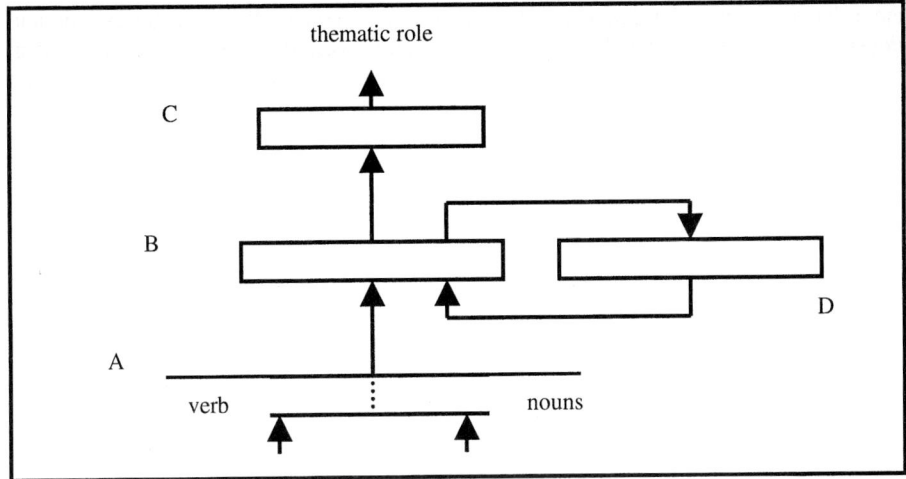

Fig. 1. The four-layer simple recurrent connectionist architecture of TRP-*BP*. To the input layer *A* the words, represented by their distributed semantic microfeatures, are entered sequentially at their specific slots according to their syntactic category: *verb* or *nouns* (subject, object, or complement). At the output layer *C*, a *thematic role* (AGENT, PATIENT, EXPERIENCER, THEME, SOURCE, GOAL, BENEFICIARY, CAUSE, INSTRUMENT, or VALUE), is displayed as soon as a word is entered in layer *A*. The context layer *D* represents the memory of the network, to which the hidden layer *B* is copied after each training step [10]

The input layer is divided in a twenty-unit slot for the verb and another twenty-unit slot for nouns. Words are presented in terms of their semantic microfeatures, one at a time, at their specific slots, until the whole sentence is completely entered. This way, besides semantics, included as part of the distributed representation employed, all kinds of natural languages with regard to word order (verb-subject-object -VSO -, as well as SVO) could be considered, since a predicate-arguments relation is established. At output layer C, thematic roles are highlighted as soon as they are assigned. For instance, when the subject of a sentence is presented, no thematic role shows up, because it is unknown which will be the main verb, the predicate that assigns such role. When the verb appears, immediately the network displays the thematic role assigned to the subject presented previously. For the other words, the correspondent thematic roles are displayed at the output, one at a time, for every input word.

3.1 The Biological Implausibility of Backpropagation

The backpropagation algorithm is largely employed nowadays as the most computationally efficient connectionist supervised learning algorithm. But backpropagation is argued to be biologically implausible [11]. The reason is that it is based on the error back propagation, that is, while the stimulus propagates forwardly, the error (difference between the actual and the desired outputs) propagates backwardly. It seems that in the cerebral cortex, the stimulus that is generated when a neuron fires, crosses the axon towards its end in order to make a synapse onto another neuron input (called dendrite). Supposing that backpropagation occurs in the brain, the error must have to propagate back from the dendrite of the post-synaptic neuron to the axon and then to the dendrite of the pre-synaptic neuron. It sounds unrealistic and improbable. Researchers believe that the synaptic "weights" have to be modified in order to make learning possible, but certainly not in this way. It is expected that the weight change uses only local information available in the synapse where it occurs. That is the reason why backpropagation seems to be so biologically implausible [8].

4 TRP-*GR*

The module TRP-*GR* (*GR* for *Generalized Recirculation*) consists of a bi-directional connectionist architecture, with three layers (A units in input layer, B units in hidden layer, and C units in output layer) and lateral inhibition occurring at the output level (figure 2). The input and the output operate in the same way as TRP-*BP*.

4.1 The Learning Procedure

The learning procedure of TRP-GR, also employed in [12] and [8], is inspired by the Recirculation [13] and GeneRec algorithms [3], and uses the two phases notion (minus and plus phases). Firstly, the inputs xi are presented to the input layer. In the minus phase, there is a propagation of these stimuli to the output through the hidden layer (bottom-up propagation). There is also a propagation of the previous actual output ok (t-1) back to the hidden layer (top-down propagation). Then, the hidden minus activation hj- is generated (sum of the bottom-up and top-down propagations – through the sigmoid activation function, represented by σ in equation 3). Finally, the current real output ok (t) is generated through the propagation of the hidden minus activation to the output layer (equation 4). The indexes i, j, and k refer to input, hidden, and output units, respectively.

$$h_j^- = \sigma(\sum_{i=0}^{A} w_{ij}.x_i + \sum_{k=1}^{C} w_{jk}.o_k(t-1)) \tag{3}$$

$$o_k(t) = \sigma(\sum_{j=1}^{B} w_{jk}.h_j^-) \tag{4}$$

In the plus phase, there is a propagation from the input x_i to the hidden layer (bottom-up). After this, there is the propagation of the desired output y_k to the hidden layer (top-down). Then the hidden plus activation $h_j^+$is generated, summing these two propagations (equation 5).

$$h_j^+ = \sigma(\sum_{i=0}^{A} w_{ij}.x_i + \sum_{k=1}^{C} w_{jk}.y_k) \tag{5}$$

In order to make learning possible, the synaptic weights w are updated, based on x_i, h_j^-, h_j^+, $o_k(t)$, and y_k, in the way shown in equations 6 and 7. Notice the presence of the learning rate (η), considered an important variable during the experiments [14].

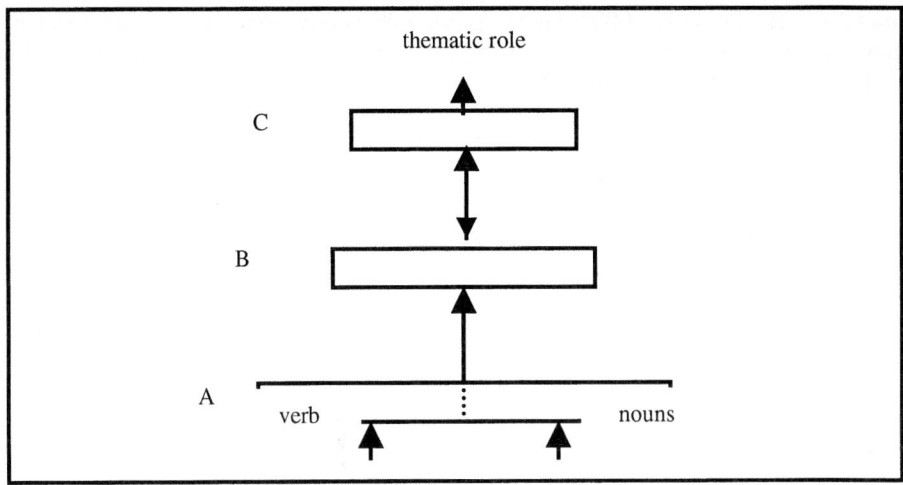

Fig. 2. The three-layer bi-directional connectionist architecture of TRP-*GR*. To the input layer *A* the words, represented by their distributed semantic microfeatures, are entered sequentially at their specific slots according to their syntactic category: *verb* or *nouns* (subject, object, or complement). At the output layer *C*, a *thematic role* (AGENT, PATIENT, EXPERIENCER, THEME, SOURCE, GOAL, BENEFICIARY, CAUSE, INSTRUMENT, or VALUE), is displayed as soon as a word is entered in layer *A*. This architecture is similar to the TRP-*BP* (figure 1), except that there is no layer D and the connections between layers B and C are bi-directional

$$\Delta w_{jk} = \eta.(y_k - o_k(t)).h_j^- \tag{6}$$

$$\Delta w_{ij} = \eta.(h_j^+ - h_j^-).x_i \tag{7}$$

5 Comparing TRP-*GR* with TRP-*BP*

Nowadays, neural network models are considered biologically impoverished, although computationally efficient. It has been proved that neurophysiologically based systems can be as computationally efficient as current connectionist systems, or even better [15]. This paper demonstrates that a connectionist system, with architecture and learning procedures based on neuroscience features, therefore biologically plausible, are also computationally efficient, more efficient than conventional systems, at least regarding a particular natural language processing application.

5.1 Training

A sentence generator supplies 364 different training sentences, presented one word at a time, according to semantic and syntactic constraints, employing a lexicon consisting of 30 nouns and 13 verbs, including thematically ambiguous verbs. It is important to emphasize here that the same training sentences are generated for both modules. After about 100,000 training cycles, which corresponds to an average output error[1] of 10^{-3}, the system is able to display, with a high degree of certainty, the thematic grid for an input sentence.

5.2 Set of Test Sentences

In order to compare TRP-*GR* with TRP-*BP*, 16 test sentences, different from training sentences, were generated by the sentence generator for both modules. Four of them are shown in figures 3 to 6, with their outputs representing thematic roles. These sentences reveal the better computational performance of the biologically plausible module TRP-*GR*, at least regarding the sentences belonging to the test set (*GR* is 11.61% more efficient than *BP*). Alternatively to the sentences generated automatically, the user can enter by hand the sentence to be tested.

On figure 3, one can see outputs of the system for the sentence *the boy fears the man*. The current word entered is in bold, while the previous words already entered are listed sequentially in parentheses. The first output line is for *BP* and the second for *GR*. The closer the output is to 1.0 the more precise is the thematic role prediction. Notice that in the *GR* module, the outputs are more accurate, at least regarding the expected thematic role for each word. Recall that the first word entered (the subject *boy*) has no thematic role displayed – that is the reason it does not appear in the figure – at least until the verb shows up. To the subject (*boy*) is assigned the thematic role EXPERIENCER, because *fear* asks for an experiencer subject it is a psychological verb.

Sentence: *the boy fears the man*

Word presented to the system: (boy) **fear**

	agent	patie	**exper**	theme	sourc	goal	benef	cause	instr	value
BP	0.001	0.004	**0.966**	0.000	0.007	0.015	0.020	0.016	0.000	0.000
GR	0.000	0.000	**0.998**	0.031	0.000	0.000	0.000	0.000	0.000	0.000

Word presented to the system: (boy-fear) **man**

	agent	patie	exper	**theme**	sourc	goal	benef	cause	instr	value
BP	0.000	0.024	0.054	**0.101**	0.044	0.049	0.034	0.001	0.003	0.001
GR	0.000	0.021	0.058	**0.168**	0.136	0.047	0.015	0.000	0.000	0.000

Fig. 3. Outputs of the system for the sentence *the boy fears the man*. Both modules arrived at the expected thematic grid [EXPERIENCER, THEME], but module *GR* values are closer to 1.0

Figure 4 displays outputs for the sentence *the girl bought a ball by a hundred dollars*. Notice again that in the *GR* module, the outputs are more precise.

Figure 5 shows the outputs of the system for the sentence *the man hit the doll*, with the thematically ambiguous verb *hit*, entered as its default reading, since it is unknown for the system which *hit* is intended. Notice that, in this case, the thematic role assigned to the subject must be AGENT instead of CAUSE, because the noun *man* has features associated with being capable of controlling the action, for instance, *human* and *animate* (see table 2). As one can see, only the *GR* module gave a suitable prediction for the subject thematic role.

---

[1] The average output error is the difference between "actual" and "desired" outputs, and it is obtained from the *average squared error energy formula* [14] for each set of different sentences presented to the network.

Sentence: *the girl bought a ball by a hundred dollars*									

Word presented to the system: (girl) **buy**

	agent	patie	exper	theme	sourc	goal	benef	cause	instr	value
BP	**0.984**	0.000	0.015	0.049	0.004	0.005	0.003	0.004	0.016	0.000
GR	**1.000**	0.000	0.000	0.002	0.000	0.000	0.000	0.000	0.000	0.000

Word presented to the system: (girl-buy) **ball**

	agent	patie	exper	**theme**	sourc	goal	benef	cause	instr	value
BP	0.011	0.036	0.010	**0.412**	0.014	0.010	0.019	0.004	0.077	0.016
GR	0.000	0.038	0.000	**0.877**	0.000	0.000	0.000	0.000	0.055	0.001

Word presented to the system: (girl-buy-ball) **hundred**

	agent	patie	exper	theme	sourc	goal	benef	cause	instr	**value**
BP	0.001	0.029	0.002	0.146	0.006	0.005	0.006	0.002	0.080	**0.928**
GR	0.000	0.000	0.000	0.046	0.000	0.000	0.000	0.000	0.002	**0.998**

Fig. 4. Outputs of the system for the sentence *the girl bought a ball by a hundred dollars*. Both modules arrived at the expected thematic grid [AGENT, THEME, VALUE], although in module *GR* the displayed values are closer to 1.0

Sentence: *the man hit the doll*									

Word presented to the system: (man) **hit**

	agent	patie	exper	theme	sourc	goal	benef	cause	instr	value
BP	0.531	0.000	0.001	0.012	0.004	0.004	0.003	**0.768**	0.003	0.000
GR	**0.542**	0.000	0.000	0.004	0.000	0.000	0.000	0.482	0.000	0.000

Word presented to the system: (man-hit) **doll**

	agent	patie	exper	**theme**	sourc	goal	benef	cause	instr	value
BP	0.020	0.082	0.001	**1.000**	0.001	0.000	0.004	0.001	0.000	0.000
GR	0.000	0.079	0.000	**0.881**	0.000	0.000	0.000	0.000	0.000	0.000

Fig. 5. Outputs of the system for the sentence *the man hit the doll*. Module *GR* arrived at the expected thematic grid [AGENT, THEME], while module *BP* arrived at [CAUSE, THEME]

Sentence: *the hammer broke the vase*									

Word presented to the system: (hammer) **break**

	agent	patie	exper	theme	sourc	goal	benef	**cause**	instr	value
BP	0.486	0.000	0.001	0.006	0.004	0.005	0.003	**0.764**	0.004	0.000
GR	0.093	0.000	0.000	0.005	0.000	0.000	0.000	**0.912**	0.000	0.000

Word presented to the system: (hammer-break) **vase**

	agent	**patie**	exper	theme	sourc	goal	benef	cause	instr	value
BP	0.001	**0.325**	0.011	0.313	0.004	0.004	0.017	0.001	0.077	0.003
GR	0.000	0.333	0.001	**0.536**	0.000	0.000	0.000	0.000	0.038	0.000

Fig. 6. Outputs for the sentence *the hammer broke the vase*. Both modules arrived at the expected thematic role CAUSE for the subject. Concerning the object, while in *BP* there is a slight preference for PATIENT, in *GR* there is an unexpected assignment of THEME

At last, figure 6 shows outputs for the sentence *the hammer broke the vase*, which employs another thematically ambiguous verb (*break*). To the subject of this sentence (*hammer*) is assigned the thematic role CAUSE instead of AGENT, because *hammer* causes the breaking, but it is not responsible for this action. Its semantic features include *non-human* and *tool/utensil*, incompatible to *control of action*, feature expected to be associated to the verb that assigns the thematic role AGENT. For the object, module *BP* worked better, assigning PATIENT to *vase*, instead of THEME.

6 Conclusion

The modules TRP-*BP* and TRP-*GR*, of the proposed system, are connectionist approaches to natural language processing, regarding the thematic role relationships between words of a sentence. The aim of this paper is to show that a biologically motivated connectionist system, with a bi-directional architecture and learning algorithm that uses only local information to update its synaptic weights, is able not only to take care of this natural language processing problem, but also to be more computationally efficient than the conventional backpropagation learning procedure through a simple recurrent connectionist architecture. This is confirmed by the outcomes for a same set of test sentences presented to both modules of the system.

References

1. Edelman, G. M., Tononi, G.: A Universe of Consciousness - How Matter Becomes Imagination. Basic Books (2000)
2. Rosa, J. L. G.: An Artificial Neural Network Model Based on Neuroscience: Looking Closely at the Brain. In: Kůrková, V., Steele, N. C., Neruda, R., Kárný, M. (eds.): Artificial Neural Nets and Genetic Algorithms – Proc. of the Intl. Conf. in Prague, Czech Republic – ICANNGA-2001. April 22-25, Springer-Verlag (2001) 138-141
3. O'Reilly, R. C.: Biologically Plausible Error-driven Learning using Local Activation Differences: The Generalized Recirculation Algorithm. Neural Comp.8:5(1996)895-938
4. Haegeman, L.: Introduction to Government and Binding Theory. Basil Blackwell Inc., Cambridge, MA (1991)
5. Dowty, D.: On the Semantic Content of the Notion of 'Thematic Role'. In Chierchia, G. *et al.* (eds.): Properties, Types and Meaning. Dordrecht, Kluwer (1989)
6. Rosa, J. L. G., Françozo, E.: Linguistic Relations Encoding in a Symbolic-Connectionist Hybrid Natural Language Processor. In Monard, M. C., Sichman, J. S. (eds.): Advances in Artificial Intelligence – Proc. of the IBERAMIA-SBIA 2000, Atibaia, São Paulo, Brazil, November 19-22. Lecture Notes in Artificial Intelligence, Vol. 1952. Springer-Verlag, Berlin (2000) 259-268
7. McClelland, J. L., Kawamoto, A. H.: Mechanisms of Sentence Processing: Assigning Roles to Constituents of Sentences. In McClelland, J. L., Rumelhart, D. E. (eds.): Parallel Distributed Processing, Vol. 2. A Bradford Book, The MIT Press (1986)
8. Rosa, J. L. G.: A Biologically Inspired Connectionist System for Natural Language Processing. In Proc. of the 2002 VII Brazilian Symposium on Neural Networks (SBRN 2002). 11-14 November. Recife, Brazil. IEEE Computer Society Press (2002) 243-248

9. Rosa, J. L. G., Françozo, E.: Hybrid Thematic Role Processor: Symbolic Linguistic Relations Revised by Connectionist Learning. In Proc. of IJCAI'99-16th. Intl. Joint Conf. on Artificial Intelligence, Vol. 2, Stockholm, Sweden, 31 July-6 August(1999) 852-857
10. Elman, J. L.: Finding Structure in Time. Cognitive Science 14 (1990) 179-211
11. Crick, F. H.: The Recent Excitement about Neural Networks. Nature 337(1989)129-132
12. Rosa, J. L. G.: A Biologically Motivated Connectionist System for Predicting the Next Word in Natural Language Sentences. In Proc. of the 2002 IEEE Intl. Conf. on Systems, Man, and Cybernetics. 06-09 October. Hammamet, Tunisia (2002)
13. Hinton, G. E., McClelland, J. L.: Learning Representations by Recirculation. In Anderson, D. Z. (ed.): Neural Information Processing Systems, 1987. New York: American Institute of Physics (1988) 358-366
14. Haykin, S.: Neural Networks - A Comprehensive Foundation. 2nd edn. Prentice Hall, Upper Saddle River, New Jersey (1999)
15. O'Reilly, R. C., Munakata, Y.: Computational Explorations in Cognitive Neuroscience - Understanding the Mind by Simulating the Brain. A Bradford Book, The MIT Press, Cambridge, MA (2000)

A Question-Answering System Using Argumentation

Emanuela Moreale and Maria Vargas-Vera

Knowledge Media Institute, The Open University,
Walton Hall, Milton Keynes MK7 6AA, England
{E.Moreale,M.Vargas-Vera}@open.ac.uk
http://kmi.open.ac.uk/

Abstract. This paper presents a novel approach to question answering: the use of argumentation techniques. Our question answering system deals with argumentation in student essays: it sees an essay as an answer to a question and gauges its quality on the basis of the argumentation found in it. Thus, the system looks for expected types of argumentation in essays (i.e. the expectation is that the kind of argumentation in an essay is correlated to the type of question). Another key feature of our work is our proposed categorisation for argumentation in student essays, as opposed to categorisation of argumentation in research papers, where - unlike the case of student essays - it is relatively well-known which kind of argumentation can be found in specific sections.

1 Introduction

A new line of research in Question Answering that was discussed at the Symposium on New directions on Question Answering (Stanford University, spring 2003) is the use of knowledge in question answering. This knowledge – which might be encoded in ontologies – would, in our view, enhance the question answering process. Such a research direction has been already taken by the AQUA project [1][2] at the Open University, England. AQUA makes extensive use of knowledge (captured in an ontology) in several parts of the question answering process, such as query reformulation and similarity algorithm (assessing similarity between name of relations in the query and in the knowledge base). Currently, AQUA is coupled with the AKT reference ontology[1], but in the future will handle several different ontologies.

This paper proposes a somewhat different approach to question answering: here we use argumentation for finding answers in the specific domain of student essays. This means that specific categories of argumentation depend on the type of question. Current work is on how argumentation could be complemented with a reasoning system which will be able to decide on action plans in case an answer is not found. We also make use of knowledge in advising students about missing categories in the essays just like in Expert Systems. It should be noted that the aim of this work is not to produce a system that understands student essays as humans do. Our goal is a

---

[1] The AKT reference ontology contains classes and instances of people, organizations, research areas, publications, technologies and events.
(http://akt.open.ac.uk/ocml/domains/akt-support-ontology/)

R. Monroy et al. (Eds.): MICAI 2004, LNAI 2972, pp. 400–409, 2004.

system that is able to locate the chunk(s) of text in which an answer to a question can be found. In our system, the user plays a key role: it is the user that performs answer validation and provides feedback to the system.

Our test bed is a set of postgraduate student essays – a type of free or non-structured text – and corresponding essay questions. Therefore, in our domain, argumentation cannot be found in specific sections of the text (as in research papers). The first contribution of this paper is the use of argumentation techniques in the question answering problem, as opposed to conventional approaches to question answering such as information retrieval. Our second contribution is our argumentation categorisation for student essays: this is loosely based on research in argumentation in academic papers, but omits categories that are not applicable to this domain. More details on our categorisation can be found in section 1 and [3].

The paper is organised as follows: section 2 presents the question answering process model. Section 3 discusses the research background on argumentation schemas in papers and argument modelling and then introduces our essay metadiscourse categorisation in the context of the reviewed background. Section 4 reports on our annotation categories and essay questions. Section 5 describes our testbed and actual matching of argumentation with essay questions. Section 6 reports preliminary results and indicates future work. Finally, section 7 draws our conclusion.

2   Question Answering Process Model

The proposed architecture (Figure 1) of our system comprises: interface, query classification, segmentation, categorization, reasoner and annotation modules.

- The interface is a window menu interface.
- The query classification module classifies queries as belonging to one of the types defined in our system.
- The segmentation module obtains segments of student essays by using a library of cue phrases and patterns.
- The categorisation component classifies the segments as one of our categories.
- The reasoner is an expert system that will reason about categories found in a student essays.
- The annotation module annotates relevant phrases as belonging to one of our defined categories. These annotations are saved as semantic tags. Future implementation may use machine learning for learning cue phrases.

Our question answering system, the *Student Essay System (SES)*, has a visual component – the *Argumentation Viewer (AV)* – which highlights instances of our argumentation categories in an essay, so as to give a visual representation of argumentation within an essay, in a shallow version of "making thinking visible"[4][5]. The intuition is that essays with considerably more "highlighting" contain more argumentation (and actual "content") and therefore attract higher grades.

The viewer can be used by tutors during assessment: they may refer to its automatic counts indicator, citation highlighting or simply use it to quickly gauge the amount and distribution of argumentation cues across an essay. *AV* can also provide formative feedback to students. Thus, if students running it on their own essay see that little argumentation is found, they are well advised to "revise" their essay before submission. An improvement in the essay (more background and reasoned argumentation) should result in more highlighting, which may increase motivation in some students.

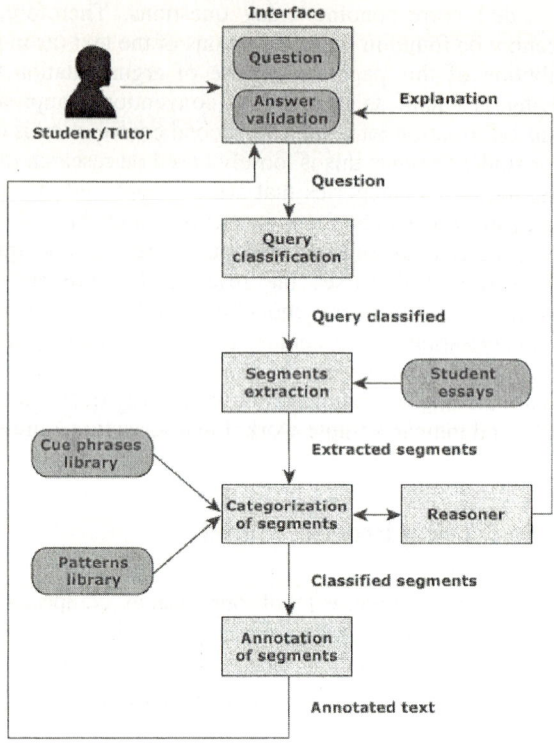

Fig. 1. Student Essay System Model

3   Argument Modelling in Papers

Relevant research background spans from articles on argumentation in research papers to knowledge representation tools supporting the construction of rhetorical arguments. An important strand of research has focused on paper structure, producing metadiscourse taxonomies applicable to research papers. In his CARS model, Swales [6] synthesised his findings that papers present three moves: authors first establish a territory (by claiming centrality, making topic generalisations and reviewing items of previous research), then they establish a niche (by counter-claiming, indicating a gap or question-raising) and finally they occupy this niche (by outlining purpose, announcing present research and principal findings and indicating paper structure). Although his analysis targeted only the introductory part of an academic research paper, his model has nevertheless been influential. For instance, Teufel [7] extended Swales's CARS model by adding new moves to cover the other sections. They classify sentences into background, other, own, aim, textual, contrast and basic categories. The authors claim that this methodology could be used in automatic text summarisation, since the latter requires finding important sentences in a source text by determining their most likely argumentative role. Their experiments showed that the annotation schema can be successfully applied by human annotators, with little training.

Hyland [8] distinguishes between textual and interpersonal metadiscourse in academic texts. The former refers to devices allowing the recovery of the writer's intention by explicitly establishing preferred interpretations; they also help form a coherent text by relating propositions to each other and to other texts. Textual metadiscourse includes logical connectives (in addition, but, therefore etc), frame markers (e.g. finally, to repeat, our aim here, endophoric markers (noted above, see Fig 2, table 1, below), evidentials (According to X, Y states) and code glosses (namely, e.g., in other words, such as). Interpersonal metadiscourse, instead, expresses the writer's persona by alerting the reader to the author's perspective to both the information and the readers themselves. Categories of interpersonal metadiscourse are hedges (might, perhaps, it is possible), emphatics (in fact, definitely, it is clear, obvious), attitude markers (Surprisingly, I agree), relational markers (Frankly, note that, you can see) and person markers (I, we, me, mine, our).

Another interesting source is ScholOnto, an Open University project aiming to model arguments in academic papers and devise an ontology for scholarly discourse[9]. As part of their project, they developed *ClaiMaker*, a tool for browsing and editing claims. Claims are classified as general (e.g. is about, uses, applies, improves on), problem-related (e.g. addresses, solves), evidence (supports/ challenges), taxonomic, similarity and causal. ClaiMaker is meant for academic research papers, whereas we want an argumentation categorisation for student essays.

3.1 Our Approach to Argumentation on Student Essays

As a first step in our research, we identified candidate categories of argumentation in student essays through a preliminary manual analysis of essay texts. Some categories were influenced by ClaiMaker and the other categorisations seen above.

Our bottom-up approach initially yielded the following argumentation categories: definition, comparison, general, critical thinking, reporting, viewpoint, problem, evidence, causal, taxonomic, content/expected and connectors. Some categories have sub-categories (e.g. connectors comprises topic introduction, inference, contrast, additive, support, reformulation and summative subcategories of connectors).

A review of this schema prompted us to reduce the number of categories (cognitive overload, clearer visualisation). We thus grouped related categories and turned them into subcategories of a new category (e.g. evidence, causal and taxonomic became subcategories of the new "link" category) or modified categories ("viewpoint" merged into "positioning", the new name for "critical thinking"). Our revised categorisation also sees comparison as part of definition, because we often define a concept by comparing it with others. The outcome of the rationalisation process is the following student essay categorisation: definition, reporting, positioning, strategy, problem, link, content/expected, connectors and general (Table 1).

Compared to Teufel's schema, ours lacks an AIM category: this is because all student essays have the implicit aim of answering the essay question. Similarly, we do not distinguish between OTHER and OWN (knowledge shared by author in other papers and this paper respectively), as this does not apply to student essays. On the other hand, our content/expected category has no counterpart in the other categorisations, since it is a student essay-specific category comprising cue phrases identifying content that the tutor expects to find in the essay. Overall, however, there are remarkable similarities across these categorisations (for a comparison, see [3]).

Table 1. Our Taxonomy for Argumentation in Student Essays

Category	Description	Cue phrases (examples)
DEFINITION	Items relating to the definition of a term. Often towards the beginning. IS_ABOUT, COMPARISONS	is about, concerns, refers to, definition; is the same; is similar /analogous to;
REPORTING	Sentences describing other research in neutral way	"X discusses", "Y suggests", "Z warns"
POSITIONING	Sentences critiquing other research; VIEWPOINTS	"I accept", "I am unhappy with", "personally";
STRATEGY	Explicit statements about the method or the textual section structure of the essay	"I will attempt to", "in section 2"
PROBLEM	Sentences indicating gap or inconsistency, question-raising, counter-claiming	"There are difficulties", "is problematic", "limitations"
LINK	Statements indicating how categories of concepts relate to others: TAXONOMIC, EVIDENCE, CAUSAL	"subclass of", "example of", "would seem to confirm", "has caused"
CONTENT/ EXPECTED	Any concept that the tutor expects students to mention in their essay. Tutor-editable	Essay-dependent
CONNECTORS	Links between propositions may serve different purposes (topic introduction, support, inference, additive, parallel, summative, contrast, reformulation)	"With regard to", "As to", "Therefore", "In fact", "In addition", "Overall", "However", "In short"
GENERAL	Generic association links	"is related to"

4   Annotation Categories and Essay Questions

Query classification gives information about the kind of answer our system should expect. The classification phase involves processing the query to identify the category of answer being sought. In particular, sentence segmentation is carried out: this reveals nouns, verbs, prepositions and adjectives. The categories of possible answers, which are listed below, extend the universal categorisation used in traditional question answering systems (by adding to the six categories: what, who, when, which, why and where). Our analysis of the essay questions in our testbed (see Table 2 for questions and Section 5 for testbed) showed that they were answered by essays with different "link profiles" (see Table 3).

Table 2. Examples of Essay Questions

	Assignment	*Example*
1. Summary + How and Why	Ass 1, part 2	"In the light of Otto Peter's ideas… say how each type can or cannot serve these ideas and why"
2. Opinion about X	Ass 2, part 1	- "Who do you think should define the learners' needs in distance education?"
	Ass 4, part 3	- "State and define your views on the questions of whether the research is adequately addressing what you regard to be the important questions or debates"
3. Describe + Discuss	Ass 2, part 2	"Imagine you are student and your teacher has a strong leaning towards the technical-vocational orientation. Describe and discuss your experiences, using concepts and examples from text book 1."
	Ass 4, part 2	"Define and discuss any cultural factors you observe in relation to each of these questions"
4. Give example of X and Critique X	Ass 4, part 1	"Provide examples of web links covering a wide range of choose aspects of open and distance education and write a short critique of each."

The basic idea is that, depending on the essay question, we expect to find a different "distribution" of links in the essay themselves. For instance, a question asking for a "summary" is usually answered by an essay containing many "reporting" links. Table 3 matches essay questions with our essay metadiscourse categories (Table 2). We ran a statistical analysis of links and question types and our findings are presented in section 5.

Table 3. Examples of Essay Questions and Expected Links

Example of Question	*Links Expected to be Important in Essay*
1. Summary of X + How and Why	Essays answering such questions have a high number of reporting, positioning, expected and contrast links.
2. Opinion about X	Essay has a high number of background, expected names, positioning links.
3. Describe and Discuss	These essays feature a high number of support and positioning links. In assignment 2, part 2, there was a low number of reporting links, as students were asked to describe a hypothetical situation; however, this may not always be the case.
4. Give an example of X and Critique X	Here, analysis and summative connector links are higher than "is about" and "contrast" links.

5   Test Bed

Our testbed consists of 193 anonymised essays (belonging to 4 different assignments), with corresponding essay questions. The essays were anonymised versions of actual essays submitted by students as part of a Masters Course at the Open University. The essays were marked by three experienced tutors, whose comments we also consulted.

We chose student essays as our domain, as essays are typically less structured than other types of documents, including academic research papers, and therefore more difficult to work with. If our approach works with student essays, it will work even better with more structured types of texts. Also, while good results have been achieved in the area of student essays classification and assessment with statistical methods, these methods have no semantics and do not provide useful feedback, which is of course of particular importance in the area of student essays.

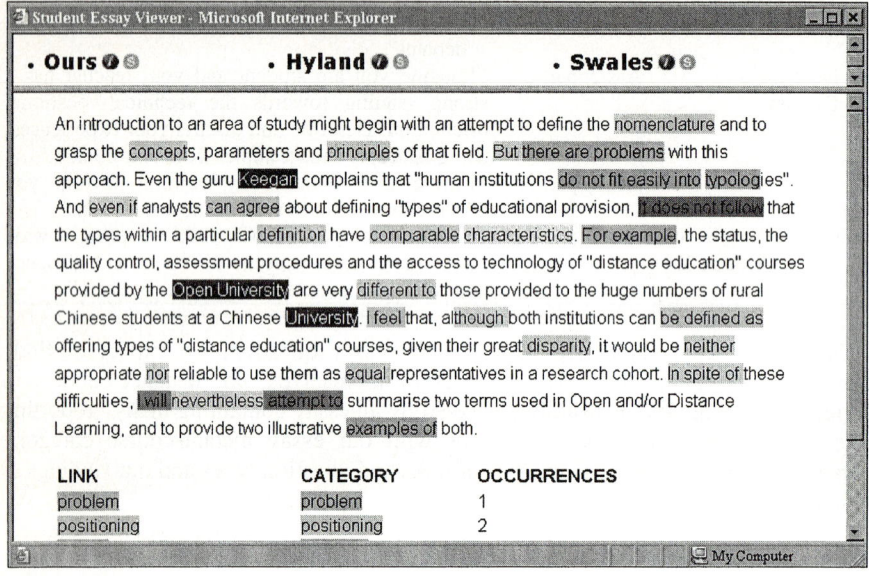

Fig. 2. Argumentation Viewer (AV) showing all annotations in an essay

Having devised an argumentation schema for essays, we decided to implement a system to visualise argumentation in student essays. The resulting AV – while being as easy to use as a webpage – can be a time-saving tool for both tutors and students to use, thanks to its quick visualisation of argumentation in an essay. However, students may particularly benefit from a question analysis module: this could analyse and classify essay questions with respect to the type of argumentation required in the essay, thus allowing alerting students to missing (or lacking) categories of argumentation. This functionality would be very useful in a formative context and would certainly get the students to stop and think about whether what they are writing is answering the question, rather than simply "waffling on". AV is thus part of SES, a question-answering tool, that tries to help create a satisfactory answer to a question and can alert the user if such satisfaction is not achieved. At this moment in time, we are working at the phrase level, but are hoping to move on to longer linguistic units (e.g. sentences and/or paragraphs) soon.

We therefore determined what "link profiles" (Tables 2, 3) could reasonably be expected in a satisfactory essay written for assignments 1 and 2 and then performed a statistical analysis on the data in our possession to verify these hypotheses and find out the specific kind of argumentation that SES should be looking for relative to each type of question. The results of this analysis are summarised in Table 4.

Table 4. Expected and Actual Argumentation links in Assignments 1 and 2

ID	Expected	Results	Analysis
Ass 1 Part 1	many reporting links	- reporting links count significant ($r=0.730$; $N=12$; $p<0.01$) - positioning links count is not - total link count significant: $r=0.624$; $N=12$; $p<0.05$ $F(1,10)= 6.385$; $p<0.05$	Both Spearman correlation and ANOVA F-statistic seems to support our expectations: reporting links are more important than positioning links in this type of essay.
Ass 1 Part 2a	high number of reporting, positioning and expected links.	- reporting more important than positioning - statistical significance for "specific reporting links": - a) "Peters" $r=0.744$;$n=12$;$p<0.01$ - b) "Peters+industrial+ODE" $r=0.717$;$n=12$;$p<0.01$ $F(1,14)=6.524$; $p<0.05$	Some students, while including sufficient reporting /expected links, managed to wander off topic (and hence their grade was not high). Better grades achieved by essays that stayed "on topic" ("specific reporting" links)
Ass 1 Part 2b		- significant correlation between score and specific reporting links: - $r=0.526$;$n=15$;$p<0.05$ ($r=0.586$ if we ignore references to "Holmberg") - no statistical significance for generic reporting or positioning links - expected not significant	Many students wandered off topic (discussed around Holmberg / expected stuff but not enough on guided didactic conversation or GDC). Hence, only reliable indicator is specific reporting links.
Ass 2 Part 1	positioning links important	- positioning links show a significant correlation with score: $r=0.538$;$n=20$;$P,0.05$	When background is not "at the forefront" in an essay question, positioning tends to be the determinant link type.
Ass 2 Part 2	-reporting (especially reporting on Schön)	- reporting links (generic): Spearman's Rho: 0.467; $n=20$; $p<0.05$; - specific reporting links $r=0.541$; $n=20$; $p<005$; - word count: $r=0.639$;$n=20$;$p<0.01$	Reporting links are important in this kind of essay, particularly links directly connected to the question (students sometimes tended to wander off topic). Word count is important, again, as this is the last part in Ass2 and some students overran their target in part 1.

While positioning links are determinant in Assignment 2 part 1, overall, the importance of reporting links is apparent: after all, essays at graduate and post-graduate level nearly always – to some extent – require showing that one has "done the reading". Where reporting links were not significantly correlated with grade, this seems to be because students wandered off topic (e.g. they talked about Holmberg and his ideas at length, but did not spend most of their time and words on guided didactic conversation, which is what the question specifically asked about). This suggests that – in order to detect if an essay is answering the question (as opposed to going off topic) – our tool should make use of both a "generic" reporting link category and a more specific one ("specific reporting links" in Table 4), with instances derived from query classification techniques (such as sentence segmentation) applied to the essay query. Examples of cues used for "specific reporting" in Assignment 1 part 2a were: Peters, industrial and Open & Distance Learning.

6 Results and Future Work

Our main contribution is the application of argumentation techniques to question answering. A second contribution of this paper is our student essay metadiscourse schema, which we have compared and contrasted with categorisations in the research paper domain (Section 1). We have analysed links between argumentation in essays and score to determine if an essay is answering the question (Section 4) and gauge its overall quality. We found that the total number of links correlates with score, that positioning and background (expected + reporting) are the variables that generally contribute the most to score prediction and that the essay question is associated with the relative importance of different link types in an essay. We also found that "specific reporting links" are often needed to detect off-topic wanderings in student essays.

We have implemented part of a question-answering system in the domain of student essays. SES is based on the idea that different essay profiles answer different types of questions and that therefore it can give useful feedback to students trying to answer an essay question. One of its components, AV, visualises the highlighted argumentation categories used in an essay: in particular, the type of argumentation and its concentration. Students may use SES to get feedback about their essay, particularly about lacking categories.

In our investigation, we have used real data, actual essays written by postgraduate students as part of their course. We believe that the results reported here are encouraging in terms of the quality and robustness of our current implementation. However, there is clearly a lot more work needed to make this technology easy enough to use for tutors and students (who are neither experts in language technologies nor 'power knowledge engineers') to use. Future implementations of the student essay viewer could categorise longer linguistic units (e.g. sentences or paragraphs) and explain the reasons why a specific categorisation is assigned to them. These explanations might be displayed in pseudo-natural language.

Future work includes implementation of an "essay question analysis module". As this paper has shown, depending on the type of essay question asked, different types of argumentation are required to answer it and this is exactly where students tend to need the most help. The module will help analyse the question, establish what type of argumentation is missing/lacking and will determine a set of "specific reporting links" for use to detect off-topic wanderings in essays. A reasoning system could then explain why the student is not answering the question and a visualisation component such as AV would be provided to display argumentation in student essays.

7   Conclusion

This paper has shown how argumentation techniques could be used successfully for finding answers to specific categories of questions. Moreover, it has briefly described our generic metadiscourse annotation schema for student essays and its links to other schemas specifying argumentation in academic papers. An argumentation visualisation tool for student essays has been introduced which uses our essay annotation schema and a cue-based approach to detect argumentation.

Finally, the paper has explored some hypotheses as to how essay assessment and creation may be aided by the student essay viewer. In particular, thanks to its argumentation and question-answering approach, this tool may help students write essays that answer the essay question and give them formative feedback during their essay-writing efforts.

References

[1] Vargas-Vera, M., Motta, E., Domingue, J.: AQUA: An Ontology-Driven Question Answering System. AAAI Spring Symposium, New Directions in Question Answering, Stanford University (2003a)
[2] Vargas-Vera, M., Motta, E., Domingue, J.: An Ontology-Driven Question Answering System (AQUA), KMI-TR-129 (2003b)
[3] Moreale, E. and Vargas-Vera, M.: Genre Analysis and the Automated Extraction of Arguments from Student Essays, 7th Int. Computer-Assisted Assessment Conference CAA-2003, Loughborough (2003)
[4] Bell, P.: Using Argument Representations to Make Thinking Visible for Individuals and Groups. In R Hall, N Miyake, & N Enyedy (Eds), Proceedings of CSCL '97: The Second International Conference on Computer Support for Collaborative Learning, Toronto: University of Toronto Press . (1997) 10–19
[5] Sharples, M. and O'Malley, C.: A Framework for the Design of a Writer's Assistant. Artificial Intelligence and Human Learning: Intelligent Computer-Aided Instruction. J Self, Chapman and Hall Ltd (1988)
[6] Swales, J.M.: Genre Analysis. Cambridge University Press (1990)
[7] Teufel, S., Carletta, J. and Moens, M.: An Annotation Schema for Discourse-Level Argumentation in Research Articles, Proceedings of EACL'99 (1999) 110–117
[8] Hyland, K.: Persuasion and Context: The Pragmatics of Academic Metadiscourse, Journal of Pragmatics 30 (1998) 437–455
[9] Buckingham Shum, S., Uren, V., Li, G., Domingue, J., Motta, E.: Visualizing Internetworked Argumentation, in Visualizing Argumentation: Software Tools for Collaborative and Educational Sense-Making. Paul A Kirschner, Simon J. Buckingham Shum and Chad S. Carr (Eds), Springer-Verlag: London (2002).

Automatic Building of a Machine Translation Bilingual Dictionary Using Recursive Chain-Link-Type Learning from a Parallel Corpus

Hiroshi Echizen-ya[1], Kenji Araki[2], Yoshio Momouchi[3], and Koji Tochinai[4]

[1] Dept. of Electronics and Information, Hokkai-Gakuen University, S26-Jo,
W11-Chome, Chuo-ku Sapporo, 064-0926 Japan
echi@eli.hokkai-s-u.ac.jp,
TEL: +81-11-841-1161(ext.7863), FAX: +81-11-551-2951
[2] Division of Electronics and Information, Hokkaido University, N13-Jo, W8-Chome,
Kita-ku Sapporo, 060-8628 Japan
araki@media.eng.hokudai.ac.jp,
TEL: +81-11-706-6534, FAX: +81-11-706-6534
[3] Dept. of Electronics and Information, Hokkai-Gakuen University, S26-Jo,
W11-Chome, Chuo-ku Sapporo, 064-0926 Japan
momouchi@eli.hokkai-s-u.ac.jp,
TEL: +81-11-841-1161(ext.7864), FAX: +81-11-551-2951
[4] Division of Business Administration, Hokkai-Gakuen University, 4-Chome,
Asahi-machi, Toyohira-ku Sapporo, 060-8790 Japan
tochinai@econ.hokkai-s-u.ac.jp,
TEL: +81-11-841-1161(ext.2753), FAX: +81-11-824-7729

Abstract. Numerous methods have been developed for generating a machine translation (MT) bilingual dictionary from a parallel text corpus. Such methods extract bilingual collocations from sentence pairs of source and target language sentences. Then those collocations are registered in an MT bilingual dictionary. Bilingual collocations are lexically corresponding pairs of parts extracted from sentence pairs. This paper describes a new method for automatic extraction of bilingual collocations from a parallel text corpus using no linguistic knowledge. We use Recursive Chain-link-type Learning (RCL), which is a learning algorithm, to extract bilingual collocations. Our method offers two main advantages. One benefit is that this RCL system requires no linguistic knowledge. The other advantage is that it can extract many bilingual collocations, even if the frequency of appearance of the bilingual collocations is very low. Experimental results verify that our system extracts bilingual collocations efficiently. The extraction rate of bilingual collocations was 74.9% for all bilingual collocations that corresponded to nouns in the parallel corpus.

1 Introduction

Recent years have brought the ability to obtain much information that is written in various languages using the Internet in real time. However, current machine

R. Monroy et al. (Eds.): MICAI 2004, LNAI 2972, pp. 410–419, 2004.

translation (MT) systems can be used only for a limited number of languages. It is important for MT systems to build bilingual dictionaries. Therefore, many methods have been studied for automatic generation of an MT bilingual dictionary. Such methods are able to produce an MT bilingual dictionary by extracting bilingual collocations from a parallel corpus. Bilingual collocations are lexically corresponding pairs of parts extracted from sentence pairs of source and target language sentences. These studies can be classified into three areas of emphasis. Some use a linguistic-based approach [1]. In a linguistic-based approach, the system requires static, large-scale linguistic knowledge to extract bilingual collocations *e.g.*, a general bilingual dictionary or syntax information. Therefore, it is difficult to apply such static large-scale linguistic knowledge to other various languages easily because developers must acquire linguistic knowledge for other languages.

Other methods for extracting bilingual collocations include statistical approaches [2, 3]. In these statistical approaches, it is difficult to extract bilingual collocations when the frequency of appearance of the bilingual collocations is very low, *e.g.*, only one time. Therefore, the system requires a large bilingual corpus, or many corpora, to extract bilingual collocations. Typically, a statistical approach extracts only bilingual collocations that occur more than three times in the parallel corpus. A third type of method emphasizes the use of learning algorithms that extract bilingual collocations from sentence pairs of source and target language sentences without requiring static linguistic knowledge. We have proposed a method using **I**nductive **L**earning with **G**enetic **A**lgorithms (GA-IL) [4]. As shown in Fig. 1, this method uses a genetic algorithm to generate two sentence pairs automatically with one different part of two source language sentences and with just one different part of two target language sentences. Unfortunately, this method requires similar sentence pairs as the condition of extraction of bilingual collocations. Therefore, these learning algorithm methods require numerous similar sentence pairs to extract many bilingual collocations, even though they require no *ex ante* static linguistic knowledge.

(1) Generation of sentence pairs by applying genetic algorithms
　(He *likes* ＼／tea.　；彼/*は* ＼／お茶/が/好き/です. [*Kare wa ocha ga suki desu.*])
　(She *likes*／＼tennis.；彼女/*は*／＼テニス/が/好き/です. [*Kanojo wa tenisu ga suki desu.*])
　　↳(She likes tea.；彼女/は/お茶/が/好き/です. [*Kanojo wa ocha ga suki desu.*])
　　⤷(He likes tennis.；彼/は/テニス/が/好き/です. [*Kare wa tenisu ga suki desu.*])
(2) Extraction of bilingual collocations by Inductive Learning
　Generated sentence pair
　(He likes **tennis**.；彼/は/**テニス**/が/好き/です. [*Kare wa **tenisu** ga suki desu.*])

　Given sentence pair
　(He likes **tea**.；彼/は/**お茶**/が/好き/です. [*Kare wa **ocha** ga suki desu.*])
　　⟹ (tennis；テニス [*tenisu*]),(tea；お茶 [*ocha*])

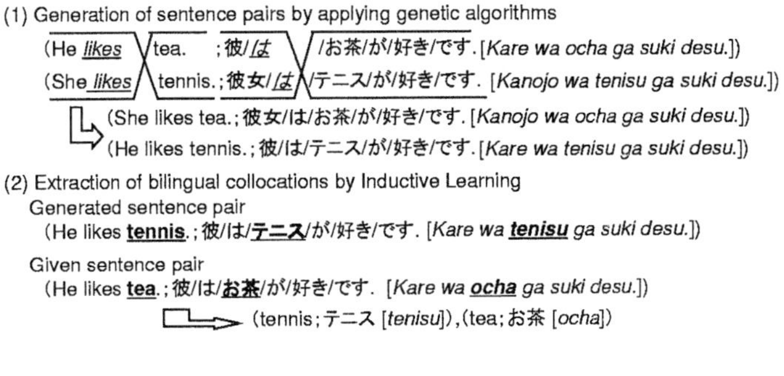

Fig. 1. Example of bilingual collocation extraction using GA-IL

We propose a new method for automatic extraction of bilingual collocations from a parallel corpus to overcome problems of existing approaches. Our method uses the learning algorithm we call **R**ecursive **C**hain-link-type **L**earning (RCL) [5] to extract bilingual collocations efficiently using no linguistic knowledge. In this RCL system, various bilingual collocations are extracted efficiently using only character strings of previously-extracted bilingual collocations. This feature engenders many benefits. This RCL system requires no static analytical knowledge, in contrast to a linguistic-based approach. Furthermore, in contrast to a statistical approach, it does not require a high frequency of appearance for bilingual collocations in the parallel corpus. This means that this RCL system can extract bilingual collocations from only a few sentence pairs. Numerous similar sentence pairs are unnecessary, in stark contrast to requirements of a learning-based approach. Evaluation experiment results demonstrate that this RCL system can extract useful bilingual collocations. We achieved a 74.9% extraction rate for bilingual collocations which correspond to nouns. Moreover, the extraction rate of bilingual collocations for which the frequency of appearance was only one in the parallel text corpus was 58.1%.

2   Overview of Our Method

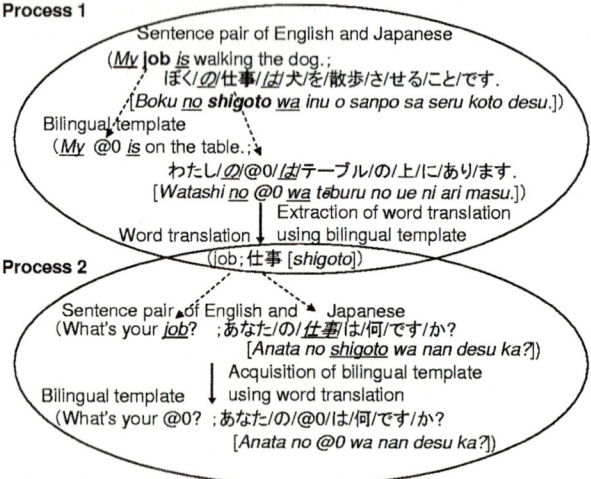

Fig. 2. Diagram of the English-Japanese collocation extraction process

The prominent feature of our method is that it does not require linguistic knowledge. We intend to realize a system based only on learning ability from the view of language acquisition of children. The RCL algorithm imitates part of that principle in language acquisition because it requires no *ex ante* static linguistic knowledge.

Figure 2 depicts the RCL process, which extracts English-Japanese collocations. This RCL system extracts two types of bilingual collocations. This is an English-Japanese collocation: (job; 仕事 [*shigoto*][5]). It can be registered in an MT bilingual dictionary as a word-level bilingual translation. Hereafter, we call this type of collocation a **word translation**. In contrast, phrases such as (What's your @0?; あなた/の/@0/は/何/です/か?[6] [*Anata no @0 wa nan desu ka?*]) are representative of an English-Japanese collocations that are used as a template for extraction of word translations. This type of collocation is called a **bilingual template**. In this paper, a word translation is a pair of source and target parts; a bilingual template is also a pair of source and target parts. Figure 2 shows a process by which a word translation (job; 仕事 [*shigoto*]) and a new bilingual template (What's your @0?; あなた/の/@0/は/何/です/か? [*Anata no @0 wa nan desu ka?*]) are extracted reciprocally.

In process 1 of Fig. 2, this RCL system extracts (job; 仕事 [*shigoto*]) as a word translation. This (job; 仕事 [*shigoto*]) corresponds to the variables "@0" in the bilingual template (My @0 is on the table.; わたし/の/@0/は/テーブル/の/上/に/あり/ます. [*Watashi no @0 wa tēburu no ue ni ari masu.*]). "My" and "is" adjoin the variable "@0" in the source part of the bilingual template. They are shared parts with the parts in the English sentence "My job is walking the dog." Moreover, "の [*no*]" and "は [*wa*]" adjoin the variable "@0" in the target part of the bilingual template; they are also shared parts with parts in the Japanese sentence "ぼく/の/仕事/は/犬/を/散歩/さ/せる/こと/です. [*Boku no shigoto wa inu o sanpo sa seru koto desu.*]" Therefore, this RCL system extracts the (job; 仕事 [*shigoto*]) by extracting "job" between the right of "My" and the left of "is" in the English sentence, and extracting "仕事 [*shigoto*]" between the right of "の [*no*]" and the left of "は [*wa*]" in the Japanese sentence.

Moreover, this RCL system acquires new bilingual templates using only character strings of the extracted (job; 仕事 [*shigoto*]). In process 2 of Fig. 2, the source part "job" of the word translation (job; 仕事 [*shigoto*]) has the same character strings as the part in the English sentence "What's your job?" In addition, the target part "仕事 [*shigoto*]" of the word translation (job; 仕事 [*shigoto*]) has the same character strings as the part in the Japanese sentence "あなた/の/仕事/は/何/です/か? [*Anata no shigoto wa nan desu ka?*]." Therefore, this RCL system acquires (What's your @0?; あなた/の/@0/は/何/です/か? [*Anata no @0 wa nan desu ka?*]) as the bilingual template by replacing "job" and "仕事 [*shigoto*]" with the variables "@0" for the sentence pair (What's your job?; あなた/の/仕事/は/何/です/か? [*Anata no shigoto wa nan desu ka?*]).

Extracted word translations and bilingual templates are applied for other sentence pairs of English and Japanese to extract new ones. Therefore, word

---

[5] Italics express pronunciation in Japanese.

[6] "/" in Japanese sentences are inserted after each morpheme because Japanese is an agglutinative language. This process is performed automatically according to this system's learning method [6], without requiring any static linguistic knowledge.

translations and bilingual templates are extracted reciprocally as a linked chain. A characteristic of our method is that both word translations and bilingual templates are extracted efficiently using only character strings of sentence pairs of the source and target language sentences. Thereby, our system can extract bilingual collocations using no linguistic knowledge, even in cases where such collocations appear only a few times in the corpus. Figure 2 shows that (job; 仕事 [*shigoto*]) was extractable even though it appears only one time.

3 Outline

Figure 3 shows an outline of this RCL system's extraction of bilingual collocations from sentence pairs of source and target language sentences. First, a user inputs a sentence pair. In the feedback process, this RCL system evaluates extracted word translations and bilingual templates using the given sentence pairs. The user does not evaluate word translations and bilingual templates directly. In the learning process, word translations and bilingual templates are extracted automatically using two learning algorithms: RCL and GA-IL. In this study, this RCL system extracts English-Japanese collocations.

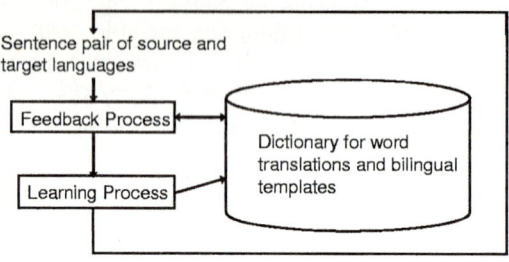

Fig. 3. Process flow

4 Process

4.1 Feedback Process

Our system extracts not only correct bilingual collocations, but also erroneous bilingual collocations. Therefore, this RCL system evaluates bilingual collocations in the feedback process. In this paper, correct bilingual collocation denotes a situation in which source parts and target parts correspond to each other; erroneous bilingual collocations are cases where source parts and target parts do not correspond to one another. In the feedback process, this RCL system first generates sentence pairs in which source language sentences have the same character strings as source language sentences of the given sentence pairs. It does so by combining bilingual templates with word translations. Consequently, this RCL system can generate sentence pairs in which the English sentences have the same character strings as the English sentences of given sentence pairs.

Subsequently, this RCL system compares Japanese sentences of the generated sentence pairs with Japanese sentences of given sentence pairs. When Japanese sentences of generated sentence pairs have the same character strings as the Japanese sentences of given sentence pairs, word translations and bilingual templates used to generate sentence pairs are determined to be correct. In this case, this RCL system adds one point to the correct frequency of the used word translations and bilingual templates. On the other hand, word translations and bilingual templates used to generate sentence pairs are designated as erroneous when Japanese sentences of generated sentence pairs have different character strings from Japanese sentences of given sentence pairs. In that case, this RCL system adds one point to the error frequency of used word translations and bilingual templates. Using the correct frequency and error frequency, this RCL system calculates the Correct Rate (CR) for the word translations and bilingual templates that were used. Following is a definition of CR. This RCL system evaluates word translations and bilingual templates automatically using CR.

$$CR\ (\%) = \frac{Correct\ frequency}{Correct\ frequency + Error\ frequency} \times 100.0 \qquad (1)$$

4.2   Learning Process

Word translations and bilingual templates are extracted reciprocally by this RCL system. We first describe the extraction process of word translations using bilingual templates as in process 1 of Fig. 2. Details of this process are:

(1) This RCL system selects sentence pairs that have the same parts as those parts that adjoin variables in bilingual templates.

(2) This RCL system obtains word translations by extracting parts that adjoin common parts, which are the same parts as those in bilingual templates, from sentence pairs. This means that parts extracted from sentence pairs correspond to variables in bilingual templates. In the extraction process, there are three patterns from the view of the position of variables and their adjoining words in bilingual templates.

Pattern 1: When common parts exist on both the right and left sides of variables in source or target parts of bilingual templates, this RCL system extracts parts between two common parts from source language sentences or target language sentences.

Pattern 2: When common parts exist only on the right side of variables in source parts or target parts of bilingual templates, this RCL system extracts parts from words at the beginning of the sentence to words of the left sides of common parts in source language sentences or target language sentences.

Pattern 3: When common parts exist only on the left side of variables in source parts or target parts of bilingual templates, this RCL system extracts parts from words of the right sides of common parts to words at the end in source language sentences or target language sentences.

(3) This RCL system yields CR that are identical to those bilingual templates used to extract word translations.

In addition, we describe the acquisition process of bilingual templates using word translations as in process 2 of Fig. 2. Details of this process are:

(1) This RCL system selects word translations in which source parts have identical character strings to those parts in source language sentences of sentence pairs, and in which target parts have the same character strings as parts in the target language sentences of sentence pairs.

(2) This RCL system acquires bilingual templates by replacing common parts, which are identical to word translations, with variables.

(3) This RCL system yields CR that are identical to those word translations used to acquire bilingual templates.

On the other hand, word translations or bilingual templates that are used as starting points in the extraction process of new ones are extracted using GA-IL. The reason for using GA-IL is that our system can extract bilingual collocations using only a learning algorithm with no static linguistic knowledge. In this study, our system uses both RCL and GA-IL.

5   Experiments for Performance Evaluation

5.1   Experimental Procedure

To evaluate this RCL system, 2,856 English and Japanese sentence pairs were used as experimental data. These sentence pairs were taken from five textbooks for first and second grade junior high school students. The total number of characters of the 2,856 sentence pairs is 142,592. The average number of words in English sentences in the 2,856 sentence pairs is 6.0. All sentence pairs are processed by our system based on the outline described in Section 3 and based on the process described in Section 4. The dictionary is initially empty.

5.2   Evaluation Standards

We evaluated all extracted word translations that corresponded to nouns. Extracted word translations are ranked when several different target parts are obtained for the same source parts. In that case, word translations are sorted so that word translations which have the highest CR described in Section 4.1 are ranked at the top. Among ranked word translations, three word-translations, ranked from No. 1 to No. 3, are evaluated by the user as to whether word translations where source parts and target parts correspond to each other are included in those three ranked translations or not.

5.3   Experimental Results

Table 1. Extraction rate of this RCL system

| Extraction | Detail | |
rate	nouns	compound nouns
74.9% (347)	75.5% (330)	65.4% (17)

There are 463 kinds of nouns and compound nouns in the evaluation data: 437 varieties of nouns and 26 varieties of compound nouns. Table 1 shows the extraction rate of this RCL system in the evaluation data. In Table 1, values in parentheses indicate the number of correct word translations extracted by this RCL system. Moreover, in this paper, a system using only GA-IL is used for comparison to this RCL system. It is difficult to make comparisons among methods [1–3] which extract bilingual collocation because they typically use various static linguistic knowledge. In the system using only GA-IL, the extraction rate for the word translations which corresponded to nouns and compound nouns was 58.7%. Therefore, using RCL, the extraction rate improved from 58.7% to 74.9%. The extraction rate of word translations for which the frequency of appearance is only one time in the parallel text corpus improved from 32.6% to 58.1% through use of RCL. Table 2 shows examples of the extracted correct word translations.

Table 2. Examples of extracted correct word translations

English	Japanese
museum	博物館 [*hakubutsukan*]
machine	機械 [*kikai*]
sumo	すもう [*sumō*]
すもう means a Japanese traditional sport.	
Statue of Liberty	自由/の/女神 [*jiyū no megami*]
Alice in Wonderland	不思議/の/国/の/アリス [*fushigi no kuni no arisu*]
electric guitar	エレキ/ギター [*ereki gitā*]

5.4   Discussion

We confirmed that this RCL system can extract word translations without requiring a high frequency of appearances of word translations. Figure 4 shows the change in extraction rates engendered by this RCL system and the system using only GA-IL for every 100 word translations that correspond to nouns and compound nouns in the 2,856 sentence pairs used as evaluation data. Figure 4 shows 463 word translations that correspond to nouns and compound nouns. The translations are arranged by appearance sequence in 2,856 sentence pairs.

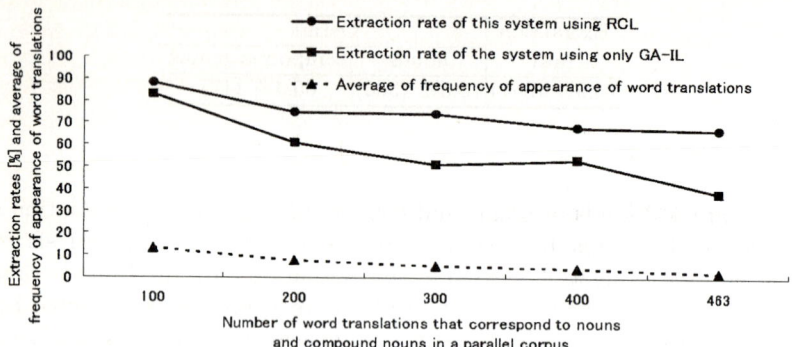

Fig. 4. Change of extraction rates and the average frequency of appearance of extracted word translations in the parallel corpus

In Fig. 4, the dotted line shows average frequencies of appearance of word translations for every 100 word translations that correspond to nouns and compound nouns in evaluation data. The average frequencies of appearance of word translations between Nos. 1 and 100 are high because such word translations appear in many other sentence pairs. The average frequency of appearance of word translations between Nos. 1 and 100 is 13.0. In general, the system extracts word translations easily when their frequency of appearance is high because the probability that the system can extract them is relatively high. Consequently, the extraction rate of word translations between Nos. 1 and 100 is higher than for those in other parts of Fig. 4. On the other hand, the average frequency of appearance of word translations between Nos. 401 and 463 is low because such word translations do not appear in any other sentence pairs. The average frequency of appearance of word translations between Nos. 401 and 463 is 2.4. In general, it is difficult for the system to extract word translations when their frequency of appearance is low because the probability that the system can extract them is relatively low.

Figure 4 depicts the extraction rate of the system using only GA-IL. The rate decreases rapidly as the frequency of appearance of word translations decreases. In contrast, the extraction rate of this RCL system is almost flat except between Nos. 1 and 100. In this RCL system, the decrement of the extraction rate is only nine points between Nos. 101 and 463. In the system using only GA-IL, the decrement of the extraction rate is 23 points between Nos. 101 and 463. These results imply that this RCL system can extract many word translations efficiently without requiring a high frequency of appearance of word translations.

On the other hand, erroneous word translations are also extracted in this RCL system. The precision of extracted word translations was 47.3%. This precision is insufficient. However, in the feedback process described in Section 4.1, this RCL system can evaluate these word translations as erroneous word translations. The rate at which the system could determine erroneous word translations for extracted erroneous word translations was 69.2%. In that case, erroneous word translations mean word translations whose CR is under 50.0%.

6   Conclusion

This paper proposed a new method for automatic extraction of bilingual collocations using **R**ecursive **C**hain-link-type **L**earning (RCL). In this RCL system, various bilingual collocations are extracted efficiently using only character strings of previously-extracted bilingual collocations. Moreover, word translations and bilingual templates are extracted reciprocally, as with a linked chain. Therefore, this RCL system can extract many word translations efficiently from sentence pairs without requiring any static linguistic knowledge or when confronting corpus which contain words with very low frequency of appearance. This study demonstrates that our method is very effective for extracting word translations and thereby building an MT bilingual dictionary.

Future studies will undertake more evaluation experiments using practical data. We also intend to confirm that this RCL system can extract bilingual collocations from sentence pairs using other languages. We infer that this RCL system is a learning algorithm that is independent of a specific language. Moreover, we will apply RCL to other natural language processing systems, *e.g.*, a dialog system, to confirm RCL effectiveness.

References

1. Kumano, A. and H. Hirakawa. 1994. Building an MT Dictionary from Parallel Texts based on Linguistic and Statistical Information. In *Proceedings of Coling '94*.
2. Smadja, F., K. R. McKeown and V. Hatzivassiloglou. 1996. Translating Collocations for Bilingual Lexicons: A Statistical Approach. *Computational Linguistics*, vol.22, no.1, pp.1-38.
3. Brown, R. D. 1997. Automated Dictionary Extraction for "Knowledge-Free" Example-Based Translation. In *Proceedings of TMI '93*.
4. Echizen-ya, H., K. Araki, Y. Momouchi, and K. Tochinai. 1996. Machine Translation Method Using Inductive Learning with Genetic Algorithms. In *Proceedings of Coling '96*.
5. Echizen-ya, H., K. Araki, Y. Momouchi, and K. Tochinai. 2002. Study of Practical Effectiveness for Machine Translation Using Recursive Chain-link-type Learning. In *Proceedings of Coling '02*.
6. Araki, K., Y. Momouchi and K. Tochinai. 1995. Evaluation for Adaptability of Kana-kanji Translation of Non-segmented Japanese Kana Sentences using Inductive Learning. In *Proceedings of Pacling '95*.

Recognition of Named Entities in Spanish Texts*

Sofía N. Galicia-Haro[1], Alexander Gelbukh[2,3], and Igor A. Bolshakov[2]

[1] Faculty of Sciences
UNAM Ciudad Universitaria Mexico City, Mexico
sngh@fciencias.unam.mx
[2] Center for Computing Research
National Polytechnic Institute, Mexico City, Mexico
{gelbukh,igor}@cic.ipn.mx, www.Gelbukh.com
[3] Department of Computer Science and Engineering, Chung-Ang University,
221 Huksuk-Dong, DongJak-Ku, Seoul, 156-756, Korea

Abstract. Proper name recognition is a subtask of Name Entity Recognition in Message Understanding Conference. For our corpus annotation proper name recognition is a crucial task since proper names appear approximately in more than 50% of total sentences of the electronic texts that we collected for such purpose. Our work is focused on composite proper names (names with coordinated constituents, names with several prepositional phrases, and names of songs, books, movies, etc.) We describe a method based on heterogeneous knowledge and simple resources, and the preliminary obtained results.

1   Introduction

A big corpus is being compiled by our research group. Since we defined its size in tenths of million words and its objective as unrestricted text analysis, the easiest and quickest manner to obtain texts was extracting electronic texts from Internet. We selected four Mexican newspapers daily published in the Web with a high proportion of their paper publication. We found that almost 50% of the total unknown words were proper names. This percentage shows the relevance of proper name recognition and it justifies a more wide analysis.

Proper names have been studied in the field of Information Extraction [15] for diverse uses. For example [5] employed proper names for an automatic newspaper article classification. Information Extraction requires the robust handle of proper names for successful performance in diverse tasks as pattern filling with correct entities that perform semantic roles [11]. The research fulfilled in the Message Understanding Conference (MUC) structure entity name task and it distinguishes three types: ENAMEX, TIMEX and NUMEX [4]. ENAMEX considers entities such as organizations (corporations names, government entities, and other type of organizations), persons (persons names, last names), and localities (localities names defined politically or geographically: cities, provinces, countries, mountains, etc.).

---

* Work done under partial support of Mexican Government (CONACyT, SNI, COFAA-IPN), Korean Government (KIPA Professorship for Visiting Faculty Positions in Korea), and ITRI of CAU. The second author is currently on Sabbatical leave at Chung-Ang University.

R. Monroy et al. (Eds.): MICAI 2004, LNAI 2972, pp. 420–429, 2004.
© Springer-Verlag Berlin Heidelberg 2004

In this paper, we are concerned with ENAMEX entity recognition but we focused our work on composite named entities: names with coordinated constituents, names with several prepositional phrases, and names of songs, books, movies, etc. We postponed name classification to future work.

NER works in MUC have been dedicated to English language, they considered complex tools or huge resources. For example, in [12] three modules were used for name recognition: List Lookup (consulting lists of likely names and name cues), Part of speech tagger, Name parsing (using a collection of specialized name entity grammars), and Name-matching (the names identified in the text are compared against all unidentified sequences of proper nouns produced by the part of speech tagger). The system of [14] recognized named entities by matching the input against pre-stored lists of named entities, other systems use gazetteers (lists of names, organizations, locations and other name entities) of very different sizes, from 110,000 names (MUC-7) to 25,000-9,000 names [6].

NER works in Language-Independent Named Entity Recognition, the shared task of Computational Natural Language Learning (CoNLL) covered Spanish in 2002 [13]. A wide variety of machine learning techniques were used and good results were obtained for name entity classification. However composite names were limited: named entities are non-recursive and non-overlapping, in case a named entity is embedded in another name entity only the top level entity was marked, and only one coordinated name appears in the training file.

Since named entities recognition is a difficult task our method is heterogeneous; it is based on local context, linguistic restrictions, statistical heuristics and the use of lists for disambiguation (very small external lists of proper names, one of similes and lists of non ambiguous entities taken from the corpus itself). In this article, we present the text analysis carried out to determine the occurrence of named entities, then we detailed our method and finally we present the obtained results.

2 Named Entities in Newspaper Texts

Two aspects should be considered in named entities recognition: known names recognizing and new names discovering. However, newspaper texts contain a great quantity of named entities; most of them are unknown names. Since named entities belong to open class of words, entities as commercial companies are being created daily, unknown names are becoming important when the entities they referred to became topical or fashioned.

We analyzed Mexican newspaper texts that were compiled from the Web. They correspond to four different Mexican newspaper, between 1998 and 2001. From the analysis, we concluded that almost 50% of total words were unknown words[1]. We found 168,333 different words that were candidates to be named entities since they were initialized or totally fulfilled with capital letters. These capitalized words represent a low percentage from all different words but they appear at least in 50% of the sentences. We present such statistics in Table 1. From those numbers we note the importance of named entities for syntactic analysis of unrestricted texts since 50% to 60% of total sentences include named entities.

---

[1] They were not recognized by our resources: a dictionary with POS and a spelling checker.

Table 1. Statistics of newspaper texts

	Newspapers			
	# 1	#2	#3	#4
# Words	87,597,168	38,387,767	5,652,358	45,702,200
# Sentences	2,927,723	1,328,157	208,298	1,696,358
# Sentences w/ named entities	1,581,225	729,496	100,602	1,007,051

The initial step, for recognition of named entities was identification of context and style. We selected one Mexican newspaper, since we supposed that all newspapers present the named entities in similar manner. We analyzed newspaper #2 and we found that named entities are introduced or defined by means of syntactic-semantic characteristics and local context. The main characteristics observed were:

Conventions. Specific words could introduce names, for example: _coordinadora del programa_ Mundo Maya (Mundo Maya program's coordinator), _subsecretario de Operación Energética de la Secretaría de Energía_ (sub secretary of…), etc.

Redundancy. Information obtained from juxtaposition of named entities and acronyms, for example: _Asociación Rural de Interés Colectivo_ (_ARIC_), two names linked for the same entity by means of specific words: _alias_, (a), for example: … _dinero de Amado Carrillo Fuentes_ **alias** _El Señor de los Cielos_…

Prepositions usage. We consider two cases:

1. Prepositions link two different named entities. For example "a" indicates direction (_Salina Cruz_ **a** _Juchitán_); "en" indicates a specific location (_Tratado sobre Armas Convencionales_ **en** _Europa_), etc.
2. Prepositions are included in the named entities (_Instituto_ **para** _la Protección al Ahorro Bancario, Monumento_ **a** _la Independencia, Centro de Investigaciones y Estudios Superiores_ **en** _Antropología Social_).

Local context. Named entities are surrounded by local context signs. They could be used for identification of book, song and movie names. For example: _Marx escribió La ideología alemana_ (Marx wrote…); …_titulado La celebración de muertos en México_ (titled…), etc. Some verbs (read, write, sing, etc.), some nouns (book, song, thesis, etc.), or proper names of authors often introduce or delimit such kind of names as those underlined.

Sets of names. Named entities could appear as sets of capitalized words. Punctuation (,;) is used to separate them, for example: _Bolivia, Brasil, Uruguay, Ecuador, Panamá,_ or … _de Charles de Gaulle y Gagarin; de Juan Pablo II; de Eva Perón_…

Flexibility. Long named entities do not appear as fixed forms. For ex.: _Instituto para la Protección al Ahorro, Instituto para la Protección al Ahorro Bancario, Instituto para la Protección del Ahorro Bancario,_ all of them correspond to the same entity. More variety exists for those names translated from foreign languages to Spanish.

Coordinated names. Some named entities include conjunctions (y, e, etc.) For example_: Luz y Fuerza del Centro, Margarita Diéguez y Armas, Ley de Armas de Fuego y Explosivos, Instituto Nacional de Antropología e Historia._

Concept names. Some capitalized words represent abstract entities. In a strict sense they could not be considered as named entities and they should be tagged with a different semantic tag. For example: *Las violaciones a la Ley en que algunos ...* (The violations to the Law in which some ...). Such kind of entities should be differentiate from those names representing an abbreviation of longer names (for example: *Ley del Seguro Social*) in a deep understanding level.

3   Named Entities Analysis

In order to analyze how named entities could be recognized by means of linguistics and context rules or heuristics we separate newspaper #2 sentences in two groups:
1. sentences with only one initial capitalized word, and
2. sentences with more than one capitalized word.

Group 1 could not contain named entities since the first word in each sentence could be name entity or one common word. [8] proposed an approach to disambiguate capitalized words when they appear in the positions where capitalization is expected. Their method utilize information of entire documents to dynamically infer the disambiguation clues. Since we have a big collection of texts we could apply the same idea.

We concentrated our analysis in group 2. We built a Perl program that extracts groups of words that we call "compounds", they really are the contexts when named entities could appear. The compounds contain no more than three non capitalized words between capitalized words. We supposed that they should correspond to functional words (prepositions, articles, conjunctions, etc.) in composite named entities (coordinated names and names with several prepositional phrases). The compounds are left and right limited by a punctuation mark and a word if they exist.

For example, for the following sentence:

Un informe oficial aseguró que Cuba invierte anualmente cerca de 100 millones de dólares en tecnologías informáticas y que en el trabajo para enfrentar al error del milenio, el país participó intensamente en el Grupo Regional de México, Centroamérica y el Caribe, con apoyo del Centro de Cooperación Internacional Y2K que funciona en Washington y que fue creado por la Organización de Naciones Unidas.

We obtained the following compounds:

- *que Cuba invierte*
- *el Grupo Regional de México, Centroamérica y el Caribe,*
- *del Centro de Cooperación Internacional Y2K que funciona en Washington y*
- *la Organización de Naciones Unidas.*

From 723,589 sentences of newspaper #2, 1348,387 compounds were obtained. We analyzed randomly approximately 500 sentences and we encountered the main problems that our method should cope with. They are described in the following sections.

3.1 Paragraph Splitting

We observed two problems in paragraph splitting: 1) sentences that should be separated and 2) sentences wrong separated. The causes of such errors were:

1. Punctuation marks. Sentences ending with quotation marks and leaders. For ex.:

"___ película personal." A pesar de ___

It is a competence error since in Spanish the point appears before quotation marks when the whole sentence is wanted to be marked.

2. Abbreviations. For ex., in the following phrase *"Arq."* corresponds to "architect":

___ ante las cámaras de televisión, el Arq. Héctor E. Herrera León ___

[9] consider several methods for determining English abbreviations in annotated corpus: combinations of guessing heuristics, lexical lookup and the document-centered approach. We only consider the first method to automatically obtain a list of abbreviations from newspaper #2. They were obtained with heuristics such as: abbreviations have length less than five characters, they appear after a capitalized word between commas, etc. They mainly correspond to professions and Mexican states.

3. Style. Some sentences show an unclear style. For example, the use of parenthesis

___ de nadie. (Y aunque muchos sabemos que los asaltos están también a la orden del día, precisamente en el día.) No hace mucho ___

The traditional Spanish use of parenthesis is the isolation of a small sentence part.

3.2 Syntactic Ambiguity

We found three main syntactic ambiguities in compounds, introduced by coordination, prepositional phrase attachment, and named entities composed of several words where only the first word is capitalized.

The last one corresponds to titles of songs, movies, books, etc. For example: *Ya en El perro andaluz, su primer filme* ... (Already in The Andalusia dog, his first movie.) The titles appearing in the electronic texts begin with one capitalized word followed by several non capitalized words, and sometimes another name entity embedded. As far as we observed, there are no use of punctuation marks to defined them. This use is different to that considered in the CoNLL-2002 training file, where the included titles are delimited by quotation marks.

Recognition of named entities related to coordination and prepositional phrase attachment is crucial for our objective: unrestricted text analysis. For all singular conjunction cases, dependency grammars assign the following structure to coordinated structures in the surface level: ($\rightarrow$) P1 $\rightarrow$ C $\rightarrow$ P2, where P1 is the sub tree root. In the simpler and more usual case, the components P1 and P2 with the conjunction cover named entities. For example *Luz y Fuerza*. However, there are other cases where the coordinated pair is a sub-structure of the entire name, for example: *Mesa de [Cultura y Derechos] Indígenas*.

The following compounds shows the ambiguity introduced by coordination (the second component is underlined):

- *Comisión Federal de Electricidad y Luz y Fuerza del Centro*, includes two organization names.
- *Margarita Diéguez y Armas y Carlos Virgilio*, includes two personal names.
- *Comunicaciones y Transportes y Hacienda* includes two organization names.

Some compound examples of single names containing coordinated words:

- *Comisión Nacional Bancaria y de Valores*
- *Subsecretario de Planeación y Finanzas*
- *Teatro y Danza de la UNAM*

Prepositional phrase attachment is a difficult task in syntactic analysis. Named entities present similar problem. We consider a diverse criterion than that considered in CoNLL: in case a named entity is embedded in another name entity or in case a named entity is composed of several entities all the components should be determined since syntactic analysis should find their relations for deep understanding in higher levels of analysis. For example:

1. *Teatro y Danza de la UNAM* (UNAM's Theater and Dance)
Teatro y Danza is a cultural department of a superior entity.
2. *Comandancia General del Ejército Zapatista de Liberación Nacional*
Comandancia General (General command) is the command of an entity (army).

A specific grammar for named entities should cope with the already known prepositional phrase attachment problem. Therefore diverse knowledge described in the following section must be included to decide the splitting or joining of named entities with prepositional phrases.

3.3 Discourse Structures

Discourse structures could be another source for knowledge acquisition. Entities could be extracted from the analysis of particular sequences of texts. We are particularly interested in

1. Enumeration that can be easily localized by the presence of similar entities, separated by connectors (commas, subordinating conjunction, etc). For example, in the following sequence:
La Paz, Santa Cruz y Cochabamba
José Arellano, Marco A. Meda, Ana Palencia García y Viola Delgado
2. Emphasizing words or phrases by means of quotation marks and capitalized words.
For example: *"Emilio Chichifet"*, *"Roberto Madrazo es el Cuello"*, *"Gusano Gracias"*, are parodies of well known names and the sentence author denote it by quotation marks.
3. Author's intension. A specific intension could be denoted by capitalized words since author chose the relation in the structure. For example, "Convent" in :
___*una visita al antiguo Convento de la Encarnación, ubicado en*___ ()
___*y así surgió el convento de Nuestra Señora de Balvanera.* ()

The first one shows the author's intension to denote the whole name of the building covering its old purpose. The author's intension in the second one is to make evident to whom is dedicated the convent.

4   Method

We conclude on our analysis that a method to identify named entities in our electronic texts collection should be based mainly on the typical structure of Spanish named entities themselves, on their syntactic-semantic context, on discourse factors and on knowledge of specific composite named entities. Then, our method consists of heterogeneous knowledge contributions.

Local context. Local context has been considered in different tasks. For example, [7] used it for semantic attribute identification in new names. We consider local context to identify names of songs, books, movies, etc. For such purpose a window of two words preceding the capitalized word was defined. In such window a word appearing in a manually compiled list of 26 items plus synonyms and variants (feminine, masculine, plural) was considered a cue that introduce a name of song, book, etc. For example:

- *En su libro La razón de mi vida (Editorial Pax)...* (In his book *The reason of my life* (Pax publisher)
- *...comencé a releer La edad de la discreción de Simone de Beauvoir,...* (I began to reread Simone de Beauvoir's *The age of discretion,*)
- *...en su programa Una ciudad para todos que...* (in his program *A city for all* that)

Some heuristics were determined to obtain the complete name: all posterior words are linked until a specific word or punctuation sign is found. Such word or punctuation sign could be: 1) a name entity, 2) any sign of punctuation in texts (period, comma, semicolon, etc.) and 3) a conjunction.

In the above examples the signs: "(", "*Simone de Beauvoir*" and the conjunction "que" delimit the names. For more complex cases, statistics are included.

The phrases delimited by quotation marks preceded by a cue were also considered as names of songs, books, movies, etc.

Linguistic knowledge. We mainly consider the preposition use, part of speech of words linking groups of capitalized words, and punctuation rules. The linguistic knowledge is settled in linguistic restrictions. For example:

1. Lists of groups of capitalized words are similar entities. Then an unknown name have similar category and the last one should be a different entity coordinated by conjunction. For example: *Corea del Sur, Taiwan, Checoslovaquia y Sudáfrica.*
2. Preposition use, considering the meaning of prepositions for localization, direction, etc. For example:

Preposition *"por"* followed by a undetermined article cannot link groups of person names. For example the compound: *Juan Ramón de la Fuente por la Federación de Colegios de Personal Académico* must be divided in *Juan Ramón de la Fuente* and *Federación de Colegios de Personal Académico.* Therefore, the compound *Alianza por la Ciudad de México* could correspond to a single name.

Two named entities joined by preposition "a" should be separated if they are preceded by preposition indicating an origin position ("de", "desde"). For example: *de Oaxaca a Salina Cruz.*

Heuristics. Some heuristics were considered to separate compounds.

1. Two capitalized words belonging to different list must be separated. For example: "*...en Chetumal Mario Rendón dijo ...*", where *Chetumal* is an item of main cities list and *Mario* is an item of personal names list.
2. One personal name should not be coordinated in a single name entity. For example: *Margarita Diéguez y Armas y Carlos Virgilio*, where Carlos is an item of personal name list.

3. A group of capitalized words with functional words followed by an acronym should be defined a single name if most of initial letters are in the acronym. For example: *FIFA Federación Internacional de la Asociación de Fútbol*; *OAA Administración Americana para la Vejez.*

4. All capitalized words grouped by quotation marks, without punctuation marks, are considered one name entity. For example: "*Adolfo López Mateos*".

Statistics. From newspaper #2 we obtained the statistics of groups of capitalized words, one single word to three contiguous words, and groups of capitalized words related to acronyms. The top statistics for such groups were used to disambiguate compounds joined by

- Functional words. For example, the compound *Estados Unidos sobre México* could be separated in *Estados Unidos* (a 2-word group with high score) and *México* (a 1-word with high score). In the same manner the compound *BP Amoco Plc* is kept as is and *ACNUR Kris Janowski* is separated in *ACNUR* and *Kris Janowski*.

- Prepositions. For example: *Comandancia General del Ejército Zapatista de Liberación Nacional* could be separated in : *Comandancia General* and *Ejército Zapatista de Liberación Nacional*.

Many NER systems use lists of names, for example [6] made extensive use of name lists in their system. They found that reducing their size by more than 90% had little effect on performance, conversely adding just 42 entries led to improved results. [10] experimented with different types of lists in an NER system entered for MUC7. They concluded that small lists of carefully selected names are as effective as more complete lists.

The lists of names used by named entity systems have not generally been derived directly from text but have been gathered from a variety of sources. For example, [2] used several name lists gathered from web sites containing lists of people first names, companies and locations. We also included lists from internet, and a hand made list of similes [1] (stable coordinated pairs) for example: *comentarios y sugerencias, noche y día, tarde o temprano*, (comments and suggestions, night and day, late or early). This list of similes was introduced to disambiguate coordinated groups of capitalized words.

The lists obtained from Internet were: 1) a list of personal names (697 items), 2) a list of the main Mexican cities (910 items) considered in the list of telephone codes.

Application of the method. Perl programs were built for the following steps that have been taken for delimiting named entities:

First step: All composite capital words with functional words are grouped in one compound. We use a dictionary with part of speech to detect functional words.

Second step. Using the previous resources (statistics of newspaper #2 and lists) and the rules and heuristics above described the program decides on splitting, delimiting or leaving as is each compound. The process is 1) look up the compound in the acronym list, 2) decide on coordinated groups using the list of similes, rules (based on enumeration and statistics), 3) decide on prepositional phrases using rules, heuristics and statistics, 4) delimit possible titles using context cues and rules, and 5) decide on the rest of groups of capitalized words using heuristics and statistics.

Table 2. Results in a testing set of sentences

	NUMBER OF:			
	COORD. GROUPS	**PREP. PHRASE GROUPS**	**TITLES**	**ALL**
Precision	56	70	55	90
Recall	49	67	32	88

5 Results

We test the results of our method in 400 sentences of newspaper#4. They were manually annotated and compared against the results obtained with our method. The results are presented in Table 2 where:

Precision: # of correct entities detected / # of entities detected

Recall: # of correct entities detected / # of entities manually labeled (eml)

The table indicates the performance for coordinated names (55 eml), prepositional groups[2] (137 eml) and titles (19 eml). The last column shows the overall performance (1279 eml) including the previous ones. The main causes of errors are: 1) foreign words, 2) personal names missing in the available list, and 3) names of cities.

The overall results obtained by [3] in Spanish texts for name entity recognition were 92.45% for precision and 90.88% for recall. But test file only includes one coordinated name and in case a named entity is embedded in another name entity only the top level entity was marked. In our work the last case was marked incorrect.

The worst result was that of title recognition since 60% of them were not introduced by a cue. Recognition of titles and named entities with coordinated words should require enlargement of current sources. The 40% of coordinated correct entities detection was based on the list of similes that could be manually enlarged.

6 Conclusions

In this work, we present a method to identify and disambiguate groups of capitalized words. We are interested in minimum use of complex tools. Therefore, our method use extremely small lists and a dictionary with part of speech. Since limited resources use cause robust and velocity of execution, important characteristics for processing huge quantity of texts.

Our work is focused on composite named entities (names with coordinated constituents, names with several prepositional phrases, and names of songs, books, movies, etc.) The strategy of our method is the use of heterogeneous knowledge to decide on splitting or joining groups with capitalized words. We confirmed that conventions are very similar in different newspapers then heuristics are applicable in the four newspapers selected.

---

[2] Where all prepositional phrases related to acronyms were not considered in this results.

The results were obtained from 400 sentences that correspond to different topics. The preliminary results shows the possibilities of the method and the required information for better results.

References

1. Bolshakov, I. A., A. F. Gelbukh, and S. N. Galicia-Haro: Stable Coordinated Pairs in Text Processing. In Václav Matoušek and Pavel Mautner (Eds.). Text, Speech and Dialogue. Lecture Notes in Artificial Intelligence, N 2807, Springer-Verlag 2003, pp. 27–35
2. Borthwick et al. Exploiting Diverse Knowledge Sources via Maximum Entropy in Named Entity Recognition Proceedings of the Sixth Workshop on Very Large Corpora (1998)
3. Carreras, X., L. Márques and L. Padró. Named Entity Extraction using AdaBoost In: Proceedings of CoNLL-2002, Taipei, Taiwan (2002) 167-170
4. Chinchor N.: MUC-7 Named Entity Task Definition (version 3.5). http://www.itl.nist.gov/iaui/894.02/related projects/muc/proceedings/muc 7 toc.html# appendices (1997)
5. Friburger, N. and D. Maurel.: *Textual Similarity Based on Proper Names.* Mathematical Formal Information Retrieval (MFIR'2002) 155–167
6. Krupka, G. and Kevin Hausman. Description of the NetOwl(TM) extractor system as used for MUC-7. In Sixth Message Understanding Conference MUC-7 (1998)
7. Mani I., McMillian R., Luperfoy S., Lusher E. & Laskowski S.: Identifying unknown proper names in newswire text. In Pustejovsky J. & Boguraev B. (eds.) Corpus processing for lexical acquisition. MIT Press, Cambridge, MA. (1996)
8. Mikheev A.: A Knowledge-free Method for Capitalized Word Disambiguation. In Proceedings of the 37th Annual Meeting of the Association for Computational Linguistics (1999) 159–166
9. Mikheev A.: Periods, Capitalized Words, etc. Computational Linguistics Vol. 28-3 (2002) 289–318
10. Mikheev A., Moens M., Grover C.: Named Entity Recognition without Gazetteers. In Proceedings of the EACL (1999)
11. MUC: Proceedings of the Sixth Message Understanding Conference. (MUC-6). Morgan Kaufmann (1995)
12. Stevenson, M. & Gaizauskas R.: Using Corpus-derived Name List for name Entity Recognition In: Proc. of ANLP, Seattle (2000) 290-295
13. Tjong Kim Sang, E. F.: Introduction to the CoNLL-2002 Shared Task: Language-Independent Named Entity Recognition. In: Proceedings of CoNLL-2002, Taipei, Taiwan (2002) 155-158
14. Wakao, T., R. Gaizauskas & Y. Wilks.: *Evaluation of an Algorithm for the Recognition and Classification of Proper Names.* In Proceedings of the 16th International Conference on Computational Linguistics (COLING96), Copenhagen (1996) 418–423
15. Wilks Y. Information Extraction as a core language technology. In M. T. Pazienza (ed.), Information Extraction, Springer-Verlag, Berlin (1997)

Automatic Enrichment of a
Very Large Dictionary of Word Combinations
on the Basis of Dependency Formalism*

Alexander Gelbukh[1,2], Grigori Sidorov[1], San-Yong Han[2],
and Erika Hernández-Rubio[1]

[1] Natural Language and Text Processing Laboratory,
Center for Computing Research, National Polytechnic Institute,
Av. Juan Dios Batiz s/n, Zacatenco 07738, Mexico City, Mexico
{gelbukh,sidorov}@cic.ipn.mx, www.gelbukh.com
[2] Department of Computer Science and Engineering, Chung-Ang University,
221 Huksuk-Dong, DongJak-Ku, Seoul, 156-756, Korea
hansy@cau.ac.kr

Abstract. The paper presents a method of automatic enrichment of a very large dictionary of word combinations. The method is based on results of automatic syntactic analysis (parsing) of sentences. The dependency formalism is used for representation of syntactic trees that allows for easier treatment of information about syntactic compatibility. Evaluation of the method is presented for the Spanish language based on comparison of the automatically generated results with manually marked word combinations.

Keywords: Collocations, parsing, dependency grammar, Spanish.

1 Introduction

There is a growing demand for linguistic resources in modern linguistics and especially in natural language processing. One of the important types of resources is the dictionary that reflects mutual combination of words.

The problem concerning the types of information about compatibility of words that should be stored in the dictionary has a rather long history – first papers appeared in 50s. Basically, the focus of attention of the researchers was the concept of collocation and its usage. The main research direction was integration of this concept into lexicographical practice and methods of teaching of foreign languages – how many examples should the dictionaries or textbooks contain, are the examples of collocations just examples of usage or essential part of knowledge of a language (language competence).

---

* Work was done under partial support of Mexican Government (CONACyT, SNI, CGPI-IPN, PIFI-IPN), Korean Government (KIPA Professorship for Visiting Faculty Positions in Korea), and ITRI of CAU. The first author is currently on Sabbatical leave at Chung-Ang University. We thank Prof. Igor A. Bolshakov for useful discussions.

R. Monroy et al. (Eds.): MICAI 2004, LNAI 2972, pp. 430–437, 2004.

After many discussions, the common point is that it is very difficult to find a concise and formal definition of collocation. Nevertheless, it seems that the majority of investigators agree that collocations are very important part of knowledge of language and they are useful for different tasks of automatic natural language processing like automatic translation, text generation, intelligent information retrieval, etc. All this causes the necessity of compilation of specialized dictionaries of collocations and even of free word combinations. See next section for more detailed discussion of the concept of collocations.

There exist many methods of extracting collocations that are based on the analysis of a large corpus [1, 3, 8, 10, 11, 18]. Still, the majority of them are oriented to searching of highly repetitive combinations of words based on measuring of their mutual information. These methods do not guarantee finding the collocations if they do not have sufficiently high frequency. Usually, the great number of collocations does not have this frequency. Besides, the corpus size for such search should be larger than the existing corpora (now measured in gigabytes).

There are several attempts to apply the results of automatic syntactic analysis (parsing) for compilation of dictionaries of collocations [3, 7]. For example, in a recent work Strzalkowski [17] uses the syntactic analysis for improving results of information retrieval by enriching the query. One of the classic works on the theme is [15]. The system *Xtract* is presented that allows for finding repeated co-occurrences of words based on their mutual information. The work consists in three stages, and, at the third stage, the partial syntactic analysis is used for filtering out the pairs that do not have a syntactic relation. Unfortunately, all these methods are applied to word pairs obtained by frequency analysis using a threshold. The aim of all these methods is collocations, and not free word combinations (see below). As far as the *Xtract* system is concerned, it is reported rather high precision (80%) and recall (94%), nevertheless, the evaluation was done by comparison of results with opinion of only one lexicographer, and what is collocation according to the system remains unclear, obviously, they did not process free word combinations.

There are already some resources of the described type available. One of the largest dictionaries of collocations and free word combinations is *CrossLexica* system [4, 5, 6]. It contains about 750,000 word combinations for Russian with semantic relations between the words and the possibilities of inference. There is also this type of resources for the English language, e.g., Oxford dictionary of collocations [14] (170,000 word combinations) or Collins dictionary [2] (140,000 word combinations), though they do not contain semantic relations. This is the lower bound of the dictionary of word combinations, which justifies the term *very large dictionary* in the title of this paper.

In the rest of the paper, we first discuss the concept of collocation and its relation with free word combination, and then we describe the method of enrichment of the dictionary based on automatic syntactic analysis with dependency representation. After this, we evaluate its performance, and finally draw some conclusions.

2   Idioms, Collocations, and Free Word Combinations

Now let us discuss the concept of collocation in more detail. Intuitively, collocation is a combination of words that has certain tendency to be used together. Still, the strength of this tendency is different for different combinations. Thus, collocations can be thought of as a scale with different grades of strength of the inter-word relation, from idioms to free word combinations.

On the one side of the scale there are complete idioms like "*to kick the bucket*", where neither the word "*to kick*", nor "*the bucket*" can be replaced without destroying the meaning of the word combination. In this case, the meaning of the whole is not related with the meaning of the components. In certain much more rare cases, the meaning of the whole has the relation with the meaning of the components, but also it has an additional part that cannot be inferred, e.g., "*to give the breast*" that means "*to feed a baby using breast*". Though the physical situation is described correctly by using the words "*to give*" and "*the breast*", the meaning of "*feeding*" is obtained from the general knowledge about the world. This case can be considered as a little shift on the scale towards free word combinations, nevertheless, this type of combinations are still idioms ("nearly-idiom" according to Mel'chuk [13]).

On the other side of the scale there are free combinations of words, like "*to see a book*", where any word of the pair can be substituted by a rather large class of words and the meaning of the whole is the sum of the meanings of the constituent words.

Somewhere in the middle on this scale, there are lexical functions[1] [13] like "*to pay attention*". In this case, the meaning of the whole is directly related only with one word (in the example above, the word *attention*), while the other word expresses a certain standard semantic relation between actants of the situation. The same relation is found, for example, in combinations like "*to be on strike*", "*to let out a cry*", etc. Usually, for a given semantic relation and for a given word that should conserve its meaning, there is a unique way to choose the word for expressing the relation in a given language. For example, in English it is *to pay*, while in Spanish it is *prestar atención* (lit. *to borrow attention*), in Russian – *obratit' vnimanije* (lit. *to turn attention to*), etc.

As far as free word combinations are concerned, it can be seen that some free word combinations are "less free" than the others, though they are still free word combinations in a sense that the meaning of the whole is sum of meanings of the constituent words. The degree of freedom depends on how many words can be used as substitutes of each word. The less is the number of substitutes, the more "idiomatic" is the word combination, though these combinations will never reach neither idioms nor lexical functions where the meaning cannot be summed.

It is obvious that the restrictions of freedom in free word combinations are the semantic constraints, for example, "*to see a book*" is less idiomatic than "*to read a book*" because there are much more words that can substitute *a book* combining with the verb *to see*, than with the verb *to read*. Namely, practically any physical object can be *seen*, while only objects that contained some written information (or its metaphoric extension, like "*to read signs of anger in his face*") can be *read*.

Another important point is that some free word combinations can have associative relations between its members, e.g., *a rabbit* can *hop*, and *a flea* also, but *a wolf* usually does not *hop*, though potentially it can move in this manner. This makes some combinations more idiomatic because the inter-word relation is strengthened by association.

---

[1] Lexical functions were discovered by Mel'čuk in 70s. Unfortunately, till now they are not reflected systematically even in good dictionaries. This is because the work of finding these functions is rather laborious and it needs very high-level lexicographic competence.

In a strict sense, only lexical functions are collocations, but the common treatment of this concept also expands it to free word combinations that are "more idiomatic". Since there is no obvious border between more idiomatic and less idiomatic, the concept of collocation finally can cover all free word combinations as well, though this makes this concept useless because its purpose is to distinguished idiomatic word combinations from the free ones. Thus, in our opinion, the difficulties related with the concept of collocations are related with impossibility to draw the exact border between it and free word combinations.

Note that the obvious solution to treat collocations only as lexical functions contradicts to the common practice. This demonstrates that, in any case, we need something to distinguish between more and less idiomatic free word combinations. If it is not collocation, then the other term should be invented.

3   Automatic Enrichment of the Dictionary

Traditionally, free word combinations are considered of no interest to linguistics, though, in fact, practically any free word combination is "idiomatic" to a certain grade, because the majority of them have certain semantic restrictions on compatibility. In our opinion, it is so, because, according to the famous Firth idea "you shall know the word by the company it keeps", any word combination is important. For example, in automatic translation, some wrong hypothesis can be eliminated using the context [16]; in language learning, the possibility to know the compatibility allows for much better comprehension of a word; not speaking about automatic word sense disambiguation, where one of the leading approaches is analysis of the context for searching of the compatible words, etc.

Note that manual compilation or enrichment of the dictionary of free word combinations is very time-consuming, for example, *CrossLexica* [5] was being complied during more than 13 years and it is very far from completion yet.

We suggest the following method of automatic enrichment of such kind of dictionaries. Obviously, the method needs some post-verification, because we cannot guarantee the total correctness of the automatic syntactic analysis, still, it is much more efficient than to do it manually.

We work with the Spanish language, but the method is easily applicable for any other language depending on the availability of a grammar and a parser. First, we apply the automatic syntactic analysis using the parser and the grammar of Spanish developed in our laboratory [9]. The results of the syntactic analysis are represented using the formalism of dependencies [12]. It is well known that the expressive power of this formalism is equal to the formalism of constituents, that is much more commonly used, but the procedure of treatment of word combinations is much more easy using dependencies.

The idea of the formalism of dependencies is that any word has dependency relations with the other words in a sentence. The relations are associated directly with word pairs, so it is not necessary to pass the constituency tree in order to obtain the relation. One word always is a head of relation, and the other one is its dependant. Obviously, one headword can have several dependencies.

The problems that are to be solved even using this formalism are the treatment of coordination conjunctions and prepositions, and filtering of some types of relations and some types of nodes (pronouns, articles, etc.).

We store the obtained combinations in the database. All members of the pairs are normalized. Still, some information about the form of the dependant is saved also. In our case, for nouns, we save the information about its number (singular or plural), say, "*play game Sg*" and "*play game Pl*" (the word combination in both cases is "*play game*", and it has an additional mark); for verbs, the information if it is a gerund or a participle is important, etc.

The coordinative conjunctions are heads in the coordinative relation; still, the word combinations that should be added to the dictionary are the combinations with their dependants. For example, *I read a book and a letter*, the combinations that should be extracted are *read book* and *read letter*. Thus, the algorithm detects this situation and generates two virtual combinations that are added to the dictionary.

Treatment of prepositional relation is different from other relations. Since the prepositions usually express grammar relations between words (for example, in other languages these relations can be expressed by grammar cases), the important relation is not relation with the preposition, but the relations between two lexical units connected by the preposition. Still, the preposition itself is also of linguistic interest, so we reflect this relation in the dictionary by the word combination that contains three members: the headword of the preposition, the preposition, and its dependant, e.g., *He plays with a child* gives the combination *play with child*.

Filtering of determined types of nodes is very easy. Since the parser uses the automatic morphological analysis, the morphological information for every word is available. It allows for filtering out the combinations without significant lexical contents, i.e., if at least one word in the combinations belongs to one of the following categories with mainly grammatical meaning. The following categories are discarded in the actual version of the algorithm: pronouns (personal, demonstrative, etc.), articles, subordinate conjunctions, negation (*not*), and numerals. Since the combinations with these words have no lexical meaning, they have no semantic restrictions on compatibility, and can be considered as "absolutely" free word combinations. These combinations are of no interest for the dictionary under consideration.

The other filter is for the types of relations. It depends on the grammar that is used. In our grammar, the following relations are present: *dobj* (direct object), *subj* (subject), *obj* (indirect object), *det* (determinative), *adver* (adverbial), *cir* (circumstantial), *prep* (prepositional), *mod* (modifying), *subord* (subordinate), *coord* (coordinative). Among these relations, the prepositional and coordinative are treated in a special mode, as mentioned above. The only relations left that are of no use for detecting of word combinations are subordinate relation and circumstantial relation.

One of the advantages of the suggested method is that it does not need corpus for its functioning, and, thus, there is no dependency of the corpus size or corpus lexical structure.

Let us have a look at the example of the functioning of the method. The following sentence is automatically parsed.

Conocía todos los recovecos del río y sus misterios.
(I knew all detours of the river and its mysteries.)

The following dependency tree corresponds to this sentence. The hierarchy of depth in the tree corresponds to the relations (number of spaces at the beginning of each line[2]). For example, V(SG,1PRS,MEAN) [*conocía*] is head of the sentence and its dependants are CONJ_C [*y*] and $PERIOD. CONJ_C has dependants N(PL,MASC) [*recovecos*] and N(PL,MASC) [*misterios*], etc. Each line corresponds to a word and contains the word form and its lemma, e.g., *conocía : conocer* (*knew : know*), etc.

```
V(SG,1PRS,MEAN) -> () // Conocía : conocer (knew : know)
   CONJ_C -> (obj) // y : y (and : and)
      N(PL,MASC) -> () // recovecos : recoveco (detours : detour)
         PR -> (prep) // del : del (of the : of the)
            N(SG,MASC) -> (prep) // río : río (river : river)
            ART(PL,MASC) -> (det) // los : el (the : the)
            #*$$todo# -> () <*$$todo> // todos : todo (all : all)
      N(PL,MASC) -> (coord_conj) // misterios : misterio (mysteries : mystery)
         DET(PL,MASC) -> (det) // sus : su (its : it)
   $PERIOD -> () // . : .
```

The following word combinations were detected:

conocer (obj) recoveco (to know detour)
conocer (obj) misterio (to know mystery)
recoveco (prep) [del] río (detour of the river)

It can be seen that the relation (*obj*) corresponds to coordinative conjunction, and then it is propagated to its dependants: *recoveco* (*detour*) and *misterio* (*mystery*). The preposition *del* is part of the 3-member word combination. The articles and pronouns are filtered out (*el, todo, su*), though the algorithm found the corresponding word combinations.

4 Evaluation

We conducted the experiments on the randomly chosen text in Spanish from Cervantes Digital Library. Totally 60 sentences were parsed that contain 741 words, average 12.4 words per sentence. For evaluation, we manually marked all dependency relations in the sentences. Then we compared the automatically added word combinations with manually marked word combinations.

Apart, we used as a baseline a method of gathering the word combinations that takes all word pairs that are immediate neighbors. Also we added certain intelligence to this baseline method – it ignores the articles and takes into account the prepositions. Totally, there are 153 articles and prepositions in the sentences, so the number of words for baseline method is 741-153 = 588.

The following results were obtained. The total number of correct manually marked word combinations is 208. From these, 148 word combinations were found by our

---

[2] Usually, the arrows are used to show the dependencies between words, but it is uncomfortable to work with arrows in text files, so we use this method of representation. Besides, this representation is much more similar to constituency formalism.

method. At the same time, the baseline method found correctly 111 word combinations. On the other hand, our method found only 63 incorrect word combinations, while the baseline method marked as a word combination 588*2 − 1 = 1175 pairs, from which 1175 − 111 = 1064 are wrong pairs.

These numbers give us the following values of precision and recall. Let us remind that precision is the relation of the correctly found to totally found, while the recall is the relation of the correctly found to the total that should have been found. For our method, precision is 148 / (148+63) = 0.70 and recall is 148 / 208 = 0.71. For the baseline method, precision is 111 / 1175 = 0.09 and recall is 111 / 208 = 0.53. It is obvious that precision of our method is much better and recall is better than these parameters of the baseline method.

5   Conclusions

A dictionary of free word combinations is very important linguistic resource. Still, compiling and enriching of this dictionary manually is too time and effort consuming task. We proposed a method that allow for enrichment of such dictionary semi-automatically. The method is based on parsing using the dependency formalism and further extraction of word combinations. Some types of relations and some types of nodes are filtered because they do not represent substantial lexical information. Special processing of coordinative and prepositional relations is performed. The method requires post-processing of obtained word combinations, but only for verification that no parser errors are present.

The results are evaluated on a randomly chosen text in Spanish. Proposed method has much higher precision and better recall than the baseline method.

References

1.   Baddorf, D. S. and M. W. Evens. Finding phrases rather than discovering collocations: Searching corpora for dictionary phrases. In: *Proc. of the 9th Midwest Artificial Intelligence and Cognitive Science Conference (MAICS'98)*, Dayton, USA, 1998.
2.   Bank of English. Collins. http://titania.cobuild.collins.co.uk/boe_info.html
3.   Basili, R., M. T. Pazienza, and P. Velardi. Semi-automatic extraction of linguistic information for syntactic disambiguation. *Applied Artificial Intelligence*, 7:339-64, 1993.
4.   Bolshakov, I. A. Multifunction thesaurus for Russian word processing. In: *Proceedings of 4th Conference on Applied Natural language Processing*, Stuttgart, October 13-15, 1994, p. 200-202.
5.   Bolshakov, I. A., A. Gelbukh. A Very Large Database of Collocations and Semantic Links. In: Mokrane et al. (Eds.) *Natural Language Processing and Information Systems, 5th International Conference on Natural Language Applications to Information Systems NLDB-2000*, Versailles, France, June 2000. Lecture Notes in Computer Science No. 1959, Springer Verlag, 2001, p. 103-114.
6.   Bolshakov, I. A., A. Gelbukh. Word Combinations as an Important Part of Modern Electronic Dictionaries. *Revista SEPLN (Sociedad Español para el Procesamiento del Lenguaje Natural)*, No. 29, septiembre 2002, p. 47-54.

7. Church, K., W. Gale, P. Hanks, and D. Hindle. Parsing, word associations and typical predicate-argument relations. In: M. Tomita (Ed.), *Current Issues in Parsing Technology*. Kluwer Academic, Dordrecht, Netherlands, 1991.

8. Dagan, I., L. Lee, and F. Pereira. Similarity-based models of word cooccurrence probabilities. *Machine Learning*, 34(1), 1999.

9. Gelbukh, A., G. Sidorov, S. Galicia Haro, I. Bolshakov. Environment for Development of a Natural Language Syntactic Analyzer. In: Acta Academia 2002, Moldova, 2002, pp.206-213.

10. Kim, S., J. Yoon, and M. Song. Automatic extraction of collocations from Korean text. *Computers and the Humanities* 35 (3): 273-297, August 2001, Kluwer Academic Publishers.

11. Kita, K., Y. Kato, T. Omoto, and Y. Yano. A comparative study of automatic extraction of collocations from corpora: Mutual information vs. cost criteria. *Journal of Natural Language Processing*, 1(1):21-33, 1994.

12. Mel'čuk, I. *Dependency syntax*. New York Press, Albany, 1988, 428 p.

13. Mel'čuk, I.Phrasemes in language and phraseology in linguistics. In: *Idioms: structural and psychological perspective*, pp. 167-232.

14. *Oxford collocation dictionary*, Oxford, 2003.

15. Smadja, F. Retrieving collocations from texts: Xtract. *Computational linguistics*, 19 (1):143-177, March 1993.

16. Smadja, F., K.R. McKeown, and V. Hatzivassiloglou. Translating collocations for bilingual lexicons: A statistical approach. *Computational Linguistics*, 22(1):1-38, 1996.

17. Strzalkowski, T. Evaluating natural language processing techniques in information retrieval. In: T. Strzalkowski (ed.) Natural language information retrieval. Kluwer, 1999, pp. 113-146.

18. Yu, J., Zh. Jin, and Zh. Wen. Automatic extraction of collocations. 2003.

Towards an Efficient Evolutionary Decoding Algorithm for Statistical Machine Translation*

Eridan Otto and María Cristina Riff

Departamento de Informática
Universidad Técnica Federico Santa María
Valparaíso, Chile
{eotto,mcriff}@inf.utfsm.cl

Abstract. In a statistical machine translation system (SMTS), decoding is the process of finding the most likely translation based on a statistical model according to previously learned parameters. This paper proposes a new approach based on evolutionary hybrid algorithms to translate sentences in a specific technical context. The tests are carried out in the context of Spanish and then translated to English. The experimental results validate the performance of our method.

1 Introduction

Machine Translation (MT) is the process of automatic translation from one natural language to another using a computer program. It is often argued that the problem of MT requires the problem of natural language understanding to be solved first. However, a number of empirical methods of translation works surprisingly well [1]. Between these methods we find Statistical-based methods which try to generate translations based on bilingual text corpora. Statistical machine translation (SMT) was first introduced by Brown et. al. [11] in the 90's. In order to design a SMT, that can translate a source sentence s (for example Spanish) into a target sentence e (for example English), the following components are required:

A *language model* (LM) that assigns a probability $P(e)$ to each English string.

A *translation model* (TM) that assigns a probability $P(s|e)$ to each pair of English and Spanish string.

A *decoder,* it uses for input a new sentence s and tries to generate as output a translated sentence e, that maximizes the translation probability $P(e|s)$, or according to the Bayes Rule, that equivalently maximizes $P(e) \cdot P(s|e)$.

There exists efficient algorithms to estimate the probabilities for a language model, like n-grams models [2]. Translations models are usually based on word replacement models developed by IBM in the early 1990s [11]. These models are referred to as (IBM) Models 1-5. In this paper, we focus our attention on the decoder. A good decoding or search algorithm is critical to the success of

---

* This research was supported by Fondecyt Project 1040364

R. Monroy et al. (Eds.): MICAI 2004, LNAI 2972, pp. 438–447, 2004.

any SMT system [8]. Knight [7] has shown that a decoding problem is a NP-complete. Thus, because of decoding problem complexity, optimal decoders, i.e. decoders that guarantee to find optimal solutions are not used in practical SMT implementation. However, some approximated decoders have been proposed in the literature, as stack or A* algorithms [4], dynamic programming based algorithms [15], and greedy heuristic based algorithms [8,5]. In this paper, we introduce an evolutionary decoding algorithm, in order to improve the efficiency of the translation task in the SMT framework. The translation is performed from Spanish to English sentences, in the context of the computer science technical area. The next section presents the SMT focusing on the IBM 4 Model and a description of the problem. In section 3 we introduce the Evolutionary Decoding Algorithm (EDA) that solves the specific decoding problem. Specialized Operators and mechanisms for parameters control included in EDA are also described. Section 4 presents the tests and results of a sets of translations from Spanish to English. Finally, we will present our conclusions and further work.

2   Statistical Machine Translation

With a few exceptions [14] most SMT systems are based on the noisy channel framework (see figure 1) that have been succesfully applied to speech recognition. In the Machine Translation framework the sentences e is written in a source language, for example English, it is then supposed to be transformed by a noisy probabilistic channel that generates the equivalent target sentences s, which in our case in Spanish. Decoding is the process to take as input any string in the target language s and to find the source e of highest probability that matches the target. The *source language* is the language into which the SMT translates. The two keys notions involved are those of the *language model* and the *translation model*. The language model provides us with probabilities for strings of words or sentences $P(e)$, this is estimated using a monolingual corpus. The source vocabulary $\mathcal{E}$ is defined by the set of all different words in the source corpus, analogously for the target vocabulary $\mathcal{S}$.

Broadly speaking the probabilities for each sentence from source corpus are independently computed. The translation model provides the conditional probabilities. In order to estimate the conditional probability $P(s|e)$, that occurs in

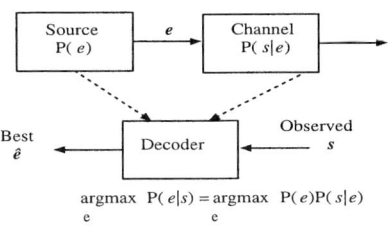

Fig. 1. The noisy channel model

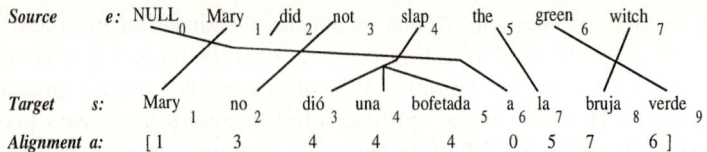

Fig. 2. An example of alignment for English and Spanish sentences

a target sentence s, the target text which translates a text containing the source sentence e requires a large bilingual aligned corpus. Usually the parameters of both the language and the translation models are estimated using traditional maximum likelihood and expectation maximization techniques [3]. Translation is the problem of finding the e that is most probable given s.

Our work is based on the IBM Model 4 translation model. Before we begin to describe this model, it is useful to introduce further notions. In a word aligned sentence-pair, it is indicated which target words correspond to each source word as shown in Figure 2.

For that, the following variables are required:

l the number of words of e, m the number of words of s

e_i the ith word of e, s_j the jth word of s

The fertility of a source word is determined by the number of corresponding words in the target string. In theory, an alignment can correspond to any set of connections. However, IBM's models are restricted to alignments where each target word is at most corresponding to one source word. It is possible to represent the alignment a as a vector $(a_1, a_2, ..., a_m)$, where the value of a_k indicates the word position in the source sentence that corresponds to the kth word in the target sentence. When a target word is not connected to any source word its a_k value is equal to zero, this is illustrated in figure 2 using a NULL symbol.

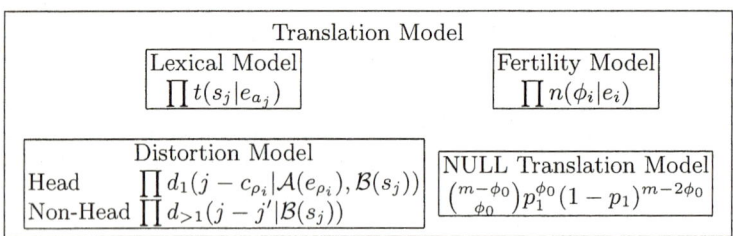

Fig. 3. Translation Model (IBM Model 4)

2.1   IBM Model 4

This model uses the following sub-models to compute the conditional probabilities $P(a, s|e)$:

Lexical Model $t(s_j|e_i)$: Word-for-word translation model, represents the probability of a word s_j corresponding to the word e_i, i.e. e_i is aligned with s_j.

Fertility Model $n(\phi_i|e_i)$: Represents the probability of a source word e_i to be aligned to ϕ_i words in the target sentence s. When a source word is not aligned to a target word ϕ_i it is equal to zero.

Distortion Model d: This model captures the probability that the position of a word in the source language matches in the target language. For this the model uses a cluster technique to define word classes $\mathcal{A}(e_i)$ for the source language and word classes $\mathcal{B}(s_j)$ for the target language. The words are clustered using some similarities criteria. The Distortion model is also broken down into two sets of parameters:

Distortion Probability for head words: A head word is the first s_j word aligned with e_i, with fertility ϕ_i not equal to zero. It is denoted by the following expression: $d_1(j - c_{\rho_i}|\mathcal{A}(e_{\rho_i}), \mathcal{B}(s_j))$, where j is the head word position, ρ_i is the position of the first word fertile to the left of e_i, c_{ρ_i} is the representative position of the word in s of its alignment with e_{ρ_i}. If the fertility of word e_{ρ_i} is greater than one, its representative position is calculated as the upper bound of the average of all words positions aligned with it.

Distortion probability for non-head words: $d_{>1}(j - j'|\mathcal{B}(s_j))$: If the word e_i has a fertility greater than one, j represents the position of a non-head word and j' is the position of the first word to the left of s_j which is aligned with e_i .

NULL Translation Model p_1: this allows for the calculation of the probability of the number of words of s aligned to NULL value in the target sentence.

Finally, the $P(a, s|e)$ is calculated by multiplying all the sub-models probabilities described above. See Brown et. al. [11] and Germann et. al. [8] for a detailed discussion of this translation model and a description of its parameters.

2.2   Decoder Problem

In this paper we focus our attention on the decoding problem. Knight in [7] has shown that for an arbitrary word-reordering, the decoding problem is NP-Complete. Roughly speaking, a decoder takes as input a new sentence s and tries to generate as output a translated sentence e, that maximizes the translation probability $P(e|s)$, where

$$P(e|s) = P(e)P(s|e) \tag{1}$$

and

$$P(s|e) = \sum_a P(a, s|e) \tag{2}$$

is the addition of $P(a, s|e)$ over all possible alignments a. In practice it is infeasible to consider all m^{l+1} alignments. Thus, an approximate value of $P(s|e) \sim P(a, s|e)$ is used to find the most probable $< e, a >$ that maximizes $P(e)P(a, s|e)$.

3   Evolutionary Decoding Algorithm

Evolutionary algorithms (EAs) [9] start by initializing a set of possible solutions called individuals. It is an iterative process that tries to improve the average

Problem s = Mary no   dio una bofetada a la   bruja verde
Chromosome = [1 3   4   4   4   0 5 7 6] (NULL, Mary,did,not,slap,the,green,witch)
    |___ Alignment structure a ___| |___ Translation structure e ___|

Fig. 4. Example of Chromosome

fitness of a set of individuals by applying a transformation procedure to a set of selected individuals to construct a new population. After some criterion is met, the algorithm returns the best individuals of the population. In this section we present the components of an evolutionary decoding algorithm (EDA), specially designed to solve the decoding problem. The goal of EDA is to find both good alignments and sentences translated.

3.1   Individuals Representation

A chromosome is composed of two related structures: An alignment structure and a translation structure. The alignment structure as defined in section 2, that is a vector of a fixed length of integers a_j. The translation structure is a string of variable length of tokens e_i and it represents a translated sentence. Figure 4 shows the representation of the example of the figure 2. This representation contains all information that the algorithm requires to do a fast evaluation and to use specialized genetic operators.

3.2   Initial Population

To generate the initial population we developed a greedy randomized construction heuristic. This method attempts to assure diversity of the initial population. The algorithm is presented in figure 5. For selection, roulette wheel method [9] is used. EDA also uses elitism.

Procedure Generate Initial-Population
Begin
For each word s_j of the sentence s to be translated
    Generate its Restricted Candidate List (RCL_j) composed by cl
    words belonging to $\mathcal{E}$, which have the higher $ti(e_i|s_j)^1$ probabilities
        For l=1 to popsize
            For j=1 to m
                $Chrom[l].e_j = random(RCL_j)$
                $Chrom[l].a_j = j$
End

Fig. 5. Structure of Initial Population Algorithm

---

[1] ti from lexical model, represents the probability of a word e_i is a translation of a word s_j

3.3   Fitness Function

In order to have a better and significant discrimination between the fitness values, we define the following evaluation function:

$$\hat{e} = \arg\min_{e} \left(-log(P(e)) - log(P(s|e))\right) \tag{3}$$

The *log* function is monotonic, thus the lowest fitness value should correspond to the best translation. It works according to the training parameters of both models. Furthermore, it simplifies the partial evaluations of all models.

3.4   Specialized Recombination Operators

We designed three different recombination operators. The goal is exchanging translation information between the parents to create a new best individual. All of these operators create two offsprings, but select the best of them to continue to the next generation. The figure 6 shows an example of applying each operator for the same sentence to be translated.

Source sentence	"La cantidad de variables es desconocida"
Parent I	[0 1 2 3 4 5] (NULL, Quantity,of,variables,is,unknown)
Parent II	[1 2 0 3 5 4] (NULL, The,amount,variables,unknown, holds)
One Point Alignment Crossover	
Offspring I	[**1 2 0** ǀ 3 4 5] (NULL,**The,amount**,variables,is,unknown)
Offspring II	[**0 1 2** ǀ 3 5 4] (NULL,**Quantity, of**,variables,unknown, holds)
Lexical Exchange Crossover	
Offspring I	[0 1 2 3 4 5] (NULL,**Amount**,of ,variables,**holds** ,unknown)
Offspring II	[1 2 0 3 5 4] (NULL,The,**quantity**,variables,unknown,**is**)
Greedy Lexical Crossover	
Offspring I	[0 1 2 3 4 5] (NULL,**Amount**,of, ,variables,is,unknown)
Offspring II	[1 2 0 3 5 4] (NULL,The,amount,variables,unknown, **is**)

Fig. 6. Example of Recombination Operators

One Point Alignment Crossover: This operator makes a crossover on the alignment part of the representation, the translation structure is changed according to the new alignment obtained in each offspring. It is shown in figure 7.
Lexical Exchange Crossover: This is a fast operator that focuses on the exchange lexical components of the chromosome. Both children inherit an alignment structure from their parents. In order to construct the child translation structure, synonymous words from both parents are interchanged according to its alignment.
Greedy Lexical Crossover: This algorithm tries to find a good alignment. Each child has the same alignment structure of each parent. In order to construct each child translation structure, the best translated word for s_j from both parents is selected using the lexical model $t(s_j|e_i)$. This word is located in each child translation structure in the position determined by its alignment.

Procedure `One Point Alignment Crossover` $(Parent_1, Parent_2)$
Begin
`Randomly select a position p in the alignment section`
`Cross the section alignment of the parents from 1 to p positions`
`Construct the translation structure of each offspring according to the new`
`alignment, inheriting the corresponding words from the parents`
End

Fig. 7. Structure of One Point Alignment Crossover

3.5 Specialized Asexual Operators

We propose two exploration operators which help the algorithm to escape from a local optima:

Mutation Word: This operator acts in the translation structure selecting a word s_k. The current word e_i that translates s_k is replaced by a randomly selected synonym word from (RCL_k).

Simple Swap: This operator randomly selects the position of two words on the translation structure and swaps their words. It modifies the alignment structure according to the new words positions.

Because it is a complex problem [6], we also include two hybrids operators which perform a local search procedure.

Language Model Local Search: It is a local search operator that works on the language model. It is a hill-climbing procedure which goal is to improve the language model probability that is calculated using trigrams partitions. The operator analyzes each sequence of three consecutive words of the translation structure. It uses a partial evaluation of the six permutations in order to select the best ordering trigram between them. Finally, when all trigrams have been analyzed and probably changed the algorithm makes a global evaluation to accept or reject the new individual.

Translation Model Local Search: This is a best improvement operator that uses the features of IBM model 4. It works with the fertility concept. The algorithm is shown in figure 8.

It is an exhaustive procedure that at the beginning tries to insert zero fertility words from the vocabulary in the translation structure. In second step deletes zero fertility words included in the translation structure which increases the evaluation function value. The next step is focused on fertility. The idea is to increase words fertility of the translation structure in order to reduce the number of words in the translation. This augmentation of fertility is accepted only if the evaluation function improves.

3.6 Parameter Control Mechanisms in EDA

The algorithm manages the most critical parameters as recombination and mutation operators probabilities with an adaptive parameter control strategy. The goal is to find a better combination of the parameters changing their values during the execution according to the state of the search [12]. In the beginning all

Procedure `Translation Model Local Search` (*Chromosome*)
Begin
For each word e_z with zero fertility in $\mathcal{E}$
    Tries to insert e_z in the position of the translation structure
    which gives the best improvement of the evaluation of the language model
For each word e_i with zero fertility in the translation structure
    Delete e_i when this action improves the evaluation function
For i_1=1 **to** l
    For $i_2 = 1$ **to** l
      If $i_1 \neq i_2$
      If $\phi_{i_1} > 1$ **and** $n(\phi_{i_1}|e_{i_1}) > 0$
        link all s_j **words aligned with** e_{i_2} **to** e_{i_1}
        delete e_{i_2} **from the translation structure**
End

Fig. 8. Structure of Translation Model Local Search

the operators probabilities are equal. The algorithm computes a ranking based on the accumulated statistical information during g generations. It classifies the operators according to their successfulness at finding good offsprings. It gives a reward to the operator that produces the better offsprings increasing its probability. Therefore, the probabilities of the worse operators are reduced. It is represented by the following equation:

$$P_{i,t+1} = (1 - \alpha) \cdot R_{i,t} + \alpha \cdot P_{i,t} \tag{4}$$

where $P_{i,t}$ is the probability of the operator i in the generation t, $R_{i,t}$ is the reward and α, a momentum parameter used to smooth the probabilities changes.

4   Experimental Results

We used articles from the bilingual ACM crossroads magazine[2] construct the corpus, shown in the table 1. We obtained 4812 bilingual sentences english-spanish in the context of computer science, of which 4732 sentences are used for training and 80 sentences for testing.

Table 1. Training and test conditions for the computational corpus.

		Spanish	English
Vocabulary		8681	6721
Training:	Sentences	4732	
	Words	92933	84650
Test:	Sentences	80	
	Words	1125	1051

---

[2] http://www.acm.org/crossroads

We used CMU-Cambridge Statistical Language Modeling Toolkit v2[3] for the training language model. GIZA++[4] The toolkit permitted to estimate the parameters of the translation model.

The algorithm works with the following tuned parameters: population size 50, maximum number of generations 50 and $cl = 15$. The more critical parameters use a dynamic adaptive parameter control mechanism described in section 3.7, with $\alpha = 0.4$, $g = 5$ and rewards matrix $0.5, 0.35, 0.15$. The hardware platform was a PC Pentium III, 870 Mhz, with 256 Mb RAM under Linux 9.0.

Performance Measures: There are two widely used metrics [13] to measure quality in MT: Word Error Rate (WER) and Position-independent Error Rate (PER). WER corresponds to the number of transformations (insert, replace, delete) to be done to the translation solution generated by EDA, in order to obtain the reference translation. PER is similar to WER, but it only takes into account the number of replace actions to do.

4.1   Tests

The algorithm is evaluated using two tests classes: the first one is a comparison between EDA and the Greedy Decoder *isi rewrite decoder v.0.7b*[5] which is based on the work of Germman et. al. [8]. Both decoders used the same language model, the same translation model and they were trained with the same corpus. Finally, from the translations obtained by using as a decoder our evolutionary algorithm is compared to other general domain public translators. Table 2 shows EDA outperforms the greedy decoder. We remarked that EDA obtains better alignments of the sentence than the greedy decoder and the translation generated by it are closest to the reference sentence. The results of EDA are more remarkable in WER than PER, because PER takes into account either the words but not the full sentence alignment. The specialized evolutionary operators enables the algorithm to do a search focused on both the words and their alignment. Finally, we compare our results with two public domain translators: Babelfish[6] and SDL International[7]. EDA outperforms their translations quality because it was especially trained and designed for computer science context.

5   Conclusions

Using an evolutionary approach to translate with the SMT framework is feasible and comparable in quality with others techniques using the same framework and other kinds of translators. General translators are powerful for a wide application areas, in contrast EDA shows a better performance due to its specific context. There are a variety of statistical translation models, all of them need a decoder for

---

[3] http://mi.eng.cam.ac.uk/ prc14/toolkit.html

[4] http://www-i6.informatik.rwth-aachen.de/web/Software/GIZA++.html

[5] http://www.isi.edu/natural-language/software/decoder/manual.html

[6] http://babelfish.altavista.com/

[7] http://ets.freetranslation.com/

Table 2. Experimental results of translations according to the length of sentences

Type of Algorithm		WER %					Avg.	PER %					Avg.
Sentence Length		8	10	12	16	18		8	10	12	16	18	
Statistical	EDA	18.7	27.6	40.2	36.5	34.8	31.5	17.2	24.8	35.4	32.0	29.1	27.7
	Greedy	29.7	41.3	51.4	44.6	47.7	42.9	20.2	31.2	37.9	33.5	30.5	30.7
General	BabelFish	43.2	57.2	58.9	56.2	47.0	52.5	32.5	41.0	47.7	41.6	34.5	39.5
Pupose	SDL Int.	40.1	60.2	61.8	67.7	50.5	56.1	29.1	45.3	48.5	52.7	43.6	43.8

translation, the results suggest that our technique is a good option to implement a decoder by adapting EDA to the features of an specific statistical model.

References

1. D. Arnold, L. Balkan, S. Meier, R.L. Humphreys, and L. Sadler. Machine Translation: an Introductory Guide. Essex University, 1995.
2. Stanley F. Chen and Joshua T. Goodman. An empirical study of smoothing techniques for language modeling. 34th Annual Meeting of the Association for Computational Linguistics, (1):3-25, 1996.
3. A. Dempster, N. Laird, and D. Rubin. Maximum likelihood from incomplete data via the em algorithm. Journal of the Royal Statistical Society, (39:1):1-38, 1977.
4. H. Ney F. Och. Statistical machine translation. EAMT Workshop, pp 39-46, 2000.
5. U. Germann. Greedy decoding for statistical machine translation in almost linear. Proceedings HLT-NAACL, pages 72-79, 2003.
6. W. Hart and R. Belew. Optimization with genetic algorithms hybrids that use local search. Addison Wesley, 1996.
7. K. Knight. Decoding complexity in word-replacement translation models. Computational Linguistics, (25:4), 1999.
8. U. Germann M. Jahr K. Knight D. Marcu and K. Yamada. Fast decoding and optimal decoding for machine translation. Proceedings of ACL 2001.
9. Z. Michalewicz. Genetics Algorithms + Data Structures = Evolution Programs. WNT, Warsaw, 1996.
10. F. Josef Och N. Ueffing and H. Ney. Conference on empirical methods for natural language processing. IBM Journal Reseach and Development, pp.156-163, 2002.
11. V. Della Pietra P. Brown, S. Della Pietra and R. Mercer. The mathematics of statistical machine translation: Parameter estimation. Computational Linguistics, (19:2):263-312, 1993.
12. M. Riff and X. Bonnaire. Inheriting parents operators: A new dynamic strategy for improving evolutionary algorithms. 13th International Symposium on Methodologies for Intelligent Systems, pp. 333-341, 2002.
13. C. Tillmann S. Vogel H. Ney H. Sawaf and A. Zubiaga. Accelerated dp-based search for statistical translation. 5th European Conference on Speech Communication and Technology, (Vol 5):2667-2670, 1997.
14. H. Ney S.Vogel and C. Tillman. Hmm-based word alignment in statistical translation. 16th Int. Conf. On Computational Linguistics,(16):836-841, 1999.
15. T. Watanabe and E. Sumita. Bidirectional decoding for statistical machine translation. 19th Int. Conf. On Computational Linguistics, pp.1079-1085, 2002.

The Role of Imperatives in Inference, Agents, and Actions

Miguel Pérez-Ramírez[1] and Chris Fox[2]

[1]Instituto de Investigaciones Eléctricas.
Reforma 113. Cuernavaca Mor., México. CP 62490.
mperez@iie.org.mx
[2]University of Essex. Computer Science Department
Wivenhoe Park, Colchester CO4 3SQ, Essex, UK.
foxcj@essex.ac.uk

Abstract. The aim of this paper is to present a model for the interpretation of imperative sentences in which reasoning agents play the role of speakers and hearers. A requirement is associated with both the person who makes and the person who receives the order which prevents the hearer coming to inappropriate conclusions about the actions s/he has been commanded to do. By relating imperatives with the actions they prescribe, the dynamic aspect of imperatives is captured and by using the idea of encapsulation, it is possible to distinguish what is demanded from what is not. These two ingredients provide agents with the tools to avoid inferential problems in interpretation.

1 Introduction

There has been an increasing tendency to formalize theories which describe different aspects of computational agents trying to emulate some features of human agents, such as reasoning, that are required to perform an autonomous interpretation of language, and to follow a course of action. Another example is to formalise relations of power among agents, where an agent makes other agents satisfy his/her goals. (e.g. [10;11]). Here we present a model for imperatives interpretation in which agents represent speakers and hearers. Once an agent has uttered an order, the main role of the agent addressed is to interpret it and decide what course of actions s/he needs to follow, so that the order given can be satisfied. Nevertheless, such autonomous reasoning behaviour might lead to wrong conclusions, derived from a weak formalization. In the specific case of the interpretation of imperatives, there is an additional problem: imperatives do not denote truth values. The term *practical inference* has been used to refer to inferential patterns involving imperatives. For instance, if an agent A is addressed with the order *Love your neighbours as yourself!* and A realizes that Alison, is one of those objects referred to as his/her neighbours, then A could infer *Love Alison as yourself.* Even though the order given cannot be *true* or *false* [9; 14; 19].

Formalizations in which imperatives are translated into statements of classical logic are problematic as they can lead an agent to draw inappropriate conclusions. In those approaches, if an agent A is given the order *Post the letter!*, s/he can

R. Monroy et al. (Eds.): MICAI 2004, LNAI 2972, pp. 448–457, 2004.
© Springer-Verlag Berlin Heidelberg 2004

erroneously infer that s/he has been ordered to *Post the letter or burn the letter!* by using the rule of introduction for disjunction.

Thus, having a choice, agent A might decide to burn the letter. In deontic approaches this is known as the Paradox of Free Choice Permission, which was thought to be an unsolved problem as recently as 1999 [18].

Here we present a model which does not suffer from this kind of paradoxical behavior. It involves the following ingredients a) *agents* with the ability to interpret imperative sentences within b) a *context*. It also captures c) *the dynamic aspect of imperatives*, so that imperatives are not translated into truth-denoting statements. Finally, d) *encapsulation* makes agents capable of distinguishing what is uttered from what is not, so avoiding 'putting words in the mouth of the speaker'.

The rest of the paper is organized as follows. First as a preamble to the model, the concepts of imperative, context and requirement are defined. Then a formalization is presented followed by examples illustrating that the model overcomes inferential problems in the interpretation of imperatives. The paper ends with some conclusions.

2   Analysis

In this section, we describe some of the main concepts which need to be addressed by the model in which agents interpret imperatives. As a first step we define imperative sentences as they are considered in this paper.

Definition: Imperative

> Imperatives are sentences used to ask someone to do or not to do something and that do not denote truth-values.

This definition introduces a distinction between different sentences used to ask someone to do something. Following the definition, *Come here!* might convey the same request as *I would like you to come here*. However the former does not denote a truth value, whereas the latter does it. The former provides an example of the kind of sentences that we shall address here. It is worth to mention that the 'something' which is requested in an imperative shall be called a *requirement*. Other examples of imperatives are: a) direct: *Come here!* ; b) negative: *Don't do that!*; c) conjunctive: *Sit down and listen carefully!*; d) disjunctive: *Shut up or get out of here!*; e) conditional: *If it is raining, close the window!*

2.1   Context

It is widely accepted that the interpretation of utterances is context dependent. For instance the imperative *Eat!*, said by a mother to her son, might be an order. However said to a guest it might be only an invitation to start eating. The real meaning depend on context.

Many authors, agree that context is related to people's view or perception of the world or a particular situation rather than the world or the situation themselves [2; 16]. That is, context is conceived in terms of what agents have in their minds. After all this is what an agent uses to interpret a sentence. This might include intentions, beliefs, knowledge etc. However we will subscribe to the following definition.

Definition: Context

> A context is a consistent collection of propositions that reflects a relevant subset of agents' beliefs.

This view will not commit us here to an ontology or classification of components or to the use of operators such as **B** for beliefs and **K** for knowledge (Turner [17]). We simply assume that all that which constitutes a context can be represented in terms of propositions so the context is viewed as a consistent set of propositions [3].

2.2 Dynamic Aspect of Imperatives

Different authors have related imperatives and actions (Ross [14], von Wright [18], Hamblin [6] p. 45 and Segerberg [15] among others). Sometimes it is said that imperatives prescribe actions. Nevertheless, it would be more precise to say that imperatives possess a dynamic aspect. For instance, *I would like you to open the door*, and *Open the door!* might convey the same request. However the former is a statement which denotes a truth value. It can be true or false within a state of affairs, but there is not a dynamic aspect in it. However the latter, does not denote a truth value, but if we assume that it is uttered in a state of affairs in which the door is closed, it demands another future and wished state of affairs in which the door is open. That is, it demands a change of states, it involves a dynamic aspect (Fig. 1). This suggests that translating imperatives into statements is the wrong approach; it does not model a basic aspect of imperatives.

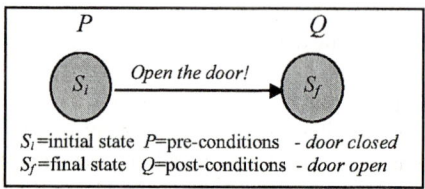

S_i=initial state P=pre-conditions *- door closed*
S_f=final state Q=post-conditions *- door open*

Fig. 1. Dynamic aspect of imperatives

2.3 Evaluation of Imperatives and Correctness

When an agent interprets an imperative, s/he also evaluates it. For instance in the example above, *Open the door!* would not make sense in a state of affairs where the door is already open. It seems that imperatives impose some pre-conditions that the agent verifies during the process of interpretation; the door must be closed. Complying with an imperative will produce a result, a post-condition which shall indicate that the order has been satisfied; the door will be open. Thus, the dynamic aspect of imperatives provides us with at least three components, namely pre-conditions, imperative, and post-conditions. This resembles what is known as Hoare's triple [8]. In 1969 Hoare proposed a logic to verify correctness of programs. He proposed to evaluate triples $P\{S\}Q$, where S is a program, P are its pre-conditions, and Q are its post-conditions. According to Hoare, the program S is correct iff the assertion P is *true* before initiation of S, and then the assertion Q is *true* on its completion. Since the interpretation of imperatives can be construed as involving a verification process, here we adopt the concept of *correctness of an imperative* which is defined analogously by using Hoare's triple $P\{Imp\}Q$.

Definition: Correctness of an Imperative

> The imperative *Imp* is correct with respect to a state of affairs Si iff P holds in S_i and Q holds w.r.t the state S_f reached after the imperative is satisfied.

An imperative is satisfied when the agent addressed, complies with the imperative, reaching the state wished by the speaker.

2.4 Encapsulation

If a person is given the order *Close all the windows!* while being in a house, and s/he realizes that the kitchen's window is open, then the agent might conclude that s/he should close that windows, as a derivation of the order given. However the person will not assume that his/her inferential derivation *Close the kitchen's window*, means that it is an imperative uttered by the speaker. An agent should also distinguish between uttered and derived requirements.

Now we will present the model, illustrating how it is able to describe the main features of imperatives and how it overcomes the paradoxical behavior faced by other approaches.

3 Model

L_{ImpA} is a dynamic language, defined along the lines of first-order dynamic logic as in Harel [7]. In this language Hoare's triples can be represented and, therefore, so can the concept of requirement. Ability of an agent (actions that an agent is able to perform) also can be represented and its semantics will allow to verify the validity of these concepts with respect to context.

3.1 Definition of Sets

We define the following sets. $C=\{c, c_1, c_2,...\}$ is a set of constant symbols. Analogously we define set for variable symbols (V); function symbols (F); regular constant symbols (C); speaker constant symbols (CS); speaker variable symbols (S); hearer constant symbols (CH); hearer variable symbols (H); atomic actions ($AtAct$); atomic predicate symbols ($AtPred$); and we assume that $AC= C \cup CS \cup CH$ and $AV= V \cup S \cup H$.

3.2 Definition of Terms

Terms are defined recursively by: $t ::= c|cs|ch|v|s|h|f(t_1, t_2, ..., t_n)$. Thus, a term is a regular constant (c), a speaker constant (cs), a hearer constant (ch), a regular variable (v), a speaker variable (s), a hearer variable (h) or a function ($f(t_1, t_2, ..., t_n)$) of arity n (n arguments), where $t_1, t_2, ..., t_n$ are terms. The expressions $ts ::= cs|s$ and $th ::= ch|h$ define the terms for speaker and hearers respectively as constants or variables.

3.3 Definition of wff of the Language L_{ImpA}

The set FOR contains all possible wffs in L_{ImpA} and the set Act contains all possible actions defined in the category of actions. The definition of the language L_{ImpA} is given by $\phi ::= p(t_1, t_2, ..., t_n)|t_1=t_2|\neg\phi\ |\phi_1 \wedge \phi_2\ |\exists x\phi\ |[\alpha]\phi$. In other words, if $p \in AtPred$, $t_1, t_2, ..., t_n$ are terms, $x \in V$, and $\alpha \in Act$, then $p(t_1, t_2, ..., t_n)$ is an atomic predicate, with arity n. $t_1=t_2$ is the equality test (=). $\neg\phi$ is the negation of ϕ. $\phi_1 \wedge \phi_2$ is the conjunction of ϕ and ψ. $\exists x\phi$ is the existential quantifier. $[\alpha]\phi$ is a modal expression indicating that ϕ holds after the action α is performed. The usual abbreviations are assumed: $\phi_1 \vee \phi_2 = \neg(\neg\phi_1 \wedge \neg\phi_2)$, $\phi_1 \rightarrow \phi_2 = \neg\phi_1 \vee \phi_2$, $\phi_1 \leftrightarrow \phi_2 = (\phi_1 \rightarrow \phi_2) \wedge (\phi_2 \rightarrow \phi_1)$, $\forall x\phi = \neg\exists x\neg\phi$ and $<\alpha>\phi = \neg[\alpha]\neg\phi$.

3.4 Category of Actions

The set Act of actions is defined as follows: $\alpha ::= a(t_1, t_2, ..., t_n)|\phi?|\alpha_1;\alpha_2|\alpha_1+ \alpha_2|(\alpha)_{ts,th}|(\alpha)_{th}$. In other words, if α, α_1, $\alpha_2 \in Act$, $t_1, t_2, ..., t_n$ are terms and ts, th are terms for speaker and hearer respectively then $a(t_1, t_2, ..., t_n)$ is the atomic action. $\alpha_1;\alpha_2$ is the sequential composition of actions. $\alpha_1+\alpha_2$ is the disjunction of actions. $\phi?$ is a test and it just verifies whether ϕ holds or not. $(\alpha)_{ts,th}$ is a *requirement*, an action requested directly or derived from a requested one by a speaker ts to a hearer th. $(\alpha)_{th}$ is an action that a hearer th is able to do. In this way it is kept track of the agents involved in a requirement, either uttered or derived.

3.5 Representation of Requirements

Requirements are represented in terms of actions with explicit reference to the speaker who demands, and the hearer addressed.

Because of the dynamic aspect of imperatives, they are associated with the actions they prescribe and therefore the dynamic operators are used among them. Thus, the sequencing operator (;) models a conjunction of requirements the choice operator (+) models a disjunction of requirements, and a conditional requirement is represented by using the symbol '$\Rightarrow$', where $(\phi \Rightarrow \alpha) = (\phi?;\alpha)$. Following Harel [7] and Gries [5] a Hoare's triple $P\{\alpha\}Q$ can be represented in L_{ImpA} as $P \rightarrow [\alpha]Q$. Thus, $P \rightarrow [(a)_{ts,th}]Q$ is an atomic requirement, $P \rightarrow [(\alpha_1;\alpha_2)_{ts,th}]Q$ is a conjunction of requirements, $P \rightarrow [(\alpha_1+\alpha_2)_{ts,th}]Q$ is a disjunction of requirements, and $P \rightarrow [(\phi?;\alpha)_{ts,th}]Q$ is a conditional requirement.

3.6 Axioms

A0) T (any tautology); **A1)** $[\phi?;\alpha]\psi \leftrightarrow \phi\rightarrow[\alpha]\psi$; **A2)** $[(\phi?;\alpha)_{ts,th}]\psi \leftrightarrow \phi\rightarrow[(\alpha)_{ts,th}]\psi$; **A3)** $[(\phi?;\alpha)_{th}]\psi \leftrightarrow \phi\rightarrow[(\alpha)_{th}]\psi$;   **A4)** $[\alpha_1;\alpha_2]\phi \leftrightarrow [\alpha_1]([\alpha_2])\phi$; **A5)** $[\alpha_1+\alpha_2]\phi \leftrightarrow [\alpha_1]\phi\wedge[\alpha_2]\phi$; **A6)** $[\phi?]\psi \leftrightarrow \phi\rightarrow\psi$; **A7)** $[\alpha](\phi\rightarrow\psi) \rightarrow [\alpha]\phi\rightarrow[\alpha]\psi$; **A8)** $\forall x\phi(x) \rightarrow \phi(t)$ provided that t is free in $\phi(x)$; **A9)** $\forall x(\phi\rightarrow\psi) \rightarrow \phi\rightarrow\forall x\psi$ provided that x is not free in ϕ. Furthermore we can relate requirements and ability of hearers: **shA1)** $[(\alpha)_{ts,th}]\psi \rightarrow [(\alpha)_{th}]\psi$; **hA2)** $[(\alpha)_{th}]\psi \rightarrow [\alpha]\psi$.

Axioms, from A0)-A7) are standard in Dynamic Logic, A2) and A3) explicitly include speakers and hearers and A8)-A9) are standard in predicate logic respectively. shA1) is analogous to Chellas (1971: p. 125) axiom where 'ought' implies 'can' in his model of imperatives through Obligation and Permission. Here shA1) expresses that if α is demanded for ts to th, is correct, that implies that there is some action, usually a sequence $\alpha=a_1;a_2; \dots ;a_n$ of actions, such that hearer is able to perform it, so that α can be satisfied. hA2) emphasizes that any action a hearer is able to do is simply an action in the nature.

3.7 Inference Rules

a) Modus Ponens **(MP)**: If ϕ and $\phi\rightarrow\phi$ then ϕ; b) Necessitation rule **(Nec)**: If ϕ then $[\alpha]\phi$; c) Universal generalization **(UG)**: If ϕ then $\forall x\phi$ provided x is not free in ϕ.

3.8 Interpretation

The interpretation for L_{ImpA} and its soundness follows Harel's (1979) semantics for first-order dynamic logic. A model ($\mathcal{M}$) for L_{ImpA} is presented elsewhere [12]. Due to the lack of space, we do not repeat the details here. The model uses a possible worlds semantics in which actions define sets of pairs of states (w, w') such that the performing of an action starting in state w reaches state w'. If a state w satisfies a formula ϕ we use the notation $w\vDash\phi$.

3.9 Truth with Respect to a Context

Let $k=\{\phi_0, \phi_1, \dots, \phi_n\}$ represent our context, where for $i=1,n$, $\phi_i\in FOR$. We may also identify the set of states defined by our context as follows. $v'(k) = \{w|$ For every $\phi\in k$, $w\vDash\phi\}$. We use the notation $k\vDash_\mathcal{M}\phi$ to indicate that ϕ is *true* in the model $\mathcal{M}$ with respect to context k, for any assignment τ. We abbreviate $k\vDash_\mathcal{M}\phi$ simply as $k\vDash\phi$. When ϕ is *not true* at k under L_{ImpA} we can write $k\nvDash\phi$. Thus, if $\phi\in FOR$, $k\vDash\phi$ iff for every w if $w\in v'(k)$ then $w\vDash\phi$. In this model we are not providing a detailed treatment of beliefs, that is why we assume that in expressions involving more than one agent, context simply represents a common set of beliefs shared by the agents involved.

3.10 Hoare Style Rules

The following are derived rules, which operate between actions and requirements. *Pre* usually indicates pre-conditions and *Pos* post-conditions. The equality $Pre\{\alpha\}Pos=$ $Pre{\to}[\alpha]Pos$ restricts both sides to hold in the same context.

(I;) Introduction for composition:
    If $\vdash Pre \to[\alpha_1]Pos'$ and $\vdash Pos'{\to}[\alpha_2]Pos$ then $\vdash Pre{\to}[\alpha_1;\alpha_2]Pos$.
(I+) Introduction for disjunction:
    If $\vdash Pre{\to}[\alpha_1]Pos$ and $\vdash Pre{\to}[\alpha_2]Pos$ then $\vdash Pre{\to}[\alpha_1+\alpha_2]Pos$.
(I⇒) Introduction for conditional:
    If $\vdash(Pre{\wedge}\phi){\to}[\alpha]Pos$ and $\vdash(Pre{\wedge}\neg\phi){\to}Pos$ then $\vdash Pre{\to}[\phi?;\alpha]Pos$.

3.11 Correctness for Imperatives

Having all this infrastructure to represent and verify requirement, we can formalize the definition of correctness for imperatives.

Definition: Correctness of an Imperative
        Given a requirement $(\alpha)_{s,h}$, prescribed by an imperative utterance Imp(k, P, $(\alpha)_{s,h}$, Q) we say that Imp is correct w.r.t context k iff $k{\models}P{\to}[(\alpha)_{s,h}]Q$ for appropriate pre and post-conditions P and Q.

Note that this definition of correctness is only a case of the more general definition $k{\models}P{\to}[\alpha]Q$, which defines the correctness of any action in L_{ImpA}. This includes requirements, ability of agents and actions in general.

3.12 Encapsulating Uttered Requirements

In order for an agent to distinguish what is uttered from what is not, we encapsulate as follows.

Definition: Set of Requirements
        Let be $\sigma_k = <(\alpha_1)_{s,h}, (\alpha_2)_{s,h}, ..., (\alpha_n)_{s,h}>$ a set of requirements demanded in context k, such that $\alpha_1, \alpha_2, ..., \alpha_n$ represent actions prescribed by imperatives sentences. s and h represents the agents playing the role of speakers and hearer respectively.

Note that σ_k allows the distinction between demanded and derived actions. On the other hand, there is the implicit assumption that all requirements in σ_k are supposed to be satisfied as long as σ_k is correct.

Definition: Correctness of a Set of Requirements
        A set σ_k is correct with respect to context k iff $k{\models}P\{(\alpha_1)_{s,h};(\alpha_2)_{s,h};$ $...;(\alpha_n)_{s,h}\}Q$ for appropriate pre and post-conditions P and Q.

4 Model at Work

In the examples below we assume that k the context, represent not the set of beliefs of a particular agent, but rather the set of common shared beliefs between the hearer and speaker involved.

a) Uttered and Derived Requirements

Let us assume that Helen says to Betty, *Love your neighbour as yourself!* Betty should be able to encapsulate the requirement such that $\sigma_k = <(Love\ your\ neighbour\ as\ yourself!)_{Helen,\ Betty}>$. We can paraphrase the order as a conditional requirement, where $\alpha(x) = Love\ x\ as\ yourself$, $\phi(x) = x\ is\ your\ neighbour$, $Q(x) = You\ love\ x\ as\ yourself$ and $P(x) = \neg Q(x)$. Thus, the Hoare's triple of the imperative is $\forall x P(x) \rightarrow [(\phi(x) \Rightarrow \alpha(x))_{Helen,\ Betty}]Q(x)$. If we assume that the requirement is correct w.r.t. k, then $k \models \forall x P(x) \rightarrow [(\phi(x) \Rightarrow \alpha(x))_{Helen,\ Betty}]Q(x)$. This means that for both Helen and Betty, the requirement according to their beliefs is acceptable. If furthermore it is the case that $\phi(Alison) = Alison\ is\ your\ neighbour$, then we can derive as follows.

1) $k \models \forall x P(x) \rightarrow [(\phi(x) \Rightarrow \alpha(x))_{Helen,\ Betty}]Q(x)$ assumption
2) $k \models \forall x\ (P(x) \wedge \phi(x)) \rightarrow [(\alpha(x))_{Helen,\ Betty}]Q(x)$ 1), axiom A1)
3) $k \models \phi(Alison)$ assumption
4) $k \models (P(Alison) \wedge \phi(Alison)) \rightarrow [(\alpha(Alison))_{Helen,\ Betty}]Q(Alison)$ 2), Univ. Inst.
5) $k \models P(Alison) \wedge \phi(Alison)$ 3), 4), Int Conj.
6) $k \models [(\alpha(Alison))_{Helen,\ Betty}]Q(Alison)$ 4), 5), MP

In 6) Betty would derive the requirement of loving Alison, from the original request by Helen, given that she is one of her neighbours. However that is not an uttered requirement, $(\alpha(Alison))_{Helen,\ Betty} \notin \sigma_k$.

b) No Choice

Let us assume that now Helen says to Betty, *Talk to the president!* Betty would distinguish this uttered requirement as follows $\sigma_k = <(Talk\ to\ the\ president)_{Helen,\ Betty}>$. We can paraphrase the order, such that $\alpha = Talk\ to\ the\ president$, $Q = You\ have\ talked\ to\ the\ president$ and $P = \neg Q$. Thus, the Hoare's triple of the imperative is $P \rightarrow [(\alpha)_{Helen,\ Betty}]Q$. If we assume that the requirement is correct w.r.t. k, then $k \models P \rightarrow [(\alpha)_{Helen,\ Betty}]Q$. This means that for both Helen and Betty, it is acceptable the requirement of talking to the president, according to their beliefs.

If we assume that $\beta = Kill\ the\ president$, Betty and Helen cannot introduce a disjunction such that Betty believes that a choice has been uttered and given to her, That is $\sigma_k = <(\alpha)_{Helen,\ Betty} + (\beta)_{Helen,\ Betty}>$. On the other hand, even a verification of a choice might be incorrect, that is $k \not\models P \rightarrow [(\alpha)_{Helen,\ Betty} + (\beta)_{Helen,\ Betty}]Q$. There might be a clash between this verification and Betty's beliefs.

c) Impossible Requirements

Let us assume that now Helen says to Betty, *Have three arms!* Betty would distinguish this uttered requirement as follows $\sigma_k = <(Have\ three\ arms)_{Helen,\ Betty}>$. We can paraphrase the order, such that α = *Have three arms*, Q = *You have three* and $P=\neg Q$. Thus, the Hoare's triple of the imperative is $P\rightarrow [(\alpha)_{\text{Helen, Betty}}]Q$. In this case, and under normal circumstances, there would be a clash between this verification and Betty's beliefs. In this case Betty's clash can be represented by the following expression, $k\nvDash P\rightarrow <(\alpha)_{\text{Helen, Betty}}>Q$, which means that there is not a state she can reach by doing something so that she can have three arms. In terms of ability we can express this as $k\nvDash P\rightarrow <(\alpha)_{\text{Betty}}>Q$, which means that Betty does not believe that she is able to perform the action of having three arms.

5 Conclusions and Future Work

We have presented a model in which agents that possess a reasoning ability are able to interpret imperative sentences. This does not suffer from the inferential problems faced by other approaches to the interpretation of imperatives.

It is assumed that by various means (order, advice, request, etc.) imperatives convey *requirements*. The dynamic aspect of imperatives allows us to envisage that the connectives between imperatives behave similarly but not identically to classical logic connectives. A set of dynamic operators is used instead (disjunction (+), composition (;), conditional imperative ($\Rightarrow$)). An introduction rule is provided for each of these operators.

The features of the model presented here, are that it captures the main aspects of imperatives (including the lack of truth-values), and that it corresponds to our intuitions about behavior of imperative sentences.

The model presented here is useful for verifying imperatives or sequences of imperatives, but it is not able to infer new utterances. This distinction between derived and uttered requirements allows us to avoid certain paradoxes.

Propositions and imperatives interact within the model. It allows us to verify the appropriate use of imperatives (correctness). Verification of correctness provides a *legitimation procedure* for imperatives, and it is able to detect impossible requirements.

There are many possible extensions for this model, for instance the explicit inclusion of time. The introduction of "contrary to duty" imperatives (Prakken and Sergot [13]; Alarcón-Cabrera [1]), would be another example.

In a near future we want to implement this model in a computer system so that it can be used in natural language interfaces. At the moment we are working on the syntactic analysis of imperatives.

References

1. Alarcón Cabrera Carlos, 1998. "*Von Wright's Deontic Logics and 'Contrary-to-Duty Imperatives.'*" Ratio Juris. Vol 11. No. 1 March 1998. pp. 67- 79.
2. Bunt. Harry "*Dialogue pragmatics and context specification*" in "*Abduction, Belief and Context in Dialogue;*" Studies in Computational Pragmatics, Amsterdam: Benjamins, Natural Language. Processing Series No. 1, 2000. pp. 81-150.

3. Buvac, Sasa. 1995. *"Resolving Lexical Ambiguity Using a Formal Theory of Context."* Visited in October 1998 in http://www-formal.Stanford.EDU/buvac/
4. Chellas, B., 1971. *"Imperatives."* Theoria. Vol 37, 1971. pp. 114-129
5. Gries, David, 1983. *"The Science of programming."* Department of Computer Science. Cornell University. Upson Hall Ithaca, NY. 1983.
6. Hamblin, C. L, 1987. *"Imperatives."* Basil Blackwell. USA. 1987
7. Harel David, 1979. *"First-Order Dynamic Logic."* Lecture Notes in Computer Science. Edited by Goos and Hartmanis. 68. Springer-Verlag.Yorktown Heights, NY. 1979.
8. Hoare. C. A. R., 1969. *"An Axiomatic Basis for Computer Programming."* Communications of the ACM, Vol. 12, No 10. October 1969. pp. 576 -580, 583.
9. Jorgensen Jorgen, 1937. *"Imperatives and logic."* Erkenntnis. Vol. 7, (1937-1938), pp. 288-296.
10. Lopez F. and Luck M., 2002. *"Empowered situations of autonomous agents"* Iberamia Springer Verlag. 2002. pp. 585-595.
11. Piwek, P., 2000. *"Imperatives, Commitment and Action: Towards a Constraint-based Model."* In: LDV Forum: Journal for Computational Linguistics and Language Technology, Special Issue on Communicating Agents, 2000.
12. Pérez-Ramírez Miguel. *Formal pragmatic model for imperatives interpretation.* Doctoral Thesis. Computer Science Department. University of Essex, Wivenhoe Park, Colchester CO4 3SQ, United Kingdom. January, 2003.
13. Prakken, Henry and Sergot, Marek, 1996. *"Contrary-to-duty Obligations."* Studia Logica 1996. 57(1/2): pp. 91-115.
14. Ross A., 1941. *"Imperatives and Logic."* Theoria (journal). Vol. 7. 1941. pp. 53-71.
15. Segerberg Krister, 1990. *"Validity and Satisfaction in Imperative Logic."* Notre Dame Journal of Formal Logic. Volume 31, Number 2, Spring 1990. pp. 203-221.
16. Sperber Dan and Wilson Deirdre, 1986. *"Relevance."* Communication and Cognition. Great Britain London. 1986.
17. Turner Raymond. *"Properties, Propositions and Semantic Theory. In Computational Linguistics and Formal Semantics."* Edited by Michael Rosner and Roderick Johnson.Cambridge University Press. Cambridge. 1992. pp. 159-180.
18. von Wright, Henrik Georg. *"Deontic Logic: A personal View"* Ratio Juris. 1999. pp. 26-38.
19. Walter Robert, 1996. *"Jorgensen's Dilemma and How to Face It."* Ratio Juris. Vol 9. No. 2 June 1996. pp. 168-171.

Automatic Multilinguality for Time Expression Resolution*

E. Saquete, P. Martínez-Barco, and R. Muñoz

Grupo de investigación del Procesamiento del Lenguaje y Sistemas de Información.
Departamento de Lenguajes y Sistemas Informáticos. Universidad de Alicante.
Alicante, Spain
{stela,patricio,rafael}@dlsi.ua.es

Abstract. In this paper, a semiautomatic extension of our monolingual (Spanish) TERSEO system to a multilingual level is presented . TERSEO implements a method of event ordering based on temporal expression recognition and resolution. TERSEO consists of two different modules, the first module is based on a set of rules that allows the recognition of the temporal expressions in Spanish. The second module is based on a set of rules that allows the resolution of these temporal expressions (which means transforming them into a concrete date, concrete interval or fuzzy interval). Both sets of rules were defined through an empirical study of a training corpus. The extension of the system, that makes the system able to work with multilingual texts, has been made in five stages. First, a direct translation of the temporal expressions in Spanish of our knowledge database to the target language (English, Italian, French, Catalan, etc) is performed. Each expression in the target language is linked to the same resolution rule used in the source language. The second stage is a search in Google for each expression so that we will eliminate all those expressions of which non exact instances are found. The third step is the obtaining of a set of keywords in the target language, that will be used to look for new temporal expressions in this language, learning new rules automatically. Finally, every new rule is linked with its resolution. Besides, we present two different kinds of evaluations, one of them measures the reliability of the system used for the automatic extraction of rules for new languages. In the other evaluation, the results of precision and recall in the recognition and resolution of Spanish temporal expressions are presented.

1   Introduction

Temporal information is one of the most relevant data you can obtain from texts, in order to establish a chronology between the events of a text. There are three different kinds of problems that are necessary to cope with when working with temporal expressions:

---

* This paper has been supported by the Spanish government, projects FIT-150500-2002-244, FIT-150500-2002-416, TIC-2003-07158-C04-01 and TIC2000-0664-C02-02.

R. Monroy et al. (Eds.): MICAI 2004, LNAI 2972, pp. 458–467, 2004.

- Identification of temporal expressions
- Resolution of the temporal expression
- Event ordering

At the moment there are different kinds of systems that try to annotate and resolve temporal expressions (TE) in different types of corpora:

- **Based on knowledge.** These systems have a previous knowledge base that contains the rules used to solve the temporal expressions.
- **Based on Machine Learning.** In this kind of system, a supervised-annotated corpus is needed to automatically generate the system rules that can have a percentage of appearance of these rules in corpus. The system is based on these rules.

Within the ones based on knowledge there are works like Wiebe et al.[6], that uses a set of defined rules. However, the corpora used in this system are scheduling dialogs, in which temporal expressions are limited. Also the system of Filatova and Hovy [4] is based on knowledge and describes a method for breaking news stories into their constituent events by assigning time-stamps to them. The system of Schilder and Habel [9] is knowledge based as well. However, it only resolves expressions that refer to the article date and not the ones that refer to a previous date in the text. By contrast, some of the most important systems based on Machine Learning are, for instance, Wilson et al.[5], Katz and Arosio [7], Setzer and Gaizauskas [10]. This latter focuses on annotating Event-Event Temporal Relations in text, using a time-event graph which is more complete but costly and error-prone.

Most of the systems described before try to resolve some of the problems related with temporal expressions, but not all of them. And, moreover, they are usually focused on one language and their adaptation to other languages is very complicated. For that reason, in this work, an approach that combines the two previous techniques for the multilinguality is presented, with the advantage that a manually annotated corpus for new rules learning in other languages is not needed.

This work uses a monolingual temporal expression resolution system based on knowledge for Spanish, described in Saquete et al.[2], to turn it into a multilingual system based on machine learning.

In order to know the performance of the system of multilingual conversion independently to the performance of the resolution system, two different measurements have been made. On one hand, precision and recall of the new expressions obtained by means of automatic translation has been measured and on the other hand, precision and recall of the monolingual system applied to a Spanish corpus is presented.

This paper has been structured in the following way: first of all, section 2 shows a short description of the monolingual system that has been presented in other articles. Then, section 3 presents the general architecture and description of the multilingual system. In section 4, two different kinds of evaluation are presented. Finally, in section 5, some conclusions are shown.

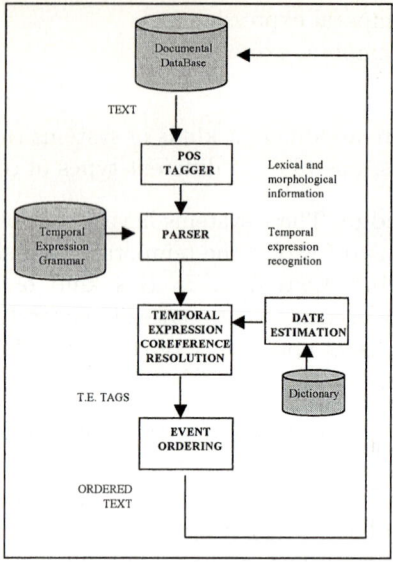

Fig. 1. Graphic representation of TERSEO

2   Description of TERSEO System

In Figure 1 the graphic representation of the monolingual system proposed for the recognition of Spanish TEs and for the resolution of its references is shown, according to the temporal model proposed. The texts are tagged with lexical and morphological information and this information is the input to the temporal parser. This temporal parser is implemented using an ascending technique (chart parser) and it is based on a temporal grammar. Once the parser recognizes the TEs in the text, these are introduced into the resolution unit, which will update the value of the reference according to the date it is referring and generate the XML tags for each expression. Finally, these tags are the input of a event ordering unit that gives back the ordered text. We can find explicit and implicit TEs. The grammar in Tables 1 and 2 is used by the parser to discriminate between them.

There are two types of temporal references that should be treated: the time adverbs (i.e. yesterday, tomorrow) and the nominal phrases that are referring to temporal relationships (i.e. the day after, the day before). In Table 2 we show some of the rules used for the detection of every kind of reference.

3   Automatic Multilinguality

In Figure 2 the graphic representation of the extension of TERSEO system is shown. The extension of the system consists of five main units:

Table 1. Sample of rules for Explicit Dates Recognition

date→ dd+'/'+mm+'/'+(yy)yy	(12/06/1975)
	(06/12/1975)
date→ dd+'de'+mm+'de'+(yy)yy	(12 de junio de 1975)
	(12th of June of 1975)
date→ ('El')+diasemana+dd+'de'+mes+'de'+(yy)yy	
	(El domingo 12 de junio de 1975)
	(Sunday, 12th of June of 1975)
time→ hh+':'+mm+(':'+ss)	*(time)*

Table 2. Sample of rules for Implicit Dates recognition

Implicit dates	reference→ 'ayer'	*(yesterday)*
referring to Document Date	reference→ 'mañana'	*(tomorrow)*
Concrete	reference→ 'anteayer'	*(the day before yesterday)*
	reference→ 'el próximo día'	*(the next day)*
Implicit Dates	reference→ 'un mes después'	*(a month later)*
Previous Date Period	reference→ num+'años después'	*(num years later)*
Imp. Dates Prev.Date Concrete	reference→ 'un día antes'	*(a day before)*
Implicit Dates	reference→ 'días después'	*(some days later)*
Previous Date Fuzzy	reference→ 'días antes'	*(some days before)*

- **Translation Unit.** This unit, using three translators (BabelFish[1], Free-Translator[2] and PowerTranslator) makes an automatic translation of all the expressions in Spanish.
- **Temporal Expression Debugger.** These translated expressions will be the input of the temporal expression debugger unit, that uses the Google resource to eliminate those expressions that have not been translated properly.
- **Keyword Unit.** These unit obtains a set of keywords in the target language.
- **New Temporal Expression Searching Engine.** These unit is able to learn new rules automatically using the keywords and an un-annotated corpus in the target language.
- **Resolution Linker.** This unit links every new rule with its resolution.

3.1 Translation Unit

The translation unit is in charge to make a direct translation of the temporal expressions in Spanish from TERSEO knowledge database to the target language (English, Italian, French, Catalan,etc). For the translation, three machine translation systems have been used (BabelFish, FreeTranslator, PowerTranslator). The use of three translators is based on a well-known multilingual technique used in many multilingual systems [8]. This unit eliminates all those expressions

---

[1] http://world.altavista.com/

[2] http://www.free-translator.com/translator3.html

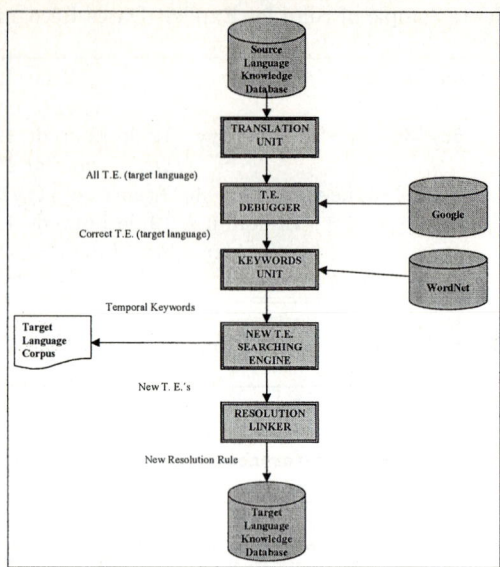

Fig. 2. Graphic representation of Automatic Multilingual Extension of TERSEO

that appear more than once after the translation. Besides, in this unit, each expression in the target language is linked to the same resolution rule used in the source language.

3.2 Temporal Expression Debugger

The confronting of the different results obtained before by the translation unit is made by this unit, in order to obtain the best translation for every expression and avoid wrong translations, because it is possible that the translator gives a wrong translation of an expression as a result.

All the translated expressions are the input of the Temporal Expression Debugger Unit, that uses Google[3] as a resource, to eliminate those expressions that have not been translated properly. Every exact expression is searched by Google, and the expression is considered wrong if Google does not return any coincidence.

3.3 Keyword Unit

A third step is the obtaining of a set of keywords in the target language, that will be used to look for new temporal expressions in this language. In order to obtain keywords, this unit uses, on one hand, all those expressions that have been previously translated to the target language and on the other hand, the lexical resource WordNet. This resource is used in order to obtain synonymous

---

[3] http://www.google.com

keywords, increasing the set of words and the possibility to obtain new temporal expressions using these words.

3.4 New Temporal Expression Searching Engine

Using the temporal words obtained before, the new temporal expression searching engine accedes to a corpus of texts in the target language, giving back new temporal expressions. These expressions are not related to any resolution rule at first.

3.5 Resolution Linker

The Resolution Linker assigns a resolution to each expression based on the characteristics of the temporal word or words that the expression contains. All these expressions are introduced in a knowledge database for the new language.The Resolution Linker increases this knowledge database with new rules found in the target language. Finally, this database will contain rules in different languages. For example, for the general rule:

```
Day(Date)-1/Month(Date)/Year(Date)
```

there is a set of expressions in the source language (Spanish in this case) that are related with this rule in the knowledge database and a set of expressions in the target language (English in this case) that are related with the same resolution rule:

- *Source set*: ayer, el pasado día, el día pasado, el último día, hace un día, hace NUM días, anteayer, anoche, de ayer, el pasado día NumDia, durante el día de ayer, durante todo el día de ayer
- *Target set*: yesterday, the past day, the last day, for a day, it does NUM days, the day before yesterday, last night, of yesterday, during the day of yesterday, the passed day, last day, a day ago, does NUM days, day before yesterday, during all the day of yesterday, the day past, makes a day, makes NUM days

3.6 Integration

Finally, it is necessary to integrate TERSEO system with the automatic extension defined, in order to have a complete multilingual system. When the corpus is in the target language, the system will use the new knowledge database in this language to identify, resolve and order temporal expressions in this corpus. The complete system is shown in Figure 3.

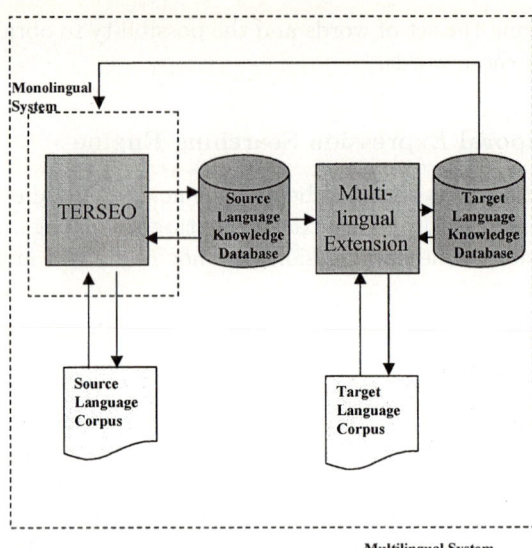

Multilingual System

Fig. 3. Graphic representation of the integration of TERSEO and the automatic extension

4   System Evaluation

In this paper, two different kinds of evaluations are presented. First of all, the monolingual system TERSEO has been evaluated, using two Spanish corpora, a training corpus and a test corpus. In addition, a second evaluation has been made in order to measure the precision and recall of the new rules obtained using automatic translation of the source knowledge database. These two evaluations have been made separately in order to measure how good the extension of the system related to the monolingual system is.

4.1   TERSEO Evaluation Using a Spanish Corpus

In order to carry out an evaluation of the monolingual system, a manual annotation of texts has been made by two human annotators with the purpose of comparing it with the automatic annotation that produces the system. For that reason, it is necessary to confirm that the manual information is trustworthy and it does not alter the results of the experiment. Carletta [3] explains that to assure a good annotation is necessary to make a series of direct measurements that are: stability, reproducibility and precision, but in addition to these measurements the reliability must measure the amount of noise in the information. The authors argue that due to the amount of agreement by chance that one can expected depends on the number of relative frequencies of the categories under test, the reliability for the classifications of categories would have to be measure

Table 3. Evaluation of the monolingual system

	TRAINING	TEST
No Art.	50	50
Real Ref	238	199
Treated Ref.	201	156
Successes	170	138
Precision	84%	91%
Recall	71%	73%
Coverage	84%	80%

using the factor *kappa* defined in Siegel and Castellan [11]. The factor *kappa (k)* measures the affinity in agreement between a set of annotators when they make categories judgments.

In our case, there is only one class of objects and there are three objects within this class: objects that refer to the date of the article, objects which refer to the previous date and objects that refer to another date different from the previous ones.

After carrying out the calculation, a value $k=0.953$ was obtained. According to the work of Carletta [3], a measurement of k like $0,68 < k < 0,8$ means that the conclusions are favorable, and if $k > 0,8$ means total reliability exists between the results of both annotators. Since our value of k is greater than $0,8$, it is guaranteed that a total reliability in the conducted annotation exists and therefore, the results of obtained precision and recall are reliable.

An evaluation of the module of resolution of TEs was carried out. Two corpora formed by newspaper articles in Spanish were used. The first set has been used for training and it consists of 50 articles, manually annotated by the two annotators named before. Thus, after making the opportune adjustments to the system, the optimal results of precision and recall were obtained that are in the table 3. Although the results in both corpora are very similar, but the scores for the test corpus are slightly higher because the number of temporal expressions was a bit smaller than in the training corpus.

4.2 Evaluation of the Automatic Multilingual Extension of the System

In this evaluation, the first two units of the automatic extension have been measured. The evaluation was to translate the temporal expressions to English. First of all, the translation unit that has an input of 380 temporal expressions in Spanish, returns an output of 1140 temporal expressions in English. But, most of these expressions are identical because the translation is the same in the three automatic translators. Therefore, the translation unit deletes these duplicate expressions, and the output of the translation unit are 563 expressions.

The debugger unit, that uses these expressions as input, returns 443 temporal expressions, that according to the Google search are correct expressions. These expressions have been checked manually in order to determine with ones are not correct. We consider two types of possible mistakes:

- The translation of the expression is wrong
- The resolution assigned to the expression is not correct

Once these possible mistakes have been analyzed, 13 temporal expressions have been classified as incorrect. In conclusion, 430 temporal expressions are considered as properly translated and resolved. Considering recall as the number of correct translated expressions divided by the number of total expressions, and precision as the number of correct translated expressions divided by the number of translated expressions, the obtained results are:

Recall= 430 / 563 = 0.76 $--> 76\%$

Precision=430 / 443 = 0.97 $--> 97\%$

Some conclusions could be deduced from these results. First of all, a precision of 97% has been obtained from the direct translation of the temporal expressions. That means the multilingual system have a 81% of precision for the training corpus and 88% of precision for the test corpus, a 3% less than the original results, which are successful values.

5   Conclusions

The approach implemented here combines the advantage of knowledge based systems (high precision) with those of systems based on machine learning (facility of extension, in this case to other languages) without the disadvantage of needing a hand annotated corpus to obtain new rules for the system.

Moreover, comparing the two evaluations that have been performed, and shows that in the precision of the translated temporal expressions only a 3% of it is lost, the results of the multilingual system are quite high.

References

1. ACL, editor. *Proceedings of the 2001 ACL-EACL, Workshop on Temporal and Spatial Information Processing*, Toulouse,France, 2001.
2. R. Muñoz E. Saquete and P. Martínez-Barco. TERSEO: Temporal Expression Resolution System Applied to Event Ordering. In TSD, editor, *Proceedings of the 6th International Conference ,TSD 2003, Text, Speech and Dialogue*, pages 220–228, Ceske Budejovice,Czech Republic, September 2003.
3. J. Carletta et al. The Reliability of a Dialogue Structure Coding Scheme. *Computational Linguistics*, 23(1):13–32, 1997.
4. E. Filatova and E. Hovy. Assigning Time-Stamps to Event-Clauses. In ACL [1], pages 88–95.
5. B. Sundheim G. Wilson, I. Mani and L. Ferro. A Multilingual Approach To Annotating And Extracting Temporal Information. In ACL [1], pages 81–87.
6. T. Ohrstrom-Sandgren J.M. Wiebe, T.P. O'Hara and K.J. McKeever. An Empirical Approach to Temporal Reference Resolution. *Journal of Artificial Intelligence Research*, 9:247–293, 1998.

7. G. Katz and F. Arosio. The Annotation of Temporal Information In Natural Language Sentences. In ACL [1], pages 104–111.

8. F. Llopis and R. Muñoz. Cross-language experiments with IR-n system. In CLEF, editor, *Proceedings CLEF-2003 Lecture Notes in Computer Science*, Tronheim, Norwey, August 2003.

9. F. Schilder and C. Habel. From Temporal Expressions to Temporal Information: Semantic Tagging of News Messages. In ACL [1], pages 65–72.

10. A. Setzer and R. Gaizauskas. On the Importance of Annotating Event-Event Temporal Relations in Text. In LREC, editor, *Proceedings of the LREC Workshop on Temporal Annotation Standards, 2002*, pages 52–60, Las Palmas de Gran Canaria,Spain, 2002.

11. S. Siegel and J. Castellan. *Nonparametric Statistics for the Behavioral Sciences.* McGraw-Hill, 2nd edition, 1988.

AQUA – Ontology-Based Question Answering System

Maria Vargas-Vera and Enrico Motta

Knowledge Media Institute (KMi),
The Open University,
Walton Hall, Milton Keynes, MK7 6AA, United Kingdom
{m.vargas-vera, e.motta}@open.ac.uk

Abstract. This paper describes AQUA, an experimental question answering system. AQUA combines Natural Language Processing (NLP), Ontologies, Logic, and Information Retrieval technologies in a uniform framework. AQUA makes intensive use of an ontology in several parts of the question answering system. The ontology is used in the refinement of the initial query, the reasoning process, and in the novel similarity algorithm. The similarity algorithm, is a key feature of AQUA. It is used to find similarities between relations used in the translated query and relations in the ontological structures.

1 Introduction

The rise in popularity of the web has created a demand for services which help users to find relevant information quickly. One such service is question answering (QA), the technique of providing precise answers to specific questions. Given a question such as "which country had the highest inflation rate in 2002?" a keyword-based search engine such as Google might present the user with web pages from the Financial Times, whereas a QA system would attempt to directly answer the question with the name of a country.

On the web, a typical example of a QA system is Jeeves[1] [1] which allows users to ask questions in natural language. It looks up the user's question in its own database and returns the list of matching questions which it knows how to answer. The user then selects the most appropriate entry in the list. Therefore, a reasonable aim for an automatic system is to provide textual answers instead of a set of documents. In this paper we present AQUA a question answering system which amalgamates Natural Language Processing (NLP), Logic, Ontologies and Information Retrieval techniques in a uniform framework.

The first instantiation of our ontology-driven Question Answering System, AQUA, is designed to answer questions about academic people and organizations. However, an important future target application of AQUA would be to answer questions posed within company intranets; for example, giving AQUA

---

[1] http://www.ask.com/

R. Monroy et al. (Eds.): MICAI 2004, LNAI 2972, pp. 468–477, 2004.

an ontology of computer systems might allow it to be used for trouble-shooting or configuration of computer systems.

AQUA is also designed to play an important role in the Semantic Web[2]. One of the goals of the Semantic Web is the ability to annotate web resources with semantic content. These annotations can then be used by a reasoning system to provide intelligent services to users. AQUA would be able to perform incremental markup of home pages with semantic content. These annotations can be written in RDF [20,13] or RDFS [5], notations which provide a basic framework for expressing meta-data on the web. We envision that AQUA can perform the markup concurrently with looking for answers, that is, AQUA can annotate pages as it finds them. In this way then, semantically annotated web pages can be cached to reduce search and processing costs.

The main contribution of AQUA is the intensive use of an ontology in several parts of the question answering system. The ontology is used in the refinement of the initial query (query reformulation), the reasoning process, and in the (novel) similarity algorithm. The last of these, the similarity algorithm, is a key feature of AQUA. It is used to find similarities between relations in the translated query and relations in the ontological structures. The similarities detected then allow the interchange of concepts or relations in the logic formulae. The ontology is used to provide an intelligent reformulation of the question, with the intent to reduce the chances of failure to answer the question.

The paper is organized as follows: Section 2 describes the AQUA process model. Section 3 describes the Query Logic Language (QLL) used in the translation of the English written questions. Section 4 presents our query satisfaction-algorithm used in AQUA. Section 5 describes the similarity algorithm embedded in AQUA. Section 6 shows output enhancements of the AQUA system. Section 7 describes a section of related work. Finally, Section 8 gives conclusions and directions for future work.

2   AQUA Process Model

The AQUA process model generalizes other approaches by providing a framework which integrates NLP, Logic, Ontologies and information retrieval. Within this work we have focused on creating a process model for the AQUA system (Figure 1 shows the architecture of our AQUA system).

In the process model there are four phases: *user interaction, question processing, document processing* and *answer extraction*.

1. **User interaction.** The user inputs the question and validates the answer (indicates whether it is correct or not). This phase uses the following components:
   - *Query interface.* The user inputs a question (in English) using the user interface (a simple dialogue box). The user can reformulate the query if the answer is not satisfactory.

---

[2] The goal of the Semantic Web is to help users or software agents to organize, locate and process content on the WWW.

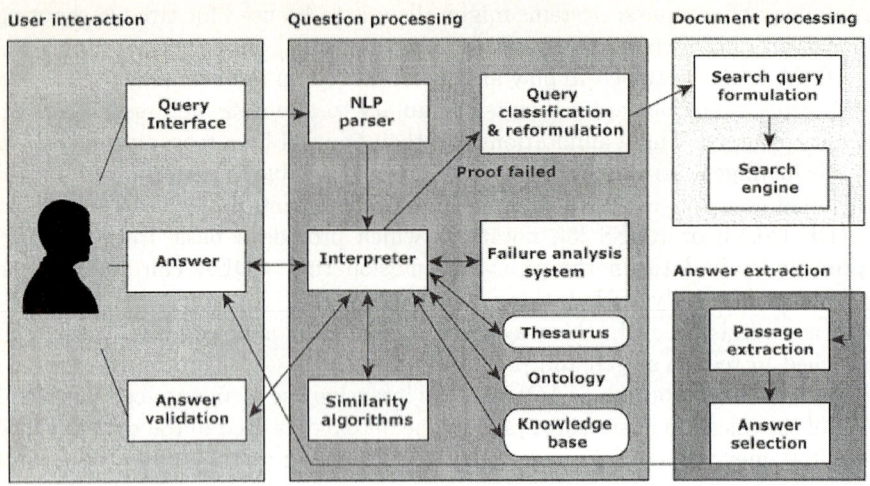

Fig. 1. The AQUA architecture

- *Answer.* A ranked set of answers is presented to the user.
- *Answer validation.* The user gives feedback to AQUA by indicating agreement or disagreement with the answer.

2. **Question processing.** Question processing is performed in order to understand the question asked by the user. This "understanding" of the question requires several steps such as parsing the question, representation of the question and classification. The question processing phase uses the following components:
    - *NLP parser.* This segments the sentence into subject, verb, prepositional phrases, adjectives and objects. The output of this module is the logic representation of the query.
    - *Interpreter.* This finds a logical proof of the query over the knowledge base using Unification and the Resolution algorithm [8].
    - *WordNet/Thesaurus.* AQUA's lexical resource.
    - *Ontology.* This currently contains people, organizations, research areas, projects, publications, technologies and events.
    - *Failure-analysis system.* This analyzes the failure of a given question and gives an explanation of why the query failed. Then the user can provide new information for the pending proof, and the proof can be re-started. This process can be repeated as needed.
    - *Question classification & reformulation.* This classifies questions as belonging to any of the types supported in AQUA, (*what, who, when, which, why* and *where*). This classification is only performed if the proof failed. AQUA then tries to use an information retrieval approach. This means that AQUA has to perform document processing and answer extraction phases.

3. **Document Processing.** A set of documents are selected and a set of paragraphs are extracted. This relies on the identification of the focus[3] of the question. Document processing consists of two components:
   - *Search query formulation.* This transforms the original question, Q, using transformation rules into a new question Q'. Synonymous words can be used, punctuation symbols are removed, and words are stemmed.
   - *Search engine.* This searches the web for a set of documents using a set of keywords.
4. **Answer processing.** In this phase answers are extracted from passages and given a score, using the two components:
   - *Passage selection.* This extracts passages from the set of documents likely to have the answer
   - *Answer selection.* This clusters answers, scores answers (using a voting model), and lastly obtains a final ballot.

3   Query Logic Language (QLL)

In this section we present the Query Logic Language (QLL) used within AQUA for the translation from of the English question into its Logic form. In QLL variables and predicates are assigned types. Also, QLL allows terms (in the standard recursively-defined Prolog sense [8,22]).

Like Prolog or OCML [25], QLL uses unification and resolution [22]. However, in the future we plan to use Contextual Resolution [28]. Given a context, AQUA could then provide interpretation for sentences containing contextually dependent constructs.

Again like Prolog QLL uses closed-world assumption. So facts that are not "provable" are regarded as "false" as opposed to "unknown". Future work needs to be carried out in order to provide QLL with three-valued logic. Once that QLL become a three-valued logic language then an evaluation of a predicate could produce *yes, no* or *unknown* as in Fril [3]. Finally, QLL handles negation as failure but it does not use cuts.

AQUA uses QLL as an inter-media language as is shown in example (section 4).

The translation rules are used when AQUA is creating the logical form of a query, i.e., from grammatical components into QLL. The set of translation rules we have devised is not intended to be complete, but it does handle all the grammatical components produced by our parser. The form of the logical predicates introduced by each syntax category is described in detail in [29].

4   The AQUA Query-Satisfaction Algorithm

This section presents the main algorithm implemented in the AQUA system. For the sake of space, we present a condensed version of our algorithm. In this

---

[3] Focus is a word or a sequence of words which defines the question and disambiguates it in the sense that it indicates what the question is looking for.

following algorithm AQUA uses steps 1-4.1 to evaluate query over the populated AKT reference ontology. [4]. Steps 4.2 to 5 are used by AQUA trying to satisfy the query using the Web as resource.

1. Parse the question into its grammatical components such as subject, verb, prepositions phrases, object and adjectives.
2. Use the ontology to convert from the QLL language to a standard predicate logic. The ontology is used by a pattern-matching algorithm [5] to instantiate type variables, and allow them to be replaced with unary predicates.
3. Re-write the logic formulae using our similarity algorithm (described in the next section)
4. Evaluate/execute the re-written logic formulae over the knowledge base.
   - 4.1 **If** the logic formulae is satisfied **then** use it to provide an answer
   - 4.2 **else**
     - Classify the question as one of the following types:
       * **what** - specification of objects, activity definition
       * **who** - person specification
       * **when** - date
       * **which** - specification of objects, attributes
       * **why** - justification of reasons
       * **where** - geographical location
     - Transform the query **Q** into a new query **Q'** using the important keywords.
     - Launch a search engine such as Google [6] with the new question **Q'**. AQUA will try to satisfy the user query using other resources such as the Web.
     - Analyze retrieved documents which satisfy the query **Q'**.
     - Perform passage extraction.
     - Perform answer selection.
     - Send answer to user for validation.

We can see from the algorithm that AQUA tries to satisfy a user query using several resources. Future implementations of AQUA could benefit from using the results obtained by the Armadillo[7] [7] information extraction engine running in the background as a complementary knowledge harvester. For instance, the user could ask the question *What publications has Yorik Wilks produced?* This is a good example of a query for which AQUA could make a request to Armadillo. Armadillo would find the publications of Yorik Wilks (for example,

---

[4] The AKT ontology contains classes and instances of people, organizations, research areas, publications, technologies and events
(http://akt.open.ac.uk/ocml/domains/akt-support-ontology/)
[5] The pattern-matching algorithm tries to find an exact match with names in the ontology.
[6] http://www.google.com
[7] Armadillo is an information extraction engine which uses resources such as CiteSeer to find a limited range of information types such as publications.

using CiteSeer[8] or his personal web site). Next, Armadillo would parse documents, retrieve the requested information and pass the set of publications back to AQUA to render an appropriate answer.

The example below shows just one aspect of use of ontology in question answering: 'ontology traversal' (i.e. generalization/specialization). Suppose we have the question: "Which technologies are used in AKT?" AQUA tries to answer question as follows.

The English question is translated into the QLL expression

use(?x : type technology, akt : type ?y)

which is then converted to the standard (Prolog-style) expression by using the AKT ontology

$\exists X : Domain$ technology(X) $\wedge$ project(akt) $\wedge$ use(X,akt).

Where the meaning of the quantifier is determined by the type of the variable it binds. For our example, let us decide that $Domain$ is the set containing the union of of each of the following congruence classes: people, projects, organizations, research areas, technologies, publications and events.

If there is a technology in the AKT project which is defined in the knowledge base then X will be bound to the name of the technology. Let us imagine the scenario where instances of technology are not defined in the AKT reference ontology. However, AQUA found in the AKT reference ontology that the relation "commercial_technology" is a subclass of "technology". Then commercial_technology is a particular kind of technology, i.e.

$commercial\_technology \subseteq technology$

By using the subsumption relation our initial formula is transformed into the following one:

$\exists X : commercial\_technology$ commercial_technology(X) $\wedge$ project(akt) $\wedge$ use(X,akt).

AQUA then tries to re-satisfy the new question over the knowledge base. This time the question succeeds with X instantiated to the name of one of the AKT technologies.

5   Concept and Relation Similarity Algorithm

The success of the attempt to satisfy a query depends on the existence of a good mapping between the names of the relations used in the query and the names of the relations used in the knowledge base/ontology. Therefore, we have embedded a similarity algorithm in AQUA. Our similarity algorithm uses both ontological structures and instances of the selected ontology, the Dice coefficient and the WordNet thesaurus.

---

[8] http://citeseer.nj.nec.com/cs

Our similarity algorithm differs from other similarity algorithms in that it uses ontological structures and also instances. Instances provide evidential information about the relations being analyzed. This is an important distinction from either the kind of similarity which can be achieved using only either WordNet or distances to superclasses (Wu et al [31]). In the former approach, WordNet returns all the synsets found, even the ones which are not applicable to the problem being solved. On the other hand, in the latter approach, the idea of a common superclass between concepts is required.

For the sake of space, we present a brief explanation of our algorithm when arguments in the user query are grounded (instantiated terms) and they match exactly (at the level of strings) with instances in the ontology. A detailed description of the algorithm and an example can be found in [30].

The algorithm uses grounded terms in the user query. It tries to find them as instances in the ontology. Once they are located, a portion of the ontology (G2) is examined, including neighborhood classes. Then an intersection[9] (G3) between augmented query G1 and ontology G2 is performed to assess structural similarity. This is done using knowledge from the ontology. It may be the case that, in the intersection G3, several relations include the grounded arguments. In this case, the similarity measure is computed for all the relations (containing elements of the user query) by using the Dice Coefficient. Finally, the relation with the maximum Dice Coefficient value is selected as the most similar relation.

AQUA reformulates the query using the most similar relation and it then tries to prove the reformulated query. If no similarity is achieved using our similarity algorithm, AQUA presents the user with the synsets obtained from WordNet. From this offered set of synsets, the user can then select the most suitable one.

6   Output Enhancements

AQUA not only provides a set of elements which satisfy the query, AQUA enhances its answer using the information from the AKT reference ontology. It provides more information about each element in the set. For instance, if the query is "who works in AKT?" then AQUA brings additional contextual information such as *AKT is a project at KMi* and *each person of the AKT team is a researcher at KMi*.

Validation of answers is a difficult task in general. Therefore, AQUA provides a visualization of proofs for supporting validation of answers. Another way, provided by AQUA, to help users in validation, could be by enhancing answers with extra information. There is ongoing work at KMi on this problem. We use Magpie [10] in this task of enhancing answers. Magpie is a semantic browser which brings information about ontological entities. For instance, it can retrieve home pages related to AKT or personal web pages of researchers working in the AKT project. All this extra information could be used by our AQUA users in answer validation.

---

[9] Intersect means to find a portion in a ontology G_2 which contains all concepts contained in G_1 (reformulated query) by applying a subsumption relation.

7   Related Work

There are many trends in question answering [16,17,18,27,4,24,14,15,2], however, we only describe the systems most closely related to the AQUA system philosophy.

MULDER is a web-based QA system [19] that extracts snippets called summaries and generates a list of candidate answers. However, unlike AQUA, the system does not exploit an inference mechanism, and so, for example, cannot use semantic relations from an ontology.

QUANDA is closest to AQUA in spirit and functionality. QUANDA takes questions expressed in English and attempts to provide a short and concise answer (a noun phrase or a sentence) [6]. Like AQUA, QUANDA combines knowledge representation, information retrieval and natural language processing. A question is represented as a logic expression. Also knowledge representation techniques are used to represent questions and concepts. However, unlike AQUA, QUANDA does not use ontological relations.

ONTOSEEK is a information retrieval system coupled with an ontology [12]. ONTOSEEK performs retrieval based on content instead of string based retrieval. The target was information retrieval with the aim of improving recall and precision and the focus was specific classes of information repositories: Yellow Pages and product catalogues. The ONTOSEEK system provides interactive assistance in query formulation, generalization and specialization. Queries are represented as conceptual graphs, then according to the authors "the problem is reduced to ontology-driven graph matching where individual nodes and arcs match if the ontology indicates that a subsumption relation holds between them". These graphs are not constructed automatically. The ONTOSEEK team developed a semi-automatic approach in which the user has to verify the links between different nodes in the graph via the designated user interface.

8   Conclusions and Future Work

In this paper we have presented AQUA - a question answering system which amalgamates NLP, Logic, Information Retrieval techniques and Ontologies [10]. AQUA translates English questions into logical queries, expressed in a language, QLL, that are then used to generate of proofs. Currently AQUA is coupled with the AKT reference ontology for the academic domain. In the near future, we plan to couple AQUA with other ontologies from our repertoire of ontologies.

AQUA makes use of an inference engine which is based on the Resolution algorithm. However, in future it will be tested with the Contextual Resolution algorithm which will allow the carrying of context through several related questions.

We have also presented our similarity algorithm embedded in AQUA which uses Ontological structures, the Dice coefficient and WordNet synsets. This algorithm is used by AQUA to ensure that the question does not fail because of

---

[10] AQUA has been implemented in Sicstus Prolog, C, OCML and PHP.

a mismatch between names of relations. Future work, intends to provide AQUA with a library of similarity algorithms.

We will also explore the automatic extraction of inference rules, since knowledge about inference relations between natural language expressions is very important for the question answering problem.

Acknowledgments. This work was funded by the Advanced Knowledge Technologies (AKT). The authors would like to thank Arthur Stutt and Mark Gaved for their invaluable help in reviewing the first draft of this paper.

References

1. Askjeeves: http://askjeeves.com/, 2000.
2. G. Attardi and A. Cisternino and F. Formica and M. Simi and A. Tommasi: Proceedings of TREC-9 Conference, NIST, pp 633-641, 2001.
3. J. F. Baldwin and T.P. Martin and B. W. Pilsworth. Fril - Fuzzy and Evidential Reasoning in Artificial Intelligence. Research Studies Press in 1995.
4. R. D. Burke and K. J. Hammond and V. A. Kulyukin and S. L. Lytinen and N. Tomuro and S. Schoenberg: Questions answering from frequently-asked question files: Experiences with the FAQ Finder System. The University of Chicago, Computer Science Department, 1997, TR-97-05.
5. D. Brickley and R. Guha: Resource Description Framework (RDF) Schema Specification 1.0. Candidate recommendation, World Web Consortium, 2000. URL:http://www.w3.org/TR/2000/CR-rdf-schema-20000327.
6. E. Breck and D. House and M. Light and I. Mani: Question Answering from Large Document Collections, AAAI Fall Symposium on Question Answering Systems, 1999.
7. F. Ciravegna and A. Dingli, D. Guthrie and Y. Wilks: Mining Web Sites Using Unsupervised Adaptive Information Extraction. Proceedings of the 10th Conference of the European Chapter of the Association for Computational Linguistic, Budapest Hungary, April 2003.
8. W. F. Clocksin and C. S. Mellish: Programming in Prolog, Springer-Verlag, 1981.
9. A. Doan and J. Madhavan and P. Domingos and A. Halevy: Learning to Map between Ontologies on the Semantic Web. In Proc. of the 11th International World Wide Web Conference (WWW2002), 2002.
10. J. Domingue and M. Dzbor and E. Motta: Semantic Layering with Magpie. Technical Report KMI-TR-125. February, 2003.
11. W. Frakes and R. Baeza-Yates: Information Retrieval: Data Structures & Algorithms, Prentice Hall, 1992.
12. N. Guarino: OntoSeek: Content-Based Acess to the Web, IEEE Intelligent Systems, pp 70-80,1999.
13. P. Hayes: RDF Model Theory, W3C Working Draft, February 2002. URL:http://www.w3.org/TR/rdf-mt/
14. E. Hovy and L. Gerber and U. Hermjakob and M. Junk and C-Y Liu: Question Answering in Webclopedia, Proceedings of TREC-9 Conference, NIST, 2001.
15. E. Hovy and L. Gerber and U. Hermjakob and C-Y Liu and D. Ravichandran: Toward Semantics-Based Answer Pinpointing, Proceedings of DARPA Human Language Technology conference (HLT), 2001.

16. B. Katz: From sentence processing to information access on the world wide web, Proceedings of AAAI Symposium on Natural Language Processing for the World Wide Web, 1997.
17. B. Katz and B. Levin: Exploiting Lexical Regularities in Designing Natural Language Systems, MIT Artificial Intelligence Laboratory, 1988, TR 1041.
18. B. Katz: Using English for Indexing and Retrieving, MIT Artificial Intelligence Laboratory, 1988, TR 1096.
19. C. Kwok and O. Etzioni and D. S. Weld: Scaling Question Answering to the Web, World Wide Web, pp 150-161, 2001.
20. O. Lassila and R. Swick: Resource Description Framework (RDF): Model and Syntax Specification. Recommendation. World Wide Web Consortium, 1999. URL: http://www.w3.org/TR/REC-rdf-syntax/.
21. D. Lin and P. Pantel: Discovery of Inference Rules for Question Answering, Journal of Natural Language Engineering, 2001.
22. J. W. Lloyd: Foundations of Logic Programming, Springer-Verlag, 1984.
23. C.D. Manning and H. Schutze: Foundations of Statistical Natural Language Processing. The MIT Press, Cambridge Massachusetts. 1999.
24. D. Moldovan and S. Harabagiu and M. Pasca and R. Mihalcea and R. Goodrum and R. Girju and V. Rus: LASSO: A Tool for Surfing the Answer Net. Proceedings of TREC-8 Conference, NIST, 1999.
25. E. Motta: Reusable Components for Knowledge Modelling. IOS Press. Netherlands, 1999.
26. N. Noy and M. Musen: PROMPT: Algorithm and Tool for Automated Ontology Merging and Alignment. In Proc. of the 17th National Conference on Artificial Intelligence (AAAI), 2000.
27. L. Plamondon and G. Lapalme and R. Diro and L Kosseim: The QUANTUM Question Answering System, Proceedings of TREC-9 Conference, NIST, 2001.
28. S. G. Pulman: Bidirectional Contextual Resolution, Computational Linguistic Vol 26/4, 497-538, 2000.
29. AQUA: An Ontology-Driven Question Answering System, AAAI Symposium on New Directions of Question Answering Stanford University, March 24-26, 2003.
30. AQUA: An Ontology-Driven Question Answering System, KMI-TR-129, KMi, The Open University, 2003.
31. Z. Wu and M. Palmer: Verb semantics and Lexical Selection. 32nd Annual Meetings of the Association for Computational Linguistics. 1994.

Phrase Chunking for Efficient Parsing in Machine Translation System

Jaehyung Yang

School of Computer and Media Engineering,
Kangnam University, Yongin-si, Kyunggi-do, 449-702, Korea
jhyang@kangnam.ac.kr

Abstract. Phrase chunking can be an effective way to enhance the performance of an existing parser in machine translation system. This paper presents a Chinese phrase chunker implemented using transformation-based learning algorithm, and an interface devised to convey the dependency information found by the chunker to the parser. The chunker operates as a preprocessor to the parser in a Chinese to Korean machine translation system currently under active development. By introducing chunking module, some of the unlikely dependencies could be ruled out in advance, resulting in noticeable improvements in the parser's performance.

1   Introduction

Traditional natural language parsers aim to produce a single grammatical structure for the whole sentence. This *full parsing* approach has not been generally successful in achieving the accuracy, efficiency and robustness required by real world applications. Therefore several *partial parsing* or *shallow parsing* techniques have been proposed, where the input sentence is partitioned into a sequence of non-overlapping *chunks*. Abney [1] introduced the notion of chunks, which denote meaningful sequences of words typically consisting of a content word surrounded by zero or more function words. Subsequent works have proposed various chunking techniques, mostly by using machine learning methods ([2], [3], [4], [5], [6], [7]). The CoNLL-2000 shared text chunking task [8] provided an opportunity to compare them with the same corpus data.

Chunkers or partial parsing systems are able to produce a certain level of grammatical information without undertaking the complexity of full parsers, and have been argued to be useful for many large-scale natural language processing applications such as information extraction and lexical knowledge acquisition ([9], [10], [11]). However, chunkers cannot be easily integrated into most practical machine translation systems. Many existing machine translation systems are based on the transfer model, where the transfer modules usually assume fully parsed structures as their input. Moreover, the output of partial parsers do not generally provide grammatical relations among words within chunks.

In this paper, we adopt chunking as a preprocessing step to full parsing. The chunking module attempts to identify useful chunks in input sentences and

R. Monroy et al. (Eds.): MICAI 2004, LNAI 2972, pp. 478–487, 2004.
© Springer-Verlag Berlin Heidelberg 2004

then provides the chunk information to the next stage by restricting the dependency relations among words. This way the chunking module could be easily integrated into the conventional parsing system while considerably improving the performance.

2   Phrase Chunking Based on Transformation-Based Learning

The target application environment of this study is an ongoing project on Chinese to Korean machine translation system, whose objective is to provide real-time online translation of general-domain web documents. The phrase chunking module is used to recognize useful chunks from Chinese text and operates as a preprocesser to the full-scale Chinese parser.

2.1   Phrase Chunk Types

Chunks are non-recursive and non-overlapping groups of continuous words. The following example shows a Chinese sentence (represented in *Pinyin* codes) whose chunks are marked by brackets with their chunk types.

[NP *gōngān xiāofáng* " *119* " *jiējǐngtái*] [NP *língchén*] [QP *2 shí 43 fēn*] [VP *jiēdào*] [NP *bàojǐng*] , [NP *9 bù xiāofángchē*] [VP *jíshí gǎndào*] [NP *huǒzāi xiànchǎng*] , [QP *3 shí 30 fēn*] [NP *dàhuǒ*] [VP *bèi pūmiè*] .

(*The "119" public fire department received a call at 2:43 early morning, 9 fire engines were immediately dispatched to the scene, and the big fire was fully under control at 3:30.*)

The chunk types are based on the phrase tags used in parse trees, and the names of the phrase tags used in this study are similar to those in Penn Chinese Treebank [12]. For example, the chunk type NP corresponds to the phrase label NP. However, since chunks are non-recursive, a phrase in parse tree will be typically broken into several chunks in many cases, and higher-level phrase tags such as S will not have corresponding chunk types. Note that it is also possible some words do not belong to any chunks.

The list of Chinese chunk types this study attempts to identify is as follows:

- ADJP : Adjectival Phrases
- ADVP : Adverbial Phrases
- NP : Noun Phrases
- QP : Quantifier Phrases
- VP : Verbal Phrases

There is always one syntactic head in each chunk: AJ (adjective) in ADJP, NN (noun) in NP, and so on. A chunk normally contains premodifiers to the left of its head, but not postmodifiers or arguments. Therefore, the syntactic head is the last element of the chunk for most cases. The exceptional cases are when a chunk is enclosed by a pair of matching parentheses or quotation marks. These symbols are regarded as part of the chunks. Some of the VP chunks can also be exceptional if two consecutive verbs form *verb-resultative* or *verb-directional* compounds where the second verbs indicate the result or direction of the first verbs. In such cases, the head can be at a position other than last. In the case of coordination, the last conjoined elements are assumed to be the syntactic heads.

QP represents quantifier phrases consisting of determiners or numbers followed by measure words. A QP can be contained in an NP chunk as a premodifier like the QP "*9 bù*" in [NP *9 bù xiāofángchē*] (*9 fire engines*) in the previous example, but a QP is considered as a chunk of its own in other cases.

Note that no chunks of type PP (prepositional phrases), for example, will be recognized. As a constituent, a prepositional phrase will consist of a preposition followed by its object phrase. Because the object phrase itself will form one or more chunk phrases, the PP chunks will almost always consist of one word which is the preposition. We chose not to include a chunk type if the chunks of the type consist of only one word, because the main objective of chunking in this study is to assist parsing and these one-word chunks will provide no useful dependency constraints. The same is true for many other phrases such as LCP (phrase headed by localizer LC), CP (relative clause headed by complementizer DE), and so on.

The chunk-annotated corpuses that were used in the experiments, were automatically constructed by extracting chunks from parse trees. For example, an NP chunk may include the syntactic head and all of its premodifiers. But if one of the premodifiers has its own NP or VP constituents, then the chunk should be broken into several smaller chunks, and some words may end up not belonging to any chunks. This automatic conversion process may introduce a certain percentage of errors, but it will not be a serious problem for a learning-based approach. Currently no chunk-annotated corpus of enough size is available.

2.2   Transformation-Based Learning

The phrase chunking system in this study was developed using transformation-based learning framework first proposed by Brill [13]. It is basically a non-statistical corpus-based learning technique, where an ordered set of transformation rules is acquired from an annotated training corpus. The idea is to start with some simple solution to the problem and apply transformations iteratively, selecting at each step the transformation which results in the largest benefit.

The chunk tags were encoded by CoNLL-2000 style representation [8] (originally from [5]) where chunk tags {I, O, B} are combined with chunk types. For example, B-NP denotes an initial word of an NP chunk, I-VP a non-initial word of a VP chunk and O a word outside any chunks.

The words in training corpus are annotated with these chunk tags as well as the part of speech tags. The learning process proceeds as follows. First, some simple baseline algorithm assigns initial chunk tags to the words in training corpus. One way to do this is to assign chunk tag Y to every word which has

POS tag X, if Y was the most frequent chunk tag of POS tag X in the training corpus. After the baseline assignment, all possible transformations that could possibly improve the current chunk tag assignment of the training corpus, are inspected. A rule that corrects a wrong chunk tag in one place of the training corpus may also change the correct tags to the wrong in other places. Therefore, the net contribution of the candidate rules should be computed. One with the largest benefit is selected, applied to the corpus and added to the sequence of learned transformation rules. The entire process is then repeated on the updated corpus, until there are no more transformations or the net contribution of the selected transformation is smaller than a pre-defined threshold.

In order to generate possible transformations at each step of the learning process, a set of *rule templates* are used to describe the kind of rules the system will try to learn. The templates determine which features are checked when a transformation is proposed. For example, the following is an example of a template, which defines a rule that will change the chunk tag based on the current chunk tag and the POS tags of three preceding words.

```
chunk_0 pos_-3 pos_-2 pos_-1 => chunk
```

The candidate transformation rules are then generated by instantiating the templates with actual values from the corpus. The features used in this study are as follows.

- neighboring words
- POS tags of neighboring words
- chunk tags of neighboring words

In the experiments, the neighboring context was limited by the range [-3, +3], that is, the features of at most three words to the left or to the right can be seen by the transformation rules. The context range defines the size of the search space for candidate rules, and therefore the amount of computation for learning is heavily dependent on the context size. Some rules also check the presence of a particular feature in a certain range. These basic features are systematically combined to produce rule templates.

2.3   Experimental Result

A Chinese phrase chunking system was implemented using the Fast Transformation-Based Learning Toolkit [14]. A total of 150 rule templates were devised that use the features explained above. Since no chunk-annotated Chinese corpus of enough size is currently available, we converted the parse trees generated by our parser into training corpus. Though the parse trees contain a certain percentage of errors, we could still expect to get a reasonably useful result by the learning process. A small-scale experimental comparison confirmed this assumption. For this purpose, two different sets of small-sized corpuses were prepared: Mtrain (45,684 tokens) and Mtest (10,626 tokens) were made from the tree-annotated corpus manually corrected by native Chinese speakers while Atrain (45,848

Table 1. Chunking result (pilot version)

Training corpus	Test corpus	Precision	Recall	$F_{\beta=1}$
Mtrain	Mtest	94.88	93.91	94.39
Atrain	Atest	93.79	92.08	92.93
Atrain	Mtest	95.07	93.91	94.49

Table 2. Chunking result

	Precision	Recall	$F_{\beta=1}$
Baseline	40.64	63.53	49.56
Final	95.75	94.13	94.93

tokens) and Atest (10,757 tokens) were directly converted from the parse trees generated by parser. The stopping threshold for the learning process was one, that is, the algorithm stopped when a rule with net score one is reached.

Table 1 shows the results measured with the usual precision, recall and $F_{\beta=1}$ rates. The first result was obtained with manually corrected training and test corpuses, while the second one was with the corpuses from the 'raw' parse trees. The numbers of acquired rules were 353 and 399, respectively. In the third experiment, the rules acquired from Atrain were applied to Mtest. Therefore, in the first and third experiments, the same Mtest was used to compare the transformation rules acquired from Mtrain and Atrain. The result does not show any serious performance drop when using the possibly inferior Atrain as training corpus. In fact, contrary to expectation, the rules acquired from Atrain performed slightly better on the Mtest corpus than the rules from Mtrain. The fact that considerably more rules were acquired from Atrain than Mtrain may be a factor here, but the difference does not seem significant. However, the result does suggest that the Mtest corpus is somehow 'easier' than Atest from the viewpoint of chunking.

For a more extensive experiment, a training corpus of 157,835 tokens and a test corpus of 45,879 tokens were used. Both corpuses consist of sentences gathered from various Chinese websites, and were automatically converted from the parse trees generated by the parser. The same 150 templates were used and the stopping threshold this time was three. The number of acquired rules was 303. Table 2 shows the baseline and final result of this experiment.

The result shows about 2% of improvement in F-measure over the earlier Atest experiment with smaller training corpus. This result is slightly better than the published result of CoNLL-2000 shared chunking task [8], but it should be noted that the results can not be directly compared since the target domain and experimental details are totally different. Moreover, the formulation of problem itself seems to be relatively easier in our case. For one thing, the number of chunk types to be identified is smaller, because the target application of this study is more restricted.

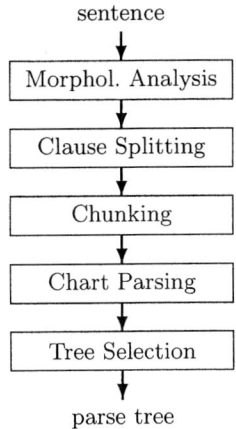

Fig. 1. Structure of parsing system

3   From Chunking to Parsing

Figure 1 shows the structure of the Chinese analysis system in our machine translation system. In order to handle the excessive length of the real world sentences, the system attempts to split the sentence into a sequence of clauses based on punctuation marks and other context information. After then, chunks are identified for each clause and the relevant information is handed over to chart-based parser module. If more than one trees are produced for a clause, the tree selection module selects one of them based on various knowledge sources.

3.1   Chunks and Dependency Information

Parser can benefit from the information obtained by phrase chunker. However, most machine learning-based chunking processes identify only the start and end positions of the chunks, without their internal structures. Therefore, it is not possible to use the chunks directly in parsing. We devised an interface that effectively conveys the dependency information made available by chunking to the parser.

Dependency relation of a sentence can be defined as $n \times n$ matrix Dep, where n is the number of words in the sentence. $Dep[i, j]$ represents the dependency between i-th and j-th words. If i-th word is a *dependent* (that is, a complement or a modifier) of k-th word, $Dep[i, k] = 1$. It implies $Dep[i, j] = 0$ for all $j \neq k$, since a word cannot have more than one *governor* in our grammar. If an identified chunk corresponds to a constituent in a parsing tree, then the words inside the chunk except its head are disallowed to have dependency relation with any words outside the chunk. More precisely, if a sentence has n words, $w_1, \ldots, w_n$, and a chunk $C[c : k]$ spanning from w_c to w_k with its head w_h, $1 \leq c \leq h \leq k \leq n$, is found, then $Dep[i, j] = 0$ for all $i, c \leq i \leq k, i \neq h$, and for all $j, 1 \leq j < c, k < j \leq n$. Figure 2 shows the status of the dependency matrix Dep when the chunk is recognized. The cells marked zero means there will be no dependency relation

	1	...	c	...	h	...	k	...	n
1	-	?	0	0	?	0	0	?	?
...	?	-	0	0	?	0	0	?	?
c	0	0	-	?	?	?	?	0	0
...	0	0	?	-	?	?	?	0	0
h	?	?	0	0	-	0	0	?	?
...	0	0	?	?	?	-	?	0	0
k	0	0	?	?	?	?	-	0	0
...	?	?	0	0	?	0	0	-	?
n	?	?	0	0	?	0	0	?	-

Fig. 2. Dependency matrix

between the two words. This matrix is consulted during parsing to prevent pairs of structures with disabled dependency from being combined.

The syntactic head of a chunk can be found in most cases by inspecting the POS tag sequence. The head of an NP chunk should be the last noun element in the chunk, the head of a QP chunk should be the last measure word (MW), and so on. Therefore, if a chunk corresponding to a constituent is recognized and its syntactic head is known, the dependency constraints can be automatically constructed.

However, there are problematic cases such as VP chunks with more than one verb elements. The simple method explained above cannot be applied to these VP chunks for two reasons. First, VP chunks do not always correspond to constituents. For example, a transitive verb may take a noun phrase as its object, which will become an NP chunk of its own. So, the VP constituent in this case will be broken into two distinct chunks: VP and NP. The VP chunks often consist of the remaining elements of verb phrases from which other chunks are extracted, and therefore do not generally correspond to any constituents. If a chunk does not correspond to a constituent, the non-head elements of the chunk can have dependency relations with words outside the chunk. Secondly, for the VP chunks with more than one verbs, the syntactic head cannot be determined just by inspecting the POS tag sequence because verbs can have post-modifiers. For example, in a VP chunk with tag sequence "AD VV VV", the first verb could be an adverbial modifier to the second one, or the second verb could be a directional or resultative modifier to the first one. For the VP chunks with more than one verb elements, the above two reasons make it impossible to construct dependency constraints such as Fig. 2.

The first problem can be avoided if we stipulate VP chunks should correspond to constituents. This approach is not desirable and inappropriate for shallow parsing application because it makes the chunk definition recursive, resulting in loss of efficiency. The second problem can also be avoided if we split verb-resultative or verb-directional constructions into two separate VP chunks. Then, the syntactic heads of VP chunks will be uniquely determined by tag sequence. However, since this verb-modifier construction is highly productive and regarded as a *lexical* process in Chinese, it is not desirable to recognize them as separate chunks.

For each sentence $[1..n]$ do the following:

1. Initialize dependency matrix Dep;
2. Apply chunking rules;
3. For each recognized chunk $C[c..k]$ do the following:

   if its chunk type $C \neq VP$, or $C = VP$ and C has only one verb then
   - Locate syntactic head h of C;
   - for all $i, c \leq i \leq k, i \neq h$, and for all $j, 1 \leq j < c, k < j \leq n$ do $Dep[i,j] = 0$;

   else (that is, $C = VP$ and C has more than one verb)
   - for all $i, c \leq i \leq k, TAG(w_i) \neq VV$, and for all $j, 1 \leq j < c, k < j \leq n$ do $Dep[i,j] = 0$.

Fig. 3. The phrase chunking algorithm

It might seem that these VP chunks are of no use for the purpose of this study. However, some of the dependency constraints, if restricted, can still be obtained for VP chunks with more than one verb elements. For the VP chunk of "AD VV VV", the head of the first word AD should be found inside the chunk. Therefore, the dependency relation between this adverb and all the other words outside the chunk can be safely set to zero. More generally, for a VP chunk with more than one verbal elements, for all non-verbal elements w_i of the chunk, $Dep[i,j]$ can be set to zero for all w_j outside the chunk.

In summary, the phrase chunker works as follows. After the input sentence goes through the morphological analysis and clause splitting stages, the chunking rules are applied and a set of chunks are recognized. For each chunk thus obtained, the dependency matrix Dep is updated according to its chunk type. This procedure is summarized in Fig. 3.

Table 3. Parsing result

	Without chunking	With chunking	Difference
Accuracy	90.35%	90.87%	+0.52%
Avg # of trees per clause	6.1	3.8	−37.8%
# of parsed words per second	866.3	1012.8	+16.9%
Avg memory usage per clause	237.2 KB	184.0 KB	−22.4%

3.2   Experimental Result

The phrase chunking module was inserted into the Chinese-Korean machine translation system right before the parser, and an experiment was performed with a test corpus (10,160 tokens) which was previously unseen by the chunking algorithm. Table 3 compares the results of parsing with and without chunking module. With chunking module added, the average number of trees was reduced drastically, and considerable improvement in both speed and memory usage was obtained. The speed measured by the number of parsed words per second increased by about 17 percent, and the average size of the total memory allocated by the parser to parse a clause decreased by about 22 percent.[1] The accuracy was calculated as the ratio of the right dependency links to the total number of links, by comparing the parsed trees to the correct trees manually prepared by native Chinese speakers. A sentence of n words has n dependency links (including the root of a tree which should have no governor), and for each word in a parsed tree, the link was regarded *right* if it has the same governor as in the corresponding correct tree. The result with chunking module showed about 0.5% improvement, which is a relatively minute improvement. We assume this is because the tree selection module currently employed in the parser is relatively reliable. Still, the improvement in efficiency alone makes the chunking module a worthwhile addition to the existing machine translation system.

4   Conclusion

This paper presented an approach to phrase chunking as a way to improve the performance of an existing parser in machine translation system. In order to accomplish this, an appropriate interface between the chunker and the parser is necessary so that the chunk information obtained by the chunker can be effectively used by the parser. We have implemented a Chinese phrase chunker using transformation-based learning algorithm, and integrated it into the Chinese-Korean machine translation system. The experimental results are promising, with improvements in parsing efficiency and accuracy. Especially, considering the excessive complexity of real world sentences that a practical general-domain natural language processing system should cope with, the noticeable improvement in parsing efficiency could be quite useful in implementing practical applications.

References

1. Abney, S.: Parsing by Chunks. in Berwick, Abney, Tenny (eds.): Principle-Based Parsing. Kluwer Academic Publishers (1991) 257–278
2. Cardie, C., Pierce, D.: Error-driven Pruning of Treebank Grammars for Base Noun Phrase Identification. in Proc of ACL/Coling (1998) 218–224
3. Cardie, C., Pierce, D.: The Role of Lexicalization and Pruning for Base Noun Phrase Grammars. in Proc of AAAI-99 (1999)
4. Abney, S.: Partial Parsing via Finite-State Cascades. in Proc of Robust Parsing Workshop ESSLLI'96 (1996) 8–15
5. Ramshaw, L. A., Marcus, M. P.: Text Chunking Using Transformation-based Learning. in Proc of 3rd ACL Workshop on ery Large Corpora (1995) 82–94
6. Argamon-Engelson, S., Dagan, I., Krymolowski, Y.: A Memory-based Approach to Learning Shallow Natural Language Patterns. in Proc of ACL/Coling, (1998) 67–73
7. Skut, W., Brants, T.: A Maximum Entropy Partial Parser for Unrestricted Text. in Proc of 6th Workshop on Very Large Corpora (1998)

---

[1] The speed and memory usage were measured on a Pentium-III 930 MHz personal computer with 192 MByte RAM. Both data were obtained by taking the average of five repeated executions.

8. Kim Sang, E. F. T., Buchholz, S.: Introduction to the CoNLL-2000 Shared Task: Chunking. in Proc of CoNLL-2000 (2000) 127–132
9. Hobbs, J., Appelt, D., Bear, J., Israel, D., Kameyama, M., Stickel, M., Tyson, M.: FASTUS: A Cascaded Finite-State Transducer for Extracting Information From Natural Language Text. in Roche, Schabes (eds.): Finite-State Language Processing (1997) 383–406
10. Briscoe, E.J., Carroll, J.: Automatic Extraction of Subcategorization from Corpora. in Proc of ACL Conference on Applied Natural Language Processing (1997)
11. Carrol, J., Minnen, G., Briscoe, T.: Corpus Annotation for Parser Evaluation. in Proc of EACL'99 Workshop on Linguistically Interpreted Corpora (1999)
12. Xue, N., Xia, F.: The Bracketing Guidelines for the Penn Chinese Treebank. IRCS Repost 00-08 available at http://www.cis.upenn.edu/~chinese/ (2000)
13. Brill, E.: Transformation-based Error-driven Learning and Natural Language Processing. Computational Linguistics, 21(4) (1995) 543–565
14. Ngai, G., Florian, R.: Transformation-Based Learning in the Fast Lane. in Proc of North American ACL 2001 (2001) 40–47

Motion Planning Based on Geometric Features

Antonio Benitez and Daniel Vallejo

Universidad de las Américas, CENTIA.
Sta. Catarina Mártir, Cholula, Puebla
72820 México
{sc098381, dvallejo}@mail.udlap.mx
http://mailweb.udlap.mx/~sc098381

Abstract. This paper describes the foundations and algorithms of a new alternative to improve the connectivity of the configuration space using probabilistic roadmap methods (PRM). The main idea is to use some geometric features about the obstacles and the robot into work-space, and to obtain useful configurations close to the obstacles to find collision free paths. In order to reach a better performance of these planners, we use the *"straightness"* feature and propose a new heuristic which allows us to solve the narrow corridor problems. We apply this technique to solve the motion planning problems for a specific kind of robots, *"free flying objects"* with six degrees of freedom (dof), three degrees used for position and the last three used for orientation. We have implemented the method in three dimensional space and we show results that allow us to be sure that some geometric features on the work-space can be used to improve the connectivity of configuration space and to solve the narrow corridor problems.

Keywords: Probabilistic roadmap methods, motion planning, geometric features, robotics.

1 Introduction

We present a new planning method which computes collision-free paths for robots of virtually any type moving among stationary obstacles (static workspace). However, our method is particularly interesting for robots with six-dof. Indeed, an increasing number of practical problems involve such robots. The main contribution in this new proposal is an heuristic which attempts to compute useful configurations close to the obstacles, searching to improve the connectivity of the PRMs. A basic definition when we are talking about probabilistic roadmap methods is the concept of *configuration*. A configuration is a tuple with a specific number of parameters which are used to determine the position and orientation of an object. The method proceeds in two phases: a construction phase and a query phase. In the construction phase a probabilistic roadmap is constructed by repeatedly generating random free configurations (using spheres which surround the robot and the obstacles) of the robot and connecting these configurations using some simple, but very fast local planner. The roadmap thus formed in the

R. Monroy et al. (Eds.): MICAI 2004, LNAI 2972, pp. 488–497, 2004.
© Springer-Verlag Berlin Heidelberg 2004

free configuration space (C-Space [12]) of the robot is stored as an undirected graph R. The configurations are the nodes of R and the paths computed by the local planner are the edges of R. The construction phase is completed by some postprocessing of R to improve its connectivity. That improving is computed using the *"straightness"* geometric feature on the workspace. This feature indicates the direction along which the object presents its long side. Following the construction phase, multiple queries can be answered. A query ask for a path between two free configurations of the robot. To process a query the method first attempt to find a path from the start and goal configurations to two nodes of the roadmap. Next, a graph search is done to find a sequence of edges connecting these nodes in the roadmap. Concatenations of the successive path segments transform the sequence found into a feasible path for the robot.

2 Related Work

Probabilistic roadmap planners (PRMs) construct a network of simple paths (usually straight paths in the configuration space) connecting collision-free configurations picked at random [1,3,4,7,15,8,10,14,13]. They have been successful in solving difficult path planning problems.

An important issue in PRM planners is the method for choosing the random configurations for the construction of the roadmaps. Recent works have considered many alternatives to a uniform random distribution of configurations as means for dealing with the narrow passage problem. A resampling step, creating additional nodes in the vicinity of nodes that are connected with a few others, is shown in [8]. Nodes close to the surface of the obstacles are added in [2]. A dilation of the configuration space has been suggested in [6], as well as an in depth analysis of the narrow passage problem. In [16] a procedure for retracting configurations onto the free space medial axis is presented. In [5] a probabilistic method for choosing configurations close to the obstacles is presented.

3 Preliminaries and Notation

The moving objects (robot) considered in this paper are rigid objects in three-dimensional space. We present configurations using six-tuples $(x,y,z,\alpha,\beta,\delta)$, where the first three coordinates define the position and the last three define the orientation. The orientation coordinates are represented in radians.

In addition to collision detection, all PRMs make heavy use of so-called *local planners* and *distance computation*. Local planners are simple, fast, deterministic method used to make connections between roadmap nodes when building the roadmap, and to connect the start and goal configurations to the roadmap during queries. Distance metrics are used to determine which pairs of nodes one should try to connect.

Let $B = \{B_0, ..., B_n\}$ be a set of obstacles in the workspace W. Let r_i be the radius associate to the sphere which involve each body in the workspace (including the robot).

Let d_i be the distance between two configurations, one of them associate to the robot and the another one associate to the obstacle B_i.

Let $c(B_i)$ be the random configuration computed by the heuristic using the obstacle B_i. Let q be the configuration $c(B_i)$ added to the roadmap and the roadmap will be denoted by R. Let v_i be the direction vector which define the "*straightness*" feature for each $B_i \in B$, and vr_i will denote the same feature on the robot. This feature indicates the direction which the body presents its long side.

The symbol $\|$ will be used to show that two configurations $c(B_i)$ and $c(B_j)$ are in parallel, that means that, the bodies associated to each configuration keep in parallel their direction vectors.

4   Algorithm Description

We now describe the planner in general terms for a specific type of robot, the free flying objects. During the preprocessing phase a data structure called the roadmap is constructed in a probabilistic way for a given scene. The roadmap is an undirected graph $R = (N, E)$. The nodes in N are a set of configurations of the robot appropriately chosen over the free C-space (C_{free}). The edges in E correspond to (simple) paths; an edge between two nodes corresponds to a feasible path connecting the relevant configurations. These paths are computed by an extremely fast, though not very powerful planner, called the local planner. During the query phase, the roadmap is used to solve individual path planning problems in the input scene. Given a start configuration q_{init} and a goal configuration q_{goal}, the method first tries to connect q_{init} and q_{goal} to some two nodes q'_{init} and q'_{goal} in N. If successful, it then searches R for a sequence of edges in E connecting q'_{init} to q'_{goal}. Finally, it transforms this sequence into a feasible path for the robot by recomputing the corresponding local paths and concatenating them.

4.1   The Construction Phase

The construction phase consists of two successive steps: first approximation of the roadmap and expanding the roadmap. The objective of the first approximation of the roadmap is to obtain an approximation using an economic and fast process. The expanding roadmap step is aimed at further improving the connectivity of this graph. It selects nodes of R which, according to some heuristic evaluator, lie in difficult regions of C_{free} and expand the graph by generating additional nodes in their neighborhoods.

First Approximation of the Roadmap. Initially the graph $R = (N, E)$ is empty. Then, repeatedly, a random free configuration is generated and added to N. For every such new node q, we select a number of nodes from the current N and try to connect q to each of them using the local planner. Whenever this planner succeeds to compute a feasible path between q and selected node q', the edge (q, q') is added to E. To make our presentation more precise:

Let LP be the local planner which return $\{0,1\}$ depending if the local planner can compute a path between two configurations given as arguments.

Let D be the *distance function*, defining a pseudo- metric in $C - space$.

The roadmap first approximation algorithm can be outlined as follows:

First Approximation
> 1. $N \longleftarrow 0$
> 2. *for* $k = 1$ *to* CTE_NODES
>> 3. $q \longleftarrow$ *a randomly chosen free configuration*
>> 4. *if (q is not in collision) then*
>>> 5. $N \longleftarrow N \cup \{q\}$
>> 6. *k=k+1*
> 7. *endfor*

Some choices for the steps of above algorithm are still unspecified. In particular, we need to define how random configurations are created in step 3, and which function is used to collision detection in 4.

Creation of random configurations. The nodes of R should constitute a rather uniform sampling of C_{free}. Every such configuration is obtained by drawing each of its coordinates from the interval of allowed values of the corresponding dof using uniform probability distribution over this interval. This sampling is computed using spheres which surround the objects. The figure 1 shows this sampling.

Collision detection. Only during this process, the collision detection function is implemented using spheres, that means that, we surround the robot and the obstacles into a sphere and the collision verification is reduced to compute if two spheres are in collision. Therefore, this process can be computed quickly.

Expanding the Roadmap. If the number of nodes computed during the first approximation of the roadmap is large enough, the set N gives a fairly uniform covering of C_{free}. In easy scenes R is well connected. But in more constrained ones where C_{free} is actually connected, R often consists of a few large components and several small ones. It therefore does not effectively capture the connectivity of C_{free}.

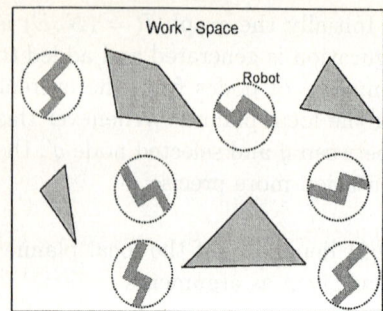

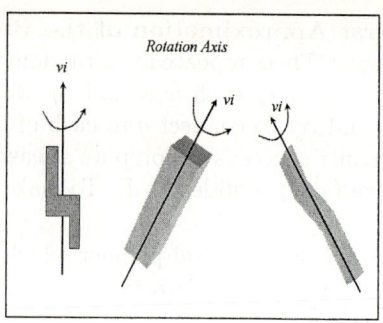

Fig. 1. First approximation using spheres surrounding the robot and computing a reduced number of configurations.

Fig. 2. The rotation axis is defined in the same direction of the *straightness* feature.

The purpose of the expansion is to add more nodes in a way that will facilitate the formation of the large components comprising as many of the nodes as possible and will also help cover the more difficult narrow parts of C_{free}. The identification of these difficult parts of C_{free} is no simpler matter and the heuristic that we propose below goes only a certain distance in this direction.

First, the heuristic attempt to take advantage of a geometric feature of the robot and the obstacles to obtain information that allows guide the search for useful configurations, and reduce the account of non-valid configurations to be calculated. In order to reach a better performance of these planners we will obtain a better representation of the connectivity of the configuration space.

The first feature used is called *"Straightness"*. This feature indicates the direction which the body presents its long side and it is given by a vector v_i, which we have used as the direction of the rotation axis. Figure 2. shows how this feature is used to define the rotation axis. Next, we begin by calculating a random configuration $c(B_i)$ near to each obstacle B_i . If the $c(B_i)$ is in collision, then the heuristic attempts to move this configuration to turn it in a free configuration, which will be close to some obstacle. (Amato and Wu in [3], propose an algorithm which compute configurations on C - *Obstacle surfaces*).

Parallel Configurations. Once the collision configuration $c(B_i)$ has been found, the first strategy is to rotate it until the rotation axis of the robot v_{ri} will be parallel to the rotation axis v_i of the obstacle B_i, that means that, $v_{ri}\|v_i$. The configuration obtained can be seen in the Figure 3., where we can see different parallel configurations. If the new $c(B_i)$ is not in collision then it is added to the roadmap, if it is in collision a process called elastic band is applied on $c(B_i)$.

Perpendicular Configurations. The second strategy is to rotate it until the rotation axis of the robot v_{ri} will be perpendicular to the rotation axis v_i of the obstacle B_i, that means that, $v_{ri} \perp v_i$. The configuration computed can be seen in the Figure 3. If the new $c(B_i)$ is not in collision then is added to the roadmap, if it is in collision the elastic band process is applied on $c(B_i)$.

The Elastic Band Heuristic. This process works as follows, first it calculates the distance vector d_i between the obstacle position and the configuration $c(B_i)$, and attempts to approach and move away the robot from the obstacle. While the band is working (scaling the d_i vector to compute the next position where the $c(B_i)$ is going to be placed) the robot is rotated on its rotation axis, searching a free configuration.

The first criteria tries to move and rotate the configuration in a smooth way, searching to keep the rotation axis of the robot parallel to the rotation axis of the obstacle where there was collision. The technique works like a band which was described in the previous section. While the elastic band process is computed, the robot is rotated on v_{ri}, this heuristic imagine that if the *"straightness"* feature was defined as in notation section then, when we try to rotate the robot about v_{ri} the swept area will be the lowest. The Figure 4. shows how the algorithm works, searching for calculating configuration around the obstacle and close to it. Into the figure, v_i and v_{ri} represents the rotation axis of the obstacle and the robot respectively, and d_i represents the distance vector which the heuristic scale to reach a free configuration. The next algorithm presents the elastic band process.

Elastic Band Heuristic

        1. r_i = *radius of i-obstacle*
        2. *ci_init = position of the i-obstacle*
        3. *scale_value = 0, angle = 0, k = 0;*
        4. d_i = *distance vector between i-obstacle and robot positions*
        5. *do*
                scale_value = random between (0.5 and 1.5)
                scale(d_i, scale_value)
                angle = random between (0,2Π)
                rotate_robot_on_rotation_axis(angle)
                c(B_i)=get_configuration_with_position (d_i)
                k = k + 1
        6. *while (c(B_i) is not free configuration and k $\leq$ CTE)*
        7. *add_configuration c(B_i) to the roadmap*

The second criteria is to get a perpendicular configuration to the obstacle, this option can be seen in Figure 3. In the same way that parallel configuration, the perpendicular configuration is added to the roadmap if and only if it is not in collision, otherwise the elastic band process is applied on it.

In the elastic band heuritic presented before, there are two undefined operations, the first one is the *scale_value* parameter, this is used to store the value

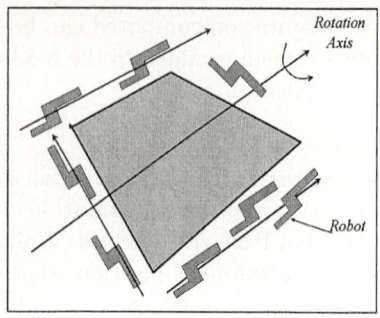

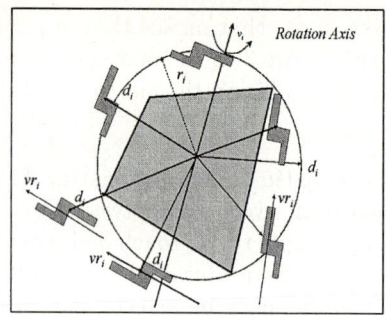

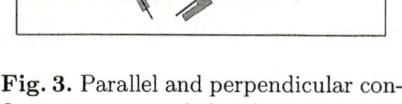

Fig. 3. Parallel and perpendicular configurations around the obstacle

Fig. 4. The elastic band heuristic

which the distance vector will be scaled to obtain the next position of the configuration $c(B_i)$, and the second on is the *scale function* which compute the product between the vector d_i, and the *scale_value*.

4.2 The Query Phase

During the query phase, paths are to be found between arbitrary input start and goal configurations q_{init} and q_{goal}, using the roadmap computed in the construction phase. Assume for the moment that C_{free} is connected and that the roadmap consists of a single connected component R. We try to connect q_{init} and q_{goal} to some two nodes of R, respectively q'_{init} and q'_{goal}, with feasible paths P_{init} and P_{goal}. If this fails, the query fails. Otherwise, we compute a path P in R connecting q'_{init} to q'_{goal}. A feasible path from q'_{init} to q'_{goal} is eventually constructed by concatenating P_{init}, the recomputed path corresponding to P, and P_{goal} reversed.

The main question is how to compute the paths P_{init} and P_{goal}. The queries should preferably terminate quasi-instantaneously, so no expensive algorithm is desired here. Our strategy for connecting q_{init} to R is to consider the nodes in R in order of increasing distance from q_{init} and try to connect q_{init} to each of them with the local planner, until one connection is succeeds or until an allocated amount of time has elapsed.

5   Experimental Results

We demonstrate the application of the planner explaining four examples. The planner is implemented in C++ and it is working in three dimensional space, for experiments reported here we used an Intel Pentium 4 CPU 2.4 GHz and 512MB in RAM.

In the following, we analyze the performance of the method (this performance is seen since the capability of the method to solve the problems) on several scenes.

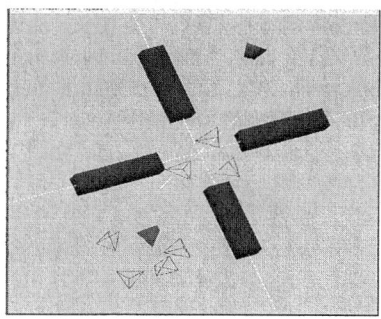

Fig. 5. Scene 1. The robot is a tetrahedro, and the obstacles are four prisms.

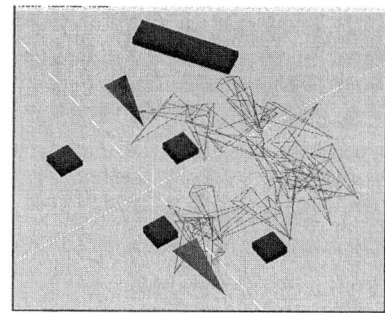

Fig. 6. Scene 2. The robot is a large tetrahedro, and the obstacles are five prisms.

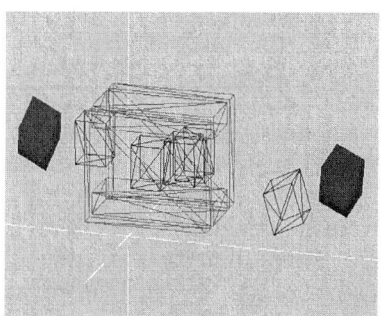

Fig. 7. Scene 3. The robot is a cube passing through a corridor

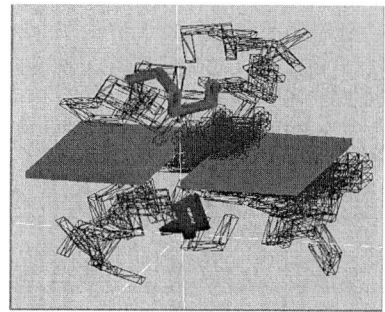

Fig. 8. Scene 4. The robot has a more complicated form

In all cases we have used a free-flying object robot with six degrees of freedom. The various environments, and some representative configurations of the robot, are shown in Figures 5,6,7 and 8. Note that the roadmap size is influenced by the number of obstacles in the work-space since a set of roadmap nodes is generated for each obstacle, i.e., the size of the network is related to the complexity of the environment. The four samples shown are presented as result of the technique applied to the problems. We present four problems, they have different difficult level. The problems are labeled as E1, E2, E3 and E4.

E1: This environment contains four obstacles and the robot is represented by a tetrahedron. The roadmap for this environment is simple, because the corridor is not very narrow, but we can see in figure 5. that the method can obtain a path between init and goal configurations.

E2: This scene is presented with five obstacles, and the robot is represented as a large tetrahedron. In the problem presented here the robot is a little bit large respect to the obstacles, nevertheless the algorithm is able to compute a path between init and goal configurations, see figure 6.

E3: This environment contains four obstacles and the robot is represented by a cube. The obstacles are placed in such a way that they form a narrow corridor. This roadmap is not easy to calculate, because the size of the robot is big, and the configuration become difficult to calculate. We can see in figure 7. that in the solution obtained there are many configurations near to the obstacles.

E4: This scene is presented with two obstacles and we can see that the form of the robot is more complex. There is a narrow corridor which becomes difficult to solve, nevertheless, the heuristic is able to find a path which goes through the corridor, see figure 8.

6   Conclusions

We have described a new randomized roadmap method for motion planning for collision free path planning. To test the concept, we implemented the method for path planning for *"free flying object"* robots in a three-dimensional space. The method was shown to perform well. We think that the heuristic could be modified so it can be used to solve motion planning problems for articulated robots. Currently, we are working on the free flying objects problems, and we are adding the *"flatness"* features on the heuristic searching to improve the connectivity. The main idea is to take advantage of the geometric features on the workspace that we can obtain a representative connection of configuration space. We would like to prove our technique to solve the so called *"alpha puzzle"* problem.

Acknowledgments. We would like to thank the Center of Research in Information and Automation Technologies (CENTIA) at the Universidad de las Américas - Puebla.

This research is supported by the project: Access to High Quality Digital Services and Information for Large Communities of Users, CONACYT.

References

1. J.M. Ahuactzin and K.Gupta. A motion planning based approach for inverse kinematics of redundant robots: The kinematic roadmap. *In Proc. IEEE Internat. Conf. Robot. Autom.*, pages 3609-3614, 1997.
2. N. Amato, B. Bayazit, L. Dale, C. Jones, and D. Vallejo. Obprm: An obstacle-based prm for 3D workspaces. *In P.K. Agarwal, L. Kavraki, and M. Mason, editors, Robotics: The Algorithm Perspective.* AK Peters, 1998.
3. N. M. Amato and Y. Wu. A randomized roadmap method for path and manipulation planning. *In Proc. IEEE Internat. Conf. Robot. Autoum,.* Pages 113-120, Mineapolis, MN, April 1996.
4. J. Barraquand and J.C. Latombe. Robot motion planning: A distributed representation approach. Internat. J. Robot. Res., 10(6):628-649,1991.

5. V. Boor, M. Overmars, and F. van der Stappen. The gaussian sampling strategy for probabilistic roadmap planners. *In Proc. IEEE Int.Conf. on Rob. and Autom.,* pages 1018-1023,1999.
6. D. Halperin, L. E. Kavraki, and J.-C. Latombe. Robotics. *In J. Goodman and J. O'Rourke, editors, Discrete and Computational Geometry.,* pages 755-778. CRC Press, NY, 1997.
7. D. Hsu, J.C. Latombe, and R. Motwani. Path planning in expansive configuration spaces. *In Proc. IEEE Internat. Conf. Robot. Autoum,.* Pages 2719-2726, 1997.
8. L. Kavraki and J. C. Latombe. Probabilistic roadmaps for robot path planning. *In K. G. and A. P. del Pobil, editor, Practical Motion Planning in Robotics: Current Approaches and Future Challenges,* pages 33-53. John Wiley, West Sussex, England, 1998.
9. L. Kavraki and J. C. Latombe. Randomized preprocessing of configuration space for fast path planning. *In Proc. IEEE Internat. Conf. Robot. Autoum,.* Pages 2138-2145, 1994.
10. L. Kavraki, P. Svestka, J.C. Latombe, and M. Overmars. Probabilistic roadmaps for path planning in high-dimensional configuration spaces. *In Proc. IEEE Internat. Conf. Robot. Autoum,.* 12(4): 566-580, August 1996.
11. J-C. Latombe. Robot Motion Planning. Kluwer Academic Publishers, Boston, MA, 1991.
12. T. Lozano-Pérez. Spatial planning: a configuration space approach. *IEEE Tr. On Computers,* 32:108-120, 1983.
13. M. Overmars. A Random Approach to Motion Planning , *Tecnical Report RUU-CS-92-32,* Computer Science, Utrecht University, the Netherlands, 1992.
14. M. Overmars and P. Svestka. A probabilistic learning approach to motion planning. *In Proc. Workshop on Algorithmic Foundations of Robotics.,* pages 19-37 1994.
15. D. Vallejo, I. Remmler, N.Amato. An Adaptive Framework for "Single Shot" Motion planning: A Selft-Tuning System for Rigid and Articulated Robots. *In Proc. IEEE Int. Conf. Robot. Autom.,* (ICRA), 2001.
16. S. A. Wilmarth, N. M. Amato, and P. F. Stiller. Maprm: A probabilistic roadmap planner with sampling on the medial axis of the freespace. *In Proc. IEEE Int. Conf. Robot. and Autom.,* Detroit, MI, 1999.

Comparative Evaluation of Temporal Nodes Bayesian Networks and Networks of Probabilistic Events in Discrete Time

S.F. Galán[1], G. Arroyo-Figueroa[2], F.J. Díez[1], and L.E. Sucar[3]

[1] Departamento de Inteligencia Artificial, UNED, Madrid, Spain
{seve,fjdiez}@dia.uned.es
[2] Instituto de Investigaciones Eléctricas, Cuernavaca, Mexico
garroyo@iie.org.mx
[3] ITESM - Campus Cuernavaca, Mexico
esucar@itesm.mx

Abstract. *Temporal Nodes Bayesian Networks* (TNBNs) and *Networks of Probabilistic Events in Discrete Time* (NPEDTs) are two different types of Bayesian networks (BNs) for temporal reasoning. Arroyo-Figueroa and Sucar applied TNBNs to an industrial domain: the diagnosis and prediction of the temporal faults that may occur in the steam generator of a fossil power plant. We have recently developed an NPEDT for the same domain. In this paper, we present a comparative evaluation of these two systems. The results show that, in this domain, NPEDTs perform better than TNBNs. The ultimate reason for that seems to be the finer time granularity used in the NPEDT with respect to that of the TNBN. Since families of nodes in a TNBN interact through the general model, only a small number of states can be defined for each node; this limitation is overcome in an NPEDT through the use of *temporal noisy gates*.

1 Introduction

Bayesian networks (BNs) [7] have been successfully applied to the modeling of problems involving uncertain knowledge. A BN is an acyclic directed graph whose nodes represent random variables and whose links define probabilistic dependencies between variables. These relations are quantified by associating a conditional probability table (CPT) to each node. A CPT defines the probability of a node given each possible configuration of its parents. BNs specify dependence and independence relations in a natural way through the network topology. Diagnosis or prediction with BNs consists in fixing the values of the observed variables and computing the posterior probabilities of some of the unobserved variables.

Temporal Nodes Bayesian Networks (TNBNs) [1] and *Networks of Probabilistic Events in Discrete Time* (NPEDTs) [5] are two different types of BNs for temporal reasoning, both of them adequate for the diagnosis and prediction of temporal faults occurring in dynamic processes. Nevertheless, the usual method of applying BNs to the modeling of temporal processes is based on the use of *Dynamic Bayesian Networks* (DBNs) [3,6]. In a DBN, time is discretized and

R. Monroy et al. (Eds.): MICAI 2004, LNAI 2972, pp. 498–507, 2004.

an instance of each random variable is created for each point in time. While in a DBN the value of a variable V_i represents the state of a real-world property at time t_i, in either a TNBN or an NPEDT each value of a variable represents the time at which a certain event may occur. Therefore, TNBNs and NPEDTs are more appropriate for temporal fault diagnosis, because only one variable is necessary for representing the occurrence of a fault and, consequently, the networks involved are much simpler than those obtained by using DBNs (see [5], Section 4). However, DBNs are more appropriate for monitoring tasks, since they explicitly represent the state of the system at each moment.

1.1   The Industrial Domain

Steam generators of fossil power plants are exposed to disturbances that may provoke faults. The propagation of these faults is a non-deterministic dynamic process whose modeling requires representing both uncertainty and time.

We are interested in studying the disturbances produced in the drum level control system of a fossil power plant. The drum provides steam to the super-heater and water to the water wall of a steam generator. The drum is a tank with a steam valve at the top, a feedwater valve at the bottom, and a feedwater pump which provides water to the drum. There are four potential disturbances that may occur in the drum level control system: a power load increase (LI), a feedwater pump failure ($FWPF$), a feedwater valve failure ($FWVF$), and a spray water valve failure ($SWVF$). These disturbances may provoke the events shown in Figure 1. In this domain, we consider that an "event" occurs when a signal exceeds its specified limit of normal functioning.

Arroyo-Figueroa and Sucar applied TNBNs to the diagnosis and prediction of the temporal faults that may occur in the steam generator of a fossil power plant [2]. In this work, we describe the development of an NPEDT for the same domain. We also present a comparative evaluation of both networks.

This paper is organized as follows. Sections 2 and 3 give some details regarding the application to our industrial domain of TNBNs and NPEDTs, respectively. Section 4 explains the process of selection of the evaluation method for the domain and presents the results obtained from it for the two systems considered. Finally, Section 5 summarizes the main achievements of this work.

2   TNBN for This Industrial Domain

Arroyo-Figueroa and Sucar developed a formalism called *Temporal Nodes Bayesian Networks* (TNBNs) [1] that combines BNs and time. They applied this formalism to fault diagnosis and prediction for the steam generator of a fossil power plant [2]. A TNBN is an extension of a standard BN, in which each node represents a temporal event or change of state of a variable. There is at most one state change for each variable in the temporal range of interest. The value taken on by the variable represents the interval in which the change occurred. Time is discretized in a finite number of intervals, allowing a different number and

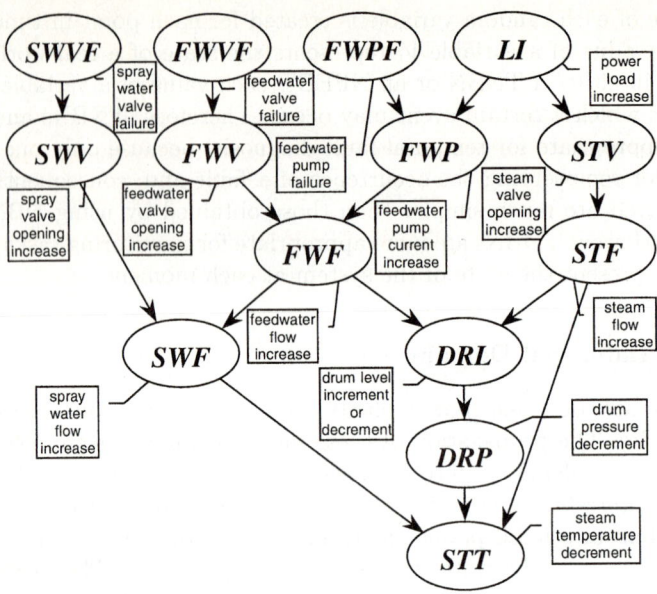

Fig. 1. Possible disturbances in a steam generator

duration of intervals for each node (multiple granularity). Each interval defined for a child node represents the possible delays between the occurrence of one of its parent events and the corresponding change of state of the child node. Therefore, this model makes use of **relative time** in the definition of the values associated to each temporal node with parents.

There is an asymmetry in the way evidence is introduced in the network: The occurrence of an event associated to a node without parents constitutes direct evidence, while evidence about a node with parents is analyzed by considering several scenarios. When an initial event is detected, its time of occurrence fixes the network temporally.

The causal model used by Arroyo-Figueroa and Sucar in the construction of their model is shown in Figure 1. The parameters of the TNBN were estimated from data generated by a simulator of a 350 MW fossil power plant. A total of more than nine hundred cases were simulated. Approximately 85% of the data were devoted to estimate the parameters, while the remaining 15% was used in the evaluation of the model, which we discuss later in the paper.

TNBNs use the general model of causal interaction, but lack a formalization of canonical models for temporal processes. Furthermore, each value defined for an effect node, which is associated to a determined time interval, means that the effect has been caused during that interval by only one of its parent events. However, this is not the general case in some domains where evidence about the occurrence of an event can be explained by several of its causes.

3   NPEDT for This Industrial Domain

In an NPEDT [5], each variable represents an event that can take place at most once. Time is discretized by adopting the appropriate temporal unit for each case (seconds, minutes, etc.); therefore, the temporal granularity depends on the particular problem. The value taken on by the variable indicates the **absolute time** at which the event occurs.

Formally speaking, a temporal random variable V in the network can take on a set of values $v[i]$, $i \in \{a, \dots, b, never\}$, where a and b are instants —or intervals— defining the limits of the temporal range of interest for V. The links in the network represent temporal causal mechanisms between neighboring nodes. Therefore, each CPT represents the most probable delays between the parent events and the corresponding child event. For the case of general dynamic interaction in a family of nodes, giving the CPT involves assessing the probability of occurrence of the child node over time, given any temporal configuration of the parent events. In a family of n parents $X_1, \dots, X_n$ and one child Y, the CPT is given by $P(y[t_Y] \mid x_1[t_1], \dots, x_n[t_n])$ with $t_Y \in \{0, \dots, n_Y, never\}$ and $t_i \in \{0, \dots, n_i, never\}$. The joint probability is given by the product of all the CPTs in the network. Any marginal or conditional probability can be derived from the joint probability.

If we consider a family of nodes with n parents and divide the temporal range of interest into i instants, in the general case the CPT associated to the child node requires $O(i^{n+1})$ independent conditional probabilities. In real-world applications, it is difficult to find a human expert or a database that allows us to create such a table, due to the exponential growth of the set of required parameters with the number of parents. For this reason, temporal canonical models were developed as an extension of traditional canonical models. In this fault-diagnosis domain, we only need to consider the *temporal noisy OR-gate* [5].

3.1   Numerical Parameters of the NPEDT

In our model, we consider a time range of 12 minutes and divide this period into 20-second intervals. Therefore, there are 36 different intervals in which any event in Figure 1 may occur. Given a node E, its associated random variable can take on values $\{e[1], \dots, e[36], e[never]\}$, where $e[i]$ means that event E takes place in interval i, and $e[never]$ means that E does not occur during the time range selected. For example, $SWF = swf[3]$ means "spray water flow increase occurred between seconds 41 and 60". As the values of any random variable in the network are exclusive, its associated events can only occur once over time. This condition is satisfied in the domain, since the processes involved are irreversible. Without the intervention of a human operator, any disturbance could provoke a shutdown of the fossil power plant.

We use the temporal noisy OR-gate as the model of causal interaction in the network. In this model, each cause acts independently of the rest of the causes to produce the effect. Independence of causal interaction is satisfied in the domain, according to the experts' opinion.

Computing the CPT for a node Y in the network requires specifying

$$c_{y[k]}^{x_i[j_i]} \equiv P(y[k] \mid x_i[j_i], x_l[never], l \neq i)$$

for each possible delay, $k - j_i$, between cause X_i and Y, when the rest of the causes are absent. Therefore, given that X_i takes place during a certain 20-second interval, it is necessary to specify the probability of its effect Y taking place in the same interval —if the rest of the causes are absent—, the probability of Y taking place in the next interval, and so on. These parameters were estimated from the same dataset used by Arroyo-Figueroa and Sucar in the construction of the TNBN.

In the NPEDT, evidence propagation through exact algorithms takes, in general, a few seconds by using Elvira[1] and the factorization described in [4]. (If that factorization is not used, evidence propagation takes almost one minute.) Consequently, this network could be used in a fossil power plant to assist human operators in real-time fault diagnosis and prediction.

4   Evaluation of the TNBN and the NPEDT

A total of 127 simulation cases were generated for evaluation purposes by means of a simulator of a 350 MW fossil power plant [8]. Each case consists of a list

$$((event_1, t_1), (event_2, t_2), \dots, (event_{14}, t_{14}))$$

where t_i is the occurrence time for $event_i$. There are 14 possible events, as Figure 1 shows. If $event_i$ did not occur then $t_i = never$. In general, among the 14 pairs included in each case, some of them correspond to evidence about the state of the steam generator.

4.1   Selection of the Evaluation Method

Our first attempt to quantify the performance of each model was carried out as follows. For each node or event X not included in the evidence:

1. Calculate $P^*(X) = P(X \mid \mathbf{e})$, the posterior probability of node X, given evidence $\mathbf{e}$.
2. For each simulated case that includes $\mathbf{e}$, obtain $ME(P^*(X), \hat{t}_X)$, a "measure of error" between the posterior probability and $\hat{t}_X$, the real (or simulated) occurrence time for X.
3. Calculate the mean and variance of the measures of error obtained in the previous step.

---

[1] Elvira is a software package for the construction and evaluation of BNs and influence diagrams, which is publicly available at http://www.ia.uned.es/~elvira

Given a *probability density function* for a variable V, $f_V(t)$, if V took place at $\hat{t}_V$, a possible measure of error is

$$ME(f_V(t), \hat{t}_V) = \int_0^{+\infty} f_V(t) \cdot |t - \hat{t}_V| \, dt. \tag{1}$$

This measure represents the average time distance between an event occurring at $\hat{t}_V$ and another one that follows distribution $f_V(t)$. For example, if $f_V(t)$ is a constant distribution between t_i and t_f (with $t_i < t_f$):

$$f_V(t) = \begin{cases} 0 & \text{if } t < t_i \\ \frac{p}{t_f - t_i} & \text{if } t_i \leq t \leq t_f \\ 0 & \text{if } t > t_f \end{cases} \tag{2}$$

then

$$ME(f_V(t), \hat{t}_V) = \begin{cases} p \cdot \left(\frac{t_i + t_f}{2} - \hat{t}_V \right) & \text{if } \hat{t}_V \leq t_i \\ \frac{p}{t_f - t_i} \cdot \left[\left(\hat{t}_V - \frac{t_i + t_f}{2} \right)^2 + \left(\frac{t_f - t_i}{2} \right)^2 \right] & \text{if } t_i \leq \hat{t}_V \leq t_f \\ p \cdot \left(\hat{t}_V - \frac{t_i + t_f}{2} \right) & \text{if } \hat{t}_V \geq t_f \end{cases}$$

Note that, if time is the variable considered, ME is equivalent to the *prediction error* (difference between the observation at time t and the *expected forecast value* for time t). The probability distribution $f_V(t)$ can be directly obtained from $P^*(V)$ in an NPEDT, while in a TNBN it is necessary to know which parent node is really causing V, which can be deduced from the information contained in the corresponding simulated case.

Two problems arise when we try to apply Equation 1 to a node of either a TNBN or an NPEDT:

- If, given a simulated case, event V does not occur, we can only assign $\hat{t}_V$ the value $+\infty$; as a consequence, the integral in Equation 1 cannot be calculated.
- If $P^*(V = v[never]) > 0$, the value t in Equation 1 cannot be precisely defined for $V = v[never]$; if we supposed that $t = +\infty$, the integral could not be computed, as in the previous problem.

In order to avoid these two problems, we adopted an alternative point of view: Instead of a *measure of error*, a *measure of proximity* between $P^*(V)$ and $\hat{t}_V$ can be used for evaluating the networks. Given a probability density function for a variable V, $f_V(t)$, if V took place at $\hat{t}_V$, a possible measure of proximity is

$$MP(f_V(t), \hat{t}_V) = \int_0^{+\infty} \frac{f_V(t)}{1 + \left(\frac{t - \hat{t}_V}{c} \right)^2} \, dt \tag{3}$$

where c is an arbitrary constant. We have selected this function because it has four desirable properties:

1. As $\int_0^{+\infty} f_V(t) \, dt = 1$, $0 \le MP \le 1$. $MP = 1$ when $f_V(t)$ is a Dirac delta function at $\hat{t}_V$.
2. Note that when $t = \hat{t}_V$, the value of the integrand is $f_V(\hat{t}_V)$; however, as $|t - \hat{t}_V| \longrightarrow +\infty$, the integrand approaches 0 regardless of the value of f_V. The two following properties deal with the two problems presented above regarding the measure of error.
3. If, given a simulated case, event V does not occur ($\hat{t}_V = +\infty$), the integrand is zero when $t \ne never$ and we consider that $MP = P^*(V = v[never])$.
4. If $P^*(V = v[never]) > 0$ and $\hat{t}_V$ takes on a finite value, we consider that the contribution of $V = v[never]$ to MP is 0.
5. When the density function is constant inside an interval, MP can be easily calculated.

Since TNBNs and NPEDTs are discrete-time models, we calculate MP (given by Equation 3) by adding the contributions of each interval associated to the values of node V and the contribution of value $never$. $P^*(V)$ defines a constant probability distribution over each of the intervals defined for V. Given the constant distribution defined in Equation 2,

$$MP\left(f_V(t), \hat{t}_V\right) = \frac{p \cdot c}{t_f - t_i} \cdot \left(\arctan\left(\frac{t_f - \hat{t}_V}{c}\right) - \arctan\left(\frac{t_i - \hat{t}_V}{c}\right)\right).$$

As expected, the maximum measure of proximity appears when $\hat{t}_V = \frac{t_i + t_f}{2}$. We have used $c = 360$ in the TNBN and the NPEDT. In the NPEDT $t_f - t_i = 20$ seconds, while in the TNBN $t_f - t_i$ is specific of each interval.

4.2 Results

By using the measure of proximity proposed in Section 4.1, we have performed tests for prediction and for diagnosis from the 127 simulation cases available.

Prediction. In order to analyze the predictive capabilities of the networks, we have carried out four different types of tests. In each of them there was only an initial fault event present: *SWVF*, *FWVF*, *FWPF* and *LI*, respectively. The states of the rest of the nodes in the networks were unknown. The time at which the corresponding initial fault event occurred defines the beginning of the global time range considered. Among the 127 simulated cases, 64 are associated to the presence of *LI*, and the rest of the initial fault events are simulated by means of 21 cases each. Tables 1 through 4 contain the means and variances of the measures of proximity obtained separately for both the TNBN and the NPEDT in the predictive tests. The average of the values shown in the last file of each table are: $\mu(\text{TNBN}) = 0.789003$, $\sigma^2(\text{TNBN}) = 2.603\text{E-}4$, $\mu(\text{NPEDT}) = 0.945778$, and $\sigma^2(\text{NPEDT}) = 1.509\text{E-}3$.

The results show that the NPEDT predicts more accurately than the TNBN. In general, the difference between the exactitude of predictions from the two networks grows as we go down in the graph. Both networks predict correctly that some events do not occur. Such events have been omitted in the tables.

Table 1. Means and variances of MP when $SWVF$ is present

Node	μ (TNBN)	σ^2 (TNBN)	μ (NPEDT)	σ^2 (NPEDT)
SWV	0.99786	2.185E-6	0.996066	3.456E-6
SWF	0.85793	4.267E-6	0.987375	4.138E-5
STT	0.55219	2.515E-3	0.874228	0.011258
Average	0.80266	8.404E-4	0.952556	3.767E-3

Table 2. Means and variances of MP when $FWVF$ is present

Node	μ (TNBN)	σ^2 (TNBN)	μ (NPEDT)	σ^2 (NPEDT)
FWV	0.99844	2.053E-6	0.995963	1.286E-6
FWF	0.88154	8.99E-5	0.957003	2.39E-4
SWF	0.71559	1.069E-6	0.818828	4.704E-4
DRL	0.85165	1.035E-3	0.914457	0.003583
DRP	0.93127	6.317E-6	0.895225	0.006293
STT	0.14576	5.724E-8	0.832621	0.001401
Average	0.754041	1.89E-4	0.902349	1.998E-3

Table 3. Means and variances of MP when $FWPF$ is present

Node	μ (TNBN)	σ^2 (TNBN)	μ (NPEDT)	σ^2 (NPEDT)
FWP	0.87001	3.522E-8	0.996962	7.425E-7
FWF	0.90496	1.478E-5	0.989113	2.018E-5
SWF	0.89533	1.537E-5	0.972282	1.598E-4
DRL	0.88665	5.776E-8	0.976043	9.658E-5
DRP	0.93262	9.382E-7	0.975946	6.43E-5
STT	0.14463	4.961E-8	0.954822	4.348E-4
Average	0.772366	5.205E-6	0.977528	1.294E-4

Table 4. Means and variances of MP when LI is present

Node	μ (TNBN)	σ^2 (TNBN)	μ (NPEDT)	σ^2 (NPEDT)
FWP	0.93043	9.377E-6	0.988255	2.594E-5
STV	0.99858	1.455E-6	0.997886	8.289E-7
FWF	0.83527	1.682E-5	0.97729	2.795E-4
STF	0.99694	8.829E-6	0.992117	1.35E-5
SWF	0.69901	2.722E-6	0.967232	6.314E-4
DRL	0.62306	5.715E-8	0.71745	2.147E-5
DRP	0.99204	1.433E-5	0.978515	1.271E-4
STT	0.540239	1.094E-7	0.986699	5.011E-5
Average	0.826946	6.712E-6	0.95068	1.437E-4

Table 5. Means and variances of MP when STT and one of its parents are present

Node	μ (TNBN)	σ^2 (TNBN)	μ (NPEDT)	σ^2 (NPEDT)
$SWVF$	0.701059	0.041	0.802444	0.118323
$FWVF$	0.449978	3.147E-3	0.742676	0.071108
$FWPF$	0.450636	3.064E-3	0.754429	0.062699
LI	0.655584	0.114252	0.995538	3.649E-5
SWV	0.762227	0.01292	0.801968	0.118188
FWV	0.446817	3.518E-3	0.742875	0.070954
FWP	0.428903	0.044449	0.688344	0.041785
STV	0.6529	0.115369	0.995781	1.091E-5
FWF	0.488658	0.04751	0.5607	0.075691
STF	0.630933	0.100964	0.999926	2.671E-9
SWF	0.609587	0.025558	0.999525	2.228E-7
DRL	0.562921	0.049913	0.510202	0.109071
DRP	0.809094	0.117564	0.662385	0.164828
Average	0.588448	0.052248	0.788984	0.064053

Diagnosis. The diagnostic capabilities of the TNBN and the NPEDT were studied on one type of test: The final fault event, STT (see Figure 1), was considered to be present. The occurrence time for STT established the end of the global time range analyzed. In this type of test, all the 127 simulated cases were used. Since in a TNBN the introduction of evidence for a node with parents requires knowing which of them is causing the appearance of the child event, in this type of test it was necessary to consider information from two nodes: STT and its causing parent. Table 5 includes the means and variances of the measures of proximity obtained in this test. Again, the NPEDT performs better than the TNBN.

Although in general the measures of proximity for diagnosis are lower than those for prediction, that does not mean that our BNs perform in diagnosis worse than in prediction. There is another reason that explains this result: If we had

- two different probability density functions, $f_V(t)$ and $f_W(t)$, the former sparser (more spread out) than the latter, and
- two infinite sets of cases, C_V and C_W, following distributions $f_V(t)$ and $f_W(t)$, respectively,

then, from Equation 3, MP would be lower on average for V than for W, since $t - \hat{t}_V$ is on average greater than $t - \hat{t}_W$. Therefore, although a BN yielded satisfactory inference results both for variable V and variable W, Equation 3 could in general produce different average MPs for V with respect to W. This is taking place in our tests. For example, in the NPEDT we calculated the mean number of states per node whose posterior probability was greater than 0.001. While in the prediction tests this number was approximately 5, in diagnosis it rose to nearly 9. Anyhow, the measure of proximity defined in Equation 3 allows us to carry out a comparative evaluation of the TNBN and the NPEDT.

5   Conclusions

Arroyo-Figueroa and Sucar applied TNBNs to fault diagnosis and prediction for the steam generator of a fossil power plant. We have recently developed an NPEDT for the same domain and have carried out a comparative evaluation of the two networks. Our evaluation method is based on a proximity measure between the posterior probabilities obtained from the networks and each of the simulated cases available for evaluation. Since the faults that may occur in the steam generator of a fossil power plant constitute dynamic processes, the proximity measure takes into account time as an important variable. We have performed different tests in order to compare the predictive as well as the diagnostic capabilities of the TNBN and the NPEDT. The results show that in general the NPEDT yields better predictions and diagnoses than the TNBN. There are two main reasons for that: Firstly, the use of temporal noisy gates in the NPEDT allows for a finer granularity than in the case of the TNBN and, secondly, the definition of the intervals in a TNBN is not so systematic as in an NPEDT and depends strongly on the domain.

Acknowledgements. This research was supported by the Spanish CICYT, under grant TIC2001-2973-C05-04. The first author was supported by a grant from the Mexican *Secretaría de Relaciones Exteriores*.

References

1. G. Arroyo-Figueroa and L. E. Sucar. A temporal Bayesian network for diagnosis and prediction. In *Proceedings of the 15th Conference on Uncertainty in Artificial Intelligence (UAI'99)*, pages 13–20, Stockholm, Sweden, 1999. Morgan Kaufmann, San Francisco, CA.
2. G. Arroyo-Figueroa, L. E. Sucar, and A. Villavicencio. Probabilistic temporal reasoning and its application to fossil power plant operation. *Expert Systems with Applications*, 15:317–324, 1998.
3. T. Dean and K. Kanazawa. A model for reasoning about persistence and causation. *Computational Intelligence*, 5:142–150, 1989.
4. F. J. Díez and S. F. Galán. Efficient computation for the noisy MAX. *International Journal of Intelligent Systems*, 18:165–177, 2003.
5. S. F. Galán and F. J. Díez. Networks of probabilistic events in discrete time. *International Journal of Approximate Reasoning*, 30:181–202, 2002.
6. U. Kjærulff. A computational scheme for reasoning in dynamic probabilistic networks. In *Proceedings of the 8th Conference on Uncertainty in Artificial Intelligence (UAI'92)*, pages 121–129, Stanford University, 1992. Morgan Kaufmann, San Francisco, CA.
7. J. Pearl. *Probabilistic Reasoning in Intelligent Systems: Networks of Plausible Inference*. Morgan Kaufmann, San Francisco, CA, 1988.
8. A. Tavira and R. Berdón. Simulador de la central termoeléctrica Manzanillo II. Technical Report 19018, Instituto de Investigaciones Eléctricas, Mexico, 1992.

Function Approximation through Fuzzy Systems Using Taylor Series Expansion-Based Rules: Interpretability and Parameter Tuning

Luis Javier Herrera[1], Héctor Pomares[1], Ignacio Rojas[1], Jesús González[1], and Olga Valenzuela[2]

[1] University of Granada, Department of Computer Architecture and Technology, E.T.S. Computer Engineering, 18071 Granada, Spain
http://atc.ugr.es
[2] University of Granada, Department of Applied Mathematics, Science faculty, Granada, Spain

Abstract. In this paper we present a new approach for the problem of approximating a function from a training set of I/O points using fuzzy logic and fuzzy systems. Such approach, as we will see, will provide us a number of advantages comparing to other more-limited systems. Among these advantages, we may highlight the considerable reduction in the number of rules needed to model the underlined function of this set of data and, from other point of view, the possibility of bringing interpretation to the rules of the system obtained, using the Taylor Series concept. This work is reinforced by an algorithm able to obtain the pseudo-optimal polynomial consequents of the rules. Finally the performance of our approach and that of the associated algorithm are shown through a significant example.

1 Introduction

The Function Approximation problem deals with the estimation of an unknown model from a data set of continuous input/output points; the objective is to obtain a model from which to get the expected output given any new input data.

Fuzzy Logic on the other hand is one of the three roots of soft-computing; it has been successfully applied to several areas in scientific and engineering sectors, due to its broad number of benefits. The simplicity of the model and its understandability, while encapsulating complex relations among variables is one of the keys of the paradigm. The other main characteristic is its capability to interpret the model, for example through the use of linguistic values to bring meaning to the variables involved in the problem.

Many authors have dealt with Fuzzy logic and Fuzzy Systems for function approximation from an input/output data set, using clustering techniques as well as grid techniques, obtaining in general good enough results. Specifically, the TSK model [7] fits better to these kind of problems due to it's computational capability.

R. Monroy et al. (Eds.): MICAI 2004, LNAI 2972, pp. 508–516, 2004.

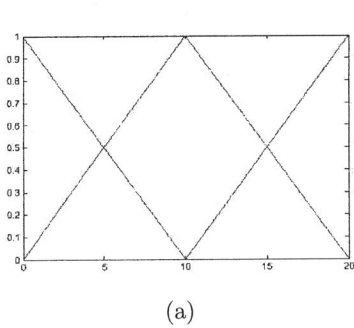
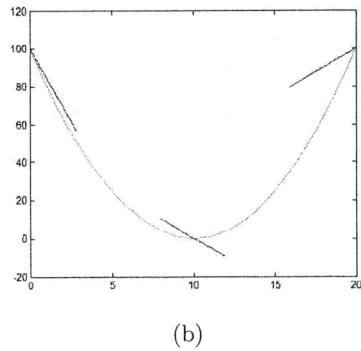

(a)   (b)

Fig. 1. a) MF distribution used for this example. Target function: y = (x - 10)2 **b)** Original function + model output + linear submodels for each of the three rules using a TSK model of order 1. We see how the global output of the TSK fuzzy system is eye-indistinguishable from the actual output, but no interpretation can be given to the three linear sub-models.

The fuzzy inference method proposed by Takagi, Sugeno and Kang, which is known as the TSK model in fuzzy systems field, has been one of the major issues in both theoretical and practical research for fuzzy modelling and control. The basic idea is the subdivision of the input space into fuzzy regions and to approximate the system in each subdivision by a simple model.

The main advantage of the TSK model is its representative power, capable of describing a highly complex nonlinear system using a small number of simple rules. In spite of this, the TSK systems suffer from the lack of interpretability, which should be one of the main advantages of fuzzy systems in general. While the general performance of the whole TSK fuzzy system give the idea of what it does, the sub-models given by each rule in the TSK fuzzy system can give no interpretable information by themselves [1]. See *Fig* 1.

Therefore, this lack of interpretability might force any researcher not to use the TSK models in problems where the interpretability of the obtained model and corresponding sub-models is a key concept.

Apart from the interpretability issue the number of rules for a working model is also a key concept. For control problems, grid-based fuzzy systems are preferable since they cover the whole input space (all the possible operation regions in which the plant to control can be stated during its operation). Nevertheless, for Mamdani fuzzy systems or even for TSK fuzzy systems of order 0 or 1, although getting pseudo-optimal solutions, they usually need an excessive number of rules for a moderated number of input variables.

In this paper we propose the use of high order TSK rules in a grid based fuzzy system, reducing the number of rules, while keeping the advantages of the grid-based approach for control and function approximation. Also to keep the interpretability of the model obtained, we present a small modification for the consequents of the high order TSK rules in order to provide the interpretability for each of the sub-models (rules) that compose the global system.

The rest of the paper is organized as follows: Section 2 presents high order TSK rules with an algorithm to obtain the optimal coefficients of the rule
consequents. Section 3 provides an introduction to the Taylor Series Expansion,
concept that will provide the key for the interpretability issue, commented in
Section 4. Finally, in section 5 it is provided a whole example that demonstrates
the suitability and goodness of our approach.

2   High-Order TSK Fuzzy Rules

The fuzzy inference system proposed by Takagi, Sugeno and Kang, known as the
TSK model in the fuzzy system literature, provides a powerful tool for modelling
complex nonlinear systems. Typically, a TSK model consists of IF-THEN rules
that have the form:

$$R^k : \text{IF } x_1 \text{ is } A_1^k \text{ AND } \ldots \text{ AND } x_n \text{ is } A_n^k \text{ THEN}$$
$$y = \alpha_0^k + \alpha_1^k x_1 + \ldots + \alpha_n^k x_n \tag{1}$$

where the A_i^k are fuzzy sets characterized by membership functions $A_i^k(x)$, α_j^k
are real-valued parameters and x_i are the input variables.

A Sugeno approximator comprises a set of TSK fuzzy rules that maps any
input data $\vec{x} = [x_1, x_2, \ldots, x_n]$ into its desired output $y \in \mathbb{R}$. The output of the
Sugeno approximator for any input vector x, is calculated as follows:

$$F(x) = \frac{\sum_{k=1}^{K} \mu_k(x) y_k}{\sum_{k=1}^{K} \mu_k(x)} \tag{2}$$

Provided that $\mu_k(x)$ is the activation value for the antecedent of the rule k,
and can be expressed as:

$$\mu_k(x) = A_1^k(x_1) A_2^k(x_2) \ldots A_n^k(x_n) \tag{3}$$

The main advantage of the TSK model is its representative power; it is capable of describing a highly nonlinear system using a small number of rules. Moreover, since the output of the model has an explicit functional expression form, it
is conventional to identify its parameters using some learning algorithms. These
characteristics make the TSK model very suitable for the problem of function
approximation; a high number of authors have successfully applied TSK systems
for function approximation. For example, many well-known neuro-fuzzy systems
such as ANFIS [4] have been constructed on the basis of the TSK model.

Nevertheless very few authors have dealt with high-order TSK fuzzy systems.
Buckley [5] generalized the original Sugeno inference engine by changing the form
of the consequent to a general polynomial, that is:

$$R^k : \text{IF } x_1 \text{ is } A_1^k \text{ AND } \ldots \text{ AND } x_n \text{ is } A_n^k \text{ THEN } y = Y_k(x) \tag{4}$$

where $Y_k(x)$ is a polynomial of any order. Taking order 2, it can be expressed as:

$$Y_k(\vec{x}) = w_0^k \cdot \vec{x} + \frac{1}{2}\vec{x}^T W^k \vec{x} \tag{5}$$

Where w_0 is a scalar, $\vec{w}$ is a column vector of coefficients with dimension n (one per each input variable) and W is a triangular matrix of dimensions $n \times n$, (W_{ij} = coefficient for quadratic factor $x_i * x_j$, $i = 1 \ldots n$, $j = i \ldots n$).

Now that we have defined how a TSK fuzzy system can be adapted to work with high-order rules, let's see, given a set of input/output data, and a configuration of membership functions for the input variables, how to adapt the consequents of the rules so that the TSK model output optimally fits the data set D. The Least Square Error (LSE) algorithm will be used for that purpose. LSE tries to minimize the error function:

$$J = \sum_{m \in D} (y_m - F(x))^2 \tag{6}$$

where F is the output of the TSK fuzzy system as in (2). Setting to 0 the first derivative (7, 8) of each single parameter (w_0 and each component of $\vec{w}$ and W) will give us a system of linear equations from which to obtain the optimal values of the parameters.

$$\frac{\partial J}{\partial w_{si}} =$$

$$2 \sum_{m \in D} \left(y_m - \frac{\sum_{k=1}^{K} \mu_k(x_m)\left(w_0^k + \vec{w}^k \vec{x}_m + \frac{1}{2}\vec{x}^T W^k \vec{x}_m\right)}{\sum_{k=1}^{K} \mu_k(x_m)} \right) \cdot \frac{\mu_s(x_m) f_{w_{si}}(x_m)}{\sum_{k=1}^{K} \mu_k(x_m)} \tag{7}$$

$$\sum_{m \in D} \frac{y_m \cdot \mu_s(x_m) \cdot f_{w_{si}}(x_m)}{\sum_{k=1}^{K} \mu_k(x_m)} =$$

$$= \sum_{k=1}^{K} \sum_i w_{ki} \sum_{m \in D} \frac{\mu_k(x_m) \cdot f_{w_{ki}} \cdot \mu_s(x_m) \cdot f_{w_{si}}(x_m)}{\sum_{j=1}^{K} \mu_j(x_m)} \tag{8}$$

Where w_{ki} -rule k, coefficient i- is the coefficient we are differentiating in each case (w_0 or any component of W or $\vec{w}$), and f_{wi} is the partial derivative of the consequent of rule k with respect to w_i, i.e., 1 for the 0-order coefficient w_0, x_i for every first-order coefficient w_i, or $x_p \cdot x_j$ for every second-order coefficient w_{pj} of W.

Once we have the system of linear equations, it only remains to obtain the optimal solution for all the coefficients of every rule. The Orthogonal Least-Square (OLS) method [6] will guarantee a single optimal solution obtaining the values for the significant coefficients while discarding the rest. We reject therefore the problems due to the presence of redundancy in the activation matrix.

Once that we have already reviewed the type of rules that we are going to operate with, now let's review the "lack of interpretability curse" that suffer TSK

Fuzzy Systems as we saw in Section 1. As polynomials are not easy interpretable as consequents of the rules, we will give now the key for the interpretability for our Taylor-Series based rules.

3   Taylor Series-Based Fuzzy Rules (TSFR)

Let $f(x)$ be a function defined in an interval with an intermediate point a, for which we know the derivatives of all orders. The first order polynomial:

$$p_1(x) = f(a) + f'(a)(x - a) \tag{9}$$

has the same value as $f(x)$ in the point $x = a$ and also the same first order derivative at this point. Its graphic representation is a tangent line to the graph of $f(x)$ at the point $x = a$.

Taking also the second derivative for $f(x)$ in $x = a$, we can build the second order polynomial

$$p_2(x) = f(a) + f'(a)(x - a) + \frac{1}{2}f''(a)(x - a)^2 \tag{10}$$

which has the same value as $f(x)$ at the point $x = a$, and also has the same values for the first and second derivative. The graph for this polynomial in $x = a$, will be more similar to that of $f(x)$ in the points in the vicinity of $x = a$. We can expect therefore that if we build a polynomial of nth order with the n first derivatives of $f(x)$ in $x = a$, that polynomial will get very close to $f(x)$ in the neighbourhood of $x = a$.

Taylor theorem states that if a function $f(x)$ defined in an interval has derivatives of all orders, it can be approximated near a point $x = a$, as its Taylor Series Expansion around that point:

$$f(x) = f(a) + f'(a)(x - a) + \frac{1}{2}f''(a)(x - a)^2 + \dots$$
$$+ \frac{1}{n!}f^{(n)}(a)(x - a)^n + \frac{1}{(n + a)!}f^{(n+1)}(c)(x - a)^{n+1} \tag{11}$$

where in each case, c is a point between x and a.

For n-dimensional purposes, the formula is adapted in the following form:

$$f(\vec{x}) = f(\vec{a}) + (\vec{x} - \vec{a})^T \left[\frac{\partial f}{\partial \vec{x}_i}(\vec{a}) \right]_{i=1\dots n} + \frac{1}{2}(\vec{x} - \vec{a})^T W(\vec{x} - \vec{a}) +$$
$$\frac{1}{3!}W^3(\vec{x} - \vec{a}, \vec{x} - \vec{a}, \vec{x} - \vec{a}) + \dots \tag{12}$$

where W is a triangular matrix of dimensions $n \times n$, and W^s is a triangular multi-linear form in s vector arguments $v^1, \dots, v^s$.

Taylor series open a door for the approximation of any function through polynomials, that is, through the addition of a number of simple functions. It is therefore a fundamental key in the field of Function Approximation Theory and Mathematical Analysis. Taylor Series Expansion will also provide us a way to bring interpretation to TSK fuzzy systems by taking a certain type of rules consequents and antecedents, as we will now see.

As noted in [3] we will use input variables in the antecedents with membership functions that form an Orderly Local Membership Function Basis (OLMF). The requirements that a set of membership functions for a variable must fulfil to be an OLMF basically are:

- Every membership function extreme point must coincide with the centre of the adjacent membership function.
- The *n-th* derivative of the membership function is continuous in its whole interval of definition.
- The *n-th* derivative of the membership function vanishes at the centre and at the boundaries.

The main advantage of using this kind of membership functions is the differentiability of the output of the TSK fuzzy system. This is not possible when we have triangular or trapezoidal membership functions, since the derivative at the centres of the membership functions does not exist, therefore not having a differentiable fuzzy system output.

These OLMF bases also have the *addition to unity property*: the addition of the activations of all the rules is always equal to unity for any point inside the input domain in a TSK fuzzy system that keeps the OLMF basis restrictions. Therefore the output of the TSK fuzzy system can be expressed as:

$$F(x) = \sum_{k=1}^{K} \mu_k(x) y_k \tag{13}$$

Then the OLS method cited in Section 2 will work well for the given system, and can identify the optimal coefficients without needing another execution of the algorithm as noticed in [6].

Finally, given that the input variables have a distribution of membership functions that form a OLMF basis, we will use high-order TSK rules in the form (4), but where the polynomial consequents are in the form:

$$Y_k(\vec{x}) = w_0^k \cdot \vec{w}^k(\vec{x} - \vec{a}_k) + \frac{1}{2}(\vec{x} - \vec{a}_k)^T \cdot W^k \cdot (\vec{x} - \vec{a}_k) \tag{14}$$

being $\vec{a}_k$ the centre of rule k, therefore forming a Taylor Series Expansions around the centres of the rules.

4   Interpretability Issues

It can be demonstrated [3] that given a Sugeno approximator $F(x)$ such that:

- 1) the input variables membership functions form a set of OLMF basis of order m (being the m-th derivative continuous everywhere);

– 2) the consequent-side is written in the rule-centred form shown in (4) and (14) and the polynomials $Y_k(x)$ are of degree n.

Then for $n \leq m$, every $Y_k(x)$ can be interpreted as a truncated Taylor series expansion of order n of $F(x)$ about the point $\vec{x} = \vec{a}_k$, the centre of the kth rule.

Supposing therefore that we have a method to obtain the optimal Taylor-Series Based TSK rules consequents coefficients for function approximation, given a data set and a membership function distribution that form a set of OLMF basis, we can interpret then the consequents of the rules $Y_k(x)$ as the truncated Taylor series expansion around the centres of the rules of the output of the system. This system also provides a pseudo-optimal approximation to the objective function. In the limit case where the function is perfectly approximated by our system, the rule consequents will coincide with the Taylor Series expansions of that function about centre of each rule, having reached total interpretability and total approximation.

In [3], Marwan Bikdash used directly the (available) Taylor Series Expansion of the function around the rule centres, for each rule, to approximate the function with the TSK fuzzy system. Notice that these rule consequents, though having strong interpretability, are not the optimal consequents in the least squares sense. Please note that the Taylor Series Expansion is an approximation for a function in the vicinity of the reference point. Therefore even using a high number of MFs, the error obtained by the method in [3] is seldom small enough (compared to a system with similar complexity with consequents optimized using LSE) and therefore the system output barely represent a good approximation of the data we are modelling.

In this paper we also suppose that the only information we have from the function to approximate are the input/output points in the initial dataset. No information is given of the derivatives of the function w.r.t. any point. Also, there is no accurate way to obtain the derivatives from the training points to perform the approximation as the method in [3] required.

5   Simulations

Consider a set of 100 randomly chosen I/O data from the 1-D function [2]:

$$F(x) = e^{-5x} sin(2\pi x) \in [0,1] \tag{15}$$

Let's try now to model those data using a fuzzy system with 5 membership functions for the single input variable x forming a OLMF basis and rule consequents of the form given by (14), being Y_k a order-2 polynomial.

The five rules obtained after the execution of the LSE algorithm using OLS are the following:

IF x is A_1 THEN $y = -26.0860x^2 + 5.3247x + 0.0116$
IF x is A_2 THEN $y = -1.6235(x - 0.25) + 0.2882$
IF x is A_3 THEN $y = 4.3006(x - 0.5)^2 - 0.5193(x - 0.5)$ (16)
IF x is A_4 THEN $y = -1.1066(x - 0.75)^2 + 0.1780(x - 0.75) - 0.0238$
IF x is A_5 THEN $y = 0$

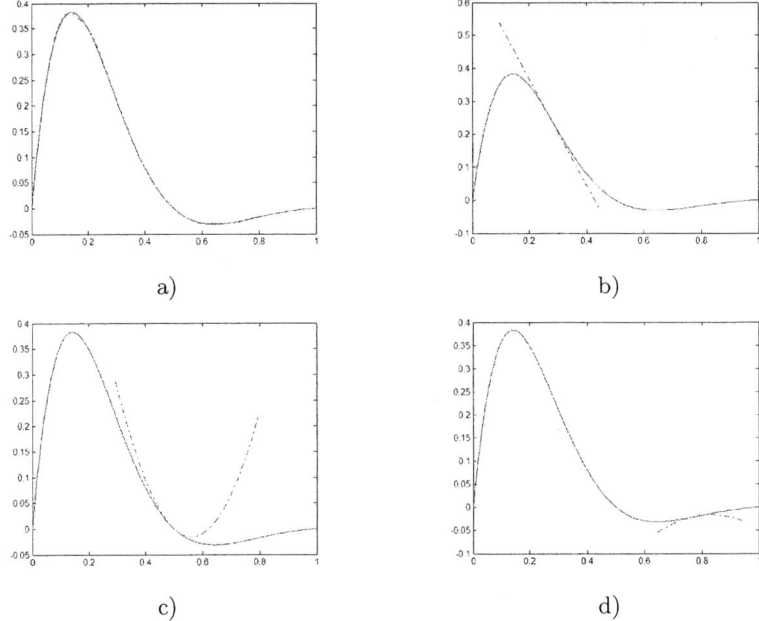

Fig. 2. a) Original function (solid line) and Taylor Series Expansion based Fuzzy System (dotted line). We see that for only 5 membership functions, the output of the system is very similar to the original function. NRMSE = 0.0154. b) Original function + model output + second membership function consequent (centered at x=0.25). c) Original function + model output + third membership function consequent (centered at x=0.5). d) Original function + model output + fourth membership function consequent (centered at x=0.75). We see clearly how these polynomials come closer to the Taylor Series Expansion around the centre of the rules of the fuzzy system output.

The interpretability comes from the fact that the function in the points near to each center of the five rules is extremely similar to the polynomial output of the rules as shown in Figure 2. These polynomials are kept expressed as Taylor Series Expansions of the function in the points in the vicinity of the centres of the rules. The system is therefore fully interpretable and also brings some more advantages as noticed below.

Figure 2 also shows clearly that the LSE finds the optimal consequents coefficients for the given input/output data set. Also it must be noted that for only five rules (one per each membership function), the error obtained is sensibly low. If we compare the system obtained for the same number of rules with a TSK fuzzy system with constant consequents, we see that the error obtained (NRMSE = 0.3493) is very high comparing to our Taylor Series Expansion based fuzzy system (NRMSE = 0.0154).

It should be remembered that the Normalized Root-Mean Square Error (NRMSE) is defined as:

$$NRMSE = \sqrt{\frac{\overline{e^2}}{\sigma_y^2}} \tag{17}$$

where σ_y^2 is the variance of the output data, and $\overline{e^2}$ is the mean-square error between the system and the dataset D output.

Also comparing using the same number of parameters, that is, 5 rules for our system, 15 rules for constant consequents TSK rules, we observe that the error obtained by our Taylor-Based rules system is much lower (NRMSE = 0.0154) than for constant consequent rule system (NRMSE = 0.0635).

6   Conclusions

In this paper we have presented a very interesting approach to the problem of function approximation from a set of I/O points utilizing a special type of fuzzy systems. Using an Orderly Local Membership Function Basis (OLMF) and Taylor Series-Based Fuzzy Rules, the proposed fuzzy system has the property that the Taylor Series Expansion of the defuzzified function around each rule centre coincides with that rule's consequent. This endows the proposed system with both the approximating capabilities of TSK fuzzy rules through the use of the OLS algorithm, and the interpretability advantages of pure fuzzy systems.

Acknowledgements. This work has been partially supported by the Spanish CICYT Project DPI2001-3219.

References

1. Yen, J., Wang, L., Gillespie, C.W.: Improving the Interpretability of TSK Fuzzy Models by Combining Global Learning and Local Learning. IEEE Trans. Fuz. Syst., Vol.6, No.4.(1998) 530–537
2. Pomares, H., Rojas, I., Gonzalez, J., Prieto, A.: Structure Identification in Complete Rule-Based Fuzzy Systems. IEEE Trans. Fuzz. Vol.10, no. 3. June (2002) 349–359
3. Bikdash, M.: A Highly Interpretable Form of Sugeno Inference Systems. IEEE Trans. Fuz. Syst., Vol.7, No.6. (1999) 686–696
4. Jang, J.-S R.: ANFIS: Adaptative-network-based fuzzy inference system. IEEE Trans. Syst. Man Cybern., vol. 23. (1993) 665–685
5. Buckley, J.J.: Sugeno-type Controllers are Universal Controllers. Fuzzy Sets. Syst., Vol.25, (1993) 299–303
6. Yen, J., Wang, L.: Simplifying Fuzzy Rule-Based Models Using Orthogonal Transformation Methods. IEEE Trans. Syst. Man Cybern., part B: cybernetics, Vol. 29, No.1. (1999) 13–24
7. Takagi, T.,Sugeno, M.: Fuzzy identification of systems and its applications to modelling and control. IEEE Trans. Syst. Man and Cyber., vol.15.(1985) 116–132

Causal Identification in Design Networks⋆

Ana Maria Madrigal and Jim Q. Smith

University of Warwick

Abstract. When planning and designing a policy intervention and evaluation, the policy maker will have to define a strategy which will define the (conditional independence) structure of the available data. Here, Dawid's extended influence diagrams are augmented by including 'experimental design' decisions nodes within the set of intervention strategies to provide semantics to discuss how a 'design' decision strategy (such as randomisation) might assist the systematic identification of intervention causal effects. By introducing design decision nodes into the framework, the experimental design underlying the data available is made explicit. We show how influence diagrams might be used to discuss the efficacy of different designs and conditions under which one can identify 'causal' effects of a future policy intervention. The approach of this paper lies primarily within probabilistic decision theory.

Keywords: Causal inference; Influence diagrams; Design interventions and strategies; Identification of Policy Effects; Directed Acyclic Graphs (DAGs); Confounders; Bayesian decision theory.

1 Introduction

Intervention has to do with 'perturbing' the dynamics of a system. If we say a system consists of components which influence each other and we say that its dynamics describe the way these components interrelate with each other in an equilibrium state, an example could be the road traffic in a town. The system at the present has some *pre-intervention* dynamics or interactions attached to it. When we intervene a system, by adding a red light in a corner, we are introducing a new component into a system that will imply new *post-intervention* dynamics. The intervention might have both qualitative effects, modifying the structure of the system (maybe by 'blocking' the interaction between two of its components) and quantitative effects, modifying the value of the components. One of the main interests consists in describing if and how the intervention is affecting the system. So, an evaluation of the intervention effects is required and it is usually measured in terms of a response variable, such as the number of accidents.

Experimental design decisions are usually made in order to assist the isolation of the intervention (causal) effects. Randomised allocation of treatments to units is a well known practice within medical clinical trials but, because of ethical, social and financial considerations, complete randomisation within an experiment

---

⋆ This work was partially funded by CONACYT.

R. Monroy et al. (Eds.): MICAI 2004, LNAI 2972, pp. 517–526, 2004.
© Springer-Verlag Berlin Heidelberg 2004

designed to evaluate a social policy will usually be infeasibly costly. Therefore, knowing the details of the policy assignment mechanism and a well planned recording of the data (choosing variables to be observed, perhaps through a survey) become very relevant issues in order to have all the information needed to measure the right 'causal' effects (see Rubin(1978)). Implementation of experimental designs and the recording mechanism will have a cost associated with them and policy makers-evaluators will question if it is worth spending certain amount of money to implement a 'proper' design of experiments.

Influence diagrams (IDs) will be used to represent the system dynamics and interventions graphically. Our interpretation of causal effects for interventions in policy programmes will follow Dawid's approach and be Bayesian decision-theoretic [3]. By including 'experimental design' decisions in what we call a Design Network (DN), in this paper, we maintain that experimental design decisions are intrinsic to any analysis of policy intervention strategies. We discuss when we can evaluate the causal effect of a class of policy intervention strategies under a design decision strategy.

2   Intervention Graphical Framework

Influence diagrams have been used for over 20 years to form the framework for both describing [see Howard and Matheson (1984), Shachter(1986), Smith(1989), Oliver and Smith(1990)] and also devising efficient algorithms to calculate effects of decisions (See Jensen(2001)) in complex systems which implicitly embody strong conditional independence assertions. However, it is only recently that they have been used to explain causal relationships (Dawid(2000), Dawid(2002)) in the sense described above, and shown to be much more versatile than Causal Bayesian Networks (Pearl (2000)).

In our context, every decision that we make when we are planning and designing an (experimental) study has an effect on the structure of the data that we are to collect. Such decisions can be included in the graphical representation of the dynamics of the system using IDs, and the structure of the data available to do the evaluation of the policy will be defined by the set of conditional independencies that are derived from the graph.

Definition 1. *If X,Y,Z are random variables with a joint distribution $P(\cdot)$, we say that X is conditionally independent of Y given Z under P, if for any possible pair of values (y,z) for (Y,Z) such that $p(y,z) > 0$, $P(x \mid y,z) = P(x \mid z)$. This can be written following Dawid (1979)[1] notation as $(X \perp\!\!\!\perp Y \mid Z)_P$.*

Dawid (2002) points out that, traditionally, in IDs conditional distributions are given for random nodes, but no description is supplied of the functions or distributions involved at the decision nodes, which are left arbitrarily and at the choice of the decision maker. If we choose to provide some descriptions about the decision rules, then any given specification of the functions or distributions at decision nodes constitutes a decision strategy, π. Decisions taken determine what we may term the partial distribution, p, of random nodes given decision nodes. If E and D denote the set of random events and decisions involved in decision strategy π, respectively, then the full joint specification p_π, conformed by decision strategy π and partial distribution of random nodes p for all $e \in E$ and $d \in D$ is given by: p_π (random,decision) $= p_\pi(e,d) = p(e:d)\pi(d:e)$

The graphical representation of the full joint specification p_π can be done by using extended IDs (see Dawid (2002)) that incorporate non-random parameter nodes (θ_E) and strategy nodes (π_D) representing the 'mechanisms' that generate random and decision nodes, respectively (i.e. $\theta_e = p(e \,|\text{pa}^0(e))$ and $\pi_d = \pi(d \,|\text{pa}^0(d))$). In what he calls augmented DAGs, Dawid(2002) incorporates 'intervention nodes' F for each of the variables in the influence diagram where $F_X = x$ corresponds to 'setting' the value of node X to x. The conditional distribution of X, given $F_X = x$ will be degenerate at the value of x (i.e. $P(X = x|F_X = x) = 1$) and he introduces a new value $\emptyset$ such that when $F_X = \emptyset$, X is left to have its 'natural' distribution, named by Pearl as the 'idle' system. Action F, in Pearl's language [10] will correspond to $F_X = do(X = x)$. Augmented DAGs, provide a very useful framework to show the differences between observation and intervention because they make explicit the structure where intervention consists in setting or 'doing' values of variables. Also, as the specification of F has to be done externally to the graph, the structure of the augmented DAG can be kept untouched for other type of specifications of F. Figure 1 shows, for a simple case, the usual representation of IDs as well as its Extended and Augmented versions, for the set (T, B, Y) where $T = (T_1, T_2, .., T_s)$ represents a set of policy variables (treatment), $B = (B_1, B_2, .., B_r)$ is a set of Background variables (potential confounders depending on its observability and the recording mechanism followed) and Y is a response variable.

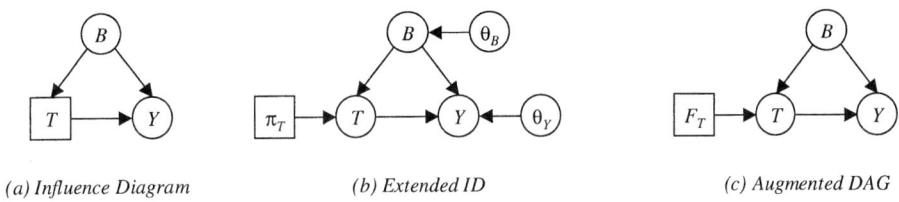

(a) Influence Diagram   (b) Extended ID   (c) Augmented DAG

Fig. 1. Extended Influence diagrams and Augmented DAGs

For causal reasoning, it is said that two augmented DAG's will represent equivalent causal assumptions if they have the same 'skeleton' and the same 'inmoralities'[3]. Causal enquiries about the 'effect of T on Y' are regarded as relating to (comparisons between) the distributions of Y given $F_T = do(T = t')$ for various settings of t'. Intervention node F of the augmented DAG is used to discuss the identifiability of atomic intervention (policy) effects under certain DAG structures and recording mechanisms of B, $R(B)$. Different structures and examples of identifiable and unidentifiable situations have been discussed by Pearl (2000), Lauritzen (2001) and Dawid (2002), each of them with their particular framework and notation.

Definition 2. *A DAG on variables* $\{X_1, ..., X_k\}$ *of a probability function* $p(\underline{x})$ *which factorises* $p(x_1, .., x_k) = \prod_i p(x_i \mid pa_{x_i})$ *where* $pa_{x_i} \subseteq \{x_1, ..., x_{i-1}\}$ $i = 2, .., k$ *is a directed acyclic graph with nodes* $\{x_1, ..., x_k\}$ *and a directed edge from* x_j *to* x_i *iff* $j \in pa_{xi}$.

It cannot be asserted in general that the effect of *setting* the value of X to x' is the same as the effect of *observing* $X = x'$. Only in limited circumstances (as when the node for X has no parents in the graph), they will coincide. Pearl asserts that, if the ID corresponds to a causal bayes net, then the intervention $F_X = do(X = x')$, transforms the original joint probability function $p(x_1, .., x_k)$ into a new probability given by

$$p(x_1, .., x_k \mid F_{X_i} = do(X_i = x_i')) = \begin{cases} \dfrac{p(x_1, .., x_k)}{p(x_i' \mid pa_i)} & \text{if } x_i = x_i' \\ 0 & \text{if } x_i \neq x_i' \end{cases}$$

On the other hand, if we were observing naturally $X_i = x_i$, the probability distribution conditional 'by observation', can be obtained by usual rules of probability following Bayes theorem, such that

$$p(x_1, .., x_k \mid X_i = x_i) = \frac{p(x_1, .., x_k)}{p(x_i)}$$

3   Policy versus Experimental Decisions

When planning and designing a policy intervention and evaluation, the policy maker will have to define a strategy that involves 'policy intervention' actions and '(pilot study) experimental design' actions. The former, will include decisions relating to how the policy will be implemented (which doses and to whom they will be provided). The latter is related to the evaluation of the policy and will include some experimental design decisions that will define the (chosen or controlled) conditions under which the study will be carried out and the data recorded. Both strategies define the (conditional independence) structure of the available data through the decision strategy, π, adopted. A decision strategy is conformed by a set of decisions or components. So, if $d_1, d_2, .., d_D$ are the components of a particular decision strategy π_D, then we are interested in describing $\pi_D (d_1, d_2, .., d_D | E)$. The set $D = \{d_1, d_2, .., d_D\}$ will contain 'policy intervention' decisions and 'experimental' decisions and one could define two subsets of D such that $D_T = \{d'; d'$ is a policy intervention$\}$ and $D_E = \{d^*; d^*$ is experimental$\}$.

Experimental design decision interventions, D_E, set the conditions under which (future) policy interventions will be evaluated. Design decisions involve treatment assignment mechanisms A, and recording mechanism $R(B)$, then $D_E = \{A, R(B)\}$. As Rubin (1978) pointed out, causal inference might be sensitive to the specification of these mechanisms or strategies. Policy assignment mechanisms define conditional independence of the data and structures in the 'experimental' graph including all observed, and unobserved nodes. Recording mechanisms determine which of the nodes are observed and available to us in the data. Both, the treatment assignments used in the experiment and the variables available to us, influence our evaluation of causal effects when we want to evaluate F_T. A broader definition of experimental design decisions could include in D_E sampling mechanisms and eligibility criteria (see Madrigal(2004)).

The way sets of factors are controlled (like randomisation and stratification) will have a qualitative effect on the conditional independence structure that the data, once recorded, will have under a given policy design strategy. Within this, each strategy will need also to quantify the levels or values at which these factors are set - e.g. doses of treatments defined. Thus, setting the value of the doses to 1 or 2, may well have a different quantitative effect on the response, but the effect of this value on the basic structure may be not altered. Most of the emphasis in practical statistical discussions is usually around the effects of these 'values', rather than about the structural consequences of the former: the focus of this paper.

When we, as 'data-collectors', approach the world, the data we observe will depend on our way of approaching it. Any dataset obtained will have been influenced by the way it was collected, so it should always be conditioned to the strategy followed in its collection. The effect each decision strategy might have on the 'available-data' structure can be qualitatively different and affect the partial distribution $p(E : D)$ in different ways. Whatever the decision strategy followed, the data we 'observe' in the database (available data) is a representation of the partial distribution of the random nodes given the set of decisions (made or deliberately 'not made'). The representation of joint partial distributions for observational and experimental data are given by $p(E : D_E = \emptyset)$ and $p(E : D_E = d_E)$, respectively. In this sense, observational data is a special type of experiment.

So, it is important that design actions and analysis assumptions are *compatible*. Setting decision strategies has as an output: 'a structure on the data available', and the ideal will be to analyse it by using statistical models that are appropriate to deal with such a structure. Within our graphical framework this requires there to be an identifiable map from the estimated experimental relationships (indexed by edges in the experimental graph) to the relationship of interest (indexed by edges in the target policy graph).

4   Introducing Experimental Nodes

Experimental design interventions, $D_E = \{A, R(B)\}$, will set the conditions under which (future) policy interventions F_T will be evaluated. These experimental actions define the recording and policy assignment mechanisms that could involve complex strategies like stratified-cluster-randomisation or some contingent-allocation rules. Similarly, policy interventions, D_T, might imply (a collection of) atomic, contingent and randomised actions.

Consider as in Section 2 the set (T, B, Y) where $T = (T_1, T_2, .., T_s)$ represents a set of policy variables (treatment), $B = (B_1, B_2, .., B_r)$ is a set of background variables and Y is a response variable. As before, let F_T be future policy intervention to be evaluated. For simplicity, suppose that T and Y are univariate; B does not contain intermediate variables between T and Y (i.e. B consists of pre-intervention variables that will not be affected by T); and the univariate future policy consists of atomic interventions $F_T = do(T = t')$.

As discussed in section 3, let $D_E = \{A, R(B)\}$ where A contains all the policy assignment mechanisms and $R(B)$ contains the recording mechanism, such that $R(B_i) = 1$, for $i = 1, 2...r$, if B_i is recorded and $R(B_i) = 0$ if B_i is either unobservable or not recorded. *Assignment nodes A* and *recording nodes R* can be included in the DAG as decision nodes to create a *design network (DN)*. Figure 2 shows a design network used for the evaluation of the future policy $F_T = do(T = t')$ under 3 possible scenarios. Note that A blocks all the paths going from B to the policy node T. This follows from the assumption that A captures *all* the allocation mechanisms for T that might be influenced by the background variables B, so that A is the only parent of the policy node T (besides the future intervention node F_T) in the design network. Recording nodes, $R(B)$, are added for each background variable B_i, introducing the decision of recording B_i versus not recording it. A double circle containing a dashed and solid line is given to each background node B_i to show its potential observability. It is assumed that policy T and response variable Y will be recorded.

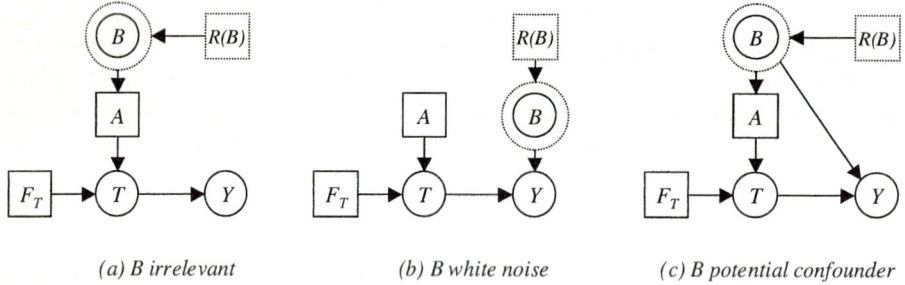

(a) B irrelevant   (b) B white noise   (c) B potential confounder

Fig. 2. Design Network for the evaluation of future policy intervention F_T

Figures 2(a) and 2(b) show cases where the background variables are irrelevant or represent white noise (respectively) for Y. In both cases, the non-confounding condition, $Y \perp\!\!\!\perp F_T \mid T$, (see Dawid 2002, section 7) holds and the future (atomic) policy intervention can be identified directly from the data available using $P(y \mid t', F_T = do(T = t')) = P(y \mid t', F_T = \emptyset)$ regardless of the knowledge we have about the policy assignment and recording mechanisms. A more interesting case to discuss experimental design effects is given by 2(c) when a potential confounder is present and $Y \perp\!\!\!\perp F_T \mid T$ does not hold. By introducing assignment nodes A, we can deduce from the design network that $Y \perp\!\!\!\perp F_T \mid (T, A)$ and $A \perp\!\!\!\perp F_T$ hold. The latter condition implies that the future policy intervention $F_T = do(T = t')$ will be done independently of the experimental design conditions chosen to allocate treatments, A. The former implies that given a known policy assignment mechanism $A = a^*$ and the value of the future policy intervention $T = t'$, learning if t' arose from that assignment mechanism $F_T = \emptyset$ or was set externally $F_T = do(T = t')$ is irrelevant for the distribution of Y, thus implying $P(y \mid t', F_T = do(T = t'), A = a^*) = P(y \mid t', F_T = \emptyset, A = a^*)$.

As the policy assignment mechanisms may involve a collection of actions, the node A might be expanded to show explicitly the mechanism underlying the assignment. This expansion will typically involve parameter and intervention nodes that are included in an *augmented-extended* version of the design network. Assignment actions A might have an effect on the original collection of conditional independence statements, S_G, and new conditional independencies, S_E, which can be derived from the *experimental DAG* will be obtained when action $A = a^*$ is taken, thus changing the structure of the original DAG. Recording decisions, will have an effect on the set of variables that will be available to us through the available (sic) experimental data. Thus $R(B)$ will not introduce any new (in)dependencies in the structure, but will be relevant when discussing potential identifiability of effects given assignment actions A and the set of conditional independencies in S_E.

The simple case of 'pure' (i.e. non-stratified) individual random allocation (contrasted to the 'no experiment' decision- i.e. observational data) will be used to introduce this procedure. When the policy assignment is done through random allocation, two control actions are performed: randomisation and intervention. So treatment t^* is set, $A_T = do(T = t^*)$, according to a probability distribution θ_T^* totally fixed and controlled by the experimenter through $A_{\theta_T} = do(\theta_T = \theta_T^*)$. Figure 3(a) shows the *augmented-extended design network* where node A from Figure 2(c) is expanded to include these two actions. Nodes A_{θ_T} and A_T stand for atomic interventions and follow the same degenerate distributions as defined for F. The parameter node θ_T denotes the probability distribution used to allocate the treatments. When no randomisation is done, so that $A_{\theta_T} = \emptyset$, θ_T is left to vary 'naturally' according to $\theta_T = p(A_T \mid B)$ (thus capturing the possibly unobserved effect of background variables on the choice of policy that will be done). When pure random allocation is done, θ_T will be set to $\theta_T = \theta_T^* = p^*(A_T)$ and by $doing(\theta_T = \theta_T^*)$ the link (r) from B to θ_T is broken, making explicit that the probability for the allocation does not depend on any background variable B, so $\theta_T^* \perp\!\!\!\perp B$. This θ_T^* will correspond to the probability of 'observing' $T = t^*$ in the experimental available data. Node A_T is used to emphasise the fact that the policy intervention value, t^*, is set externally by the experimenter. Although A_T and F_T have the same form, $A_T = do(T = t^*)$ represents an action that was done according to θ_T^* (in the past, when allocating policy) that define the structure of the data available (in the present), and F_T will be used to represent the atomic action of a (future) intervention $F_T = do(T = t')$ to address identifiability of causal effects $P(Y \mid do(T = t'), \cdot)$. In general, the set $\{t^*\}$ of policy-intervention-values assigned in the experiment through A_T is not necessarily the same as the set of future-policy-values $\{t'\}$ defined by future policy F_T. However, if $\{t'\} \subset \{t^*\}$, the positivity condition (see Dawid 2002) is satisfied. When this is not the case, some parametric assumptions need to be made for $P(Y \mid T, \cdot)$ before the policy effects can be identified from the data available.

Although the whole information required is contained in the augmented-extended design network, an experimental augmented ID is shown in Figure 3 to make explicit the different structures of the (experimental) data available obtained for both situations, namely when random allocation is performed 3(b)

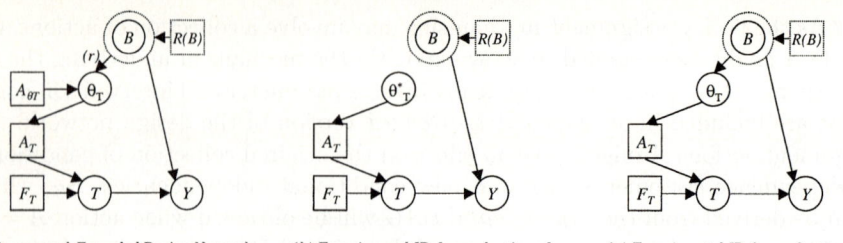

(a) Augmented-Extended Design Network   (b) Experimental ID for evaluation of   (c) Experimental ID for evaluation of
for Random Allocation   Future Policy F_T under $A_{\theta_T} = \theta^*_T$ Future Policy F_T under $A_{\theta_T} = \varnothing$

Fig. 3. Augmented-Extended Design Network and Experimental Influence Diagrams

and when no random allocation is carried out $3(c)$. From Figure $3(b)$, we can see that after random allocation is performed, the conditional independence $(T \perp\!\!\!\perp B)_E$ and $(Y \perp\!\!\!\perp F_T \mid T)_E$ are additional to the independencies in the original observational graph O included in S_O. The structure of this experimental graph is the same as the one in Figure $2(b)$ and it is easily shown that the causal effect is directly identified by $P(y \mid t', F_T = do(T = t'), A_{\theta_T} = do(\theta_T = \theta^*_T)) = P(y \mid t', F_T = \emptyset, A_{\theta_T} = do(\theta_T = \theta^*_T))$. In this case, the recording or not of B, $R(B)$, is irrelevant for both identifiability and the type of effect measured. From $3(c)$, we can see that if no random allocation is done and it is decided to use an observational study by setting $A_{\theta_T} = \emptyset$, no 'extra' conditional independencies are gained. In this case, identifiability of the average effect will depend on the recording of B. Thus, if $R(B) = 1$ and B is recorded in the data available, the policy intervention effect on Y could be estimated using the 'back-door formula' (see Pearl (2000), Lauritzen (2001) and Dawid (2002)), such that $P(y \mid F_T = do(T = t'), A_{\theta_T} = \emptyset, R(B) = 1) = \int_B P(y \mid t', B) P(B) dB$. However, if $R(B) = 0$ and B is not recorded, the treatment effect on Y is not identifiable from the available data.

In general, we will say that the 'causal' effect of T on Y is identifiable *directly* from available (experimental) data collected under $D_E = d_E$, if learning the value of F_T (i.e. learning if the future policy was set to a value or left to vary 'naturally') does not provide any 'extra' information about the response variable Y given the value of T and experimental conditions $D_E = d_E$ (i.e. if $Y \perp\!\!\!\perp F_T | T, D_E$) then $P(y \mid t', F_T = do(T = t'), D_E = d_E) = P(y \mid t', F_T = \emptyset, D_E = d_E)$. Note that this will hold (or not) regardless of $R(B)$. However, when identifiability cannot be obtained directly from data defined by D_E, identifiability can still hold for a particular configuration of $R(B)$. Then, we say that the causal effect is identifiable through an 'adjustment' procedure if $P(y \mid t', F_T = do(T = t'), D_E = d_E) = h(y, t', B^* \mid D_E = d_E)$ such that $R(B^*_i) = 1$ for all $B^*_i \in B^* \subseteq B$ and h is a function of known probabilistic distributions of recorded variables under d_E. In this latter case, the design d_E is said to be ignorable (see Rosenbaum and Rubin(1983) and Rubin(1978)).

The efficacy of experimental design interventions D_E could then be measured in terms of making the (causal) effects of $F_T = do(T = t')$ identifiable and then two (or more) experiments can be compared in these terms. A general algorithm for the evaluation of design decisions D_E, using design networks is:

1. Build the complete ID including all influences between policy nodes, background variables (observable and unobservable) and the response. (e.g. Fig 1(a))

2. Construct the (extended) design network, adding all potential treatment assignment mechanisms A, recording mechanisms $R(B)$, and future policy to be evaluated F. (e.g. Fig 3(a))

3. For each potential treatment assignment mechanism A construct its correspondent experimental ID. (e.g. Fig 3(b) and 3(c))

4. Using S_E and identifiability conditions, construct a set of possible *design consequences* (in terms of (type of) identifiability of $F_T = do(T = t')$) for each different set of experimental $D_E = \{A, R(B)\}$.

5. Define some utility function over the set of design consequences.

6. Among the experimental decisions D_E, choose the one with highest utility.

To illustrate steps 4-6, imagine we could establish that the utilities associated with obtaining direct identifiability, adjusted (back-door) identifiability and unidentifiability are given by U_D, U_A and U_U, respectively. Then for the pure random allocation vs. observational case we have that for the four possible combinations of $(A, R(B))$:

	Experimental Decisions		Design Consequence	Utility
D_E	A_{θ_T}	$R(B)$	$P(y \mid F_T = t', D_E)$	U
1	$do(\theta_T = \theta_T^*)$	1	direct identifiablity	U_D
2	$do(\theta_T = \theta_T^*)$	0	direct identifiablity	U_D
3	$A_{\theta_T} = \emptyset$	1	adjusted identifiability	U_A
4	$A_{\theta_T} = \emptyset$	0	No identifiable	U_U

Both experimental decisions that include random allocation, $A_{\theta_T} = do(\theta_T = \theta_T^*)$, have the same utility associated in terms of identifiability and are equivalent in these terms. However, performing an experiment (randomising and/or recording) will typically have a cost associated that should be included in the utility for a complete evaluation of the designs. Making a difference between the utility associated with direct and adjusted identifiability might sound suspicious. However, although policy effects can be identified in both situations, some maximum likelihood estimates will not generally have the same efficiency (see Lauritzen(2001)). A broader discussion can be found in Madrigal (2004).

5   Conclusions

Design networks and experimental influence diagrams were introduced by incorporating explicitly nodes for policy assignment A and recording mechanisms R. This demonstrates to be very useful to show clearly the experimental design intervention consequences in the graph. In particular, certain policy assignment mechanisms, such as randomised allocation, will add 'extra' independencies to the ID defining a new collection of conditional independencies. The relevance of A to assist identification and the equivalence of two different mechanisms A_1 and A_2 in terms of identifiability can be adressed under this framework for diverse types of assignment (for a broader discussion (see Madrigal (2004)). Recording mechanisms show to be relevant to assist non-direct identification of effects. Identifiability of effects, although a very important issue, is not the only thing needed when we face the inferential problem. The general idea was introduced for 'pure' random allocation of policies in this paper, extensions of this to stratified and clustered assigments can be found in Madrigal (2004).

References

1. Dawid, A.P. (1979). *Conditional independence in statistical theory.* Journal of the Royal Statistical Society (Series B), vol. 41, pp. 1–31.
2. Dawid, A. P. (2000). *Causal Inference Without Counterfactuals.* Journal of the American Statistical Association 95: 407–48.
3. Dawid, A.P.(2002) *Influence Diagrams for Causal Modelling and Inference,* International Statistical Review , 70, 2, 161189, Printed in The Netherlands
4. Howard, R. and Matheson, J. (1981). *Influence diagrams.* In Howard, R. and Matheson, J., editors, Readings on the Principles and Applications of Decision Analysis,volume II, pages 721–762. Strategic Decisions Group, Menlo Park, CA.
5. Jensen,F.V.(2001) *Bayesian Networks and Decision Graphs.* Springer, New York, 2001.
6. Lauritzen, S. L. (2001). *Causal inference from graphical models.* In: Complex Stochastic Systems, eds. O. E. Barndorff-Nielsen, D. R. Cox and C. Kluppelberg, pp. 63–107. Chapman and Hall/CRC Press. London/Boca Raton.
7. Lauritzen, S. L., Dawid, A. P., Larsen, B. N. and Leimer, H.-G. (1990), *Independence properties of directed Markov fields.* Networks 20, 491–505
8. Madrigal, A.M.(2004) *Evaluation of Policy interventions under Experimental conditions using Bayesian Influence Diagrams.* PhD Thesis. University of Warwick.UK
9. Oliver,R. M. and Smith,J. Q.(1990). *Influence Diagrams, Belief Nets and Decision Analysis.* Series in probability and methematical statistics. Wiley, Chichester.
10. Pearl, J. (2000) *Causality.* Cambridge University Press.
11. Rosenbaum, Paul R. and Rubin, Donald B. (1983) *The central role of the propensity score in observational studies for causal effects,* Biometrika 70: 41–55
12. Rubin, D. (1978). *Bayesian inference for causal effects: The role of randomization.* Annals of Statistics, 6:34–58.
13. Shachter,R. D.(1986). *Evaluating influence diagrams.* Operation Research 34(6): 871–882.
14. Smith, J. Q. (1989). *Influence diagrams for Bayesian decision analysis,* European Journal of Operational Research 40, 363–376.
15. Verma,T. and Pearl J. (1990). *Causal networs: Semantics and expressiveness.* In Uncertainty in Artificial Intelligence 4, (ed. R.D. Shachter, T.S. Levitt, L.N. Kanal, and J.F.Lemmer), pp. 69–76. North-Holland, Amsterdam.

Bayes-N: An Algorithm for Learning Bayesian Networks from Data Using Local Measures of Information Gain Applied to Classification Problems

Manuel Martínez-Morales[1], Nicandro Cruz-Ramírez[2], José Luis Jiménez-Andrade[1], and Ramiro Garza-Domínguez[1]

[1] Facultad de Física e Inteligencia Artificial, Universidad Veracruzana,
Xalapa, Veracruz, México.
manumartinez@uv.mx
[2] Laboratorio Nacional de Informática Avanzada (LANIA),
Xalapa, Veracruz, México.
ncruz@lania.mx

Abstract. Bayes-N is an algorithm for Bayesian network learning from data based on local measures of information gain, applied to problems in which there is a given *dependent* or *class* variable and a set of *independent* or *explanatory* variables from which we want to predict the class variable on new cases. Given this setting, Bayes-N induces an ancestral ordering of all the variables generating a directed acyclic graph in which the class variable is a sink variable, with a subset of the explanatory variables as its parents. It is shown that classification using this variables as predictors performs better than the naive bayes classifier, and at least as good as other algorithms that learn Bayesian networks such as K2, PC and Bayes-9. It is also shown that the MDL measure of the networks generated by Bayes-N is comparable to those obtained by these other algorithms.

Keywords: Bayesian networks, data mining, classification, MDL, machine learning.

1 Introduction

There are several problems in scientific research in which there is a particular structure in the relationship between the variables under consideration. In problems of this type there is a *dependent* or *response* variable, and a set of *independent* or *explanatory* variables (for example in experimental design, regression models, prediction, classification problems, and so on). The underlying hypothesis is that the behaviour of the dependent variable can be explained as a result of the action of the independent variables. Although in some contexts a causal relationship is assumed, usually the assumption is restricted to state that there is some sort of association or covariation between variables. Probabilistic models (discrete, continuous or mixed) are applied when uncertainty is present. Bayesian networks [1][2][3] provide appropriate models in many of such cases, particularly when we are looking not only for the structure of the relationship as in the case of learning the network topology,

R. Monroy et al. (Eds.): MICAI 2004, LNAI 2972, pp. 527–535, 2004.
© Springer-Verlag Berlin Heidelberg 2004

but also when we want to use the model as an inference machine, like for example in classification problems. The application of Bayesian networks to this kind of problems is not new [4], but there are several problems to be addressed, in particular those related to learning Bayesian networks from data and assessing their performance when applied to classification problems.

In this paper we present Bayes-N, an algorithm for learning a Bayesian network from data, that takes advantage of the asymmetric relationship (dependent vs. independent covariation be *discrete* variables) in problems of the type just described, generating an ancestral ordering among variables based on local measures of information gain [5][6][7][8] and controlled statistical tests of conditional independence. We show that the algorithm performs well compared with similar algorithms, and that for classification problems its performance is better than the naive bayes classifier [4] and performs at least as well as K2 [9], Pc [7] and Bayes9 [8]. Also the MDL measure of goodness of fit of the network to the data from which it was obtained compares to the MDL of networks obtained by other well known algorithms as the ones just mentioned.

2 A Statistical Test for Conditional Independence

In 1959 S. Kullback proposed a statistical test for conditional independence based on information measures [10] which was later generalized [11] and has been widely used in association with loglinear models [12]. It has also been used in the context of undirected graphical models related to multivariate statistical analysis [13]. Here, a simple variant of the test is applied to induce the structure of directed acyclic graphs as explained below. For the case of testing marginal independence for two discrete variables, Kullback's test is equivalent to the usual chi-square test.

Kullback's Test for Conditional Independence. Let X, Y, Z, be discrete random variables with given joint, conditional and marginal probability distributions. The information gain on X given by Y is defined as $I(X/Y) = H(X) - H(X|Y)$, and the conditional information on X given Y and Z is defined by $I(X/Z,Y)=H(X/Z)-H(X|Z,Y)$. H(X), H(X/Y),and H(X/Z,Y) are the entropy and the conditional entropies defined as usual [14].

By $X \perp Y$ we mean X and Y are marginally independent. By $X \perp Y,Z$ we mean X is conditionally independent of Y given Z.

A test for marginal independence between X and Y can be set up in terms of information gain measures as follows:

$$H_0 : I(X \mid Y) = 0, (X \perp Y)\qquad(1)$$

$$H_1 : I(X \mid Y) > 0, (X \not\perp Y)$$

Let $K(X|Y)$ denote the estimator of $I(X|Y)$ obtained from the sample, and let N be the sample size. Kullback shows that under H_0, the statistic $T=2NK(X|Y)$ is asymptotically distributed as a chi-square variable (with appropriate degrees of freedom). Under H_1, T will have a non-central chi-square distribution. Thus we can perform a test of independence based on $K(X|Y)$. In fact T is closely related to the statistic G^2, frequently used in test related to loglinear and graphical models [12][15]. T is used here to emphasize the particular application we have in mind.

A test for conditional independence of X and Y given Z, as proposed by Kullback, is based on the information gain on X given by Y once Z is known. The hypotheses to be tested are:

$$H_0 : I(X \mid Z,Y) = 0, (X \perp Y,Z) \tag{2}$$

$$H_1 : I(X \mid Z,Y) > 0, (X \not\perp Y,Z)$$

The statistic $T=2NK(X|Z,Y)$, where N is the sample size and $K(X|Z,Y)$ is the estimator of $I(X|Z,Y)$, is asymptotically distributed as a chi-square variable under H_0. Under H_1, T has a non-central chi-square asymptotic distribution.

The proposed algorithm performs test for conditional independence as just described above, in an order that depends on measures of information gain, making Bonferri`s adjustment and defining a threshold for the information gain as described below.

Bonferroni's Adjustment. In general, if we have k independent tests, each with level of significance of α and all null hypotheses are true, the probability of obtaining significant results by chance is $1 - (1 - \alpha)^k$. This probability is called the global significance level , α_g, when many tests of hypothesis are made. [16][17]

Bonferroni's Adjustment consists of choosing the global significance level α_g = 0.05, say, and computing the significance level for each individual test:

$$\alpha = 1 - \left(1 - \alpha_g\right)^{\frac{1}{k}} \tag{3}$$

where k is the number of independence tests made by the algorithm and is calculated as:

$$k = \sum_{i=1}^{n} \sum_{j=0}^{p} (n-i) + j, \text{ with } j < (n-i) \tag{4}$$

Please note that $\alpha < \alpha_g$, which reduce the risk of overfitting when the number of tests is large, i.e. the network will have more arcs than necessary.

Percentage of Information Gain. Most algorithms for learning Bayesian networks based on marginal and conditional independence tests, use a threshold to determine if the variables at issue are independent or not. For large databases, small values of the information statistic will appear to be significant, even after Bonferroni's adjustment has been performed [16]. Bayes-N includes an additional criterion to decide if two variables are independent based on the percentage of information gain, defined by:

$$\%I = \frac{I(X \mid Y)}{H(X)} \text{ in the case of testing marginal independence} \tag{5}$$

$$\%I = \frac{I(X \mid Z,Y)}{H(X \mid Z)} \quad \text{in the case of testing conditional independence} \qquad (6)$$

This measure defines an indifference region [16] for deciding what amount of information is relevant, specifying an information gain threshold that must be exceeded before declaring two variables to be (or not to be) marginally independent or conditionally independent.

3 The Algorithm

Bayes-N belongs to a family of algorithms with which we have been working for some time[6], [8], [18]. We make the following assumptions:
  a) The variables in the database are discrete.
  b) There are no missing values in all the cases of the database
  c) Given the true probabilistic distribution (the true model), the cases occur independently
  d) The number of cases in the databases is enough to make the independence and conditional independence tests reliable.

Basically the algorithm works as follows. Let X be the dependent variable, and $Y = \{Y_1, Y_2..., Y_n\}$ the set of independent variables. Let p be the depth of the tests; i.e. the maximum number of variables in the conditional set. Be α_G the global significance as defined previously. The total number of independence tests to be performed is k. Let α be the local significance, and I_{min} the threshold for information gain. $\%I$ is the percentage of information of the dependent variable provided by the independent variable being tested. During the first iteration it performs tests for marginal independence between the dependent variable (X) and the independent variables $(Y_1, Y_2..., Y_n)$. Next, the independent variables are ordered in terms of $I(X|Y_i)$. If the hypothesis of independence is rejected then a directed arc is drawn from $Y_{(1)}$, the variable with greatest $I(X|Y)$, to X and then tests of conditional independence based on $I(X|Y_i, Y_{(1)})$ $((1) \neq i$) are performed to decide if any other arcs are to be drawn from some $Y_i's$ to X. Next we condition on the two variables with greatest $I(X|Y)$, and repeat the test of conditional independence applied only to those variables connected to X in the previous step and decide which arcs, if any, are to be deleted. The procedure is repeated until we have conditioned on p variables. We make $X=Y_{(1)}$, repeat the procedure and iterate until no more variables are available. Bonferroni's adjustment and the information threshold criterion are embedded in the statistical tests.

Remark. The global significance, α_g, the depth p, and the minimal percentage of information, I_{min}, are parameters defined by the user.

4 Classification

A classifier is a function that maps a set of instances (attributes) into a specific label (class) [19][4]. In the data mining terminology, it is commonly accepted that the term *classification* refers to the prediction of discrete, nominal or categorical variables' values while the term *prediction* refers to the prediction of continuous variables' values [20].

There exist different methods to test the performance, in terms of accuracy, of any classifier such as *holdout, cross-validation* and *bootstrap* [19][20]. In this paper, the holdout and cross-validation methods are used to check the accuracy of the model built by Bayes-N.

In the holdout method, the common practice is to randomly partition the data in two different mutually exclusive samples: the training and the test sets. The test set is also called the holdout set. The size of the training set is usually 2/3 of the data and the remaining 1/3 of the data corresponds to the size of the test set. The accuracy of the model built by the induction algorithm (in this case Bayes-N) is the percentage of the test set cases that are classified to the correct category they belong by the model. In other words, the class to which each case in the test set truly belongs is compared to the prediction, made by the model, for that same instance. The reason for partitioning the data this way is to avoid overfitting the data since, if the accuracy of the model were estimated taking into account only the training set, then some possible anomalous features which are not representative of the whole data could be included in this subset and the estimate may possibly not reflect the true accuracy. Thus, a test set has to be selected and used to test the robustness of the model, in the sense of making correct classifications given noisy data.

Thus, the overall number of correct classifications divided by the size of the test set is the accuracy estimate of the holdout method. Formula 7 [19] shows how to calculate the accuracy using the holdout approach.

$$acc_h = \frac{1}{h} \sum_{(v_i, y_i) \in D_h} \delta(I(D_t, v_i), y_i) \tag{7}$$

where $I(D_t, v_i)$ denotes the instance v_i built by inducer I on data set D_t (the training set) which is assigned the label y_i and tested on the test set D_h; h is the size of the test set. $\delta(i,j)=1$ if i=j and 0 otherwise. This means that the loss function used for calculating the accuracy in the holdout method is a 0/1 loss function, which considers equal misclassification costs.

The variance of the holdout method is estimated as follows [19]:

$$Var = \frac{acc \times (1 - acc)}{h} \tag{8}$$

where h is the size of the test set.

Another common approach, which is also used to measure classification accuracy and which will also be used here to calculate the accuracy of the classifier induced by Bayes-N, is the *k-fold* cross-validation. In the k-fold cross-validation method, as described in [19][20], the complete dataset is randomly partitioned in k mutually exclusive subsets (called also the folds) D_1, D_2, ..., D_k of approximately equal size. The induction algorithm is trained and tested k times in the following way: in the first iteration, this algorithm is trained on subsets D_2, ..., D_k and tested on subset D_1; in the second iteration, the algorithm is trained on subsets D_1, D_3, ..., D_k and tested on subset D_2 and so on. The overall number of correct classifications from the k iterations divided by the size of the complete dataset is the accuracy estimate of the k-fold cross-validation method. Formula 9 shows how to calculate the accuracy of the cross-validation approach.

$$acc_{cv} = \frac{1}{n} \sum_{(v_i, y_i) \in D_{(i)}} \delta(I(D \setminus D_{(i)}, v_i), y_i) \qquad (9)$$

where $I(D \setminus D_{(i)}, v_i)$ denotes the instance v_i built by inducer I on data set $D \setminus D_{(i)}$, which is assigned the label y_i and tested on the test set $D_{(i)}$; n is the size of the complete dataset D. $\delta(i,j)=1$ if i=j and 0 otherwise. As in equation 7, this means that the loss function used for calculating the accuracy in the cross-validation method is a 0/1 loss function, which considers equal misclassification costs.

Equation 10 shows the formula for the estimation of the variance in this method [16]:

$$Var_{cv} = \frac{acc_{cv} \times (1 - acc_{cv})}{n} \qquad (10)$$

where n is the size of the complete dataset D.

It is very important to stress the advantage of Bayes-N against some search and scoring algorithms regarding the performance in classification tasks. In the case of Bayes-N, the Bayesian network is built by adding or deleting arcs (according to which is the case) taking into account only a pair of nodes and the nodes in the conditional set; i.e., the rest of the nodes are not considered in the analysis. This is why the information gain measures used in Bayes-N are called local. In other words, the construction of the network does not depend on a global scoring function, such as MDL (minimum description length) or BIC (Bayesian information criterion), that evaluates the entire network every time an application of an operator (such as adding, deleting or reversing arcs) is carried out. In cases where there are many attributes, these global scoring functions fail to minimize local errors that have to do with the classification performance of the resultant network. That is to say, although this network produces a good MDL score, it may perform poorly as a classifier [4].

5   Results

Three different databases were used to test the performance of five different algorithms. The first one is called ALARM. ALARM stands for "A Logical Alarm Reduction Mechanism". This database was constructed from a network that was built by Beinlich [9], [21] as an initial research prototype to model potential anaesthesia problem in the operating room. ALARM has 37 variables (nodes) and 46 arcs. From these 37 variables, 8 variables represent diagnostic problems, 16 variables represent findings and 13 variables represent intermediate variables that connect diagnostic problems to findings. Each node (variable) has from 2 to 4 different possible values. The size of the sample of the ALARM database is 10,000 cases. The class node is Blood Pressure (Node 5).

The second database is a real-world database that comes from the field of pathology and has to do with the cytodiagnosis of breast cancer using a technique called fine needle aspiration of the breast lesion (**FNAB**) [22], [23](Stephenson et al. 2000), which is the most common confirmatory method used in the United Kingdom for this purpose[23]. It contains 692 consecutive specimens of FNAB received at the Department of Pathology, Royal Hallamshire Hospital in Sheffield during 1992-1993 [23]. 11 independent variables and 1 dependent variable form part of such a dataset. The independent variables are: age, cellular dyshesion, intracytoplasmic lumina, "three-dimensionality" of epithelial cells clusters, bipolar "naked" nuclei, foamy macrophages, nucleoli, nuclear pleomorphism, nuclear size, necrotic epithelial cells and apocrine change. All these variables, except age, are dichotomous taking the values of "true" or "false" indicating the presence or absence of a diagnostic feature. Variable age was actually sorted into three different categories: 1 (up to 50 years old), 2 (51 to 70 years old) and 3 (above 70 years old). The dependent variable "outcome" can take on two different values: benign or malignant. In the case of a malignant outcome, such a result was confirmed by a biopsy (where available).

The third database is called ASIA [24]. ASIA has 8 variables and 8 arcs. This database comes from a very small Bayesian network for a fictitious medical example about whether a patient has tuberculosis, lung cancer or bronchitis, related to their X-ray, dyspnoea, visit-to-Asia and smoking status; it is also called "Chest Clinic". Each node (variable) has 2 different possible values. The probability distributions for each node are described at the Norsys Software Corporation web site[24]. The size of the sample of the ASIA database is 1,000 cases.

Table 1 shows the classification performance, using the holdout method [16], of five different algorithms: Naïve Bayes[4], Bayes-N, K2 [9], Pc [7] and Bayes9 [8]. Table 2 shows the classification performance, using the 5-fold cross-validation method, of the same five different algorithms. Accuracy and standard deviation are shown in these tables. Table 3 shows the MDL for the networks as used for the holdout method.

Table 1. Classification performance for the holdout method of Naïve Bayes, Bayes-N, Tetrad and Bayes9.

Dat	Naïve	Bayes-N	K2	Tetrad (Pc)	Bayes9
Alar	62.65 ±	82.57 ±	82.57 ±	82.57 ±	82.57 ±
Can	92.80 ±	95.34 ±	95.34 ±	92.80 ±	95.34 ±
Asia	93.53 ±	96.18 ±	96.18 ±	95.01 ±	96.18 ±

Table 2. Classification performance for the 5-fold cross-validation method of Naïve Bayes, Bayes-N, K2, Tetrad and Bayes9

Data	Naïve	Bayes-N	K2	Tetrad (Pc)	Bayes9
Alar	61.52 ±	82.25 ±	82.25 ±	82.13 ±	82.79 ± 0.38
Canc	93.00 ±	94.65 ±	94.51 ±	94.36 ±	94.36 ±
Asia	89.63 ±	94.30 ±	94.20 ±	95.80 ±	95.80 ±

Table 3. MDL scores for the networks as used for the holdout method

Data set	Naïve	Bayes-N	K2	Tetrad (Pc)	Bayes9
Alarm	143730.14	78010.91	71590.66	78845.10	79352.5
Cancer	2685.40	2679.55	2648.20	2746.72	2759.91
Asia	2387.20	2213.34	2215.23	2211.79	2211.34

6 Discussion

As can be seen from Tables 1 and 2, the classification performance of Bayes-N is much better than that of naive Bayesian classifier and produces comparable results of those given by K2, Tetrad and Bayes9. The advantage of Bayes-N over naive bayes, besides from accuracy, is that it performs a correct subset feature selection getting rid, for the analysis, of variables that are not significant. Also, Bayes-N does not make the strong assumption, made by naive bayes, that the attribute variables are conditionally independent given the class variable. That is to say, Bayes-N considers that there may well be interactions among attributes, which in turn, can give more richness in the modelling and understanding of the phenomenon under investigation. In the case of the breast cancer dataset, the pathologists use the 11 independent variables in order to decide whether the patient has cancer or not (class variable) achieving a high overall classification performance [22]. Our initial hypothesis was that the naive Bayesian classifier, which by definition takes into account all these variables to make the final diagnosis, would produce much better results than those produced by the algorithms that only take a subset of these variables such as Bayes-N. However, as the results show, this was surprisingly not the case; i.e., Bayes-N outperforms naive bayes even when the former uses a subset of the whole set of attributes used by the latter. This can give indication that the local information gain measures used by Bayes-N represent a robust and accurate approach when building Bayesian network classifiers. Thus, with the reduction of redundant attributes, these measures also lead to the construction of parsimonious models.

Compared to K2, a very notable feature of Bayes-N is that it does not need an ancestral ordering to build the network while K2 indeed does. In fact, Bayes-N induces this ancestral ordering using local information gain measures. In the case of K2, an ancestral ordering must be externally provided and the resultant network constructed by such a procedure is highly sensitive to this order; i.e., if the optimal ancestral ordering is not the one provided to K2, then the resultant network might be extremely inaccurate [9], [25].

Compared with Tetrad and Bayes9, Bayes-N gives direction to all the arcs in the network whereas the other two procedures may produce undirected arcs. Although this problem can be alleviated more or less easily in some problems, it still needs a certain amount of knowledge elicitation in order to direct these arcs. Even in large domains, as in the case of ALARM, Bayes-N seems to induce correct ancestral orderings, which allow to direct all the arcs among variables.

Some limitations of Bayes-N can be mentioned. First of all, for the Bonferroni's adjustment, it is necessary to make, a priori, the calculation of the number of independence or conditional independence tests for this adjustment to be included in the procedure. And finally, the percentage of significant gain is a parameter that has to be manually tuned. Unfortunately, as usually happens in the definition of a threshold, certain values for this parameter can lead to inaccurate results.

As future work, we want to look for criteria that may allow for the automatic assignment of the percentage of significant information gain.

References

1. J. Pearl, *Probabilistic Reasoning in Intelligent Systems: Networks of Plausible Inference.* Second edition. Morgan Kauffman Pub., Inc. (1988).
2. R. G. Cowell, A. P. Dawid, S.L. Lauritzen. *Probabilistic Networks and Expert Systems.* Springer Verlag. (1999)
3. F.V. Jensen. *Bayesian Networks and Decision Graphs.* Springer Verlag. (2001)
4. N. Freidman, D. Geiger, S. Goldszmidt, Bayesian Networks classifiers. *Machine Learning,* 29 (pp 131-161), (1997)
5. J.R.Quinlan, *C4.5: Programs for Machine Learning.* Morgan Kaufmann Publishers. (1993)
6. M. Martinez-Morales, An Algorithm for the Induction of Probabilistic Networks from Data. *XII Reunion Nacional de Inteligencia Artificial, ITESM,* Cuernavaca, Morelos, Mexico, Limusa. (1995).
7. Spirtes, P., Glymour, C. and Scheines, R., An algorithm for fast recovery of sparse causal graphs, *Social Science Computer Review,* 9, 62-72, (1991).
8. N. Cruz-Ramirez, Building Bayesian Networks From Data: a Constraint Based Approach. *Ph D Thesis.* Department of Psychology. The University of Sheffield. (2001).
9. G.F. Cooper, and E. Herskovits, A Bayesian Method for the induction of probabilistic networks from data. *Machine Learning,* 9 (pp. 309-347), (1992).
10. S. Kullback, *Information Theory and Statistics.* Dover, New York, (1949).
11. H. H. Ku, R. N. Varner and S. Kullback. *Analysis of Multidimensional Contingency Tables.* J. Amer. Statist. Assoc., 66, 55-64, (1971).
12. S. E. Feinberg. *The Analysis of Cross-Classified Categorical Data.* The MIT Press. Cambridge Mass., (1981).
13. J. Whittaker, *Graphical Models in Applied Multivariate Analysis.* John Wiley, Chichester, (1990).
14. Shannon, C. E. and W. Weaver (1949). The mathematical theory of communication. Urbana, University of Illinois Press.
15. P. Spirtes, and C. Glymour, *Causation, Prediction and Search,* Springer-Verlag. (1993).
16. P.J. Bickel, K.A. Doksum. Mathematical Statistics: Basic Ideas and Selected Topics. Holden Day, Inc. Oakland, Cal. 1977.
17. J.M. Bland, and D.G. Altman, Multiple significance tests: the Bonferroni method. BMJ; 310: 170, (1995).
18. N. Cruz-Ramirez, and M. Martinez-Morales. Un algoritmo para generar redes Bayesianas a partir de Datos estadísticos. *Primer Encuentro Nacional de Computación, ENC 97,* Querétaro. (1997).
19. R. Kohavi, A Study of Cross-Validation and Bootstrap for Accuracy Estimation and Model Selection. *14th International Joint Conference on Artificial Intelligence IJCAI'95,* Montreal, Canada, Morgan Kaufmann. (1995).
20. J. Han, and M. Kamber, *Data Mining. Concepts and Techniques,* Morgan Kaufmann, (2001).
21. G. F. Cooper, *An Overview of the Representation and Discovery of Causal Relationships using Bayesian Networks.* Computation, Causation & Discovery. C. Glymour and G. F. Cooper, AAAI Press / MIT Press: 3-62. (1999).
22. S. S. Cross, A. K. Dube, et al. Evaluation of a statistically derived decision tree for the cytodiagnosis of fine needle aspirates of the breast *(FNAB). Cytopathology* **8:** 178-187. (1998).
23. S. S. Cross, J. Downs, et al. Which Decision Support Technologies Are Appropriate for the Cytodiagnosis of Breast Cancer? Artificial Intelligence Techniques in Breast Cancer Diagnosis and Prognosis. A. Jain, A. Jain, S. Jain and L. Jain, World Scientific. **39:** 265-295. (2000).
24. Norsys. Norsys Software Corporation, Electronic source: http://www.norsys.com. (2001).
25. D. Heckerman, D. Geiger, et al. Learning Bayesian Networks: The combination of knowledge and statistical data, *Technical Report MSR-TR-94-09,* Microsoft Research, Redmond, Washington, (1994).

Methodology for Handling Uncertainty by Using Interval Type-2 Fuzzy Logic Systems

Germán Montalvo and Rogelio Soto

Center for Intelligent Systems, Tecnológico de Monterrey, Campus Monterrey, México
{gmontalvo,rsoto}@itesm.mx

Abstract. This paper proposes a methodology that is useful for handling uncertainty in non-linear systems by using type-2 Fuzzy Logic (FL). This methodology works under a training scheme from numerical data, using type-2 Fuzzy Logic Systems (FLS). Different training methods can be applied while working with it, as well as different training approaches. One of the training methods used here is also a proposal —the One-Pass method for interval type-2 FLS. We accomplished several experiments forecasting a chaotic time-series with an additive noise and obtained better performance with interval type-2 FLSs than with conventional ones. In addition, we used the designed FLSs to forecast the time-series with different initial conditions, and it did not affect their performance.

1 Introduction

In this paper, we propose a general methodology for designing fuzzy logic systems (FLS) based on input-output pairs. The proposed methodology provides a way to handle uncertainty through the use of type-2 FLSs. Next, we will give a brief introduction to type-2 fuzzy logic (FL) and its fuzzy sets.

Frequently, the knowledge that is used to construct the rules in a FLS is uncertain. This uncertainty leads to rules with uncertain antecedent and/or consequent, which in turns translates into uncertain antecedent and/or consequent membership functions (mf). The main sources of such uncertainties are: (1) When the meaning of the words that are used in the antecedents and consequents of the rules can be uncertain (words mean different things to different people). (2) When we do a survey to a group of experts, we might get different consequents for the same rule, because the experts not necessarily agree. (3) When we use noisy measurements to activate FLSs. (4) When the data that are used to tune the parameters of FLS are also noisy. All of these sources of uncertainty translate into uncertainties about the mf of fuzzy sets. Ordinary fuzzy sets (henceforth type-1 fuzzy sets), are not able to directly model such uncertainties because their mfs are totally crisp. Whereas type-2 fuzzy sets are able to model those uncertainties because their mfs are themselves fuzzy. In our experiments we had cases (3) and (4) (due to noisy data for training and testing), so we used type-2 fuzzy sets to correctly handle these uncertainties.

General type-2 fuzzy sets are three-dimensional and the amplitude of their secondary mfs (called the secondary grade) can be in $[0, 1]$. When the domain

R. Monroy et al. (Eds.): MICAI 2004, LNAI 2972, pp. 536–545, 2004.

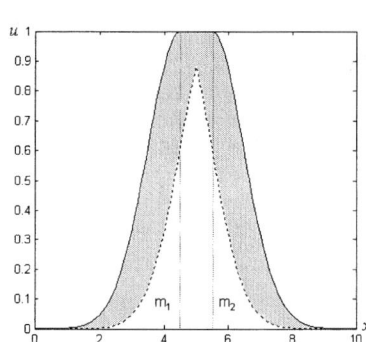

Fig. 1. FOU for Gaussian primary membership function with uncertain mean

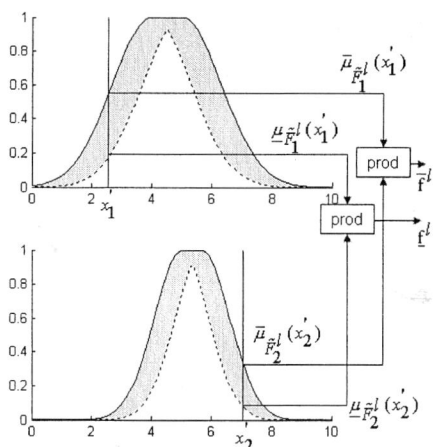

Fig. 2. Input and antecedent operations for an interval singleton type-2 FLS using product t-norm

of a secondary mf (called the primary membership) bounds a region (called the footprint of uncertainty, FOU) whose secondary grades all equal one, the resulting type-2 fuzzy set is called interval type-2 fuzzy set, which can easily be depicted in two dimensions instead of three, see Fig. 1, where the solid line denotes the upper mf, and the dashed line denotes the lower mf. Moreover, since working with general type-2 fuzzy sets is computationally very intensive, we only used interval type-2 fuzzy sets, because they are not that intensive and they still can handle noisy data by making use of an interval of uncertainty. Systems using interval type-2 fuzzy sets are called interval type-2 FLSs [1], and they were used for illustrating the proposed methodolgy. We also used type-1 FLSs in order to have a reference of performance.

2   FLSs with Different Fuzzifiers

According to the type of fuzzification [2], FLSs can be divided into singleton and non-singleton, which are described below.

2.1   Singleton FLS

In a singleton type-1 FLS, the fuzzifier maps a crisp point into a fuzzy singleton, which is a set that only has one element, the unit, i.e., $\mu_A(x) = 1$ for $x = x'$ and $\mu_A(x) = 0$ for $x \neq x'$. Thus, a singleton type-1 FLS can directly map the crisp inputs (i.e., the fuzzy singletons) into the membership values of the antecedents. With these membership values, the system computes a firing level by using a t-norm (minimum or product). Then, it applies a composition (max-min or max-product) to the firing level of each rule and its corresponding consequent (note

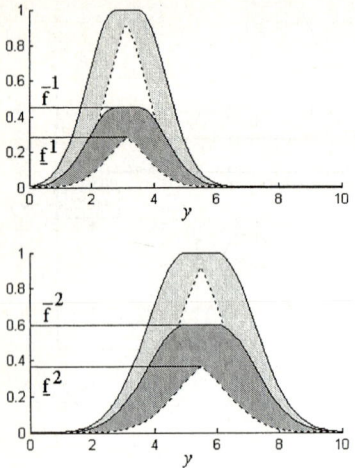
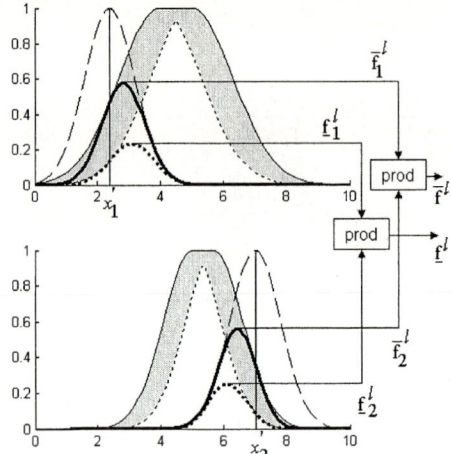

Fig. 3. Consequent operations for an interval type-2 FLS, with its fired output sets using product t-norm

Fig. 4. Input and antecedent operations for an interval non-singleton type-2 FLS using product t-norm

that the firing level is crisp value). Later, it combines the weighted consequents through the s-norm (max) in order to obtain an output fuzzy set, which is defuzzified to compute a crisp value that will be the system output.

In an interval singleton type-2 FLS [1], the process of fuzzy inference can be briefly described as follows. First, fuzzification process is accomplished as shown in Fig. 2, which depicts input and antecedent operations for a two-antecedent single-consequent rule, singleton fuzzification, and, in this case, product t-norm. It is worth mentioning that, regardless the t-norm, the firing strength is an interval type-1 set F^l, represented by its lower and upper mfs as $[\underline{f}^l, \overline{f}^l]$.

Figure 3 depicts the weighted consequents $\mu_{\tilde{B}^l}$ for a two-rule ($l = 1, 2$) singleton type-2 FLS, where $\overline{f}^1$ is t-normed with the upper mf $\overline{\mu}_{\tilde{G}^1}$ —$\mu_{\tilde{G}^l}$ is the consequent of the rule R^l—, and $\underline{f}^1$ is t-normed with the lower mf $\underline{\mu}_{\tilde{G}^1}$.The primary membership of $\mu_{\tilde{B}^l}(y)$ $\forall y \in Y$ [i.e., the $FOU(\tilde{B}^l)$] is the darkened area. Figure 5 depicts the combined type-2 output set for the two-rule singleton type-2 FLS, where the fired output sets are combined using the maximum t-conorm. The upper solid curve corresponds to $\left[\overline{f}^1 \star \overline{\mu}_{\tilde{G}^1}\right] \vee \left[\overline{f}^2 \star \overline{\mu}_{\tilde{G}^2}\right]$ for $\forall y \in Y$, the lower dashed curve corresponds to $\left[\underline{f}^1 \star \underline{\mu}_{\tilde{G}^1}\right] \vee \left[\underline{f}^2 \star \underline{\mu}_{\tilde{G}^2}\right]$ for $\forall y \in Y$. The primary membership of $\mu_{\tilde{B}}(y)$ $\forall y \in Y$ [i.e., the $FOU(\tilde{B})$] is the darkened area between these two functions, and it is also an interval set.

The next step, after fuzzy inference, is type-reduction. Regardless the type-reduction method we choose, and because of the fact that we are now dealing with interval sets, the type-reduced set is also an interval set, and it has the structure $Y_{TR} = [y_l, y_r]$. We defuzzify it using the average of y_l and y_r; hence, the defuzzified output of an interval singleton type-2 FLs is $y(\mathbf{x}) = [y_l + y_r]/2$.

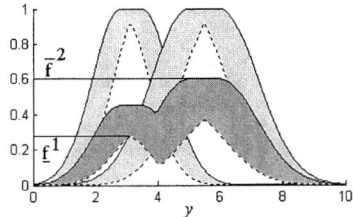

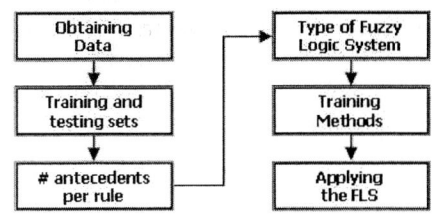

Fig. 5. Combined output sets for the two fired output sets shown in Fig. 3

Fig. 6. Block diagram of the methodology proposed for designing FLS

2.2 Non-singleton FLS

A non-singleton FLS has the same structure as a singleton FLS (fuzzifier + inference engine + defuzzifier), and they share the same type of rules; the difference lies on the fuzzification. In a non-singleton FLS, the fuzzifier treats the inputs as fuzzy numbers; in other words, a non-singleton FLS models its inputs into fuzzy sets by associating mfs to them.

Conceptually, the non-singleton fuzzifier implies that the given input value x_i' is the most likely value to be the correct one from all the values in the immediate neighborhood; however, because the input is corrupted by noise, neighboring points are also likely to be the correct value, but to a lesser degree.

Within the fuzzification process in a non singleton type-1 FLS, the crisp inputs to the system x_k establish the centers of the mfs of the input fuzzy sets μ_{X_k}; i.e., they are modeled as fuzzy numbers. These fuzzy numbers are used to compute the firing level of each rule by using a t-norm (minimum or product). Here, as in a singleton type-1 FLS, the firing level of a rule is again a crisp value, so that the process of inference and defuzzification described for that system can also be applied for a non-singleton type-1 FLS.

In an interval non-singleton type-2 FLS [1], the process of fuzzy inference can be briefly described as follows. First, as part of the process to obtain the output from the system, it is necessary to determine the *meet* operation between an input type-1 set and an antecedent type-2. This task just involves the t-norm operation between the input mf and the lower and upper mfs of the antecedent. The result is an interval set denoted as $\mu_{\tilde{Q}_k^l}(x_k)$, and depicted by the thick (solid and dashed) lines in Fig. 4, where we show input and antecedent operations for a two-antecedent single-consequent rule, non-singleton fuzzification, and product t-norm. Regardless the t-norm used, the firing strength is an interval type-1 set $[\underline{f}^l, \overline{f}^l]$, where $\underline{f}^l = \underline{f}_1^l \star \underline{f}_2^l$ and $\overline{f}^l = \overline{f}_1^l \star \overline{f}_2^l$. Observe that $\underline{f}_k^l$ is the supremum of the firing strength between the t-norm of $\mu_{X_k}(x_k)$ and the lower mf $\underline{\mu}_{\tilde{F}_k^l}(x_k)$; and that $\overline{f}_k^l$ is the supremum of the firing strength between the t-norm of $\mu_{X_k}(x_k)$ and the upper mf $\overline{\mu}_{\tilde{F}_k^l}(x_k)$ ($k = 1, 2$). Note that $\mu_{X_k}(x_k)$ is centered at $x_k = x_k'$. These t-norms are shown as heavy curves in Fig. 4. From these heavy curves it is easy to pick off their suprema.

As we can see, the result of input and antecedent operations is again an interval —the firing interval—, as in Fig. 2. Consequently, the process of inference and defuzzification described for the singleton type-2 FLS can also be applied for a non-singleton type-2 FLS, i.e., the results depicted in Fig. 3 and Fig. 5 remain the same for an interval non-singleton type-2 FLS.

3   Proposed Methodology

The proposed methodology is oriented to model non-linear systems by learning from numerical data, not from human knowledge. In other words, it is specifically for designing FLS from input-output pairs. Note that, as the methodology is for handling uncertainty in non-linear systems, it focuses mostly on type-2 FLSs (since they can model the noise from the training set by means of interval type-2 mfs); however, it can also be applied with type-1 FLSs, but their performance is not quite as good as when there are no sources of uncertainty. Figure 6 shows the block diagram of this methodolgy. The steps are described below:

1. **Obtaining data.** First, you have to obtain the input-output pairs from which the FLS is going to be trained. Usually these data pairs are given in advance (e.g., from historical data of a process), but if they are not provided, it is necessary to obtain them by doing simulations (as in our experiments, where we forecasted a time-series).
2. **Defining the training and testing sets.** The data (obtained in the previous step) should be divided into two groups in order to form the training set and the testing set.
3. **Setting the number of antecedents per rule.** The   number   of   antecedents that each rule will have is equal to the number of inputs to the FLS.
4. **Defining the type of FLS.** Here, you specify the characteristics of the system that will be used, such as the type of the fuzzifier (singleton, non-singleton), the shapes of the mfs (triangular, trapezoidal, Gaussian), the type of composition (max-min, max-product), the type of implication (minimum, product), and the type of defuzzifier (centroid, center average)
5. **Training methods.** The training of the system and the elaboration of its rules depend on the training method used, see Section 4.
6. **Applying the FLS.** When the system has already been trained with the training set, it can be used for obtaining the ouputs from FLS by using now the testing set. The output of the trained system and the desired output are used to compute the system performance.

Note that while working with FLSs of the same type (i.e., systems with the same definition in step 4), but with different training methods (e.g., one-pass method or gradient descent method), the systems share the first four steps, which allows us to make a more reliable comparison.

4   Training Methods

The methods used here for training the FLSs were the one-pass method and the gradient descent method (also called steepest descent method).

4.1   One-Pass Method

In this method the system parameters are not tuned, because once the rules have been obtained from the training set, they will not change at all. In fact, the data establish directly the centers of the fuzzy sets in both the antecedents and consequent of each rule (typically, the remaining parameters of the mfs are preset by the designer). Hence, the number of rules is equal to the number of training data pairs N.

The procedure for training a type-2 FLS with the one-pass method is very similar to the exposed above (which is for a type-1 FLS); but now, the mfs used in the antecedents and consequents are interval type-2 fuzzy sets, instead of the conventional ones. In this case, the training set is going to be employed to establish the interval of uncertainty, or more specifically, to define the left and right means of each mf, see Fig. 1. Since the training of the system is still directly done from the N noisy input-output pairs, the total of rules will be N, as in the type-1 FLSs.

Note that, when training a system with this method, the type of fuzzifier is irrelevant, because the method only focus on establishing the parameters of the rules, whereas the mf parameters modeling the inputs (which are not considered as part of the rules) are simply preset by the designer. In other words, rules produced in a singleton FLS are exactly the same as those from a non-singleton, as long as they both are type-1 FLSs or type-2 FLSs.

4.2   Gradient Descent Method

Unlike the one-pass method, this method does tune the system parameters, by using a gradient descent algorithm and N training data pairs. Its objective is to minimize the function error: $e^{(i)} = \frac{1}{2}[f(\mathbf{x}^{(i)}) - y^{(i)}]^2$ $i = 1, \ldots, N$ where $f(\mathbf{x}^{(i)})$ is the value obtained by training the system with the input-output pair $(\mathbf{x}^{(i)} : y^{(i)})$. In this case, all the parameters of the rules will be tuned according to this error [2]. These parameters should be initialized with values that have a physical meaning (as suggested in [1], see Table 1) so that the algorithm converges faster. The parameters are tuned as the epochs increase —here, an epoch is defined as the adjustment made to the parameters in a cycle that covers the N training pairs only once. The algorithm stops when a predefined number of epochs have been reached or when the error has become smaller than an arbitrary value.

Typically, when using the gradient descent method, the parameters to be tuned depend on the type of fuzzifier employed. For example, when using a singleton fuzzifier, the parameters to be tuned are those concerning only the mfs of the antecedents and consequents of the rules. Whereas when using a non-singleton fuzzifier the parameters to be tuned are those concerning the mfs that model the inputs (typically the spread) in addition to the ones mentioned above.

Besides, with this method we can apply different training approaches —or tuning approaches. In this way, the *dependent approach* uses parameters from another FLS already designed (with the best performance) to update a new FLS (for example, using a singleton FLS to design a non-singleton). This is done by keeping all of the parameters that are shared by both FLSs fixed at the values already adjusted, and tuning only the remaining parameter(s) of the new system. On the other hand, in the *independent approach* all the parameters of the new FLS are tuned. If a FLS has already been designed, then we can use its parameters as initial values or *seeds*; we called this case the *partially independent approach*, and the one with no seeds, the *totally independent approach*.

5   Experiments

In order to illustrate the methodology proposed in Section 3, we did some experiments forecasting the Mackey-Glass time series [4], represented as:

$$\frac{ds(t)}{dt} = \frac{0.2s(t-\tau)}{1 + s^{10}(t-\tau)} - 0.1s(t) \tag{1}$$

For $\tau > 17$, (1) exhibits chaos. In our simulations we used $\tau = 30$. Next, we will give a short description of each step.

1. **Obtaining data.** In order to generate the data for the training and testing sets, (1) was transformed into a discrete time equation, and we applied the Euler's approximation method with a step size equal to 1. Then, we corrupted those data with a 0 dB additive noise. We generated 50 sets of this uniformly distributed noise $n(k)$, and added them to the noise-free time series $s(k)$; so, we got 50 noisy data sets $x(k) = s(k) + n(k)$, where $k = 1001, 1002, \ldots, 2000$.
2. **Defining the training and testing sets.** We formed the training and testing sets from the 1000 data obtained in the previous step. The training set was formed by the first 504 data, i.e, $x(1001), x(1002), \ldots, x(1504)$. The testing set was formed by the remaining 496 data.
3. **Setting the number of antecedents per rule.** The number of antecedents per rule that we used for forecasting the time-series was $p = 4$, i.e., $x(k-3), x(k-2), x(k-1), x(k)$, from which we obtained $x(k+1)$. Note that we only designed single-stage forecasters (with four-antecedent single-consequent rules), since, even though the system error may be very tiny, iterative forecasts might increase that error in every iteration, up to undesired values [5], [6].
4. **Defining the type of FLS.** As we did several experiments, there are different definitions of FLSs, but all of them used product implication, max-product composition. Type-1 FLSs used type-1 Gaussian mfs for the rule

Table 1. Initial values of the parameters using the gradient descent method. Each antecedent is described by two fuzzy sets ($i = 1, \ldots, M$ and $k = 1, \ldots, p$)

FLS	Input	For each antecedent	Consequent
ST1FLS	N/A	mean: $m_x - 2\sigma_x$ or $m_x + 2\sigma_x$; $\sigma_{F_k^i}$	$\bar{y}^i \in [0, 1]$
NST1FLS	$\sigma_X = \sigma_n$	mean: $m_x - 2\sigma_x$ or $m_x + 2\sigma_x$; $\sigma_{F_k^i}$	$\bar{y}^i \in [0, 1]$
ST2FLS	N/A	mean: $[m_x - 2\sigma_x - 0.25\sigma_n, m_x - 2\sigma_x + 0.25\sigma_n]$ or $[m_x + 2\sigma_x - 0.25\sigma_n, m_x + 2\sigma_x + 0.25\sigma_n]$; $\sigma_k^i = 2\sigma_x$	$\bar{y}_l^i = \bar{y}^i - \sigma_n$ $\bar{y}_r^i = \bar{y}^i + \sigma_n$
NST2FLS	$\sigma_X = \sigma_n$	mean: $[m_x - 2\sigma_x - 0.25\sigma_n, m_x - 2\sigma_x + 0.25\sigma_n]$ or $[m_x + 2\sigma_x - 0.25\sigma_n, m_x + 2\sigma_x + 0.25\sigma_n]$; $\sigma_k^i = 2\sigma_x$	$\bar{y}_l^i = \bar{y}^i - \sigma_n$ $\bar{y}_r^i = \bar{y}^i + \sigma_n$

fuzzy sets, center-average defuzzifier, and whether singleton fuzzifier or Gaussian non-singleton fuzzifier. Type-2 FLSs used Gaussian primary mfs with uncertain mean for the rule fuzzy sets, interval weighted average type-reducer, and whether singleton defuzzifier or Gaussian non-singleton fuzzifier (modeling the inputs as type type-1 Gaussian mfs because the additive noise was stationary).

5. **Training methods.** According to the definitions made in the previous step, we applied both the one-pass method and the gradient descent method in order to train the FLSs. In the former, we obtained systems with 500 rules (because the training set was formed by N=500 input-output data pairs); whereas in the latter, we obtained systems of only 16 rules (i.e. 2 fuzzy sets per antecedent, 4 antecedents per rule, giving a total $2^4 = 16$ rules). Note that the number of rules in the gradient descent method did not depend on the size of the training set; it was prefixed at 16 rules. In this method, the parameters were initialized using the formulas of the Table 1.

6. **Applying the FLS.** Once the systems were trained, we checked their performance with the testing set. This performance was evaluated by computing the following RMSE (root mean-squared error):

$$RMSE = \sqrt{\frac{1}{496} \sum_{k=1504}^{1999} \left[s(k+1) - f(\mathbf{x}^{(k)}) \right]^2} \tag{2}$$

As we did 50 simulations for each experiment, we obtained 50 values of $RMSE$; so in order to display an overall performance of each system, we calculated the average and the standard deviation of these 50 $RMSE$s. Table 2 shows the performance of the FLSs trained with the one-pass method.

Figure 7 displays the performance of the FLSs trained with the gradient descent method. Note that, because of space matter, we only show the performance obtained with the totally independent approach; but in the experiments that we did with the other two approaches, we observed that the error could attain its minimum faster (i.e., in earlier epochs), and that the *gap* be-

Table 2. Mean and standard deviation of the *RMSE*s from FLSs trained with the one-pass method in 50 simulations

FLS	$\overline{RMSE}$	σ_{RMSE}
Singl. T1FLS	0.1954	0.0082
Singl. T2FLS	0.1784	0.0077
Non-singl. T1FLS	0.1371	0.0075
Non-singl. T2FLS	0.1370	0.0075

Table 3. Mean and standard deviation of the *RMSE*s obtained in 50 simulations forecasting the original time series and a second time series, both with additive noise

FLS	$\overline{RMSE}$	σ_{RMSE}	$\overline{RMSE_2}$	σ_{RMSE_2}
S. T1FLS	0.1566	0.0129	0.1566	0.0112
N-s. T1FLS	0.1553	0.0123	0.1553	0.0107
S. T2FLS	0.1486	0.0107	0.1486	0.0091
N-s. T2FLS	0.1486	0.0106	0.1486	0.0089

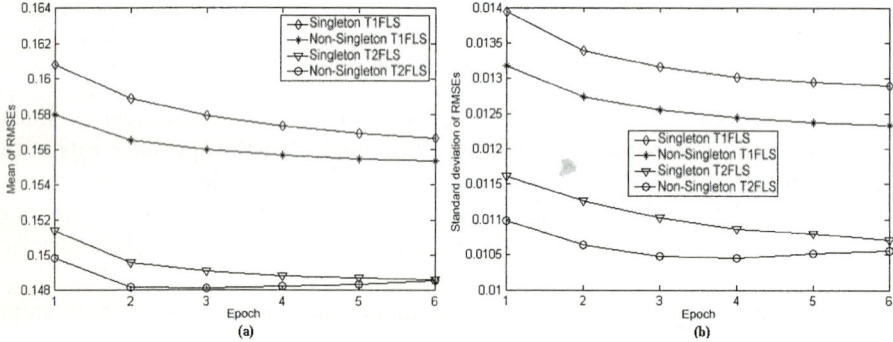

Fig. 7. Mean (a) and standard deviation (b) of the *RMSE*s from FLSs trained with the gradient descent method in 50 simulations. Parameters were tuned for six epochs in each simulation

tween the type-1 and type-2 FLSs was enlarged (since these approaches are benefited from parameters tuned in previous systems).

In addition, after being designed, FLSs trained with the gradient descent method were used for forecasting the Mackey-Glass time series, but now with noise in the initial conditions (for practical purposes, it is the same as simply having different initial conditions). The resultant time series was also corrupted by a 0 dB additive noise. Table 3 shows the performance obtained in those FLSs. Note that, since there was no tuning in this case, we do not illustrate the error per epoch; we only exhibit the performance in the sixth epoch (from Fig. 7), as well as the performance obtained with this second noisy time series. Observe that the behavior of the systems is very similar in both time series, i.e., the averages of the *RMSE*s obtained in the first time series coincide with those obtained here; what's more, the standard deviations were smaller.

6   Conclusions and Further Work

The methodology proposed here, was easily applied for designing different types of FLS forecasters with distinct methods and different approaches. Furthermore, it can be directly extended for working not only with time-series forecasters but also to process modeling.

In the experiments, the gradient descent method generated systems with a small number of rules, and we obtained very good results, even when experiments with the time-series were proved for robustness. In these latter experiments, the trained systems were robust enough as to handle the noise in the initial conditions and the additive noise in the testing data sets. On the other hand, the system with the smallest error was that designed with the one-pass method; however, it does not mean that it was the best one, because if we had an environment where a quick time response is crucial, this system would not be very satisfactory, because it has many rules (which make it extremely slow for doing only one forecast). In contrast, the gradient descent method typically generates FLSs with fewer rules, consequently the time to produce a single output value is shortened. This feature encourages its use in real-time applications over the one-pass method.

As a futher work, the systems designed with the one-pass method might reduce their number of rules generated by using the Wang's *Table Look-up* scheme [3], adapting it to work with type-2 fuzzy sets. In systems designed with the gradient descent method, the total of rules can be reduced (if necessary) by applying the Mendel's SVD–QR method [2]. In the case that the additive noise in the environment is not stationary, we can use a non-singleton fuzzifier that models the inputs by means of type-2 fuzzy sets (remember that we only modeled the inputs with type-1 fuzzy sets, because of a stationary additive noise).

References

1. Q. Liang, J.M. Mendel: Interval Type-2 Fuzzy Logic Systems: Theory and Design. IEEE Trans. on Fuzzy Syst. (2000) vol. 8, 535–550
2. J.M. Mendel: Uncertain Rule-Based Fuzzy Logic Systems: Introduction and New Directions. Prentice-Hall, Upper Saddle River, N.J. (2001)
3. L.–X. Wang, J.M. Mendel: Generating Fuzzy Rules by Learning from Examples. IEEE Trans. on Systems, Man, and Cybernetics. (1992) vol. 22, 1414–1427
4. M.C. Mackey, L. Glass: Oscillation and Chaos in Physiological Control Systems. Science (1977) vol. 197 287–289
5. T.D. Sanger: A Tree-Structured Adaptive Network for Function Aproximation in High-Dimensional Spaces. IEEE Trans. Neural Networks (1991) vol. 2, 285–293
6. A.L. Schiavo, A.M. Luciano: Powerful and Flexible Fuzzy Algorithm for Nonlinear Dynamic System Identification. IEEE Trans. on Fuzzy Syst. (2001) vol. 9, 828–835

Online Diagnosis Using Influence Diagrams

Baldramino Morales Sánchez and Pablo H. Ibargüengoytia

Instituto de Investigaciones Eléctricas
Av. Reforma 113, Palmira
Cuernavaca, Mor., 62490, México
baldra2k@hotmail.com, pibar@iie.org.mx

Abstract. This paper presents the utilization of influence diagrams in the diagnosis of industrial processes. The diagnosis in this context signifies the early detection of abnormal behavior, and the selection of the best recommendation for the operator in order to correct the problem or minimize the effects. A software architecture is presented, based on the *Elvira* package, including the connection with industrial control systems. A simple experiment is presented together with the acquisition and representation of the knowledge.

1 Introduction

In recent years, the power generation industry has faced important problems that require the modernization of current installations, principally in both the instrumentation and control systems. The current trend consists in increasing the performance, availability and reliability of the actual installations. The performance refers to the amount of mega watts that can be generated with a unit of fuel. The availability refers to the hours that the central stops generating, and the reliability refers to the probability of counting with all the equipment of the plant. Additionally, modern power plants are following two clear tendencies. First, they are very complex processes working close to their limits. Second, they are highly automated and instrumented, leaving the operator with very few decisions. However, the classic control systems are programmed to stop the plant under the presence of abnormal behavior. Some decisions can be taken in the supervisory level that control systems are unable to make, i.e., to *reason* about the abnormal behavior and the probable consequences.

This research group at Electrical Research Institute or IIE, has been working in the design of On-line intelligent diagnosis systems for gas turbines of power plants [5,3]. This project includes two special challenges. First, the management of uncertainty given the thermodynamic conditions of the gas turbine and the difficulty of constructing accurate analytical models of the process. Second, the continuous acquisition of the turbine parameters. The problem here is the interconnection with different data networks, different proprietary databases, and probably different field buses. in order to from the correct state of the turbine. This allows the early detection of small deviations and defines the recommended actions for maintaining the generation of electricity in optimal condition.

R. Monroy et al. (Eds.): MICAI 2004, LNAI 2972, pp. 546–554, 2004.
© Springer-Verlag Berlin Heidelberg 2004

Diagnosis is the technique utilized in several fields, devoted to find faults that explain abnormal behavior in a system. Several approaches have been proposed and they can be classified in three kinds [1].

Data–driven : based on large amount of data given by modern control and instrumentation systems, from which meaningful statistics can be computed.

Analytical : based on mathematical models often constructed from physical first principles.

Knowledge–based : based on causal analysis or expert knowledge, conclusions and inferences are made given information of the process. They can be found in several kinds of models and inference methods [7].

The selection of the best approach for a given problem depends on the quality and type of available models, and on the quality and quantity of data available.

This paper presents a knowledge based diagnosis system that manages the natural uncertainty found in real applications. The model is composed by Influence diagrams, i.e., a Bayesian network representing the probabilistic relationship of all the important variables, plus additional nodes that utilize decision theory for the selection of the best corrective action.

The diagnosis architecture presented in this paper is part of a larger system formed by a monitor, an optimizer, and a diagnosis module. When the monitor detects that the process works normally, it runs the optimizer in order to increase the performance of the process, e.g., the generation of more mega watts per unit of gas. On the opposite, when the diagnosis module detects an abnormal behavior, it identifies the faulty component and generates advices to the operator in order to return the plant to its normal state. This optimizer and diagnosis system are devoted to enhance the performance and availability indices.

This paper is organized as follows. First, section 2 introduces the influence diagrams and presents a very simple example of their use in industrial applications. Section 3 describes the software architecture developed for the construction of a prototype of the on-line diagnosis system (DX). Next, section 4 presents an application example running coupled with a gas turbine simulator and discusses the results obtained. Finally, section 5 concludes the paper and addresses the future work in this area.

2   Influence Diagrams

An influence diagram is a directed acyclic graph consisting of three types of nodes [6]:

1. Zero or more chance nodes that represent propositional variables. For example, *turbine_normal* that can be true or false, or *temperature_gas* that can be {*high, medium, low*}. They are represented by circles in the diagram.
2. Zero or more decision nodes that represent the possible choises available to the decision maker. They are represented by squares in the diagram.
3. One utility node whose value is the expected utility of the outcome. This node is represented by a diamond in the diagram.

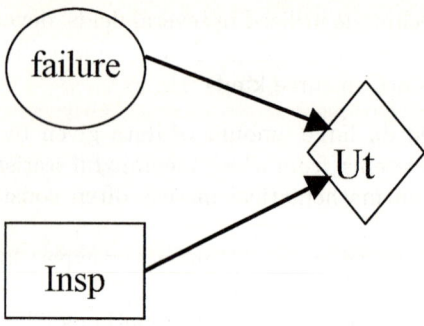

Fig. 1. Example of influence diagram.

An influence diagram can be seen as a typical Bayesian network (the chance nodes) plus the decision and utility nodes. Thus, the arcs into chance nodes represent the variables from which the nodes are conditionally dependent. The arcs into decision nodes represent the variables that will be known by the decision maker at the time the decision is made. The arcs into the utility node show which variables participate in the calculation of the utility values. Figure 1 shows a basic influence diagram. Node *failure* is a Boolean variable representing the chance of having a failure in the turbine. Node *Insp* is a two value decision: to make or not to make an inspection. Node *Ut* considers the values of node *failure* and node *Insp* to calculate the utility value of the possible scenarios. Table 1 describes an example of the four possible scenarios and their utility values. Every scenario corresponds to the combination of the node *Ut*'s parents, i.e., nodes *failure* and *Insp*. $+d$ stands for the decision of making the inspection and $+f$ stands for existence of a failure. $-d$ and $-f$ represents the opposite. The domain experts calculate the utility values considering the cost of executing the inspection and the possible problems caused if the inspection is not carried out. For example, the lowest value (3) corresponds to the combination of presence of the failure but the decision of no inspection to the turbine $(Ut(+f, -d))$. On the contrary, the highest value (10) corresponds to the decision of no inspection but without failure $(Ut(-f, -d))$.

Consider the following a priori probabilities of failure node: $P(+f = 0.86, -f = 0.14)$. The expected utility value for a decision is calculated as follows:

$$Ut(+d) = [P(+f) \times u(+d, +f)] + [P(-f) \times u(+d, -f)]$$
$$= (0.14 \times 8) + (0.86 \times 9) = 8.86$$

where $u(x)$ is the utility value of the scenario x established in the utility node as in Table 1. Similarly, $Ut(-d) = 9.02$. Therefore, the maximum expected utility, given the current knowledge about the state of the turbine is obtained as the $max(Ut(+d), Ut(-d)) = 9.02$. The best decision is not interrupt the functioning of the turbine with an inspection. However, if the probability of failure vector of node *failure* changes, then the expected utility would change accordingly.

Table 1. Example of values for the utility node.

Ut	+f	−f
+d	8	9
−d	3	10

Influence diagrams represent an appropriate technique to provide the maximum expected utility, i.e., the optimal decision, given the current knowledge about the state of the process.

The next section describes the software architecture implemented for a experiment in a gas turbine simulator using this influence diagram.

3   Software Architecture

A typical knowledge based, on–line diagnosis system utilizes a general structure as shown in Fig. 2. First, the acquisition of the model is required. This can be obtained with an automatic learning algorithm and historical data. Also, the model is complemented utilizing expert knowledge about the operation of the gas turbines. Once that the model has been obtained, it is inserted in the on-line diagnosis system (DX in the figure). The DX reads real time values of the variables that participate in the diagnosis. This variables act as the evidence from which the posterior probabilities will be calculated. Figure 2 shows also an utility function entering the DX. This is required since the calculation of the utility values may depend on some parameters that may change continuously. For example, some utility function may require the cost of the MW/hour or the cost of the fuel in dollars or Mexican pesos. This utility function can be evaluated and updated every time is needed. Finally, a graphic user interface (GUI) is needed so the notification of the optimal decision can be given to the operator. Also, commands can be asserted to the system or the introduction of new operation parameters.

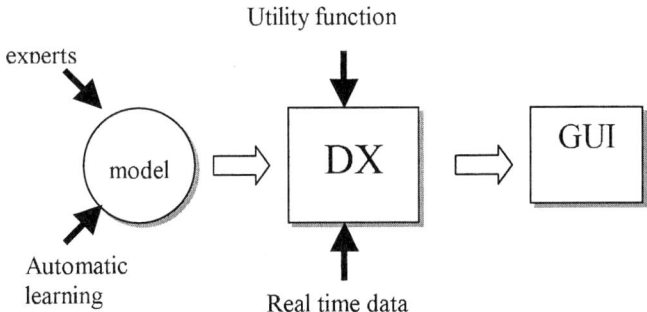

Fig. 2. General diagram of the diagnosis system architecture.

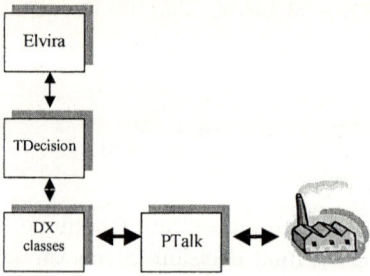

Fig. 3. Internal architecture of the diagnosis system.

The DX module shown in Fig. 2 is the main program of the prototype. As mentioned before, the program utilizes the Elvira package [4]. The Elvira system is a Java tool to construct probabilistic decision support systems. Elvira works with Bayesian networks and influence diagrams and it can operate with discrete, continuous and temporal variables. However, Elvira was designed to work off-line with its specific GUI. Thus, one of the contributions of this work is the development of the interface class that allows utilizing the elemental classes of Elvira for influence diagrams capture and propagation. Figure 3 describes the internal architecture of the DX module. The DX classes module represents all the classes written at this location. They read the models, read the variables information (e.g. valid ranges of continuous variables), and control the exchange of information with the GUI. This module also controls the main loop of the diagnosis with the following steps:

1. read the real time information,
2. generate the evidence
3. propagate probabilities
4. update utility values
5. get the maximum expected utility, i.e., generate a recommendation

The module Ptalk implements a data client over an OPC server (OPC stands for Object linking and embedding). This class can exchange data with commercial controllers and data bases like Siemens or SQL servers.

The module Tdecision is the main contribution in this research project. It allows utilizing all the Elvira's algorithms in an embedded program for the on-line diagnosis. This module prepares the information that elvira requires to load evidence, propagate probabilities and obtain results. The most important methods of Tdecision are the following:

Constructor: reads and compile the file with the model.
SetEvidence: writes the values of the known nodes.
SetUtilityValues: write an update of the utility values.
Propagate: commands the execution of the propagation of probabilities.
GetUtilityValues: calculates the expected utility values according to the propagation.

GetMaxUtility: calculates the maximum expected utility value and responds with the optimal decision.

The next section describes a simple example executed in the prototype.

4   Application Example

The architecture has been utilized in diagnosis experiments in a gas turbine simulator at the laboratory. The simulation executed for this experiment consists in a increasing of load from 2 MW to 23 MW. Six analog signals were sampled every half second, so a number of 2111 records were obtained during the 20 minutes.

The learning module of *elvira* with the K2 algorithm [2] were executed utilizing the data table with seven variables and 2111 records. The K2 algorithm was chosen since it permits to *suggest* the structure of the network through the ordering of the variables in the table. This ordering was obtained with expert advice. For example, the demanded power *causes* the position of the gas valve and this parameter *causes* the generation of power. Table 2 explain the identifiers, their description, and the number of intervals in the discretization. The number of intervals was chosen according to the value range and the requirements of granularity in the experiments. The Decision node can take three values: $in - line\ revision$, $off - line\ revision$, and do *nothing*. Figure 4 shows the resulting influence diagram involving the six variables, obtained by $elvira's$ learning modules. The $MWdem$ variable represents the power demanded by the operator. In an automatic control system, this is the only set-up that the operator manipulate. The rest of the variables will move according to this signal. The position of gas control valve $Vgas$ is the control variable that represents the aperture of the gas valve. Thus, if more power is demanded, more aperture will be read in this variable. Variable MW is the measure of the mega watts generated. If the gas valve is opened, then the mega watts will increase. Finally, the $TTXDi$ variables represent the exhaust gas temperature in the turbine, in different parts of the circumference. The Utility node has 24 values corresponding to all the combinations between 8 values of $MWdcm$ and 3 values of Decision. Summarizing, the power demand causes the aperture of the gas valve, and this

Table 2. Variables participating in the experiments.

ID	Description	Num. states
MWdem	Demanded power	8
Vgas	Valve of gas position	10
MW	Generated power	8
TTXD1	Exhaust gas temperature 1	10
TTXD2	Exhaust gas temperature 2	10
TTXD3	Exhaust gas temperature 3	10
Decision	decision	3
Utility	Utility	24

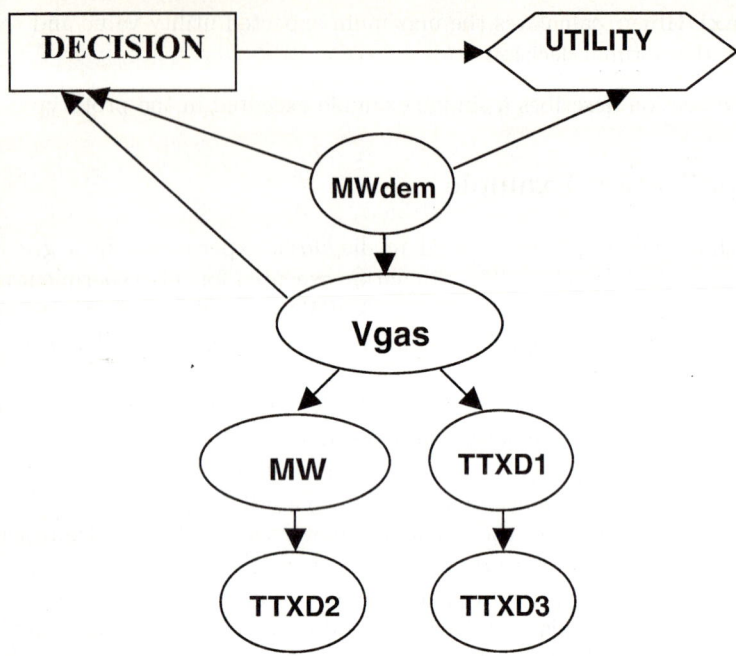

Fig. 4. Influence diagram obtained with automatic learning and experts advice.

aperture causes the generation of mega watts. The generation also produces an increment (or decrement) of temperature gases. Several tests were made with different discretization values in order to see the best result in the learning process. Also, different information was provided to K2 algorithm for different structures as explained above.

This experiment considers that if the value of power demand $MWdem$ and the aperture of the valve $Vgas$ is known, then a diagnosis of the turbine can be made and the decision of $in - line$ revision, or $off - line$ revision of *nothing* can be obtained. Also, the calculation of the utility values can be made using the decision and the power demand values. The utility function considers the *cost* of taking a decision and the *gain* obtained if this decision is made in the current situation. For example, if more power is demanded, the associated cost of stopping the turbine for an off-line revision is much higher and the benefit may not be high since full power were demanded. On the contrary, if there were a fault detected and the decision is to make a major revision, then the cost is high but the benefit is also very high. In this case, do nothing can be cheap but the benefits can be negative, e.g., a major malfunctioning of the turbine.

Therefore, the utility function defined in this experiments consists on an equation depending on the parents of the utility node, i.e., the decision made and the demand of power. The equation relates the cost of the decision made and the gain obtained. More experiments are being carried out to define the best equation that produces the optimal results according to controlled scenarios.

Table 3. Results obtained in ten executions of the prototype.

MWdem	Vgas	MW	TTXD1	TTXD2	TTXD3	Decision		
						Off – line	In – line	nothing
16,5	38,2	22,7	353,5	331,5	503,8	10.0	11.0	5.0
14,4	41,2	12,3	370,6	224,2	454,7	8.0	9.0	4.0
15,4	59,5	13,4	217,2	156,1	433,7	8.0	9.0	4.0
17,5	77,9	12,3	183,1	401,6	435,7	10.0	11.0	5.0
9,2	47,3	4,1	302,4	525,9	234,3	4.0	5.0	2.0
15,4	65,7	12,3	424,7	107,0	510,9	8.0	9.0	4.0
2,0	48,4	19,6	141,1	392,6	180,1	0.0	1.0	0.0
2,0	47,3	18,5	214,2	268,3	325,5	0.0	1.0	0.0
11,3	60,6	8,2	384,6	453,7	417,7	6.0	7.0	3.0
23,7	69,7	16,5	284,4	376,6	417,7	0.0	15.0	0.0

Table 3 shows the results obtained when the program carries out ten different cycles of execution (at random). The first six columns describe the current value of the corresponding variables and their assigned interval. The value at the left is the real value read by the system, and the value at the right represents the number of discretization interval corresponding to the value. For example, in the first cell, variable *MWdem* has 16 MW that corresponds to the interval 5 in the discretization. The last three columns correspond to the expected utility values for each possible decision. For example, in the first row, the best decision to recommend is the execution of an in-line revision (value of 11), and the worst decision is to do nothing (value of 5). The rest of the rows also *decide* the in-line revision but with different levels of intensity. For example, the last row suggests in-line revision with 15 to 0, in contrast to 11 to 10 units in the first row.

These results of course depend on the knowledge captured by the experts in two aspects. First, the structure of the influence diagram, and second the numerical parameters required in the reasoning. They are, the *a − priori* and conditional probabilities of the chance nodes, and the utility values stored in the utility node. These ten runs of the prototype demonstrated the advantage of performing an in-line diagnosis together with the recommendation of the optimal action in the current situation.

5   Conclusions and Future Work

This paper has presented an on-line diagnosis system for gas turbines. The system utilizes influence diagrams that use probabilistic reasoning and decision theory techniques. The probabilistic models are constructed with automatic learning algorithms inspired with expert knowledge. The system is implemented based on Elvira package and other classes designed by this research group. The main strength of the influence diagrams is the formal representation and manipulation of the models: probabilistic and decision/utility. An optimal recommendation is issued based on the current information of the state of the turbine. One of the contributions of this work is the design of the Tdecision class. It allows to insert new evidence, to change utility values if needed and to call the propagation routines of *elvira*. This propagation produces two different results. One, the maximum expected utility that defines the optimal action and second, the posterior probability of all the chance nodes that may describe the behavior of the turbine.

Experiments on a gas turbine simulator have shown the feasibility for the use of this technique and this prototype in more complex and real applications. The next task will be to acquire real data from a real turbine in a power plant, to run the automatic learning algorithms for obtaining more accurate models and question the experts to recognize which information is required to take a decision, and which information is required to calculate the utility value of the decisions. These two steps will provide a better influence diagram for a specific turbine.

Future work is going in this direction.

References

1. L.H. Chiang, E.L. Russell, and R.D. Braatz. *Fault Detection and Diagnosis in Industrial Systems*. Springer, London, Great Britain, 2001.
2. G.F. Cooper and E. Herskovits. A bayesian method for the induction of probabilistic networks from data. *Machine Learning*, 9(4):309–348, 1992.
3. Luis de Jesús González-Noriega and Pablo H. Ibargüengoytia. An architecture for on–line diagnosis of gas turbines. In M. Toro F.J. Garijo, J.C. Riquelme, editor, *Advances in Artificial Intelligence - IBERAMIA 2002, LNAI 2527*, pages 795–804, Sevilla, Spain, 2002. Springer.
4. The Elvira Consortium. Elvira: An environment for creating and using probabilistic graphical models. In *Proceedings of the First European Workshop on Probabilistic graphical models (PGM'02)"*, pages 1–11, Cuenca, Spain, 2002.
5. Pablo H. Ibargüengoytia, L.Enrique Sucar, and Sunil Vadera. Real time intelligent sensor validation. *IEEE Transactions on Power Systems*, 16(4):770–775, 2001.
6. R.E. Neapolitan. *Probabilistic resoning in expert systems*. John Wiley & Sons, New York, New York, U.S.A., 1990.
7. V. Venkatasubramanian, R. Rengaswamy, K. Yin, and S. N. Kavuri. Review of process fault diagnosis. *Computers and Chemical Engineering*, 27(3):293–346, 2003.

Toward a New Approach for Online Fault Diagnosis Combining Particle Filtering and Parametric Identification

Rubén Morales-Menéndez[1], Ricardo Ramírez-Mendoza[1], Jim Mutch[2], and Federico Guedea-Elizalde[3]

[1] ITESM campus Monterrey, Center for Industrial Automation
Monterrey NL, México
{rmm,ricardo.ramirez}@itesm.mx
[2] University of British Columbia, Dept. of Computer Science
Vancouver, BC, Canada
mutch@cs.ubc.ca
[3] University of Waterloo, Systems Design Engineering
Waterloo, ON, Canada
fguedea@pami.uwaterloo.ca

Abstract. This paper proposes a new approach for online fault diagnosis in dynamic systems, combining a Particle Filtering (PF) algorithm with a classic Fault Detection and Isolation (FDI) framework. Of the two methods, FDI provides deeper insight into a process; however, it cannot normally be computed online. Our approach uses a preliminary PF step to reduce the potential solution space, resulting in an online algorithm with the advantages of both methods. The PF step computes a posterior probability density to diagnose the most probable fault. If the desired confidence is not obtained, the classic FDI framework is invoked. The FDI framework uses recursive parametric estimation for the residual generation block and hypothesis testing and Statistical Process Control (SPC) criteria for the decision making block. We tested the individual methods with an industrial dryer.

1 Introduction

Fault diagnosis is increasingly being discussed in literature [1] and is the subject of international workshops and special journal issues [13,14]. Industrial applications require adequate supervision to maintain their required performance. Performance can decrease due to faults, which generate malfunctions. Malfunctions of plant equipment and instrumentation increase the operating costs of any plant and can sometimes lead to more serious consequences, such as an explosion.

Supervision of industrial processes has become very important. Usually this supervision is carried out by human operators. The effectiveness of human supervision varies with the skills of the operator.

In this paper, we consider processes that have a number of discrete modes or operating regions corresponding to different combinations of faults or regions of

R. Monroy et al. (Eds.): MICAI 2004, LNAI 2972, pp. 555–564, 2004.

qualitatively different dynamics. The dynamics can be different for each discrete mode. Even if there are very few faults, exact diagnosis can be quite difficult. However, there is a need to monitor these systems in real time to determine what faults could have occurred. We wanted to investigate whether we could do real-time fault diagnosis by combining a principled, probabilistic PF approach with classic FDI techniques.

Particle Filtering [4] is a Markov Chain Monte Carlo (MCMC) algorithm that approximates the belief state using a set of samples, called *particles*, and updates the distribution as new observations are made over time. PF and some variants have been used for fault diagnosis with excellent results [2,16,11,12].

Our FDI framework uses a recursive Parametric Estimation Algorithm (PEA) for the residual generation block and hypothesis testing and Statistical Process Control (SPC) criteria for the decision making block.

PEA is used for online identification in time-varying processes [10], identifying the current discrete mode of the process [19,20]. A supervision block ensures robustness and correct numerical performance, specifically, initialization by means of the adaptation algorithm, parameter estimate bounds checking, input-output persistent detection, oscillation detection, disturbances and set-point changes, signal saturation, and bumpless transfer (mode transition).

The paper is organized as follows: Section 2 describes the industrial process, mathematical models and experimental tests. Section 3 presents the PF algorithm as a fault diagnosis approach and discusses its performance. Section 4 describes the residual generation and decision making blocks and their incorporation into the FDI framework. Section 5 discusses the strengths and weaknesses of both methods and describes the combined approach. Lastly, we suggest future directions.

2   Processes Monitored

To test the fault diagnosis algorithms, we worked with a common, real-world process. An industrial dryer was adapted for experimental purposes, allowing faulty points to be repeatedly implemented. The industrial dryer is a thermal process that converts electricity to heat. The dryer is able to control the exit air temperature by changing its shooting angle. The generated faults were implemented using the fan speed (low/high), fan grill (closed/open), and dryer exit vent (clear/obstructed). Using only measurements taken with a temperature sensor, we wanted to diagnose the most probable faulty point online. Fig. 1 shows an actual photo and a schematic diagram of a dryer with potential faulty points.

Mathematical model. Normal operation corresponds to low fan speed, an open airflow grill, and a clean temperature sensor. We denote this discrete mode $z_t = 1$. We induced different types of faults: $z_t = 2$ (faulty fan), $z_t = 3$ (faulty grill), $z_t = 4$ (faulty fan and grill), etc. We applied an open-loop step test for each discrete mode [18]. Using the monitored data (y_t, u_t) and a PEA [15], an Auto-Regressive with eXogenous variable model, $ARX(n_a, n_b, d)$, was proposed for each discrete mode z_t,

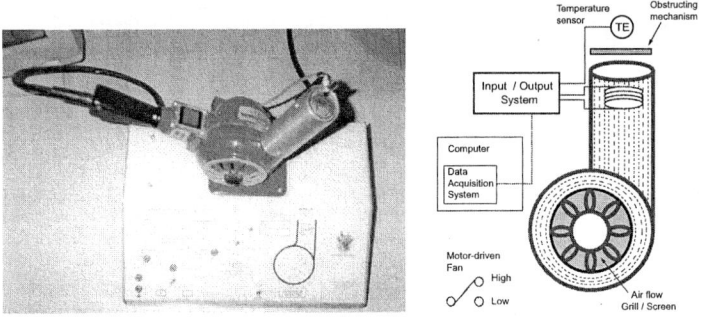

Fig. 1. Industrial dryer. This dryer uses a motor-driven fan and a heating coil to transform electrical energy into convective heat. The diagram shows the sensor and potential faulty points.

$$y_n = a_1(z_t)y_{n-1} + \cdots + a_{n_a}(z_t)y_{n-n_a} + b_1(z_t)u_{n-1-d} + \cdots + b_{n_b}(z_t)u_{n-n_b-d} \tag{1}$$

where n_a and n_b are the number of coefficients $a(\cdot)$ and $b(\cdot)$; d represents the discrete *dead time*. From the ARX model we can get the deterministic state space representation using a standard control engineering procedure:

$$x_t = A(z_t)x_{t-1} + B(z_t)\gamma_t + F(z_t)u_t \tag{2}$$

$$y_t = C(z_t)x_t + D(z_t)v_t. \tag{3}$$

y_t denotes the measurements, x_t denotes the unknown continuous states, and u_t is a known control signal. $z_t \in \{1, \ldots, n_z\}$ denotes the discrete modes (normal operation, faulty fan, faulty grill, etc)[1] at time t. The process and measurement noises are *i.i.d* Gaussian: $\gamma_t \sim \mathcal{N}(0, I)$ and $v_t \sim \mathcal{N}(0, I)$. The parameters $A(\cdot)$, $B(\cdot)$, $C(\cdot)$, $D(\cdot)$, and $F(\cdot)$ are matrices with $D(\cdot)D(\cdot)^T > 0$. $z_t \sim p(z_t|z_{t-1})$ is a Markov process. This model is known as a *jump Markov linear Gaussian* (JMLG) model [2], and combines the Hidden Markov and State Space models. The noise matrices $B(\cdot)$ and $D(\cdot)$ are learned using the Expectation-Maximization (EM) algorithm [7]. The left plot of Fig. 2 shows a graphical representation of the JMLG model.

Experimental tests. We physically inserted a sequence of faults, according to a Markov process, and made appropriate measurements. The right plot of Fig. 2 compares the real data with that generated by the JMLG model. The upper graph shows the discrete mode of operation over time, and the lower graph makes the comparison. The JMLG model successfully represents the dynamics of the system.

The aim of the analysis is to compute the marginal posterior distribution of the discrete modes $p(z_{0:t}|y_{1:t}, u_{1:t})$. This distribution can be derived from

---

[1] There is a single linear Gaussian model for each realization of z_t.

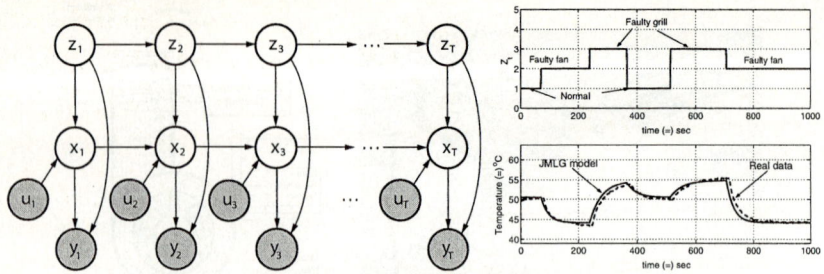

Fig. 2. JMLG model. The left plot is a graphical representation of the model. The right plot demonstrates its ability to model the system.

the posterior distribution $p\left(x_{0:t}, z_{0:t}|y_{1:t}, u_{1:t}\right)$ by standard marginalization. The posterior density satisfies the following recursion[2]:

$$p\left(x_{0:t}, z_{0:t}|y_{1:t}\right) = p\left(x_{0:t-1}, z_{0:t-1}|y_{1:t-1}\right) \frac{p\left(y_t|x_t, z_t\right) p\left(x_t, z_t|x_{t-1}, z_{t-1}\right)}{p\left(y_t|y_{1:t-1}\right)}. \quad (4)$$

Equation (4) involves intractable integrals; therefore numerical approximations such as Particle Filtering (PF) are required.

3   Particle Filtering Algorithm

In the PF setting, we use a weighted set of *particles* $\{(x_{0:t}^{(i)}, z_{0:t}^{(i)}), w_t^{(i)}\}_{i=1}^N$ to approximate the posterior with the following point-mass distribution:

$$\widehat{p}_N\left(x_{0:t}, z_{0:t}|y_{1:t}\right) = \sum_{i=1}^{N} w_t^{(i)} \delta_{x_{0:t}^{(i)}, z_{0:t}^{(i)}}\left(x_{0:t}, z_{0:t}\right), \quad (5)$$

where $\delta_{x_{0:t}^{(i)}, z_{0:t}^{(i)}}\left(x_{0:t}, z_{0:t}\right)$ is the well-known Dirac-delta function. At time $t-1$, N particles are given $\{x_{0:t-1}^{(i)}, z_{0:t-1}^{(i)}\}_{i=1}^N$, approximately distributed according to $p(x_{0:t-1}^{(i)}, z_{0:t-1}^{(i)}|y_{1:t-1})$. PF allows us to compute N particles $\{x_{0:t}^{(i)}, z_{0:t}^{(i)}\}_{i=1}^N$ approximately distributed according to $p(x_{0:t}^{(i)}, z_{0:t}^{(i)}|y_{1:t})$ at time t. Since we cannot sample from the posterior directly, the PF update is accomplished by introducing an appropriate importance proposal distribution $q(x_{0:t}, z_{0:t})$ from which we can obtain samples. Fig. 3 shows a graphical representation of this algorithm[3], which consists of two steps: Sequential Importance Sampling (SIS) and selection. This algorithm uses the transition priors as proposal distributions, $q(x_{0:t}, z_{0:t}|y_{1:t}) = p(x_t|x_{t-1}, z_t)p(z_t|z_{t-1})$, so the important weights w_t simplify to the likelihood function $p(y_t|\hat{x}_t, \hat{z}_t)$.

---

[2] For clarity, we omit the control signal u_t from the argument lists of the various probability distributions.

[3] For simplicity, $\hat{x}_t$ was omitted

The earliest PF implementations were based only on SIS, which degenerates with time. [9] proposed a selection step which led to successful implementations. The selection step eliminates samples with low importance weights and multiplies samples with high importance weights.

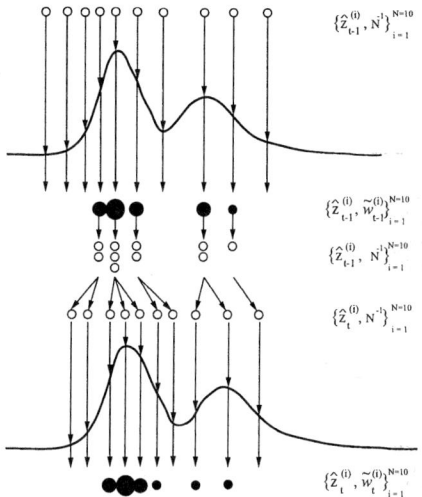

Fig. 3. PF algorithm. An approximation of $p(z_{t-1}|y_{1:t-2})$ is obtained through un-weighted measure $\{\hat{z}_{t-1}^{(i)}, \frac{1}{N}\}_{i=1}^{N}$ at time $t-1$. For each particle the importance weights are computed at time $t-1$, $\{\hat{z}_{t-1}^{(i)}, \tilde{w}_{t-1}^{(i)}\}_{i=1}^{N}$, which generates an approximation of $p(z_{t-1}|y_{1:t-1})$. The selection step is applied and an approximation of $p(z_{t-1}|y_{1:t-1})$ is obtained using unweighted particles $\{\hat{z}_{t-1}^{(i)}, \frac{1}{N}\}_{i=1}^{N}$. Note that this approximated distribution and the previous one are the same. The *SIS* step yields $\{\hat{z}_{t}^{(i)}, \frac{1}{N}\}_{i=1}^{N}$ which is an approximation of $p(z_t|y_{1:t-1})$ at time t.

Fault diagnosis results. Given the real observations over time, we tested the PF algorithm with different numbers of particles N, left graph in Fig. 4. We define *diagnosis error* as the percentage of time steps during which the discrete mode was not identified properly. We use *Maximum A Posteriori (MAP)* to define the most probable discrete mode over time. There is a baseline error rate resulting from human error in timing the discrete mode changes (these changes were manually implemented).

The right graphs in Fig. 4 compare the true discrete modes with the *MAP* estimates generated by the PF algorithm. The overall diagnosis error is shown in the left graph. As we can see, PF improves as the number of particles grows.

To test the stability of our PF algorithm, we engineered some variations in the transition matrix $p(z_t|z_{t-1})$. Despite these changes, the diagnosis error remained the same. This is predicted by Bayes' theorem. All inference is based on the posterior distribution which is updated as new data becomes available.

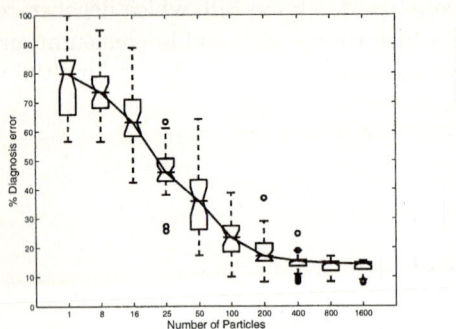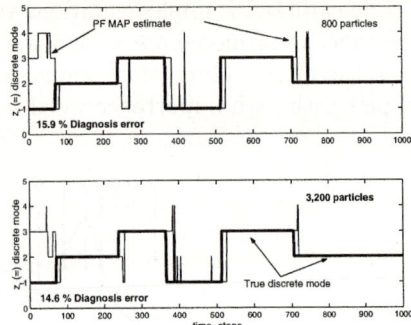

Fig. 4. Diagnosis error for the industrial dryer. The left graph is a box and whisker plot of the diagnosis error for different numbers of particles. The right graphs compare the true mode with the MAP estimate over time for two runs of 800 and 3,200 particles.

4   FDI Approach

FDI is a set of techniques used to detect and isolate faults, sometimes with incomplete information. An FDI system has 3 stages [6]: *fault detection* (noticing an abnormal condition), *fault isolation* (locating the fault), and *fault identification* (determining the fault's size). A *residual generator* block receives the input/output process signals and generates the residual[4]. There are different methods for residual generation; we use parametric estimation. A *decision making* block performs the fault isolation and identification. We use hypothesis tests and Statistical Process Control (SPC) criteria for the decision making block.

Residual Generation block. Parametric Estimation Algorithm (PEA) as a residual generation block is an analytical redundancy method [17]. First it is necessary to learn a reference model of the process in a fault-free situation (discrete mode $z_t = 1$). Afterwards, model parameters are learned recursively. The behavior of these estimates allow the detection of an abnormal situation and fault isolation.

Assuming that faults are reflected in physical parameters, the basic idea of this detection method is that parameters of the real process are learned recursively; then the current learned parameters are compared with the parameters in a fault-free discrete mode. Any substantial difference indicates a change in the process which may be interpreted as a fault. One advantage of the PEA is that it gives the size of the deviations, which is important for fault analysis. However, the process requires a persistent excitation in order to learn the parameters online. Additionally, the determination of physical parameters from mathematical ones generally is not unique and is only possible for low-order models.

Decision Making block. This block is implemented using hypothesis tests and Statistical Process Control (SPC) criteria. In hypothesis testing, a null hy-

---

[4] Inconsistency between real signals and synthetic signals.

pothesis (H_0) and an alternative hypothesis (H_1) are defined in relation to the parameters of a distribution. The null hypothesis must be accepted or rejected based on the results of the test. Two types of error can occur. α and β are the probability of error type I and II respectively. The hypothesis tests most likely to be used in the FDI context are shown in Table 1[5].

Table 1. Hypothesis tests for FDI.

Null hypothesis	Alternative hypothesis	Rejection criteria	Statistical test
$H_0 : \mu = \mu_0$ σ^2 known	$H_1 : \mu \neq \mu_0$ $H_1 : \mu > \mu_0$ $H_1 : \mu < \mu_0$	$\|Z_0\| > Z_{\alpha/2}$ $Z_0 > Z_\alpha$ $Z_0 < Z_\alpha$	$Z_0 = \frac{\bar{x}-\mu_0}{\sigma/\sqrt{n}}$
$H_0 : \mu = \mu_0$ σ^2 unknown	$H_1 : \mu \neq \mu_0$ $H_1 : \mu > \mu_0$ $H_1 : \mu < \mu_0$	$\|t_0\| > t_{\alpha/2,\nu}$ $t_0 > t_{\alpha,\nu}$ $t_0 < t_{\alpha,\nu}, \nu = n-1$	$t_0 = \frac{\bar{x}-\mu_0}{S/\sqrt{n}}$
$H_0 : \sigma^2 = \sigma_0^2$	$H_1 : \sigma^2 \neq \sigma_0^2$ $H_1 : \sigma^2 > \sigma_0^2$ $H_1 : \sigma^2 < \sigma_0^2$	$\chi_0^2 > \chi_{\alpha/2,\nu}^2$ or $\chi_0^2 < \chi_{1-\alpha/2,\nu}^2$ $\chi_0^2 > \chi_{\alpha,\nu}^2$ $\chi_0^2 < \chi_{\alpha,\nu}^2, \nu = n-1$	$\chi_0^2 = \frac{(n-1)S^2}{\sigma_0^2}$

According to the SPC criteria [5], an out-of-control situation may be detected when from 7 consecutive points, all 7 fall on the same side of the central limit. Alternatively, we can make the same determination when 10 of 11, 12 of 14, 14 of 17, or 16 of 20 consecutive points are located on the same side of the central limit.

Fault Diagnosis approach. The residual generation block is implemented by an online PEA. ARX parameters ($\{a(.)_i\}_{i=1}^{n_a}, \{b(.)_j\}_{j=1}^{n_b}$) are associated with each discrete mode z_t. Given this, it is possible to define hypothesis tests for the fault-free model ($z_t = 1$) versus the faulty discrete modes hypothesis ($z_t > 1$). Under this interpretation [5], H_0 is the fault-free discrete mode, H_1 is a faulty discrete mode, α is the probability of a false alarm, i.e. detecting a faulty discrete mode when there is no fault, and β is the probability of failing to detect a faulty discrete mode. When any of the null hypotheses are rejected, a faulty discrete mode will be declared. It will be necessary to test the hypotheses for every faulty discrete mode.

This characterization of faults allows fault isolation, because the most likely fault will be the one that does not reject (accepts) the greatest number of null hypotheses (the greatest number of parameters) corresponding to it. In other words, for fault isolation, we implement a voting scheme based on the number of non-rejected null hypotheses. Table 1 shows the SPC criteria.

Assuming a normal distribution for the parameter behavior, hypothesis tests can now be performed using the known mean values and variance for the normal discrete mode $z_t = 1$; see Table 2.

---

[5] Symbols used in this table are standard.

Table 2. Hypothesis tests for each parameter, where $i = 1, \ldots, n_a$ and $j = 1, \ldots, n_b$.

H_0	$\mu_{a_i} = \mu_{a_i}(z_t = 1)$	$\sigma^2_{a_i} = \sigma^2_{a_i}(z_t = 1)$	$\mu_{b_j} = \mu_{b_j}(z_t = 1)$	$\sigma^2_{b_j} = \sigma^2_{b_j}(z_t = 1)$
H_1	$\mu_{a_i} \neq \mu_{a_i}(z_t = 1)$	$\sigma^2_{a_i} \neq \sigma^2_{a_i}(z_t = 1)$	$\mu_{b_j} \neq \mu_{b_j}(z_t = 1)$	$\sigma^2_{b_j} \neq \sigma^2_{b_j}(z_t = 1)$

If one hypothesis is rejected, it will be understood that there is at least an incipient fault. To avoid false alarms, SPC criteria should be applied to these tests, so a behavior, rather than a single test, indicates the presence of a fault. It should be noted that there will be a propagation error in fault isolation, because testing the estimated parameters against each set of values corresponding to each faulty discrete mode involves having α and β errors for each test.

5   Combined Approach

PF algorithms have several advantages in the fault diagnosis context. They perform online diagnosis dealing with several potential discrete modes, thereby giving low diagnosis error. Nevertheless, PF has some problems:

- Diagnosis results have some degree of uncertainty because PF is a numerical approximation. This uncertainty depends on many factors. If the posterior probability distribution shows more than one mode, there is uncertainty in the model selection.
- The MAP estimate only gives the most probable fault. There is no allowance for the second most probable fault, etc.
- The JMLG model is not updated online. Individual parameter changes cannot be detected because the global effect could be masked by the model structure.

The FDI approach also has important advantages, namely that it provides a deeper insight into the process. If the relationship between model parameters and physical parameters is unique, the fault isolation is easy, and it provides direct fault identification. FDI's primary limitations are:

- The diagnosis is mainly offline; there is a lag of "n" time steps in the computing of statistics.
- The procedure for recursively learning parameters is expensive and impractical because the process must be persistently excited.

We propose a combined system, incorporating both the online speed of PF and the insight available from FDI. The system consists of two sequential stages:

Stage 1: PF. Using PF, a posterior probability density is computed given the observations online. If the diagnosis confidence is high enough (see the left example distribution in Fig. 5), a diagnosis can be made (discrete mode 6 in the example). However, if the density does not permit a confident diagnosis (see the right example distribution), we proceed to the FDI stage. Note that even in this case, PF has reduced the size of the potential solution space.

Stage 2: FDI. Considering only the most likely discrete modes from the PF stage (modes 5, 6, and 7 in the right example distribution, Fig. 5), a hypothesis test is computed with respect to the current learned discrete mode given by the PEA block. These hypothesis tests use a detailed model parameter analysis in order to find the right model.

Stage 1 significantly reduces the number of candidate discrete modes, allowing stage 2 to diagnose online.

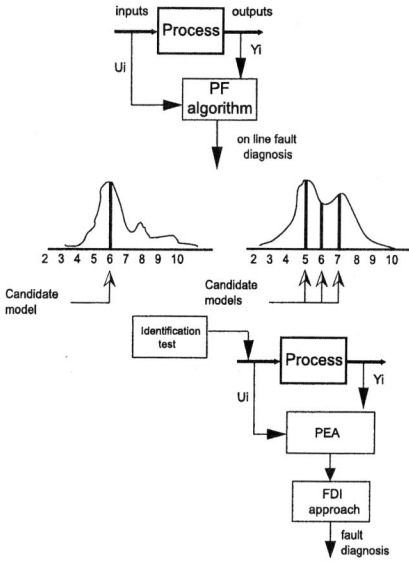

Fig. 5. Robust fault diagnosis sequence.

5.1 Conclusions and Future Work

The PF and FDI approaches complement each other. The combined system generates less uncertainty than PF alone, yet unlike pure FDI it can still be computed online.

Some important future improvements would be a method for detecting new faults (discrete modes) and a better method for recursive learning of the JMLG model. There have been some advances along these lines [8,3], but more research is needed to obtain reliable solutions.

References

1. F Caccavale and L Villani. *Fault Detection and Fault Tolerance for Mechatronics Systems: Recent Avances*. Springer-Verlag, Berlin Heidelberg New York, 2003.
2. N de Freitas. Rao-Blackwellised particle filtering for fault diagnosis. In *IEEE Aerospace Conference*, 2001.
3. A Doucet and Tadic V B. B parameter estimation in general state-space models using particle methods,. *to appear Annals of the Institute of Statistical Mathematics, 2003*, 2003.
4. A Doucet, N de Freitas, and N J Gordon. *Sequential Monte Carlo Methods in Practice*. Springer-Verlag, New York, 2001.
5. J D Gabano. Détection de defauts sur entraînement électrique. Technical report, Université de Poitiers, Poitiers, France, 1993.
6. J Gertler. *Fault detection and diagnosis in engineering systems*. Marcel Dekker, Inc., 1998.
7. Z Ghahramani and G E Hinton. Parameter estimation for linear dynamical system. Technical Report CRG-TR-96-2, Department of Computer Science, University of Toronto, Toronto, 1996.
8. Z Ghahramani and G E Hinton. Variational learning for switching state-space models. *Neural Computation*, 12(4):963–996, 1998.
9. N Gordon, D Salmond, and Smith. Novel approach to nonlinear/non-Gaussian Bayesian state estimation. *IEEE Proceedings-F*, 140(2):107–113, April 1993.
10. T. Hägglund and K. Aström. Supervision of adaptive control algorithms. *Automatica*, 36(1).
11. F Hutter and R Dearden. Efficient on-line fault diagnosis for non-linear systems. In 7th *International Symposium on Artificial Intelligence, Robotics and Automation in Space*, 2003.
12. F Hutter and R Dearden. The Gaussian particle filter for diagnosis of non-linear systems. In 14th *International Workshop on Principles of Diagnosis*, Washington, DC, 2003.
13. International Federation of Automatic Control. *Fault detection, supervision and safety for technical process*, Baden Baden,Germany, September 1992. Pergamon.
14. International Federation of Automatic Control. *Fault detection, supervision and safety for technical process*, Espoo,Finland, June 1994. Pergamon.
15. L Ljung. *System Identification: Theory for the User*. Prentice-Hall, 1987.
16. R Morales-Menéndez, N de Freitas, and D Poole. Real-time monitoring of complex industrial processes with particle filters. In *Advances in Neural Information Processing Systems 16*, Cambridge, MA, 2002. MIT Press.
17. R Patton and J Chen. Parity space approach to model-based fault diagnosis. a tutorial survey and some results. *IFAC SAFEPROCESS Symposium Baden-Baden*, 1:239–255, 1991.
18. C A Smith and A B Corripio. *Principles and Practice of Automatic Process Control*. John Wiley & Sons, second edition, 1997.
19. F. Valle. Fault detection and isolation applied to the supervision of adaptive control systems; a neural network approach. Villa Erba, Italy, August 2001. International Federation of Automatic Control.
20. F. Valle. Statistical hypothesis neural network approach for fault detection and isolation an adaptive control system. Merida, Mexico, Abril 2002. MICAI.

Power Plant Operator Assistant: An Industrial Application of Factored MDPs

Alberto Reyes, Pablo H. Ibargüengoytia, and L. Enrique Sucar

Instituto de Investigaciones Eléctricas / ITESM Cuernavaca
Av. Reforma 113, Palmira
Cuernavaca, Mor., 62490, México
{areyes,pibar}@iie.org.mx, esucar@itesm.mx

Abstract. Markov decision processes (MDPs) provide a powerful framework for solving planning problems under uncertainty. However, it is
difficult to apply them to real world domains due to complexity and representation problems: (i) the state space grows exponentially with the
number of variables; (ii) a reward function must be specified for each
state-action pair. In this work we tackle both problems and apply MDPs
for a complex real world domain -combined cycle power plant operation.
For reducing the state space complexity we use a factored representation
based on a two–stage dynamic Bayesian network [13]. The reward function is represented based on the recommended optimal operation curve
for the power plant. The model has been implemented and tested with
a power plant simulator with promising results.

1 Introduction

Markov Decision Processes (MDP) [5,12] and Partially Observable Markov Decision Processes (POMDP) [10] provide a solution to planning problems under
uncertainty as they base its strength in the computation of an optimal policy,
in accessible and stochastic environments. In these approaches, an agent can
do observations, starting from which, it computes a probabilistic distribution of
states where the system can be. Based on this position, it designs the optimal
sequence of actions to reach a specific goal.

However, in this formalism, the state space grows exponentially with the
number of problem variables, and its inference methods grow in the number
of actions. Thus, in large problems, MDPs become impractical and inefficient.
Recent solutions like those shown in [7,8] introduce the use of featured-based
(or factored) representations to avoid enumerating the problem state space and
allow to extend this formalism to more complex domains.

In recent years, the power generation industry has faced important problems
that require the modernization of current installations, principally in both the
instrumentation and control systems. The current trend consists in increasing
the performance, availability and, reliability of the actual installations. The performance refers to the amount of mega watts that can be generated with a unit of
fuel. The availability refers to the hours that the central is out of service, and the

R. Monroy et al. (Eds.): MICAI 2004, LNAI 2972, pp. 565–573, 2004.
© Springer-Verlag Berlin Heidelberg 2004

reliability refers to the probability of counting with all the equipment of the plant. Additionally, modern power plants are following two clear tendencies. First, they are very complex processes working close to their limits. Second, they are highly automated and instrumented, leaving the operator with very few decisions.

However, there still exist some unusual maneuvers that require the experience and ability of the operator. Some examples are load rejection or responses to failures [1]. A current strategy is the use of intelligent systems for the support in the decision process that the operator carries out. The intelligent system may learn the actions of an experimented operator and may advice and train the new operators in the decision processes that are required in special occasions. Unexpected effects of the actions, unreliable sensors and incompleteness of the knowledge suggest the use of uncertainty management techniques.

This paper first explains the disturbances presented in a combined cycle power plant due to a load rejection and other similar situations, and states a possible solution by using an intelligent operator assistant. In section 3, the heart of the intelligent system is shown describing the main elements of the MDP formalism and its most popular inference methods. Section 4 illustrates a feature-based representation extending MDPs to deal with real-world problem complexity. In section 5, the implementation details of the operator assistant are shown. Finally, in section 6, experimental results and test cases are described.

2   Problem Domain

A heat recovery steam generator (HRSG) is a process machinery capable of recovering residual energy from a gas turbine exhaust gases, and use it for steam generation purposes (Fig.1). Its most important components are: steam drum, water wall, recirculation pump, and afterburners. The final control elements associated to its operation are: feedwater valve, afterburner fuel valve, main steam valve, bypass valve, and gas valve.

During normal operation, the conventional three-element feedwater control system commands the feedwater control valve to regulate the steam drum level. However, when a partial or total electric load rejection is presented this traditional control loop is not longer capable to stabilize the drum level. In this case, the steam-water equilibrium point moves, causing an enthalpy change of both fluids (steam and water). Consequently, the enthalpy change causes an increment in the water level because of a strong water displacement to the steam drum. The control system reacts closing the feedwater control valve. However a water increase is needed instead of a feedwater decrease. A similar case is presented when a sudden high steam demand occurs.

Under these circumstances, the participation of a human operator is necessary to help the control system to decide the actions that should be taken in order to overcome the transient. A practical solution to this problem is the use of an intelligent operator assistant providing recommendations to operators about how to make the best action on the process that corrects the problem. The operator assistant should be able to find an action policy according to the crisis

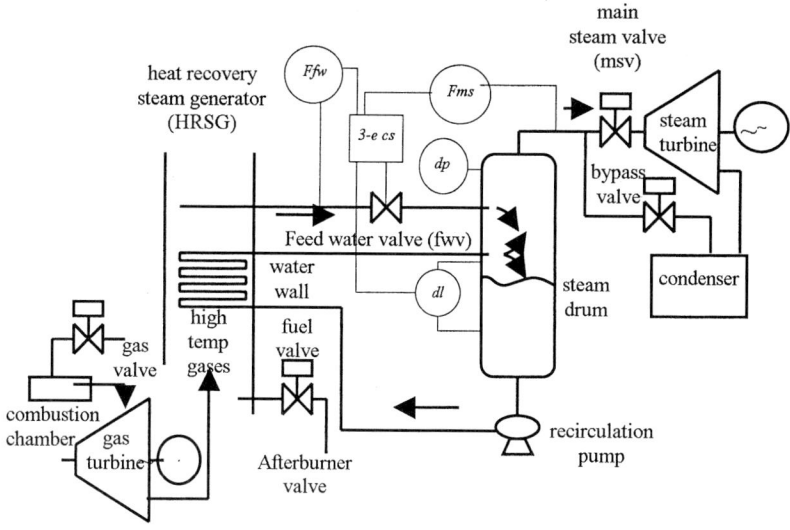

Fig. 1. Feedwater and main steam systems simplified diagram. Ffw refers to feedwater flow, Fms refers to main stream flow, dp refers to drum pressure, dl refers to drum level, and $3 - ecs$ refers to flow controller.

dimension, take into account that actuators are not perfect and can produce non-desired effects, and consider the performance, availability and reliability of the actual plant installations under these situations.

3   Markov Decision Processes

Markov Decision Processes (MDP) [12] seems to be a suitable solution to this kind of problems as they base its strength in the computation of an optimal policy in accessible and stochastic environments.

An MDP M is a tuple $M =< S, A, \Phi, R >$, where S is a finite set of states of the system. A is a finite set of actions. $\Phi : A \times S \to \Pi(S)$ is the state transition function, mapping an action and a state to a probability distribution over S for the possible resulting state. The probability of reaching state s' by performing action a in state s is written $\Phi(a, s, s')$. $R : S \times A \to \Re$ is the reward function. $R(s, a)$ is the reward that the system receives if it takes action a in state s.

A policy for an MDP is a mapping $\pi : S \to A$ that selects and action for each state. Given a policy, we can define its finite-horizon value function $V_n^\pi : S \to \Re$, where $V_n^\pi(s)$ is the expected value of applying the policy π for n steps starting in state s. The value function is defined inductively with $V_0^\pi(s) = R(s, \pi(s))$ and $V_m^\pi(s) = R(s, \pi(s)) + \Sigma_{s' \in S} \Phi(\pi(s), s, s') V_{m-1}^\pi(s')$. Over an infinite horizon, a discounted model γ is frequently used to ensure policies to have a bounded expected value. For some γ chosen so that $0 < \gamma < 1$, the value of any reward from the transition after the next is discounted by a factor of γ, and the one after that γ^2, and so on. Thus, if $V^\pi(s)$ is the discounted expected value in state s following policy π forever, we must have $V^\pi(s) = R(s, \pi(s)) + \gamma \Sigma_{s' \in S} \Phi(\pi(s), s, s') V^\pi_{m-1}(s')$, which yields a set of linear equations in the values of $V^\pi()$.

A solution to an MDP is a policy that maximizes its expected value. For the discounted infinite–horizon case with any given discount factor γ in (0,1) range, there is a policy V^* that is optimal regardless of the starting state [9] that satisfies the following equation: $V^*(s) = max_a \{R(s, a) + \gamma \Sigma_{s' \in S} \Phi(a, s, s') V^*(s')\}$.

Two popular methods for solving this equation and finding an optimal policy for an MDP are: (a) value iteration and (2) policy iteration [12].

In policy iteration, the current policy is repeatedly improved by finding some action in each state that has a higher value than the action chosen by the current policy for the state. The policy is initially chosen at random, and the process terminates when no improvement can be found. This process converges to an optimal policy [12].

In value iteration, optimal policies are produced for successively longer finite horizons until they converge. It is relatively simple to find an optimal policy over n steps $\pi^*_n(.)$, with value function $V^*_n(.)$ using the recurrence relation: $\pi^*_n(s) = arg\ max_a \{R(s, a) + \gamma \Sigma_{s' \in S} \Phi(a, s, s') V^*_{n-1}(s')\}$ with starting condition $V^*_0(.) = 0$ $\forall\ s \in S$, where V^*_m is derived from the policy π^*_m as described earlier. The algorithm to the optimal policy for the discounted infinite case in a number of steps that is polynomial in $|S|, |A|, log\ max_{s,a} |R(s, a)|$ and $1/(1 - \gamma)$.

4   Factored MDPs

The problem with the MDP formalism is that the state space grows exponentially with the number of domain variables, and its inference methods grow in the number of actions. Thus, in large problems, MDPs becomes impractical and inefficient. Factored representations avoid enumerating the problem state space and allow that planning under uncertainty in more complex domains to be tractable.

In a factored MDP, the set of states is described via a set of random variables $\mathbf{X} = \{X_1, \ldots, X_n\}$, where each X_i takes on values in some finite domain $Dom(X_i)$. A state $\mathbf{x}$ defines a value $x_i \in Dom(X_i)$ for each variable X_i. Thus, the set of states $S = Dom(X_i)$ is exponentially large, making it impractical to represent the transition model explicitly as matrices. Fortunately, the framework of dynamic Bayesian networks (DBN) [14,4] gives us the tools to describe the transition model function concisely. In these representations, the post-action nodes (at the time $t + 1$) contain matrices with the probabilities of their values given their parents' values under the effects of an action.

These representations can have two types of arcs: *diachronic* and *synchronic*. *Diachronic* arcs are those directed from time t variables to time $t + 1$ variables, while *synchronic* arcs are directed between variables at time $t + 1$. Figure 2 shows a simple DBN with 5 binary state variables and diachronic arcs only, to illustrate the concepts presented.

A Markovian transition model Φ defines a probability distribution over the next state given the current state. Let X_i denote the variable X_i at the current time and X'_i the variable at the next step. The *transition graph* of a DBN is a

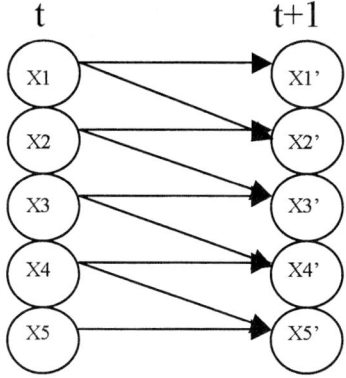

Fig. 2. A simple DBN with 5 state variables.

two–layer directed acyclic graph G_T whose nodes are $\{X_1, \ldots, X_n, X'_1, \ldots, X'_n\}$. In the graph, the parents of X'_i are denoted as $Parents(X'_i)$. Each node X'_i is aso-ciated with a *conditional probability distribution* (CPD) $P_\Phi(X'_i \mid Parents(X'_i))$. The transition probability $P_\Phi(\mathbf{x'_i} \mid \mathbf{x_i})$ is then defined to be $\Pi_i P_\Phi(x'_i \mid \mathbf{u_i})$ where $\mathbf{u_i}$ is the value in $\mathbf{x}$ of the variables in $Parents(X'_i)$. Because there are not syn-chronic arcs in the graph, the variables are conditionally independent at the time $t + 1$. So, for an instantiation of variables at time t, the probability of each state at the time $t + 1$ can be computed simply by multiplying the probabilities of the relevant variables at the time $t + 1$.

The transition dynamics of an MDP can be expressed by a separated DBN model $\Phi_a = \langle G_a, P_a \rangle$ for each action a. However, in many cases, different actions have similar transition dynamics, only differing in their effect on some small set of variables. In particular, in many cases, a variable has a default evolution model, which only changes if an action affects it directly. Koller and Parr [3] use the notion of a *default transition model* $\Phi_d = \langle G_d, P_d \rangle$. For each action a, they define $Effects[a] \subseteq X'$ to be the variables in the next state whose local probability model is different from Φ_d, i.e., those variables X'_i such that $P_a(X'_i \mid Parents_a(X'_i)) \neq P_d(X'_i \mid Parents_d(X'_i))$. Note that d can be an action in our model where $Effects[d] = \phi$. If we define 5 actions $a_1, \ldots, a_5$ and a default action d in the example of the DBN, the action a_i changes the CPD of variable X'_i and so $Effects[a_i] = X'_i$.

5   A FMDP for the Steam Generation System

In this section, the components and the implementation details of the FMDP–based model for assisting operators during manual operations in the steam gen-eration system will be explained. First, a knowledge module that manages the transition, the reward and the observation matrices is required, i.e., the knowl-edge base. These matrices can be established once that a finite set of actions on

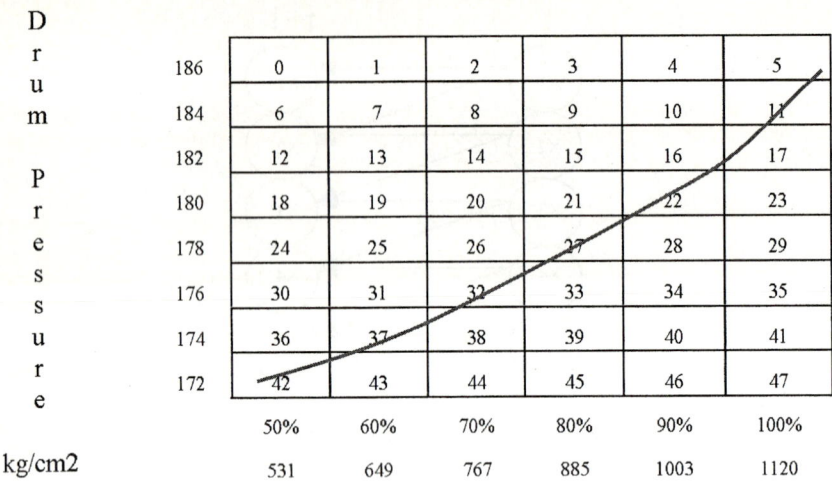

D r u m P r e s s u r e	186	0	1	2	3	4	5
	184	6	7	8	9	10	11
	182	12	13	14	15	16	17
	180	18	19	20	21	22	23
	178	24	25	26	27	28	29
	176	30	31	32	33	34	35
	174	36	37	38	39	40	41
	172	42	43	44	45	46	47
		50%	60%	70%	80%	90%	100%
kg/cm2		531	649	767	885	1003	1120

Main steam flow (T/H)

Fig. 3. Recommended operation curve for a Heat Recovery Steam Generator.

each state and a finite set of observations are defined. Second, a decision process module is required where the MDP algorithm is implemented and interfaced with the knowledge and actors modules. Third, an actor module is the direct interface with the environment. In this case, the steam generator of a power plant is the environment and the operator is the actor. The actor provides the goals required and executes the commands that modify the environment.

The set of states in the MDP are directly obtained from the steam generator operation variables: *feedwater flow (Ffw)*, *main steam flow (Fms)*, *drum pressure (Pd)* and *power generation (g)*, as the controlled variables; and the *disturbance (d)*, as the uncertain exogenous event. Initially we consider the case of a "load rejection" as the disturbance. These variables are discretized in a number of intervals, so the state of the plant (a part of it) is represented by the combination of the state variables.

For optimal operation of the plant, a certain relation between the state variables must be maintained, specified by a *recommended operation curve*. For instance, the recommended operation curve that relates the *drum pressure* and the *main steam flow* is shown in Fig.3. The reward function for the MDP is based on the optimal operation curve. The states matching the curve will be assigned a positive reward and the reminding states a negative one. Given this representation, the objective of the MDP is to obtain the optimal policy for getting the plant to a state under the optimal operation curve.

The set of actions is composed by the opening and closure operations in the feedwater *(fwv)* and main steam valves *(msv)*. It is assumed that *fwv* and *msv* respectively regulates *Ffw* and *Fms*. Thus, *Ofwv* (+), *Ofwv* (−), denote the

Table 1. Set of control actions.

Process Operations	
a_0	$Ofwv(+)$
a_1	$Ofwv(-)$
a_2	$Omsv(+)$
a_3	$Omsv(-)$
a_4	0

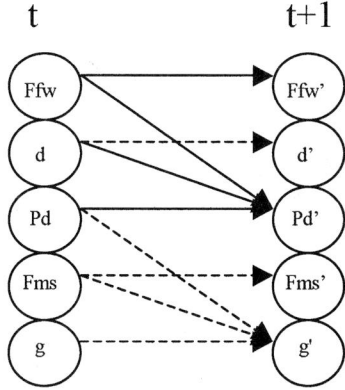

Fig. 4. Two–stage Dynamic Bayesian Network for the actions a0 and a1.

action of opening/closing the *fwv* and, *Ofms* (+), *Ofms* (−), the action of opening/closing *msv*. The null action (0) indicates no changes in these valves. Table 1 shows the whole set of actions. Initially, only five actions will be used, however the formalism can be applied to greater set of actions and their combinations.

The state variables are discretized as follows: *Pd* can take 8 values, *Fms* can take 6, and *Ffw*, *d*, and *g* can take two values, so the state dimension is $8^1 \times 6^1 \times 2^3 = 384$. To reduce the number of states, we use a factorized representation based on two-stage dynamic Bayesian network [4].

The transition model in this work is represented through a two-stage Bayesian network with 5 state variables as shown in Fig.4. The effects over the relevant nodes during the application of an action are denoted through solid lines. Dashed lines represent those nodes with no effect during the same action. In these approach the action effects are denoted by: *Effects*[a0, a1] = {*ffw'*, *pd'*}, *Effects*[a2, a3] = {*fms'*, *g'*}, and *Effects*[a4] = {∅} for the null action.

6   Experimental Results

In order to test the factored MDP-based operator assistant, a simplified version of a linear steam generation simulator was built using Java2 [11]. The probabilistic state transition model was implemented based on Elvira [6], which was extended to compute Dynamic Bayesian Networks. The tests were made using a Pentium PC.

We first constructed a transition model extensionally with the idea of comparing its compilation time versus a factored model. The first case is a $| S |^2$ dimension conditional probability matrix with 384 probability values/action where S is the state space. With this model it took 4.22 minutes to build a probability table for one state and one action only. So that, the model for one state and four actions would take 16.87 minutes, and a complete model would take almost two hours for S (384 possible states). The number of parameters enumerated is 737,284.

On the other hand, the factored model is composed by two 32x16 tables (512 parameters) for the actions a0 and a1, and two 96x16 tables (1,536 parameters) for the actions a2 and a3. The null action model in both cases (a4) was built very easily assuming deterministic transition from one state to itself (probability=1.0). The results were as expected, from the factorized representation the complete transition model was obtained in less than two minutes. In this case the number of enumerated parameters was $512(2) + 1,536(2) = 4,096$. If we expressed the space saving as the relation: number of non factored parameters enumerated / number of factored parameters enumerated, we would have for our example a model 180 times simpler. Symmetrically, if the time saving were expressed as non-factored execution time / factored execution time we would have a model 3,240 times faster.

According to this technique, it is not necessary to enumerate all domain literals, neither evidence variables (time t) nor interest variables (time $t+1$). This simplification makes easier and more efficient the transition model construction. For example, in the case of actions a0 and a1 the characteristic state only requires enumerating the variables Ffw, d and pd, with which $2^2 \times 8^1 = 32$ states. In the same way, the states affected by the action a0 or a1 only need $2^1 \times 8^1 = 16$ combinations. We also obtain computational savings in the reward specification, given that we do not need to specify a reward value for each state, but only for characteristic states, composed in this case by Pd and Fms.

The factored MDP converged in 3 iterations (for a $\gamma = 0.3$) using value iteration in less than 1 second.

7   Conclusions

Markov decision processes (MDPs) provide a powerful framework for solving planning problems under uncertainty. However, it is difficult to apply them to real world domains due to complexity and representation problems. In this work, we have applied the factored MDP formalism as a framework for solving these problems in industrial real-world domains. We described the features of an FMDP-based operator assistant for the treatment of transients in a HRSG. For reducing the state space complexity we use a factored representation based on a two-stage dynamic Bayesian network. For representing the reward function we have taken advantage of recommended optimal operation curve for the power plant. The model has been implemented and tested with a power plant simulator with promising results.

Some authors [7] recommend to split a big problem in small pieces solving them separately by a set of cooperative agents. Those multi-agent approaches in fact solve several simpler problems but need domain-dependant coordination strategies that in some cases are practically impossible to specify.

Currently, we are exploring extensions to the FMDPs formalism based on symbolic representations from classical planning [2] to have additional reductions in the problem complexity. The main idea is avoid using multiagent approaches and preserve standard dynamic programming algorithms in the inference side.

References

1. Mario E. Agueda and Pablo H. Ibargüengoytia. An architecture for planning in uncertain domains. In *Proc. ICTAI-01 Thirteen International Conference on Tools with Artificial Intalligence*, pages 152–159, Dallas, Tex., USA, 2001.
2. Boutilier C., Reiter R., and Price B. Simbolic dynamic programming for first order MDPs. In *Proc. International Joint Conf. on Artificial Intelligence, IJCAI-2001*, 2001.
3. Koller D. and Parr R. Policy iteration for factored MDPs. In *Proceedings of the Sixteenth Conference on Uncertainty in Artificial Intelligence, UAI-00*, pages 326–334, Stanford, CA, USA, 2000.
4. A. Darwiche and Goldszmidt M. Action networks: A framework for reasoning about actions and change under understanding. In *Proceedings of the Tenth Conference on Uncertainty in Artificial Intelligence, UAI-94"*, pages 136–144, Seattle, WA, USA, 1994.
5. Bellman R. E. *Dynamic Programming*. Princeton University Press, Princeton, N.J., U.S.A., 1957.
6. The Elvira Consortium. Elvira: An environment for creating and using probabilistic graphical models. In *Proceedings of the First European Workshop on Probabilistic graphical models (PGM'02)"*, pages 1–11, Cuenca, Spain, 2002.
7. Guestrin, Koller, and Parr. Multiagent planning with factored MDPs. In *Advances in Neural Information Processing Systems NIPS-14*, 2001.
8. J. Hoey, St-Aubin R., A. Hu, and Boutilier C. Spudd: Stochastic planning using decision diagrams. In *Proceedings of the 15th Conference on Uncertainty in Artificial Intelligence, UAI-99*, pages 279–288, 1999.
9. R. A. Howard. *Dynamic Programming and Markov Processes*. MIT Press, Cambridge, Mass., U.S.A., 1960.
10. Astrom K.J. Optimal control of Markov processes with incomplete state information. *J. Math. Anal. Applications*, 10:174–205, 1965.
11. Patrick Naughton and Herbert Schildt. *Java 2: The Complete Reference*. Osborne/Mc Graw Hill, 3rd Edition, London, Great Britain, 2000.
12. Martin L. Puterman. *Markov Decision Processes: Discrete Stochastic Dynamic Programming*. Wiley, New York, N.Y., U.S.A., 1995.
13. Dearden R. and Boutillier C. Abstraction and approximate decision-theoretic planning. *Artificial Intelligence*, 89:219–283, 1997.
14. Dean T. and Kanazawa K. A model for reasoning about persistence and causation. *Computational Intelligence*, 5(3):142–150, 1989.

Scene Modeling by ICA and Color Segmentation

J. Gabriel Aviña-Cervantes[1,2]* and Michel Devy[1]

[1] Laboratoire d'Analyse et d'Architecture des Systèmes
7, Avenue du Colonel Roche, 31077 Toulouse Cedex 4, FRANCE
{gavina,michel}@laas.fr
http://www.laas.fr/laasve/index.htm
[2] Facultad de Ingeniería Mecánica, Eléctrica y Electrónica,
Universidad de Guanajuato.
Avenida Tampico 912. Salamanca, Guanajuato. 36730, México.
avina@salamanca.ugto.mx
http://www.ugto.mx

Abstract. In this paper, a method is proposed for the interpretation of outdoor natural images. It fastly constructs a basic 2-D scene model that can be used in the visual systems onboard of autonomous vehicles. It is composed of several processes: color image segmentation, principal areas detection, classification and verification of the final model. The regions provided by the segmentation phase are characterized by their color and texture. These features are compared and classified into predefined classes using the Support Vector Machines (SVM) algorithm. An Independent Component Analysis (ICA) is used to reduce redundancy from the database and improve the recognition stage. Finally, a global scene model is obtained by merging the small regions belonging to the same class. The extraction of useful entities for navigation (like roads) from the final model is straightforward. This system has been intensively tested through experiments on sequences of countryside scenes color images.

1 Introduction

The construction of a complete model of an outdoor natural environment is one of the most complex tasks in Computer Vision [1]. The complexity lies on several factors such as the great variety of scenes, the absence of structures that could help visual process and the low control in the variation of the current conditions (as illumination [2], temperature and sensor motion). Only some of these factors can be easily overcome or compensated. Moreover, real time algorithms are generally required. Image segmentation [3], i.e. the extraction of homogeneous regions in the image, has been the subject of considerable research activity over the last three decades. Many algorithms have been elaborated for gray scale images. However, the problem of segmentation for color images, which convey much

---

* The author thanks the support of the CONACyT. This work has been partially funded by the French-Mexican Laboratory on Computer Science (LAFMI, Laboratoire Franco-Mexicain d'Informatique)

R. Monroy et al. (Eds.): MICAI 2004, LNAI 2972, pp. 574–583, 2004.
© Springer-Verlag Berlin Heidelberg 2004

more information about the objects in the scene, has received lower attention, primarily due to the fact that computer systems were not powerful enough, until recently, to display and manipulate large, full-color data sets.

In [4], an approach for image interpretation in natural environments has been proposed. It consists in several steps: first, a color segmentation algorithm provides a description of the scene as a set of the most representative regions. These regions are characterized by several attributes (color and texture) [5], so that to identify a generic object class they may belong to. Murrieta [4] has evaluated this approach to recognize rocks, trees or grassy terrains from color images. In [6], a pre-classification step was used in order to select the database according to some global classification based on the images: this step allows to use the best knowledge database depending on the season (winter or summer), the weather (sunny or cloudy) or the kind of environment (countryside or urban).

This paper is an extension of Murrieta's works. In particular, we focus on two issues dealing with scenes modeling. The first issue is the fast and correct segmentation of natural images. It is a fact that a good segmentation is fundamental to get a successful identification. The second issue is the information redundancy in the database. We aim to reduce it with an Independent Component Analysis (ICA). The ICA [7] of a random vector is the task of searching for a linear transformation that minimizes the statistical dependence between the output components [8]. The concept of ICA may be seen as an extension of the principal component analysis (PCA). ICA decorrelates higher-order statistics from signals while PCA imposes independence up to the second order only and defines orthogonal directions. Besides, ICA basis vectors are more spatially related local than the PCA basis vectors and local features give better object (signal) representation. This property is particularly useful for recognition.

The organization of this paper is as follows. Section 2 describes the color segmentation algorithm. The process to characterize the regions obtained by the segmentation step is described in the section 3. In sections 4 and 5, we discuss the application of ICA to the pattern recognition tasks in particular with the SVM classification method. Final scene models and some experimental results are presented in the section 6. Finally, we give our conclusions and hints for future work.

2   Color Image Segmentation

Image segmentation is an extremely important and difficult low-level task. All subsequent interpretation tasks including object detection, feature extraction, object recognition and classification rely heavily on the quality of the segmentation process. Image segmentation is the process of extracting the principal connected regions from the image. These regions must satisfy a uniformity criterion derived from its spectral components.

The segmentation process could be improved by some additional knowledge about the objects in the scene such as geometrical, textural, contextual or optical properties [3,9]. It is essentially a pixel-based processing. There are basically two different approaches to the segmentation problem: region-based and edge-based methods. Region-based methods take the basic approach of dividing the image into regions and classifying pixels as inside, outside, or on the boundary of a structure based on its location and the surrounding 2D regions. On the other hand, the edge-based approach classifies pixels using a numerical test for a property such as image gradient or curvature. Each method has its pros and cons. Indeed, region-based methods are more robust, but at expense of poorer edge localization. Edge-based methods achieve good localization but are sensitive to noise. Our segmentation method belongs to the former category. Then, the *color space* selection is an important factor to take into account in the implementation since this defines the useful color properties [2]. Two goals are generally pursued: first, the selection of uncorrelated color features and second, the selection invariance to *illumination changes*. To this purpose, color segmentation results have been obtained and compared using several color representations. In our experiences, the best color segmentation was obtained using the $I_1 I_2 I_3$ representation (Ohta's space) [2], defined as:

$$I_1 = \frac{R+G+B}{3} \ ,$$

$$I_2 = \frac{R-B}{2} \ , \tag{1}$$

$$I_3 = \frac{2G-R-B}{4} \ .$$

The components of this space are uncorrelated, so statistically it is the best way for detecting color variations. They form a linear transformation [9] of the RGB space where I_1 is the intensity component, I_2 and I_3 are roughly orthonormal color components[1]. To cope with low saturation images, we use a hybrid space. In this case, under-segmentation is expected due to poor colorimetric features. However, we have maintained good results in segmentation, by slightly reinforcing the contours over each color component before segmentation. In order to avoid to implement a complex edge detector, an alternative consist in using the color space $l_1 l_2 l_3$ proposed by Gevers [10] formulated as:

$$l_1 = \frac{|R-G|}{|R-G|+|R-B|+|G-B|} \ ,$$

$$l_2 = \frac{|R-B|}{|R-G|+|R-B|+|G-B|} \ , \tag{2}$$

$$l_3 = \frac{|G-B|}{|R-G|+|R-B|+|G-B|} \ .$$

These color features present a very good behavior to illumination changes. Moreover, their advantages are particularly important in edge detection and pattern recognition.

Our segmentation algorithm is a combination of two techniques: the thresholding or clustering and region growing techniques. The advantage of this hybrid

---

[1] I_2 and I_3 are somewhat similar to the chrominance signal produced by the opponent color mechanisms of human visual system

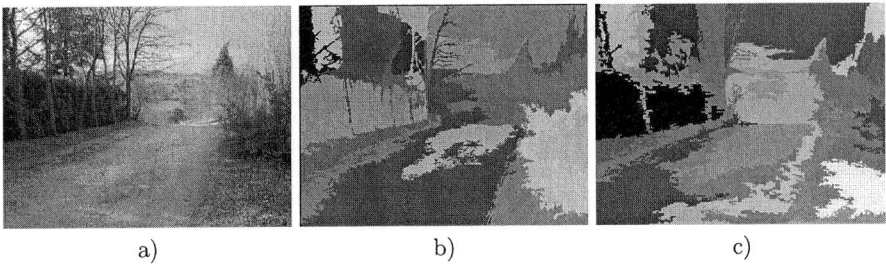

Fig. 1. Color image segmentation. a) Original low saturated color image, b) segmentation using Ohta's color space and c) Segmentation using an hybrid color space(Gevers/Ohta) used only for low saturated color images.

method is that it allows to achieve the process of region growing independently of the starting point and of the scanning order on the adjacent cells. This segmentation is carried out in a bottom-up way: dividing small regions first and then, combining them to form greater regions. The method does the grouping of the pixels in the 3-D spatial domain of square cells and gives them the same label. The division of the image into square cells provides a first arbitrary partition. Several classes are defined by the analysis of the *color histograms*. Thus, each square cell in the image is associated with a class. The fusion of the neighboring square cells belonging to the same class is done by using an adjacency graph (adjacency-8). Finally, to avoid over-segmented images the regions smaller than a given threshold are merged to the nearest adjacent region using a color distance criterion. We have adopted the method suggested by Kittler [11] to get the principal thresholds from the histograms. It assumes that the observations come from mixtures of Gaussian distributions and uses the Kullback-Leibler criterion from information theory to estimate the thresholds[11]. In our implementation, this approach is generalized to get the optimal number of thresholds. Next section explains the features we use to characterize each of the segmented region.

3   Color and Texture Object Features

Texture is the characteristic used to describe the surface of a given object, and it is undoubtedly one of the main features employed in image processing and pattern recognition. This feature is essentially a neighborhood property. Haralick provides a comprehensive survey of most classical, structural and statistical approaches to characterize texture [12].

In our approach, each region obtained by the previous segmentation algorithm is represented by a color and texture vector. The texture operators we use are based on the sum and difference histograms proposed by M. Unser [5], which are a fast alternative to the usual co-occurrence matrices used for texture analysis. This method requires less computation time and less memory storage than the conventional spatial texture methods. Then, a region can be characterized by a collection of sum and difference histograms that have been estimated for different relative displacements δx and δy. For a given region into the image $I(x, y) \in [0, 255]$, the sum and difference histograms are defined as:

$$h_s(i) = Card(i = I(x, y) + I(x + \delta x, y + \delta y)) ,$$
$$h_d(j) = Card(j = | I(x, y) - I(x + \delta x, y + \delta y) |) , \qquad (3)$$

where $i \in [0, 510]$ and $j \in [0, 255]$. Sum and difference images can be built for all pixel (x, y) of the input image I,

$$I_s(x, y) = I(x, y) + I(x + \delta x, y + \delta y) ,$$
$$I_d(x, y) = | I(x, y) - I(x + \delta x, y + \delta y) | . \qquad (4)$$

Furthermore, normalized sum and difference histograms can be computed for selected regions of the image, so that:

$$H_s(i) = \frac{Card(i = I_s(x,y))}{m} ,$$

$$H_d(j) = \frac{Card(j = I_d(x,y))}{m} , \qquad (5)$$

$$H_s(i) \in [0, 1] \text{ and } H_d(j) \in [0, 1] ,$$

where m is the number of points belonging to the considered region. These normalized histograms may be interpreted as probabilities. $\hat{P}_{s(i)} = H_s(i)$ is the estimated probability that the sum of the pixels $I(x, y)$ and $I(x + \delta x, y + \delta y)$ will have the value i and $\hat{P}_{d(j)} = H_d(j)$ is the estimated probability that the absolute difference of the pixels $I(x, y)$ and $I(x + \delta x, y + \delta y)$ will have value j. Several *statistics* are applied to these probabilities to generate the texture features.

We have chosen seven texture operators from these histograms: *Energy, Correlation, Entropy, Contrast, Homogeneity, Cluster shade and Cluster prominance.* This selection has been based on the Principal Component Analysis over all texture features proposed by Unser [5]. In this way we obtain a probabilistic characterization of the spatial organization of an image. Although, the histograms change gradually in function of the viewpoint, the distance from the sensor to the scene and the occlusions, these features are rather reliable. Additionally, the statistical means of I_1, I_2 and I_3 over each region are used to characterize the color into the region.

4   Classification Using Support Vector Machines

For our object recognition problem, the classifier input is composed of several numerical attributes (color and texture) computed for each objet (region) in the image. SVM [13,14] is one of the most efficient classification methods, because the separation between classes is optimized depending of *kernel* functions (linear, polynomials, Gaussian radial basis function, etc.). Like NNs, SVMs are a discriminative supervised machine learning technology, i.e. they need training with labeled empirical data in order to learn the classification.

The region attributes we described in section 3 ($\mathbb{R}^{10}$ vector) were used to build the training sets (classes) considering the selected texture operator along the eight basic possible directions $\{(i,j)\}_{(i,j)\in\{-1,0,1\}/\{(0,0)\}}$ for the δx and δy relative displacements. The final texture value is obtained by the mean of those eight values. The idea is to avoid any preferential direction in the construction of the training set. However, in the classification step, we have chosen only one direction, $\delta x = \delta y = 1$, in order to speed up the identification stage.

The database we get is pre-processed and filtered by the Independent Component Analysis technique. The Support Vector Machines[13] technique has been efficiently evaluated and gave very good results. However, we have found that it is not very versatile to cope with periodic database updates due to its slow learning convergence with our database. Last, note that for our specific problem, we have used a third degree polynomial optimization kernel function into the SVM implementation.

5 Independent Component Analysis

Recently, blind source separation by ICA has attracted a great deal of attention because of its potential applications in medical signal processing (EEG and MEG Data), speech recognition systems, telecommunications, financial analysis, image processing and *feature extraction*. ICA assumes that signals are generated by several (independent) sources, whose properties are unknown but merely assumed non-Gaussian distributed. The goal of this statistical method is to transform an observed multidimensional random vector into components that are statistically as independent from each other as possible [15]. In other words, "ICA is a way of finding a linear non-orthogonal co-ordinate system in any multivariate data". Theoretically speaking, ICA has a number of advantages over PCA and can be seen as its generalization.

Definition 1. *ICA feature extraction of random data vector* $\mathbf{x} = (x_1, x_2, ..., x_d)^t$ *of size d consists in finding a transform matrix* $W \in \mathbb{R}^{m \times d}$ *such that the components of transformed vector are as independent as possible. We assume that* $\mathbf{x}$ *is the linear mixture of m independent sources* $\mathbf{s} = (s_1, s_2, ..., s_m)^t$ *without loss of generality,*

$$\mathbf{x} = \mathbf{As} = \sum_{i=1}^{m} a_i s_i \ , \tag{6}$$

$\mathbf{A} \in \mathbb{R}^{d \times m}$ *is an unknown matrix called mixing/feature matrix and the source* s_i *has zero mean. The columns of* $\mathbf{A}$ *represent features; we denote them by* a_j *and* s_i *signals the amplitude of the ith feature in the observed data x.*

If we choose the independent components s_i *to have a unit variance,* $E\{S_i S_i^t\} = 1$, $i = 1, 2, ..., n$, *it will make independent components unique, except for their signs. So the problem of ICA feature extraction can be seen as to estimate both A and s by the following linear transform from* $\mathbf{x}$,

$$\mathbf{s} = \mathbf{Wx} \ . \tag{7}$$

The statistical model in equation 7 is called independent component analysis, or ICA model. Indeed, it is sufficient to estimate A because the estimate of W is the pseudoinverse of A.

Generally, it is very useful to apply some preprocessing techniques to the data in order to make the ICA estimation simpler and better conditioned:

1. Centering x, i.e. subtract its mean vector $x = x - E\{x\}$.
2. Whitening x, by which we linearly transform x into a "white" vector $\tilde{x}$ which has uncorrelated components and with unitary variances $E\{\tilde{x}\tilde{x}^t\} = I$.

Singular Valor Decomposition (SVD) is usually used to obtain the whitened matrices in ICA procedures. Lately, there have been considerable research interest and many fundamental algorithms [15,7] have been proposed to extract efficiently the ICA basis from the data features. Hyvärinen et al. [8], introduce a fixed-point iteration scheme to find the local extrema of the kurtosis $(kurt(x) = E\{x^4\} - 3\left(E\{x^2\}\right)^2)$ of a linear combination of the observed variables x. This algorithm has evolved (fastICA algorithm) using a practical optimization on the contrast functions. These are derived by the maximization of the negentropy [2] relationship. Negentropy of a random vector x with probability density $f(x)$ is defined as follows

$$J(x) = \int f(x) log f(x) dx - \int f(x_{gauss}) log f(x_{gauss}) dx \ , \qquad (8)$$

where $x_g auss$ is a Gaussian random variable of the same covariance matrix as x. FastICA can also be derived as an approximative Newton iteration, see [8] for further details. This fixed point approach was adopted in this paper.

SVM method has been trained using the ICA representation of all database classes. ICA-based recognition procedure is fairly similar to the PCA application methodology. Initially, the unlabeled vector (color and texture attributes) computed for each region in the segmented image is normalized (centered, whitened). It is projected into each ICA subspace (ICA representation for each predefined database class must be available). The projection is simply an inner product between the input vector and each projection bases,

$$\mathbf{s} = \mathbf{W}\left(\mathbf{x} - \mathbf{E}\{\mathbf{x}\}\right) \ . \qquad (9)$$

Thus, the input projected vectors can be identified comparing them with the ICA database basis using the Support Vector Machines classifier. Next section presents some experimental results obtained for natural scene modeling.

6   Scene Model Generation

The user must define a priori how many classes will be interesting for his application. Obviously, this class selection depends on the environment type. In

---

[2] This measure of nongaussianity is always non-negative and it has the additional interesting property that is invariant for invertible linear transformations.

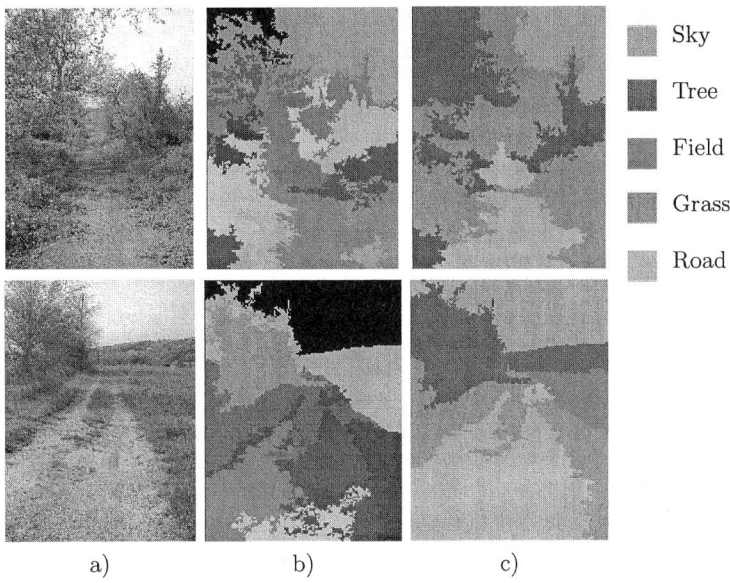

Sky

Tree

Field

Grass

Road

Fig. 2. Natural scene modeling. a) Outdoor color image, b) Region based segmented image and c) 2-D Final scene model.

our experiments, we have selected 7 classes, Sky, Field, GRASS, Tree, ROCKS, Water and Wood. These database classes have been carefully filled up using the color and texture information obtained from the learning images. Moreover, this supervised database was processed using ICA in order to feed up the training SVM procedure.

Usually, the color segmentation methods generates over-segmented images thus a fusion phase is needed. In our methodology, that phase must merge all the neighbor regions with the same texture and color characteristics (same nature). In order to complete the fusion, we need to use the results from the characterization and classification stages. This process gives us an image with only the most representative regions in the scene.

In the table 1 is shown the confusion matrix for the most representatives label classes in our experiments. These results have been computed using ICA and SVM recognition procedures. It is important to notice that large regions are more reliably classified than small regions.

In the evaluation stage, we have analyzed 2868 regions obtained from 82 test images. In these images, 2590 regions were identified as belonging to one of the proposed classes, i.e. 462 regions were correctly labeled as "road", 43 "road" regions are incorrectly detected as "Tree" and 17 "Rocks" regions were mislabeled. Furthermore, 2242 regions were correctly identified and 278 regions were non-classified (outliers) by the SVM technique. Apart from the classes "Wood" and "Water", for which there are very few samples available, all the classes were classified very accurately. Using a preprocessing stage with ICA gives us a relative better score than PCA. In training and testing the classifier we have

Table 1. Confusion Matrix for Region Classification Using Color and Texture.

Classes	Tree	Sky	Grass	Road	Field	Water	Rocks	Success
Tree	613	7	64	58	3	0	32	78.89 %
Sky	12	163	0	0	0	1	0	92.61 %
Grass	69	0	934	8	1	2	0	92.11 %
Road	43	0	0	462	5	0	1	90.41 %
Field	0	0	1	3	23	0	0	85.18 %
Water	2	2	1	0	0	6	0	54.55 %
Rocks	11	5	0	17	0	0	41	55.41 %

only used regions corresponding to the 7 classes. In systems having less set of classes it would be necessary to include a further class for unknown objects.

In our experiments, a standard 400×300 pixels color image was processed by the color segmentation algorithm in about 80 ms on a Sparc Station 5. Some preliminary results are shown in the figure 2 where the classification ICA/SVM was applied to it. The recognition results using the SVM method are the following: a recognition rate of 80%, without data pre-processing, 83.35% using with PCA and 86.56% using ICA preprocessing. The total execution time including all the stages has taken less than 1.0 s per image. The test images were taken in spring scenes with different illumination conditions. It is particularly important in applications as automatic vehicles and robotics to dispose of a visual model of the environment. Thus, the good recognition rate obtained with the road zones may be exploited to complement the visual navigation systems.

7   Conclusions

We have presented an approach for the detection of navigation zones in outdoor natural images (earthed roads, planar regions, etc) relying on a robust, modular, fast color image interpretation scheme in the Ohta/Gevers color space. Using color segmentation, we get the principal components (regions, objects) of the image. These regions are characterized by their color and texture distribution. Independent Component Analysis allows us to construct and filter a robust database so that redundancy is reduced and recognition rate is improved.

We have used the SVM and ICA methods to classify the representative vector ($\mathbb{R}^{10}$) extracted from each region in the image. A complete 2-D model of the outdoor natural images is built with very good results (success of 86.56%). We have also observed that using ICA instead of PCA leads to better recognition rates. Using PCA with SVM also gave us good results because SVMs are relatively insensitive to the representation space. Moreover, ACI algorithm is more computationally demanding than PCA.

In the future work, we will use powerful shape descriptors and contextual scene analysis in order to add robustness to the recognition phase of objects into the image.

References

1. O. Duda, P.H., Stork, D.G.: Pattern Classification and Scene Analysis. Wiley & sons (1998)
2. Ohta, Y.: Knowledge-Based Interpretation of Outdoor Natural Color Scenes. Research Notes in Artificial Intelligence 4, Pitman Advanced Publishing Program (1985)
3. Comaniciu, D., Meer, P.: Mean shift: A robust approach toward feature space analysis. IEEE Transactions on Pattern Analysis and Machine Intelligence **24** (2002) 603–619
4. Murrieta, R., Parra, C., Devy, M., Briot, M.: Scene modeling from 2d and 3d sensory data acquired from natural environments. In: IEEE The 10th International Conference on Advanced Robotics, Hungary (2001) 221–228
5. Unser, M.: Sum and difference histograms for texture classification. IEEE Transactions on Pattern Analysis and Machine Intelligence **8** (1986) 118–125
6. Murrieta, R., Parra, C., Devy, M., Tovar, B., Esteves, C.: Building multi-level models : From landscapes to landmarks. In: IEEE International Conference on Robotics and Automation, Washington, D.C. (2002) 4346–4353
7. Common, P.: Independent component analysis, a new concept? Signal Processing **36** (1994) 287–314
8. Hyvärinen, A.: Fast and robust fixed-point algorithms for independent component analysis. IEEE Transactions on Neural Networks **10** (1999) 626–634
9. Altunbasak, Y., Eren, P.E., Tekalp, A.M.: Region-based parametric motion segmentation using color information. Graphical Models and Image Processing **60** (1998) 13–23
10. Gevers, T., Smeulders, W.M.: Color based object recognition. Pattern Recognition **32** (1999) 453–464
11. Kittler, J., Illingworth, J.: Minimum error thresholding. Pattern Recognition **19** (1986) 41–47
12. Haralick, R.M.: Statistical and structural approaches to texture. Proceedings of the IEEE **67** (1979) 786–804
13. Boser, B.E., Guyon, I.M., Vapnik, V.N.: A training algorithm for optimal margin classifiers. In: IEEE Transactions on Neural Networks, Fifth Annual Workshop on Computational Learning Theory, PA:ACM (1992) 144–152
14. Vapnik, V.N., Golowich, S.E., Smola, A.J.: Support vector method for function approximation, regression estimation, and signal processing. Advances in Neural Information Processing Systems (NIPS) **9** (1996) 281–287
15. Yuen, P.C., Lai, J.H.: Face representation using independent component analysis. Pattern Recognition **35** (2002) 1247–1257

Non–parametric Registration as a Way to Obtain an Accurate Camera Calibration

Félix Calderón and Leonardo Romero

División de Estudios de Postgrado
Facultad de Ingeniería Eléctrica
Universidad Michoacana de San Nicolás de Hidalgo
Santiago Tapia 403 Morelia. Michoacán. México
{calderon,lromero}@zeus.umich.mx

Abstract. We present the SSD–ARC, a non–parametric registration technique, as an accurate way to calibrate a camera and compare it with some parametric techniques. In the parametric case we obtain a set of thirteen parameters to model the projective and the distortion transformations of the camera and in the non–parametric case we obtain the displacement between pixel correspondences. We found more accuracy in the non–parametric camera calibration than in the parametric techniques. Finally, we introduce the parametrization of the pixel correspondences obtained by the SSD–ARC algorithm and we present an experimental comparison with some parametric calibration methods.

1   Introduction

Most algorithms in 3-D computer vision rely on the pinhole camera model because of its simplicity, whereas video optics, specially wide-angle lens, generate a lot of non–linear distortion. Camera calibration consists in finding the optimal transformation between the 3-D space of the scene and the camera plane. This general transformation can be separated in two different transformations: first, the projective transformation [15] and the distortion transformation [2].

This paper focuses in automatic camera calibration method based on a non–parametric registration technique, named SSD–ARC. We compare our approach with recent parametric techniques given in [17] and [12], obtaining more accurate calibrations with the SSD–ARC approach.

2   Registration Algorithm

Let I_1 and I_2 be a couple of images with gray level pixels. Individual pixels of image I_t are denoted by $I_t(r_i)$ where $r_i = [x_i, y_i]^T$ and r_i is over the lattice L of the image. Let I_1 be a synthetic calibration pattern and I_2 be this pattern viewed by the camera under calibration. We can model the calibration process as finding a set of displacements $V = \{V_1, V_2, \cdots\}$ where $V_i = [u_i, v_i]^T$ is a

R. Monroy et al. (Eds.): MICAI 2004, LNAI 2972, pp. 584–591, 2004.

displacement for one pixel at position $r_i \in I_2$. The goal is to match I_2, after the application of the displacement set V, with I_1:

$$I_1(x_i, y_i) = I_2(x_i + u_i, y_i + v_i) \tag{1}$$

In the literature the are many methods, to solve equation (1), based in first derivatives [3,7,4] and others are based on second derivatives [8,19,20]. They compute the Optical Flow (OF) using Taylor's expansion of (1). In [4] a linear approximation of (1) and a smoothness constrain are used over the magnitude of the displacement gradient $|\nabla V_i|$.

Others use the Sum of Squared Differences (SSD), a measure of proximity between two images which depends on the displacement set V as:

$$SSD(V) = \sum_{i \in L} [I_1(x_i, y_i) - I_2(x_i + u_i, y_i + v_i)]^2 \tag{2}$$

In [16] the authors use the SSD function and an interpolation model based on Splines, they compute the OF and use it in the registration task. Minimization of their function is accomplished using Levenberg–Marquardt's algorithm [13]. In [6] they add, to the SSD function, the same smoothness constrain as in [4] and additionally they normalize the derivatives with respect to the magnitude of the displacement gradient.

In this paper we proposed to use a variant of the SSD function to solve equation (1) and therefore calibrate the camera. First we review briefly, the parametric calibration method presented in [12], then in section 4 we describe our approach. In section 5 we compute a parametric representation of the displacement set V and finally we show an experimental comparison between all these methods.

3   Parametric Camera Calibration

Let $V_i = T(\theta_p, \theta_d, r_i)$ be a parametric representation of the displacement of pixel at location r_i. Where $\theta_p = [\theta_0, ..., \theta_7]$ represents a projective transformation and $\theta_d = [\theta_8, ..., \theta_{12}]$ represents a distortion transformation. Tamaki et al [17] compute the complete transformation in two steps, first they asume a given distortion transformation and then compute the projective transformation that match I_2 into I_1, minimizing a SSD metric. In the second step, they find the inverse distortion transformation minimizing another SSD metric. Finally they apply an iterative procedure in order to find the right distortion transformation. In [18] they do a new presentation of this algorithm, they continue computing the transformation in two steps and introduce the implicit function theorem in order to find the right distortion instead of the inverse distortion transformation. They minimize their SSD function using the Gauss-Newton algorithm. Because they made some approximations in the way to compute the first derivatives of the projective model and they solve the problem in two isolated steps, their method is very sensitive to the initial values.

In [12] they find the complete transformation in one step, thirteen parameters for distortion and projective model using a SSD metric and solve it using the known algorithm Gauss–Newton–Levembert–Maraquart [9]. Their method is more robust, simple and accurate than Tamaki's approaches [17,18].

4   Non–parametric Camera Calibration

In [1] Calderon and Marroquin present an approach based on a physic analogy of the equation SSD which represents the potential energy kept in a set of springs, where the error between the images is represented by the spring deformations. They focus on minimizing the total potential energy given as the sum of the energy in each one of the springs. Because the image noise increase the total energy, they introduce a way to disable the outlier contribution to the global energy, based on the image's gradient magnitude.

They proposed an energy function which is based on a coupling system of springs with an Adaptive Rest Condition(ARC) [10]. The SSD–ARC energy function is:

$$U_{SSD-ARC}(V, l) = \sum_{i \in L} [E(V_i) - l_i H(V_i)]^2 + \frac{\lambda \mu}{4} \sum_{i \in L} |\nabla V_i|^2 + \mu \sum_{i \in L} l_i^2 \quad (3)$$

with

$$H(V_i) = |\nabla I_2 (x_i + u_i, y_i + v_i)|$$

$$E(V_i) = I_1(x_i, y_i) - I_2(x_i + u_i, y_i + v_i)$$

$$l_i = \frac{E(V_i)H(V_i)}{\mu + H^2(V_i)}$$

where $E(V_i)$ is the error term between image I_1 and I_2 which depends of the displacement $V_i = [u_i, v_i]^T$. $H(V_i)$ is the magnitude of the gradient of the image I_2 for a given displacement. The parameter l_i implements the way to exclude the outliers, in other words, exclude pixels with a hight errors. The behavior of this energy function depends on the regularization parameter μ and λ. The parameter μ controls the exclusion of outliers and parameter λ controls the displacement similarity between neighbors.

To minimice $U_{SSD--ARC}$ in equation (3) they used Richardson's iteration (see [5]) and the final solution scheme is :

$$V_i^{k+1} = \overline{V}_i^k - \frac{1}{\lambda} \frac{E(V_i^k)}{\mu + H^2 V_i^k} \nabla E(V_i^k) \quad (4)$$

$$+ \frac{1}{\lambda} \frac{\left[E(V_i^{(k)})\right]^2 H(V_i^{(k)})}{\left[\mu + H^2(V_i^{(k)})\right]^2} \nabla H(V_i^{(k)})$$

Fig. 1. Synthetic image pattern (left) and the correspondent camera image (right)

Where $\overline{V}_i$ is the average displacement computed as: $\overline{V}_i = V(x_{i+1}, y_i) + V(x_{i-1}, y_i) + V(x_i, y_{i+1}) + V(x_i, y_{i-1})$ (see [1] for details).

In order to have a better performance, for the SSD–ARC, they use the scale-space (coarse to fine strategy) [11].

We propose to use SSD–ARC as a non–parametric calibration technique. In some applications the set of displacement V is enough to solve the calibration problem. However if you want to correct only the distortion of the image, without the projective transformation, a further step is needed. In the following section we use the displacement set V to compute a parametric representation for the distortion transformation and then we are able to undistort the images.

5   Point Correspondences Method

To find the thirteen parameters of the projective and distortion transformation, given the set of displacement V computed by SSD–ARC, we use the Point Correspondences Method (PC), described in [12]. They use a SSD metric based on the Euclidian distance and minimice the resulting error function using the Gauss–Newton–Levenberg–Marquard method [9]. We name this algorithm SSD–ARC–pc.

The algorithm is as follows:

1.- Compute the set of displacements V using the SSD–ARC.

2.- Estimate θ_d using the PC method. Discard θ_p

An interesting variant of this method is to take a subset of V instead of the whole set V. Since the calibration pattern has a regular pattern (rectangles) a natural choice is to select only conner points. We denoted this variant of the method as SSD–ARC–pc*.

6   Experimental Results

We test a Fire-i400 firewire industrial color camera from Unibrain with 4.00 mm C-mount lens. This camera acquire 30 fps with resolution of 640x480 pixels.

Table 1. SSD errors for the parametric and the non–parametric algorithms

Algorithm	Scales	Time (sec.)	Error
SSD–ARC-pc	1	92.469	15456.726
Tamaki	3	163.844	15263.134
Romero	1	57.000	14820.000
SSD–ARC–pc*	1	79.469	14512.966
SSD–ARC	4	60.469	11847.001

Table 2. Calibration results from the parametric approaches

Parameter	SSD − ARC − pc	Tamaki	Romero	SSD − ARC − pc*
θ_0	1.056	1.0560	1.0431	1.0447
θ_1	0.0408	0.0586	0.0433	0.0427
θ_2	-22.6761	-20.7956	-19.5562	-18.4801
θ_3	-0.0156	-0.0108	-0.0172	-0.0144
θ_4	1.0488	1.0696	1.0470	1.0515
θ_5	3.7795	0.8944	4.3369	3.4368
θ_6	3.4405e-5	-5.3654e-5	2.8627e-5	4.1702e-5
θ_7	6.2721e-5	-1.2009e-4	6.7935e-5	6.7851e-5
θ_8	-8.2396e-7	4.9466e-7	-7.8158e-7	-8.0626e-7
θ_9	1.2537e-12	3.1922e-12	7.1399e-13	9.9604e-13
θ_{10}	311.12427	320.71564	307.9092	313.8008
θ_{11}	203.4334	236.0663	208.59712	208.0083
θ_{12}	1.0092	1.0089	0.9983	0.9916

The pattern calibration showed in the figure 1 was made using xfig program under Linux and the image taken by the camera is shown in the same figure.

In order to have a reference about the performance of our methods we tested the parametric algorithms described by Tamaki [17], Romero [12] versus SSD–ARC (section 4), SSD–ARC–pc and SSD–ARC–pc* (section 5) using the two images showed in figure 1.

The error measure, in all cases, was the SSD function given by equation (2). Table 1 shows results for these algorithms including the number of scales used by the algorithm and the computation time (Pentium IV 1.6 Ghz). The final parameters computed by each method are showed in table 2. Note that Tamaki [17] algorithm compute the inverse transformation and you can observe this fact in the sign of parameter θ_8. Note that the least error was given by the non–parametric algorithm SSD–ARC. Nevertheless, when we parameterized this solution (SSD–ARC–pc* algorithm) we have a significant increment in the total error. You can check this fact in the table 1 in the rows for SSD–ARC and SSD–ARC–pc. Also observe that SSD–ARC–pc* algorithm gives better results than SSD–ARC–pc, because displacement of corners are more reliable than other displacement of pixels. In other words, corners are good feature points to track [14].

A visual comparison for all these methods is showed in figure 2. Each image is formed by the squared differences between the calibration pixels of the pattern

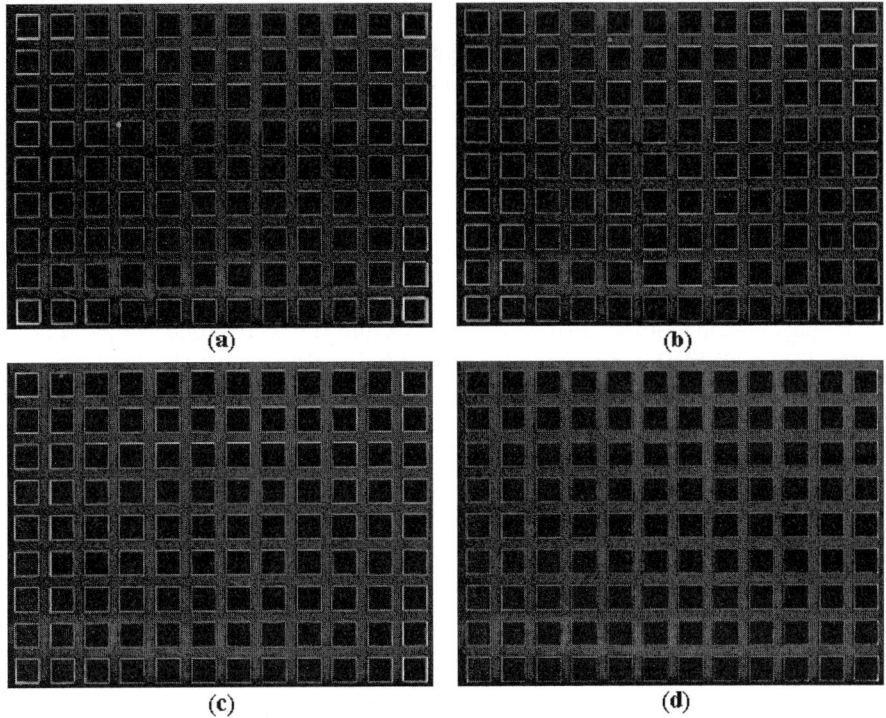

Fig. 2. Error images for the algorithms a) SSD–ARC–pc, b) Tamaki, c) SSD–ARC–pc* and d) SSD–ARC

Fig. 3. Images from our laboratory. Original image taken by the camera (left), and undistorted image computed by SSD–ARC (right)

image and the corrected camera image. A perfect match would give a black image and lighter pixels correspond to higher differences. The best match is given by SSD–ARC followed by SSD–ARC–pc*. The worst match is given by SSD–ARC–pc specially on the corners of the image. The SSD–ARC non–parametric approach has a better correction of the non–linear distortion introduced by the lens, than parametric approaches presented in this paper.

Finally figure 3 show an image of our laboratory taken by the camera and results applying the SSD–ARC approach described in this paper. Note the correction specially at the top of the image and left and right sites.

7   Conclusions

We have presented two methods to solve the calibration problem, the first one is a non–parametric method, named SSD–ARC, and the second one is a parametric method, named SSD–ARC–pc. The SSD–ARC method gave the least error in the comparison with other methods. The SSD–ARC–pc* merges the parametric and non–parametric calibration methods. We found more accurate results using the corners points of the images instead of all the points and also a slightly error reduction compared with results from [12].

In some application, for instance in stereo vision systems, the images corrected by SSD–ARC could be the images of rectified cameras (the optical axes are parallel and there are not rotations). The SSD–ARC approach is specially valuable when you use cheap lens with a high non–linear distortion, where, the parametric approaches could have a poor accuracy. The non–parametric approach also could be used with wide angle lens or even with eye fish lens. In contrast, parametric approaches need to increase the number of parameters with cameras using large wide angle lens or eye fish lens.

We plan to use the SSD–ARC algorithm with cameras, using large wide angle lens, in order to build a stereo vision system for a mobile robot.

Acknowledgements. This research has been supported in part by CIC-UMSNH grants 10.6 and 10.9.

References

1. Felix Calderon and Jose Luis Marroquin. Un nuevo algoritmo para calculo de flujo optico y su aplicación al registro de imagenes. *Computacion y Sistemas*, 6(3):213–226, 2003.
2. Oliver Faugeras. *Three-Dimensional Computer Vision*. MIT Press., 1999.
3. C. Fennema and W. Thompson. Velocity determination in scenes containing several moving objects. *Comput. Graph. Image Process*, 9:301–315, 1979.
4. Berthold Klaus Paul Horn. *Robot Vision*. MIT Press, Cambridge, Massachusetts, second edition, 1986. Chapter 12.
5. C. T. Kelley. *Iterative Methods for Linear and Nonlinear Equations*, volume 16. Society for Industrial and Applied Mathematics. SIAM, Philadelphia. USA, 1995.
6. Shang-Hong Lai and Baba C. Vemuri. Reliable and efficient computation of optical flow. *International Journal of Computer Vision*, 29(2):87–105, 1998.
7. H. H. Nagel. Displacement vectors derived from second-order intensity variations in image sequences. *Comput. Graph. Image Process*, 21:85–117, 1983.

8. H H Nagel. On the estimation of optical flow: Relations between different approaches and some new results. *Artificial Intelligence*, 33:299–324, 1987.

9. W. Press, B. Flannery, S. Teukolsky, and W. Vetterling. *Numerical Recipies, the Art of Scientific Computing.* Cambrige University Press., 1986.

10. Mariano Rivera and Jose L. Marroquin. The adaptive rest-condition spring system: An edge-preserving regularization techique. *IEEE Int. Conf. on Image Processing (ICIP-2000), IEEE Signal Processing Society, Vancouver, BC, Canada*, II:805–807, September 2000.

11. Bart M. Ter Haar Romeny. *Geometry-Driven Diffusion in Computer Vision.* Kluwer Academic Publishers, Dordrecht, The Netherlands, 1994.

12. Leonardo Romero and Felix Calderon. Correcting radial lens distortion using image and point correspondece. In *CIARP 2003*, La Havana, Cuba, November 2003. Springer Verlag.

13. L. E. Scales. *Introduction to Non-Linear Optimization.* Department of Computer Science University of Liverpool, Liverpool. UK, 1984.

14. Jianbo Shi and Carlo Tomasi. Good features to track. *IEEE Conference on Computer Vision and Pattern Recognition CVPR94*, pages 593–600, 1994.

15. Richard Szeliski. Video mosaic for virtual enviornmests. *IEICE computer Graphics Application*, 16:22–30, 1996.

16. Richard Szeliski and James Coughlan. Spline-based image registration. Technical Report 94/1, Harvard University, Department of Physics, Cambridge, Ma 02138, April 1994.

17. Toru Tamaki, Tsuyoshi, and Noburu Ohnishi. An automatic camera calibration method with image registration technique. In *SCI2000*, pages 317–322, 2000.

18. Toru Tamaki, Tsuyoshi Yamamura, and Noboru Ohnishi. An automatic camara calibration methos with image registration thecnique. In *ACCV2002*, volume 1, pages 23–25, 2002.

19. O Tretiak and L Pastor. Velocity estimation from image sequences with second order differential operators. *Proc. 7th Intern. Conf. Patt. Recog. Montreal*, pages 20–22, 1984.

20. S Uras, F Girosi, A Verri, and V Torre. A computational approach to motion perception. *Biol. Cybern*, 60:79–97, 1988.

A Probability-Based Flow Analysis Using MV Information in Compressed Domain

N.W. Kim, T.Y. Kim, and J.S. Choi

Department of Image Engineering, Graduate School of
Advanced Imaging Science, Multimedia, and Film, Chung-Ang University
{mysope,kimty,jschoi}@imagelab.cau.ac.kr

Abstract. In this paper, we propose a method that utilizes the motion vectors (MVs) in MPEG sequence as the motion depicter for representing video contents. We convert the MVs to a uniform MV set, independent of the frame type and the direction of prediction, and then make use of them as motion depicter in each frame. To obtain such uniform MV set, we proposed a new motion analysis method using Bi-directional Prediction-Independent Framework (BPIF). Our approach enables a frame-type independent representation that normalizes temporal features including frame type, MB encoding and MVs. Our approach is directly processed on the MPEG bitstream after VLC decoding. Experimental results show that our method has the good performance, the high validity, and the low time consumption.

1 Introduction

A huge volume of information requires the concise feature representations. The motion feature of them provides the easiest access to its temporal features, and is hence the key significance in video indexing and video retrieval. That is the reason that the motion-based video analysis has received large attention in video databases research [1, 2, 3].

In the area of motion-based video analysis, many researchers have followed methods of motion analysis such as optical flow popular in computer vision and block matching popular in image coding literature. Cherfaoui and Bertin [4] have suggested the shot motion classification scheme that computes global motion parameters for the camera following an optical flow computation scheme. An example of block matching based motion classification scheme is the work of Zhang et al. [5] that carry out motion classification by computing the direction of motion vectors and the point of convergence or divergence. Noting that using the motion vectors embedded in P and B frames can avoid expensive optic flow or block matching computation, several researchers have stated exploring shot motion characterization of MPEG clips [6][7]. Kobla [8] have proposed the use of flow information to analyze the independent frame-type pattern (i.e., the pattern of I, P, and B frames) in the MPEG stream. But, it has a problem that flow estimation is considered by only single-directional prediction in most frames.

In this paper, we propose the motion analysis method that normalizes MVs in MPEG domain using Bi-directional Prediction-Independent Framework. The

R. Monroy et al. (Eds.): MICAI 2004, LNAI 2972, pp. 592–601, 2004.

normalized MVs (N-MVs) enable accurate video analysis which is useful in contexts where motion has a rich meaning. We have a purpose in constructing an effective and comprehensive motion field by making up for the week point in current sparse motion field. From such process, the N-MVs by *BPIF* can be utilized as motion depicter to efficiently characterize motion feature of video, and as feature information for global camera motion estimation in each frame, video surveillance system, video indexing and video retrieval.

The remainder of the paper is organized as follows. In the next section, we propose the motion analysis method using *BPIF* in compressed domain and establish the active boundary for the proposed one. In Section 3, experimental results will be demonstrated to corroborate the proposed method. Finally, we conclude this paper in Section 4.

2 Motion Analysis Using Bi-directional Prediction-Independent Framework

An MB in MPEG sequence can have zero, one, or two MVs depending on its frame type and its prediction direction [9]. Moreover, these MVs can be forward-predicted or backward-predicted with respect to reference frames which may or may not occur adjacent to the frame including the MB. We therefore require the more uniform set of MVs, independent of the frame type and the direction of prediction. Our approach in this paper involves representing each MV as the backward-predicted vector with respect to the next frame, independent of the frame type.

2.1 Motion Flow Estimation

Let us consider two consecutive reference frames, R_i and R_j. Let the B frames between them be denoted by $B_1,...,B_n$, where n is the number of B frames between two reference frames (typically, $n=2$). From the mutual relation among frames, we can represent each MV as a backward-predicted vector with respect to the next frame, independent of the frame type [8][10]. Roughly, this algorithm consists of following two steps.

Motion Flow for R_i and B_n Frame. We derive the flow between the first reference frame R_i and its next frame B_1 using the forward-predicted MVs of B_1. Then, we can derive the flow, B_n, using the backward-predicted MVs between the second reference frame R_j and the previous frame B_n. Intuitively, if the MB in the B_1 frame, $B_{1(u,v)}$, is displaced by the MV (x, y) with respect to the MB in the R_i frame, $R_{i(u,v)}$, then it is logical to conjecture that the latter MB is displaced by the MV (-x, -y) with respect to $B_{1(u,v)}$, where u and v denote the indices of the current MB in the array of MBs. Therefore, the flow for the R_i frame is obtained by the MV with respect to the MB in the B_1 frame. Also, the motion flow in the B_n frame is estimated by using the similar method as described above [8].

But, these algorithms have the problem that the number of extracted N-MVs is not enough to represent each frame. The motion flow for the R_i frame uses only forward-predicted vectors in B frames and the motion flow for the B_n frame uses only backward-predicted vectors in R_j frames. It means that this method has considered only single-directional prediction to estimate the motion flow for R_i and B_n frames.

Our approach to compensate the above problem is to implement a bi-directional motion analysis algorithm using forward-predicted motion vector from R_i to R_j, free from the limitation of single-directional motion analysis (see Fig. 1). The number of N-MVs in motion flow for the R_i frame can be improved by using both the backward-predicted MV from the R_j frame to the B_1 frame and the forward-predicted MV from the R_i frame to the R_j frame, in contrast with the conventional algorithm which only uses the forward-predicted MV in the B_1 frame to estimate the motion flow in the R_i frame. To derive the motion flow for B_n is almost similar to the estimation method in R_i frame.

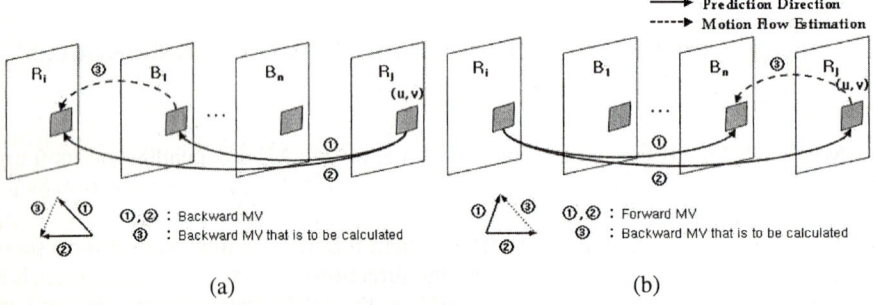

Fig. 1. Flow estimation. (a) Flow estimation of MVs in R_i frames. (b) Flow estimation of MVs in B_n frames.

The numerical formula is expressed in Eq. (1) and Eq. (2). Let the backward-predicted MV in $B_{1(u,v)}$ be denoted by $\overrightarrow{B_1R_j}$. And let the forward-predicted MV from $R_{i(u,v)}$ to $R_{j(u,v)}$ be denoted by $\overrightarrow{R_iR_j}$. Then, we can calculate $\overrightarrow{R_iB_1}$, the motion flow in R_i frame, as

$$\overrightarrow{R_iR_j} \equiv \overrightarrow{R_iB_1} + \overrightarrow{B_1R_j} . \tag{1}$$

And, if we denote the forward-predicted MV in $B_{n(u,v)}$ by $\overrightarrow{R_iB_n}$, then, we can obtain the motion flow, $\overrightarrow{B_nR_j}$, from the relationship as follows :

$$\overrightarrow{R_iR_j} \equiv \overrightarrow{R_iB_n} - \overrightarrow{B_nR_j} . \tag{2}$$

Fig. 1-(a) and Fig. 1-(b) show motion analysis method using *BPIF* in R_i and B_n frame, respectively. The solid line represents the direction of the real MV, and the dotted line shows the direction of the re-estimated MV. We derive the more elaborate motion flow in R_i and B_n frame by using Eq. (1) and Eq. (2).

Motion Flow for $B_1 \sim B_{n-1}$ Frame. The motion flow between successive B frames is derived by analyzing corresponding MBs in those B frames and their motion vectors with respect to their reference frames. Since each MB in each B frame can be of one of three types, namely forward-predicted (*F*), backward-predicted (*B*), or bidirectional-predicted (*D*), there exist nine possible combinations. Here, we represent these nine pairs by FF, FB, FD, BF, BB, BD, DF, DB, and DD. Each of these nine combinations is considered individually, and flow is estimated between them by analyzing each of the MVs with respect to the reference frame. The algorithm is divided into following four parts by combinations of corresponding MBs in successive *B* frames.

> *Case 1*) when corresponding MBs have forward- + forward-predicted MV
>   : FF, FD, DF, DD ;
> *Case 2*) when corresponding MBs have backward- + backward-predicted MV
>   : BB, BD, DB ;
> *Case 3*) when corresponding MBs have forward- + backward-predicted MV : FB ;
> *Case 4*) when corresponding MBs have backward- + forward-predicted MV : BF ;

The motion flow estimation method in Case 1 and Case 2 of above four cases is obtained by similar method to it in R_i or B_n frame. Let the forward-predicted MV in $B_{k(u,v)}$ be denoted by $\overrightarrow{R_iB_k}$, and let the backward-predicted MV in $B_{k+1(u,v)}$ be denoted by $\overrightarrow{B_{k+1}R_j}$. Fig. 2-(a) and Eq. (3) expresses the motion flow in Case 1. The figure and the numerical formula in Case 2 are described in Fig. 2-(b) and Eq. (4), respectively.

$$-\overrightarrow{B_{k+1}R_i} \equiv \overrightarrow{R_iB_k} + \overrightarrow{B_kB_{k+1}} \tag{3}$$

$$\overrightarrow{B_kR_j} \equiv \overrightarrow{B_kB_{k+1}} + \overrightarrow{B_{k+1}R_j} . \tag{4}$$

To derive the motion flow in Case 3 and Case 4, we reuse the forward-predicted MV from the R_i frame to the R_j frame, $\overrightarrow{R_iR_j}$. In Case 3, the motion flow, $\overrightarrow{B_kB_{k+1}}$, is derived by $\overrightarrow{B_{k+1}R_j}$, $\overrightarrow{R_iB_k}$, and $\overrightarrow{R_iR_j}$. This case is shown in Fig. 2-(c) and expressed in Eq. (5).

$$\overrightarrow{R_iR_j} - \overrightarrow{R_iB_k} \equiv \overrightarrow{B_kB_{k+1}} + \overrightarrow{B_{k+1}R_j} . \tag{5}$$

And, if we denote the motion flow between $R_{i(u,v)}$ and $B_{k+1(u,v)}$ by $\overrightarrow{R_iB_{k+1}}$, and between $B_{k(u,v)}$ and $R_{j(u,v)}$ by $\overrightarrow{B_kR_j}$, we can calculate $\overrightarrow{B_kB_{k+1}}$, by using $\overrightarrow{R_iB_{k+1}}$ and $\overrightarrow{B_kR_j}$, which is the motion flow in Case 4. This structure is shown in Fig. 2-(d). We can obtain Eq. (6) and Eq. (7) by the analysis of the flow and Eq. (8) is deducted from these equations.

$$\overrightarrow{R_iR_j} \equiv \overrightarrow{R_iB_k} + \overrightarrow{B_kR_j} \tag{6}$$

$$\overrightarrow{R_iB_{k+1}} \equiv \overrightarrow{B_kB_{k+1}} + \overrightarrow{R_iB_k} \tag{7}$$

$$\overrightarrow{R_iR_j} - \overrightarrow{R_iB_{k+1}} \equiv \overrightarrow{B_kR_j} - \overrightarrow{B_kB_{k+1}} . \tag{8}$$

2.2   Active Boundary of the Proposed Method

The flow estimation method in this paper works on the assumption that 'if $Q_{(u1,v1)}$ which is the MB in the non-reference frame Q has the MV (x, y), it is equivalent that $R_{(u2,v2)}$ which is the MB in the reference frame R is moved by the MV (x, y) to $Q_{(u1,v1)}$'.

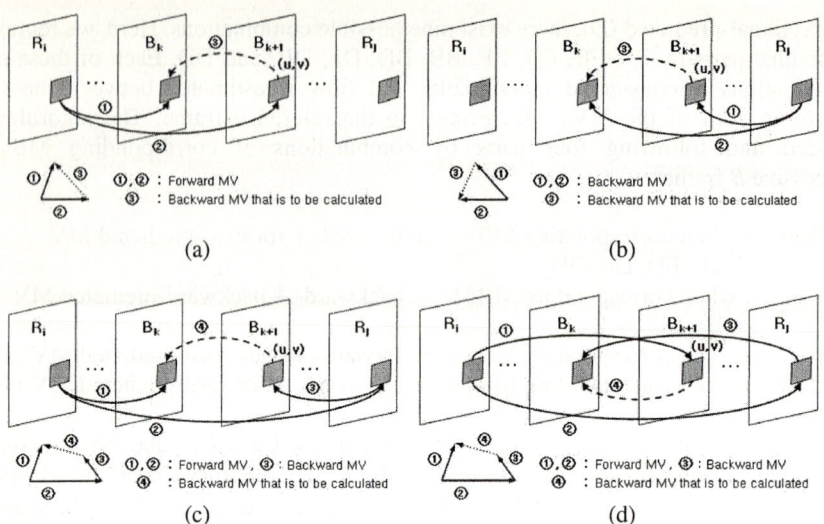

Fig. 2. Flow estimation of MVs in $B_1 \sim B_{n-1}$ frames. (a)~(d) Flow estimation of MVs from case 1 to case 4, successively.

However, it should be mentioned that it may always not be appropriate to use the MVs in same MB (u_1, v_1) over Q and R frames. That is, a problem is occurred by the following fact; if $Q_{(u1,v1)}$ has the MV (x, y), it is the MV predicted not by $R_{(u2,v2)}$, but by $R_{(u1,v1)}$ as Fig. 3-(a). When $R_{(u2,v2)}$ moves to Q frame by the MV (x, y), the corresponding MB is actually $Q_{(u2,v2)}$. Therefore, to satisfy the above assumption, the error distance, $\mathfrak{D}$, should be minimized as shown Fig. 3-(b). Namely, most of the MVs in compressed domain should be within the error distance, $\mathfrak{D}$. To verify this supposition, we calculate the MV histogram and the normal distribution of MV from various types of video scenes. A random variable $\mathfrak{D}$ has a normal distribution if its probability density function is

$$p(\mathfrak{D}) = (2\pi\sigma^2)^{-\frac{1}{2}} exp\left[-(\mathfrak{D}-M)^2 / 2\sigma^2\right] \qquad for \ -\infty < \mathfrak{D} < \infty.$$

The normal probability density function has two parameters M(mean) and σ(standard deviation). Fig. 4 shows the result of the normal distribution in various sequence such as news, movies, and music videos. Table 1 represents the numerical result. The normal distribution is differently calculated by the maximum value of the error distance which is smaller than the block size ($-8 \leq \mathfrak{D} \leq 8$) or the MB size ($-16 \leq \mathfrak{D} \leq 16$). If the error distance is within the block size, the distance between $R_{(u1,v1)}$ and $R_{(u2,v2)}$ which is the corresponding MB of $Q_{(u1,v1)}$ will be smaller than the block size. Therefore, any neighbor MBs except $R_{(u2,v2)}$ doesn't include the area of $R_{(u1,v1)}$ as much as $R_{(u2,v2)}$ (Fig. 3-(c)). For this case, our assumption for the corresponding MBs can be regarded as appropriate.

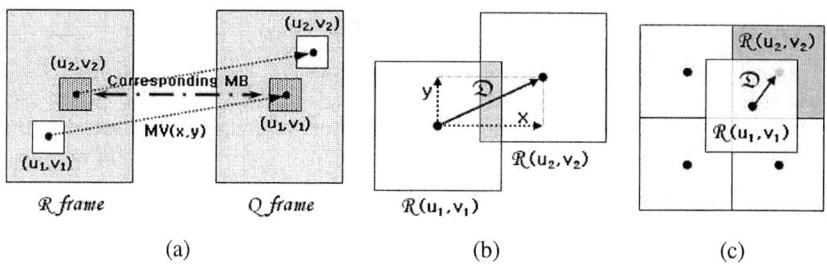

Fig. 3. Error estimation. (a) MB mismatching. (b) Error distance. (c) MB matching.

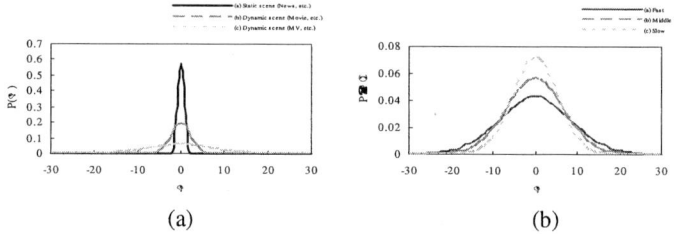

Fig. 4. Normal Distribution. (a) Various scenes. (b) Music video scenes.

As described in Table 1, most of compressed videos have the small motion under the block size. Except the fast scenes like as music videos, the probability that the MVs in sequence are less than the block size is more than 99%. In music videos, in case of the middle speed scenes, the probability that the MVs are smaller than the block size is over 80%. But, as shown in Table 1, the probability that motion is smaller than the block size is under 70% in music videos with fast scenes. That is, the application of the proposed method in fast scenes has the limitation, when standard deviation is approximately over 7. Nevertheless, the proposed method is clearly available for the image analysis in global motion characterization, not in the local motion characterization in each frame. That is because the maximum motion of MVs hardly strays off MB size.

Table 1. Normal distribution of MV.

		M	σ	$P(-8 \leq \mathcal{D} \leq 8)$	$P(-16 \leq \mathcal{D} \leq 16)$
	News	0.03	0.69	0.99	0.99
	Movies	0.05	2.04	0.99	0.99
Music Videos	Fast	−0.98	9.05	0.68	0.94
	Middle	−0.53	6.99	0.79	0.98
	Slow	−0.38	5.48	0.89	0.99

3 Experimental Results

In this chapter, we present the effectiveness and performance for the proposed motion flow method. As for the test sequences, our experimental database consists of MPEG-1 coded video sequences, which have the various camera work and object motion.

Comparison of the Number of N-MVs. To evaluate the effectiveness of the estimation, we provide ground truth and compare it to the results from the flow estimation steps. Using the original uncompressed image frames, we encode the frames into MPEG files, which all B frames are replaced by P frames using a MPEG encoder. IBBPBB ordering (IPB encoded frame), for example, then becomes IPPPPP ordering (IPP encoded frame). We apply our flow estimation steps to the files in IPB format, and we compare the flow vectors of the frames between the two encodings.

The number of N-MVs in our approach has increased over 18% than it in [8] as listed in Table 2. In detail, the number of N-MVs in R_i, $B_1 \sim B_{n-1}$ and B_n obtained by the proposed method has increased over 8%, 6%, and 44%, respectively. Especially, the number of N-MVs has markedly increased in B_n frame. This result originates in the fact that most of the MBs in B_n frames have forward-predicted motion vector from R_i rather than backward-predicted motion vector from R_j. The more the B_n frame has a lot of forward-predicted motion vectors, the better the performance of the proposed algorithm is.

$$MV\ Detected\ Ratio = \frac{Number\ of\ MV\ in\ IPB\ frame}{Number\ of\ MV\ in\ IPP\ frame}$$

MV detected ratio (MDR) has been calculated by the comparison of the number of N-MVs between IPP encoded frames and IPB encoded frames. This is not considered whether the MVs extracted from the two encodings are identical in the directions of the corresponding MBs or not.

The Verification of the Validity for N-MVs. The effectiveness of the proposed method isn't verified by the increase of the number of N-MVs. For the verification, we have compared the directions of the corresponding MBs. At first, we quantize the vectors of the two encodings in the several principal directions (presently 4 bins), and compare them. If they have the identical principle direction, we regard them in IPB encoded frame as the effective MVs. Using these effective MVs, we can obtain the MV effective ratio (MER).

$$MV\ Effective\ Ratio = \frac{Number\ of\ Effective\ MV\ in\ IPB\ frame}{Number\ of\ MV\ in\ IPP\ frame}$$

The result of the experiments that verifies the validity of N-MVs is numerically summarized in Table 3. Examples of flow estimation are shown in Fig. 5. Fig. 5-(b) is a MB image that is derived from re-encoded IPP format files. Fig. 5-(c) and Fig. 5-(d) are its corresponding MB images from the IPB encoded streams. Fig. 5-(c) and Fig. 5-(d) show the MV flows in the proposed method and in Kobla's method, respectively. Being compared with Fig. 5-(b) which is the ground truth, we can see that the more accurate flow estimation is accomplished in the proposed method, not in Kobla's method. The shade of the MB in Fig. 5 represents the direction of the flow vector. Fig. 6 is the comparison result of the MV histogram in IPB sequence and IPP sequence. To investigate the accurate result, we quantize the MVs in more fine directions. The simulation result shows our approach is closer to the ground truth sequence which is IPP encoded frame.

Table 2. Comparison of MDR.

	Proposed method		Kobla's method [8]	
	Avg. MV num	MDR	Avg. MV num	MDR
R_i frame	198	0.71	176	0.63
B_i frame	216	0.78	199	0.71
B_n frame	219	0.79	98	0.35
Total frame	212	0.76	163	0.58

Table 3. Comparison of MER.

	Proposed method	Kobla's method [8]
R_i frame	0.88	0.81
B_i frame	0.75	0.60
B_n frame	0.82	0.43
Total frame	0.81	0.61

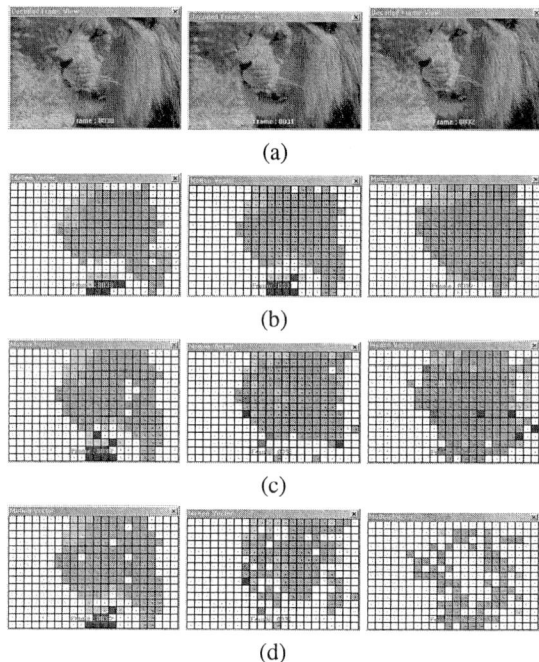

(a)

(b)

(c)

(d)

Fig. 5. Examples of flow estimation (From left to right : R_i, B_j, B_n frames). (a) Original Image. (b) MV vector in IPP encoded frame. (c) Estimated MV vector in IPB encoded frame (Proposed method). (d) Estimated MV vector in IPB encoded frame (Kobla's method).

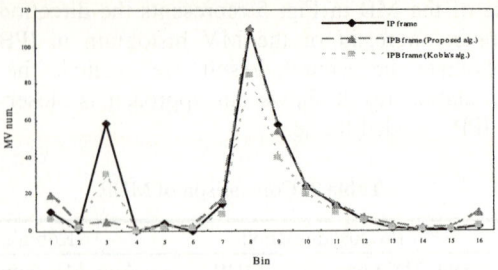

Fig. 6. Histogram comparison in N-MV field.

The Application of N-MVs. Finally, we show the object tracking method as one of applications using the N-MV field. Fig. 7 depicts the effective object tracking in the proposed motion flow and, at once, attests the validity of the proposed N-MVs representation by comparing with the tracking method using MV field in IPP encoded frames. The object tracking using only forward-predicted MV in P frame on IPP encoded sequence is shown in Fig. 7-(a). This differs little from Fig. 7-(b) using the motion flow by our *BPIF*; rather, it has lither curve in the aspect of the moving tracking. This means that the proposed motion analysis method doesn't seriously transform and distort the real MVs on MPEG domain and is sufficiently reasonable. The object tracking method in this paragraph has referred to [11].

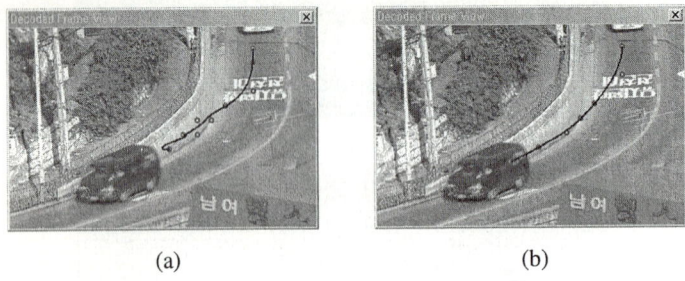

(a)   (b)

Fig. 7. Comparison of object tracking. (a) Object tracking in IPP encoded frame. (b) Object tracking in N-MV field.

4   Conclusions

In this paper, we have proposed the motion analysis method on the ground of normalizing the MVs on MPEG compressed domain. We have proposed the Bi-directional Predicted-Independent Framework for generating the structure in which I, P, and B frames can be considered equivalently. Simulation results show that our frame-type-independent framework enables to represent the dense and comprehensive motion field. These N-MVs can be used as the motion depicter for video indexing, which have the strong point of computational efficiency and low storage space.

Acknowledgement. This research was supported in part by the Ministry of Education, Seoul, Korea, under the BK21 Project, and by the Ministry of Science and Technology, Seoul, Korea, under the NRL Project (M10204000079-02J0000-07310).

References

[1]   H.L. Eng and K.K. Ma: Bidirectional motion tracking for video indexing. Multimedia Signal Processing, pp. 153-158, 1999.

[2]   N.V. Patel and I.K. Sethi: Video shot detection and characterization for video databases. Pattern Recognition, vol. 30, no. 4, pp. 583-592, 1997.

[3]   J.G. Kim, H.S. Chang, J.W. Kim and H.M. Kim: Efficient camera motion characterization for MPEG video indexing. IEEE International Conference on Multimedia and Expo, vol. 2, pp. 1171-1174, 2000.

[4]   M. Cherfaoui and C. Bertin: Temporal segmentation of videos: A new approach. in IS & T and SPIE Proc.: Digital Video Compression Algorithm and Technology, vol. 2419, San Jose, 1995.

[5]   H. Zhang, A. Kankanhalli and S. Smoliar: Automatic partitioning of full-motion video. Multimedia Systems I, 10-28, 1993.

[6]   H. Zhang, C.Y. Low, Y. Gong and S. Smoliar: Video parsing using compressed data. in Proc. of SPIE Conf. on Image and Video Processing II, vol. 2182, pp. 142-149, 1994.

[7]   Y. Juan and S.F. Chang: Scene change detection in a MPEG compressed video sequence. in IS & T and SPIE Proc.: Digital Video Compression Algorithm and Technology, vol. 2419, San Jose, 1995.

[8]   V. Kobla: Indexing and Retrieval of MPEG Compressed Video. Journal of Electronic Imaging, Vol.7 (2), 1998.

[9]   ISO/IEC/JTC1/SC29/WG11, 13812-2, 1995.

[10]   O. Sukmarg and K.R. Rao: Fast object detection and segmentation in MPEG compressed domain. Proc. of IEEE TENCON 2000, vol. 3, pp. 364-368, 2000.

[11]   N.W. Kim, T.Y. Kim and J.S. Choi: Motion analysis using the normalization of motion vectors on MPEG compressed domain. ITC-CSCC2002, vol.3, pp.1408-1411, 2002.

How Does the Hue Contribute to Construct Better Colour Features?

Giovani Gomez Estrada[1], Eduardo Morales[2], and Huajian Gao[1]

[1] Max-Planck-Institute, Heisenbergstraße 3, D-70569, Stuttgart, Germany,
{giovani,hjgao}@mf.mpg.de
[2] ITESM Cuernavaca, Reforma 182-A, Temixco, 62589, Morelos, Mexico,
eduardo.morales@itesm.mx

Abstract. We explore the impact of including hue in a feature construction algorithm for colour target detection. Hue has a long standing record as a good attribute in colour segmentation, so it is expected to strengthen features generated by only RGB. Moreover, it may open the door to infer compact feature maps for skin detection. However, contrary to our expectations, those new features where hue participates tend to produce poor features in terms of recall or precision. This result shows that (i) better features can be constructed without the costly hue, and (ii) unfortunately a good feature map for skin detection is still evasive.

1 Introduction

It is well-known that pixel based skin detection plays an important step in several vision tasks, such as gesture recognition, hand tracking, video indexing, face detection, and computer graphics, see e.g. [3,4,9,14,23,25]. Although colours may vary due to ambient light, brightness, shadows or daylight, skin detection is computationally tractable. Practitioners had traditionally used just existing off-the-shelf colour models, like HSV, YUV, raw RGB or normalised RGB, which however often yields poor precision[1] to upper layers in their vision systems.

We know there is no single colour model suitable for skin detection [6], and that traditional models are not so useful [1,21] for this task. Fortunately, machine learning community had developed the concept of attribute construction, which in this context means to override all existing attributes and infer new ones for the task at hand. However, *which attributes should be used to infer a good model for skin detection?*

We present a computational study where R, G, B and hue participate within an attribute construction approach. Guided by existing literature, we expect a clear improvement over features generated with only R, G, and B. Hereafter, we shall refer to "attribute" as raw input variables, and "feature" to any combination of attributes.

---

[1] Precision = $\frac{TP}{TP+FP} \times 100\%$, where TP = true positives; and FP = false positives, where the prediction is incorrectly set as *skin*

R. Monroy et al. (Eds.): MICAI 2004, LNAI 2972, pp. 602–611, 2004.
© Springer-Verlag Berlin Heidelberg 2004

This report will review, in section 2, the crossroads of colour detection and machine learning. Then, in section 3, the main premise and expectations are presented. Two influential tools from machine learning, attribute construction and attribute selection, are described in sections 4 and 5, respectively. Experimental settings and findings appear in section 6, while conclusions to this work are found in section 7.

2   Improving Colour Detection

Although eliminating the illumination components has been a popular practice for skin detection, it has not really improved our vision systems. What is even worst, it has been reported that this practice actually decreases the separability in some models [21]. The other way around, adding components in a stepwise procedure have the same problems. For instance, what you gain with C_r or hue is lost by adding its second element, C_b and Saturation, respectively. In this direction there are some bad news, see e.g. [1,21], that many practitioners have sadly noticed, no matter which existing colour model we use, the separability of skin and non-skin points is independent of the colour model employed.

Of course, we may argue that a long term solution would be to look at different wavelengths. But, for the time being, red-green-blue response prevails as the standard input value. Thus, if existing general colour models do not help for target detection one may be tempted to create *synthetic* ones. Say, these may not be reversible, not useful for other tasks, nor adding anything new to Colour Science. Of course, those synthetic models have not to be created by guessing combinations in unsound way but with a systematic procedure. In general, any feature space tuned for this purpose will hereafter be cited as "skin colour model".

2.1   Learning and Colour

Since our raw attributes are not very helpful for skin and non-skin discrimination, we may therefore transform RGB into a nonlinear mapping. Projecting RGB into higher spaces may result in easier decision boundaries. A line in these new spaces is in fact a non-linear one in the original space. It is known from Statistical Learning Theory that a hypothetical polynomial of sufficiently high degree do approximate any arbitrary decision boundary, no matter of how complex it is. Nevertheless, for our purposes two practical questions arise, (1) how do you create such a non-linear features in a constructive manner, and (2) how do you get *only few* of them to describes a good decision boundary.

Two recent steps have been done to bring machine learning approaches to help colour detection [5,29]. While in both cases colour targets were fed into a decision tree induction system (c4.5 [19]), the main difference is the attribute construction step. In [29] the RGB stimulus was directly transformed into hue, saturation, and average values of R, G, and B. Resulting decision trees use those attributes, e.g. moment of inertia, to classify colour targets.

Since their work uses pre-existing models, it is more in the sense of the Michalski's view of pattern discovery in computer vision [15]. However, under this idea, we assume that the current description language is good enough to describe our colour targets. A different path was adopted in [5], and no pre-existing models were assumed. Then, as their induction systems progress, new and more specific features are constructed. In each cycle, current features are passed to an attribute selection step, and only those which exhibit good performance are allowed to continue in the process. Although both approaches are bit costly in terms of computing time (e.g. attribute selection and tree induction), it is worthwhile to explore machine learning ideas to automate colour detection.

3   Why Not Hue?

As mentioned before, authors in [5] did use RGB to create new features. However, we may criticise why they did not include hue in their initial set. Hue has a long standing record of good colour attribute. Moreover, it has been recently assessed as one of the most influential attributes in a survey [6]. Thus, it seems quite normal to include hue and propose two questions:

1. does Hue contribute to infer better colour spaces for skin detection?
2. whether or not is possible to infer a 2D skin space.

The intuition behind adding hue is far clear. Hue may be used as a short-cut to get more compact features. It is an obvious candidate for any induction system. Many other colour attributes are easily derived as a linear combination of RGB, meanwhile Hue is quite more complex to infer. By allowing hue to participate in the attribute construction, one may expect powerful features with better recall, precision and success measures [2]. Further, as a by-product, one may therefore expect to find out a good 2D model. Many current approaches to skin detection use three components (e.g. [5,6,14]), or a 2D where the illumination one has been just removed.

4   Attribute Construction

Most constructive induction systems use boolean combinations of existing attributes to create new ones, e.g. [18,20,27,28]. Say, their constructive operators can form conjunctions and/or disjunctions of attributes (e.g. [11,12,18,20]) or even use more sophisticated operators such as M-of-N [16] and X-of-N [27]. M-of-N answers whether at least M of the conditions in the set are true. X-of-N answers how many conditions in this set are true. Although a large number of studies have been devoted to boolean combinations of attributes (e.g. [28]), there are very few systems that use arithmetic combinations of real-value ones, which normally occur in vision. Most notably is the Bacon system [13] which

---

[2] Recall $= \frac{TP}{TP+FN} \times 100\%$, where TP = true positives.
   Success rate $= \frac{TP+TN}{TP+FP+TN+FN}$, where FN = false negatives.

searches for empirical laws relating dependent and independent variables. Bacon finds increasing and decreasing monotonic relations between pairs of variables that take on numeric values and calculates the slope by relating both terms to create a new attribute. Once a functional relation between variables is found, it is taken as a new dependent variable. This process continues until a complex combination is found relating *all* the primitive attributes.

In this paper we start with hue and the three basic color components RGB in a normalised form, and a simple set of arithmetic operators to produce a suitable model for pixel based colour detection. Once a new set of attributes is produced, a restricted covering algorithm (RCA, [5]), is used to construct single rules of no more than a small number of easy to evaluate terms with a minimum accuracy. We are interested in inducing simple models as they are relevant to applications which require fast response times, such as, semi-automatic calibration of colour targets, gesture recognition, face and human tracking, etc.

The general approach followed in this paper for constructive induction is shown in Table 1. The idea, is to start with some primitive attributes and a set of constructive operators, create a new representation space, run an inductive learning algorithm, and select the best attributes of this new space. This process continues until a predefined stopping criterion.

Table 1. General constructive induction idea. (i) the machine learning algorithm, (ii) the constructive induction module, and (iii) an evaluation component.

CurrentAttrib = original attributes, i.e. $\{\frac{r}{r+g+b}, \frac{g}{r+g+b}, \frac{b}{r+g+b}, Hue\}$
Operators = set of constructive operators, i.e. $\{+,-,*,/\}$
UNTIL termination criterion
  • NewAttrib = CurrentAttrib ∪ new attributes
    constructed with Operators on CurrentAttrib
  • Run a machine learning algorithm on NewAttrib
  • CurrentAttrib = Select the best attributes
    from NewAttrib

The constructive induction algorithm starts with hue, $\frac{r}{r+g+b}$, $\frac{g}{r+g+b}$, and $\frac{b}{r+g+b}$. All of them were used to create new attributes by seven constructive operators: $A + B, A * B, A - B, B - A, A/B, B/A$, and A^2, where A and B can be any pair of distinct attributes.

5   Attribute Selection

While it is relatively easy to create new features, their evaluation is a very time consuming step. It is the internal loop in these induction systems, say, every new hypothesis or features have to be assessed in their goodness to discriminate the target classes. There are basically two main approaches in attribute selection: filters and wrappers. Filters rank variables independently of their later usage. Conversely, wrappers guide their attribute selection process specifically for the machine learning algorithm employed. Generally speaking, filters are faster than wrappers. However, it is commonly assumed that wrappers do offer better predicting performance, i.e. the selected subset is tightly tuned for the machine learning algorithm and thus for the predictor too. Additional information on attribute selection can be found in one recent survey [8], and a special issue on Variable and Feature Selection in [10].

In this paper we adopt a wrapper approach using an information gain heuristics. The resulting representation is a tree-like structure, generated by RCA, which is chosen because of two main advantages: (i) simplicity in both representation and computing requirements, and (ii) able to produce a range of models for *the target* class. The algorithm is briefly described within the next paragraphs.

5.1   RCA

The general strategy of RCA is to favour attributes which cover a large number of true positives and attributes with small number of false positives. We are interested in single rules, so we shall talk about the total number of true positives (TTP) which will be used to increase the measure of recall and the total number of false positives (TFP) which will be used to increase precision.

Since we are dealing with real-value attributes, RCA creates binary splits using an information gain heuristics (as C4.5 does, [19]). RCA considers two possible attributes in parallel when constructing rules. On its first cycle, RCA constructs two rules which have as LHS the attribute with larger TTP in one rule and the attribute with larger $TTP - TFP^2$ in the other rule. The following cycle produces two rules out of each original rule (4 in total) following the same criterion, again adding to the LHS of each rule one attribute with large coverage and one which is heavily penalized by the number of misclassifications. This process continues until the rules produced have a certain number of predetermined terms. The upper bound of rules to be produced is 2^n, where n is the number of terms on each rule. RCA builds 2^n rules in parallel aiming for a large coverage with small errors on the same example set. This idea handles two objectives, thus it produces a range of alternatives, potentially from *high recall-poor precision* to *high precision-poor recall*, and balanced intermediate states, of course. An overall description of RCA is given in table 2.

5.2   Connection to Other Methods

The idea of improving features on-the-fly is not new. To our best knowledge, it appeared in the MOLFEA project, an inductive database system, e.g. [11,12]. However, they use a boolean conjunction of predefined attributes to generate new ones. We share the aim to generate features not in advance but "on demand", by detecting the need for a representation change, but nevertheless we do use arithmetic instead of boolean combinations.

Other works [17,22] did use genetic programming as a preprocessing step. They construct new features from the initial dataset, generating "potentially" useful features in advance. A genetic algorithm is then used to control the attribute selection step. Here, a binary chromosome represents attributes, say, the

Table 2. Overall description of RCA. Two intermixed criteria to induce rules with complementary attributes.

For each class C
    Let $E =$ training examples
    Let $N =$ maximum number of terms per rule
    Create a rule $R(0)$ with empty LHS and class C
    Let depth $D = 1$
    Until $D = N$ **do**
        For each attribute A create a split (Sp_A)
            with greater information gain
        For each existing rule $R(D-1)$
            create two new rules $(R_1(D)$ and $R_2(D))$ by
            adding to its LHS, a Sp_i with larger TTP
            $(R_1(D))$ and a Sp_j with larger $TTP - TFP^2$
            (R_2)
        Let $D \to D + 1$
        For each $R_i(D)$ continue with its own
            covered examples from E
    Output all $R_i(D)$

0/1 or (false/true) slot means whether the corresponding attribute does participate in the wrapper process. This idea does not introduce any bias in the feature construction in a class-depending or goal-driven fashion, as previously mentioned.

Although an open avenue would be to use other (e.g. evolutive) ideas for attribute construction and selection, which may suits well in this context, we feel that our proposed technique is rather straightforward (see table 2) and avoid unnecessary costly operations.

6   Experimental Settings and Results

We create ten subsets with skin and non-skin elements. The dataset is described in [6], which is based on real skin images, from different input sources, illumination conditions and races, with no photographic manipulation. For each data set, we selected 33000 skin and 67000 non-skin elements uniformly at random. We perform 10-fold cross validation in the attribute selection step, the inner loop. The covering algorithm, RCA, wraps c4.5 for attribute selection, which ran with the usual pruning and confidence thresholds. In addition, we request a minimum number (500) of elements per leaf to force fewer leaves. Final results of each induced model were calculated on large and balanced unseen data: 12.2 million points for each skin and non-skin targets.

Table 3 shows the best bi-dimensional models found by RCA. RCA is designed in such a way that one feature can appear twice in the same branch. Hence, it introduces a double threshold. Only two leaves were generated with this concept. To our surprise, the best precision on both 2D and 3D models is

Table 3. Only two models had two variables, yet one of them has the higher precision among all experiments.

colour models (two components)		recall (%)	precision (%)	success rate (%)
$\frac{gb}{(r+g+b)^2}$	h	80	**92.6**	86.3
$\frac{gb}{(r+g+b)^2}$	$\frac{h*(r+g+b)}{b}$	97	74.8	82.7

Table 4. Best features generated by the attribute selection procedure. Only the last row exhibits a well-balanced performance.

color model (three components)			recall (%)	precision (%)	success rate (%)
$\frac{gb}{(r+g+b)^2}$	h	$\frac{r}{b}$	95.6	88.6	91.7
$\frac{gb}{(r+g+b)^2}$	$\frac{h*(r+g+b)}{b}$	$\frac{r}{g}$	**98.2**	77.9	85.2
$\frac{h*(r+g+b)}{b}$	$\frac{r}{g}$	h	98.1	82.9	88.9
h	$\frac{gb}{(r+g+b)^2}$	$\frac{rg}{(r+g+b)^2}$	98	78.8	85.3
h	$\frac{gb}{(r+g+b)^2}$	$\frac{b-r}{(r+g+b)}$	98	64.1	72
h	$\frac{gb}{(r+g+b)^2}$	$\frac{h*(r+g+b)}{g}$	98.1	65.3	73.4
h	$\frac{r}{b}$	$\frac{r-b}{(r+g+b)}$	94	90.5	92.4

the first model in table 3. Normally, what is expected is a high recall, but in this case $\frac{gb}{(r+g+b)^2}$ and hue contributed to achieve 92.6% of precision.

The same features in table 3 were selected in other branches, as shown in first two lines of table 4. Interestingly, better models were found by removing these double thresholds and selecting a new variable instead. Thus, the overall effect does eliminate a threshold on $\frac{gb}{(r+g+b)^2}$ and increases the recall. We should be critic with the second row in table 4, in which recall is rather high. It is not a surprise since even a plain ratio like $\frac{r}{g}$ can achieve more than 95% in recall, but at expenses of poor precision, as in this case. Interesting point should have a balance in both recall and precision, which in turn will lead a good success rate.

We should compare tables 3 and 4 to state of the art models, shown as table 5. An attribute construction and selection approach appears in [5], and its finding is listed in table 5-top. The second row (from [6]) shows a model found by a stepwise forward selection method, and consists of hue, GY and W_r, which are defined as:

Table 5. State of the art models: (top) Automatic feature construction from RGB, (middle) Step-wise forward selection on several colour components. (bottom) Skin Probability Map, which is extremely fast.

other models (three components)			recall (%)	precision (%)	success rate (%)
$\frac{r}{g}$	$\frac{rb}{(r+g+b)^2}$	$\frac{rg}{(r+g+b)^2}$	93	91.5	92.2
h	GY	W_r	93.2	92.1	**92.6**
	SPM on raw RGB		95.8	77.3	91

$$GY = -0.30 * r + 0.41 * g - 0.11 * b$$

$$W_r = (\frac{r}{r+g+b} - \frac{1}{3})^2 + (\frac{g}{r+g+b} - \frac{1}{3})^2$$

Unfortunately, features like W_r are very difficult to infer with the existing attribute construction scheme. Third row in table 5 shows a pragmatic and well-known approach, so called Skin Probability Map (SPM), working on raw RGB values. The SPM has a threshold variable which is tuned for this comparison. The learning procedure used all ten subsets, instead of only one. This is somehow an unfair comparison, but that is why SPMs work, see [6,14], e.g. skin in RGB has a very sparse distribution. As a common practice in SPMs, we used the God given parameter [14] of 32 equally sized histogram bins, i.e. 32^3.

6.1 Discussion

With those results on hand we may come back to the original questions. How does the hue contribute to new colour features? Essentially, there is no real impact of including hue in new features.

Although some good features have been found, we expected better results, say, by consistently exceeding a mark of 90% in both recall and precision. Two existing models, shown in table 5 do achieve this mark, and one of them does not use hue at all. Only one model in table 4 (last one, top to bottom), exhibit competitive results. And, at best, it is comparable to table 5-top, which does not use hue and thus faster to compute. Moreover, some doubts may arise with the inclusion of $\frac{r}{b}$, a noisy feature, which nevertheless was selected in two models.

Although promising features appear in table 3, a good enough 2D skin space is unfortunately still evasive. The success of this study relies in creating strong features, which were not produced using hue. In fact, the attribute selection shows a strong bias to $\frac{h*(r+g+b)}{g}$ and $\frac{h*(r+g+b)}{b}$. Nonetheless, their associated models show regular to poor performance.

7   Conclusions

We report an attribute construction experience with the aim of finding good colour features for pixel based skin detection by including hue in the initial subset. Unfortunately, with our methodology, we found that hue has a minor contribution in novel features. Moreover, only one model is at best comparable to the existing literature in this field, which does not use hue. Thus, it indicates that (i) better features may be constructed without the costly hue, and (ii) unfortunately a 2D skin colour model is still evasive.

Skin colour processing is an active field. We encourage other people to verify and extend this line by including different features (e.g. texture) in the attribute construction scheme or, perhaps, developing novel attribute selection methods that overcome the initial bias to terms with hue.

References

1. A. Albiol, L. Torres, Edward Delp, *Optimum Color Spaces for Skin Detection*, Proc. of ICIP, Color and Multispectral Processing I, Thessaloniki, 2001.
2. J. Brand, J. S. Mason, *A comparative assessment of three approaches to pixel-level human skin-detection*, Proc. of ICPR, Vol. I, pp. 1056-1059, Barcelona, 2000.
3. J. Brand, J. S. Mason, M. Roach, M. Pawlewski, *Enhancing face detection in colour images using a skin probability map*, Int. Conf. on Intelligent Multimedia, Video and Speech Processing, pp. 344-347, Hong Kong, 2001.
4. M. Fleck, D. A. Forsyth, C. Bregler, *Finding naked people*, Proc. of ECCV, Buxton and Cipolla, eds., Vol. II, LNCS, vol. 1064, pp. 592-602, Cambridge, 1996.
5. G. Gomez, E. Morales, *Automatic Feature Construction and a Simple Rule Induction Algorithm for Skin Detection*, Proc. of the ICML Workshop on Machine Learning in Computer Vision, pp. 31-38, A. Sowmya and T. Zrimec (editors), July 2002, Sydney.
6. G. Gomez *On selecting colour components for skin detection*, Proc. of the ICPR, vol. II, pp. 961-964, Québec, Aug. 2002.
7. I. Guyon, A. Elisseeff, *An introduction to variable and feature selection*, JMLR, vol. 3, pp. 1157-1182, 2003.
8. M. Hall, H. Holmes, *Benchmarking attribute selection techniques for discrete class data mining*, to appear in IEEE Trans. on Knowledge and Data Engineering, 2003.
9. E. Hjelmås and B. K. Low, *Face detection: A survey*, CV&IU, 83(3), pp. 236-274, 2001.
10. Special Issue on Variable and Feature Selection, *Journal of Machine Learning Research*, vol. 3, Mar. 2003.
11. S. Kramer, *Demand-driven construction of structural features in ILP*, In Rouveirol and Sebag, editors, Proc. of the Int. Conf. on ILP, vol. 2157, LNAI, pp. 132-141, Springer-Verlag, Strasbourg, Sept. 2001.
12. S. Kramer, L. De Raedt, *Feature construction with version spaces for biochemical applications*, Prof. of the ICML 2001, pp. 258-265, MA, USA, 2001.
13. P. Langley, G. L. Bradshaw, H. A. Simon, *Rediscovering chemistry with the BACON system*, in Machine Learning, R. S. Michalski, J. Carbonell and T. M. Mitchell (eds.), pp. 307-329, Morgan Kaufmann, 1983.

14. M. J. Jones, J. Regh, *Statistical color models with applications to skin detection*, Proc. of CVPR, Vol. I, pp. 274-280, CO, USA, 1999.

15. R. S. Michalski, A. Rosenfeld, Y. Aloimonos, Z. Duric, M. Maloof, Q. Zhang, *Progress On Vision Through Learning: A Collaborative Effort of George Mason University and University of Maryland*, Proc. of the Image Understanding Workshop, Palm Springs, Feb., 1996.

16. P. M. Murphy, M. J. Pazzani, *ID2-of-3: Constructive induction of M-of-N concepts for discriminators in decision trees*, Int. Workshop on Machine Learning, pp. 183-187, Illinois, June 1991.

17. F.E.B. Otero, M.M.S. Silva, A.A. Freitas, J.C. Nievola, *Genetic Programming for Attribute Construction in Data Mining*, in EuroGP 2003, C. Ryan et al. (editor), LNCS vol. 2610, pp. 384-393, Springer-Verlag, Essex, 2003.

18. G. Pagallo, *Adaptive decision tree algorithm for learning from examples*, Ph.D. thesis, University of California at Santa Cruz, 1990.

19. J.R. Quinlan, C4.5: Programs for Machine Learning. Morgan Kaufmann, San Mateo, CA, 1993.

20. H. Ragavan, L. Rendell, *Lookahead feature construction for learning hard concepts*, Proc. of the ICML, pp. 252-259, Amherst, June 1993.

21. M. C. Shin, K. I. Chang, L. V. Tsap, *Does Colorspace Transformation Make Any Difference on Skin Detection?*, IEEE Workshop on Applications of Computer Vision, pp. 275-279, Orlando, Dec. 2002.

22. M. G. Smith, L. Bull, *Feature construction and selection using genetic programming and a genetic algorithm*, in EuroGP 2003, C. Ryan et al. (editor), LNCS vol. 2610, pp. 229-237, Springer-Verlag, Essex, 2003.

23. M. Soriano, B. Martinkauppi, S. Huovinenb, M. Laaksonenc, *Adaptive skin color modeling using the skin locus for selecting training pixels*, Pattern Recognition, 36(3), pp. 681-690, March 2003.

24. J.C. Terrillon, M. Shirazit, H. Fukamachi, S. Akamatsu, *Comparative performance of different skin chrominance models and chrominance spaces for the automatic detection of human faces in color images*, Proc. of Automatic Face and Gesture Recognition, 54-61, Grenoble, Mar. 2000.

25. N. Tsumura, N. Ojima, K. Sato, M. Shiraishi, H. Shimizu, H. Nabeshima, S. Akazaki, K. Hori, Y. Miyake, *Image-based skin color and texture analysis/synthesis by extracting hemoglobin and melanin information in the skin*, ACM Trans. on Graphics, 22(3), pp. 770-779, 2003.

26. B. Zarit and B. J. Super and F. K. H. Quek, *Comparison of Five Color Models in Skin Pixel Classification*, Workshop on Recognition, Analysis, and Tracking of Faces and Gestures in Real-Time Systems, pp. 58-63, Corfu, 1999.

27. Z. Zheng, *Constructing nominal X-of-N attributes*, Proc. of the IJCAI, pp. 1064-1070, Québec, Aug. 1995.

28. Z. Zheng, *A comparison of constructing different types of new feature for decision tree learning*, in Feature Extraction,Construction and Selection: A data mining perspective, Liu and Motoda (eds.), Kluwer Academic, 1998.

29. T. Zrimec, A. Wyatt, *Learning to recognize objects - Toward automatic calibration of color vision for Sony robots*, Proc. of the ICML Workshop on Machine Learning in Computer Vision, A. Sowmya and T. Zrimec (editors), Sydney, July 2002.

Morphological Contrast Measure and Contrast Mappings: One Application to the Segmentation of Brain MRI

Jorge D. Mendiola-Santibañez[1], Iván R. Terol-Villalobos[2], and
Antonio Fernández-Bouzas[3]

[1] Doctorado en Instrumentación y Control Automático,
Universidad Autónoma de Querétaro, 76000, Querétaro, México
[2] CIDETEQ,S.C., Parque Tecnológico Querétaro, S/N,
San Fandila-Pedro Escobedo, 76700, Querétaro México,
famter@ciateq.net.mx
[3] Instituto de Neurobiología, UNAM Campus Juriquilla,
Juriquilla, 76001, Qro. México

Abstract. In this paper, the use of morphological contrast mappings and a method to quantify the contrast for segmenting magnetic resonance images (MRI) of the brain was investigated. In particular, contrast transformations were employed for detecting white matter in a frontal lobule of the brain. Since contrast mappings depend on several parameters (size, contrast, proximity criterion), a morphological method to quantify the contrast was proposed in order to compute the optimal parameter values. The contrast quantifying method, that employs the gradient luminance concept, enabled us to obtain an output image associated with a good visual contrast. Because the contrast mappings introduced in this article were defined under partitions generated by the flat zone notion, these transformations are connected. Therefore, the degradation of the output images by the formation of new contours was avoided. Finally, the ratio between white and grey matter was calculated and compared with manual segmentations.

1 Introduction

In mathematical morphology contrast enhancement is based on morphological contrast mappings as described by Serra [17]. The main idea of these transformations is the comparison of each point of the original image with two patterns; subsequently, the nearest value with respect to the original image is selected. The first works dealing with contrast theory were carried out by Meyer and Serra [12]. Indirectly, a special class of contrast mappings denominated morphological slope filters (MSF) were introduced by Terol-Villalobos [20][21][22]. Here a gradient criterion was used as a proximity criterion. Moreover, in Terol-Villalobos [22], the flat zone concept on the partition was introduced in the numerical case and the morphological slope filters were defined as connected transformations. Once the basic flat zone operations were defined on the partition in the numerical

R. Monroy et al. (Eds.): MICAI 2004, LNAI 2972, pp. 612–621, 2004.
© Springer-Verlag Berlin Heidelberg 2004

case, the morphological contrast mappings were proposed as connected transformations by Mendiola and Terol [10][11]. One important difference between the contrast mappings proposed by Serra[17] and those proposed by Mendiola and Terol [10][11] was that for the latter the size of the structuring element was considered a variable parameter in the primitives as well as in the proximity criterion. However, this originates a problem since, appropriate values for these parameters must be calculated. This problem is solved in the present paper by the proposal of a morphological quantitative contrast method, which is used to determine some adequate values for the parameters involved in the morphological contrast mappings. Numerous models of contrast metric based on the human visual system have been proposed, they are mostly concerned with predicting our ability to perceive basic geometrical shapes and optical illusions. Few of these models work properly; mainly because the human visual system is enormously complex. Nevertheless, there have been several attempts providing reasonable successful models, some examples can be found in [2], [3], [6], [15], and [19]. In our case, the main purpose of introducing a morphological quantitative contrast model is to have a contrast measure useful in the determination of the output images presenting an enhancement in the contrast from the point of view of visual contrast. The morphological quantitative contrast measure introduced in this work uses the concept denominated luminance gradient (see [1]); the contrast model will be used to determine some optimal parameters associated with contrast mappings, which will be applied to detecting white matter located in a frontal lobule of the brain. On the other hand, several techniques of image processing have been employed for segmenting MRI of the brain. A complete description dealing with this subject is presented in [5], [7], and [14]. At the present time, the most widely applied technique is manual segmentation of the brain, which has several disadvantages: (i) it generally requires a high level of expertise, (ii) it is time and labor consuming, and (iii) it is subjective and therefore not reproducible. The advantages of employing an automatic or semi-automatic segmentation approach are its reproducibility and readiness, which are useful when the specialist in the area needs to measure, diagnose and analyze, an image in a study. Some works on MRI segmentation of the brain related to mathematical morphology can be found in [4],[8], [13], among others. In this paper we propose a mophological contrast measure and the application of contrast mappings in order to segment white and grey matter in a frontal lobule of the brain. The quantification of white and grey matter in frontal lobule provides to experts in the area important information concerning memory impairment related to aging. This paper is organized as follows. Section 2, briefly presents the basic morphological transformations defined on the partition and the morphological contrast mappings. In section 3, a morphological method to quantify the contrast is introduced. Finally, in section 4 an application of brain MRI is presented. In this case white and grey matter are segmented in a frontal lobule and their ratio is quantified and compared with manual segmentations obtained by experts from the Institute of Neurobiology, UNAM Campus Juriquilla.

2   Morphological Basic Transformations on the Partition

2.1   Connectivity

Serra [18] established connectivity by means of the concept of connected class.

Definition 1 (Connected class). *A connected class C in $\wp(E)$ is a subset of $\wp(E)$ such that:*

(i) $\emptyset \in C$
(ii) $\forall x \in E, \{x\} \in C$
(iii) *For each family $\{C_i\}$ in C,* $\bigcap C_i \neq \emptyset \Rightarrow \bigcup C_i \in C$

where $\wp(E)$ represents the set of all sets of E. An element of C is called a con-nected set. An equivalent definition to the connected class notion is the opening family expressed by the next theorem [18].

Theorem 1 (Connectivity characterized by openings). *The definition of a connectivity class C is equivalent to the definition of a family of openings $\{\gamma_x, x \in E\}$ such that:*

(a) $\forall x \in E, \gamma_x(x) = \{x\}$
(b) $\forall x, y \in E$ and $A \subseteq E, \gamma_x(A) = \gamma_y(A)$ or $\gamma_x(A) \bigcap \gamma_y(A) = \emptyset$
(c) $\forall A \subseteq E$ and $\forall x \in E, \forall x \notin A \Rightarrow \gamma_x(A) = \emptyset$

When the transformation γ_x is associated with the usual connectivity (arc-wise) in Z^2 (Z is the set of integers), the opening $\gamma_x(A)$ can be defined as the union of all paths containing x that are included in A. When a space is equipped with γ_x, the connectivity can be expressed using this operator. A set $A \subset Z^2$ is connected if and only if $\gamma_x(A) = A$. In Fig. 1 the behavior of this opening is illustrated. The connected component of the input image X (Fig. 1(a)), where point x belongs, is the output of the opening $\gamma_x(X)$, while the other components are eliminated.

Definition 2 (Partition). *Given a space E, a function $P : E \rightarrow \wp(E)$ is called a partition of E : (a) if $x \in P(x), x \in E$, (b) if $P(x) = P(y)$ or $P(x) \bigcap P(y) = \emptyset$ with $x, y \in E$.*

$P(x)$ is an element of the partition containing x. If there is a connectivity defined in E and $\forall x$, the component $P(x)$ belongs to this connectivity, then the partition is connected.

Definition 3. *The flat zones of a function $f : Z^2 \rightarrow Z$ are defined as the connected components (largest) of points with the same value of the function.*

The operator $F_x(f)$ will represent the flat zone of a function f at point x.

Definition 4. *An operator is connected if and only if it extends the flat zones of the input image.*

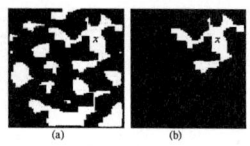

Fig. 1. Connected components extraction.(a)Binary image X, (b) The opening $\gamma_x(X)$ extracts the connected component in X where point x belongs.

Definition 5. *Let x be a point of Z^2 equipped with γ_x . Two flat zones $F_x(f)$ and $F_y(f)$ in Z^2 are adjacent if $F_x(f) \bigcap F_y(f) = \gamma_x(F_x(f) \bigcup F_y(f))$*

Note that, (a) $x \in F_x(f)$, and (b) $\forall x, y, F_x(f) = F_y(f)$ or $F_x(f) \bigcap F_y(f)) = \emptyset$. Therefore, the flat zone notion generates a partition of the image. Thus, the use of both concepts, flat zone and partition, were used for the introduction of morphological transformations in the grey level case.

Definition 6. *Let x be a point in Z^2 equipped with γ_x. The set of flat zones adjacent to F_x is given by, $A_x = \{F_{x'} : x' \in Z^2, F_x \bigcup F_{x'} = \gamma_x(F_x \bigcup F_{x'})\}$.*

In Fig. 2 the adjacent flat zone concept is illustrated. Two adjacent flat zones are presented (see Fig. 2(b) and 2(c)), and the adjacency of the expression $F_x(f) \bigcup F_y(f) = \gamma_x(F_x(f) \bigcup F_y(f))$ is also illustrated in Fig. 2(d).

In the case of working on the partition, the transformations should be operated on the pair (f, P_f) and the element $(f, P_f)(x)$ is taken as the grey level value of the connected component $F_x(f)$. The morphological dilation and erosion applied over the flat zones are given by:

$$\delta(f, P_f)(x) = max\{(f, P_f)(y) : F_y \in A_x \bigcup \{F_x\}\}, \tag{1}$$

$$\varepsilon(f, P_f)(x) = min\{(f, P_f)(y) : F_y \in A_x \bigcup \{F_x\}\}, \tag{2}$$

The dilation δ_μ and erosion ε_μ of size μ are obtained iterating μ times the elemental dilation and erosion given in equations (1) and (2):

$$\delta_\mu(f, P_f)(x) = \underbrace{\delta\delta\cdots\delta(f, P_f)(x)}_{\mu\ times} \tag{3}$$

$$\varepsilon_\mu(f, P_f)(x) = \underbrace{\varepsilon\varepsilon\cdots\varepsilon(f, P_f)(x)}_{\mu\ times} \tag{4}$$

The opening and closing on the partition of size μ induced by f are:

$$\gamma_\mu(f, P_f)(x) = \delta_\mu(\varepsilon_\mu(f, P_f), P_f)(x), \tag{5}$$

$$\varphi_\mu(f, P_f)(x) = \varepsilon_\mu(\delta_\mu(f, P_f), P_f)(x), \tag{6}$$

The morphological external gradient of size μ on the partition is defined as:

$$grade_\mu(f, P_f)(x) = \delta_\mu(f, P_f)(x) - (f, P_f)(x) \tag{7}$$

The basic morphological transformations defined in this section enable us to present the three states morphological contrast mappings in the next section.

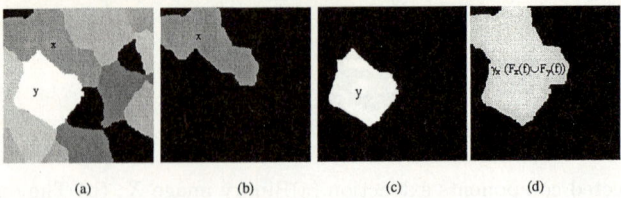

Fig. 2. Adjacent flat zone concept.(a) Image f with 14 flat zones, (b) Flat zone in point x, $F_x(f)$, (c) Flat zone in point y, $F_y(f)$, (c) Two adjacent flat zones, i.e, $F_x(f) \bigcup F_y(f) = \gamma_x(F_x(f) \bigcup F_y(f))$.

2.2 Morphological Contrast Mappings

As was expressed in the introduction, the contrast mappings consist of the selection of some patterns (primitives) for each point of the image in accordance with a proximity criterion. The selection of the primitives is very important, since the degradation of the output images can be attenuated if the primitives are idempotent transformations as described by Serra(see [17]). On the other hand, in Mendiola and Terol (see [10][11]) two and three states morphological contrast mappings with size criteria on the partition were proposed. The proximity criterion with size criteria basically allows a different performance of the morphological contrast mappings, hence providing an alternative way of modifying the contrast in an image. As follows three states contrast mappings with size criteria on the partition are considered. These contrast mappings are composed by three primitives, opening and closing on the partition and original image (see equations (5) and (6)). The proximity criterion $\rho(x)$ (see equation (8)) considers the bright and dark regions of the image. Note in equation (8) that a ratio factor in each point of the image is calculated.

$$\rho(x) = \frac{\varphi_{\mu_1}(f, P_f)(x) - (f, P_f)(x)}{\varphi_{\mu_1}(f, P_f)(x) - \gamma_{\mu_2}(f, P_f)(x)} \tag{8}$$

Expession (9) establishes a three states contrast mapping with size criteria on the partition .

$$W^3_{\mu_1,\mu_2,\beta,\alpha}(f, P_f)(x) = \begin{cases} \varphi_{\mu_1}(f, P_f)(x) & 0 \le \rho(x) < \beta \\ (f, P_f)(x) & \beta \le \rho(x) < \alpha \\ \gamma_{\mu_2}(f, P_f)(x) & \alpha \le \rho(x) \le 1 \end{cases} \tag{9}$$

The main advantage of working on the partition is that the flat zones of the image will never be broken during their processing, and the generation of new contours into the output image will be avoided. The former situation occurs because the employed transformations are connected. From equations (8) and (9) notice that four parameters exist to determine, μ_1, μ_2, α and β. Parameters μ_1 and μ_2 are obtained from equation (10) by means of a graphic method. The traditional way of studying structures sizes constituting the image is by means of the granulometric study of the image (see [16]).

The graphic method for determining the structures sizes of the processed images in this work consists in calculating the volume point by point in the image processed by means of the equation (10), in this case the closing size is fixed while the opening size changes. Expression (10) works similar to granulometric density and allows obtaining of the size of the opening or closing on the partition when one of the index is fixed, while the other index changes.

$$\eta(x) = \frac{\gamma_{\mu_i}(f, P_f)(x) - \gamma_{\mu_{i+1}}(f, P_f)(x)}{\varphi_{\mu_j}(f, P_f)(x) - \gamma_{\mu_i}(f, P_f)(x)} \tag{10}$$

An estimation of the parameters α and β involved in equation (9) is obtained by means of the morphological contrast method proposed in section (3).

3   Contrast Metric

Given a two-dimensional luminance distribution across a surface, the luminance gradient is defined as (see [1]):

$$\frac{\triangle L}{\triangle x} = \left| \frac{L_b - L_a}{b - a} \right|$$

where L_a and L_b are the luminances at two closely spaced points a and b on the surface separated by a distance $\triangle x = b - a$ (the absolute value is necessary to eliminate any directional dependence). When $\triangle x \to 0$:

$$\frac{\triangle L}{\triangle x} \bigg|_{lim \triangle x \to 0} = \left| \frac{dL}{dx} \right|$$

The changes in luminance are associated with the contours of the image, since they produce changes on the scene. One transformation that enables us to work directly with the contours of the image is the morphological external gradient (see equation 7). The next expression is proposed in order to have an indirect measure of the variations of the luminance gradient (VLG).

$$VLG = \sum_{x \in D_f} [maxgrade(f, P_f)(x) - mingrade(f, P_f)(x)] \tag{11}$$

Where, $maxgrade(f, P_f)(x) = max\{grade_\mu(f, P_f)(y); F_y(f) \in A_x(f) \bigcup \{F_x(f)\}\}$ and $mingrade(f, P_f)(x) = min\{grade_\mu(f, P_f)(y); F_y(f) \in A_x(f) \bigcup \{F_x(f)\}\}$; the element x belongs to the definition domain denoted by D_f. The idea of this morphological quantitative contrast method consists of the selection of the best parameters associated with some value of VLG obtained from the graph *VLG vs. parameters*. The analysis of the graph will be mainly focused on its maxima and minima, since they are associated with substantial changes in intensity. The following steps are employed for the selection of the local maximum and minimum producing good visual contrast.

- **Step 1**.- Calculate and draw the graph *VLG values vs. parameters* for a set of output enhanced images.
- **Step 2**.- A smooth visual contrast will correspond to the value of VLG associated with the global minimum in the graph *VLG values vs. parameters*.
- **Step 3**.- A higher visual contrast will correspond to the value of VLG associated with the global maximum in the graph VLG values vs. parameters.

The performance of this quantitative morphological contrast measure method is illustrated in the next section.

4   MRI Segmentation

In this section an application of contrast mappings (see section(2.2)) and morphological quantifying contrast method(see section(3)) is presented. In particular the detection of white matter in a frontal lobule of the brain was carried out. The brain MRI-T1 presented in this paper belongs to the MRI-T1 bank of the Institute of Neurobiology, UNAM Campus Juriquilla. The file processed and presented in this article comprised 120 slices, in which 17 belonged to a frontal lobule. The selection of the different frontal lobule slices was carried out by a specialist in the area of the same institute. The segmentation of the skull for each brain slice was carried out by means of the transformation proposed in [9], in such a way that our interest lies only on the segmentation of white and grey matter. The first five slices without skull of a frontal lobule are presented in Fig. 3(a). By means of equation (10), the size of the opening was calculated just for the first slice of the frontal lobule and applied to other brain slices. This approximation was made to avoid a large an inadequate process. The size of the closing on the partition was fixed with $\mu = 15$. Note that several values for the closing on the partition can be tested; however greater size for the closing will give adequate segmentations. The graph of the volume of equation (10), when the closing size is $\mu = 15$ and the opening size varies within the interval $[1,12]$, is presented in Fig. 3(b). This graph shows that $\mu = 7$ is an adequate value for the size of the opening, since an important changes in the internal structures of the image may be appreciated. Once the adequate sizes for the opening and closing on the partition were determinate , the parameters α and β involved in the contrast mapping transformation defined in equation (9) must be found. The obtention of α and β was carried out by means of the morphological contrast method proposed in section (3). In order to simplify the procedure to find the adequate values for α and β, only the first slice of the frontal lobule was analyzed, and once such values were found, they were applied to the remainder slices. This supposition was considered as an approximation to detect white matter in the different slices, without undertaking an impractical analysis. In accordance with step 1 of the morphological contrast method, the graph *VLG vs. parameters* must be obtained. In this work 12 values for VLG were generated, where parameters α and β took their values within the interval $[0, 1]$. The graph *VLG vs. parameters* is presented in Fig. 3(c). In accordance with step 2 and step 3 of the proposed morphological contrast method , the maximum of interest can

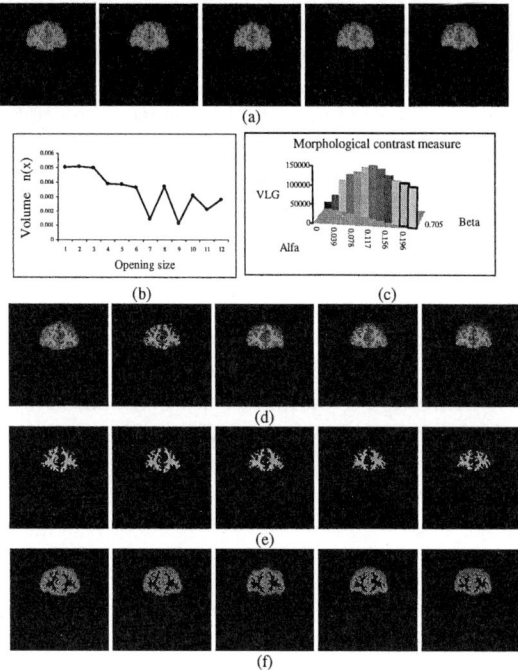

Fig. 3. MRI Segmentation. (a) First five slices of a frontal lobule; (b)Graph of the volume of equation (10), the opening size varies within the interval [1,12]; (c) Graph *VLG vs parameters*; (d) First five output images in which white matter is detected; (e) Separation of the white matter detected from the images in Fig. 3(d) ; (f) First five slices where grey matter is segmented

be obtained from graph in Fig.3(c), its value is 140248, corresponding to the parameters $\alpha = 0.117$ and $\beta = 0.47$. Such values are associated with the image presenting the best visual contrast. The parameters $\alpha = 0.117$ and $\beta = 0.47$ were applied in equation (9) together with the opening size $\mu = 7$ and closing size $\mu = 15$ for detecting white matter in the slices of the frontal lobule. The first five output images where white matter was detected are presented in Fig. 3(d). In order to segment white and grey matter the next algorithm was applied.

Algorithm to Segment White and Grey Matter

(i)   Get the threshold of the images in Fig. 3(d) between 90–255 sections.

(ii) Introduce a mask between the original image in Fig 3(a) and the image obtained in step (i).

(iii) Establish a point by point difference between the original image in Fig.3(a) and the image in step (ii).

(iv) Get the thereslhold of the images obtained in step (iii) between 70–255 sections.

(v)   Introduce a mask between the images in Fig. 3(a) and the images obtained in step (iv). In this step the grey matter is segmented.

In Fig. 3(e) and 3(f) the segmentation of white and grey matter are presented. On the other hand, the quantification of white and grey matter was carried out slice by slice from images in Figs.3(e) and 3(f). In this case, the pixels different from zero were counted. The volume of white matter amounted to 17614 pixels and that of grey matter to 22384 pixels; the ratio between grey and white matter was 1.270. The relation between white and grey matter was compared with a manual segmentation achieved by an expert in the area, the comparison gave a variation of +5% with respect to the manual segmentation. In this paper the segmentation of only one frontal lobule is presented, however, the same procedure was applied for segmenting four frontal lobules. In these segmentations, the ratios between white and grey matter presented a variation of ±5% with respect to the manual segmentations. The segmentation of white and grey matter, as well as the ratios between white and grey matter were validated by an expert of the Institute of Neurobiology, UNAM Campus Juriquilla, Querétaro.

5   Conclusion

In the present work, morphological contrast mappings and a proposed morphological quantitative contrast method were used to segment MRI of the brain in order to obtain a segmentation of white and grey matter located in a frontal lobule. The morphological contrast method was useful to determine some important parameters that define the action interval of the proximity criterion utilized in the morphological contrast mappings. The ratio between grey and white matter was compared with a manual segmentation carried out in the Institute of Neurobiology, UNAM Campus Juriquilla, obtaining an adequate result. The procedure proposed to segment white and grey matter has the disadvantage of not being completely automatic.

Acknowledgements. The author Jorge D. Mendiola Santibañez thanks CONACyT México for financial support. The author I. Terol would like to thank Diego Rodrigo and Darío T.G. for their great encouragement. This work was partially funded by the government agency CONACyT (Mexico) under the grant 41170. We also thank M. Sánchez-Alvarez for proof reading the english version of this manuscript.

References

1. Ashdown, I.:Luminance gradients: photometric analysis and perceptual reproduction. Journal of the Illuminating Engineering Society, **25** (1996) 69–82.
2. Barten, P. G. J.: Physical model for the contrast sensitivity of the human eye. Proceedings of SPIE, **1666** (1992) 57–72.
3. Blommaert, F. J. J., and Martens, J.:An object-oriented model for brightness perception. Spatial Vision, **1** (1990) 15–41.
4. Dogdas, B,D., Shattuck, D., and Leahy R,M. :Segmentation of the skull in 3D human MR images using mathematical morphology. Proceedings of SPIE Medical Imaging Conference, **4684** (2002) 1553–1562.

5. Haralick, R. and Shapiro, L.: Survey: Image segmentation techniques. Computer Vision, Graphics and Image Processing, **29** (1985) 100–132.
6. Horn, B. K. P.:Determining lightness from an image. Computer Graphics and Image Processing, **3** (1977) 277–299.
7. Jasjit, S., Sameer, S., and Reden, L.: Computer vision and pattern recognition techniques for 2-D and 3-D MR cerebral cortical segmentation (part I): a state of the art review. Pattern Analysis and Applications, **5** (2002) 46–76.
8. Lemieux, L., Hagemann, G., Krakow, K., and Woermann, FG.: Fast, accurate and reproducible automatic segmentation of the brain in T1-weighted volume magnetic resonance image data. Magnetic Resonance in Medicine, **1**, (1999) 127–135.
9. Mendiola-Santibañez, J,D. and Terol-Villalobos, I. R. : Markers propagation through morphological gradient for segmenting MRI . Avances Recientes en Análisis de Imágenes y Reconocimiento de Patrones TIARP 2001 México D.F, (2001) 85–96.
10. Mendiola-Santibañez, J.D. and Terol-Villalobos, I. R. :Morphological contrast enhancement using connected transformations. Proceedings of SPIE, **4667** (2002a) 365–376.
11. Mendiola-Santibañez, J.D and Terol-Villalobos, I. R. : Morphological contrast mappings on partition based on the flat zone notion. Computación y Sistemas, **6** (2002b) 25–37.
12. Meyer, F. and Serra, J.: Activity mappings. Signal Processing,**16** (1989) 303–317.
13. Ortuño, J,E. and Malpica,N. and Reig, S. and Martínez, R. and Desco, M. and Santos, A.: Algoritmo morfológico de segmentación de imágenes de resonancia magnética normales ponderados en T1, Madrid, España, Congreso Anual de la Sociedad de Ingeniería Biomédica CASEIB2001, (2001) 205–208.
14. Pal, N, R. and Pal, S, K.: A review of image segmentation techniques. Pattern Recognition, **9** (1993) 1277–1294.
15. Peli, E.:Contrast in complex images. J. Optical Society of America , **7** (1990) 2032–2040.
16. Serra, J.: Image Analysis and Mathematical Morphology, J. Serra, Ed., Vol. I, Academic, New York, (1982).
17. Serra, J.: Toggle mappings. Technical report N-18/88/MM, Centre de Morphologie Mathematique, ENSMP, Fontainebleau, France, (1988a)
18. Serra, J.: Image Analysis and Mathematical Morphology, J. Serra, Ed., Vol. II, Academic, New York, (1988b).
19. Stockham, T. G. Jr.:Image processing in the context of a visual model. Proc. IEEE, **60** (1972) 828–842.
20. Terol-Villalobos, I. R.:Nonincreasing filtres using morphological gradient criteria. Optical Engineering, **35** (1996) 3172-3182.
21. Terol-Villalobos, I. R. and Cruz-Mandujano, J.A. : Contrast enhancement and image segmentation using a class of morphological nonincreasing filters. Journal of Electronic Imaging, **7** (1998) 641–654.
22. Terol-Villalobos, I.R.:Morphological Image Enhancement and Segmentation. Advances in Imaging and Electron Physics, P. W. Hawkes Editor, Academic Press, (2001) 207–273.

Gaze Detection by Dual Camera and Dual IR-LED Illuminators

Kang Ryoung Park[1] and Jaihie Kim[2]

[1] Division of Media Tech., SangMyung Univ.,
7 Hongji-Dong, JongRo-Gu, Seoul, Republic of Korea
[2] Dept. of Electrical and Electronic Engineering, Yonsei University,
Seoul, Republic of Korea

Abstract. Gaze detection is to locate the position (on a monitor) of where a user is looking. This paper presents a new and practical method for detecting the monitor position where the user is looking. In general, the user tends to move both his head and eyes in order to gaze at certain monitor position. Previous researches use one wide-view camera, which can capture a whole user's face. However, the image resolution is too low with such a camera and the fine movements of user's eye cannot be exactly detected. So, we implement the gaze detection system with dual camera system(a wide and a narrow-view camera). In order to locate the user's eye position accurately, the narrow-view camera has the functionalities of auto focusing/pan/tilting based on the detected 3D facial feature positions from the wide-view camera. In addition, we use IR-LED illuminator in order to detect facial features and especially eye features. To overcome the problem of specular reflection on a glasses, we use dual IR-LED illuminators and detect the accurate eye position with escaping the glasses specular reflection. From experimental results, we implement the real-time gaze detection system and obtain the gaze position accuracy between the computed positions and the real ones is about 3.44 cm of RMS error.

Keywords: Gaze Detection, Dual Camera, Glasses Specular Reflection, Dual IR-LED Illuminators

1   Introduction

Gaze detection is to locate the position where a user is looking. This paper presents a new and practical method for detecting a point on the monitor where the user is looking. In human computer interaction, the gaze point on a monitor screen is a very important information. Gaze detection system has numerous fields of application. They are applicable to the interface of man-machine interaction, such as the view control in three dimensional simulation programs. Furthermore, they can help the handicapped to use computers and are also useful for those whose hands are busy doing other things[18]. Previous studies were mostly focused on 2D/3D head rotation/translation estimation[1][14], facial gaze detection[2-8][15][16][18][23] and eye gaze detection[9-13][17][21][24-29].

R. Monroy et al. (Eds.): MICAI 2004, LNAI 2972, pp. 622–631, 2004.

However, the gaze detection considering head and eye movement simultaneously has been rarely researched. Ohmura and Ballard et al.[4][5]'s methods have the disadvantages that the depth between camera plane and feature points in the initial frame must be measured manually and it takes much time(over 1 minute) to compute the gaze direction vector. Gee et al.[6] and Heinzmann et al.[7]'s methods only compute gaze direction vector whose origin is located between the eyes in the head coordinate and do not obtain the gaze position on a monitor. In addition, if 3D rotations and translations of the head happen simultaneously, they cannot estimate the accurate 3D motion due to the increase of complexity of least-square fitting algorithm, which requires much processing time. Rikert et al.[8]'s method has the constraints that the distance between a face and the monitor must be kept same for all training and testing procedures and it can be cumbersome to user. In the methods of [10][12][13][15][16], a pair of glasses having marking points is required to detect facial features, which can be inconvenient to a user. The methods of [2][3][20] shows the gaze detection by head movements, but have the limits that the eye movements do not happen. The method of [19] shows the gaze detection by head and eye movements, but uses only one wide-view camera, which can capture the whole face of user. However, the image resolution is too low with such a camera and the fine movements of user's eye cannot be exactly detected. So, we implement the gaze detection system with dual camera(a wide-view and a narrow-view camera). In order to detect the positions of user's eye changed by head movements, the narrow-view camera has the functionalities of auto focusing/pan/tilting based on the detected 3D facial feature positions from the wide-view camera. In addition, we use IR-LED illuminator in order to detect facial features and especially eye features. To detect the exact eye positions in case of users with glasses, we use dual IR-LED illuminators. In section 2, I explain the method for extracting facial features using our gaze detection system. In section 3, I show the method of estimating the 3D facial feature positions and capturing eye image by narrow view camera. In section 4, the method for estimating 3D head rotation and translation is shown and the method for detecting final gaze position is explained in section 5. In section 6, the performance evaluation is provided and the conclusion is shown in section 7.

2 Extraction of Facial Features

In order to detect gaze position on a monitor, we first locate facial features(both eye centers, eye corners, nostrils and lip corners) in an input image. There have been so many researches for detecting face and facial features. One of them is to use facial skin color[22], but their performance may be affected by the environmental light or race, etc. To overcome such problems and detect the facial features robustly in any environment, we use the method of detecting specular reflection on the eyes[19]. It requires a camera system equipped with some hardware as shown in Fig.1.

In Fig.1, the IR-LED(1) is used to make the specular reflections on eyes[19]. The HPF(2)(High Pass Filter) in front of camera lens can only pass the infrared

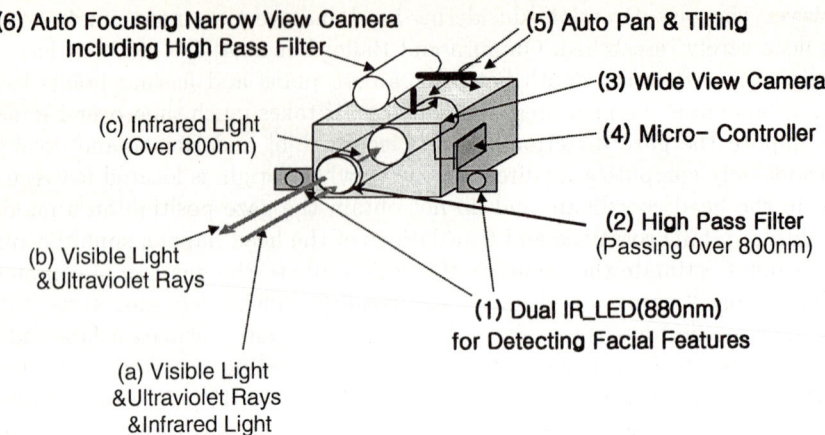

(6) Auto Focusing Narrow View Camera Including High Pass Filter

(5) Auto Pan & Tilting

(3) Wide View Camera

(c) Infrared Light (Over 800nm)

(4) Micro- Controller

(2) High Pass Filter (Passing 0ver 800nm)

(b) Visible Light &Ultraviolet Rays

(1) Dual IR_LED(880nm) for Detecting Facial Features

(a) Visible Light &Ultraviolet Rays &Infrared Light

Fig. 1. The Gaze Detecting Camera with Dual IR-LED illuminators

lights(over 700 nm) and the input images are only affected by the IR-LED(1) excluding external illuminations. So, it is unnecessary to normalize the illumination of the input image. We use a normal interlaced wide-view(3) and narrow-view(6) CCD sensor and a micro-controller(4) embedded in camera system which can detect every VD(Vertical Drive, which means the starting signal of even or odd field) from CCD output signal. From that, we can control the Illuminator[19]. In general, the normal CCD sensor shows lower sensitivity for IR-LED light compared to visible light and the input image is darker with IR-LED light. So, we use the several IR-LEDs(880nm) as the illuminator for detecting facial features. The reason of using 880nm as illuminator is that general human eye can perceive the visible and the near infrared light(below 880nm). So, our illuminators are not uncomfortable to user's eye. When a user starts our gaze detection system, the starting signal is transferred into the micro-controller in camera via the RS-232C. Then, the micro-controller turns on the IR-LED during the even field and turns off it during the odd field, successively[19]. From that, we can get a difference image between the even and the odd image and the specular points of both eyes can be easily detected, because its gray level is higher than any other region[19]. In addition, we use the Red-Eye effect in order to detect more accurate eye position[19] and use the method of changing Frame Grabber decoder value. The output signal of wide/narrow-view camera(as shown in Fig.1) is NTSC format and we use a 2 channel Frame Grabber to convert the NTSC analog signal into digital image. We have implemented the PCI interfaced Frame Grabber with 2 decoders and 1 multimedia bridge. Each decoder can A/D convert(analog to digital convert) the NTSC signal from narrow-view and wide-view camera. The multimedia bridge chip interfaces the 2 decoder with PCI bus of computer. In general, the NTSC signal has high resolution($0 \sim 2^{10} - 1$), but the ability of A/D converting with general decoder is low resolution($0 \sim 2^8 - 1$). So, the input NTSC signal cannot be fully represented with such decoder and some signal range may be cut off. The NTSC signal in high saturated range are represented as $255(2^8-1)$ level of image. So, both the specular reflection on eye and the some reflection region on facial skin may be represented as same image level($2^8 - 1$). In such case, we have the difficulties to discriminate the specular reflection from the other reflection with image information. However, the NTSC analog signal level of each region is different(the analog level of specular reflection on eye is higher than that of other reflection. We can identify such phenomena checking the NTSC analog level with oscilloscope equipment). So, if we change the decoder brightness setting(making the brightness value lower), then the A-D converting range with decoder can be shifted to the upper direction. In such case, there may not be the high saturated range and the specular reflection on eye and the other reflection can be discriminated easily. When the specular points on eye are detected, we can restrict the eye region around the detected specular points. With the restricted eye searching region, we locate the accurate eye center by the circular edge matching method. Because we search the restricted eye region, it does not take much time to detect the exact eye center(almost $5 \sim 10$ ms in Pentium-II 550MHz). After locating the eye center, we detect the eye corner by using eye corner shape template and SVM(Support Vector Machine)[19]. We get 2000 successive image frames(100 frames $\times$ 20 persons in various sitting positions) and from that, 8000 eye corner samples (4 eye corners $\times$ 2000 images) are obtained and additional 1000 images are used for testing. Experimental results show the classification error from training data is 0.11% (9/8000) and that from testing data is 0.2%(8/4000) and our algorithm is valid on the users with glasses or contact lens. In our experimental results, MLP(Multi-Layered Perceptron) shows the error of 1.58% from training data and 3.1% from testing data. In addition, the classification time of SVM is so small as like 13 ms in Pentium-II 550MHz[21]. After locating eye centers and eye corners, the positions of both nostrils and lip corners can be detected by anthropometric constraints in a face and SVM similar to eye corner detection. Experimental results show that RMS error between the detected feature positions and the actual positions(manually detected positions) are 1 pixel (of both eye centers), 2 pixels (of both eye corners), 4 pixels (of both nostrils) and 3 pixels (of both lip corners) in 640×480 image[19]. From the detected feature positions, we select 7 feature points (left/right eye corners of left eye, left/right eye corners of right eye, nostril center, left/right lip corners)[19] and compute 3D facial motion based on the 2D movement of them.

3   Estimating the Initial 3D Facial Feature Positions and Capturing Eye Image by Narrow View Camera

After feature detection, we take 4 steps in order to compute a gaze position on a monitor[2][3][19]. At the first step, when a user gazes at 5 known positions on a monitor, the 3D positions(X, Y, Z) of initial 7 feature points(selected in the section 2) are computed automatically. In such case, if we use more calibration points, the computation accuracy of initial feature positions will be somewhat increased, but the user's inconvenience is also increased accordingly. At the second and third step, when the user rotates/translates his head in order to gaze at one position on a monitor, the new 3D positions of those 7 features can be computed from 3D motion estimation. At the 4th step, one facial plane is determined from the new 3D positions of those 7 features and the normal vector of the plane represents a gaze vector by head movements. Here, if the changed 3D positions of initial 7 feature points can be computed at the 2nd and 3rd step, they can be converted into the positions of monitor coordinate. From that, we can also convert those feature positions into those of camera coordinate based on the camera parameter which can be obtained at the 1st step. With this information, we can pan/tilt the narrow-view camera in order to capture the eye image. In general, the narrow-view camera has a small viewing angle(large focal length of about 30 - 45mm) with which it can capture large eye image. So, if the user moves(especially rotates) his head severely, one of his eyes may disappear in camera view. So, we track only one visible eye with auto pan/tile narrow-view camera. For pan/tilting, we use 2 stepping motors with 420 pps(pulses per second). In addition, general narrow-view camera has small DOF(Depth of Field) and the input image can be easily defocused according to user's Z movement. The DOF is almost the Z distance range in which the object can be clearly captured in the camera image. The DOF shows the characteristics that if the size of camera iris is smaller, or the Z distance of object to be captured is larger in front of camera, the DOF is bigger. However, in our case, we cannot make the user's Z distance bigger on purpose because the users sits in $50 \sim 70$ cm in front of monitor in general. In addition, making the camera iris size smaller lessens the input light to camera CCD sensor and the input image is much darker. So, we use the narrow-view camera with iris size of 10mm, an auto focusing lens and a focusing motor(420 pps) in order to capture clearer(more focused) eye image. These auto pan/tilt/focusing are manipulated by micro-controller(4) in camera of Fig.1. For focusing of narrow-view eye image, the Z distance information between the eye and a camera is required. In our research, the Z distance can be computed at the 2nd and 3rd step and we can use such information as the seed of auto focusing for eye image. However, the auto focusing in narrow-view camera is reported to be difficult due to small DOF and exact auto focusing cannot be achieved only with Z distance. So, we contrive a simple auto focusing algorithm which checks the pixel disparity in an image. That is, the auto pan/tilt of narrow-view camera is achieved according to the detected eye position from the wide-view camera and the preliminary auto focusing for eye image is accomplished based on the computed Z distance of the 3rd step. After that, the captured eye image is transferred to PC and our simple focusing algorithm checks the focus quality of image. If the quality does not meet our threshold, then we send the controlling command of focus lens to camera micro-controller(4) in Fig.1. Here, when the defocused eye image is captured, it is difficult to determine the movements of focus lens(move forward or backward). For that, we use various heuristic information(for example, image brightness and blind/pyramid lens searching, etc). With this auto focusing mechanism, we can get the focused eye image from narrow-view camera. In this stage, we consider the specular reflection on glasses. The surface of glasses can reflect the IR-LED light into narrow-view camera and the eye image may be covered with large reflection region. In such case, the eye region cannot be detected and we cannot compute the consecutive eye gaze position. The surface of glasses is mainly affected by the user's vision. The weaker the vision becomes, the flatter the surface of glasses may be. In such flatter surface, the reflection region tends to be larger in eye image and it is more difficult to detect eye region. So, we use dual IR-LED illuminators like Fig.1(1). The dual illuminators turn on alternately. When the large specular reflection happens from one illuminator(right or left illuminator), then it can be detected from image. As mentioned before(section 2), the NTSC analog level of specular reflection region is higher than any other region and they can be detected by changing decoder brightness setting. When the large specular region proves to exist with the changed decoder brightness value, then our gaze detection system automatically change the illuminator(from left to right or right to left). In such case, the specular reflection may not happen. With these procedures, if the focused eye image can be captured, we use a trained neural network(multi-layered perceptron) to detect the gaze position by eye's movement. Then, the facial and eye gaze position on a monitor is calculated from the geometric sum between the facial gaze position and the eye gaze. The detail explanations about the first step including the camera calibration can be referred to [2] and experimental results show that the RMS error of between the real 3D feature positions(measured by 3D position tracking sensor) and the estimated one is 1.15 cm(0.64cm in X axis, 0.5cm in Y axis, 0.81cm in Z axis) for 20 person data which were used for testing the feature detection performance.

4   Estimating the 3D Head Rotation and Translation

This section explains the 2nd step shown in section 3. Considering many limitations or problems of previous motion estimation researches[19], we use the EKF for 3D motion estimation algorithm and the moved 3D positions of those features can be estimated from 3D motion estimations by EKF and affine transform[2][19]. Detail accounts can be referred to[1]. The estimation accuracy of EKF is compared with 3D position tracking sensor. Our experimental results show the RMS errors are about 1.4 cm and 2.98° in translation and rotation.

5   Detecting the Gaze Position on the Monitor

5.1   By Head Motion

This section explains the 3rd and 4th step explained in section 3. The initial 3D positions of the 7 features computed in monitor coordinate in section 3 are converted into the 3D feature positions in head coordinate and using these converted 3D feature positions, 3D rotation and translation matrices estimated by EKF and affine transform, we can obtain the new 3D feature positions in head and monitor coordinate when a user gazes at a monitor position[2]. From that, one facial plane is determined and the normal vector of the plane shows a gaze vector. The gaze position on a monitor is the intersection position between a monitor and the gaze vector[2][3][20].

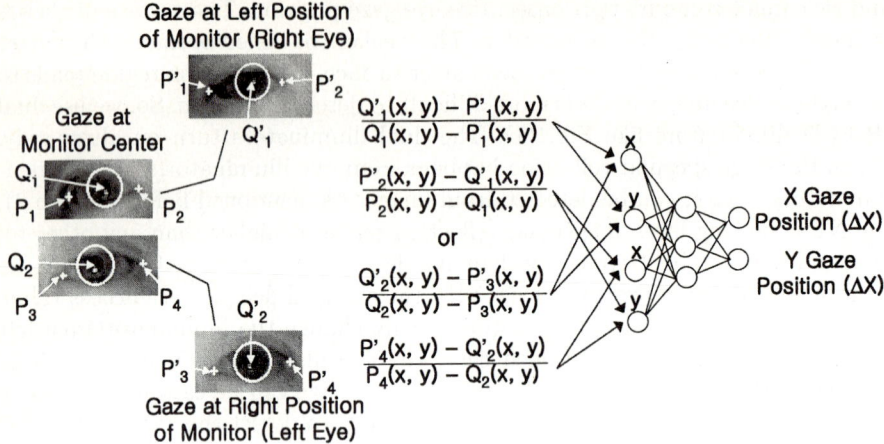

Fig. 2. The neural network for detecting gaze position by eye movements

5.2   By Eye Motion

In section 5.1, the gaze position is determined only by head movement. As mentioned before, when a user gazes at a monitor position, both the head and eyes can be easily moved simultaneously. So, we compute the eye movements from the detected iris center and eye corner points as shown in Fig.2. Here, we use the circular edge detection and the eye corner template with SVM in order to detect iris and corner. This method is almost same to those for detecting eye position in wide-view camera mentioned in section 2. As mentioned before, when a user rotates his head severely, one of his eyes may disappear in narrow-view camera. So, we detect both eyes in case the user gazes at a monitor center and when the user rotates his head severely, we track only one eye. In general, the eye positions and shape are changed according to a user gaze position. The distance between the iris center and left or right eye corner is changed according to user's gaze positions. We use a neural network(Multi-layered Perceptron) to train the relations between the eye movements and gaze positions as shown in Fig.2.

Here, the input values for neural network are normalized by the distance between the eye center and the eye corner, which are obtained in case of gazing monitor center. That is why we use only auto focusing lens for narrow-view camera without zoom lens. Without zoom lens, the eye size and the distance between the iris center and the eye corner in image plane(pixel) are affected by the user's Z position. That is, the more the user approaches the monitor, the larger the eye size and the distance between the eye ball and eye corner become. In our research, the Z distances of user are varied between $50 \sim 70$cm. So, the distance normalizations for neural network are required like Fig.2.

5.3   Detecting Facial and Eye Gaze Position

After detecting eye gaze position based on the neural network, we can locate final gaze positions on a monitor by both head and eye movements based on the vector summation of each gaze position(face and eye gaze)[19].

6   Performance Evaluations

The gaze detection error of proposed method is compared to our previous methods[2][3][18][19] like Table 1. The researches[2][3] use the 4 steps mentioned in section 3, but compute facial gaze position without consider the eye movements. The research[18] does not compute 3D facial feature positions/motions and calculates the gaze position by mapping the 2D feature position into the monitor gaze position by linear interpolation or neural network. In addition, they consider only head movements without eye movements. The method[19] computes the gaze positions considering both head and eye movements, but uses only one wide-view camera. The test data are acquired when 10 users gazed at 23 gaze positions on a 19" monitor. Here, the gaze error is the RMS error between the actual gaze position and the computed ones. The reason that we use the RMS error as the criterion for gaze detection accuracy is that we calculate the gaze position on a monitor with X and Y position and the accuracy in two axises should be considered at the same time. Shown in Table 1, the gaze errors are calculated in two cases. The case I means that gaze error about test data including only head movements. In the meanwhile, it is often the case that the head and eye movements happen simultaneously, when a user gazes at. So, we tested the gaze error including head and eye movements in the case II.

Shown in Table 1, the gaze error of the proposed method is the smallest in any case. At the second experiment, points of radius 5 pixels are spaced vertically and horizontally at 150 pixel intervals(2.8 cm) on a 19" monitor with 1280×1024 pixels. The test conditions are almost the same as Rikert's research[8][19]. The RMS error between the real and calculated gaze position is 3.43 cm and it is superior to Rikert's method(almost 5.08 cm). This gaze error is correspondent to the angular error of 2.41 degrees on X axis and 2.52 degrees on Y axis. In addition, Rikert has the constraints that user's Z distance must be always the same, but we do not. For verification, we tested the gaze errors according to the Z distance(55, 60, 65cm). The RMS errors are 3.38cm in the distance of 55cm, 3.45cm in 60cm, 3.49cm in 65cm. It shows that our method can permit the user to move about in the Z direction. And Rikert's method takes much processing

Table 1. Gaze error about test data including only head movements (cm)

Method	Linear interpol.[18]	Single neural net[18]	Combined neural nets[18]	[2] method	[3] method	[19] method	Proposed method
case I	5.1	4.23	4.48	5.35	5.21	3.40	2.98
case II	11.8	11.32	8.87	7.45	6.29	4.8	3.44

time(1 minute in alphastation 333MHz), compared to our method(about 700ms in Pentium-II 550MHz). Our system only requires the user to gaze at 5 known monitor positions at the initial calibration stage (as shown in the section 3) and after that, it can track/compute the user's gaze position without any user's intervention at real-time speed.

7   Conclusions

This paper describes a new gaze detecting method. The gaze error is about 3.44 cm and the processing time is about 700ms in Pentium-II 550MHz. Whereas, Rikert's method shows the RMS error of almost 5.08 cm and it takes processing time of 1 minute in alphastation 333MHz. Our gaze detection error can be compensated by the additional head movement(like mouse dragging). In future works, we have plans to research more accurate method of detecting eye image and it will increase the accuracy of final gaze detection. In addition, the method to increase the auto panning/tilting/focusing speed of narrow view camera should be researched to decrease total processing time.

Acknowledgment. This work was supported by Korea Science and Engineering Foundation (KOSEF) through Biometrics Engineering Research Center(BERC) at Yonsei University.

References

1. A. Azarbayejani., 1993, Visually Controlled Graphics. IEEE Trans. PAMI, Vol. 15, No. 6, pp. 602-605
2. K. R. Park et al., Apr 2000, Gaze Point Detection by Computing the 3D Positions and 3D Motions of Face, IEICE Trans. Inf.&Syst.,Vol. E.83-D, No.4, pp.884-894
3. K. R. Park et al., Oct 1999, Gaze Detection by Estimating the Depth and 3D Motions of Facial Features in Monocular Images, IEICE Trans. Fundamentals, Vol. E.82-A, No. 10, pp. 2274-2284
4. K. OHMURA et al., 1989. Pointing Operation Using Detection of Face Direction from a Single View. IEICE Trans. Inf.&Syst., Vol. J72-D-II, No.9, pp. 1441-1447
5. P. Ballard et al., 1995. Controlling a Computer via Facial Aspect. IEEE Trans. on SMC, Vol. 25, No. 4, pp. 669-677
6. A. Gee et al., 1996. Fast visual tracking by temporal consensus, Image and Vision Computing. Vol. 14, pp. 105-114
7. J. Heinzmann et al., 1998. 3D Facial Pose and Gaze Point Estimation using a Robust Real-Time Tracking Paradigm. Proceedings of ICAFGR, pp. 142-147
8. T. Rikert, 1998. Gaze Estimation using Morphable Models. ICAFGR, pp.436-441
9. A.Ali-A-L et al., 1997, Man-machine interface through eyeball direction of gaze. Proc. of the Southeastern Symposium on System Theory, pp. 478-82
10. A. TOMONO et al., 1994. Eye Tracking Method Using an Image Pickup Apparatus. European Patent Specification-94101635
11. Eyemark Recorder Model EMR-NC, NAC Image Technology Cooperation

12. Porrill-J et al., Jan 1999, Robust and optimal use of information in stereo vision. Nature. vol.397, no.6714, pp.63-6

13. Varchmin-AC et al., 1998, image based recognition of gaze direction using adaptive methods. Gesture and Sign Language in Human-Computer Interaction. Int. Gesture Workshop Proc. Berlin, Germany, pp. 245-57.

14. J. Heinzmann et al., 1997. Robust real-time face tracking and gesture recognition. Proc. of the IJCAI, Vol. 2, pp. 1525-1530

15. Matsumoto-Y, et al., 2000, An algorithm for real-time stereo vision implementation of head pose and gaze direction measurement. Proc. the ICAFGR. pp. 499-504

16. Newman-R et al., 2000, Real-time stereo tracking for head pose and gaze estimation. Proceedings the 4th ICAFGR 2000. pp. 122-8

17. Betke-M et al., 1999, Gaze detection via self-organizing gray-scale units. Proc. Int. Workshop on Recog., Analy., and Tracking of Faces and Gestures in Real-Time System. pp. 70-6

18. K. R. Park et al., 2000. Intelligent Process Control via Gaze Detection Technology. EAAI, Vol. 13, No. 5, pp. 577-587

19. K. R. Park et al., 2002, Facial and Eye Gaze detection. LNCS, Vol.2525, pp. 368-376

20. K. R. Park et al., 2002. Gaze Position Detection by Computing the 3 Dimensional Facial Positions and Motions. Pattern Recognition, Vol. 35, No.11, pp. 2559-2569

21. J. Wang and E. Sung, 2002. Study on Eye Gaze Estimation, IEEE Trans. on SMC, Vol. 32, No. 3, pp.332-350

22. http://www.is.cs.cmu.edu/mie/modelgaze-tracking.html

23. Y. Matsumoto, 2000. An Algorithm for Real-time Stereo Vision Implementation of Head Pose and Gaze Direction Measurement, ICFGR, pp.499-505

24. http://www.iscaninc.com

25. http://www.seeingmachines.com

26. B Wolfe, D. Eichmann, 1997. A neural network approach to tracking eye position, International Journal Human Computer Interaction, Vol. 9, No.1, pp. 59-79

27. David Beymer and Myron Flickner, 2003. Eye Gaze Tracking Using an Active Stereo Head, IEEE Computer Vision and Pattern Recognition

28. J. Zhu et al., 2002. Subpixel eye gaze tracking, International Conference on Face and Gesture Recognition

29. R. Stiefelhagen, J. Yang, and A. Waibel, 1997. Tracking eyes and monitoring eye gaze, Proceedings of Workshop on Perceptual User Interfaces, pp. 98-100

Image Processing and Neural Networks for Early Detection of Histological Changes

J. Ramírez-Niño[1], M.A. Flores[2], C. Ramírez[1], and V.M. Castaño[3]

[1] Instituto de Investigaciones Eléctricas,
apartado postal 1-475, Cuernavaca, Morelos 62000, México
[2] Centro Nacional de Investigación y Desarrollo Tecnológico,
apartado postal 5-164, Cuernavaca, Morelos 62000, México
[3] Centro de Física Aplicada y Tecnología Avanzada, U.N.A.M.,
apartado postal 1-1010, Querétaro, Querétaro 76000, México

Abstract. A novel methodology for the histological images characterisation taken from the microscopic analysis of cervix biopsies is outlined. First, the fundament of the malignancy process is reviewed in order to understand which parameters are significant. Then, the analysis methodology using equalisation and artificial Neural Networks is depicted and the step by step analysis output images are shown. Finally, the results of the proposed analysis applied to example images are discussed.

1 Introduction

Cervical Uterine Cancer (CUC) is the most common type of cancer in women at reproductive age, in Mexico, where around 4,300 deceases were recorded in 2001 alone [1] and it represents a serious public health problem worldwide. Enormous effort has been dedicated towards designing adequate diagnosis techniques in order to detect CUC in its early stage and there are massive campaigns to apply diagnosis tests. The challenge is not only having a reliable testing technology, but also a simple and inexpensive in order to be used in a massive scale. Accordingly, the aim of this work is to develop a practical, low-cost tool that allows measuring the nucleus/cytoplasm ratio (N/C) a long the epithelium layer, to help distinguish normal tissue from abnormal. First, the fundamental medical concepts are reviewed to provide a clear idea about the parameters involved in pathological images analysis. Then, the method developed is described in detail and, finally, some actual results on real cases are explained, as well.

2 Medical Background

2.1 Epithelium Structure

Different layers known as basal, parabasal, intermediate and superficial are typical of a healthy cervix epithelium. The cervix is the lower part of the uterus and is often

R. Monroy et al. (Eds.): MICAI 2004, LNAI 2972, pp. 632–641, 2004.

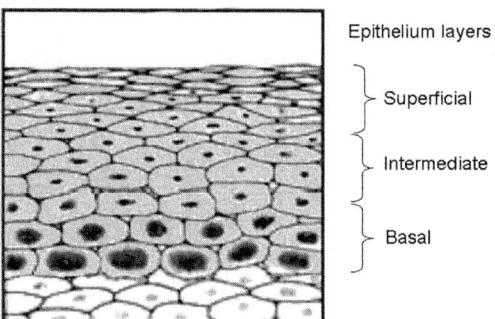

Epithelium layers

Superficial

Intermediate

Basal

Fig. 1. Schematic diagram of the cervix epithelium layers.

called the neck of the cervix. The epithelial cells are produced in the basal layer and they move through the superficial layer in about 15 days. For this reason, when a biopsy (small sample of cells) is analysed, a view of the epithelium cells evolution along the time is shown. As the cells mature, the cell nucleus get smaller and the cytoplasm amount increases. The parabasal, intermediate and superficial layers are the areas of the images where the mathematical analysis will be focused. These structures are shown in Figure 1.

2.2 Cervical Uterine Cancer

Although cells in different parts of the body may look and work differently, most of them repair and reproduce by themselves within the same way. Normally, this division of cells takes place in an orderly and controlled manner. If, for some reason, the process gets out of control, the cells will continue to divide, developing into a lump that is called a tumour. Tumours can be either benign or malignant. A malignant tumour is characterised by uncontrolled growth, alterations of varying extent in the structural and functional differentiation of its component cells, and the capacity to spread beyond the limits of the original tissue.

The CUC can take many years to develop. Before it does, early changes occur in the cells of the cervix. The name given to these abnormal cells, which are not cancerous but may lead to cancer is Cervical Intra-epithelial Neoplasia (CIN). This is not precisely a cancer, but frequently woman can develop it into cancer over a number of years provided it is left untreated. Some doctors call these changes pre-cancerous, meaning that the cells have the potential to develop into cancer. Thus, The CIN occurs only when the cells lose their normal appearance. When the abnormal cells are looked under the microscope, they may be divided into three categories, according to the thickness of the cervix epithelium affected, namely:

- CIN 1 – only one third is affected and is called mild dysphasia.
- CIN 2 – two thirds is affected and is called moderate dysphasia.
- CIN 3 – the full thickness of the cervix epithelium is affected, it is referred as severe dysphasia (frank cancer that has not invaded the surrounding tissues).

The CIN 3 is also known as carcinoma-in-situ. Although this may sound like cancer, CIN 3 is not strictly a cervix cancer, but it must be treated as soon as possible. The progression of CIN from one stage to the next takes years and, in some cases of

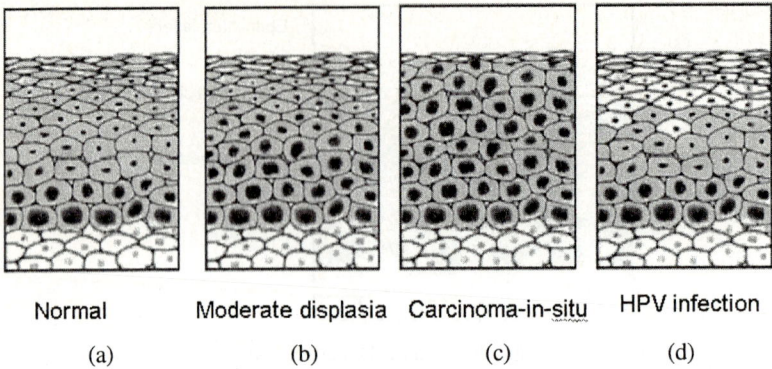

Normal   Moderate displasia Carcinoma-in-situ   HPV infection

(a)   (b)   (c)   (d)

Fig. 2. Normal epithelium a, moderate displasia b, carcinoma-in-situ c and HPV infection d.

CIN 1 may even go back to normal tissue. However, as they are part of a progressive disease, all cases of abnormal smears should be investigated and cases of CIN2 and CIN3 must be treated. [1-2]. Schematic samples of different epithelium alterations as moderate displasia, carcinoma-in-situ and the HPV infection compared with a normal epithelium are shown in Figure 2.

3 Analysis Technique

The approach proposed is based on the classification of the cellular structures obtained from biopsy microscopy images and then, its digital analysis over defined areas. An efficient neural network approach is selected and used to classify benign and malignant structures, based on the extracted morphological features. This technique consists of the identification of pre-malignant conditions, which may progress to malignancy. Friendly and easy-to-use software in order to help the pathologist on the diagnosis of cervix cancer was developed. The software input consists of microscopy images taken from the cervix biopsy stained by the standard procedure. The software performs a quantitative analysis on the nucleus/cytoplasm ratio and the structural analysis of the cellular tissue at its different layers.

3.1 Neural Networks

The first problem finding out the biopsy image structures is to classify the pixels according with its colour characteristics. The classification problem requires labelling each pixel as a belonging to one of "n" classes (nucleus, epithelial cytoplasm, sub-epithelial cytoplasm and white zones).

Artificial neural networks can separates the classes by a learning process that gradually adjust a parameters set of a discriminant function and it is the heart of the image analysis process.

When a plane can separate two classes, the classes are said to be linearly separable and a neural network without hidden units or layers can learn such problem. This property can be applied to our classification problem because the stain used in the biopsy allows colorizing the epithelium structures substantially different.

For multinomial classification problems, a neural network with n outputs, one for each class, and target values of 1 for correct class, and 0 otherwise, is used. The correct generalisation of the logistic sigmoid to the multinomial case is the Softmax activation function:

$$y_i(x) = \frac{e^{x_i}}{\sum_C e^{x_i}} \quad i = 1, 2, \ldots, C \tag{1}$$

where $y_i(x)$ is the activation function of the ith output node and C is the number of classes. Notice that $y_i(x)$ is always a number between 0 and 1.

The error function is defined as:

$$E = \sum_{j=1}^{C} t_j \ln(y_j) \tag{2}$$

Equation 2 is the so-called Cross-Entropy error, where t_j is the target; y_j is the output "j".

$$\frac{\partial E}{\partial W_{rs}} = (t_r - y_r)x_s \tag{3}$$

$$W(new) = W(old) + \mu(t - y)x \tag{4}$$

Equation 3 represents the error change rate when the weights are altered; Equation 4 allows to get the new weights W(new) in terms of the olds weights W(old) and μ is the learning rate between 0 and 1. Since all the nodes in a Softmax output layer interact. The output value of each node depends on the values of all the others.

Preconditioning Network Criteria. There are two main factors to consider during the learning process of the neural network:

• If μ (the learning rate) is too low, convergence will be very slow; set it too high, and the network will diverge. The ill conditioning in neural networks can be caused by the training data, the network's architecture, and initial weights. The ill conditioning can be avoided by using preconditioning techniques.

• Inputs and targets normalization. To normalize a variable, first subtract its average and then, divide it over its standard deviation.

Before training, the network weights are initialised to small random values. The random are usually chosen from a uniform distribution over the range [-r,r]. This type of learning is referred to as "supervised learning" (or learning with teacher) because target values are taken from known images structures. In this type of supervised training, both the inputs "x_i "and outputs "t_i "are provided. The network then processes the inputs and compares its resulting outputs against the desired outputs. The error function is then calculated by the system, causing the system to adjust the weights, which control the network. Sets of pixels values are taken from a known image structure (reference image). The pixel values are used as the inputs or the decision values, and the output structures in the image structures are established as classes. There will be a values range for the decision values that map to the same class. If the

Inputs   Activation   Outputs
                           Function

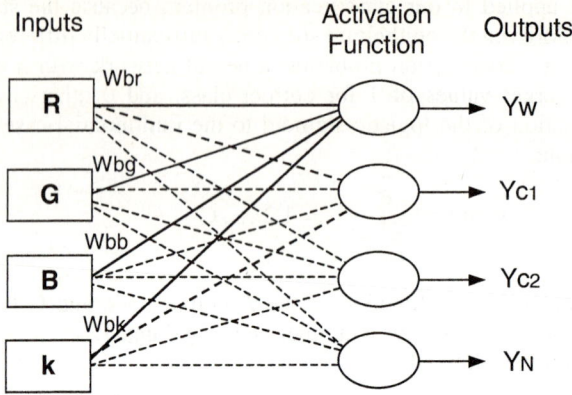

Fig. 3. Neural network structure used by the proposed method.

values of the decision variables are plotted, different regions or point clusters will correspond to different classes [3-5].

A single layer network was selected for the network topology and the so-called Perceptron algorithm trains it. The selected topology is shown in Figure 3.

One layer, 5 inputs, 4 nodes, activation function Softmax, error function cross-entropy, type of learning algorithm perceptron are the complete neural network specifications. The five inputs are conformed by RGB pixel's characteristics and an input constant "k".

Perceptron algorithm. The Perceptron algorithm is a step-wise method, which allows finding out the weights set that can classify appropriately the image pixels. The steps are the following:
1. Initialise the weights with small random values
2. Pick a learning rate μ as a number between 0 and 1
3. Compute the output activation for each training pattern by the Equation 1
4. Compute the error function by the Equation 2
5. Updating the weights W by the Equation 4 until stopping condition is satisfied (a specific error function value)

It is important that the step four considers all the pixels set from all structures or classes and provides them to the algorithm in random order to assure an appropriate algorithm convergence. The $y_i(x)$ is interpreted as the probability that "i" is the correct class. This means that:

• The output of each node must be between 0 and 1.
• The sum of the outputs over all nodes must be equal to 1.

In other words, $y_i(x)$ values indicates the probability that a particular pixel belongs to nucleus Y_N, epithelial cytoplasm Y_{C1}, sub-epithelial cytoplasm Y_{C2} or white zones Y_W structures. Once the neural network is trained, it has the ability to predict the output for an input that has not be seen and this is called "generalization". [6-11]

4 Practical Image Analysis Procedure

Two operation modes are considered:

Learning mode. The software learns the reference values that will be used by the neural network in the image analysis. This is done only once. A reference image is selected and it is analysed in order to get the basic parameters used later in the image possessing.

Two parameter sets are considered in this stage:

- Colour deviations usually are produced by differences in the stain procedure and by differences in the slide illumination at the image acquisition process. An equalisation process helps to reduce the colour deviation between images. One image is selected as a reference and its RGB colour histogram is taken separately. The digital value of the red colour pixels of the image, for example goes from 30 to 240, green goes from 25 to 218 and blue from 10 to 250. These values are taken as reference parameters (RL, RH, GL, GH, BL and BH,) and are used to modify the respective levels of further images.
- Little samples images from the reference image are taken. Samples of pixels from the nucleus, cytoplasm and white zones are normalized and used as inputs and outputs (x,t) array when the neuronal network is trained. Thus, the final weights W_{rs} are obtained applying the perceptron algorithm.

Normal mode. When the pathologist selects an image, the image processing is started. Figure 4 shows a typical example of a normal biopsy. The images most have all of structures shown in Figure 1 and preferably at the same arrange position.

a).- The first step is the equalisation process using the parameters obtained from the learning stage. This is done by a linear conversion for each pixel and for its RGB component colour. By applying this conversion, a new image is built. Tree equations, like the equation 5, for the equalisation process are used.

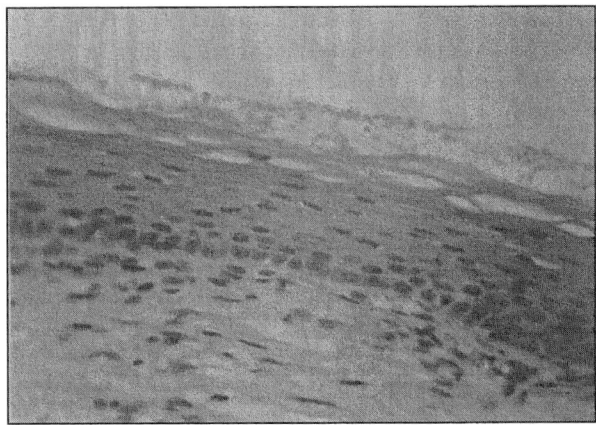

Fig. 4. A biopsy Image taken from the microscope digital camera.

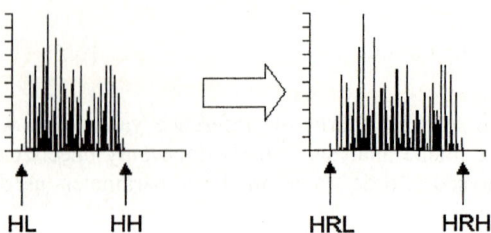

HL   HH   HRL   HRH

Fig. 5. Histogram transformation by the equalization process.

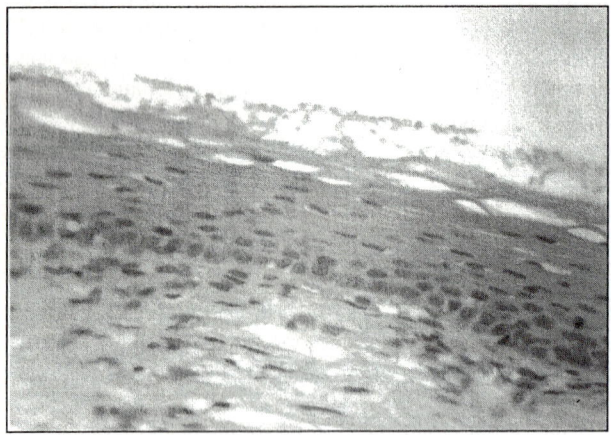

Fig. 6. Image after the equalization process.

$$PR_{New} = (RH - RL) + PR_{Old}\left[\frac{RH - RL}{HRH - HRL}\right] \qquad (5)$$

Where PR_{New} is the new value of the red component for each pixel, PR_{Old} is the old value of the red component. RH and RL are the higher and lower components of the red histogram taken from the reference image. HRH and HRL are the higher and lower components of the red histogram taken from the image to be processed. Similar equations are used for the green and blue components of the pixel transformation. The equalization process produces a change in the histogram and it is represented in Figure 5. The new transformed image is shown in Figure 6.

b).- Using the neural network weights, as obtained from the learning mode, the program builds a new image where each pixel is classified into four categories: nucleus, epithelial cytoplasm, sub-epithelial cytoplasm and white zones or external zone. Four different grey levels are assigned to each zone as the new image is built. The structures classified from the image in Figure 6 are shown in Figure 7.

Fig. 7. Image transformed is classified in four different grey levels.

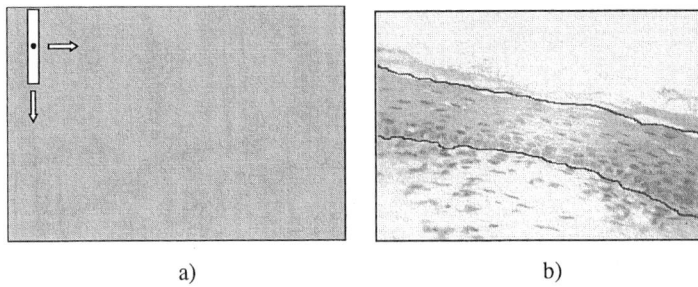

a)   b)

Fig. 8. Schematic diagram that shows how the analysis window moves over the image in order to find out the epithelium limits a) and how the epithelial layer limits are found b).

c).- The epithelium zone is then established using a moving rectangular window, which helps to find where the epithelium begins and ends. The window is first moved vertically and in the horizontal path as is shown in Figure 8. The central window point is evaluated in order to find out the epithelium limits. Within a rectangular window, nucleus (N), epithelial cytoplasm (C1), sub-epithelial cytoplasm (C2) and white zones (W) structure areas or number of pixels for each zone inside the window are computed.

If the sign of [C1-C2] changes when the window moves vertically and $C1 \neq 0$ and $C2 \neq 0$ then, the beginning of the epithelium edge is found and drawn over the image. If the sign of [W −(N+C1+C2)] change then the external limit is also found. A view of one screen output of the software, showing the epithelial layer limits can be seen in Figure 9.

d).- The nucleus/cytoplasm ratio (N/C1) and white halos/cytoplasm ratio (W/C1) are evaluated only in the epithelial layer and plotted. Selecting an area over the image does this by means of a rectangular window. The N/C1 ratio of a normal epithelium has an exponential behaviour that is also plotted and used as a reference. The areas

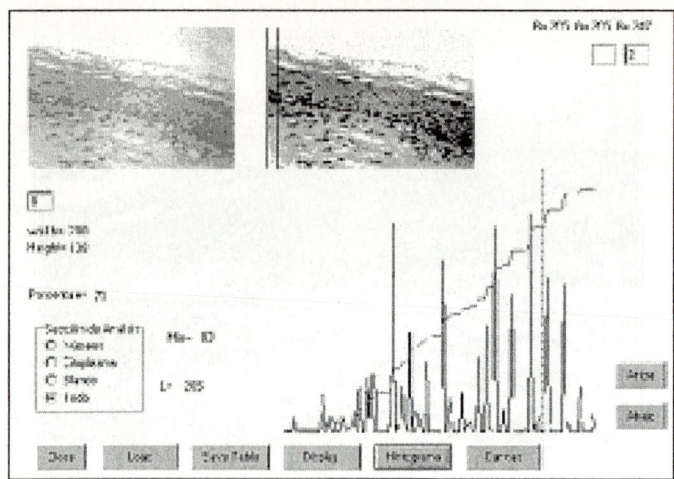

Fig. 9. A view of one screen software output showing an epithelial typical analysis.

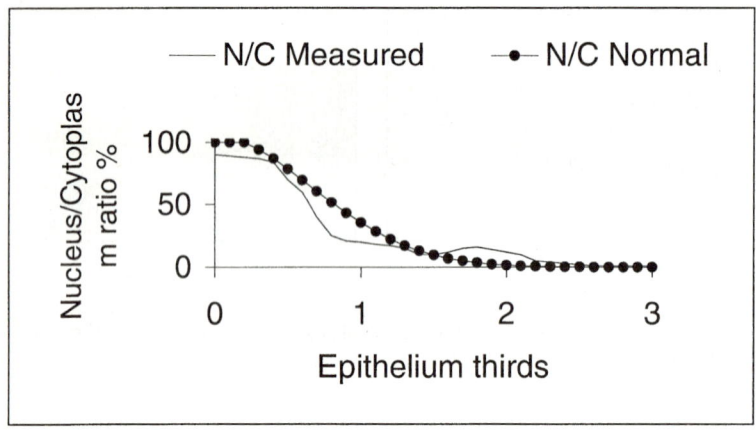

Fig. 10. Normal and measured the Nucleus/Cytoplasm ratio along the epithelium thirds.

where the N/C1 have abnormal behaviour are contrasted in order to provide a warning signal to the pathologist. An example of this output is shown in Figure 10.

The computer program was developed on Delphi language and it runs on windows platform. It was conceived as an easy tool for pathologists. The system has a digital camera coupled to microscope and a personal computer. The software allows loading images from files and saving or printing the analysis results. The user interface provides a selection window on top of the image that gives the numerical or graphical nucleus/cytoplasm ratio for any selected area. The microscope should have the magnification power fixed at 10X preferably, in order to cover a large epithelium area. The image digital resolution should be such that nucleus diameter average pixels size being around 10 pixels and must be save in bitmap file type.

When the neural network is trained, one hundred of teaching interactions are enough to reach an error magnitude of 10^{-11}.

5   Conclusions

Around 30 different images were tested with satisfactory results and the effectiveness of the image analysis proposed was demonstrated. It is mandatory that the images have the complete epithelium basic structures in order to assure reliable results.

The results indicate that the use of intelligent computational techniques along with image densitometry can provide useful information for the pathologists. It can provide quantitative information that may support the diagnostic reports.

Although the developed software is easy to use and provides valuable information about the histological images, it is at laboratory prototype stage. Novel algorithms have been developed as a nucleus size measurement and the basal line is analysed in order to find out if the malign cells infiltrate it.

Details of the software are available from the authors, upon request.

Acknowledgment. The authors thank **Dr. Arturo Ramírez Niño** for his valuable medical support and for his photographic material, which was used to develop and test this image processing technique.

References

1. Registro Histopatológico de Neoplasias Malignas en México, Epidemiología, Dirección General de Epidemiologóa, S.S.A., ISBN 968-811-620-3, 1998, p 43-53.
2. Ackerma's Surgical Pathology, Eighth edition Vol two, Mosby, 1996, ISBN-0-8016-7004-7, p 1353-1391.
3. National Health Service Executive Guidance on Commissioning Cancer Services. Improving Outcomes in Gynaecological Cancers. July 1999.
4. D. Maravall Gómez-Allende, Reconocimiento de Formas y Visión Artificial. Addison-Wesley Iberoamericana. 1994, p 1-13, pp311-340.
5. G. A. Capenter, and S. Grossberg, "The ART of Adaptive Pattern Recognition by a Self-Organizing Neural Networks", Computer, March, 1988.
6. G. A. Capenter, and S. Grossberg, "A Massively Parallel Architecture for a Self-Organizing Neural Pattern Recognition Machine", Computer Vision, Graphics and Image Processing,p 37,1987.
7. K. Fuksushima, "Analysis of the Process of Visual Pattern Recognition by the Meocognitron", Neural Networks, Volume 2, 1989.
8. D. J. Foran et al. "Histological slides evaluated using statistical image processing", Proceedings of the 12th Annual International; 12; Philadelphia, PA, USA; IEEE Engineering in Medicine and Biology Society; p1-4 November 1990.
9. R. C. González and R. E. Woods. Tratamiento Digital de Imágenes. USA, Addison – Wesley. 1996.
10. D. Maravall y Gómez-Allende. Reconocimiento de Formas y Visión Artificial. USA, Addison – Wesley Iberoamericana, 1994.
11. M. K. Schneider et al. "Multi-scale Methods for the Segmentation and Reconstruction of Signals and Images" IEEE Transactions on image processing, 9 (3), March 2000, pp. 456-468.

An Improved ICP Algorithm Based on the Sensor Projection for Automatic 3D Registration

Sang-Hoon Kim[1], Yong-Ho Hwang[1], Hyun-Ki Hong[1], and Min-Hyung Choi[2]

[1] Dept. of Image Eng., Graduate School of Advanced Imaging Science, Multimedia and Film, Chung-Ang Univ., 221 Huksuk-dong, Dongjak-ku, Seoul, 156-756, KOREA
ksh1974@imagelab.cau.ac.kr, hwangyongho@hotmail.com,
honghk@cau.ac.kr
[2] Dept. of Computer Science and Eng., Univ. of Colorado at Denver, Colorado, USA
minchoi@acm.org

Abstract. Three-dimensional (3D) registration is the process aligning the range data sets form different views in a common coordinate system. In order to generate a complete 3D model, we need to refine the data sets after coarse registration. One of the most popular refinery techniques is the iterative closest point (ICP) algorithm, which starts with pre-estimated overlapping regions. This paper presents an improved ICP algorithm that can automatically register multiple 3D data sets from unknown viewpoints. The sensor projection that represents the mapping of the 3D data into its associated range image and a cross projection are used to determine the overlapping region of two range data sets. By combining ICP algorithm with the sensor projection, we can make an automatic registration of multiple 3D sets without pre-procedures that are prone to errors and any mechanical positioning device or manual assistance. The experimental results demonstrated that the proposed method can achieve more precise 3D registration of a couple of 3D data sets than previous methods.

1 Introduction

Range imagery is increasingly being used to model real objects and environments, and the laser sensors have simplified and automated the process of accurately measuring three-dimensional (3D) structure of a static environment [1]. Since it is not possible to scan an entire volumetric object at once due to topological and geometrical limitations, several range images showing only partial views of the object must be registered. Therefore, registration to align multiple 3D data sets in a common coordinate system is one of the most important problems in 3D data processing. For the registration process, each input data set consists of 3D points in the camera's local coordinate system. In order to register all input sets, a local coordinate of each 3D data set is transformed to a common coordinate, and the transformation between two data sets can be represented with a homography matrix. More specifically, the process provides a pose estimate of the input views that is a rigid body transformation with the six rotation and translation parameters. In general the relative sensor positions of several range sets can be estimated by mounting the sensor on a robot arm or keeping the sensor fixed and moving like an object on a turn-table [2].

R. Monroy et al. (Eds.): MICAI 2004, LNAI 2972, pp. 642–651, 2004.

The registration problem is composed of two phases: coarse registration and fine registration. In general, the coarse process obtains a rough estimation of 3D transforms by using mechanical positioning devices and manual processing. In order to refine the 3D estimate and make a complete 3D model, the fine registration is applied after coarse registration. The iterative closest point algorithm (ICP) is most widely used as the refinement method and calculates 3D rigid transformation of the closest points on the overlapping regions [3]. The two main difficulties in ICP, determining the extent of overlap in two scans and extending the method for multiple scans, have been a focus of the further research [4]. Namely, ICP requires *a priori* knowledge about an approximate estimation of the transformations, so starts with pre-estimated overlaps. Otherwise ICP tends to converge monotonically to the nearest local minimum of a mean square distance metric.

This paper presents an improved ICP algorithm that can automatically register multiple 3D data sets from unknown viewpoints. For a full automatic registration without an initial estimation process, we use the sensor projection matrix that is the mapping of the 3D data into its associated range image. The sensor projection matrix consists of the extrinsic and the intrinsic parameters as the camera projection does. The extrinsic parameters describe the position and the orientation of the sensor, and the intrinsic parameters contain measurements such as focal length, principal point, pixel aspect ratio and skew [5]. Since all range data is obtained with one range sensor, in general, the intrinsic parameters always remain unchanged. Then we use the covariance matrix to roughly obtain the extrinsic parameters that represent the relative 3D transformations between two inputs. The improved ICP method iteratively finds the closest point on a geometric entity to a given point on the overlapping regions based on the sensor projections. By combining ICP algorithm with the sensor projection constraint, we can solve the local minimum problem.

The remainder of the paper is organized as follows. In Sec. 2, previous studies are explained. In Sec. 3, an improved ICP algorithm is presented, and in Sec. 4, we demonstrate the experimental results and compare with previous methods. Finally, the conclusion is described in Sec. 5.

2 Previous Studies

In the last few years, several algorithms for 3D registration have been proposed and can be classified into the semiautomatic and the automatic methods. Semiautomatic approaches require manual assistance including specification of initial pose estimates or rely on external pose measurement systems, so they have a couple of limitations and setting of equipments is needed [6]. For example, a mechanical positioning device can only deal with indoor-sized objects and a manual assistance may be inaccurate. On the contrary, automatic registration is to automatically recover the viewpoints from which the views were originally obtained without *a prior* knowledge about 3D transformation. The main constraint of most automatic methods is that many pre-processes including feature extraction, matching and surface segmentation are required. In order to calculate the pose for arbitrary rotation and translation parameters, we need to know at least 3 corresponding feature points between the 3D data sets. Once correspondences have been established, numerical minimization is used to determine the object's rotation and translation [7]. However, automatically detecting suitable features and matching them are very difficult, and currently no reliable methods exist. Furthermore, another approach is to ask the user to supply the features, but this is very labor intensive and often not very accurate.

From the viewpoints of constructing a complete 3D model, the registration problem is divided into the coarse registration and the fine. In the coarse process we use usually mechanical positioning devices or manual processing to obtain a rough estimate of 3D transforms. B. Horn proposed a closed-form solution to find the relationship between two coordinate systems of 3D points by using a unit quaternion from covariance matrix [8]. In addition, a refinery technique is needed to improve the 3D estimate and make a complete 3D model. After that P.J. Besl., *et. al.* presented ICP that optimizes 3D parameters based on Horn's method by using the closest points matching between two sets [3].

3 Proposed Algorithm

This paper presents an improved ICP algorithm for automatic registration of multiple 3D data sets without *a prior* information about 3D transformations. The proposed iterative method uses the eigenvector of the covariance matrix and the sensor projection in an initial estimation. The eigenvector represents the direction of an object and defines a new axis at the centroid of the object. The analysis of the eigenvectors provides the relative sensor position in a common coordinate system. By using a cross projection based on the senor position, the overlapping regions can be detected. Finally, the improved ICP method iteratively finds the closest point on a geometric entity to a given point on the overlapping regions, and refines the sensor position.

3.1 Finding Overlapping Regions by Cross Projection

If an initial pose of the object differs so much from the real one, generally, it is difficult to construct a precise model due to self-occlusions. The more overlapping regions in 3D data sets we have, the more precise registration can be performed. Therefore, we assume that multiple-view range images have significant overlaps with each other [9]. By using an initial estimation of the relative sensor position and the sensor projection constraint, the proposed method finds the overlapping regions between two range data sets. The overlaps, which can be detected by two sensors at a time, are located in both 3D data sets. Fig. 1 shows overlapping regions on the first range data sets (R_1) at the sensor S_1 and the second (R_2) at S_2.

The overlapping regions on R_1 are measured at the second sensor pose (S_2), and those on R_2 are also measured at the first (S_1). So we can define the overlapping regions according to the visibility from two viewpoints. In order to find the overlapping regions, we propose a cross projection method that projects the first data set R_1 into the second sensor position S_2, and R_2 into S_1, respectively. Our method examines whether there are occlusions (scan errors) and self-occlusion. By analyzing the relation of the sensor direction vector and the vertex normal vector, we can find the overlapping regions. For example, when the angle between the sensor direction and the vertex normal vector (V_n) is lower than 90 degree, it is possible to scan the point by the sensor. Otherwise, we determine that the vertices are occluded, and those are not detected by the sensor.

$$(S_2 - V_1) \cdot V_{n1} > 0: \text{Overlap region in the } R_1 \tag{1}$$

$$(S_1 - V_2) \cdot V_{n1} > 0: \text{Overlap region in the } R_2 , \tag{2}$$

where V_1 and V_2 are vertex in R_1 and R_2, respectively. In short, the overlap in R_1 is found by S_2 and that in the R_2 is by S_1.

In the case of a concave object, there may be self-occlusion regions in the 3D data sets. As described in Fig. 2, the self-occlusion vertices are projected to the same pixel of the second range image by the second sensor projection. In this case, we examine the distance of the sensor position between vertices, and select the closest vertex from the sensor. The proposed cross projection can exclude the occlusion vertices and the self-occlusions, and find the overlapping regions between two views.

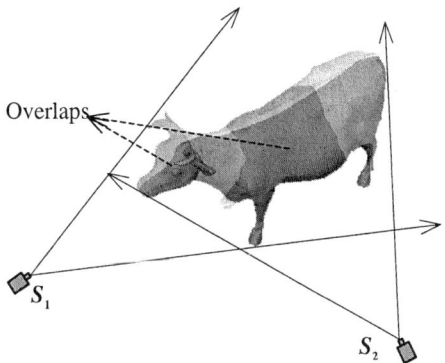

Fig. 1. Overlaps between two range sensors

3.2 Sensor Projection Matrix and Sensor Position

The sensor projection matrix is almost similar to the camera projection matrix. In general, the range sensor provides 3D range data sets (X) and the range image (x) corresponding to the range data sets. We can compute easily the sensor projection (P) and the sensor pose (S) using n corresponding points between range image and 3D range data sets [5]. The process is summarized as follows:

a. For each correspondence (x and X), A_i matrix (2×12) is computed.
b. Assemble n of A_i into a single A matrix ($2n \times 12$).
c. Obtain the SVD (Singular Value Decomposition) of A. A unit singular vector corresponding to the smallest singular value is the solution p. Specifically, if $A = UDV^T$ with D diagonal with positive diagonal entries, arranged in descending order down the diagonal, then p is the last column of V.
d. The P matrix is determined from p, and the sensor pose (S) is computed as follow:

$$S = M^{-1}p_4 , \tag{3}$$

where p_4 is the last column of P, and $P = M[\ I\ |\ M^{-1}p_4\ ] = KR[\ I\ |\ -S\ ]$.

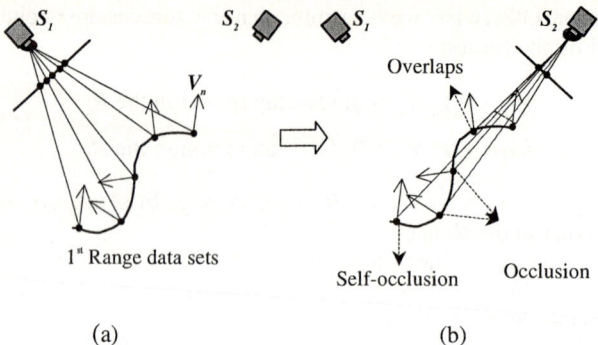

Fig. 2. The overlaps by cross-projection. (a) 1st range data from 1st sensor (b) 1st range data from 2nd sensor: the overlaps, occlusion and self-occlusion through the 2nd sensor and 1st range data

Since a range data is defined in its local coordinate system, all initial sensor positions obtained from multiple data sets are almost constant. For registration, we should find an accurate sensor pose in a common coordinate system. An accurate initial estimate can reduce the computation load and make the result of registration more reliable. By using a unit quaternion from closed-form covariance with the given corresponding point pairs in the two data sets, Horn suggested a method for registration of two different coordinate system [8]. Although our method is mathematically similar to Horn's, we do not use the corresponding point pairs, which are usually obtained in pre-processing or geometric limitation of 3D views. The proposed algorithm uses a similarity of 3D range data sets of an object from different views instead of feature correspondences. More specifically, we use the orthonormal (rotation) matrix that can be easily computed by eigenvalue decomposition of the covariance matrix instead of a unit quaternion. The eigenvector of the covariance matrix provides the major axis and the minor of 3D point clouds, so that it defines a new coordinate of the object. Three eigenvectors of the covariance matrix represent x, y, and z axes of the 3D data set, respectively. The obtained covariance matrix is used to define the object's local coordinate, and the centroid of the data sets is an origin of a new coordinate system.

In the first stage, the centroid (**C**) of each range data sets is calculated as follows:

$$C = \frac{1}{N} \sum_{j=0}^{N-1} V_j , \qquad (4)$$

where **V** and N represent 3D vertex in the range data sets and the number of vertices, respectively. In addition, we compute the covariance matrix (**Cov**) of each range data sets as follows:

$$Cov = \frac{1}{N} \sum_{j=0}^{N-1} (V_j - C)(V_j - C)^T . \qquad (5)$$

Let, Cov_1 and Cov_2 be covariance matrices of two range data sets (R_1 and R_2) respectively. We find two object coordinates by using eigenvalue decomposition of both covariance matrixes from R_1 and R_2.

$$Cov_1 = U_1 D_1 U_1^T$$
$$Cov_2 = U_2 D_2 U_2^T , \qquad (6)$$

where the diagonal matrices $(\mathbf{D})$ and orthonormal matrices $(\mathbf{U})$ represent eigenvalue and eigenvector of covariance matrices, then $\mathbf{U}$ provides a new object's coordinate. $\boldsymbol{R}_1$ and $\boldsymbol{R}_2$ are defined again in the new coordinate by $\mathbf{U}_1$, $\mathbf{U}_2$ and the centroids of two range sets $(\mathbf{C}_1, \mathbf{C}_2)$. In addition, a rigid transformation (T) is found by $\mathbf{U}_1$ and $\mathbf{U}_2$, and an initial relative sensor position is approximated by the rigid transformation (T).

$$T = \begin{bmatrix} \mathbf{U}_1\mathbf{U}_2^{-1} & \mathbf{C}_2 - \mathbf{C}_1 \\ 0_3^T & 1 \end{bmatrix}. \tag{7}$$

3.3   3D Registration by Improved ICP Algorithm

In general, ICP algorithm finds a rigid transformation to minimize the least-squared distance between the point pairs on the pre-determined overlapping regions. By using the sensor constraints and the cross projection, we can define the overlaps from the transformed data sets and the sensor positions, and then calculate 3D rigid transformation of the closest points on overlaps. More specifically, two range data sets are cross-projected into an initial position of the sensor, so an overlapping region is found. On the overlaps we find the closest point pairs, and calculate the transformations that can minimize the square distance metric between the points. The obtained transformations are used to optimize the initial sensor position for a more precise location. Our iterative method repeats the estimation of the sensor position and the detection of the overlapping regions. This process is repeated until the distance error value of closest point pair is minimized (Eq. 8), and we can optimize the sensor pose and 3D transformations of the range data.

$$\mathbf{E} = \sum_{i=1}^{n} \left\| \mathbf{V}_{1i} - \boldsymbol{R}(\mathbf{V}_{2i} - \mathbf{C}_2) - T \right\|^2, \tag{8}$$

where $\mathbf{V}_1$ and $\mathbf{V}_2$ are the closest point pairs of overlaps in two range sets and $\mathbf{C}_2$ is the centroid of $\mathbf{V}_2$. Rotation parameters $(\boldsymbol{R})$ is found by eigenvalue decomposition of two covariance matrices and translation (T) is the displacement between the centroids of the points $\mathbf{V}_1$ and $\mathbf{V}_2$. Our method automatically finds the closest point pairs $(\mathbf{V}_1$ and $\mathbf{V}_2)$ on the overlapping regions between two 3D sets from unknown viewpoints. Fig. 3 provides the block diagram of the proposed algorithm.

4   Experimental Results

We have demonstrated that the proposed algorithm can more precisely and efficiently register 3D data sets from unknown viewpoints than ICP method. The proposed algorithm has been tested on various 3D range images, which contain from 60K to 100K data points. The simulation is performed on PC with Intel Pentium 4 1.6GHz. In order to compare performance of each method, we use the virtual range scanning system and the real laser scanner with the calibrated turntable. We fixed the virtual sensor and acquired the "COW" range data sets by rotating the object with +60 degrees along Y-axis. "FACE" data is actually acquired by Minolta Vivid 700 laser scanner and the calibrated turntable with the same degrees. Consequently, we can compare precisely performance of the previous method with that of the proposed because 3D transformations are known.

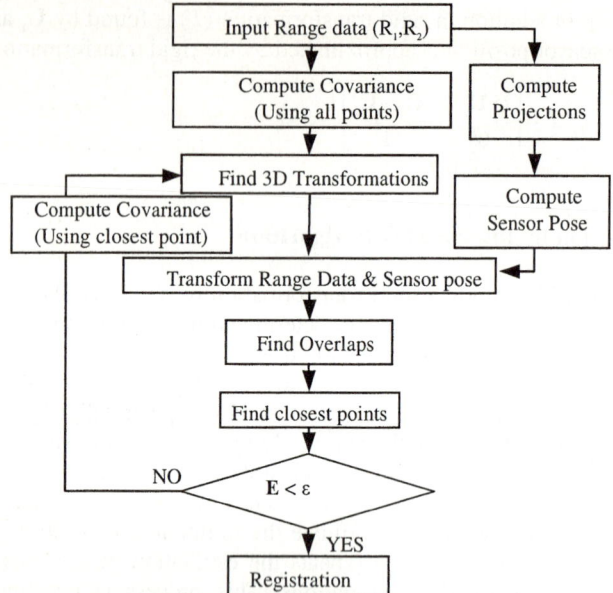

Fig. 3. Block diagram of the proposed method

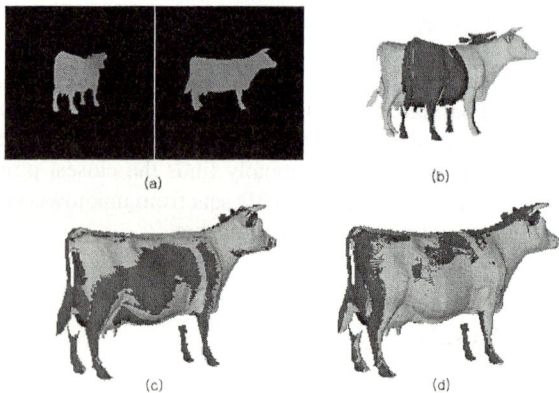

Fig. 4. Registration results of "COW" data sets. (a) Input range data sets (b) initial pose (c) registration by ICP (d) registration by improved ICP

Fig. 4 and 5 show the experimental results on two range data sets. As shown in Table 1, our method can make a precise registration without a precision milling machine or *a prior* 3D transformation between views. ICP algorithm computes 3D parameters of the closest points on the surface regions based on the sensor projection. On the contrary, the proposed method finds firstly the overlapping regions, and the points on these regions are considered. Therefore, the computation time for iteration

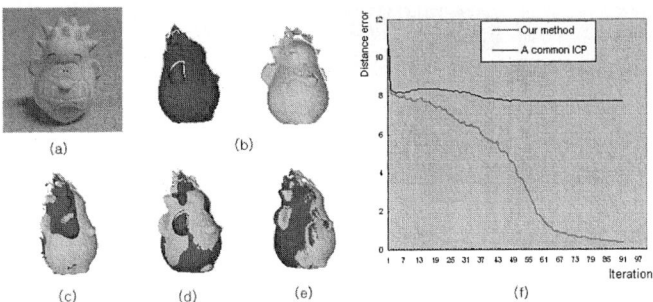

Fig. 5. Registration results of "FACE" data sets. (a) Real object (b) range data sets (c) initial pose (d) (e) registration by improved ICP (f) distance errors of the closest point pairs

Table 1. The experimental results on two range data sets

		Previous ICP	**Proposed Method**
C O W	Iterations (times)	93	15
	CPU time (sec)	1867	87
	Rotation parameter	θ_x:-2.392, θ_y: 58.95, θ_z: 0.709	θ_x: -0.052, θ_y: 59.91, θ_z: 0.067
	Translation parameter	T_x: -0.352, T_y: 0.036, T_z: 0.047	T_x: 0.109, T_y: -0.12, T_z: 0.945
	Registration Error	θ_x: 2.392, θ_y: 1.051, θ_z: -0.709 T_x: 0.352, T_y: -0.036, T_z: -0.047	θ_x: 0.052, θ_y: 0.09, θ_z: 0.067 T_x: -0.109, T_y: 0.12, T_z:-0.945
F A C E	Iterations (times)	92	87
	CPU time (sec)	694	123
	Rotation parameter	θ_x: 5.624, θ_y: 15.77, θ_z: 7.469	θ_x: 0.125, θ_y: 60.07, θ_z: -0.100
	Translation parameter	T_x: -4.31, T_y: 1.173, T_z: 1.895	T_x: 0.224, T_y: -0.03, T_z: -0.142
	Registration Error	θ_x: -5.624, θ_y: 44.23, θ_z: -7.469 T_x: 4.31, T_y: -1.173, T_z: -1.895	θ_x: -0.125, θ_y: 0.07, θ_z: 0.100 T_x: -0.224, T_y: 0.03, T_z: 0.142

in ICP is much longer than that in the proposed method. ICP converged to the local minimum of a mean square distance metric on "FACE" data, so the results on "FACE" data have much more errors than those on "COW". In the results by the proposed, the iteration times of "COW" is much less than those of "FACE", because "COW" has more obviously the major and the minor axis than "FACE". The results by the improved ICP show very small errors in each axis as shown in table 1, and these can be further vanished through an integration process. The proposed method obtains the major axis and the minor axis of 3D data sets to analyze the relative transformation, so it is difficult to register a totally spherical object.

Feature point extraction algorithm and ICP are generally combined to make an automatic registration of 3D data sets from unknown viewpoints. In this paper, the spin image is used as feature point extraction for registration [10]. Fig. 6 shows the comparison of the registration results by three methods. Because the overlaps between two data sets in "WATCH" are too small, it is difficult to find the corresponding points. As shown in Fig. 6 (a), only the proposed method accurately registered two data sets. The shape of "COPTER" has a bilateral symmetry, so the spin image is hard to establish the correspondence between two views. On the other hand, the proposed method computes the major and the minor axis of the object, and can cope with its symmetry in Fig. 6 (b). Since "DRIVER" has little overlap regions and its hilt is

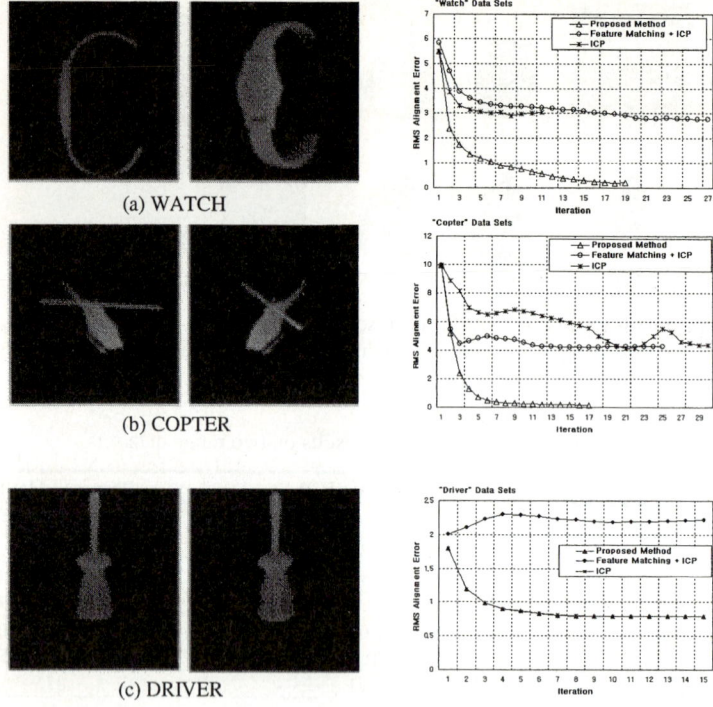

Fig. 6. Comparison of previous methods and the proposed method

cylindrically symmetric, the spin image is impossible to match the points between views. The shapes of hilt in "DRIVER" from different viewpoints are almost alike, so our method is difficult to determine uniquely the minor axis of the hilt Fig. 6 (c) shows both methods failed to achieve a precise 3D registration.

5   Conclusions

This paper presents an improved ICP algorithm that can automatically register multiple 3D data sets from unknown viewpoints without the preliminary processes including feature extraction and matching. The proposed method uses the sensor projection and the covariance matrix to estimate an initial position of the sensor. By using the cross projection based on the obtained senor position, we can find the overlapping regions. Finally, the improved ICP algorithm iteratively finds the closest point on a geometric entity to the given point on the overlapping regions, and refines the sensor position. The experimental results demonstrated that the proposed method can achieve a more precise 3D registration than previous methods. Further research includes a study on application to cylindrical or spherical objects. In addition, we will create photorealistic scene through 2D/3D alignment by using projections such as texture mapping.

Acknowledgment. This research was supported by the Ministry of Education, Korea, and under the BK21 project, and the Ministry of Science and Technology, Korea, under the NRL(2000-N-NL-01-C-285) project.

References

1. L. Nyland, D. McAllister, V. Popescu, C. McCue, and A. Lastra, "The Impact of Dense Range Data on Computer Graphics," *In Proceedings of IEEE Workshop on Multi-View Modeling and Analysis of Visual Scenes* (1999) 3-10
2. D. F. Huber and M. Herbert, "Fully Automatic Registration of Multiple 3D Data Sets," *In Proceedings of IEEE Computer Society Workshop on Computer Vision Beyond the Visible Spectrum*, Dec. (2001)
3. P. J. Besl and N. D. Mckay, "A Method for Registration of 3-D Shapes," *IEEE Trans, Patt. Anal. Machine Intell.*, vol. 14, no. 2, Feb. (1992) 239-256
4. K. Pulli, "Multiview Registration for Large Data Sets," In Proceedings of the Second International Conference on 3-D Digital Imaging and Modeling (1999) 160 – 168
5. R. Hartley and A. Zisserman, *Multiple View Geometry in Computer Vision*, Cambridge Univ. Press (2000)
6. P. Neugebauer, "Geometrical Cloning of 3D Objects via Simultaneous Registration of Multiple range images," *In Proceedings of the 1997 International Conference on Shape Modeling and Applications*, Mar. (1997) 130 – 139
7. S. F. El-Hakim, P. Boulanger, F. Blais and J. A. Berladin, "A system for indoor 3-D mapping and virtual environments," *In Proceedings of Vidiometrics V (SPIE vol. 3174)*, July (1997) 21-35
8. Horn, Berthold K. P., "Closed-Form Solution of Absolute Orientation Using Unit Quaternions," *Journal of the Optical Society of America.* A, vol. 4, no 4, April (1987) 629-642
9. G. Roth, "Registering Two Overlapping Range Image," *In Proceedings of the Second International Conference on 3-D Digital Imaging and Modeling*(1999) 191-200
10. A. E. Johnson, M. H. Herbert, "Using spin images for efficient object recognition in cluttered 3D scenes," *IEEE Trans. on pattern analysis and machine intelligence*, vol.21, no.5, may (1999)

Structure and Motion Recovery Using Two Step Sampling for 3D Match Move

Jung-Kak Seo, Yong-Ho Hwang, and Hyun-Ki Hong

Dept. of Image Eng., Graduate School of Advanced Imaging Science, Multimedia and Film, Chung-Ang Univ., 221 Huksuk-dong, Dongjak-ku, Seoul, 156-756, KOREA
pikei@imagelab.cau.ac.kr, hwangyongho@hotmail.com, honghk@cau.ac.kr

Abstract. Camera pose and scene geometry estimation is a fundamental requirement for match move to insert synthetic 3D objects in real scenes. In order to automate this process, auto-calibration that estimates the camera motion without prior calibration information is needed. Most auto-calibration methods for multi-views contain bundle adjustment or non-linear minimization process that is complex and difficult problem. This paper presents two methods for recovering structure and motion from handheld image sequences: the one is key-frame selection, and the other is to reject the frame with large errors among key-frames in absolute quadric estimation by LMedS (Least Median of Square). The experimental results showed the proposed method can achieve precisely camera pose and scene geometry estimation without bundle adjustment.

1 Introduction

Computer vision techniques have been applied for visual effects from 1990's, and image composition that combines an actual shot image with a virtual object is a representative research area. Applications involving synthesis of real scenes and synthetic objects require image analysis tools that help in automating the synthesis process. One such application area is match move in which the goal is to insert synthetic 3D objects in real but un-modeled scenes and create their views from the given camera positions so that they appear to move as if they were a part of the real scene. [1] For stable 3D appearance change of the object from the given camera position, 3D camera pose estimation is needed. At the same time, an accurate 3D structure of the scene is used for placement of the objects with respect to the real scene. In order to automate this process, reliable camera pose estimation and 3D scene geometry recovery without prior calibration knowledge are necessary. This paper is a study on automated end-to-end multi-view pose and geometry estimation that work with auto-calibration.

Multi-view pose and geometry analysis has attracted much attention in the past few years [2,3,4]. H. S. Sawhney represents the method to estimate an accurate relative camera pose from the fundamental matrix over extend video sequence [1]. M. Pollefeys proposes 3D modeling technique over image sequence from handheld camera, and then extends that for AR-system [4,5]. S. Gibson describes an improved feature tracking algorithm, based on the widely used in KLT tracker, and presents a

R. Monroy et al. (Eds.): MICAI 2004, LNAI 2972, pp. 652–661, 2004.

robust hierarchical scheme merging sub-sequence together to form a complete projective reconstruction, then finally describes how RANSAC based random sampling can be applied to the problem of self-calibration [6]. After projective reconstruction process, however, most algorithms require bundle adjustment or nonlinear minimization that is a very complex and difficult problem.

This paper presents two sampling methods to estimate camera positions and scene structure from video sequences. The first step is key-frame selection. Reconstruction of 3D structure is achieved by first selecting a set of key-frames with which to build small, sub-sequence reconstructions. Key-frame selection has several benefits. The most important benefit is that 3D camera pose estimation and 3D scene geometry recovery processing, which are the relatively expensive processes, can be performed with smaller number of views. Another benefit is that video sequences with different amounts of motion per frame become more isotropic after frame decimation [7]. The second step is to reject the frame with large errors among key-frames in the absolute quadric estimation by LMedS (Least Median of Square). LMedS algorithm chooses from the entire tested hypothesis the one with least median squared residual on the entire absolute quadric sets [8]. In order to upgrade the projective structure to metric reconstruction in auto-calibration, an unknown projective transformation can be acquired by decomposition of absolute quadric [3]. Absolute quadric estimation can achieve a precise upgrade to metric reconstruction. This paper presents a novel approach to auto-calibration, by using LMedS based random sampling algorithm to estimate absolute quadric. A schematic diagram (Fig. 1) shows the workflow based on two steps for 3D match move.

To begin with, Sec. 2 describes auto-calibration using absolute quadric, and Sec. 3 discusses key-frame selection. After details of our LMedS based on absolute quadric estimation are given in Sec. 4, we show the experimental results for synthetic and real scenes in Sec. 5. Finally, the conclusion is described in Sec. 6.

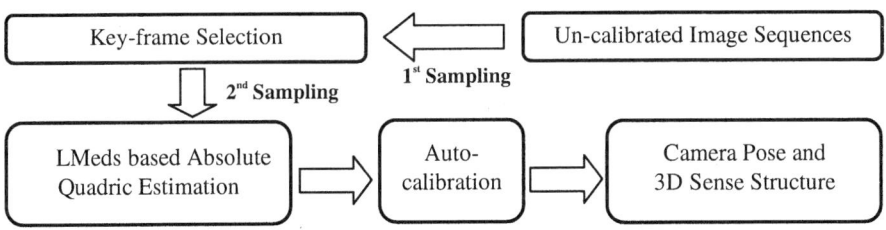

Fig. 1. Two steps for camera pose and 3D scene structure estimation

2   Auto-calibration

The resulting projective structure and motion are given up an unknown projective transformation. To upgrade the projective structure to Euclidean reconstruction, traditional methods first calibrate a camera by using an object with a calibration pattern. Then, a metric structure of the scene can be acquired from the correspondence between images. A well designed calibration object with known 3D Euclidean geometry is necessary for a precise camera calibration. Recently auto-calibration algorithms have been actively researched to avoid setting of the calibration object in the scene because pre-procedures for calibration have a couple of limitations and setting of equipments. On the contrary, because auto-calibration algorithms can estimate the camera parameters without prior information, many methods have been widely studied up to present. Among them, Heyden and Astrim, Trigg and Pollefeys used explicit constraints that relate the absolute conic to its images [3,9].

2.1 Projective Reconstruction

Projective structure and motion can be computed without camera parameters when point matches are given from more than two perspective images [9]. For two images the bilinear constraint expressed by the fundamental matrix is called the epipolar constraint. For three and four images, the trilinear and quadrilinear constraints are expressed by the trifocal and quadrifocal tensor, respectively. For more image than four images, P. Sturm presented factorization methods that suffer less from drift and error accumulation by calculating all camera projection matrices and structure at the same time [10]. The drawback of factorization methods relying on decomposition of matrix is that all corresponding points must remain in all views from the first frame to the last. To solve overcome this problem, a merging based projective reconstruction method is proposed [11,12]. Sequential merging algorithms are heavily dependent on a good initial estimate of structure, and susceptible to drift over long sequences. Therefore, the resultant error increases cumulatively over time. The hierarchical merging methods are proposed to reduce the error. The hierarchical merging has an advantage that the error can be more evenly distributed over an entire sequence [6]. In the experiment results, we have evaluated accuracy of the proposed auto-calibration algorithm on the sequential and the hierarchical approach.

2.2 Auto-calibration Algorithm

The process of projection of a point in 3D to the image plane can be represented as follows:

$$P_{euc} = KP_oT = \begin{bmatrix} f_x & s & x_o \\ & f_y & y_o \\ & & 1 \end{bmatrix} \begin{bmatrix} 1 & 0 & 0 & 0 \\ 0 & 1 & 0 & 0 \\ 0 & 0 & 1 & 0 \end{bmatrix} \begin{bmatrix} R_{3\times3} & t \\ 0'_3 & 1 \end{bmatrix}, \tag{1}$$

where T represents the transformation of coordinate systems from world to the camera, P_o is the perspective projection and K is the intrinsic parameter. We can reconstruct a scene up to a projective transformation by using the corresponding points on the images.

$$m = P_{proj}M_{proj} = P_{proj}HH^{-1}M_{proj}, \tag{2}$$

where m denotes the point in the image, P_{proj} and M_{proj} are the projective projection matrix and the projective structure of the scene point corresponding to the image point m, respectively. The projective structure M_{proj} is related to the transformation H. Calibration is the process to find the transformation H, which can be obtained by decomposition of absolute quadric. Absolute quadric is estimated as follows:

$$P_{proj}\Omega_{proj}P^T_{proj} = \omega^* = KK^T ,$$ (3)

where Ω is absolute quadric in the projective coordinate frame.

We assume that zero-skew and unit aspect ratio, and the principle point is known. Then the linear equations on Ω are generated from the zero entries in Eq. (3). This is represented as:

$$(P_{proj}\Omega_{proj}P^T_{proj})_{12} = 0$$
$$(P_{proj}\Omega_{proj}P^T_{proj})_{13} = 0$$ (4)
$$(P_{proj}\Omega_{proj}P^T_{proj})_{23} = 0$$
$$(P_{proj}\Omega_{proj}P^T_{proj})_{11} = (P_{proj}\Omega_{proj}P^T_{proj})_{22}$$

where $(\ )_{ij}$ is the element of i-th row and j-th column. Absolute quadric can be estimated from at least three images by Eq.(4). When Ω_{proj} is known, we can easily obtain the intrinsic parameter by using Choleski decomposition of ω^*. Absolute quadric can be decomposed by EVD (Eigen Value Decomposition) as:

$$EVD(\Omega_{proj}) = UDU^T = U\sqrt{D}\Omega_{euc}\sqrt{D}U^T = H\Omega_{euc}H^T ,$$ (5)

where Ω_{euc} is absolute quadric in Euclidean coordinate frame. Zero eigenvalue of D is replaced by 1. Finally, from Eq. (5) Euclidean camera motion and structure are obtained by applying H to the projective coordinate frame [5,6]. Fig. 2 shows relation of projective and Euclidean coordinate.

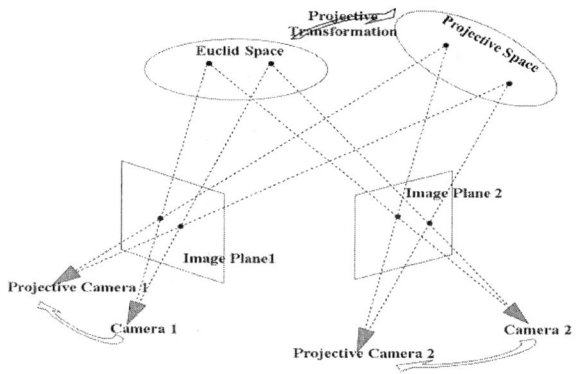

Fig. 2. Relation of projective and Euclidean coordinate

3   Key-Frame Selection

In general, the motion between frames has to be fairly small so that a precise correspondence can be established by using automatic matching, while significant parallax and large baseline is desirable to get a well-conditioned problem. A good choice of the frame from a video sequence can produce a more appropriate input to pose and geometry recovery and thereby improve the final result [7]. So the goal of key-frame selection is to select a minimal subsequence of feature views from video, such that co-respondence matching still works for all pairs of adjacent in the subsequence.

To achieve this goal, we consider three measures: (i) ratio of the number of corresponding points about feature points, (ii) distribution of corresponding points about the frame, and (iii) the homography error. Eq. (6) is combination of three measures:

$$S = w_1(1 - \frac{N_c}{N_F}) + w_2\sigma_c + w_3 H_{err} \tag{6}$$

where S is the score to select the key-frame, N_c and N_F are the number of corresponding points and that of feature points. σ_c is a standard deviation of the point density, and H_{err} is a homography error. w_i is the weight used to alter the relative significance of each score. Typically, the homography error is small when there is little camera motion between frames. Homograhpy error is used to evaluate the baseline length between two views. Standard deviation of the point density represents the distribution of corresponding points. If the corresponding points are evenly distributed on the image, we can obtain a more precise fundamental matrix [13]. Because the fundamental matrix contains all available information of the camera motion, evenly distributed corresponding points set improves final estimation results. To evaluate whether points are distributed evenly about image, we divide the entire image uniformly into sub-regions based on the number of corresponding points, and then calculate the point density of sub-region and that of the image. Standard deviation can be represented as:

$$\sigma_c = \sqrt{\frac{1}{N_S} \sum_{i=1}^{N_S} \left(N_{Ci} - \frac{N_C}{N_S} \right)} \,, \tag{7}$$

N_S is the number of sub-regions, N_C and N_{Ci} are the number of inliers and that in the i-th sub-region, respectively.

The selection process starts by positioning the key-frame at the first frame. All possible pairings of the first frame with the consecutive frames in the sequence are then considered. Assuming that key-frame has already been placed at frame i, key-frame selection is achieved by evaluating the score for a pairing of a current frame with the subsequent frame. This is continued until the ratio of the number of corresponding points to that of feature points goes down 50%. The frame with the lowest score is then marked as the next key-frame.

4 LMedS Based Absolute Quadric Estimation

Absolute quadric can be estimated by Eq. (4) from at least three images. For a more precise absolute quadric estimation, we present a novel approach by using LMedS-based random sampling algorithm. The random sets of projection matrices are selected from the key-frame set, and the linear equations by Eq. (4) are derived. We automatically reject the frame with large errors among key-frames, causing absolute quadric estimation to fail. The estimated absolute quadric is projected to each camera matrix, and computes each residual:

$$r_i = \left(P_{proj}^F \Omega_{proj} P_{proj}^{F\,T} - P_{proj}^i \Omega_{proj} P_{proj}^{iT} \right)_{norm}, \tag{8}$$

where P^F is the foundation camera matrix that is an initial projection matrix $[\ I\ |\ 0\ ]$. We iterate the sampling process and the computing residuals by an arbitrary number, and then find absolute quadric with a minimum median residual. From the minimum residual, a threshold for rejecting the camera matrix that causes absolute quadric estimation to fail can be computed as follows [8]:

$$\tau = 2.5 \times 1.4826 \left[1 + 5/(n-q) \right] \sqrt{r_{median}} \ , \tag{9}$$

where n and q are the number of the camera and that of the selected camera, respectively. r_{median} is the median residual with the minimum.

This is summary of LMedS based absolute quadric estimation.
1. Projective reconstruction process.
2. Random sampling two camera matrices except the foundation camera matrix.
3. Estimate absolute quadric by Eq. (4) and compute the residual of each camera matrix by Eq. (8).
4. Repeat 2-3 by an arbitrary number, and find absolute quadric having the minimum median residual.
5. Reject camera matrix by Eq. (9)
6. Re-estimate absolute quadric from the inlier camera matrix set.

Camera matrices of the rejected frames in two sampling processes are recovered by the camera resection algorithm that estimates the camera projection matrix from corresponding 3D points and image entities [9]. Corresponding 3D points can be easily obtained by matching process over neighboring frames.

5 Experimental Results

5.1 Key-Frame Selection

The proposed method has been tested on four video sequences and compared with Nister's method (**A**) and S. Gibson's (**B**) [6,7]. The simulation is performed on PC with Intel Pentium 4 2.3GHz, RAM 1Gbytes. Table 1 shows the number of key-frames and the computation time. In the results by Nister's method, the computation time is much dependent on the size of image, because it computes sharpness of the image over all frames. Gibson's method estimates the fundamental matrix on every frame, and selects relatively the smaller number of key-frames than Nister's. However, Gibson's computation time is almost same that of the Nister's, since much computation loads are required in the estimation of a precise fundamental matrix. On the contrary, the proposed method (**C**) considers the distribution of corresponding points on the frame instead of estimating the fundamental matrix directly. Therefore, the proposed algorithm is faster than previous methods and the position and the number of the selected key-frame is almost alike with those by Gibson's. Because camera pose and scene geometry are estimated on the key-frames, selection of fewer and precise those provides computational efficiency and accuracy.

Table 1. Numbers of the selected key-frame and the computation time

Video sequences			Number of the selected key frame			Computation time (sec)		
Type	Number of total frame	Size of frame	A	B	C	A	B	C
Box	621	720 × 480	23	14	15	412	416	179
Desk	407	720 × 480	17	13	13	201	200	76
Fountain	134	320 × 240	28	12	12	1023	38	10
Cottage	100	720 × 576	27	27	24	74	102	42

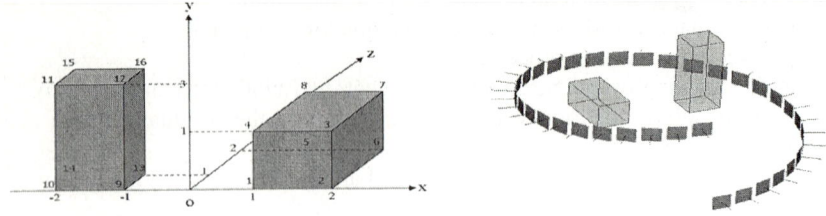

Fig. 3. Synthetic model and camera pose

5.2 Synthetic Data

We have experimented on the synthetic object to evaluate the proposed auto-calibration algorithm. Fig. 3 shows the synthetic model and the camera pose. The camera is rotated around the model and moved along positive y-axis at the same time. The intrinsic parameters are fixed, and noise is added to the synthetic data. We have estimated absolute quadric with the linear method, bundle adjustment [9] and the proposed algorithm on two merging approaches: sequential merging [10] and hierarchical merging algorithm [6]. Fig. 4 and 5 represent an accumulation error of camera intrinsic parameters by an absolute quadric, and the comparison of camera poses recovery. The sequential merging algorithm is dependent on an initial estimate of structure, and the error is propagated more and more over time. On the other hand, the hierarchical merging algorithm distributes the error over an entire sequence evenly. Therefore, the performance of hierarchical merging algorithm is better than that of sequential merging algorithm. In addition, bundle adjustment merges better than the linear method, and the proposed method achieve much more precise results than bundle adjustment at the sequential merging as shown in Fig. 4 and 5.

5.3 Real Image Sequences

We have tested the proposed method and previous methods on the real video sequence. The number of the frame is 621 and the image size is 720×480. Three frames among the video sequence are shown in Fig. 6(a). (b) represents in a graph form 15 frames selected by the proposed method. The graph shows the homography error in every frame. 6(c) gives the results by the linear method, bundle adjustment and the proposed method, respectively, on two merging algorithms, which are the sequential and the hierarchical merging. The results are obtained from accumulating

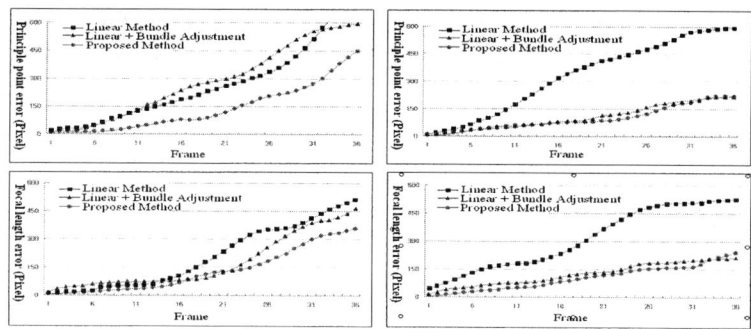

Sequential merging based projection reconstruction   Hierarchical merging based projection reconstruction

Fig. 4. Intrinsic parameter error graph

	Linear Method	Linear + Bundle adjustment	Proposed Method
Sequential Merging based Projective Reconstruction			
Hierarchical Merging Reconstruction			

Fig. 5. Recovered camera motion and scene geometry

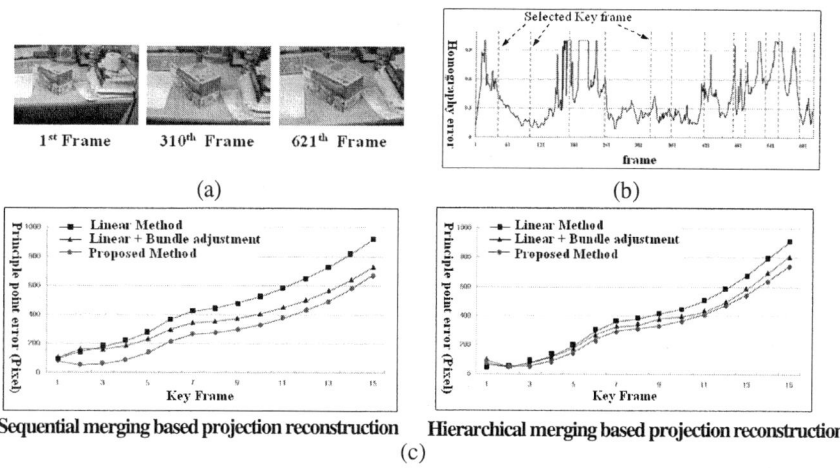

Fig. 6. (a) Real video sequence, (b) the selected key-frames and (c) principle point accumulation error graph

the distance error of the original principle points and the obtained. Fig. 6(c) shows the proposed method can achieve precise camera pose estimation without bundle adjustment.

5.4 Match Move

The proposed algorithm has been tested on two real image sequences. The number of the first image sequence is 16 and the image size is 800×600. The virtual object is combined with the real scene by using the recovered camera motion and the scene geometry. Fig. 7 shows the recovered camera motion and the textured scene geometry from the first image sequence. In the second images, the number of frames on the real video sequence is 407 and the image size is 720×480. Fig. 8 shows augmented video sequences of two images.

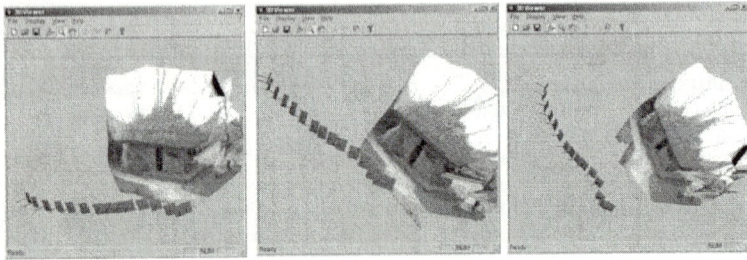

Fig. 7. Recovered camera pose and textured scene geometry

Fig. 8. Augmented video sequences

6 Conclusion

3D structure and motion recovery is important for video sequence processing. Previous methods use bundle adjustment or non linear minimize process that is complex and difficult problem. This paper proposes a new algorithm for camera motion estimation and scene geometry recovery based on two processes: key-frame selection and an absolute quadric estimation by LMedS. The experimental results demonstrated that the proposed method can achieve a more precise estimation of camera and scene structure of a couple of image sequences than previous methods. For resolving virtual-real occlusion or collision, further research about a precise modeling of scene is needed.

Acknowledgment. This research was supported by the Ministry of Education, Korea, and under the BK21 project, and the Ministry of Science and Technology, Korea, under the NRL(2000-N-NL-01-C-285) project.

References

1. H. S. Sawhney, Y. Guo, J. Asmuth, and R. Kumar, "Multi-View 3D Estimation and Applications to Match Move", *In proc. IEEE MVIEW* (1999) 21-28
2. O. Faugeras, Q-T. Luong, and S. Maybank, "Camera Self-Calibration: Theory and Experiments", *In proc. ECCV'92, Lecture Notes in Computer Science*, vol. 588 (1992) 321-334
3. W. Triggs, "Autocalibration and The Absolute Quadric", *In proc. IEEE CVPR* (1997) 609-614
4. M. Pollefeys and L.Van Gool, "Self-Calibration from the Absolute Conic on the Plane at Infinity", *In proc. CAIP'97*, vol.1296 (1997) 175-182
5. K. Cornelis, M. Pollefeys, M. Vergauwen, and L.V. Gool, "Augmented Reality from Uncalibrated Video Sequences.", *In proc. SMILE 2000, Lecture Notes in Computer Science*, vol. 2018 (2001) 144-160
6. S. Gibson, J. Cook, T. Howard, R. Hubbold, and D. Oram, "Accurate Camera Calibration for Off-line, Video-Based Augmented Reality", *In proc. IEEE and ACM ISMAR*, Darmstadt, Germany, Sep. (2002)
7. D. Nister, "Frame Decision for Structure and Motion", *In proc. SMILE 2000, Lecture Notes in Computer Science*, vol. 2018, (2001) 17-34
8. Z. Zhang., R. Deriche , O. Faugeras and Q. Loung, *A robust technique for matching two uncalibrated images through the recover of the unknown epipolar geometry*, Tech.Rep. 2273, Institut National de Recherche en Informatique et Automatique, (1994)
9. R. Hartley and A. Zisserman, *Mutiple View Geometry in Computer Vision*, Cambrige Univ. Press. (2000)
10. P. Sturm, B. Triggs, "A Factorization Based Algorithm for Muti-Image Projective Structure and Motion", *ECCV'96, Lecture notes in Computer Science*, vol 1065 (1996) 709-720
11. A. Chiuso, P. Favaro, H. Jin, and S. Soatto, "Motion and Structure causally integrated over time.", *IEEE Trans. On Pattern Matching and Machine Intelligence*, vol 24, no 4 (2002) 523-535
12. A. Fitzgibbon and A. Zisserman, "Automatic camera recovery for closed or open image sequences.", *In proc. ECCV* (2001) 144-160
13. R. Hartley, "In Defence of The 8-Point Algorithm", *In proc. IEEE ICCV* (1995) 1064-1070

Multiscale Image Enhancement and Segmentation Based on Morphological Connected Contrast Mappings

Iván R. Terol-Villalobos

CIDETEQ,S.C., Parque Tecnológico Querétaro, S/N,
SanFandila-Pedro Escobedo, 76700, Querétaro Mexico,
`famter@ciateq.net.mx`

Abstract. This work presents a multiscale image approach for contrast enhancement and segmentation based on a composition of contrast operators. The contrast operators are built by means of the opening and closing by reconstruction. The operator that works on bright regions uses the opening and the identity as primitives, while the one working on the dark zones uses the closing and the identity as primitives. To select the primitives, a contrast criterion given by the connected tophat transformation is proposed. This choice enables us to introduce a well-defined contrast in the output image. By applying these operators by composition according to the scale parameter, the output image not only preserves a well-defined contrast at each scale, but also increases the contrast at finer scales. Because of the use of connected transformations to build these operators, the principal edges of the input image are preserved and enhanced in the output image. Finally, these operators are improved by applying an anamorphosis to the regions verifying the criterion.

1 Introduction

Image enhancement is a useful technique in image processing that permits the improvement of the visual appearance of the image or provides a transformed image that enables other image processing tasks (image segmentation, for example). Methods in image enhancement are generally classified into spatial methods and frequency domain ones. The present work is focused on the spatial methods, and in particular, to the use of morphological image transformations. The methods presented here, not only have the objective of improving the visualization, but also to be used as a preprocessing step for image segmentation. In mathematical morphology (MM), several works have been focused on the contrast enhancement ([1],[2], [3], [4], [5],[6]). Among them, some interesting works concerning multiscale contrast enhancement were made by Toet ([1]), and Mukhopadhyay and Chanda ([2]). Toet proposes an image decomposition scheme based on local luminance contrast for the fusion of images. In particular, the use of the alternating sequential morphological filters as a class of low-pass filters was proposed in [1]. On the other hand, Mukhopadhyay and Chanda [2] propose a decomposition

R. Monroy et al. (Eds.): MICAI 2004, LNAI 2972, pp. 662–671, 2004.

of the image based on the residues obtained by the tophat transformation. However, the first formal work in morphological contrast was made by Meyer and Serra [6] who propose a framework theory for morphological contrast enhancement based on the activity lattice structure. In their work, the original idea of Kramer and Bruckner (KB) transformation [7] was used. This transformation, which sharpens the transitions between the object and background, changes the gray value of the original image at each point of the image for the closest of the dilation and erosion values. The contrast operators proposed by Serra and Meyer progress in the way suggested by KB, but the hypotheses are modified. They not only assume that the transformations are extensive and anti-extensive, but also that the transformations must be idempotent. The use of this last hypothesis to build contrast operators, avoids the risk of degrading the image. Another form that allows an attenuation of the image degradation problem in the KB algorithm was proposed by Terol-Villalobos [8]. In his work, the dilation and erosion transformations are also used as in the KB transformation, but in a separated way to build a class of non-increasing filters called morphological slope filters (MSF). On the other hand, the proximity criterion is not used, and a gradient criterion is introduced. An extension of this class of filters was proposed in [5]. In this case, the MSF are sequentially applied rendering a selection of features at each level of the sequence of filters. Recently, in [9], a class of connected MSF was proposed by working with the flat zone notion. The present work progresses in the same way suggested in [6], but using the opening and closing by reconstruction as primitives. However, in a similar manner for the dilatation and erosion in MSF, the opening and closing by reconstruction will be used separately. On the other hand, the proximity criterion will be avoided and a contrast criterion, given by the tophat transformation will be used for selecting the primitives. Furthermore, the use of a tophat criterion is combined with the notion of multiscale processing to originate a powerful class of contrast mappings. The use of filters by reconstruction, that form a class of connected filters, will allow the definition of a multiscale approach for contrast enhancement.

2   Some Basic Concepts of Morphological Filtering

2.1   Basic Notions of Morphological Filtering

The basic morphological filters ([10]) are the morphological opening $\gamma_{\mu B}$ and the morphological closing $\varphi_{\mu B}$ with a given structuring element ; where, in this work, B is an elementary structuring element (3x3 pixels) that contains its origin. $\check{B}$ is the transposed set ($\check{B} = \{-x : x \in B\}$) and μ is an homothetic parameter. The morphological opening and closing are given, respectively, by:

$$\gamma_{\mu B}(f)(x) = \delta_{\mu \check{B}}(\varepsilon_{\mu B}(f))(x) \quad \text{and} \quad \varphi_{\mu B}(f)(x) = \varepsilon_{\mu \check{B}}(\delta_{\mu B}(f))(x) \quad (1)$$

where the morphological erosion $\varepsilon_{\mu B}$ and dilation $\delta_{\mu B}$ are expressed by: $\varepsilon_{\mu B}(f)(x) = \wedge\{f(y) : y \in \mu \check{B}_x\}$ and $\delta_{\mu B}(f)(x) = \vee\{f(y) : y \in \mu \check{B}_x\}$. $\wedge$ is the inf operator and $\vee$ is the sup operator. In the following, we will avoid the elementary structuring element B. The expressions $\gamma_\mu, \gamma_{\mu B}$ are equivalent (i.e. $\gamma_\mu = \gamma_{\mu B}$). When the homothetic parameter is $\mu = 1$, the structuring element B will also be avoided (i.e. $\delta_B = \delta$). When $\mu = 0$, the structuring element is a set made up of one point (the origin).

Another class of filters is composed by the opening and closing by reconstruction. When filters by reconstruction are built, the basic geodesic transformations, the geodesic dilation and the geodesic erosion of size 1, are iterated until idempotence is reached [11]. Where the geodesic dilation and the geodesic erosion of size one are given by $\delta_f^1(g) = f \wedge \delta(g)$ with $g \leq f$ and $\varepsilon_f^1(g) = f \vee \varepsilon(g)$ with $g \geq f$, respectively. When the function g is equal to the erosion or the dilation of the original function, we obtain the opening and the closing by reconstruction:

$$\tilde{\gamma}_\mu(f) = \lim_{n \to \infty} \delta_f^n(\varepsilon_\mu(f)) \quad \tilde{\varphi}_\mu(f) = \lim_{n \to \infty} \varepsilon_f^n(\delta_\mu(f)) \tag{2}$$

2.2   Connectivity and Connected Tophat Transformations

An interesting way of introducing connectivity for functions is via the flat zone notion and partitions. Concerning the flat zone notion, one says that the flat zones of a function are the largest connected components of points with the same gray-level value. On the other hand, a partition of a space E is a set of connected components $\{X_i\}$ which are disjoint ($X_i \cap X_j = \emptyset$) and the union is the entire space ($\cup X_i = E$). Thus, since the set of flat zones of a function constitutes a partition of the space, a connected operator for functions can be defined as follows.

Definition 1 *An operator ψ acting on gray-level functions is said to be connected if, for any function f, the partition of flat zones of $\psi(f)$, is less fine than the partition f.*

The openings and closings by reconstruction (eqn. (2)) are the basic morphological connected filters. When applying these filters the flat zones increase the size with μ; the flat zones are merged. Based on these transformations, other connected transformations can be defined. In particular the connected tophat transformation is computed by the arithmetic pointwise difference of the original function from the opened one (or the difference of the closed function from the original one): $Thw_\lambda(f)(x) = f(x) - \tilde{\gamma}_\lambda(f)(x)$ (and $Thb_\lambda(f)(x) = \tilde{\varphi}_\lambda(f)(x) - f(x)$). Below, the opening (closing) by reconstruction will be used as primitive to built the contrast operator, while the connected tophat transformation will be used as criterion to select the primitives.

3   Contrast Mappings Based on Tophat Criteria

In this section, a study of the contrast mappings, using a contrast criterion given by the tophat transformation, is made. The interest in the use of this type of criterion consists in knowing strictly the contrast introduced in the output image. Consider the two-state contrast mappings defined by the following relationships:

$$\kappa_{\mu,\phi}^{\gamma}(f)(x) = \begin{cases} \widetilde{\gamma}_{\mu}(f)(x) \; if[f - \widetilde{\gamma}_{\mu}(f)](x) \le \phi \\ f(x) \quad if[f - \widetilde{\gamma}_{\mu}(f)](x) > \phi \end{cases}$$

$$\kappa_{\mu,\phi}^{\varphi}(f)(x) = \begin{cases} \widetilde{\varphi}_{\mu}(f)(x) \; if[\widetilde{\varphi}_{\mu}(f) - f](x) \le \phi \\ f(x) \quad if[\widetilde{\varphi}_{\mu}(f) - f](x) > \phi \end{cases} \tag{3}$$

Both operators $\kappa_{\mu,\phi}^{\gamma}$ and $\kappa_{\mu,\phi}^{\varphi}$ are connected; the partitions of the output images computed by these operators are composed by flat zones of f and other flat zones merged by $\widetilde{\gamma}_{\mu}$ and $\widetilde{\varphi}_{\mu}$. The first operator works on bright structures, whereas the second one on the dark regions. The use of a contrast criterion to build these operators permits the classification of the points in the domain of definition of f in two sets. A set $S_{\mu,\phi}(f)$ composed by the regions of high contrast, where for all points $x \in S_{\mu,\phi}(f)$

$$[f - \widetilde{\gamma}_{\mu}(f)](x) > \phi \quad for \quad \kappa_{\mu,\phi}^{\gamma} \quad and \quad [\widetilde{\varphi}_{\mu}(f) - f](x) > \phi \quad for \quad \kappa_{\mu,\phi}^{\varphi}$$

and the set $S_{\mu,\phi}^{c}(f)$ composed of weak contrast zones (the complement of $S_{\mu,\phi}(f)$), where for all points $x \in S_{\mu,\phi}^{c}(f)$

$$[f - \widetilde{\gamma}_{\mu}(f)](x) \le \phi \quad for \quad \kappa_{\mu,\phi}^{\gamma} \quad and \quad [\widetilde{\varphi}_{\mu}(f) - f](x) \le \phi \quad for \quad \kappa_{\mu,\phi}^{\varphi}$$

Remark 1 *In general, the operator $\kappa_{\mu,\phi}^{\gamma}$ using the opening as pattern will be analyzed. Then, for convenience, the notation $\kappa_{\mu,\phi}$ will be used instead of $\kappa_{\mu,\phi}^{\gamma}$. When it is required, the type of primitive (opening or closing) will be specified.*

Now, let us show how the contrast is modified for obtaining the output image. By construction, the contrast mapping $\kappa_{\mu,\phi}^{\gamma} = \kappa_{\mu,\phi}$ is an anti-extensive transformation. Thus, the following inclusion relation is verified: $\gamma_{\mu}(f) \le \kappa_{\mu,\phi}(f) \le f$. Then, the operator increases the contrast of a region by attenuating the neighboring regions with the opening by reconstruction. On the other hand, the contrast operators based on a tophat criterion not only classify the high and weak contrast regions ($S_{\mu,\phi}(f)$ and $S_{\mu,\phi}^{c}(f)$) of the input image, but also impose a well defined contrast to the output image, as expressed by the following property:

Property 1 *The output image computed by $\kappa_{\mu,\phi}$ has a well-defined contrast. For all point x of its domain of definition, the tophat transformation value of $\kappa_{\mu,\phi}(f)(x)$ is:*

$$[\kappa_{\mu,\phi}(f)(x) - \widetilde{\gamma}_{\mu}(\kappa_{\mu,\phi}(f))](x) > \phi \quad for\ all\ points\ x \in S_{\mu,\phi}(f) \quad and$$
$$[\kappa_{\mu,\phi}(f)(x) - \widetilde{\gamma}_{\mu}(\kappa_{\mu,\phi}(f))](x) = 0 \quad for\ all\ points\ x \in S_{\mu,\phi}^{c}(f)$$

Now, since $S_{\mu,\phi}(\kappa_{\mu,\phi}(f)) = S_{\mu,\phi}(f)$, one has:

Property 2 *The two-state contrast operator $\kappa_{\mu,\phi}$ is an idempotent transformation; $\kappa_{\mu,\phi}\kappa_{\mu,\phi}(f) = \kappa_{\mu,\phi}(f)$.*

Similar results can be expressed for the contrast operator using the closing by reconstruction and the original function as primitives. Finally, in a composition of two-state contrast mappings based on the parameter ϕ the strongest operator imposes its effects: $\kappa_{\mu,\phi_i}\kappa_{\mu,\phi_j} = \kappa_{\mu,\phi_j}\kappa_{\mu,\phi_i} = \kappa_{\mu,max\{\phi_i,\phi_j\}}$

4   Multiscale Morphological Contrast

In this section, the different scales (sizes) of the image will be taken into account for increasing the contrast of the output image. To introduce the scale parameter, a composition of contrast operators depending on the size parameter will be applied. In order to generate a multiscale processing method some properties are needed. Between them, causality and edge preservation are the most important ones [12]. Causality implies that coarser scales can only be caused by what happened at finer scales. The derived images contain less and less details: some structures are preserved; others are removed from one scale to the next. Particularly, the transformations should not create new structures at coarser scales. On the other hand, if the goal of image enhancement is to provide an image for image segmentation, one requires the edge preservation; the contours must remain sharp and not displaced. It is clear that openings and closings by reconstruction preserve contours and regional extreme. In fact, they form the main tools for multiscale morphological image processing. Consider the case of a composition of two contrast operators, and defined by the update equation:

$$\kappa_{\mu_2,\phi}\kappa_{\mu_1,\phi}(f)(x) = \begin{cases} \widetilde{\gamma}_{\mu_2}(\kappa_{\mu_1,\phi}(f))(x) \; if[\kappa_{\mu_1,\phi}(f) - \widetilde{\gamma}_{\mu_2}(\kappa_{\mu_1,\phi}(f))](x) \leq \phi \\ \\ \kappa_{\mu_1,\phi}(f)(x) \quad if[\kappa_{\mu_1,\phi}(f) - \widetilde{\gamma}_{\mu_2}(\kappa_{\mu_1,\phi}(f))](x) > \phi \end{cases} \tag{4}$$

Figure 1 illustrates an example of a composition of two-state contrast mappings with parameters $\mu_1 < \mu_2$ and ϕ. In Fig. 1(b) the opening size of the function in Fig. 1(a) is illustrated in dark gray color, whereas the regions removed by the opening are shown in bright gray color. In Fig. 1(c) the output funtion $\kappa_{\mu_1,\phi}(f)$ is shown. Finally, in Figs. 1(d) and 1(e) the opening $\widetilde{\gamma}_{\mu_2}(\kappa_{\mu_1,\phi}(f))$ and the output image computed by the composition $\kappa_{\mu_2,\phi}\kappa_{\mu_1,\phi}$ are illustrated. Observe that the high contrast regions of $\widetilde{\gamma}_{\mu_1}$ are not modified by $\widetilde{\gamma}_{\mu_2}$ as shown in Fig. 1(e). In the general case, when a family $\{\kappa_{\mu_k,\phi}\}$ of contrast operators is applied by composition, the following property is obtained.

Property 3 *The composition of a family of contrast operators* $\{\kappa_{\mu_k,\phi}\}$ *, with* $\mu_1 < \mu_2 < \cdots < \mu_n$ *, preserves a well-defined contrast at each scale. For a given* μ_i*, such that* $1 \leq i \leq n$*, and for all points* $x \in S_{\mu_i,\phi}(\kappa_{\mu_n,\phi}\cdots\kappa_{\mu_2,\phi}\kappa_{\mu_1,\phi}(f))$;

$$[\kappa_{\mu_n,\phi}\cdots\kappa_{\mu_2,\phi}\kappa_{\mu_1,\phi}(f) - \widetilde{\gamma}_{\mu_i}(\kappa_{\mu_n,\phi}\cdots\kappa_{\mu_2,\phi}\kappa_{\mu_1,\phi}(f))](x) > \phi;$$

and for all points $x \in S^c_{\mu_i,\phi}(\kappa_{\mu_n,\phi}\cdots\kappa_{\mu_2,\phi}\kappa_{\mu_1,\phi}(f))$,

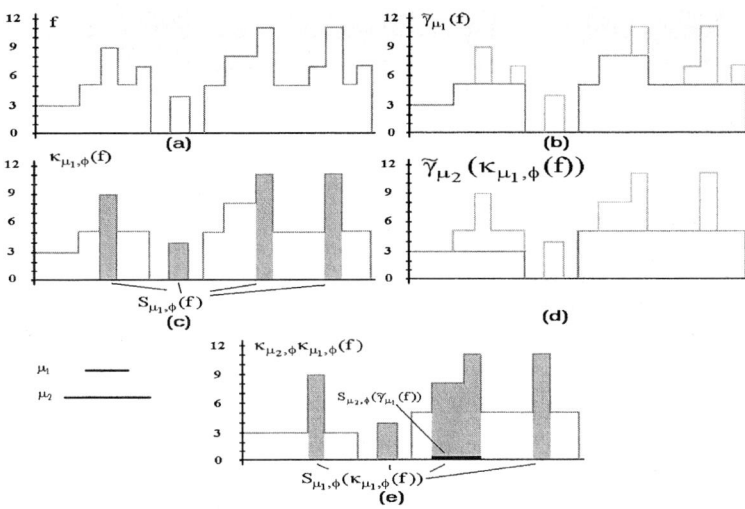

Fig. 1. a) Original function, b) Opening by reconstruction $\widetilde{\gamma}_{\mu_1}(f)$, c) Output function $\kappa_{\mu_1,\phi}(f)$, d) Opening by reconstruction $\widetilde{\gamma}_{\mu_2}(\kappa_{\mu_1,\phi}(f))$, e) Output function $\kappa_{\mu_2,\phi}\kappa_{\mu_1,\phi}(f)$

$$[\kappa_{\mu_n,\phi}\cdots\kappa_{\mu_2,\phi}\kappa_{\mu_1,\phi}(f)-\widetilde{\gamma}_{\mu_i}(\kappa_{\mu_n,\phi}\cdots\kappa_{\mu_2,\phi}\kappa_{\mu_1,\phi}(f))](x)=0;$$

and the structures at scale μ_i *are preserved,* $S_{\mu_i,\phi}(\kappa_{\mu_n,\phi}\cdots\kappa_{\mu_2,\phi}\kappa_{\mu_1,\phi}(f))=$ $S_{\mu_i,\phi}(\kappa_{\mu_i,\phi}\cdots\kappa_{\mu_2,\phi}\kappa_{\mu_1,\phi}(f))$

For a composition of a family $\{\kappa_{\mu_k,\phi_k}\}$ of contrast operators the structures at scale μ_i are preserved under the condition $\phi_1\geq\phi_2\geq\cdots\geq\phi_n$. Finally, the composition of contrast operators increases the contrast at finer scales as expressed by the following property:

Property 4 *In a composition of a family of contrast operators* $\{\kappa_{\mu_k,\phi}\}$ *, with* $\mu_1<\mu_2<\cdots<\mu_n$, *the following inclusion relation can be established. For a given* μ_i *such that* $1\leq i\leq n$, *and for all points* $x\in S_{\mu_i,\phi}(\kappa_{\mu_n,\phi}\cdots\kappa_{\mu_2,\phi}\kappa_{\mu_1,\phi}(f))$;

$$[\kappa_{\mu_n,\phi}\cdots\kappa_{\mu_2,\phi}\kappa_{\mu_1,\phi}(f)-\widetilde{\gamma}_{\mu_i}(\kappa_{\mu_n,\phi}\cdots\kappa_{\mu_2,\phi}\kappa_{\mu_1,\phi}(f))](x)\geq$$
$$[\kappa_{\mu_i,\phi}\cdots\kappa_{\mu_2,\phi}\kappa_{\mu_1,\phi}(f)-\widetilde{\gamma}_{\mu_i}(\kappa_{\mu_i,\phi}\cdots\kappa_{\mu_2,\phi}\kappa_{\mu_1,\phi}(f))](x)$$

Figure 2(b) shows the output image $\kappa_{\mu_2,\phi}\kappa_{\mu_1,\phi}(f)$, with $\mu_1=64$, $\mu_2=96$, and $\phi=15$, while Fig. 2(d) and 2(e) illustrate the binary images computed by a threshold between 10 and 255 gray-levels of the internal gradients of the original image and the output image $\kappa_{\mu_2,\phi}\kappa_{\mu_1,\phi}(f)$. Figures 2(c) and 2(f) show the output image $\kappa_{\mu_3,\phi}\kappa_{\mu_2,\phi}\kappa_{\mu_1,\phi}(f)$ with $\mu_1=32$, $\mu_2=64$, $\mu_2=96$, $\phi_1=10$, $\phi_2=\phi_3=15$, and its binary image computed by means of a threshold between 10 and 255 gray-levels of its internal gradient. Finally, Figs. 2(g)-(i) illustrate the segmented images obtained from the images in Figs. 2(d)-(f). By comparing Figs. 2(h) and 2(i) observe the structures at scale $\mu_1=32$ introduced in the

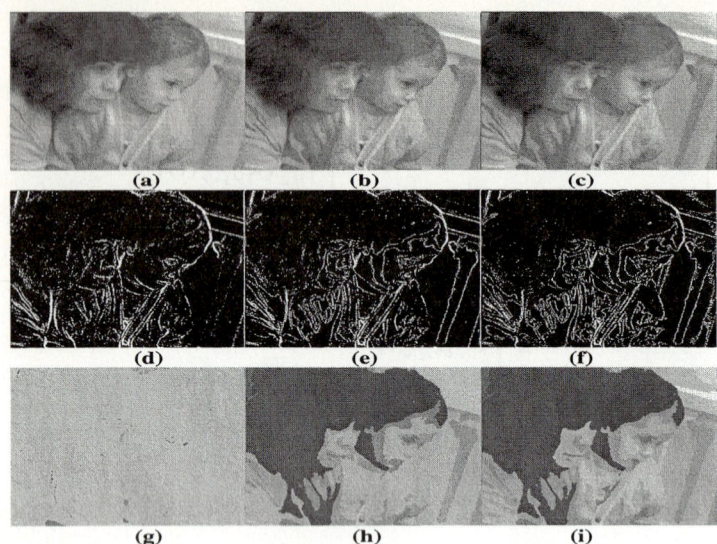

Fig. 2. a) Original image, b), c) Output images $\kappa_{\mu_2,\phi}\kappa_{\mu_1,\phi}(f)$, $\kappa_{\mu_3,\phi}\kappa_{\mu_2,\phi}\kappa_{\mu_1,\phi}(f)$ d), e), f), Gradient contours of images, (a),(b),(c), and g), h), i) Segmented images

output image 2(f). For a complete study of image segmentation in mathemathical morphology see [13].

5   Some Improved Multiscale Contrast Algorithms

The above-described approach presents a main drawback; this approach does not permit to increase the gray-levels of the image. To attenuate this inconvenience, some modifications to the multiscale contrast operator above-proposed are studied. On the other hand, when a family of contrast operators is applied by composition, one begins with a smallest structuring element. Here, one also illustrates the case of a composition of contrast mappings beginning with the greatest structuring element.

5.1   Linear Anamorphosis Applied on the Tophat Image

Consider the following residue: $a_{\mu,\phi}(f)(x) = 0$ if $f - \widetilde{\gamma}_\mu(f) \leq \phi$ and $a_{\mu,\phi}(f)(x) = [f - \widetilde{\gamma}_\mu(f)](x)$ if $f - \widetilde{\gamma}_\mu(f) > \phi$. Then, the output image $\kappa_{\mu,\phi}(f)$ can be expressed in the form: $\kappa_{\mu,\phi}(f) = \widetilde{\gamma}_\mu(f) + a_{\mu,\phi}(f)$ Now, let us take the linear anamorphosis: $\alpha a_{\mu,\phi}(f)$, where α is a positive integer. Then, a new two-state contrast mapping will be defined by;

$$\kappa'_{\mu,\phi}(f)(x) = \widetilde{\gamma}_\mu(f)(x) + \alpha a_{\mu,\phi}(f)(x) \tag{5}$$

When the parameter α is equal to one, we have $\kappa'_{\mu,\phi} = \kappa_{\mu,\phi}$. Take α as the minimum integer value that enables us to increase the contrast ($\alpha = 2$). Let us consider some conditions for this last operator. If the parameter ϕ takes the zero value, the extensive operator $\kappa'_{\mu,\phi} = [f + (f - \widetilde{\gamma}_\mu(f))]$ is obtained, and if ϕ takes the maximum value of function $a_{\mu,\phi}(f)$, one has that for all points in the domain of definition of f, $\kappa'_{\mu,\phi} = \widetilde{\gamma}_\mu(f)$. Now, for other ϕ values, one can define the set of high contrast points $S_{\mu,\phi}(\kappa'_{\mu,\phi}(f))$ that satisfy: for all points $x \in S_{\mu,\phi}(\kappa'_{\mu,\phi}(f))$, $\kappa'_{\mu,\phi}(f)(x) = [f + a_{\mu,\phi}(f)](x)$ and $\kappa'_{\mu,\phi}(f)(x) - \widetilde{\gamma}_\mu(f)(x) = 2a_{\mu,\phi}(f)(x) \geq \phi$. With regard to the set of weak contrast points $S^c_{\mu,\phi}(\kappa'_{\mu,\phi}(f))$, one has: for all points $x \in S^c_{\mu,\phi}(\kappa'_{\mu,\phi}(f))$, $\kappa'_{\mu,\phi}(f)(x) = \widetilde{\gamma}_\mu(f)(x)$ and $\kappa'_{\mu,\phi}(f)(x) - \widetilde{\gamma}_\mu(f)(x) = 0$. Thus, the operator $\kappa'_{\mu,\phi}$ increases twice the contrast of the output image with respect to the operator $\kappa_{\mu,\phi}$. If a composition of two contrast operators $\kappa'_{\mu_2,\phi_2}\kappa'_{\mu_1,\phi_1}(f)$ $(\mu_1 < \mu_2)$ is applied, the parameter ϕ_2 can take twice the value of ϕ_1 without affecting the structures preserved by the first operator. But this is not the only advantage, because this operator increases the contrast of a region using two ways: by attenuating the neighboring regions and by increasing its gray-levels. The images in Fig. 3 (b) and 3(c) illustrate the performance of this operator. A composition of three contrast mappings $\kappa'_{\mu_3,\phi_3}\kappa'_{\mu_2,\phi_2}\kappa'_{\mu_1,\phi_1}$, with $\mu_1 = 8$, $\mu_2 = 16$, $\mu_2 = 48$, and $\phi_1 = 0$, $\phi_2 = 3$, $\phi_3 = 7$ was applied to the original image in Fig. 3(a) to obtain the image in Fig. 3(b), whereas the composition $\kappa'_{\mu_1,\phi_1}\kappa'_{\mu_2,\phi_2}\kappa'_{\mu_3,\phi_3}$, with the same parameters was used to compute the image in Fig. 3(c).

5.2   Contrast Operator on Bright and Dark Regions

All the contrast operators, introduced in this paper, work separately with bright or dark regions. Here, the main interest is to introduce a contrast operator that permits the process of both regions. Consider the following operators

$$\kappa'^{\gamma}_{\mu,\phi}(f)(x) = \widetilde{\gamma}_\mu(f)(x) + \alpha a^{\gamma}_{\mu,\phi}(f)(x) \quad \kappa'^{\varphi}_{\mu,\phi}(f)(x) = \widetilde{\varphi}_\mu(f)(x) - \alpha a^{\varphi}_{\mu,\phi}(f)(x)$$

These contrast operators will be used as the primitives for building a new contrast operator. Observe that symbols γ and φ are now introduced in the contrast operators. In order to build such an operator, another criterion to choose the primitives must be introduced. The natural criterion is the comparison between the tophat on white regions with that on black regions. Thus, the contrast operator, working on bright and dark regions, will be given by:

$$\kappa^{\gamma\varphi}_{\mu_1,\mu_2,\phi}(f)(x) = \begin{cases} \kappa'^{\gamma}_{\mu_1,\phi}(f)(x) \; if [\widetilde{\varphi}_{\mu_2}(f) - f](x) \leq [f - \widetilde{\gamma}_{\mu_1}(f)](x) \\ \\ \kappa'^{\varphi}_{\mu_2,\phi}(f)(x) \qquad\qquad otherwise \end{cases} \qquad (6)$$

Figure 3(d) shows the output image computed from the image in Fig. 3(a) by the contrast mapping $\kappa^{\gamma\varphi}_{\mu'_1,\mu'_2,\phi_2}\kappa^{\gamma\varphi}_{\mu_1,\mu_2,\phi_1}$. The selected sizes for the primitives were $\mu_1 = 16$, $\mu_2 = 8$ for the first operator and $\mu'_1 = 48$, $\mu'_2 = 16$ for the second one, while the parameter values ϕ_1, ϕ_2 were taken equal to zero. A similar composition of contrast operators was applied on Fig. 3(a) for obtaining the image in Fig. 3(e), but in this case the parameter values ϕ_1 and ϕ_2 were selected as $\phi_1 = 0$ and $\phi_2 = 7$. Compare this last image with that in Fig. 3(d), and observe how the

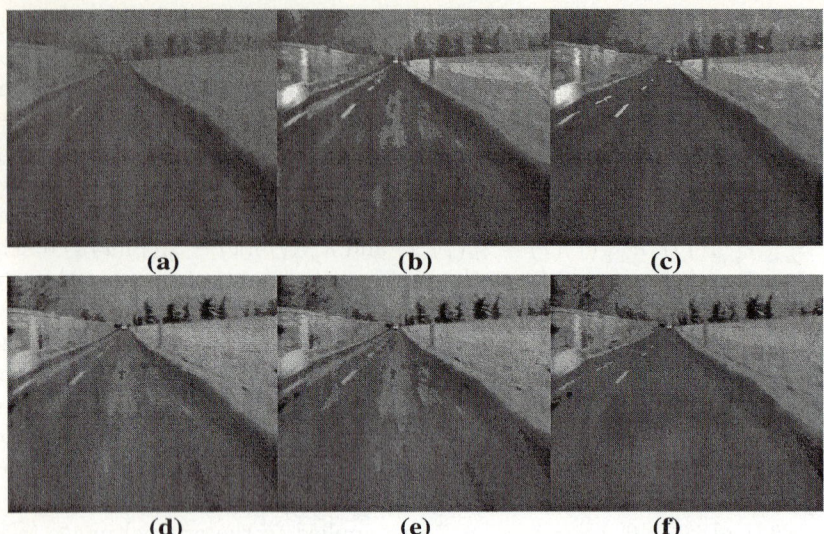

Fig. 3. a) Original image f, b), c) Output images $\kappa'_{\mu_3,\phi_3}\kappa'_{\mu_2,\phi_2}\kappa'_{\mu_1,\phi_1}(f)$ and $\kappa'_{\mu_1,\phi_1}\kappa'_{\mu_2,\phi_2}\kappa'_{\mu_3,\phi_3}(f)$, with parameters $\mu_1 = 8$, $\mu_2 = 16$, $\mu_2 = 48$, and $\phi_1 = 0$, $\phi_2 = 3$, $\phi_3 = 7$, d), e) Output images $\kappa^{\gamma\varphi}_{\mu'_1,\mu'_2,\phi_2}\kappa^{\gamma\varphi}_{\mu_1,\mu_2,\phi_1}(f)$ with parameters $\mu_1 = 16$, $\mu_2 = 8$, $\mu'_1 = 48$, $\mu'_2 = 16$ using $\phi_1 = \phi_2 = 0$ for (d) and $\phi_1 = 0$, $\phi_2 = 7$ for (e), f) Output image $\kappa^{\gamma\varphi}_{\mu_1,\mu_2,\phi_1}\kappa^{\gamma\varphi}_{\mu'_1,\mu'_2,\phi_2}(f)$ with the same parameters of (e).

contrast is increased when the gray-level of some regions is attenuated by the opening or closing. Finally, Fig. 3(f) illustrates the output image computed by $\kappa^{\gamma\varphi}_{\mu_1,\mu_2,\phi_1}\kappa^{\gamma\varphi}_{\mu'_1,\mu'_2,\phi_2}$. with the same parameter values used to compute the image in Fig. 3(e).

6   Conclusion and Future Works

In this work, a multiscale connected approach for contrast enhancement and segmentation based on connected contrast mappings has been proposed. For building the contrast operators, a contrast criterion given by the tophat transformation was used. This type of criterion permits the building of new contrast operators which will enable us to obtain images with a well-defined contrast. When applying by composition a family of contrast operators depending on a size parameter, a multiscale algorithm for image enhancement was generated. The output image computed by a composition of contrast operators preserves a well-defined contrast at each scale of the family. Finally, the use of anamorphoses was introduced to propose some improved multiscale algorithms. Future works on the multiscale contrast approach will be in the direction to extend the approach to the morphological hat-transform scale spaces proposed in [14].

Acknowledgements. The author I. Terol would like to thank Diego Rodrigo and Darío T.G. for their great encouragement. This work was funded by the government agency CONACyT (41170), Mexico.

References

1. Toet, A.: Hierarchical image fusion, Machine Vision and Applications, **3** (1990) 1–11
2. Mukhopadhyay, S., Chanda, B.: Multiscale morphological approach to local contrast enhancement, Signal Process., **80**(4) (2000) 685–696
3. Schavemaker, J.G.M., Reinders, M.J.T., Gerbrands, J.J., Backer, E.: Image sharpening by morphological filters, Pattern Recognition, **33** (2000) 997–1012
4. Potjer, F.,K.: Region adyacency graphs and connected morphological operators. Mathematical Morphology and Its Applications to Image and Signal Processing P. Maragos, Schafer R.W., M.A. Butt,(Eds.), Kluwer, (1996) pp. 111–118
5. Terol-Villalobos, I.R., Cruz-Mandujano, J.A.: Contrast enhancement and image segmentation using a class of morphological nonicreasing filters, Journal Electronic Imaging, **7**, (1998) 641–654
6. Meyer, F., Serra, J.: Contrast and activity lattice, Signal Process., **16**(4) (1989) 303–317
7. Kramer, H.P.,Bruckner, J.B.: Iteration of non-linear transformations for enhancement of digital image, Pattern Recognition, **7**(4) (1975) 53–58
8. Terol-Villalobos, I.R.: Nonincreasing filters using morphological gradient criteria, Opt. Engineering, **35**, (1996) 3172–3182
9. Terol-Villalobos, I.R.: Morphological image enhancement and segmentation. Advances in Imaging and Electron Physics. Hawkes, P.W. (Ed.), Academic Press,**118**, (2001) pp. 207–273
10. Serra, J.: Image analysis and mathematical morphology vol. 2. Academic Press, (1988)
11. Vincent, L.: Morphological grayscale reconstruction in image analysis: Applications and efficient algorithms, IEEE Transactions on Image Processing, **2** (1993) 176–201
12. Meyer, F., Maragos, P.: Nonlinear scale-space representation with morphological levelings, J. Vis. Comm. Image Represent., **11**(3) (2000) 245–265
13. Meyer, F., Beucher, S.: Morphological segmentation, J. Vis. Comm. Image Represent., **1** (1990) 21–46
14. Jalba, A.C., Roerdink, J.B.T.M., Wilkinson, M.H.F.: Morphological hat-transform scale spaces and their use in texture classification. In Proc. Int. Conf. Image Proc., Barcelona, Spain, Vol. **I** (2003) 329–332

Active Object Recognition Using Mutual Information

Felipe Trujillo-Romero[1], Victor Ayala-Ramírez[1], Antonio Marín-Hernández[2],
and Michel Devy[2]

[1] Universidad de Guanajuato FIMEE Tampico 912
36730 Salamanca, Gto.
Mexico
[2] LAAS-CNRS
7, Av. du Col. Roche
31077 Toulouse Cedex
France

Abstract. In this paper, we present the development of an active object
recognition system. Our system uses a mutual information framework in
order to choose an optimal sensor configuration for recognizing an unknown object. System builds a conditional probability density functions
database for some observed features over a discrete set of sensor configurations for a set of interesting objects. Using a sequential decision
making process, our system determines an optimal action (sensor configuration) that augments discrimination between objects in our database.
We iterate this procedure until a decision about the class of the unknown
object can be made. Actions include pan, tilt and zoom values for an active camera. Features include the color patch mean over a region in our
image. We have tested on a set composed of 8 different soda bottles and
we have obtained a recognition rate of about 95%. Sequential decision
length was of 4 actions in the average for a decision to be made.

1 Introduction

Object recognition is a very important task in robot navigation because it is one
of the aspects that enable a system to behave autonomously. This capability is
essential when identifying a pre-planified path or when avoiding an obstacle [1].

An active sensor is very useful in robot navigation because enables the robot
to look for objects known to be in its proximity without needing to change its
path. Active sensing tasks have been studied by Mihaylova [2].

Some recent works use mutual information frameworks to determine the
best actions to command an active camera in order to recognize some objects
[3][4]. Some others deal with sensor control for path servoing in robot navigation
[5][6][7].

In this paper we develop a system to actively recognize a set of objects by
choosing a sequence of actions for an active camera that helps to discriminate
between the objects in a learned database. Rest of this paper is organized as

R. Monroy et al. (Eds.): MICAI 2004, LNAI 2972, pp. 672–678, 2004.
© Springer-Verlag Berlin Heidelberg 2004

follows: In section 2, we state our problem formulation using mutual information. A description of our system implementation is given in section 3. In section 4, we present our test and results. Finally, we present our conclusion and the work to be done in the future in section 5.

2   Problem Formulation

An active sensor can be very useful when recognizing an object. Denzler[3][4] has proposed to use an information theoretic approach for the object recognition problem. His approach consists in using a smart sensor and to choose successive configuration steps in order to discriminate between objects in a learned database.

Uncertainty and ambiguity between objects are reduced by a camera action that maximizes mutual information. The key point of his work is the integration of the probabilistic models for active sensors with the effect of the different actions available.

Let us define x_t as the estimated state for recognition of Ω_k classes, $k \in \{1, n\}$ at iteration t. At each step, we are interested in computing the true state given an observation o_t. According to the information theory, framework optimal estimation is given by an action a_t that optimizes mutual information. Mutual information is defined as

$$I(x_t; a_t|o_t) = H(x_t) - H(x_t|o_t, a_t) \qquad (1)$$

where $H(\cdot)$ denotes the entropy of a probability distribution. Considering

$$H(x_t) = - \int_{x_t} p(x_t) \log p(x_t) dx_t \qquad (2)$$

and

$$I(x_t; a_t|o_t) = \int_{x_t} \int_{o_t} p(x_t)p(o_t|x_t, a_t) \log \frac{p(o_t|x_t, a_t)}{p(o_t, a_t)} do_t dx_t, \qquad (3)$$

the optimal action a_t^* that maximizes mutual information is given by

$$a_t^* = \max_{a_t} I(x_t|o_t, a_t). \qquad (4)$$

3   System Implementation

We can divide the implementation of active object recognition system in two parts: the learning phase and the recognition phase.

3.1   Learning Phase

Objective of the learning phase is to create a conditional probability density function database linking actions in the configuration space of the active sensor and objects in our database.

We consider actions like pan, tilt and zoom configuration values for an active camera. We divide the full range of every configurable action into a set of discrete values, that is, every action a_t is defined as:

$$a_t = (p_{k,t} \; t_{k,t} \; z_{k,t})^T \tag{5}$$

where p_k, $k \in \{1, n_p\}$ is a pan value, t_k, $k \in \{1, n_t\}$ is a tilt value and z_k, $k \in \{1, n_z\}$ is a zoom value, with n_p, n_t, n_z being respectively the number of discrete steps for the ranges of pan, tilt and zoom values.

We can use different properties of an object to characterize it. Among these properties we can find the chromatic or grayscale intensity, size, form, edges, etc. In this work, we considered the chromatic intensity of the object as the feature to use for the active object recognition. Chromatic intensities for objects in our database were modelled using gaussian probability density functions.

During the learning phase, we compute an RGB intensity mean vector using Equation 1. These values characterize the objects in our database at a given sensor configuration. We assume a normal distribution of intensities for illumination variations. To obtain the parameters we compute mean and variance for several runs under the same sensor configuration.

$$I_p \begin{pmatrix} I_r(p) \\ I_g(p) \\ I_b(p) \end{pmatrix} = \frac{1}{n} \sum_{i=0}^{n-1} I_i \begin{pmatrix} I_r(i) \\ I_g(i) \\ I_b(i) \end{pmatrix} \tag{6}$$

In Equation 1, I_p represents the mean intensity for each image. I_i represents the intensity for each pixel of that image. And n is the total number of pixels of the image. With these values we can compute the probability of observing some characteristic of the object when the sensor shows a given configuration state.

We have then the conditional probability for observing a feature c_t given some action a_t as:

$$P(c_t|a_t) = \int_{x_t} P(c_t|x_t, a_t) P(x_t) dx_t. \tag{7}$$

We used 8 different objects with similar properties for our database. These objects are shown in Figure 1. We obtained 30 different images for each object. The process was repeated 8 times, each time in a different position of the object. This procedure let us to capture an object model including distinctive properties. As we have taken images from different viewpoints of each object, we can recognize objects even if they show a different aspect from the learned ones.

In Figure 2, we can observe the different graphs of the RGB mean intensities for each object for a range of pan values at a fixed setup for tilt and zoom values. These features let us to discriminate the correct class for the unknown item among all the objects in our database.

3.2   Recognition Phase

The objective of this phase is the active object recognition. That is the main part of this work. When an unknown object from our database is presented to

Fig. 1. Images of the objects in our database.

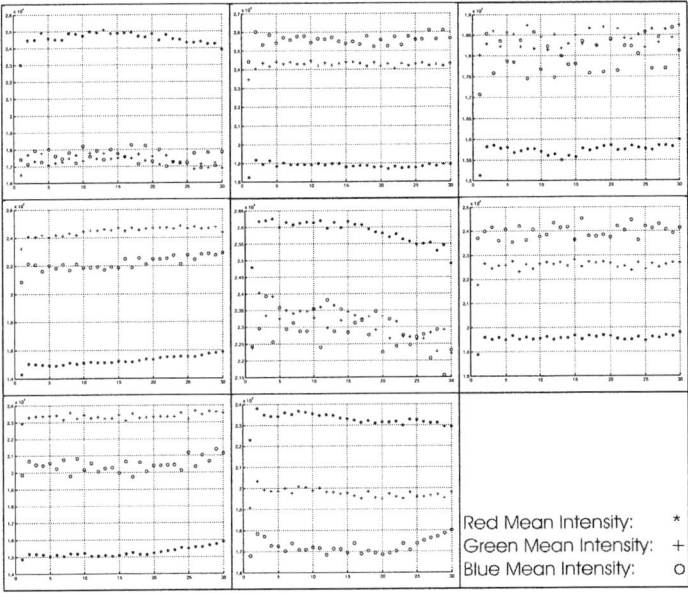

Fig. 2. Red, green and blue mean intensities for the color patches of the objects over a range of pan values.

the system, a sequential process is started. We assume equal *a priori* probability of the unknown object belonging to each class Ω_k.

Firstly, mutual information is computed as follows:

$$I_0(\Omega, c|a) = \sum_{k=1}^{K} e_k(a) P_k \tag{8}$$

where entropies e_k are defined as:

$$e_k(a) = \sum_{c_i} P(c_i|\Omega_k, a) \log \frac{P(c_i|\Omega_k, a)}{P(c_i|a)} \tag{9}$$

Mutual information will provide us the best matching between current estimated state and the observation made at this step. Then we look for the action a_0^* that maximizes mutual information:

$$a_0^* = \max_a I_0(\Omega, c|a) \tag{10}$$

We need to execute this action on the sensor and also it is required to update a priori probabilities P_k for each possible class. This process will reinforce probability of maybe ambiguous classes for the unknown object and in the other hand, it will weaken probabilities of the unknown object belonging to non-similar classes.

$$P_k = \frac{P(c_0|\Omega_k, a_0) P(\Omega_k|a_0)}{P(c_0|a_0)} \tag{11}$$

We iterate this procedure in a sequential way until the probability of the most probable class to which the unknown object belongs exceeds a given certainty threshold.

4   Test and Results

We present tests and results of our implementation in this section.

We present temporal evolution of a posteriori probabilities for each class when an object of type 2 was presented to our system as a unknown object. The graphs that we can see in Figure 4 show the sequential decision process results. In this case, our system identifies correctly the object under test. We can see also the number of iterations needed by the system in order to identify the object. We start from an equal probability hypothesis for all the object classes, mutual information let us to choose actions that make converge our decision process in a scenario where only one class is correct as a label for the unknown object. In Figure 3, we show another run of the system with a different object. In this graph, we can see that the number of iterations to decide a label for the unknown object depends on the actual view of the object and the initial setting for the camera action. In both cases, the number of iterations needed to choose a label for the object under test is different and depends on the unknown object.

A recognition rate of 95% was achieved under the following conditions: Illumination should be similar during both the learning and recognition phases. The acquisition of the images should be done to the same distance between the camera and the object, even if the object could be turned around the vertical symmetry axis of the bottles with respect to the original position.

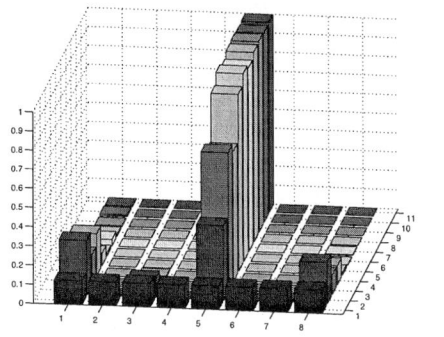

Fig. 3. Recognition of object 5.   **Fig. 4.** Recognition of object 2.

5   Conclusions and Perspectives

We have presented a system that can perform an active object recognition task. It achieves a good recognition rate (95 %) even if it is sensible to illumination changes. The acquired image of the unknown object has not been learnt in advance. We acquire an image of one of the objects in our database but not necessarily under the same environment conditions where the learning phase has been carried out. Nevertheless, our system is robust to rotation around the vertical symmetry axis.

If we could take some more robust features that do not depend on illumination variability as the objects features, recognition rate for our system could be improved.

Our future work will be directed towards:

Increasing the number of features to take into account. We can recognize objects in a more reliable way.

To combine the active sensor with some kind of active handler (like a turntable). Action will be then composed by the states of the active sensor augmented by the state of the turntable. This setup will help in the recognition phase because we could choose view-action pairs where the object can be recognized more easily.

Modelling the conditional probability functions of normal distributions by using fuzzy logic rules. This will save amounts of memory because we will store probability density functions as a set of fuzzy rules. That also will enable us to implement non parametric conditional probability density functions for the object-action pairs.

Acknowledgements. This work has been partially funded by Mexican CONA-CyT project I39328A and the LAFMI project "Concepción de funciones de percepción y planificación para la navegación topológica de un robot móvil en ambiente semi-estructurado interior o natural".

References

1. de Souza, G., Kak, A.C.: Vision for mobile robot navigation: a survey. IEEE Trans. on Pattern Analysis and Machine Intelligence **24** (2002) 237–267
2. Mihaylova, L., Lefevbre, T., Bruyincxx, H., Gadeyne, K., Schutter, J.D.: A comparison of decision making criteria and optimization techniques for active robot sensing. In: Proc. of the Fifth Int. Conf. on Numerical Methods and Applications NMA'02, Borovets, Bulgaria (2002)
3. Denzler, J., Brown, C.: Optimal selection of camera parameters for state estimation of static systems: An information theoretic approach. Technical Report 732, The University of Rochester, New York (2000)
4. Denzler, J., Brown, C., Niemann, H.: Optimal Camera Parameters for State Estimation with Applications in Object Recognition. In: Pattern Recognition – 23rd DAGM Symposium. Springer, Berlin (2001) 305–312
5. Ayala-Ramírez, V., Hayet, J.B., Lerasle, F., Devy, M.: Visual localization of a mobile robot in indoor environnements using planar landmarks. In: Proc. of the IEEE/RSJ Int. Conf on Intelligent Robots and Systems IROS'2000. Volume 1., IEEE/RSJ, IEEE Press (2000) 275–280
6. Ayala-Ramírez, V., Devy, M.: Active selection and tracking of multiple landmarks for visual navigation. In: Proc. of the 2nd Int. Symp. on Robotics and Automation (ISRA-200), Monterrey, Mexico (2000) 557–562
7. Trujillo-Romero, F., Ayala-Ramírez, V., Marín-Hernández, A., Devy, M.: Control de modalidades en un modelo de funcionalidad visual: aplicación a una tarea de localización de un robot móvil. In: Actas de Conielecomp-03, Puebla, México (2003) 206–211

An Approach to Automatic Morphing of Face Images in Frontal View

Vittorio Zanella[1,2] and Olac Fuentes[2]

[1]Universidad Popular Autónoma del Estado de Puebla
21 sur #1103 Col. Santiago Puebla 72160, México
vzanella@upaep.mx
[2]Instituto Nacional de Astrofísica Optica y Electrónica
Luis Enrique Erro #1 Sta. María Tonantzintla Puebla 72840, México
fuentes@inaoep.mx

Abstract. Image metamorphosis, commonly known as morphing, is a powerful tool for visual effects that consists of the fluid transformation of one digital image into another. There are many techniques for image metamorphosis, but in all of them there is a need for a person to supply the correspondence between the features in the source image and target image. In this paper we describe a method to perform the metamorphosis of face images in frontal view with uniform illumination automatically, using a generic model of a face and evolution strategies to find the features in both face images.

1 Introduction

Image metamorphosis is a powerful tool for visual effects that consists of the fluid transformation of one digital image into another. This process, commonly known as *morphing* [1], has received much attention in recent years. This technique is used for visual effects in films and television [2, 3], and it is also used for recognition of faces and objects [4].

Image metamorphosis is performed by coupling image warping with color interpolation. Image warping applies 2D geometric transformations to images to retain geometric alignment between their features, while color interpolation blends their colors.

The quality of a morphing sequence depends on the solution of three problems: feature specification, warp generation and transition control. Feature specification is performed by a person who chooses the correspondence between pairs of feature primitives. In actual morphing algorithms, meshes [3, 5, 6], line segments [7, 8, 9], or points [10, 11, 12] are used to determine feature positions in the images. Each primitive specifies an image feature, or landmark. Feature correspondence is then used to compute mapping functions that define the spatial relationship between all points in both images. These mapping functions are known as warp functions and are used to interpolate the positions of the features across the morph sequence. Once both images have been warped into alignment for intermediate feature positions, ordinary color interpolation (cross-dissolve) is performed to generate image morphing.

R. Monroy et al. (Eds.): MICAI 2004, LNAI 2972, pp. 679–687, 2004.

Transition control determines the rate of warping and color blending across the morph sequence.

Feature specification is the most tedious aspect of morphing, since it requires a person to determine the landmarks in the images. A way to determine the landmarks automatically, without the participation of a human, would be desirable. In this sense, evolution strategies could be an efficient tool to solve this problem.

In this work, we use evolutionary strategies and a generic model of the face to find the facial features and the spatial relationship between all points in both images, without the intervention of a human expert. We initially chose work with images of faces in frontal view with uniform illumination and without glasses and facial hair to simplify the problem.

2 Feature Specification

Many methods have been developed to extract facial features. Most of them are based on neural nets [13], geometrical features of images [14], and template matching methods [15, 16].

Unfortunately, most methods require significant human participation; for example in [14] a total of 1000 faces were measured, and the locations of 40 points on each face were recorded, to build the training set of faces. In this work we do not need a training set of faces to find the model, instead, we use a model of 73 points based on a simple parameterized face model [17], (Figure 1). The model does not rely on color or texture, it only uses information about the geometrical relationship among the elements of the face. For example, we use the fact that the eyes are always at the same level and above the mouth in a face in frontal view.

The components of the face model that we used are the eyes, eyebrow, nose, mouth, forehead and chin.

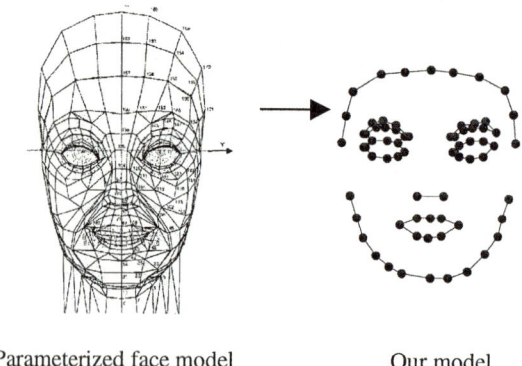

Parameterized face model   Our model

Fig. 1. The Face Model

2.1 Evolution Strategies

Evolutionary strategies are algorithms based on Darwin's theory of natural evolution, which states that only the best individuals survive and reproduce. The procedure starts by choosing randomly a number of possible solutions within the search space in order to generate an initial population. Based on a fitness function calculated for each solution, the best members of the population are allowed to take part in reproduction, this procedure is called selection. Genetic operations are performed on individuals with the idea that evolved solutions should combine promising structures from their ancestors to produce an improved population. Usually two types of genetic operations are utilized: *crossover* and *mutation*. Crossover is the combination of information of two or more individuals and mutation is the modification of information from an individual.

Our algorithm is a (1+1)-ES algorithm [18], i.e. the initial population is formed only by one individual (a face model) then mutation is the only operation utilized.

The form of the individual is $i = ((x_1, y_1), (x_2, y_2), \ldots, (x_{73}, y_{73}))$, that corresponds to the 73 points in the model. The mutation operation corresponds to an affine transformation with parameters s_x, s_y, t_x, t_y, where s_x and s_y are the scale parameters in x and y respectively, and t_x and t_y are the translation parameters in x and y. Rotation in this case is not used because we assume that the images are in frontal view and not rotated.

The mutation operation consists of modifying the translation and scale parameters. It adds normal random numbers with mean μ and standard deviation σ, $N(\mu, \sigma)$, in the following way:

$$t'_x = t_x + N(0,1) \tag{1}$$

$$t'_y = t_y + N(0,1) \tag{2}$$

$$s'_x = s_x + N(1,0.5) \tag{3}$$

$$s'_y = s_y + N(1,0.5) \tag{4}$$

Scale and translation are performed using the following matrix:

$$S = \begin{pmatrix} s'_x & 0 & 0 \\ 0 & s'_y & 0 \\ 0 & 0 & 1 \end{pmatrix} \tag{5}$$

and

$$T = \begin{pmatrix} 1 & 0 & 0 \\ 0 & 1 & 0 \\ t'_x & t'_y & 1 \end{pmatrix} \tag{6}$$

In this way, we perform the following operations for each point in the model $(x', y', 1) = (x, y, 1) \cdot S$ by the scale and $(x', y', 1) = (x, y, 1) \cdot T$ by the translation.

For the fitness function we need to find the binary image, and the contour image, corresponding to the source and target images. We use the fact that the images have uniform illumination; in this case most of the points in the image depict skin and then we can find the regions in the face that are darker than skin, for example the eyes or mouth. We segment the image using a threshold near the mean intensity of the pixels representing skin, for this, first we convert the original image into a gray scale image I, after that the threshold Th is calculated from the image histogram as follows:

$$Th = \frac{\sum_{i=1}^{255} h(i) \cdot i}{\sum_{i=1}^{255} h(i)} \tag{7}$$

where $h(i)$ corresponds to the number of points with gray intensity i in the histogram of the image. The value of Th corresponds to the average value of the gray intensity of the image. With Th we find the eyes and mouth regions in the points with values less than Th, to find a binary image $\phi(I)$.

(a)   (b)

Fig. 2. (a) Contours image (b) Binary image

Once we have the binary image and the contour image $\phi(I)$, obtained with the Canny operator, (Figure 2), we compute the following function:

$$Fitness = \max(A_{eyes} + A_{mouth}). \tag{8}$$

Where

$$A_{eyes} = \iint\limits_{R_{El}} (\phi(I)) dI + \iint\limits_{R_{Er}} (\phi(I)) dI . \tag{9}$$

and

$$A_{mouth} = \iint\limits_{R_M} (\phi(I)) dI . \tag{10}$$

The symbols R_{El}, R_{Er} and R_M, correspond to the left eye, right eye and mouth regions respectively, (see Figure 3).

After the Fitness is found, we adjust the chin, forehead and the eyebrows, so that:

$$S = \max(NP_{eyebrows} + NP_{chin+forehead}) \qquad (11)$$

here

$$NP_{eyebrows} = \int_{B_{EBl}} \varphi(I)ds + \int_{B_{EBr}} \varphi(I)ds \qquad (12)$$

$$NP_{chin+forehead} = \int_{B_{FH}} \varphi(I)ds + \int_{B_C} \varphi(I)ds \qquad (13)$$

Here B_{EBl}, B_{EBr}, B_{FH} and B_C are the left eyebrow, right eyebrow, forehead and chin edges, ds, respectively and $\varphi(I)$ is the contour image of image I, Figure 3.

This process is performed with the source image and the target image. The results are shown in Figures 4 and 5.

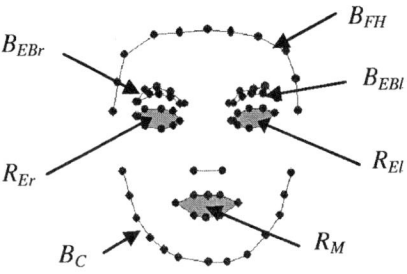

Fig. 3. Regions and edges of the face model

Fig. 4. The best individual adjusted to the segmented image

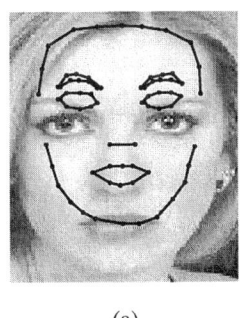

(a)   (b)   (c)

Fig. 5. (a) First individual, (b) Intermediate individual and (c) The best individual

3 Warp Generation

Once the model has been adjusted to the images, the next step is to perform image deformation, or warping, by mapping each feature in the source image to its corresponding feature in the target image. When we use point-based feature specification, we must deal with the problem of scattered data interpolation.

The problem of scattered data interpolation is to find a real valued multivariate function interpolating a finite set of irregularly located data points [19]. For bivariate functions, this can be formulated as:

Input: n data points (x_i, y_i), $x_i \in \Re^2$, $y_i \in \Re$, i=1, ..., n.
Output: A continuous function $f: \Re^2 \to \Re$ interpolating the given data points, i.e.
$f(x_i) = y_i$, i =1, ..., n.

In this work we use the inverse distance weighted interpolation method.

3.1 Inverse Distance Weighted Interpolation Method

In the inverse distance weighted interpolation method [19], for each data point $\mathbf{p}_i$, a local approximation $f_i(\mathbf{p}):\Re^2 \to \Re$ with $f_i(\mathbf{p}_i) = y_i$, i=1,..,n is determined. The interpolation function is a weighted average of these local approximations, with weights dependent on the distance from the observed point to the given points,

$$f(\mathbf{p}) = \sum_{i=1}^{n} w_i(\mathbf{p}) f_i(\mathbf{p}) \tag{14}$$

Where $f_i(\mathbf{p}_i) = y_i$, i=1,..,n. $w_i:\Re^2 \to \Re$ is the weight function:

$$w_i(\mathbf{p}) = \frac{\sigma_i(\mathbf{p})}{\sum_{j=1}^{n} \sigma_j(\mathbf{p})} \tag{15}$$

with

$$\sigma_i(\mathbf{p}) = \frac{1}{\left\| \mathbf{p} - \mathbf{p}_i \right\|^\mu} \tag{16}$$

The exponent μ controls the smoothness of the interpolation.

4 Transition Control

To obtain the transition between the source image and the target image we use linear interpolation of their attributes. If I_s and I_T are the source and target images we generate the sequence of images I_λ, $\lambda \in [0,1]$, such that

$$I_\lambda = (1-\lambda) \cdot I_S + \lambda \cdot I_T \qquad (17)$$

This method is called cross-dissolve.

5   Results

We tested the method with images of faces in frontal view with uniform illumination without glasses and facial hair. The run time on average is 30 seconds to perform the metamorphosis on a 2.0 Ghz Pentium IV machine with 128 Mb of RAM.

The method finds a satisfactory individual in around 500 iterations. The results models are shown in Figures 6, 8 and 10 while Figure 7, 9 and 11 shows the morphing process between these images

6   Conclusions

We developed a method to perform the automatic morphing of face images using evolutionary strategies and a generic face model. We do not need a training set of faces to obtain the model because we use a model based on a simple parameterized face model. The results are good although we worked with a simplified problem using only images of faces in frontal view and with uniform illumination. As to future work we plan to generalize the method working with images with non-uniform illumination or with rotated face images using, for example, symmetry-based algorithms [20, 21] to supply more information about the position of the face.

Fig. 6. Final individuals over the source and target images

Fig. 7. Resulting Face Image Morphing for images in Figure 6

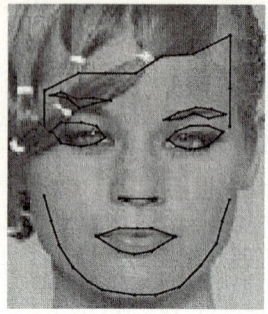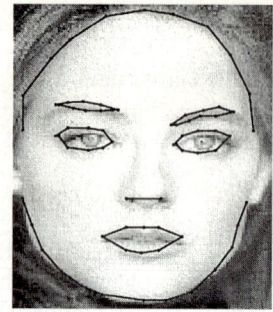

Fig. 8. Example 2

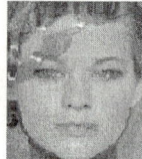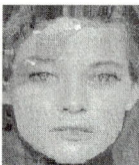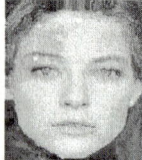

Fig. 9. Resulting Face Image Morphing for images in Figure 8

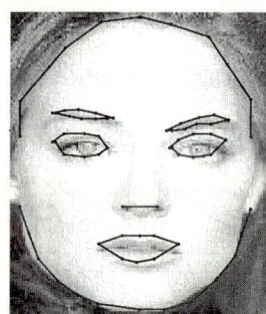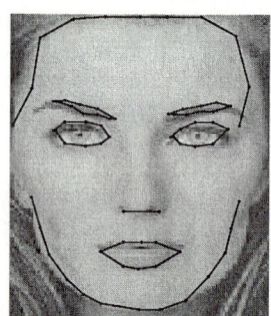

Fig. 10. Example 3

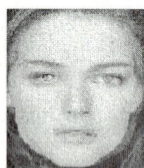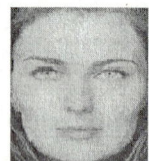

Fig. 11. Resulting Face Image Morphing for images in Figure 10

References

1. G. Wolberg, Image Morphing: a Survey, The Visual Computer Vol. 14, 360-372,1998
2. P. Litwinowicz, & L.Williams, Animating Images with Drawings, Proceedings of the SIGGRAPH Annual Conference on Computer Graphics, 409-412, 1994
3. G. Wolberg, Digital Image Warping, IEEE Computer Society Press, Los Alamitos CA., 1990
4. Bichsel, Automatic Interpolation and Recognition of Face Images by Morphing, The 2nd International Conference on Automatic Face and Gesture Recognition. IEEE Computer Society Press, Los Alamitos, CA, 128-135, October 1996
5. W. Aaron, et al., Multiresolution Mesh Morphing, Proceedings of the SIGGRAPH Annual Conference on Computer Graphics, 343-350, August 1999.
6. G. Wolberg, Recent Avances in Image Morphing, Computer Graphics International, Pohang Korea, June 1996
7. T. Beier, & N. Shawn, Feature-Based Image Metamorphosis, Proceedings of the SIGGRAPH Annual Conference on Computer Graphics,Vol. 26, No. 2, 35-42, July 1992.
8. S. Lee, K. Chwa, & S. Shin, Image Metamorphosis Using Snakes and Free-Form Deformations, In Robert Cook, editor, SIGGRAPH 95 Conference Proceedings, Annual Conference Series, pages 439–448. ACM SIGGRAPH, Addison Wesley, August 1995.
9. S. Lee et al., Image Metamorphosis with Scattered Feature Constraints, IEEE Transactions on Visualization and Computer Graphics, 2:337–354, 1996.
10. Nur, et al., Image Warping by Radial Basis Functions: Aplications to Facial Expressions, CVGIP: Graph Models Image Processing, Vol.56, No. 2, 161-172, 1994
11. S. Lee, et al., Image Morphing Using Deformable Surfaces, Proceedings of the Computer Animation Conference, IEEE Computer Society, 31-39, May 1994
12. S. Lee, et al., Image Morphing Using Deformation Techniques, J. Visualization Comp. Anim. No.7, 3-231, 1996
13. N. Intrator, D. Reisfeld, & Y. Yeshurun, Extraction of Facial Features for Recognition using Neural Networks, Proceedings of the International Workshop on Automatic Face and Gesture Recognition, Zurich, 260-265, 1995.
14. Craw, D. Tock and A. Bennett, Finding Face Features, Proceedings of the European Conference on Computer Vision, ECCV-92, Ed. G. Sandini, 92-96, Springer-Verlag 1992
15. M. J. T. Reinders. Model Adaptation for Image Coding. PhD thesis, Delft University of Technology, Delft, The Netherlands, Dec. 1995.
16. T.Cootes, A.Hill, C.Taylor and J.Haslam, Use of Active Shape Models for Locating Structures in Medical Images. Image and Vision Computing, 12(6):1994, 355-366.
17. Parke Federic I. and Waters Keith, Computer Facial Animation, AK Peters Wellesley, Massachusetts, 1996.
18. Back T., Rudolph Gunter, Schwefel Hans-Paul, Evolutionary Programming and Evolution Strategies: Similarities and Differences, Proccedings of the second Annual Conference on Evolutionary Programming, pp 11-22, Evolutionary Programming Society, San Diego CA. 1993
19. D. Ruprecht and H. Muller, Image warping with scattered data interpolation. IEEE Computer Graphics and Applications, 15(2), 37-43. 1995.
20. D. O'Mara, & R. Owens, Measuring Bilateral Symmetry in Digital Images, TENCON Digital Signal Processing Applications, Piscataway, U.S.A., IEEE 1996.
21. D. Reinsfeld, H. Wolfson, & Y. Yeshrum, Context Free Attentional Operators: The Generalized Symmetry Transform, International Journal of Computer Vision, Vol 14, 119-130,1995.

A Study of the Parallelization of a Coevolutionary Multi-objective Evolutionary Algorithm

Carlos A. Coello Coello and Margarita Reyes Sierra

CINVESTAV-IPN (Evolutionary Computation Group)
Departamento de Ingeniería Eléctrica, Sección de Computación
Av. IPN No. 2508. Col. San Pedro Zacatenco, México D.F. 07300, MÉXICO
ccoello@cs.cinvestav.mx, mreyes@computacion.cs.cinvestav.mx

Abstract. In this paper, we present a parallel version of a multi-objective evolutionary algorithm that incorporates some coevolutionary concepts. Such an algorithm was previosly developed by the authors. Two approaches were adopted to parallelize our algorithm (both of them based on a master-slave scheme): one uses Pthreads (shared memory) and the other one uses MPI (distributed memory). We conduct a small comparative study to analyze the impact that the parallelization has on performance. Our results indicate that both parallel versions produce important improvements in the execution times of the algorithm (with respect to the serial version) while keeping the quality of the results obtained.

1 Introduction

The use of coevolutionary mechanisms has been scarce in the evolutionary multiobjective optimization literature [1]. Coevolution has strong links with game theory and its suitability for the generation of "trade-offs" (which is the basis for multiobjective optimization) is, therefore, rather obvious. This paper extends our proposal for a coevolutionary multi-objective optimization approach presented in [2]. The main idea of our coevolutionary multi-objective algorithm is to obtain information along the evolutionary process as to subdivide the search space into n subregions, and then to use a subpopulation for each of these subregions. At each generation, these different subpopulations (which evolve independently using Fonseca & Fleming's ranking scheme [3]) "cooperate" and "compete" among themselves and from these different processes we obtain a single Pareto front. The size of each subpopulation is adjusted based on their contribution to the current Pareto front (i.e., subpopulations which contributed more are allowed a larger population size and viceversa). The approach uses the adaptive grid proposed in [4] to store the nondominated vectors obtained along the evolutionary process, enforcing a more uniform distribution of such vectors along the Pareto front.

This paper presents the first attempt to parallelize a coevolutionary multi-objective optimization algorithm. The main motivation for such parallelization is because the proposed algorithm is intended for real-world applications (mainly in engineering) and therefore, the availability of a more efficient version of the algorithm (in terms of CPU time required) is desirable. In this paper, we compare the serial version of our algorithm (as reported in [2]) with respect to two parallel versions (one that uses Pthreads and another one that uses MPI). A comparison with respect to PAES [4] is also included to

R. Monroy et al. (Eds.): MICAI 2004, LNAI 2972, pp. 688–697, 2004.

give a general idea of the performance of the serial version of our algorithm with respect to other approaches. However, for a more detailed comparative study the reader should refer to [2]. The main aim of this study is to compare the performance gains obtained by the parallelization of the algorithm. Such performance is measured both in terms of the computational times required as well as in terms of the quality of the results obtained.

2   Statement of the Problem

We are interested in solving problems of the type:

$$\text{minimize } [f_1(\boldsymbol{x}), f_2(\boldsymbol{x}), \dots, f_k(\boldsymbol{x})] \tag{1}$$

subject to:

$$g_i(\boldsymbol{x}) \geq 0 \quad i = 1, 2, \dots, m \tag{2}$$

$$h_i(\boldsymbol{x}) = 0 \quad i = 1, 2, \dots, p \tag{3}$$

where k is the number of objective functions $f_i : R^n \to R$. We call $\boldsymbol{x} = [x_1, x_2, \dots, x_n]^T$ the vector of decision variables. We thus wish to determine from the set $\mathcal{F}$ of all the vectors that satisfy (2) and (3) to the vector $x_1^*, x_2^*, \dots, x_n^*$ that are *Pareto optimal*. We say that a vector of decision variables $\boldsymbol{x}^* \in \mathcal{F}$ is *Pareto optimum* if there does not exist another $\boldsymbol{x} \in \mathcal{F}$ such that $f_i(\boldsymbol{x}) \leq f_i(\boldsymbol{x}^*)$ for every $i = 1, \dots, k$ and $f_j(\boldsymbol{x}) < f_j(\boldsymbol{x}^*)$ for at least one j. The vectors $\boldsymbol{x}^*$ corresponding to the solutions included in the Pareto optimal set are called *nondominated*. The objective function values corresponding to the elements of the Pareto optimal set are called the *Pareto front* of the problem.

3   Coevolution

Coevolution refers to a reciprocal evolutionary change between species that interact with each other. The relationships between the populations of two different species can be described considering all their possible types of interactions. Such interaction can be positive or negative depending on the consequences that such interaction produces on the population. Evolutionary computation researchers have developed several coevolutionary approaches in which normally two or more species relate to each other using any of the possible relationships, mainly competitive (e.g., [5]) or cooperative (e.g., [6]) relationships. Also, in most cases, such species evolve independently through a genetic algorithm. The key issue in these coevolutionary algorithms is that the fitness of an individual in a population depends on the individuals of a different population.

4   Description of the Serial Version of Our Algorithm

The main idea of our approach is to try to focus the search efforts only towards the promising regions of the search space. In order to determine what regions of the search

```
1. gen = 0
2. populations = 1
3. while (gen < Gmax) {
4.          if(gen = Gmax/4 or Gmax/2 or 3 * Gmax/4)
            {
5.                      check_active_populations()
6.                      decision_variables_analysis()
                        (compute number of subdivisions)
7.                      construct_new_subpopulations()
                        (update populations)
            }
8.          for (i = 1; i ≤ populations; i + +)
9.                      if (population i contributes
                        to the current Pareto front)
10.                                 evolve_and_compete(i)
11.         elitism()
12.         reassign_resources()
13.         gen + + }
```

Fig. 1. Pseudocode of our algorithm.

space are promising, our algorithm performs a relatively simple analysis of the current Pareto front. The evolutionary process of our approach is divided in 4 stages. Our current version equally divides the full evolutionary run into four parts (i.e., the total number of generations is divided by four), and each stage is allocated one of these four parts.

First Stage. During the first stage, the algorithm is allowed to explore all of the search space, by using a population of individuals which are selected using Fonseca and Fleming's Pareto ranking scheme [3]. Additionally, the approach uses the adaptive grid proposed in [4]. At the end of this first stage, the algorithm analyses the current Pareto front (stored in the adaptive grid) in order to determine what variables of the problem are more critical. This analysis consists of looking at the current values of the decision variables corresponding to the current Pareto front (line 6, Figure 1). This analysis is performed independently for each decision variable. The idea is to determine if the values corresponding to a certain variable are distributed along all the allowable interval or if such values are concentrated on a narrower range. When the whole interval is being used, the algorithm concludes that keeping the entire interval for that variable is important. However, if only a narrow portion is being used, then the algorithm will try to identify portions of the interval that can be discarded from the search process. As a result of this analysis, the algorithm determines whether is convenient or not to subdivide (and, in such case, it also determines how many subdivisions to perform) the interval of a certain decision variable. Each of these different regions will be assigned a different population (line 7, Figure 1).

Second Stage. When reaching the second stage, the algorithm consists of a certain number of populations looking each at different regions of the search space. At each generation, the evolution of all the populations takes place independently and, later on, the nondominated elements from each population are sent to the adaptive grid where they "cooperate" and "compete" in order to conform a single Pareto front (line 10, Figure 1). After this, we count the number of individuals that each of the populations contributed to the current Pareto front. Our algorithm is *elitist* (line 11, Figure 1), because after the first generation of the second stage, all the populations that do not provide any individual to the current Pareto front are automatically eliminated and the sizes of the other populations are properly adjusted. Each population is assigned or removed individuals such that its final size is proportional to its contribution to the current Pareto front. These individuals to be added or removed are randomly generated/chosen. Thus, populations compete with each other to get as many extra individuals as possible. Note that it is, however, possible that the sizes of the populations "converge" to a constant value once their contribution to the current Pareto front does not change any longer.

Third Stage. During the third stage, we perform a check on the current populations in order to determine how many (and which) of them can continue (i.e., those populations which continue contributing individuals to the current Pareto front) (line 5, Figure 1). Over these (presumably good) populations, we will apply the same process from the second stage (i.e., they will be further subdivided and more populations will be created in order to exploit these "promising regions" of the search space). In order to determine the number of subdivisions that are to be used during the third stage, we repeat the same analysis as before. The individuals from the "good" populations are kept. All the good individuals are distributed across the newly generated populations. After the first generation of the third stage, the elitist process takes place and the size of each population will be adjusted based on the same criteria as before. Note however, that we define a minimum population size and this size is enforced for all populations at the beginning of the third stage.

Fourth Stage. During this stage, we apply the same procedure of the third stage in order to allow a fine-grained search.

Decision Variables Analysis. The mechanism adopted for the decision variables analysis is very simple. Given a set of values within an interval, we compute both the minimum average distance of each element with respect to its closest neighbor and the total portion of the interval that is covered by the individuals contained in the current Pareto front. Then, only if the set of values covers less than 80% of the total of the interval, the algorithm considers appropriate to divide it. Once the algorithm decides to divide the interval, the number of divisions gets increased (without exceeding a total of 40 divisions per interval), as explained next. Let's define $range^i$ as the percentage of the total of $interval^i$ that is occupied by the values of the variable i. Let $\bar{d}^i_{min}$ be the minimum average distance between individuals (with respect to the variable i) and let $divisions^i$ be the number of divisions to perform in the interval of the variable i:

```
if (range^i <0.8*interval^i)
     while (d̄^i_min <0.2*interval^i)
        { divisions^i + +; interval^i =0.2*interval^i; }
```

Parameters Required. Our proposed approach requires the following parameters:

1. Crossover rate (p_c) and mutation rate (p_m).
2. Maximum number of generations ($Gmax$).
3. Size of the initial population ($popsize_{init}$) to be used during the first stage and minimum size of the secondary population ($popsize_{sec}$) to be used during the further stages.

5   Description of the Parallelization Strategy

The topology adopted in this work consisted of a master-slave scheme. As we indicated before, the evolutionary process of our algorithm is divided in **4 stages**. Next, we will briefly describe the part of each of these stages that was parallelized.

First Stage. In the case of Pthreads, this first stage is performed by the master thread. In the case of MPI, the corresponding work is performed by each of the slave processes. Since the master slave is the only one with access to the adaptive grid, upon finishing each generation, each slave process must send its full population to the master process. The master process receives all the populations and applies the corresponding filters to send the nondominated individuals (of each population) to the adaptive grid.

Second Stage. From this stage, the algorithm uses a certain number of populations so that it can explore different regions of the search space. Thus, in the case of Pthreads, given a fixed number of threads, a dynamic distribution of the total number of population takes place: the threads evolve the next available population. At each generation, each thread evolves its corresponding populations and, then, it sends the nondominated individuals from each population to the adaptive grid (line 10, Figure 1). The grid access was implemented with mutual exclusion. After accessing the adaptive grid, the master thread is on charge of counting the number of individuals provided by each population to constitute the current Pareto front, and also on charge of reassigning the resources corresponding to each of the populations (lines 11 and 12, Figure 1). In the case of MPI, given a fixed number of slave processes, we assigned a fixed and equitative number of populations to each process. Once the master process has decided which populations will be assigned to each slave process, it proceeds to transfer them. In order to decrease the sending and/or reception of messages peer-to-peer between processes, we created *buffers*. Thus, each time that one or more full populations need to be sent or received, a buffer is created to pack (or receive) all the necessary information and later on, such information is sent (or unpacked). This is done with all the slaves, such that all can receive their corresponding populations. Finally, each slave sends back all its populations to the master process, such that the master can use them in any procedures required.

Third and Fourth Stages. The main mechanism of these stages, represented by lines 4–7 in Figure 1 is performed by the master thread (process). Then, we continue with the evolutionary process and with the resources reassignment described in the second stage.

Synchronization. In the case of Pthreads, at each generation we must wait until all the threads have finished their corresponding evolutionary processes and grid accesses. Each finished process waits until the continuation signal is received. Once all the processes have finished, the last thread to arrive takes care of the necessary processes and when it finishes, it sends the required signal to awaken all the other threads and continue with the evolutionary process. In the case of MPI, we use barriers at each generation for the synchronization. Such barriers are adopted after sending all the populations to all the slaves and after the reception of all the corresponding populations. This was done such that all the slaves could start the evolutionary process and corresponding evaluations of their individuals at the same time.

6 Comparison of Results

The efficiency of a parallel algorithm tends to be measured in terms of its correctness and its speedup. The speedup (SP) of an algorithm is obtained by dividing the processing time of the serial algorithm (T_s) by the processing time of the parallel version (T_p): $SP = T_s/T_p$. In all the experiments performed, we used the following parameters for our approach: crossover rate (p_c) of 0.8, mutation rate (p_m) of $1/codesize$ and size of the initial population ($popsize_{init}$) equal to the minimum size of the secondary population ($popsize_{sec}$) = 20. The maximum number of generations ($Gmax$) was adjusted such that the algorithms always performed an average of 40000 fitness function evaluations per run. The maximum number of allowable populations was 200. The experiments took place on a PC with 4 processors. In order to give an idea of how good is the performance of the proposed algorithm, we will also include a comparison of results with respect to the Pareto Archived Evolution Strategy (PAES) [4] (PAES was run using the same number of fitness function evaluations as the serial version of our coevolutionary algorithm), which is an algorithm representative of the state-of-the-art in the area. To allow a quantitative comparison of results, the following metrics were adopted:

Error Ratio (ER): This metric was proposed by Van Veldhuizen [7] to indicate the percentage of solutions (from the nondominated vectors found so far) that are not members of the true Pareto optimal set: $ER = (\sum_{i=1}^{n} e_i)/n$ where n is the number of vectors in the current set of nondominated vectors available; $e_i = 0$ if vector i is a member of the Pareto optimal set, and $e_i = 1$ otherwise.

Inverted Generational Distance (IGD): The concept of generational distance was introduced by Van Veldhuizen & Lamont [8,9] as a way of estimating how far are the elements in the Pareto front produced by our algorithm from those in the true Pareto front of the problem. This metric is defined as: $GD = (\sqrt{\sum_{i=1}^{n} d_i^2})/n$ where n is the number of nondominated vectors found by the algorithm being analyzed and d_i is the Euclidean distance (measured in objective space) between each of these and the nearest member of the true Pareto front. In our case, we implemented an "inverted" generational distance metric (IGD) in which we use as a reference the true Pareto front, and we compare each of its elements with respect to the front produced by an algorithm.

For each of the examples shown below, we performed 30 runs per algorithm. The Pareto fronts that we will show correspond to the median of the 30 runs performed with respect to the ER metric.

6.1 Test Function 1

Table 1 shows the values of SP and the metrics ER and IGD for each of the versions compared.

$$\text{Min } f_1(x_1, x_2) = x_1, \quad \text{Min } f_2(x_1, x_2) = (1.0 + 10.0x_2)$$

$$(1.0 - \frac{x_1^2}{1.0 + 10.0x_2} - \frac{x_1}{1.0 + 10.0x_2}\sin(2\pi 4x_1))$$

$$0.0 \leq x_1, x_2 \leq 1.0 \quad (4)$$

Table 1. Comparison of results for the first test function. SP refers to the speedup achieved.

		PAES	Serial	Pthreads $SP=2.9541$	MPI $SP=2.5185$
ER	best	0.01	0.22	0.16	0.09
	median	0.06	0.40	0.36	0.39
	worst	0.12	0.57	0.57	0.56
	average	0.057	0.39	0.37	0.36
	std. dev.	0.0301	0.1164	0.1215	0.1283
IGD	best	0.001030	0.000596	0.000606	0.000564
	median	0.001305	0.000818	0.000807	0.000875
	worst	0.003224	0.003277	0.003277	0.002906
	average	0.001382	0.001062	0.001061	0.001204
	std. dev.	0.000409	0.000638	0.000638	0.000637

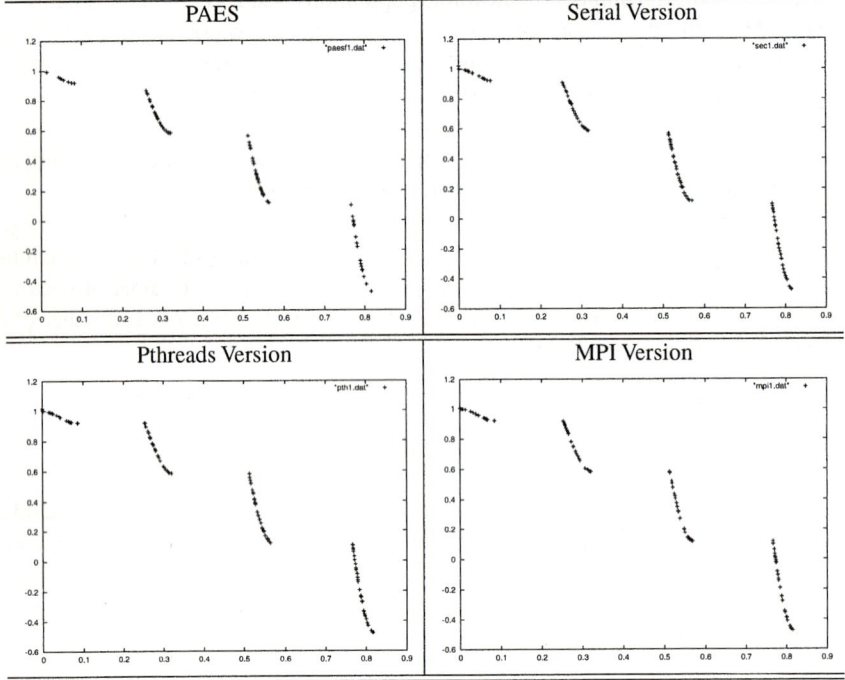

Fig. 2. Pareto fronts obtained by the serial versions of PAES and our coevolutionary algorithm, the Pthreads version and the MPI version for the first test function.

6.2 Test Function 2

Table 2 shows the values of SP and the metrics ER and IGD for each of the versions compared.

$$\text{Min } f_1(x_1, x_2) = x_1, \quad \text{Min } f_2(x_1, x_2) = \frac{g(x_2)}{x_1}$$

$$g(x_2) = 2.0 - e^{-(\frac{x_2-0.2}{0.004})^2} - 0.8e^{-(\frac{x_2-0.6}{0.4})^2}, \quad 0.1 \le x_1, x_2 \le 1.0$$

Table 2. Comparison of results for the second test function. SP refers to the speedup achieved.

		PAES	Serial	Pthreads SP=2.2486	MPI SP=2.5639
	best	0.01	0.06	0.03	0.07
	median	0.11	0.17	0.16	0.16
ER	worst	1.0	0.56	0.56	0.77
	average	0.26	0.14	0.14	0.14
	std. dev.	0.3390	0.1191	0.1197	0.1842
	best	0.005430	0.002321	0.002611	0.002882
	median	0.009875	0.003642	0.003648	0.003444
IGD	worst	0.023626	0.007876	0.007876	0.010387
	average	0.010495	0.003747	0.003791	0.003914
	std. dev.	0.004310	0.001035	0.000984	0.001431

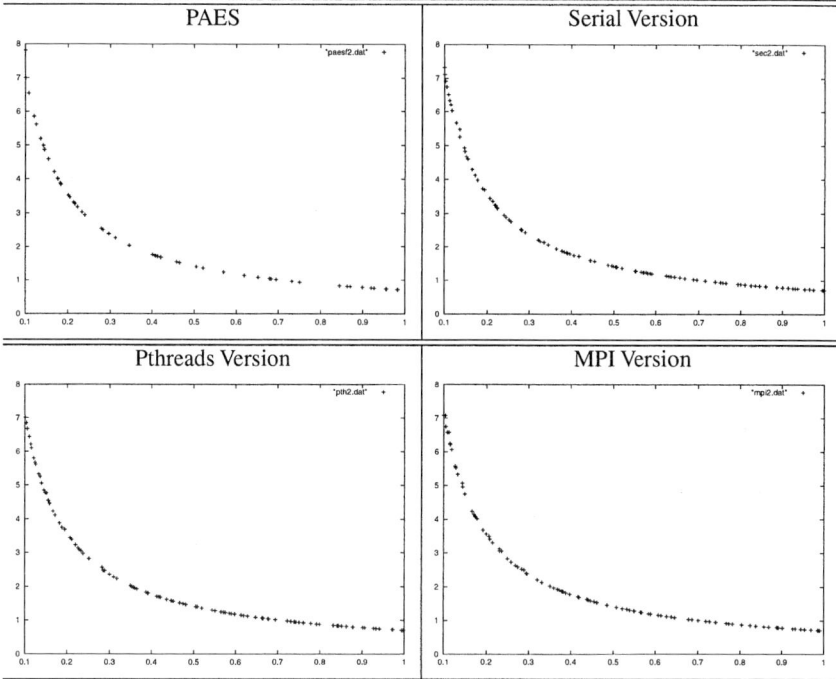

Fig. 3. Pareto fronts obtained by the serial versions of PAES and our coevolutionary algorithm, the Pthreads version and the MPI version for the second test function.

7   Discussion of Results

In the case of the first test function, when comparing results with respect to the ER metric, PAES considerably improves the results achieved by our coevolutionary approach in all of its versions. However, note that with respect to the IGD metric, our approach presents a better average performance than PAES. On the other hand, it is very important to note that, despite the fact that the use of Pthreads improves the results of the serial version (with respect to the ER metric), the MPI version does even better. With respect to the

IGD metric, the three versions of the coevolutionary algorithm have a similar behavior in all the test functions. In general, the results when using Pthreads are very similar than those obtained with the serial version. In contrast, the MPI version produces (marginally) better results than the other two versions in the case of the first function, and (marginally) poorer results in the case of the second function.

In the second test function, our coevolutionary approach had a better average performance than PAES with respect to the ER metric. In fact, note that the worst solutions achieved by PAES totally missed the true Pareto front of the problem (therefore the value of 1.0 obtained). Regarding the IGD metric, the results of the three versions of our coevolutionary algorithm are approximately three times better than those obtained by PAES. In the case of the second test function, the mere use of Pthreads improves on the results obtained using the serial version of the algorithm (when measured with respect to the ER metric). On average, however, the results obtained by our MPI approach are of the same quality as those obtained with the serial version of the algorithm.

In general, regarding the ER metric, the four algorithms reach the true Pareto front of each problem, and the first test function is the only one in which PAES is found to be superior to our approach (in any of its versions). However, regarding the IGD metric, we can see that the results of our coevolutionary algorithm are better than those obtained by PAES. Graphically, we can see that this is due to the fact that PAES has problems to cover the entire Pareto front of the problem. Regarding the speedups achieved, in the first test function, the Pthreads implementation was superior to the MPI version. In the second example, the best speedup was achieved by our MPI strategy. The speedup values that we obtained are considered acceptable if we take into account that the parallelization strategy adopted in this study is rather simple and does not adopt the best possible workload for the 4 processors available.

8   Conclusions and Future Work

We presented a simple parallelization of a coevolutionary multi-objective optimization algorithm. The main idea of our algorithm is to obtain information along the evolutionary process as to subdivide the search space into subregions, and then to use a subpopulation for each of these subregions. At each generation, these different subpopulations "cooperate" and "compete" among themselves and from these different processes we obtain a single Pareto front. The size of each subpopulation is adjusted based on their contribution to the current Pareto front. Thus, those populations contributing with more nondominated individuals have a higher reproduction probability. Three versions of the algorithm were compared in this paper: the serial version and two parallel versions: one using Pthreads and another one using MPI. We also included a comparison of results with respect to PAES to have an idea of the performance of the serial version of our algorithm. The results obtained indicate that, despite the simplicity of the parallel strategy that we implemented, the gains in execution time are considerably good, without affecting (in a significant way) the quality of the results with respect to the serial version. As part of our future work we are considering the use of a more efficient parallelization strategy that can improve the $speedup$ values achieved in this paper. We are also considering certain structural engineering applications for our proposed approach.

Acknowledgments. The first author acknowledges support from CONACyT through project number 34201-A. The second author acknowledges support from CONACyT through a scholarship to pursue graduate studies at CINVESTAV-IPN's Electrical Engineering Department.

References

1. Coello Coello, C.A., Van Veldhuizen, D.A., Lamont, G.B.: Evolutionary Algorithms for Solving Multi-Objective Problems. Kluwer Academic Publishers, New York (2002) ISBN 0-3064-6762-3.
2. Coello Coello, C.A., Reyes Sierra, M.: A Coevolutionary Multi-Objective Evolutionary Algorithm. In: Proceedings of the Congress on Evolutionary Computation, IEEE Press (2003) (accepted for publication)
3. Fonseca, C.M., Fleming, P.J.: Genetic algorithms for multiobjective optimization: formulation, discussion and generalization. In Forrest, S., ed.: Proceedings of the Fifth International Conference on Genetic Algorithms, San Mateo, California, University of Illinois at Urbana-Champaign, Morgan Kauffman Publishers (1993) 416–423
4. Knowles, J.D., Corne, D.W.: Approximating the Nondominated Front Using the Pareto Archived Evolution Strategy. Evolutionary Computation **8** (2000) 149–172
5. Paredis, J.: Coevolutionary algorithms. In Bäck, T., Fogel, D.B., Michalewicz, Z., eds.: The Handbook of Evolutionary Computation, 1st supplement. Institute of Physics Publishing and Oxford University Press (1998) 225–238
6. Potter, M., Jong., K.D.: A cooperative coevolutionary approach to function optimization. In: Proceedings from the Fifth Parallel Problem Solving from Nature, Jerusalem, Israel, Springer-Verlag (1994) 530–539
7. Van Veldhuizen, D.A.: Multiobjective Evolutionary Algorithms: Classifications, Analyses, and New Innovations. PhD thesis, Department of Electrical and Computer Engineering. Graduate School of Engineering. Air Force Institute of Technology, Wright-Patterson AFB, Ohio (1999)
8. Van Veldhuizen, D.A., Lamont, G.B.: Multiobjective Evolutionary Algorithm Research: A History and Analysis. Technical Report TR-98-03, Department of Electrical and Computer Engineering, Graduate School of Engineering, Air Force Institute of Technology, Wright-Patterson AFB, Ohio (1998)
9. Van Veldhuizen, D.A., Lamont, G.B.: On Measuring Multiobjective Evolutionary Algorithm Performance. In: 2000 Congress on Evolutionary Computation. Volume 1., Piscataway, New Jersey, IEEE Service Center (2000) 204–211

Reactive Agents to Improve a Parallel Genetic Algorithm Solution

Ana Lilia Laureano-Cruces[1], José Manuel de la Cruz-González[1],
Javier Ramírez-Rodríguez[1], and Julio Solano-González[2]

[1] Universidad Autónoma Metropolitana, Unidad Azcapotzalco, CBI, Departamento de
Sistemas, Av. San Pablo 180, Col. Reynosa, Azcapotzalco, DF 02200, México.
{clc,jararo}@correo.azc.uam.mx
josman75@yahoo.com.mx
[2] DISCA-IIMAS-, Universidad Nacional Autónoma de México, P.O. Box 20-726,. Álvaro
Obregón, DF 01000, México.
julio@uxdea4.iimas.unam.mx

Abstract. One of the distributed artificial intelligence objectives is the
decentralization of control. Multi-agent architectures distribute the control
among two or more agents, which will be in charge of different events. In this
paper the design of a parallel Multi-agent architecture for genetic algorithms is
described, using a bottom-up behavior design and reactive agents. Such design
tries to achieve the improvement solution of parallel genetic algorithms. The
purpose of incorporating a reactive behavior in the parallel genetic algorithms is
to improve the overall performance by up-dating the sub-populations according
to the general behavior of the algorithm avoiding getting stuck in local minima.
Two kinds of experiments were conducted for each one of the algorithms and
the results obtained with both experiments are shown.

1 Introduction

A kind of Multi-agent (MA) architecture is the one designed with reactive agents,
which were first studied by Brooks [1] in the early 80s. Their main characteristic is
that they have no exhaustive representation of the real world. Their behavior is
emergent, i. e., it is to a great extent dependent on the perception of the environment
at a given instant.

Reactive agents are also known as agents based on behavior. Their main features are:
1) a constant interaction with the environment, and 2) a control mechanism allowing
them to work with limited resources and incomplete information [3,4,6]

The chief advantage of the use of reactive agents lies in the speed of adaptation to
unforeseen situations This advantage has a high cost, since reactive design leaves a
great deal of deliberative tasks to the designer.

In this paper a proposal for the analysis and design of reactive agents based on the
bottom-up design mechanism proposed by Maes [7] and Laureano, de Arriaga and

R. Monroy et al. (Eds.): MICAI 2004, LNAI 2972, pp. 698–706, 2004.
© Springer-Verlag Berlin Heidelberg 2004

García-Alegre [5] is developed, in order to improve on the results obtained in [10] by means of a parallel genetic algorithm whose domain is centered on the efficiency of the classification of a universal set in two independent subsets. The balance between the capacity to converge to an optimum and the ability to explore new regions is dictated by p_m, p_c and the type of crossover employed. In this work p_m, p_c are varied adaptively occording to the fitness values of the solutions [9].

Such architecture is implemented by establishing a similarity between the desires expressed by Maes: eating, exploring and fleeing, with the desire to: interchange individuals and improve the quality of the solution.

2 Design of the Reactive Genetic Algorithm

2.1 Control Mechanism for a Reactive Agent

Pattie Maes [7] proposes a reactive mechanism for choosing a given behavior among a set of them.

Maes simulates the behavior of a not very complex artificial creature, which has a set of ten different behaviors: eating, drinking, exploring, going-towards-food, going-towards-water, sleeping, fighting, fleeing-from-creature, going-towards-creature, and dodging-obstacle. Besides, it has a set of seven motivations: thirst, hunger, sleepiness, fear, tiredness, safety and agressiveness. Such creatures are placed in a virtual environment, inside which can be found some *elements* such as: water, food, another creature, an obstacle. The quantities of those *elements* are variables.

Each behavior is associated with: a) an activation level represented by a real number; b) a set of conditions, and c) a threshold, represented as well by a real number. For a given behavior to be executed, its activation level must surpass the threshold level, as well as fulfilling a number of conditions related to the environment. For instance: for the eating behavior to be executed, there must be food near the creature.

As for behavior activation mechanisms, they are represented by 1) the creature's desire to perform a given behavior; 2) the present situation: the environment influences the creature's desires; 3) activation through the precedent: When a behavior is executed, the value of the activation level goes down to almost zero. The same happens to all the values of activation levels associated to the desires related to that behavior.

2.2 Parallel Genetic Algorithm with Reactive Characteristics

The Parallel Genetic Algorithm (PGA) performance is based on the interchange of individuals among different sub-populations. Plans best known for individuals interchange are migration and diffusion. Those mechanisms have as input data a previous knowledge of: 1) the generation, and 2) the sub-populations involved.

The purpose of incorporating a reactive behavior in the PGA, is improve the overall performance by up-dating the sub-populations according to the general behavior of the algorithm avoiding getting stuck in local minima. An emergent behavior is proposed that, as has been already stated, is the main feature of reactive agents. The Reactive Parallel Genetic Algorithm (RPGA) will be able to send and receive individuals from and to any other sub-population. The former, at the time required, by observing the stimuli presented by the environment at a given time, without affecting its performance. In what follows a more detailed description is made of the characteristics and elements that will substitute the traditional migration mechanism:

1. A sub-population might send individuals to another sub-population in any generation,. There is no need for both sub-populations to be synchronized. The sender does not know in what generation, nor to whom will it send individuals, until the very moment they are sent.

2. Due to the reactive migration plan, several cases can arise in the individuals interchange stages. These go from the minimal case in which in a given generation no population sends any individuals, to the maximum one in which, given a generation, all the populations send individuals to the $n - 1$ remaining ones. All the subsets of ordered pairs of the set of sub-populations must be considered.

3. In each generation, each genetic algorithm GA (sub-population) must verify if individuals from other sub-populations have arrived. The former due to the lack of synchronization and migration topology. For that reason, all the sub-populations, represented by their GA, must check a special buffer, which will be called the *station*. It is in this *station* where all arriving individuals are temporarily stored. If the station is empty, the GA continues on its task; if it is not, the individuals are extracted and added to the sub-population.

4. The sending of individuals from one sub-population to another is determined by certain non-deterministic impulses assigned to each GA. Those impulses would be controlled by a mechanism similar to the one used by Maes [7] to simulate the behavior of simple creatures in a dynamic environment. The mechanism proposed here borrows some concepts from Maes, adding some new ones in order to be able to adapt it to the field of GAs. The new concepts are defined below.

   – *Migration Limit:* is a value representing the limit that the *migration impulse* must surpass for the GA to be able to send a group of individuals to some of the $n - 1$ remaining sub-populations. The *migration limit* can remain constant during the population evolution.

   – *Migration Impulse:* is a value representing the GA's desire of sending individuals to a specific sub-population. It allows each GA to have a *migration impulse* for each one of the $n - 1$ remaining sub-populations. When this value surpasses the *migration limit*, the GA selects a group of individuals and sends them to the corresponding sub-population. The migration impulse is cut down to 10% of its present value after they are sent.

–   *Stimulus Range:* is an interval comprising the allowed values of the stimulus in order to increment the *migration impulse*. In other words, all the GA (sub-populations) in each generation produce a random value for each one of the n-1 remaining sub-populations. Such value is within the production range of the stimulus. The generated value will be called *stimulus* and it will be added to the present value of the *migration impulse*.

Given the characteristics described above and knowing the optimal solution, The purpose is to keep a high diversity in the sub-populations to prevent premature convergence.

An important aspect of the GA is the quality of the solution. For that reason, a mechanism is included in which each population requests to the n-1 remaining sub-populations the sending of individuals. Such request will be made based on the time elapsed from the last time the former best solution was improved. The time interval (number of generations) elapsed without improvement will be called *improvement limit*.

When in a GA a number of generations have passed and the *improvement limit* did not change, it sends a message to the other n-1 GAs. This message is interpreted as a request for individuals from the sender. The former will allow the rest of the GAs (sub-populations) to send their own individuals. Once they are sent, the value of the *migration impulse* of the receiving sub-population is decreased. The value of the migration impulse is stored in each sending sub-population. The decrease of that value is in order to prevent such sub-population from receiving individuals on a short period of time.

All these characteristics, together in the same GA, constitute what we hereafter will call Reactive Parallel Genetic Algorithm (RPGA), which is presented in Fig. 1.

As can be perceived in the Fig. 1, the RPGA works in the following fashion: initially, it generates randomly a population of individuals, and enters the evolution cycle of that population, where for each iteration (generation) it finds out the aptitude of the individuals. It chooses the individuals that will survive, according to the selection plan used [2]. Individuals are crossed and mutated. Later, starts the reactivity stage, where, to begin with, the value of the *migration impulse* of each remaining sub-population is increased. A check is made to see if an individuals' request have arrived, in which case the value of the *migration impulse* is increased again in each sub-population that sent a request. The value of each migration impulse is looked over, and individuals are sent to the sub-populations whose migration impulses are greater than the *migration limit*.

Later on, the *station* is verified to look for individuals that just arrived; if they did, those individuals are added to the sub-population; otherwise, the iterative process continues. The last step is to verify which one is the best element found in this

> *Generate Initial Population*
> **Do While** *Population Evolution Criterion not Fulfilled*
> > *Find Aptitude*
> > *Select Individuals*
> > *Cross Individuals*
> > *Mutate Individuals*
> > *Increment Migration Impulse*
> > *If (Requests Arrived),* **Then**
> > > *Increment Migration Impulse*
> >
> > **End If**
> > *If (Impulse > Limit),* **Then**
> > > *Send Individuals*
> >
> > **End If**
> > *If (individuals arrived),* **Then**
> > > *Add Individuals to Population*
> >
> > **End If**
> > *If (solution not Improved in given time)* **Then**
> > > *Send Individuals Request*
> >
> > **End If**
>
> **End Do**

Fig. 1. Reactive Genetic Algorithm

generation. If that element is better than the global optimum, the former is substituted by the new best element. Otherwise, a counter is incremented. If the value of that counter is greater than or equal to the *improvement limit*, then the GA sends an individuals request to the other GAs. This cycle is repeated until the result complies with the convergence criterion or with the number of iterations agreed upon.

Communication between sub-populations is represented by sending and receiving individuals. This is accomplished by perceiving the local environment through three independent agents in each sub-population. Such perception is meant to find stimuli allowing them to communicate with the n-1 sub-populations. The interaction between agents is local for the sub-population and its purpose is to reach its goals: request, sending and reception of individuals. Fig. 2 shows the types of communication, considering two agents; that is, two populations.

3 Experiments

3.1 Objective Function

For this research we had available a set of 201 samples, belonging to a universal set, of whom 49 belong to Group 1, and 152 to Group 2. The comparison between genetic algorithms was carried out by measuring the effectiveness of each one, in order to classify accurately each individual in its proper group.

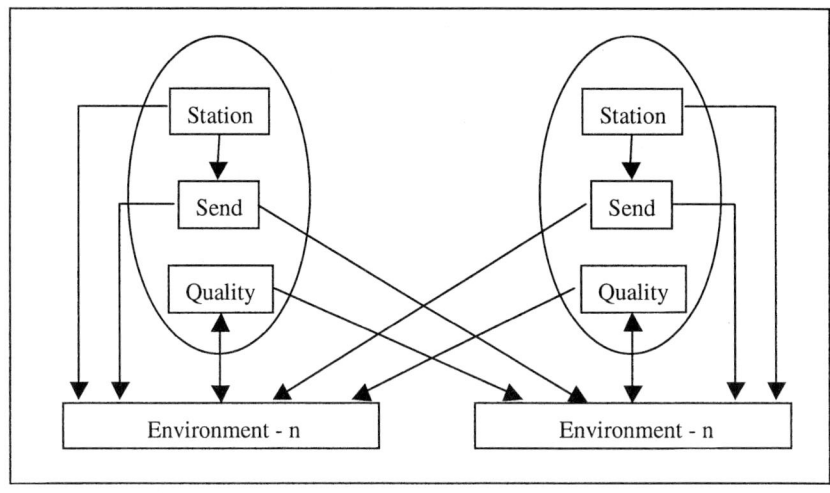

Fig. 2. Types of Communication using 2 agents

An objective function was designed for this purpose, determining the number of successes for each individual in the population, in such way that the best individual will be the one having 201 successes, or 100% effectiveness, while the worst would be the one with 0 successes, or 0% effectiveness when classifying:

$$f(x) = C\sum_{i=1}^{n} a_i + \sum_{j=1}^{m} b_j \tag{1}$$

where:

n is the number of samples from group 1.

m is the number of samples from group 2.

$$a_i = \begin{cases} 1 & if \quad classifies \quad correctly \quad sample \quad i \quad from \quad group \quad 1 \\ 0 & otherwise \end{cases}$$

$$b_j = \begin{cases} 1 & if \quad classifies \quad correctly \quad sample \quad j \quad from \quad group \quad 2 \\ 0 & otherwise \end{cases}$$

C: a constant, used to assign a greater weight to successes in samples from group 1.

In this work two types of mutation were used: static and dynamic. The dynamic one was defined in a similar way to the one used by Pal and Wang [10] where individuals whose fitness is equal to the best in generation have a $P_m = 0$. This avoid the mutation of high quality individuals giving as a result a high probability of premature convergence. Therefore in this case a more aggressive mutation rate can be used, that is,

$$p_m = \frac{k_1(A_{max} + A_{avg} - A_{ind})}{A_{max}} \qquad for \ A_{ind} > A_{avg} \tag{2}$$

$$p_m = k_2 \qquad\qquad \text{for A}_{ind} <= \text{A}_{avg} \qquad\qquad (3)$$

where:

p_m	= mutation probability.
A_{max}	= aptitude of the best individual of the population in that generation.
A_{avg}	= average aptitude of all individuals of the population in the generation.
A_{ind}	= aptitude of the individual for which p_m is being estimated.
k_1	= 0.5
k_2	= 0.25

3.2 Parameters and Configuration

The RPGA uses a maximum of 2000 generations. The universal stochastic selection method of reproduction is applied. The crossing mechanism is a discrete one with a probability of 1.0. The mutation mechanism is based on the one proposed by Mühlenbein and Schilerkamp-Voosen [8] and the mutation probability is dynamic, based on the work of Pal and Wang [9].

A real codification is used for the chromosome structure, since the alleles of each individual have values in the interval [0, 1]. An adjusted aptitude plan is used to map the aptitudes of the individuals as values in the interval [0, 1].

Table 1. Results of tests for parallel and reactive genetic algorithms when using static mutation.

Run	Parallel Genetic Algorithm			Reactive Genetic Algorithm		
	Time	Aptitude	Effect	Time	Aptitude	Effect
1	370	0.9813	93.58	409	0.9798	93.08
2	372	0.9829	94.06	407	0.9829	94.06
3	368	0.9844	94.56	410	0.9829	94.06
4	369	0.9829	94.06	412	0.9813	93.58
5	375	0.9782	92.58	413	0.9798	93.08
6	375	0.9813	93.58	411	0.9844	94.56
7	389	0.9798	93.08	408	0.9813	93.58
8	371	0.9782	92.58	407	0.9844	94.56
9	372	0.9798	93.08	410	0.9844	94.56
10	371	0.9844	94.56	415	0.9829	94.06
Average	373.2	0.9813	93.57	410.2	0.9824	93.92

Table 2. Results of tests for parallel and reactive genetic algorithms when using dynamic mutation.

	Parallel Genetic Algorithm			Reactive Genetic Algorithm		
Run	**Time**	**Aptitude**	**Effect**	**Time**	**Aptitude**	**Effect**
1	670	0.9829	94.06	707	0.9860	95.06
2	679	0.9875	95.55	710	0.9891	96.04
3	673	0.9860	95.06	711	0.9829	94.06
4	672	0.9813	93.58	709	0.9844	94.56
5	670	0.9860	95.06	710	0.9891	96.04
6	669	0.9860	95.06	708	0.9813	93.58
7	671	0.9829	94.06	700	0.9891	96.04
8	675	0.9813	93.58	710	0.9860	95.06
9	679	0.9829	94.06	712	0.9875	95.55
10	673	0.9829	95.55	715	0.9891	96.04
Average	673.1	0.9840	94.56	709.2	0.9864	95.20

The RPGA has available a population of 800 individuals, the best results were obtained when it was divided into 8 sub-populations of 100 each. Members of the population migrate using the reactive mechanism with a migration percentage of 10%. The best individuals of each population are selected to migrate to others, and the incoming individuals substitute the worst ones.

In order to implement a reactive migration scheme, several runs were conducted. The best results were obtained for migration rates of: 10, 15 and 20, to save communications we choose 20 as migration limit. Therefore, migration impulses are set to zero and progressively increased in each generation randomly, with a stimulus value included in the interval [0.0, 2.0]. The *improvement limit* has a value of 20 generations.

3.3 Experiments and Results

Two kinds of experiments were performed for each one of the algorithms: a) a parallel, and b) a reactive one. The first experiment was made using static mutation, and the second one, dynamic. For each algorithm 10 trials were made. At the end of those experiments information was obtained about: 1) best percentage of classification, and 2) the classification average. The results obtained with both experiments are shown above (Table 1 and Table 2).

As can be seen in the Table 1, the reactive genetic algorithm obtained a classification average slightly higher than the parallel one. Even so, both algorithms achieved a best classification percentage of 94.56%.

Table 2, shows that the reactive genetic algorithm obtained a classification average of 95.20%, while the parallel one is slightly lower, at 94.56%. On the other hand, the reactive algorithm achieved classification with an effectiveness of 96.04% while the parallel one reached 95.55%.

4   Conclusions

In this paper, a migration mechanism for genetic algorithms controlled by reactive agents is presented. Such agents were inspired by the bottom-up design of the behavior proposed by Maes [7] and Laureano et al. [5].

The results obtained show that both algorithms present their best results when dynamic mutation is used, the RGA being the best for classifying, with a mean effectiveness percentage of 95.20%, while the PGA reaches 94.55%.

In that way the RGA can be considered as an efficient method for the solution of complex problems. In the case we deal with, slightly better results are found from those of the PGA. Even if the computing time of the RGA is larger, it has however a practical advantage, a higher classification average.

References

1.   Brooks, R. 1991. Intelligence without Reason. *Artificial Intelligence*, **47**:139-159.
2.   Goldberg. D. 1989. *Genetic Algorithms in Search, Optimization and Machine Learning.* (ed.) Addison-Wesley.
3.   Laureano, A., 1998. Los Sistemas Reactivos: Un Nuevo Acercamiento a la Inteligencia Artificial Distribuida. *NOVATICA.* **132**:51-55. (Spain.)
4.   Laureano, A., and de Arriaga, F. 1998. Multi-Agent Architecture for Intelligent Tutoring Systems. *Interactive Learning Environments,* (ed.) Swets & Zeitlinger, **6**(3):225-250.
5.   Laureano, A., and de Arriaga, F. and García-Alegre, M. 2001. Cognitive Task Analysis: a Proposal to Model Reactive Behaviours. *Journal of Experimental & Theoretical Artificial Intelligence.* (ed.) Taylor & Francis, Ltd.
6.   Laureano, A., and Barceló, A. 2003. Formal verification of multi-agent systems behaviour emerging from cognitive task analyisis. *Journal of Experimental & Theoretical Artificial Intelligence.* (ed.) Taylor & Francis, Ltd. (to appear).
7.   Maes, P. February 1991. A Bottom-Up Mechanism for Action Selection in an Artificial Creature. From Animals to Animats: *Proceedings of the Adaptive Behavior Conference'91.* Edited by S. Wilson and J. Arcady-Meyer. MIT-Press.
8.   Mühlenbein, H. Schlierkamp-Voosen, D. 1993. Predictive Models for the Breeder Genetic Algorithm, I: Continuous Parameter Optimization. *Evolutionary Computation.* **1**(1):25-49.
9.   Patniak, L., Mandavilli, S. 1996. Adaptation in Genetic Algorithms, pp. 45-63. In Pal, S. and Wang, P. (Editors). *Genetic Algorithms for Pattern Recognition.* CRC Press.
10. Quintana Hernández, M. I., Solano González, J., A Genetic Algorithm Approach to Auxiliary Diagnosis of Neurocysticerosis, *Proceedings of the 2000 Genetic and Evolutionary Computation Congress Workshop Programm,* Las Vegas, Nevada, pp 301-304.

Simple Feasibility Rules and Differential Evolution for Constrained Optimization

Efrén Mezura-Montes[1], Carlos A. Coello Coello[1], and Edy I. Tun-Morales[2]

[1] CINVESTAV-IPN
Evolutionary Computation Group (EVOCINV)
Departamento de Ingeniería Eléctrica
Sección de Computación
Av. Instituto Politécnico Nacional No. 2508
Col. San Pedro Zacatenco
México D.F. 07300, MÉXICO
emezura@computacion.cs.cinvestav.mx
ccoello@cs.cinvestav.mx
[2] Instituto Tecnológico de Villahermosa
Carretera Villahermosa-Frontera Km. 3.5 Cd. Industrial
Villahermosa Tabasco
eltedy@hotmail.com

Abstract. In this paper, we propose a differential evolution algorithm to solve constrained optimization problems. Our approach uses three simple selection criteria based on feasibility to guide the search to the feasible region. The proposed approach does not require any extra parameters other than those normally adopted by the Differential Evolution algorithm. The present approach was validated using test functions from a well-known benchmark commonly adopted to validate constraint-handling techniques used with evolutionary algorithms. The results obtained by the proposed approach are very competitive with respect to other constraint-handling techniques that are representative of the state-of-the-art in the area.

1   Introduction

Evolutionary Algorithms (EAs) are heuristics that have been successfully applied in a wide set of areas [1,2], both in single and in multiobjective optimization. However, EAs lack a mechanism able to bias efficiently the search towards the feasible region in constrained search spaces. This has triggered a considerable amount of research and a wide variety of approaches have been suggested in the last few years to incorporate constraints into the fitness function of an evolutionary algorithm [3,4].

The most common approach adopted to deal with constrained search spaces is the use of penalty functions. When using a penalty function, the amount of constraint violation is used to punish or "penalize" an infeasible solution so that feasible solutions are favored by the selection process. Despite the popularity of penalty functions, they have several drawbacks from which the main one is that they require a careful fine tuning of the penalty factors that accurately estimates the degree of penalization to be applied as to approach efficiently the feasible region [5,3].

R. Monroy et al. (Eds.): MICAI 2004, LNAI 2972, pp. 707–716, 2004.

Differential Evolution (DE) is a relatively new EA proposed by Price and Storn [6]. The algorithm is based on the use of a special crossover-mutation operator, based on the linear combination of three different individuals and one subject-to-replacement parent. The selection process is performed via deterministic tournament selection between the parent and the child created by it. However, as any other EA, DE lacks a mechanism to deal with constrained search spaces.

The constraint-handling approach proposed in this paper relies on three simple selection criteria based on feasibility to bias the search towards the feasible region. We have used the same approach implemented on different types of Evolution Strategies in which the results were very promising [7,8]. The main motivation of this work was to analyze if the use of the selection criteria that we successfully adopted in evolution strategies would also work with differential evolution. This is an important issue to us, because it has been hypothesized in the past that evolution strategies are a very powerful search engine for constrained optimization when dealing with real numbers [9]. However, no such studies exist for differential evolution nor other related heuristics that operate on real numbers (as evolution strategies). We thus believe that the search power of other heuristics such as differential evolution has been underestimated and therefore our interest in analyzing such search power.

The paper is organized as follows: In Section 2, the problem of our interest is stated. In Section 3 we describe the previous work related with the current algorithm. A detailed description of our approach is provided in Section 4. The experiments performed and the results obtained are shown in Section 5 and in Section 6 we discuss them. Finally, in Section 7 we establish some conclusions and we define our future paths of research.

2   Statement of the Problem

We are interested in the general nonlinear programming problem in which we want to:Find x which optimizes $f(x)$ subject to: $g_i(x) \leq 0$, $i = 1, \dots, n$ $h_j(x) = 0$, $j = 1, \dots, p$ where x is the vector of solutions $x = [x_1, x_2, \dots, x_r]^T$, n is the number of inequality constraints and p is the number of equality constraints (in both cases, constraints could be linear or nonlinear). If we denote with $\mathcal{F}$ to the feasible region and with $\mathcal{S}$ to the whole search space, then it should be clear that $\mathcal{F} \subseteq \mathcal{S}$. For an inequality constraint that satisfies $g_i(x) = 0$, we will say that is active at x. All equality constraints h_j (regardless of the value of x used) are considered active at all points of $\mathcal{F}$.

3   Previous Work

DE is a population-based evolutionary algorithm with an special recombination operator that performs a linear combination of a number of individuals (normally three) and one parent (which is subject to be replaced) to create one child. The selection is deterministic between the parent and the child. The best of them remain in the next population. DE shares similarities with traditional EAs. However it does not use binary encoding as a simple genetic algorithm [2] and it does not use a probability density function to self-adapt its parameters as an Evolution Strategy [10]. The main differential evolution algorithm [6] is presented in Figure 1.

```
Begin
   G=0
   Create a random initial population xᵢ_G ∀i, i = 1, ... , NP
   Evaluate f(xᵢ_G) ∀i, i = 1, ... , NP
   For G=1 to MAX_GENERATIONS Do
      For i=1 to NP Do
         Select randomly r₁ ≠ r₂ ≠ r₃ :
         j_rand = randint(1, D)
         For j=1 to D Do
            If (rand_j[0, 1) < CR or j = j_rand) Then
               uⁱ_{j,G+1} = x^{r3}_{j,G} + F(x^{r1}_{j,G} − x^{r2}_{j,G})
            Else
               uⁱ_{j,G+1} = xⁱ_{j,G}
            End If
         End For
         If (f(uⁱ_{G+1}) ≤ f(xⁱ_G)) Then
            xⁱ_{G+1} = uⁱ_{G+1}
         Else
            xⁱ_{G+1} = xⁱ_G
         End If
      End For
      G = G + 1
   End For
End
```

Fig. 1. DE algorithm. randint(min,max) is a function that returns an integer number between min and max. rand$[0, 1)$ is a function that returns a real number between 0 and 1. Both are based on a uniform probability distribution. "NP", "MAX_GENERATIONS", "CR" and "F" are user-defined parameters.

The use of tournament selection based on feasibility rules has been explored by other authors. Jiménez and Verdegay [11] proposed an approach similar to a min-max formulation used in multiobjective optimization combined with tournament selection. The rules used by them are similar to those adopted in this work. However, Jiménez and Verdegay's approach lacks an explicit mechanism to avoid the premature convergence produced by the random sampling of the feasible region because their approach is guided by the first feasible solution found. Deb [12] used the same tournament rules previously indicated in his approach. However, Deb proposed to use niching as a diversity mechanism, which introduces some extra computational time (niching has time-complexity $O(N^2)$). In Deb's approach, feasible solutions are always considered better than infeasible ones. This contradicts the idea of allowing infeasible individuals to remain in the population. Therefore, this approach will have difficulties in problems in which the global optimum lies on the boundary between the feasible and the infeasible regions. Coello & Mezura [13] used tournament selection based on feasibility rules. They also adopted nondominance checking using a sample of the population (as the multiobjective optimization approach called NPGA [14]). They adopted a user-defined parameter S_r, to control the diversity in the population. This approach provided good results in some well-known engineering problems and in some benchmark problems, but presented problems when facing high dimensionality [13].

Some previous approaches have been proposed to solve constrained optimization problems using DE. Storn [15] proposed an adaptive mechanism that relaxes the constraints of the problem in order to make all the initial solutions feasible. This pseudo-feasible region is shrunk each generation until it matches the real feasible region. Also, Storn [15] proposed to use an aging concept in order to avoid that a solution remains in the population too many generations. Furthermore, he modified the original DE algorithm because when a child is created and it is not better than the parent subject-to-replace, another child is created. The process is repeated NT times. If the parent is still better, the parent remains in the population. Both, the aging parameter and NT are defined by the user. Storn [15] used a modified "DE/rand/1/bin" version. The approach showed a good performance in problems with only inequality constraints but presented problems when dealing with equality constraints. Moreover, only two test functions (out of seven used to test the approach) are included in the well-known benchmark for constrained optimization proposed by Koziel & Michalewicz [16] and enriched by Runarsson & Yao [9]. The main drawback of the approach is that it adds two user-defined parameters and that the NT parameter can cause an increase in the number of evaluations of the objective function without any user control.

Lampinen & Zelinka [17] used DE to solve engineering design problems. They opted to handle constraints using a static penalty function approach that they called "Soft - constraint". The authors tested their approach using three well-known engineering design problems [17]. They compared their results with respect to several classical techniques and with respect to some heuristic methods. The main drawback of the approach is the careful tuning required for the penalty factors which is in fact mentioned by the authors in their article. The last two methods discussed also lack of a mechanism to maintain diversity (to have both, feasible and infeasible solutions in the population during all the evolutionary process), which is one of the most important aspects to consider when designing a competitive constraint-handling approach [8].

4   Our Approach

The design of our approach is based on the idea of preserving the main DE algorithm and just adding a simple mechanism, which has been found to be successful with other EAs. Moreover, our constraint-handling approach does not add any extra parameter defined by the user (other than those required by the original DE algorithm).

The modifications made to the original DE are the following:

1. The simple mechanism to deal with constraints are three simple selection criteria which guide the algorithm to the feasible region of the search space:
   – Between 2 feasible solutions, the one with the highest fitness value wins.
   – If one solution is feasible and the other one is infeasible, the feasible solution wins.
   – If both solutions are infeasible, the one with the lowest sum of constraint violation is preferred.
   These criteria are applied when the child is compared against the parent subject to be replaced.
2. In order to accelerate the convergence process, when a child replaces its parent, it is copied into the new generation but it is also copied into the current generation. The goal of this change is to allow the new child, which is a new and better solution,

to be selected among the three solutions (r_1, r_2 or r_3) and contribute to create better solutions. In this way, a promising solution does not need to wait for the next generation to share its genetic code.

3. When a new decision variable of the child is created and it is out of the limits established (lower and upper) by an amount, this amount is subtracted or added to the limit violated to shift the value inside the limits. If the shifted value is now violating the other limit (which may occur), as a last option, a random value inside the limits is generated.

Our proposed version of the DE algorithm, called CHDE (Constraint Handling Differential Evolution) is shown in Figure 2.

Begin
  G=0
  Create a random initial population x_G^i $\forall i, i = 1, \ldots, NP$
  Evaluate $f(x_G^i)$ $\forall i, i = 1, \ldots, NP$
  For G=1 to MAX_GENERATIONS **Do**
    For i=1 to NP **Do**
      Select randomly $r_1 \neq r_2 \neq r_3$:
      $j_{rand} = \text{randint}(1, D)$
      For j=1 to D **Do**
        If $(rand_j[0, 1) < CR$ **or** $j = j_{rand})$ **Then**
          $u_{j,G+1}^i = x_{j,G}^{r3} + F(x_{j,G}^{r1} - x_{j,G}^{r2})$
        Else
          $u_{j,G+1}^i = x_{j,G}^i$
        End If
      End For
$\Longrightarrow$ **If** $(u_{G+1}^i$ is better than x_G^i (based on the three selection criteria)) **Then**
          $x_{G+1}^i = u_{G+1}^i$
$\Longrightarrow$ $x_G^i = u_{G+1}^i$
        Else
          $x_{G+1}^i = x_G^i$
$\Longrightarrow$ $x_G^i = x_G^i$
        End If
      End For
        $G = G + 1$
    End For
  End

Fig. 2. CHDE algorithm. The modified steps are marked with an arrow. randint(min,max) is a function that returns an integer number between min and max. rand[0, 1) is a function that returns a real number between 0 and 1. Both are based on a uniform probability distribution. "NP", "MAX_GENERATIONS", "CR" and "F" are user-defined parameters

5 Experiments and Results

To evaluate the performance of the proposed approach we used the 13 test functions described in [9]. The test functions chosen contain characteristics that are representative of what can be considered "difficult" global optimization problems for an evolutionary algorithm. Their expressions can be found in [9].

To get a measure of the difficulty of solving each of these problems, a ρ metric (as suggested by Koziel and Michalewicz [16]) was computed using the following expression: $\rho = |F|/|S|$, where $|F|$ is the number of feasible solutions and $|S|$ is the total number of solutions randomly generated. In this work, $S = 1,000,000$ random solutions.

Table 1. Values of ρ for the 13 test problems chosen.

Problem	n	Type of function	ρ	LI	NI	LE	NE
g01	13	quadratic	0.0003%	9	0	0	0
g02	20	nonlinear	99.9973%	2	0	0	0
g03	10	nonlinear	0.0026%	0	0	0	1
g04	5	quadratic	27.0079%	4	2	0	0
g05	4	nonlinear	0.0000%	2	0	0	3
g06	2	nonlinear	0.0057%	0	2	0	0
g07	10	quadratic	0.0000%	3	5	0	0
g08	2	nonlinear	0.8581%	0	2	0	0
g09	7	nonlinear	0.5199%	0	4	0	0
g10	8	linear	0.0020%	6	0	0	0
g11	2	quadratic	0.0973%	0	0	0	1
g12	3	quadratic	4.7697%	0	9^3	0	0
g13	5	nonlinear	0.0000%	0	0	1	2

The different values of ρ for each of the functions chosen are shown in Table 1, where n is the number of decision variables, LI is the number of linear inequalities, NI the number of nonlinear inequalities, LE is the number of linear equalities and NE is the number of nonlinear equalities.

We performed 30 independent runs for each test function. Equality constraints were transformed into inequalities using a tolerance value of 0.0001 (except for problems g03, g11 and g13 where the tolerance was 0.001). The parameters used for the CHDE are the following: $NP = 60$, $MAX\_GENERATIONS = 5,800$. To ensure that there is no sensitivity to "F" and "CR" parameters, F was generated randomly (using a uniform distribution) per run between $[0.3, 0.9]$ and CR was also randomly generated between $[0.8, 1.0]$. The intervals for both parameters were defined empirically.

The results obtained with the CHDE are presented in Table 2. A comparison of the performance of CHDE with respect to three techniques that are representative of the state-of-the-art in the area: the Homomorphous maps [16], Stochastic Ranking [9] and the Adaptive Segregational Constraint Handling Evolutionary Algorithm (ASCHEA) [18] are presented in Tables 3, 4 and 5, respectively.

6   Discussion of Results

As can be seen in Table 2, CHDE could reach the global optimum in the 13 test problems. The apparent improvement to the optimum solutions (or the best-known solutions) for problems g03, g05, g11 and g13 is due to the tolerance value adopted for the equality constraints. However, the statistical measures suggest that the proposed approach presents premature convergence in some cases. This seems to be originated by the high selection pressure provided by the deterministic selection. It also causes that infeasible

Table 2. Statistical results obtained by the CHDE for the 13 test functions with 30 independent runs.

Problem	Optimal	Best	Mean	Median	Worst	St. Dev.
			Statistical Results of the CHDE Algorithm			
g01	−15	−15.000	−14.792134	−15.000	−12.743044	0.401
g02	0.803619	0.803619	0.746236	0.800445	0.302179	0.081
g03	1	1.00	0.640326	0.702939	0.029601	0.239
g04	−30665.539	−30665.539	−30592.154435	−30665.539	−29986.214382	108.779
g05	5126.498	5126.496714	5218.729114	5231.557639	5502.410392	76.422
g06	−6961.814	−6961.814	−6367.575424	−6961.814	−2236.950336	770.803
g07	24.306	24.306	104.599221	24.482980	1120.541494	176.761
g08	0.095825	0.095825	0.091292	0.095825	0.027188	0.012
g09	680.63	680.6300	692.472322	680.639178	839.782911	23.575
g10	7049.25	7049.248021	8442.656946	7137.415303	15580.370333	2186.49
g11	0.75	0.749	0.761823	0.749	0.870984	0.020
g12	1	1	1	1	1	0
g13	0.053950	0.053866	0.747227	0.980831	2.259875	0.313

Table 3. Comparison of our approach (CHDE) with respect to the Homomorphous Maps (HM) NA = Not Available.

Problem	Optimal	Best Result		Mean Result		Worst Result	
		CHDE	HM	CHDE	HM	CHDE	HM
g01	−15	−15.000	−14.7886	−14.792134	−14.7082	−12.743044	−14.6154
g02	0.803619	0.803619	0.79953	0.746236	0.79671	0.302179	0.79119
g03	1	1.00	0.9997	0.640326	0.9989	0.029601	0.9978
g04	−30665.539	−30665.539	−30664.5	−30592.154435	−30655.3	−29986.214382	−30645.9
g05	5126.498	5126.496714	−	5218.729114	−	5502.410392	−
g06	−6961.814	−6961.814	−6952.1	−6367.575424	−6342.6	−2236.950336	−5473.9
g07	24.306	24.306	24.620	104.599221	24.826	1120.541494	25.069
g08	0.095825	0.095825	0.0958250	0.091292	0.0891568	0.027188	0.0291438
g09	680.63	680.6300	680.91	692.472322	681.16	839.782911	683.18
g10	7049.25	7049.248021	7147.9	8442.656946	8163.6	15580.370333	9659.3
g11	0.75	0.749	0.75	0.761823	0.75	0.870984	0.75
g12	1	1	0.999999857	1	0.999134613	1	0.991950498
g13	0.053950	0.053866	NA	0.747227	NA	2.259875	NA

Table 4. Comparison of our approach (CHDE) with respect to the Stochastic Ranking (SR)

Problem	Optimal	Best Result		Mean Result		Worst Result	
		CHDE	SR	CHDE	SR	CHDE	SR
g01	−15	−15.000	−15.000	−14.792134	−15.000	−12.743044	−15.000
g02	0.803619	0.803619	0.803515	0.746236	0.781975	0.302179	0.726288
g03	1	1.00	1.000	0.640326	1.000	0.029601	1.000
g04	−30665.539	−30665.539	−30665.539	−30592.154435	−30665.539	−29986.214382	−30665.539
g05	5126.498	5126.496714	5126.497	5218.729114	5128.881	5502.410392	5142.472
g06	−6961.814	−6961.814	−6961.814	−6367.575424	−6875.940	−2236.950336	−6350.262
g07	24.306	24.306	24.307	104.599221	24.374	1120.541494	24.642
g08	0.095825	0.095825	0.095825	0.091292	0.095825	0.027188	0.095825
g09	680.63	680.6300	680.630	692.472322	680.656	839.782911	680.763
g10	7049.25	7049.248021	7054.316	8442.656946	7559.192	15580.370333	8835.655
g11	0.75	0.749	0.750	0.761823	0.750	0.870984	0.750
g12	1	1	1	1	1	1	1
g13	0.053950	0.053866	0.053957	0.747227	0.057006	2.259875	0.216915

solutions close to the boundaries of the feasible region do not remain in the population. Therefore, our CHDE requires a diversity mechanism (i.e., some infeasible solutions must remain in the population to avoid premature convergence) that does not increase its computational cost in a significant way.

With respect to the three state-of-the-art approaches, some facts require discussion: With respect to the Homomorphous Maps [16], our approach obtained a better "best" solution in nine problems (g01, g02, g03, g05, g06, g07, g09, g10 and g12) and a similar "best" results in other three (g04, h08 and g11). Also, CHDE provided a better "mean" result in five problems (g01, g05, g06, g08 and g12) and a better "worst" result for two problems (g05 and g12). It is clear that CHDE was superior in quality of results than the Homomorphous Maps and it was competitive based on statistical measures.

Table 5. Comparison of our approach (CHDE) with respect to the Adaptive Segregational Constraint Handling Evolutionary Algorithm (ASCHEA). NA = Not Available.

Problem	Optimal	Best Result		Mean Result		Worst Result	
		CHDE	ASCHEA	CHDE	ASCHEA	CHDE	ASCHEA
g01	−15	−15.000	−15.0	−14.792134	−14.84	−12.743044	NA
g02	0.803619	0.803619	0.785	0.746236	0.59	0.302179	NA
g03	1	1.00	1.0	0.640326	0.99989	0.029601	NA
g04	−30665.539	−30665.539	30665.5	−30592.154435	30665.5	−29986.214382	NA
g05	5126.498	5126.496714	5126.5	5218.729114	5141.65	5502.410392	NA
g06	−6961.814	−6961.814	−6961.81	−6367.575424	−6961.81	−2236.950336	NA
g07	24.306	24.306	24.3323	104.599221	24.66	1120.541494	NA
g08	0.095825	0.095825	0.095825	0.091292	0.095825	0.027188	NA
g09	680.63	680.6300	680.630	692.472322	680.641	839.782911	NA
g10	7049.25	7049.248021	7061.13	8442.656946	7193.11	15580.370333	NA
g11	0.75	0.749	0.75	0.761823	0.75	0.870984	NA
g12	1	1	NA	1	NA	1	NA
g13	0.053950	0.053866	NA	0.747227	NA	2.259875	NA

With respect to the Stochastic Ranking [9], CHDE was able to find a better "best" result in three problems (g02, g07 and g10) and a similar "best" result in the remaining ten problems (g01, g03, g04, g05, g06, g08, g09, g11, g12 and g13). Besides these, our approach got a similar "mean" and "worst" result for problem g12. CHDE found either similar or best quality results than the Stochastic Ranking, which is one of the most competitive approaches for evolutionary constrained optimization. However, SR is still more robust than CHDE. This is because SR has a good mechanism to maintain diversity in the population (keep both, feasible and infeasible solutions during all the process).

With respect to the Adaptive Segregational Constraint Handling Evolutionary Algorithm (ASCHEA) [18], our approach found better "best" results in three problems (g02, g07 and g10) and a similar "best" in eight functions (g01, g03, g04, g05, g06, g08, g09 and g11). Finally, CHDE could find a better "mean" result in problem g02. Our approach showed a competitive performance based on quality and showed some robustness compared to ASCHEA. However, the analysis was incomplete because the worst results found by ASCHEA were not available.

From the previous comparison, we can see that the CHDE produced competitive results based on quality with respect to three techniques representative of the state-of-the-art in constrained optimization. CHDE can deal with highly constrained problems, problems with low (g06 and g08) and high (g01, g02, g03, g07) dimensionality, with different types of combined constraints (linear, nonlinear, equality and inequality) and with very large (g02) or very small (g05, g13) or even disjoint (g12) feasible regions. However, our approach presented some robustness problems and more work is required in that direction.

It is worth emphasizing that CHDE does not require additional parameters. In contrast, the Homomorphous Maps require an additional parameter (called v) which has to be found empirically [16]. Stochastic ranking requires the definition of a parameter called P_f, whose value has an important impact on the performance of the approach [9]. ASCHEA also requires the definition of several extra parameters, and in its latest version, it uses niching, which is a process that also has at least one additional parameter [18].

Measuring the computational cost, the number of fitness function evaluations (FFE) performed by our approach is lower than the other techniques with respect to which it was compared. Our approach performed 348,000 FFE. Stochastic ranking performed 350,000 FFE, the Homomorphous Maps performed 1,400,000 FFE, and ASCHEA performed 1,500,000 FFE.

7   Conclusions and Future Work

A novel approach based on the simplest version of the Differential Evolution algorithm, coupled with three simple criteria based on feasibility (CHDE) was proposed to solve constrained optimization problems. CHDE does not require a penalty function or any extra parameters (other than the original parameters of the DE algorithm) to bias the search towards the feasible region of a problem. Additionally, this improved approach has a low computational cost and it is easy to implement. Our algorithm was compared against three state-of-the-art techniques and it provided a competitive performance. Our future work consists on adding a diversity mechanism which does not increase its computational cost [8] in order to avoid premature convergence.

Acknowledgments. The first author acknowledges support from the Mexican Consejo Nacional de Ciencia y Tecnología (CONACyT) through a scholarship to pursue graduate studies at CINVESTAV-IPN's Electrical Engineering Department. The second author acknowledges support from (CONACyT) through projects number 32999-A and 34201-A.

References

1. Coello Coello, C.A., Van Veldhuizen, D.A., Lamont, G.B.: Evolutionary Algorithms for Solving Multi-Objective Problems. Kluwer Academic Publishers, New York (2002) ISBN 0-3064-6762-3.
2. Goldberg, D.E.: Genetic Algorithms in Search, Optimization and Machine Learning. Addison-Wesley Publishing Co., Reading, Massachusetts (1989)
3. Coello Coello, C.A.: Theoretical and Numerical Constraint Handling Techniques used with Evolutionary Algorithms: A Survey of the State of the Art. Computer Methods in Applied Mechanics and Engineering **191** (2002) 1245–1287
4. Michalewicz, Z., Schoenauer, M.: Evolutionary Algorithms for Constrained Parameter Optimization Problems. Evolutionary Computation **4** (1996) 1–32
5. Smith, A.E., Coit, D.W.: Constraint Handling Techniques—Penalty Functions. In Bäck, T., Fogel, D.B., Michalewicz, Z., eds.: Handbook of Evolutionary Computation. Oxford University Press and Institute of Physics Publishing (1997)
6. Price, K.V.: An Introduction to Differential Evolution. In Corne, D., Dorigo, M., Glover, F., eds.: New Ideas in Optimization. Mc Graw-Hill, UK (1999) 79–108
7. Mezura-Montes, E., Coello Coello, C.A.: A Simple Evolution Strategy to Solve Constrained Optimization problems. In: Proceedings of Genetic and Evolutionary Computation Conference(GECCO'2003), Heidelberg, Germany, Chicago, Illinois, USA, Springer-Verlag (2003) 641–642 Lecture Notes in Computer Science No. 2723.
8. Mezura-Montes, E., Coello Coello, C.A.: Adding a Diversity Mechanism to a Simple Evolution Strategy to Solve Constrained Optimization Problems. In: Proceedings of IEEE International Congress on Evolutionary Computation (CEC'2003), Canberra, Australia, IEEE Neural Networks Society (2003) (Accepted for Publication).
9. Runarsson, T.P., Yao, X.: Stochastic Ranking for Constrained Evolutionary Optimization. IEEE Transactions on Evolutionary Computation **4** (2000) 284–294
10. Schwefel, H.P.: Evolution and Optimal Seeking. John Wiley & Sons Inc., New York (1995)
11. Jiménez, F., Verdegay, J.L.: Evolutionary techniques for constrained optimization problems. In Zimmermann, H.J., ed.: 7th European Congress on Intelligent Techniques and Soft Computing (EUFIT'99), Aachen, Germany, Verlag Mainz (1999) ISBN 3-89653-808-X.

12. Deb, K.: An Efficient Constraint Handling Method for Genetic Algorithms. Computer Methods in Applied Mechanics and Engineering **186** (2000) 311–338

13. Coello Coello, C.A., Mezura-Montes, E.: Handling Constraints in Genetic Algorithms Using Dominance-Based Tournaments. In Parmee, I., ed.: Proceedings of the Fifth International Conference on Adaptive Computing Design and Manufacture (ACDM 2002). Volume 5., University of Exeter, Devon, UK, Springer-Verlag (2002) 273–284

14. Horn, J., Nafpliotis, N., Goldberg, D.E.: A Niched Pareto Genetic Algorithm for Multiobjective Optimization. In: Proceedings of the First IEEE Conference on Evolutionary Computation, IEEE World Congress on Computational Intelligence. Volume 1., Piscataway, New Jersey, IEEE Service Center (1994) 82–87

15. Storn, R.: System Design by Constraint Adaptation and Differential Evolution. IEEE Transactions on Evolutionary Computation **3** (1999) 22–34

16. Koziel, S., Michalewicz, Z.: Evolutionary Algorithms, Homomorphous Mappings, and Constrained Parameter Optimization. Evolutionary Computation **7** (1999) 19–44

17. Lampinen, J., Zelinka, I.: Mechanical Engineering Design Optimization by Differential Evolution. In Corne, D., Dorigo, M., Glover, F., eds.: New Ideas in Optimization. Mc Graw-Hill, UK (1999) 127–146

18. Hamida, S.B., Schoenauer, M.: ASCHEA: New Results Using Adaptive Segregational Constraint Handling. In: Proceedings of the Congress on Evolutionary Computation 2002 (CEC'2002). Volume 1., Piscataway, New Jersey, IEEE Service Center (2002) 884–889

Symbolic Regression Problems by Genetic Programming with Multi-branches

Carlos Oliver Morales and Katya Rodríguez Vázquez

DISCA, IIMAS, National Autonomous University of Mexico, Circuito Escolar Ciudad Universitaria, Mexico City, 04510, Mexico.
oliver_carlos@hotmail.com.mx, katya@uxdea4.iimas.unam.mx

Abstract. This work has the aim of exploring the area of symbolic regression problems by means of Genetic Programming. It is known that symbolic regression is a widely used method for mathematical function approximation. Previous works based on Genetic Programming have already dealt with this problem, but considering Koza's GP approach. This paper introduces a novel GP encoding based on *multi-branches*. In order to show the use of the proposed multi-branches representation, a set of testing equations has been selected. Results presented in this paper show the advantages of using this novel multi-branches version of GP.

1 Introduction

Genetic Programming (GP) is an evolutionary paradigm that has been used for solving a wide range of problems belonging to a variety of domains. Some examples of these applications are robot control, pattern recognition, symbolic regression, generation of arts (music and visual arts) [18], circuit design amongst others. Function approximation problem is based on a symbolic regression process. Symbolic regression by means of genetic programming has been already studied in previous works [7, 22]. However, this paper introduces a multi-branches encoding scheme for GP in order to deal with this sort of function approximation. The multi-branches encoding has been successfully applied for predicting climatological variables [16] and designing combinatorial circuits [19].

The aim of this work is then to approximate a set of equations by means of genetic programming with a multi-branches encoding proposed in this paper.

The structure of this work is as follows. Section 2 presents a review of different proposals for representing executable structures. A detailed description of our muti-branches genetic programming approach is given in section 3. An important fact in genetic programming encoding is the concept of introns. This is described in section 4. Problem definition is stated in section 5 and section 6 contains experiments details. Finally, section 7 gives results analysis, discussion and conclusions.

R. Monroy et al. (Eds.): MICAI 2004, LNAI 2972, pp. 717–726, 2004.
© Springer-Verlag Berlin Heidelberg 2004

2   Representation of Executable Structure

An important aspect of evolutionary algorithms performance is the individual representation. Angeline [1] mentioned that representation in Evolutionary Algorithms plays an important role in order to get a successful search.

The work by Cramer in 1985 introduced the representation of computer programs. Cramer represented individuals by means of strings of constant size. However, representations of fixed size reduce the flexibility and applicability of these implementations. In 1992, Koza introduced the Genetic Programming paradigm. This uses representations of variable size, hierarchical tree structures. In Koza's proposal these are S-expression (Koza described GP based on LISP programming language). This GP tree representation requires a set of primitives. Selecting the adequate primitives determines the efficiency of using this encoding [1].

New representation proposals followed Koza's initial work. One of these was the use of modular structures (sub-routines). In this area, Angeline and Pollack [2] introduced the GLIB. GLIB used specialized operators dedicated to modules acquisition. These are mutation operators (compression and expansion) which modified the individual structures (genotypes) but not the individual evaluation (phenotypes). The GLIB operator of compression works by substituting a selected branch by a function. This is, the set of nodes contained in selected branch composes a module which is defined as a new function. The GLIB operator of expansion is the inverse process. A selected acquired module is substituted in the individual structure by the set of node contained in selected module. Then, the expanded module is deleted from the set of function.

A similar version of GLIB approach are the ADF's (Automatically Defined Functions). The aim of ADF's is to protect branches with an important genetic value from the destruction of the genetic operators: mutation and recombination [10]. Rosca and Ballard [20] have also proposed an Adaptative Representation which defines heuristics for detecting useful branches.

In some cases, alternative representations have been proposed for solving specific problems. In symbolic regression, an alternative is to use a representation by means of different types of polynomials. An example of this sort of representations is the GMDH (Group Method of Data Handling) proposed by Ivakhnenko [6], which uses a network of transfer polynomials for pruning a layer and the outputs of a previous layer are the inputs of subsequent ones. Nikolaev and Iba [15] introduced the Accelerated Genetic Programming of Polynomials which also considers the use of transfer polynomials combined with a recursive least squares algorithm. The set of polynomials used in these approaches are discrete version of Volterra series known as polynomial of Gabor-Kolmogorov. Others problems have been also solved by using genetic programming and polynomials as it is the case of modelling chemical process [5]. Using polynomials has the advantage of estimating associated coefficients by means of diverse forms. In Koza's proposal [9], coefficients and constants values are obtaining by means of evolution process. Other GP versions compute coefficients by means of Least Squares algorithms [15] [17].

The multi-branches representation presented in this paper also states the use of polynomials. This approach searches a solution by dividing the problem into sub-problems (branches) and solving each of these sub-problems individually. Once sub-problems are solved, partial solutions of branches are integrated in order to obtain a global solution of the problem [19].

3   Multi-branches GP Representation

The multi-branches (MB) representation used in this work consists of four parts: a root node, N branches, $N+1$ coefficients and an output. The number of coefficients are $N+1$, a coefficient for each branch plus the constant term. Figure 1 shows a diagram of this multi-branches structure.

The two main genetic operators are crossover and mutation. Crossing over consists of selecting a pair of parent structures. Then, a branch is randomly selected in each parent and finally selected branches are exchanged between them. Mutation operator randomly selects an individual. A branch is then selected, deleted and substituted by a new branch randomly generated. Mutation and crossover processes are graphically shown in Figures 2 and 3, respectively.

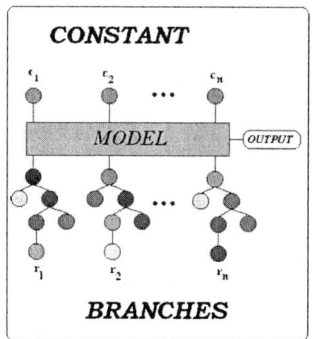

Fig. 1. Multi-Branches GP structure representation

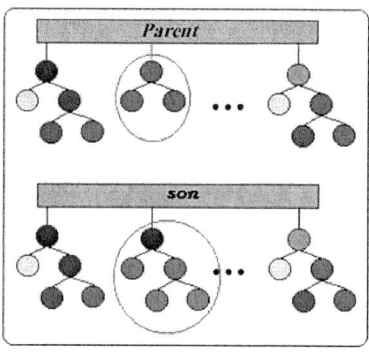

Fig. 2. Mutation operator

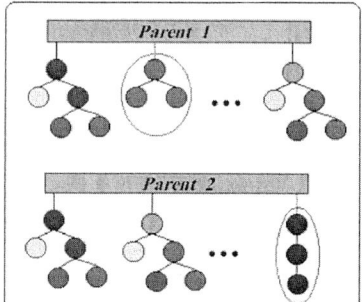

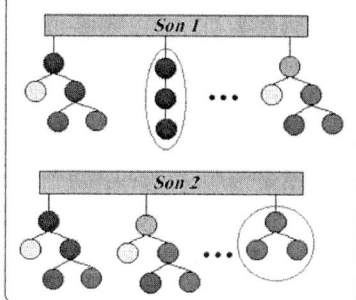

Fig. 3. Croosover operator: i) Branches selection and ii) Exchange of branches.

The GP parameters used in this version of genetic programming are similar to the ones used by Koza's GP approach, except to parameters regarding maximum number of nodes (or maximum tree depth or size). In this MB version, the individual structure (expression) size is bounded by the number of branches and the maximum depth of these branches.

4 Introns

In GP, the individuals growth in size without any improvement in performance is known as bloat [12]. Some of the identified causes that produces bloating are the fitness functions [12] and the presence of introns [4][14][23]. Introns are parts of a chromosome that do not affect the individual evaluation (phenotype).

Introns are considered as a sort of structures that protects part of the chromosome from destructive effects produced by genetic operators [13]. However, some researchers argue that introns have more negative effects than beneficial. In the literature, diverse mechanisms for destructing introns are reported: remove of redundant code (introns) by means of an edition operator [9], penalization of individual size [14][26], constraint operators [11][25] and alternatives selection schema [4].

Comparing the Koza's GP version and the GP with multi-branches [16] for symbolic regression of climatological data, it was observed that GP with multiple branches produced solutions possessing a better precision and lower complexity [17]. The improvement in complexity is due to GP with multi-branches takes advantages of the definition of introns as it will be explain later on.

5 Problem Statement

Fitting data points (curves) can be performed by means of a combination of known functions. The function approximation $g(x)$ is obtained by estimating the set of coefficients a_i, one for each of the n known functions $f(x)$ and a_0 (the independent coefficient), as given by equation 1.

$$g(x) = a_0 + a_1 f_1(x) + \cdots + a_n f_n(x) \qquad (1)$$

$$= a_0 + \sum_{i=1}^{n} a_i f_i(x)$$

Determining a priori which is the set of more adequate functions is not an easy task. The set of known functions can be larger and the value of some coefficients can be so small that the associated function is insignificant and estimating coefficients for all possible functions is computationally expensive. A better approximation method should consider only the most significant functions and coefficients and also computational costs must be low. Thus, the central point is to find such functions $p(x)$ and associated coefficients which are the most significant in order to better approximate a curve. This is as shown in equation (2).

$$Q = \{ \; g : g \; is \; a \; known \; function \; \}$$
$$P = \{ p : p \in Q, \, p \; is \; significant \; for \; approximation \; to \; g(x) \; \}$$
$$\forall p_i(x) \in P$$

$$g(x) = b_0 + b_1 p_1(x) + \cdots + b_n p_n(x) \tag{2}$$

$$= b_0 + \sum_{i=1}^{n} b_i p_i(x)$$

Using genetic programming, a given finite set of primitives (functions and terminals or argument) bounds the problem of function approximation. The set of primitives can then build a wide range of functions. The only restriction presented in GP is the maximum size of the hierarchical tree structure.

6 Experiments

A set of equations was considered in order to have a wide range of symbolic regression (function approximation) problems. These equations were based on Keijzer's work [7]. The set of functions used in all these approximations is defined in Table 1. Based on Keijzer's study, it was defined a maximum number of evaluations. From this parameter, maximum number of generations and population size can vary but without exceeding the number of evaluations. For each equation, a different domain range is specified as described in Table 2.

The set of functions for testing this multi-branches genetic programming approach is given as follows:

$$[8] \quad f(x) = 0.3 \, x \, sin(\, 2 \, \pi \, x \,) \tag{3}$$

$$[21] \quad f(x) = x^3 \, exp^{-x} \, cos(\, x \,) \, sin(\, x \,)(sin^2(\, x \,) * cos(\, x \,) - 1 \,) \tag{4}$$

$$[7] \quad f(x, y, z) = \frac{30 \, x \, z}{(\, x - 10 \,) \, y^2} \tag{5}$$

$$[22] \quad f(x) = \sum_{i}^{x} 1 / i \tag{6}$$

$$[22] \quad f(x) = arcsinh(\, x \,) \tag{7}$$

$$[22] \quad f(x) = arcsinh(\, x \,) \tag{8}$$

$$[22] \quad f(x) = arcsinh(\, x \,) \tag{9}$$

$$[24] \quad f(x, y) = x^y \tag{10}$$

$$[24] \quad f(x, y) = xy + sin((\, x - 1 \,)(\, y - 1)) \tag{11}$$

$$[24] \quad f(x, y) = x^4 - x^3 + y^2 / 2 - y \tag{12}$$

$$[24] \quad f(x, y) = 6 \sin(x) \cos(x) \tag{13}$$

$$[24] \quad f(x, y) = 8 / (2 + x^2 + y^2) \tag{14}$$

$$[24] \quad f(x, y) = x^3 / 5 + y^3 / 2 - y - x \tag{15}$$

Table 1. Parameter settings for genetic programming with multi-branches.

Parameters	Values
Function set	{ x + y, x * y, 1/x, -x, sqrt(x)
Number of evaluations	10000
Maximun Genome size	400
Population Size	50
% of Crossover	95
% of Mutation	15
Number of branches	6

Table 2. Problem settings.

Problem	Equation	Range train	Range test	note
1	3	x=[-1:0.1:1]	[-1:0.001:1]	25000 evals
2	3	x=[-2:0.1:2]	[-2:0.001:2]	25000 evals
3	3	x=[-3:0.1:3]	[-3:0.001:3]	
4	4	x=[0:0.05:10]	[0.5:0.05:10.5]	{exp, log, sin, cos} 60000 evals
5	5	x,z = rnd(-1,1)	idem	train 1000 cases
		y = rand(1,2)	idem	test 10000 cases
6	6	x=[1:1:50]	[1:1:120]	extrapolation
7	7	x=[1:1:100]	[1:0.1:100]	
8	8	x=[0:1:100]	[0:0.1:100]	
9	9	x=[0:1:100]	[0:0.1:100]	
10	10	x,y = rnd(0,1)	x,y=mesh([0:0.01:1])	train 100 cases
11	11	x,y = rnd(-3,3)	x,y=mesh([-3:0.01:3])	train 20 cases
12	12	x,y = rnd(-3,3)	x,y=mesh([-3:0.01:3])	train 20 cases
13	13	x,y = rnd(-3,3)	x,y=mesh([-3:0.01:3])	train 20 cases
14	14	x,y = rnd(-3,3)	x,y=mesh([-3:0.01:3])	train 20 cases
15	15	x,y = rnd(-3,3)	x,y=mesh([-3:0.01:3])	train 20 cases

7 Result Analysis, Discussion, and Conclusions

7.1 Results

In Table 3, the normalized mean squared error (*NRMS*) of results from previous work [7] the same set of functions and the multi-branches genetic programming is shown. MB genetic programming is compared to Keijzer's approach, GP with scaling and interval definition. Note that same set of functions are used in both cases.

The *NRMS* value is computed by means of equation (16), where N is the number of fitness cases (data points), *MSE* is the mean squared error and σ_t is the standard deviation of the target values. The best individual for each problem is then evaluated using testing data. Testing performance results are presented in Table 4. Finally, Table 5 shows the average complexity and the best solution complexity of each run for the genetic programming with multi-branches approach. Complexity is here measured as the number of nodes contained in evolved solutions. This includes both function nodes and terminal nodes. The amount of destructive overfitting was defined by Keijzer [7].

$$NRMS = 100 * \frac{\sqrt{\frac{N}{(N-1)} * MSE}}{\sigma_T} \qquad (16)$$

Table 3. Main training information of the best of run individuals produced by each version

Problem	1	2	3	4	5	6	7	8	9	10	11	12	13	14	15
no interval	20	54	76	22	2	2	2	2	2	11	12	4	30	15	10
no scaling	50	78	88	46	22	49	50	56	93	54	19	4	63	91	23
interval + scaling	8	34	62	15	1	1	1	1	1	7	11	1	25	1	7
multi branches	2	24	85	19	1	0	0	1	0	3	8	7	19	13	1

Table 4. Amount of destructive overfitting for each of the problems

Problem	1	2	3	4	5	6	7	8	9	10	11	12	13	14	15
no interval	6	11	25						1		49	31	30	36	23	40
no scaling			2										1	15		1
interval + scaling													1	3		1
Multi branches										2	194			0	

Table 5. Mean and the best solution complexity for each problem

Problem	1	2	3	4	5	6	7	8	9	10	11	12	13	14	15
Mean	62	77	61	39	40	39	38	54	39	44	39	37	43	40	30
Best solution	74	83	124	39	58	42	48	83	40	58	53	26	47	48	36

8   Discussion

Results generated by means of genetic programming with multi-branches showed to be better, in terms of performance (NRMS), than the ones obtained by means of GP without scaling or no-interval presented by Keijzer [7]. In the case of GP+scaling+interval, results showed to be similar but multi-branches GP gave slightly better performance in many cases. However, there were three cases (equations (3), (4) and (14)) where the combined use of scaling + interval exhibited a better performance than multi-branches GP. In the case of equation (3) and using scaling+interval, error values were also high. Regarding overfitting values, observations are quite similar in both methods, as mentioned previously. It is important to mention that computational cost required to obtain these results, was less in the case of the present paper. The number of evaluations considered for the multi-branches genetic programming were 10000, except for cases indicated in Table 2 where the number of evaluations coincided with previous work (25000 evaluations). In terms of maximum genome size, multi-branches GP used a maximum of 400 nodes, whereas 1024 were used for others approaches. It is observed in Table 5 that the number of nodes of best solutions were in the range of [26, 124] nodes.

Introns can be classified into four groups: hierarchical, horizontal, asymptotical and incremental fitness [4]. Genetic programming with multi-branches presents a kind of introns which do not fall into any of these four groups. This new type of introns shows a beneficial effect during evolution. An intron can occur when two or more branches produce the same partial output. Coefficients values of branches that produce same partial output are zero, except one whose value is computed by means of a Least Squares algorithm. If these similar branches belongs to a higher fitness individuals, then they are kept; otherwise they will be destroyed during evolution process. Other type of introns presented in multi-branches representation are the branches whose coefficient is zero. These branches do not contribute in the final solution and complexity can be reduced.

9   Conclusions

The multi-branches representation for genetic programming introduced in this paper has proved to be powerful. It has been tested on function approximation problems and results showed to be promising. It was also observed that computational cost tends to be reduced by using this representation. It is also relevant to note that introns in multi-branches representation are easily detected and show beneficial effects.

Further studies will focused on both the flexibility of this representation in diverse domains and the effects and control of introns.

Acknowledgements. Authors would like to thank the financial support of Consejo Nacional de Ciencia y Tecnología (CONACyT), México, under the project 40602-Y, PAPPIT-UNAM under the project ES100201.

References

1. Angeline P.J. (1996). Parse trees. *Evolutionary Computation 1, basic algorithms and operators.* Edited by T. Back, D.B. Fogel and T. Michalewickz.
2. Angeline P.J. and Pollack J.B. (1994). Co – evolving high level representation *Artificial life III* ed. C.G. Langton. Addison Wesley. Pp 55 – 71.
3. Cramer N.L. (1985) A representation for the adaptative generation of simple sequencial programs. in *Proc. 1ˢᵗ. Int. Conference on Genetic Algorithms. Pittsburg, PA, July 1985.* ed. J.J. Grefenstette. Hillsdale, NJ: pp 183 – 187.
4. Harries K. and P. W. H. Smith (1998). Code Growth, Explicitly Defined Introns and Alternative Selection Schemes. *Evolutionary Computation* Vol. 6, No 4. pp 346-364.
5. Hinchiffe, M.; Hiden, H.; McKay, B.; Willis, M.; Tham, M. and Barton, G.(1996). Modelling Chemical Process System using multi-gene Programming Algorithm. In Koza, J.R., editor, *Late Breaking Papers at the Genetic Programming* 1996 Conference, pp 56-65, Stanford University, C.A. Stanford Bookstore, Stanford, C.A.
6. Ivakhnenko A. G., (1971) Polynomial theory of complex systems, *IEEE Transactions on Systems, Man, and Cybernetics*, pp. 364--378.
7. Keijzer M. (2003). Improving Symbolic Regression with Interval Arithmetic and Linear Scaling. in *Genetic Programming, 6ᵗʰ European Conference, EuroGP 2003. Essex, UK April 2003 proceedings.* Eds. Ryan C., Soule T., Keijzer M., Tsang E., Poli R. and Costa E
8. Keijzer M. and V. Babovic.(2002). Genetic Programming, Ensemble Methods and the Bias/Variance Tradeoff – introductory Investigations. in *Genetic Programming, European Conference, EuroGP 2003. (Edinburgh).* Poli R., Banzhaf W., Langdom W.B., Miller J.F., Nordin P. and Fogarty T.C. eds. LNCS vol. 1802, Springer Verlag. 15-16 April 2000, pp. 76 – 90.
9. Koza, J.R. (1992). *Genetic Programming: on the Programming of Computers by Means of Natural Selection.* Cambridge Massachuset. MIT press.
10. Koza, J.R. (1994*). Genetic Programming II: Automatic Discovery of Reusable Programs.* Cambridge Massachuset. MIT press.
11. Langdon W. B. (1999). Size Fair and Homologous Tree Genetic Programming Crossovers. in *Proceedings of the Genetic and Evolutionary Computation Conference*, vol. 2. Morgan Kaufmannm eds.Wolfgang Banzhaf and Jason Daida and Agoston E. Eiben and Max H. Garzon and Vasant Honavar and Mark Jakiela and Robert E. Smith, pp 1092-1097.
12. Langdon W.B. and R. Poli (1997) Fitness Causes Bloat. *Second On-line World Conference on Soft Computing in Engineering Design and Manufacturing.* Springer-Verlag London. eds. P. K. Chawdhry and R. Roy and R. K. Pan. pp 13-22.
13. Nordin P., Francone F., and Banzhaf W.(1996). Explicitly defined introns and destructive crossover *in genetic programming.* In Peter J. Angeline and K. E. Kinnear, Jr., editors, Advances in Genetic Programming 2, chapter 6, pages 111{134. MITPress, Cambridge, MA, USA.
14. Nordin, J.P. and Banzhaf, W. (1995) Complexity Compression and Evolution. In Proceedings of Sixth International Conference of Genetic Algorithms, Pittsburgh, 1995. L. Eshelman (ed.). Morgan Kaufmann, San Mateo, CA.
15. Nikolaev I.N and H.Iba. (2001). Accelerated Genetic Programming of Polynomials. in Genetic Programming and Evolvable Machines. Vol. 2. number 3, sept. 2001. pp 231 – 258.
16. Oliver M.C. (2002). Programación Genética Multi - Ramas en el Modelado y Predicción de Datos Climatológicos. Tesis de Maestría. Universidad Autonoma de México, D.F., México (spanish)
17. Oliver M.C. y K.V. Rodríguez (2002). Estructuta de Arbol vs Estructura Polinomial con Programación Genética en el Modelado de Variables Climatológicas. en el 1er Congreso Español de Algoritmos Geneticos y Bioinspirados. Del 6 al 8 de Febrero de 2002, Merida, España.

18. Poli R. (1996). Genetic programming for image analysis. In John R. Koza, David E. Goldberg, David B. Fogel, and Rick L. Riolo, editors, Proc. Genetic Programming 1996, pages 363--368. MIT Press, 1996.
19. Rodríguez V.K. and Oliver M.C. (2003). Divide and Conquer: Genetic Programming Based on Multiple Branches Encoding. in Genetic Programming, 6th European Conference, EuroGP 2003. Essex, UK April 2003 proceedings. Eds. Ryan C., Soule T., Keijzer M., Tsang E., Poli R. and Costa E.
20. Rosca J.P. and Ballard D.H. (1996). Discovery of subroutines in genetic programming. Advances in Genetic Programming. Vol. 2, ed. P.J. Angeline and K. Kinnear. Cambridge Massachuset. MIT press. pp 177 – 202.
21. Salustowicks, R.P., J. Schmidhuber. (1997). Probabilistc Incremental Program Evolution. in Evolutionary Computation vol. 5, number 2. pp. 123 – 141.
22. Streeter M. and L.A. Becker. (2001). Automated Discovery of Numerical Aproximation Formulae via Genetic Programming. in Proceedings of the Genetic and Evolutionary Conference (GECCO 2001), San Francisco CA. Spector L., Goodman E.D., Wu A., Langdom W.B.,Voigth H.M., Gen M., Sen S., Dorigo M., Pezeshk S., Garzon M.H. and Burke E. eds., Morgam Kaufmann, 7 – 11 July 2001, pp 147 – 154.
23. Soule T, J. A. Foster, and J. Dickinson (1996). Code growth in genetic programming. In John R. Koza, David E. Goldberg, David B. Fogel, and Rick L. Riolo, editors, Genetic Programming 1996: Proceedings of the First Annual Conference, pages 215--223, Stanford University, CA, USA, 28--31July 1996. MIT Press.
24. Topchy A. and W.F. Punch. (2001). Faster Genetic Based on Local Gradient Search of Numeric Leaf Values. in Proceedings of the Genetic and Evolutionary Conference (GECCO 2001), San Francisco CA. Spector L., Goodman E.D., Wu A., Langdom W.B.,Voigth H.M., Gen M., Sen S., Dorigo M., Pezeshk S., Garzon M.H. and Burke E. eds., Morgam Kaufmann, 7 – 11 July 2001, pp 155 – 162.
25. Sims K. (1993) Interactive Evolution of Equations for Procedural Models. The Visual Computer, v9, pp. 466-476.
26. Zhang, B.-T. and Muhlenbein, H., Balancing Accuracy and Parsimony in Genetic Programming, in Evolutionary Computation, vol.3, no.1, pp.17-38.

A Preprocessing That Combines Heuristic and Surrogate Constraint Analysis to Fix Variables in TSP

M. Osorio and D. Pinto

School of Computer Science,
Universidad Autónoma de Puebla,
72560, Puebla, México
{aosorio,dpinto}@cs.buap.mx

Abstract. A preprocessing procedure that uses a local guided search defined in terms of a neighborhood structure to get a feasible solution (UB) and the Osorio and Glover [18], [20] exploiting of surrogate constraints and constraint pairing is applied to the traveling salesman problem. The surrogate constraint is obtained by weighting the original problem constraints by their associated dual values in the linear relaxation of the problem. The objective function is made a constraint less or equal than a feasible solution (UB). The surrogate constraint is paired with this constraint to obtain a combined equation where negative variables are replaced by complemented variables and the resulting constraint is used to fix variables to zero or one before solving the problem.

Keywords: TSP problem, Surrogate Constraint Analysis, Preprocessing.

1 Introduction

The TSP has received great attention from the operations research and computer science communities because is very easy to describe but very hard to solve [2]. The problem can be formulated saying that the traveling salesman must visit every city in his territory exactly once and then return to the starting point. Given the cost of travel between all cities, he should plan his itinerary for a minimum total cost of the entire tour.

Space solution for TSP is the n-cities permutation, $n!$. Any simple permutation is a different solution. The optimum is the permutation that correspond to a travel with the minimum cost. The evaluation function is very simple, because we only need to add the cost profit associated with each segment in the itinerary, to obtain the total cost for that itinerary.

The TSP is a relatively old problem. It was already documented in 1759, with a different name, by Euler. The term 'traveling salesman' was first used in 1932 in a German book written by a veteran traveling salesman. The TSP, in the way we know it now, was introduced by the RAND Corporation in 1948. The

R. Monroy et al. (Eds.): MICAI 2004, LNAI 2972, pp. 727–734, 2004.
© Springer-Verlag Berlin Heidelberg 2004

Corporation's reputation helped to make the TSP a well known and popular problem. The TSP also became popular at that time due to the apparition of linear programming and the attempts to solve combinatorial problems.

In 1979, it was proved that the TSP is NP-hard, a special kind of NP-complete problems (see Garey et al, [1]). All NP problems can be reduced polynomialy to them. It means that if one can find a solution in polynomial time to one of them, with a deterministic procedure, it may find it for all NP and then, P=NP. Nobody has been able to find efficient algorithms for NP-complete problems until now, and nobody has demonstrated that such algorithms do not exist.

The TSP can be symmetric or asymmetric. In the symmetric case, departure and return costs are the same and can be represented with an undirected graph. For the asymmetric case, the more common one, the departure and return costs are different and can only be represented by a directed graph. Because the symmetric problem is usually harder than the asymmetric one, this research was directed to the symmetric case.

The TSP has become a classic problem because it serves to represent a great number of applications in real life, as the coloring sequence in textile industry, the design of insulating material and optic filters, the impression of electronic circuits, the planning of trajectories in robotics and many other examples that can be represented using sequences (see Salkin [21]). Besides, it may represent a big number of combinatorial problems that cannot be solved in polynomial time and are NP hard.

The exponential nature of the time needed to solve this problem in an exact way has originated, during the last decades, the development of heuristic algorithms to approximate its optimal solution (see Gass [2]).

To relate the experience obtained in this research, we structured the present paper in the following way. In section 2, we present the Integer Programming formulation for TSP. In section 3, we describe the Dual Surrogate Constraint, and the Paired Constraint in section 4. In Section 5 we present an example solved with our approach. Section 6, shows experimental results and Section 7, the Conclusion.

2   Integer Programming Formulation

As we mentioned before, a traveling salesman must visit n cities, each exactly once. The distance between every pair of cities ij, denoted by $d_{ij}, (i \neq j)$, is known and may depend on the direction traveled (i.e., d_{ij} does not necessarily equal d_{ij}). The problem is to find a tour which commences and terminates at the salesman"s home city and minimizes the total distance traveled.

Suppose we label the home city as city 0 and as city $n + 1$. (Then we may think of the salesman"s initial location as city 0 and the desired final location as city $n + 1$). Also, introduce the zero-one variables $x_{ij}, (i = 0, 1, \ldots, n, j = 1, \ldots, n + 1, i \neq j)$, where $x_{ij} = 1$ if the salesman travels from city i to j, and $x_{ij} = 0$ otherwise. To guarantee that each city (except city 0) is entered exactly once, we have $\sum_{i=0}^{n} x_{ij} = 1, (j = 1, \ldots, n + 1, i \neq j)$.

Similarly, to ensure that each city (except city $n + 1$) is left exactly once, we have $\sum_{j=1}^{n+1} x_{ij} = 1, (i = 0, \ldots, n, i \neq j)$. These constraints, however, do not eliminate the possibility of subtours or "loops". One way of eliminating the subtour possibility is to add the constraints $\alpha_i - \alpha_j + (n + 1)x_{ij} \leq n, (i = 0, \ldots, n, j = 1, \ldots, n + 1, i \neq j)$.

Where α_i is a real number associated with city i. To complete the model we should minimize the total distance between the cities. An integer programming formulation of the traveling salesman problem is to find variables x_{ij} and arbitrary real numbers α_i which:

$$
\begin{array}{lll}
\text{Minimize} & \sum_{i=0}^{n} \sum_{j=1}^{n+1} d_{ij} x_{ij} & \\
\text{Subject to} & \sum_{i=0}^{n} x_{ij} = 1 & (j = 1, \ldots, n + 1, i \neq j) \\
& \sum_{j=1}^{n+1} x_{ij} = 1 & (i = 0, \ldots, n, i \neq j) \\
& \alpha_i - \alpha_j + (n + 1)x_{ij} \leq n & (i = 0, \ldots, n, j = 1, \ldots, n + 1, i \neq j) \\
& \alpha_i \geq 0 & (i = 0, \ldots, n + 1) \\
& x_{ij} \in \{0, 1\} & (i = 0, \ldots, n, j = 1, \ldots, n + 1, i \neq j)
\end{array}
$$

Where $x_{0,n+1} = 0$ (since $x_{ij} = 0$ for $i = j$). This formulation originally appeared in Tucker [22], and avoids subtours successfully, but enlarge considerable the model that now has $(n + 1)^2 + 2$ variables with $(n + 1)^2 - n$ binaries and $(n + 2) + (n + 1)^2$ constraints.

3 Dual Surrogate

As defined by Glover [4], a surrogate constraint is an inequality implied by the constraints of an integer program and designed to capture useful information that cannot be extracted from the parent constraints individually, but which is nevertheless a consequence of their conjunction. The integer program can be written as:

$$
\begin{array}{ll}
\text{Minimize} & \mathbf{cx} \\
\text{Subject to} & \mathbf{Ax} \leq \mathbf{b}, 0 \leq \mathbf{x} \leq \mathbf{e} \\
\text{and} & \mathbf{x} \text{ integer}
\end{array}
$$

Since $\mathbf{Ax} \leq \mathbf{b}$ implies $\mathbf{b} - \mathbf{Ax} \geq \mathbf{0}$, we have for a nonnegative weighting vector $\mathbf{u}$ that $\mathbf{u}(\mathbf{b} - \mathbf{Ax}) \geq 0$ is a surrogate constraint. A value of $\mathbf{u}$ is selected which satisfies a most useful or a "strongest" surrogate constraint definition as given in [4], [5]. It has been shown by Glover [5] that $\mathbf{u}$ comprises the optimal values of the variables of the dual linear program of the corresponding relaxed LP and that the weighting vector in a strongest constraint consists of the optimal dual variables of the associated linear program.

Optimality conditions for surrogate duality are the requirements that the surrogate multiplier vector $\mathbf{u}$ is nonnegative, $\mathbf{x}$ is optimal for the surrogate problem, and $\mathbf{x}$ is feasible for the primal problem. "Strong" optimality conditions add the requirement of complementary slackness. A complete derivation of this theory can be seen in Glover [5]. The methodology proposed here relies on these fundamental results.

4   Paired Constraint

The main ideas about constraint pairing in integer programming were exposed by Hammer et al. [9]. Based on the objective of getting bounds for most variables, the strategy is to pair constraints in the original problem to produce bounds for some variables.

Based on the results exposed about surrogate constraints, the dual surrogate constraint provides the most useful relaxation of the constraint set, and can be paired with the objective function. If we name $K = (n+1)^2 + (n+2)$, the total number of constraints and $L = (n+1)^2 + 2$, the total number of variables, the resulting surrogate is:

$$\sum_{k=1}^{K} u_k(a_{kl}z_k) \le \sum_{k=1}^{K} u_k b_k, l = 1, ..., L \tag{1}$$

Where u_k are the dual values for every surrogate, a_{kl}, the coefficient in row k and column l, z_k the kth variable (it may be x_{ij} or α_i), b_k the kth right hand side. Now, we define

$$s_l = \sum_{k=1}^{K} u_k(a_{kl}z_k), l = 1, ..., L \tag{2}$$

Besides, we made the objective function less or equal than a known feasible integer solution (UB). This integer solution was obtained using a guided local search defined in terms of neighborhood structure, where tour B is a neighbor of tour A and it can be obtained from A by specific type of perturbation or move. It takes infinitesimal CPU times to get a feasible tour with this procedure [14].

The paired constraint between the surrogate and the objective function will be,

$$\sum_{l=1}^{L} (c_l - s_l)z_l \le UB - \sum_{k=1}^{K} u_k b_k \tag{3}$$

To be able to use constraint 3 to fix variables in both bounds, all coefficients must be positive or zero. We substitute $y_l = 1 - z_l$ in the negative coefficients $(c_l - s_l)$ to get positive ones $(c_l - s_l)'$ and add the equivalent value in the right hand side. The right hand side of the surrogate is the LP optimal solution (LB), and the right hand side of this paired constraint becomes the difference between the best known solution, the upper bound (UB), and the LP solution, the lower bound (LB). The resultant paired constraint used to fix variables to zero or one, is

$$\sum_{l=1,(c_l-s_l\ge 0)}^{L} (c_l - s_l)z_l + \sum_{l=1,(c_l-s_l<0)}^{L} (c_l - s_l)'y_l \le UB - LB \tag{4}$$

If coefficients $(c_l - s_l)$ of z_l are greater to the difference (UB-LB), those variables must be zero in the integer solution; if the coefficients $(c_l - s_l)'$ of y_l are greater to the same difference, those variables must be one in the integer solution because its complement, y_l must be zero. Variables whose coefficients are smaller than the difference remain in the problem. Because we depend on the gap UB-LB and LB can not be changed because it is the LP continuous relaxed solution of the problem, a better UB given by the best integer solution known, can increase the number of integer variables fixed.

5   Example

We illustrate the procedure in the following example. Table 1 shows the distances for a traveling salesman problem with 3 cities.

Table 1. Distances for the 3-cities example

From/To	1	2	3
1	∞	26	82
2	134	∞	117
3	38	13	∞

The Integer Programming formulation for this example is:

Minimize $26x_{12} + 82x_{13} + 134x_{21} + 117x_{23} + 38x_{31} + 13x_{32}$

Subject to $x_{01} + x_{02} + x_{03} + x_{04} = 1$

$$x_{12} + x_{13} + x_{14} = 1$$
$$x_{21} + x_{23} + x_{24} = 1$$
$$x_{31} + x_{32} + x_{34} = 1$$
$$x_{01} + x_{21} + x_{31} = 1$$
$$x_{02} + x_{12} + x_{32} = 1$$
$$x_{03} + x_{12} + x_{23} = 1$$
$$x_{04} + x_{14} + x_{24} + x_{34} = 1$$
$$4x_{01} + \alpha_0 - \alpha_1 \leq 3$$
$$4x_{02} + \alpha_0 - \alpha_2 \leq 3$$
$$4x_{03} + \alpha_0 - \alpha_3 \leq 3$$
$$4x_{04} + \alpha_0 - \alpha_4 \leq 3$$
$$4x_{12} + \alpha_1 - \alpha_2 \leq 3$$
$$4x_{13} + \alpha_1 - \alpha_3 \leq 3$$
$$4x_{14} + \alpha_1 - \alpha_4 \leq 3$$
$$4x_{21} + \alpha_2 - \alpha_1 \leq 3$$
$$4x_{23} + \alpha_2 - \alpha_3 \leq 3$$
$$4x_{24} + \alpha_2 - \alpha_4 \leq 3$$
$$4x_{31} + \alpha_3 - \alpha_1 \leq 3$$
$$4x_{32} + \alpha_3 - \alpha_2 \leq 3$$
$$4x_{34} + \alpha_3 - \alpha_4 \leq 3$$
$$\alpha_i \geq 0, (i = 0, ..., 4)$$
$$x_{ij} \in \{0,1\}, (i = 0, ..., 3, j = 1, ...4, i \neq j)$$

The relaxed LP problem substitutes $x_{ij} \in \{0,1\}$ by $0 \leq x_{ij} \leq 1$. The LP optimal solution is 64 and the dual values for the constraints (not including the bounds) are:

$$u_i = \{-51, 0, 0, -13, 51, 26, 51, 0, 0, 0, 0, 0, 0, 0, 0, 0, 0, 0, 0, 0, 0\}$$

The surrogate constraint, the paired constraint and the variables fixed can be seen in Table 2.

Table 2. Surrogate and Paired Constraints

	x_{01}	x_{02}	x_{03}	x_{04}	x_{12}	x_{13}	x_{14}	x_{21}	x_{23}	x_{24}	x_{31}	x_{32}	x_{34}		RHS	
c_l	0	0	0	0	26	82	0	134	117	0	38	13	0	$\leq$	80	UB
s_l	0	-25	0	51	26	51	0	51	51	0	38	13	-13	$\leq$	64	LB
$c_l - s_l$	0	25	0	51	0	31	0	83	66	0	0	0	13	$\leq$	16	UB-LB
x_{ij}		0		0		0		0	0						fixed	

6   Experimental Results

We tested our procedure with 30 symmetric instances generated with a random exponential distribution that produces specially hard instances [19]. The average values obtained for every set of five instances with the same number of cities but generated with different seeds, are reported in Table 3. The problems were solved in a Pentium III with 1066 MHz and 248 MB in RAM. To obtain the LP solution and to solve the problem to optimality, we utilized ILOG CPLEX 8.0. The feasible solution used as UB was obtained with a guided local search defined in terms of neighborhood structure [16].

Table 3. Results for Hard Instances

Number of Cities	Best Known	Fixed Variables	%Fixed Variables	%Rel.Dif between Soln's	CPU Secs.	Optimal Solution
10	1696	57.8	51.88	7.17	0.758	1582
20	2321	174.4	37.67	20.62	7.525	1924
30	3095	205.8	20.72	58.78	97.17	1949

6.1   Hard Problem Generation for TSP

We developed a generator that produces challenging TSP problems. Following the ideas presented in Osorio and Glover [19], our approach uses independently exponential distributions over a wide range to generate the distances between the cities. This kind of instances takes at least 10 times the number of CPU seconds and 100 times the number of nodes in the searching tree, required for CPLEX to get optimality than the instances generated with a random uniformly distribution. The problem generator used to create the random instances of TSP is designed as follows. The distances between the cities, d_{ij}, are integer numbers drawn from the exponential distribution $d_{ij} = 1.0 - -1000ln(U(0,1))$.

7   Conclusions

Our procedure is a very easy way to fix binary variables to their bounds in TSP instances. It can be seen as an effective preprocessing that reduces the binary number of variables to be fixed in a searching tree. The procedure is simple and utilizes a local guided search defined in terms of neighborhood structure to get a feasible tour and surrogate analysis with results from the solution of the LP relaxed problem. The results obtained shows that a percentage of variables can be fixed in a short amount of time for many different instances.

References

1. Garey, M. and D. Johnson, *Computers and Intractability*, Computers and Intractability, W.H. Freeman, San Francisco (1979).
2. Gass, S. (ed.), *Encyclopedia of Operations Research and Management Sciences*, Kluwer Academic Publishers, New York (1997).
3. Glover, F., *Flows in Arborescences. Management Science*, 17 (1971) 568-586.
4. Glover, F., *Surrogate Constraints*, Operations Research 16 (1968) 741-749.
5. Glover, F., *Surrogate Constraint Duality in Mathematical Programming*, Operations Research 23 (1975) 434-451.
6. Glover, F., Sherali, H., Lee, Y., *Generating Cuts from Surrogate Constraint Analysis for Zero-One and Multiple Choice Programming*, Computational Optimization and Applications 8 (1997) 151-172.
7. Greenberg, H. and W. Pierskalla, W., *Surrogate Mathematical Programs*, Operations Research 18 (1970) 924-939.
8. Granot, F., Hammer, P. L., *On the use of boolean functions in 0-1 linear programming*, Methods of Operations Research (1971) 154-184.
9. Hammer, P., Padberg, M. and Peled, U.,*Constraint Pairing in Integer Programming*, INFOR 13 (1975) 68-81.
10. Hooker, J.N., *Logic-based methods for optimization*, In: Borning, A. (ed.): Principles and Practice of Constraint Programming. Lecture Notes in Computer Science Vol. 874 Springer-Verlag, Berlin Heidelberg New York (1994) 336-349.
11. Hooker, J.N., *A Framework for combining solution methods*, Working Paper, Carnegie Mellon University (2003).
12. Hooker, J. N., Osorio, M. A., *Mixed Logical/Linear Programming*, Discrete Applied Mathematics 96-97 (1999) 395-442.
13. Jeroslow, R. E., and J. K. Lowe, *Modeling with integer variables*, Mathematical Programming Studies 22 (1984) 167-184.
14. Johnson, D.S., *Local Optimization and the Traveling Salesman Problem*, in Proceedings of the 17th International Colloquium on Automata, Languages and Programming, pp. 446-461, Springer, Berlin, 1990.

15. Johnson, D. S., McGeoch, L.A., *The Traveling Salesman Problem: A Case Study in Local Optimization*, In: E. H. L. Aarts, E.H.L, Lenstra, J.K. (eds.): Local Search in Combinatorial Optimization. John Wiley and Sons, Ltd., (1997) 215-310.
16. Johnson, D.S., Gutin, G., McGeoch, L.A., Yeo, A., Zhang,W., Zverovich, A., *Experimental Analysis of Heuristics for the ATSP*, In: G. Gutin, G. and A. Punnen, A. (eds.): The Traveling Salesman Problem and its Variations. Kluwer Academic Publishers, Dordrecht (2002) 445-487 .
17. Karwan, M. H., Rardin, R. L., *Some relationships between Lagrangean and surrogate duality in integer programming*, Mathematical Programming 17 (1979) 230-334.
18. Osorio, M.A., Glover, F., Hammer, P., *Cutting and Surrogate Constraint Analysis for Improved Multidimensional Knapsack Solutions*, Annals of Operations Research 117(2002), 71-93.
19. Osorio, M.A., Glover, F., *Hard Problem Generation for MKP*, Proceedings of the XI CLAIO. Concepción, Chile (2002).
20. Osorio, M.A., Glover, F., *Exploiting Surrogate Constraint Analysis for Fixing Variables in both bounds for Multidimensional Knapsack Problems*, In: Chávez, E., Favela, J., Mejía, M., Oliart, A. (eds.): Proceedings of the Fourth Mexican International Conference on Computer Science. IEEE Computer Society. New Jersey (2003) 263-267.
21. Salkin, M., *Integer Programming*, Adisson-Wesley Publishing Company. New York (1975).
22. Tucker, A., *On Directed Graphs and Integer Programs*, IBM Mathematical Research Projecft Technical Report, Princeton University (1960).

An Evolutionary Algorithm for Automatic Spatial Partitioning in Reconfigurable Environments

P. Pratibha, B.S.N. Rao, Muthukaruppan, S. Suresh, and V. Kamakoti

Digital Circuits and VLSI Laboratory,
Department of Computer Science and Engineering,
Indian Institute of Technology, Madras
Chennai - 600036, India
kama@iitm.ernet.in

Abstract. This paper introduces a CAD tool, ASPIRE (Automatic Spatial Partitioning In Reconfigurable Environments), for the spatial partitioning problem for Multi-FPGA architectures. The tool takes as input a HDL (Hardware Description Language) model of the application along with user specified constraints and automatically generates a task graph G; partitions the G based on the user specified constraints and maps the blocks of the partitions onto the different FPGAs (Field Programmable Gate Arrays) in the given Multi-FPGA architecture, all in a single-shot. ASPIRE uses an evolutionary approach for the partitioning step. ASPIRE handles the major part of the partitioning at the behavioral HDL level making it scalable with larger complex designs. ASPIRE was successfully employed to spatially partition a reasonably big cryptographic application that involved a 1024-bit modular exponentiation and to map the same onto a network of nine ACEX1K based Altera EP1K30QC208-1 FPGAs.

1 Introduction

Functional specifications of semiconductor products change frequently in compliance with market requirements and evolving standards. This necessitates a hardware environment that can be programmed dynamically. Reconfigurable systems provide a viable solution to this problem. But, such reconfigurable systems demand expensive and tedious initialization phases that in turn entail concepts like temporal [1] and spatial partitioning [3]. A given application that is too large to fit into the reconfigurable system, all at once, is passed through the temporal partitioning phase, which ensures a break up of the application into temporal segments that maximize on resource utilization and minimize on execution time. Each of the temporal segments is further spatially partitioned, in order to establish a mapping of the tasks and the memory segments within a specific temporal segment onto the available FPGAs, in a manner that enhances the efficiency of the implemented logic. An evolutionary approach to solve the spatial partitioning problem is presented in [3]. The concepts presented in [2],

R. Monroy et al. (Eds.): MICAI 2004, LNAI 2972, pp. 735–745, 2004.

though not directly related to the theme of this paper, provide significant insight on the utilization of primitive genetic algorithms to solve the problem of hardware software partitioning and hardware design space exploration.

1.1 Previous Work

The genetic search procedure was developed by John Holland [4] in 1975 and since then it has been successfully employed to provide solutions for the various combinatorial problems in VLSI design automation [5,6]. The genetic algorithms help the solutions to get out of local optima, particularly where multiple constraints are involved like the spatial partitioning problem solved in this paper. One of the latest papers published in the area of spatial partitioning is by Jose Ignacio Hidalgo [7]. The GA algorithm employed here [7] does not capture all the constraints for e.g. memory constraints, speed of execution, routing constraints etc. The crossover operators are not so effective. The CPU time required for getting desirable results is large. The partitioning done in [7] is at net-list (cell) level making it less scalable with increasing design size. The algorithm developed by Iyad Quaiss [3] considers the partitioning at behavioral level.

1.2 Contributions of This Paper

ASPIRE takes as input a HDL model of the application along with user specified constraints and automatically generates a task graph G; partitions the G based on the user specified constraints and maps the blocks of the partitions onto the different FPGAs in the given Multi-FPGA architecture, all in a single-shot. The crux of our contribution is a genetic approach for the spatial partitioning problem for FPGAs which is employed by ASPIRE in the partitioning step. One of the most notable feature of this paper is that the spatial partitioning problem not only maps different tasks in a temporal segment to the multiple FPGAs, but also routes the pin to pin inter-FPGA connections between the multi-FPGAs such that, some critical parameters of the routing are taken care of. These parameters include time-critical nets, routing congestion on interconnection devices and the overall inter-FPGA signal propagation delay.

2   Overview of ASPIRE

The ASPIRE tool follows a three-phased approach, as shown in Figure 2.1 to meet the desired objectives. The first phase of ASPIRE verifies whether the given module can be fit onto single FPGA.If it is not possible to map the module onto a single FPGA, the tool splits the module depending on the instantiations and various constructs in the module into smaller independent modules taking care of all interactions between the modules arising from splitting the bigger Parent module. This process is carried over recursively for every module. An example of a generation of task graph is shown in the Figure 2.2, where a module is split into 16 modules until each can be fit onto a single FPGA. The shaded ovals

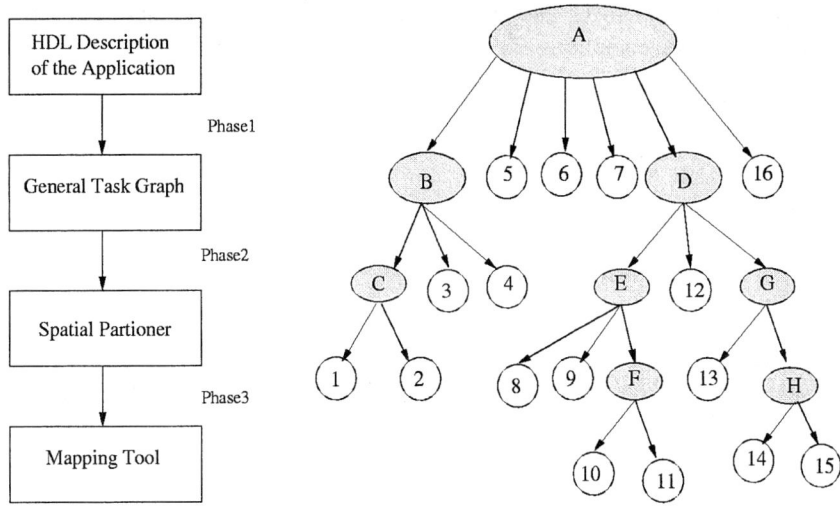

Fig. 2.1. Three Phase Approach   **Fig. 2.2.** Task graph

shown are the modules that cannot fit into a single FPGA and that need to be split and the leaves of the graph gives the final modules that can fit onto a single FPGA.

After obtaining the modules that can be fit onto a single FPGA, the second phase of the tool employs a genetic approach to agglomerate the modules efficiently satisfying the constraints so that they can be fit into minimum number of FPGAs. The third phase does mapping onto the FPGAs.

3   Spatial Partitioning

The target architecture onto which the application is to be mapped is assumed to be a network of N FPGAs, each possessing a local memory, and all of them having access to a global shared memory [3]. Throughout this paper, let N refer to the total number of FPGAs available on the target architecture. During the process of spatial partitioning, we are required to assign a particular FPGA from the set of N FPGAs to every task that is a part of a particular temporal segment. Apart from that, the spatial partitioning phase also addresses the problem of mapping logical memory segments to local or shared memory. The complexity of the problem increases due to various constraints associated with spatial partitioning [1].

- **Area Constraint:** The logic of the different tasks mapped on to the N FPGAs dictates the amount of area required on each FPGA. As the available area for each FPGA is fixed, this imposes a constraint on the logic that could be realized.

- **Speed Constraint:** The speed with which the implemented circuit works is of utmost importance. It is required to use certain heuristics to determine an implementation with good speed of execution else it is not practically feasible.
- **Memory Constraint:** The memory segments of the tasks of a spatial partition should not exceed the memory resources available.
- **Connection Constraint:** The Multi-FPGA system would be required to establish a connection between specified FPGAs within it, and also to the external world. Hence, the utilization of the pin resources should be done judiciously at this stage.

3.1   Phase I: The Task Graph Generation

The first phase of ASPIRE involves splitting a given application, specified in a HDL format, into smaller modules that can fit into the FPGAs.

Definition 1 (Definition): *Given a set of n HDL modules $M = (m_1, m_2, ..m_n)$ and k distinct pairs of edges $E = (e_1, e_2..e_k)$ between modules such that each e_i is an ordered pair of vertices $< m_x, m_y >$, then the circuit can be represented as a graph $G = (M, E)$ which is called a task graph. A graph $G' = (M', E')$ is a subgraph of $G = (M, E)$ if and only if $M' \subseteq M, E' \subseteq E$.*

A given module can be fit into a given single FPGA as long as the logic blocks and the number of pins required by the module does not surpass the maximum number of the available logic blocks and pins in the FPGA. The algorithm for the construction of the task graph is as follows:

Function TaskGraph (HDL description M)
begin
            If M fits in a single FPGA
                then return
            else
            begin
                Split M into smaller modules
                $(m_1, m_2, ...m_n)$
                Add nodes $m_1, m_2..m_n$ to task graph
                Update the task graph to capture the
                relationships
                For each m_i call TaskGraph(m_i)
            end
End Function

The task array generated by this phase is given as an input to the genetic algorithm, which computes an optimal mapping of the tasks onto the FPGAs considering all the constraints imposed by the architecture.

3.2   Phase II: The Genetic Approach

The second phase of the tool ASPIRE takes it's input from the first phase. The input is in the form of a task graph. This phase provides an optimal mapping of the tasks on to the given FPGA architecture using an evolutionary strategy.

ENCODING. The encoding used is identical to the one utilized in [1]. Two arrays are maintained, a task array *Task* and a memory array *Memory*. The length of Task is equal to the number of tasks in the task graph, t, while the length of Memory is equal to the number of memory segments, m. For $1 \leq i \leq t$, the variable *Task[i]*, ranging from 1 to N, represents the FPGA number to which task i is assigned to. Similarly for $1 \leq i \leq m$, the variable *Memory[i]*, ranging from 1 to N, represents the memory bindings. *Memory[i]=0* implies that the memory segment i is mapped to he shared memory. The *Task* and *Memory* arrays together constitute a chromosome.

INITIAL POPULATION. The task arrays for all chromosomes in the initial population are set to random legal values. Then based on task assignments, for each chromosome, we map the logical memory segments to local/global physical memories. If the majority of the tasks, which access a given logical memory segment M, are assigned to a FPGA f, then M is mapped onto the local memory present in f. Through a lot of experimentation, we decided to start with an initial population of size N.

MATING. The following genetic operators are used in the mating phase of the proposed genetic algorithm. We present a new approach to the Area and Memory Constraint operators. We introduce Speed Constraint Operator and Routing Crossover Operator which are not considered by previous approaches.

- **Area Constraint Operator (ACO):** This operator takes in two parents, Parent1 and Parent2, and produces a total of two offspring that are, with a high probability, better off as far as area constraints are concerned. Note that ACO only acts on the *Task* arrays of the parents and not on the *Memory* arrays. The ACO has been framed in a manner that retains all the information regarding the tasks up till the first violation of the area constraint. The parents are then crossed over in an attempt to reorganize the tasks in a manner that would progressively reduce the number of area conflicts, as the population evolves. Cross over at point i means the child gets the mapping of tasks from 1 to i from first parent and from i to end of tasks from second parent.

```
Function ACO (Parent P1, Parent P2)
   • Obtain the index, i1, of the first task in the Task array
     of P1, that causes an area constraint violation.
   • If such a conflict does not exist, then randomly choose
     a index.
```

- Obtain the index, i2, of the first task in the Task array of P2, that causes an area constraint violation.
- If such a conflict does not exist, then randomly choose a index.
- Obtain Child1 by crossing over the two parents at i1.
- Obtain Child2 by crossing over the two parents at i2.

End Function

- **Pin Constraint Operator (PCO):** The PCO attempts to optimize on the delay caused by the pin connections and hence reduce the communication time of the circuit when it is up and running. The reasoning behind the PCO is to minimize the inter-FPGA communication. The time required for a signal to propagate from one FPGA to another is much more than the time taken for intra-FPGA information transmission. Hence, in the PCO, the task that uses the greatest number of pins is chosen, since that task might have been placed in the wrong FPGA. By moving the task to another FPGA, one might be able to drastically cut down on the number of pins used, and hence the total time required for the signals to propagate.

Function PCO (Parent P1, Parent P2)
- Obtain the index, i1, of the task that utilizes the maximum number of pins in P1. Break ties arbitrarily.
- Obtain the index, i2, of the task that utilizes the maximum number of pins in P2. Break ties arbitrarily.
- Obtain Child1 by crossing over the two parents at i1.
- Obtain Child2 by crossing over the two parents at i2.

End Function

- **Memory Constraint Operator (MCO):** MCO requires two chromosomes, Parent1 and Parent2, and produces two offspring that are hopefully better off as far as memory constraints are concerned. Since the amount of memory available is of a finite quantity, one has to ensure the judicious allocation of the memory resources. MCO initially checks for memory conflicts, and if they do not exist, it then checks for the memory segment that is most accessed by tasks in other FPGAs. Such a segment, if placed in another FPGA, would reduce the number of accesses to it from other FPGAs, as a consequence of which, the speed with which the circuit executes would be made more efficient.The Function MCO is similar to ACO with the Task array replaced by Memory array and area violation by memory violation.
- **Default Crossover Operator (DCO):** Most chromosomes in the population would already be valid solutions, but they may not be close to the optimal, hence we utilize the DCO in an attempt to bring the solution as close as possible to the optimal solution. The DCO chooses random locations in the Task and Memory arrays and crossover the two parents to obtain the required offspring.

```
Function DCO (Parent P1, Parent P2)
```
- Choose a random index, i1, in the Task array.
- Choose a random index, i2, in the Memory array.
- Crossover P1 and P2 at i1 in the Task array and at i2 in
  the Memory array.
```
End Function
```

For the process of mating, the best of the population is chosen along with a few random selections as well. The chosen chromosomes are paired up, and one of the above four operators are applied randomly. Note that applying ACO to a solution that does not violate the area constraint would not be possible, in such cases the algorithm simply returns and the DCO is used.

MUTATION. The mutation operator is an attempt to save characteristics that have been lost over several generations. This operator randomly chooses a value from the Task and the Memory array and changes it to another legal value. A probability of mutation is associated with each chromosome in the population, which is basically inversely proportional to its fitness value. We choose *Nmutation* number of chromosomes during every iteration for the mutation process.

FITNESS FUNCTION. The fitness function has been divided into five distinct sections. For each section we obtain a fitness value in the range $[0..10]$, where 0 indicates a bad solution, and 10 indicates an excellent solution. We weigh the five fitness values and scale them up appropriately to a value in the range $[0..10]$. The five sections are as follows:

1. **Area Fitness Value (AFV):** Obtain the number of FPGAs, C, in which the area required by the logic exceeds the area provided by the FPGA. AFV is determined by computing $((N - C)/N) * 10$. The higher the value, the better the chromosome is with respect to the area constraint.
2. **Pin Connection Fitness Value (PFV):** Obtain the total number of FPGAs, E, in which the number of pins available is less than the total number of pins required by the logic and memory mapped on to it. PFV is determined by computing $((N - E)/N) * 10$.
3. **Memory Fitness Value (MFV):** Obtain the number of local memory and shared memory resource violations, V. MFV is determined by computing $((N-V)/N)*10$. The equation has been framed in a manner such that a high value indicates a better solution with respect to the memory constraints.
4. **Speed Fitness Value (SFV):** The speed with which the implemented circuit operates is greatly dependent on the location of a task t, with respect to the variables it interacts with. The speed would be greatly enhanced if most of the variables used by t were mapped onto the local memory of the FPGA in which t is mapped. The fitness value is a function of the proximity between the FPGAs mapping a task t and those storing the variables that interact with t. Closer are the variables to t, the higher is the fitness value.

The critical interacting paths between the tasks should be short for faster execution, so such tasks should be mapped close enough, this takes care of critical paths This fitness function depends on the architecture of the multi-FPGA system.

5. **Routing Fitness Value (RFV):** The routing fitness value tries to minimize on various routing factors such as the total length of wires used to route, and the total number of segments used for routing. It ensures that the spatial partition is such that it is possible to find a routing on the target architecture.

The final fitness value is determined by weighing the above five fitness values in the required proportions and scaling the final value to a range of $[0..10]$. Such an approach of computing the fitness value takes into account all the factors associated with the most important one being given higher priority. It can also be easily extended to include other constraints as well.

3.3   The Final Genetic Algorithm

The sequential genetic algorithm, which provides a solution to the spatial partitioning problem, is provided below.

```
SpatialGeneticSequential (Problem Specification)
```

- Create initial population;
- while (solution with the required fitness value has not been found) do
    - Choose Parents for mating process
    - Pair up Parents Randomly and Carry Out Mating
    - Add Offspring to population
    - Carry out Mutation
- return (the chromosome C with maximum fitness value)

```
End Function
```

The third phase of the tool ASPIRE is a simple mapping tool which requires an iterative algorithm and is hence not explicitly discussed here.

4   Experimental Results

We have tested ASPIRE on many large circuits and obtained very good results. An implementation of modular exponentiation based architecture proposed by Thomas Blum and C.Paar [8] was chosen to illustrate the efficiency of spatial partitioning algorithm proposed in this paper. The application has large utilization in the area of cryptography. It is a resource efficient architecture and suitable for implementation in FPGAs. The design of this architecture is based

Table 4.1. Comparison of results with existing GA [3]

S.No	Number of tasks	Run-times (in secs) using normal GA as in [3]	Run-times using using algorithm (ASPIRE)
1	5	2.46	1.1
2	8	14.48	10.1
3	10	46.2	12.46
4	18	102.1	20.3
5	20	153.1	25.5
6	40	228.4	130.6
7	60	456.2	150.8
8	100	761.1	200.7

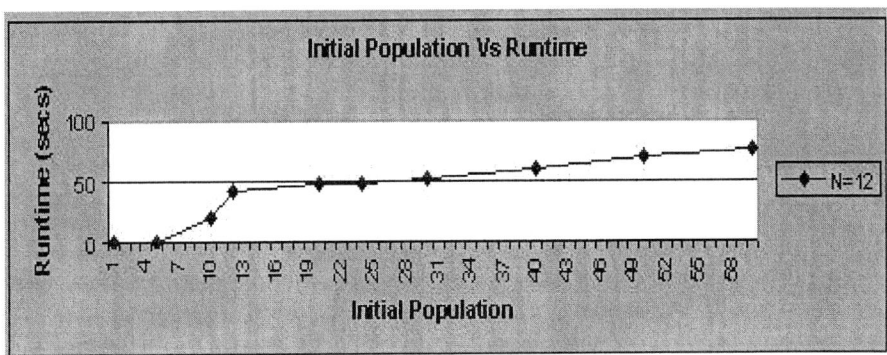

Graph 4.1. Initial population versus Runtime

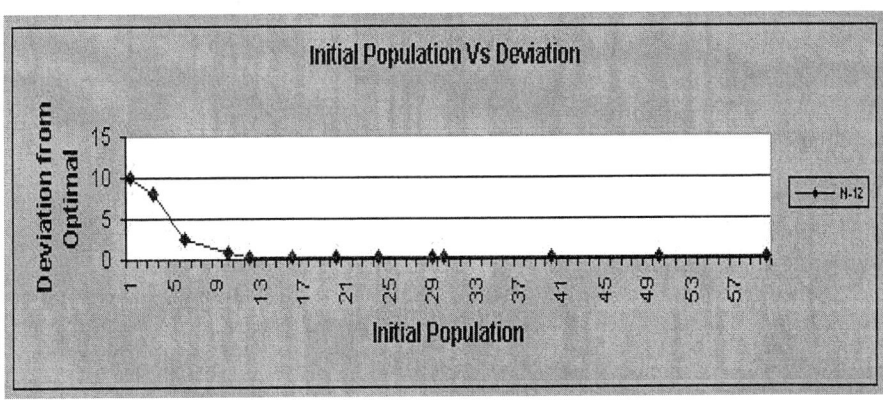

Graph 4.2. Initial population versus deviation from optimal.

on a systolic array, which computes the modular exponentiation. The total number of logic blocks required by the circuit was 14365, certainly more than the maximum present in a single ACEX1K FPGA. Given the Verilog description of the architecture, ASPIRE generated a task graph of 151 nodes and mapped the same onto a network of nine FPGAs of the ACEX1K type of Altera (Number EP1K30QC208-1). Each ACEX1K FPGA has 1728 logic blocks and 147 I/O pins. The proposed genetic approach was implemented on a 1.2 GHz dual processor Intel Xeon server.

In addition, our approach was tested on randomly generated task graphs and the results are shown in Table 4.1. Table 4.1 shows that our program takes one-third of the time that is taken by the approach in [3], even for task graphs with small number (for e.g., 20) of tasks. Our approach becomes faster with more number of tasks, implying its scalability with increasing number of tasks. An initial population in the range N to 2N, where N is the number of tasks in the task graph, assisted in attaining an optimal balance between the runtimes and fitness values (Graphs 4.1 and 4.2). Similar experiments were conducted to fix the rates of mating and mutation. A rate of mating in the range of N/4 to N/8 and a rate of mutation of N/8 proved to be ideal for our algorithm.

5   Conclusion

In this paper we have presented a completely automatic spatial partitioner, which takes a HDL description of a big application and maps onto a given Multi-FPGA architecture. The crux of our approach is a spatial partitioner, which uses an evolutionary approach to solve the problem. ASPIRE was successfully employed to spatially partition a reasonably big cryptographic application that involved a 1024-bit modular exponentiation. The genetic spatial partitioner was also experimented on random task graphs and shown to work efficiently and scalable with larger task graphs. Future work in this field may be oriented in enhancing the crossover operators and the fitness functions. We are currently working in parallel simulations of the genetic approach to further reduce the time complexity of our algorithm.

References

1. Kenneth A. De Jong and William M. Spears, Optimal Temporal Partitioning and Synthesis for Reconfigurable Architectures, In the Proceedings of Design Automation and Test in Europe (DATE), Feb. 23-26, 1998, page 389.
2. Vinoo Srinivasan, Shankar Radhakrishnan, and Ranga Vemuri, Hardware Software Partitioning with Integrated Hardware Design Space Exploration, in the Proceedings of Design Automation and Test in Europe (DATE), Feb. 23-26, 1998, page 28.
3. Iyad Ouaiss, Sriram Govindarajan, Vinoo Srinivasan, Meenakshi Kaul, and Ranga Vemuri, An Integrated Partitioning and Synthesis System for Dynamically Reconfigurable Multi-FPGA Architectures, In the Proceedings Reconfigurable Architecture Workshop, RAW 1998.

4. D. E. Goldberg, Genetic algorithms in Search, Optimization, and Machine Learning, Addison-Wesely, ISBN,1989
5. Ram Vemuri, Genetic Algorithms for Partitioning, Placement and Layer Assignment for Multichip Modules, PhD thesis, University of Cincinnati, USA, July 1994
6. Pinaki Mazumder and Elizabeth Rudnick, Genetic Algorithms for VLSI Design, Layout and Test Automation, Prentice Hall PTR, (2002).
7. Jose Ignacio Hidalgo, Juan Lanchares, Roman Hermida, Partitioning and placement for Multi-FPGA systems using genetic algorithm, Euromicro conference 2000, vol. 1, pg. 209.
8. Thomas Blum, C.Paar, High Radix Montgomery modular exponentiation on reconfigurable hardware, IEEE transactions on computers, 2001.

GA with Exaptation: New Algorithms to Tackle Dynamic Problems

Luis Torres-T

Centro de Sistemas Inteligentes
ITESM, Campus Monterrey
CETEC Torre Sur, 5° Nivel
Ave. Eugenio Garza Sada 2501 Sur, Col. Tecnológico
Phone (0181) 8328 - 4258
Nuevo Leon, Mexico.

Abstract. It is propose new evolutionary algorithms with exaptive properties to tackle dynamic problems. Exaptation is a new theory with two implicit procedures of retention and reuse of old solutions. The retention of a solution involves some kind of memory and the reuse of a solution implies the adaptation of the solution to the new problem. The first algorithm proposed uses seeding techniques to reuse a solution and the second algorithm proposed uses memory with seeding techniques to retain and reuse solutions respectively. Both algorithms are compared with a simple genetic algorithm (SGA) and the SGA with two populations, where the first one is a memory of solutions and the second population is searching new solutions. The Moving Peak Benchmark (MPB) was used to test every algorithm.

1   Introduction

In recent years the optimization of dynamic problems has become a growing field of research. The real-world problems are not static, they exist in a dynamic environment and it is necessary to modify the current solution when a change is detected. We need evolutionary algorithms that do not re-start in every change; these algorithms must take advantage of the population information to obtain a valid solution in a short time. It is expected a similar solution when there are a minimum change of the problems and a dissimilar solution when there are an important change of the problem.

Some examples of dynamic problems are job shop problems where there are changes in due time, changes in the number of machines, processing times, etc., and these changes imply a re-schedule in the job shop. Learning in dynamic environments is a desirable quality for mobile robots. Navigation represents a simultaneous problem of path planning and movement to the goal along the path. Finally consider an electric company where in some periods there is high demand of energy and in another periods there is low demand. Usually it is necessary an optimization algorithm to manage and control sources efficiently with this dynamic demand. All of these dynamic problems can be modeled with

R. Monroy et al. (Eds.): MICAI 2004, LNAI 2972, pp. 746–753, 2004.

variables, the optimization function and a set of constrains. Every one of them can changes through time [1]. Many authors have suggested some extension in the simple genetic algorithm to tackle these dynamic problems. Branke has suggested the following categories to group the algorithms proposed [2,3]:

- Evolutionary algorithms detect every change in the environment. If it is detected some change, then new individuals are injected into the population to increase diversity.
- Evolutionary algorithms which have an implicit memory. These algorithms use double or more complex representations (diploid, haploids) [4,5]. In a given moment just one representation is active.
- Evolutionary algorithms which have an explicit memory to store useful information of the past and it is recalled when the dynamic problem returns to a similar situation presented in the past [6,7].
- Evolutionary algorithms avoid every time the convergence. Genetic algorithms with sharing and random immigrants are examples of these kinds of algorithms.
- Evolutionary algorithms use a multiple subpopulations to search the optimum or search a new optimum.

Many authors have suggested dynamic problems to test algorithms, but some of them are too simple or too complex to use in the research area. Branke suggested a problem with a multidimensional landscape consisting of several peaks. The width, the height and the position of each peak can be altered slightly or abruptly when a change of the environment occur [8]. This benchmark will be used to test all the algorithms.

The following sections will present the comparison between two new evolutionary algorithms inspired in exaptation, the simple genetic algorithms (SGA), and the SGA with two populations of Branke [8] to optimize the dynamic problem presented in the moving peaks benchmark. Section II reviews the exaptation theory. Section III proposes two genetic algorithm inspired in exaptation ideas. Section IV reports some experiments and some results of the comparisons. Finally, it is discussed some conclusions and future work in section V.

2 Exaptation

Gould and Vrba [9,10] proposed the term exaptation, which refers to a trait that current provides fitness, but originally arose for some other reason. Every entity (species) tries to survive in a continuous non-static environment. The entity has traits which lets survive in the environment. Some traits are useful because provide high fitness but another ones do not provide fitness, they are useless or redundants. Some traits may have evolved in one context of the environment but later, such a trait may be co-opted for use in a different role. In other words, the exaptation is a change in the function of an old trait to solve a new problem.

Exaptation has three procedures. First, when there is a change in the environment it is detected a set of possible traits with high fitness. The second procedure reuse the possible useful traits with high fitness and adapt them to the new environment. The third procedure retains a useful trait for future references but the useless traits do not disappear completely, they are stored as redundant or useless structures.

The initial population of a genetic algorithm is random. The SGA solves a problem and it takes several cycles to get an optimum or an individual with high fitness for the optimization function. In the end of the run the population have individuals that are very similar between them. If there is a change of the environment and some individuals are useless maybe some of them have useful traits. If the SGA runs again with a changed function and the same population, the useful traits may arise and they can let to get a new optimum quickly. In the SGA is possible to reuse the last population if the function does not change too much. If the change is important then the reuse of the last population can be useless. It is necessary to modify the SGA in order to get some features of exaptation and it can be used to solve dynamic problems.

3   Genetic Algorithms with Exaptation

The first algorithm proposed is the SGA with seeding techniques; this algorithm is inspired in exaptation because it cause the reuse of structures when the algorithm detects any change in the optimization function. If one change is detected then some variations or neighbors of the best solution found are injected into the actual population. The variations or neighbors replace a percent of the total population. It could be that some components (genes) of the best individual can be reused in the new function. The neighbors of the solution can give the appropriate solution if the problem changes slightly. The variations (mutations) of the solution can give a key if the problem changes abruptly. This algorithm can be grouped to genetic algorithms that detect a change and they apply an injection.

The second algorithm is inspired in exaptation and it is implanted from the point of view of learning by analogy; this learning mechanism has a memory of useful solutions of the past, a storing procedure of solutions, a search mechanism and a modification procedure. The second algorithm applies similar procedures: A recognition procedure where it is used the evaluation of the best individual to be compared again the best evaluation found in the past. If there is a degradation of the past solution then there is a change in the objective function. Storing procedure saves the best individual found into the memory. It avoids to save the same individual in the memory two times. First it locates the most similar individual of the memory to the best individual found and if the best individual found has better evaluation than the individual of the memory then the best individual is stored into the memory. In another case, there is not change in the memory. This procedure tries to apply the exaptive property of retention of solutions. The modification procedure is based in seeding techniques.

The algorithms implemented are the SGA, the SGA with elitism, the SGA with two populations, the SGA with seeding and the SGA with memory and seeding. In the SGA that reuse the last population of the search, the population is initialized just at the beginning of the run. The algorithm is shown below. P is the population, F_E retains the evaluation value of every individual in the population. I is an auxiliary variable and it retains the best individual of the population per generation. The evaluation value of the Individual I is saved in e.

Simple Genetic Algorithms
1) $P \leftarrow$ Random initialization
2) $F_E \leftarrow$ Evaluation(P)
3) Get the best individual I and its evaluation e from F_E
4) $P \leftarrow$ Selection(P, F_E)
5) $P \leftarrow$ Reproduction(P) (crossover and mutation)
6) If end condition is not satisfied, then go to step (2)
7) End

Simple genetic algorithm with elitism reuse the last population of the search. This algorithm has the same features of the SGA, the difference is the elitism procedure included. The algorithm is the following:

Simple genetic algorithm with elitism
1) $P \leftarrow$ Random initialization
2) $F_E \leftarrow$ Evaluation(P)
3) Get the best individual I and its evaluation e from F_E
4) $P \leftarrow$ Selection(P, F_E)
5) $P \leftarrow$ Reproduction(P) (crossover and mutation)
6) Apply elitism inyecting I in P
7) If end condition is not satisfied, then go to step (2)
8) End

The SGA with two populations proposed by Branke includes two populations, the memory population M and the search population P. Every k generations it is saved the best solution found. It searchs the minimum distance between the individual I_g and the individuals stored in the the memory, then the more fit individual is storing into the memory M. The detection of a change in the objective function is by the comparison between the best evaluation value of the memory e_m, the actual search population e and the past evaluation value detected e_a. The algorithm re-initialize the search population P when a change is detected.

Genetic algorithm based in memory proposed by Branke
1) $P \leftarrow$ Random initialization
2) $M \leftarrow$ Random initialization or empty memory
3) Get the best past evaluation e_a
4) $FE \leftarrow$ Evaluation(P)
5) Get the best individual I and its evaluation value e from F_E
6) $F_{EM} \leftarrow$ Evaluation(M)
7) Get the best individual I_m and its evaluation value e_m from F_{EM}
8) Detect the best individual I_g between I and I_m
9) If $\max(e_m, e) < e_a$ then $P \leftarrow$ random inicialization
10) Every k generations the best individual I_g is storing into the memory M
11) $P \leftarrow$ Selection(P, F_E)
12) $P \leftarrow$ Reproduction(P) (crossover and mutation)
13) Includes elitism inyecting I_g in P
14) If end condition is not satisfied, then go to step (3)
15) End

The genetic algorithm with seeding injects neighbors of the best individual I when it detects a change in the objective function.

Genetic algorithm with seeding techniques
1) $P \leftarrow$ Random initialization
2) Get the best past evaluation e_a
3) $FE \leftarrow$ Evaluation(P)
4) Get the best individual I and its evaluation value e from F_E
5) If $e < e_a$ then apply seeding of 50% of neighborn and variations of I in P
6) $P \leftarrow$ Selection (P, F_E)
7) $P \leftarrow$ Reproduction (P) (crossover and mutation)
8) Includes Elitism inyecting I in P
9) If end condition is not satisfied, then go to step (2)
10) End

The SGA with memory and seeding has a memory to save the best solution found. The procedure is similar to the algorithm of Branke. The algorithm uses a SGA with seeding of neighbors and variations of 50%. The condition to make a seeding is when the evaluation value of the memory e_m is lower than the best past evaluation value e_a. When the memory detects a lower evaluation in the individuals of the memory this is an indication that the function changes and there is an unknown solution, so it is necessary to find a new one just with the information of the memory.

Genetic algorithm with memory and seeding techniques
1) $P \leftarrow$ Random initialization
2) $M \leftarrow$ Random initialization or empty memory
3) Get the best past evaluation value e_a
4) $FEM \leftarrow$ Evaluation(M)
5) Get the best individual I_m and its evaluation value e_m from F_{EM}
6) If $em < e_a$ then applies seeding of 50% of Neighborn and variations of I in P
7) $FE \leftarrow$ Evaluation(P)
8) Get the best individual I and its evaluation value e from F_E
9) $P \leftarrow$ Selection(P, F_E)
10) $P \leftarrow$ Reproduction(P) (crossover and mutation)
11) Every k generations saves in memory M the best individual I
12) If end condition is not satisfied, then go to step (3)
13) End

4   Experimentation and Results

For the experiment it is used a SGA with crossover probability of 0.8 and mutation rate of 0.025, a total population size of 100 individuals. The benchmark has
five variables. Every variable is coded into a binary vector of size 8, consequently
the chromosome has the size of 40 bits. It is used a selection tourment of size 2.
Every generation involves 100 evaluations. For dynamic fitness function is useless
to report the best solution found. It is reported on the offline-performance, which
is the average of the best solutions at each time step T ($e_p(T) = \frac{1}{T} \cdot \sum_{t=1}^{T} e(t)$),
$e(t)$ is the best solution per generation at time t. The number of values that are
used for the average grows with time, so the curves tend to be smoother. For
the comparison will be implanted the five algorithms of the last section. The
memory of the algorithms is empty.

The fitness function changes every 50 generations. There are two cases for
testing. In the first one the location of every peaks stay at the same place but
there are changes in the height and the weight of every peak (set $s = 0$, $\lambda = 1$ in
MPB). The following figure 1 shows the offline performance of four algorithms,
the SGA (sga), the SGA with two populations (sga2p), the SGA with memory
and seeding (sgams)and the SGA with seeding (sgas). The SGA with elitism
(sgae) is not shown because has the same performance as the SGA. The performance of the algorithms suggest a minimum difference between the algorithm of
two populations and the SGA with memory and seeding, so there are not a clear
out-performance of one algorithm over other one. Nevertheless both algorithms
are better than the SGA and the SGA with seeding.

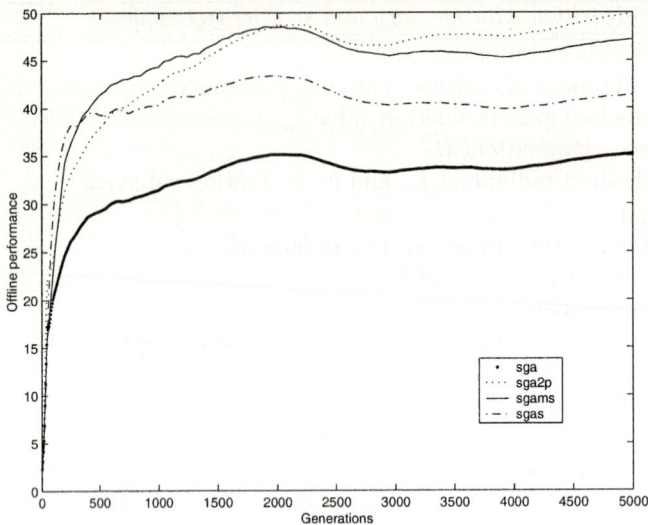

Fig. 1. Offline Performance of several approaches. The peaks location stay at the same place.

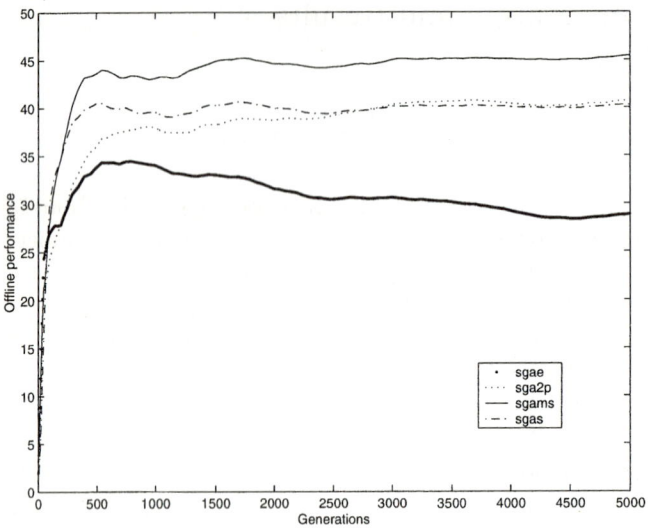

Fig. 2. Offline Performance of several approaches. The peaks location changes of position.

In the second case the peaks locations changes of position (set $s = 0.5$, $\lambda = 1$ in MPB). The figure 2 shows the offline performance of four algorithms, the SGA is not shown because it has similar performance of the SGA with elitism. The SGA with memory and seeding suggests better performance than SGA with two populations.

5   Conclusion

In this paper I propose two algorithms inspired in exaptation ideas. The algorithms make intensive use of seeding techniques of the best solution useful in the moment. Both algorithms were tested in the Moving Peaks Benchmark suggested by Branke. it was implemented other algorithms to make comparisons between them. It was shown that the algorithms proposed are competitive solving dynamic problems because they have similar performance.

In future work there are two tendencies, first we want to get pure exaptive algorithms with retention and reuse implicit properties and the use of more controlled seeding techniques. The second tendency is to find more dynamic problems to test these algorithms like the problems found in dynamic learning.

References

1. K. Trojanowski and Z. Michalewicz. Evolutionary algorithms for non-stationary environments. In: Proc. of 8th Workshop: Intelligent Information systems, ICS PAS Press, (1999) 229–240
2. J. Branke: Evolutionary approaches to dynamic optimization problems; a survey. In: GECCO Workshop on Evolutionary Algorithms for Dynamic Optimization Problems, (1999) 134–37
3. J. Branke: Evolutionary approaches to dynamic optimization problems - Updated survey. In: GECCO Workshop on Evolutionary Algorithms for Dynamic Optimization Problems (2001), 27–30
4. David E. Goldberg: Genetic algorithms in search, optimization, and machine learning. Addinson - Wesley. Pub. Co., Reading MA (1989).
5. D. Dasgupta and D. McGregor: Nonstationary function optimization using the structured genetic algorithm. In: R. Männer and B. Manderick, editors, Parallel Problem Solving from Nature, Elsevier Science Publisher (1992) 145–154
6. Sushil J. Louis and Judy Johnson: Robustness of Case-Initialized Genetic Algorithms. FLAIRS-99, Orlando, FL, AAAI Press. (1999)
7. Connie Loggia Ramsey and John J. Grefenstette: Case-Based Initialization of Genetic Algorithms. Proc. of the Fifth Int. Conf. on Genetic Algorithms, Morgan Kaufmann, San Mateo, CA. (1993) 84–91.
8. J. Branke: Memory-enhanced evolutionary algorithms for dynamic optimization problems. In: Congress on Evolutionary Computation (CEC'99), IEEE, Band 3, (1999) 1875-1882
9. S. J. Gould and S. Vrba, Exaptation: A missing term in the science of form, Paleobiology, volume 8 (1982) 4–15
10. Stephen Jay Gould, A crucial Tool for an Evolutionary Psychology", Journal of Social Issues", volume 47, (1991) 43–65

Intelligent Control Algorithm for Steam Temperature Regulation of Thermal Power Plants

A. Sanchez-Lopez, G. Arroyo-Figueroa, and A. Villavicencio-Ramirez

Instituto de Investigaciones Electricas
Calle Reforma No.113 Colonia Palmira
62490 Cuernavaca, Morelos, Mexico
{garroyo,jasl}@iie.org.mx

Abstract. Artificial intelligence techniques have been developed through extensive practical implementations in industry in form of intelligent control. One of the most successful expert-system techniques, applied to a wide range of control applications, has been fuzzy logic technique. This paper shows the implementation of a fuzzy logic controller (FLC) to regulate the steam temperature in a 300 MW Thermal Power Plant. The proposed FLC was applied to regulate superheated and reheated steam temperature. The results show that the fuzzy controller has a better performance than advanced model-based controller, such as Dynamic Matrix Control (DMC) or a conventional PID controller. The main benefits are the reduction of the overshoot and the tighter regulation of the steam temperatures. Fuzzy-logic controllers can achieve good result for complex nonlinear processes with dynamic variation or with long delay times.

1 Introduction

Over the last 15 years the complexity of the operation of thermal power plants has been increased significantly. Mainly by two factors: changes in the operating conditions and the increment of the age of the plants. Today, the operation of thermal power plants must be optimal considering higher productions profits, safer operation and stringent environment regulation. In addition, the reliability and performance of the plants is affected by its age. These factors increase the risk of equipment failures and the number of diagnoses and control decisions which the human operator must take [1, 2].

As a result of these changes, the computer and information technology have been extensively used in thermal plant process operation. Distributed control systems (DCS) and management information systems (MIS) have been playing an important role to show the plant status. The main function of DCS is to handle normal disturbances and maintain key process parameters in pre-specified local optimal levels. Despite their great success, DCS have little function for abnormal and non-routine operation because the classical Proportional-integral-derivative (PID) control is widely used by the DCS. PID controllers exhibit poor performance when applied to process containing unknown non-linearity and time delays. The complexity of these problems and the difficulties in implementing conventional controllers to eliminate

R. Monroy et al. (Eds.): MICAI 2004, LNAI 2972, pp. 754–763, 2004.

variations in PID tuning motivate the use of other kind of controllers, such as model based controllers and intelligent controllers.

This paper proposes a model based controller such as Dynamic Matrix Controller and an intelligent controller based on fuzzy logic as an alternative control strategy applied to regulate the steam temperature of the thermal power plant. The temperature regulation is considered the most demanded control loop in the steam generation process. The steam temperature deviation must be kept within a tight variation rank in order to assure safe operation, improve efficiency and increase the life span of the equipment. Moreover, there are many mutual interactions between steam temperature control loops that have been considered. Other important factor is the time delay. It is well know that the time delay makes the temperature loops hard to tune. The complexity of these problems and difficulties to implement PID conventional controllers motivate to research the use of model predictive controllers such as the dynamic matrix controller or intelligent control techniques such as the fuzzy logic controller as a solution for controlling systems in which time delays, and non-linear behavior need to be addressed [3,4].

The paper is organized as follows. A brief description of the Dynamic Matrix Controller (DMC) is presented in Section 2. The fuzzy logic controller (FLC) design is described in Section 3. Section 4 presents the implementation of both controllers DMC and FLC to regulate the superheated and reheated steam temperature of a thermal power plant. The performance of the FLC controller was evaluated against two other controllers, the conventional PID controller and the predictive DMC controller. Results are presented in Section 5. Finally, the main set of conclusions according to the analysis and results derived from the performance of controllers is presented in Section 6.

2 Dynamic Matrix Control

The Dynamic Matrix Control (DMC) is a kind of model based predictive control. This controller was developed to improve control of oil refinement processes [5]. The DMC and other predictive control techniques such as the Generalized Predictive Control [6] or Smith predictor [6] algorithms are based on past and present information of controlled and manipulated variables to predict the future state of the process.

The Dynamic Matrix Control is based on a time domain model. This model is utilized to predict the future behavior of the process in a defined time horizon. Based on this precept the control algorithm provides a way to define the process behavior in the time, predicting the controlled variables trajectory in function of previous control actions and current values of the process [7].

The control technique includes the followings procedures:

a) Obtaining the Dynamic Matrix model of the process. In this stage, a step signal is applied to the input of the process. The measurements obtained with this activity represent the process behavior as well as the coefficients of the process state in time. This step is performed just once before the operation of the control algorithm in the process.

b) Determination of deviations in controlled variables. In this step, the deviation between the controlled variables of the process and their respective set points is measured.

c) Projection of future states of the process. The future behavior of each controlled variable is defined in a vector. This vector is based on previous control actions and current values of the process.

d) Calculation of control movements. Control movements are obtained using the future vector of error and the dynamic matrix of the process. The equation developed to obtain the control movements is shown below:

$$\underline{\Delta}^+_m = [\ \underline{A}^T \underline{A} + f^2 \underline{I}\ ]^{-1} \underline{A}^T \underline{X}^+ \tag{1}$$

where $\underline{A}$ represents the dynamic matrix, $\underline{A}^T$ the transposed matrix of $\underline{A}$, $\underline{X}$ the vector of future states of the process, f a weighting factor, $\underline{I}$ the image matrix and $\underline{\Delta}$ the future control actions. Further details about this equation are found in [5].

e) Control movements' implementation. In this step the first element of the control movements' vector is applied to manipulated variables.

A DMC controller allows designers the use of time domain information to create a process model. The mathematical method for prediction matches the predicted behavior and the actual behavior of the process to predict the next state of the process. However, the process model is not continuously updated because this involves recalculations that can lead to an overload of processors and performance degradation.

Discrepancies in the real behavior of the process and the predicted state are considered only in the current calculation of control movements. Thus, the controller is adjusted continuously based on deviations of the predicted and real behavior while the model remains static.

3   Fuzzy Logic Control

Fuzzy control is used when the process follows some general operating characteristic and a detailed process understanding is unknown or process model become overly complex. The capability to qualitatively capture the attributes of a control system based on observable phenomena and the capability to model the nonlinearities for the process are the main features of fuzzy control. The ability of Fuzzy Logic to capture system dynamics qualitatively and execute this qualitative schema in a real time situation is an attractive feature for temperature control systems [8].

The essential part of the fuzzy logic controller is a set of linguistic control rules related to the dual concepts of fuzzy implication and the compositional rule of inference [9].

Essentially, the fuzzy controller provides an algorithm that can convert the linguistic control strategy, based on expert knowledge, into an automatic control strategy. In general, the basic configuration of a fuzzy controller has four main modules as it is shown in the figure 1.

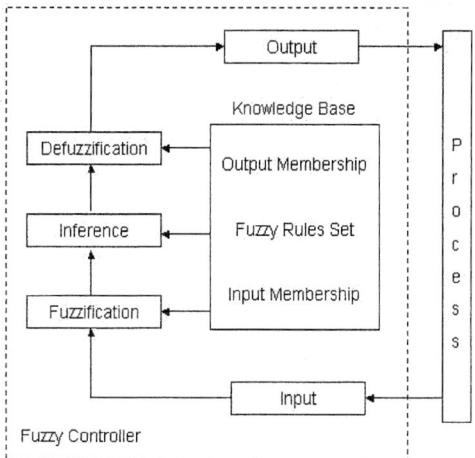

Fig. 1. Architecture of a Fuzzy Logic Controller.

In the first module, a quantization module converts to discrete values and normalizes the universe of discourse of various manipulated variables (Input). Then, a numerical fuzzy converter maps crisp data to fuzzy numbers characterized by a fuzzy set and a linguistic label (Fuzzification). In the next module, the inference engine applies the compositional rule of inference to the rule base in order to derive fuzzy values of the control signal from the input facts of the controller. Finally, a symbolic-numerical interface known as defuzzification module provides a numerical value of the control signal or increment in the control action.

Thus the necessary steps to build a fuzzy control system are [10,11]: (a) Input and output variables representation in linguistic terms within a discourse universe; (b) Definition of membership functions that will convert the process input variables to fuzzy sets; (c) Knowledge base configuration; (d) Design of the inference unit that will relate input data to fuzzy rules of the knowledge base; and (e) Design of the module that will convert the fuzzy control actions into physical control actions.

4 Implementation

The control of the steam temperature is performed by two methods. One of them is to spray water on the steam flow, mainly in the super-heater. The sprayed water must be strictly regulated in order to avoid the steam temperature to exceed the design temperature range of ±1% (±5 °C). This makes sure the correct operation of the process, improvement of the efficiency and extension of lifetime of the equipment. The excess of sprayed water in the process can result in degradation of the turbine. The water in liquid phase impacts strongly on the turbine's blades. The other process to control the steam temperature is to change the burner slope in the furnace, mainly in the reheated. The main objective of this manipulation is to keep constant the steam temperature when a change in load is made.

The DMC, fuzzy logic and PID controllers were implemented in a full model simulator to control the superheated and reheated steam temperature. The simulator simulates sequentially the main process and control systems of a 300 MW fossil power plant.

4.1 Dynamic Matrix Control (DMC)

The matrix model of the process is the main component of the Dynamic Matrix Controller. In this case the matrix model was obtained by a step signal in both the sprayed water flow and the burners' position.

Figure 2 shows a block diagram of the DMC implementation in the steam superheating and reheating sections. The temperature deviations were used as the controller's input. The sprayed water flow and slope of burners were used as the manipulated variables or controller's output.

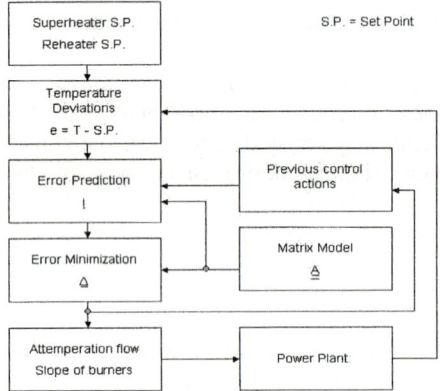

Fig. 2. Implementation of DMC controller

4.2 Fuzzy Logic Control (FLC)

Seven fuzzy sets were chosen to define the states of the controlled and manipulated variables. The triangular membership functions and their linguistic representation are shown in figure 4. The fuzzy sets abbreviators belong to: NB=Negative Big, NM=Negative Medium, NS=Negative Short, ZE=Zero, PS=Positive Short, PM=Positive Medium and PB=Positive Big.

The design of the rule base in a fuzzy system is a very important part and a complex activity for control systems. Li et al [11] proposed a methodology to develop the set of rules for a fuzzy controller based on a general model of a process rather than a subjective practical experience of human experts. The methodology includes analyzing the general dynamic behavior of a process, which can be classified as stable or unstable (figure 4).

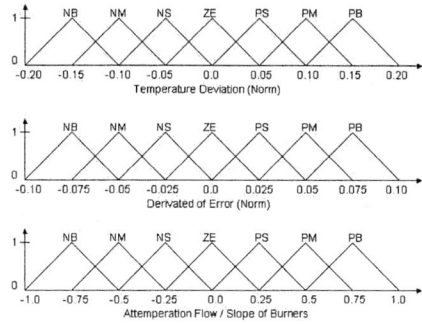

Fig. 3. Fuzzy sets of FLC

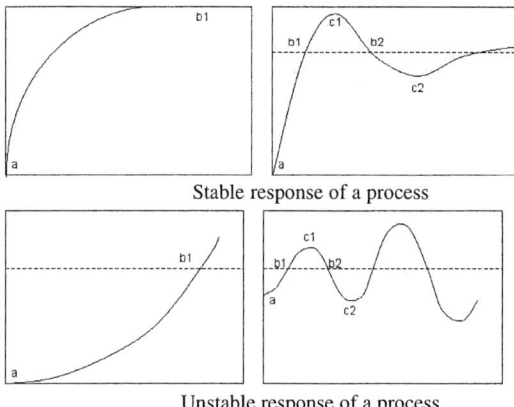

Stable response of a process

Unstable response of a process

Fig. 4. Common step response of a process

In figure 3 the range of fuzzy sets are normalized to regulate the temperature within the 20% above or below the set point, the change of error within the ± 10 %, and the control action are considered to be moved from completely close or 0° inclination to completely open or 90° of inclination in water flow valve and slope of burners respectively. In the case of regulation of temperature, if the requirements change to regulate the temperature within a greater range, the methodology proposed by Li et al [11] considers to apply a scale factor in the fuzzy sets.

Characteristics of the four responses are contained in the response show by the second stable response. The approach also uses an error state space representation to show the inclusion of the four responses in the second stable one (figure 5).

A set of general rules can be built by using the general step response of a process (second order stable system):

1. If the magnitude of the error and the speed of change is zero, then there is not necessary to apply any control action (keep the value of the manipulated variable).
2. If the magnitude of the error is close to zero in a satisfactory speed, then there is no necessary any control action (keep the value of the manipulated variable).
3. If the magnitude of the error is not close to the system equilibrium point (origin of the phase plane diagram) then the value of the manipulated variable is modified in function of the sign and magnitude of the error and speed of change.

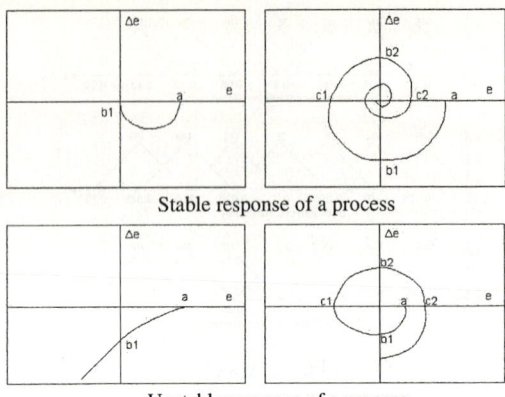

Fig. 5. Time domain response in error state space representation.

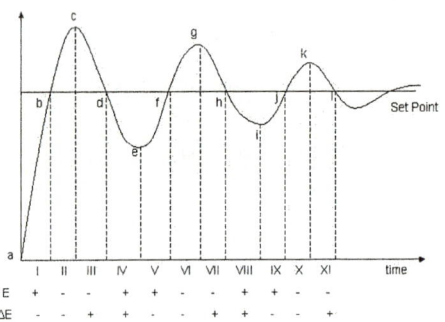

Fig. 6. Step response of a second order system.

The fuzzy control rules were obtained observing the transitions in the temperature deviations and their change rates considering a general step response of a process instead of the response of the actual process to be controlled. The magnitude of the control action depends on the characteristics of the actual process to be controlled and it is decided during the construction of the fuzzy rules. A coarse variable (few labels or fuzzy regions) produces a large output or control action, while a fine variable produces small one.

Figure 6 shows a representative step response of a second-order system. Based on this figure, a set of rules can be generated. For the first reference range (I), it is necessary to use a fuzzy rule in order to reduce the rise time of the signal:

$$IF\ E=PB\ and\ \Delta E=NS\ THEN\ OA=PM \tag{2}$$

Where E means the deviation, ΔE denotes the change rate and OA determines the output action required to regulate the controlled variable. Another rule can be obtained for this same region (I). The objective of this rule will be to reduce the overshoot in the system response:

$$IF\ E=PS\ and\ \Delta E=NB\ THEN\ OA=NM \tag{3}$$

Table 1. Set of Rules of a FLC.

Rule	E	ΔE	Control Action	Reference Point
1	PB	ZE	PB	a
2	PM	ZE	PM	e
3	PS	ZE	PS	i
4	ZE	NB	NB	b
5	ZE	NM	NM	f
6	ZE	NS	NS	j
7	NB	ZE	NB	c
8	NM	ZE	NM	g
9	NS	ZE	NS	k
10	ZE	PB	PB	d
11	ZE	PM	PM	h
12	ZE	PS	PS	l
13	ZE	ZE	ZE	set point
				Reference Range
14	PB	NS	PM	I (rise time)
15	PB	NB	NM	I (overshoot)
16	NS	PS	NM	III
17	NS	PB	PM	III
18	PS	NS	ZE	IX
19	NS	PS	ZE	XI

Analyzing the step response is possible to generate the fuzzy rule set for each region and point in the graph. Table 1 shows the set of rules obtained using this methodology. The second and third columns represent the main combinations between the error and its change rate of each variable. The forth column indicates the necessary control action to control the process condition. The last column shows the reference points and ranges that belong to each fuzzy rule.

5 Controllers Performance

In every case, the system was submitted to an increment in load demand [12]. The disturbance was a kind of ramp from 70% to 90% in the load. The load change rate was 10 MW/min, which represents the maximum speed of change in the load. The performance parameters evaluated belong to overshoot amplitude, response time, maximum value, integral error square, integral absolute error.

Figure 7 shows the graphic results obtained by each controller in the super-heater and re-heater respectively. In both cases the stability of the steam temperature is

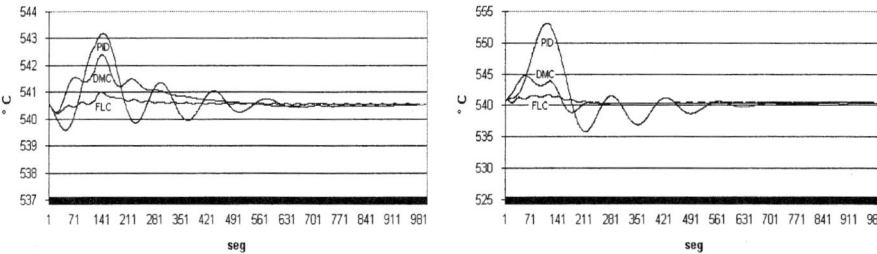

Fig. 7. Superheated and reheated steam temperature response .

widely improved by the advanced control algorithms. In the same way, the steam temperature deviation from the set point is tightly regulated.

The DMC reduced the superheated steam temperature overshoot almost 30% and the response time 15% in relation to the PID controller response. The maximum deviation observed with respect to the reference is reduced 30% in relation to the PID controller. In the re-heater, the DMC reduced the steam temperature deviation almost 65% and the response time 60% in relation to the PID controller. The maximum value reached by the steam temperature is reduced significantly in the same comparison (65%).

When a fuzzy controller is applied to the superheated steam temperature with the same disturbance described before, the overshoot is reduced almost 80% in relation to the PID controller performance or 70% in relation to the DMC performance. There is no response time because the fuzzy controller keeps the steam temperature within a tight variation rank. The maximum deviation observed with respect to the reference is strongly reduced in relation to both the PID controller (80%) and the DMC (70%).

There is no overshoot using the fuzzy controller because of the kind of the process response. There is also not response time because the fuzzy controller keeps the steam temperature within a tight variation rank.

6   Conclusions

The Dynamic Matrix Control algorithm has shown significant reduction and better stability in the superheated and reheated steam temperatures. However, the use of fuzzy logic theory to control the steam temperatures achieved better performance in the characteristics before mentioned. Moreover, the response time of the signals were considered as insignificant because the fuzzy controller kept the steam temperatures within a tight variation rank.

The Dynamic Matrix controller includes the execution of matrix calculations that are in function of the number of inputs in the process. The speed of the DMC performance can be affected by this parameter. The fuzzy logic controller is based on solving arithmetic and logic equations independently of the number of inputs.

Both Fuzzy and Dynamic Matrix controllers are suitable to use when there is not a model that represents the process. In the case of the DMC algorithm, it has the disadvantage of keeping the process out of the control point in order to get the matrix model. On the other hand, the fuzzy controller implementation is based on approximated reasoning and knowledge representation of the experience. The fuzzy controller considers the expert reasoning and knowledge from operators as well as a general model or dynamic behavior of a process. The main benefits of the fuzzy control are the reduction of the overshoot and the tight regulation of steam temperature.

References

1. Arroyo-Figueroa G., Sucar L. E., Solis E., and Villavicencio A. SADEP – a fuzzy diagnostic system shell – an application to fossil power plant operation. Expert Systems with Applications 1998; 14 (1/2): 43-52.
2. Abdennour A. An intelligent supervisory system for drum type boilers during severe disturbances. Electrical Power and Energy Systems 2000;22:381-387.
3. Verbruggen H. B., and Bruijn P.M. Fuzzy control and conventional control: what is (and can be) the real contribution of fuzzy systems?. Fuzzy Sets and Systems 1997; 90: 151-160.
4. Babuska R. and Verbruggen H.B. An Overview of Fuzzy modeling for control. Control Engineering Practice 1996;4(11):1593-1606.
5. Luyben William L. Process modeling, simulation and control for chemical engineers. McGraw-Hill International Editions, 1990.
6. Eaton, J.W. & J.B. Rawlings. Model- Predictive Control of Chemical Processes, Chemical Engineering. Science 1992;47: 705-725.
7. Sanchez-Lopez A., Arroyo-Figueroa G., and Villavicencio A. Dynamic Matrix Control of Steam Temperature in Fossil Power Plant. Proceedings of the IFAC Symposium on Control of Power Plants and Power Systems, December 1995. p 275-280.
8. Fuzzy Logic Control Advances in Applications. In Verbruggen H.B. and Babuska R., editors. World Scientific Series in Robotics and Intelligent Systems, 1999.
9. Yen V.C. Rule selections in fuzzy expert systems. Expert Systems with Applications 1999;16(1):79-84.
10. Lee Chien Chuen. Fuzzy logic in control systems: fuzzy logic controller - Part I and II. IEEE Transactions On Systems, Man, And Cybernetics 1990; 20: 404-435.
11. Han-Xiong Li, and Gatland H.B. A new methodology for designing a fuzzy logic controller, IEEE Transactions on Systems, Man and Cybernetics 1995; 25:505-512.
12. Sanchez-Lopez A., Arroyo-Figueroa G., and Villavicencio A. Advanced Control Algorithms for Steam Temperature Control in Fossil Power Plants. Proceedings of the IFAC/CIGRE Symposium on Control of Power Systems and Power Plants, Beijing, China 1997, p. .198-204.

A Fed-Batch Fermentation Process Identification and Direct Adaptive Neural Control with Integral Term

Ieroham S. Baruch[1], Josefina Barrera-Cortés[2], and Luis A. Hernández[1]

CINVESTAV-IPN,
Ave. IPN No 2508,
A.P. 14-470 Mexico D.F., C.P. 07360 MEXICO
[1] Department of Automatic Control
baruch@ctrl.cinvestav.mx
[2] Department of Biotechnology and Bioengineering
jbarrera@mail.cinvestav.mx

Abstract. A nonlinear mathematical model of a feed-batch fermentation process of *Bacillus thuringiensis (Bt.)*, is derived. The obtained model is validated by experimental data. Identification and direct adaptive neural control systems with and without integral term are proposed. The system contains a neural identifier and a neural controller, based on the recurrent trainable neural network model. The applicability of the proposed direct adaptive neural control system of both proportional and integral-term direct adaptive neural control schemes is confirmed by comparative simulation results, also with respect to the λ-tracking control, which exhibit good convergence, but the I-term control could compensate a constant offset and proportional controls could not.

1 Introduction

The recent advances in understanding of the working principles of artificial neural networks has given a tremendous boost to the application of these modeling tools for control of nonlinear systems, [1], [2], [3], [4]. Most of the current applications rely on the classical NARMA approach; here a feedforward network is used to synthesize the nonlinear map, [2], [4]. This approach is powerful in itself but have some disadvantages, [2]: the network inputs are a number of past system inputs and outputs, so to find out the optimum number of past values, a trial and error must be carried on; the model is naturally formulated discrete time with fixed sampling period, so if the sampling period is changed, the network must be trained again; the problem associated with the stability, convergence and the rate of convergence of this networks are not clearly understood and there is not a framework available for analysis in vector-matricial form, [4]; the necessary condition of the plant order to be known. Besides to avoid this difficulties, a new recurrent Neural Networks (NN) topology, and a Backpropagation (BP) learning algorithm, [5], derived in a vector-matricial form, has been proposed, and its convergence, has been studied.

The adaptive control by Neural Networks (NNs) is of interest in Biotechnology for controlling *metabolite production*, [6], due to its adaptation to time varying process characteristics. A *metabolite* is a product of the microbial activity during the

R. Monroy et al. (Eds.): MICAI 2004, LNAI 2972, pp. 764–773, 2004.
© Springer-Verlag Berlin Heidelberg 2004

microorganism metabolism. The microbial cultivation can be carried out in *batch, fed-batch* or *continuous* fermentation, [7]. In some references, the nonlinear mathematical model of this fermentation process is linearized and a classical control is designed based on this linear equations, [8]. The major disadvantage of this approach is that it is not adaptive and could not respond to the changing process characteristics. In [9] a comparative study of linear, nonlinear and neural-network-based adaptive controllers for a class of fed-batch baker's and brewer's yeast fermentation is done. The paper proposed to use the method of neural identification control, given in [4], and applied Feedforward (FF) NNs (Multilayer Perceptron – MLP and Radial Basis Functions NN – RBF). The proposed control gives a good approximation of the nonlinear plants dynamics, better with respect to the other methods of control, but the applied static NNs have a great complexity, and the plant order has to be known. The application of Recurrent NNs (RNN) could avoid this problem and could reduce significantly the size of the applied NNs. For the bioprocess of interest (fermentation of *Bacillus thuringiensis*), RNN has been applied only for systems identification, [10], process prediction, [11], and an inverse plant model feedforward neural control, [12]. In the present paper, it is proposed to apply a direct adaptive recurrent neural control with integral term, transforming the control scheme, given in [12], which seems to be appropriate to capture the nonlinear dynamics, given by a mathematical model of the *fed-batch fermentation* of *Bacillus thuringiensis (Bt.)*, and to track the system reference in presence of noise.

2   Fed-Batch Fermentation Process Description

List of symbols used.

u(t)	Nutrient feeding rate at a *t* time, h^{-1}.
S_f	Substrate concentration in the feeding *g/l*.
S(t)	Substrate concentration in the culture at *t*, *g/l*.
X(t)	Biomass concentration in the culture at *t*, *g/l*.
V(t)	Culture volume into the fermentor at *t*, *l*.

Sketch of the Fed-batch fermentor is shown on Fig.1. The fed-batch fermentation model described a microorganism cultivation in a sterile reactor, [7], [11], maintained under operational conditions, adequate for microorganism growth at a desired specific growth rate (μ). The operational conditions considered are: temperature of 30°C, pH of 7.1 and dissolved oxygen in a concentration greater than 40%, [11]. The nutrients are supply during the exponential phase of *Bt.* growth.

To derive the model, the following considerations have been taken into account:

1) Yield coefficient (Y) is constant during all the fermentation; 2) The substrate consumption for the maintenance cells is negligible; 3) The increase volume in the fermentor is equal to the nutrient volume fed; 4) Cell dead is considered negligible during the fermentation. The model is based on the derivation of the Mass balance equations of the fermentor, [9], which are as follows:

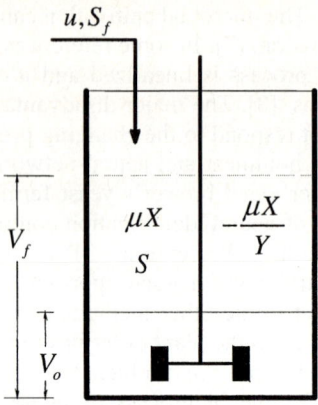

Fig.1. Fed-batch fermentation process of Bt.

- Evolution of the culture volume:

$$\frac{dV}{dt} = u(t) \tag{1}$$

- Evolution of the total microorganism mass in the fermentor:

$$\frac{d(VX)}{dt} = \mu(S(t)) X(t) V(t) \tag{2}$$

- Evolution of the limiting substrate in the fermentor:

$$\frac{d(SV)}{dt} = u(t) S_f - \frac{\mu(S(t)) X(t) V(t)}{Y} \tag{3}$$

- The current specific growth rate $\mu(S(t))$ is described by the Monod equation, [11]:

$$\mu(S(t)) = \frac{\mu_{max} S(t)}{K_m + S(t)} \tag{4}$$

Where: μ_{max} is the maximal growth rate; K_m is a Michaelis-Menten constant. The derivation of (2) and (3) gives:

$$\dot{V}(t) = u(t) \tag{5}$$

$$\dot{X}(t) = X(t) \left[\mu(s(t)) - \frac{u(t)}{V(t)} \right] \tag{6}$$

$$\dot{S}(t) = \frac{u(t)}{V(t)} (S_f - s(t)) - \frac{\mu(s(t)) X(t)}{Y} \tag{7}$$

Where: V(t): $\Re_{\geq 0} \rightarrow \Re_{>0}$ is a growth function, representing the culture volume in the fermentor at t (t is the current time); $u(t)$: $\Re_{\geq 0} \rightarrow \Re_{>0}$ is the input to the fermentor at t; S_f >0 is the substrate concentration in $u(t)$ at t; $S(t)$ is the substrate concentration in the culture at t; $X(t)$ is the cell concentration in the culture at t; finally, $Y>0$ and $\mu(t,S)$: $\Re_{\geq 0} \times \Re_{\geq 0} \rightarrow \Re_{\geq 0}$ are continuous functions for $\mu(t,0)=0$ $\forall$ $t\geq 0$. The existence of positive solution of the equations (5), (6), (7) has been proved by a theorem, [13].

3   Topology and Learning of the Recurrent Neural Network

A *Recurrent Trainable Neural Network* model (RTNN), and its learning algorithm of dynamic *Backpropagation-type*, (BP), together with the explanatory figures and stability proofs, are described in [5]. The RTNN topology, given in vector-matricial form, is described by the following equations:

$$X(k+1) = AX(k) + BU(K) \tag{8}$$

$$Z(k) = S[X(k)] \tag{9}$$

$$Y(k) = S[CZ(k)] \tag{10}$$

$$A = \text{block-diag}\,(a_{ii})\,;|a_{ii}|<1 \tag{11}$$

Where: Y, X, and U are, respectively, output, state and input vectors with dimensions l, n, m; A = block-diag (a_{ii}) is a (nxn)- state block-diagonal weight matrix; a_{ii} is an i-th diagonal block of A with (1x1) dimension. Equation (11) represents the local stability conditions, imposed on all blocks of A; B and C are (nxm) and (lxn)- input and output weight matrices; S is vector-valued sigmoid or hyperbolic tangent-activation function, [5]; the sub-index k is a discrete-time variable. The stability of the RTNN model is assured by the activation functions and by the local stability condition (11). The most commonly used BP updating rule applied, [5], is given by:

$$W_{ij}(k+1) = W_{ij}(k) + \eta\Delta W_{ij}(k) + \alpha\Delta W_{ij}(k-1) \tag{12}$$

Where: W_{ij} is a general weight, denoting each weight matrix element (C_{ij}, A_{ij}, B_{ij}) in the RTNN model, to be updated; ΔW_{ij}, (ΔC_{ij}, ΔJ_{ij}, ΔB_{ij}), is the weight correction of W_{ij}; while; η and α are learning rate parameters. The weight updates are computed by the following equations:

$$\Delta C_{ij}(k) = [T_j(k) - Y_j(k)]S'_j(Y_j(k))Z_i(k) \tag{13}$$

$$\Delta A_{ij}(k) = R\ X_i(k-1) \tag{14}$$

$$R = C_i(k)[T(k) - Y(k)]S'_j(Z_i(k)) \tag{15}$$

$$\Delta B_{ij}(k) = R\ U_i(k) \tag{16}$$

Where: ΔA_{ij} , ΔB_{ij} , ΔC_{ij} are weight corrections of the weights J_{ij}, B_{ij}, C_{ij}, respectively; (T-Y) is an error vector of the output RTNN layer, where T is a desired target vector and Y is a RTNN output vector, both with dimensions l; X_i is an i-th element of the state vector; R is an auxiliary variable; S_j' is derivative of the activation function. Stability proof of this learning algorithm, is given in [5]. The described above RTNN is applied for identification and adaptive control of a feed-batch fermentation process.

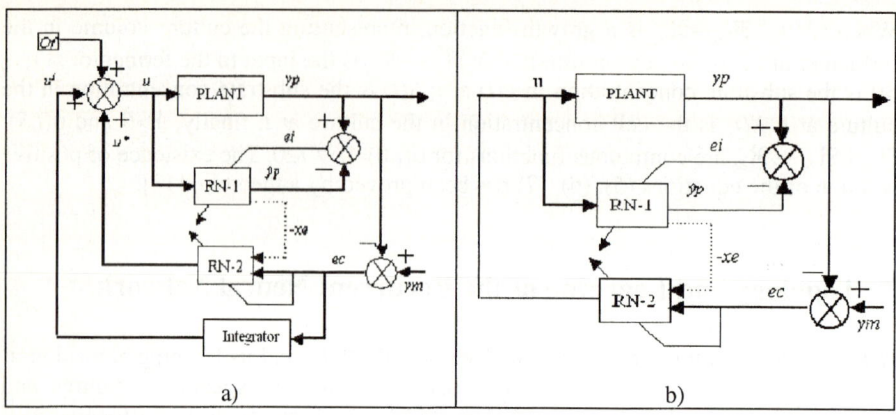

Fig.2. a) Block-diagram of the direct adaptive neural control with I-term. **b)** Block-diagram of the direct adaptive neural control without I-term.

4   A Direct Adaptive Neural Control System with Integral Term

Block-diagrams of the proposed direct adaptive control system with and without I-term are given on Fig.2.a), b). The control scheme, given on Fig.2.a), contains two RTNNs and a discrete-time integrator. The first RTNN is a neural identifier which delivers a state estimation vector as an entry to the second RTNN which is a neural controller. An additional entry to the neural controller is the control error $e_c(k) = y_m(k) - y_p(k)$. The integral of the control error $e_c(k)$ is an additional part of the control. The neural identifier RN-1 is learned by the identification error $e_i(k) = y_p(k) - \hat{y}_p(k)$ and the neural controller is learned by the control error $e_c(k)$ using the backpropagation algorithm, given by equations (12). The linear approximation of the neural identifier RN-1 is given by the equations:

$$x_e(k+1) = Ax_e(k) + Bu(k) \tag{17}$$

$$\hat{y}_p(k) = Cx_e(k) \tag{18}$$

The neural controller RN-2 equations also could be expressed in linear form, as it is:

$$u^*(k) = C^* x^*(k)$$

$$x^*(k+1) = A^* x^*(k) - B_1^* x_e(k) + B_2^* e_c(k) ; \tag{19}$$

$$e_c(k) = y_m(k) - y_p(k)$$

Where: $x^*(k)$ is n_c-dimensional state vector of the neural controller; $u^*(k)$ is an input vector with dimension m; $e_c(k)$ is a control error with dimension 1. The reference signal $y_m(k)$ is a train of pulses and the control objective is that the control error tends to zero when k tends to infinity. The control action is the sum of two components:

$$u(k) = u^i(k) + u*(k) \tag{20}$$

$$u^i(k+1) = u^i(k) + T_0 K_i e_c(k) \tag{21}$$

Where: $u^i(k)$ is the output of the integrator with dimension l (here l = m is supposed); Of is an offset variable with dimension m, which represents the plant's imperfections; T_0 is the period of discretization; K_i the integrator (lxl) gain matrix. Applying the z-transformation we could obtain the following expressions and z-transfer functions:

$$u^i(z) = (z-1)^{-1} T_0 K_i e_c(z) \tag{22}$$

$$q_1(z) = C^*(zI - A^*)^{-1} B_1^* \tag{23}$$

$$q_2(z) = C^*(zI - A^*)^{-1} B_2^* \tag{24}$$

$$p(z) = (zI - A)^{-1} B \; ; \; x_e(z) = p(z)u(z) \tag{25}$$

$$W^p(z) = C_p(zI - A_p)^{-1} B_p \; ;$$
$$y_p(z) = W^p(z)[u(z) + Of(z)] \tag{26}$$

Where: the equation (22) define the I-term dynamics; the equation (25) describes the dynamics of the hidden layer of the neural identifier RN-1, derived from the equation (17); the equation (26) represents the plant dynamics, derived in linear form, by means of a state-space model. The linearized equation (19) of the RN-2 also could be written in z-operator form, using the transfer functions (23) and (24), which yields:

$$u*(z) = -q_1(z)x_e(z) + q_2(z)e_c(z) \tag{27}$$

Substituting $x_e(z)$ from (25) in (27), and then the obtained result, together with (22) in the z-transformed equation (20), after some mathematical manipulations, we could obtain the following expression for the control signal:

$$u(z) = [I + q_1(z)p(z)]^{-1}[(z-1)^{-1} T_0 K_i + q_2(z)]e_c(z) \tag{28}$$

The substitution of the error $e_c(z)$ from (19) and the control $u(z)$ from (28) in the plant's equation (26) after some mathematical manipulation finally give:

$$\{(z-1)I + W^p(z)[I + q_1(z)p(z)]^{-1}[T_0 K_i + (z-1)q_2(z)]\} y_p(z)$$
$$= W^p(z)[I + q_1(z)p(z)]^{-1}[T_0 K_i + (z-1)q_2(z)]y_m(z) + \tag{29}$$
$$+ (z-1)W^p(z)Of(z)$$

From the equation (29), which describes the dynamics of the closed-loop system with I-term neural control, we could conclude that if the plant (26) is stable with minimum phase and the neural networks RN-1, 2 are convergent, which signifies that the transfer functions from (23) to (25) are also stable with minimum phase, so the closed-loop system, described by (29) will be stable. The term (z-1) is equivalent of a discrete-time derivative, so that a constant offset $O_f(k)$ could be compensated by the I-term and the control error tends to zero ($e_c(k) \rightarrow 0$).

5 Simulation Results

The fed-batch fermentation process model, given in part two, together with the initial condition values of the variables are used for simulation. These parameters are: $V(0) = 3l$, minimal volume required to operate the fermentor; $X(0) = 3.58 g/l$ bacillus concentration contained in the inoculate used for starting the *Bacillus thuringiensis* fermentation; $S(0) = 15.6 g/l$, initial concentration of glucose, which was taken as the limiting substrate; $S_f = 34.97 g/l$, ; $\mu_{max} = 1.216h^{-1}$, maximal specific growth rate reached for the applied operating conditions (X(0) and S(0), principally); $Km = 5$ and $Y = 7.5$ are average values calculated from the experimental data available and obtained for the applied operating conditions previously indicated. The topology and learning parameters of the neural identifier RN-1 are: (1, 7, 1), $\eta = 0.1$, and $\alpha = 0.01$. The neural identification is done in closed loop where the input of the plant $u(t)$ is the same as the input of the RN-1, and it is computed applying the λ-tracking method, [13], which is as follows:

$$e(t) = y_p(t) - y_m(t)$$

$$u(t) = sat_{[0,u_{max}]}(k(t)e(t))$$

$$\dot{k}(t) = \delta \begin{cases} (|e(t)| - \lambda)^r & si \ |e(t)| > \lambda \\ 0 & si \ |e(t)| \leq \lambda \end{cases}$$

(30)

Where: $u_{max} = 0.65$, $\lambda = 0.0025$, $\delta = 33$ and $r = 1$. The period of discretization is chosen as $To = 0.01$, which signifies that it is equivalent to 1 hour of the real process time. After the identification is completed the neural controller RN-2 changes the λ-tracking controller and both RTNNs continue with its learning. There are simulated 2 continuous operation cycles of 21 hours each. The neural controller RN-2 has the topology (8, 7, 1) and the learning parameters are: $\eta = 0.75$; $\alpha = 0.01$. The plant output $y_{p(k)}$ is normalized so to be compared with the output of the neural identifier RN-1, $\hat{y}_p(k)$, and to form the identification error $e_i(k)$, utilized to learn its weights. The graphical simulation results obtained applying an I-term neural control are given on Fig.3 A) from a) to h) and that using only a proportional control, are given on Fig. 3 B), from a) to d). For sake of comparison, both control results are compared with the results of λ-tracking control. In the three cases a 10% constant offset is added to the control signal. For all these cases of control used here: a) represents the output of the plant (biomass concentration), $y_p(k)$, compared with the reference signal, $y_m(k)$, in two cycles of 21 hour each; b) compare the output of the

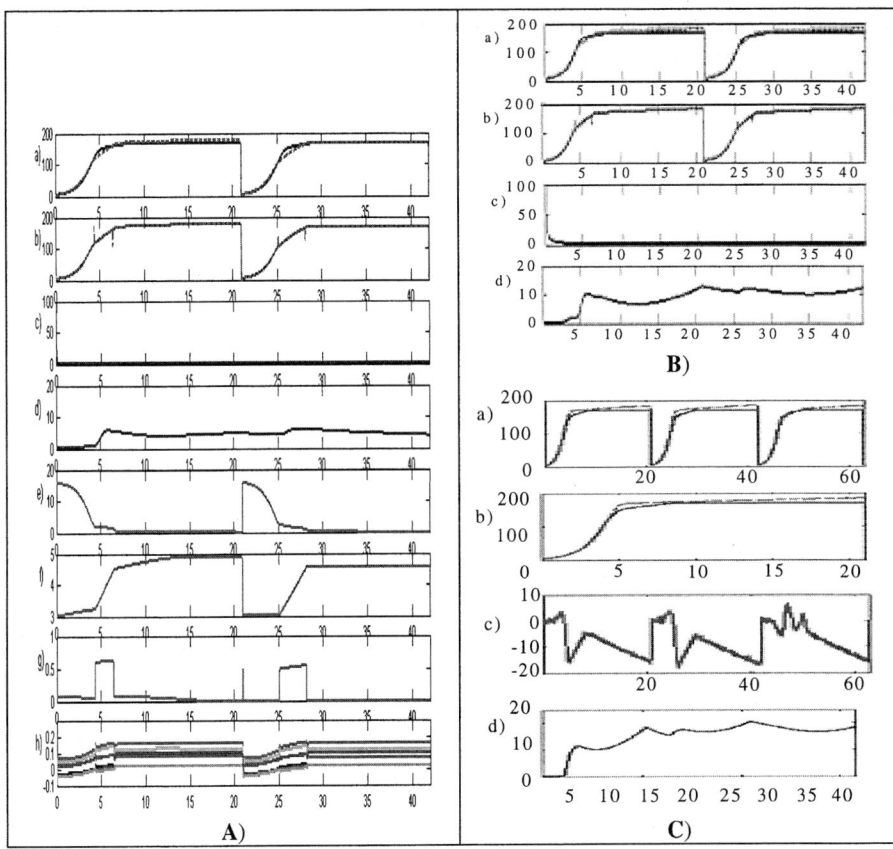

Fig.3. A). Simulation results with direct adaptive control containing I-term. a) comparison between the plant output *yp(k)* and the reference signal *ym(k)* [*g/l*]; b) comparison between the plant output *yp(k)y* and the output of neural identifier RN-1; c) MSE% of approximation; d) MSE% of control; e) evolution of the substrate consumption in the bioreactor S(k) [*g/l*]; f) evolution of the operation volume in the bioreactor V(k) [*l*] ; g) control signal, generated by RN-2, u(k) [*l/h*]; h) states of the RN-1, used for control. **B).** Simulation results using only direct adaptive proportional control. **C).** Simulation results using λ-tracking control. For the three control schemes figures a) to d) signifies the same thing and could not be repeated.

plant, $y_p(k)$, with the output of the neural identifier RN-1, $\hat{y}_p(k)$; c) represents the Means-Squared-Error (MSE %) of approximation, which is about 1% in the end of the learning; d) represents the MSE % of control. Only for the case A) - e) shows the S(k) substrate evolution on time; f) represents the volume of operation V(k) in the bioreactor which increments from the fourth hour of operation, due to the control input influent introduced in the bioreactor; g) is the alimentation flux in the bioreactor u(k); h) represents the state variables of the neural identifier RN-1, used for control. The comparison of the graphical results, obtained with the control, containing I-term (Fig. 3A), the control which not contain I-term (Fig. 3B), and the λ-tracking control (Fig. 3C), shows that the 10% offset caused an displacement of the plant output with respect of the reference and a substantial increment of the MSE% of control (from 4% to 8% for the proportional neural control and to 12% for the λ-tracking control), which means that proportional control systems could not compensate the offset at all and have static errors.

6 Conclusions

A nonlinear mathematical model of a feed-batch fermentation process of *Bacillus thuringiensis (Bt.)*, is derived. The obtained model is validated by experimental data. Schemes of direct adaptive neural control system with and without integral term are proposed. The system contains a neural identifier and a neural controller, based on the recurrent trainable neural network model. The applicability of the proposed direct adaptive neural control system of both proportional and integral-term direct adaptive neural control schemes is confirmed by comparative simulation results, also with respect to the λ-tracking control, which exhibit good convergence, but the I-term control could compensate a constant offset and proportional controls could not.

Acknowledgements. We want to thank CONACYT-MEXICO for the scholarship given to Alberto Hernández, MS student at the CINVESTAV-IPN and for the partial financial support of this research, through the project 42035-Z (SEP-CONACYT).

References

1. Hunt, K.J., Sbarbaro, D., Zbikowski, R., and Gawthrop, P.J. : Neural Networks for Control Systems - A Survey, Automatica, **28** (1992), 1083-1112.
2. Chen, S., and Billings, S. A. : Neural Networks for Nonlinear Dynamics System Modeling and Identification, International Journal of Control, **56** (1992), 263-289.
3. Pao, S.A., Phillips, S.M., and Sobajic, D. J. : Neural Net Computing and Intelligent Control Systems, International Journal of Control, **56** (1992), 263-289.
4. Narendra, K.S., and Parthasarathy, K. : Identification and Control of Dynamic Systems using Neural Networks, IEEE Transactions on NNs, **1** (1990), 4-27.
5. Baruch, I., Flores, J.M., Nava, F., Ramirez, I.R., and Nenkova, B. : An Adavanced Neural Network Topology and Learning, Applied for Identification and Control of a D.C. Motor. In: Proc. 1-st. Int. IEEE Symp. on Intelligent Systems, Varna, Bulgaria, (2002), 289-295.
6. Kumar, PA, Sharma, RP, and Malik, VS. : The Insecticidal Proteins of *Bacillus thuringiensis*. Advances in Applied Microbiology, 42 (1997), 1-43.
7. Dulmage, H.T. : Production of Bacteria for Biological Control of Insects, Biological Control in Crop Production. In: G.G. Papavisas, ed. Allenheld Osmun, Totowa, (1981), 129-141.
8. Levisauskas, D., Simutis, R., Botvitz, D., and Lubbert, A. : Automatic control of the specific growth rate in fed-batch cultivation processes, based on an exhaust gas analysis, Bioprocess Engineering, 15 (1996), 145-150.
9. Boskovic, J. D., and Narendra K. S. : Comparison of Linear, Nonlinear and Neural-network-based Adaptive Controllers for a Class of Fed-batch Fermentation Processes, Automatica, 31 (1995), 817-840.

10. Zhang, Q., Reid, J.F., Litchfield, J.B., Ren, J., and Wu, Chang S.: A Prototype Neural Network Supervised Control System for *Bacillus thuringiensis* fermentations, Biotechnology and Bioengineering, 43 (1994), 483-489.
11. Valdez-Castro, L., Baruch, I., and Barrera-Cortes, J. : Neural networks applied to the prediction of fed-batch fermentation kinetics of *Bacillus thuringiensis*, Bioprocess and Biosystems Engineering, 25 (2003), 229-233.
12. Baruch, I., Barrera Cortes, J., Medina, J.P., and.Hernandez, L.A : An Adaptive Neural Control of a Fed-Batch Fermentation Processes. In: Proc. of the IEEE Conference on Control Applications, Istanbul, Turkey, June 23-25, 2 (2003), 808-812.
13. Giorgieva, P., and Ilchmann A. : Adaptive λ-tracking control of activated sludge processes, International Journal of Control, **74** (2001), 1247-1259.

A Fuzzy-Neural Multi-model for Mechanical Systems Identification and Control

Ieroham S. Baruch, Rafael Beltran L, Jose-Luis Olivares, and Ruben Garrido

CINVESTAV-IPN, Ave. IPN No 2508,
A.P. 14-470 Mexico D.F., C.P. 07360 MEXICO
{baruch,lolivares,garrido}@ctrl.cinvestav.mx,
rbeltran_1976@yahoo.com.mx

Abstract. The paper proposed a new fuzzy-neural recurrent multi-model for systems identification and states estimation of complex nonlinear mechanical plants with friction. The parameters and states of the local recurrent neural network models are used for a local direct and indirect adaptive trajectory tracking control systems design. The designed local control laws are coordinated by a fuzzy rule based control system. The applicability of the proposed intelligent control system is confirmed by simulation and comparative experimental results, where a good convergent results, are obtained.

1 Introduction

In the recent decade, the *Neural Networks* (*NN*) became universal tool for many applications. The *NN* modeling and application to system identification, prediction and control was discussed for many authors [1], [2], [3]. Mainly, two types of *NN* models are used: *Feedforward* (*FFNN*) and *Recurrent* (*RNN*). All drawbacks of the described in the literature *NN* models could be summarized as follows: 1) there exists a great variety of *NN* models and their universality is missing, [1], [2], [3]; 2) all *NN* models are sequential in nature as implemented for systems identification (the *FFNN* model uses one or two tap-delays in the input, [1] and *RNN* models usually are based on the autoregressive model, [2], which is one-layer sequential one); 3) some of the applied *RNN* models are are not trainable in the feedback part; 4) most of them are dedicated to a *SISO* and not to a *MIMO* applications, [2]; 5) in more of the cases, the stability of the *RNN* is not considered, [2], especially during the learning; 6) in the case of *FFNN* application for systems identification, the plant is given in one of the four described in [1] plant models, the linear part of the plant model, especially the system order, has to be known and the *FFNN* approximates only the non-linear part of this model, [1]; 7) all these *NN* models are nonparametric ones, [3], and so, not applicable for an adaptive control systems design; 8) all this *NN* models does not perform state and parameter estimation in the same time, [3]; 9) all this models are appropriate for identification of nonlinear plants with smooth, single, odd, nonsingular nonlinearities, [1]. *Baruch et all*, [4], in their previous paper, applied the state-space approach to describe *RNN* in an universal way, defining a Jordan canonical two - or three-layer *RNN* model, named *Recurrent Trainable Neural Network* (*RTNN*), and a *dynamic Backpropagation(BP) algorithm of its learning*. This

R. Monroy et al. (Eds.): MICAI 2004, LNAI 2972, pp. 774–783, 2004.

NN model is a parametric one, permitting the use of the obtained parameters and states during the learning for control systems design. Furthermore, the *RTNN* model is a system state predictor/estimator, which permits to use the obtained system states directly for state-space control. For complex nonlinear plants, *Baruch et al*, [5], proposed to use a fuzzy-neural multi-model, which is also applied for systems with friction identification, [6], [7]. In [8] a wide scope of references using fuzzy-neural approach for nonlinear plants approximation is given and the RNN architecture of *Frasconi-Gori-Soda*, is used. The main disadvantage of this work is that the applied *RNN* model there is sequential in nature. Depending on the model order, this *RNN* model generates different computational time delays, which makes difficult the fuzzy system synchronization. So, the aim of this paper is to go ahead, using the *RTNN* as an identification and state estimation tool in direct and indirect adaptive fuzzy-neural multi-model based control systems of nonlinear plants, illustrated by representative simulation and comparative experimental results.

2 Models Description

2.1 Recurrent Neural Model and Learning

The *RTNN* model is described by the following equations, [4]:

$$X(k+1) = JX(k)+BU(k) \tag{1}$$

$$Z(k)=S[X(k)] \tag{2}$$

$$Y(k) = S[CZ(k)] \tag{3}$$

$$J = \text{block-diag } (J_i); \; |J_i| < 1 \tag{4}$$

Where: $X(k)$ is a N - state vector; $U(k)$ is a M- input vector; $Y(k)$ is a L- output vector; $Z(k)$ is an auxiliary vector variable with dimension L; $S(x)$ is a vector-valued activation function with appropriate dimension; J is a weight-state diagonal matrix with elements J_i ; equation (4) is a stability conditon; B and C are weight input and output matrices with appropriate dimensions and block structure, corresponding to the block structure of J. As it can be seen, the given *RTNN* model is a completely parallel parametric one, with parameters - the weight matrices J, B, C, and the state vector $X(k)$, so it is useful for identification and control purposes. The *controllability* and *observability* of this model are considered in [4]. The general *BP* learning algorithm is given as:

$$W_{ij}(k+1) = W_{ij}(k) +\eta \, \Delta W_{ij}(k) +\alpha \, \Delta W_{ij}(k-1) \tag{5}$$

Where: W_{ij} (C, J, B) is the ij-th weight element of each weight matrix (given in parenthesis) of the *RTNN* model to be updated; ΔW_{ij} is the weight correction of W_{ij}; η, α are learning rate parameters. The updates ΔC_{ij} , ΔJ_{ij}, ΔB_{ij} of C_{ij} , J_{ij}, B_{ij} are given by:

$$\Delta C_{ij}(k) = [T_j(k) - Y_j(k)] \, S_j'(Y_j(k)) \, Z_i(k) \tag{6}$$

$$\Delta J_{ij}(k) = R_1 \, X_i(k-1) \tag{7}$$

$$\Delta B_{ij}(k) = R_1 \, U_i(k) \tag{8}$$

$$R_1 = C_i(k) \, [T(k)-Y(k)] \, S_j'(Z_j(k)) \tag{9}$$

Where: T is a target vector with dimension L; [T-Y] is an output error vector also with the same dimension; R_1 is an auxiliary variable; S'(x) is the derivative of the activation function, which for the hyperbolic tangent is $S_j'(x) = 1-x^2$. The stability of the learning algorithm and its applicability for systems identification and control, are proven in [4], where the results of a *DC* motor neural control, are also given.

2.2 Fuzzy-Neural Multi-model

For complex dynamic systems identification, the Takagi-Sugeno fuzzy rule, cited in [8], admits to use in the consequent part a crisp function, which could be a static or dynamic (state-space) model. Some authors, referred in [8], proposed as a consequent crisp function to use a *NN* function. *Baruch et all.* [5], [6], [7], proposed as a consequent crisp function to use a *RTNN* function model, so to form a fuzzy-neural multi-model. The fuzzy rule of this model is given by the following statement:

$$R_i: \quad \text{IF x is } A_i \text{ THEN } y_i \,(k+1)= N_i\,[x(k), u(k)], \; i=1,2,.., P \tag{10}$$

Where: $N_i(.)$ denotes the *RTNN* model, given by equations (1) to (3); i -is the model number; P is the total number of models, corresponding *Ri*. The output of the fuzzy neural multi-model system is given by the following equation:

$$Y= \Sigma_i \, w_i \, y_i = \Sigma_i \, w_i \, N_i(x,u) \tag{11}$$

Where w_i are weights, obtained from the membership functions, [9]. As it could be seen from the equation (11), the output of the approximating fuzzy- neural multi-model is obtained as a weighted sum of *RTNN* functions, [9], given in the consequent part of (10). In the case when the intervals of the variables, given in the antecedent parts of the rules are not overlapping, the weights obtain values one and the weighted sum (11) is converted in a simple sum, and this simple case, called fuzzy-neural multi-model, [7], [8], [11], will be considered here.

3 An Adaptive Fuzzy-Neural Control System Design

3.1 A Direct Adaptive Fuzzy-Neural Control

The structure of the entire identification and control system contains a *fuzzyfier,* a *Fuzzy Rule-Based System (FRBS),* and *a set of RTNN models.* The system does not need a *defuzzyfier,* because the *RTNN* models are *crisp limited nonlinear state-space models.* The direct adaptive neural multimodel control system incorporates in its *FRBS* a set of *RTNN* controllers. The control fuzzy rules are:

$$R_i:\quad \text{If x is } A_i \text{ then } u_i = U_i(k), \text{ i=1, 2 ,.., L} \tag{12}$$

$$U_i(k) = -N_{fb,i}[x_i(k)] + N_{ff,i}[r_i(k)] \tag{13}$$

Where: r(k) is the reference signal; x(k) is the system state; $N_{fb,i}[x_i(k)]$ and $N_{ff,i}[r_i(k)]$ are the feedforward and feedback parts of the fuzzy-neural control. The total control, issued by the fuzzy neural multi-model system is described by the following equation:

$$U(k) = \Sigma_i \, w_i \, U_i(k) \tag{14}$$

Where w_i are weights, obtained from the membership functions, [9], corresponding to the rules (12). As it could be seen from the equation (14), the control could be obtained as a weighted sum of controls, [11], given in the consequent part of (12). In the case when the intervals of the variables, given in the antecedent parts of the rules, are not overlapping, the weights obtain values one and the weighted sum (14) is converted in a simple sum, and this particular multi-model case will be considered here. Block-diagram of a direct adaptive multi-model control system is given on Fig. 1. The block-diagram contains a fuzzy-neural identifier and a fuzzy-neural controller.

3.2 An Indirect Adaptive Fuzzy-Neural Control

The block diagram of the indirect adaptive fuzzy-neural control system is given in Fig. 2. The structure of the system contains a fuzzy-neural identifier, which contains two neural models *RTNN-1,2* issuing a state $(x_i(k))$ and parameter (Ji, Bi, Ci) information to local linear controllers. The multimodel control is given by the same rule (12), but here the local control, [11], is given by:

$$U_i(k) = (C_i\,B_i)^{-1}\{C_i\,J_i\,X_i(k) + r_i(k+1) + \gamma\,[r_i(k) - Y_i(k)]\};\ i=1,2,..,P \tag{15}$$

In this particular case, we use only two neural nets for process identification. The RTNN-1 corresponds to the positive part of the plant output signal, and the RTNN-2 corresponds to the negative one. For this two neural models – two correspondent controls $U_1(k)$ and $U_2(k)$ are computed by equation (14), where the control parameter γ is a real number between 0.999 y 0.999 and $r_i(k)$ is the correspondent local reference signal. If the RTNN is observable and controllable, then the local matrix product $C_i\,B_i$ is different from zero $(C_i\,B_i \neq 0)$.

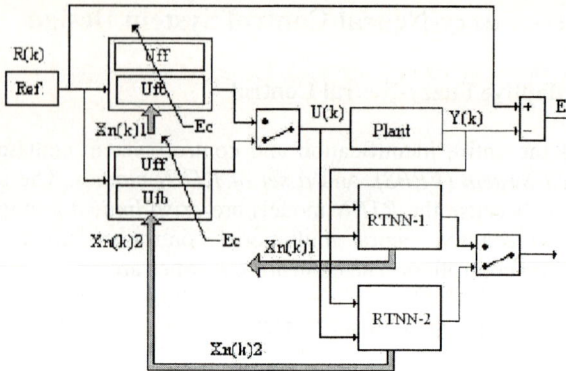

Fig.1. Block-diagram of the direct adaptive fuzzy-neural multimodel control system.

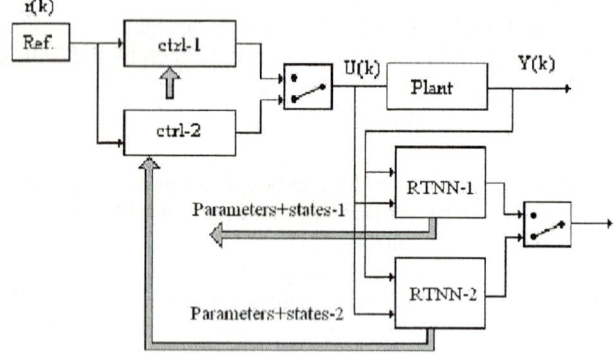

Fig.2. Block-diagram of the indirect adaptive fuzzy-neural multimodel control system.

Next both adaptive control schemes using the multi-*RTNN* model will be applied for a real-time identification and control of nonlinear mechanical system. It is expected that the application of a learning adaptive model like the fuzzy-neural *RTNN* multi-model will be well suited for identification and control of such nonlinear process with unknown variable parameters and dynamic effects.

4   Simulation Results

Let us consider a *DC*-motor - driven nonlinear mechanical system with friction (see [9] for more details about the friction model), to have the following friction parameters: $\alpha = 0.001$ m/s; $F_s^+ = 4.2$ N; $F_s^- = -4.0$ N; $\Delta F^+ = 1.8$ N ; $\Delta F = -1.7$ N ; $v_{cr} = 0.1$ m/s; $\beta = 0.5$ Ns/m. Let us also consider that position and velocity measurements are taken with period of discretization To = 0.1 s, the system gain ko = 8, the mass m = 1 kg, and the load disturbance depends on the position and the velocity, $(d(t) = d_1 q(t) + d_2 v(t); d_1 = 0.25; d_2 = -0.7)$. So the discrete-time model of the 1-DOF mass mechanical system with friction is obtained in the form, [6], [7]:

$$x_1(k+1) = x_2(k) \qquad (16)$$

$$x_2(k+1)=-0.025x_1(k)-0.3x_2(k)+0.8u(k)-0.1fr(k) \qquad (17)$$

$$v(k) = x_2(k) - x_1(k) \qquad (18)$$

$$y(k) = 0.1\,x_1(k) \qquad (19)$$

Where: $x_1(k)$, $x_2(k)$ are system states; $v(k)$ is system velocity; $y(k)$ is system position; fr(k) is a friction force, taken from [9], with given up values of friction parameters. The graphics of the simulation results, obtained with the direct adaptive control system, given on Fig. 1, are shown on Fig. 3.a,b,c,d. The graphics on Figure 3.a compare the output of the plant with the reference which is r(k)= 0.8 sin(2πk). To form the local neural controls, this reference signal is divided in two parts – positive and negative. The time of learning is 60 sec. The two identification *RTNNs* have architectures (1, 5, 1) and the two feedback control *RTNNs* have architectures (5, 5, 1). The two feedforward *RTNNs* architectures are (1, 5, 1). The learning parameters are η = 0.1, α = 0.2. Fig. 3.b shows the results of identification, where the output of the plant is divided in two parts, which are identified by two *RTNNs*. The combined control signal and the *MSE%* of control are given on Fig. 3. c, d. As it could be seen from the last graphics, the *MSE%* rapidly decreases, and reached values below 1%.

The graphics of the simulation results, obtained with the indirect adaptive control system, given on Fig. 2, are shown on Fig. 4.a,b,c,d. Fig. 4.a compare the output of the plant with the reference signal (r(k)= 10 sin(2πk)), which is divided in two parts – positive and negative. The time of learning is 100 sec. The two identification and the two *FF* control *RTNNs* have topologies (1, 5, 1). The learning rate parameters are η = 0.001, α = 0.01, and the control parameter is γ=0.1. Fig. 4.b shows the results of identification, where the output of the plant is divided in two parts, identified by two *RTNNs. The state and parameter information, issued by the identification multimodel is used to design a linear control law.* The combined control signal and the *MSE%* of control are given on Fig. 4.c,d. As it could be seen from the last graphics, the *MSE%* rapidly decreases, and reached values below 1.5 %.

5   Experimental Results

In this section, the effectiveness of the multi-model scheme is illustrated by a real-time *DC*-motor position control, [4], using two *RTNNs*, (positive and negative) for the systems output, control and reference signals. A 24 Volts, 8 Amperes *DC* motor, driven by a power amplifier and connected by a data acquisition control board *(Multi-Q*[TM] *)* with the *PC,* has been used. The *RTNN* was programmed in *MatLab*[TM]-*Simulink*[TM] and *WinCon*[TM] , which is a real-time *Windows 95* application that runs *Simulink* generated code using the real-time *Workshop* to achieve digital real-time control on a *PC.* The load is charged and discharged on the *DC* motor shaft by means of electrically switched clutch. The control signal is designed in two parts – feedback and feedforward. For sake of simplicity, the feedback part is realized as a P-controller (Kp=5) and only a feedforward part of the fuzzy-neural control scheme is applied, which allow us to omit the system identification.

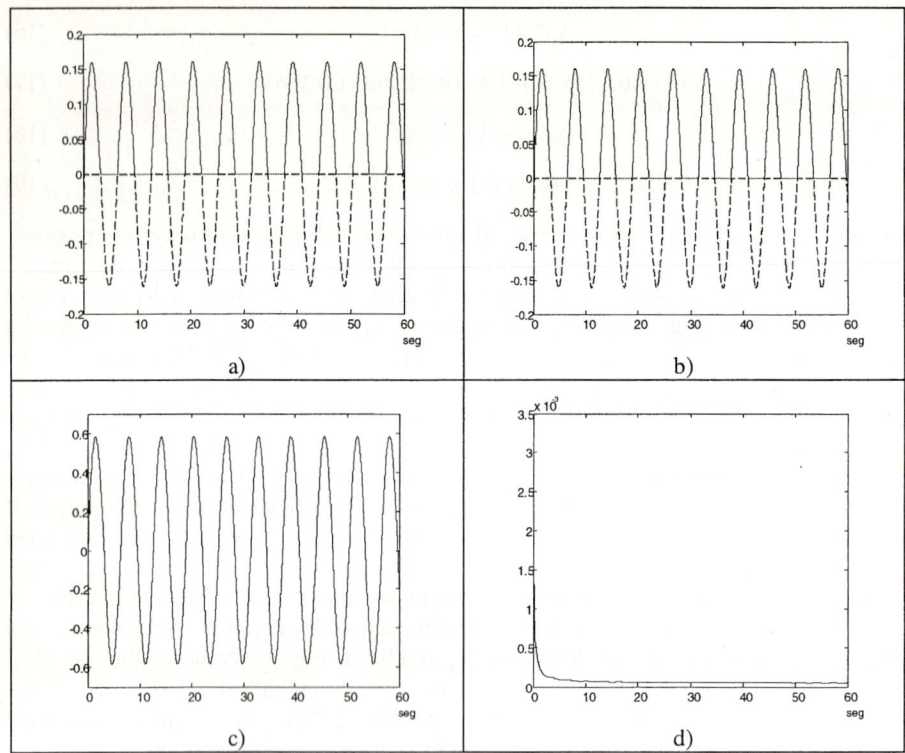

Fig. 3. Graphical results of simulation using direct adaptive fuzzy-neural multimodel control. a) Comparison of the output of the plant and the reference signal; b) Comparison of the output of the plant and the outputs of the identification RTNNs; c) Combined control signal; d) Mean Squared Error of control (MSE%).

So, the neural multimodel feedforward controller is realized by means of two *RTNNs* – positive and negative. The graphics of the experimental results, obtained with this control are given on Fig. 5.a-e. Fig. 5.a, b compare the DC motor shaft position with the reference signal ($r(k) = 1.5 * [\sin(0.2 * k)]$) in the absence of load (Fig. 5a) (0-45 sec) and in the presence of load (Fig. 5b) (70-150 sec.). The control signal and the *MSE%* of reference tracking are given on Fig.5c, d, respectively for the complete time of the experiment (0-200 sec.). The architectures of the two feed-forward *RTNNs* are (1, 5, 1). The learning rate parameters are η = 0.003, α = 0.0001 and the period of discretization is To = 0.001 sec. The *MSE%* exhibits fast convergence and rapidly reached values below 1%. For sake of comparison, the same experiment was repeated for DC-motor position control with PD controller (Kp=3, Kd=0.05). The results obtained without load are almost equal to that of Fig. 5a, but when the load is charged on DC-motor shaft, a lack of tracking precision is observed (see Fig. 5e, 45-100 sec.).

The obtained values of the *MSE%* for both control experiments (with a neural multimodel control – 0.761% and with a PD control – 0.286%) show that the precision of tracking of the neural multimodel control is about two times greater that

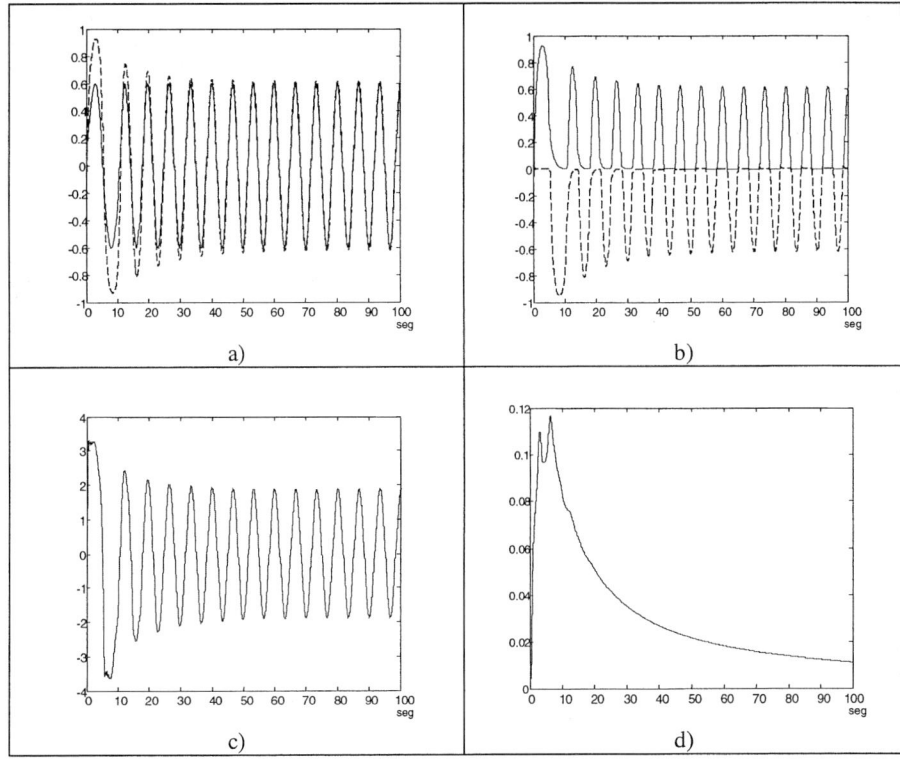

Fig. 4. Graphical results of simulation using indirect adaptive fuzzy-neural multimodel control. a) Comparison of the output of the plant and the reference signal; b) Comparison of the output of the plant and the outputs of the identification RTNNs; c) Combined control signal; d) Mean Squared Error of control (MSE%).

that, obtained by means of the PD control. Furthermore, the neural multimodel control could adapt to a load variation and the PD control needs gain update.

6 Conclusions

A two-layer Recurrent Neural Network *(RNN)* and an improved dynamic Backpropagation method of its learning, is described. For a complex nonlinear plant identification and control, a fuzzy-neural multi-model, is used. The fuzzy-neural multi-model, containing two *RNNs*, is applied for real-time identification and direct adaptive control of nonlinear mechanical system with friction, where the simulation results exhibit a good convergence. The obtained comparative experimental results of a *DC*-motor control are also acceptable, which confirms the applicability of the proposed fuzzy neural multi-model control scheme.

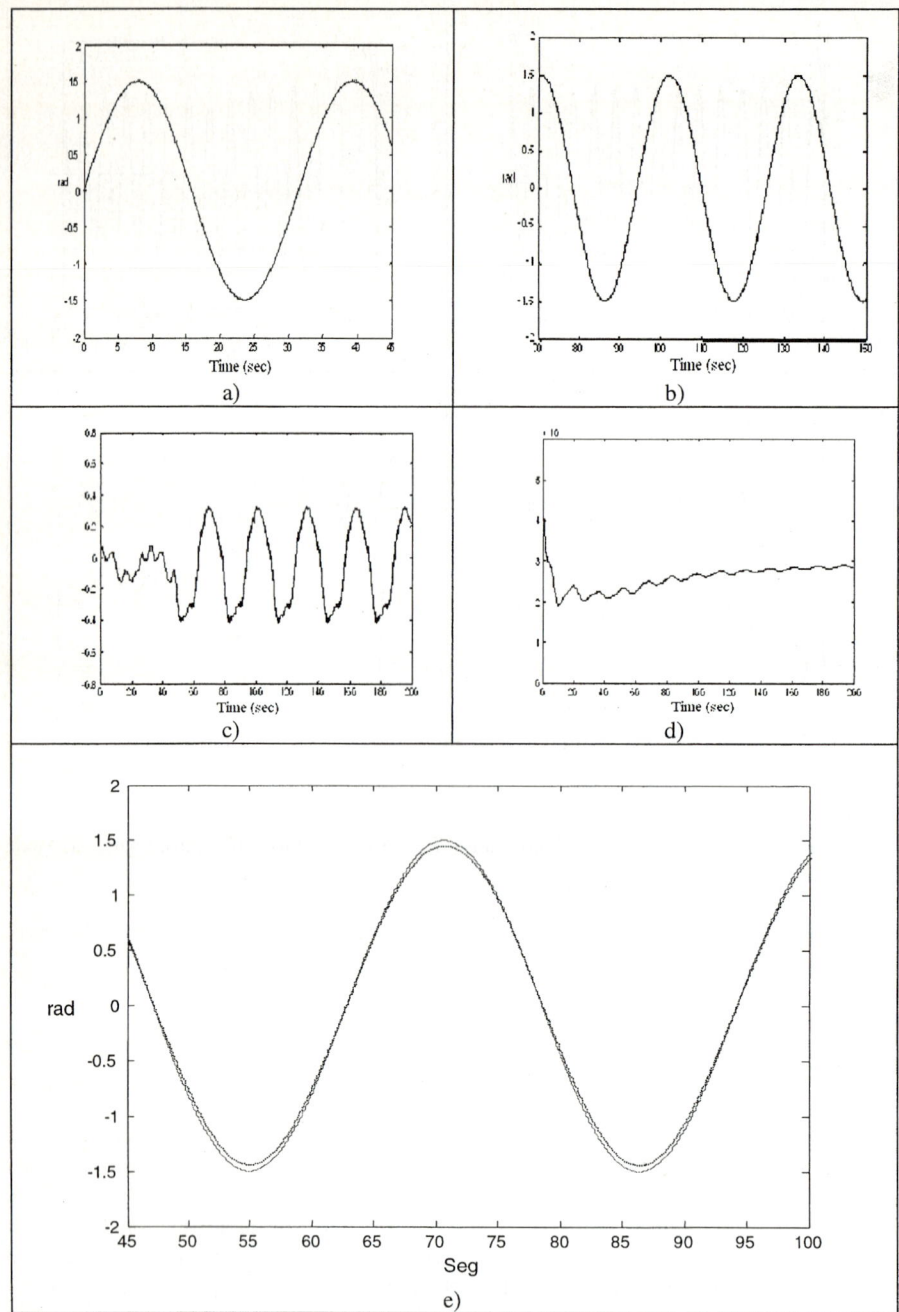

Fig. 5. Experimental results of a DC motor position control using direct adaptive neural multimodel control scheme. Comparison of the output of the plant and the reference signal: a) without load (0-45 sec.); b) with load (70-150 sec.); c) Combined control signal (0-200 sec.); d) Mean Squared Error of control; e) Comparison of the output of the plant and the reference signal for control with PD controller and load on a DC-motor shaft (45-100 sec.).

References

1. Narendra K. S., Parthasarathy K. : Identification and Control of Dynamic Systems using Neural Networks. IEEE Transactions on NNs, 1 (1990), 4-27.
2. Sastry P. S., Santharam G., Unnikrishnan K.P. : Memory Networks for Identification and Control of Dynamical Systems. IEEE Transactions on NNs, 5 (1994), 306-320.
3. Hunt K.J., Sbarbaro D., Zbikowski R., Gawthrop P. J. : Neural Network for Control Systems-A Survey. Automatica, **28** (1992), 1083-1112.
4. Baruch I., Flores J.M., Nava F., Ramirez I.R., Nenkova B.: An Adavanced Neural Network Topology and Learning, Applied for Identification and Control of a D.C. Motor. Proc. of the First Int. IEEE Symposium on Intelligent Systems, Sept. (2002), Varna, Bulgaria, 289-295.
5. Baruch I., Gortcheva E. : Fuzzy Neural Model for Nonlinear Systems Identification, Proc. of the IFAC Worshop on Algorithms and Architectures for Real-Time Control, AARTC'98, 15-17 April, (1998), Cancun, Mexico, 283-288.
6. Baruch I., Garrido R., Mitev A., Nenkova B.: A Neural Network Approach for Stick-Slip Model Identification. Proc. of the 5-th Int. Conf. on Engineering Applications of Neural Networks, EANN'99, 13-15 Sept, (1999), Warsaw, Poland, 183-188.
7. Baruch, I., Flores, J.M., Martinez, J.C., Nenkova, B.: Fuzzy- Neural Models for Real-Time Identification and control of a Mechanical System. (St.Cerri, D.Dochev-Eds.) Artificial Intelligence: Methodology, Systems and Applications, 9-th International conference, AIMSA 2000, Varna, Bulgaria, September 2000. Lecture Notes in Artificial Intelligence 1904, Springer, Berlin, (2000), 292-300.
8. Mastorocostas P.A., Theocharis J.B.: A Recurrent Fuzzy-Neural Model for Dynamic System Identification. IEEE Trans. on SMC – Part B: Cybernetics, 32 (2002), 176-190.
9. S.W. Lee, J.H. Kim.: Robust adaptive stick-slip friction compensation. IEEE Trans. on Ind. Electr., **42** (1995), 474-479.

Tuning of Fuzzy Controllers

Eduardo Gómez-Ramírez and Armando Chávez-Plascencia

Laboratory of Advance Technology Research and Development
LIDETEA
La Salle University
Benjamín Franklin 47 Col. Condesa
06140, México, D.F. México
egr@ci.ulsa.mx, al980576@ulsa.edu.mx

Abstract. The fuzzy controllers could be broadly used in control processes thanks to their good performance, one disadvantage is the problem of fuzzy controllers tuning, this implies the handling of a great quantity of variables like: the ranges of the membership functions, the shape of this functions, the percentage of overlap among the functions, the number of these and the design of the rule base, mainly, and more even when they are multivariable systems due that the number of parameters grows exponentially with the number of variables. The importance of the tuning problem implies to obtain fuzzy system that decrease the settling time of the processes in which it is applied. In this work a very simple algorithm is presented for the tuning of fuzzy controllers using only one variable to adjust the performance of the system. The results will be obtained considering the relationship that exists between the membership functions and the settling time.

1 Introduction

The methodology for tuning a controller some times is a heuristic work. Some elements are important to consider in the tuning, like the bandwidth, the error in steady state, or the speed of response. It is possible to use this information or to make different tests to find the optimal parameters. In the case of a PID controller it is necessary to find three parameters (proportional gain, derivative time, and integral parameters). In the case of fuzzy controllers, there are many parameters to compute like, number of membership functions, ranges of every function, the rules of membership functions, the shape of this functions, the percentage of overlap, etc. [1–3]. Many people prefer to use a very well known PID controller that a fuzzy controller with all these parameters to estimate. This is a very important reason that in the industry this intelligent controller is not used.

The tuning of any controller's type implies the adjustment of the parameters to obtain a wanted behavior or a good approach with a minimal error to the desire response. The different methods published in the area for the problem of fuzzy controllers' tuning use methodologies like evolutionary computation [4–6] and artificial neural networks [7–9]. This methods search the solution according to objective functions, parameter estimation, gradient error, etc., but in many cases these

R. Monroy et al. (Eds.): MICAI 2004, LNAI 2972, pp. 784–793, 2004.

alternatives have serious convergence problems, either a very complex mathematical representation, the computation time is very big, or it is possible that the solution computed is only a local minima of the solution.

In this paper a very simple method for tuning fuzzy controllers is presented using only one parameter. In this case the paper is based in the relation between the stabilization time and the range of the membership functions. To explain the paper is structured in the following way: In section 2 of this work the relationship that exists among the location of the membership functions with the transfer characteristic is presented. In section 3 the system used is described and the controller's description for the tuning is presented. The section 4 outlines an algorithm of parametric tuning that modifies the operation points that define the group of membership functions. In the section 5 the results of the simulations are shown for different values of the tuning factor and different graphics that show the behavior of the settling time in function of the tuning factor. The simulations were carried out using Simulink of Matlab. Finally, some conclusions end this paper.

2 Transfer Characteristic of a Fuzzy Controller

The transfer characteristic allows defining the fuzzy controller's behavior in its answer speed, sensitive and reaction under disturbances, using the location of the operation points. As it will be described later on, this is related with the election of the fuzzy controller's gain dy/dx where y is the output and x is the input of the system, in different regions of the domain x, since given a domain x, the localization of the operation points determines the slopes of the transfer characteristic in different parts of the domain x.

Case 1. For a flat slope in the middle of the domain x and increasing slopes toward increasing $|x|$ values, choose larger distances between operations points in the middle of domain (see figure 1). This means:

$$\text{For } |x_2| > |x_1| \quad \Rightarrow \quad |dy/dx|_{x_2} > |dy/dx|_{x_1}$$

Case 2. For a steep slope in the middle of the domain x and decreasing slopes toward increasing $|x|$ values, choose smaller distances between operations points in the middle of domain (see figure 2). This means:

$$\text{For } |x_2| > |x_1| \quad \Rightarrow \quad |dy/dx|_{x_2} < |dy/dx|_{x_1}$$

Option 1 should be chosen if for small errors a slow reaction to disturbances of the system under control is required and option 2 should be chosen if for small errors the system is supposed to be sensitive with respect to disturbances.

Note that in the previous figures the values for the intervals of the membership function are important for the slopes and the speed of the controller response. If the membership functions "expand" (figure 1) then the response is slower than a compress group of membership functions (figure 2).

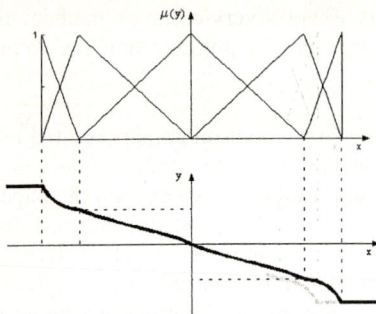
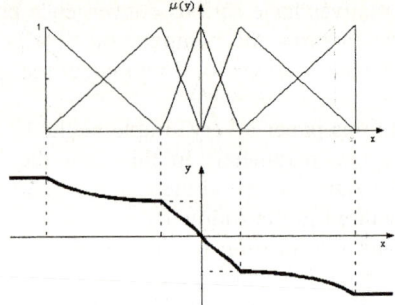

Fig. 1. Relationship between the location of the membership functions and the transfer characteristic for the case 1.

Fig. 2. Relationship between the location of the membership functions and the transfer characteristic for the case 2.

3 Fuzzy Controller

For the analysis and simulations with the tuning algorithm a second order system has been considered:

$$\frac{1}{0.45\,s^2 + 2\,s + 1} \tag{1}$$

overdamped with a damping ratio $\xi = 1.4907$ and a natural frequency $\omega_n = 1.4907\ rad\,/\,s$.

The fuzzy controller designed for the control of the plant described previously is a system TISO (two inputs-one output) where the inputs are the error and the change of error while the output is the control action. Each one of the controller's variables has been divided in 5 fuzzy regions. The fuzzy associative memory, integrated by 25 rules, it is shown in the figure 4.

The membership functions were defined in triangular shape for the middle and in a trapezoidal shape in the extremes, such that always have it overlap in the grade of membership $\mu(x) = 0.5$ (figures 5, 6 and 7). These membership functions will be considered later on as the initial conditions for the proposed algorithm. The control surface for the fuzzy controller under its initial conditions is shown in the figure 8.

4 Tuning Algorithm

The objective of the tuning algorithm is to be able to manipulate, by means of a single variable and in a simple way, the settling time of the system, from the answer without controller until the response equivalent to 1/5 of the settling time of the answer without controller. The response must be fulfilled too with the constraints of small overshoots and without persistent oscillations, which means, a very smooth response.

Table 1. Fuzzy variables for the controller

Input variables		Output variable
error	*change of error*	*control action*
GN: Big negative	GN: Big negative	DG: Big diminution
MN: Medium negative	MN: Medium negative	DP: Small diminution
Z: Zero	Z: Zero	M: Hold
MP: Medium positive	MP: Medium positive	AP: Small increase
GP: Big positive	GP: Big positive	AG: Big increase

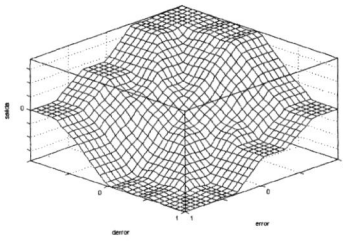

e $\dot{e}$	GN	MN	Z	MP	GP
GN	AG	AG	AP	DP	DG
MN	AG	AP	M	M	DG
Z	AG	AP	M	DP	DG
MP	AG	M	M	DP	DG
GP	AG	AP	DP	DG	DG

Fig. 3. Example of control surface of a fuzzy controller

Fig. 4. Fuzzy associative memory for the control system

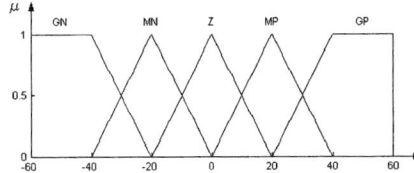

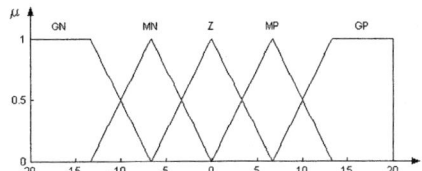

Fig. 5. Membership functions for the input variable *error*

Fig. 6. Membership functions for the input variable *change of error*

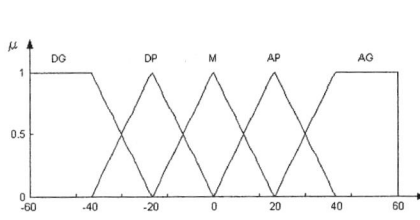

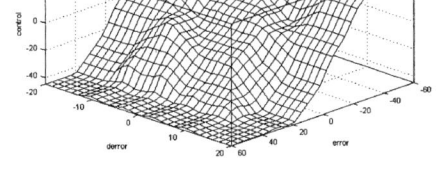

Fig. 7. Membership functions for the output variable *control action*

Fig. 8. Control surface for the fuzzy controller with the membership functions under their initial conditions

This algorithm is based on the properties of the transfer characteristic or, in this case, of the control surface that it allows to modify the controller's behavior by means of modifications in the position and support of the membership functions maintaining fixed the fuzzy controller's structure. Obtaining a slower answer for configurations with wide or expanded membership functions in the center and reduced in the ends, and the other way, a faster answer for configurations with reduced or compressed membership functions in the center and wide in the ends.

The tuning algorithm only modifies the membership functions of the input variables since the disposition of the membership functions of the output fuzzy variable remains constant since this disposition is only in function of a proportion of the range of the control action, this is, they always remain uniformly spaced.

4.1 Tuning Factor Selection

The tuning factor is a number $k \in [0, 1]$ that determines the grade of tuning adjustment obtaining for $k = 0$ the biggest settling time and for $k = 1$ the smallest settling time.

4.2 Normalization of the Ranges of the Fuzzy Controller's Variables

In this step the range of each input fuzzy variable is modified so that their limits superior and inferior are equal to +1 and -1, respectively.

4.3 Tuning Factor Processing

To expand and compress the values in the x-axis of the membership function it is necessary to use a function that fulfill this condition such that the new vector of operation points will be given by:

$$Vop_{final} = (Vop_{initial})^{r(k)} \qquad (2)$$

Where $Vop_{initial}$ are the values normalized of the membership function in the x-axis and $r(k)$ is a polynomial.

Table 2. Important values of $r(k)$

K	r
0	1/40
0.5	1
1	3

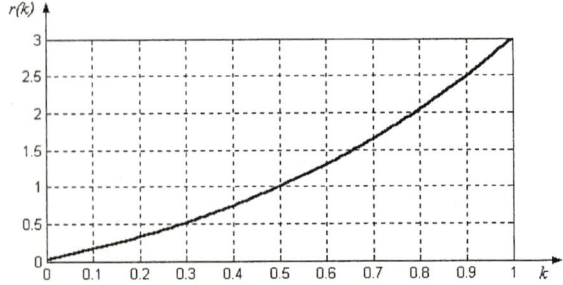

Fig. 9. Plot of function $r(k)$

The initial coefficients of the polynomial were obtained using mean square method. The values of k were defined in this way to be able to make an estimate over all their range $k \in [0, 1]$. The values of r, since it is an exponent, they were defined considering the increasing or decreasing of a number that is powered to the exponent r. Remember that the goal is to expand (slow response) for $k=0$ and to compress (fast response) $k=1$. For values below $r = 1/40$ the answer of the system was not satisfactory and in the same way, for values more than $r = 3$. The polynomial obtained was:

$$r(k) = \frac{30k^3 + 37k^2 + 52k + 1}{40} \tag{3}$$

This $r(k)$ was found testing the optimal response for different dynamical systems and finding the optimal parameters of the polynomial that fix the function for different values of k ($k = 0, 0.5, 1$) (figure 11).

4.4 Denormalization of the Ranges of the Fuzzy Variables

In this step it is necessary to convert the normalized range to the previous range of the system. This can be computed only multiplying the *Vop* vector by a constant factor.

5 Results of the Simulation

The cases will be analyzed for 3 values different of k, $k = 0, 0.5, 1$, showing the effect in the membership functions of the fuzzy variables, the control surface and the graph result of the simulation. For all the analyzed cases it will be used as input a step function with amplitude 40, the parameters that allow to evaluate the quality of the tuning are the settling time (considered to 98% of the value of the answer in stationary state), the overshoots and the oscillations. Also for all the analyzed cases the controller's structure is fixed, that means, the fuzzy associative memory is the same in all the examples. In the simulations it is included (on-line dotted) the answer of the system without controller to compare with the response using different tunings of the controller. The controller's fuzzy variables and the membership functions for the initial conditions are shown in the figures 5, 6 and 7: *error, change of error* and *control action* respectively.

5.1 Case 1: Adjusting the Membership Functions with a Tuning Factor $k = 0$

The function $r(k)$ takes the value $r(0) = 1/40$. With the tuning process the vectors of operation points for the fuzzy input variables are the following ones:

$$Vop\ error_{final} = [-59.3947, -58.3743, 0, 58.3473, 59.3947]$$
$$Vop\ d/dt(error)_{final} = [-19.7982, -19.4581, 0, 19.4581, 19.7982]$$

Making the simulation with the controller's characteristics shown in the figure 10 the following answer was obtained:

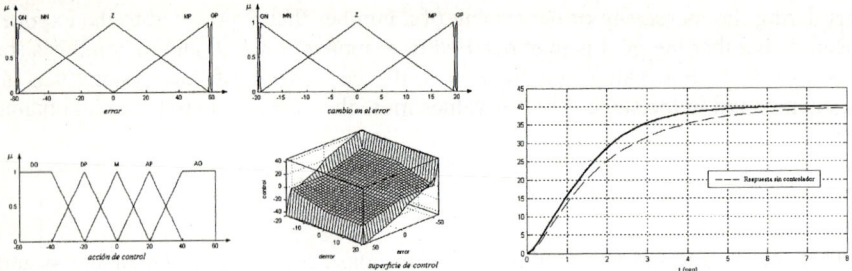

Fig. 10. Membership functions of the fuzzy variables **Fig. 11.** Answer of the system for the
and control surface for $k=0$ case 1 with $k = 0$

In the figure 11 it is shown that with the tuning factor $k = 0$ the controller's effect on the answer of the system, due to the tuning, is small, approaching to the answer without controller. In this case the settling time is the biggest that can be obtained, $t_s = 4.96\ s$.

5.2   Case 2: Adjusting the Membership Functions with a Tuning Factor $k = 0.5$

The function $r(k)$ takes the value $r(0.5) = 1$. Computing the simulation with the controller's characteristics shown in the figure 12 the following answer was obtained:

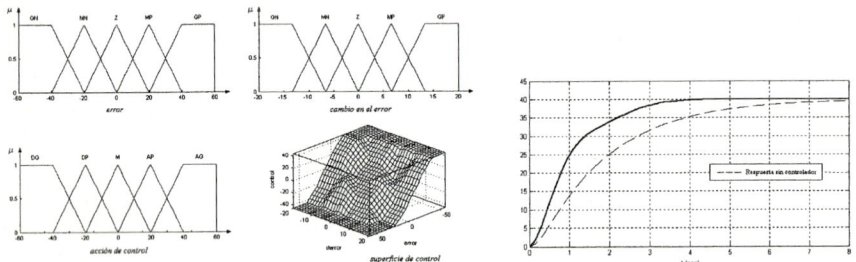

Fig. 12. Membership functions of the fuzzy variables **Fig. 13.** Answer of the system for the
and control surface for $k = 0.5$ case 2 with $k=0.5$.

This case, with the tuning factor $k = 0.5$, is equal to operate with the initial conditions of the membership functions. The settling time is $t_s = 3.36\ s$.

5.3   Case 3: Adjusting the Membership Functions with a Tuning Factor $k = 1$

The function $r(k)$ takes the value $r(1) = 3$. Computing the simulation with the controller's characteristics shown in the figure 14 the answer was obtained in figure 15, where the settling time is $t_s = 1.6\ s$ and it is the less value that can be obtained.

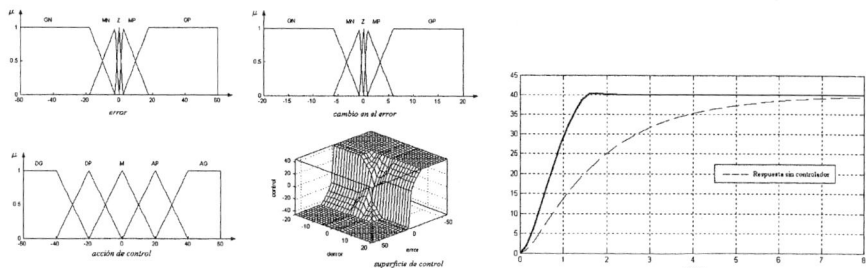

Fig. 14. Membership functions of the fuzzy variables and control surface for $k=1$

Fig. 15. Answer of the system for the case 3 with $k = 1$

The controller's effect on the answer of the system has begun to cause a small overshoot, due the bigger compression of the membership functions. If the value of $r(k)$ is increased, the settling time is not reduced and it only causes bigger overshoots and oscillations around the reference.

To visualize the effect of different values of the tuning factor k over the settling time of the answer of the system simulations with increments $\Delta k = 0.05$ in the interval $[0, 1]$ were computed. The result is shown in figure 16.

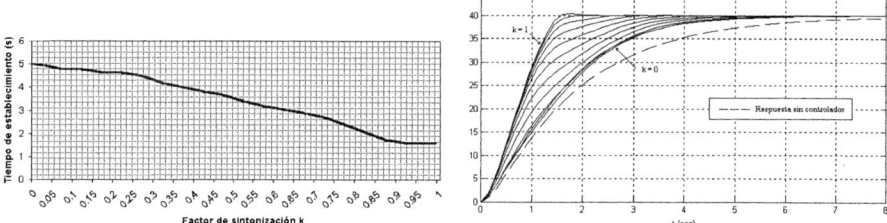

Fig. 16. Settling time versus tuning factor k

Fig. 17. Comparative graph of the answers of the system for different values of k

Making use of the simulations, and the graphs in figures 16 and 17, it is possible to see that the optimal value of k for the tuning is $k = 0.9$. this value generates a settling time $t_s = 1.6\ s$ without a great overshoot and without oscillations (figure 18).

Additionally, the fuzzy controller's performance was compared with that of a controller PID (Proportional-integral-derivative) whose parameters are the following ones $K_p = 25$, $T_i = 1.35$ and $T_d = 5$, and being that the differences are minimum as for time of establishment and general behavior (figure 19).

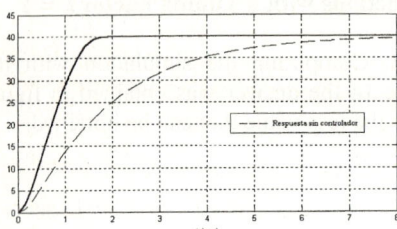

Fig. 18. Answer of the system with $k = 0.9$

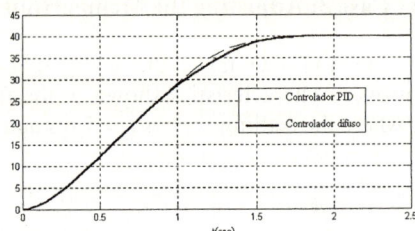

Fig. 19. Comparative graph of fuzzy controller answer versus PID answer

The disadvantage found in the controller PID is its inefficiency in comparison with the fuzzy controller since the control action generated by the PID can take very big values that are impossible to consider in a real implementation. On the other hand, the fuzzy controller uses real range of values.

Considering that this is the fastest answer that can be gotten with the controller PID, limited to the nature of the system, that is to say, limiting the range of the values that can take the control action to same values that those considered in the fuzzy controller's definition, it can be said that the tuning made on the fuzzy controller is satisfactory since it allows to vary the time of answer with very good behavior in the whole range of the tuning factor. Note that it is not evident to find three parameters of the PID for the optimal tuning and in the case of the fuzzy controllers it is necessary to increase or decrease the parameter k depending the settling time desired.

6   Conclusions

The tuning methods of fuzzy controllers include the handling of a great quantity of variables that makes very difficult, and many times non satisfactory the search of structures and good parameters. The method proposed uses only one variable and operates considering the transfer characteristic, or in this case the control surface that is the fuzzy controller's property that defines their behavior allowing that the system can response with bigger or smaller speed and precision.

The function $r(k)$ can be generalized to any system that uses a fuzzy controller varying the values $r(0)$ and $r(1)$ as well as the coefficients of the function $r(k)$ depending on the desired behavior.

Another perspective is to create a self tuning algorithm that modifies by itself the factor k to find the desired response. In this point, the use of fuzzy controllers presents attractive aspects for its implementation in real systems.

References

[1] Cox, Earl; Fuzzy Fundamentals, IEEE Spectrum, USA, October (1992).

[2] Palm, R., Fuzzy control approaches, General design schemes, Structure of a fuzzy controller, Handbook of Fuzzy Computation. Institute of Physics, Bristol. USA. (1998)

[3] Palm R, Fuzzy control approaches, Sliding mode fuzzy control, Handbook of Fuzzy Computation. Institute of Physics, Bristol. USA. (1998)

[4] Kinzel, J, Klawoon F y Kruse R. Modifications of genetic algorithms for designing and optimizing fuzzy controllers. 1st IEEE Conf. N Evolutionary Computations, ICEC'94. Orlando, FL, USA. (1994)

[5] Lee, M. A. y Tagaki H. Integrating design stages of fuzzy systems using genetic algorithms. 2nd IEEE Int. Conf. On Fuzzy Systems, Fuzz-IEEE'93pp 612-617. San Francisco, CA, USA, (1993)

[6] Bonissone, P. P., Kedhkar P. & Chen Y. Genetic algorithms for automated tuning of fuzzy controllers: a transportation application. 5th IEEE Conf. On Fuzzy Systems, Fuzz-IEEE'96, New Orleans, LA, USA, (1996)

[7] Lee, S. C. and Lee E. T. Fuzzy sets and neural networks. J. Cabernet.. USA. **4** (1974) 83-103

[8] Jang, J. S. R. ANFIS: adaptive-network-based-fuzzy-inference-system. IEEE Trans. Syst. Man Cybernet, SMC-23 . USA. (1993) 665-685

[9] Kawamura A, Watanabe N, Okada H y Asakawa K. A prototype of neuro-fuzzy cooperation systems. 1st IEEE Int. Conf. On Fuzzy Systems, Fuzz-IEEE'92, San Diego, CA, USA. (1992)

Predictive Control of a Solar Power Plant with Neuro-Fuzzy Identification and Evolutionary Programming Optimization

Mahdi Jalili-Kharaajoo

Young Researchers Club, Islamic Azad University, Iran
P.O. Box: 14395/1355, Tehran, Iran
mahdijalili@ece.ut.ac.ir

Abstract. The paper presents an intelligent predictive control to govern the dynamics of a solar power plant system. This system is a highly nonlinear process; therefore, a nonlinear predictive method, e.g., neuro-fuzzy predictive control, can be a better match to govern the system dynamics. In our proposed method, a neuro-fuzzy model identifies the future behavior of the system over a certain prediction horizon while an optimizer algorithm based on EP determines the input sequence. The first value of this sequence is applied to the plant. Using the proposed intelligent predictive controller, the performance of outlet temperature tracking problem in a solar power plant is investigated. Simulation results demonstrate the effectiveness and superiority of the proposed approach.

1   Introduction

Model based predictive control (MBPC) [1,2] is now widely used in industry and a large number of implementation algorithms due to its ability to handle difficult control problems which involve multivariable process interactions, constraints in the system variables, time delays, etc. Although industrial processes especially continuous and batch processes in chemical and petrochemical plants usually contain complex nonlinearities, most of the MPC algorithms are based on a linear model of the process and such predictive control algorithms may not give rise to satisfactory control performance [3,4]. If the process is highly nonlinear and subject to large frequent disturbances, a nonlinear model will be necessary to describe the behavior of the process. In recent years, the use of neuro-fuzzy models for nonlinear system identification has proved to be extremely successful [5-9]. The aim of this paper is to develop a nonlinear control technique to provide high-quality control in the presence of nonlinearities, as well as a better understanding of the design process when using these emerging technologies, i.e., neuro-fuzzy control algorithm. In this paper, we will use an Evolutionary Programming (EP) algorithm [10,11] to minimize the cost function and obtain the control input. The paper analyzes a neuro-fuzzy based nonlinear predictive controller for a solar power plant, which is a highly nonlinear process [12]. The procedure is based on construction of a neuro-fuzzy model for the process and the proper use of that in the optimization process. Using the proposed intelligent predictive controller, the performance of outlet temperature tracking

R. Monroy et al. (Eds.): MICAI 2004, LNAI 2972, pp. 794–803, 2004.
© Springer-Verlag Berlin Heidelberg 2004

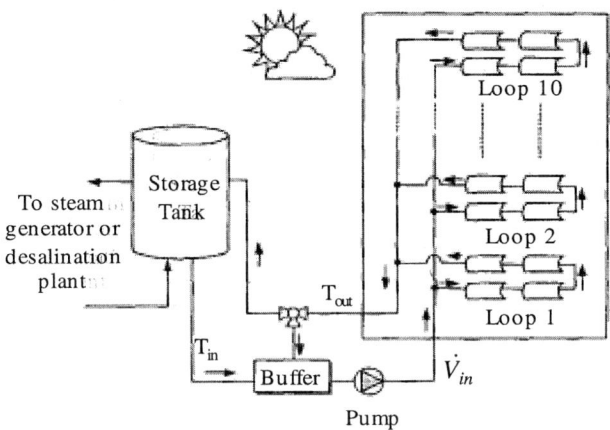

Fig. 1. Distributed solar collector field schematic.

problem in a solar power plant is investigated. Some simulations are provided to demonstrate the effectiveness the proposed control action.

2   The Solar Thermal Power Plant

The schematic diagram of the solar power plant used in this work is depicted in Fig. 1 [13-15]. Every solar collector has a linear parabolic-shaped reflector that focuses the sun's beam radiation on a linear absorber tube located at the focus of the parabola. Each of the loops is 142m, while the reflective area of the mirrors is around 264m2. The heat transfer fluid used to transport the thermal energy is the Santotherm 55, which is synthetic oil with a maximum film temperature of 318°C and an autoignition temperature of 357°C. The thermal oil is heated as it circulated through the absorber tube before entering the top of the storage tank. A three way valve located at the field outlet enables the oil reeyeling (by passing the storage tank) unit is outlet temperature is high enough to be sent to the storage tank. The thermal energy storage in the tank can be subsequently used to produce electrical energy in a conventional steam turbine/generator or in the solar desalination plant operation. In this work the input-output data available in [16] is used for the identification of the plant.

3   Neuro-Fuzzy Identification and Predictive Control of the Plant

In predictive control approach, control system anticipates the plant response for a sequence of determined control action in future time horizon [1,2]. The optimal control action in this time horizon is a good choice to minimize the difference between desired and predicted responses. MPC takes advantage of this prediction. It is originally developed for linear model of the plant that provides the prediction formulation. The MPC was developed for limited classes of nonlinear systems. In

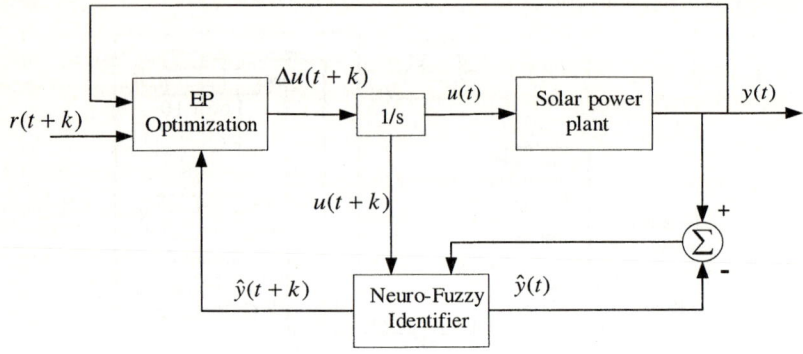

Fig. 2. Neuro-fuzzy predictive control scheme.

some cases, on-line estimation provides parametric estimation of nonlinear process that can be used for an MPC methodology. Neuro-fuzzy system, as universal approximator, may be considered for identification of nonlinear systems. This nonlinear mapping is used for process output prediction in future time horizon.

The structure of intelligent adaptive predictive control is shown in Fig. 2. Prediction system is formed by Neuro-Fuzzy Identifier (NFI) to generate the anticipated plant output for a future time window, $N_1 \leq t \leq N_2$. The fuzzy rules and membership functions of this identifier can be trained off-line by the actual measured data of solar power plant system. The future control variable for this prediction stage is determined in an optimization algorithm for the time interval of $N_1 \leq t \leq N_u$, such that $N_u \leq N_2$, minimizing the following cost function:

$$J = \sum_{k=N_1}^{N_2} \left\| \hat{y}(t+k) - r(t+k) \right\|_R^2 + \sum_{k=N_1}^{N_u} \left\| \Delta u(t+k) \right\|_Q^2 + \left\| y(t) - r(t) \right\|_R^2 \tag{1}$$

where $\hat{y}(t+k)$ is predicted plant output vector which is determined by NFI for time horizon of $N_1 \leq k \leq N_2$, $r(t+k)$ is desired set-point vector, $\Delta u(t+k)$ is predicted input variation vector in time range of $N_1 \leq k \leq N_u$, $y(t)$ and $r(t)$ are present plant output and set-point vectors, respectively. The optimization block finds the sequence of inputs to minimize cost function in (1) for future time, but only the first value of this sequence is applied to the plant. This predictive control system is not model-based and is not using the mathematical model of the plant. Therefore, the optimization cannot be implemented by conventional methods in MPC. The search engine based on EP is used to determine the optimized control variable for the finite future horizon. The competition search is performed on initial randomly chosen vectors of input deviation in a population and their mutated vectors. The mutation and competition continues to achieve desirable cost value.

We use the neuro-fuzzy network proposed in [9], a four-layer network, for the objective of predictive control. The first layer of identifier network represents the input stage that provides the crisp inputs for the fuzzification step. The second layer performs fuzzification. The weights and biases respectively represent the widths and means of input membership functions. Using exponential activation function, the outputs of the second layer neurons are the fuzzified system inputs. Weighting matrix of the third layer input represents antecedent parts of rules, and is called the Premise Matrix. Each row of the premise matrix presents a fuzzy rule such as:

$$R_{Premise} : IF \ x_1 \ is \ T^1_{x_1} \ AND... \ AND \ x_m \ is \ T^1_{x_m} \ THEN...$$

where $T^j_{x_i}$ is the jth linguistic term of the ith input.

The neuron output is determined by the min composition to provide the firing strength of rules. The fourth layer consists of separate sections for every system output. Each section represents consequent parts of rules for an output, such as:

$$R_{Consequent} :... \ THEN... \ y_i \ is \ T^1_{y_i} ...$$

where $T^j_{y_i}$ is the jth linguistic term of the ith output. Layer 5 makes the output membership functions. Combination of the fifth and sixth layers provides defuzzification method. Weighting matrix of the fifth layer for each output section is a diagonal matrix that contains width of the output membership functions. The activation value of each neuron provides one summation term in defuzzified output. The linear activation function determines output of each output section. The sixth layer completes defuzzification, and provides crisp output. The weighting vector of each neuron contains means of the output membership functions. The crisp output is derived by using activation function to implement the Center of Gravity approximation. Identification process may not perform desirably if it does not include the input/output interaction. For this purpose, series-parallel configuration [17] is chosen. This identification structure considers the past output states in conjunction with the present inputs to determine the present output. The identifier with augmented inputs is represented by

$$\hat{y}(k+1) = \hat{f}\big(y(k),..., y(k-i); u(k),..., u(k-j)\big) \tag{2}$$

such that $\hat{y}(k)$ is the estimated output at time step k, $\hat{f}$ is identifier function, $u(k)$ and $y(k)$ are plant input and output vectors, respectively, at time step k.

Adaptation of neuro-fuzzy identifier to a solar power plant system is essential to extract an identifier that truly models the system. Training algorithms enable identifier to configure fuzzy rules and adjust membership functions to model a solar power plat system with certain error penalty. Training of neuro-fuzzy identifier is taking place in two phases of configuration and tuning. Configuration phase determines fuzzy rules automatically based on available data from the system operation. For this purpose Genetic Algorithm (GA) training is chosen [18], because of specific structure of the neuro-fuzzy identifier. Fuzzy membership functions are adjusted during tuning to reduce modeling error. Error backpropagation method is used for this tuning.

In the start of training, the identifier is initialized with default input/output membership functions and fuzzy rules. Positions of '1's in the premise and consequence weighting matrices of the third and fourth layers define fuzzy rules. These matrices are encoded in the form of GA chromosome. We recall that the fourth layer consists of several sub-sections because of multiple outputs. Therefore, a GA chromosome has a compound structure with one section as the number of system outputs. In this work, GA with non-binary alphabet [19] will be the training method.

Alphanumeric size of each section is equal to the membership function number of the output. The GA will act separately on these sub-chromosomes to find the best fit. Having a set of experimental input/output plant data points, GA can be applied to find optimal set of fuzzy rules.

The fitness function, based on the least squares principle, provides evaluation of population individuals. To complete the GA iteration, it is necessary to prepare the next generation of population with applying three GA operators: selection, crossover and mutation. The weighted roulette wheel is used as selection operator that assigns a weighted slot to each individual [20]. Crossover operator generates two offspring strings from each pair of parent strings, chosen with probability of ρ_c. Crossover takes place in every sub-chromosome of parents. Crossover points are determined randomly with uniform distribution. Mutation operator changes value of a gene position with a frequency equal to mutation rate ρ_m. The new value of a chosen gene will be randomly determined with uniform distribution. Tuning the parameters of fuzzy membership functions completes training of the neuro-fuzzy system. Adjusting the membership function increases the accuracy of the identifier, since the initial membership functions have been chosen in the beginning of the training. Error back-propagation is used for training self-organized NF. More details about this method of identification can be found in [9]. The learning rates should be chosen appropriately. A small value of learning rate provides slow convergence. Moreover, stability may not be achieved with using large learning rate. Training ends after achieving specified error or reaching the maximum iteration number. Mean and width of the input/output membership functions are updated with final values of weighting matrices and bias vectors. For input-output data [16] the proposed neuro-fuzzy identification is performed and will be used for the objective of predictive control.

4   Control Input Optimization

The intelligent predictive control system does not depend on the mathematical model of the plant. Therefore, the optimization cannot be implemented by conventional methods in MPC. The search engine-based on evolutionary programming (EP) is used to determine the optimized control variables for a finite future time interval. The EP performs a competition search in a population and its mutation offspring. The members of each population are the input vector deviations that are initialized randomly. The mutation and competition continue making new generations to minimize value of a cost function. The output of the optimizer block is the control valve deviations that are integrated and applied to the identifier and solar power plant unit. The EP population consists of the individuals to present the deviation of control inputs. This population is represented by the following set

$$U_n = \{\Delta U_{1,n}, \Delta U_{2,n}, ..., \Delta U_{n_p,n}\} \tag{3}$$

such that U_n is the nth generation of population, and n_p is the population size. The ith individual is written by

$$\Delta U_{i,n} = [\Delta u_1^{i,n}, ..., \Delta u_m^{i,n}], for \ i = 1, 2, ..., n_p \tag{4}$$

where m is number of inputs. The $\Delta u_j^{i,n}$ is the jth vector of the ith generation as in the following

$$\Delta u_j^{i,n} = [\Delta u_j^{i,n}(1)...\Delta u_j^{i,n}(n_u)]^T, \, for \, j = 1,...,m \tag{5}$$

such that n_u is the number of steps in the discrete-time horizon for the power unite input estimation that is defined by

$$n_u = N_u - N_1 \tag{6}$$

where N_1 is the start time of prediction horizon and N_u is the end time of the input prediction. The individuals of input deviation vector belongs to a limited range of real numbers

$$\Delta u_j^{i,n}(.) \in [\Delta u_{j,min}, \Delta u_{j,max}] \tag{7}$$

In the beginning of EP algorithm, population is initialized randomly chosen individuals. Each initial individual is selected with uniform distribution from the above range of corresponding input.

The EP with adaptive mutation scale has shown a good performance in locating the global minima. Therefore, this method is used as it is formulated in [11]. The fitness value of each population is determined with a cost function to consider the error of predicted input and output in prediction time window. The cost function of the ith individual in the population is defined by

$$f_{i,n} = \sum_{k=1}^{n_y} \left\| r(t+k) - \hat{y}_{i,n}(t+k) \right\|_R^2 +$$

$$\sum_{k=1}^{n_u} \left\| \Delta U_{i,n}(k) \right\|_Q^2 + \left\| r(t) - \hat{y}(t) \right\|_R^2 \tag{8}$$

where $r(t+k)$ is the desired reference set-point at sample time of $t+k$, and $\hat{y}_{i,n}(t+k)$ is the discrete predicted plant output vector which is determined by applying $\Delta U_{i,n}(k)$ into the locally-linear fuzzy identifier for time horizon of $n_y = N_2 - N_1$.

The $\Delta U_{i,n}(k)$ in (8) is the kth of the ith individual in the nth generation. The input deviation vectors is determined in a smaller time window of n_u as in (6) such that $n_u \le n_y$. The inputs of the identifier stay constants after $t + n_u$.

The maximum, minimum, sum and average of the individual fitness in the nth generation should be calculated for further statistical process by

$$f_{max}\big|_n = \{f_{i,n}\big|f_{i,n} \ge f_{j,n} \; \forall f_{j,n}, j = 1,...,n_p\} \tag{9}$$

$$f_{min}\big|_n = \{f_{i,n}\big|f_{i,n} \le f_{j,n} \; \forall f_{j,n}, j = 1,...,n_p\} \tag{10}$$

$$f_{sum}\big|_n = \sum_{i=1}^{n_p} f_{i.n} \tag{11}$$

$$f_{avg}\big|_n = \frac{f_{sum}\big|_n}{n_p} \tag{12}$$

After determining the fitness values of a population, the mutation operator performs on the individuals to make a new offspring population. In mutation, each element of the parent individual as in (5) provides a new element by adding a random number such as

$$\Delta u_j^{i+n_p,n}(k) = \Delta u_j^{i,n}(k) + N(\mu, \sigma_{i,j}^2(n)) \tag{13}$$

$$for \quad i = 1,2,...,n_p \quad j = 1,2,...,m \quad k = 1,2,...,n_u$$

such that $N(\mu, \sigma_{i,j}^2(n))$ is Gaussian random variable with mean $\mu = 0$ and variance of $\sigma_{i,j}^2(n)$. The variance of the random variable in (13) is chosen to be

$$\sigma_{i,j}^2(n) = \beta(n)(\Delta u_{j,\max} - \Delta u_{j,\min}) \frac{f_{i,n}}{f_{\max}|_n} \tag{14}$$

where $\beta(n)$ is the mutation scale of the population such that $0 < \beta(n) \leq 1$. After mutation, the fitness of offspring individuals are evaluated and assigned to them.

The generated new individuals and old individuals produce a new combine population whit size of $2n_p$. Each member of the combined population competes with some other members to determine which one is valuated to survive to the next generation. For this purpose, the ith individual $\Delta U_{i,n}$ competes with jth individual $\Delta U_{j,n}$, such that $j = 1,2,...,p$. The number of individuals to compete whit is a fixed number p. The p individuals are selected randomly whit uniform distribution. The result of this competition is a binary number $v_{ij,n} \in \{0,1\}$ to represent lose or win, and is determined by

$$v_{ij,n} = \begin{cases} 1 & if \lambda_{j,n} < \dfrac{f_{j,n}}{f_{j,n} + f_{i,n}} \\ 0 & otherwise \end{cases} \tag{15}$$

such that $\lambda_{j,n} \in [0,1]$ is a randomly selected number with uniform distribution, and $f_{j,n}$ is the fitness of the jth selected individual. The value of $v_{ij,n}$ will be set to 1 if according to (15) the fitness of the ith individual is relatively smaller than the fitness of the jth individual. To select the survived individual, a weight value is assigned to each individual by

$$w_{i,n} = \sum_{k=1}^{p} v_{ij,n} \quad for \quad i = 1,2,...,2n_p \tag{16}$$

The n_p individuals whit the highest competition weight $w_{i,n}$ are selected to form the (n+1)th generation. This newly formed generation participates in the next iteration. To determine the convergence of the process, the difference of maximum and minimum fitness of the population is checked against a desired small number $\varepsilon > 0$ as in

$$f_{\max}|_n - f_{\min}|_n \leq \varepsilon \tag{17}$$

If this convergence condition is met, the mutation scale with the lowest fitness is selected as sequence of n_u input vectors for the future time horizon. The first vector is applied to the plant and the time window shifts to the next prediction step.

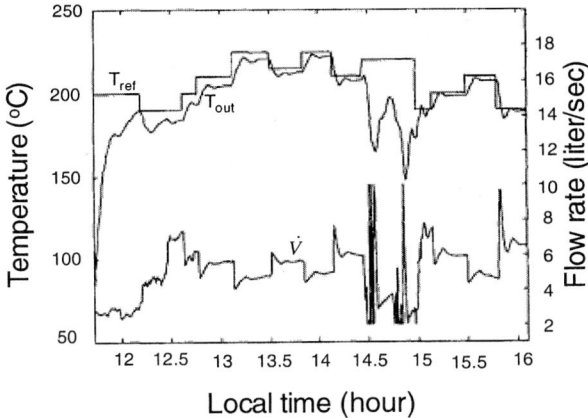

Fig. 3. Simulation results of set point, outlet oil temperature and oil flow rate.

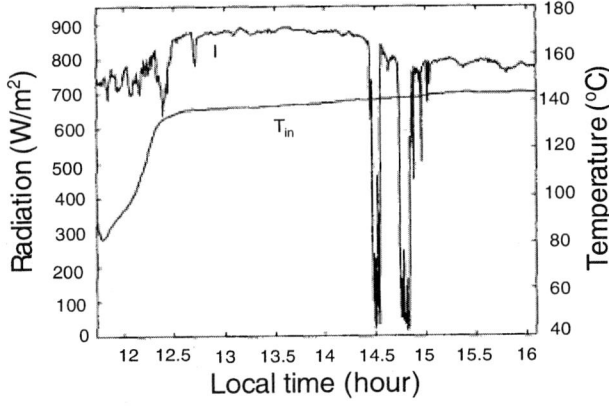

Fig. 4. Simulation results of solar radiation and inlet oil temperature.

Before starting the new iteration, the mutation scale changes according to the newly formed population. If the mutation scale is kept as a small fixed number, EP may have a premature result. In addition, a large fixed mutation scale will raise the possibility of having a non-convergence process. An adaptive mutation scale provides a change of mutation probability according to the minimum fitness value of n_p individuals in the (n+1)th generation. The mutation scale for the next generation is determined by

$$\beta(n+1) = \begin{cases} \beta(n) - \beta_{step} & if\ f_{\min}\big|_n = f_{\min}\big|_{n+1} \\ \beta(n) & if\ f_{\min}\big|_n < f_{\min}\big|_{n+1} \end{cases} \qquad (18)$$

where n is generation number, β_{step} is the predefined possible step change of the mutation scale in each iteration.

5 Simulation Results

The proposed intelligent predictive control is tested on a real solar power plant with input-output data available in [16]. In order to maintain (or drive) the outlet oil temperature at the pre-specified level despite variations in the sun's beam radiation and in inlet oil temperature, the control system manipulates the thermal oil flow rate pumped to the solar collector field. After the initial training, identifier is engaged in the closed loop of the predictive control as in Fig. 1. The parameters of prediction horizon is selected to be $n_y = 50$, $\left(n_y = N_2 - N_1\right)$, and $n_u = 20$, with time step of $\Delta t = 6 \sec$. Population size is chosen to be $n_p = 15$. The crossover and mutation rates are chosen to be $\rho_c = 0.75$ and $\rho_m = 0.002$, respectively, in GA training.

Figs. 3 and 4 show the outlet oil temperature (T_{out}), set point (T_{ref}), oil flow rate $(\dot{V})$ and the inlet oil temperature (T_{in}), the solar radiation (I), respectively. As it can be seen, the proposed intelligent predictive control provides a very interesting dynamic response of the outlet oil temperature, being the control system quiet stable in all the operating points.

6 Conclusion

In this paper, an intelligent predictive control was applied to solar power plant system. This system is a highly nonlinear process; therefore, a nonlinear predictive method, e.g., neuro-fuzzy predictive control, can be a better match to govern the system dynamics. In our proposed method, a neuro-fuzzy model identified the future behavior of the system over a certain prediction horizon. An optimizer algorithm based on EP used the identifier-predicted outputs and determined input sequence in a time window. Using the proposed neuro-fuzzy predictive controller, the performance of outlet temperature tracking problem in a solar power plant was investigated. Simulation results demonstrated the effectiveness and superiority of the proposed approach.

References

1. Camacho, E.F. Model predictive control, Springer Verlag, 1998.
2. Garcia, C.E., Prett, D.M., and Morari, M. Model predictive control: theory and practice- a survey, Automatica, 25(3), pp.335-348, 1989.
3. Badgwell, A.B., Qin, S.J. Review of nonlinear model predictive control applications, In Nonlinear predictive control theory and practice, Kouvaritakis, B, Cannon, M (Eds.), IEE Control Series, pp.3-32, 2001.
4. Parker, R.S., Gatzke E.P., Mahadevan, R., Meadows, E.S., and Doyle, F.J. Nonlinear model predictive control: issues and applications, In Nonlinear predictive control theory and practice, Kouvaritakis, B, Cannon, M (Eds.), IEE Control Series, pp.34-57, 2001.
5. Babuska, R., Botto, M.A., Costa, J.S.D., and Verbruggen, H.B. Neural and fuzzy modeling on nonlinear predictive control, a comparison study, Computatioinal Engineering in Systems Science, July, 1996.

6. Arahal, M.R., Berenguel, M., and Camacho, E.F. Neural identification applied to predictive control of a solar plant, Con. Eng. Prac. 6(3), pp.333-344, 1998.
7. Lennox, B., and Montague, G. Neural network control of a gasoline engine with rapid sampling, In Nonlinear predictive control theory and practice, Kouvaritakis, B, Cannon, M (Eds.), IEE Control Series, pp.245-255, 2001.
8. Petrovic, I., Rac, Z., and Peric, N. Neural network based predictive control of electrical drives with elastic transmission and backlash, Proc. EPE2001, Graz, Austria, 2001.
9. Ghezelayagh, H. and Lee, K.Y. Application of neuro-fuzzy identification in the predictive control of power plant, in preprints of 15th IFAC World Congress, Barcelona, Spain, June, 2002.
10. Fogel, L.J., The future of evolutionary programming. Proc. 24th Asilomar Conference on Signals, Systems and Computers. Pacific Grove, CA, 1991.
11. Lai, L.L., Intelligent system application in power engineering: Evolutionary programming and neural networks. John Wiley & Sons Inc., New York, USA, 1998.
12. Camacho, E.F. and Berenguel, M., Robust adaptive model predictive control of a solar power plant with bounded uncertainties, Int. Journal of Adaptive Control and Signal Processing, 11, pp.311-325, 1997.
13. Pickhardt, R. and Silva, R., Application of a nonlinear predictive controller to a solar power plant, IEEE Conference on Control Application, Trieste, Italy, 1998.
14. Coito, F., Lemones, J., Silva, R. and Mosca, E., Adaptive control of a solar energy plant: Exploiting accessible disturbances, Int. Journal of Adaptive Control and Signal Processing, 11, pp.326-342, 1997.
15. Henriques, J., Cardoso, A. and Dourado, A., Supervision and C-means clustering of PID controllers for a solar power plant, Int. Journal of Approximate Reasoning, 22, pp.73-91, 1999.
16. ftp://ftp.esat.kuleuven.ac.be/pub/SISTA/espinosa/datasets/cstr.dat
17. Narandra, K.S. and K. Parthasarathy, Identification and control of dynamical systems using neural networks. IEEE Trans. on Neural Networks, vol. 1, no. 1, pp. 4-27, 1990.
18. Goldberg, D.E. Genetic Algorithm in Search, Optimization, and Machine Learning. Reading, MA: Addison-Wesley, 1989.
19. Mason, A.J. Partition coefficients, static deception and deceptive problems for nonbinary alphabets. Proceedings of the 4th International Conference on Genetic Algorithms, pp. 210-214, 1991.
20. Dimeo, R. and K.Y. Lee Boiler-turbine control system design using a Genetic Algorithm. IEEE Trans. Energy Conversion, 10(4), pp.752-759, 1995.

Modeling of a Coupled Industrial Tank System with ANFIS

S.N. Engin[1], J. Kuvulmaz[1], and V.E. Ömürlü[2]

[1]Department of Electrical Engineering, Yildiz Technical University,
34800 Besiktas, Istanbul Turkey
{nengin,janset}@yildiz.edu.tr
[2]Department of Mechanical Engineering, Yildiz Technical University,
34800 Besiktas, Istanbul, Turkey
omurlu@yildiz.edu.tr

Abstract. Since liquid tank systems are commonly used in industrial applications, system-related requirements results in many modeling and control problems because of their interactive use with other process control elements. Modeling stage is one of the most noteworthy parts in the design of a control system. Although nonlinear tank problems have been widely addressed in classical system dynamics, when designing intelligent control systems, the corresponding model for simulation should reflect the whole characteristics of the real system to be controlled. In this study, a coupled, interacting, nonlinear liquid leveling tank system is modeled using ANFIS (Adaptive-Network-Based Fuzzy Inference System), which will be further used to design and apply a fuzzy-PID control to this system. Firstly, mathematical modeling of the system is established and then, data gathered from this model is employed to create an ANFIS model of the system. Both mathematical and ANFIS model is compared, model consistencies are discussed, and flexibility of ANFIS modeling is shown.

1 Introduction

Artificial Neural Networks (ANNs) and Fuzzy Logic (FL) have been increasingly in use in many engineering fields since their introduction as mathematical aids by McCulloch and Pitts, 1943, and Zadeh, 1965, respectively. Being branches of Artificial Intelligence (AI), both emulate the human way of using past experiences, adapting itself accordingly and generalizing. While the former have the capability of learning by means of parallel connected units, called neurons, which process inputs in accordance with their adaptable weights usually in a recursive manner for approximation; the latter can handle imperfect information through linguistic variables, which are arguments of their corresponding membership functions.

Although the fundamentals of ANNs and FL go back as early as 1940s and 1960s, respectively, significant advancements in applications took place around 1980s. After the introduction of back-propagation algorithm for training multi-layer networks by Rumelhart and McClelland, 1986, ANNs has found many applications in numerous inter-disciplinary areas [1-3]. On the other hand, FL made a great advance in the mid 1970s with some successful results of laboratory experiments by Mamdani and

R. Monroy et al. (Eds.): MICAI 2004, LNAI 2972, pp. 804–812, 2004.

Assilian [4]. In 1985, Takagi and Sugeno [5] contributed FL with a new rule-based modeling technique.

Operating with linguistic expressions, fuzzy logic can use the experiences of a human expert and also compensate for inadequate and uncertain knowledge about the system. On the other hand, ANNs have proven superior learning and generalizing capabilities even on completely unknown systems that can only be described by its input-output characteristics. By combining these features, more versatile and robust models, called "neuro-fuzzy" architectures have been developed, [6-7].

In a control system the plant displaying nonlinearities has to be described accurately in order to design an effective controller. In obtaining the model, the designer has to follow one of two ways. The first one is using the knowledge of physics, chemistry, biology and the other sciences to describe an equation of motion with Newton's laws, or electric circuits and motors with Ohm's, Kirchhoff's or Lentz's laws depending on the plant of interest. This is generally referred to as *mathematical modeling*. The second way requires the experimental data obtained by exciting the plant, and measuring its response. This is called *system identification* and is preferred in the cases where the plant or process involves extremely complex physical phenomena or exhibits strong nonlinearities.

Obtaining a mathematical model for a system can be rather complex and time consuming as it often requires some assumptions such as defining an operating point and doing linearization about that point and ignoring some system parameters, etc. This fact has recently led the researchers to exploit the neural and fuzzy techniques in modeling complex systems utilizing solely the input-output data sets. Although fuzzy logic allows one to model a system using human knowledge and experience with if-then rules, it is not always adequate on its own. This is also true for ANNs, which only deal with numbers rather than linguistic expressions. This deficiency can be overcome by combining the superior features of the two methods, as is performed in ANFIS architecture introduced by Jang, 1993 [8-11].

In the literature, ANFIS applications are generally encountered in the areas of function approximation, fault detection, medical diagnosis and control, [12-17]. In this study, ANFIS architecture was used to model the dynamic system, which is taken as a black-box, i.e. described by its observed responses to the introduced inputs.

2 Fuzzy Modeling and ANFIS Architecture

In fuzzy system identification, first, system parameters should be determined. In this study, while modeling coupled nonlinear liquid leveling tank system, the ANFIS architecture based on Takagi - Sugeno fuzzy modeling is employed. With a hybrid learning procedure, ANFIS can learn an input – output mapping combining the complimentary features of Neural Networks and Fuzzy Logic. The regression vector is chosen as NARX model as follows.

$$\varphi = \left[u(t-k), \ldots \ldots u(t-n), \ y(t-k), \ldots \ldots y(t-m) \right] \tag{1}$$

For simplicity, fuzzy inference system is to be considered as having two inputs (x, y) and one output (z) (MISO). A first order Sugeno model [5] can be expressed with two rules as follows and the related inference method is shown in Fig.1.

Rule 1 IF $x A_1$ and $y B_1$ then $f_1 = p_1 x + q_1 y + r_1$

Rule 2 IF $x A_2$ and $y B_2$ then $f_2 = p_2 x + q_2 y + r_2$

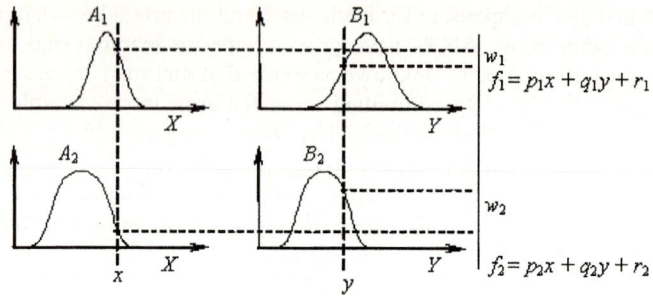

Fig. 1. The inference method of Sugeno model

Using the f_1 and f_2 membership functions the output function for this Sugeno model is expressed as,

$$f = \frac{w_1 f_1 + w_2 f_2}{w_1 + w_2} \\ = \overline{w_1} f_1 + \overline{w_2} f_2 \tag{2}$$

The corresponding ANFIS model for Sugeno's fuzzy structure is given in Fig.2.

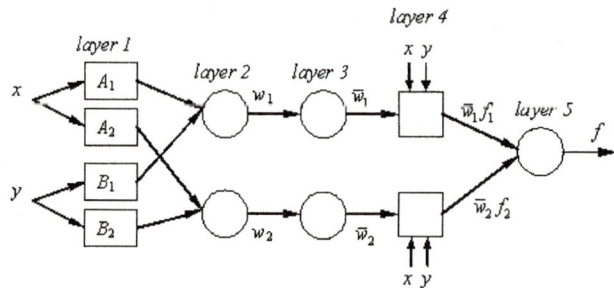

Fig. 2. The ANFIS model Sugeno's fuzzy inference method

As it is seen from Fig.2, ANFIS has 5 layers and functions of these layers are explained below:

Layer 1:   In this layer where the fuzzification process takes place, every node is adaptive. Outputs of this layer form the membership values of the premise part.

Layer 2:   In contrary to Layer 1 the nodes in this layer are fixed. Each node output represents a firing strength of a rule.

Layer 3:   In this layer where the normalization process is performed, the nodes are fixed as they are in Layer 2. The ratio of the ith rule's firing strength to the sum of all rule's firing strength is calculated for the corresponding node.

Layer 4:   Since the nodes in this layer operate as a function block whose variables are the input values, they are adaptive. Consequently the output of this layer forms TSK outputs and this layer is referred to as the consequent part.

Layer 5:   This is the summation layer. Which consist of a single fixed node. It sums up all the incoming signals and produces the output.

3 Modeling a Nonlinear Coupled-Tank System with ANFIS

In this part, an ANFIS model of a nonlinear coupled tank system is obtained. Fig.3. shows a simple double tank liquid-level system with a valve between [18]. Each tank has and outlet port with Q_2 and Q_4 flowrates. First tank is fed with Q_1 flowrate. The system is configured as a SISO system, Q_1 – input and h_2 – output. By formulizing mass input-output balance for each tank and Bernoulli equations, following nonlinear equations are obtained:

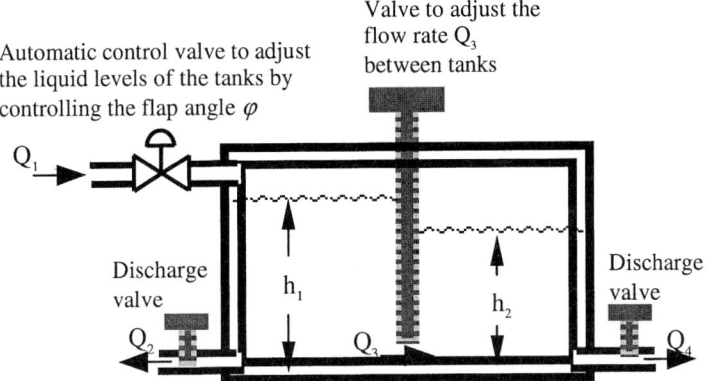

Fig. 3. A simple schematic for an interacting coupled-tank level control system.

$$A_1 \frac{dh_1}{dt} = Q_1 - a_1\sqrt{h_1} - a_3\sqrt{h_1 - h_2}$$
$$A_2 \frac{dh_2}{dt} = -a_2\sqrt{h_2} - a_3\sqrt{h_1 - h_2} \tag{3}$$

Q_1 is the volumetric flow rate and can reach maximum 0.12 m³/sec and adjusted by a valve. A_1 and A_2 are the base surface area of each tank which are 1 m². a_1, a_2 and a_3 are proportionality constants. The values of these constants are dependent on the discharge coefficients, cross-section area of the outlets and the gravitational constants. Outlet area of tank I and II are 0.01 m² and outlet area between two tanks is 0.05 m². Q_1 is the controlled input liquid flow rate and given as

$$q_{in} = Q_{in} \cdot \sin(\varphi(t)) \qquad \varphi(t) \in [0, \pi/2] \tag{4}$$

An excitation signal which represents input valve angel values between 0 and π/2 radian is created by means of adding two sinusoidal signals, Fig.4. The output data set is produced using the expressions above in MATLAB SIMULINK, Fig.4. The data set obtained is fed to the ANFIS in order to approximate a model of the system to be controlled. All these computations are carried out in MATLAB SIMULINK.

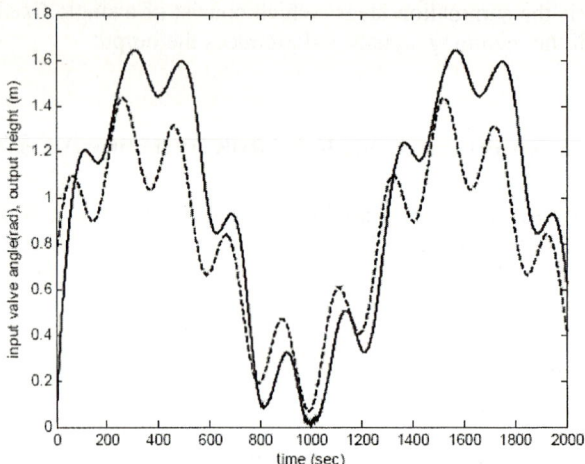

Fig. 4. Training data for ANFIS from the double tank system illustrated (input data - dashed, output data – solid)

4   Simulation Results

This section presents the simulation results of proposed ANFIS model for the tank liquid-level system and its control. In order to obtain an input – output data set, an input data set which represents the changes of the control valve's flap angle, φ, in the range of 0 (no flow in) to $\pi/2$ (full flow) radians for 2000 samples, is produced analytically as plotted in Fig.4. This input is applied to the system and the corresponding liquid level outputs in meters are obtained.

In the modeling, regression vector is chosen as NARX model, which involves past input and output to approximate the system's input-output relationship, shown below.

$$\varphi = [u(t-1) \quad y(t-1)]$$

Here, the system is modeled as a MISO system having two inputs and one output. Each input variable is represented by five membership functions, which make 25 rules. The membership functions for this Takagi-Sugeno fuzzy model are chosen as a generalized bell function. The input-output data is processed by ANFIS and hence the proposed model is obtained. Below in Fig.5, the outputs of mathematical and ANFIS models are plotted for comparison. The time axes for simulation results are plotted in terms of discrete index number. The corresponding time scale in second is selected automatically by MATLAB. Fig.6 shows the actual difference between the two models at each sample.

As an actual evaluation process of the proposed ANFIS model, nonlinear double tank system is evaluated through set of input data either similar to or different from training data and compared with the mathematical model of the original system. First, original training data which is the combination of sinusoidal and step signals, is applied to both ANFIS and mathematical models and the response of the systems are gathered, Fig.5. Comparison of these two in Fig.6. shows that general conformity of the ANFIS model to the mathematical model is very successful. Only around zero input value does the system represent the maximum discrepancy which is around 8 cm. Second, system evaluation is continued with the unit step input application and input and output of the models are illustrated in Fig.7 and conformance between mathematical and ANFIS models is shown. Lastly, the ANFIS model is forced against a random input which is again combination of more complex functions in Fig.8. Again, general agreement of two signals is successful but around zero input value, Fig. 9. and Fig.10.

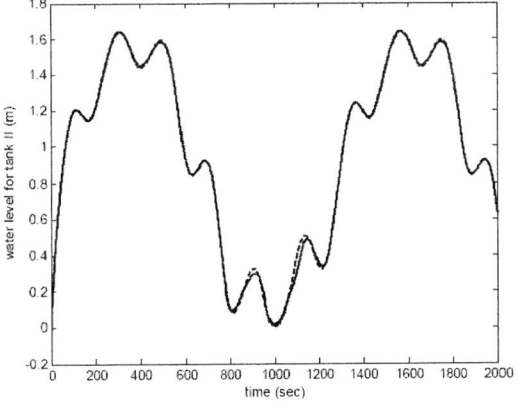

Fig. 5. Responses of the ANFIS and mathematical model of double tank system to the training input data (mathematical model output - dashed, ANFIS model output – solid).

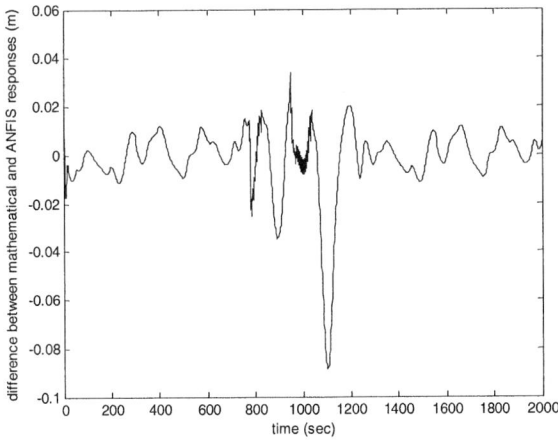

Fig. 6. Difference between mathematical and ANFIS model of double tank system for the training input response.

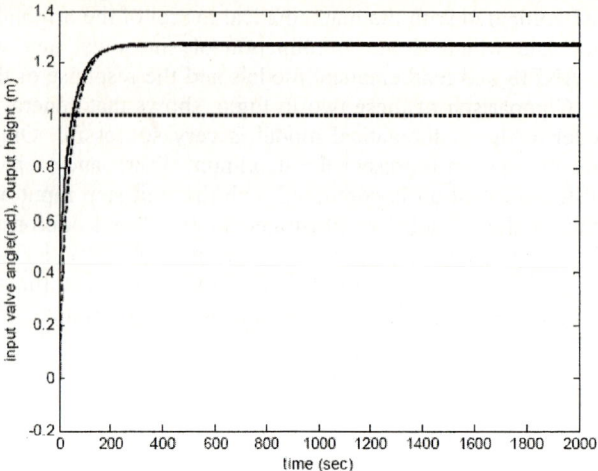

Fig. 7. Mathematical and ANFIS model response of double tank system to a unit step input (input step - dotted, math response - dashed, ANFIS response – solid)

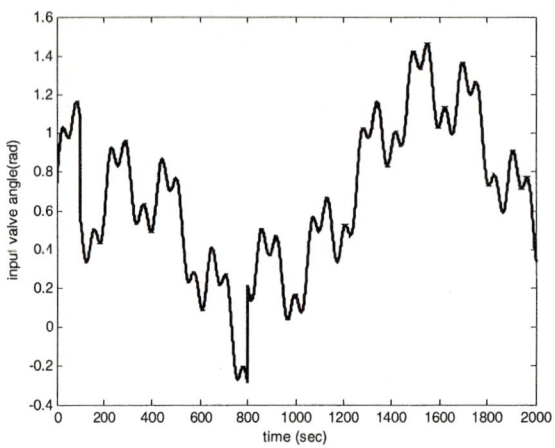

Fig. 8. A non-uniform, random input for evaluation of double tank system ANFIS model

Conclusions

It is generally not possible to derive an accurate model of a process or plant especially with nonlinearities. If a reliable model is not available, it is quite difficult to design a controller producing desired outputs. On the other hand, traditional modeling techniques are rather complex and time consuming. However, using input-output data set, ANFIS can approximate the system. When the data set does not represent the whole operating range adequately, the model to be obtained will not be as robust.

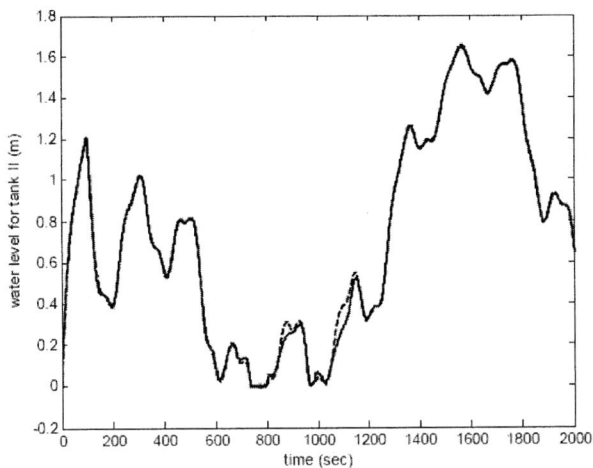

Fig. 9. Double tank system ANFIS and mathematical model responses to a random input data (math - dashed, ANFIS – solid)

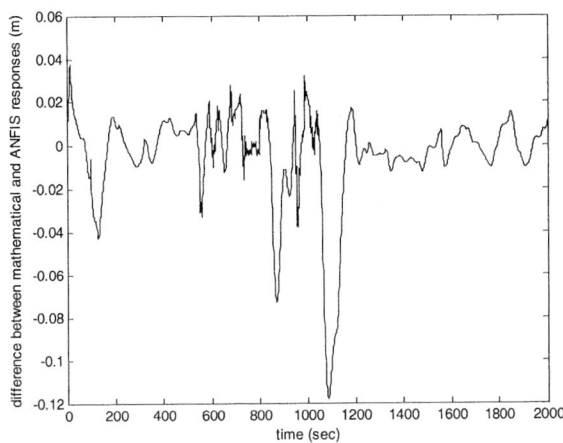

Fig. 10. Difference between mathematical and ANFIS model of double tank system for random input data.

During modelling stage, ANFIS, using Sugeno model with two inputs and one output, each having five membership functions, is employed and a nonlinear coupled-tank liquid-level system is modelled successfully. Model evaluations are performed through various forms of input data and comformance between mathematical and ANFIS models is represented and ability of ANFIS to model a nonlinear system is shown.

References

1. Patterson, D. W. Artificial Neural Networks – Theory and Applications, Prentice Hall, 1996.
2. Engin, S. N., and Gulez, K. "A Wavelet Transform – Artificial Neural Networks (WT-ANN) based Rotating Machinery Fault Diagnostics Methodology", IEEE NSIP' 99, Falez Hotel, Antalya, Turkey, 1-3 June 1999
3. Staszewski, W. J. and Worden, K. Classification of Faults in Gearboxes - Pre-processing Algorithms and Neural Networks. Neural Computing and Applications 5(3): 160-183, 1997
4. Mamdani, E. H. and Assilian, S., An Experiment in Linguistic Synthesis with a Logic Controller, Int. J. Man – Machine Studies 8, pp. 1 – 13, 1975
5. Takagi, S. and Sugeno, M. Fuzzy identification of fuzzy systems and it's application to modelling and control, IEEE Trans. Systems Man Cybern., 15 pp 116-132, 1985
6. Culliere, T., Titli, A., Corrieu, J. Neuro-fuzzy modelling of nonlinear systems for control purposes, In Proc. IEEE INT. Conf. on Fuzzy Systems, pp 2009-2016, Yokohama, 1995
7. Nauck, D, Fuzzy neuro systems: An overview, In R. Kruse, J. Gebhardt and R. Palm, eds, Fuzzy Systems in Computer Science, pp 91-107, Vieweg, Braunschweig, 1994
8. Jang, J. ANFIS: Adaptive-Network Based Fuzzy Inference System. IEEE Trans. on Systems, Man and Cybernetics, Vol. 23. No. 3 pp. 665-685, 1993
9. Jang, J. and Sun. C. T. Neuro-Fuzzy Modeling and Control. IEEE Proc., Vol. 83. No. 3, pp 378 – 406, 1995
10. Jang, J., Input Selection for ANFIS Learning, IEEE Fuzzy Systems, pp. 1493 – 1499, 1996
11. Jang, J., Neuro – Fuzzy Modeling for Dynamic System Identification, IEEE Fuzzy Systems Symposium, pp. 320 – 325, 1996
12. Altug, S. and Chow, M. Fuzzy Inference Systems Implemented on Neural Architectures for Motor Fault Detection and Diagnosis IEEE Trans. on Ind. Electronics, Vol. 46, No. 6, December 1999
13. Zhou, C. and Jagannathan, K., Adaptive Network Based Fuzzy Control of a Dynamic Biped Walking Robot IEEE 1996 Int. Joint Symposia on Intelligence and Systems (IJSIS'96) Nov. 04 – 05 1996
14. Djukanović, M.B. and Ćalović, M.S. and Veśović, B.V. and Šobajć, D.J., Neuro – Fuzzy Controller of Low Head Hydropower Plants Using Adaptive – Network Based Fuzzy Inference System IEEE Trans. on Energy Conversion, Vol. 12, No. 4, December 1997
15. Niestroy. M., The use of ANFIS for Approximating an optimal controller World Cong. on Neural Networks, San Diego, CA, Sept. 15- 18, pp 1139 – 1142, 1996
16. Jensen, E. W. and Nebot, A., Comparision of FIR and ANFIS Methodologies for Prediction of Mean Blood Pressure and Auditory Evoked Potentials Index During Anaesthesia Proceedings of the IEEE Engineering in Medicine and Biology Society, Vol. 20, No. 3, 1998
17. Oonsivilai, A. and El – Hawary, M.E., Power System Dynamic Modeling using Adaptive – Network Based Fuzzy Inference System Proceedings of the 1999 IEEE Canadian Conf. on Electrical and Computer Engineering Canada May 9 – 12 1999
18. Lian, S.T., Marzuki, K., Rubiyah, M., Tuning of a neuro-fuzzy controller by genetic algorithms with an application to a coupled-tank liquid-level control system, Engineering Application of Artificial Intelligence, 517-529, 1998

Robust Bootstrapping Neural Networks[*]

Héctor Allende[1,2], Ricardo Ñanculef[1], and Rodrigo Salas[1]

[1] Universidad Técnica Federico Santa María; Dept. de Informática;
Casilla 110-V; Valparaíso-Chile;
{hallende,jnancu,rsalas}@inf.utfsm.cl
[2] Universidad Adolfo Ibañez; Facultad de Ciencia y Tecnología.

Abstract. Artificial neural networks (ANN) have been used as predictive systems for a variety of application domains such as science, engineering and finance. Therefore it is very important to be able to estimate the reliability of a given model. Bootstrap is a computer intensive method used for estimating the distribution of a statistical estimator based on an imitation of the probabilistic structure of the data generating process and the information contained in a given set of random observations. Bootstrap plans can be used for estimating the uncertainty associated with a value predicted by a feedforward neural network.

The available bootstrap methods for ANN assume independent random samples that are free of outliers. Unfortunately, the existence of outliers in a sample has serious effects such as some resamples may have a higher contamination level than the initial sample, and the model is affected because it is sensible to these deviations resulting on a poor performance. In this paper we investigate a robust bootstrap method for ANN that is resistant to the presence of outliers and is computationally simple. We illustrate our technique on synthetic and real datasets and results are shown on confidence intervals for neural network prediction.

Keywords: Feedforward Artificial Neural Networks, Bootstrap, Robust theory, Confidence Interval.

1 Introduction

Feedforward neural networks (FANN) with nonlinear transfer functions offer universal approximation capabilities based wholly on the data itself, i.e., they are purely empirical models that can theoretically mimic the input-output relationship to any degree of precision.

Our estimations about the characteristics of a population of interest relay on the treatment of a sample or a set of prototypes that are realizations of an unknown probability model. The source of confidence about these estimations are the result of the fact that we are trying to generalize based on a limited set of samples that are contaminated by the process of data acquisition. The question

---

[*] This work was supported in part by Research Grant Fondecyt 1010101 and 7010101, and in part by Research Grant DGIP-UTFSM.

R. Monroy et al. (Eds.): MICAI 2004, LNAI 2972, pp. 813–822, 2004.

is how to do an estimate of the probabilistic behaviour of our estimates, which are functionally dependent on the unknown probabilistic model of the data.

The traditional way to treat this problem has been by imposing strong assumptions over the probabilistic laws on the data generating process or by taking the asymptotic approach (see [7] and [9]).

Computationally intensive methods based on bootstrap techniques [3] have been used for evaluating the performance of ANN [6], but no care is taken under contaminated data. The existence of outliers in a sample is an obvious problem in inference which can become worse when the usual bootstrap is applied, because some resamples may have higher contamination levels than the initial samples [10]. Bootstrapping robust estimators has some drawbacks, namely, numerical stability and high computational cost. Usually, real data is contaminated by outliers, i.e., observations that are substantially different to the bulk of data, with different sources of variation yielding exceptions of different nature, so rejection of outliers is not an acceptable treatment.

In this paper we propose a modification of the bootstrap procedure applied to neural networks that is resistant to the presence of outliers in the data and is computationally simple and feasible. The paper is organized as follows: in section 2 we introduce the notation and architecture of feedforward neural networks (FANN); in section 3 we present the bootstrap and its application to neural networks; in section 4 we develop our robust version of the bootstrap procedure; finally in section 5 we present a simulation study on datasets and the conclusions are drawn in the last section.

2   Feedforward Artificial Neural Networks

A FANN consists of elementary processing elements called neurons, organized in layers: the input, the hidden and the output layers. The links of the neurons are from one layer to the successive without any type of bridge, lateral or feedback connections. For simplicity, a single-hidden-layer with only one output architecture is considered in this paper, so the different class of neural models can be specified by the number of hidden neurons by $S_\lambda = \{g_\lambda(\underline{x}, \underline{w}) \in \mathbb{R}, \ \underline{x} \in \mathbb{R}^m, \ \underline{w} \in \mathcal{W}\}$, where $\mathcal{W} \subseteq \mathbb{R}^d$ is the parameter space and is assumed that is convex, closed and bounded, m is the dimension of the input space, $g_\lambda(\underline{x}, \underline{w})$ is a non-linear function of $\underline{x}$ with $\underline{w} = (w_1, w_2, ..., w_d)^T$ being its parameter vector, λ is the number of the hidden neurons and $d = (m + 2)\lambda + 1$ is the number of free parameters.

Given the sample of observations $\chi = \{\underline{x}_k, y_k\}_{k=1}^n$, where we suppose a noisy measured output y_k which is considered as the realization of the random variable $Y = Y|\underline{x}$ conditioned to $\underline{x}_k$. We assume that there exists an unknown regression function $\varphi(\underline{x}) = \mathbb{E}[Y|\underline{x}]$ such that for any fixed value of $\underline{x}$, the stochastic process is determined by $Y|\underline{x} = E[Y|\underline{x}] + \varepsilon$, where ε is a random variable with zero expectation and variance σ_ε^2. The task of neural learning is to construct an estimator $g_\lambda(\underline{x}, \underline{w})$ of the unknown function $\varphi(\underline{x})$ by

$$\hat{y} = g_\lambda(\underline{x}, \underline{w}) = \gamma_2 \left(\sum_{j=1}^{\lambda} w_j^{[2]} \gamma_1 \left(\sum_{i=1}^{m} w_{ij}^{[1]} x_i + w_{m+1,j}^{[1]} \right) + w_{\lambda+1}^{[2]} \right) \qquad (1)$$

where $\underline{w}$ is a parameter vector to be estimated, λ is a control parameter (number of hidden units) and, an important factor in the specification of neural models, is the choice of the 'activation' function γ_s', these can be any non-linear functions as long as they are continuous, bounded and differentiable. The activation function of the hidden neurons γ_1 typically is a logistic function $\gamma_1(z) = [1 + exp\{-z\}]^{-1}$. For the output neuron the function γ_2 could be a linear function $f(z) = z$, or a nonlinear function.

3   Bootstrap and Bootstrapping Neural Networks

The Bootstrap of Efron [3] is a method for estimating the distribution of an estimator or test statistic by resampling the data or a model estimated from the data. Bootstrap is actually a well tested tool in many areas of parametrtic and nonparametric statistics and a field of intensive research over the last two decades.

In the context of regression models, two types of bootstrap have taken force: the residual and the pairwise bootstrap. Both approaches attempt to respect the dependence between predictors and targets. The approach named *residual bootstrapping* applies a bootstrap plan over the residuals of the model, this plan is usually nonparametric but can be smoothed or parameterized if we have enough information. To obtain the set of residuals $\{\varepsilon_1, \varepsilon_2, \ldots, \varepsilon_n\}$ we adjust the model $g(\underline{x})$ to the data and obtain the set of parameters for the model, where the entities under study can be these parameters or a function of theses parameters. Applying the bootstrap plan to the set of residuals we can obtain a bootstrap residual set, say $\{\varepsilon_1^*, \varepsilon_2^*, \ldots, \varepsilon_n^*\}$. To generate a bootstrap data set we follow the recursive scheme $y_k = g(\underline{x}_k) + \varepsilon_k^*$. We repeat the procedure several times and for each bootstrap data set we adjust the model again. In the case of *Pairwise Bootstrap* the idea is resampling directly the training pairs $\{\underline{x}_k, y_k\}_{k=1}^{n}$ taking both predictors and target simultaneously. The bootstrap samples obtained with both methods are used to adjust the models and generate an estimate of the distribution of the quantity of interest.

Unfortunately several problems arise with the FANN models, they are neither globally nor locally identified due to the fact that the parameterization of the network function is not unique (for example, we can permute the hidden units), the possible symmetry of the activation function and the presence of irrelevant hidden units. However we can always infer about a distinguishable function of the weight vector such as the network output.

4   Robust Bootstrap Procedure in Neural Networks

In this section we construct a robust bootstrap plan for neural networks based on a robust resampling algorithm and robust estimators for the models. Robust estimations are designed to produce estimates that are immune to serious distortions up to certain number of outliers. However, this approach remains insufficient because the resampling procedure can break even an estimator with a high breakdown point.

To address the potentially harmful replication of outliers in the bootstrap samples, we work directly over the estimated distribution that draws the observations. In [2], they introduce a perturbation of the resampling probabilities ascribing more importance to some sample values than others using the influence function (see [5]) to compute those selection probabilities. This procedure leads to resampling less frequently those observations that affect mostly the initial model while assigning higher probabilities to the observations forming the main structure.

4.1   Robust Learning Algorithm

First, we deal with the problem of a robust model that is resistant to outlying observations. In some earlier works it is shown that FANN models are affected with the presence of outlying observations, in the way that the learning process and the prediction performance are deteriorated (See [1]).

Let the data set $\chi = \{\underline{x}_k, y_k\}_{k=1}^n$ consist of an independent and identically distributed (i.i.d) sample of size n coming from the probability distribution $F(\underline{x}, y)$. A nonlinear function $y = \varphi(\underline{x}) + \epsilon$ is approximated from the data by a FANN model $y = g_\lambda(\underline{x}, \underline{w}^*) + \varepsilon$. An M-estimator $\hat{\underline{w}}_n^M$ is defined by $\hat{\underline{w}}_n^M = arg\ min\{RL_n(\underline{w}) : \underline{w} \in \mathcal{W}\}$, where $RL_n(\underline{w})$ is a robust functional cost given by the following equation,

$$RL_n(\underline{w}) = \frac{1}{n} \sum_{k=1}^n \rho \left(\frac{y_k - g_\lambda(\underline{x}_k, \underline{w})}{\sigma_\varepsilon} \right) \tag{2}$$

where ρ is the robust function that introduces a bound to the influence due to the presence of outliers in the data. Assuming that ρ is differentiable and its derivative is given by $\psi(r, \underline{w}) = \frac{\partial \rho(r, \underline{w})}{\partial r}$, an M-estimator $\hat{\underline{w}}_n^M$ can be defined implicitly by the solution of

$$\sum_{k=1}^n \psi \left(\frac{y_k - g_\lambda(\underline{x}_k, \underline{w})}{\sigma_\varepsilon} \right) Dg_\lambda(\underline{x}_t, \underline{w}) = \underline{0}$$

where $\psi : \mathbb{R} \times \mathcal{W} \to \mathbb{R}$, $r_t = y_t - g_\lambda(\underline{x}^t, \hat{\underline{w}}_n^M)$ is the residual error and

$$Dg_\lambda(\underline{x}, \underline{w}) = \left(\frac{\partial}{\partial w_1} g_\lambda(\underline{x}, \underline{w}), \ldots, \frac{\partial}{\partial w_d} g_\lambda(\underline{x}, \underline{w}) \right)^T \tag{3}$$

is the gradient of the FANN. We will denote $Dg_\lambda = Dg_\lambda(\underline{x}, \underline{w})$ for short.

4.2   Robust Resampling

When we resample the original set of observations, at least in the non-parametric bootstrap case, we assign equal selection probabilities to all observations, but the bootstrap samples can be harmfully altered by outliers. The bad behaviour of the bootstrap when there are outliers in the mother sample have been referenced in several papers [10] [2] [11]. We will adapt their proposal for robustifying bootstrap resampling algorithm presented in [2].

To obtain the selection probabilities of the observations, we measure the influence of the particular data over the parameters. The IF is a local measure introduced by Hampel [5] and describes the effect of an infinitesimal contamination on the estimate at the point $(\underline{x}, y)$. The IF of the M-estimator applied to the FANN model calculated at the distribution function $F(\underline{x}, y)$ is given by,

$$IF(\underline{x}, r; \underline{w}^*, F) = -\psi(r, \underline{w}^*)M^{-1}Dg_\lambda(\underline{x}, \underline{w}^*)^T \tag{4}$$

where $r = r(\underline{x}, y) = y - g_\lambda(\underline{x}, \underline{w})$ is the residual, $Dg_\lambda(\underline{x}, \underline{w}^*)$ is given by equation (3) and M is given by $M = \int_{\mathbb{R}} H(\underline{x}, r, \underline{w}^*)dF(\underline{x}, y) = \mathbb{E}_F[H]$, where H is the Hessian of $\rho(\cdot)$ with respect to the parameters $\underline{w}$, i.e. , $H(\underline{x}, r, \underline{w}) = (\psi'(r, \underline{w})Dg_\lambda Dg_\lambda^T - \psi(r, \underline{w})D^2g_\lambda)$, and $D^2g_\lambda = \left[\frac{\partial^2 g_\lambda(\underline{x}, \underline{w})}{\partial w_i \partial w_j}\right]$ is the Hessian matrix of the FANN of side $d \times d$. In practice, M is not observable and must be estimated. White [12] demonstrated that a consistent estimator of M is

$$\widehat{M_n} = \frac{1}{n}\sum_{k=1}^{n} H(\underline{x}_k, r_k, \hat{\underline{w}}_n^M) \tag{5}$$

where $\hat{\underline{w}}_n^M$ are the parameters obtained from the data by the minimization of the risk function (2). With this result, we can estimate the influence at the point $(\underline{x}^*, y^*)$ by $\widehat{IF}(\underline{x}^*, r^*; \hat{\underline{w}}_n^M) = \psi(r^*, \hat{\underline{w}}_n^M)\hat{M}_n^{-1}Dg_\lambda(\underline{x}^*, \hat{\underline{w}}_n^M)^T$.

Instead we used the standardized influence function as a measure of the impact (or the distance) of the observation to the model:

$$SIF(r, \underline{x}, \underline{w}^*, F) = \sqrt{IF(r, \underline{x}, \underline{w}^*, F)^T V(\underline{w}^*)^{-1}IF(r, \underline{x}, \underline{w}^*, F)} \tag{6}$$

where the variance of the estimator is given by,

$$\begin{aligned}V(\underline{w}^*) &= \int IF(\underline{x}, y; \underline{w}^*, F)IF(\underline{x}, y; \underline{w}^*, F)^T dF(\underline{x}, y) \\ &= M(\psi, F)^{-1}Q(\psi, F)M(\psi, F)^{-T}\end{aligned} \tag{7}$$

and

$$Q(\psi, F) := \int \psi(r, \underline{w}^*)^2 Dg_\lambda(\underline{x}, \underline{w}^*)Dg_\lambda(\underline{x}, \underline{w}^*)^T dF(\underline{x}, y)$$

$$= \mathbb{E}_F[\psi(r, \underline{w}^*)^2 Dg_\lambda(\underline{x}, \underline{w}^*)Dg_\lambda(\underline{x}, \underline{w}^*)^T]$$

A consistent estimator of Q is given in [12] by

$$\hat{Q}_n = \frac{1}{n}\left\{\sum_{t=1}^{n}\psi(r_t,\hat{\underline{w}}_n^M)^2 Dg_\lambda(\underline{x}_t,\hat{\underline{w}}_n^M)Dg_\lambda(\underline{x}_t,\hat{\underline{w}}_n^M)^T\right\}$$

With this result, we can estimate the variance of the estimator $\hat{V}(\hat{\underline{w}}_n^M) = \hat{M}_n^{-1}\hat{Q}_n\hat{M}_n^{-T}$, where $r^* = y^* - g_\lambda(\underline{x}^*,\hat{\underline{w}}_n^M)$.

Now we introduce our proposal of the robust version of the resampling procedure that will be the basis for the Robust FANN Algorithm that we will propose.

Robust Resampling Algorithm

1. Compute the estimated , $\widehat{SIF}_k = \widehat{SIF}(r_k,\underline{x}_k,\hat{\underline{w}},F)$, at each data point $k = 1,2,\dots,n$.
2. Compute the resampling distribution $P = (p_1,p_2,\dots,p_n)$ where, $p_k = \frac{w_k}{\sum_{j=1}^{n}w_j}$ and

$$w_k = I_{[0,c]}\left(\left|\widehat{SIF}\right|\right) + \eta\left(c,\left|\widehat{SIF}_k\right|\right)\times I_{[c,\infty]}\left(\left|\widehat{SIF}_k\right|\right) \qquad k = 1..n \quad (8)$$

where $I_{[a,b]}$ is the indicator function of the interval $[a,b]$, $c > 0$ is the tuning constant, and η is the attenuating function activated at c, non-negative, $\lim_{t\to\infty}t^2\eta(c,t) = 0$ for c fixed and $\frac{\partial\eta(c,t)}{\partial t}\big|_{t=c} = 0$. The first condition is evident because the function $\eta(\cdot)$ is only attenuating the probability of resampling of an observation proportional to its influence; second, guarantees that the outliers don't introduce a significative bias. Last is a smoothness condition that preserves the efficiency of the procedure with few outliers.
3. Apply a bootstrapping plan starting with this modified empirical distribution $P = (p_1,p_2,\dots,p_n)$.

To choose the $\eta(\cdot)$ function, a first election can be (See A. Pires et.al. [2]) a member of the family

$$\eta(x,c,s,\tau) = \begin{cases}\left[1+\frac{(x-c)^2}{\gamma s^2}\right]^{\frac{-\tau+1}{2}} & 1 < \tau < \infty \\ \exp\left[-\frac{(x-c)^2}{2s^2}\right] & \tau = \infty\end{cases} \qquad (9)$$

where c is the location parameter (equal to the tuning constant c of expression (8)), s is the scale parameter and τ is a shape parameter, a reasonable choice could be $\tau = 2$.

4.3   Robust Bootstrap FANN Algorithm (RB-FANN)

In this section we introduce our Robust bootstrap algorithm for feedforward neural networks (RB-FANN) that introduce a robust sampling and robust learning algorithm for several neural networks created.

Robust Bootstrap Algorithm for FANN

1. Choose a FANN architecture by fixing the number of hidden parameters λ, and denote the model by $g_\lambda(\underline{x}, \underline{w})$.
2. Train the neural networks with the robust learning algorithm presented in section 4.1 with the whole training dataset $\{\underline{x}_k, y_k\}_{k=1}^n$, obtaining the robust model $g_\lambda(\underline{x}, \hat{\underline{w}}_n^M)$
3. Calculate the residuals $\hat{\varepsilon}_k = y_k - g_\lambda(\underline{x}, \hat{\underline{w}}_n^M)$, for all the training set $\{\underline{x}_k, y_k\}_{k=1}^n$.
4. Bootstrap loop $(b = 1, \ldots, B)$.
   a) Apply a robust bootstrap resampling plan presented in section 4.2 over the center residuals $(\tilde{\varepsilon}_1, \ldots, \tilde{\varepsilon}_n)$ generating independently the bootstrap errors $(\tilde{\varepsilon}_1^*, \ldots, \tilde{\varepsilon}_n^*)$.
   b) Apply a bootstrap resampling plan over the input vectors $(\underline{x}_1, \ldots, \underline{x}_n)$ generating independently the bootstrap input vectors $(\underline{x}_1^*, \ldots, \underline{x}_n^*)$.
   c) Generate the b-th training data set $\{\underline{x}_i^*, y_i^*\}$, where $y_i^* = g_\lambda(\underline{x}_i^*, \hat{\underline{w}}_n^M) + \tilde{\varepsilon}_i^*$
   d) Train the boostrap FANN with a robust learning algorithm to obtain the weight vector $\tilde{\underline{w}}_n^{b*}$ and the model $g_\lambda(\underline{x}, \tilde{\underline{w}}_n^{b*})$.
   e) Let b=b+1, if there are sufficient (B) bootstrap replications exit loop go to 5, else go to 4(a)
5. For each bootstrap weight vector $\tilde{\underline{w}}_n^{b*}$ that represents a trained network, we evaluate the function of interest $f^{*b} = f(\tilde{w}_n^{*b})$. For example, if we are studying the response of the network to a given input $\underline{x}$ we evaluate the output of the b-th trained network to this input $\underline{x}$, i.e., $g_\lambda^{*b}(\underline{x}) = g_\lambda(\underline{x}, \tilde{\underline{w}}_n^{b*})$.
6. From the set of bootstrap replications $\{f^{*1}, \ldots, f^{*B}\}$ we can make our inferences.

5   Simulation Results

In this section we show two experimental results where we compare the classical bootstrap for FANN [4] with our robust version. We make inference based on the bootstrap results, in particular we are interested in the mean and in the the $\alpha\%$ confidence interval information extracted from the empirical distribution of the bootstraps predictions. We center our attention in the prediction of a syntethic and a real data set.

In order to make the simulations we need to choose the robust estimators for the learning process of the FANN. In this section we select the Huber function, which are given by $\psi_H(r, c) = sgn(r)min\{|r|, c\}$.

5.1   Example #1: Computer Generated Data

In this section the procedure is applied to computer generated data of a one-dimensional input and output space as in [8], where the true underlying function $\varphi(x), x \in \mathbb{R}$ is known and given by:

$$\varphi(x) = \sin(w_\alpha x) \sin(w_\beta x), \qquad w_\alpha = 2.5, w_\beta = 1.5, x \in [0, \pi] \qquad (10)$$

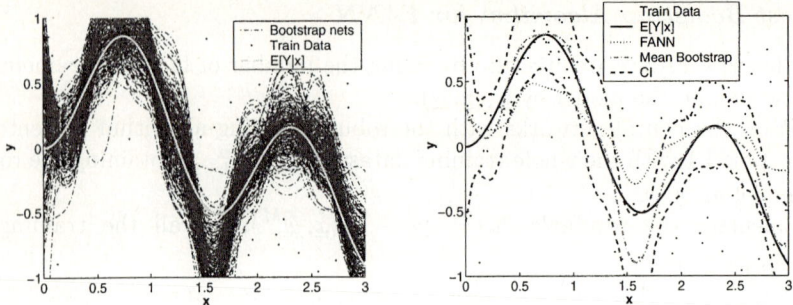

Fig. 1. Bootstrap Inference: Left, several bootstrap approximating the regression function. Right, prediction and confidence interval for the regression function by bootstrap replications

The target values are generated by adding noise $a(x) \sim N(0, \sigma_a^2(x))$, where $\sigma_a^2(x) = 0.01 + 0.25 \times [1 - \sin(w_\alpha x)]^2$ and by adding additive outliers. The observational process z_t is obtained by $z = \varphi(x) + a + uv$, where v is a zero-one process with $P[v \neq 0] = \beta$, u has distribution $F_u = N(0; \sigma_u^2)$ and $0 < \beta << 1$. We generated 200 random samples in $[0, \pi]$ to train the FANN and we test the model with equally spaced 315 data from 0 to π separated by intervals of 0.01, the parameters chosen are $\sigma_u^2 = 1$ and $\beta = 0\%, 5\%, 10\%, 20\%$. In the right side of figure 1 the regression function and the training data are shown.

A single-input-single-output (SISO) FANN model with one hidden layer with ten hidden neurons and logistic activation function for the hidden layer and linear activation function for the output neuron was implemented to model the data. Two bootstrap algorithms were used, the classical (B) and our robust version (RB) with the Huber estimator. To obtain the parameters of the several networks the backpropagation with momentum algorithm was used (see [12]).

The result of both procedure are summarized in table 1, where the performance of the training and test set was measured with the mean square error and for the quality of the confidence interval, the probability coverage (PC) and the mean length ($\overline{L}$) of the interval in the training and test set was computed. The PC is the proportion of points of the real data that fall inside the interval and the mean length is defined as $\overline{L} = \sum_{k=1}^{n} \frac{1}{n}(L_k^{sup} - L_k^{inf})$, where L_k^{sup} and L_k^{inf} are the superior and inferior limit of the CI at the point $(\underline{x}_k, y_k)$.

As can be noted in table 1, the mean of the bootstrap estimates improves the performance of the prediction obtained by the initial net, moreover, the robust version (RB) performs better than the classical (B) in most of the cases. If we look to the confidence interval, the difference between the coverage probability (PC) and the desired confidence α are almost the same for both cases, but the robust bootstrap CI size are smaller than the classical bootstrap. In the figure 1 it is noted how the Bootstrap mean prediction improves the accuracy of the initial net, and how the C.I. contains the regression function when the robust bootstrap is applied.

Table 1. Performance of the model on the computer generated data, probability coverage (PC, $\alpha = 95\%$ declared) and mean length ($\overline{L}$) of the Confidence Interval results for the Synthetic dataset with 200 Bootstrap replications, 200 training patterns and 315 testing ones with $\beta\%$ of additive outliers

Bootstrap Type	$\beta\%$ Outliers	net MSE Test set	Boots. MSE Test set	PC Test set	$\overline{L}$ Test set
B	0	0.0209	0.0188	81.71	0.5774
RB	0	0.0182	0.0158	90.47	0.4217
B	5	0.0098	0.0112	93.41	0.5002
RB	5	0.0139	0.0113	93.96	0.4868
B	10	0.0164	0.0131	98.73	0.6233
RB	10	0.0140	0.0095	97.14	0.4943
B	20	0.0310	0.0269	100.00	0.7849
RB	20	0.0263	0.0196	93.97	0.6580

5.2   Example #2: Real Data, Boston Housing Dataset

We now apply our method to a set of observed data, the Boston housing dataset. This dataset contains information collected by the U.S. Census Service concerning housing in the area of Boston Mass. It was obtained from the StatLib archive (http://lib.stat.cmu.edu/datasets/boston), and has been used extensively throughout the literature to benchmarks algorithms. The dataset is small in size with only 506 cases, it has 13 input attributes (crime, residential land, non-retail business, river, nitric oxides concentration, etc.) and the task is to predict the median value of owner-occupied homes. This dataset is characterized by the high level of contaminated data.

The results are shown in table 2. As can be appreciated the robust bootstrap always improve the performance of the initial net, this is not the case of the classical bootstrap, and the robust version are always better than the classical. If we look to the confidence interval, we obtain similar results in the PC, but the robust bootstrap has smaller mean length of CI.

Table 2. Performance of the model on the real data, probability coverage (PC, $\alpha = 95\%$ declared) and mean length ($\overline{L}$) of the Confidence Interval results for the Boston dataset with 200 and 20 Bootstrap replications. The sizes of the training set, validation set and testing set are 308, 200 and 200 respectively

Bootstrap Type	B	net MSE Train	Val.	Test	Boots. MSE Train	Val.	Test	PC Train	Val.	Test	$\overline{L}$ Train	Val.	Test
B	200	73	2242	3018	69	1326	1450	77	94	97	20.36	168.33	267.37
RB	200	173	1724	1782	194	743	601	68	90	99	22.67	69.17	99.43
B	20	73	2242	3018	76	3511	4614	67	83	88	20.56	177.73	275.93
RB	20	172	1724	1782	182	617	364	56	88	94	17.09	55.74	78.45

6   Concluding Remarks

In this paper we introduce a robust bootstrap technique for estimating confidence and prediction intervals for FANN. The Intervals incorporate a significantly improved estimate of the underling model uncertainty. The bootstrap distribution might be a very poor estimator of the distribution of the regression estimates because the proportion outliers in the bootstrap sample can be higher than the original sample.

The robust bootstrap plan for FANN based on a robust resampling is easy to implement in terms of stability and computational cost (speed of convergence) in situations involving multiple dimensional problems.

The algorithm shown here generates an alteration of the original empirical distribution that gives a robust resampling scheme for whole bootstrap procedure; but it leaves some unsolved problems, as for example, introduce bias to the distribution. The performance of our algorithm can be improved by applying other inference techniques for the bootstraps results. The results presented in this paper can be easily extended to FANN with a higher number of layers and output neurons. Further studies are needed in order to apply this technique to nonlinear time series, where the data are correlated.

References

1. H. Allende, C. Moraga, and R. Salas, *Robust estimator for the learning process in neural networks applied in time series*, ICANN. LNCS **2415** (2002), 1080–1086.
2. C. Amado and A. Pires, *Robust bootstrapping using influence functions*, Proceedings in Computational Statistics 2000: Short Communications and Posters, Statistics Netherlands, Voorburg, 2000, pp. 83–84.
3. B. Efron, *Bootstrap methods: another look at the jacknife*, The Annals of Statistics **7** (1979), 1–26.
4. J. Franke and M. Neumann, *Bootstrapping neural networks*, Neural Computation **12** (2000), 1929–1949.
5. F.R. Hampel, E.M. Ronchetti, P.J. Rousseeuw, and W.A. Stahel, *Robust statistics*, Wiley Series in Probability and Mathematical Statistics, 1986.
6. Tom Heskes, *Practical confidence and prediction intervals*, Advances in Neural Information Processing Systems. MIT Press **9** (1997), 176–182.
7. J. Hwang and A. Ding, *Prediction intervals for artificial neural networks*, J. American Statistical Association **92** (1997), no. 438, 748–757.
8. D. Nix and A. Weigend, *Estimating the mean and the variance of the target probability distribution*, IEEE, in Proceedings of the IJCNN'94 (1994), 55–60.
9. R. Salas, R. Torres, H. Allende, and C. Moraga, *Robust estimation of confidence interval in neural networks applied to time series*, IWANN. LNCS **2687** (2003), 441–448.
10. M. Salibián-Barrera and R. Zamar, *Bootstrapping robust estimates of regression*, The Annals of Statistics **30** (2002), 556–582.
11. K. Singh, *Breakdown theory for bootstrap quantiles*, The annals of Statistics **26** (1998), 1719–1732.
12. Halbert White, *Artificial neural networks: Approximation and learning theory*, Basil Blackwell, Oxford, 1992.

A Kernel Method for Classification

Donald MacDonald[1], Jos Koetsier[1], Emilio Corchado[1],
Colin Fyfe[1], and Juan Corchado[2]

[1] School of Information and Communication Technologies
The University of Paisley, High Street, Paisley, PA1-2BE, Scotland.
corc-ci0@paisley.ac.uk
[2] Departamento de Informática y Automática, Universidad de Salamanca, Spain.

Abstract. Kernel Maximum Likelihood Hebbian Learning Scale Invariant Maps is a novel technique developed to facilitate the clustering of complex data effectively and efficiently and that is characterised for converging remarkably quickly. The combination of Maximum Likelihood Hebbian Learning Scale Invariant Map and the Kernel Space provides a very smooth scale invariant quantisation which can be used as a clustering technique. The efficiency of this method have been used to analyse an oceanographic problem.

1 Introduction

Kernel Maximum Likelihood Hebbian Learning Scale Invariant Map (K-MLSIM) is based on a modification of a new type of topology preserving map that can be used for scale invariant classification [6]. Kernel models were first developed within the context of Support Vector Machines [16]. Support Vector Machines attempt to identify a small number of data points (the support vectors) which are necessary to solve a particular problem to the required accuracy. Kernels have been successfully used in the unsupervised investigation of structure in data sets [15], [11], [9]. Kernel methods map a data set into a Feature space using a nonlinear mapping. Then typically a linear operation is performed in the feature space; this is equivalent to performing a nonlinear operation on the original data set. The Scale Invariant Map is an implementation of the negative feedback network to form a topology preserving mapping. A kernel method is applied in this paper to an extension of the Scale Invariant Map (SIM) which is based on the application of the Maximum Likelihood Hebbian Learning (MLHL) method [4] and its possibilities are explored. The proposed methodology groups cases with similar structure, identifying clusters automatically in a data set in an unsupervised mode.

2 Kernel Scale Invariant Map

This section reviews the techniques used to construct the K-MLSIM method.

R. Monroy et al. (Eds.): MICAI 2004, LNAI 2972, pp. 823–832, 2004.

2.1 Scale Invariant Map

Consider a network with N dimensional input data and having M output neurons. Then the activation of the ith output neuron is given by:

$$act_i = \sum_{j=1}^{N} w_{ij} x_j \tag{1}$$

Now if we invoke a competition between the output neurons, it is possible to have a number of different competitions between output neurons, two obvious examples are:

Type A: The neuron with greatest activation wins.

Type B: The neuron closest to the input vector wins.

The Kohonen network typically uses the second since the first requires specific renormalisation to ensure that all neurons have a chance of winning a competition. We have shown that the scale invariant mapping produced by the new network does not require any additional competition limiting procedure when using the first criterion. In both cases, the winning neuron, the pth, is deemed to be maximally firing (=1) and all other output neurons are suppressed(=0). Its firing is then fed back through the same weights to the input neurons as inhibition.

$$e_j \leftarrow x_j - w_{pj}.1\_for\_all\_j \tag{2}$$

where p is the winning neuron. Now the winning neuron excites those neurons close to it i.e. we have a neighbourhood function $\Lambda(p, j)$ which $\Lambda(p, j) \leq \Lambda(p, k)$ for all $j, k : \|p - j\| \geq \|p - k\|$ where $\|.\|$ is the Euclidean norm. In the simulations described in this paper, we use a Gaussian whose radius is decreased during the course of the simulation. Then simple Hebbian learning gives

$$\Delta w_{ij} = \eta_t \Lambda(p, i).e_j = \eta_t \Lambda(p, i).(x_j - w_{pj}) \tag{3}$$

where we have used x_j as the activation of the jth input neuron and w_{ij} is the weight between this and the ith output neuron. For the pth winning neuron, the network is performing simple competitive learning but note the direct effect the pth output neuron's weight has on the learning of other neurons. This algorithm introduces competition into the same network used in [5] to perform a Principal Component Analysis (PCA) and in [7] to perform an Exploratory Projection Pursuit (EPP).

2.2 Kernel K-Means Clustering

We will follow the derivation of [14] who has shown that the k means algorithm can be performed in Kernel space. The basic idea of the set of methods known as kernel methods is that the data set is transformed into a nonlinear feature space $(\phi : x \rightarrow \phi(x))$. Any linear operation now performed in this feature space is equivalent to a nonlinear operation in the original space.

The aim is to find k means, m_μ, so that each point is close to one of the means. First we note that each mean may be described as lying in the manifold spanned by the observations, $\phi(\mathbf{x}_i)$ i.e. $m_\mu = \sum_i w_{\mu i} \phi(x_i)$. Now the k means algorithm chooses the means, $\mathbf{m}_\mu$, to minimise the Euclidean distance between the points and the closest mean

$$\left|\phi(\mathbf{x}) - m_\mu\right|^2 = \left|\phi(\mathbf{x}) - \sum_i w_{\mu i} \phi(\mathbf{x}_i)\right|^2 = k(\mathbf{x},\mathbf{x}) - 2\sum_i w_{\mu i} k(\mathbf{x},\mathbf{x}_i) + \sum_{i,j} w_{\mu i} w_{\mu j} k(\mathbf{x}_i,\mathbf{x}_j)$$ (4)

i.e. the distance calculation can be accomplished in Kernel space by means of the K matrix alone. Let $M_{i\mu}$ be the cluster assignment variable. i.e. $M_{i\mu}=1$ if $\phi(\mathbf{x}_i)$ is in the μth cluster and is 0 otherwise. [14] initialises the means to the first training patterns and then each new training point, $\phi(\mathbf{x}_{t+1}), t+1 > k$, is assigned to the closest mean and its cluster assignment variable calculated using

$$M_{t+1,\alpha} = \begin{cases} 1 \_ if \_ \|\phi(x_{t+1}) - m_\alpha\| < \|\phi(x_{t+1}) - m_\mu\|, \forall \mu \ne \alpha \\ 0 \_ otherwise \end{cases}$$ (5)

In terms of the kernel function (noting that $k(\mathbf{x},\mathbf{x})$ is common to all calculations) we have

$$M_{t+1,\alpha} = \begin{cases} 1 \_ if \_ \sum_{i,j} w_{\alpha i} w_{\alpha j} k(\mathbf{x}_i,\mathbf{x}_j) - 2\sum_i w_{\alpha i} k(\mathbf{x},\mathbf{x}_i) \\ < \sum_{i,j} w_{\mu i} w_{\mu j} k(x_i,x_j) - 2\sum_i w_{\mu i} k(\mathbf{x},\mathbf{x}_i), \forall \mu \ne \alpha \\ 0 \_ otherwise \end{cases}$$ (6)

We must then update the mean, $\mathbf{m}_\alpha$ to take account of the $(t+1)^{th}$ data point

$$\mathbf{m}_\alpha^{t+1} = \mathbf{m}_\alpha^t + \zeta\left(\phi(x_{t+1}) - \mathbf{m}_\alpha^t\right)$$ (7)

where we have used the term $\mathbf{m}_\alpha^{t+1}$ to designate the updated mean which takes into account the new data point and

$$\zeta = M_{t+1,\alpha} \Big/ \sum_{i=1}^{t+1} M_{i,\alpha}$$ (8)

Now (7) may be written as

$$\sum_i w_{\alpha i}^{t+1} \phi(\mathbf{x}_i) = \sum_i w_{\alpha i}^t \phi(\mathbf{x}_i) + \zeta\left(\phi(\mathbf{x}_{t+1}) - \sum_i w_{\alpha i} \phi(\mathbf{x}_i)\right)$$ (9)

which leads to an update equation of

$$w_{\alpha i}^{t+1} = \begin{cases} w_{\alpha i}^t (1-\zeta) \_ for \_ i \ne t+1 \\ \zeta \_ for \_ i = t+1 \end{cases}$$ (10)

2.3 Kernel Self Organising Map

We have previously used the above analysis to derive a Self Organising Map [10] in Kernel space. The SOM algorithm is a k means algorithm with an attempt to distribute the means in an organised manner and so the first change to the above algorithm is to update the closest neuron's weights and those of its neighbours. Thus we find the winning neuron (the closest in feature space) as above but now instead of (6), we use

$$M_{t+1,\mu} = \Lambda(\alpha,\mu), \forall \mu \tag{11}$$

where α is the identifier of the closest neuron and $\Lambda(\alpha,\mu)$ is a neighbourhood function which in the experiments reported herein was a gaussian. Thus the winning neuron has a value of M=1 while the value of M for other neurons decreases monotonically with distance (in neuron space) away from the winning neuron. For the experiments reported in this paper, we used a one dimensional vector of output neurons numbered 1 to 20 or 30. The remainder of the algorithm is exactly as reported in the previous section.

2.4 The Kernel Scale Invariant Map

We will, in this Section, consider only linear kernels though the extension to other kernels is straightforward. Since every point in data space can be represented by a linear combination of the training data set $\{\mathbf{x}_i, i=1,...,N\}$, we have $\exists v_i : x = \sum_{i=1}^{N} v_i \mathbf{x}_i$ for all x in the data space. Similarly the weight vectors can be represented in the same way. Thus we can represent

$$y_\mu = \sum_{j=1}^{N} w_{\mu j} \mathbf{x}_j \tag{12}$$

as

$$y_\mu = \sum_j \sum_i v_{\mu i} x_i x_j = \sum_j \sum_i v_{\mu i} k(\mathbf{x}_i \mathbf{x}_j) \tag{13}$$

Now we wish to have a competition to find out which output will win for a particular input, $\mathbf{x}_l$, and so the first question to be addressed is the nature of the competition. If we are working in data space with the above overcomplete basis, then every member of the training set is representable as a vector which is all zeros except for the lth position which is set to 1. Therefore we identify the lth column of the kernel matrix, and determine the output which wins the competition to represent x_l as

$$\alpha = \arg\max_\mu y_\mu = \arg\max_\mu \sum_i v_{\mu i} x_i x_l = \arg\max_\mu \mathbf{k}_l \mathbf{v}_\mu \tag{14}$$

where we have used k_l as the vector from the lth column of the kernel matrix.

We have experimented with two methods:
1. The Kernel method of the previous section. With the notation above, we have

$$v_{\alpha i} = \begin{cases} v_{\alpha i}(1-\zeta)\_ for \_ i \neq l \\ \zeta \_ for \_ i = l \end{cases} \tag{15}$$

with ζ defined as for the Kernel SOM. This continues to be one-shot learning with a subsequent gradual decay.
2. The neural method used with the standard SIM. Note that since we are working in the space spanned by the data as basis vectors, the input vector has a zero

everywhere but the lth position and we are subtracting $\mathbf{v}$ (α being the winning neuron). Thus

$$\mathbf{e} = \mathbf{x} - \mathbf{v}_\alpha \qquad (16)$$

in this basis. We then apply the standard learning rule so that

$$\Delta v_{\mu i} = \eta \Lambda(\alpha, \mu) e_i \qquad (17)$$

Even though this method is an iterative method as is usual in neural methods, we find that only a few (less than 10, often just 2 or 3) iterations through a data set are enough to form the mapping.

3   Maximum Likelihood Hebbian Learning

We have previously [2, 10] considered a general cost function associated with a negative feedback PCA network.

$$J = 1^T E\{(\mathbf{x} - Wy)^2\} \qquad (18)$$

If the residual after the feedback has probability density function

$$p(\mathbf{e}) = \frac{1}{Z}\exp(-|\mathbf{e}|^p) \qquad (19)$$

Then we can denote a general cost function associated with this network as

$$J = -\log p(\mathbf{e}) = |\mathbf{e}|^p + K \qquad (20)$$

where K is a constant. Finding the minimum of J corresponds to finding the maximum of $p(\mathbf{e})$ i.e. we are maximising the probability that the residual comes from a particular distribution. We do this by adjusting the weights. Therefore performing gradient descent on J we have

$$\Delta W \propto -\frac{\partial J}{\partial W} = -\frac{\partial J}{\partial \mathbf{e}}\frac{\partial \mathbf{e}}{\partial W} \approx y(p|\mathbf{e}|^{p-1} sign(\mathbf{e}))^T \qquad (21)$$

We would expect that for leptokurtotic residuals (more kurtotic than a Gaussian distribution), values of p < 2 would be appropriate, while platykurtotic residuals (less kurtotic than a Gaussian), values of p > 2 would be appropriate. We have previously [8], [3], [13] shown that this network can perform EPP.

3.1   Application to Kernel Scale Invariant Map

Now the SIM was originally derived by introducing competition to the negative feedback PCA network. Therefore we introduce the MLHL concept of the last section to the Scale Invariant Map (SIM). Consider the feedback in 16. Let us present a particular input, $\mathbf{x}_i = (0,..,0,1,0,..0)$ which has 1 in the lth position, to the network. Then if neuron α wins the competition, it is because the weights $\mathbf{v}$ have a high dot product with the elements of l's column of the k matrix; either $\mathbf{v}_{\alpha l}$ is large or $\mathbf{v}_{\alpha k}$ (for input k which will be grouped with l) is large. Thus the residuals after feedback will have a bimodal distribution - either the residuals will tend towards 0 or the residuals will be large.

This suggests maximising the likelihood that the residuals come from a sub-gaussian distribution; therefore, we proposed the learning rules

$$\Delta v_{\mu j} = \eta \Lambda(\alpha, \mu) sign(e_j) |e_j|^2 \tag{22}$$

This has an interesting effect on the learning rules in that a pie slice of the data is learned but the actual positions of the neuron centres themselves (when transformed back into data space) lie outside the data set. This enables a very smooth scale invariant quantisation as shown in Figure 1. The **v** weight vectors are shown in Figure 2. The data set, drawn uniformly from [-1,1]*[-1,1], is shown by the crosses. The weights of the converged Kernel Scale Invariant Map have been joined to form almost a circle. The corresponding vector in data space based on the data as basis vectors is shown in Figure 2 each line of the diagram represents the weights of one output neuron in terms of the data points (the **v** weights in fact).

Fig. 1. The data set is shown by the red crosses. It was drawn uniformly from[-1,1]*[-1,1]. The weights of the converged KSIM have been joined to form almost a circle.

Fig. 2. The **v** weights as represented in the data basis. Each line is the weight vector into an output neuron and is shown.

We have found that even a very small departure from the standard K-SIM parameter (with p=2) gives a visible change to the representation of the data set. In the top left of Figure 3, we show the converged weights after 7 iterations of the K-SIM algorithm when p=1.8; the weights are well enclosed in the data. In the top right of that figure, we show the weights when p=2.1 was used; the weights are beginning to move outside the data set. In the bottom figure, we show what happens when p=2.5. Now the weights are well outside the data.

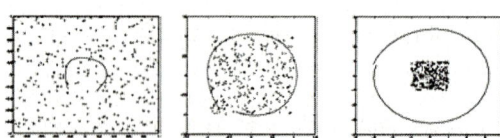

Fig.3. The left figure shows the weights after 7 iterations of the K-SIM algorithm with p=1.8 on the standard artificial data set. The one in the middle shows the weights with p=2.1. The right figure shows the weights when p=2.5.

Consider the situation in which there are n points in the pie slice won by y. Without loss of generality let us write $w = (a_1, a_2, ..., a_n, 0, 0, ..., 0)$ i.e. the vector w has non-zero components corresponding to the points (in the training set), $x_1, ..., x_n$ while its components corresponding to $x_{n+1} ... x_N$ are all zero. Then

$$\Delta w_\alpha = \eta \Lambda(\alpha, \mu) sign(e)|e|^{p-1} \tag{23}$$

Let us consider only the situation in which the points $x_1, \ldots, x_n$ are presented to the network and so the output y_α is the winner; thus $\Lambda(\alpha, \mu) = 1$. Let point x_1 be presented and so $x = (1, 0, 0, \ldots, 0)$. Then

$$e = (1 - a_1, -a2, \ldots, -a_n, 0, \ldots, 0) \tag{24}$$

When point x_2 is presented, $x = (0, 1, 0, \ldots, 0)$ and

$$e = (-a_1, 1 - a2, \ldots, -a_n, 0, \ldots, 0) \tag{25}$$

We will consider the effect of the update rules on this weight vector for different values of p.

p=1. Focus now on the first element of w_α, the element of the weight vector linking input x_1 to output y_α, then at convergence $E(\Delta w_{\alpha 1}) = E(sign(e_1)) = 0$. Clearly if $a_1 < 0$, $sign(e_1)$ is always positive. Therefore $a_1 > 0$. Thus there can only be two non-zero elements in this vector. Impossible.

p=2. This is the standard K-SIM. Then at convergence $E(\Delta w_{\alpha 1}) = E\left(sign(e_1)|e_1|^{1}\right) = 0$ and so

$$1 - a_1 + (n-1) * (-a_1) = 0 \tag{26}$$

Thus $a_1 = 1/n$. This argument applies equally to all non-zero elements of w_α and so $w_\alpha = \left(\dfrac{1}{n}, \dfrac{1}{n}, \ldots, \dfrac{1}{n}, 0, \ldots, 0\right)$ which when we translate back to the original basis means that the centre of the KSIM is given by

$$c_\alpha = \frac{1}{n} x_1 + \frac{1}{n} x_2 + \ldots + \frac{1}{n} x_n \tag{27}$$

the mean of the data points for which neuron α is responsible for representing.

p=3. At convergence $E(\Delta w_{\alpha 1}) = E\left(sign(e_1)|e_1|^{2}\right) = 0$ and so, for $0 < a_1 < 1$,

$$(1 - a_1)^2 - (n-1) * (a_1)^2 = 0 \tag{28}$$

Solving this, we find that $a_1 = \dfrac{-1 \pm \sqrt{(n-1)}}{n-2}$. Thus for $n = 10$, $a_1 = \dfrac{1}{4}$ or $-\dfrac{1}{2}$. In practise, we have never seen the latter result but it seems, in principle, possible. Note that the solution is an equally weighted sum of the data points where the weights are greater than $\dfrac{1}{n}$. Thus the centre, $c_\alpha^* = C * c_\alpha$ where C is a constant and c_α is the mean of the data points defined in 26.

This gives the broad picture. Intermediate values of p will give solutions somewhere between the results given above. In general, at convergence $E(\Delta w_{\alpha 1}) = E\left(sign(e_1)|e_1|^{p-1}\right) = 0$ and so

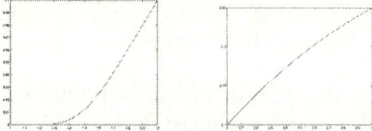

Fig. 4. As we vary p from 1 to 2, a_1 climbs slowly to 0.1 (left figure) and grows more slowly subsequently (right figure).

$$(1-a_1)^{p-1} - (n-1)*(a_1)^{p-1}=0 \tag{29}$$

if $a_1>0$. This implies

$$a_1 = \frac{1}{1+(n-1)^{\frac{1}{p-1}}} \tag{30}$$

The effect of varying p with n=10 is shown in Figure 4. We see that for values close to 1, a_1 remains close to 0, while for values approaching 2, we reach the 1/10 value. Subsequently, a_1 continues to rise but shows signs of levelling off (right figure).

4   Experiments Using Real Data Using the K-MLSIM and Conclusions

In the following section we detail the results of the K-MLSIM on the red tides data. The K-MLSIM is specially suited to be used on the red tides data because of the flexibility of the p-parameter. Changing this parameter affects the update of the centres and it determines how far each centre will move. This property allows the selection of different clustering combinations, penalising, or accentuating the representation of outliers in the clustering. In the case of the red tides data, as each instance of a red tide would be considered an outlier, it is necessary for us to use an algorithm to deal with these important data points in an appropriate manner. In this section we will show that the K-MLSIM is a powerful method that can extract the relevant clustering information.

We have shown previously that the ε-insensitive SIM [12] in data space, which is equivalent to using a p value of 0, will place each centre in the median of the cluster. This property was extended by [1] to use different values of p to achieve different clustering combinations. The larger the value of p the greater the contribution outliers will have in the clustering.

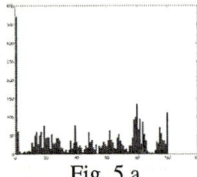
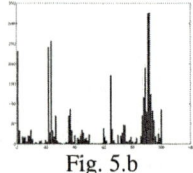
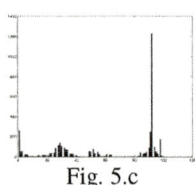

Fig. 5.a   Fig. 5.b   Fig. 5.c

Fig. 5. Clustering of K-SIM on red tides data using 100 centres and a value of $p = 0$ (Fig.5a), a value of p = 0.5 (Fig 5b) and a value of p = 2 (Fig 5c).

The effect that this parameter has on the clustering is important as it allows us to change the clustering to be more representative of the properties of the red tides data as it contains small numbers of outliers which are very important for the classification. If we were to cluster with a contemporary algorithm, we would likely be left with fewer centres that identify instances of red tides than we would like. In contrast the K-SIM can be tailored to give us more centres identifying red tides, resulting in a more expressive clustering.

Figure 5 shows the clusters produced by the K-MLSIM with different values of the p parameter. This parameter will penalize the effect of outliers in the data. This results in the centres being placed in the median of the data cloud.

As we can see from Figure 5a, the clustering is a compact coding with at most 800 data samples being assigned to one centre. This coding is less interesting for the red tides data as the abnormal points are those which are important, and so we wish to find a clustering which promotes rather than penalises them. In the figure 5b we use a value of p = 0.5 which places more emphasis on the larger changes in the weights, which in turn means that outliers, or abnormal data, will have greater effect on the learning. Thus we can ensure that the data points representing red tides will be strongly represented in the clustering, which is ideal for this problem. In Figure 5b we can see that there is a more sparse representation as there is a greater emphasis placed on large differences between the winner and the input data. In this figure we can see that the dense clusters are assigned fewer centres and that less dense clusters that contain outliers are more favoured. Assigning more centres to the less dense clusters also allows us to get a better representation within clusters.

Figure 5c. shows the clustering of the K-MLSIM on the red tides data using a p value of 2. The K-MLSIM is more penalizing to small changes in the weights than with p = 0.5. As can be seen from figure 5c it has provided an even more sparse representation of the clustering. This is a far more suitable clustering of the red tides data where we used smaller values of p. By changing the value of p in the weight update rule the K-MLSIM can be adapted to penalize or promote outliers in its clustering.

We have demonstrated a new technique for clustering. Of interest too is the fact that the method allows investigation of the nonlinear projection matrix K that readily reveals when a new situation behaves similarly, which may be very important in the identification of toxin episodes in coastal water.

References

1. Corchado E. and Fyfe C. The Scale Invariant Map and Maximum Likelihood Hebbian Learning. KES2002. Sixth International Conference on Knowledge-Based Intelligent Information Engineering Systems. Italy. (2002)
2. Corchado E. and Fyfe C. Relevance and kernel self-organising maps. In International Conference on Artificial Neural Networks, ICANN2003. (2003)
3. Corchado E., MacDonald D. and Fyfe C. Optimal projections of high dimensionald data. *In IEEE International Conference on Data Mining, ICDM02.* (2002)
4. Corchado E., MacDonald D. and Fyfe C. Maximum and Minimum Likelihood Hebbian Learning for Exploratory Projection Pursuit. *Data Mining and Knowledge Discovery. In Press.*

5.   Fyfe C. PCA properties of interneurons. In From Neurobiology to Real World Computing, ICANN 93, (1993) pp. 183-188.
6.   Fyfe C. A scale-invariant feature map. *Network:Computation in Neural Systems,* 7: 269-275,1996.
7.   Fyfe C. and Baddeley R. Non-linear data structure extraction using simple hebbian networks. Biological Cybernetics, (1995) 72(6):533-541.
8.   Fyfe C., Baddeley R. and McGregor D.R. Exploratory Projection Pursuit: An Artificial Neural Network Approach, University of Strathclyde Research report/94/160. (1994).
9.   Fyfe C. and Corchado J. M. Automating the construction of CBR Systems using Kernel Methods. International Journal of Intelligent Systems. Vol 16, No. 4, April 2001. ISSN 0884-8173.
10. Fyfe C. and MacDonald D. Epsilon-insensitive Hebbian Learning. Neurocomputing, (2002) 47:35-57.
11. Fyfe, C., MacDonald, D., Lai, P. L., Rosipal, R. and Charles, D. Unsupervised Learning with Radial Kernels in Recent Advances in Radial Basis Functions, Editors R. J. Howlett and L. C. Jain, Elsevier. (2000).
12. MacDonald D. Unsupervised Neural Networks for the Visualisation of Data. PhD Thesis, University of Paisley. (2002).
13. MacDonald D., Corchado E., Fyfe C. and Merenyi E. Maximum and Minimum Likelihood Hebbian Learning for Exploratory Projection Pursuit. In International Conference on Artificial Neural Networks, ICANN2002. (2002).
14. Scholkopf B.,The Kernel Trick for Distances. Technical report, Microsoft Research, May 2000.
15. Scholkopf B., Smola A. and Muller K. R. Nonlinear component analysis as a kernel eigenvalue problem. Neural Computation, (1998) 10:1299-1319.
16. Vapnik V. The nature of statistical learning theory, Springer Verlag. (1995)

Applying Genetic and Symbolic Learning Algorithms to Extract Rules from Artificial Neural Networks

Claudia R. Milaré, Gustavo E.A.P.A. Batista,
André C.P.L.F. de Carvalho, and Maria C. Monard

University of São Paulo - USP
Institute of Mathematics and Computer Science - ICMC
Department of Computer Science and Statistics - SCE
Laboratory of Computational Intelligence - LABIC
P. O. Box 668, 13560-970, São Carlos, SP, Brazil
{claudia,gbatista,andre,mcmonard}@icmc.usp.br

Abstract. Several research works have shown that Artificial Neural Networks — ANNs — have an appropriate inductive bias for several domains, since they can learn any input-output mapping, *i.e.*, ANNs have the universal approximation property. Although symbolic learning algorithms have a less flexible inductive bias than ANNs, they are needed when a good understating of the decision process is essential, since symbolic ML algorithms express the knowledge induced using symbolic structures that can be interpreted and understood by humans. On the other hand, ANNs lack the capability of explaining their decisions, since the knowledge is encoded as real-valued weights and biases of the network. This encoding is difficult to be interpreted by humans. Aiming to take advantage of both approaches, this work proposes a method that extract symbolic knowledge, expressed as decision rules, from ANNs. The proposed method combines knowledge induced by several symbolic ML algorithms through the application of a Genetic Algorithm — GA. Our method is experimentally analyzed in a number of application domains. Results show that the method is able to extract symbolic knowledge having high fidelity with trained ANNs. The proposed method is also compared to TREPAN, another method for extracting knowledge from ANNs, showing promising results.

1 Introduction

Artificial Neural Networks — ANNs — have been successfully employed in several application domains. However, the comprehensibility of the induced hypothesis is as important as its performance in many of these applications. This is one of the main criticism about ANNs: the lack of capability for explaining their decisions since the knowledge is encoded as real-valued weights and biases. On the other hand, the comprehensibility of the induced hypothesis is one of main

R. Monroy et al. (Eds.): MICAI 2004, LNAI 2972, pp. 833–843, 2004.
© Springer-Verlag Berlin Heidelberg 2004

characteristics of symbolic Machine Leaning — ML — systems. This work explores the lack of comprehensibility of the models induced by ANNs, proposing solutions for the following problem:

> *Given a model produced by a learning system, in this case* ANNs, *and represented in a language that is difficult to be understood by the majority of the users, how to re-represent this model in a language that improves comprehensibility in order to be easily understood by an user.*

Several research works have investigated how to convert hypotheses induced by ANNs to more human comprehensible representations, as surveyed in [1]. The majority of the proposed methods has several limitations, such as: can only be applied to specific network models or training algorithm; do not scale well with the network size; and are restricted to problems having exclusively discrete-valued features.

This work proposes the use of symbolic ML systems and GAs to extract comprehensible knowledge from ANNs. The main goal of this work is to obtain a symbolic description of an ANN that has a high degree of fidelity with the knowledge induced by the ANN. The proposed method can be applied to any type of ANN. In other words, the method does not assume that the network has any particular architecture, nor that the ANN has been trained in any special way. Furthermore, the induction of symbolic representations is not directly affected by the network size, and the method can be used for applications involving both real-valued and discrete-valued features.

This paper is organized as follows: in Section 2 is described the proposed method to extract comprehensible knowledge from ANNs; in Section 3 the method is experimentally evaluated on several application domains; and finally, in Section 4 the main conclusions of this work are presented, as well as some directions for future work.

2   Proposed Method

The method proposed in this work uses symbolic ML algorithms and GAs to extract symbolic knowledge from trained ANNs. In this method, an ANN is trained over a data set E. After the training phase, the ANN is used as a "black box" to classify the data set E creating a new class attribute. The values of the new class attribute reflect the knowledge learned by the ANN, *i.e.*, these values reflect the hypothesis **h** induced by the ANN. The data set labelled by the trained ANN is subsequently used as input to p symbolic ML systems, resulting in p symbolic classifiers $\mathbf{h}'_1, \mathbf{h}'_2, \ldots \mathbf{h}'_p$. Each classifier $\mathbf{h}'_i$, $1 \leq i \leq p$ approximates the hypothesis **h** induced by the ANN.

Unfortunately, each symbolic ML system represents the induced concept in a different language, hindering the integration of these classifiers. Thus, it is necessary to translate the representation of these classifiers to a common language. In order to make such translation, we used the work of Prati [7], which proposes a standard syntax called $\mathcal{PBM}$ to represent rules. Thus, each symbolic classifier is translated to the $\mathcal{PBM}$ format. After the classifiers $\mathbf{h}'_1, \mathbf{h}'_2, \ldots \mathbf{h}'_p$ are converted to the $\mathcal{PBM}$ syntax, they are integrated into a rule database. An unique natural number is assigned to each rule in the rule database in order to identify each rule.

The rules stored in the rule database are used to form the individuals of the GA population. Each individual is formed by a set of rules. The representation of each individual is a vector of natural numbers, where each number is the identifier of a rule in the rule database. The initial population of the GA is composed by vectors with random numbers, representing sets of random rules from the rule database.

During the GA execution, the individuals, *i.e.* the rule sets, are modified by the mutation and crossover operators. The mutation operator randomly exchanges a rule from one of the rule sets by another rule from the rule database. The crossover operator implemented is asymmetric, *i.e.*, given two rule sets, two crossover points are chosen. The sub-vectors defined by the two crossover points are exchanged. It is important to note that as the crossover operator is asymmetric, even though all initial individuals have the same number of rules, the selection of the most adapted individuals may conduct to the survival of larger or smaller rule sets. The GA fitness function calculates the infidelity rate between the ANN and each individual. Thus, the objective of the GA is to minimize the infidelity rate. Infidelity rate is the percentage of instances where the classification made by an ANN disagrees with the classification made by the method used to explain the ANN.

Another important issue is how to classify a new instance given a rule set. The strategies employed to classify an instance given a set of rules are: *SingleRule*, that uses the classification given by the rule with highest prediction power; and *MultipleRules* that uses all fired rules in order to classify an instance. After the execution of the GA, one individual winner is obtained. The set of rules is usually composed by rules obtained from classifiers induced by different symbolic ML systems. This set of rules is then used to explain the behavior of the ANN. A post-processing phase may be applied to the winner. The objective of this post-processing is to remove those rules from the winner that are not fired for any instance in the training and validation sets. Additional details about the GA implementation can be found in [6].

3   Experimental Evaluation

Several experiments were carried out in order to evaluate the proposed method. Experiments were conducted using six data sets, collected from the UCI repository [2]. These data sets are related to classification problems in different application domains. Table 1 shows the corresponding data sets names and summarizes some of their characteristics. The characteristics are: `#Instances` – the total number of instances; `#Features` – the total number of features as well as the number of continuous and nominal features; `Class and Class %` – the class values and distribution of these values; `Majority Error` – the majority error; and, `Missing Values` – if the data set has missing values.

Table 1. Data sets summary description.

Data Set	#Instances	#Features (cont.,nom.)	Class	Class %	Majority Error	Missing Values
breast	699	9(9,0)	benign	65.52%	34.48%	yes
			malignant	34.48%		
crx	690	15(6,9)	−	55.50%	44.50%	yes
			+	44.50%		
heart	303	13(6,7)	absence	54.13%	45.87%	yes
			presence	45.87%		
pima	768	8(8,0)	0	65.02%	34.98%	no
			1	34.98%		
sonar	208	60(60,0)	M	53.37%	46.63%	no
			R	46.63%		
votes	435	16(0,16)	republican	54.80%	45.20%	no
			democrat	45.20%		

Table 2. Error rate obtained by the ANNs — mean and standard deviation.

breast	2.98 (0.46)
crx	13.47 (1.01)
heart	17.78 (2.12)
pima	22.92 (1.15)
sonar	20.14 (3.21)
votes	3.69 (0.86)

The experiments were divided into three phases. In the following sections these phases are described in the same order that they were conducted and the results obtained in each phase are also presented.

3.1   Phase 1

The objective of Phase 1 is to train the ANNs, whose knowledge will be extracted in the next phases. Phase 1 was performed as follows:

1. Each of the six data sets was divided using the 10-fold stratified cross-validation resampling method [10]. Each training set was divided in two subsets: training set (with 90% of instances) and validation set (with 10% of instances).
2. All the networks were trained using the Backpropagation with Momentum algorithm [9] and a validation set was used to decide when the training should stop. After several experiments, the architectures chosen were: breast (9-3-1), crx (43-7-1), heart (22-1-1), pima (8-2-1), sonar (60-12-1) and votes (48-1).
3. The error rate for each data set was measured on the test set. Table 2 shows the mean error rates obtained in the 10 folds, and their respective standard deviation between parenthesis.

3.2   Phase 2

In this phase, the ANNs trained in Phase 1 are used to label the data sets, i.e., they are used to create a new class-attribute. The results obtained by the proposed method are compared with another method for extracting knowledge from ANNs, the TREPAN [4]. Given a trained ANN, and the training set used for its training, the TREPAN method builds a decision tree to explain the ANN behavior. TREPAN uses the trained ANN to label the training set and builds a decision tree based on this data set. TREPAN can also generate artificial data automatically, using the trained ANN to label the new instances. Unlike most decision tree algorithms, which separate the instances of different classes by using

Table 3. Parameter values employed in the experiments with TREPAN.

	MinSample	SplitTest
simple0	0	simple
simple1000	1000	simple
mofn0	0	mofn
mofn1000	1000	mofn

Table 4. GA's parameter values employed in the experiments.

parameters	values
n_g	20
n_i	20
t_i	10
p_c	0.25
p_m	0.01

a single attribute to partition the input space, TREPAN uses m-of-n expressions for its splits. A m-of-n expression is a boolean expression which is satisfied when at least m (an integer threshold) of its n conditions (boolean conditions) are satisfied. Phase 2 was performed as follows:

1. TREPAN was executed with different values assigned to its main parameters, including its default parameters, as showed in Table 3. The **MinSample** parameter of TREPAN specifies the minimum number of instances (*i.e.* training instances plus artificial instances) to be considered before selecting each split. The default value is 1000. When this parameter is set to 0, no artificial instance is generated by TREPAN. The **SplitTest** parameter defines if the splits of the internal nodes are m-of-n expressions (mofn) or simple splits (simple). The option mofn1000 is the default option used by the TREPAN method, that is, m-of-n expressions are employed and 1000 instances must be available in a node for this node to be either expanded or converted into a leaf node.
2. The infidelity rate between TREPAN and the ANN was measured on the test set.
3. The syntactic comprehensibility of the knowledge extracted by TREPAN was measured. In this work, the syntactic comprehensibility was measured considering the number of induced rules and the average number of conditions per induced rule.
4. The training, validation and test sets used to train the ANNs in Phase 1 were labelled by the corresponding ANNs.
5. The symbolic ML systems C4.5, C4.5rules [8] and CN2 [3] were chosen to be used in the experiments. These systems are responsible for generating the rules for the proposed method, *i.e.*, the rules that will be integrated by the GA. The C4.5, C4.5rules and CN2 were executed with their default parameters.
6. The infidelity rate between the symbolic ML systems (C4.5, C4.5rules, and CN2) and the ANN was measured on the test set, as well as the syntactic comprehensibility of the models induced by the symbolic inducers.

3.3   Phase 3

In this phase, the classifiers produced in Phase 2 by the symbolic ML systems C4.5, CN2 e C4.5rules on the training set labelled by the ANNs are used to form the GA individuals. Phase 3 was carried out as follows:

1. The classifiers induced by the symbolic ML systems C4.5, C4.5rules e CN2 were converted to the $\mathcal{PBM}$ syntax.
2. For each of the six data sets employed in this experiment, a GA was executed several times, varying their parameters as well as the strategies used to classify an instance given a set of rules. Table 4 shows the values used for the parameters: n_g (number of gerations); n_i (number of individuals); t_i (initial size of individual, that is, the number of rules of each individual); p_c (probability of crossover) and p_m (probability of mutation), used with the approaches *SingleRule* and *MultipleRules* in the GA. The values $n_g = 40$, $n_i = 15$ and $p_c = 0.4$ were also used with the approach *SingleRule*.
3. Finally, the infidelity rate and the syntactic comprehensibility for the individual winner were measured.

Table 5 shows the infidelity rate (mean and standard deviation) obtained by the symbolic ML systems, TREPAN and GA. Table 6 shows the number of induced rules and Table 7 shows the average number of conditions per rule. The results of infidelity rate, number of induced rules and mean number of conditions per induced rule, for the symbolic ML systems and TREPAN, were obtained in Phase 2. SingleRule means that the GA was executed with the *SingleRule* strategy and SingleRulePP refers to the same strategy followed by the post-processing; MultipleRules means the *MultipleRules* strategy and MultipleRulesPP refers to the same strategy followed by the post-processing. The GA was executed with the parameters $n_g = 20$, $n_i = 20$, $t_i = 10$, $p_c = 0.25$ and $p_m = 0.01$ to SingleRule, SingleRulePP, MultipleRules and Multiple-RulesPP. In *SingleRule and *SingleRulePP the parameters are $n_g = 40$, $n_i = 15$, $t_i = 10$, $p_c = 0.4$ and $p_m = 0.01$

In what follows, the best results are shown in boldface. The *10-fold cross-validated paired t* test [5] was used to compare the infidelity rate and comprehensibility. According to the *10-fold cross-validated paired t* test, the difference between two algorithms is statistically significant with 95% of confidence if the result of this test is greater than 2.262 in absolute value. The ↑ symbol indicates that a difference is significant with 95% of confidence when the method in boldface is compared to the other methods.

Table 8 shows the methods in ascending order of infidelity rate. Table 9 presents the methods in ascending order of mean number of induced rules, and Table 10 shows the methods in ascending order of mean number of conditions per induced rule. The numbers in the right side of the method's name indicate how many significant results, with 95% of confidence, the method obtained when compared with the remaining methods. It can be observed that:

– For the breast data set, even though the method SingleRule obtained the best result for the infidelity rate with 3 significant results when compared

Table 5. Infidelity rate (mean and standard deviation).

	breast	crx	heart	pima	sonar	votes
C4.5	↑ 2.93 (0.53)	**2.91 (0.81)**	↑ 14.07 (1.54)	8.85 (1.07)	22.98 (3.21)	3.21 (0.97)
C4.5rules	2.48 (0.53)	3.06 (0.72)	10.00 (1.11)	8.46 (1.01)	23.43 (3.25)	2.98 (1.07)
CN2	1.90 (0.62)	↑ 5.82 (0.75)	↑ 13.70 (1.99)	9.12 (0.94)	22.57 (3.35)	2.75 (0.95)
simple0	↑ 3.37 (0.44)	3.36 (0.71)	↑ 14.07 (1.81)	↑ 10.81 (0.65)	24.90 (3.06)	3.67 (1.03)
simple1000	↑ 4.39 (0.95)	5.37 (1.85)	12.22 (2.53)	8.86 (1.15)	22.14 (2.91)	**2.30 (0.96)**
mofn0	2.78 (0.63)	3.83 (0.84)	12.22 (1.75)	10.42 (1.31)	25.57 (3.15)	2.99 (0.97)
mofn1000	3.07 (0.80)	4.75 (1.49)	**7.04 (1.40)**	**7.95 (1.01)**	↑ 27.36 (2.73)	2.76 (0.75)
	GA: $n_g = 20,\ n_i = 20,\ t_i = 10,\ p_c = 0.25,\ p_m = 0.01$					
SingleRule	**1.61 (0.55)**	3.52 (0.65)	12.22 (1.57)	8.85 (1.00)	22.05 (3.24)	2.76 (0.66)
SingleRulePP	2.20 (0.70)	4.44 (0.66)	12.59 (1.58)	10.42 (1.06)	↑ 24.93 (3.36)	3.91 (1.07)
MultipleRules	2.04 (0.58)	3.22 (0.67)	13.33 (1.48)	8.20 (0.97)	↑ 25.00 (2.11)	2.99 (0.83)
MultipleRulesPP	2.04 (0.58)	3.22 (0.67)	13.33 (1.48)	8.20 (0.97)	↑ 25.00 (2.11)	2.99 (0.83)
	GA: $n_g = 40,\ n_i = 15,\ t_i = 10,\ p_c = 0.4,\ p_m = 0.01$					
*SingleRule	1.75 (0.64)	3.68 (0.66)	8.89 (0.99)	8.60 (1.10)	23.05 (2.74)	2.98 (1.32)
*SingleRulePP	2.63 (0.71)	4.90 (0.60)	11.48 (2.24)	8.34 (1.21)	**21.07 (2.24)**	4.15 (1.37)

Table 6. Number of induced rules (mean and standard deviation).

	breast	crx	heart	pima	sonar	votes
C4.5	↑ 8.90 (0.91)	↑ 14.10 (3.44)	↑ 17.40 (1.33)	↑ 25.00 (0.92)	↑ 13.50 (0.34)	↑ 9.40 (1.07)
C4.5rules	↑ 8.00 (0.54)	↑ 8.70 (1.58)	↑ 11.40 (0.8)	↑ 18.30 (1.16)	↑ 8.10 (0.38)	5.80 (0.44)
CN2	↑ 12.10 (0.55)	↑ 13.50 (1.42)	↑ 16.00 (0.75)	↑ 24.40 (0.97)	↑ 25.20 (0.53)	↑ 13.30 (0.67)
simple0	↑ 9.40 (0.48)	↑ 31.50 (4.81)	↑ 18.10 (0.99)	↑ 26.10 (1.48)	↑ 12.40 (0.60)	↑ 13.60 (0.90)
simple1000	↑ 10.60 (0.73)	↑ 31.00 (8.03)	↑ 20.00 (1.92)	↑ 29.30 (2.01)	↑ 9.50 (1.10)	↑ 11.00 (1.61)
mofn0	↑ 7.40 (0.78)	↑ 11.10 (1.76)	↑ 9.20 (0.83)	↑ 23.30 (1.38)	↑ 6.90 (0.53)	↑ 7.10 (0.53)
mofn1000	2.40 (0.31)	↑ 9.90 (1.94)	**5.30 (0.83)**	↑ 26.00 (1.55)	**4.10 (0.67)**	6.50 (0.72)
	GA: $n_g = 20,\ n_i = 20,\ t_i = 10,\ p_c = 0.25,\ p_m = 0.01$					
SingleRule	↑ 14.60 (1.12)	↑ 16.20 (3.15)	↑ 21.50 (2.26)	↑ 18.40 (1.97)	↑ 20.80 (3.86)	↑ 15.00 (1.62)
SingleRulePP	↑ 7.00 (0.47)	**4.50 (0.96**	7.90 (0.74)	**9.60 (1.37)**	↑ 7.60 (1.24)	**5.30 (0.67)**
MultipleRules	↑ 14.50 (1.92)	↑ 19.80 (4.29)	↑ 18.40 (3.06)	↑ 30.20 (3.39)	↑ 22.60 (2.91)	↑ 14.00 (1.29)
MultipleRulesPP	↑ 14.50 (1.92)	↑ 18.80 (4.08)	↑ 18.10 (2.98)	↑ 30.20 (3.39)	↑ 21.60 (2.71)	↑ 12.90 (1.22)
	GA: $n_g = 40,\ n_i = 15,\ t_i = 10,\ p_c = 0.4,\ p_m = 0.01$					
*SingleRule	↑ 17.60 (1.33)	↑ 20.30 (5.08)	↑ 24.30 (2.03)	↑ 42.00 (3.71)	↑ 31.60 (2.09)	↑ 14.40 (0.95)
*SingleRulePP	↑ 7.60 (0.56)	↑ 5.70 (1.07)	↑ 10.80 (0.87)	↑ 19.60 (1.65)	↑ 11.80 (1.45)	6.10 (0.64)

with the remaining methods, this method did not obtain good results for the number of induced rules and for the mean number of conditions per induced rule. The method SingleRulePP, even obtaining only 1 significant result related to the infidelity rate, obtained 8 significant results for the number of induced rules and 7 significant results for the mean number of conditions per induced rule.

– For the crx data set, the method C4.5rules obtained good results for the number of induced rules and for the mean number of conditions per induced rule. For the infidelity rate, this method obtained only one significant result. However, the other methods were not able to obtain many significant results.

Table 7. Average number of conditions per induced rule (mean and standard deviation).

	breast	crx	heart	pima	sonar	votes
C4.5	↑ 3.63 (0.17)	2.62 (0.46)	↑ 3.25 (0.06)	↑ 5.66 (0.11)	↑ 4.27 (0.11)	2.68 (0.20)
C4.5rules	2.57 (0.05)	**2.17 (0.10)**	**2.41 (0.04)**	**2.92 (0.05)**	↑ 2.84 (0.13)	2.52 (0.11)
CN2	2.56 (0.07)	↑ 2.84 (0.08v)	↑ 2.92 (0.10)	3.02 (0.05)	**2.03 (0.02)**	2.64 (0.05)
simple0	↑ 3.54 (0.11)	↑ 2.78 (0.10)	↑ 3.05 (0.11)	↑ 5.58 (0.13)	↑ 3.93 (0.13)	2.83 (0.10)
simple1000	↑ 4.00 (0.19)	2.61 (0.27)	↑ 3.27 (0.12)	↑ 5.94 (0.17)	↑ 3.81 (0.24)	2.61 (0.18)
mofn0	↑ 6.74 (0.54)	↑ 7.62 (0.75)	↑ 9.47 (0.59)	↑ 10.23 (0.49)	↑ 9.35 (0.49)	↑ 5.46 (0.41)
mofn1000	↑ 7.49 (0.48)	↑ 10.10 (0.91)	↑ 10.17 (0.41)	↑ 10.73 (0.32)	↑ 23.41 (1.51)	↑ 9.04 (0.90)
GA: $n_g = 20, n_i = 20, t_i = 10, p_c = 0.25, p_m = 0.01$						
SingleRule	2.78 (0.11)	↑ 2.97 (0.14)	2.83 (0.08)	3.73 (0.16)	2.87 (0.09)	2.55 (0.11)
SingleRulePP	2.54 (0.08)	2.25 (0.27)	2.75 (0.12)	2.96 (0.09)	2.94 (0.14)	**2.28 (0.16)**
MultipleRules	↑ 2.79 (0.10)	↑ 3.00 (0.16)	2.89 (0.11)	↑ 3.79 (0.08)	2.91 (0.07)	2.54 (0.11)
MultipleRulesPP	↑ 2.79 (0.10)	↑ 2.96 (0.16)	2.88 (0.11)	↑ 3.79 (0.08)	2.95 (0.08)	2.47 (0.09)
GA: $n_g = 40, n_i = 15, t_i = 10, p_c = 0.4, p_m = 0.01$						
*SingleRule	2.65 (0.13)	↑ 2.86 (0.15)	2.78 (0.10)	↑ 3.83 (0.07)	2.94 (0.11)	2.59 (0.12)
*SingleRulePP	**2.46 (0.08)**	2.41 (0.20)	2.75 (0.08)	3.14 (0.09)	2.91 (0.05)	2.31 (0.08)

Table 8. Methods ordered by infidelity rate.

	breast	crx	heart	pima	sonar	votes
1	SingleRule[3]	C4.5[1]	mofn1000[3]	mofn1000[1]	*SingleRulePP[4]	simple1000
2	*SingleRule[3]	C4.5rules[1]	*SingleRule[6]	MultipleRules[1]	SingleRule[1]	CN2
3	CN2[1]	MultipleRules[2]	C4.5rules[1]	MultipleRulesPP[1]	simple1000	SingleRule
4	MultipleRules[2]	MultipleRulesPP[2]	*SingleRulePP	*SingleRulePP	CN2	mofn1000
5	MultipleRulesPP[2]	simple0[1]	SingleRule[1]	C4.5rules[1]	C4.5	C4.5rules
6	SingleRulePP[1]	SingleRule	mofn0	*SingleRule	*SingleRule	*SingleRule
7	C4.5rules	*SingleRule	simple1000	SingleRule	C4.5rules	MultipleRulesPP
8	*SingleRulePP[1]	mofn0[1]	SingleRulePP	C4.5	simple0	MultipleRules
9	mofn0	SingleRulePP	MultipleRules	simple1000	SingleRulePP	mofn0
10	C4.5	mofn1000	MultipleRulesPP	CN2	MultipleRulesPP	C4.5
11	mofn1000	*SingleRulePP	CN2	SingleRulePP	MultipleRules	CN2
12	simple0	simple1000	C4.5	mofn0	mofn0	SingleRulePP
13	simple1000	CN2	simple0	simple0	mofn1000	*SingleRulePP

- For the heart data set, the methods *SingleRule and mofn1000 obtained the best results for the infidelity rate. However, for the number of induced rules, the method *SingleRule did not obtain good results, and the method mofn1000 did not obtain good results for the mean number of conditions per induced rule.
- For the pima data set, the methods *SingleRulePP and C4.5rules obtained good results for the syntactic complexity. For the infidelity rate, the maximum number of significant results obtained by the methods was 1, thus none of them can be considered the best.
- For the sonar data set, the method *SingleRulePP obtained very good results for the infidelity rate and the number of induced rules.
- For the votes data set, none of them presented significant results for the infidelity rate. However, the methods SingleRulePP, *SingleRulePP and C4.5rules presented good results for the syntactic complexity.

Table 9. Methods ordered by number of induced rules.

	breast	crx	heart	pima	sonar	votes
1	mofn1000^{12}	SingleRulePP^{11}	mofn1000^{11}	SingleRulePP^{12}	mofn1000^{12}	SingleRulePP^9
2	SingleRulePP^8	*SingleRulePP^{10}	SingleRulePP^{10}	C4.5rules^7	mofn0^8	C4.5rules^8
3	mofn0^5	C4.5rules^3	mofn0^8	SingleRule^6	SingleRulePP^7	*SingleRulePP^8
4	*SingleRulePP^7	mofn1000^3	*SingleRulePP^7	*SingleRulePP^8	C4.5rules^7	mofn1000^6
5	C4.5rules^4	mofn0^3	C4.5rules^6	mofn0^2	simple1000^6	mofn0^6
6	C4.5^4	CN2^2	CN2	CN2^2	*SingleRulePP^4	C4.5^4
7	simple0^3	C4.5^2	C4.5	C4.5	simple0^5	simple1000
8	simple1000^1	SingleRule^1	simple0	mofn1000^1	C4.5^3	MultipleRulesPP^2
9	CN2	MultipleRulesPP^1	MultipleRulesPP	simple0^1	SingleRule^1	CN2
10	MultipleRules	MultipleRules^1	MultipleRules	simple1000	MultipleRulesPP^2	simple0
11	MultipleRulesPP	*SingleRule^1	simple1000	MultipleRules	MultipleRules	MultipleRules
12	SingleRule	simple1000	SingleRule	MultipleRulesPP	CN2	*SingleRule
13	*SingleRule	simple0	*SingleRule	*SingleRule	*SingleRule	SingleRule

Table 10. Methods ordered by average number of conditions per induced rule.

	breast	crx	heart	pima	sonar	votes
1	*SingleRulePP^7	C4.5rules^8	C4.5rules^6	C4.5rules^8	CN2^6	SingleRulePP^2
2	SingleRulePP^7	SingleRulePP^2	*SingleRulePP^2	SingleRulePP^5	C4.5rules^5	*SingleRulePP^2
3	CN2^4	*SingleRulePP^2	SingleRulePP^2	CN2^8	SingleRule^1	MultipleRulesPP^3
4	C4.5rules^5	simple1000^2	*SingleRule^2	*SingleRulePP^9	MultipleRules^2	C4.5rules^3
5	*SingleRule^7	C4.5^2	SingleRule^2	SingleRule^5	*SingleRulePP^1	MultipleRules^2
6	SingleRule^5	simple0^2	MultipleRulesPP^2	MultipleRules^5	*SingleRule^1	SingleRule^3
7	MultipleRules^5	CN2^2	MultipleRules^2	MultipleRulesPP^5	SingleRulePP^1	*SingleRule^2
8	MultipleRulesPP^5	*SingleRule^2	CN2^4	*SingleRule^5	MultipleRulesPP^1	simple1000^2
9	simple0^3	MultipleRulesPP^2	simple0^2	simple0^3	simple1000^2	simple0^2
10	C4.5^3	SingleRule^2	C4.5^2	C4.5^2	simple0^3	CN2^2
11	simple1000^2	MultipleRules^2	simple1000^2	simple1000^2	C4.5^2	C4.5^2
12	mofn0	mofn0^1	mofn0	mofn0	mofn0^1	mofn0^1
13	mofn1000	mofn1000	mofn1000	mofn1000	mofn1000	mofn1000

Finally, analyzing the results in a general way, it is possible to conclude that the use of GAs for extracting comprehensible knowledge from ANNs is promising and should be explored in more deep. One of the aspects that should be better investigated refers to the good results obtained by the strategy *SingleRule* compared to the strategy *MultipleRules*. Apparently, a GA builds better classifiers considering the best rule to classify a new instance, instead of considering all the rules that cover an instance and to decide the classification of this instance based on the global quality of these rules.

4   Conclusion

In this work, we propose a method based on symbolic ML systems and GAs in order to extract comprehensible knowledge from ANNs. The main advantage of the proposed method is that it can be applied to any supervised ANN. The use of GAs allows the integration of the knowledge extracted by several symbolic ML systems in a single set of rules. This set of rules should have a high fidelity with the ANN due to the fact that this set of rules will be used to explain the ANN. This task is not trivial, since in order to obtain a high degree of fidelity, the rules have to complement themselves. In the experiments carried out, the proposed method achieved satisfactory results, and should be further explored.

Several ideas for future works will be evaluated, such as:

- More symbolic ML systems can be used to increase the diversity of rules. Another strategies are to vary the parameters of these systems and to induce classifiers on different samples.
- In the current implementation, we chose to generate the individuals of GA by randomly selecting rules from the whole set of classifiers. As the individuals of the initial population are not necessarily "good" classifiers, there is a higher chance of stopping in a local maxima. In this work, we opted for building the initial population randomly, with the objective of verifying the potential of the proposed method without favoring the GA. We intend to investigate the behavior of the GA when each initial individual of the population is a "good" classifier. This can be accomplished by using the induced classifiers as initial individuals.
- Another important aspect regarding the set of generated rules is that this set should cover an expressive region of the instance space. In other words, it is of little use to have a set of rules in which each individual rule is highly fidel to an ANN if all these rules cover the same instances. If a set of rules has several redundant rules, then several instances might be classified by the *default* rule. In the current implementation, the default rule classifies every instance as belonging to the majority class. A strategy to create individuals with complementary covering rules is to introduce this information in the GA fitness function.

Acknowledgements. This research is partially supported by Brazilian Research Councils CNPq and FAPESP.

References

[1] R. Andrews, J. Diederich, and A. B. Tickle. A Survey and Critique of Techniques for Extracting Rules from Trained Artificial Neural Networks. *Knowledge-Based Systems*, 8(6):373–389, 1995.

[2] C. Blake, E. Keogh, and C. J. Merz. UCI Repository of Machine Learning Datasets, 1998.

[3] P. Clark and T. Niblett. The CN2 Induction Algorithm. *Machine Learning*, 3:261–284, 1989.

[4] M. W. Craven. *Extracting Comprehensible Models from Trained Neural Networks*. PhD thesis, University of Wisconsin - Madison, 1996.

[5] T. G. Dietterich. Approximate Statistical Tests for Comparing Supervised Classification Learning Algorithms. *Neural Computation*, 10(7):1895–1924, 1997.

[6] C. R. Milaré. *Extraction of Knowledge from Artificial Neural Networks Using Symbolic Learning Systems and Genetic Algorithms (in Portuguese)*. PhD thesis, University of São Paulo, 2003.

[7] R. C. Prati, J. A. Baranauskas, and M. C. Monard. A Proposal for Unifying the Representation Language of Symbolic Machine Learning Algorithms (in Portuguese). Technical Report 137, ICMC-USP, 2001.

[8] J. R. Quinlan. *C4.5 Programs for Machine Learning*. Morgan Kaufmann, 1988.

[9] D. Rumelhart, G. Hilton, and R. Williams. Learning Internal Representations by Error Propagation. In *Parallel Distributed Processing: Explorations in the Microstructure of Cognition*, volume 1. MIT Press, 1986.

[10] S. M. Weiss and C. A. Kulikowski. *Computer Systems that Learn*. Morgan Kaufmann, 1991.

Combining MLP and RBF Neural Networks for Novelty Detection in Short Time Series

A.L.I. Oliveira[1,2], F.B.L. Neto[1,2], and S.R.L. Meira[2]

[1] Polytechnic School, Pernambuco University
Rua Benfica, 455, Madalena, Recife – PE, Brazil, 50.750-410
[2] Center of Informatics, Federal University of Pernambuco
P.O. Box 7851, Cidade Universitaria, Recife – PE, Brazil, 50.732-970
{alio,fbln,srlm}@cin.ufpe.br

Abstract. Novelty detection in time series is an important problem with application in different domains such as machine failure detection, fraud detection and auditing. In many problems, the occurrence of short length time series is a frequent characteristic. In previous works we have proposed a novelty detection approach for short time series that uses RBF neural networks to classify time series windows as *normal* or *novelty*. Additionally, both normal and novelty random patterns are added to training sets to improve classification performance. In this work we consider the use of MLP networks as classifiers. Next, we analyze (a) the impact of validation and training sets generation, and (b) of the training method. We have carried out a number of experiments using four real-world time series, whose results have shown that under a good selection of these alternatives, MLPs perform better than RBFs. Finally, we discuss the use of MLP and MLP/RBF committee machines in conjunction with our previous method. Experimental results shows that these committee classifiers outperform single MLP and RBF classifiers.

1 Introduction

Novelty detection – the process of finding novel patterns in data – is very important in several domains such as computer vision, machine fault detection, network security and fraud detection [14,5]. A novelty detection system can be regarded as a classifier with two possible outcomes, one for *normal* and the other for *novelty* patterns. However, in most cases, there is only normal data available to train the classifier [14,5]. Hence, novelty detection systems must be properly designed to overcome this problem.

The behavior of many systems can be modeled by time series. Recently, the problem of detecting novelties in time series has received great attention, with a number of different techniques being proposed and studied, including techniques based on time series forecasting with neural networks [8,9], artificial immune system [5], wavelets [13] and Markov models [7]. These techniques have been applied in areas such as machine failure detection [5] and auditing [8,9].

R. Monroy et al. (Eds.): MICAI 2004, LNAI 2972, pp. 844–853, 2004.

Forecasting-based time series novelty detection has been criticized because of the not so good performance [7,5]. Alternatively, a number of classification-based approaches have been recently proposed [5,13,7]. However, none of them is devoted to short time series. This has motived us to design a method devoted to short time series novelty detection [10]. Our method is designed to classify time series windows as normal or novelty. It is based on the negative samples approach, which consists of generating artificial samples to be used to represent novelty [14,5]. In order to improve classification performance on test sets, our method also adds artificial normal samples to the training sets. We have used RBF neural networks trained with the DDA algorithm as our classifier [2].

In this work we study how the use of different classifiers impact the system performance. The classifiers considered are Multi-Layer Perceptrons neural networks (MLPs), RBFs, committees of MLPs and committees of MLP and RBF networks. Training MLPs requires the use of some method to avoid overfitting. We consider two approaches: early stopping [6] and weight decay with Bayesian regularization [4,6]. In order to use early stopping it is necessary to further divide data available for training into training and validation sets. We also evaluate two ways of creating training and validation sets from time series.

Next section presents the proposed approach and the alternative methods to generate training and validation sets. Section 3 presents the classification algorithms considered in this work. Section 4 describes experiments carried out with real-world time series in order to compare the performance of the classifiers. Finally, in section 5 conclusions and suggestions for further research are presented.

2   The Proposed Approach

Our novelty detection system works by classifying time series windows as normal or novelty [10]. The system requires fixed length windows, with window size w. A window is formed by w consecutive datapoints extracted from the time series under analysis. The first training pattern will have the first w datapoints from the time series as its attributes values. To obtain the second pattern we start with the second datapoint and use the next w datapoints. The remaining patterns are obtained by sliding the window by one and taking the next w datapoints. So, if we have a time series with l datapoints and use window size w, we will have $l - w + 1$ patterns. These patterns will later be separated to obtain training and test sets.

Given a window from the time series, the idea is to define an *envelope* around it as shown in figure 1. Any time series window with all values inside the envelope is considered normal. Windows with points outside the envelope are considered novelty. We use a threshold p_1 to define the envelope. Normal patterns are defined by establishing the maximum percent deviation p_1 above and below each datapoint of a given original pattern.

We suppose that the time series represent the normal behaviour and so the training set will have only normal patterns. Thus, in order to train a classifier for

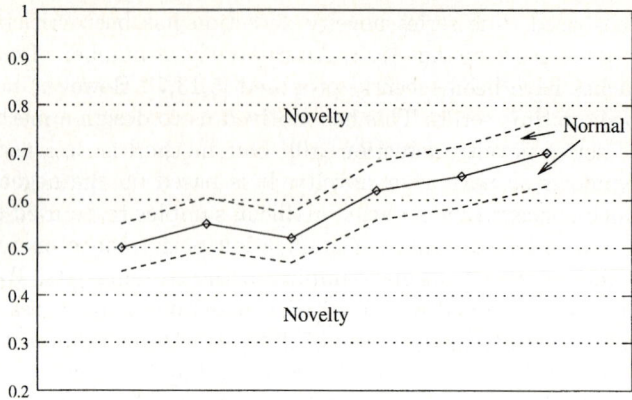

Fig. 1. Definition of normal and novelty regions.

the novelty detection task, we need to generate *novelty random patterns*. These patterns are windows with values in the novelty regions shown in figure 1. We need to generate sufficient random patterns for each window in the series, in order to represent adequately the novelty space. We also generate a number of *normal random patterns* whose datapoints are inside the envelope. In order to improve classification performance, random patterns should be added in a way that the resulting data set have equal numbers of normal and novelty patterns [6]. The training set with the original patterns and the random normal and random novelty patterns is called augmented training set.

In many problems of interest, such as auditing, where novelty is related to possibility of fraud, we are mainly interested in testing network performance in detection of patterns whose deviation from normality is not too big. So, we also define a second threshold p_2 to limit the novelty regions. For example, in the experiments presented below, we use $p_1 = 0.1$ and $p_2 = 0.5$, meaning that patterns whose attributes are at most 10% from the normal pattern are considered normal and patterns whose attributes deviates from a normal pattern from 10% to 50% are considered novelty or fraudulent patterns. After generating the augmented training set, we train a classifier to discriminate normal and novelty windows in the time series.

2.1   Generation of Training and Validation Sets

Early stopping is a common method used to avoid overfitting in neural network training [6], specially with MLP neural networks. In this technique, data available for training is further divided into training and validation sets. In time series forecasting it is common to separate data into training, validation and test sets using the natural time order [15,6]. If we use this approach in our system, augmented training, validation and test sets would be generated from the respective training, validation and test sets.

We argue that dividing data in time order means loosing important information for training. We propose a new form of division that we call *distributed division*. In distributed division the original time series is also divided into training, validation and test sets in time order. However, a number of the random patterns generated from the training set are added to form the augmented validation set and vice versa. In this way, the resulting augmented training and validation sets will have information from all the period available for training.

Generation of augmented training and validation sets in distributed division works as follows:

1. Divide the original time series into disjoint training and test periods in the natural time order;
2. For each set, generate normal patterns with window size w length, according to the procedure previously stated;
3. For each normal pattern available in the training set, generate n normal random patterns, according to the criterion previously stated. Put a percentage of these patterns in the augmented training set and the remaining patterns in the augmented validation set;
4. For each normal pattern available in the training set, generate $n + 1$ novelty random patterns, according to the criterion previously stated; Put a percentage of these patterns in the augmented training set and rest in the augmented validation set.

3   The Classification Algorithms

This work aims at studying a number of alternative classifiers for the proposed short time series novelty detection system. In a previous paper we have used RBFs trained with the DDA [10]. In this work we consider Multi-Layer Perceptron (MLP) neural networks and committee machines formed either by MLPs only or by MLP and RBF-DDA. The number of inputs for each classifier corresponds to the window size w. Each classifier has two outputs, one used to indicate normal patterns and the other, novelties. All networks have a single hidden layer.

3.1   Radial Basis Functions Networks – RBFs

The DDA algorithm is a constructive algorithm used to build and train RBF networks [2]. It does not need a validation set and so, all training data can be more effectively used for training. RBF-DDA has often achieved classification accuracy comparable to MLPs trained with Rprop [12] but training is significantly faster.

3.2   Multi-layer Perceptrons – MLPs

The second kind of classifiers considered in this work are Multi-Layer Perceptron (MLP) neural networks. We have used four alternative MLP classifiers: 1)

MLP trained with Rprop using time order validation sets; 2) MLP trained with Rprop using distributed validation sets; 3) MLP trained with RpropMAP using distributed validation sets; 4) A committee machine with MLPs trained with RpropMAP.

The two first MLP classifiers are trained with the *resilient backpropagation* (Rprop) [12] and early stopping with the GL_5 criterion from Proben1 [11].

The third MLP classifier is trained with Rprop with adaptive weight decay (RpropMAP) [4]. This is an extended version of the Rprop algorithm that uses regularization by adaptive weight decay [6]. The weighting parameter λ for the weight-decay regularizer is computed automatically within the Bayesian framework, during training. RpropMAP has two parameters besides those of Rprop: the initial weighting λ of the weight decay regularizer and the update frequency of the weighting parameter. In our experiments we have used the default values for these parameters, which are 1 and 50, respectively.

RpropMAP does not need a validation set, which is a very important advantage for our problem. All data available for training are effectively used to adjust the network weights. Training is carried out in two phases. The first phase uses a validation set in order to discover the number of epochs to be used in the second phase. The second phase uses the full training set. In the experiments we start by dividing training data into training and validation sets using distributed validation. Next, we randomly initialize the network weights and bias and train it by using RpropMAP and early stopping with the GL_5 criterion. At the end of training, we take note of the number of epochs needed, e_{max}. Finally, we use the same random weights and bias initialization and train the network, this time with the full training set. Training stops when the number of epochs reaches e_{max}.

The fourth MLP classifier is a committee machine of MLP classifiers. Experiments with the third classifier are carried out ten times with different random initializations of weights and bias. Next, we obtain the mean and standard deviation of the classification error across executions. On the other hand, the fourth MLP classifier uses *ensemble mean* to compute the classification error [6]. In this case we will have, for each augmented training set, ten MLPs with two output neurons trained with RpropMAP, as described previously. For each MLP j, the value of output i is given by y_{ij}. Given a pattern p in the test set, we compute the output i of the committee classifier as $\sum_{j=1}^{10} y_{ij}$. Next, pattern p is classified according to the winner-takes-all criterion [6]. This is done for each pattern in the test set, in order to compute the classification error in this set.

3.3 MLP/RBF Committee

MLP and RBF networks have different characteristics, mainly due to their different activation functions [6]. The experiments carried out in this work show that these networks have different performance regarding false positive and false negatives. This has motivated us to propose the use of a MLP/RBF committee in order to further improve the novelty detection system performance. The committee uses RBF trained with DDA and MLPs trained with RpropMAP.

For each augmented training set we need to train the RBF only once because DDA does not depends on weights initialization. On the other hand, we need ten MLPs for each augmented training set. RBF-DDA outputs can be greater than 1. MLPs using sigmoid logistic activation functions produce outputs from 0 to 1. So, in order to integrate the information from these classifiers we must transform their results. We use the *softmax* transformation for this propose [6]. Firstly, we combine the results of MLPs trained with RpropMAP to form the MLP committee described previously. Next, we apply the softmax transformation $g_i = e^{y_{ij}} / \sum_{i=1}^{2} e^{y_{ij}}$ to each committee output i. The softmax transformation is also applied independently to the outputs of the trained RBF-DDA. Finally, the softmax transformed outputs of the MLP committee and of the RBF are combined to obtain an ensemble mean. The winner-takes-all criterion is applied for classification.

4   Experiments

We performed some experiments using real-world data in order to compare the performance of the different classifiers on our novelty detection approach. The time series used in the experiments have been used in our previous work with RBF-DDA as classifiers [10]. The series are shown in figure 2. All have 84 values corresponding to the months from January 1996 to December 2002. The first series was extracted from a real payroll and was used previously in a study of a payroll auditing system based on neural networks forecasting [9]. The remaining series are sales time series with values in the same period of the first series. Each series had their values normalized between 0 and 1.

It is clear that these series are non-stationary. So, in order to use a focused TLFN (*Time Lagged Feedforward Networks*), it is important to pre-process the time series in order to work with their stationary versions [6]. We have used the classic technique of differencing to obtain stationary versions of the time series [3]. For each original time series $\{x_1, \ldots, x_N\}$ a differenced time series $\{y_2, \ldots, y_N\}$ was formed by $y_t = x_t - x_{t-1}$. Note that the differenced time series does not have the first datapoint. In fact, we have shown in our previous work that differencing the time series has a great influence on novelty detection with RBF-DDA [10]. Hence, in this study we consider only differenced versions of time series.

We have used a window size $w = 12$. The patterns are generated from each time series according to the procedure described in section 2. For differenced time series we will have 72 patterns with 12 attributes each. We have used the last 12 patterns as the test set and the remaining patterns as training set. It is important to emphasize that normalization is carried out only after the generation of the random patterns.

The normal and novelty regions were defined using thresholds $p_1 = 0.1$ and $p_2 = 0.5$. For each original pattern we have added 9 normal random patterns and 10 random novelty patterns. With this, our training and test sets increases by a factor of 20, having, respectively, 1200 and 240 patterns for differenced

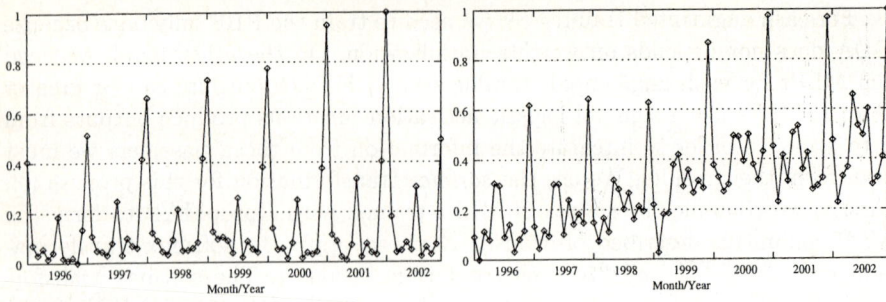

(a) Series 1: earning from a Brazilian pay-roll.

(b) Series 2: sales from a Brazilian company.

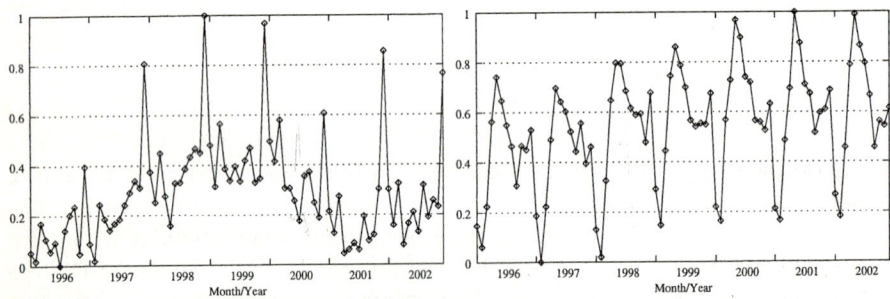

(c) Series 3: USA computer and software stores sales.

(d) Series 4: USA hardware stores sales.

Fig. 2. Time series used in the experiments. Series 3 and 4 are available at the URL http://www.census.gov/mrts/www/mrts.html.

time series. For classifiers that need a validation set, we further divide training data into training and validation sets using either time order or distributed validation, according to section 2. In both cases, the training set will have 80% of the patterns (960) and the validation set will have 20% of them (240 patterns).

4.1 Networks Topologies and Training

The number of hidden units in the RBF classifier is obtained automatically during training by the DDA algorithm [2]. We have used MLPs with one hidden layer. The number of units in the hidden layer has a great impact on classifier performance. For MLPs, experiments were carried out with 2, 6, 12, 18, 24, 36 and 48 units in the hidden layer. We present only the results corresponding to the topology that has performed better.

For each time series we have trained the network with ten different versions of the augmented training set generated from different seeds, to take into account the variability of the random patterns added to form them. DDA algorithm for RBF training is constructive and its result does not depend on weights initialization. Thus, for each augmented training set, experiments are executed only once.

On the other hand, MLPs performance depends on weights and bias initializations, therefore, in this case, for each augmented training set, we train and test the network ten times, to take into account the weight initialization influence on results.

4.2   Results and Discussion

Table 1 presents results obtained after training the networks for series 1, 2, 3, and 4. It contains the mean number of epochs used in training, the mean number of hidden units in the resulting network and the network performance on its test set, i.e., the classification error, the false alarm rate and the undetected novelty rate. A false alarms happens when the network classifies a normal pattern as novelty. An undetected novelty happens when a novelty pattern is misclassified.

In table 1 MLP(1) means MLP trained with Rprop using time order validation sets; MLP(2) means MLP trained with Rprop using our distributed validation sets generation; MLP(3) means MLP trained with RpropMAP; MLP(4) means MLP committee with ensemble mean; MLP/RBF is the classifier built by combining MLP and RBF results. Finally, we also present our former RBF-DDA results for comparison [10].

Results show that the use of the proposed distributed validation set approach improves MLP performance on test sets for all series considered. It can also be seen that using all data available for training to form the training set and training with RpropMAP greatly improves performance. Results also show that the committee of MLPs and the MLP/RBF committee further improve classification performance on test sets, for all time series considered. These committee machines outperform both MLP and RBF-DDA. RBF-DDA obtained 8.35% mean classification error across the four series, while the MLP committee and the MLP/RBF committee obtained, respectively, 2.24% and 3.03%.

The MLP and MLP/RBF committees have produced comparable results for the classification error. MLP committee outperformed MLP/RBF committee in two series and produced worse results for the remaining two series. However, these classifiers produced very different results regarding false alarm and undetected novelty rates. RBF-DDA and the MLP/RBF committee have produced 0% false alarm on all experiments. On the other hand, pure MLP classifiers tend to produce false alarm rates greater than undetected novelty rates. This is due to the different nature of MLPs and RBFs. MLPs build global input-output mappings while RBFs build local mappings [6].

5   Conclusions

In this work we have analyzed a number of alternative classifiers to be used in conjunction with our method for novelty detection in short time series [10]. Our method works by generating both novelty and normal random patterns and adding than to training sets in order to improve classification performance. In this paper we compare performance of RBF-DDA, MLPs and committee machines of these classifiers. The classifiers were compared using four real-world

Table 1. Performance of the novelty detection approach on test sets for each time series

Classifier	Epochs	Hidden Units	Class. error mean	Class. error s.dev	False alarm rate mean	False alarm rate s.dev	Undetec. novelty rate mean	Undetec. novelty rate s.dev
			Series 1					
MLP (1)	224.10	6	30.08%	3.53%	21.52%	2.75%	8.55%	2.09%
MLP (2)	584.35	24	10.10%	1.68%	8.60%	2.08%	1.50%	1.44%
MLP (3)	3552.65	48	1.37%	0.56%	0.91%	0.44%	0.46%	0.24%
MLP (4)	3552.65	48	0.04%	0.13%	0.00%	0.00%	0.04%	0.13%
MLP/RBF	3552.65/4	48/623.2	3.25%	1.33%	0.00%	0.00%	3.25%	1.33%
RBF-DDA	4	623.2	11.00%	2.86%	0.00%	0.00%	11.00%	2.86%
			Series 2					
MLP (1)	150.10	12	33.17%	1.57%	22.86%	1.96%	10.31%	1.93%
MLP (2)	988.75	12	22.41%	1.56%	19.80%	2.01%	2.61%	0.97%
MLP (3)	7033.55	36	7.09%	2.26%	6.44%	2.21%	0.65%	0.34%
MLP (4)	7033.55	36	3.58%	2.42%	3.37%	2.34%	0.21%	0.41%
MLP/RBF	7033.55/4	36/621.7	3.08%	1.27%	0.00%	0.00%	3.08%	1.27%
RBF-DDA	4	621.7	6.50%	1.86%	0.00%	0.00%	6.50%	1.86%
			Series 3					
MLP (1)	450.55	12	29.90%	1.41%	25.24%	1.95%	4.66%	0.90%
MLP (2)	710.95	24	29.26%	3.00%	26.65%	3.28%	2.61%	0.92%
MLP (3)	7869.75	48	8.35%	2.88%	6.78%	2.74%	1.57%	0.38%
MLP (4)	7869.75	48	4.54%	3.29%	3.71%	2.90%	0.83%	0.52%
MLP/RBF	7869.75/4	48/656.1	3.04%	0.92%	0.00%	0.00%	3.04%	0.92%
RBF-DDA	4	656.1	8.79%	1.93%	0.00%	0.00%	8.79%	1.93%
			Series 4					
MLP (1)	205.00	48	20.36%	3.22%	13.43%	1.86%	6.93%	2.53%
MLP (2)	640.45	48	11.46%	2.71%	8.48%	2.87%	2.98%	1.03%
MLP (3)	6948.30	36	2.09%	0.58%	1.02%	0.47%	1.07%	0.45%
MLP (4)	6948.30	36	0.79%	0.69%	0.21%	0.35%	0.58%	0.53%
MLP/RBF	6948.30/4	36/644.4	2.75%	1.09%	0.00%	0.00%	2.75%	1.09%
RBF-DDA	4	644.4	7.13%	1.32%	0.00%	0.00%	7.13%	1.32%

non-stationary time series and the experiments have shown that the machine committees formed by MLPs and the MLP/RBF machine committees achieve similar performance, with 2.24% and 3.03% mean classification errors, respectively. This represent a considerable improvement over RBF-DDA, which has produced a mean classification error of 8.35% across these series. [10].

The classifiers have been compared using cyclic non-stationary time series which appear in many important problems, such as auditing [10]. However, we are aware of the importance of assessing system performance on other kinds of time series. Our future works include studying the impact of the window size on system's performance and applying neural networks with more powerful temporal processing abilities such as TDRBF [1], TDNN, FIR and recurrent networks [6]. They will be used to classify directly non-stationary time series and will be applied in conjunction to the method proposed here on real auditing problems, such as accountancy auditing [8] and payroll auditing [9].

References

1. M. R. Berthold. A time delay radial basis function network for phoneme recognition. In *Proc. of the IEEE International Conference on Neural Networks*, volume 7, pages 4470–4473, 1994.
2. Michael R. Berthold and Jay Diamond. Boosting the performance of RBF networks with dynamic decay adjustment. In G. Tesauro, D. Touretzky, and J. Alspector, editors, *Advances in Neural Information Processing*, volume 7. 1995.
3. C. Chatfield. *The Analysis of Time Series – An Introduction*. Chapman & Hall, fourth edition, 1989.
4. A. Zell et al. *SNNS - Stuttgart Neural Network Simulator, User Manual, Version 4.2*. University of Stuttgart and University of Tubingen.
5. F. Gonzalez, D. Dasgupta, and R. Kozma. Combining negative selection and classification techniques for anomaly detection. In *Proc. of the Congress on Evolutionary Computing*, 2002.
6. Simon Haykin. *Neural Networks: A Comprehensive Foundation*. Prentice Hall, 2nd edition, 1998.
7. E. Keogh, S. Lonardi, and W. Chiu. Finding surprising patterns in a time series database in linear time and space. In *Proc. ACM Knowledge Discovery and Data Mining - SIGKDD'02*, pages 550–556, 2002.
8. Eija Koskivaara. Artificial neural network models for predicting patterns in auditing monthly balances. *Journal of Operational Research Society*, 51(9):1060–1069, Sept 2000.
9. A. L. I. Oliveira, G. Azevedo, A. Barros, and A. L. M. Santos. A neural network based system for payroll audit support (in portuguese). In *Proceeding of the IV Brazilian National Artificial Intelligence Meeting*, 2003.
10. A. L. I. Oliveira, F. B. L. Neto, and S. R. L. Meira. Novelty detection for short time series with neural networks. In A. Abraham, M. Köppen, and K. Franke, editors, *Design and Application of Hybrid Intelligent Systems*, volume 104 of *Frontiers in Artificial Intelligence and Applications*. IOS Press, 2003.
11. L. Prechelt. Proben1 – a set of neural networks benchmark problems and benchmarking rules. Technical Report 21/94, Universität Karlsruhe, Germany, 1994.
12. M. Riedmiller and H. Braun. A direct adaptive method for faster backpropagation learning: The RPROP algorithm. In *Proceedings of the IEEE International Conference on Neural Networks (ICNN 93)*, 1993.
13. C. Shahabi, X. Tian, and W. Zhao. TSA-tree: A wavelet-based approach to improve the efficiency of multi-level surprise and trend queries on time-series data. In *Proc. of 12th International Conference on Scientific and Statistical Database Management*, 2000.
14. S. Singh and M. Markou. An approach to novelty detection applied to the classification of image regions. *IEEE Transactions on Knowledge and Data Engineering*, 15, 2003.
15. J. Yao and C. L. Tan. A case study on using neural networks to perform technical forecasting of forex. *Neurocomputing*, (34):79–98, 2000.

Treatment of Gradual Knowledge Using Sigma-Pi Neural Networks

Gerardo Reyes Salgado[1] and Bernard Amy[2]

[1] Centro Nacional de Investigación y Desarrollo Tecnológico (CENIDET), Mexico
greyes@cenidet.edu.mx, http://www.cenidet.edu.mx
[2] Laboratoire LEIBNIZ-IMAG, Grenoble, France
amy@imag.fr, http://www-leibniz.imag.fr/RESEAUX/

Abstract. This work belongs to the field of hybrid systems for Artificial Intelligence (AI). It concerns the study of "gradual" rules, which makes it possible to represent correlations and modulation relations between variables. We propose a set of characteristics to identify these gradual rules, and a classification of these rules into "direct" rules and "modulation" rules. In neurobiology, pre-synaptic neuronal connections lead to gradual processing and modulation of cognitive information. While taking as a starting point such neurobiological data, we propose in the field of connectionism the use of "Sigma-Pi" connections to allow gradual processing in AI systems. In order to represent as well as possible the modulation processes between the inputs of a network, we have created a new type of connection, "Asymmetric Sigma-Pi" (ASP) units. These models have been implemented within a pre-existing hybrid neuro-symbolic system, the INSS system, based on connectionist nets of the "Cascade Correlation" type. The new hybrid system thus obtained, INSS-Gradual, allows the learning of bases of examples containing gradual modulation relations. ASP units facilitate the extraction of gradual rules from a neural network.

1 Introduction

Artificial intelligence (AI) very early concerned with the concept of learning which is the basis of all experience, with the goal to develop methods that allow machines to acquire some expert knowledge. Two main ways have been explored then exploited, that drove to knowledge systems of a very different natures: the symbolic method used at the basis of classic AI, and more recently the use of connectionism methods based on the implementation of artificial neuron networks (A.N.N.) permitting a more numeric type learning. First studied separately, these two approaches of learning have been combined in hybrid systems that integrate the symbolic and the neuronal while trying to pull the best part of every technique.

One of the problems was the expression power of such systems. If the classic AI succeeded in the implementation of some methods that permit the representation and treatment of some high-level knowledge, it didn't happen the same in the connectionism AI that permitted the representation mainly of the rules of relatively low-level knowledge. On the other hand, the hybrid systems were limited by their expression power by the capacities of their neuronal part.

R. Monroy et al. (Eds.): MICAI 2004, LNAI 2972, pp. 854–861, 2004.

The neuro-symbolic hybrid systems (NSHS) as K.BA.N.N. [18], SYNHESYS [7] or INSS [9], generally use a set of symbolic rules of order 0 or 0+ of the type:

"IF <premise 1> AND/OR <premise 2>, THEN conclusion"
"IF attribute/variable (>, <, =) AND/OR value..., THEN conclusion"   (1)

They do not permit the treatment of the knowledge a type employed by the experts, the knowledge called gradual:

"The MORE (or LESS) x is A, the MORE (or LESS) y is B"   (2)

The main characteristics of the rules of this type are: the dynamic and gradual relation between the premise and the conclusion, and the imprecision of the treated knowledge. They have been much studied by the linguists that proposed to represent the graduality with the help of "topoi", relations that associate some gradual variables [11]. The logicians on their side used the theory of the possibilities and the fuzzy sets to figure out gradual rules equivalent to "topoi" ([2], [5]). Our approach to the problem remained near to the fuzzy logic.

With regard to the implementation, the starting point of our work was the neuro-symbolic hybrid system INSS developed by Fernando Osório [9]. INSS permits the compilation, the learning and the explicitation of classic rules. Our system is an extension of INSS. We called it INSS-Gradual (Gradual Incremental Neuro-Symbolic System). It contains a module connectionist that permits the learning of example bases possessing the gradual relations and modulation, and a second module that permits the gradual rule explicitation from an artificial neural network. The connectionist module of INSS-Gradual is provided with a new type of neuronal connection, the "Asymmetric Sigma-Pi" units, derived of the "Sigma-Pi" units proposed by Rumerlhart [13]. In the continuation of this article, we will describe the stages to the development of INSS-Gradual.

2 Characteristics and Classification of Gradual Rules

The gradual knowledge (Davis [3], Després [4]) describes a continuous dynamic and singular relationship among some variables with an orderly domain: For example, the influence or modulation of a variable on another variable. This knowledge only indicates the address of the change and not its width. Symmetry does not exist: "*x exercises influence on y*", it does not imply that "*y exercises influence on x*". During our work, we identify two kinds of gradual rules :

- Direct Gradual Rules (DGR) of the type "*The MORE x is A, The MORE y is B*". They describe the progressive and direct influence of the premise on the conclusion. For example: "*An INCREASE of motor power, results in An INCREASE in fuel-consumption*", or "$\uparrow$ *power* $\Rightarrow \uparrow$ *fuel-consumption*" (where the symbols $\uparrow$ and $\downarrow$ indicate "*an increase*" or "*a decrease*", respectively).

- Modulation Gradual Rules (MGR) of the type "*The MORE x is A, The MORE [DGR]*". In these, the premise exerts a modulation (inhibition or excitation) on the "force" of the DGR. For example: "*The MORE the model of a car is old, The MORE [An INCREASE of the car weight, resulting in A DECREASE in the miles-per-gallon of fuel]*", or "(+) *model* $\downarrow \Rightarrow [\uparrow weight \Rightarrow \downarrow miles-per-gallon]$.

In both cases, The MORE can be changed to The LESS, without forgetting that the relationships are not symmetrical, and that to change MORE for LESS can imply a different sense in the graduality relationship.

3   Modelling of the Neurobiological Phenomena of Modulation

The concept modulation present in the gradual rule has foundations in the neurobiological phenomena. According to Smyth [14], one of the means of integrating an activity in the cerebral cortex of mammals is the modulation of the transmission of information through "processors" present in the system. These "processors" accentuate or inhibit the consistency of information dealt with the one that, at the same time, is transmitted by the other "processors". This process is a useful strategy because the information of a variable of the environment can be transmitted through several other lines of treatment. If different lines of information are concerned with different variables of the environment, then several of these variables will be taken statistically into account. These statistical relations (or correlations) can be used for the discovery of some important variables of the environment, and especially of their reciprocal influences.

In his works of modelling of the cortical column and analysis of its operating and learning laws, F. Alexander [1] identifies some behaviours of "modulation". He shows that "the columns receive and can modulate information coming from columns of other cortical areas or the same area, from other maxi-columns (set of columns that receive more than a receptive field)".

This type of behaviour is the basis of some transmission phenomena of information putting in plays at least two input variables and an output variable, and in which an input modulates the completed treatment. The input charged of the modulation is called "variable that modulates" and the other input is called "variable modulated".

3.1   The Behaviour of Modulation in a Neurobiological Connection

In the classical neurobiological connections a neuron fires its signal on the dendrite of another neuron. However, there exists another type of connection corresponding to modulation phenomena: the pre-synaptic connections (see Fig. 1.a). In this type of connection, the neuron that modulates establishes its discharge on a synapse and not on a dendrite: by this synapse, a neuron controls another synapse having an inhibition or excitation effect on the latter.

3.2   The Sigma-Pi Units, a Way to Represent the Pre-synaptic Connections

As previously said, the majority of neuro-symbolic hybrid systems only make the learning and/or the explicitation of symbolic rules of the type IF... THEN... For this, they use some A.N.N. based on the "Sigma" classic units (S units) where in each unit the sum pondered of outputs of other units is presented. In Sigma connection, the neural connection inhibits or excites a dendrite. This type of unit does not take into

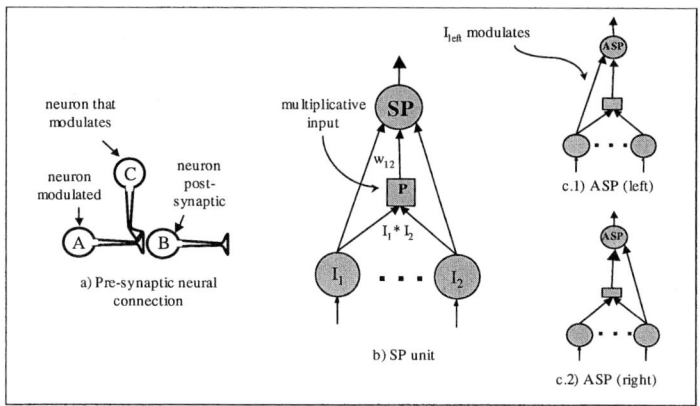

Fig. 1. Pre-synaptic neural connection, Sigma-Pi unit and Asymmetric Sigma-Pi units.

account the behaviour of present modulation in the gradual rules. This is why we were interested in the "Sigma-Pi" units (SP units - see Fig. 1.b).

The "Sigma-Pi" units permit, for a particular unit, a multiplication of certain inputs before passing to the Sigma unit. These multiplicative units [13] allow an input to control the other unit or units. These units are a way to represent the neurobiological pre-synaptic connections where the effectiveness of the synapse between the axon 1 and the dendrite would be modulated by the activity between the axon 1 and the axon 2 [8]. However, the Sigma-Pi units do not take into account the characteristic of asymmetry that is present in the pre-synaptic connections and in the modulation behaviours of gradual rules: in the product of the x and y variable we do not know if x modulates y or the inverse. Multiplying the two variables we lose information. It is for that reason that we proposed the "Asymmetric Sigma-Pi" units (ASP units - see Fig. 1.c). These units allow us to establish a relation of modulation between two inputs of the A.N.N. and at the same time to show what the input that modulates is.

The "Asymmetric Sigma-Pi" units permit a "more natural" representation of the modulation relationships between the inputs of the A.N.N. without losing the corresponding information. These units were implemented in the neural module of INSS-Gradual.

4   Learning of Gradual Rules with Asymmetric Sigma-Pi Units

The ASP units were implemented in the neural module of INSS-gradual using the "Cascade-Correlation" (CasCor) paradigm [6]: To each phase of the learning, the neural module proposes a set of ASP-left and ASP-right candidate units, which will be exposed to a competitive learning using CasCor. Among them, the winning unit will be that that maximizes the correlation between the residual error of the global output and the output of the candidate unit. This winning unit will be incorporated into the net, and one will continue the learning of the base of examples. In the end, we will obtain an A.N.N. made up of S and ASP units (see Fig. 2).

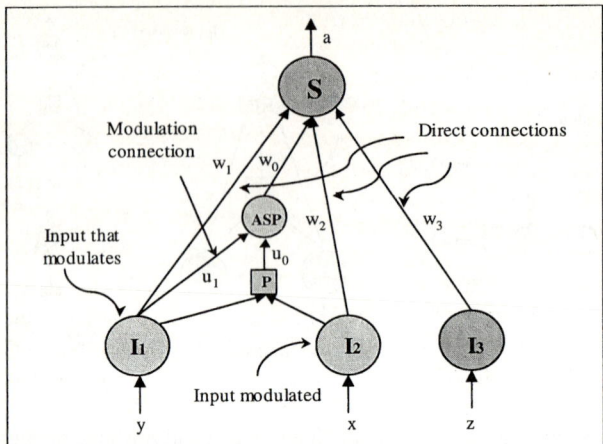

Fig. 2. Neural network with a Sigma-Pi unit and an Asymmetric Sigma-Pi unit created for the neural module of INSS-Gradual used later on for the explicitation.

We proved the neural module on two bases of examples (in the first one, we knew about the existence of gradual relationships, and in the second one, we ignored it):

a) "Gradual Monk's Problem". (256 examples, 4 inputs, 1 output). This was created from "Monk's Problem" [16]. The task is to classify the entities in the gradual class robot (real value): $\{0,..., 6\}$. For that we used the attributes : angles-that-form-the-head (ordered by the number of angles) : $\{3, 4, 5, 6\}$; body-size: $\{0, 1, 2, 3\}$; smile (a bigger value indicates a defined smile: $\{1, 2, 3, 4\}$) and brain-size: $\{0, 1, 2, 3\}$. The Table 1 present the type of examples used.

b) "Miles per Gallon Problem". (392 examples, 7 inputs, 1 output) [9]. The goal is to predict the performance in "miles per gallon" (mpg) of diverse cars starting from three qualitative attributes (cylinders-number, model, origin) and four quantitative attributes (displacement, power, weight, acceleration).

After the learning process, the topologies of the neural networks are as follows:

a) "Gradual Monk's Problem": three ASP units, of which two relate the attributes angles-that-form-the-head and body-size, and another unit that relates smile and brain-size.

b) "Miles per Gallon Problem": 4 ASP units, of which two relate the attributes model and weight, another unit that relates origin with cylinders-number, and one that relates origin with acceleration, and lastly another for origin and number of cylinders. The type of neuron network created is shown in the Figure 2.

5   Eclectic Explicitation of Gradual Rules

After the learning process, the INSS-Gradual system allows an explicitation of new rules starting from the A.N.N. We consider that the graduality is present in the direct connections, and that the ASP units represent the modulation relationships. Therefore, we built the DGR by means of the analysis of the direct connections and the MGR by the analysis of the derivative of the A.N.N.'s global output with regard to the inputs of the ASP unit. For this, a new method of eclectic explicitation [17] was implemented. The method combines two stages: an analysis of the interior of A.N.N. (decompositional stage) and an analysis of the outputs of A.N.N. (pedagogical stage):

1) Decompositional. The weights of the direct connections are examined (see Fig. 2). For each direct connection, we calculate the percentage that represents their weight with regard to all the other connections. For the most important connections, we build a DGR depending on the weight sign. In addition, the ASP units are analysed, and it is determined which of the inputs modulates, and which one is modulated.

2) Pedagogical. For each ASP, we calculate the derivative of the global output of the neural network with relationship to the modulated input of the ASP relationship ($\delta a/\delta x$) (see Fig. 2). To build a MGR we analyse the sign of the derivative, the weight of the connection of the ASP unit toward the output (w_0), the weight of the connection of the P unit toward the ASP unit (u_0), the weight of the connection of the input modulated toward the output (w_2), as well as the topology of the ASP unit. The relationship between w2 and the output will allow us to define the DGR (for example, "The MORE x, the MORE a" - see Fig. 2). The signs of the other weights and the derivative (w_0, u_0, and $\delta a/\delta x$) will allow us to build the MGR completely (for example, "The MORE y, The MORE [DGR]" - see Fig. 2).

5.1 Results of the Explicitation by Using the Eclectic Method

The results of the explicitation on the two bases of examples are as follows:

a) "Gradual Monk's Problem".

a.1) Direct Gradual Rules:

DGR1: $\uparrow$ *body-size* $\Rightarrow$ $\uparrow$ *class-robot;*

DGR2: $\uparrow$ *smile* OR $\uparrow$ *brain-size* OR $\uparrow$ *angles-that-form-the-head* $\Rightarrow$ $\downarrow$ *class-robot.*

a.2) Modulation Gradual Rules:

MGR1: (+) *angles-that-form-the-head* $\uparrow$ $\Rightarrow$ (–) [$\uparrow$ *body-size* $\Rightarrow$ $\uparrow$ *class-robot];*

MGR2: (+) *angles-that-form-the-head* $\uparrow$ $\Rightarrow$ (–) [$\uparrow$ *body-size* $\Rightarrow$ $\uparrow$ *class-robot];*

MGR3: (+) *smile* $\uparrow$ $\Rightarrow$ (+) [$\uparrow$ *brain-size* $\Rightarrow$ $\downarrow$ *class-robot].*

The explicitation allows us to recover the two MGR with which one had created the base of examples.

b) "Miles per Gallon".

b.1) Direct Gradual Rules:

DGR1: ($\uparrow$ *model* OR $\uparrow$ *acceleration* OR $\uparrow$ *displacement*) $\Rightarrow$ $\uparrow$ *mpg;*

DGR2: ($\uparrow$ *weight* OR $\uparrow$ *power* OR $\uparrow$ *cylinders-number*) $\Rightarrow$ $\downarrow$ *mpg.*

b.2) Modulation Gradual Rules:

MGR1: (+) *model* $\uparrow$ $\Rightarrow$ (–) [$\uparrow$ *weight* $\Rightarrow$ $\downarrow$ *miles-per-gallon*];

MGR2: (+) *model* $\uparrow$ $\Rightarrow$ (–) [$\uparrow$ *weight* $\Rightarrow$ $\downarrow$ *miles-per-gallon*];

MGR3: (+) *origin* $\uparrow$ $\Rightarrow$ (–) [$\uparrow$ *cylinders-number* $\Rightarrow$ $\downarrow$ *mpg*];

MGR4: (+) *origin* $\uparrow$ $\Rightarrow$ (–) [$\uparrow$ *acceleration* $\Rightarrow$ $\uparrow$ *mpg*].

For "Miles per Gallon Problem", we observe that some rules are similar to those obtained by Thimm [15] who used an "intuitive and informal" explicitation method. For example, he obtained *"The MORE weight, the LESS mpg"* and *"However, the newer the cars are, the LESS they consume"*. These two rules are represented in the MGR1: "The *MORE the model of a car is new, the LESS [An INCREASE of the car weight, resulting in A DECREASE in the miles-per-gallon of fuel]*" or "(+) *model* ↑ ⇒ (–) [↑ *weight* ⇒ ↓ *miles-per-gallon*]". One of the advantages of our method is the automation of this process and the possibility of obtaining DGR and MGR.

6 Conclusions

The gradual rules permit the representation and the treatment of the gradual or modulation knowledge. During our research work, we identified their characteristics and their representation of these gradual rules. We proposed a classification of them in two kinds: direct gradual rules and modulation gradual rules. The first one permits the representation of an immediate gradual link between the premise and the conclusion of a rule. The second one corresponds just where a premise would exercise an effect of modulation on another already established relation.

In neurobiology, the pre-synaptic synapses permit certain modulation effects that have a similar consequence to the behaviours that we named gradual or of modulation. Based on this neurobiological information, we proposed for the neural networks the units of a new type, the Asymmetric Sigma - Pi units, witch that permits the representation of the modulation processes and the learning of gradual knowledge. It drove us to the INSS-Gradual system. To extract this knowledge, we added a method of explicitation of gradual rules that permits the extraction of this rule type from an A.N.N. that includes the Asymmetric Sigma-Pi units.

The INSS-Gradual system permits a "fine" analysis of the mechanisms for the treatment of high-level knowledge and the limits of these mechanisms in the automatic knowledge acquisition systems (see the problem of representation of qualitative variables in [12]). The new connectionist units that it implements permit a re-balancing between the two methods of learning combined in the classical hybrid system this while allowing to one and another method to take into account the same high-level knowledge type.

References

1. Alexandre, F.: Intelligence Neuromimétique. Mémoire pour l'obtention de l'habilitation à diriger des recherches. Henri Poincaré University - Nancy I. France (June 1997).
2. Bouchon-Meunier, B.: La Logique Floue et ses Applications. Addison-Wesley France, S.A. Paris. (October 1995).
3. Davis, H.: Using Models of Dynamic Behaviour in Expert Systems. Neuvième Journées Internationales sur Les Systèmes Experts et leurs Applications. Avignon, France. (29 May - 2 June 1989).
4. Després, S.: Chapter 5 of Topoi et Gestion des Connaissances. Edit. Raccah, P.-Y. Masson, Paris (1996).
5. Dubois, D., Prade, H.: Prédicats Graduels et Modalités Nuancées. Le Courrier du CNRS. Sciences Cognitives. CNRS. N° 79 (October 1992).
6. Fahlman, S.E., Lebiere, C.: The Cascade-Correlation Learning Architecture. Carnegie Mellon University. Technical Report. CMU-CS-90-100. (1990).

7. Giacometi, A.: Modèles Hybrides de l'Expertise. PhD Thesis, LIFIA-IMAG, Grenoble - France (November 1992).
8. Gurney, K.: Alternative Node Types. Notes in http ://pikas.inf.tu-dresden.de/~ihle/NNcourse/ NOTES/18/18.html. Dept. Human Sciences, Brunel University Uxbridge, Middx (1997).
9. Osório, F. S.: INSS - Un Système Hybride Neuro-Symbolique pour l'Apprentissage Automatique Constructif. PhD Thesis, LEIBNIZ-IMAG, Grenoble – France (February 1998).
10. Quinlan, R.: Combining Instance-Based and Model-Based Reasoning. In Proceedings on the Tenth International Conference of Machine Learning. University of Massachusetts. Amherst. Morgan Kauffmann (1993).
11. Raccah, P-Y.: Chapter 10 of Sémantique et Cognition : Catégories, Prototypes et Typicalité. Dubois, D. (Ed). Edit. CNRS (1991).
12. Reyes-Salgado G.: Connaissances de haut niveau dans les systèmes hybrides neuro-symboliques. PhD Thesis, LEIBNIZ-IMAG, Grenoble – France (June 2001).
13. Rumelhart, D.E., McClelland, J.L.: PDP Research Group. Parallel Distributed Processing : Explorations in the Microstructure of Cognition. Vol. 1 : Foundations. The MIT Press, Cambridge, Massachusetts (1986).
14. Smyth, D., Phillips, W. A., Kay, J.: Measures for Investigating the Contextual Modulation of Information Transmission. In: Network : Computation in Neural Systems" Vol. 7, pp. 307-316. UK (1996).
15. Thimm, G.: Optimisation of High Order Perceptrons. PhD Thesis. École Polytechnique Fédérale de Lausanne, Switzerland (1997).
16. Thrun, S. B. et al: The Monk's Problem – A Performance Comparison of Different Learning Algorithms. Carnegie Mellon University - CMU, Technical Report CMU-CS-91-197. Web : http://www.cs.cmu.edu/~thrun/, Ftp : ftp://archive.cis.ohio-state.edu/pub/neuroprose (December 1991).
17. Tickle, A. B., Andrews, R., Golea, M., Diederich, J.: The Truth Will Come to Light : Directions and Challenges in Extracting the Knowledge Embedded Within Trained Artificial Neural Networks. IEEE Transactions on Neural Networks, Vol. 9, No. 6 (November 1998).
18. Towell, G.: Symbolic Knowledge and Neural Networks : Insertion, Refinement and Extraction. Ph.D. Thesis. Univ. of Wisconsin - Madison. USA (1991).

A Method to Obtain Sensing Requirements in Robotic Assemblies by Geometric Reasoning

Santiago E. Conant-Pablos[1], Katsushi Ikeuchi[2], and Horacio Martínez-Alfaro[3]

[1] Center for Intelligent Systems, ITESM Campus Monterrey, México
sconant@itesm.mx, http://www-csi.mty.itesm.mx/~sconant
[2] Institute of Industrial Science, The University of Tokyo, Japan
ki@iis.u-tokyo.ac.jp, http://www.cvl.iis.u-tokyo.ac.jp/~ki
[3] Center for Intelligent Systems, ITESM Campus Monterrey, México
hma@itesm.mx, http://www-csi.mty.itesm.mx/~hma

Abstract. This paper presents a method for determining sensing requirements for robotic assemblies from a geometrical analysis of critical contact-state transitions produced among mating parts during the execution of nominal assembly plans. The goal is to support the reduction of real-life uncertainty through the recognition of assembly tasks that require force and visual feedback operations. The assembly tasks are decomposed into assembly skill primitives based on transitions described on a taxonomy of contact relations. Force feedback operations are described as a set of force compliance skills which are systematically associated to the assembly skill primitives. To determine the visual feedback operations and the type of visual information needed, a backward propagation process of geometrical constraints is used. This process defines new visual feedback requirements for the tasks from the discovery of direct, and indirect, insertion and contact dependencies among the mating parts. A computational implementation of the method was developed and validated with test cases containing assembly tasks including all the combinations of sensing requirements. The program behave as expected in every case.

1 Introduction

This paper presents a method for determining sensing requirements for robotic assembly from an analysis of critical contact-state transitions produced among assembled parts during the execution of nominal assembly plans. The goal is to support the reduction of real-life uncertainty, through the recognition of assembly tasks that require force and visual feedback. Force feedback is proposed to be used during the execution of assembly operations that involve objects in contact. Visual feedback is proposed to be used before the assembly operations to detect errors and deviations from the original plan that could require of preventive adjustments in the configurations of the mating parts [1]. Plans considered are restricted to binary plans, which are also linear and sequential, that describe a totally ordered sequence of assembly steps.

R. Monroy et al. (Eds.): MICAI 2004, LNAI 2972, pp. 862–871, 2004.

The information about the contacts formation is obtained by analyzing geometric models of the objects [2], and are classified in accordance to a taxonomy used by Ikeuchi and Suehiro in the *Assembly Plan from Observation* (APO) method [3]. The assembly tasks are decomposed into assembly skill primitives based on transitions described on this taxonomy.

The assembly parts considered in this work are rigid mechanical pieces modeled as polyhedral objects. Very small errors in the assembly operations involving objects in contact could generate great forces that could damage the assembly parts, the robot, and/or the workcell. Such operations are determined as including critical contact transitions that require force control [4]. Force feedback operations prescribed by the method for these operations are described as a set of force compliance skills which are systematically associated to the assembly skill primitives.

To determine the visual feedback operations and the type of visual information needed, a backward propagation process of geometrical constraints is used. This process defines new visual feedback requirements for the tasks from the discovery of direct, and indirect, insertion and contact dependencies among the mating parts. The method extends the approach proposed by Miura and Ikeuchi [5] to determine preventive visual feedback requirements for the environmental objects (stationary objects that configure the environment during an assembly operation) including cases of multiple motions of the same object, tasks that do not modify the contact state, and tasks that break previous contact formations.

2   Contact State Analysis

The use of sensors and sensing operations is needed only in tasks where the amount of uncertainty with respect to some dimensions is big enough to put in risk its successful execution. Such dimensions are what we call the *critical dimensions of an assembly task*. In this paper, the *dimensions of an assembly operation* are defined as the least number of independent coordinates required to specify the pose of the manipulated object and the poses of the objects in the environment that participate in contact relations with the manipulated object.

Contacts are directional phenomenons with a constraining motion effect over the manipulated object that depend on the contact's direction and can be represented by $N \cdot \triangle T \geq 0$, where N denotes the contact direction (constraint vector) and $\triangle T$ the possible translational motion vectors. The frictional resistance to motion generated among the contacting features is ignored by this analysis under the assumption of applying enough force to defeat the existent resistance.

To represent the contact relations formed during the execution of an assembly plan, we use the taxonomy shown in Fig. 1. This taxonomy identifies all possible assembly relations based on the directions of the contact surface normals. The contact directions and possible movement directions are represented on the Gaussian sphere.

The three digits in the labels of the states in Fig. 1 denotes the number of *maintaining DOF*, *detaching DOF*, and *constraining DOF*, respectively. A maintaining DOF indicates that there is not a constraint component in that direction

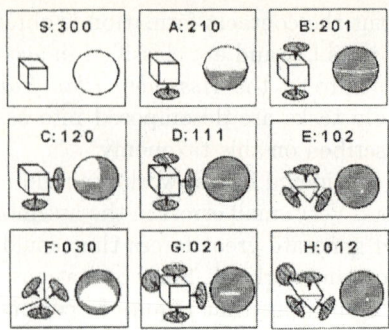

Fig. 1. Contact-state relations taxonomy.

and then a very small movement is not expected to modify the contact state. A detaching DOF indicates that a constraining component exists in that direction and then a conveniently selected motion can eliminate the contact. A constraining DOF indicates that there is no possibility of movement in that direction.

The changes in the contact-state relations that characterize a task are identified by the transitions of DOF in the manipulated object. There are six possible types of transitions between DOF: maintaining to detaching (M2D), maintaining to constraining (M2C), detaching to constraining (D2C), detaching to maintaining (D2M), constraining to maintaining (C2M), and constraining to detaching (C2D). It is also possible that an assembly plan includes some steps that do not modify the category of any DOF of the manipulated object. These steps including maintaining to maintaining (M2M), detaching to detaching (D2D), and constraining to constraining (C2C) *pseudo-transitions* of DOF have to be considered since some of them could require of sensing information.

3   Assembly Skill Primitives

Every assembly task comprise some kind of motion. From an analysis on the effect of this motion over the manipulated object's DOF, the following four assembly skill primitives were extracted: **move (M)** - an assembly skill primitive required by tasks including M2M and D2M DOF transitions to displace an object in a completely unconstrained manner; **make-contact (C)** - a move assembly skill primitive required by tasks including M2D DOF transitions that ends when a new contact is produced between the manipulated object and the environment; **insert (I)** - an assembly skill primitive required by tasks including M2C transitions to move the manipulated object into a low-tolerance region where the completely unconstrained DOF finishes completely constrained; and **slide (S)** - an assembly skill primitive required by tasks including the rest of the DOF transitions – D2D, D2C, C2M, C2D, and C2C – to move an object while maintaining the contact with at least one constraining surface (c-surface).

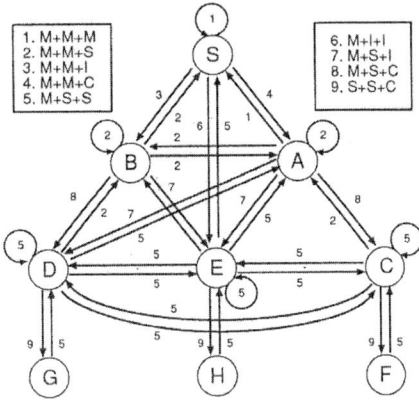

Fig. 2. Procedure graph including the assembly skill primitives.

Taking the DOF transition analysis to the procedure graphs, it is realized that the execution of some assembly operations require the concurrent use of multiple assembly skill primitives. Figure 2 depicts the required skills for the assembly operations in the procedure graphs.

4   Force Sensing Strategies

To implement the assembly skill primitives, force and torque information is used to detect new contacts and to react to tactile stimuli. All the skills with exception of the move manipulation skill require of force compliance capabilities. The move assembly skill primitive requires position control, but not necessarily of any kind of sensing.

From an analysis of the make-contact, slide, and insert assembly skill primitives three force compliance skills are recognized: **detect-contact** - a force compliance skill that moves an object until a new contact is produced against the assembly environment; **configuration-control** - a force compliance skill that corrects the configuration of the features in contact through rotations of the manipulated object; and **keep-contact** - a force compliance skill that moves an object while maintaining contact with constraining surfaces.

Table 1 presents the force compliance skills needed to implement every assembly skill primitive.

5   Visual Sensing Strategies

The problem of determining the geometrical relations among objects in contact is inherently related to recognizing and locating objects in the scene. The typical way to detect contact relations among objects by vision is through a process of geometric reasoning and the use of threshold values.

Table 1. Force compliance skills required by each assembly skill primitive.

Assembly skill primitive	Force Compliance skill
move	
make-contact	detect-contact
	configuration-control
slide	keep-contact
	detect-contact
insert	keep-contact
	configuration-control

Since the present work is interested in using vision with preventive intentions, the sensing planner has to take advantage of the periods when the manipulator has control over the assembly parts to perform some convenient adjustments in their pose configurations. The best sensor configuration to perform a proposed visual sensing strategy should be obtained by a sensor planner [6].

The analysis to identify the assembly skill primitives that require preventive use of vision is divided in two parts: one that analyses an assembly operation isolated from the rest of the plan, and another, that analyses the roll of an assembly operation as part of the full plan. In the first case, visual sensing requirements are determined considering only the new contact relations produced by the task when an object is manipulated. In the second case, visual sensing requirements are determined considering the contact relations produced by tasks where an object participates as part of the environment.

5.1   Visual Sensing for a Manipulated Object

Not all the assembly skill primitives require the use of preventive vision. Due to the assumption of bounded error, a move primitive is not expected to fail, and the cost of using vision is not considered worth its marginal benefit. Although vision could be of assistance to the make-contact primitive for discriminating among potential contact surfaces, determining the approach configuration, and evaluating subassembly stability risks; those situations are also considered of marginal benefit during the assembly planning. In addition, vision is not used also for the slide primitive because vision is not good to detect actual contacts, and then, it is not a good idea to use it for keeping contacts while moving.

The insertion primitive is a low-tolerance operation where small errors typically cause failure. Insertion fails when the inserting features enters in contact with faces adjacent to the inserting slot, instead of penetrating the target region. This failure can be realized by monitoring the insertion process until a first contact is detected. Force and torque data can be used to determine success or failure. The absence of contacts before the insertion operations makes force feedback useless and vision adequate to verify the fulfillment of the alignment constraints imposed by the M2C DOF transitions. Consequently, an assembly step will require of using preventive vision on the manipulated object only if it includes any of the following five of the 36 possible transitions: $S \Rightarrow B$, $S \Rightarrow E$, $A \Rightarrow D$, $A \Rightarrow E$, or $B \Rightarrow E$.

5.2 Visual Sensing for an Environmental Object

The sensing planner considers the use of vision in order to achieve two goals: first, to succeed in insertion operations because, as explained before, the success depends not only in the positional control of the manipulated object; it is also important that the environmental conditions for the insertion exist. Second, to succeed in producing all the prescribed contacts among the assembly elements during the execution of every operation.

Sensing for insertion condition. To succeed in insertions, the insert features of the environment have to correspond and be aligned with the insert features of the manipulated object. When the environment includes insert features of one object, there is no need to add new visual sensing requirements for it; only the manipulated object's configuration would have to be adjusted to compensate for any observed error with respect to the environmental object's pose. Instead, when the environment includes insert features of two or more objects, an *indirect insert dependency* is defined among them. If any of these environmental objects was pre-assembled, it is possible that new visual sensing requirements need to be included into its preventive visual sensing strategy. These sensing requirements must be fulfilled when this object is manipulated.

Sensing for contact prescription. In the present work, the execution of an assembly operation is considered successful if all the expected contacts are achieved. To achieve all the expected contacts the configuration of the contacting features on the environment has to correspond with the configuration of the contacting features on the manipulated object. When the environment includes features of one object, there is not need to add new visual sensing requirements for it; only the manipulated object's configuration would have to be adjusted, using force sensing, to compensate for any sensed error in the force and torque patterns. Instead, when the environment includes contact features of two or more objects, an *indirect contact dependency* is defined among them. If any of these environmental objects was pre-assembled, it is possible that new visual sensing requirements need to be included into its preventive visual sensing strategy. These sensing requirements must be fulfilled when this object is manipulated.

5.3 The Insert and Contact Dependency Graph

An *insert and contact dependency graph* (ICdg) is introduced to express direct and indirect dependencies among assembly elements caused by make-contact and insert assembly skill primitives. An ICdg is a graph where nodes represent objects and arcs represent alignment constraints extracted from an analysis of insert relations and contact relations resulting from operations described into a nominal assembly plan. The direction of the arcs answer to the assembly order, and then, describes a dependency of one object's configuration (the arc's source) on the configuration of another (the arc's target). The root arrowed node is the current manipulated object, while the end arrowed nodes are environmental objects.

The ICdg is used, during the sensing planning stage, as a tool for determining the critical dimensions for the manipulation of objects. The ICdg is also used, during the sensing execution stage, for adjusting the observed configurations of the objects to conform with all the alignment constraints defined by past, current, and future contact-state relations.

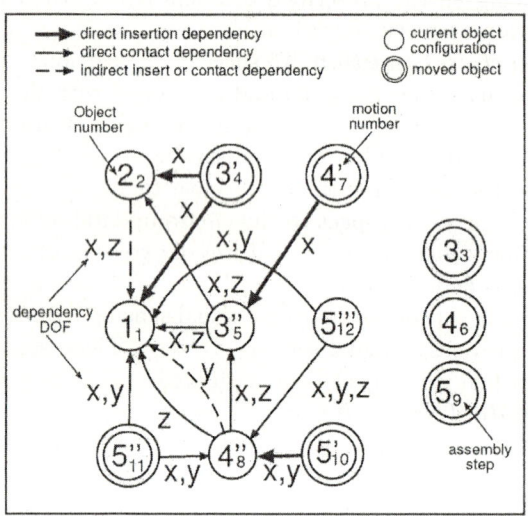

Fig. 3. ICdg.

Elements of an ICdg

An ICdg could include two types of nodes and three types of arcs. One type of nodes is added for each environmental object that is not moved during the full assembly process. A second type of node is added for each manipulated object. The object related to nodes of the first type does not need to be observed because their poses are usually known from the starting of the assembly, e.g. a work table. They can act like fixed constraining references for the other objects. When an assembly operation requires of using vision, the pose of some environmental objects related to the nodes of the second type would need to be observed.

The three types of arcs were devised to record the nature of the dependency between the objects they link. Two types of arcs (solid in Fig. 3) record alignment constraints that describe direct relations originated from contacts and insertions produced during current and past manipulations of the objects involved. These arcs are generated between the manipulated object and one or more environmental objects. A third arc type (dashed in Fig. 3) records alignment constraints that describe both indirect insert dependencies and indirect contact dependencies among environmental objects. The labels of the arcs indicate the constrained DOF of the source node that can be described as a function of the DOF of the target node. Between two nodes not linked by any arc, do not hold any alignment dependency, which means that errors in the pose of one of the objects is not expected to affect the mating operation of the other.

Propagation of Alignment Constraints

New contact formations depicted as solid arcs in an ICdg could reveal new alignment constraints among environmental objects. Such environmental objects could already participate in alignment constraints with other objects, which could reveal further constraints. This situation defines a backward propagation pattern that starts from a currently manipulated object up to pre-assembled environmental objects.

This constraint propagation scheme involves at least three objects and is fired up by three conditions: **(C1)** an object is inserted or enters in contact with multiple environmental objects making its object configuration to depend upon theirs and the defined dependencies include common constrained DOF (*joining constraint*); **(C2)** an object is inserted or enters in contact with an environmental object, while this environmental object already depends on another environmental object, and in both cases the dependencies include common constrained DOF (*inherited constraint*); and **(C3)** an object is inserted or enters in contact with an environmental object, and this environmental object has another environmental object depending on it, and both dependencies on this object include common constrained DOF (*shared constraint*).

Not all the indirect dependencies are relevant for visual sensing. The indirect dependencies that are relevant are only those that relate with critical dimensions for a future assembly task, when these critical dimensions are not enforced by any direct dependency existing before the manipulation of the environmental objects were performed.

Since an environmental object could be manipulated several times before the task that made an indirect dependency relevant, the constraint propagation method has to determine the manipulation step where vision will be useful for correcting any possible error with respect to the critical dimensions. Such step is the most recently effected on the environmental object where the critical dimension was not constrained. Since the assembly skill primitives are defined for each task dimension, the manipulation step selected is the last step where such critical dimension required of a move or an insert assembly skill primitive.

The constraint propagation method is applied for each assembly step. It starts determining all the face contacts in which the manipulated object participates, and finishes when all the direct dependencies for the manipulated object and the new indirect dependencies for the environmental objects are deduced. Since the indirect dependencies are deduced for pre-assembled environmental objects, a record of the sensing plan evolution is maintained to allow going back to a manipulation step for an environmental object and modify its indirect dependencies.

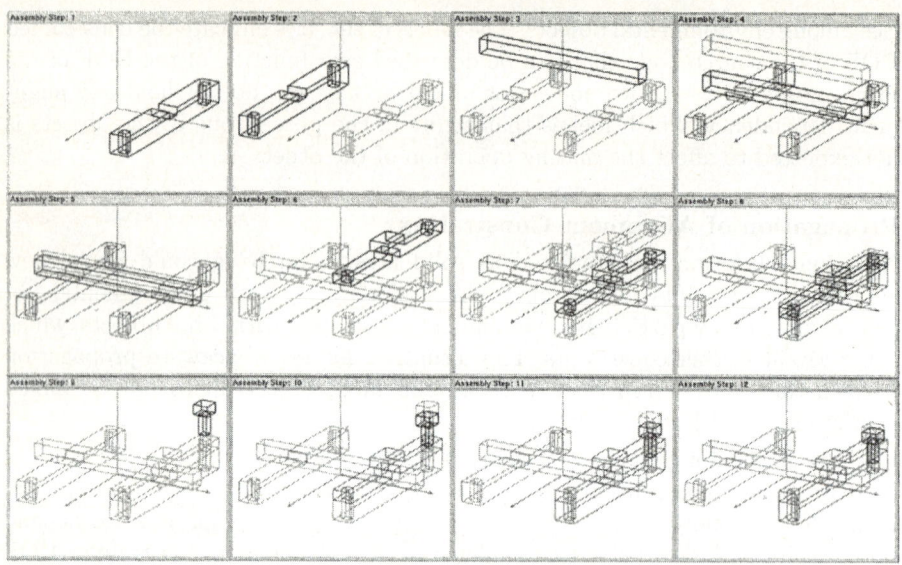

Fig. 4. Sequence of assembly steps.

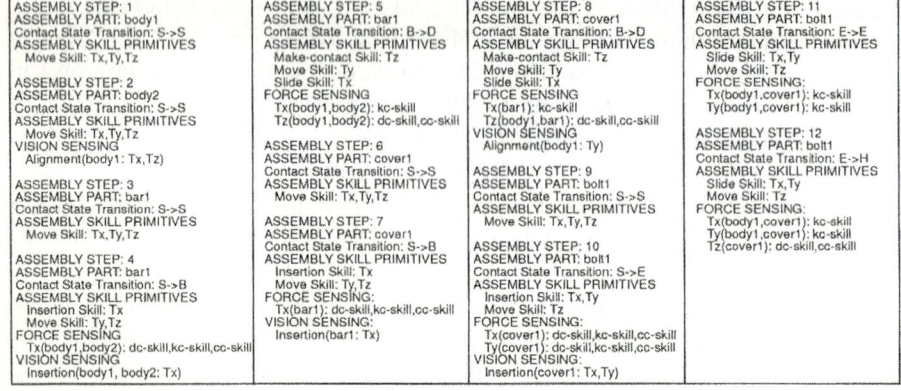

Fig. 5. Assembly plan with sensing operations.

6   A Computational Implementation of the Method

We implemented the proposed method as a C++ computer application. The CAD models of the objects are created with a CSG modeling tool known as VANTAGE [7].

A nominal assembly plan is composed by a sequence of assembly steps. Every step specifies the type of assembly operation, the name of an assembly part to be manipulated, the name of the VANTAGE object that represent the model of the part, and the motion parameters as a list of six values (three for translation and three for rotation).

Next, we present a case solved using the proposed method. Fig. 4 illustrates the steps specified in the nominal assembly plan; Fig. 3 depicts the final ICdg for the case; and finally, Fig. 5 shows the resulting assembly plan including the sensing feedback operations. Force sensing is specified by relating force compliance skills with critical DOF and assembly parts. Visual sensing is specified as `Insertion` for steps that include such assembly skill primitive and as `Alignment` for steps that have indirect dependecies.

7 Conclusions

In this paper we have introduced a geometric reasoning method to determine force and vision sensing requirements for robotic assemblies. The characterization of assembly steps as transitions of contact states allowed the additional segmentation of tasks into assembly skill primitives. These primitives together with the polyhedral form of the assembly parts allowed the systematic association of tasks with force compliance skills that conform force sensing requirements for the execution of the assembly steps. Also, from the discovery of insert assembly skill primitives and make-contact skill primitives where two or more environmental object participate new visual sensing requirements are deduced.

We have implemented the method as a computational program, tested and verified its effectiveness to determine all the expected sensing requirements. The method is limited to objects modeled as polyhedra and it is oriented to preventive sensing. Future research directions include its extension to objects with curved surfaces and the inclusion of sensing for verification and correction.

References

1. Conant-Pablos, S. E., Ikeuchi, K.: Preventive sensing planning for robotic assembly. In Proc. 1999 IEEE Intl. Conf. on Multisensor Fusion and Integration for Intelligent Systems. Taipei, Taiwan (1999) 171–176
2. Zhang, L., Xiao, J.: Derivation of contact states from geometric models of objects. In IEEE Proc. Intl. Symp. on Assembly and Task Planning. (1995) 375–380
3. Ikeuchi, K., Suehiro, T.: Towards an assembly plan from observation. part i: Assembly task recognition using face-contact relations (polyhedral objects). In Proc. 1992 IEEE Intl. Conf. on Robotics and Automation. (1992) 2171–2177
4. Mason, M. T.: Compliance and force control for computer controlled manipulators. IEEE Trans. on Systems, Man, and Cybernetics. **SMC-11**(1981) 418–432
5. Miura, J., Ikeuchi, K.: Task-oriented generation of visual sensing strategies in assembly tasks. IEEE Trans. on Pattern Analysis and Machine Intelligence (PAMI) **20(2)** (1998) 126–138
6. Allen, P. K., Tarabanis, K. A., Tsai, R. Y.: A survey of sensor planning in computer vision. IEEE Trans. on Robotics and Automation. **11(1)** (1995) 86–104
7. Hoffman, R., Ikeuchi, K., Balakumar, P., Robert, J. C., Kanade, T.: Vantage: A frame-based geometric/sensor modeling system - programmer/user's manual v1.0. Tech. Rep. Carnegie Mellon University (1991)

Intelligent Task Level Planning for Robotic Assembly: Issues and Experiments

Jorge Corona Castuera and Ismael Lopez-Juarez

Mechatronics and Intelligent Manufacturing Systems Research Group (MIMSRG)
CIATEQ, A.C. Advanced Technology Centre,
Manantiales 23-A, Parque Industrial Bernardo Quintana
76246 El Marqués, Qro., México
{jcorona,ilopez}@ciateq.mx
http://www.ciateq.mx/

Abstract. Today's industrial robots use programming languages that do not allow learning and task knowledge acquisition and probably this is one of the reasons of its restricted used for complex task in unstructured environments. In this paper, results on the implementation of a novel task planner using a 6 DOF industrial robot as an alternative to overcome this limitation are presented. Different Artificial Neural Networks (ANN) models were assessed first to evaluate their learning capabilities, stability and feasibility of implementation in the planner. Simulations showed that the Adaptive Resonance Theory (ART) outperformed other connectionist models during tests and therefore this model was chosen. This work describes initial results on the implementation of the planner showing that the manipulator can acquire manipulative skills to assemble mechanical components using only few clues.

1   Introduction

Time and cost in industrial production are the factors that had contributed to the dedication of the manufacturers of manipulators to improve the speed and precision of the systems they offer. Although, the kinematics of manipulators has been deeply developed, their sensorial abilities are still poorly developed. Vision systems are common in quality control and inspection, whilst Force/Torque sensors (F/T) at robot's wrists are limited to —excluding a few exceptions— researching. Sensorial ability seems to be absolutely necessary to provide more flexibility, efficiency, and a higher level of autonomy to industrial robots [1].

Contact force modeling is very complex within a tridimensional environment subject to many uncertainties. Uncertainties in the production line can be originated from assembly components' geometry and location, the position of the manipulated object in respect to the final effector, the stiffness matrix of the final compensation point, sensors' noise, and not modeled friction and flexibility [2].

Several alternatives have been proposed to solve the problems caused by such uncertainties [2]:

R. Monroy et al. (Eds.): MICAI 2004, LNAI 2972, pp. 872–881, 2004.

1. To reduce uncertainties by improving the accuracy of the environment and of the robot. This is normally a very expensive process.
2. To improve the design of the parts to be assembled in such a way that it simplifies the assembly process. This is not always possible and rarely enough.
3. To apply active compensation techniques. The programmed path is modified by an algorithm that uses sensed contact forces as input.

Two classes of active compensation can be distinguished: fine movement planning and reactive control. The latter is the foundation of the assembling methodologies to be employed as a result of the task planning.

Next sections will present some academic research, the planner, tested neural networks, and results. Finally, conclusions and comments will be given.

2   Background

Several research efforts have been carried out about reactive control using manipulators to the execution of the canonic assembly *peg-in-hole* [3,4,6,7]. Due to the complex nature of the behavior of contact forces, researchers have recurred to the utilization of artificial neural networks (ANN).

Taking the previous work of Lopez-Juarez [3] as a reference, our proposal consists in the design of a superior controller or task planner which receives the features of the components to be assembled (tasks descriptor) —by means of a vision system— as input. The planner is based upon the use of neural networks which allows us to take the decision about the kind of methodology that the manipulator shall employ when the pieces come into contact.

The assembly paths will be solved by the tasks planner. These rely upon the features of the assembly components (i.e. shape, size, chamfer existence, and others). The information source for the tasks descriptor proceeds from a vision system, which includes the location and orientation of the assembly components needed to complete the assembly process.

3   Related Work

A few researchers have applied neural networks to assembly operations with manipulators and force feedback. Vijaykumar Gullapalli [7] used BackPropagation (BP) and Reinforcement Learning (RL) to control a Zebra robot. Its neural controller was based on the location error reduction beginning from a know location. Enric Cervera [6] employed Self-Organizing Map (SOM) and RL to control a Zebra robot, but the location of the destination piece was unknown. Martin Howarth [4] utilized BP and RL to control a SCARA robot, without knowing the location of assembly. Howarth also propounded the employment of tasks level programming, using a BP-based neural controller. It was not implemented within a manipulator, but the simulation showed acceptable results [5]. Ismael Lopez-Juarez [3] implemented Fuzzy ARTMAP to control a PUMA robot, also

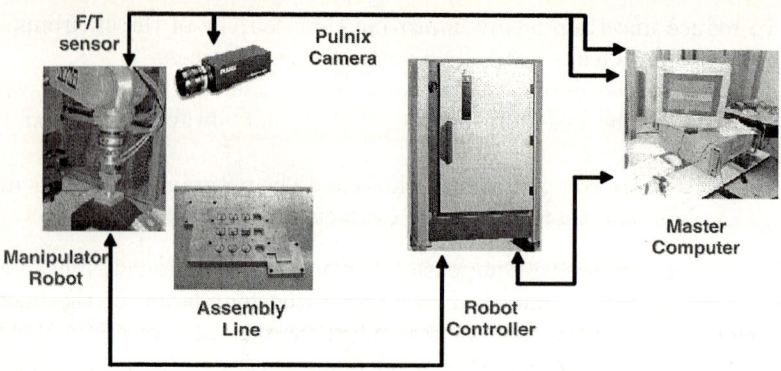

Fig. 1. KUKA KR15 Manipulator Control Architecture

with an unknown location. Jörg [1] presents the employment of vision systems and force feedback in the assembly of moving components.

We have seen in neural controllers with force feedback, which are part of our proposal at the lower level of the planner, that the movements of the manipulator are constrained: the maximum number is 12 (corresponding to the spatial coordinate system, linear and angular movements). When the F/T-sensor indicates similar forces in two directions, the controller will chose any direction; so diagonal movements (4) will facilitate such a decision, by having a total of 16 movements. We are currently working to include those movements in the assembly neural controller.

Besides, taking into account the mechanical devices' error compensation function for assembly, we propose the reduction on stiffness of the manipulator's joints in order to diminish the contact forces during assembly.

We realized that a common characteristic among the reviewed research efforts was the employment of neural networks for the force feedback control. Many of these works demonstrated that using neural networks was adequate for execution; even when there were different kinds of neural network architectures involved. This reason motivated a new experiment to observe the behavior of the most known neural architectures.

4   Planner Design

The main task of the planner is to perform mechanical assembly operations —explicitly peg-in-hole insertions, given that this is one of the most studied problems. The planner will operate within an industrial environment.

4.1   Hardware Architecture

The planner is designed for an assembly architecture as shown in Fig. 1. It consists of a manipulator of 6 DOF, the robot controller, the F/T-sensor mounted

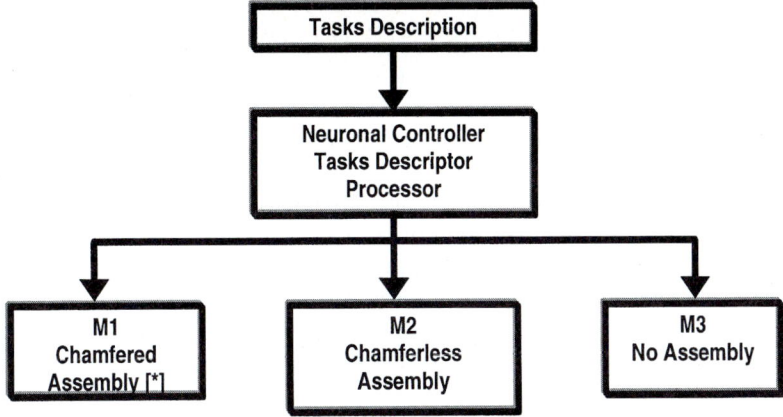

Fig. 2. Schematics of the Task Planner

at the robot's wrist, the camera and the master computer. The robot controller contains the components that provide and control the robotic arm power. The master computer has serial communication with the controller, and with the vision system. It receives and processes F/T-signals and hosts the Tasks Planner and the assembly methodologies (Knowledge Bases). When the planner is executed, the master computer sends low-level commands to the robot controller. The camera is mounted over the manipulator's working area.

4.2   Tasks Level Planner

The idea of a planner arises due to the nature and behavior of the contact forces in different conditions of the parts to be assembled, e.g. the assembly of parts in presence of chamfer shows an obviously different behavior to the assembly in absence of chamfer. Besides, shape and size features can also produce different behavior of the contact force at the moment of performing the assembly, giving greater flexibility to the robotic system to the assembly of different piece under different conditions.

Figure 2 shows the general schematics of the tasks planner. The indicated tasks (chamfered assembly, charmferless assembly, and no assembly) are some of the tasks that the robotic system must perform. Deciding which task to perform is the fundamental work of the planner.

The task to perform depends on the physical features of the component and the environment. Inside the process of feature acquisition, a vision system results useful to automate this process.

The test components were aluminum bars with three different sections (circular, squared, and composite —from the two previous) and with three different sizes (24.8, 24.9, and 25.0 mm). The holed components (25mm) were also made of aluminum, with chamfered and chamferless versions.

The steps of the Planner:

1. Feature acquisition. Obtain the physical features of the components to be assembled and their environment (location and orientation within the manipulator's working space). The acquisition of such features could be automated by means of a vision system, in order to remove the need of a rigid component fixation system.
2. Collection of the component to be assembled. With the received information from the vision system, the manipulator situates itself at the location of the component, and orientates its gripper to pick the component up.
3. Placing of the component to the assembly location. The component is taken to the assembly location with the aid of the vision system.
4. Planner's input conversion. Every feature is codified in an associated vector to be supplied the Tasks Planner.
5. Knowledge Base selection. The planner will provide the predicted knowledge base to be employed to perform the assembly, as long as the assembly is possible.
6. Performing of the assembly. The selected knowledge base is used by the neural controller at the lowest level of the planner.

4.3   Artificial Neuronal Networks

The use of Artificial Neural Networks in robotics is an alternative approach for force feedback control. The type of connectionist network has to be decided on the basis of network performance and a previous analysis should be carried out.

It was decided to make an assessment of connectionist models with suitable characteristics in order to be implemented in the Task Planner. The chosen models were the Hopfield Network, Backpropagation, Adaptive Resonance Theory and Self-Organising Maps (SOM).

The Hopfield network it is known as a fixed weight network, single layer [11]. The Backpropagation is based on the multi layer *Perceptron*. Once the network is trained and if new input becomes available to retrain the network, then it has to be trained with all old patterns and new ones. The training has to be made off-line and the number of epochs could easily reach hundreds or thousands. The Adaptive Resonance Theory is a model developed by Stephen Grossberg at the Boston University. It allows unsupervised learning as well as supervised learning [12]. The Self-Organising Map was developed by Teuvo Kohonen and consists of neurons organized on a regular low-dimensional grid. Each neuron is a d-dimensional weight vector (prototype vector, codebook vector) where d is equal to the dimension of the input vectors. The neurons are connected to adjacent neurons by a neighborhood relation, which dictates the topology, or structure, of the map [10].

4.4   Simulation Results

Simulation results on the different ANN performance were obtained implementing the above network algorithms using MATLAB running on a Pentium III PC

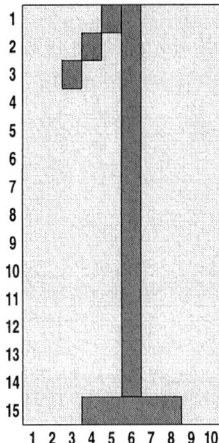

Fig. 3. Example of input representation

at 650 MHz. In all cases the basic algorithm was employed except for the SOM where a ToolBox was also used.

There were used 10 binary patterns like the one shown in Figure 3. These patterns represented the characters corresponding to the values 0-9 using a [15 x 10] matrix and the same test was run for all the networks.

Hopfield Network. This network was limited and unable to classify more than two patterns. It took 0.16 s to train and test the learning of the two patterns. It was decided also to test its convergence time (learning and testing) in order to compare this timing with the other networks. It was found that for 100 thousand epochs, the timing was 298.18 seconds.

Backpropagation. There were used different topologies: 150-300-150, 150-300-10, 150-75-10 for the input layer, middle layer and output layer respectively. For the topology of 150-300-10 the learning took place at 500 epochs with 2200 s (36 min, 40 sec.). The chosen topology was 140-40-10 that after 2200 epochs showed satisfactory results with a maximum error of 15%. For the testing phase, the network responds in 1.56 s.

ARTMAP. The network learnt very quickly. Using a learning rate of 0.9, the network learned all patterns in two epochs in 0.23 s, even a noise form (0.1 to 0.3)% was added.

Self-Organizing Map (SOM). Using the Toolbox from the Helsinki University. The network was tested for the proposed input patterns. The time response was of 1.75 seconds. The simulation resulted in coarse learning for 5 epochs and 18 for fine learning, with a final quantization error of 0.396.

ART-1. The network learned all the patterns in two epochs. With this architecture the response was 9.38 s, which included the display of the patterns. In later test of this network using C programming, the learning time resulted very short and about 6 ms only for processing without considering the display of the patterns.

These results can be summarized in the Table 1:

Table 1. ANN Performance

FEATURES	HOPFIELD	B.P.	ARTMAP	ART1	SOM
No. Epochs	100,000	2200	2	2	5, 18
Convergence time (s)	298.18 Does not converge	216 per 100 epochs	0.4	9.373	1.572
Topology	Single layer [150, 150]	150-40-10			150-[13,5] Hexagonal
Learning	Fixed	Supervised	Supervised	Unsupervised	Unsupervised

5   Implementation Results

The formation of the initial knowledge in the robot consists of showing the robot how to react to individual components of the Force/Torque vector at the wrist of the manipulator. The influence of each vector component requires a motion opposite to the direction of the applied force to diminish its effect. The procedure is illustrated in Figure 4.

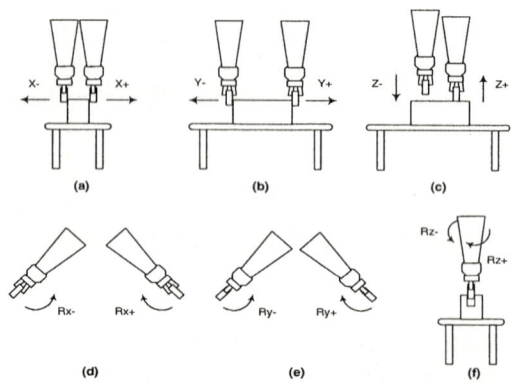

Fig. 4. Training Procedure

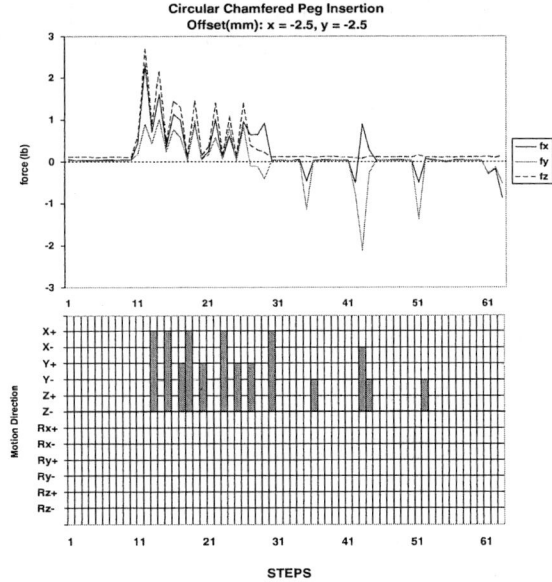

Fig. 5. Insertion with learning enabled

The Intelligent assembly was carried out using aluminium pegs with different cross-sectional geometry. The Fuzzy ARTMAP network parameters during experiments were set for fast learning (learning rate = 1). The base vigilance $\overline{\rho_a}$ had a low value since it has to be incremented during internal operations. ρ_{map} and ρ_b were set much higher to make the network more selective creating as many clusters as possible.

Figure 5 shows data collected during the insertion directed by the Task Planner and with learning enabled, this meant that the Planner was allowed to learn new patterns. For comparison purposes, another insertion with the same offset was carried out, but in this case the robot's learning capability was inhibited (See Figure 6). This means that the robot uses solely the initial learning and no patterns are allowed to be learned during the operation. In both Figures, the upper graph represents the force traces whereas the motion directions commanded by the Task Planner are given in the lower graph. In the Motion Direction graph, the horizontal axis corresponds with the Z- direction. Bars above the horizontal axis represent linear alignments and below the horizontal axis represent angular alignments.

Despite that the offset was the same, the number of alignment motions and insertion time were higher. With the learning inhibited, the robot was not allowed to learn contact states within the chamfer hence the Task Planner generated motions based only on its initial knowledge. The robot was ultimately able to insert the workpiece component, however the performance was poorer in terms of alignment and consequently speed.

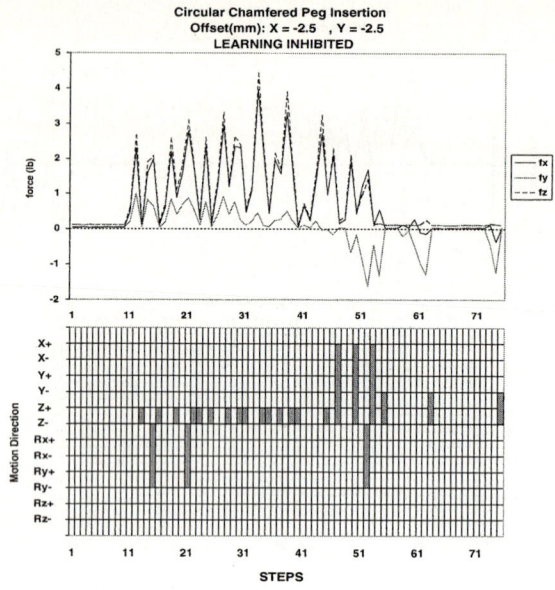

Fig. 6. Insertion with learning inhibited

6   Conclusions and Comments

In this paper a intelligent task-level planner for robotic assembly was proposed. After deciding that a connectionist network could offer the appropriate features for learning and recognition, it was planned performance analysis for different candidate model. Our results showed that in terms of speed both ART and SOM networks showed suitable characteristics to be employed in the task planner. The use of ART was chosen mainly because of its fast learning response (typically 1 to 2 epochs) and its robustness against noise. Initial results on the implementation with a robot demonstrates the usefulness of our approach. The planner has been tested on the lower level and further work is needed. Is it envisaged for future work that the planner has to acquire is initial knowledge on-line that is that the knowledge base formation should be constructed autonomously. Having this feature, the robot could perform operations autonomously without prior knowledge of the task. The robot would then be instructed with simple orders, i.e. insert, thus creating truly Task level programming.

Acknowledgments. The authors wants to thank to the Consejo Estatal de Ciencia y Tecnologia (CONCYTEQ) and Deutscher Akademischer Austausch Dienst (DAAD) for partially funding this project.

References

1. Jörg, S., Langwald, J., Stelter, J., Natale, C., Hirzinger, G.: Flexible Robot-Assembly using a Multi-Sensory Approach. In: Proc. IEEE Int. Conference on Robotics and Automation. San Francisco, CA (2000) 3687-3694
2. Nuttin, M., Van Brussel, H., Peirs, J., Soembagijo, A.S., Sonck, S.: Learning the Peg-into-Hole Assembly Operation with a Connectionist Reinforcement Technique. Katholieke Universiteit Leuven. Belgium
3. I Lopez-Juarez, I.: On-line learning for Robotic Assembly Using artificial Neural Networks and Force Sensing. PhD Thesis. The Nottingham Trent University (2000)
4. Howarth, M.: An Investigation of task Level Programming for Robotic Assembly. PhD Thesis. The Nottingham Trent University (1998)
5. Howarth, M., Sivayoganathan, K., Thomas, P.D., Gentle C.R.: Robotic Task Level Programming Using Neural Networks. Artificial Neural Networks. Conference Publication **409**. IEE (1995)
6. Cervera, E., Del Pobil, A.P.: Programming and learning in real-world manipulation tasks. In: Int. Conference on Intelligent Robot and Systems (IEEE/RSJ). Proc. **1** (1997) 471-476
7. Gullapalli, V., Franklin, J.A., Benbrahim, H.: Control Under Uncertainty Via Direct Reinforcement Learning. Robotics and Autonomous Systems. (1995) 237–246
8. Serrano-Gotarredonda, T., Linares-Barranco B., Andreou A.G.: Adaptive Resonance Theory Microchips. Kluwer Academic Publisher. USA (1998)
9. Aguado, B.A.: Temas de Identificación y Control Adaptable. Instituto de Cibernética, Matemática y Física. La Habana, Cuba (2000)
10. Kohonen, T.: Self-Organizing Maps. Springer Series in Information Sciences, Vol. 30. 3 edn. (2001)
11. Arbib, M.A.: The Handbook of Brain theory and Neural Networks. Part 1: Background: The elements of brain theory and neural networks I. 2 edn. MIT Press, Cambridge, Massachusetts (2003) 17-18
12. Carpenter, G.A., Grossberg, S.: Adaptive Resonance Theory (ART). In: Arbib, M.A., ed.: The Handbook of Brain theory and Neural Networks. 2 edn. MIT Press, Cambridge, Massachusetts (2003) 79-82

Wrapper Components for Distributed Robotic Systems

Federico Guedea-Elizalde[1], Ruben Morales-Menéndez[1], Rogelio Soto[1],
Insop Song[2], and Fakhri Karray[2]

[1] ITESM, Campus Monterrey
Center for Intelligent Systems and Center for Industrial Automation
fguedea@pami.uwaterloo.ca, rmm@itesm.mx, r.soto@ieee.org
[2] University of Waterloo
Systems Design Engineering
Waterloo, Ontario, Canada.
{isong,karray}@pami.uwaterloo.ca

Abstract. Nowadays, there is a plethora of robotic systems from different vendors and with different characteristics that work in specific tasks. Unfortunately, most of the robotic operating systems come in a closed control architecture. This fact represents a challenge to integrate these systems with other robotic components, such as vision systems or other types of robots. In this paper, we propose an integration methodology to create or to enhance robotic systems by combining tools from computer vision, planning systems and distributed computing areas. In particular we are proposing the use of CORBA specification to create Wrapper Components. They are object-oriented modules that create an abstract interface for a specific class of hardware or software components. Furthermore, they have several connectivity and communication properties that make easy to interconnect with each other.

Keywords: CORBA, Distributed Components, Robotics.

1   Introduction

Nowadays there are many types of robotic systems, and each one is designed with a specific task in mind. However, there are some tasks that can be improved by using new tools. Integration with more sensory systems is necessary; also, better algorithms that increase the dexterity of the robot are needed. This is a challenge, and a time-consuming task for the robot designer, mainly because of the closed controller architecture in the robotic components.

Distributed Robotic Systems (DRS) is a very wide and multi-disciplinary research area. It is expected that DRS will be able to perform tasks that are impossible for a single robot, i.e moving a big load, and will be more reliable and efficient. Next robot generation must deal with a wide range of complex and uncertain situations. Thus, robot control systems must provide the resources

R. Monroy et al. (Eds.): MICAI 2004, LNAI 2972, pp. 882–891, 2004.

for *intelligent* performances. Isolated resources have appeared in the modern robotics literature; however, there are few frameworks for combine them coherently into an integrated system [1]. Because of the large number of components, it is easy to see that many problems arise when designing a DRS. Specifically, the following problems are the most often considered:

- Construction of the robotic components (hardware implementation).
- Communication among intelligent robotic components.
- Reconfiguration of the system to deal with changing environments.
- Methods of distributing intelligence and control among the components.

This paper addresses the *Communication and Integration problem*. We propose the use of modular components based on the standard middleware *Common Object Request Broker Architecture* (CORBA) specification formulated by the Object Management Group (OMG) [2]. This specification defines a middleware component that alleviates the hard task of communicating objects from different platform, operating systems and programming languages. The main idea is to hide the internal details of the robotic components, meanwhile they offer a standard interface according to the class of component they belong. We named our approach as *Wrapper Components*.

2   Related Work

There are several approaches to create solutions for distributed intelligent robotic. One of the first approaches was the Task Control Architecture (TCA) [3], created at CMU. TCA provides a general control framework for building task-level control systems for mobile robots. TCA provides a high-level machine independent method for passing messages between distributed machines. Its main drawback is the centralized aspect of this communication scheme. In **CAMPOUT** [4], which stands for Control Architecture for Multi-robot Planetary OUTposts, there is a set of key mechanisms and architectural components to facilitate the development of multi-robot systems. The mechanisms are *Modular Task Decomposition, Behavior Coordination Mechanisms, Group Coordination*, and *Communication Infrastructure*. The communication facilities are provided using UNIX-style sockets. This is a low-level communication protocol compared to our approach using CORBA. **TelRIP** [5] is a protocol that allows the building of modular tele-robotics networks. TelRIP is a mechanism that uses the *producer/consumer* approach to deliver data objects. The main contribution of TelRIP is the capability for measuring and monitoring the communication performance, but this is based in data management. Our approach follows the object-oriented paradigm.

Sanz *et.al.*,used CORBA as the middleware for their multi-mobile robot research project called ARCO, Architecture for COoperation of mobile platforms [6]. *Integration* is one of the biggest problems to tackle in the development of large and complex systems using artificial components [7]. Similar to us, ARCO

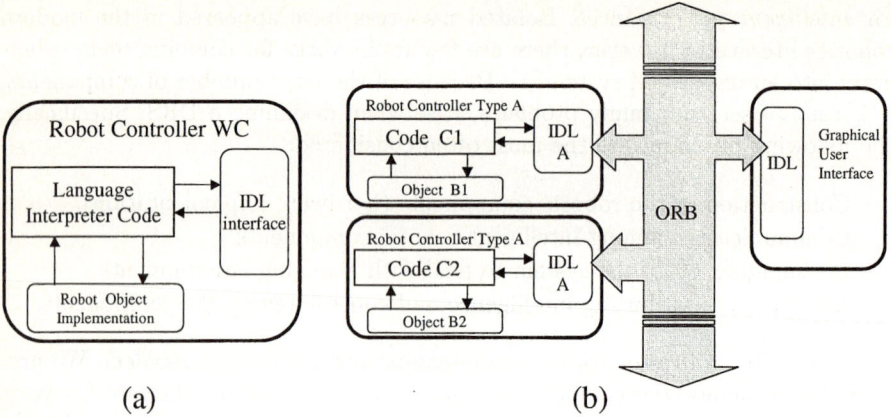

Fig. 1. (a)Basic elements in a Wrapper Component, (b) Two Robot Controller Wrapper Components of type A accessed through the same type of interface in the Graphic User Interface module.

addressed the integration problem by using modular, generic, flexible and compatible components. However, ARCO is more oriented to the control issue meanwhile we are oriented to the construction of robotic applications.

3   Wrapper Components

We adopted some ideas from the aforementioned works to construct modular DRS. We defined the Wrapper Components using the Interface Definition Language (IDL) provided in CORBA specification.

3.1   Wrapper Component Definition

As the name suggests, a wrapper component is a programming module that encapsulates an abstract functionality for specific hardware or software modules in the system. The basic configuration consists of three main parts: IDL interface, Transformation/Interpreter Code and Hardware/Software Object/Library Implementation. Fig. 1(a) shows these parts.

IDL Interface. It is an interface definition for a particular class of components; its actual definition is a key issue for constructing reusable and easy to connect components. We define three basic functionalities for this interface: *Abstraction, Monitoring*, and *Configuration*. By **Abstraction** we refer to the particular functions set (methods) that a specific component class must have without taking into account for implementation details. For example, in Fig. 1(b) there are two robot controllers which belong to the same class; however, the hardware/software components are different. Code modules C1 and C2 are different because of the different implementation B1 and B2, but both have the same IDL A definition, so client users of this component can use either without change in their code. By **Monitoring** we refer to the general functions set that every component must have to query its internal states. By **Configuration** we refer to the capability of changing the internal range of the component according to external requirements. To illustrate the previous two concepts we provide a simple gripper example. Suppose we have a robot with a servo-gripper which current range is from -10 volts when the gripper is totally closed to +10 volts when the gripper is totally open. In the design of the system, the range for the gripper was set up to the range of [0,100] for an aperture of 10 cm, from totally close(0 cm) to totally open (10 cm). If the robot is grasping an object which its width size is 7.2cm, then the response for a query of the gripper's current position must be 72, instead of +4.4 volts.

Transformation/Interpreter Code. This is the element that requires more effort when implementing the wrapper component. The *component builder* has to do all the data transformation and data interpretation. These steps are required to match the data types and data structure from the IDL interface to the Hardware/Software object implementation, and viceversa.

Hardware/Software Object Implementation. Integration into the whole system is demanded for this element. Usually, it is defined for a specific hardware or it is supplied by a specific vendor. Most of the cases, this component is provided "as it is" with an Application Program Interface (API) definition. However, it is difficult, if not impossible, to access the low level code.

3.2   Wrapper Component Features

We found the following conventional properties: *Reusability, Connectivity, Generality* and *Flexibility*. However, we are also interested in *Abstraction*, and *Manipulation*.

By using CORBA specification we achieved connectivity at least for three aspects: a) platform, i.e. actual computational architecture, b) Operating Systems and c) Programming languages. Abstraction and reusability are two related properties. While reusability looks for making inter-changeable modules; Abstraction helps to create these modules. The more abstract a module is the more general its definition is. In the other hand, if we can manipulate a component on-the-fly, then we can achieve certain degree of flexibility. Fig. 2 shows the conceptual scheme of using Wrapper Components to create application modules. The bold line shown resembles the concept of a special interface among the components so they can connect each other easily.

3.3   Design Guidelines for Creating a Wrapper Component

There is not general technique that can solve every problem that arises during the development stage; however, we must consider some aspects before starting the development of any module. Some guidelines are opposite among them, so a tradeoff must be set according to the requirements on the application or the flexibility on the system.

Module : Mobile Robot

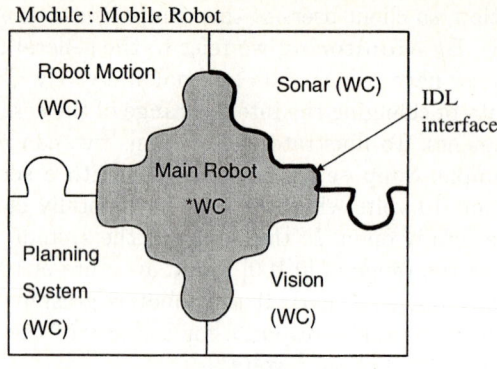

*WC=Wrapper Component

Fig. 2. Conceptual scheme to create a Module using Wrapper Components.

The smaller number of functions, the easier to connect. Defining a small but powerful number of functions in the interfaces between the different components will give more chances for a good connectivity; however, the required effort for good communication is a time-consuming task. Consider the example shown below.

```
interface Robot {
    void do_action{in string action};
    void get_status{out string status};
}
```

In this example the interface is text-oriented, in both ways, no more functions. Indeed, we can construct a complete interface using these functions but the effort is really tremendous.

Data Oriented versus Message Oriented. Usually, in control and robotic systems, if we have a heavy data transmission, in data size and in frequency, we prefer to use a data oriented rather than a message oriented approach.

Manipulation and Configuration. The Wrapper Components must allow certain level of manipulation or reconfiguration in order to be flexible. This is accomplished by means of configuration functions defined in the IDL interface.

Abstract function, an user oriented approach. By an abstract function, we refer to the way the component is conceived. For example, an arm manipulator can be visualized as a set of axis where each axis has a set of properties, such as minimum/maximum range of movement, type of movement (rotational vs translational), etc. This is a generic approach that applies to almost all types of arm manipulators but the effort to make an application is passed to the next level of design. On the other hand, an arm manipulator can be visualized as an equipment that can realize a set of functions, such as, Extend/Retract the arm, Turn wrist or arm base, Move Up/Down, etc. This is also a generic approach where the major effort is in the development of the component but the complexity in the next high level is reduced.

3.4   CORBA Services in Wrapper Components

CORBA Services play an important role when designing Wrapper Components. In this research we are exploiting two services: Naming Service [8] and Event Service [9].

Naming Service: Every time a component starts its execution, it registers into a defined Naming Server with a specific *name*. This is a standard feature for all components. If another component appears and it needs communication with the previous component, the only action to do is to "resolve" the *name*.

Event Service: This is an advance communication scheme. Usually, it is used in a *publisher/suscriber* scheme to communicate 1 to n anonymous components; also for sending data in an asynchronous way.

4   Application

We developed several wrapper components for our robotic system. Due to limited space, we will only present part of the Vision System. The Vision System has representative features. It is a very important component to improve the performance of the robotic units. However, its integration has been accomplished traditionally as a module tied to the robot software bundle. Mainly to improve the response time of the whole system. In our equipment we account for two stereo cameras mounted in similar pan-tilt units. See [10] for more details, also Fig. 4 shows a partial view of this setup.

4.1   Vision System Abstraction

We want some characteristics for this system without focusing to a particular hardware. For example, it is desirable that the vision system captures images periodically. In the high level, it is expected that the vision system can realize an object recognition process or a complex task, such as object tracking. Meanwhile in the middle level, it could be a specific image processing task, such as edge detection or blob-motion detection. Based on these features we define the following points for the Vision System:

IDL definition. The following interface definition assumes certain properties from the low level control, such as, a maximum frame rate available from the framegrabber. The functions defined are biased to manipulate the vision system in a high level aspect.

```
interface vision {
    void Learn(in short x, in short y, in string name);
    void Find(in string name);
    void Track(in string name);
    void End_Track(void);
    void GetObj(void);
}
```

Learn is an abstract function that invokes a learning process in the vision system. In our current implementation, this task is based on the feature extraction of a solid object whose approximated center position (x, y) is passed as an argument, i.e. an user can select the object by clicking inside of it from an image displayed through a graphic user interface. **Learn** is an abstract function, the way it is implemented can vary from one vision system to other. For example, one system can use the external shape of the object to identify some invariant properties, other system can use points of interest and the correlation between them, while other system can identify some correlations between specific parts of the object, but all implementations must have a method to save the name of the object with the features associated to it. The function **Find** looks for the object passed with argument *name*. First the function **Find** searches in the object database to check if the specific *name* object has been learned. If the object exists in the database, the next step is a searching procedure in the current image captured on the framegrabber. If the object is found, an approximated center position point is returned. Other implementation could return the top-left position of the object with an accuracy metric. **GetObj** is a function that returns a list of previous learned objects. **Track** and **End_Track** are explained in the next section.

Communication Channels. From the previous IDL definition it can be observed that none of the functions return a value, neither as an argument or as a type returned value. This is decided in this way because of the functionality required from the vision system and to take advantage of the CORBA services. Thus, the response of the system is captured through other communication channels based on Event Channels or Event Service. Fig. 3 depicts this idea. The Event Channel for images is used to send compressed image frame data. This information is sent periodically based on the velocity of the framegrabber. For example, from Fig. 3 the graphic user interface (GUI) is connected at any time to the Image Event Channel to receive images and to display them in a screen monitor. Next the user can select one object from this interface as an object to be learned by the vision system. The Response Event Channel is used to send a

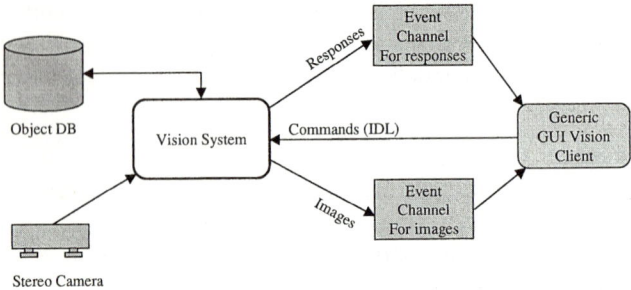

Fig. 3. Communication channels for the Vision System

Table 1. Command Response Format for Vision Feedback.

Command	Response
LEARN	(LEARN "Tag_name" OK)
	(LEARN "Tag_name" FAIL)
FIND	(FIND "Tag_name" OK (x,y))
	(FIND "Tag_name" FAIL)
TRACK	(TRACK number_of_objects ("Tag_name_1" OK (x,y, z)) ...
	("Tag_name_n" FAIL))
END_TRACK	stop all messages of the tracking procedure.
GET_OBJ	(GET number_of_objects ("Tag_name_1", ...,"Tag_name_n"))

feedback of the central position of certain objects. This activity is started using the function **Track**. The response message uses a LISP-like format to send a variable number of tracked objects. Table 1 shows part of the message format for the commands mentioned in this article. The message transmission is ended by the command **End_Track**.

4.2   Experimental Tests

In our current configuration we used the vision system component together with the robot controller component to move the arm manipulator so it can be able to grasp an specific object. This object was previously learned by the system. Fig. 4 shows the setup for this experiment. There is a "robot's brain controller", as it is shown in Fig. 2. This component interacts with the user or operator to receive the next action or activity to execute. When it receive the order to grasp an object, it realizes the following sequence of activities.

1. Ask to the vision system for the list of learned objects. If the object exists, go to next step, but if the object doesn't exist it responses to the user indicating that such object name is not recognized.
2. Send command Find object. This is to assure that the previous learned object can be found in the current image. If the object is found it proceeds to next step. Otherwise it replies with a object-not-found message.
3. Send a Track command for two objects: End-Effector and the object to grasp.
4. Get into a conditional loop to move the arm manipulator according to the position error between the End-Effector and the object. The position error is calculated with the information received through the response event channel.
5. When the error is below a specific threshold the Track procedure is ended and an End_Track command is issued. Next, the brain controller sends the close_gripper command to the robot controller.

This sequence of activities follows a natural path similar to what a human being could do. Also, our design follows a *non-blocking* communication scheme by using the *producer/consumer* approach. This is a very important aspect due to there are distributed components. So, if one of the components fails or is

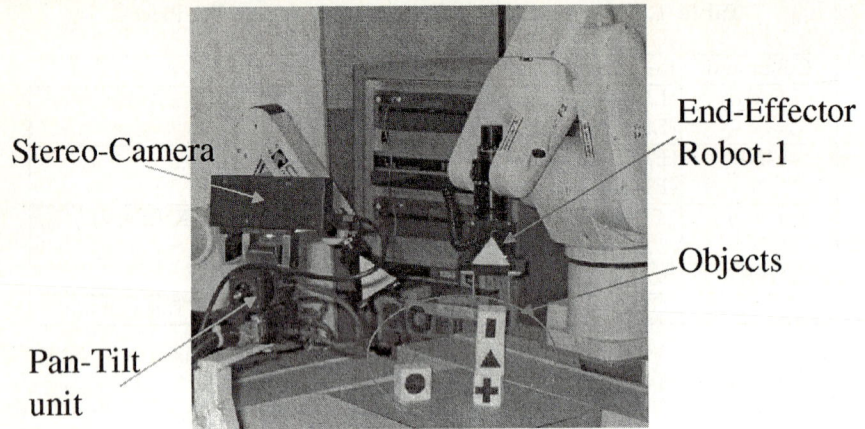

Fig. 4. Experimental setup for the integration of wrapper components. Left, a stereo-camera is taking visual information about the arm manipulator and the objects to identify and to grasp.

missing, the component's designer has several alternative paths to conclude the task.

Following we enumerate some comparison between distributed non-abstract (DNA) approach vs distributed abstract approach (DA).

1. **Modularity.** Both approaches offer modularity, but DA offer a better performance in the high level of design.
2. **Development time.** For small project DNA offer a quick response, but for long projects DA evolves better.
3. **Reusability.** In this case DNA could suffer with small changes but in DA the impact of the change is isolated.
4. **Maintenance.** DNA works fine for small projects but it will suffer for large projects.

5   Conclusions

In order to provide an effective solution for the *Integration* and *Communication* problems when designing a Distributed Robotic System (DRS), we proposed the use of Commercial-of-the-Shelf (COTS) middleware **components** to construct a communication framework for designing DRS. We named these elements **Wrapper Components**, because of the properties they must have to hide the internal details of their particular implementations while offering a set of communication facilities to connect the components into the whole system.

We presented a Vision System as a Wrapper Component to illustrate the communication and integration aspects.

Acknowledgments. This work was supported by the TEC de Monterrey, Campus Monterrey, CONACYT-Mexico and the University of Waterloo in Ontario, Canada.

References

1. G. Beni and J. Wang, "Theoretical problems for the realization of distributed robotic systems.," in *Proceedings of the International Conference on Robotics and Automation*, Sacramento, California, 9-11 April 1991, vol. 3, pp. 1914–1920.
2. OMG, "Common Object Request Broker Architecture and Specification (CORBA)," Tech. Rep., Object Management Group, Fall Church, USA, 2000.
3. R. Simmons, L.-J. Lin, C. Fedor, "Autonomous task control for mobile robots," in *Proceedings of 5th IEEE International Symposium on Intelligent Control, 1990.*, 5-7 Sept. 1990, vol. 2, pp. 663–668.
4. P. Pirjanian, T.L. Huntsberger, A. Trebi-Ollennu, H. Aghazarian, H. Das, S. Joshi, and P.S. Schenker, "CAMPOUT: A Control Architecture for Multi-robot Planetary Outposts," in *Proceedings of the SPIE Sensor Fusion and Decentralized Control in Robotic Systems III*, Boston, MA, Nov. 2000, vol. 4196, pp. 221–230.
5. M. Skubic, G. Kondraske, J. Wise, G. Khoury, R. Volz and S. Askew, "A telerobotics construction set with integrated performance analysis," in *Proceedings of the 1995 IEEE/RSJ Intl. Conf. on Intelligent Robots and Systems*, Pittsburgh, PA, August 1995, vol. 3, pp. 20–26.
6. R. Sanz, J.A. Clavijo, A. de Antonio and M. Segarra, "ICa: Middleware for Intelligent Control," in *Proceedings of the 1999 IEEE International Symposium on Intelligent Control/Intelligent Systems and Semiotics*, Cambridge, MA, 15-17 Sept 1999, pp. 387–392.
7. R. Sanz, M. Alonso, I. Lopez and C.A. Garcia, "Enhancing Control Architectures using CORBA," in *Proceedings of the 2001 IEEE International Symposium on Intelligent Control*, Mexico City, Mexico, 5-7 Sept 2001, pp. 189–194.
8. OMG, "CORBA Naming Service Specification, v1.2," Object Management Group, Inc. 2002.
9. OMG, "CORBA Event Service Specification, v1.1," Object Management Group, Inc. March 2001.
10. F. Guedea, R. Soto, F. Karray, and I. Song, "Enhancing Distributed Robotics Systems using CORBA," in *Proceedings of the First International Conference on Humanoid, Nanotechnologies, Information Technology, Communication and Control, Environment and Management 2003 (HNICEM'03)*, , Manila, Philippines, March 27-29 2003.

Fuzzy Sliding Mode Control of Robotic Manipulators Based on Genetic Algorithms

Mahdi Jalili-Kharaajoo and Hossein Rouhani

Young Researchers Club, Islamic Azad University, Iran
P.O. Box: 14395/1355, Tehran, Iran
mahdijalili@ece.ut.ac.ir

Abstract. In this paper, fuzzy sliding mode controller based on genetic algorithms is designed to govern the dynamics of rigid robot manipulators. When fuzzy sliding mode control is designed there is no criterion to reach an optimal design. Therefore, we will design a fuzzy sliding mode controller for the general nonlinear control systems as an optimization problem and apply the optimal searching algorithms and genetic algorithms to find the optimal rules and membership functions of the controller. The proposed approach has the merit to determine the optimal structure and the inference rules of fuzzy sliding mode controller simultaneously. Using the proposed approach, the tracking problem of two-degree-of-freedom rigid robot manipulator is studied. Simulation results of the close-loop system with the proposed controller based on genetic algorithms show the effectiveness of that.

1 Introduction

Several well-known difficulties must be overcome in the Fuzzy Logic Control (FLC) design as follows: (1) Converting the experts' knowledge how into if–then rules is difficult and the results are often incomplete and unnecessary, since operators and control engineers are not capable of specific details or cannot express all their knowledge including intuition and inspiration. (2) Characteristics of fuzzy control systems cannot be pre-specified. (3) It is hard to search optimal parameters of controller to achieve maximum performance. To overcome (1) and (2), the fuzzy sliding mode (FSM) control [1,2] schemes are proposed. Essentially, the FSM control design can be considered as an optimization problem for multi-parameters to ease difficulty (3) [3-5]. For improving performance of the sliding mode control (SMC) [6-12], based fuzzy controller, we adopt optimal searching algorithms, that is, the genetic algorithms (GAs). The GAs have been demonstrated to be a powerful tool for automating the definition of the fuzzy control rule base and membership functions, because that adaptive control, learning, and self-organization can be considered in a lot of cases as optimization or searching processes. The advantages have extended the GA in development of a wide range of approaches for designing fuzzy sliding mode controllers over the last few years. This work presents a Fuzzy Sliding Mode Based on Genetic Algorithms (FSMBGA) control design applied to tracking problem of two-degree-of-freedom rigid robot manipulator. The simulation results show that the FSMBGA controller exhibit better and faster response in comparison with FSM control action.

R. Monroy et al. (Eds.): MICAI 2004, LNAI 2972, pp. 892–900, 2004.

2 Fuzzy Sliding Mode Control Design Based on Genetic Algorithms

2.1 Sliding Mode Control Design

A Sliding Mode Controller is a Variable Structure Controller (VSC). Basically, a VSC includes several different continuous functions that map plant state to a control surface, and the switching among different functions is determined by plant state that is represented by a switching function.

Consider the design of a sliding mode controller for the following system

$$\dot{z}(t) = A(z(t) - z_d) + Bu(t) + f(z, u, t) \tag{1}$$

where z_d is reference trajectory and $u(t)$ is the input to the system. We choose m switching functions as follows

$$s_i(z) = c_i z = c_{i1} z_1 + c_{i2} z_2 + \dots + c_{in} z_n \tag{2}$$

where $c_i = [c_{i1}, c_{i2}, \dots, c_{in}]$, c_i is a sliding vector and n is the number of states. We rewrite Equation (2) in the form

$$s(z) = cz \tag{3}$$

where $c = [c_1, \dots, c_m]^T$.

The following is a possible choice of the structure of a sliding mode controller [13]

$$u = u_h + u_{eq} \tag{4}$$

where

$$u_{eq} = -(cB)^{-1} cAz$$

$$u_h = -(cB)^{-1} (\gamma + \sigma) \frac{s}{\|s\|} \tag{5}$$

The control strategy adopted here will guarantee a system trajectory move toward and stay on the sliding surface $s = 0$ from any initial condition if the following condition meets

$$\dot{s} s \le -\sigma |s| \tag{6}$$

where η is a positive constant that guarantees the system trajectories hit the sliding surface in finite time [13].

It is proven that if k is large enough, the sliding model controllers of (2) are guaranteed to be asymptotically stable [13].

2.2 Fuzzy Sliding Mode Control Design

The fuzzy control rule is the spirit of fuzzy control design. However, when the fuzzy variables are more than two, establishing a complete fuzzy rule set becomes difficult. The SMC guarantees the stability and robustness of the resulting control system, which can be systematically achieved but at the cost of chattering effect. The FSM controller is a hybrid controller, which combines the advantages of the fuzzy controller and the sliding mode controller. The combination becomes a feasible approach to rectify the shortcomings and preserve the advantages of these two approaches. The structure of fuzzy sliding mode controller is described as follows: According to the control law (4) with one switching function, we have the fuzzy control rule j [3] as

$$R^j: \text{If } s \text{ is } A^j, \text{ then } u \text{ is } u_j,$$

where $j=-q,-q+1,\ldots,q$, s is obtained from Equation (3) for one switching function, and Aj is a linguistic value with respect to s of rule j. The definition of membership function is

$$\mu_{A^j}(s) = \begin{cases} \dfrac{s-\sigma_{j-1}}{\sigma_j - \sigma_{j-1}}, & \sigma_{j-1} < s < \sigma_j \\[2mm] \dfrac{\sigma_{j+1}-s}{\sigma_{j+1}-\sigma_j}, & \sigma_j < s < \sigma_{j+1} \end{cases} \tag{7}$$

where σ_j is the centre of jth membership function. The triangle membership function is determined by three parameters, σ_{j-1}, σ_j and σ_{j+1}. The definition of membership functions is symmetrical, that is, $\sigma_o = 0$, $\sigma_{-1} = -\sigma_1$,..., $\sigma_{-q} = -\sigma_q$. The control law u_j is

$$u_j = k_j \operatorname{sgn}(s_j) + u_{eqj} \tag{8}$$

where

$$u_{eqj} = G_j z \tag{9}$$

in which $G_j = [g_{j,1}, g_{j,2}, \ldots, g_{j,n}]$, and $j=-q,-q+1,\ldots,q$. With respect to the SMC, the parameters are assumed as follows:

$$q = 1 \qquad \sigma_o = 0 \qquad \sigma_{-1} = \sigma_1 = \varepsilon \qquad \text{with } \varepsilon \to 0$$
$$G_{-1} = Go = G_1 = -(cB)^{-1} cA \tag{10}$$
$$k_{-1} = (cB)^{-1}(\gamma + \sigma) \qquad k_o = 0 \qquad k_1 = -(cB)^{-1}(\gamma + \sigma)$$

2.3 Fuzzy Sliding Mode Control Based on Genetic Algorithms

In the previous studies [3-7], the structures and parameters of control rules decide the performance of fuzzy control. From the control point of view, the parameters of structures should be modified automatically by evaluating the results of fuzzy control. In this section, we will introduce the GAs to the problem of determining and optimizing the FSM control for a given system. The key to put a genetic search for the FSM control into practice is that all design variables to be optimized are encoded as a finite length string. Each design is represented by a binary string, which consists various smaller strings that can be decoded to the value for each design variable. According to the structure and parameters of the FSM controller in previous section, individual multivariable binary coding is arranged in the following form

c_1	c_2	...	c_{2n}	σ_1	σ_2	...	σ_q	k_{-q}	k_{-q+1}	...	k_q	G_{-q}	G_{-q+1}	...	G_q

where $\sigma_j, j = 1,2,...q$ are parameters of membership functions in antecedent fuzzy sets as shown in Equation (7), kj and Gj are parameters of the consequent part as shown in Equations (8), (9). The binary string of this FSMC has $1 + 4n+3q +4nq$ variables.

Fitness as a qualitative attribute measures the reproductive efficiency of living creatures according to the principle of survival of the fittest. In the FSM controller design, the parameters of controller are determined and optimized through assessing the individual fitness. In order to employ the GAs to optimize the FSM controller for the system, we establish the fitness function according to the objective of active vibration control. Thus the FSMC design based on the GAs can be considered as an optimization search procedure over a large parameter space. For the active vibration control, we define the performance index [4] as

$$ J = \frac{1}{M} \sum_{k=1}^{M} |s_k| \tag{11} $$

where s_k is the value of switching function s at the kth time step, $M = \text{int}(t_{\max} / \Delta t)$ denotes the number of computing steps, $t_{\max}$ is the running time, and Δt is the sampling period. The fitness function can then be defined as

$$ F = \frac{1}{J + \tau} \tag{12} $$

where τ is a small positive constant used to avoid the numerical error of dividing by zero.

The GAs control parameters play an important role in the procedure of optimizing the parameters of the fuzzy logic controller. Some worthwhile discussions of the GAs parameters are made as follows:

- *Encoding form:* The linear encoding form is used. The length of binary coding string for each variable is important for the GAs. There is always a compromise between complexity and accuracy in the choice of string length. Here, a 16-bit binary coding is used for each parameter.
- *Crossover and mutation rates:* Crossover and mutation rates are not fixed during evolution period. At the beginning, crossover and mutation rates are, respectively, fixed to 0.9 and 0.1, then decrease 10 percent in each generation until crossover rate is 0.5 and mutation rate is 0.01.
- *Population size:* The population size has to be an even number and is kept fixed throughout. Generally, the bigger the population size, the more design features are included. The population size should not be too small, but the procedure of optimizing will be slow when the population size is big.

3 Two-Degree-of-Freedom Robot Manipulator Model

We begin with a general analysis of an n-joint rigid robotic manipulator system whose dynamics may be described by the second-order nonlinear vector differential equation [14-17]

$$ M(q)\ddot{q} + h(q,\dot{q}) = u(t) \tag{13} $$

where $\dot{q}(t)$ is the $n \times 1$ vector of joint angular positions, M(q) is the $n \times n$ symmetric positive definite inertia matrix, $h(q, \dot{q})$ is the $n \times 1$ vector containing Coriolis, centrifugal forces and gravity torques, u(t) is the $n \times 1$ vector of applied joint torques (control inputs).

The dynamic equations of the two-link robotic manipulator are expressed in state variable form as $x_1 = q_1, x_2 = \dot{q}_1$, $x_3 = q_2, x_4 = \dot{q}_2$ with x=[x1 x2 x3 x4]T. The dynamics of this specific system is given by the equations

$$\dot{x}_1 = x_2 \tag{14-a}$$

$$\dot{x}_2 = \frac{1}{a_1}[bx_2(x_2 + x_4)\left(1 + \frac{a_2^2}{a_1 a_2 - a_2^2}\right) + \gamma_1 g + u_1 \tag{14-b}$$

$$-\frac{a_2}{(a_1 a_2 - a_2^2)^2}(a_1(\gamma_2 g - bx_4 + u_2) - a_1(\gamma_1 g + u_2)))]$$

$$\dot{x}_3 = x_4 \tag{14-c}$$

$$\dot{x}_4 = \frac{1}{a_1 a_2 - a_2^2}[a_1(\gamma_2 g - bx_4^2 + u_2) - a_2(bx_2(x_2 + x_4) + \gamma_1 g + u_2)] \tag{14-d}$$

where

$$a_1 = (m_1 + m_2)r_1^2 + m_2 r_2^2 + 2m_2 r_1 r_2 \cos(x_3) + J_1 \tag{15-a}$$

$$a_2 = m_2 r_2^2 + 2m_2 r_1 r_2 \cos(x_3) \tag{15-b}$$

$$b = m_2 r_1 r_2 \sin(x_3) \tag{15-c}$$

$$\gamma_1 = -((m_1 + m_2)r_1 \cos(x_3) + m_2 r_2 \cos(x_1 + x_3)) \tag{15-d}$$

$$\gamma_1 = -(m_2 r_2 \cos(x_1 + x_3)) \tag{15-e}$$

4 Simulation Results

To assess the FSMC based on GAs, simulation results of a two-degree-of-freedom robot manipulator with proposed control action are obtained. For simulation the following parameters are considered

$$r_1 = 1.0m, r_2 = 0.8m, J_1 = 5Kgm, J_2 = 5Kgm$$

$$m_1 = 0.5Kg, m_2 = 1.5kg, g = 9.8Kgm / s^2$$

$$p_1 = 50, p_2 = 50, p_3 = 1, p_4 = 1$$

Using the proposed method the nonlinear optimal control law for u_1 and u_2 can be obtained. In this section the MATLAB simulation highlights the operation of the manipulator when tracking to an oscillatory reference signal is considered. Here the desired trajectory reference signals are defined as

$$\tilde{x}_1 = \begin{cases} -0.75 \sin(\pi / 20), & 0 \le t \le 10 \\ -0.75, & t \ge 10 \end{cases}$$

$$\tilde{x}_3 = \begin{cases} 2\pi \sin(\pi / 20), & 0 \le t \le 10 \\ 2\pi, & t \ge 10 \end{cases}$$

The initial state values of the system are selected as

$$[x_1 \ x_2 \ x_3 \ x_4]^T = [-0.15 \ -0.2 \ 0.349 \ 0.987]^T$$

4.1 SMC Design

At first stage, we choose one switching function as

$$s = cz = c_1 z_1 + ... + c_6 z_6 \quad \text{in which} \quad c = [1 \ 1 \ 1 \ 1].$$
$$u_{eq} = [2.3955 \quad -8.4554 \quad 3.0288 \quad 5.595]$$
$$u_h = 25 sign(s)$$

4.2 FSMS Design

In this case we choose the switching function as the case of SMC.
Then, we have the following three control rules $(q=1)$

R^{-1}: If s is NB, then u is $G_{-1} z + k_{-1}$.

R^o: If s is NB, then u is $G_o z + k_o$.

R^1: If s is NB, then u is $G_1 z + k_1$.

where the membership functions with respect to fuzzy sets NB, ZO, and PB are shown in Fig. 1. In this paper, the design parameters of the FSMC are selected as follows:

$$\sigma_1 = 0.12 \quad k_{-1} = 25 \quad k_o = 0 \quad k_1 = -25$$
$$G_{-1} = G_o = G_1 = [2.3955 \quad -8.4554 \quad 3.0288 \quad 5.595]$$

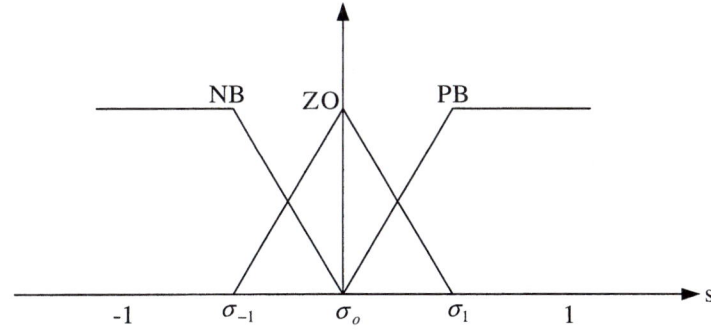

Fig. 1. The membership function of fuzzy sets.

4.3 Design of FSMC Based on GAs

The design parameters of the FSMC based on the GAs associated with the above three control rules (q=1) are specified as follows: sampling time interval = 0.02sec, population size = 50, initial crossover probability = 0.9, initial mutation probability

= 0.1, bit length for parameter =16, generations = 60, σ, k, c and G are [0,1], [25,25], [0,15] and [0,15], respectively. The optimal parameters of the FSMC are generated after 60 generations, namely,

$$c = \begin{bmatrix} 3.381 & 2.157 & 7.670 & 4.671 \end{bmatrix}$$

$$\sigma_1 = 0.0316 \quad k_{-1} = 24.6 \quad k_o = 9.37 \quad k_1 = -22.74$$

$$G_{-1} = \begin{bmatrix} -12.750 & 9.305 & 5.765 & -9.857 \end{bmatrix}$$

$$G_o = \begin{bmatrix} 3.208 & -1.4712 & -4.643 & -1.4772 \end{bmatrix}$$

$$G_1 = \begin{bmatrix} 5.472 & 2.361 & -6.706 & -1.2082 \end{bmatrix}$$

4.4   Results and Discussion

The closed-loop system responses using the Fuzzy Sliding Mode (FSM) and Fuzzy Sliding Mode Based on Genetic Algorithms (FSMBGA) are shown in Fig. 2 where $y = x_1$ and $e_1 = y - y_d$ (y_d is the desired reference). As it can be seen, the responses using FSMBGA is better with less error than that of FSM. Also, the tracking time, Tt, for FSMBGA is 1.879sec while it is 4.43sec for FSM. It is observed that employing FSMBGA can provide a faster tracking response in comparison with the response obtained by employing FSM. Generally, a faster response will require more control effort. It is inherent in the present controllers that fast tracking response is associated with larger peak values of the control force u_1.

   In the other simulation the performance of the controllers is in response to the case of parameter variations. Indeed, assume that the system is now suffering from a varying payload with the mass m_2 within the range of $m_{2\,min} = 0.5kg$ and $m_{2\,max} = 3kg$. The control responses obtained by employing the controllers at $m_2 = 2kg$ are shown in Fig. 3. As it can be seen in this case the FSMBGA performs better and faster than FSM.

5   Conclusion

In this paper, the FSMBGA controller for tracking control of two-degree-of-freedom robot manipulator has been developed. First, the FSM controller is introduced. Designing an equivalent control and a hitting control give the membership functions of consequent part. The membership functions of antecedent part are defined for stability requirement. Secondly, a FSM controller is developed through the GAs, i.e. we design the optimal parameters of the FSM without any experts' knowledge. Simulation results of the system with the proposed FSM and FSMBGA controllers showed that FSMBGA has better and faster response than FSM. Also, the robustness of FSMBGA controller against parameter uncertainty was better than that of FSM one.

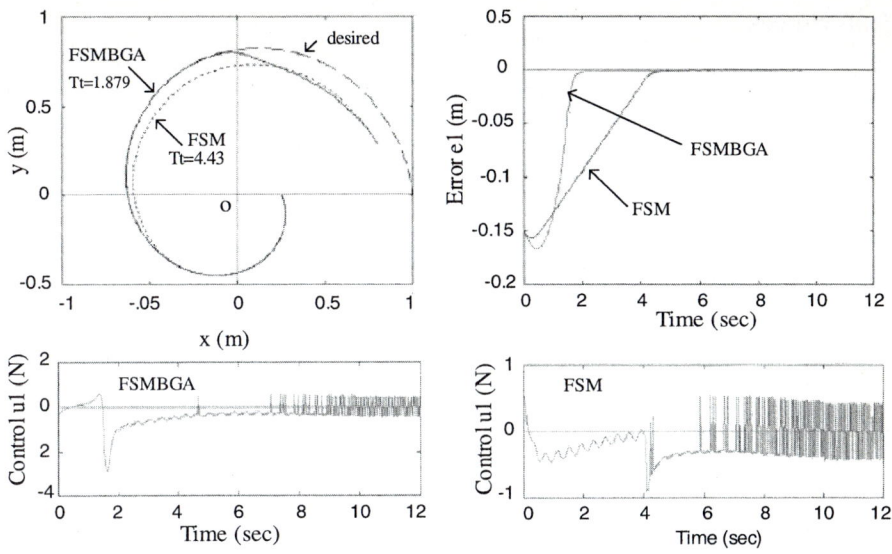

Fig. 2. Closed-loop system response using FSM and FSMBGA controllers.

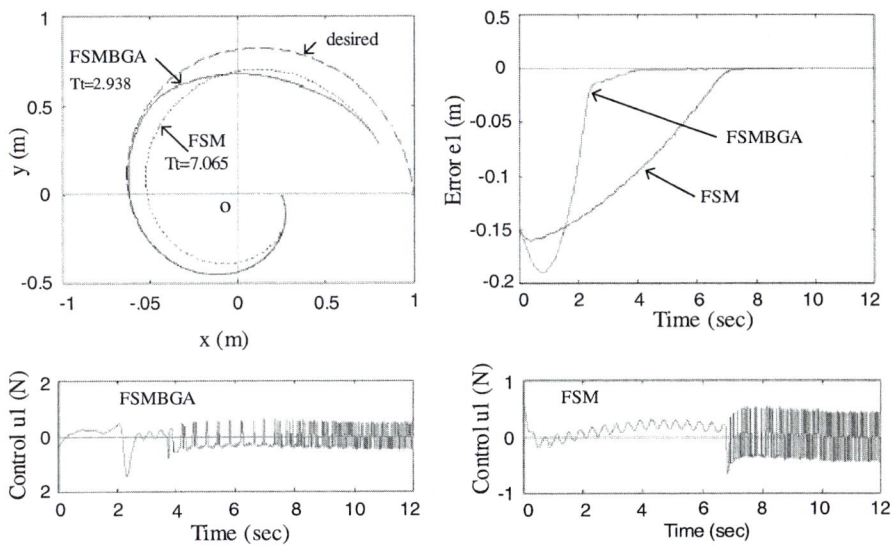

Fig. 3. Closed-loop system response using FSM and FSMBGA controllers with $m_2 = 2kg$.

References

1. Lin SC, Chen YY. Design of adaptive fuzzy sliding mode for nonlinear system control, in Proc. IEEE International Conference on Fuzzy Systems, Orlando, Wiley: New York, pp.35–39, 1994.
2. Lu YS, Chen JS. A self-organizing fuzzy sliding mode controller design for a class of nonlinear servo systems. IEEE Transactions of Industrial Electronics, 41, pp.492– 502, 1994.
3. Chen JY. Expert SMC-based fuzzy control with genetic algorithms. Journal of the Franklin Institute, 6, pp.589–610, 1999.
4. Lin SC, Chen YY. Design of self-learning fuzzy sliding mode controllers based on genetic algorithms. Fuzzy Sets and Systems, 86, pp.139 –153, 1997.
5. Chen CL, Chang MH. Optimal design of fuzzy sliding-mode control: a comparative study. Fuzzy Sets and Systems, 93, pp.37– 48, 1998.
6. Edwards, C. & Spurgeon, S. K., Sliding mode control. Taylor & Francis Ltd, 1998.
7. Young, D. K., Utkin,V. I. & Özgüner, A control engineer's guide to sliding mode control. IEEE Transaction on Control System Technology, 7(3), May, 1999.
8. Bhatti A. I. Advanced sliding mode controllers for industrial applications. PhD thesis, university of Leicester, 1998.
9. Drakunov, S.V. & Utkin, V. I. Sliding mode control in dynamic systems. International Journal of Control, 55(4), pp.1029-1037, 1992.
10. Utkin, V. I. Sliding modes in control optimization. New York, Springer- Verlag, 1992.
11. Jalili-Kharaajoo, M., Yazdanpanah, M.J., Ebrahimirad, H. Digital sliding mode control of position control of induction motors, in Proc. 4th IFAC Int. Sym. Robust Control Design, Italy, 2003.
12. Jalili-Kharaajoo, M., Yazdanpanah, M.J., Ebrahimirad, H. Feedback linearization with sliding mode control of current and arc length in GMAW systems, in Proc. 4th IFAC Int. Sym. Robust Control Design, Italy, 2003.
13. John Y. Hung, W. Gao and James C. Hung, Variable Structure Control: A Survey, IEEE Transactions on Industrial Electronics, 40(1), pp.2-21, 1993.
14. Spong, M.W. On the robust control of robot manipulators, IEEE Trans. Automatic Control, 37(11), pp.1782-1786, 1992.
15. Zhihong, M. and Yu, X. Adaptive terminal Sliding Mode Tracking Control for Rigid Robotic Manipulators with Uncertain Dynamics. Journal of S. Mechanical Engineering, Series C., 40(3), 1997.
16. Keleher, P.G. and Stonier, R.J. Adaptive terminal sliding mode control of a rigid robot manipulator with uncertain dynamics incorporating constrain inequalities. J. ANZIAM, 43(E), pp.102-157, 2002.
17. Battoliti, S. and Lanari, L. Tracking with disturbance attenuation for rigid robots. Proc. IEEE International. Conference on Robotics and Automation, pp. 1578-1583, 1996.

Collective Behavior as Assembling of Spatial Puzzles

Angélica Muñoz Meléndez[1], Alexis Drogoul[2], and Pierre-Emmanuel Viel[2]

[1] INAOE, Luis Enrique Erro No. 1
72840 Tonantzintla Puebla, México
munoz@inaoep.mx
[2] LIP6 - UPMC, Case 169 - 4, place Jussieu
75252 Paris Cedex 05
alexis.drogoul@lip6.fr

Abstract. This paper describes how collective behavior can be achieved using simple mechanisms based on local information and low-level cognition. Collective behavior is modeled and analyzed from the spatial point of view. Robots have a set of internal tendencies, such as association and repulsion, that enable them to interact with other robots. Each robot has a space around its body that represents a piece of the puzzle. The robots' goal is to find other pieces of the puzzle, associate with them and remain associated for as long as possible. Experiments on queuing using this puzzle-like mechanism are analyzed.

Keywords: Collective robotics, spatial coordination, proxemics.

1 Introduction

This research focuses on the design of collective behavior for autonomous mobile robots based on simple mechanisms. By simple mechanisms we denote those that depend on local information and low-level cognition, *i.e.* mechanisms used by robots that have limited capabilities and limited knowledge of the environment. The kind of collective behavior we are interested in involves the arrangement and maintaining of spatial patterns by a multi-robot system, such as formation and flocking. These behaviors are useful for a number of applications such as material transportation, hazardous material handling and terrain coverage. The central idea of our work is to implement collective behavior using a domain independent mechanism [4].

The paper presents the proxemic coordination, a situated distributed method for collective problem solving. It is situated because it relies mainly on the information perceived by robots, instead of on a description of the environment. As robots determine their actions locally, the model is distributed. This mechanism is based on the spatial coordination of a group of robots in approximate patterns. For that, each robot has a space around its body called the *proxemic space*, that should be preserved from contact with objects and kin. Robots also have a set of internal tendencies, such as association and repulsion, that enable them to

R. Monroy et al. (Eds.): MICAI 2004, LNAI 2972, pp. 901–910, 2004.

interact with others. A robot looks for its kin in order to associate with them and remain associated for as long as possible. But if the internal tendencies are modified, it can then avoid its kin. The association is performed by assembling the frontiers of proxemic spaces. In contrast, the repulsion supposes the moving away of robots. Robots and their territories are the pieces of a puzzle whose shape is defined by the application: a column for queuing or a square for formations.

The paper is organized as follows: section 2 addresses related work. Section 3 presents our proposal. Sections 4 and 5 describe various experiments and give some technical details. Section 6 examines results, and section 7 discusses conclusions and perspectives.

2   Related Work

Spatial coordination in groups of agents has mainly been studied in simulation [3,14]. Interesting experiments where several agents [6] or robots [9] coordinate and synchronize their movements have also been reported. Spatial organization and flocking have been largely studied in the literature and a variety of simulated experiments has been presented [12,14].

Social potential field [15] are very close to our research. In this, artificial force laws between robots producing both attraction and repulsion are defined. The method is robust and efficient, it relies on a certain amount of global information and on a direct communication between robots. Thus, robots have to exchange their absolute positions in order to perform force calculations and to coordinate their movements. The method has been applied to model collective behaviors such as clustering and guarding, but only using simulated robots. This is due to the difficulties to calculate social potential fields in real-time.

A similar method using motor-shema instead of force laws has also been explored [1]. In this approach, modular behaviors are composed in order to achieve spatial formations such as lines, columns and diamonds. The method has been tested using simulated and physical robots. More recent results of this work [2] describe robots with attachments sites in their body that determine the spatial structure formed by robots.

Self-assembling robots is a very active research avenue in the robotics community [10]. Mechanisms composed of simple robots that are able to adopt various shapes and reconfigure themselves have been physically built [5,17] and simulated [13]. The design and implementation of these systems, which combine a lot of computing and engineering skills, are beyond of the goals of our current research. However, the general principle that enables robot-pieces to attract and assemble, has inspired us to propose a puzzle-like mechanism to display collective behavior in robotics.

The research reported in this paper is similar to social potential fields and to spatial formation with attachments sites. Our approach is different from the first in the application of repulsion and attraction forces. Whereas in the work mentioned these forces are used to avoid obstacles and guide robots to the goal, in ours they are directed to the spatial dynamic coordination of robots. Our work is also different in that our robots do not exchange information about their positions. In contrast with the second method, we use hierarchical behaviors instead of motor schema and the attachment sites of our robots are not fixed. These sites can be modified during an experiment resulting in a different global behavior.

3   Proposal

Coordination is at the core of puzzle-like mechanisms. But if self-assembling demands a lot of exactness, queuing and formations are less demanding as to the precision of the movements executed by participants. From a global point of view, the area formed by a group of robots coordinating their movements can be considered as a shape that robots are trying to preserve. This shape is of course non-fixed, it can be reconfigured according to the rules of assembling applied by robots.

We propose a method to coordinate approximately the movements of a group of mobile robots that have to organize themselves spatially. Neither direct communication nor centralized control is involved in this strategy. Instead, a robot must be able to delimit a space around itself, a proxemic space, and perceive its kin. Both capabilities are necessary to define the internal tendencies of robots. This method is called proxemic coordination.

The notions of proxemic space, kin recognition and internal tendency are discussed below.

3.1   Proxemic Space

The proxemics is a notion introduced by the anthropologist Edward Hall [7]. According to him, the space plays an essential role in social systems. Individuals define and organize the space around their bodies. Their behavior is then closely related with the interactions perceived within this space.

The idea that an individual moves surrounded by a *bubble* and that the bubble arrangement influences his behavior, inspired us to propose a method of proxemic coordination for a group of robots. The proxemic space is for us, a virtual space defined by a robot as an extension of its body.

3.2   Kin Perception

Kin recognition is a requirement for the generation of complex behavior in groups of robots [8]. Spatial coordination needs often mechanisms of kin perception and recognition. Robots should be able to distinguish not only their environment, but also their kin.

Being able to recognize their kin is considered a basic skill to apply proxemic coordination. In order to recognize themselves, robots may use a set of features, such as colors or visual cues, to distinguish between their kin and other elements of the environment. These mechanisms are, as we see below, based on local robots' perception.

3.3 Tendencies

In addition to the ability to delimit a proxemic space, robots must be able to assemble their spaces in specific manners. Like in puzzles, where the shape of the pieces determines how they are assembled, the robots have attachment labels. These labels may be viewed as plus $(+)$ and minus $(-)$ polarities that are used by robots to connect their spaces.

Robots are guided by two internal tendencies: association and repulsion. Association is defined as the attachment of opposite labels $(+/-$ or $-/+)$, and repulsion as the avoidance of similar labels $(+/+, -/-)$.

Attachment labels may also change during an experiment according to specific situations. A robot with flat-battery taking part in a formation, for instance, has the right to change its polarities and withdraw from collective formation.

4   Simulated Experiments

We have programmed a virtual environment using Starlogo©[1] in order to implement our proposal. The rules of proxemic coordination are used in this experiment to enable a group of robots to reach a global formation. Robot's goal is to form a line in front of a predefined landmark, but the landmark location is not known by robots.

4.1   Proxemic Space

The proxemic space is a rectangle in face of a robot. A robot can perceive if this one-unit dimension space is clear or not. The proxemic space is clear if neither a robot nor a border of the environment is perceived there. This condition is used by robots in order to decide which behavior to execute.

The robots are able to execute three behaviors: `wander`, `avoid obstacles` and `queue`. A robot can move 0.1 steps forward in the direction that it is facing and turn right by 5 degrees.

4.2   Kin Perception

A robot can detect if another robot is located one unit directly in front of its proxemic space. If a partner is detected, the robot can also detect its orientation. The partner orientation is useful to determine if an attachment label is "visible" or not.

---

[1] Starlogo is a programming environment of decentralized systems, developed at the *Massachuset Institute of Technology*, available at:
http://education.mit.edu/starlogo/

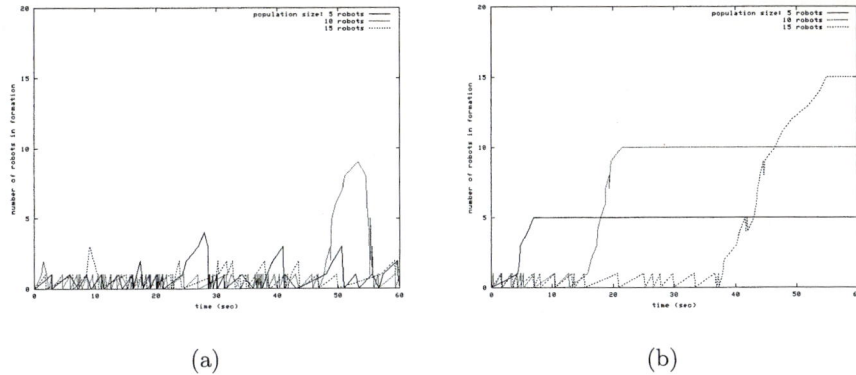

(a)   (b)

Fig. 1. Number of robots in formation in two groups of robots during 60 sec. The experiments were performed using subgroups of 5, 10 and 15 robots that were randomly located in the environment. The attachment labels of the first group (a) were fixed whereas those of the second group (b) were modified during experiments. The second group managed to solve conflicts when two robots are attracted by a same third robot.

4.3   Tendencies

Two attachments labels were defined. A label plus was situated on the robot's head and a label minus on the robot's rear. Robots are attracted by attachments labels minus and by the landmark indicating the beginning of the line.

Depending on the distance between attachments labels, robots assemble their proxemic spaces in three different manners: approximate, standard and accurate. That is, a robot can be attracted by an attachment label situated, respectively, $\pm 20^0$, $\pm 10^0$ and $\pm 5^0$ away from its own attachment label. The quality of a formation depends on this assembling precision.

This tendency enables robots to follow themselves and to form *breakable* lines. That is, lines that are easily unarranged when an object is perceived within proxemic space, what happens often in an environment where various robots are wandering (see figure 1(a)). In order to remain still and form static lines robots change their attachment labels once they are assembled. This modification acts as a blocking mechanism that protect formations and contribute to solve conflictive situations (see figure 1(b)).

Figure 2 shows some snapshots of our system. As we can see, the robots did not form fine lines, but they reached global formations using only local information.

5   Physical Experiments

We have used the rules of proxemic coordination in order to enable a group of physical mobile robots to form a line in front of a landmark. The experiments described in this section were conducted using three Pioneer 2-DX mobile robots

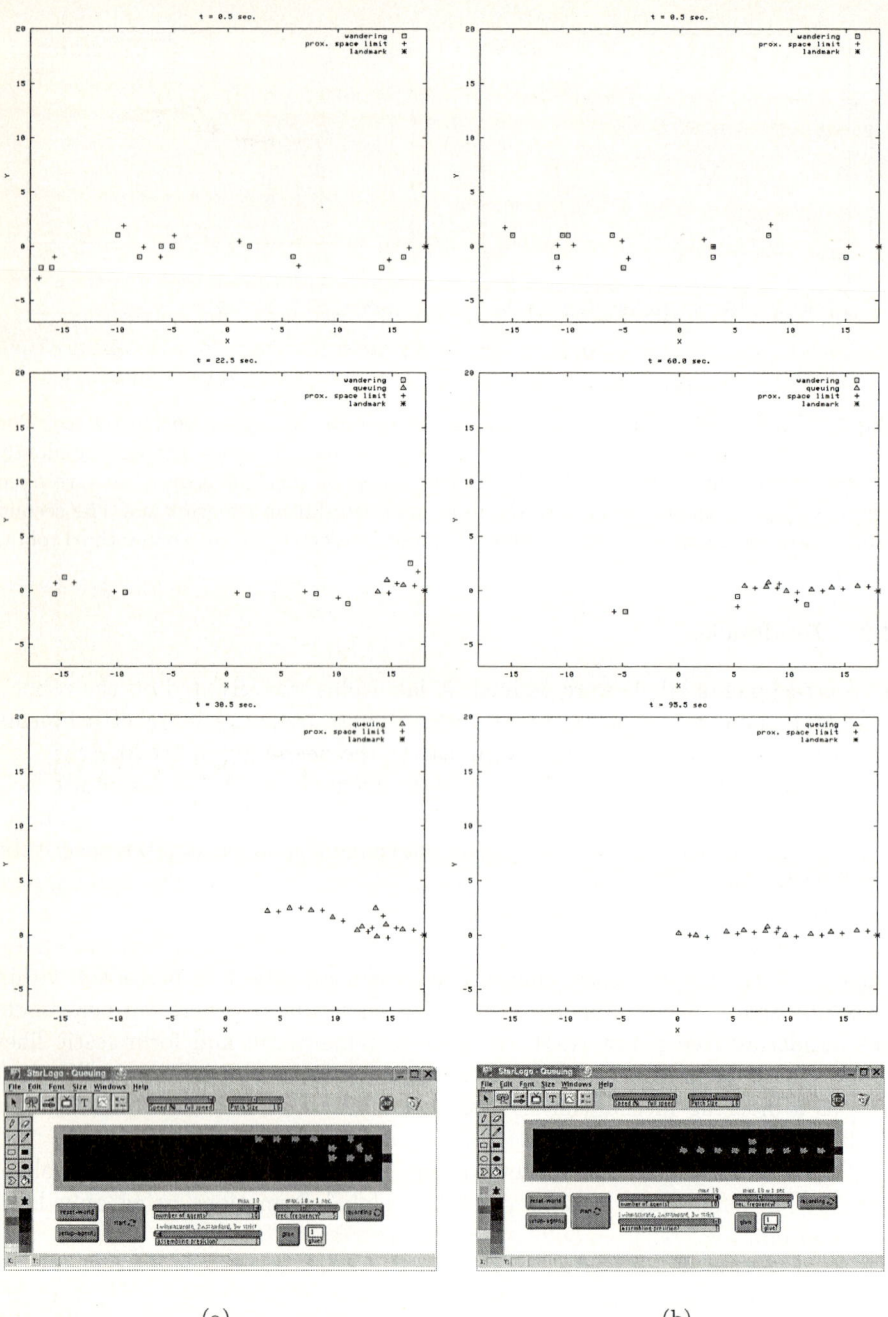

Fig. 2. Two snapshots of our system with 10 robots that were randomly placed. Robots assembled their proxemic spaces using approximate (a) and accurate (b) precision. The location and the state of the robots at three different instants are also shown. During these experiments the attachment labels changed once robots were assembled.

of Active Media©, provided with odometers, bumpers, sonars, radio modems, video-cameras and onboard computer.

5.1   Proxemic Space

A robot uses two sonar arrays to delimit its proxemic space. Based on sonar readings, the robot can determine whether or not its proxemic space is clear (see figure 3). The sonars' sensitivity ranges from 10 centimeters to more than 5 meters and can be adjusted in order to see small objects at great distances. The sensors' sensitivity determines the possible limits of proxemic spaces.

Robots are able to execute four behaviors: `wander`, `avoid obstacles`, `queue` and `adjust position`. The last behavior enables robots to assemble the frontiers of their proxemic spaces as accurate as possible.

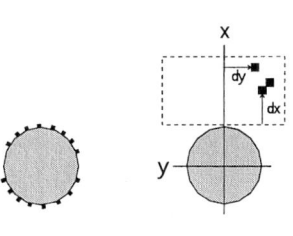

Fig. 3. A robot is equipped with 2 sonar arrays of 8 sonar each (left). In our experiments, proxemic space is a virtual rectangle situated ahead of the robot (right). Sonars are used to calculate the distances along x, dx, or along y, dy, to the nearest object within this rectangle.

Fig. 4. An environmental landmark (right) and a robot with a cylinder covered by a visual cue set horizontally (left).

5.2   Kin Perception

We have developed a cue-based recognition system in order to differentiate visually the environment and the kin using the CCD cameras of the robots [16]. A cue consists of black bars on a white background. This system is based on the recognition of two kinds of cues: environmental landmarks and robots cues. The former distinguish elements of the environment, such as objects and walls, the latter are worn by the robots as identity cues (see figure 4).

Recognition is based on a picture analysis method that we call the railroad method. This name comes from the following analogy: when someone who is wandering comes upon a railroad, he follows it. As he follows the rails, he counts the railway sleepers. Similarly, in our method the pictures are scanned and if a succession of three black bars are encountered (the rails) we follow their direction and count the bits (the railway sleepers). For details see [16].

This system can obtain the position of the cues in the picture, their own identifiers, the distance between the cues and the camera, and their orientation. Additionally, the system enables us to distinguish correctly eight angles of identity cues worn by robots in movement $(0^o, 45^o, \ldots, 315^o)$. These angles are used to put virtual attachment labels on our robots

5.3   Tendencies

As in line-formation simulated experiments, two attachment labels were defined: a label plus on the angle 0^0 and a label minus on the angle 180^0 of identity cues. Robots are attracted by labels minus and by an specific environmental landmark indicating the beginning of the line.

Once a robot has assembled its proxemic space, it changes its attachment labels in order to remain still. Since attachment labels are virtual, robots communicate and update the state of their labels continually.[2]

Figure 5 illustrates the environment and the robots in action. Figure 6 illustrates the trajectories followed by robots during this experiment.

Fig. 5. Snapshots of three mobile robots wandering in a corridor and assembling their proxemic spaces in line.

---

[2] Although physical robots communicate, this communication is not intended to improve their coordination efforts, but to inform about the polarities of their proxemic spaces

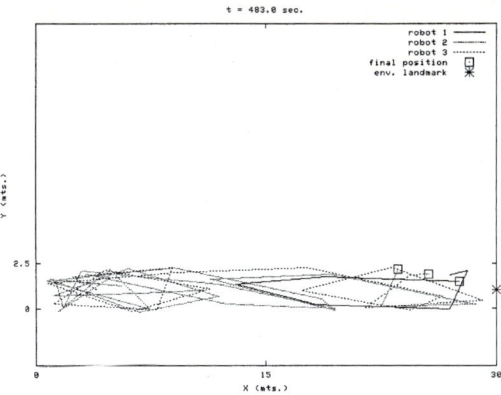

Fig. 6. Trajectories followed by three physical robots that form a line using the method of proxemic coordination.

6   Discussion

Reproducing simulated experiments using physical robots is a major challenge for roboticists. Most of the rules used in simulation are poorly situated and are only useful for idealized robots that are equipped with perfect sensors and actuators, and are able to perform actions without fault.

Our method of proxemic coordination is well adapted for solving problems of spatial coordination using simulated and physical robots. As we could see, robots reached global spatial structures taking into account local information.

Robots using the rules of proxemic coordination depend mainly on their sensors in order to operate. If the landmark indicating the beginning of the line is moved, for example, robots are able to unarranged the formation and to redo it in front of a new location.

Proxemic coordination is not intended to solve problems of coordination involving fine assembling, but it has been applied to a number of collective robotics applications, such as collective box-pushing and dynamic formations (for preliminary results see [11]).

7   Conclusions and Perspectives

In this paper we have described proxemic coordination, a simple method to enable mobile robots to coordinate their movements in order to reach a global spatial formation. Spatial coordination is important for solving problems of collective robotics such as material transportation and terrain coverage.

The experiments described are in progress and future work will focus on defining more flexible proxemic spaces. We are working on various shapes of proxemic spaces, as well as on resizable proxemic spaces.

We are also using the method of proxemic coordination in the design of the behavior of self-assembling robots.

References

1. Balch T., Arkin R.: Behavior-based formation control for multi-robot teams. In: IEEE Transactions on Robotics and Automation 14(6) (1998) 926-939
2. Balch T., Hybinette M.: Social potentials for scalable multi-robot formations. In: Proc. of the IEEE Int. Conf. on Robotics and Automation, Vol. 1. (2000) 73-80
3. Di Paolo E.A.: Social coordination and spatial organization: steps towards the evolution of communication. In: Husbands P., Harvey J. (eds): Proceedings of the 4th European Conference on Artificial Life. MIT Press, Cambridge MA (1997)
4. Ferber J., Jacopin E.: The framework of eco-problem solving. In: Demazeau Y., Müller J.-P. (eds): Decentralized A.I. 2. Proceedings of the 2nd European Workshop on Modeling Autonomous Agents in a Multi-Agent World. North-Holland, Elsevier, Amsterdam (1991) 181-194
5. Fukuda T., Nakagawa S., Kawauchi Y., Buss M.: Structure decision method for self-organizing robots based on cell structure-CEBOT. In: Proceedings of the 5th IEEE International Conference on Robotics and Automation, Vol. 2 (1989) 695-700
6. Gervasi V., Prencipe G.: Flocking by a set of autonomous mobile robots. Technical report TR-01-21, University of Pisa (2001)
7. Hall E.T.: The hidden dimension. Anchor Books Doubleday, New York (1966)
8. Mataric M.: Kin recognition, similarity and group behavior. In: Proc. of the 15th Annual Cognitive Science Society Conf. Lawrence Erlbaum Ass. (1993) 705-710
9. Mataric M., Zordan V., Williamson M.: Making complex articulated agents dance: an analysis of control methods drawn from robotics, animation and biology. In: Autonomous Agents and Multi-Agent Systems 2(1) (1999) 23-44
10. Mondada F., Guignard A., Bonani M., Floreano D., Bär D., Lauria M.: Swarm-bot: from concept to implementation. In: Lee G., Yuj J. (eds): Proc. of the IEEE/RSJ International Conference on Intelligent Robot and Systems (2003) 1626-1631
11. Muñoz-Meléndez A.: Coopération située : une approche constructiviste de la conception de colonies de robots. PhD thesis, Université Pierre et Marie Curie, Paris (2003)
12. Reynolds C.W.: Flocks, herds and schools: a distributed behavioral model. In: Computer Graphics 21(4) (1987) 25-34
13. Théraulaz G., Bonabeau E.: Modelling the collective building of complex architectures in social insects with lattice swarms. In: Journal of Theoretical Biology 177 (1995) 381-400
14. Ünsal C., Bay J.S.: Spatial self-organization in large populations of mobile robots. In: IEEE International Symposium on Intelligent Control (1994) 249-254
15. Reif J.H., Wang H.: Social potential field: a distributed behavioral control for autonomous robots. In: Goldberg K., Halperin D., Latombe J.-C., Wilson R. (eds): International Workshop on Algorithmic Foundations of Robotics. A.K. Peters (1995) 431-459
16. Viel P.-E.: Reconnaissance individualisée de robots et de zones. MSc. thesis (DEA de Robotique et Systèmes Intelligents), Université Pierre et Marie Curie, Paris (2001)
17. Yim M., Zhang Y., Roufas K., Duff D., Eldershaw C.: Connecting and disconnecting for chain self-reconfiguration with PolyBot. In: IEEE/ASME Transactions on mechatronics, special issue on Information Technology in Mechatronics (2003)

Towards Derandomizing PRM Planners

Abraham Sánchez[1] and René Zapata[2]

[1] Facultad de Ciencias de la Computación, BUAP
14 Sur esq. San Claudio, CP 72550
Puebla, Pue., México
asanchez@cs.buap.mx
[2] LIRMM, UMR5506 CNRS, 161 rue Ada 34392,
Montpellier Cedex 5, France
zapata@lirmm.fr

Abstract. Probabilistic roadmap methods (PRM) have been successfully applied in motion planning for robots with many degrees of freedom. Many recent PRM approaches have demonstrated improved performance by concentrating samples in a nonuniform way. This work replace
the random sampling by the deterministic one. We present several implementations of PRM-based planners (multiple-query, single-query and
Lazy PRM) and lattice-based roadmaps. Deterministic sampling can be
used in the same way than random sampling. Our work can be seen as
an important part of the research in the uniform sampling field. Experimental results show performance advantages of our approach.

1 Introduction

The complexity of motion planning for robots with many degrees of freedom
(more than 4 or 5) has led to the development of computational schemes that
attempt to trade off completeness against time. One such scheme, randomized
planning, avoids computing an explicit geometric representation of the free space
$\mathcal{F}$. Instead, it uses an efficient procedure to compute distances between bodies
in the workspace.

It samples the configuration space $(\mathcal{CS})$ by selecting a number of configurations at random and retaining only the free configurations as *nodes*. It then
checks if each pair of nodes can be connected by a collision-free path in configuration space. This computation yields the graph $G = (V, E)$, called a *probabilistic
roadmap* [1], where V is the set of nodes and E is the set of pairs of nodes that
have been connected.

The default sampling approach for PRM planners samples $\mathcal{F}$ in a random
way. Samples from the uniform distribution are usually obtained by generating
the so-called *pseudo-random numbers*. Random sampling often generates clusters
of points; in addition, gaps appears in the sample space. Recent research has
focussed on designing efficient sampling and connection strategies [2], [3], [4], [5].

Recent works replace the random sampling by the deterministic one [6], [7].
The work presented in [7] for non-holonomic motion planning, proposes the use

R. Monroy et al. (Eds.): MICAI 2004, LNAI 2972, pp. 911–920, 2004.
© Springer-Verlag Berlin Heidelberg 2004

of other sequences, Sobol', Faure, Niederreiter and generalized Halton. Lavalle and Branicky [6] only use two low-discrepancy sequences, the Halton and Hammersley. The sampling is seen as an optimization problem in which a set of points is chosen to optimize some criterion of uniformity. Also, deterministic sampling can be thought of as a sophisticated form of stratified sampling.

2   Deterministic Sampling

The historical origin of discrepancy theory is the theory of uniform distribution developed by H. Weyl and other mathematicians in the early days of the 20th century. While the latter deals with the uniformity of infinite sequences of points, the former deals with the uniformity of finite sequences. Finite sequences always have some irregularity from the ideal uniformity due to their finiteness. *Discrepancy* is a mathematical notion for measuring such irregularity. Let $X = [0,1]^d \subset \mathbb{R}^d$ define a space over which to generate samples. Consider designing a set, P, of n d-dimensional sample points $\{x_0, x_1, \ldots, x_n\}$ in way that covers X. Let $\mathcal{R}$ be a collection of subsets of X, called a *range space*. Let $R \in \mathcal{R}$ denote one such subset. The formal definition of discrepancy is as follows:

$$D_n(P, \mathcal{R}) = \sup_{R \in \mathcal{R}} \left| \frac{P \cap R}{n} - \lambda(R) \right|, \tag{1}$$

where λ denotes the Lebesgue measure on X and the supremum is taken over all axis-parallel boxes R. A detailed analysis of the discrepancy can be found in [8] and in the references therein.

Similarly to the notion of discrepancy, it is possible to quantify the denseness of n points, the *dispersion*, which is defined by

$$d_n(P, \delta) = \max_{x \in X} \min_{1 \leq i \leq n} \delta(x, x_i), \tag{2}$$

It was introduced by Hlawka (1976) and later investigated in more general form in [8]. Above δ denotes any metric. For any particular range space, the dispersion is clearly bounded by the discrepancy. The relation

$$d_n(P, \delta) \leq \sqrt{d} \, D_n(P, \mathcal{R})^{1/d} \tag{3}$$

is established in [8] for the Euclidean metric. For the maximum metric one obtains

$$d'_n(P, \delta) \leq D_n(P, \mathcal{R})^{1/d} \tag{4}$$

according to [8]. Thus every low-discrepancy point set (or sequence) is a low-dispersion point set (or sequence), but no conversely.

Although dispersion has been given less consideration in the literature than discrepancy, and it is more suitable for motion planning. Dispersion has been deve-loped to bound optimization error; however, in PRM-based planners, it can be used to ensure that any corridor of a certain width will contain sufficient samples [6].

2.1 Finite Point Sets and Sequences

For practical use, there are three different types of low-discrepancy sequences or point sets : Halton sequences, lattice rules, and (t, k)-sequences. The last one includes almost all important sequences such as Sobol'sequences, Faure sequences, and Niederreiter-xing sequences between others.

Many of the relevant low-discrepancy sequences are linked to the van der Corput sequence. The Halton sequence is a d dimensional generalization that uses van der Corput sequences of d different bases, one for each coordinate. The Hammersley point set is an adaptation of the Halton sequence, using only $d - 1$ distinct primes. A different approach was used by Sobol' who suggested a multi-dimensional (t, s)-sequence using a base 2. The Sobol' idea was further developed by Faure, who suggested alternative multi-dimensional (t, s)-sequences with base $b \geq d$. A general construction principle for (t, s)-sequences has been proposed by Niederreiter. We refer to [6], [7], [9] and [8] for the construction of low-discrepancy sequences.

In general, slightly better distributions are possible if the number of sample points needed is known in advance. One effective way to obtaining such sets is to use the lattice point method. Good lattice point sets are an important kind of low-discrepancy points for multi-dimensional quadrature, simulation, experimental design, and other applications [10].

Let n be an integer ≥ 2 and $\mathbf{a} = (a_1, \cdots, a_d)$ be an integer vector modulo n. A set of the form

$$P_n = \{\{ak/n\} = (\{a_1 k/n\}, \cdots, \{a_d k/n\}) \mid k = 1, \ldots, n\} \tag{5}$$

is called a lattice point set, where $\{x\}$ denotes the fractional part of x. The vector $\mathbf{a}$ is called a lattice point or generator of the set.

The advantage of the lattice point set, as defined in (5), is that it has a simple form and is easy to program. A disadvantage is that the number of points, n, is fixed and the good lattice points, $\mathbf{a}$, typically depend on n. This is the contrast case of (t, m, s)-nets, which can be extended in size by drawing them from a (t, s)-sequence [8]. This deficiency in lattice point sets can be overcome by replacing k/n in (5) by the van der Corput sequence. Tables $\mathbf{a}$ for extensible lattice point sets are given by Hickernell et al. [11].

We considered a particular type of lattice called *the Sukharev grid*, is constructed for some n such that $k = n^{1/d}$ is an integer. X is decomposed into n cubes of width $1/k$ so that a tiling of $k \times k \times \times \cdots \times k$ is built. Classical grid places a vertex at origin of each region, the Sukharev grid places a vertex at the center of each region.

2.2 Uniformity of Low-Discrepancy Sequences

For numerical integration and many other purposes, Monte Carlo methods have been used for a long time. Newer developments replace the pseudo-random sequences by deterministic sequences (quasi-random or low-discrepancy sequences). Although motion planning is an approach different to the integration one, it is worth evaluating these carefully constructed and well analyzed samples. Their potential use in motion planning is no less reasonable than using pseudo-random sequences, which were also designed with a different intention in mind.

We generated points of the sequences up to $d = 100$ and $n = 100000$ and observed their uniformities in two-dimensional planes selected at random, using Halton, Faure, Sobol' and Niederreiter sequences.

The Halton sequences give uniform distributions for lower dimensions $(1-7)$. As the number of dimensions increases, the quality of this sequence rapidly decreases because two-dimensional planes within the hypercube are sampled in cycles with increasing periods. For dimensions larger than 8 the sample points generated by Halton sequence are ordered into lines. To avoid the line ordering for the points generated by Halton sequence, we used the generalized Halton sequences. The specific characteristics of the generalized Halton sequences are still unknown (a certain degree of local non-uniformity is introduced).

The Faure sequence is an example of a less successful (t, s)-sequence, that gives a different distribution. While it achieves a high degree of local uniformity, the unit square projections of the hypercube are sampled in strips, and the new points fall into the vicinity of those generated previously.

The Sobol' sequence preserves its uniformity as d increases.

The Niederreiter sequences are (t, s)-sequences defined for any base $b \geq d$, where b is a power of a prime number, they only make a light improvement on the Faure sequences in certain dimensions.

These experiments consolidate two ideas: 1) With a larger base, a low-discrepancy sequence can present certain pathologies, and 2) the minimal size of a low-discrepancy sample that has better equidistribution properties than a pseudo-random sequence grows exponentially with the dimension [9].

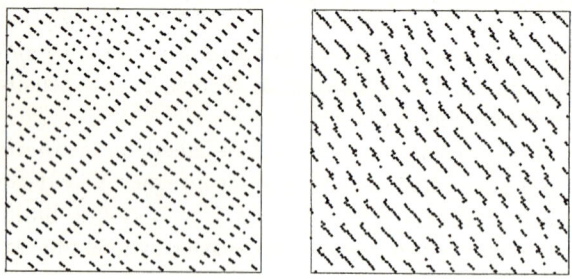

Fig. 1. Projection of the first 1000 points of the Halton $(d = 8)$ and Faure $(d = 50)$ sequences.

3   Deterministic Roadmap Methods

In the last few years, the PRM approach has been studied by many researchers [1], [2], [3], [4], [14]. This had led to a large number of variants of this approach, each one with its own merits. It is difficult to compare PRM variants, because it is hard to maintain congruence when each variant has been tested on different types of scenes, has been used different underlying libraries, and has been executed on different machines.

The philosophy behind the classic PRM was to perform preprocessing (the learning phase) so that *multiple-queries* for the same environment could be handled efficiently. Once the PRM has been constructed, the query phase attempts to solve motion planning problems: q_i and q_g are treated as new nodes in the PRM, and connections are attempted. Then, standard graph search is performed to connect q_i to q_g. If the method fails, then either more nodes are needed in the PRM, or there is no solution.

The classic PRM [1] was chosen because it eases the comparison between its deterministic variants; the samples from the pseudo-random number generator appear directly as nodes in the roadmap (except those in collision).

We can consider two variants of the PRM, a *deterministic roadmap*, DRM, and a *lattice roadmap*[1], LRM, by applying the deterministic sampling techniques described in Section II.

The main problem with classical grid search is that too many points per axis are typically required. The PRM was proposed to reduce the exponential number of samples needed for this approach. If we generalize the grid to a lattice (which is essentially a nonorthogonal grid), one can consider this method as a special kind of the lattice roadmap.

We used the following scenes (see Figure 2) to compare different deterministic sampling methods. All techniques were integrated in the MSL library (University of Illinois) implemented in C++ under Linux, and uses the PQP collision detection package from University of North Carolina. All experiments were run on a 866 Mhz Pentium 3 with 128 MB of internal memory.

The number of nodes required to find a path that travels through the corridors is shown in Table 1 for all sampling strategies. We also compared two PRM variants, Gaussian and Visibility.

Table 1. Comparisons of the number of nodes

Prob.	PRM	DRM	LRM	GS	VS
2 narrows	4316	3175	2322	700	35
1 narrow	2480	1840	1239	656	39

---

[1] The costly neighborhood structure is implicitly defined by the lattice rules.

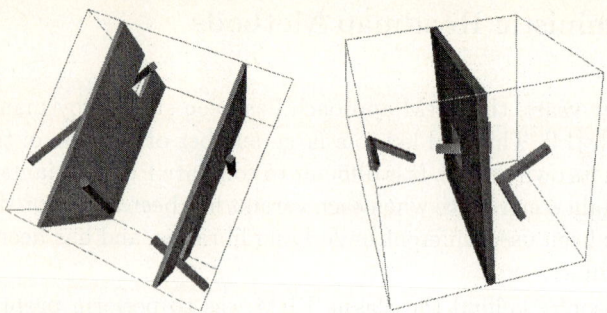

Fig. 2. A 6-dof planning problem in which an object passes through two small opening; and an L-shaped object that must rotate to get through the hole.

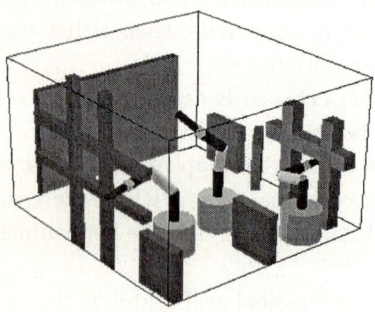

Fig. 3. A 8-dof mobile manipulator.

Sanchez et al [7] have proposed the use of low-discrepancy sequences in the nonholonomic motion planning context. Figure 3 present an example for mobile manipulators.

In all our experiments, pseudo-random numbers were generated using the linear congruential and Mersenne Twister generator for PRM. We have used Halton, generalized Halton, Hammersley, Faure, Sobol' and Niederreiter sequences as inputs for DRM.

We chose the best result among all deterministic sequences for DRM. The construction time is obviously smaller for the deterministic case; this is due to the fact that the number of nodes necessary to answer correctly a query is smaller. It is important to mention that in the case of very cluttered environments, the construction time is similar for both methods PRM and DRM. For the number of generated arcs and the calls to collision checking, the difference between the two is enormous.

Analyzing the obtained results, we can affirm that the use of the deterministic sampling offers additional advantages: the number of nodes require to find a path is always inferior in the deterministic sampling case, the collision test calls diminishes considerably, as well as the number of configurations generated during the construction phase. All these results confirm that the coverage of the free space is better using determinist sampling.

These results confirm that the deterministic sampling approach does not require an important adaptation of the classic PRM algorithm.

4   Hsu and SBL Planners

While multi-query planners use a sampling strategy to cover the whole free-space, a single-query planner applies a strategy to explore the smallest portion of free-space needed to find a solution path. For example, see the planners presented in [14] and [15].

The planner in [14] constructs two trees of nodes (the roadmap) rooted at q_i and q_g respectively. It samples new configurations first in the neighborhoods of q_i and q_g, and then iteratively, in the neighborhoods of newly-generated nodes. It stops as soon as the two trees become one connected component, and a path between q_i and q_g can be extracted from the roadmap. The current implementation of the algorithm uses a fixed-size neighborhood around an existing node to sample new configurations. The size of neighborhoods has a big impact on the distribution of nodes. If the size is too small, the nodes tend to cluster around the initial and the goal configuration and leave large portions of the free space with no samples. If the size is very large, the samples likely distribute more evenly in the free space, but the rejection rate also increases significantly.

The planner in [15] searches $\mathcal{F}$ by building a roadmap made of two trees of nodes, T_i and T_g. The root of T_i is the initial configuration q_i, and the root of T_g is the goal configuration q_g (bi-directional search). Every new node generated during planning is installed in either one of the two trees as the child of an already existing node. The link between the two nodes is the straight-line segment joining them in $\mathcal{CS}$. This segment will be tested for collision only when it becomes necessary to perform this test to prove that a candidate path is collision-free (lazy collision checking). The planner is given two parameters: s - the maximum number of nodes that can generate and ρ, - a distance threshold. In this implementation ρ is set between 0.1 and 0.2.

These algorithms can be derandomized by using a deterministic low-discrepan-cy sequences, such as generalized Halton, Sobol', Faure, or Niederreiter. We simply replace random samples with deterministic ones. Table 2 shows the results of experiments performed on two difficult scenes for articulated robots. The planners were implemented in Java.

The first results obtained with the derandomization of these algorithms are very interesting. The run time is smaller in the case of the use of deterministic sampling, like the calls to collision checking. Also we noticed that the intrinsic parameters of the algorithms are not easy to choose.

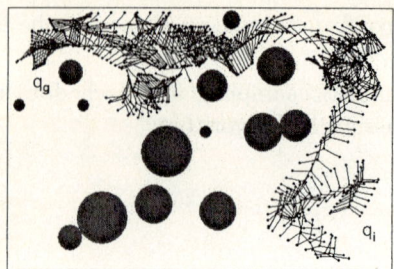 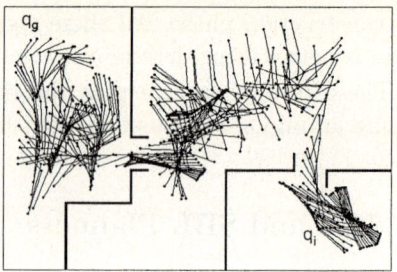

Fig. 4. Two paths found by Hsu and SBL planners for a 11-dof and 8-dof manipulators.

Table 2. Statistics for the two environments

11-dof Prob.	Hsu	SBL	Hsu/DRM	SBL/DRM
Nodes in roadmap	1156	6831	805	4416
Nodes in path	37	61	42	65
Running time	17.77	3.45	9.46	2.29
Collision checks	56877456	5676136	28966459	4045502
8-dof Prob.	Hsu	SBL	Hsu/DRM	SBL/DRM
Nodes in roadmap	447	2343	413	2210
Nodes in path	33	53	26	44
Running time	3.27	0.84	2.99	0.78
Collision checks	8893118	1560958	8097380	1277984

5   Discussion

Low-discrepancy samples were developed to perform better than random samples for numerical integration (using an inequality due to Koksma-Hlawka). Low-dispersion samples were developed to perform better than random samples in numerical optimization (using an inequality due to Niederreiter). We can obtain a bound that expresses the convergence rate in terms of dispersion and the width of the narrowest corridor in $\mathcal{F}$. The corridor thickness appears to be a measure of difficulty.

We used low-discrepancy sequences to bridge the gap between the flexibility of pseudo-random number generators and the advantages of a regular grid. They are designed to have a high level of uniformity in multi-dimensional space, but unlike pseudo-random numbers they are not statistically independent. The trouble with the grid approach is that it is necessary to decide in advance how fine it should be, and all the grid points need to be used. It is therefore not possible to sample until some convergence criterion has been met. Recently, Lindemann and Lavalle [16] proposed a new sampling method in the PRM framework. This grid sampling satisfies the desirable criteria uniformity, lattice structure and incremental quality. It is an arbitrary-dimensional generalization of the van der Corput sequence.

The results indicate an advantage of deterministic sampling, lattices, and grids over pseudo-random sampling, particularly in a lazy PRM approach. Classic PRM attempts to reduce the exponential number of samples needed for a grid-based approach by using random sampling. But, given the Sukharev criterion [8], we know that an exponential number of samples is needed in any case. Lazy PRM provides a link between grid search and classic PRM. DRM is definitely an improvement over the PRM by using deterministic sampling.

The results reported in [12], [13] bound the number of nodes generated by probabilistic roadmap planners, under the assumption that the free space $\mathcal{F}$ satisfies some geometric properties. One such property, so called *expansiveness*, measures the difficulty caused by the presence of narrow passages. If $\mathcal{F}$ is expansive, the probability that a probabilistic roadmap planner fails to find a free path between two given configurations, tends exponentially to zero while the number of nodes increases.

Deterministic sampling enables all deterministic roadmap planners to be *resolution complete* (see [6] for more details), in the sense that if it is possible to solve the query at a given sampling resolution, they will solve it. The resolution can be increased arbitrarily to ensure that any problem can be solved, if a solution exists.

6   Conclusions

We know that contemporary motion planning algorithms (many of which use randomization) are very efficient to solve many difficult problems. This can lead to the conclusion, that randomization is the key for its effectiveness.

Although randomization can become a "black box", which hides the reasons for success in an algorithm. Therefore, the attempts to derandomize popular motion planning algorithms do not reflect antipathy towards randomization, but rather the desire to understand fundamental insights of these algorithms.

Hsu and SBL algorithms are properly partially-randomized versions, in which deterministic and randomized strategies are combined. We hope that more works that investigate partially-randomized and deterministic variants of contemporary motion planning algorithms will be considered in the future. As we have already mentioned, our work can be seen as part of the efforts proposed in [6] to derandomize PRMs.

We will need to demonstrate that the performance of determinist sampling in dimension superior to 10 will be equivalent to that obtained in the case of inferior dimensions. In section 2,2 we discussed the uniformity of low-discrepancy sequences.

Randomization is a common algorithmic technique, and it is of great value in many contexts. In the robot motion planning context, randomization is the most effective technique for reducing the high cost associated with moving objects with many degrees of freedom. The usefulness of randomization for this purpose has been challenged.

References

1. Kavraki, L., Švestka, P., Latombe, J-C., Overmars, M. H. "Probabilistic roadmaps for path planning in high-dimensional configuration spaces", IEEE Transactions on Robotics and Automation. Vol 12, No. 4 (1996) 566-579
2. Amato, N., Burchan, B., Dale, L., Jones, C., Vallejo, D. "OBPRM: An obstacle-based prm for 3D workspaces", Proc. of Workshop on Algorithmic Foundation of Robotics, (1998) 155-168
3. Boor, V., Overmars, M., Van der Steppen, F. "The gaussian sampling strategy for probabilistic roadmap planners", IEEE Int. Conf. on Robotics and Automation, (1999) 1018-1023
4. Nissoux, C., Siméon, T., Laumond, J. P.: "Visibility based probabilistic roadmaps". IEEE Int. Conf. on Intelligent Robots and Systems (1999)
5. Bohlin, R., Kavraki, L. "Path planning using lazy PRM", IEEE Int. Conf. on Robotics and Automation, (2000)
6. Lavalle, S., Branicky, M. "On the relationship between classical grid search and probabilistic roadmaps", Proc. of Workshop on Algorithmic Foundation of Robotics, (2002)
7. Sánchez, A., Zapata, R., Lanzoni, C. "On the use of low-discrepancy sequences in non-holonomic motion planning", IEEE Int. Conf. on Robotics and Automation, (2003)
8. Niederreiter, H. "Random number generation and quasi-Monte Carlo methods". Society for Industrial and Applied Mathematics, Philadelphia, Pennsylvania (1992)
9. Sánchez, L. A. "Contribution à la planification de mouvement en robotique: Approches probabilistes et approches déterministes", PhD thesis, Université Montpellier II, 2003.
10. Sloan, I. H., Joe, S. "Lattice methods for multiple integration", Oxford University Press (1994)
11. Hickernell, F. J., Hong, H. S., L'Écuyer, P., Lemieux, C. "Extensible lattice sequences for quasi-Monte Carlo quadrature", SIAM, Journal on Scientific Computing, Vol 22, No. 3 (2001) 117-138
12. Kavraki, L., Latombe, J-C., Motwani, R., Raghavan, P. "Randomized query processing in robot motion planning", Journal of Computer and System Sciences, Vol. 57, No. 1, (1998) 50-60
13. Hsu, D., Latombe, J-C., Motwani, R. "Path planning in expansive configuration spaces", Int. J. of Computational Geometry and Applications, Vol. 9 (1999) 495-512
14. Hsu, D.. "Randomized single-query motion planning in expansive spaces", PhD thesis, Stanford University, 2000.
15. Sánchez, A. G., Latombe, J-C. "A single-query bi-directional probabilistic roadmap planner with lazy collision-checking", Int. Symposium on Robotics Research, 2001.
16. Lindemann S., LaValle S. "Incremental low-discrepancy lattice methods for motion planning", Proc. IEEE Int. Conf. on Robotics and Automation, 2003.

Author Index

Lecture Notes in Artificial Intelligence (LNAI)

Vol. 2684: M.V. Butz, O. Sigaud, P. Gérard (Eds.), Anticipatory Behavior in Adaptive Learning Systems. X, 303 pages. 2003.

Vol. 2671: Y. Xiang, B. Chaib-draa (Eds.), Advances in Artificial Intelligence. XIV, 642 pages. 2003.

Vol. 2663: E. Menasalvas, J. Segovia, P.S. Szczepaniak (Eds.), Advances in Web Intelligence. XII, 350 pages. 2003.

Vol. 2661: P.L. Lanzi, W. Stolzmann, S.W. Wilson (Eds.), Learning Classifier Systems. VII, 231 pages. 2003.

Vol. 2654: U. Schmid, Inductive Synthesis of Functional Programs. XXII, 398 pages. 2003.

Vol. 2650: M.-P. Huget (Ed.), Communications in Multi-agent Systems. VIII, 323 pages. 2003.

Vol. 2645: M.A. Wimmer (Ed.), Knowledge Management in Electronic Government. XI, 320 pages. 2003.

Vol. 2639: G. Wang, Q. Liu, Y. Yao, A. Skowron (Eds.), Rough Sets, Fuzzy Sets, Data Mining, and Granular Computing. XVII, 741 pages. 2003.

Vol. 2637: K.-Y. Whang, J. Jeon, K. Shim, J. Srivastava, Advances in Knowledge Discovery and Data Mining. XVIII, 610 pages. 2003.

Vol. 2636: E. Alonso, D. Kudenko, D. Kazakov (Eds.), Adaptive Agents and Multi-Agent Systems. XIV, 323 pages. 2003.

Vol. 2627: B. O'Sullivan (Ed.), Recent Advances in Constraints. X, 201 pages. 2003.

Vol. 2600: S. Mendelson, A.J. Smola (Eds.), Advanced Lectures on Machine Learning. IX, 259 pages. 2003.

Vol. 2592: R. Kowalczyk, J.P. Müller, H. Tianfield, R. Unland (Eds.), Agent Technologies, Infrastructures, Tools, and Applications for E-Services. XVII, 371 pages. 2003.

Vol. 2586: M. Klusch, S. Bergamaschi, P. Edwards, P. Petta (Eds.), Intelligent Information Agents. VI, 275 pages. 2003.

Vol. 2583: S. Matwin, C. Sammut (Eds.), Inductive Logic Programming. X, 351 pages. 2003.

Vol. 2581: J.S. Sichman, F. Bousquet, P. Davidsson (Eds.), Multi-Agent-Based Simulation. X, 195 pages. 2003.

Vol. 2577: P. Petta, R. Tolksdorf, F. Zambonelli (Eds.), Engineering Societies in the Agents World III. X, 285 pages. 2003.

Vol. 2569: D. Karagiannis, U. Reimer (Eds.), Practical Aspects of Knowledge Management. XIII, 648 pages. 2002.

Vol. 2560: S. Goronzy, Robust Adaptation to Non-Native Accents in Automatic Speech Recognition. XI, 144 pages. 2002.

Vol. 2557: B. McKay, J. Slaney (Eds.), AI 2002: Advances in Artificial Intelligence. XV, 730 pages. 2002.

Vol. 2554: M. Beetz, Plan-Based Control of Robotic Agents. XI, 191 pages. 2002.

Vol. 2543: O. Bartenstein, U. Geske, M. Hannebauer, O. Yoshie (Eds.), Web Knowledge Management and Decision Support. X, 307 pages. 2003.

Vol. 2541: T. Barkowsky, Mental Representation and Processing of Geographic Knowledge. X, 174 pages. 2002.

Vol. 2533: N. Cesa-Bianchi, M. Numao, R. Reischuk (Eds.), Algorithmic Learning Theory. XI, 415 pages. 2002.

Vol. 2531: J. Padget, O. Shehory, D. Parkes, N.M. Sadeh, W.E. Walsh (Eds.), Agent-Mediated Electronic Commerce IV. Designing Mechanisms and Systems. XVII, 341 pages. 2002.

Vol. 2527: F.J. Garijo, J.-C. Riquelme, M. Toro (Eds.), Advances in Artificial Intelligence - IBERAMIA 2002. XVIII, 955 pages. 2002.

Vol. 2522: T. Andreasen, A. Motro, H. Christiansen, H.L. Larsen (Eds.), Flexible Query Answering Systems. X, 383 pages. 2002.

Vol. 2514: M. Baaz, A. Voronkov (Eds.), Logic for Programming, Artificial Intelligence, and Reasoning. XIII, 465 pages. 2002.

Vol. 2507: G. Bittencourt, G.L. Ramalho (Eds.), Advances in Artificial Intelligence. XIII, 417 pages. 2002.

Vol. 2504: M.T. Escrig, F. Toledo, E. Golobardes (Eds.), Topics in Artificial Intelligence. XI, 427 pages. 2002.

Vol. 2499: S.D. Richardson (Ed.), Machine Translation: From Research to Real Users. XXI, 254 pages. 2002.

Vol. 2484: P. Adriaans, H. Fernau, M. van Zaanen (Eds.), Grammatical Inference: Algorithms and Applications. IX, 315 pages. 2002.

Vol. 2479: M. Jarke, J. Koehler, G. Lakemeyer (Eds.), KI 2002: Advances in Artificial Intelligence. XIII, 327 pages. 2002.

Vol. 2475: J.J. Alpigini, J.F. Peters, A. Skowron, N. Zhong (Eds.), Rough Sets and Current Trends in Computing. XV, 640 pages. 2002.

Vol. 2473: A. Gómez-Pérez, V.R. Benjamins (Eds.), Knowledge Engineering and Knowledge Management. Ontologies and the Semantic Web. XI, 402 pages. 2002.

Vol. 2466: M. Beetz, J. Hertzberg, M. Ghallab, M.E. Pollack (Eds.), Advances in Plan-Based Control of Robotic Agents. VIII, 291 pages. 2002.

Vol. 2464: M. O'Neill, R.F.E. Sutcliffe, C. Ryan, M. Eaton, N.J.L. Griffith (Eds.), Artificial Intelligence and Cognitive Science. XI, 247 pages. 2002.

Vol. 2448: P. Sojka, I. Kopecek, K. Pala (Eds.), Text, Speech and Dialogue. XII, 481 pages. 2002.

Vol. 2447: D.J. Hand, N.M. Adams, R.J. Bolton (Eds.), Pattern Detection and Discovery. XII, 227 pages. 2002.

Vol. 2446: M. Klusch, S. Ossowski, O. Shehory (Eds.), Cooperative Information Agents VI. XI, 321 pages. 2002.

Vol. 2445: C. Anagnostopoulou, M. Ferrand, A. Smaill (Eds.), Music and Artificial Intelligence. VIII, 207 pages. 2002.

Vol. 2443: D. Scott (Ed.), Artificial Intelligence: Methodology, Systems, and Applications. X, 279 pages. 2002.

Vol. 2432: R. Bergmann, Experience Management. XXI, 393 pages. 2002.

Vol. 2431: T. Elomaa, H. Mannila, H. Toivonen (Eds.), Principles of Data Mining and Knowledge Discovery. XIV, 514 pages. 2002.

Vol. 2430: T. Elomaa, H. Mannila, H. Toivonen (Eds.), Machine Learning: ECML 2002. XIII, 532 pages. 2002.

Vol. 2427: M. Hannebauer, Autonomous Dynamic Reconfiguration in Multi-Agent Systems. XXI, 284 pages. 2002.

Vol. 2424: S. Flesca, S. Greco, N. Leone, G. Ianni (Eds.), Logics in Artificial Intelligence. XIII, 572 pages. 2002.